T0137359

Lecture Notes in Artificial Intelligence   10868

Subseries of Lecture Notes in Computer Science

More information about this series at http://www.springer.com/series/1244

Malek Mouhoub · Samira Sadaoui
Otmane Ait Mohamed · Moonis Ali (Eds.)

Recent Trends and Future Technology in Applied Intelligence

31st International Conference
on Industrial Engineering and Other Applications
of Applied Intelligent Systems, IEA/AIE 2018
Montreal, QC, Canada, June 25–28, 2018
Proceedings

 Springer

Editors
Malek Mouhoub
University of Regina
Regina, SK
Canada

Otmane Ait Mohamed
Concordia University
Montreal, QC
Canada

Samira Sadaoui
University of Regina
Regina, SK
Canada

Moonis Ali
Texas State University
San Marcos, TX
USA

ISSN 0302-9743   ISSN 1611-3349 (electronic)
Lecture Notes in Artificial Intelligence
ISBN 978-3-319-92057-3   ISBN 978-3-319-92058-0 (eBook)
https://doi.org/10.1007/978-3-319-92058-0

Library of Congress Control Number: 2018944379

LNCS Sublibrary: SL7 – Artificial Intelligence

Printed on acid-free paper

This Springer imprint is published by the registered company Springer International Publishing AG
part of Springer Nature
The registered company address is: Gewerbestrasse 11, 6330 Cham, Switzerland

Preface

There has been a steady increase in demand for efficient, dynamic, and intelligent systems for solving complex real-world problems. Applied intelligence technologies have been used to build smart machines that can solve such problems of significant complexity. The International Conference on Industrial, Engineering and Other Applications of Applied Intelligent Systems (IEA/AIE), sponsored by the International Society of Applied Intelligence (ISAI), concentrates on applied intelligence as well as its applications to complex problem-solving. The annual conference has become an important international event in the field of applied intelligence, where researchers and industrial communities communicate with each other and promote the development of advanced research in applied intelligence.

The 31st International Conference on Industrial, Engineering and Other Applications of Applied Intelligent Systems (IEA/AIE 2018) was organized by Concordia University and sponsored by the International Society of Applied Intelligence (ISAI). It is with great pleasure that we present to you the proceedings of IEA/AIE 2018. The conference was held in the vibrant city of Montreal during June 25–28, 2018. Montreal is becoming an artificial intelligence hub with the recent large provincial and federal funding in the area of machine learning in addition to investments from tech giants such as Google, Microsoft, and Facebook.

IEA/AIE 2018 received 146 submissions from Canada and the following 44 countries: Algeria, Argentina, Australia, Austria, Belgium, Brazil, Chile, China, Cuba, Czech Republic, Egypt, France, Germany, Greece, Hong Kong, India, Iran, Iraq, Italy, Japan, Jordan, Luxembourg, Malaysia, Morocco, The Netherlands, New Zealand, Nigeria, Norway, Oman, Pakistan, Poland, Portugal, Saudi Arabia, Singapore, Spain, Sweden, Switzerland, Taiwan, Tanzania, Tunisia, Turkey, UAE, UK and the USA. Each submission was carefully reviewed by three members of the Program Committee. For the final conference program and for inclusion in these proceedings, 35 regular papers, with allocation of 12 pages each, were selected. Additionally, 29 short papers, with allocation of six to eight pages each, were accepted. These papers cover a wide range of artificial intelligence topics, including data mining and machine learning, knowledge representation, natural language processing, robotics, planning and scheduling, constraint programming, and evolutionary computation. Finally, 22 papers accepted in the following four special tracks are also included in these proceedings: Artificial Intelligence, Law and Justice Track; Data Science, Privacy, and Security Track; Intelligent Systems Approaches in Information Extraction Track; and Internet of Things and Ubiquitous Computing and Big Data Track.

The conference program was enriched by three keynote presentations and tutorials. The keynote speakers were Behrouz Far, University of Calgary, Wahab Hamou-Lhadj, Concordia University, and Guy Lapalme, University of Montreal. We would like to thank the Program Committee members for their time, dedication, and effort in providing valuable reviews. We thank all the authors for submitting their contributions and the authors of accepted papers for preparing the final version of their papers and presenting their work at the conference. We would like to thank both Concordia University and ISAI, as well as every member of the organization team for their help and support. Finally, we are very grateful to the development team of the EasyChair conference system. This system made the process of paper submission and evaluation, as well as the preparation of the proceedings, easy for us and saved us a significant amount of time.

April 2018   Malek Mouhoub
                                                         Samira Sadaoui
                                                  Otmane Ait Mohamed
                                                             Moonis Ali

The original version of the book was revised:
For detailed information please see Erratum.
The Erratum to this book is available at
https://doi.org/10.1007/978-3-319-92058-0_87

Organization

General Co-chairs

Otmane Ait Mohamed	Concordia University, Canada
Moonis Ali	Texas State University, USA

International Advisory Committee

Hamido Fujita (Chair)	Iwate Prefectural University, Japan
Enrique Herrera-Viedma	University of Granada, Spain
Francisco Chiclana	De Montfort University, UK
Yinglin Wang	Shanghai Jiao Tong University, China
Love Ekenberg	Stockholm University, Sweden
Imre Rudas	Óbuda University, Hungary
Shiliang Sun	East China Normal University, China
Vincenzo Loia	University of Salerno, Italy
Ali Selamat	Universiti Teknologi Malaysia, Malaysia
Bipin Indurkhya	AGH University of Science and Technology, Poland
Chris Bowman	University of Technology Sydney, Australia
Jun Sasaki	Iwate Prefectural University, Japan
Ligang Zhou	Macao University of Science and Technology, SAR China
Rajendra Acharya	Singapore University of Social Science, Singapore
Levente Kovacs	Obuda University, Hungary

Program Co-chairs

Malek Mouhoub	University of Regina, Canada
Samira Sadaoui	University of Regina, Canada

Organization Co-chairs

Ghaith Bany Hamad	Concordia University, Canada
Malek Mouhoub	University of Regina, Canada

Special Sessions Chair

Mohamed El Bachir Menai	King Saud University, Saudi Arabia

Social Events and Local Arrangements Co-chairs

Leila Kosseim   Concordia University, Canada
Marie-Jean Meurs   Concordia University, Canada

Web Co-chairs

Marwan Ammar   Concordia University, Canada
Paulo R. M. de Andrade   University of Regina, Canada
Shubhashis Kumar Shil   University of Regina, Canada

Publicity Co-chairs

Fatiha Sadat   Université du Québec à Montréalal, Canada
Paulo R. M. de Andrade   University of Regina, Canada

Sponsoring Institutions

IEA/AIE 2018 was organized by Concordia University, Montréal, Canada.

Sponsored by
Concordia University, Canada
International Society of Applied Intelligence (ISAI)
Regroupement Stratégique en Microsystèmes du Québec
Springer
Texas State University, USA
University of Regina, Canada

Organized in cooperation with

Association for the Advancement of Artificial Intelligence (AAAI)
Association for Computing Machinery (ACM/SIGART)
Austrian Association for Artificial Intelligence (OEGAI)
Canadian Artificial Intelligence Association (CAIAC)
Catalan Association for Artificial Intelligence (ACIA)
International Neural Network Society (INNS)
Italian Artificial Intelligence Association (AI*IA)
Japanese Society for Artificial Intelligence (JSAI)
Lithuanian Computer Society, Artificial Intelligence Section (LIKS-AIS)
Spanish Society for Artificial Intelligence (AEPIA)
Society for the Study of Artificial Intelligence and the Simulation of Behaviour (AISB)
Taiwanese Association for Artificial Intelligence (TAAI)
Taiwanese Association for Consumer Electronics (TACE)
Texas State University, USA
University of Regina, Canada

Program Committee

Sultan Ahmed	University of Regina, Canada
Yamine Ait Ameur	IRIT/INPT-ENSEEIHT
Otmane Ait Mohamed	Concordia University, Canada
Wolfgang Alschner	University of Ottawa, Canada
Abdelmalek Amine	University of Saida, Algeria
Abdelkrim Amirat	University of Nantes, France
Xiangdong An	UT Martin, USA
Yacine Atif	Skövde University, Sweden
Xavier Aurey	University of Essex, UK
Ebrahim Bagheri	Ryerson University, Canada
Olivier Barsalou	Université du Québec à Montréal (UQAM), Canada
Ghalem Belalem	Université d'Oran, Algeria
Hafida Belbachir	USTOMB Oran, Algeria
Ladjel Bellatreche	LIAS/ENSMA, France
Jamal Bentahar	Concordia University, Canada
Marc Bertin	Université du Québec à Montréal, Canada
Ismail Biskri	Université du Québec à Trois-Rivières, Canada
Jean-Francois Bonastre	Université d'Avignon et des Pays de Vaucluse, France
Leszek Borzemski	Wroclaw University of Technology, Poland
Karim Bouamrane	University of Oran 1 Ahmed Benbella, Algeria
Adel Bouhoula	Ecole superieure des communications de Tunis, Tunisia
Kamel Boukhalfa	USTHB University, Algeria
Mourad Bouneffa	LISIC ULCO, France
Lars Braubach	University of Hamburg, Germany
Andres Bustillo	University of Burgos, Spain
Cory Butz	University of Regina, Canada
Francisco Campa	University of the Basque Country, UPV/EHU, Spain
Joao Paulo Carvalho	Instituto Superior Tecnico/INESC-ID, Portugal
Celine Castets Renard	Toulouse Capitole University, France
Allaoua Chaoui	University Mentouri Constantine, Algeria
Eric Charton	Yellow Pages, Canada
Shyi-Ming Chen	National Taiwan University, Taiwan
Salim Chikhi	University of Constantine 2
Samira Chouraqui	LAMOSI, France
Flavio S. Correa Da Silva	University of São Paulo, Brazil
Hugo Cyr	Université du Québec à Montréal (UQAM), Canada
Rozita Dara	University of Guelph, Canada
Abdelkader Dekdouk	Dhofar University, Oman
Mahieddine Djoudi	University of Poitiers, France
Liang Dong	Clemson University, USA
Richard Dosselmann	University of Regina, Canada
Georgios Dounias	University of the Aegean, Greece
Gerard Dreyfus	École Supérieure de Physique et de Chimie Industrielles (ESPCI Paris), France

Mohamed El-Darieby	University of Regina, Canada
Zakaria Elberrichi	EEDIS/UDL SBA, Algeria
Maher Elshakankiri	University of Regina, Canada
Larbi Esmahi	Athabasca University, Canada
Ahmed Esmin	Federal University of Lavras, Brazil
Jocelyne Faddoul	Saint Mary's University, Canada
Rim Faiz	University of Carthage, Tunisia
Behrouz Far	University of Calgary, Canada
Atefeh Farzindar	University of Southern California, USA
Laurence-Léa Fontaine	Université du Québec à Montréal, Canada
Kim Fontaine-Skronski	Montreal Institute of International Studies, Canada
Enrico Francesconi	ITTIG-CNR, Italy
Hamido Fujita	Iwate Prefectural University, Japan
Michel Gagnon	Polytechnique Montreal, Canada
Sebastien Gambs	Université du Québec à Montréal, Canada
Yong Gao	The University of British Columbia, Canada
Nicolás García-Pedrajas	University of Córdoba, Spain
Vincent Gautrais	University of Montreal, Canada
Nadia Ghazzali	Université du Québec à Trois-Rivières, Canada
Nacira Ghoualmi-Zine	Badji Mokhtar University and Networks and Systems Laboratory, Algeria
Iker Gondra	St. Francis Xavier University, Canada
Maciej Grzenda	Orange Labs Poland and Warsaw University of Technology, Poland
Hans W. Guesgen	Massey University, New Zealand
Zahia Guessoum	Université de Paris 6, France
Abhishek Gupta	McGill University and District 3 Innovation Center, Concordia University, Canada
Adlane Habed	University of Strasbourg, France
Allel Hadjali	LIAS/ENSMA, France
Tarfa Hamed	University of Guelph, Canada
Sofiane Hamrioui	University of Mulhouse, France
Tim Hendtlass	Swinburne University, Australia
Francisco Herrera	University of Granada, Spain
Mark Hoogendoorn	Vrije Universiteit Amsterdam, The Netherlands
Wen-Juan Hou	National Taiwan Normal University, Taiwan
Jimmy Huang	University of York, UK
Diana Inkpen	University of Ottawa, Canada
Aminul Islam	University of Louisiana at Lafayette, USA
Adel Jebali	Concordia University, Canada
He Jiang	Dalian University of Technology, China
Christophe Jouis	Université Pierre et Marie Curie, France
Vicente Julian	Universitat Politècnica de València, Spain
Richard Khoury	Laval University, Canada
Tetsuo Kinoshita	Tohoku University, Japan
Frank Klawonn	Ostfalia University of Applied Sciences, Germany

Leila Kosseim	Concordia University, Canada
Lars Kotthoff	University of Wyoming, USA
Dariusz Krol	Wrocław University of Technology, Poland
Adam Krzyzak	Concordia University, Canada
Binod Kumar	JSPM's Jayawant Institute of Computer Applications, India
Philippe Langlais	University of Montreal, Canada
Guy Lapalme	University of Montreal, Canada
Daniel Le Métayer	Inria, France
Florence Le Priol	Paris-Sorbonne University, France
Fuhua Lin	Athabasca University, Canada
Pawan Lingras	Saint Mary's University, Canada
Samir Loudni	Université de Caen Basse-Normandie, France
Dominic Martin	McGill University, Canada
Mohamed El Bachir Menai	King Saud University, Saudi Arabia
Robert Mercer	University of Western Ontario, Canada
Marie-Jean Meurs	Université du Québec à Montréal (UQAM), Canada
Shamima Mithun	Concordia University, Canada
Abidalrahman Moh'D	Dalhousie University, Canada
Malek Mouhoub	University of Regina, Canada
Ayahiko Niimi	Future University Hakodate, Japan
Roger Nkambou	Université du Québec À Montréal (UQAM), Canada
Seyednaser Nourashrafeddin	Dalhousie University, Canada
Samir Ouchani	University of Luxembourg, Luxembourg
Anca Pascu	University of Brest, France
Barbara Pes	Università degli Studi di Cagliari, Italy
Eric Poirier	Université du Québec à Trois-Rivières, Canada
Dilip Pratihar	Indian Institute of Technology, India
Amine Rahmani	University of Saida, Algeria
Sheela Ramanna	University of Winnipeg, Canada
Hamou Reda Mohamed	Université Dr Moulay Taher Saïda, Algeria
Robert Reynolds	Wayne State University, USA
Louis Rompré	Université du Québec à Montréal, Canada
Kaushik Roy	North Carolina A&T State University, USA
Samira Sadaoui	University of Regina, Canada
Fatiha Sadat	UQAM, Canada
Mehdi Sadeqi	University of Regina, Canada
Gregorio Sainz-Palmero	Universidad de Valladolid, Spain
Eugene Santos	Dartmouth College, USA
Khaled Shaalan	The British University in Dubai, UAE
Weiming Shen	National Research Council Canada
Shubhashis Kumar Shil	University of Regina, Canada
Marina Sokolova	University of Ottawa and Institute for Big Data Analytics, Canada
Joao Sousa	TU Lisbon, IST, Portugal

Contents

Evolutionary Computation

Expert Systems and Robotics

Knowledge Representation

Machine Learning

Meta-Heuristics

Multi-Agent Systems

Natural Language Processing

Neural Networks

Data Science, Privacy, and Security

Intelligent Systems Approaches in Information Extraction

Artificial Intelligence, Law and Justice

Constraint Solving and Optimization

A Method for the Online Construction of the Set of States of a Markov Decision Process Using Answer Set Programming

Leonardo Anjoletto Ferreira[1]([✉]), Reinaldo A. C. Bianchi[2], Paulo E. Santos[2], and Ramon Lopez de Mantaras[3]

[1] Accesstage Tecnologia S.A., São Paulo, Brazil
leonardo.ferreira@accesstage.com.br
[2] Artificial Intelligence in Automation Group, Centro Universitário FEI,
São Bernardo do Campo, Brazil
{rbianchi,psantos}@fei.edu.br
[3] Institut d'Investigació en Intelligéncia Artificial,
Spanish National Research Council, Barcelona, Spain
mantaras@iiia.csic.es

Abstract. Non-stationary domains, that change in unpredicted ways, are a challenge for agents searching for optimal policies in sequential decision-making problems. This paper presents a combination of Markov Decision Processes (MDP) with Answer Set Programming (ASP), named *Online ASP for MDP* (oASP(MDP)), which is a method capable of constructing the set of domain states while the agent interacts with a changing environment. oASP(MDP) updates previously obtained policies, learnt by means of Reinforcement Learning (RL), using rules that represent the domain changes observed by the agent. These rules represent a set of domain constraints that are processed as ASP programs reducing the search space. Results show that oASP(MDP) is capable of finding solutions for problems in non-stationary domains without interfering with the action-value function approximation process.

1 Introduction

A key issue in Artificial Intelligence (AI) is to equip autonomous agents with the ability to operate in changing domains by adapting the agents' processes at a cost that is equivalent to the complexity of the domain changes. This ability is called *elaboration tolerance* [1,2]. Consider, for instance, an autonomous robot learning to navigate in an unknown environment. Unforeseen events may happen that could block passages (or open previously unavailable ones). The agent should be able to find new solutions in this changed domain using the knowledge previously acquired plus the knowledge acquired from the observed changes in

P. E. Santos—Supported by PITE FAPESP-IBM grant 2016/18792-9.
R. L. de Mantaras—Partially supported by Generalitat de Catalunya 2017 SGR 172.

the environment, without having to operate a complete code-rewriting, or start a new cycle of domain-exploration from scratch.

Reinforcement Learning (RL) is an AI framework in which an agent interacts with its environment in order to find a sequence of actions (a policy) to perform a given task [3]. RL is capable of finding optimal solutions to Markov Decision Processes (MDP) without assuming total information about the problem's domain. However, in spite of having the optimal solution to a particular task, a RL agent may still perform poorly on a new task, even if the latter is similar to the former [4]. Therefore, Reinforcement Learning alone does not provide elaboration-tolerant solutions. Non-monotonic reasoning can be used as a tool to increase the generality of domain representations [1] and may provide the appropriate element to build agents more adaptable to changing situations. In this work we consider Answer Set Programming (ASP) [5,6], which is a declarative non-monotonic logic programming language, to bridge the gap between RL and elaboration tolerant solutions. The present paper tackles this problem by introducing a novel algorithm: *Online ASP for MDP* (oASP(MDP)), that updates previously obtained policies, learned by means of Reinforcement Learning (RL), using rules that represent the domain changes as observed by the agent. These rules are constructed by the agent in an *online* fashion (i.e., as the agent perceives the changes) and they impose constraints on the domain states that are further processed by an ASP engine, reducing the search space. Tests performed in non-stationary non-deterministic grid worlds show that, not only oASP(MDP) is capable of finding the action-value function for an RL agent and, consequently, the optimal solution, but also that using ASP does not hinder the performance of a learning agent and can improve the overall agent's performance.

To model an oASP(MDP) learning agent (Sect. 3), we propose the combination of Markov Decision Processes and Reinforcement Learning (Sect. 2.1) with ASP (Sect. 2.2). Tests were performed in two different non-stationary non-deterministic grid worlds (Sect. 4), whose results show a considerable increase in the agent's performances when compared with a RL base algorithm, as presented in Sects. 4.1 and 4.2.

2   Background

This section introduces Markov Decision Processes, Reinforcement Learning and Answer Set Programming that are the foundations of the work reported in this paper.

2.1   MDP and Reinforcement Learning

In a sequential decision making problem, an agent is required to execute a series of actions in an environment in order to find the solution of a given problem. Such sequence of actions, that forms a feasible solution, is known as a policy (π) which leads the agent from an initial state to a goal state [7,8]. Given a set of feasible solutions, an optimal policy π^* can be found by using Bellman's Principle of Optimality [8], which states that "an optimal policy has the property that whatever the initial state and initial decision are, the remaining decisions must constitute an optimal policy with regard to the state resulting from the first decision"; π^* can be defined as the policy that maximises/minimises a desired reward/cost function.

A formalisation that can be used to describe sequential decision making problems is a Markov Decision Process (MDP) that is defined as a tuple $\langle \mathcal{S}, \mathcal{A}, \mathcal{T}, \mathcal{R} \rangle$, where:

- $\mathcal{S}$ is the set of states that can be observed in the domain;
- $\mathcal{A}$ is the set of actions that the agent can execute;
- $\mathcal{T} : \mathcal{S} \times \mathcal{A} \times \mathcal{S} \mapsto [0, 1]$ is the transition function that provides the probability of, being in $s \in \mathcal{S}$ and executing $a \in \mathcal{A}$, reaching the future state $s' \in \mathcal{S}$;
- $\mathcal{R} : \mathcal{S} \times \mathcal{A} \times \mathcal{S} \mapsto \mathbb{R}$ is the reward function that provides a real number when executing $a \in \mathcal{A}$ in the state $s \in \mathcal{S}$ and observing $s' \in \mathcal{S}$ as the future state.

One method that can be used to find an optimal policy for MDPs, which does not need *a priori* knowledge of the transition and reward functions, is the reinforcement learning model-free off-policy method known as Q-Learning [3,9].

Given an MDP $\mathcal{M}$, Q-Learning learns while an agent interacts with its environment by executing an action a_t in the current state s_t and observing both the future state s_{t+1} and the reward r_{t+1}. With these observations, Q-Learning updates an action-value function $Q(s, a)$ using $Q(s_t, a_t) \leftarrow Q(s_t, a_t) + \alpha.(r_{t+1} + \gamma \cdot \max_a Q(s_{t+1}, a) - Q(s_t, a_t))$, where α is the learning rate and γ is a discount factor. By using these reward values to approximate a $Q(s, a)$ function that maps a real value to pairs of states and actions, Q-Learning is capable of finding π^* which maximises the reward function. Since Q-Learning is a well-known and largely used RL method, we omit its detailed description here, which can be found in [3,9].

Although Q-Learning does not need information about $\mathcal{T}$ and $\mathcal{R}$, it still needs to know the set $\mathcal{S}$ of states before starting the interaction with the environment. For finding this set, this work uses Answer Set Programming.

2.2 Answer Set Programming

Answer Set Programming (ASP) is a declarative non-monotonic logic programming language that has been successfully used for NP-complete problems such as planning [6,10,11].

An ASP rule is represented as $A \leftarrow L_1, L_2, \ldots, L_n$ where A is an atom (the head of the rule) and the conjunction of literals $L_1, L_2, \ldots, L_n$ is the rule's body.

An ASP program Π is a set of rules in the form of Formula 2.2. ASP is based on the stable model semantics of logic programs [12]. A stable model of Π is an interpretation that makes every rule in Π true, and is a minimal model of Π. ASP programs are executed by computing stable models, which is usually accomplished by inference engines called answer set solvers [12].

Two important aspects of ASP are its third truth value for *unknown*, along with *true* and *false*, and its two types of negation: strong (or classical) negation and weak negation, representing *negation as failure*. As it is defined over stable models semantics, ASP respects the rationality that *one shall not believe anything one is not forced to believe* [5].

Although ASP does not allow explicit reasoning with or about probabilities, ASP's choice rules are capable of generating distinct outcomes for the same input. I.e., given a current state s and an action a, it is possible to describe in an ASP logic program states $s1$, $s2$ and $s3$ as possible outcomes of executing a in s as "1{ s1, s2, s3 }1 :- a, s." Such choice rules can be read as "given that s and a are true, choose at least one and at maximum of one state from $s1$, $s2$ and $s3$". Thus, the answer sets [s, a, s1], [s, a, s2] and [s, a, s3] represent the possible transitions that are the effects of executing action a on state s.

This work assumes that for each state $s \in S$ there is an ASP logic program with choice rules describing the consequences of each action $a \in \mathcal{A}_s$ (where $\mathcal{A}_s \subseteq \mathcal{A}$ is the set of actions for the state s). ASP programs can also be used to represent domain constraints: the allowed or forbidden states or actions. In this context, to find a set S of an MDP and its $Q(s, a)$ function is to find every answer set for every state that the agent is allowed to visit, i.e. every allowed transition for each state-action pair. In this paper ASP is used to find the set of states S of an MDP and Q-Learning is used to approximate $Q(s, a)$ without assuming prior knowledge of $\mathcal{T}$ and $\mathcal{R}$. The next section describes this idea in more detail.

3   Online ASP for MDP: oASP(MDP)

Given sets S and $\mathcal{A}$ of an MDP, a RL method M can approximate an action-value function $Q(s, a)$. If S is constructed state by state while the agent is interacting with the world, M is still able to approximate $Q(s, a)$, as it only uses the current and past states for that. By using choice rules in ASP, it is possible to describe a transition $t(s, a, s')$ in the form 1{s'}1 :- s, a for each action $a \in \mathcal{A}_s$ and each state $s \in S$. By describing possible transitions for each action in each state as a logic program, an ASP engine can be used to provide a set of observed states S_o, a set of actions $\mathcal{A}_s$ for each state and, finally, an tabular action-value function defined from the interaction with the environment, that can be used to further operate in this environment and can be used by a RL method to find the optimal policy. This is the essence of the oASP(MDP) method, represented in Algorithm 1.

Although the example that follows and the experiments being performed with a simple description of states, actions and transitions, ASP can be used to describe more complex domains, such as the ones used by [4,13] which may have a set of restrictions. However, the gridworld used in this work allows the complete control over the parameters used for the experiments and the environment's behaviour, thus allowing the observation of different aspects of the algorithm and how it responds to different changes in the non-stationary environment.

Input: The set of actions $\mathcal{A}$, an action-value function approximation method M and a number of episodes n.
Output: The approximated $Q(s, a)$ function.

1   Initialize the set of observed states $\mathcal{S}_o = \varnothing$
2   **while** *number of episodes performed is less than n* **do**
3   **repeat**
4   Observe the current state s
5   **if** $s \notin \mathcal{S}_o$ **then**
6   Add s to the set of states $\mathcal{S}_o$.
7   Choose and execute a random action $a \in \mathcal{A}$.
8   Observe the future state s'.
9   Update state s logic program with observed transition adding a choice rule.
10   Update $Q(s, a)$'s description by finding every answer set for each state s added to $\mathcal{S}_o$ in this episode.
11   **else**
12   Choose an action $a \in \mathcal{A}$ as defined by M.
13   Execute the chosen action a.
14   Observe the future state s'.
15   Update $Q(s, a)$'s value as defined by M.
16   Update the current state $s \leftarrow s'$.
17   **until** *the end of the episode*

Algorithm 1. The oASP(MDP) Algorithm.

In order to illustrate oASP(MDP) (Algorithm 1), let's consider the grid world in Fig. 1, and an oASP(MDP) agent, initially located at the state "S" (blue cell in the grid), that is capable of executing any action in the following set: $\mathcal{A} =\{$ *go up, go down, go left, go right*$\}$. This grid world has walls (represented by the letter "W"), that are cells where the agent cannot occupy and through which it is unable to pass. If an agent moves toward a wall (or toward an external border of the grid) it stays at its original location. When the interaction with the environment starts, the agent has only information about the set of actions $\mathcal{A}$. The set of observed states $\mathcal{S}_o$ is initially empty.

At the beginning of the agent's interactions with the environment, the agent observes the initial state $s0$ and verifies if it is in $\mathcal{S}_o$. Since $s0 \notin \mathcal{S}_o$, the agent adds $s0$ to $\mathcal{S}_o$ (line 6 of Algorithm 1) and executes a random action, let this action be *go up*. As a consequence of this choice, the agent moves to a new state $s1$ (the cell above S) and receives a reward $r0$. At this moment, the agent has information about the previous state, allowing it to write the choice rule "$1\{s1\}1 : - s0, go\ up$" as an ASP logic program. In this first interaction, the only answer set that can be found for this choice rule is "$[s0, go\ up, s1]$". With this information the agent can initialize a $Q(s0, go\ up)$ and update this value using the reward $r0$ (line 15).

After this first interaction, the agent is in the state $s1$ (the cell above S). Again, this is an unknown state ($s1 \notin \mathcal{S}_o$), thus, as with the previous state, the agent adds $s1$ to $\mathcal{S}_o$, chooses a random action, let it be *go up* again, and executes this action in the environment. By performing *go up* in this state, the agent hits a wall and stays in the same state. With this observation, the agent writes the choice rule "$1\{s1\}1 : -s1, go\,up$" and updates the value of $Q(s1, go\,up)$ using the received reward $r1$.

Since the agent is in the same state as in the previous interaction, it knows the consequence of the action *go up* in this state, but has no information about any other actions for this state. At this moment, the agent selects an action using the action-selection function defined by the learning method M and executes it in the environment. For example, let it choose *go down*, returning to the blue cell (S). The state $s1$ has now two choice rules: "$1\{s1\}1 : -s1, go\,up$" and "$1\{s0\}1 : -s1, go\,down$" which lead to the answer sets "$[s1, go\,up]$" and "$[s1, go\,down, s0]$" respectively. Once again, the agent updates the $Q(s1, go\,up)$ function using the method described in M with the reward $r2$ received. After this transition, the agent finds itself once again in the initial state and continues the domain exploration just described. If, for example, the agent chooses to execute the action *go up* again, but due to the non-deterministic nature of the environment, the agent goes to the state on the right of the blue square, then a new state $s2$ is observed and the choice rule for the previous state is updated to "$1\{s1, s2\}1 : -s0, go\,up$". The answer sets that can be found considering this choice rule are "$[s0, go\,up, s1]$" and "$[s0, go\,up, s2]$". With the reward $r3$ received, the agent updates the value of $Q(s0, go\,up)$.

The learning process of oASP(MDP) continues according to the chosen action-value function approximation method (from line 11 onwards). After a number of interactions with the environment, the oASP(MDP) agent has executed every possible action in every state that *is possible to be visited* and has the complete environment description. Note that this method excludes states of the MDP that are unreachable by the agent, which improves the efficiency of a RL agent in cases that the environment imposes state constrains (as we shall see in the next section).

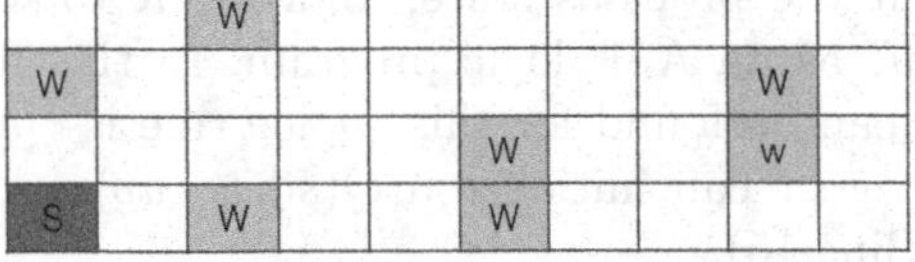

Fig. 1. Example of a randomly generated grid world. (Color figure online)

The next section presents the tests applied to evaluate oASP(MDP) implemented with Q-Learning as the action-value function approximation method M.

4   Tests and Results

The oASP(MDP) algorithm was evaluated with tests performed in non-deterministic, non-stationary, grid-world domains. Two test sets were considered where, in each set, one of the following domain variables was randomly changed: *the number and location of walls in the grid* (Sect. 4.1), and *the transition probabilities* (Sect. 4.2).

Four actions were allowed in the test domains considered in this work: *go up, go down, go left* and *go right*. Each action has a predefined probability of conducting the agent in the desired direction and also for moving the agent to an orthogonal (undesired) location. The transition probability for each action depends on the grid world and will be defined for each test, as described below. In all tests, the initial state was fixed at the lower-leftmost square (e.g., cell 'S' in Fig. 1) and the goal state fixed in the upper-rightmost square (e.g., cell 'G' in Fig. 1).

In the test domains, walls were distributed randomly in the grid as obstacles. For each grid, the ratio of walls per grid size is defined. The initial and goal states are the only cells that do not accept obstacles. Wall's placement in the grid changed at the 1000th and 2000th episodes during each test trial. An example of a grid used in this work is shown in Fig. 1.

Results show the data obtained from executing Q-Learning and oASP(MDP) (with Q-Learning as the action-value function approximation method) in the same environment configuration. The values used for the RL variables were: learning rate $\alpha = 0.2$, discount factor $\gamma = 0.9$, exploration/exploitation rate for the ϵ-greedy action selection method: $\epsilon = 0.1$ and the maximum number of steps in an episode is 1000.

For Q-Learning, the agent starts the interaction with a priori knowledge of the complete $Q(s, a)$ table and it only approximates the values. When the environment changes, the agent is presented with a new $Q(s, a)$ table describing the new environment and the learning process starts all over. For ASP(Q-Learning), the agent starts knowing only the set of actions, with the set of states, transition function and $Q(s, a)$ table being constructed during the interaction. When a change occurs in the environment, the agent doesn't receive any information about the change or how it changed and continues the learning process with the same $Q(s, a)$ table from the previous interaction, modifying it as necessary.

In each test, three variables were used to compare Q-Learning and oASP(MDP). First, the root-mean-square deviation (RMSD), that provides information related to the convergence of the methods by comparing values of the $Q(s, a)$ function in the current episode with respect to that obtained in the previous episode. Second, we considered the return (sum of the rewards) received in an episode. Third, the number of steps needed to go from the initial state to the goal state was evaluated. The results obtained were also compared with that of an agent using the optimal policy in a deterministic grid world (the best performance possible, shown as a red-dashed line in the results below).

For oASP(MDP), the number of state-action pairs known by the agent was also measured and compared with the size of Q-Learning's fixed $Q(s,a)$ tabular implementation. This variable provides information of how far an oASP(MDP) agent is from knowing the complete environment along with how much the $Q(s,a)$ function could be reduced.

The test domains and related results are described in detail in the next sections.

4.1   First Test: Changes in the Wall–Free-Space Ratio

In the first test, the size of the grid was fixed to 10×10 and the transition probabilities were assigned at 90% for moving on the desired direction and 5% for moving in each of the two directions that are orthogonal to the desired. In this test, changes in the environment occurred in the number and location of walls in the grid. Initially the domain starts with no walls (0%), then it changes to a world where 10% of the grid is occupied by walls placed at random locations and, finally, the grid world changes to a situation where 25% of the grid is occupied by walls. Each change occurs after 1000 episodes.

The results obtained in the first test are represented in Fig. 2. Figure 2a shows that the RMSD values of oASP(MDP) decrease faster than those of Q-Learning, thus converging to the optimal policy ahead of Q-Learning. It is worth observing that when a change occurs in the environment (at episodes 1000 and at 2000) there is no increase in oASP(MDP) RMSD values, contrasting with the significant increase in Q-Learning's values. A similar behaviour is shown in Fig. 2e, where there is no change in the number of steps of oASP(MDP) after a change occurs, at the same time that Q-learning number of steps increase considerably at that point.

The return values obtained in this test are shown in Fig. 2c, where it can be observed that both oASP(MDP) and Q-learning reach the maximum value together during the initial episodes, but there is no reduction in the return values of oASP(MDP) when the environment changes, whereas Q-learning returns drop to the initial figures.

Figure 2g shows the number of state-action pairs that oASP(MDP) has found for the grid world. Values obtained after the 15th episode were omitted since they presented no variation. This figure shows that oASP(MDP) has explored every state of the grid world and performed every action allowed in each state, resulting in a complete description of the environment. Since oASP(MDP) has provided the complete description of the environment, the agent that uses oASP(MDP) optimizes the same action-value function as the agent that uses Q-Learning, thus the optimal policy found by both agents is the same. Due to the exploration of the environment performed in the beginning of the interaction, before the 10th episode the agent has executed every action in every possible state at least once and, as can be seen in line 6 of Algorithm 1, the agent then uses the underlying RL procedure to find the action-value function.

4.2   Second Test: Changes in the Transition Probabilities

In this test, the grid was fixed at a 10×10 size, with wall–free-space ratio fixed at 25%. Changes in the environment occurred with respect to the transition probabilities. Initially, the agent's actions had 50% of probability for moving the agent in the desired direction and 25% for moving it in each of the two orthogonal directions. The first change set the probabilities at 75% (assigned to the desired action effect) and 12.5% (for the directions orthogonal to the desired). The final change assigned 90% for moving in the desired direction and 5% for moving in each of the orthogonal directions.

The RMSD values for oASP(MDP), in this case, decreased faster than those of Q-Learning, reaching zero before the first change occurred, while Q-Learning at that point had not yet converged, as shown in Fig. 2b. Analogously to the first test, there is no change in RMSD values of oASP(MDP) when the environment changes, whereas Q-learning presents re-initializations. In the results on return and the number of steps, shown in Figs. 2d and f respectively, the performance of oASP(MDP) improves faster than the Q-Learning performance when there is a change in the environment. This is explained by the fact that, after oASP(MDP) approximates the action-value function (in the periods between the changes), when a change occurs, the information about it, acquired by the agent, is used to find solutions in the new world situation. In this case, the current action-value function is simply updated. Q-Learning, on the other hand, is restarted at each time a change occurs, resulting in the application of an inefficient policy in the new environment.

The number of state-action pairs that oASP(MDP) was able to describe is shown in Fig. 2h. Once more, values obtained after the 15th episode were omitted, as they present no variation after this point. Analogous to the results obtained in the first experiment, oASP(MDP) was capable of executing at least once every allowed action in every state possible to be visited. As before, by exploring the environment oASP(MDP) could efficiently find the set of allowed states, defining the complete $Q(s, a)$.

In summary, the tests performed in the domains considered show that the information previously obtained is beneficial to an agent that learns by interacting with a changing environment. The action-value function obtained by oASP(MDP) before a change occurs accelerates the approximation of this function in a new version of the environment, avoiding the various re-initializations observed in Q-learning alone (as shown in Fig. 2). However, as the action-value function approximation method used in oASP(MDP) (in this work) was Q-Learning, the policies learnt by oASP(MDP) and Q-Learning alone were analogous. This can be observed when comparing the curves for oASP(MDP) and Q-Learning in Fig. 2 after convergence, noticing also that they keep the same distance with respect to the best performance possible (red-dashed lines in the graphs).

Tests were performed in virtual machines in AWS EC2 with t2.micro configuration, which provides one virtual core of an Intel Xeon at 2.4 GHz, 1 GB of RAM and 8 GB of SSD with standard Debian 8 (Jessie). oASP(MDP) was

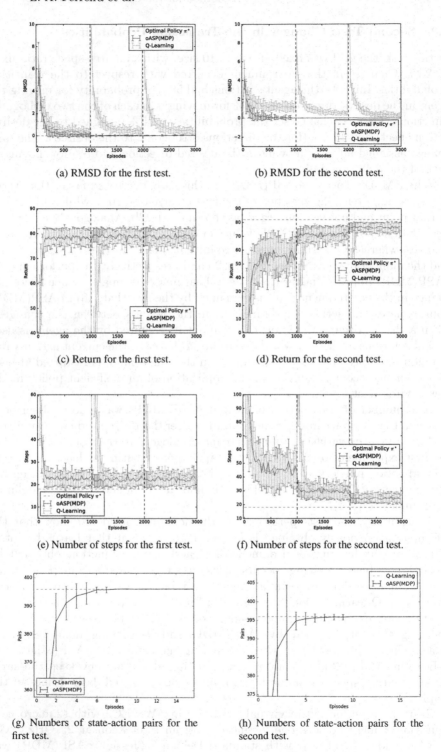

(a) RMSD for the first test.

(b) RMSD for the second test.

(c) Return for the first test.

(d) Return for the second test.

(e) Number of steps for the first test.

(f) Number of steps for the second test.

(g) Numbers of state-action pairs for the first test.

(h) Numbers of state-action pairs for the second test.

Fig. 2. Results for the first and second tests. (Color figure online)

implemented in Python 3.4 using ZeroMQ for providing messages exchanges between agent and environment and Clingo [14] was used as the ASP Engine. The source code for the tests can be found in the following (anonymous) URL: http://bit.ly/2k03lkl.

5   Related Work

Previous attempts at combining RL with ASP include [10], which proposes the use of ASP to find a pre-defined plan for a RL agent. This plan is described as a hierarchical MDP and RL is used to find the optimal policy for this MDP. However, changes in the environment, as used in the present work, were not considered in [10].

Analogous methods were proposed by [11,15], in which an agent interacts with an environment and updates an action's cost function. While [15] uses the action language BC, [11] uses ASP to find a description of the environment. Although both methods consider action costs, none of them uses Reinforcement Learning and they do not deal with changes in the action-value function description during the agent's interaction with the environment.

An approach to non-deterministic answer set programs is P-Log [16,17]. While P-Log is capable of calculating transition probabilities from sampling, it is not capable of using this information to generate policies. Also P-Log does not consider action costs. Thus, although P-Log can be used to find the transition function, it cannot find the optimal solution, as proposed here.

Works related to non-stationary MDPs such as [18,19], which deal only with changes in reward function, are more associated with RL alone than with a hybrid method such as oASP(MDP), since RL methods are already capable of handling changes in the reward and transition functions. The advantage of ASP is to find the set of states so that it is possible to search for an optimal solution regardless of the agent's transition and reward functions.

A proposal that resembles oASP(MDP) is [4]. This method proposes the combination of deep learning to find a description to a set of states, which are then described as rules to a probabilistic logic program and, finally, a RL agent interacts with the environment using the results and learns the optimal policy.

The closest proposal to oASP(MDP) is DARLING [13]. Both methods combine ASP and RL in order to find a policy in planning domain by using ASP to represent and reason about the environment and RL to learn by interacting with this environment. But while oASP(MDP)'s approach is towards finding the optimal solution regarding action costs, DARLING uses a plan's length as an evaluation criteria and the policy with the minimum length considered the solution to DARLING may not be the optimal policy when considering Bellman's Optimality Policy. Furthermore, oASP(MDP) interacts with a mostly unknown environment (only the set of actions is known a priori), while DARLING needs sets of states and action along with the transition function to reason about the environment. However, a detailed comparison of all aspects of DARLING and oASP(MDP)'s approach is still needed.

6   Conclusion

This paper presented the method oASP(MDP) for approximating action-value functions of Markov Decision Processes, in non-stationary domains, with unknown set of states and unknown transition and reward functions. This method is defined on a combination of Reinforcement Learning (RL) and Answer Set Programming (ASP). The main advantage of RL is that it does not need *a priori* knowledge of transition and reward functions, but it relies on having a complete knowledge to the set of domain states. In oASP(MDP), ASP is used to construct the set of states of an MDP to be used by a RL algorithm. ASP programs representing domain states and transitions are obtained as the agent interacts with the environment. This provides an efficient solution to finding optimal policies in changing environments.

Tests were performed in two non-stationary non-deterministic grid-world domains, where each domain had one property of the grid world changed over time. In the first domain, the ratio of obstacles and free space in the grid was changed, whereas in the second domain changes occurred in the transition probabilities. The changes happened in intervals of 1000 episodes in both domains. Results show that, when a change occurs, oASP(MDP) (with Q-learning as the action-value function) is capable of approximating the $Q(s, a)$ function faster than Q-learning alone. Therefore, the combination of ASP with RL was effective in the definition of a method that provides more general (or more elaboration tolerant) solutions to changing domains than RL methods alone.

Future works are directed to working with both oASP(MDP) and DARLING in order to understand how one method can benefit with the other's approach and a new algorithm that combines ASP and MDP results from this combination.

References

1. McCarthy, J.: Generality in artificial intelligence. Commun. ACM **30**(12), 1030–1035 (1987)
2. McCarthy, J.: Elaboration tolerance. In: Proceedings of the Fourth Symposium on Logical Formalizations of Commonsense Reasoning (Common Sense 98), vol. 98, London, UK (1998)
3. Sutton, R.S., Barto, A.G.: Reinforcement Learning: An Introduction, 2nd edn. MIT Press, Cambridge (2015)
4. Garnelo, M., Arulkumaran, K., Shanahan, M.: Towards deep symbolic reinforcement learning. arXiv preprint arXiv:1609.05518 [cs], September 2016
5. Gelfond, M., Lifschitz, V.: The stable model semantics for logic programming. In: Kowalski, R., Bowen, K. (eds.) Proceedings of International Logic Programming Conference and Symposium, pp. 1070–1080. MIT Press, Cambridge (1988)
6. Lifschitz, V.: Answer set programming and plan generation. Artif. Intell. **138**(1), 39–54 (2002)
7. Bellman, R.: A Markovian decision process. Indiana Univ. Math. J. **6**(4), 679–684 (1957)
8. Bellman, R.E., Dreyfus, S.E.: Applied Dynamic Programming, 4th edn. Princeton University Press, Princeton (1971)

9. Watkins, C.J.C.H.: Learning from delayed rewards. Ph.D. thesis, University of Cambridge, England (1989)
10. Zhang, S., Sridharan, M., Wyatt, J.L.: Mixed logical inference and probabilistic planning for robots in unreliable worlds. IEEE Trans. Robot. **31**(3), 699–713 (2015)
11. Yang, F., Khandelwal, P., Leonetti, M., Stone, P.: Planning in answer set programming while learning action costs for mobile robots. In: AAAI Spring 2014 Symposium on Knowledge Representation and Reasoning in Robotics (AAAI-SSS) (2014)
12. Gelfond, M.: Answer sets. In: van Harmelen, F., Lifschitz, V., Porter, B. (eds.) Handbook of Knowledge Representation, pp. 285–316. Elsevier (2008)
13. Leonetti, M., Iocchi, L., Stone, P.: A synthesis of automated planning and reinforcement learning for efficient, robust decision-making. Artif. Intell. **241**, 103–130 (2016)
14. Gebser, M., Kaminski, R., Kaufmann, B., Schaub, T.: Answer Set Solving in Practice. Morgan & Claypool Publishers, San Rafael (2013)
15. Khandelwal, P., Yang, F., Leonetti, M., Lifschitz, V., Stone, P.: Planning in action language BC while learning action costs for mobile robots. In: Proceedings of the Twenty-Fourth International Conference on Automated Planning and Scheduling, ICAPS 2014, 21–26 June 2014, Portsmouth, New Hampshire, USA (2014)
16. Baral, C., Gelfond, M., Rushton, N.: Probabilistic reasoning with answer sets. Theory Pract. Log. Program. **9**(1), 57 (2009)
17. Gelfond, M., Rushton, N.: Causal and probabilistic reasoning in P-log. In: Heuristics, Probabilities and Causality. A Tribute to Judea Pearl, pp. 337–359 (2010)
18. Even-Dar, E., Kakade, S.M., Mansour, Y.: Online Markov decision processes. Math. Oper. Res. **34**(3), 726–736 (2009)
19. Yu, J.Y., Mannor, S., Shimkin, N.: Markov decision processes with arbitrary reward processes. Math. Oper. Res. **34**(3), 737–757 (2009)

Hardware/Software Co-design for Template Matching Using Cuckoo Search Optimization

Alexandre de Vasconcelos Cardoso[1,2], Nadia Nedjah[2],
and Luiza de Macedo Mourelle[3(✉)]

[1] Brazilian Navy Weapons Systems Directorate, Brazilian Navy,
Rio de Janeiro, Brazil
alexvcardoso@yahoo.com.br
[2] Department of Electronics Engineering and Telecommunication,
Engineering Faculty, State University of Rio de Janeiro, Rio de Janeiro, Brazil
nadia@eng.uerj.br
[3] Department of Systems Engineering and Computation, Engineering Faculty,
State University of Rio de Janeiro, Rio de Janeiro, Brazil
ldmm@eng.uerj.br

Abstract. Template matching is an important method used for object tracking in order to find a given pattern within a frame sequence. Pearson's Correlation Coefficient is applied to each image pixel to quantify the degree of similarity between two images. To reduce the processing time, a dedicated co-processor, responsible of performing the correlation computation, is used. Cuckoo Search is applied to improve the search for the maximum correlation point between the image and the template. The search process is implemented in software and is run by an embedded general purpose processor. Results are compared to those previously obtained when using Particle Swarm Optimization for the search process, while keeping the same hardware.

1 Introduction

Template Matching [1,2] is one of the most used techniques for tracking patterns in images. It consists of finding a pre-defined small image, termed as the template, inside a larger image. The normalized cross correlation is widely used because of its properties of invariance to linear brightness and contrast variations [3]. Template matching is computationally expensive, especially when using large templates with an extensive image set [4].

This work uses a hardware/software co-design system implementation of template matching for tracking application. The software part consists of an optimized search for the maximum correlation point between the image and the template, using Cuckoo Search (CS) approach. The required computation of Pearson's Correlation Coefficient (PCC) is implemented in hardware via a dedicated co-processor in two different configurations: serial and pipeline [5,6].

© Springer International Publishing AG, part of Springer Nature 2018
M. Mouhoub et al. (Eds.): IEA/AIE 2018, LNAI 10868, pp. 16–21, 2018.
https://doi.org/10.1007/978-3-319-92058-0_2

Section 2 presents the template matching, correlation and CS concepts. In Sect. 3, there is the description of the hardware employed. In Sect. 4, the experiments to be executed are described and the obtained results are presented. Finally, in Sect. 5, we draw some conclusions and some new directions for future works.

2 Theoretical Background

Template matching (TM) is used in image processing to measure the degree of similarity between two images. The method compares selected portions of a main image against another [1]. After similarity evaluation considering all the possible images, the position inside the main image, where the pixels provide the highest correlation degree, is identified as the location of the pattern.

Among the similarity measures for template matching, the normalized cross correlation is often used [2,3]. PCC is a dimensionless measure of similarity between two variables due to a normalized cross-correlation process. For two images P and A, the PCC can be computed as defined in Eq. 1:

$$PCC(A, P) = \frac{\sum_{i=1}^{N}(p_i - \overline{p}) \times (a_i - \overline{a})}{\sqrt{\sum_{i=1}^{N}(p_i - \overline{p})^2 \times \sum_{i=1}^{N}(a_i - \overline{a})^2}}, \tag{1}$$

wherein N is the number of pixels, p_i is the intensity of each pixel i in the template P, $\overline{p}$ is the average intensity of the pixels of the template, a_i is the intensity of each pixel i in the patch A from the analyzed image and $\overline{a}$ is the average intensity of the pixels in the patch of the image A. The subtraction of the mean image from each pixel value causes invariance to global linear brightening changes. It is important that template P and patch A of the image must have the same dimensions.

CS is an optimization algorithm proposed by Yang [7], based on an aggressive strategy performed by some species of cuckoo birds. A female cuckoo invades a communal nest and lays its egg in it, where it can match the color of the eggs of the host [8]. As soon little cuckoo is born, it eliminates the other eggs to improve its chance to survive and it grows as if it were the only offspring of the host bird.

In Algorithm 1, all nests positions represent solutions in the search space, because the cuckoo lays its egg in a randomly chosen nest [8]. The best cuckoos are kept during generations to maintain the information of best fitness positions. Random walk is implemented via Lévy flights, used as global search strategy, whose step length is controlled by Lévy probability distribution, instead of Gaussian distribution. The length of step can also be scaled by an adjustable factor L, regarding the dimensionality of the problem, as shown in Eq. 2:

$$x_i^{t+1} = x_i^t + L \cdot Levy(\lambda), \tag{2}$$

wherein the parameters to be adjusted are Lévy flight scale factor L, number of cuckoos N, maximum number of generations M, discovering probability P_a and stop criterion.

Algorithm 1. Cuckoo Search Algorithm

Define objective function f(x);
Define L, N, M, P_a and stop criterion;
Generate initial population of N host nests x_i;
while $(t < M)$ or (stop criterion) **do**
    Get a cuckoo (say, i) randomly by Lévy flights and evaluate its quality/fitness;
    Choose a nest among n (say, j) randomly;
    if $(F_i > F_j)$ **then**
        Replace j by the new solution;
    end if;
    Abandon fraction (P_a) of worse nests and build new ones;
    Keep $(1 - P_a)$ best nests with high quality solutions;
    Rank the nest and find the best one;
end while;
Return best nest position.

Walia and Kapoor [9] used CS with Particle Filter (PF) to improve target recognizing process, despite of target rotations or scale changes. Merad *et al.* presented a multiple target tracking system to track customers in stores using Particle Filter [10].

3 Hardware Architecture

In hardware/software co-design [11], the final target architecture usually has software components executed by a soft processor, which is aided by dedicated hardware components developed especially for the application to implement some time consuming tasks [12,13].

Obtaining PCC values is the most time consuming computation of template matching. Therefore, it is implemented via a dedicated co-processor, in order to reduce the processing time and allow a real-time execution [5,6]. The pipeline version consists of three stages: the first one is responsible for computing the pixels average of the images to be compared; the second one is responsible for computing the three sums in Eq. 1; the third one is responsible for computing the main multiplication, the square-root and the division in Eq. 1. Furthermore, the search for the location with the maximum correlation degree is assisted by CS, executed as a software, by a general purpose processor.

4 Results

The proposed system is implemented using the *Smart Vision Development Kit* rev 1.2 (SVDK) of *Sensor to Image* [14] and it requires 11% of flip-flops, 39%

of LUTs, 25% of buffers and 69% of block RAMs. Because of synthesis time
constraints associated to the project, the co-processor runs at 25 MHz.

Figure 1 shows the images used in this work and the corresponding templates, highlighted by the inner square [15]. The number of cuckoos N is 50,
the discovering probability P_a is 25%, Lévy flight scale factor L is 15 and, as
stopping criterion, we set up to either establish an acceptable PCC threshold of
0.95 or a maximum of 10 iterations. This CS configuration was applied to find
templates with TM in less then 33 ms when using serial and parallel hardware
configurations.

   (a) Cars   (b) Pickup   (c) Sedan   (d) IR1

   (e) IR2   (f) IR3   (g) Truck   (h) Rcar

Fig. 1. Reference images used in the tests

The performance of the proposed system is evaluated using two scenarios:
CS_{HS}, which is the intelligent search using CS implemented in software whereby
PCCs are calculated by the proposed co-processor working in serial mode, with
a search window size of 101×101 pixels; CS_{HP}, which is the co-processor working in pipeline mode, also with a search window size of 101×101 pixels. In [5,6],
the same serial and pipeline hardware approaches were used with Particle Swarm
Optimization (PSO) as the search method, wherein PSO_{HS} and PSO_{HP} were the
serial mode and the parallel mode, respectively. In the present work, CS tracking
co-design approach performance is compared to PSO's in terms of execution time
and success rate.

The results obtained for CS_{HS} are given in Fig. 2. CS execution time was less
then PSO for all images. All average times obtained using this serial hardware
co-processor were under 33 ms, then accomplishing the necessary time to work in
real-time video tracking. During this approach, CS success rate was worse than
the one obtained by PSO for all images analyzed.

The results obtained for CS_{HP} are given in Fig. 3. The same configuration of
CS applied on CS_{HS} was used in CS_{HP}. CS results for execution time were the
best for seven of the eight pictures, and only one (*Sedan*) was similar to PSO_{HP}.

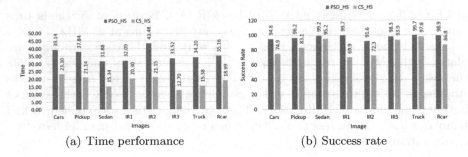

(a) Time performance   (b) Success rate

Fig. 2. Time (ms) and success rate performances for serial approach

For image $IR3$, CS had the lowest necessary time, but less than PSO average execution time for this image and for image $Cars$ it had the worst. The success rate obtained for CS_{HP} was similar to results obtained for CS_{HS}. For seven images, the results were lower than PSO_{HP} approach, the exception was $Truck$. The worst CS accuracy performance obtained was for $IR1$.

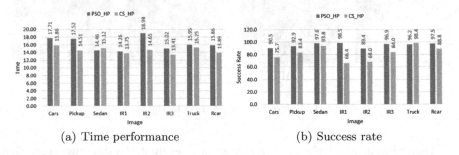

(a) Time performance   (b) Success rate

Fig. 3. Time (ms) and success rate performances for pipeline approach

5   Conclusion

CS time performance, obtained with co-processor using serial and pipeline approaches, was faster than that obtained using the same hardware and PSO, but was worse in accuracy. Both CS hardware approaches returned time performances fast enough to operate with 30 fps videos for all test images. Obtained success rates were similar in all CS configurations and normally worse than obtained by PSO approaches. When the size of the search window was reduced to simulate more components of the swarm looking for the target, CS in pipeline mode improved the success rate to values closer to 100%, with better results than PSO using the same search window.

As a future work, and in order to further improve the performance of the process, the co-processor design could be examined as to increase the operation frequency and the number of components of the swarm. Other intelligent search techniques could be implemented to obtain higher success rate when reaching real-time performance.

Acknowledgement. We thank the State of Rio de Janeiro Research Funding Agency (FAPERJ, http://www.faperj.br) and the Brazilian Navy (https://www.marinha.mil.br/) for funding this study.

References

1. Ahuja, K., Tuli, P.: Object recognition by template matching using correlations and phase angle method. Int. J. Adv. Res. Comput. Commun. Eng. **2**(3), 1368–1373 (2013)
2. Yilmaz, A., Javed, O., Shah, M.: Object tracking: a survey. ACM Comput. Surv. (CSUR) **38**(4), 13 (2006)
3. Perveen, N., Kumar, D., Bhardwaj, I.: An overview on template matching methodologies and its applications. IJRCCT **2**(10), 988–995 (2013)
4. Sharma, P., Kaur, M.: Classification in pattern recognition: a review. Int. J. Adv. Res. Comput. Sci. Softw. Eng. **3**(4), 3 (2013)
5. Tavares, Y.M.: Sistema integrado de hardware software para rastreamento de alvos. Master's thesis, UERJ, Rio de Janeiro, Brazil (2016)
6. Tavares, Y.M., Nedjah, N., de Macedo Mourelle, L.: Co-design system for template matching using dedicated co-processor and particle swarm optimization. In: Latin American Symposium on Circuits and Systems (2017)
7. Yang, X.S., Deb, S.: Cuckoo search via lévy flights. In: World Congress on Nature and Biologically Inspired Computing, NaBIC 2009, Coimbatore, India, pp. 210–214. IEEE (2009)
8. Fister Jr., I., Fister, D., Fister, I.: A comprehensive review of cuckoo search: variants and hybrids. Int. J. Math. Model. Numer. Optim. **4**(4), 387–409 (2013)
9. Walia, G.S., Kapoor, R.: Intelligent video target tracking using an evolutionary particle filter based upon improved cuckoo search. Expert Syst. Appl. **41**(14), 6315–6326 (2014)
10. Merad, D., Aziz, K.E., Iguernaissi, R., Fertil, B., Drap, P.: Tracking multiple persons under partial and global occlusions: application to customers behavior analysis. Pattern Recogn. Lett. **81**, 11–20 (2016)
11. Schelle, A., Stütz, P.: Visual communication with UAS: recognizing gestures from an airborne platform. In: Lackey, S., Chen, J. (eds.) VAMR 2017. LNCS, vol. 10280, pp. 173–184. Springer, Cham (2017). https://doi.org/10.1007/978-3-319-57987-0_14
12. Jarrah, A., Jamali, M.M., Hosseini, S.S.S.: Optimized FPGA based implementation of particle filter for tracking applications. In: NAECON IEEE National Aerospace and Electronics Conference, Dayton, USA, pp. 233–236. IEEE (2014)
13. Liu, W., Chen, H., Ma, L.: Moving object detection and tracking based on ZYNQ FPGA and ARM SOC. In: IET International Radar Conference 2015, Hangzhou, China, pp. 1–4. IET (2015)
14. SensorToImage: SVDK Hardware User Guide, revision 1.1. SensorToImage (2015)
15. Collins, R., Zhou, X., Teh, S.K.: An open source tracking testbed and evaluation web site. In: IEEE International Workshop on Performance Evaluation of Tracking and Surveillance, vol. 2, no. 6, p. 35 (2005)

Optimziation Methods for Beacon Based Foraging Algorithms

Christopher Sanford[✉] and Jae Oh

Syracuse University, Syracuse, NY 13203, USA
{clsanfor,jcoh}@syr.edu

Abstract. Beacon-based Robotic foraging is inspired by nature's ability to create efficient explorers and gatherers, and imposes a number of constraints on how agents can interact. In decentralized models, the robots must maintain chains of communication, effectively explore areas, and start collecting from discovered targets. Previous approaches have used a beacon-based technique, which is dependent on swarm size to environment size ratios, and do not have guarantees on finding all targets. This paper outlines the issues in these approaches and offers solutions to finding targets reliably, robust task allocations, and efficient beacon network. We verify our techniques by providing metrics of successful swarm size to environment size ratios, robot congestion improvement, and target utility independent measurements for gathering.

Keywords: Multi-agents · Foraging

1 Introduction

Robotic or automated foraging has become an interesting problem recently and combines many multi-disciplinary techniques to accomplish its goals. Automated foraging is given an unknown environment (structure, layout, existing entities, and desirable resources unknown) and is required to explore this environment to find targets. The robots are to navigate, map out, and efficiently cover the environment so that target collection can be done. Robots must repeatedly deliver items from discovered targets to the home base.

This continuous foraging is not a trivial problem, especially when there are no localization techniques. When localization is absent, robots must maintain a network of communication in some form. We assume no localization method, and thus we need to make up for this lack of navigational luxury.

The second aspect of foraging, continuous item retrieval, requires orienting and allocating robots to discovered targets. Some techniques utilize robots to create static waypoints for the retrieval process for navigation. However, static waypoints may waste the robots for the retrieval task. For this paper, we assume that we can feasibly create an optimal static waypoint network for robots to navigate, thus eliminating the need for mobile networks.

© Springer International Publishing AG, part of Springer Nature 2018
M. Mouhoub et al. (Eds.): IEA/AIE 2018, LNAI 10868, pp. 22–33, 2018.
https://doi.org/10.1007/978-3-319-92058-0_3

We look at a beacon based foraging algorithm proposed by Hoff et al. [6], and its multi-target extension done by Jiao et al. [4]. The approach Hoff et al. uses two types of agents (the extension uses three) Beacon, Walker (Explorer in the extension), and Worker (in [4]). The beacons work to map out the area by creating routes in the environments with themselves. The explorers search along the currently established network to find targets, or to become beacons to extend the network, and workers specifically only gather from found targets.

The previous algorithms solves the problem rudimentally, therefore has a number of fundamental issues such as task allocation (target assignment), congestion, and poorly utilized beacons. We present two algorithms: Rostering for controlling how robots are assigned to targets for gathering, and NetOpt for better utilizing beacons for discovering targets and possible reallocating as workers.

2   Related Work

Many Robotic foraging models are inspired by biological examples such as ants. Using ants as a primary example, they work in a rather stochastic way which can coordinate when necessary to accomplish food gathering. Though stochastic models have been studied in Adler and Gordon [1], we focus on a deterministic approach using only a minimal amount of random walking.

Below we outline the progression of foraging techniques and analysis that has proceeded this work. Generally foraging has been concerned with single targets, with only recently multiple targets becoming a topic of concern.

- Svennebring and Koenig have used visual markings to identify explored terrain [7]. This has the advantage of not necessarily needing additional robots to maintain mapping information, but physical markings can be unreliable depending on the material, and the visual identification capabilities of the robot.
- O'Hara et al. use statically deployed networks in their G.N.A.T.S. system to create potential fields to guide multi-agent systems perform distributed path planning [5]. Theirs has the advantage of being able to plan out the network, but not allowing optimized searching. Specifically, if the network has not been deployed optimally, or the area has been unexplored, their method will not work well.
- Barth [2] studied the deployable network, which allows beacons to be placed as the robots explore. This method has the advantage of having a more dynamic setup with the mapping data and doesn't rely on known information about the environment.
- Hoff et al. proposed two techniques to forage for a single target: A modified virtual pheromone and a multi-state beacon algorithm [6]. In the multi-state beacon algorithm, robots can either be a Beacon, an Explorer or a Worker. Each of these 'types' has a different task assigned to it. Robots can switch between 'types' according to instructions in the algorithm to accomplish their task of finding targets and moving between their targets and the home base.

Explorers explore the area for their target and have a chance to become beacons under the right circumstances. Beacons transmit information across the network of robots, and workers move between the base and the target using the beacon network. The algorithm assumes that the robots spawn out of the base one by one over a period. The first robots to spawn quickly become Beacons marking the location of the base. As more robots spawn out of the base, they begin to explore the map, indexing themselves based on the *cardinality* of Beacon robots in their vicinity. Over time the robots will spread out and create a network of beacons, and once the robots locate a target, they can use that network of beacons to move to and from the base and targets. These beacon type robots index themselves in two ways, ascending and descending from the home base. This creates a network which can relay information to the robots and also serves to create a path for the robots to follow once they find their target (food). Once the 'food' has been found some robots transition into worker types and move up the indexed beacons until they gather the 'food' and then return it to the home base. The algorithms handle dynamic foraging as with Barth's beacon setup and allow parameter tuning with the beacon based approach. We focus on an extension to the beacon method and analyze some of its parameter tunings.

– Jiao et al. provide an extension to Hoff's beacon based algorithm to deal with multiple targets [4]. The changes create the network into a tree like structure branching to each target and allow for workers to individually select targets to work with. The algorithm suffers from problems such as congestion and low beacon utilization, also present in Hoff's, but provides an initial effort to deal with multiple targets.

The above algorithms take advantage of storing mapping information somewhere and use this information to navigate without localization. Our approach will not use localization techniques, such as GPS, either; our algorithm relies on local communication for distributing navigation information as well as coordinating resource gathering.

Both Hoff's [6] and Jiao's [4] algorithms suffer three fundamental problems which will be addressed by our optimizations.

1. Target allocation: We need to ensure that targets have an adequate number of workers allocated when discovered. Since worker allocation is done via probability parameters ($Pr(Explorer \rightarrow Worker) = wprob$), robots can often be allocated too quickly to early targets or not quickly enough and most explorers become beacons.
2. Robot congestion: There tend to be too many robots converging to a target that can impede robots motion. This happens due to no control flow or coordination done between robots assigning themselves to targets.
3. Beacon optimization: The previous algorithms can use beacons inefficiently and lack the ability to reuse beacons when not being utilized.

3   The Rostering Technique

The multi-target extension [4] does not make any guarantees about target allocation, often having workers flock to the first target found, and any subsequent targets have little or no gathering workers. The parameter tuning for this algorithm does not add any guarantees to it as well, and thus needs more control. Due to the same occurrence, too many workers flocking to one target causes traffic congestion impeding the traffic of mobile robots and slowing down the gathering process. Lastly, beacons are not necessarily allocated optimally, either not heading towards a target, or deploys themselves nearby other beacons when the network could spread out further.

We propose the rostering algorithm to help with both target allocation and robot congestion, with beacon optimization handled in a later section. To elaborate on what these issues entail, we need to see what happen when targets are found. As soon as a target is found, the cardinality information will propagate across the network and will be broadcasted to explorers. Explorers will check to become a worker at each iteration at a fixed problem probability ($P(Exp \rightarrow Worker) = wprob$), and if $wprob$ of too large most of the explorers will quickly become workers. Large probabilities ($wprob \geq 0.001$) will lead to explorers becoming workers far too quickly and prevents further exploration.

To remedy both congestion and target allocation we propose the rostering algorithm that can control the number of robots going between different targets. Taking advantage that beacons already broadcast target information, they now use a new structure to allocate robots to particular targets shown below.

```
class RosteringRobot extends Robot {
    map<target, set<Robot>> roster;
}
```

The structure assigns for each target a set of robots to work on it. When a beacon broadcasts its cardinality information, it will also broadcast roster openings, and nearby explorers can choose to join in on these rosters. As these rosters fill up, they are broadcasted throughout the network to maintain a global structure. To use this structure when an explorer hears an open roster with a given fixed probability, it will assign itself to a target on that roster. To prevent too many robots assigning themselves to a specific target every robot has a maximal roster size that it will ignore. This maximal amount is fixed before the foraging starts and is done as such since global synchronization of these decisions is costly. This process is demonstrated below.

---

function ROSTERINGEXPLORER()
    Let *robots* ← set of nearby robots;
    Let *bcasts* ← set of heard broadcasts;
    Let *targets* ← set of nearby targets;
    Let *map* ← $\bigcup_{m \in bcasts} m$;
    if (*targets* $\neq \emptyset$ and $\exists t \in targets, map[t] \neq START$) or $|bcasts| = 1$ **then**
        type ← *BEACON*;
    else if $|keys(map)| > 0$ and *open_roster*() **then**
        With the probability of p, *type* ← *WORKER*
        assignSelfToRoster();
    else
        RandomWalk();

One thing to note is the **assignSelfToRoster()** procedure; The explorer broadcasts a message and if a beacon hears this message the algorithm will function correctly. To see how this works we look at the modified beacon procedure below.

---

function ROSTERBEACON()
    Beacon();
    Broadcast *roster*
    Let *bcasts* ← set of heard broadcasts;
    Let *bots* ← set of nearby robots;
    for $t \in knownTargets()$ **do**
        if $t \notin keys(roster)$ **then**
            $roster[t] = \{\}$;
    for $(t \mapsto assigned) \in roster$ **do**
        $roster[t] = roster[t] \cup assigned$;

First note that it does what the multi-target beacons do by using the **Beacon** procedure by Jiao et al. [4]. It first updates its roster list as necessary for initialization. Secondly it listens to all broadcasts; These broadcasts now contain roster information and more important roster information from workers. Within these broadcast if there is a worker assigned to a target it doesn't know about, the beacon will add the worker to the list of known workers. In practical situations this broadcast will most likely be more than just a simple procedure call for an explorer, and its possible workers can continue to broadcast this information for a short time before stopping to guarantee the information is heard entirely.

We should note that this doesn't guarantee a certain amount of workers will be allocated, usage of a high assignment probability will guarantee assignments, but the rostering may allow assignments of higher than the desired value. However, as long as network latency is low and a good probability is chosen, then the actual assignment population will be very close the desired amount.

4   Rostering Experimental Analysis

We want to analyze how the rostering technique improves performance. We measure a few different factors, such as congestion improvements, the number of targets found, and average time lost due to congestion. These metrics represent vital issues that are present in the multi-target extension; the multi-target extension suffered from the lack of ability to find all the targets in a given environment, which can be undesirable when different targets represent different needs. The multi-target extension can also suffer from the congestion issue due to the lack of control in sending robots to particular targets; Specifically, too many robots converge to the first target found.

For these experiments we will be maintaining a few fixed parameters; time, an import factor to allow robots to work, is measured in no specific units and the speed of robots is constant, relative to those units. We also fix the size of the population as 100 robots. This value was chosen through experimentation on finding the disc shape of the robots coverage area and chose an appropriate target location distribution similarly described by Jiao et al. [4]. Lastly, we provide the worker assignment bound to be 5.

Fist we will compare how we improve upon congestion; We compare performance by measuring the average time lost on each trip for each worker. This is done by computing the minimal time required to reach the target (given a known maximal speed of each robot) and find the difference between each trip time that minimal time, we then average these trip times for each robot to compute the average time loss for each robot. We compare our rostering algorithm against the multi-target *hoff* algorithm with two different probability parameters on worker conversion.

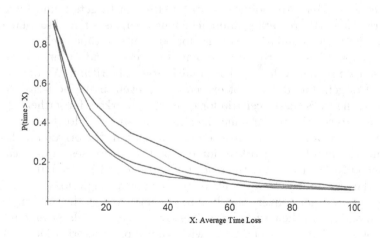

Fig. 1. Congestion metrics

Figure 1 shows the cumulative probabilities of a particular average time loss. The x-axis represents the average time loss for robots, and the y axis represents the probability of having at least X average lost time. By definition, as $X \to 0$ $Y \to 1$ and $X \to \infty$ as $Y \to 0$. So we choose a significant section of the data to display. Our experimental setup has that the minimal amount of time required to direct move to each target is at most 20 units of time. Figure 1 shows the improvement of our algorithm compared to the original multi-target. Specifically for some chosen values, we have the following values:

	$X = 10$	$X = 20$	$X = 30$	$X = 40$
Hoff(p = 0.001)	0.6764	0.4218	0.2775	0.21286
Hoff(p = 0.01)	0.6901	0.4534	0.3508	0.2803
Roster(p = 0.001)	0.5542	0.2820	0.1985	0.1445
Roster(p = 0.01)	0.5048	0.2990	0.1632	0.1333

Fig. 2. Sample results of congestion

Figure 2 demonstrates some of the results of improvement. For $X = 10$ Not much improvement is demonstrated (at most 27%). However, as X increases we start seeing at most 52% improvements. Qualitatively we can view the simulations and check that robots are assigned correctly, but here we have better quantified demonstrations on how well the rostering approach helps deal with traveling time and improves congestion conditions.

The second metric we want to look at for improvement is the number of targets found. In Jiao et al. they had looked at how many targets were found when varying the worker conversion parameter and had demonstrated that while the parameter can be tweaked to do better often, it will cripple the ability to do the retrieval. Here we look at the distribution of targets found for the hoff multi-target and the rostering approach. Our setup is similar to that of Jiao et al. [4], where the simulation will last for 600 units of time each.

Figure 3a and b shows the distribution of targets found for one of the better and worse case scenarios for the base multi-target algorithm. We note that the number of targets found does not exceed seven, even in the best-case scenario. This also is the worst case scenario for converting workers for gathering.

We want to see the performance increase for using this for finding new targets; Since when workers are converted very quickly in the original multi-target algorithm, the number of workers for exploration decreases dramatically and instantaneously. We then take the rostering approach with $p = 0.01$. Here we do not vary the probability, as we want to see how much the performance improves due to a fewer worker conversions. Figure 3c demonstrates the performance.

As demonstrated, the performance does not increase by a large amount, but it does so comparatively to experiments with similar parameterization. The multi-target algorithm with $p = 0.0001$ performs similarly. However, we should note that is because no gathering is being done (generally, only a few robots become workers), whereas the rostering approach almost all targets will have workers and early targets are essentially guaranteed at least five gathering workers (this is due to the high probability with worker conversion). So while the target distribution has not improved by much, it does improve slightly with more guarantees on gathering.

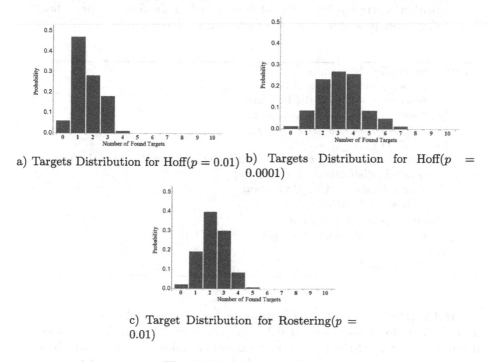

a) Targets Distribution for Hoff($p = 0.01$)

b) Targets Distribution for Hoff($p = 0.0001$)

c) Target Distribution for Rostering($p = 0.01$)

Fig. 3. Rostering comparison

5   Network Optimizaiton

In this section, we attempt to resolve the issue of how effectively the beacons are used. There are two focus areas: Beacon placement and beacon recycling. Both in Hoff's and the multi-target extension, beacon placement is not effective: Often there are two beacons almost right next to each other due to the condition for becoming a beacon. Secondly, we design an algorithm for reusing the beacons, which is non-existent in the previous two algorithms. We assume that the robots can check the distance between beacons by using infrared detection or similar methods. For this section, we use the term **NetOpt** to denote the extended algorithm using these two methods.

First, we consider the minimal distance checking which is a minor extension to the algorithm; This check is inspired by other techniques that mimic the molecular model–a technique that seeks to find a spread equilibrium for the robots to perform a coverage of the map as in Batalin [3]. The area coverage problem is a subproblem of foraging, though in general, it is not necessary to cover the entire environment in foraging. Batalin's algorithm creates an equilibrium by treating the robots as molecules and uses distance checks. Our algorithm does indeed use distance checks, but instead of creating an equilibrium it forces the robots to spread out farther and thus covering more region. This addition to the algorithm is straight forward and is captured in the following modification to the **Explorer** procedure from the multi-target algorithm.

---

function MINDISTEXPLORER()
 Let *robots* ← set of nearby robots;
 Let *beacons* ← set of nearby beacons;
 Let *bcasts* ← set of heard broadcasts;
 Let *targets* ← set of nearby targets;
 Let *map* ← $\bigcup_{m \in bcasts} m$;
 if (*targets* $\neq \emptyset$ and $\exists t \in targets, map[t] \neq START$) or $|bcasts| = 1$ **then**
  Let $D = \{dist(b, this) : b \in beacons\}$
  if $\forall d \in D, d < MAX\_DIST$ **then**
   type ← *BEACON*;
 else if $|keys(map)| > 0$ **then**
  With the probability of p, *type* ← *WORKER*;
 else
  RandomWalk();

MAX_DIST is a configurable constant for all robots; We use the constant as a fixed ratio of the physical detection distance. This check maintains the desired properties of the multi-target extension and ensures that new beacons will not cluster around a target and only become beacons if they detect exactly one beacon.

Secondly, we'll look at beacon recycling beacons that are not used or used inefficiently. One problem with the previous beacon-based methods is that when beacons are placed, they will always be there, thereby creating un-utilized beacons. We want to be able to identify unused and viable beacons to be recycled. One property of the network we will use for this is that our network is a tree-like structure, and captured more succinctly in the following theorem.

Theorem 1. *Given a configuration of the beacon network N, then any beacon which does not detect a larger nest cardinality can be removed without disconnecting the network.*

This theorem tells us that beacons only need to check this condition in broadcasts to determine if they are a **leaf** beacon. More explicitly the two condition we check for are:

1. Is the beacon a leaf?
2. Is the beacon allocated as an initial beacon for a target?

The first condition is just the leaf condition; the second is to make sure that no beacon that has found a target will leave the network. When a beacon decides to leave and become an explorer, it may use the beacon network to navigate back to the nest and restart its search. The decision on whether or not to recycle oneself for each leaf beacon depends highly on the knowledge given the region; We assume the most general case where the targets can be placed in an arbitrary distribution, so our beacons wait a fixed amount of time before recycling themselves.

Care must be taken for this process; if a beacon was to leave the network when an explorer was nearby, then its possible that the explorer will become loose the sight of the network. This could happen only with the minimal distance checks algorithm. Without minimal distance checks, the leaf-time being checked against should not be incremented when there are explorers within range. Otherwise, explorers can just end up replacing that beacon immediately and can stunt the growth of the network.

6   NetOpt Experimental Analysis

NetOpt is designed to improve target finding performance, so in this section, we provide insight on the improvements that NetOpt brings on the distribution of targets found. We keep the same setup as in the rostering experiments and apply NetOpt with rostering simultaneously. Figure 4a shows the distribution of targets found using the NetOpt addition to the algorithm.

As can be seen, NetOpt provide a large improvement, reaching targets found that the previous two algorithms could not achieve, as well as being able to maintain a centered distribution about more than 70% of targets found. While this shows a vast improvement given some of the resources available, one might question the performance should requirements change in robot population and gathering necessities.

Figure 4d shows the performance with only 50 robots and five workers. The distribution is less spread but has much better performance than the original. Next, we take the previous setup and decrease the worker factor to show how much performance can increase by reducing the worker count. Figure 4b shows the distribution by reducing the worker bound to 2, thereby allowing for more explorers. A large percentage still find only four targets, but vastly less find less. Shifting much of the distribution towards five and six targets found. Though neither of these still find all ten targets.

On the other side of the spectrum, we provide a better scenario for our robots by increasing the population to 125. Figure 4c shows the results with a worker bound of 5. With only a 25% increase in population the performance increases drastically from the 100-5 configuration. Though ten targets are not guaranteed, the performance increase is noticeable.

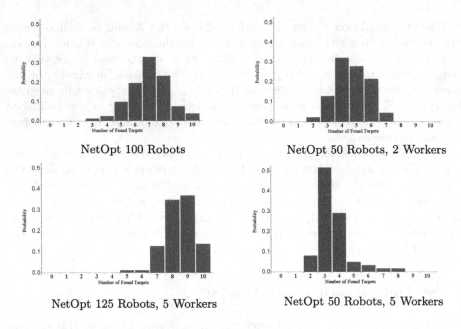

Fig. 4. NetOpt Comparisons

7 Future Work

Our algorithm does demonstrate nice improvements on the old ones but still only works under certain assumptions. To reiterate some of these assumptions:

1. Local communication for global knowledge;
2. Random walking is sufficient to eventually reach all targets;
3. Quantity of robots is enough to fulfill the previous.

Having no localization is the requirement that forces to have a beacon network; Though the beacon network is not necessary, local communication and connectivity are important in general. The other two requirements are what allows to make the simplifying tests of allowing beacons to remain static once they have positioned themselves. Future work would be to address these constraints which could allow for more dynamic beacons. Our NetOpt algorithm handles recycling beacons once they have found themselves to be not helpful, but if targets existed much farther past the random walk trajectory, then even the NetOpt algorithm would do very poorly.

The other issues are related to how exploration is done; since our algorithm uses random walking, it may travel to already explored regions. Since a global localization is not employed there would need to be a way to maintain relative regions of exploration to each beacon, and communicate desired regions of unexplored areas.

8   Conclusions

Foraging algorithms have been explored by many researchers and have taken various approaches. Statistical models have been developed through the inspiration from biological foragers such as ants. More deterministic approaches have been developed assuming both localization and lack of localization methods. These older methods focused more on single target foraging, whereas the more recent work considers a multi-target extension.

Our work solves a number of problems with the multi-target extension. The older algorithms suffered from many defects, specifically the naive probability parameterization leading to the lack of ability to effectively control exploration and target item delivery, congestion due to uncontrolled worker conversion, and lack of guarantees on gathering properties.

We demonstrate the efficacy of our work in a few ways. We develop a way of measuring congestion which was absent in previous work. We continue the measurements from older work that computes the distribution of targets found, and demonstrate the improvements from older work. We also outline the assumptions that facilitate these metrics as well as allow the algorithm to perform well. We presented an algorithm to utilize beacon robots more effectively, consequently improving the exploration capability. Lastly outlining what needs to be accomplished to break away from these assumptions for future work.

References

1. Adler, F.R., Gordon, D.M.: Information collection and spread by networks of patrolling ants. Am. Nat. **140**(3), 373–400 (1992)
2. Barth, E.J.: A dynamic programming approach to robotic swarm navigation using relay markers. In: Proceedings of the American Control Conference, vol. 6, pp. 5264–5269, July 2003
3. Batalin, M.A., Sukhatme, G.S.: Spreading out: a local approach to multi-robot coverage. In: Asama, H., Arai, T., Fukuda, T., Hasegawa, T. (eds.) Distributed Autonomous Robotic Systems, vol. 5, pp. 373–382. Springer, Tokyo (2002). https://doi.org/10.1007/978-4-431-65941-9_37
4. Jiao, Z., Sanford, C., Oh, J.: Multi-target extension for beacon based foraging methods. Technical report, Syracuse University, November 2017. https://surface.syr.edu/eecs/250/
5. O'Hara, K.J., Walker, D.B., Balch, T.R.: The GNATS — low-cost embedded networks for supporting mobile robots. In: Parker, L.E., Schneider, F.E., Schultz, A.C. (eds.) Multi-robot Systems. From Swarms to Intelligent Automata Volume III, pp. 277–282. Springer, Dordrecht (2005). https://doi.org/10.1007/1-4020-3389-3_24
6. Hoff, N.R., Sagoff, A., Wood, R.J., Nagpal, R.: Two foraging algorithms for robot swarms using only local communication. In: 2010 IEEE International Conference on Robotics and Biomimetics, ROBIO 2010, pp. 123–130, January 2011
7. Svennebring, J., Koenig, S.: Building terrain-covering ant robots: a feasibility study. Auton. Robots **16**(3), 313–332 (2004)

On Using "Stochastic Learning on the Line" to Design Novel Distance Estimation Methods

Jessica Havelock[1], B. John Oommen[1,2], and Ole-Christoffer Granmo[2(✉)]

[1] School of Computer Science, Carleton University, Ottawa, Canada
[2] Centre for Artificial Intelligence Research, University of Agder, Grimstad, Norway
ole.granmo@uia.no

Abstract. In this paper, we consider the problem of Distance Estimation (DE) when the inputs are the x and y coordinates of the points under consideration. The aim of the problem is to yield an accurate value for the real (road) distance between the points specified by the latter coordinates. This problem has, typically, been tackled by utilizing parametric functions called Distance Estimation Functions (DEFs). The parameters are learned from the training data (i.e., the true road distances) between a *subset* of the points under consideration. We propose to use Learning Automata (LA)-based strategies to solve the problem. In particular, we resort to the Adaptive Tertiary Search (ATS) strategy, proposed by Oommen *et al.*, to affect the learning. By utilizing the information provided in the coordinates of the nodes and the true distances from this *subset*, we propose a scheme to estimate the inter-nodal distances. In this regard, we use the ATS strategy to calculate the best parameters for the DEF. Traditionally, the parameters of the DEF are determined by minimizing an appropriate "Goodness-of-Fit" (GoF) function. As opposed to this, the ATS uses the current estimate of the distances, the feedback from the Environment, and the set of known distances, to determine the unknown parameters of the DEF. While the GoF functions can be used to show that the results are competitive, our research shows that they are rather not *necessary* to compute the parameters themselves. The results that we have obtained using artificial and real-life datasets demonstrate the power of the scheme, and also validate our hypothesis that we can completely move away from the GoF-based paradigm that has been used for four decades, demonstrating that our scheme is novel and pioneering.

Keywords: Road distance estimation · Estimating real-life distances
Learning Automata · Adaptive Tertiary Search
Stochastic Point Location

The second author gratefully acknowledges the partial support of NSERC, the Natural Sciences and Engineering Council of Canada.

1   Introduction

There are many well-studied problems whose solutions depend upon the distances between points in the Cartesian plain or in a geographic region. The traveling salesman problem, and vehicle scheduling problems are common examples of real-life scenarios that rely on distance information. The input to these Distance Estimation (DE) problems are, typically, the start and end locations in the form of x and y co-ordinates of the locations in the Cartesian plain, or the latitude and longitude in the geographic region. To determine the direct distance (i.e., as the bird flies), that must be traveled between a pair of known locations, is trivial. However, determining the actual "road distances", which are the *physical* distances to be traveled on the "roads" built in the community, is much more challenging, and far from trivial. These road distances (also synonymously known as traveling distances, or "true" distances) can depend on the network, the terrain, the geographical impediments like rivers or canyons, and of course, the direct distance between the respective points – which serves as a lower bound for the "true" distances. The problem of DE involves finding the best estimator for the true distances. This problem has been studied for over four decades, and its solutions have been put to use in many practical applications, such as in developing vehicle scheduling software, vehicle routing, and in the partitioning of districts for firefighters [1,5]. Indeed, as alluded to earlier, this is a central issue in designing GISs and GPSs.

Legacy Methods: Distance Estimation Functions. Any system that consists of inter-connected points, like a road network, can utilize DE to model and estimate the inter-point distances. To achieve this, historically, one typically resorts to Distance Estimating *Functions* (DEFs). These functions can take on any form, but the ideal ones are those that are simultaneously good estimators, and that are also characterized by low computational requirements. Love and Morris first introduced the concept of using simple parametric functions that employ the x and y co-ordinates for approximating distances [3]. The first DEFs were based on common norms, most of which are still used. All these DEFs involved parameters whose values are obtained by a "training" phase in order for them to best fit the data of the system being characterized. Consequently, some "true" road distances in the system must be known *a priori*, and they are used to "learn" the parameters associated with the DEFs. The accuracy of the estimations depends on the DEF, the system and the available data.

Our Proposed Approach. In this paper, we will contribute to the field of DE by applying a new method for determining the DEF. This method is called the Adaptive Tertiary Search (ATS) which was derived by Oommen and Raghunath [4]. To date, it has been central to two related problems (and their respective applications), namely, the continuous Stochastic Point Location problem, and the problem of parameter learning from a stochastic teacher or a stochastic compulsive liar. Both of these problems work within a stochastic domain analogous to that of DE. The ability of the ATS to perform ϵ-optimally in these stochastic domains renders it an ideal search strategy which can be used in DE.

The ATS is a search method that uses Learning Automata (LA) to perform a stochastic search "on a line" to determine the parameter sought for. The most "daring" step that we have taken in DE is that we have *completely moved away from invoking Goodness-of-Fit (GoF) criteria for the DEFs*, thus proposing a marked departure from the methods that have been used for more than four decades. These concepts will be explained presently.

2   Distance Estimation: Core Concepts

The prediction or DE, is typically done by determining or discovering the appropriate DEF. A DEF is a mapping from $R^d \times R^d$ to R, and returns the estimate of the true distance. The inputs to the DEF are the locations of the two points, and it produces an estimate of the distance between them by incorporating the set of parameters into the DEF. Clearly, the set of parameters alluded to must be *learnt* in order for the DEF to best represent the space.

Definition 1. *A **Distance Estimation Function (DEF)** is defined as a function $\pi(P_1, P_2|\Lambda) : R^d \times R^d \longrightarrow R$, in which $P_1 = \langle x_1, x_2, ..., x_d \rangle$ and $P_2 = \langle y_1, y_2, ..., y_d \rangle$ are points in R^d, and Λ is a set of parameters whose values characterize π, and which must be learnt using a set of training points with known true inter-point distances.*

The set of parameters, Λ, is typically learnt by minimizing a GoF function, which, in turn, is used to measure how well a network or region is represented by the DEF. Central to the legacy methods of DE is the above-mentioned concept of GoF functions. GoF functions are measures of how good a DEF estimates the true (but unknown) distances. Several GoF functions have been consistently utilized in the literature pertaining to the field of DE. The most commonly-used GoF function is the sum of Square Deviation (SD).

2.1   Distance Estimation Functions (DEFs)

The most common types of DEFs are those based on the family[1] of L^p norms, traditionally used for computing distances:

$$L_p(X) = \left(\sum_{i=1}^{n} (|x_i|^p) \right)^{1/p}. \tag{1}$$

The various L^p norms have been used as stepping stones to design DEFs, and some of the most common DEFs have, indeed, been derived from the L^p norms [3]. The input to these functions are the co-ordinates of the input vectors,

---

[1] The cases for $p = 1$, $p = 2$ and $p = \infty$ represent the Taxi-Cab, Euclidean and Largest Absolute Value norms respectively. The L^p norms for other values of p ($p \in R$) also have significance in DE.

X_1 and X_2. In practice, these DEFs are first trained on the subset of the coordinates of the cities and *their* known inter-point distances for the specific region under consideration. This training is done so as to obtain the "best" parameters for the DEF given the training data. Once these parameters have been determined, the DEF can thereafter be invoked for estimating distances for other cities whose inter-city distances are unknown.

3   The Adaptive Tertiary Search and Its Use in DE

The solution that we propose for DE is based on a scheme relevant to the Stochastic Point Location (SPL) problem. To formulate the SPL, we assume that there is a Learning Mechanism (LM) whose task is to determine the optimal value of some variable (or parameter), λ. We assume that there is an optimal choice for λ - an unknown value, say $\lambda^* \in [0, 1]$. In this paper, we shall use the ATS [4] to solve the DE problem, although any of the other reported solutions could have been used just as well. The advantage of the ATS is that it is not a hill climbing search, and therefore overcomes the problems of being dependent on a starting point and a step size.

To determine λ^* within the resolution of accuracy, the original search interval is divided into three equal and disjoint subintervals, Δ^i, where $i = 1...3$. The subintervals are searched using a two-action LA. The LA returns the $\lambda(n)$, the estimated position of λ^* from that subinterval, $O^i \in \{Left, Right, Inside\}$. From these outputs, a new search interval is obtained which is based on the decision table given in Table 1. This is repeated until the search interval is smaller than the resolution of accuracy. The search interval will be reduced to yield the required resolution within a finite number of epochs because the size of the search interval is decreasing [4]. After the search interval has been sufficiently reduced, the midpoint of the final interval is returned as the estimate for λ^*.

Table 1. The decision table for the ATS scheme.

O^1	O^2	O^3	New sub-interval
Inside	Left	Left	Δ^1
Left	Left	Left	Δ^1
Right	Inside	Left	Δ^2
Right	Left	Left	$\Delta^1 \cup \Delta^2$
Right	Right	Inside	Δ^3
Right	Right	Left	$\Delta^2 \cup \Delta^3$
Right	Right	Right	Δ^3

The ATS proposed by Oommen and Raghunath [4] was initially used to solve the SPL problem, and subsequently for parameter learning when interacting with a stochastic teacher or a stochastic compulsive liar. For both of these problems, one had to determine only a single unknown parameter. Our aim is to utilize these core concepts in DE where one has to learn/estimate many parameters simultaneously. In order to adapt the ATS to find more than a single parameter, we must specify the corresponding "Environment", and also both the process of updating multiple search intervals and the issue of how the set of LA interact with it.

3.1 Updating Search Intervals

Let us first consider the case where the DEF has two parameters, say k and p. The strategy for our search will be to use the ATS to determine the best value for k and p, say k^* and p^*, respectively. However, it is crucial that the *order* of updating the search intervals in the k and p spaces is considered when determining these multiple unknown parameters. If this is not done correctly, it may result in the premature reduction of a search interval. In the SPL problem, the subintervals were first searched using the LA, after which the search interval was updated. This order of executing the searching, and the pruning of the intervals must also be maintained while searching for the two parameters, k and p, simultaneously. In other words, all the subintervals must be searched before any interval is updated. Each search interval must undergo the same search process as in the case of the single-parameter ATS. The only difference is that the search intervals must be updated simultaneously. The order (or sequence) for achieving this is shown in Algorithm 1.

Algorithm 1. TwoDimensionalATS

Input: The Resolutions ρ_k and ρ_p

Output: Estimates of k^* and p^*

Method:

1: **repeat**
2:     **for** $j \leftarrow 1$ to 3 **do**
3:         Execute LA^j for k
4:         Execute LA^j for p
5:     **end for**
6:     GetNewInterval for k - From Table 1
7:     GetNewInterval for p - From Table 1
8: **until** (Size_of_Interval(k) $< \rho_k$) $\wedge$ (Size_of_Interval(p) $< \rho_p$)
9: $k^* \leftarrow$ Midpoint(FinalInterval(k))
10: $p^* \leftarrow$ Midpoint(FinalInterval(p))
End Algorithm

The set of LA operate in the same manner as in [4], except for how it deals with the additional parameters. When the LA is learning information about how it should update the value for k, it uses values of p from within its *current* search interval and vice versa. As a result, each LA operates with the knowledge of the *current* search interval of *all* the other parameters.

This process of searching for multiple parameters can be done in parallel by assuming that for each learning loop, the other parameter's value is either the maximum or the minimum of its current search interval. This is a consequence of the monotonicity of the DEFs, as discussed in Sect. 3.3.

3.2   The Corresponding LA

Each LA is provided with two inputs, namely the parameter that it is searching for, and all the search intervals. Each LA is required to yield as its output the relative location of the parameter in question. It does this by producing a decision (Left, Right or Inside) based on *its* final belief after communicating with its specific Environment.

The LA starts out with a uniform belief, 50% for both "Left" and "Right". It then makes a decision based on its current belief. If the decision is "Left", then the LA picks a point in the left half of the interval at random; otherwise (i.e., the decision is "Right") the point is chosen from the right half of the interval. Once the decision is made, the LA asks the Environment for a response. The LA uses a Linear Reward Inaction (L_{RI}) update scheme, and so the current belief is only updated if the Environment's response is positive.

The LA and the Environment repeat this loop for a large number, say N_∞, iterations. After they are done communicating, the LA produces its output as per the LA algorithm briefly described below. This is omitted here in the interest of space but found in [2]. If the LA's belief of "Right" is greater than $1 - \epsilon$, the parameter in question is to the right side of the current search interval, and so its output is "Right". Conversely, if the belief of "Left" is greater than $1 - \epsilon$, the LA's final decision is "Left". If neither of these cases emerge, the LA does not have a belief greater than $1 - \epsilon$ that the parameter is to the "Right" or "Left", and in this case, the LA decides that the parameter's optimal value is "Inside" the present interval. The entire algorithm is formally given in [2] (omitted here in the interest of space).

3.3   The Corresponding Environment

Each LA requires feedback from a specific Environment. This feedback informs the LA if it has made the correct decision, i.e., choosing the right or left half of the subinterval. It is easy to obtain this answer because it only involves a single parameter at a time. To further explain this, consider the DEFs below:

$$F(k, p) = k \cdot F_1(X_1, X_2, p), \text{ and where,} \tag{2}$$

$$F_1(X_1, X_2, p) = \left(\sum_{i=1}^{d} |x_{1i} - x_{2i}|^p \right)^{1/p} . \tag{3}$$

Although nothing specific can be said about the monotonicity characteristics of $F(k, p)$, we see from Eq. (2) that by virtue of the fact that it is always positive and that it can be factored, it is monotonically *increasing* with k for any fixed value, p. Similarly, from Eq. (3), since $F_1(X_1, X_2, p)$ is not a function of k, it is monotonically *decreasing* with p for any fixed value of k. These properties allow the Oracle to respond accordingly when finding k, and for the corresponding LA to move in the desired direction (i.e., "Left" or "Right") in the space that only involves the single parameter k. The contrary monotonicity properties allow the Oracle to respond according to a corresponding algorithm (*EnvironmentResponseP*, found in [2]) when determining p, and for the corresponding LA to move in the desired direction (i.e., "Left" or "Right") in the space that involves only p.

4   Testing and Results: 2-Dimensional Environments

In this section[2], we present the results for the 2-dimensional DE using the ATS. We show that this method of estimation works for three different DEFs where, the first two DEFs each contained only a single parameter that had to be determined, k or p respectively. The last DEF contained two parameters, k and p. To compare the results we used four typical GoF measures.

Experimental Setup: Our test for the ATS was done on real-world data sets, since the "proof of the pudding is, indeed, in the eating". This data consisted of three sets, which in turn involved 29, 97, and 561 cities each. The data sets involving 29 and 561 cities were obtained from the MP-TESTDATA (the TSPLIB Symmetric Traveling Salesman Problem Instances) [6]. Observe that for data of this type, there are no "Known" values of k and p. This is because the data was not *created* and therefore did not depend on any "Known" values. "Benchmark" values were therefore used for comparison, determined using a hill-climbing search.

Weighted L^p DEF: When the ATS was used in conjunction with the Weighted L^p DEF, the ATS out-performed the hill-climbing search, as shown in results in Table 2. While the ATS and the hill-climbing search performed very similarly, the ATS had a slight improvement over the hill-climbing search. Both the data set with 29 points and the data set with 97 points had a p value that was close to 2.0. As a result, the Weighted L^p DEF had a similar performance to the Weighted Euclidean DEF. For the data set with 561 points, the ATS produced an average p value of about 1.2, whereas the hill-climbing search's p value was 1.74. This change in p value resulted in a larger difference in the accuracy of the estimation of the distances between the ATS using the Weighted L^p DEF and the Weighted Euclidean DEF. Finally, the ATS using the Weighted L^p DEF, out-performed the previous two DEFs. The most significant contribution of this work was that the ATS did not require the use of GoF functions, which we believe is pioneering and novel.

---

[2] The experimental results that we have obtained are extensive and involve two artificial and two real-life data sets. The results presented here constitute only a small subset; additional details of the experimental results are found in [2].

Table 2. Results for 100 runs of the ATS with the Weighted L^p DEF on the real-world data sets.

Data set size	N = 29		N = 97		N = 561	
Error	Average	Standard	Average	Standard	Average	Standard
Type	Error	Deviation	Error	Deviation	Error	Deviation
	Estimated		Estimated		Estimated	
K Value	0.2220	9.4600×10^{-4}	1.3517	0.0164	0.1410	0.0022
P Value	1.9935	0.0353	1.8022	0.0932	1.1517	0.0437
SD	22.93	0.28	20118.81	226.04	17756.97	364.02
NAD	1.79	0.01	83.28	0.22	2227.20	19.61
RAD	0.0402	0.0003	0.1253	0.0004	0.1423	0.0016
EP	0.0496	0.0004	0.2051	0.0005	0.1569	0.0014
	Benchmark		Benchmark		Benchmark	
K Value	0.2203	8.1873×10^{-8}	1.2326	0.0053	0.1550	4.9035×10^{-8}
P Value	1.9200	9.0190×10^{-8}	1.5071	0.0221	1.7400	6.0445×10^{-8}
SD	23.71	0.00	19922.21	62.01	20522.75	0.05
NAD	1.83	0.00	86.27	0.16	2418.51	0.00
RAD	0.0412	0.0000	0.1381	0.0005	0.1598	0.0000
EP	0.0508	0.0000	0.2125	0.0004	0.1704	0.0000

5   Conclusions

In this paper, we considered the Distance Estimation (DE) problem that has been studied for almost four decades. It involves estimating the real-life distances between points in the Cartesian plain or in a geographic region. Our solution differs significantly from the legacy methods in that we depart from the use of so-called "Goodness-of-Fit" (GoF) functions. Rather, we have used the field of Learning Automata (LA) and in particular, the Adaptive Teriary Search (ATS) to solve the Stochastic Point Location (SPL) problem. This paper has made some major contributions. Firstly, it extended the ATS application to the DE problem. In this regard, we defined both the new environments and the corresponding LA for this problem for three simple DEFs. Using these newly-defined Environments and LA, the ATS was shown to produce parameters competitive to those obtained by the hill-climbing search for all of these DEFs – without utilizing GoFs. The other contribution that we made (with regards to the ATS) was to successfully search for multiple parameters *simultaneously*.

References

1. Erkut, H., Polat, S.: A simulation model for an urban fire fighting system. OMEGA Int. J. Manage. Sci. **20**(4), 535–542 (1992)
2. Havelock, J., Oommen, B.J., Granmo, O.-C.: Novel Distance Estimation Methods Using "Stochastic Learning on the Line" Strategies. Unabridged version

3. Love, R.F., Morris, J.G.: Modelling inter-city road distances by mathematical functions. Oper. Res. Q. **23**(1), 61–71 (1972)
4. Oommen, B.J., Raghunath, G.: Automata learning and intelligent tertiary searching for stochastic point location. IEEE SMC **28**(6), 947–954 (1998)
5. Oommen, J., Altnel, I.K., Aras, N.: Discrete vector quantization for arbitrary distance function estimation. IEEE SMC **28**(4), 496–510 (1998)
6. Skorobohatyj, G.: MP-TESTDATA - The TSPLIB symmetric traveling salesman problem instances (2011). http://elib.zib.de/pub/mptestdata/tsp/tsplib/tsp/index.html. Accessed 12 Sept 2011

Data Mining and Knowledge Discovery

Person Re-identification Using Masked Keypoints

Diego Reyes and John Atkinson[(✉)]

Universidad Adolfo Ibañez, Santiago, Chile
diegoreyesmo@gmail.com , john.atkinson@uai.cl

Abstract. In this work, a method for person re-identification from surveillance videos is proposed. In this approach, person detection is based on moving objects from sequences of images, and on incorporating a feature extraction technique that can distinguish distinct persons according to their physical appearance by using masked images that reduce noise from the background. Our approach uses keypoints to build an image's descriptor so that the best discriminative keypoints can be identified between different persons. Experiments using our masked re-identification method show significant improvements in the recognition rate when masked frames are used to reduce noise of the second plane.

1 Introduction

Video surveillance has usually focused on the development of systems that can automatically detect and track people. In many video-surveillance applications, the interest is to determine if a presently visible person has already been observed somewhere else in the cameras network, task usually referred to as *Person Re-identification* (Re-ID), which aims to correctly identify all instances of the same visual object (i.e., person) at any given location and at any given time instant in an image or video. Re-ID can be a useful tool for people analysis in security as a data association method for long-term tracking in surveillance. However, current identification techniques show many difficulties. They rely on the exploitation of visual cues such as color, texture, and the object's shape.

Despite the many advances to address the Re-ID task, it is still an open problem as the appearance of individuals varies greatly through the scenes, due to possibly different acquisition devices and ambient lighting, changes in viewpoints, illumination conditions, shadows, etc, as well as the presence of other similar individuals in the scenes. In addition, depending on the location of the cameras, the *Field of View* (FOV) may be overlapped with close cameras so that distance between the objects captured by every camera can be used to automatically infer the topology of the camera network.

Formally, Re-ID can be defined as the task of tagging the same identification to all the instances of a person in an image by using visual features extracted

© Springer International Publishing AG, part of Springer Nature 2018
M. Mouhoub et al. (Eds.): IEA/AIE 2018, LNAI 10868, pp. 45–56, 2018.
https://doi.org/10.1007/978-3-319-92058-0_5

from images or videos [1] so different key questions can be answered by using a camera network: *Where has a person previously been seen?*, *Where was a person after being seen in a certain location?*, etc. However, a key open problem is to perform a Re-ID task within a single FOV, this is, determining when an individual re-enters a place monitored by a camera.

Accordingly, this work describes a novel Re-ID method for detecting and comparing persons using features extracted from their movement observed in videos. In addition, the approach incorporates a multiple-scene plane segmentation step by using masked images from videos so as to improve the person detection task. Unlike other approaches using single images, a keypoint-based Re-ID method is proposed to detect persons from videos by using changes on sequences of images to accurately calculate the area where a person is located based on keypoints [3,6,7,9,12].

2   Person Re-identification

Person Re-Identification (Re-ID) is the task of matching persons images observed in different camera views with visual features [4]. It aims at matching a query image with images of a large number of candidate persons in a gallery in order to recognize the object of the query. A typical Re-ID system is composed of two major steps:

1. **Extracting Person Descriptors:** in this step a person is detected and tracked from multiple images or videos, and features and descriptors are extracted:

    (a) *Person Detection:* it identifies a person in a single scene. For this, automatic classifiers are used to train and detect two kind of objects in a scene: person and non-person. However, there are several consecutive images (frames) in video scenes so that persons can be detected without using training data and supervised learning methods as changes in every pixel are tracked every time there is a movement within a scene (i.e., a person walking down). The task of pixel classification for static and moving areas is known as *first plane* and *second plane* segmentation, respectively. Second-plane detection from images can remove all the information that is part of a moving person, hiding pixels that remain unchanged.

    (b) *Person Tracking:* it tracks a person within a FOV by using multiple cameras. Furthermore, during a single tracking, additional information of a person can be inferred such as direction, starting and ending location, etc.

    (c) *Feature Extraction:* the effectiveness of a Re-ID method is strongly dependent on the type of extracted feature, which is assessed by using the *Cumulative Matching Characteristic* (CMC) metric. This estimates the probability that a Re-ID method correctly extracts a descriptor that matches the query image and those descriptors in an image gallery. Since the method can extract several answers, every outcome is composed of a group of selected images based on their similarity with the target query. Thus, for the first answer the method extracts one image; for the second one, the method gets two images and so on, up to the $k-th$ answer composed of k images. An answer is correct if the image of the query (person) is one of the k selected images, so the detection (recognition) rate can be calculated as follows:

$$\text{Detection Rate} = \frac{\#\text{ Correct Answers}}{\#\text{ Queries}} \times 100$$

In order to compare different Re-ID methods, standard datasets are used including $ViPER$ that contains 600 unique person images taken from outdoor environments from different angles and locations, and $CAVIAR4REID$[1] that collects an average of 10 to 20 images per person taken from video-surveillance cameras in shopping centers.

Furthermore, the types of features typically extracted from the standard $VIPeR$ dataset include *Color* such as RBG, HSV and histogram channels, *Shape*, *Location* (i.e., the movement captured by each camera is equivalent to each other), *Texture* [2,8,11,13].

(d) *Descriptor Generation:* In order to build a person's descriptor, keypoints are calculated by using the SIFT (*Scale-Invariant Feature Transform*) algorithm for feature transformation, achieving a higher detection rate of 70.4% for $k = 20$. This improvement can partially be due to more descriptive features being incorporated such as the color difference between a pixel and its neighborhood, which makes a person's physical appearance more explicit.

2. **Match Descriptors:** this step associates two or more descriptors so as to determine if they correspond to the same person or not (i.e., descriptor matching). To find a match, the methods usually compute some distance between the target descriptor (*query*) and all the candidate neighborhood descriptors. The k closest candidates are then selected by using the *k-Nearest Neighbor* (KNN) method or statistic-based metrics [13,15].

3   A Keypoint-Based Re-ID Method

In this work, an improved model for Re-ID from surveillance videos is proposed. For this, an SVM-based detection method selects candidate image areas to contain a person by filtering detected silhouettes based on their shape. Unlike other Re-ID approaches for person detection and image segmentation, our keypoint-based Re-ID method contributes as follows:

1. Person descriptors are extracted from sequences of images which may provide additional information to efficiently select image areas containing a person, by applying plane segmentation techniques.

---

[1] http://homepages.inf.ed.ac.uk/rbf/CAVIAR/.

2. Masked keypoints are applied to build an image's descriptor so that key areas can be identified so to provide more discriminant information between images containing different persons [10].
3. Descriptors are matched by using simple direct distance metrics as training image datasets are not always available (or enough) so as to use supervised learning.

Accordingly, our Re-ID method consists of two main tasks: *Person detection* from video images and *Person Re-identification* from previously generated images.

3.1   Person Detection

The overall Re-ID method takes videos captured from multiple static cameras. This allows it to distinguish parts of an image corresponding to the background (i.e., fixed points) from those in the first plane (i.e, mobile points).

Detected persons are only identified from the first (`DetectFirstPlane(Frame)`) plane which is composed of one or more isolated segments within a frame (`CaptureVideoFrame(CameraData)`), caused by moving objects located at different positions in a scene. Hence the method should only select segments that may potentially contain persons (aka. *keypoints*). To this end, an algorithm that segments first and second planes from multiple cameras (`CameraData`) was used to identify pixels contained in moving areas, as follows:

```
PersonDetection (CameraData):

While (There are frames to be captured) Do
    Frame  = CaptureVideoFrame(CameraData)
    CreateBackgroundSubtractor(CameraData)
    ForegroundMask = DetectFirstPlane(Frame)
    CleanMask = RemoveShadows(ForegroundMask)
    Enmasked = TripleChannelsRGB(CleanMask)
    Enmasked = BitwiseMask(Frame,Enmasked)
    InitialContours = FindContours(Enmasked)
    Contours = FindPolynomyContour(InitialContours)
    Area = FindIndexOfLargestContour(Contours)
End-While
Return Area
```

The method is based on changes produced between each adjacent frame of video by using a Gauss probability distribution, generating a new bitmap having the same dimension as the query image, and containing white and black pixels for moving and static areas, respectively.

Plane Segmentation. Shadows can become part of the a scene's first plane if they are not detected, so a keypoint might contain pixels that do not belong to a person body. To address this issue, shadows are identified by applying the same previously-mentioned segmentation method. For this, bitmaps containing grayscale pixels are generated, where shadows are represented with grey values (`RemoveShadows(ForegroundMask)`). Since the second plane is only represented with black pixels, keeping shadows in this plane is enabled by transforming color pixels into black pixels according to certain thresholds (`TripleChannelsRGB(CleanMask)`). The resulting bitmap is then used as a *mask* overlapping the frame, hiding the second plane (aka. *background subtraction* in `CreateBackgroundSubtractor(CameraData)`). Each frame's pixels (i.e., mask and initial pixel) are represented as sequences of logical values that are AND-operated (`BitwiseMask(Frame,Enmasked)`). Once the second plane is removed by using masked frames, the keypoints of the image are identified. These masked images are used to remove background noise, which may improve the effectiveness of the Re-ID task as they avoid extracting and comparing background's features, so reducing the noise contained in an image's descriptor. Unlike isolated images, creating masked frames in videos does not require additional calculation as this is the result of the segmentation task itself.

Keypoint Selection. The extracted bitmap is used to calculate the contours of the shapes contained in the first plane by using a tracking edges algorithm that generates those points belonging to the edges of the detected contours (`FindContours(Enmasked)`). Polygons are then generated so they approximately match target areas by using the *Ramer Douglas Peucker* (RDP) method. Finally, they become approximate edges for the moving silhouette (`FindPolynomyContour(InitialContours)`). In order to estimate whether a polygon is associated to a person or not, two features are calculated:

1. *The ratio between objects and detected persons* (aka. *Aspect Ratio* as the polygon's ratio may become a good discriminant factor to select keypoints containing persons as its calculation has a low computational cost.
2. *The size of the image (i.e., pixels' area)* as it allows the method to rule out an area whose dimension exceeds some threshold independently defined for each scenario.

For videos where the path followed by a target person is known, the search is restricted to certain frame's areas so as to analyse a few number of candidate keypoints only. Hence for each camera, a rectangular area is established so that regions not containing persons are avoided (i.e., vehicles avenues). Finally, a person is selected from each analyzed frame, which corresponds to a keypoint with the largest area that meets three conditions: minimum aspect ratio, area within some threshold and location within an established area.

Feature Extraction. Features used to describe images (i.e., keypoints) were extracted by applying a SIFT-based method which is robust to changes of scale and rotation. Every keypoint corresponds to an image's round area and is composed of its center's coordinates (x, y), the size (i.e., scale) and direction.

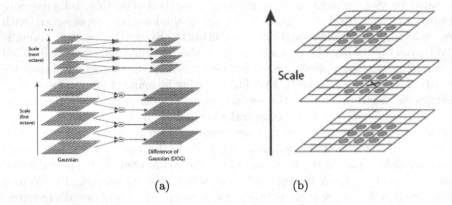

(a)   (b)

Fig. 1. SIFT: (a) Scale Space of Octaves and Difference of Gaussians. (b) Searching for local minimum and maximum in Scale Space: pixel x is marked as a keypoint as long as it is lower or higher than its 26 neighbors (green circles) (Color figure online)

In order to detect keypoints, SIFT generates several images from the initial query, gradually reducing its size. Eight different sizes are usually suggested to be generated (i.e., octaves), so that a Gaussian Blur (GB) operator can be then applied 5 times, each more intense than the previous one. For each pair of consecutive Gaussians, the difference is obtained (i.e., Difference of Gaussians or DoG) by calculating an approximate second partial derivative (i.e., Laplacian) for each GB-operated image (aka. *Laplacian of Gaussian* or LoG) as seen in example of Fig. 1(a). From these, keypoints located in pixels of a DoG exceeding a maximum threshold or minimum value among neighbors are selected, which includes keypoints within an octave, and the neighbors of the current image, the next one and the previous one (see Fig. 1(b)). Keypoints that are not good features (i.e., low contrast, borderline) are then ruled out, and the remaining objects are used to calculate their orientation from direction and magnitude data provided by the Gradient of the keypoint's neighborhood, based on its most frequent direction.

Extracting keypoints contained in the second plane is avoided by creating masked images so that keypoints being matched against are those exclusively obtained from a person's clothes and not from the background.

3.2   Person Re-identification

In order to compare a target image (query) against another one in the gallery, their respective keypoints are used and matched. The best candidate keypoint is the nearest neighbor contained in a gallery's image based on the minimum Euclidean distance, which generates a vector of distances between each pair of associated keypoints (`FindIndexOfLargestContour(Contours)`). Unlike voting mechanisms [5], Re-ID is performed by summing up the distance between pairs of keypoints, and then selecting that image of the gallery, with the minimum sum.

Storing and Matching Persons. Our keypoints-based Re-ID model can be in one of the following states:

1. *Storing:* It aims at creating an image gallery containing information about the detected persons. Every time a moving area is detected, a person object is looked for by extracting physical appearance features, and then stored into the gallery, otherwise the detected area is discarded and the video processing goes on.
2. *Searching:* It aims at searching and matching new persons and those contained in the gallery. A detected person's features are matched against those in the gallery in order to select the best candidate images. Note that a target person is assumed to be previously stored so the method might try to re-identify a person not contained in the gallery.

4   Experiments

In this work, a computer prototype of the proposed method for person detection and video-based Re-ID was implemented. In order to assess the effectiveness of our keypoints-based Re-ID approach, several setting experiments were conducted and different comparisons with state-of-the-art approaches were carried out. Overall, experiments aimed at exploring two main claims:

1. Person detection can be improved by using additional information provided by a person's sequence of images (video).
2. Re-ID can be improved by incorporating a plane segmentation task using masked images and keypoints selection based on the *Aspect Ratio*.

4.1   Data Collection

Experiments used the standard $CAVIAR$ dataset[2] consisting of 26 video sequences captured from two cameras with different locations and angles within a shopping center, and using a size of each frame's image of 384×288 pixels. Both cameras form an angle of app. $90°$, with part of FOV being overlapped, and include the videos contain persons who enter and leave the place. Built up from persons contained in these videos, a new image dataset is provided: $CAVIAR4REID$. Out of 72 different individuals (i.e., images ranging from 17×39 to 72×144 pixels), 50 of them are captured by both cameras

---

[2] http://homepages.inf.ed.ac.uk/rbf/CAVIAR.

whereas 22 of them were captured in one of the cameras. In addition, each camera provided 10 images per person, with different resolution, lighting, gestures, and occlusion.

Note that videos are not suitable to assess the ability of our keypoint-based Re-ID method to correctly select keypoints containing persons as any moving object in the video corresponds to a person. In order to deal with this issue, surveillance videos containing additional moving objects were used (i.e., car traffic, buses, bikes, etc). These videos (928 × 420 pixels) were obtained from two security cameras of an outdoor parking close to a street intersection and recorded for 3 h, showing other moving objects.

4.2   Parameters Setting

Since a method for person detection is based on the moving object's geometrical shape, its effectiveness (i.e., recognition rate) directly depends on the minimum *Aspect Ratio* used to segment the first plane's areas, whereas person Re-ID depends on the maximum number of keypoints used to match person descriptors.

Person Detection According to the *Aspect Ratio*. In order to determine the *Aspect Ratio* (AR) that maximizes the effectiveness of a person detection task, several systematic tests were conducted by using different minimum values for AR so that the following frequencies can be registered: number of detected moving areas that exceed the minimum AR (aka. detections), number of detections not containing persons (aka. error), and the number of persons who were never detected (aka. misses).

The experiments used videos containing 8 distinct persons and results show that as the minimum AR for a keypoint to be detected as a person increases, the detection error drops, being this less than 12% whenever the AR is at least 1.125. Note that as the AR increases too much, frame areas containing persons are ruled out, increasing the number of non-detected persons, so the best minimum AR becomes 1.125.

Re-identification According to Keypoints. The number of pairs of keypoints to be included in the sum of distances may affect the performance of the detection task so the best number of pairs should be determined. To this end, recognition rates for calculating distances by using 1 to 15 pairs of keypoints are compared. These experiments were conducted on the *CAVIAR4REID* dataset (see Fig. 2), and their results indicate that when using less than 2 or more than 12 pairs, the recognition rate is lower than when using a mean number of the extreme values.

Re-identification According to Masked Images. In order to assess the impact of masked images on the features extraction task, *CAVIAR* videos were used to create a dataset similar to *CAVIAR4REID*. However, it creates a masked background as our proposed approach requires consecutive frames of

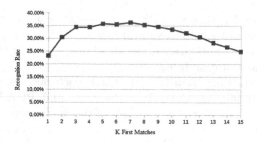

Fig. 2. Recognition rate vs. pairs of keypoints

a video in order to create the mask. Accordingly, the Re-ID task was evaluated by measuring the detection rate on the CMC curve based on the proportion of correctly detected persons from an answer with k candidate images, using the best number of keypoints. Hence two kind of assessments were performed: one using the raw images within $CAVIAR4REID$ (i.e., *unmasked*) and other using similar images (i.e., same persons) but using masked background (*masked*). Results in Fig. 3 indicate that as the background is masked, the recognition rate gets improved for nearly 25%, suggesting the mask avoids extracting features (keypoints) from the background, which might be close between persons obtained from the same location.

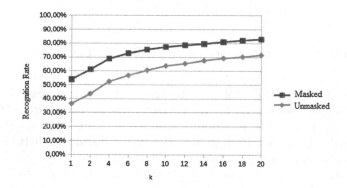

Fig. 3. Comparing the Re-ID task with and without mask.

4.3 Comparing Our Method

The impact of the masks on methods using other feature extraction techniques and descriptors matching was also measured by using the $CAVIAR4REID$ dataset. Compared methods included those using masks to remove the second plane and those not using masks (but using a different technique for feature extraction and descriptors matching) so three approaches were finally used:

1. **Histogram Plus Epitome (HPE):** each person's descriptor is represented as a color histogram built from several images, which can remove the second plane by using masks. Similarity is measured by calculating the direct distance between each pairs of descriptors [2].
2. **Principal Component Analysis (PCA):** each descriptor is composed of an histogram containing some HSV channels, and PCA-based supervised learning is used to reduce the dimensions of the descriptors, but no masks are used [13].
3. **Local Coordinate Coding (LCC):** each descriptor is composed of a color and gradient histogram with no masks. Similarity is measured by using tagged samples [14].

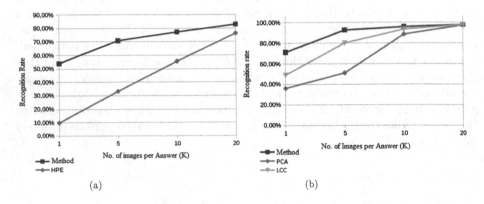

(a)   (b)

Fig. 4. Our proposed method vs. (a) HPE. (b) LCC and PCA

Like our approach, HPE applies a direct metric to compare descriptors, but it uses mask to hide features. HPE was assessed by using images from 50 persons (see Fig. 4(a)), getting low recognition rate for $k < 10$. This may be due to features based only on color histograms which do not distinguish between persons having a physical appearance with similar color [8].

On the other hand, PCA and LCC do not use masks so they build person's descriptors that include the second plane's features. Since these methods apply supervised learning to compare descriptors, only a part of the dataset was used for training and testing purposes. Our method was assessed by randomly selecting 36 persons from the dataset, and comparing its recognition rate against that of PCA and LCC as shown in Fig. 4(b). Results indicate that using gradients improves the recognition rate over 30% for $k = 5$.

While PCA did not use masks to remove the background, it got better results than HPE due to the number of trials and the comparison technique. In addition, the proposed method was observed to get the best Re-ID recognition rate for all the experiments, suggesting that the combination of second plane masks and feature extraction (i.e., SIFT) significantly affects the performance of the person detection task.

5 Conclusions

In this research, a method for person re-identification from surveillance videos was proposed. For this, an SVM-based detection method selects candidate image areas to contain a person by filtering detected silhouettes based on their shape. Person descriptors are extracted from videos which provide addition information to efficiently select the image areas containing a person, by applying plane segmentation techniques and masked frame so that an object's second plane can be removed.

Experiments using real videos obtained from surveillance camera containing persons and other moving objects, show the promise of our person detection method using the aspect ratio to select persons from several moving objects, achieving a detection rate of over 90%, but using less resources than supervised learning methods. Furthermore, results using masked images to remove the second plane and incorporating gradient-based features showed an increase in the recognition rate of 10% for $k < 5$. This suggests that using masked frames can indeed reduce an image's noise, avoiding matching keypoints of areas that do not contain a target person.

Acknowledgements. This research was supported by FONDECYT (Chile) under grant number 1170002: *"An effective Linguistically-motivated computational model for opinion retrieval in sentiment analysis tasks"*.

References

1. Bauml, M., Stiefelhagen, R.: Evaluation of local features for person re-identification in image sequences. In: 10th IEEE International Conference on Advanced Video and Signal-Based Surveillance, Klagenfurt, Austria (2011)
2. Bazzani, L., Cristani, M., Perina, A., Murino, V.: Multiple-shot person re-identification by chromatic and epitomic analyses. Pattern Recogn. Lett. **33**(7), 898 903 (2012). Special Issue on Awards from ICPR 2010
3. Cheng, D.S., Cristani, M.: Person re-identification by articulated appearance matching. In: Gong, S., Cristani, M., Yan, S., Loy, C.C. (eds.) Person Re-Identification. ACVPR, pp. 139–160. Springer, London (2014). https://doi.org/10.1007/978-1-4471-6296-4_7
4. Farenzena, M., Bazzani, L., Perina, A., Murino, V., Cristani, M.: Person re-identification by symmetry-driven accumulation of local features. In: IEEE Computer Vision and Pattern Recognition, San Francisco, CA (2010)
5. Hamdoun, O., Moutarde, F., Stanciulescu, B., Steux, B.: Person re-identification in multi-camera system by signature based on interest point descriptors collected on short video sequences. In: Second ACM/IEEE International Conference on Distributed Smart Cameras (ICDSC), pp. 1–6 (2008)
6. Karanam, S., Yang, L., Richard, J.: Person re-identification with discriminatively trained viewpoint invariant dictionaries. In: IEEE International Conference on Computer Vision (2015)
7. Khedher, M., El-Yacoubi, M., Dorizzi, B.: Fusion of appearance and motion-based sparse representations for multi-shot person re-identification. Neurocomputing **248**, 94–104 (2017)

8. Kviatkovsky, I., Adam, A., Rivlin, E.: Color invariants for person re-identification. IEEE Trans. Pattern Anal. Mach. Intell. **35**, 1622–1634 (2013)
9. Lisanti, G., Masi, I., Bagdanov, A., Del Bimbo, A.: Person re-identication by iterative re-weighted sparse ranking. IEEE Trans. Pattern Anal. Mach. Intell. **37**, 1629–1642 (2015)
10. Liu, C., Gong, S., Loy, C.C., Lin, X.: Person re-identification: what features are important? In: Fusiello, A., Murino, V., Cucchiara, R. (eds.) ECCV 2012. LNCS, vol. 7583, pp. 391–401. Springer, Heidelberg (2012). https://doi.org/10.1007/978-3-642-33863-2_39
11. Mazzon, R., Tahir, S., Syed, F., Cavallaro, A.: Person re-identification in crowd. Pattern Recogn. Lett. **33**(14), 1828–1837 (2012)
12. Munaro, M., Ghidoni, S., Tartaro, D., Menegatti, E.: A feature-based approach to people re-identification using skeleton keypoints. In: IEEE International Conference on Robotics and Automation, Hong Kong, China (2014)
13. Pedagadi, S., Orwell, J., Velastin, S., Boghossian, B.: Local fisher discriminant analysis for pedestrian re-identification. In: IEEE Conference on Computer Vision and Pattern Recognition (CVPR), pp. 3318–3325, June 2013
14. Xiao, L., Mingli, S., Dacheng, T., Xingchen, Z., Chen, C., Jiajun, B.: Semi-supervised coupled dictionary learning for person re-identification. In: IEEE Conference on Computer Vision and Pattern Recognition (CVPR), pp. 3550–3557, June 2014
15. Zheng, W., Gong, S., Xiang, T.: Reidentification by relative distance comparison. IEEE Trans. Pattern Anal. Mach. Intell. **35**(3), 653–668 (2013)

Knowledge Discovery Process
for Detection of Spatial Outliers

Giovanni Daián Rottoli[1,2,3(✉)] ⓘ, Hernán Merlino[3],
and Ramón García-Martínez[3]

[1] PhD Program on Computer Sciences, Universidad Nacional de La Plata,
La Plata, Argentina
[2] PhD Scholarship Program to Reinforce R+D+I Areas,
Universidad Tecnológica Nacional, Ciudad Autónoma de Buenos Aires, Argentina
rottolig@frcu.utn.edu.ar
[3] Information Systems Research Group, National University of Lanús,
Remedios de Escalada, Argentina
hmerlino@unla.edu.ar

Abstract. Detection of spatial outliers is a spatial data mining task aimed at discovering data observations that differ from other data observations within its spatial neighborhood. Some considerations that depend on the problem domain and data characteristics have to be taken into account for the selection of the data mining algorithms to be used in each data mining project. This massive amount of possible algorithm combinations makes it necessary to design a knowledge discovery process for detection of local spatial outliers in order to perform this activity in a standardized way. This work provides a proposal for this knowledge discovery process based on the Knowledge Discovery in Database process (KDD) and a proof of concept of this design using real world data.

Keywords: Spatial outliers · Local outliers · Spatial data mining
Knowledge discovery process · Spatial clustering

1 Introduction

Spatial outlier discovery is a knowledge discovery and data mining trend that has been used for many applications in fields such as climatology, geology, medicine, ecology and chemistry, among others [1–3].

Given a spatially referenced dataset $SD = \{d_i\}, i = 1..|SD|$, with each spatial object $d_i = [s_{i1}, s_{i2}, \ldots, s_{im}, v_{i1}, v_{i2}, \ldots, v_{in}]$, with spatial attributes $s_{ij} \in d_i, j = 1..m$ and non-spatial attributes $v_{ik} \in d_i, k = 1..n$, a spatial outlier is defined as an observation $d \in SD$, whose non-spatial attributes values differ from the non-spatial attributes values of its spatial neighbors [4]. For example, a new house

© Springer International Publishing AG, part of Springer Nature 2018
M. Mouhoub et al. (Eds.): IEA/AIE 2018, LNAI 10868, pp. 57–68, 2018.
https://doi.org/10.1007/978-3-319-92058-0_6

in an old neighborhood of a growing metropolitan area is a spatial outlier based on the non-spatial attribute "house age". Because of this, spatial outliers are considered *local outliers* [5].

Many methods have been developed for spatial outlier mining, such as Local Outlier Factor (LOF), Spatial Local Outlier Measure (SLOM), Novel Local Outlier Detection Method (NLOD), etc. [6–13], but some considerations should be taken into account.

First, according to Chandola et al. (2009) [14] and Liu et al. (2017) [15], it is a challenge nowadays to select the way in which neighborhoods are defined for local outlier detection without previous knowledge about the data domain. The contextual dependency of spatially referenced data causes that a spatial object may or may not be considered an outlier, according to the way in which neighborhoods were built. Then, a non-spatial attribute may vary in the space without it representing an abnormality. According to the given example, in a metropolitan area, the age of the buildings decreases gradually, with oldest ones located in the historical center. Lastly, a certain neighborhood may represent a spatial abnormality in relation to other neighborhoods, without spatial points being outliers.

Some of the methods proposed in the bibliography allow us to deal with some of the aforementioned considerations, but this shows the need to have several methods for outlier detection specialized in particular cases that can be varied to approach different situations, depending on the problem domain.

In this work, we propose a knowledge discovery process for detection of spatial outliers in order to have a standard procedure to perform this activity, regardless of the problem domain, the characteristics of the data and therefore, the data mining methods to be used.

This paper is organized as follows. Section 2 contains the knowledge discovery process for detection of spatial outliers. Section 3 shows how the process works using real-world data. Finally, conclusions and futures lines of work are presented in Sect. 4.

2   Knowledge Discovery Process for Detection of Spatial Outliers

In this paper we propose a knowledge discovery process for detection of spatial outliers based on the Knowledge Discovery on Database process (KDD) [16], designed as a pipeline with well defined and separate activities to be able to use different data mining approaches for each of these tasks, in order to adapt the process to the particular data mining problem (Fig. 1).

This process includes steps for data preparation, neighborhood definition and description, with a proposal to be used in case of not having a predefined method to perform this activity; outlier detection; group outlier detection; and information analysis. All steps of the process are described in the following subsections.

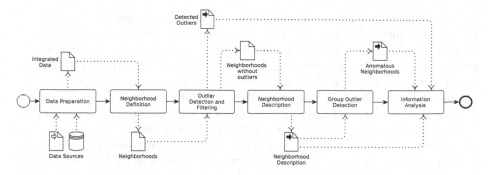

Fig. 1. Knowledge discovery process for detection of local spatial outliers, in Business Process Model Notation (BPMN)

2.1 Data Preparation

The first step for outlier detection is to integrate all the data, obtained from different sources into one single record of spatial objects consisting of spatial attributes, relative to the space, such as latitude and longitude, and non-spatial attributes, relevant to the problem domain (Table 1).

Table 1. Integrated data format

Id	Spatial attributes	Non-spatial attributes
id_1	s_{1j}	v_{1j}
id_2	s_{2j}	v_{2j}
$\vdots$	$\vdots$	$\vdots$
id_n	s_{nj}	v_{nj}

Each data source usually has its own format for data representation. For this reason all the sources must be integrated, cleaning errors, dealing with inconsistencies, and normalizing the attributes values if necessary. Also, it can be useful to use attribute selection algorithms such as Boruta [17] on non-spatial attributes if the number of columns is too large. Data preparation is a well-known activity of the KDD process [16].

2.2 Neighborhood Definition

After the construction of a unique data table, it is necessary to select a criterion for the construction of neighborhoods: as mentioned before, depending on the way in which neighborhoods are defined, some spatial points may or may not be considered outliers.

This criterion is related to the problem domain; in some cases, there might be a predefined method to consider two or more points as neighbors, and in other cases the business intelligence and data analysts might ignore it. Because of this, we propose the use of unsupervised learning using spatial clustering techniques to perform this activity if the criterion to group the data is unknown.

In previous works [12,15], spatial clustering techniques were used for outlier detection considering the points that do not belong to any cluster (or single-point clusters) as anomalous. In this work, on the other hand, different clustering algorithms can be used for definition of the regions that presents a homogeneous behavior in relation to the non-spatial attributes of the spatial data. The points that differ from the normal behavior of its neighborhood will be considered outliers.

This work proposes the use of REDCAP algorithms for spatial clustering. This graph-based algorithm family is aimed at discovering clusters of arbitrary shape with all its elements contiguous to each other. This contiguity criterion, as mentioned before, depends on the problem domain [18–20].

As result of this activity a new column with the neighborhood to which each spatial object belongs is added to the original data table (Table 2).

Table 2. Integrated data format with neighborhoods

Id	Spatial attributes	Non-spatial attributes		Neighborhood
id_1	s_{1j}	v_{1j}		N_1
id_2	s_{2j}	v_{2j}		N_2
$\vdots$	$\vdots$	$\vdots$	$\vdots$	
id_n	s_{nj}	v_{nj}		N_l

2.3 Outlier Detection and Filtering

The spatial data with the spatial neighborhoods is used as input in order to discover spatial objects that do not have a normal behavior in relation to other spatial objects in its neighborhood. Those abnormal points will be considered outliers.

To perform this analysis a measure of outlierness must be calculated for each spatial point in each neighborhood using its non-spatial attributes to discover the deviations in each cluster, considering that these attributes were used to group similar spatial points. Different algorithms can be used, such as LOF, SLOM, different distance measures like Euclidean or Mahalanobis, among others.

This work proposes the use of Mahalanobis Distance [21,22] to calculate how much do the non-spatial values of a spatial object differ from the median values of their neighbors. The reason for using this method is the fact that this distance takes into account the correlations of the data set, but a few different methods can be used depending on the problem domain. For example, LOF-based algorithm can be used to consider density between points, or even more complex methods can be applied, such as the ones proposed by Kuna et al. (2012) [23].

After calculating the outlierness value, the spatial points with a value higher than a user-specified threshold must be filtered and two different tables will be generated: one with the anomalous points and one with the non-anomalous points.

2.4   Neighborhood Description

In this step, after filtering the outliers from the database, it is necessary to describe the normal behavior of each neighborhood in order to use it later in the analysis step to find out the characteristics of the abnormal data objects.

Unsupervised learning discovers implicit patterns from data, but they must be described according to the values of its non-spatial attributes to provide an easy understanding of the process results to analysts.

Several methods can be used to perform this activity and all of them can be complemented. For example, the application of rule-based classification algorithms such as C4.5 [24, 25] or CART [26, 27] is a good tool to find out the decision rules that describe each neighborhood [20], as well as classical statistical measures such as mean and standard deviation of each non-spatial data attribute. The selection of the tools and algorithms also depends on the problem domain and the data characteristics.

The result of this step is a description of each spatial neighborhood which will be used later to detect outlier clusters.

2.5   Group Outlier Detection

As mentioned before, some spatial clusters could have very different behavior to its spatial neighbors. No progression can be noticed between adjacent clusters. An example of this is shown in Fig. 2.

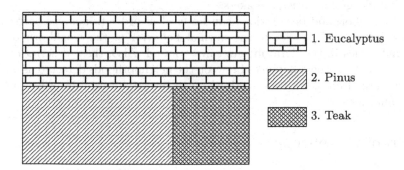

Fig. 2. Example of tree plantation distribution.

Consider this image as a tree plantation where each pattern corresponds to a spatial cluster or spatial area with a different kind of tree: Eucalyptus, Pinus and Teak. The description of each cluster will be based on the spatial object attribute Species, but, if we consider another attribute such as the rotation age of each kind of tree, we can know that the Teak tree cluster is anomalous in relation to its neighbors because of its old age (63.3 years in average) compared to its neighbors: an average of 8.2 years in the case of eucalyptus, and 20.16 years for the pinus species [28].

Because of this, it is possible to model each spatial cluster as spatial objects with its non-spatial attributes equal to the description data obtained in the last step and using the adjacency between them as neighboring criteria. The example shown above is modeled in Table 3.

In this spatial clusters model, any of the data outlierness values mentioned in Sect. 2.3 can be used to assess whether any cluster deviates too much from its neighbors. In the same way as in the previous cases, the model depends on the problem domain and the analyst should select the methods they deem more appropriate.

Table 3. Description table for the data cluster examples (may not be correct).

Id	Species	Rotation length avg.	Rotation length S.D.	...
1	Eucalyptus	8.2	0.83	...
2	Pinus	20.16	3.43	...
3	Teak	63.3	5.77	...

2.6   Information Analysis

At this point of the process, many information resources were created. These resources are (i) the list of the spatial data objects marked as outliers, (ii) the description of the normal behavior of the neighborhoods, and (iii) the oulierness level of each neighborhood. This information has to be analyzed to generate useful knowledge for decision makers.

The neighborhood descriptions can be used in order to analyze each of the outliers detected: if you know the normal behavior of the neighborhood, the abnormal values in the data objects can be found. Also, these descriptions can be used to find out the differences between the neighborhoods detected as outliers and the normal ones. All these activities can be automatized in order to speed up the analysis.

3   Proof of Concept

In this section a real dataset and simple data mining algorithms were used to show how the proposed process works in a real scenario, not with an emphasis on the results of the outlier search, but on the operation of the proposed process using real data.

The real dataset used in this proof of concept corresponds to county population data from the United States of America [29]. From this data file, only counties from 5 states were used in order to reduce the dataset size: Illinois, Indiana, Kentucky, Missouri and Tennessee. Also, only four non-spatial attributes were selected from the original data file, and two new spatial attributes were generated from geographical data: 'POPESTIMATE2016', 7/1/2016 total resident population estimate, renamed as 'Pop'; 'BIRTHS2016', Births in period 7/1/2015 to 6/30/2016, renamed as 'Births'; 'DEATHS2016', Deaths in period 7/1/2015 to 6/30/2016, renamed as 'Deaths'; 'INTERNATIONALMIG2016', Net international migration in period 7/1/2015 to 6/30/2016, renamed as 'Mig'; 'Lat', generated attribute with the Latitude of the county centroid, and 'Long', generated attribute with the longitude of the county centroid. Records with empty fields were also removed, resulting in 524 rows.

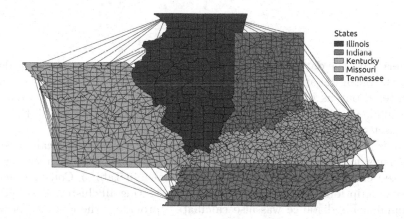

Fig. 3. Delaunay triangulation as contiguity criterion between counties centroids.

This integrated dataset was used as input for REDCAP first-order single-linkage regionalization algorithm [18] considering two counties as contiguous if their centroids are linked with an edge in the county centroid's Delaunay triangulation (Fig. 3). This algorithm is not the most efficient from the REDCAP family, but it was chosen because of its simplicity to carry out the proof of concept. This activity resulted in nine clusters or neighborhoods (Fig. 4). It should be noted that the Haversine formula was used to calculate the distance between spatial points.

After neighborhood definition, the Mahalanobis distance was calculated for each object as an outlierness measure using only its non-spatial attributes , as shown in Formula 1, where s_j is the vector of non-spatial values of the evaluated point, μ is the vector of non-spatial mean values from the neighborhood, and C is the covariance matrix.

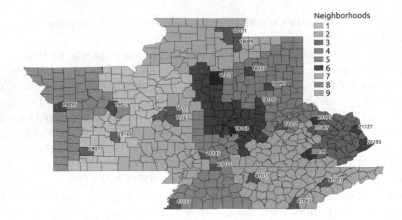

Fig. 4. Detected neighborhoods in USA Counties. Shaded counties were detected as outliers.

$$\sqrt{(s_j - \mu)'\mathbf{C}^{-1}(s_j - \mu)} \qquad (1)$$

Afterwards, the data records with a distance higher than one standard deviation of the mean distance of the other spatial objects in the same neighborhood were filtered out as outliers(Fig. 4). As a result of this activity, two datasets were available: one with only outlier counties (Table 4), and one with the original dataset without the outliers.

The dataset without outliers was described using simple statistical measures: for each neighborhood, the mean and standard deviation of each non-spatial attribute were calculated, yielding the values shown in Table 5. Considering each of these descriptions as a spatial object and considering all clusters as neighbors, the Mahalanobis distance was also calculated, providing the distance between each description in order to discover anomalous clusters. Neighborhoods with a distance that differs from the mean distance by more than 1 standard deviation are considered outliers.

Using all the information obtained, it is possible to acquire knowledge about the anomalous data behavior using the filtered outliers and the neighborhood descriptions: for example, counties with GEOId 29077 and 29183 are two of the outliers discovered in neighborhood 1 (Table 4), these outliers have values considerably greater than the values of the description of the neighborhood. On the other hand, it must be highlighted that the other outlier in this neighborhood also has bigger attribute values than its neighborhood description, with the exception of the number of deaths, which is smaller. This knowledge could be of interest for the business intelligence.

Additionally, using the neighborhood description data with the Mahalanobis distances, it can be seen that outlier clusters 3 and 8 are mainly characterized by a small number of migrations compared to the other clusters.

Table 4. Outliers discovered using the proposed process, ordered by neighborhood and GeoID

GeoID	Non-spatial attributes				Spatial attributes		Neighborhood
	Pop	Births	Deaths	Mig	Long	Lat	
29077	288690	3590	2753	341	−93.34199	37.25805	1
29169	52654	780	271	233	−92.20766	37.82463	1
29189	998581	11591	10027	2186	−90.44341	38.64068	1
17031	5203499	68049	42297	18434	−87.64616	41.8954	2
18089	485846	5918	4908	324	−87.37636	41.4722	2
21097	18646	215	205	21	−84.33139	38.44181	3
21127	15863	200	210	21	−82.73475	38.06788	3
21195	60555	623	831	11	−82.39587	37.46903	3
21199	63956	716	795	38	−84.57718	37.10393	3
18105	145496	1305	894	1019	−86.52314	39.16092	4
18097	941229	14433	8015	3033	−86.13847	39.78171	4
18157	188059	2356	1138	1716	−86.8941	40.38862	4
29019	176594	2119	1064	698	−92.30966	38.99062	5
29095	691801	9423	6473	895	−94.34609	39.0085	5
17019	208419	2413	1345	1798	−88.19919	40.14008	6
18163	181721	2188	1887	186	−87.58578	38.02514	6
17119	265759	3032	2814	148	−89.90517	38.82985	7
17163	262759	3282	2678	127	−89.92841	38.4703	7
29510	311404	4547	3070	981	−90.24512	38.63581	7
21035	38437	407	408	119	−88.2722	36.6211	8
21145	65162	728	848	9	−88.71272	37.05408	8
47157	934603	13448	8326	1258	−89.8956	35.184	8
21067	318449	4107	2231	1350	−84.45873	38.04233	9
21111	765352	9918	7513	2460	−85.65916	38.18719	9
47037	684410	10438	5461	3091	−86.78482	36.16944	9
47065	357738	4227	3529	527	−85.16479	35.18086	9
47093	456132	5285	4321	598	−83.93709	35.99322	9

Also, combining this information it can be noticed that the anomalous neighborhood 8 has three outlier counties, but only one of them has a number of migrations in the same order than its description, in spite of having higher values for its other attributes. These characteristics can be valuable for decision making.

Lastly, a look at the outlier distribution on the map may be worthwhile (Fig. 4): the majority of the outliers discovered are located at the borders of the

Table 5. Neighborhood description using statistical measures with the distance between them. Outlier clusters are shown in bold.

N	Mean				Standard deviation				M. Dist
	Pop	Births	Deaths	Mig	Pop	Births	Deaths	Mig	
1	33754.67	385.57	331.81	29.22	56192.63	653.11	441.8	85.29	6.93
2	136820.51	1601.74	1092.69	219.86	206767.29	2403.60	1390.69	527.26	7.07
3	**18862.3**	**223.78**	**234**	**3.25**	**12602.97**	**153.18**	**151.7**	**4.71**	**2.52**
4	51439.08	624.69	473.85	56.08	59744.4	787.73	466.96	132.15	5.86
5	30888.16	377.32	291.58	32.88	43050.14	553.7	332.66	67.98	6.78
6	29718.71	351.25	305.15	29.3	32312.55	387.77	276.28	99.9	6.93
7	28076.34	316.02	314.86	17.15	34015.47	387.5	314.68	42.58	4.51
8	**25599.76**	**293.5**	**304.91**	**10.91**	**18538.67**	**234.24**	**203.67**	**17.11**	**2.61**
9	45742.36	538.35	455.56	50.61	49057.77	640.15	381.33	112.18	4.74

generated regions. A refinement of the definition of these neighborhoods can be performed by going back to this stage of the proposed process and repeating the detection of outliers, in case they are caused by an error of the regionalization algorithm.

4 Conclusion

This work describes a knowledge discovery process for detection of spatial outliers. This process is designed as a pipeline based on the KDD Process with properly divided activities that include data preparation, neighborhood definition and description, outlier detection and filtering, group outlier detection, and information analysis using the data obtained in each step. These activities are independent from data mining algorithms, allowing data scientists to use the algorithms they deem appropriate to solve the problems related to the problem domain or the data they are working with.

A proof of concept of this knowledge discovery process was provided using real world data, basic algorithms for neighborhood definition, and statistical measures for outlier detection and outliers and neighborhood description, in order to show how the process works in a real setting.

An evaluation for different data mining algorithms must be carried out to find a good combination thereof for well-known problems, in order to have a battery of configurations ready to be used as a starting point in spatial outlier analysis. Also, it is possible to generate a heuristic approach for data mining algorithm selection using problem domain metadata. Lastly, the use of this process into an iterative methodology such as CRISP-DM [30] or MoProPEI [31] must be assessed.

Acknowledgments. The research presented in this paper was partially funded by the PhD Scholarship Program to reinforce R&D&I areas (2016-2020) of the Universidad

Tecnológica Nacional, Research Project 80020160400001LA of National University of Lanús, and PIO CONICET-UNLa 22420160100032CO of National Research Council of Science and Technology (CONICET), Argentina. The authors also want to extend their gratitude to Kevin-Mark Bozell Poudereux, for proofreading the translation, and the anonymous reviewers of this work for their valuable comments and suggestions.

References

1. Araki, S., et al.: Effect of spatial outliers on the regression modelling of air pollutant concentrations: a case study in Japan. Atmos. Environ. **153**, 83–93 (2017)
2. Bakon, M., et al.: A data mining approach for multivariate outlier detection in postprocessing of multitemporal InSAR results. IEEE J. Sel. Topics Appl. Earth Obs. Remote Sens. **10**, 2791–2798 (2017)
3. Michel, B., et al.: Spatial outlier detection in the air quality monitoring network of Normandy (France). In: GRASPA Working Papers (2014)
4. Deepak, P.: Anomaly detection for data with spatial attributes. In: Celebi, M.E., Aydin, K. (eds.) Unsupervised Learning Algorithms, pp. 1–32. Springer, Cham (2016). https://doi.org/10.1007/978-3-319-24211-8_1
5. Shekhar, S., Chang-Tien, L., Zhang, P.: A unified approach to detecting spatial outliers. GeoInformatica **7**(2), 139–166 (2003)
6. Breunig, M.M., et al.: LOF: identifying density-based local outliers. ACM SIGMOD Rec. **29**(2), 93–104 (2000)
7. Chawla, S., Sun, P.: SLOM: a new measure for local spatial outliers. Knowl. Inf. Syst. **9**(4), 412–429 (2006)
8. Schubert, E., Weiler, M., Zimek, A.: Outlier detection and trend detection: two sides of the same coin. In: 2015 IEEE International Conference on Data Mining Workshop (ICDMW). IEEE (2015)
9. Kamble, B., Doke, K.: Outlier detection approaches in data mining. Int. Res. J. Eng. Technol. (IRJET) **4**(3), 634–638 (2017)
10. Ernst, M., Haesbroeck, G.: Comparison of local outlier detection techniques in spatial multivariate data. Data Min. Knowl. Discov. **31**(2), 371–399 (2017)
11. Tang, B., He, H.: A local density-based approach for outlier detection. Neurocomputing **241**, 171–180 (2017)
12. Du, H., et al.: Novel clustering-based approach for local outlier detection. In: 2016 IEEE Conference on Computer Communications Workshops (INFOCOM WKSHPS). IEEE (2016)
13. Liu, X., Lu, C.-T., Chen, F.: Spatial outlier detection: Random walk based approaches. In: Proceedings of the 18th SIGSPATIAL International Conference on Advances in Geographic Information Systems. ACM (2010)
14. Chandola, V., Banerjee, A., Kumar, V.: Anomaly detection: a survey. ACM Comput. Surv. (CSUR) **41**(3), 15 (2009)
15. Liu, Q., et al.: Unsupervised detection of contextual anomaly in remotely sensed data. Remote Sens. Environ. **202**, 75–87 (2017)
16. Fayyad, U., Piatetsky-Shapiro, G., Smyth, P.: The KDD process for extracting useful knowledge from volumes of data. Commun. ACM **39**(11), 27–34 (1996)
17. Kursa, M.B., Jankowski, A., Rudnicki, W.R.: Borutaa system for feature selection. Fundam. Inf. **101**(4), 271–285 (2010)
18. Guo, D.: Regionalization with dynamically constrained agglomerative clustering and partitioning (REDCAP). Int. J. Geogr. Inf. Sci. **22**(7), 801–823 (2008)

19. Mennis, J., Guo, D.: Spatial data mining and geographic knowledge discovery: an introduction. Comput. Environ. Urban Syst. **33**(6), 403–408 (2009)
20. Rottoli, G.D., Merlino, H., García-Martínez, R.: Knowledge discovery process for description of spatially referenced clusters. In: International Conference on Software Engineering & Knowledge Engineering. Ed. USA KSI Research Inc. and Knowledge Systems Institute, 410415 (2017). https://doi.org/10.18293/SEKE2017-013
21. De Maesschalck, R., Jouan-Rimbaud, D., Massart, D.L.: The Mahalanobis distance. Chemom. Intell. Lab. Syst. **50**(1), 1–18 (2000)
22. Hodge, V., Austin, J.: A survey of outlier detection methodologies. Artif. Intell. Rev. **22**(2), 85–126 (2004)
23. Kuna, H., García-Martínez, R., Villatoro, F.: Automatic outliers fields detection in databases. J. Model. Simul. Syst. **3**(1), 14–20 (2012)
24. Quinlan, J.R.: Improved use of continuous attributes in C4. 5. J. Artif. Intell. Res. **4**, 77–90 (1996)
25. Quinlan, J.R.: C4. 5: Programs for Machine Learning. Elsevier, New York (2014)
26. Breiman, L., et al.: Classification and Regression Trees. CRC Press, Boca Raton (1984)
27. Bel, L., et al.: CART algorithm for spatial data: application to environmental and ecological data. Comput. Stat. Data Anal. **53**(8), 3082–3093 (2009)
28. Luis, U., Pérez, O.: Table 1: Productivity and rotation lengths for main forest plantation trees in selected tropical countries. Mean Annual Volume Increment of Selected Industrial Forest Plantation Species. Forest Plantations Thematic Papers. Forestry Department of Food and Agriculture Organization of the United Nations (2001)
29. United States Census Bureau: Population, population change and estimated components of population change, 1 April, 2010 to 1 July, 2016. (CO-EST2016-alldata), County Population Totals Datasets: 2010–2016. On-Line: https://www.census.gov/data/datasets/2016/demo/popest/-counties-total.html. Accessed 17 Oct 2017
30. Wirth, R., Hipp, J.: CRISP-DM: towards a standard process model for data mining. In: Proceedings of the 4th International Conference on the Practical Applications of Knowledge Discovery and Data Mining (2000)
31. Martins, S., Pesado, P., García-Martínez, R.: Intelligent systems in modeling phase of information mining development process. In: Fujita, H., Ali, M., Selamat, A., Sasaki, J., Kurematsu, M. (eds.) IEA/AIE 2016. LNCS (LNAI), vol. 9799, pp. 3–15. Springer, Cham (2016). https://doi.org/10.1007/978-3-319-42007-3_1

Text Modeling Using Multinomial Scaled Dirichlet Distributions

Nuha Zamzami[1,2][✉] and Nizar Bouguila[1]

[1] Concordia Institute for Information Systems Engineering,
Concordia University, Montreal, QC, Canada
n_zamz@encs.concordia.ca, nizar.bouguila@concordia.ca
[2] Faculty of Computing and Information Technology, King Abdulaziz University,
Jeddah, Saudi Arabia

Abstract. The Dirichlet Compound Multinomial (DCM), the composition of the Dirichlet and the multinomial, is a widely accepted generative model for text documents that takes into account burstiness. However, recent research showed that the Dirichlet is not the best to be chosen as a prior to multinomial. In this paper, we propose a novel model called the Multinomial Scaled Dirichlet (MSD) distribution that is the composition of the scaled Dirichlet distribution and the multinomial. Moreover, we investigate the Expectation Maximization (EM) with the MSD mixture model as a new clustering algorithm for documents. Experiments show that the new model is competitive with the best state-of-the-art methods on different text data sets.

1 Introduction

Given the rapid growth of on-line information, developing efficient methods to access, sort and search through various sources of data is becoming more crucial. Handling and organizing data in textual format using text categorization techniques are essential for classifying new documents and finding interesting information within World Wide Web, digital libraries, and electronic mail [1]. The applications of text Modeling include a number of tasks such as document organization and browsing, corpus summarization and document classification [2]. Due the sparse and high dimensional representation of the textual data, many interesting and powerful contributions to improve the accuracy through designing text-specific algorithms have been proposed in the literature over the last two decades.

Multinomial models are popular in text classification [2,3], as they have been shown to outperform other probabilistic models for text classification which were implemented within the naive Bayes framework, namely, Poisson, Bernoulli, and negative binomial [4]. However, the multinomial independency assumption, *i.e.,* each word of the document is generated independently from every other, is not valid for word emissions in natural text where words tend to appear in bursts [5]. Recently, machine learning researchers have detected several technical problems associated with the multinomial assumption [6,7].

© Springer International Publishing AG, part of Springer Nature 2018
M. Mouhoub et al. (Eds.): IEA/AIE 2018, LNAI 10868, pp. 69–80, 2018.
https://doi.org/10.1007/978-3-319-92058-0_7

The most popular solution is the Dirichlet Compound Multinomial (DCM) which is the composition of the Dirichlet and the multinomial [7]. The hierarchical approach of DCM considers the count vector for each document to be generated by a multinomial distribution whose parameters are generated by the Dirichlet distribution. The model can be interpretted as a bag-of-bags-of words [7]. Numerous computational advantages can be obtained using such composition that is based mainly on the fact that the Dirichlet is conjugate to the multinomial [8]. The Dirichlet, however, has some drawbacks, including its very restrictive negative covariance structure, inconsiderate relations between categories, and its poor parameterization [9–11]. Thus, different interesting alternatives to the DCM have been lately proposed, namely, the Multinomial Generalized Dirichlet Distribution (MGDD) [12], and the Multinomial Beta-Liouville Distribution (MBLD) [13].

This paper proposes another alternative model called the Multinomial Scaled Dirichlet (MSD) distribution, which is the composition of the scaled Dirichlet distribution and the multinomial in the same way that the DCM, MGDD, MBLD are the compositions of the Dirichlet, the generalized Dirichlet and the Beta-Liouville, respectively, with the multinomial. The scaled Dirichlet is a generalization of the Dirichlet distribution, which is the best known distribution for categorical data modeling. Scaled Dirichlet includes the Dirichlet as a special case, and is shown to be an interesting prior to the multinomial.

Concerning the parameters learning for the multinomial scaled Dirichlet mixture model, we propose the use of the Expectation Maximization (EM) algorithm. By modeling different document collections, we show that the mixture of MSD is better suited than the mixtures of multinomial and the DCM for modeling text data. Although the focus here is on modeling text documents, the MSD is applicable in many other domains also where burstiness is important, such as several tasks in computer vision.

This paper is organized as follows. First, Sect. 2 briefly reviews the Multinomial and DCM distributions. Next, Sect. 3 discusses the MSD distribution in detail where we propose a new prior to the multinomial, namely, the scaled Dirichlet. Section 4 applies the expectation-maximization approach with the MSD mixture to obtain a new clustering algorithm for modeling text documents. Section 5 is devoted to experimental results aiming to evaluate the performance of the proposed model. Finally, Sect. 6 concludes the paper.

2   Multinomial and Dirichlet Compound Multinomial

Multinomial distribution, the multivariate generalization of the Binomial distribution, is widely used in text clustering. In modeling text documents using multinomial distribution, an individual document is represented as a vector of word counts (bag-of-words representation). The assumptions for Multinomial model are the length of document n (in tokens) is known, and the words occurrences are independent from each other. Define $\mathbf{X} = (x_1, \ldots, x_D)$ as a random vector of counts where x_d represents the number of times a word w_d appears in the document.

Then the probability of a document $\mathbf{X}$, represented as a vector of counts, that it follows a multinomial distribution with parameters $\boldsymbol{\rho} = (\rho_1, \ldots, \rho_D)$, is given by:

$$\mathcal{M}(\mathbf{X}|\boldsymbol{\rho}) = \frac{n!}{\prod\limits_{d=1}^{D} x_d!} \prod_{d=1}^{D} \rho_d^{x_d} \tag{1}$$

where D is the size of the vocabulary, and $n = \sum_{d=1}^{D} x_d$.

The multinomial models are simple and convenient to use, thus, they are very popular. However, their main drawback is that they make a naive Bayes assumption: that the probability of each word event in a document is independent of the words context and its position in the document [4], which is not very accurate. Indeed, various heuristics to address this issue have been proposed in the literature to improve the classification accuracy. Examples include: log-normalizing counts [6], exponential family fit [14], and the mixture model [15].

In natural languages, the word frequencies have been shown to be affected by the phenomenon of burstiness [5,16]. Modeling the probabilities of repeat occurrences of words improves the classification performance and information retrieval accuracy. Multinomial distributions fail to capture this phenomenon well as was shown in [7]. An appropriate and efficient solution to address this issue is the hierarchical model called Dirichlet Compound Multinomial (DCM), where for a specific document, the multinomial is linked to particular sub-topics, and thus, it makes the emission of some words more likely than others. This gives it the ability to handle *burstiness* even for rare words, *i.e.*, if a rare word appears once in a document, it is much more likely to appear again. The hierarchical approach of DCM introduces the prior information into the construction of the statistical model, where the Dirichlet is generally taken as a prior to the multinomial distribution. The Dirichlet distribution, with a set of parameters $\boldsymbol{\alpha} = (\alpha_1, \ldots, \alpha_D)$, is defined as:

$$\mathcal{D}(\boldsymbol{\rho}|\boldsymbol{\alpha}) = \frac{\Gamma(A)}{\prod\limits_{d=1}^{D} \Gamma(\alpha_d)} \prod_{d=1}^{D} \rho_d^{\alpha_d - 1} \tag{2}$$

where $A = \sum_{d=1}^{D} \alpha_d$. Then, the DCM is the marginal distribution given by the following integration [7]:

$$\mathcal{DCM}(\mathbf{X}|\boldsymbol{\alpha}) = \int_{\rho} \mathcal{M}(\mathbf{X}|\boldsymbol{\rho})\mathcal{D}(\boldsymbol{\rho}|\boldsymbol{\alpha})d\rho$$

$$= \frac{n!}{\prod\limits_{d=1}^{D} (x_d)!} \frac{\Gamma(A)}{\Gamma(\sum\limits_{d=1}^{D} x_d + \alpha_d)} \prod_{d=1}^{D} \frac{\Gamma(x_d + \alpha_d)}{\Gamma(\alpha_d)} \tag{3}$$

We can note that compared to the multinomial, the DCM has one extra degree of freedom, since its parameters are not constrained to sum up to one, which makes it more practical [6,9]. Using this prior information, we can show that the $\hat{\rho}_d$ estimates are given by:

$$\hat{\rho}_d = \frac{\alpha_d + x_d}{\sum\limits_{d=1}^{D} \alpha_d + \sum\limits_{d=1}^{D} x_d}, \qquad d = 1, \ldots, D \tag{4}$$

Although the Dirichlet distribution is a natural conjugate prior for the multinomial likelihood and it exhibits many convenient mathematical properties, it is not the most appropriate solution. Dirichlet does not take into account relative positions between categories or multinomial cells [11]. Moreover, it has a poor parameterization that limits its ability to better model variance and covariance [10]. A more flexible choice of a prior to mutinomial, that can help resolving these issues, is a generalization of the Dirichlet called the scaled Dirichlet distribution [11,17].

3   Multinomial Scaled Dirichlet (MSD) Distribution

The scaled dirichlet is a generalization of the Dirichlet distribution, which is the distribution of a random vector obtained after applying the perturbation and powering operations to a Dirichlet random composition. These operations define a vector-space structure in the simplex, and play the same role as sum and product by scalars in real space [17].

The scaled Dirichlet has a set of parameters; $\boldsymbol{\alpha} = (\alpha_1, \ldots, \alpha_D)$ which is the shape parameter, and $\boldsymbol{\beta} = (\beta_1, \ldots, \beta_D)$ which is the scale parameter. The probability density of the probability vector $\boldsymbol{\rho} = (\rho_1, \ldots, \rho_D)$, is given by [17]:

$$\mathcal{SD}(\boldsymbol{\rho}|\boldsymbol{\alpha}, \boldsymbol{\beta}) = \frac{\Gamma(A)}{\prod\limits_{d=1}^{D} \Gamma(\alpha_d)} \frac{\prod\limits_{d=1}^{D} \beta_d^{\alpha_d} \rho_d^{\alpha_d - 1}}{\left(\sum\limits_{d=1}^{D} \beta_d \rho_d \right)^A} \tag{5}$$

where Γ denotes the Gamma function.

The shape parameter $\boldsymbol{\alpha}$ simply describes the form or shape of the scaled Dirichlet distribution, and its flexibility is very significant in finding patterns and shapes inherent in a data set. The scale parameter $\boldsymbol{\beta}$ controls how the density plot is spread out where the shape of the density is invariant, irrespective of the value of a constant or uniform scale parameter.

Note that the Dirichlet distribution is a special case of the scaled Dirichlet that can be obtained when all elements of the vector $\boldsymbol{\beta}$ are equal to a common constant. Thus, the scaled Dirichlet includes the Dirichlet as a special case. Compared to the Dirichlet, the scaled Dirichlet has D extra parameters, which enhances the model flexibility [18,19].

Integrating over ρ gives the marginal distribution of $\mathbf{X}$, as follows:

$$\mathcal{MSD}(\mathbf{X}|\boldsymbol{\alpha},\boldsymbol{\beta}) = \int_\rho \mathcal{M}(\mathbf{X}|\boldsymbol{\rho})\mathcal{SD}(\boldsymbol{\rho}|\boldsymbol{\alpha},\boldsymbol{\beta})d\rho$$

$$= \int_\rho \frac{n!}{\prod_{d=1}^D x_d!} \prod_{d=1}^D \rho_d^{x_d} \frac{\Gamma(A)}{\prod_{d=1}^D \Gamma(\alpha_d)} \frac{\prod_{d=1}^D \beta_d^{\alpha_d} p_d^{\alpha_d-1}}{\left(\sum_{d=1}^D \beta_d\rho_d\right)^A} d\rho$$

$$= \frac{n!}{\prod_{d=1}^D x_d!} \frac{\Gamma(A)}{\prod_{d=1}^D \Gamma(\alpha_d)} \prod_{d=1}^D \beta_d^{\alpha_d} \int_\rho \frac{\prod_{d=1}^D \rho_d^{x_d+\alpha_d-1}}{\left(\sum_{d=1}^D \beta_d\rho_d\right)^A} d\rho$$

$$= \frac{n!}{\prod_{d=1}^D x_d!} \frac{\Gamma(A)}{\prod_{d=1}^D \Gamma(\alpha_d)} \prod_{d=1}^D \beta_d^{\alpha_d} \frac{\prod_{d=1}^D \Gamma(x_d+\alpha_d)}{\Gamma(\sum_{d=1}^D x_d+\alpha_d)\prod_{d=1}^D \beta_d^{x_d+\alpha_d}}$$

$$= \frac{n!}{\prod_{d=1}^D x_d! \, \Gamma(n+A)} \frac{\Gamma(A)}{\prod_{d=1}^D \beta_d^{x_d}} \prod_{d=1}^D \frac{\Gamma(x_d+\alpha_d)}{\Gamma(\alpha_d)} \qquad (6)$$

The last step of Eq. (6) is obtained by using the fact that $\int_\rho \mathcal{SD}(\boldsymbol{\rho}|\boldsymbol{\alpha},\boldsymbol{\beta}) = 1$, and applying the following empirically tested approximation:
$\left(\sum_{d=1}^D \beta_d \, \rho_d\right)^{\sum_{d=1}^D x_d} \simeq \prod_{d=1}^D \beta_d^{x_d}$, given a common constant value for β.

By setting $\beta_1 = \beta_2 = \cdots = \beta_D = 1$, Eq. (6) is reduced to (3), which is the DCM.

4 MSD Mixture Model Learning

In mixture modeling, we assume that our data population is generated from a mixture of sub populations. Given an observed data set $\mathcal{X}$ with N data instances $\{\mathbf{X}_1,\ldots,\mathbf{X}_N\}$, each D-dimensional vector $\mathbf{X}_i = (x_{i1},\ldots,x_{iD})$ is drawn from a superposition of K multinomial scaled Dirichlet densities of the form:

$$p(\mathbf{X}_i|\boldsymbol{\pi},\boldsymbol{\alpha},\boldsymbol{\beta}) = \sum_{k=1}^K \pi_k \, \mathcal{MSD}(\mathbf{X}_i|\boldsymbol{\alpha}_k,\boldsymbol{\beta}_k) \qquad (7)$$

where π_k ($0 < \pi_k < 1$ and $\sum_{k=1}^K \pi_k = 1$) are the mixing proportions. Each $\mathcal{MSD}$ $(\mathbf{X}_i|\boldsymbol{\alpha}_k,\boldsymbol{\beta}_k)$ is called a component of the mixture, and has its own parameters $\theta_k = \{\boldsymbol{\alpha}_k,\boldsymbol{\beta}_k\}$, where $\boldsymbol{\alpha}_k = (\alpha_{k1},\ldots,\alpha_{kD})$, and $\boldsymbol{\beta}_k = (\beta_{k1},\ldots,\beta_{kD})$.

Next, we introduce a K-dimensional binary random vector $\mathbf{Z_i} = (z_{i1}, \ldots, z_{iK})$ to each data vector $\mathbf{X_i}$, where $z_{ik} \in \{0,1\}$ and $\sum_{k=1}^{K} z_{ik} = 1$. Here, the latent variable $\mathbf{Z_i}$ works as an indicator variable, where:

$$z_{ik} = \begin{cases} 1 & \text{if } \mathbf{X_i} \text{ belongs to component k} \\ 0 & \text{otherwise,} \end{cases} \tag{8}$$

The distribution of the latent variable $\mathcal{Z} = \{\mathbf{Z_1}, \ldots, \mathbf{Z_N}\}$ is conditioned on the mixing coefficients π as:

$$p(\mathcal{Z}|\pi) = \prod_{i=1}^{N} \prod_{k=1}^{K} \pi_k^{z_{ik}} \tag{9}$$

The complete data at this case are $(\mathcal{X}, \mathcal{Z}|\Theta)$, where $\mathcal{X}$ represents a set of observed variables, and $\Theta = (\alpha_1, \ldots, \alpha_K, \beta_1, \ldots, \beta_K, \pi_1, \ldots, \pi_K)$ denotes the set of all latent variables and parameters. For learning a mixture model, Expectation Maximization (EM) algorithm can be used to obtain the maximum likelihood estimates of the mixture parameters. In the **E-step** of the EM algorithm, we compute the posterior probabilities (*i.e.*, the probability that a vector $\mathbf{X_i}$ belongs to cluster k), as:

$$\hat{z}_{ik} = p(k|\mathbf{X}_i, \theta_k) = \frac{\pi_k \, p(\mathbf{X}_i|\theta_k)}{\sum_{k=1}^{K} \pi_k \, p(\mathbf{X}_i|\theta_k)} \tag{10}$$

In the **M-step**, we update the model parameter estimates according to:

$$\Theta = \arg \max_{\Theta} \{\mathcal{L}(\mathcal{X}, \mathcal{Z}|\Theta)\}$$
$$= \arg \max_{\Theta} \sum_{i=1}^{N} \sum_{k=1}^{K} z_{ik} \, \log \left(p(\mathbf{X}_i|\theta_k)\pi_k\right) \tag{11}$$

when maximizing (11) we obtain:

$$\pi_k = \frac{1}{N} \sum_{i=1}^{N} z_{ik} \tag{12}$$

We can obtain the maximum likelihood parameter estimates for the MSD by taking the derivative of the log-likelihood function and find Θ_{MLE} when the derivative is equal to zero. The complete data log likelihood corresponding to a K-component mixture is given by:

$$\mathcal{L}(\mathcal{X}, \mathcal{Z}|\Theta) = \sum_{k=1}^{K} \sum_{i=1}^{N} z_{ik} \left(\log \pi_k + \log p(\mathbf{X}_i|\theta_k)\right) \tag{13}$$

where: $\log p(\mathbf{X}_i|\theta_k) = \log(n_i!) - \sum_{d=1}^{D} \log \Gamma(x_{id} + 1) + \log \Gamma(A) - \log \Gamma(n_i + A)$

$$- \sum_{d=1}^{D} x_{id} \log(\beta_{kd}) + \sum_{d=1}^{D} \left(\log \Gamma(x_{id} + \alpha_{kd}) - \log \Gamma(\alpha_{kd}) \right)$$

$$(14)$$

The derivative with respect to α_{kd}, $d = 1, \ldots, D$, is:

$$\frac{\partial \mathcal{L}(\mathcal{X}, \mathcal{Z}|\Theta)}{\partial \alpha_{kd}} = \sum_{i=1}^{N} z_{ik} \frac{\partial}{\partial \alpha_{kd}} \log(p(\mathbf{X}_i|\theta_k))$$

$$= \sum_{i=1}^{N} z_{ik} \left(\Psi(A) - \Psi(n_i + A) + \Psi(x_{id} + \alpha_{kd}) - \Psi(\alpha_{kd}) \right) \quad (15)$$

and the derivative with respect to β_{kd}, $d = 1, \ldots, D$, is:

$$\frac{\partial \mathcal{L}(\mathcal{X}, \mathcal{Z}|\Theta)}{\partial \beta_{kd}} = \sum_{i=1}^{N} z_{ik} \frac{\partial}{\partial \beta_{kd}} \log(p(\mathbf{X}_i|\theta_k))$$

$$= \sum_{i=1}^{N} z_{ik} \left(\frac{-x_{id}}{\beta_{kd}} \right) \quad (16)$$

where Ψ is the digamma function (the logarithmic derivative of the Gamma function). However, we do not obtain a closed-form solution for the α_k and β_k parameters. We therefore use the Newton-Raphson method expressed as:

$$\theta_k^{new} = \theta_k^{old} - H^{-1}G$$
$$\approx [\alpha_k^{old} - H^{-1}G; \beta_k^{old} - H^{-1}G] \quad (17)$$

Where H is the Hessian matrix associated with $\mathcal{L}(\mathcal{X}, \mathcal{Z}|\Theta)$, and G is the first derivatives vector. To calculate the Hessian matrix, we have to compute the second and mixed derivatives of the log likelihood function.

By computing the second and mixed derivatives of $\mathcal{L}(\mathcal{X}, \mathcal{Z}|\Theta)$ with respect to α_{kd}, $d = 1, \ldots, D$, we obtain:

$$\frac{\partial^2 \mathcal{L}(\mathcal{X}, \mathcal{Z}|\Theta)}{\partial \alpha_{kd1} \partial \alpha_{kd2}} = \begin{cases} \sum_{i=1}^{N} z_{ik} \left(\Psi'(A) - \Psi'(n_i + A) + \Psi'(x_{id} + \alpha_{kd}) - \Psi'(\alpha_{kd}) \right) \\ \qquad\qquad\qquad\qquad\qquad\qquad\qquad\qquad\qquad \text{if} \quad d_1 = d_2 = d \\ \sum_{i=1}^{N} z_{ik} \left(\Psi'(A) - \Psi'(n_i + A) \right) \\ \qquad\qquad\qquad\qquad\qquad\qquad\qquad\qquad\qquad\qquad \text{otherwise,} \end{cases}$$

$$(18)$$

where Ψ' is the trigamma function.

By computing the second and mixed derivatives of $\mathcal{L}(\mathcal{X}, \mathcal{Z}|\Theta)$ with respect to β_{kd}, $d = 1, \ldots, D$, we obtain:

$$
\frac{\partial^2 \mathcal{L}(\mathcal{X}, \mathcal{Z}|\Theta)}{\partial \beta_{kd1} \partial \beta_{kd2}} = \begin{cases} \sum_{i=1}^{N} z_{ik} \left(\frac{x_{id}}{\beta_{kd}^2} \right) & \text{if } d_1 = d_2 = d \\ 0 & \text{otherwise,} \end{cases} \tag{19}
$$

The second and mixed derivatives of $\mathcal{L}(\mathcal{X}, \mathcal{Z}|\Theta)$ with respect to α_{kd} and β_{kd}, $d = 1, \ldots, D$, is 0. The complete block Hessian matrix H_k has to be transformed to its inverse before it can be used in the Newton-Raphson maximization. The Hessian matrix for MSD is as follows:

$$
\begin{bmatrix} \mathbf{H}_{(\alpha_{kd1}\alpha_{kd2})} & 0 \\ 0 & \mathbf{H}_{(\beta_{kd1}\beta_{kd2})} \end{bmatrix} \tag{20}
$$

To achieve an optimal performance, a proper initialization is needed to avoid converging to a local maxima. To initialize the π_k parameter, we use the K-means algorithm, and to initialize the model parameters we make use of the method of moments.

In the case of the multinomial scaled Dirichlet distribution, a closed form solution for its moment equations does not exist. Thus, we will initialize the α_k vector using the moments equations of the DCM distribution [20], while the β_k vector will be initialized with equal scaling (a vector of ones). Parameters will be then updated during the EM iterations to take their natural values in relation to the observed data. The complete algorithm for learning the MSD mixture parameters is summarized in (Algorithm 1).

5   Experimental Results

The goal of our experiments is to compare the performance of MSD mixture to the previously proposed generative models widely used for text categorization, DCM and multinomial mixture (MM). We use datasets that have been considered in the past (see for example, [13,21]), namely WebKB4[1], the ModApte version of the Reuters-21578[2] and NIPS[3].

The WebKB4 data set which is a subset of the WebKB data set, containing 4,199 Web pages gathered from computer science departments of various universities. The considered subset is limited to the four most common categories: Course, Faculty, Project, and Student.

The first step in our experiment is removing all stop and rare words (less than 50 occurrences in our experiments) from the vocabularies. Then, we perform the feature selection using the Rainbow package [22], where we select the

---

[1] http://www.cs.cmu.edu/afs/cs.cmu.edu/project/theo-20/www/data.
[2] http://kdd.ics.uci.edu/databases/reuters21578.
[3] https://cs.nyu.edu/~roweis/data.html.

Algorithm 1. EM for estimating the MSD mixture parameters

Input: Dataset $\mathcal{X}$ with N D-dimensional vectors, a specified number of clusters K
Apply the K-means on the ND-dimensional vectors to obtain initial K clusters
Initialize the shape parameters α_k using method of moments
Initialize the scale parameter vector β_k with a vector of ones
repeat
{The Expectation Step(E-step)}
   for $i = 1$ to N **do**
      for $k = 1$ to K **do**
         Compute the posterior probabilities $p(k|\mathbf{X}_i, \theta_k)$ using equation (10)
      end for
   end for
{The Maximization Step(M-step)}
   for $k = 1$ to K **do**
      Update the mixing proportion π_k using equation(12)
      Update the θ_k using equation (17)
   end for
until *convergence*

---

top 300 words. The second step is to represent each web page histogram as a vector containing the frequency of occurrence of each word from the term vector (complete set of words occurring in all the Web pages).

The ModApte data set is a subset of the well-known corpus Reuters-21578, which is composed of 135 classes with a vocabulary of $15,996$ words. The documents in this data set are multilabeled, as they may belong to $0, 1$, or many categories. For our experiments, we consider a subset which is composed of the 10 categories having the highest number of class members ($6,775$ and $2,258$ training and testing documents are considered for this subset, respectively). Since stop words have already been removed in this collections, we are not removing any additional words.

NIPS collection contains the OCRed text of all papers published in the 2002 and 2003 NIPS proceedings. This collection has 391 documents in 9 different topics. Following [21], we use only papers from 2002 and 2003 since earlier and later years papers are organized into different research areas. This data set is characterized by $6,871$ words. Papers that are less than 700 words long were eliminated, and stop words were removed.

We run each algorithm MM, DCM and MSD 100 times with different random initialization and report the average classification accuracy, precision, recall and mutual information with standard errors for each data set. As a rule of thumb, differences between methods are significant at around the 5% level if their (mean $\pm$ standard error) ranges do not overlap. The categorization results for the three data sets are given in Table 1 reported as the average of performance metrics with standard errors.

Note that the experiments are done directly here (*i.e.,* we do not separate the data set into training and testing sets). In case of using separate training

Table 1. Classification results for the three data sets (average ± standard error)

Data set	Model	Accuracy	Precision	Recall	MI
WebKb4	MM	81.90 ± 0.66	81.32 ± 0.44	82.46 ± 0.50	73.30 ± 0.35
	DCM	84.30 ± 0.39	83.72 ± 0.21	84.44 ± 0.27	76.51 ± 0.43
	MSD	$\mathbf{88.50 \pm 0.07}$	$\mathbf{89.17 \pm 0.05}$	$\mathbf{88.27 \pm 0.06}$	$\mathbf{89.43 \pm 0.03}$
ModApte	MM	85.44 ± 0.06	72.17 ± 0.04	91.76 ± 0.02	83.32 ± 0.03
	DCM	87.13 ± 0.05	74.84 ± 0.05	$\mathbf{93.56 \pm 0.02}$	88.32 ± 0.02
	MSD	$\mathbf{90.04 \pm 0.02}$	$\mathbf{75.59 \pm 0.01}$	90.85 ± 0.01	$\mathbf{98.14 \pm 0.02}$
NIPS	MM	69.34 ± 0.17	65.45 ± 0.74	75.31 ± 0.33	79.33 ± 0.16
	DCM	74.11 ± 0.04	72.58 ± 0.07	75.31 ± 0.27	84.06 ± 0.07
	MSD	$\mathbf{80.56 \pm 0.04}$	$\mathbf{78.02 \pm 0.03}$	$\mathbf{83.96 \pm 0.04}$	$\mathbf{92.55 \pm 0.17}$

and test sets, it would be necessary to smooth or regularize the distributions found by maximum likelihood [21]. Moreover, we set the number K of clusters to be found to be the same as the number of prespecified classes.

The performance of the model is compared on each document collection using accuracy, precision and recall average at macro level to evaluate how the models perform overall across the sets of data. For the WebKB4 collection, the average accuracies achieved are 81.90 ± 0.66 and 84.30 ± 0.39 (mean plus/minus standard error), by multinomial mixtures and DCM respectively, and by MSD is 88.50 ± 0.07.

For the ModApte data set, MSD outperforms other models with accuracy of 90.04 ± 0.02 compared to 85.44 ± 0.06 for MM and 87.13 ± 0.05 for DCM. NIPS document collection has relatively longer documents than the other used data sets. The average accuracy for classifying NIPS using MSD is 80.56 ± 0.04, which is also better than the previously reported results using MM or DCM. All differences are statistically significant as shown by a Student's t-test.

We have also considered the Mutual Information (MI) [21,23], to quantify how much the assigned classes by an algorithm agrees with the prespecified ones. Let m_i be the number of documents assigned to class i, and n_j the number of documents with prespecified label j, and c_{ij} the number of documents in class i but misclassifed and assigned to class j. With N total documents, define $p_i = m_i/N$, $q_j = n_j/N$, and $r_{ij} = c_{ij}/N$. The MI is then given by:

$$MI = \sum_i \sum_j r_{ij} \log \frac{r_{ij}}{p_i q_j} \tag{21}$$

According to mutual information reported as MI in Table 1, it is clear that MSD is outperforming the other two models (*i.e.*, a Student's t-test shows that the differences in MI between the MSD, DCM and MM models are statistically significant). The mutual information gained by classifying the WebKB4 data set using MSD is 89.43 ± 0.03, which is statistically significantly superior to the 73.30 ± 0.35 and 76.51 ± 0.43 by the MM and DCM, respectively.

Similarly, for the modApte document collection, the MSD outperforms other models with 98.14 ± 0.02 average mutual information compared to 83.32 ± 0.03 by MM, and 88.32 ± 0.02 by DCM. The average mutual information achieved by MSD clustering with NIPS document collection is 92.55 ± 0.17, and by DCM clustering is 84.06 ± 0.07, but only 79.33 ± 0.16 in case of using the mixture of multinomials.

6 Conclusion

In this paper we have proposed a novel mixture of distributions to model text data based on the scaled Dirichlet and the multinomial distributions. The approach proposed is motivated by the hierarchical framework for modeling text data that can be understood as a bag-of-bags-of words. In such models, a document is not generated directly, instead, a suitable prior is used to generate a multinomial and this mutinomial is then used to generate the document.

The scaled Dirichlet, a generalization of the Dirichlet, has many convenient properties that make it more useful and practical than the Dirichlet as a prior to the multinomial. The multinomial scaled Dirichlet mixture allows more modeling flexibility than mixtures of DCM, or multinomials as it remains D extra degrees of freedom. We estimated the parameters of this mixture using the EM algorithm.

The experimental results show that mixtures of MSD distributions mostly achieve higher performance compared to the mixtures of multinomials and DCM when modeling document collections. The model presented in this paper would be also applicable to many other problems with categorical data, such as image database summarization, image classification and handwritten digit recognition.

References

1. Cerchiello, P., Giudici, P.: Dirichlet compound multinomials statistical models. Appl. Math. **3**(12), 2089–2097 (2012)
2. Aggarwal, C.C., Zhai, C.: An introduction to text mining. In: Aggarwal, C., Zhai, C. (eds.) Mining Text Data, pp. 1–10. Springer, Boston (2012). https://doi.org/10.1007/978-1-4614-3223-4_1
3. Sebastiani, F.: Machine learning in automated text categorization. ACM Comput. Surv. (CSUR) **34**(1), 1–47 (2002)
4. McCallum, A., Nigam, K.: A comparison of event models for Naive Bayes text classification. In: Proceedings of the AAAI-98 Workshop on Learning for Text Categorization, vol. 752, pp. 41–48. Citeseer (1998)
5. Church, K.W., Gale, W.A.: Poisson mixtures. Nat. Lang. Eng. **1**(2), 163–190 (1995)
6. Rennie, J.D.M., Shih, L., Teevan, J., Karger, D.R.: Tackling the poor assumptions of Naive Bayes text classifiers. In: Proceedings of the Twentieth International Conference on Machine Learning ICML, vol. 3, pp. 616–623 (2003)
7. Madsen, R.E., Kauchak, D., Elkan, C.: Modeling word burstiness using the Dirichlet distribution. In: Proceedings of the 22nd International Conference on Machine Learning, pp. 545–552. ACM (2005)

8. Margaritis, D., Thrun, S.: A Bayesian multiresolution independence test for continuous variables. In: Proceedings of the Seventeenth Conference on Uncertainty in Artificial Intelligence, pp. 346–353. Morgan Kaufmann Publishers Inc. (2001)

9. Mosimann, J.E.: On the compound multinomial distribution, the multivariate β-distribution, and correlations among proportions. Biometrika **49**(1/2), 65–82 (1962)

10. Migliorati, S., Monti, G.S., Ongaro, A.: E-M algorithm: an application to a mixture model for compositional data. In: Proceedings of the 44th Scientific Meeting of the Italian Statistical Society (2008)

11. Lochner, R.H.: A generalized Dirichlet distribution in Bayesian life testing. J. Royal Stat. Soc. Ser. B (Methodol.) **37**, 103–113 (1975)

12. Bouguila, N.: Clustering of count data using generalized Dirichlet multinomial distributions. IEEE Trans. Knowl. Data Eng. **20**(4), 462–474 (2008)

13. Bouguila, N.: Count data modeling and classification using finite mixtures of distributions. IEEE Trans. Neural Netw. **22**(2), 186–198 (2011)

14. Teevan, J., Karger, D.R.: Empirical development of an exponential probabilistic model for text retrieval: using textual analysis to build a better model. In: Proceedings of the 26th Annual International ACM SIGIR Conference on Research and Development in Information Retrieval, pp. 18–25. ACM (2003)

15. Jansche, M.: Parametric models of linguistic count data. In: Proceedings of the 41st Annual Meeting on Association for Computational Linguistics, vol. 1, pp. 288–295. Association for Computational Linguistics (2003)

16. Katz, S.M.: Distribution of content words and phrases in text and language modelling. Nat. Lang. Eng. **2**(1), 15–59 (1996)

17. Monti, G.S., Mateu-Figueras, G., Pawlowsky-Glahn, V.: Notes on the scaled Dirichlet distribution. In: Compositional Data Analysis: Theory and Applications. Wiley, Chichester (2011)

18. Hankin, R.K., et al.: A generalization of the Dirichlet distribution. J. Stat. Softw. **33**(11), 1–18 (2010)

19. Oboh, B.S., Bouguila, N.: Unsupervised learning of finite mixtures using scaled Dirichlet distribution and its application to software modules categorization. In: Proceedings of the 2017 IEEE International Conference on Industrial Technology (ICIT), pp. 1085–1090. IEEE (2017)

20. Bouguila, N., Ziou, D.: Unsupervised learning of a finite discrete mixture: applications to texture modeling and image databases summarization. J. Vis. Commun. Image Representation **18**(4), 295–309 (2007)

21. Elkan, C.: Clustering documents with an exponential-family approximation of the Dirichlet compound multinomial distribution. In: Proceedings of the 23rd International Conference on Machine Learning, pp. 289–296. ACM (2006)

22. McCallum, A.K.: Bow: A Toolkit for Statistical Language Modeling, Text Retrieval, Classification and Clustering (1996). http://www.cs.cmu.edu/mccallum/bow

23. Banerjee, A., Dhillon, I.S., Ghosh, J., Sra, S.: Clustering on the unit hypersphere using von Mises-Fisher distributions. J. Mach. Learn. Res. **6**, 1345–1382 (2005)

A Comparison of Knee Strategies
for Hierarchical Spatial Clustering

Brian J. Ross[✉]

Department of Computer Science, Brock University, 500 Sir Isaac Brock Way,
St. Catharines, ON L2S 3A1, Canada
bross@brocku.ca
http://www.cosc.brocku.ca/~bross/

Abstract. A comparative study of the performance of knee detection
approaches for the hierarchical clustering of 2D spatial data is under-
taken. Knee detection is usually performed on the dendogram generated
during cluster generation. For many problems, the knee is a natural indication of the ideal or optimal number of clusters for the given problem.
This research compares the performance of various knee strategies on
different spatial datasets. Two hierarchical clustering algorithms, single
linkage and group average, are considered. Besides determining knees
using conventional cluster distances, we also explore alternative metrics such as average global medoid and centroid distances, and F score
metrics. Results show that knee determination is difficult and problem
dependent.

Keywords: Knee · Hierarchical clustering · Spatial clustering

1 Introduction

Clustering is a classification technique which automatically groups data according to shared characteristics. Hierarchical clustering is a method in which a hierarchy of clusters is incrementally generated for a dataset. Hierarchical clustering
requires the determination of an appropriate number of clusters after the cluster
hierarchy has been generated. Often, the clustering dendogram is used for making this decision. Each dendogram node denotes a clustering step in which two
clusters were merged together. The node is labeled with the distance between
the two clusters that were combined. Often, the knee can be visually identified
within the dendogram, using a plot of the distance measures. The knee has been
defined as the point of maximal marginal rate of return [11]. When it exists, the
knee corresponds to the optimal number of clusters.

Although knees can be effective for determining optimal clusterings, there is
no canonical rule for specifying the knee point, nor prescribed distance metric
on which to apply knee analyses [5]. Knee identification is not a general solution
to cluster optimization. Clustering is intractable; the determination of optimal

© Springer International Publishing AG, part of Springer Nature 2018
M. Mouhoub et al. (Eds.): IEA/AIE 2018, LNAI 10868, pp. 81–87, 2018.
https://doi.org/10.1007/978-3-319-92058-0_8

clusters for even K = 2 is NP-complete [3]. For real-world datasets, the identification of "optimality" may be ill-defined or subjective. The dendogram's utility for knee analysis depends upon the quality of the underlying clustering, which can be fallible.

This paper compares various knee strategies and distance metrics on different datasets. We use both single-linkage and group average clustering in our trials, and consider alternative distance measurements for dendograms. Our results will confirm that many problem cases do not exhibit identifiable knees, and hence knees can be a useful heuristic method, but not a solution, for cluster optimization.

Section 2 reviews the clustering algorithms and knee strategies used in the experiments. The spatial data and its preparation is described in Sect. 3. Results are presented and discussed in Sect. 4. Conclusions and future directions for the research are in Sect. 5. See [7] for more details of this research.

2   Background

2.1   Hierarchical Clustering

Hierarchical clustering generates a complete clustering of a dataset [9]. Initially, all data points are considered individual clusters. A distance table *Distance* records the distances between all existing clusters. Using this table, the closest clusters are determined. They are joined together to form a new cluster, which replaces the two merged clusters. The distance table is updated to reflect this change. This iteratively continues until a single cluster has been created. Clustering steps are modelled by a dendogram. Each node denotes the incremental merging of two clusters. The node is labelled with the distance between these joined clusters, which the clustering algorithm used in order to select them for merging.

The feature that defines different hierarchical clustering algorithms is the method which is used to measure distances between clusters. We consider two methods. In single linkage clustering, a distance between a cluster C_w and new cluster $C_{p \cup q}$ is updated as:

$$Distance(C_w, C_{p \cup q}) = minimum(Distance(C_w, C_p), \ Distance(C_w, C_q))$$

The group average method uses:

$$Distance(C_w, C_{p \cup q}) = average(Distance(C_w, C_p), \ Distance(C_w, C_q))$$

2.2   Distance Measures

We apply knee detection to 3 distance measurements associated with dendogram nodes.

(i) *Standard distance (Std):* This is the distance used by the clustering algorithm (Sect. 2.1). Each node of the dendogram indicates this distance, which is always the minimum between all the clusters at that point in the clustering.

(ii) *Global average medoid distance (Avg Med):* Letting C_i be cluster i ($1 \leq i \leq K$), MD_i be the total distance between the medoid (the member that is on average closest to the other members) and other elements of C_i, and T be the total number of elements in all clusters. Then: $AvgMed = (\Sigma_{i=1}^{K} MD_i)/T$.

(iii) *Global average centroid distance (Avg Cent):* Like (ii), but let CD_i be the total distance of all elements in C_i to the centroid (average coordinate of all elements): $AvgCent = (\Sigma_{i=1}^{K} CD_i)/T$.

2.3   Knee Determination

There are a number of proposals for identifying knees in dendogram plots. Let n_i be node i in the dendogram ($1 \leq i \leq K$), and d_i be the distance measure associated with n_i. We assume that dendogram nodes are numbered in the *inverse* order they were created; the root of the dendogram is therefor n_1. The knee methods considered are:

(i) **Magnitude:** Node with maximum magnitude $d_{i+1} - d_i$.

(ii) **Ratio:** Node with maximum ratio d_{i+1}/d_i [1].

(iii) **Second derivative:** Node with greatest second derivative.

(iv) **Minimum:** Node with minimal distance.

(v) **L-method, L-method D, L-method S:** Two lines segments are iteratively fit to the plot using linear regression [8]. The ideal placement minimizes the root mean square error between the regression lines and the plot points. Two L-method variations are included:

- L-method D (distance): If line 1 uses nodes 1 to n, then line 2 uses nodes $n + 1$ to $2n$.
- L-method S (sampling): If line 1 uses nodes 1 to n, then line 2 will evenly sample n nodes between $n + 1$ through k (last node).

(vi) **F score A, F score B:** The F score is based on the F test of a one-way analysis of variance (ANOVA) [4]. We plot the F score at all nodes in the dendogram. We then find the point furthest from the root showing a significant drop in F score, which suggests a decline in measurable cohesion in the clustering. We use two methods for finding this knee in the F score plot.

- F score A: This finds the highest i in which $(f_{i+1} - f_i) > \delta_{1...i}^2$, where $\delta_{1..i}^2$ is the standard deviation of the plotted F scores 1 to i.
- F score B: The highest i in which $(f_{i+1} - f_i) > \delta_{1...k}^2$, where $\delta_{1..k}^2$ is the standard deviation of all k F scores on the plot.

3   Spatial Data and Preparation

Sixteen spatial datasets with different data sizes, shapes, complexities, and target cluster sizes were selected from [2, 6] (see [7] for details). Due to the computational overhead of hierarchical clustering, datasets with more than 800 points were randomly downsampled. Those with less than 800 points were left intact.

Target cluster sizes were obtained as follows. The datasets were each evaluated with single linkage (Min) and group average (Gavg) clustering at the supplied clustering target values. Any clusters of size ≤ 3 are discarded. The size of the remaining clustering will denote the target clustering for that dataset and cluster algorithm. Before knee analysis, the size of each dendogram is reduced to its final 100 nodes. Knee solutions will therefore never exceed 100 clusters.

The L methods require a minimal number of points for linear regression. For all datasets with target cluster numbers above 5, we set this minimum to 5. We set the minimum to 2 for smaller target datasets.

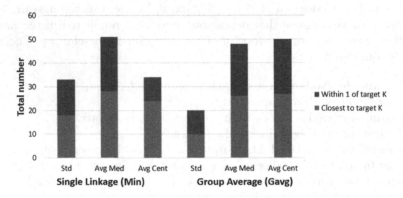

Fig. 1. Summary of knee performance with respect to clustering algorithm and distance metric. *Within 1 of target* tallies when a knee strategy generated a clustering size at, or within 1, of the target K. *Closest to target* tallies when a knee strategy generated a clustering size closest to the target K value. A single result can be tallied as both within 1 of target, and closest to target.

4   Results

Figure 1 compares the quality of knee evaluations with respect to the distance measurement used by the clustering algorithm. The summary shows that alternative distance metrics such as average global medoid and centroid distance are effective for knee identification.

Figure 2 shows how frequently difference knee strategies found the nearest value to the target K associated with the dataset and clustering algorithm. The chart shows separate tallies for single linkage and group average clusterings, and the tallies sum the results of all datasets and distance measures. The Mag, Ratio, and 2nd Deriv knee strategies were the most successful, followed by the F score at the Min strategies.

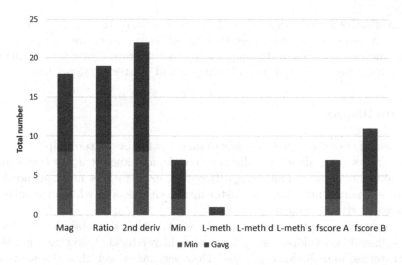

Fig. 2. Frequency that knee strategies were closest to target cluster size. The nearest result for a dataset is selected from results of all knee strategies and distance measurements obtained.

Table 1. Breakdown of performance of knee strategies with respect to clustering algorithm and distance metric. Values denote the number of times each knee strategy produced clusterings that were the closest to the target cluster size for a given dataset and clustering algorithm (ties are possible).

Knee	Std		Avg Med		Avg Cent		Total
	Min	Gavg	Min	Gavg	Min	Gavg	
Mag	5	4	3	1	0	4	18
Ratio	5	2	3	3	1	5	19
2nd deriv	5	4	3	5	0	5	22
Min	0	0	1	2	1	3	7
L-meth	0	0	0	1	0	0	1
L-meth D	0	0	0	0	0	0	0
L-meth S	0	0	0	0	0	0	0
F score A	-	-	1	2	1	3	7
F score B	-	-	2	5	1	3	11

Table 1 show the performance of knee strategies with respect to the distance metric and clustering algorithm. The table tallies the number of times when knee strategies produced the closest clustering to the target size for that dataset and clustering algorithm. Standard distances were only useful for the Mag, Ratio and 2nd deriv knee methods. The non-standard average medoid/centroid distances were also effective for knee detection. If this table were further deconstructed over all the datasets used, one would see that the effectiveness of knee strategies and distance metrics is problem-dependent. No specific knee strategy and distance metric is universally effective for all datasets and clustering algorithms.

5   Conclusion

The success of knee strategies depends upon many factors. A serendipitous match of dataset, clustering algorithm, distance metric, and knee strategy can result in high quality hierarchical clusterings. However, expectations must acknowledge the computational limitations of clustering algorithms, and whether identifiable knees exist in given problem cases.

There are many directions for future work. Other data besides 2D spatial datasets should be explored, as well as other hierarchical clustering algorithms, knee strategies, and distance metrics. However, we expect that the same conclusions as above will apply. More generally, a study of mathematical transformations of distance plots, with a goal towards effective knee detection, should be investigated. Another avenue of research is to use machine learning for knee detection [10]. Machine learning might be used to match datasets, clustering algorithms, dendogram distance transformations, and knee strategies.

Acknowledgements. This research was supported by NSERC Discovery Grant RGPIN-2016-03653.

References

1. Breaban, M., Iftene, A.: Dynamic objective sampling in many-objective optimization. Proc. Compt. Sci. **60**, 178–187 (2015)
2. Franti, P.: Clustering Datasets (2015). http://cs.uef.fi/sipu/datasets/. Accessed 31 Oct 2017
3. Garey, M., Johnson, D.: Computers and Intractability. W.H. Freeman, New York (1979)
4. Hayter, A.: Probability and Statistics for Engineers and Scientists. Duxbury, Pacific Grove (2007)
5. Ketchen, D.J., Shook, C.: The application of cluster analysis in strategic management research: an analysis and critique. Strateg. Manag. J. **17**, 441–458 (1996)
6. Online (2017). https://github.com/deric/clustering-benchmark. Accessed 31 Oct 2017
7. Ross, B.: A comparison of knee strategies for hierarchical spatial clustering. Technical report TR18-01, Brock U, Department of Computer Science, February 2018
8. Salvador, S., Chan, P.: Determining the number of clusters/segments in hierarchical clustering/segmentation algorithms. In: Proceedings of IEEE International Conference on Tools with Artificial Intelligence (ICTAI), pp. 576–584. IEEE (2004)
9. Suh, S.C.: Practical Applications of Data Mining. Jones & Bartlett Learning, Sudbury (2012)

10. Xie, J., Girshick, R., Farhadi, A.: Unsupervised deep embedding for cluster analysis. In: Proceedings of 33rd International Conference on Machine Learning. JMLR: W&CP (2008)
11. Zhang, Y., Zhang, X., Tang, J., Luo, B.: Decision-making strategies for multi-objective community detection in complex networks. In: Pan, L., Păun, G., Pérez-Jiménez, M.J., Song, T. (eds.) BIC-TA 2014. CCIS, vol. 472, pp. 621–628. Springer, Heidelberg (2014). https://doi.org/10.1007/978-3-662-45049-9_102

Credit Card Default Prediction as a Classification Problem

Makram Soui[1(✉)], Salima Smiti[1], Salma Bribech[1], and Ines Gasmi[2]

[1] University of Gabes, Gabes, Tunisia
smakram.isgg@gmail.com, salima.smiti92@gmail.com,
bribech.salma@gmail.com
[2] University of Manouba, Manouba, Tunisia
gasmioines@gmail.com

Abstract. Nowadays, the use of credit card becomes an integral part of modern economies. Still, predicting credit card defaulters is considered as the most important. So, its assessment becomes a crucial task. In this context, a few Data mining and intelligent artificial techniques were used for extracting meaningful patterns from a given dataset. In this study, we consider credit card risk assessment as a classification problem based on genetic programming (GP) algorithm, where the goal is to maximize the accuracy of the generated model. We evaluate our proposal using customers default payments dataset of Taiwan, and, we compared it with some existing works. The performance of our finding leads to the assumption that GP is able to generate an effective assessment model based on IF-THEN rules. The result confirms the efficiency of our algorithm with an average of more than 86% of precision, recall, and accuracy.

Keywords: Credit card · Credit card defaulters · Classification rules
Genetic programming

1 Introduction

Nowadays, the credit card becomes the most popular mode of payment for both online and regular purchase. According to statistics compiled by the Financial Supervisory Commission, in 2015, 36 banks issued a credit card in Taiwan and the number of cards in circulation was 38 million [1]. However, with the increasing use of credit-card, the credit-card defaults has also increased. Therefore, the implementation of an efficient prediction model for credit card defaults has become essential for banks and financial institutions to reduce losses.

Hence, research on predicting credit card defaulters has focused on defining and developing a predictive model for credit-card defaults. In this way, the predictive model of credit card defaulters has gained increasing attention and has been considerable. However, most of the existing works about the prediction of credit-card defaulters rely on a classification of customers' credit card payments. In fact, it is difficult to classify the nature of a customer into "defaulter" or "not defaulter" for many reasons. The customer has many characteristics (age, education, sex, repayment status, etc.) that would be taking into account in the prediction of the credit-card defaulters.

© Springer International Publishing AG, part of Springer Nature 2018
M. Mouhoub et al. (Eds.): IEA/AIE 2018, LNAI 10868, pp. 88–100, 2018.
https://doi.org/10.1007/978-3-319-92058-0_9

The diversity of these credit cardholders' characteristics makes the decision task very difficult [2].

Recent research works have focused to increase the accuracy of the prediction model for credit card defaults. For this reason, many classification techniques are used for building accurate classification models for predicting defaulters credit cardholders. These techniques can be grouped into three categories, statistical techniques, artificial intelligence techniques and hybrid techniques. The popular statistical techniques used for the prediction of credit card defaulters are the discriminant analysis and logistic regression [3, 4]. Several others artificial intelligence including support vector machine, neural network, and decision tree have been widely used in the prediction of credit card defaulters [5–7]. In addition, an important number of effective hybrid techniques have been proposed [8–10]. However, existing works on this domain has highlighted complex and black-box models, which can be not understandable by customers and financial experts.

To this end, rules-based techniques remain popular, due to its ability on extracting practical knowledge from a given dataset and transforming it into usable and understandable information. A useful predictive model for credit-card defaulters achieves a good balance between accuracy and comprehensibility. Therefore, using rules allows a financial institution to generate transparent decision model capable to predict and to detect easily the default payments of credit card customers.

In this context, we propose in this paper to use the GP for automatically synthesizing a set of rules for solving customers' default payments problem. In addition, our proposal aims to find the best rules in terms of accuracy, precision, and recall. The performance of our proposed method is assessed using customers' default payments dataset of Taiwan and compared with similar works used others classifiers.

The remainder of this paper is organized as follows: Sect. 2 illustrates the related works on the Taiwan dataset. Section 3 represents the research methodology. Section 4 highlights the experimental setup. Empirical study and outcomes are discussed in Sect. 5. Finally, Sect. 6 draws conclusions and future works.

2 Related Works

Recently, the default payments of credit card customers have become one of the major issues for financial institutions. It provokes great losses for banks. Due to the importance of the analysis of credit card customers, several works have focused on detecting the credit card defaulters using different data mining techniques.

[1] Proposed the neural network to predict the default of credit card customers. The experiments over the Taiwan dataset prove the effectiveness of this model. In a continuous work, [11] applied the neural network which integrated with grey incidence analysis and Dempster-Shafer theory to predict the default cases of Taiwan dataset. The implementation of this model includes two stages. The first stage applies the neural network to perform the training and test process. The second stage integrates both the grey incidence analysis and Dempster-Shafer for feature selection in order to choose the significant independent variables for the input of the neural network. The experimental

results show the integrated model has a better prediction accuracy if compared to the model, which applied neural network only.

In a similar work, [12] compared the predictive accuracy of the probability of default among six data mining methods: K-nearest neighbor, logistic regression, discriminant analysis, Naïve Bayes, artificial neural network and classification trees, using the case of customers' default payments in Taiwan. The classification results show the artificial neural network is the only one that can accurately estimate the probability of default. In another study, [13] compared the performance of various data-mining algorithms such as BayesNet, Meta-stacking, Naïve Bayes, Random Forest, Sequential minimal optimization (SMO) and ZeroR in predicting the credit card defaulters using customers' default payments dataset of Taiwan. The experimental results showed that Random Tree and Random Forest achieved the highest accuracy compared with the other models. In addition, [2] compared the predictive accuracy of customers' default payments using six data mining techniques: Fisher linear discriminant analysis (FLDA), Naïve Bayes, J48, Logistic Regression, Multilayer Perceptron (MLP) and k-nearest neighbor. The results show that the neural network gives a good performance and better accuracy to predict the default of credit card customers.

Most of the methods and techniques mentioned above can be considered as important and powerful data mining techniques predictive modeling. However, they are still difficult to interpret because of their black-box nature such as neural network classifier. That makes them less accurate. Furthermore, these classification methods are based on the discriminate equation, which takes into account the values of both defaults and not defaults payments. However, the function-based approach is hard for a human to understand.

To this end, [14] reported that rules are one of the most popular, transparent and interpretable symbolic representations of knowledge discovered from data. For this reason, we propose to generate automatically classification rules by using the GP in order to build an accurate and transparent model to predict credit card defaulters.

3 Proposed Credit-Card Default Prediction Approach

Our contribution aims to define a set of classification rules as a combination of customer credit card characteristics. The goal of our approach is to generate the best classification rules among all possible rules that maximize the accuracy of the classification model in predicting credit-card defaulters. The rule generation process aims to find the best combination of the characteristics of customer credit card.

As showed in Fig. 1, rules generation process takes as inputs the credit card default dataset and the characteristics of the customer and generates as output a set of classification rules. During the rules generation process, our approach combines randomly the characteristics of the customer credit card within logical expressions (intersection AND) to create rules. A fitness function calculates the quality of each rule by comparing the list of classification rule with the instances from the dataset.

We use the Genetic programming (GP) as a branch of Genetic Algorithm that can be used to generate classification rules. The proposed method has four phases: (1) generation and evaluation of the initial population, (2) selection of parents,

(3) generation of the population of children and (4) merge parents and children and evaluation of the new population. The pseudo code for the algorithm is given in Fig. 2.

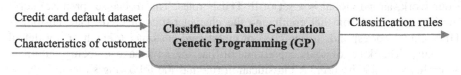

Credit card default dataset

Characteristics of customer

Classification Rules Generation Genetic Programming (GP)

Classification rules

Fig. 1. The proposed approach overview.

```
Input:  Set of credit card customer's characteristics.
Input:  Credit card default dataset.
Output: Set of classification rules.
1: Initial_population (P, Max_size);
2: P: =set_of (I);
3: I: =classification_rule (R, class type);
4: repeat
5: For all R∈ P do;
6: Generated rule: =execute_rules(R, I)
7: Fitness (I):= compare (generated rule, examples)
8: End for
9: Best_solution:= best_fitness(I) ;
10: P:=generate_new_population(P);
11: it:=it+1;
12: until it=max_it
13: return best_solution
```

Fig. 2. High-level pseudo code for GP adaptation to our problem.

As the Fig. 2 shows, the algorithm takes as input set of credit card customer's characteristics and credit card default dataset. Lines 1–3 construct an initial GP population, which is a set of the individual that define possible classification rules. Lines 4–13 encode the main GP loop, which searches for the best classification rules. During each iteration, the quality of each individual is evaluated, and the solution having the best fitness (line 9) is saved. Then, a new population of solutions is generated using the crossover operator (line 10) to the selected solutions; each pair of parent solutions produces two new solutions. We include the parent and child variants in the population and then apply the mutation operator to each variant; this will provide the population for the next generation. Steps 4 to 12 are performed repeatedly until maximum iteration is fulfilled. The output of the algorithm is the set of best-extracted classification rules (Fig. 3).

4   Classification Rules Generation

4.1   Creation of Initial Population

In our work, an individual is a set of IF-THEN rules. The IF clause (premise) corresponds to the condition that combining the characteristics of credit card customers. THEN clause corresponds to the class of credit card customer (default or not default payments). This kind of rules representation has the advantage of being intuitively comprehensible for the user. A classification rule has the following structure:

IF (combination of credit cardholders characteristics) THEN (class of credit cardholders payments)

The rules will undergo a process of improvement; they must be presented as a tree. For instance, let us consider the following example of classification rules generated by a Taiwan credit card dataset:

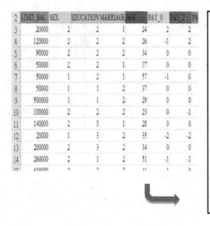

R1: IF (Pay_Amt3=1) and (Pay_4=2) and (Pay_3=2) and (Pay_Amt5=1) and (Pay_Amt6=0) and (Limit_Ball=2) **THEN** Class Default Payment.

R2: IF (Pay_Amt5=0) and (Pay_Amt3=4) and (Pay_2=1) and (Pay_Amt2=2) and (Limit_Ball=1) and (Pay_0=4) **THEN** Class Not Default Payment.

R3: IF (Pay_Amt3=3) and (Pay_Amt2=1) and (Pay_Amt5=0) and (Pay_6=2) and (Pay_Amt6=0) and (Pay_5=1) **THEN** Class Default Payment.

R4: IF (Limit_Ball=2) and (Pay_Amt2=1) and (Pay_Amt5=0) and (Pay_3=1) and (Pay_Amt6=0) and (Pay_4=2) **THEN** Class Default Payment.

Fig. 3.   Example of classification rules.

This step takes as input the characteristics of customers' credit card (Age, Pay_Amt, Education, Marriage, etc.), and class type (default or not default payments) and generates, as output, a random initial population from a possible combination of customer's credit card characteristics. Our solution is modeled as a tree representation, when, the terminals (leafs nodes of a tree) correspond to different customer's characteristics with their threshold values. Figure 4 represents an example of an individual (solution) represented as a tree. This representation corresponds to an OR composition of three sub-trees, each sub-tree represents a rule:

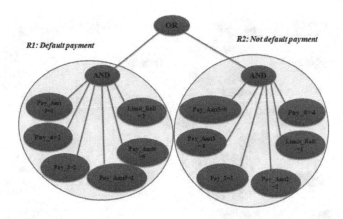

Fig. 4. A tree representation of an individual.

4.2 Genetic Operator

To better explore the search space, we use this three genetic operator: crossover, mutation, and selection:

- **Crossover:** this operator aims at generating offspring. To this end, the proposed algorithm starts by selecting randomly two parents. These parents will be split into two sub-trees. After that, they are combined to generate two new individuals (offspring). Each child combines information coming from both parents. An example of crossover process is shown in Fig. 5.
- **Mutation:** Normally, after crossover has occurred, each child produced by the crossover undergoes mutation with a low probability. This phase consists of changing randomly one or more rules in the solution. The modification of rule aims to change randomly the value of customer characteristic. Figure 6 shows a new solution derived from the one of Fig. 5.
- **Selection:** In this phase, the set of solution that will participate in the crossover and mutation operators are selected. Two parents (individuals) are selected from the initial population. Thus, proposed algorithm uses binary tournament selection to guide the selection process. In fact, this step aims to select the best individuals to be reproduced in the child population.

4.3 Evaluation of Individuals of the Initial Population

In this step, we evaluate the generated solutions of the initial population (Pt) in order to estimate and discover the interesting classification rules. In fact, generated individual should be validated with a fitness function that a quantifies the quality of generated rules. So, it is crucial to use an efficient and performant fitness function in order to reduce computational complexity and maximize the accuracy. This evaluation is based on the calculation of the fitness function F_{score} Quality given in Eq. (1) which will evaluate the quality of classification rules. It aims to generate a set of best rules that can be used in the decision process to correctly classify the customer credit card as defaulter

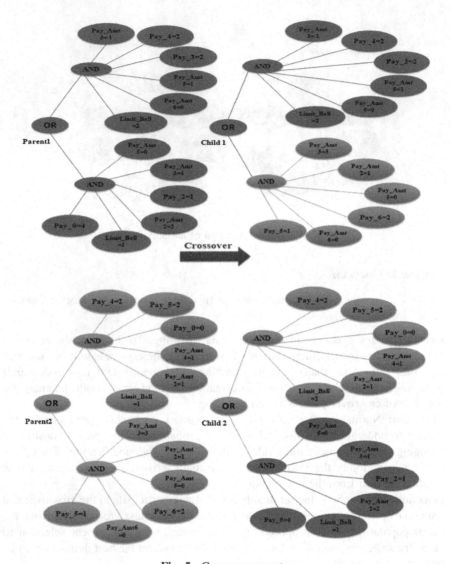

Fig. 5. Crossover operator.

or not-defaulter. The idea is to improve the accuracy, precision, and recall of classification rules by maximizing the Quality function.

$$\mathbf{Q(Solution_i)} = \frac{\sum_{i=1}^{s} \frac{\text{Number of rule detecting Problem}_j}{\text{Occurrence of Problemj in the base of examples}}}{\text{Number of problems type}} \tag{1}$$

We suggested integrating the feature selection in the rules generation process. In fact, the credit card default dataset is often large and characterized by redundant and irrelevant features. However, the irrelevant and redundant features in the training set

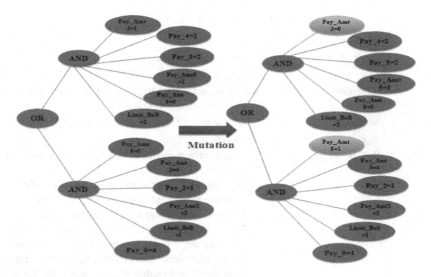

Fig. 6. Mutation operator.

can produce less accurate results. This difficulty can be solved by using feature selection methods. It is the most basic step in data pre-processing as it reduces the dimensionality of the data. Feature selection aims to filter out redundant and irrelevant variables in order to increase the performance of rule-based classifiers and reduce the high complexity of the model. In this work, the selected feature was performed by Information gain feature selection algorithm, which is commonly used in the machine learning community, to refine the attributes of origin Taiwan dataset. According to [14], the information gain is the most useful feature selection method in predicting the credit card defaulters.

5 Experimental Setup

5.1 Description of the Experimental Dataset

The performance of the proposed GP classifier is evaluated using a published Taiwan credit card dataset. This dataset is obtained from the University of California, Irvine (UCI) Machine Learning Repository [15]. The total numbers of instances are 30000 divided into two classes: 6 636 "default payment" and 23 364 "not default payment" and used 24 predictive attributes. An overview of this dataset has been presented in the following Table 1.

Taiwan credit card dataset is randomly partitioned into two parts, training set, and testing set. In this study, 70% of the data are used for training and the remaining 30% are exclusively used to evaluate the performance of the model.

Table 1. Description of the Taiwan dataset

	Attribute	Description
X1	Limit_Ball	Amount of the given credit
X2	Sex	Gender (1 = male; 2 = female)
X3	Education	Education (1 = graduate school; 2 = university; 3 = high school; 4: others)
X4	Marriage	Marital status (1 = married; 2 = single; 3 = others)
X5	Age	Age (year)
X6–X11	Pay_0-Pay_6	History of past payment (from April to September 2005) as follows: X6 = the repayment status in September, 2005; X7 = the repayment status in August, 2005;...; X11 = the repayment status in April, 2005 The measurement scale for the repayment status is: -1 = pay duly; 1 = payment delay for one month; 2 = payment delay for two months;. ...; 8 = payment delay for eight months; 9 = payment delay for nine months and above
X12–X17	Bill_Amt1-Bill_Amt17	Amount of bill statement (NT dollar) X12 = amount of bill statement in September, 2005; X13 = amount of bill statement in August, 2005;...; X17 = amount of bill statement in April, 2005
X18–X23	Pay_Amt1-Pay_Amt6	Amount of previous payment (NT dollar) X18 = amount paid in September, 2005; X19 = amount paid in August, 2005;...; X23 = amount paid in April, 2005
X24	Default payment	Default payment (Yes = 1, No = 0)

5.2 Evaluation Criteria

To assess the performance of our approach, we computed three measures: precision, recall, and accuracy that are originally defined in the domain of prediction default payments and widely used when comparing search algorithms results. The definition of these metrics can be explained with respect to a 2×2 confusion matrix as that given in the following Table 2.

Table 2. A confusion matrix

	Positive (Default)	Negative (Not-default)
Positive (Default)	True Positive (TP)	False Negative (FN)
Negative (Not-default)	False Positive (FP)	True Negative (TN)

As shown the Eq. (2), the precision denotes the number of true positive (Default) case prediction among the total number of positive predictions:

$$\text{Precision} = \frac{TP}{TP + FP} \tag{2}$$

The recall (Eq. 3) indicates the number of true positive (Default) predictions compared to the total number of defaulters payments:

$$\text{Recall} = \frac{TP}{FN + TP} \tag{3}$$

However, most credit card prediction defaulters' studies employ the accuracy as the criteria for performance evaluation. It presents the proportion of the correctly predicted cases (default and not default) on a particular dataset. The accuracy can be defined by the following equation:

$$\text{Accuracy} = \frac{TP + TN}{TP + FP + TN + FN} \tag{4}$$

In general, the precision calculates the probability that detected classification rules are correct, the recall is the probability that expected classification rules are detected and the accuracy calculates the probability of the correctly classified instances (both default and not-default customers). Thus, their values are between 0 and 1, and the higher value the better it is. The expected rules were reported by the collected instances of the testing dataset.

6 Empirical Analysis

Our study addresses two main experiments, which are defined below. In this section, we explain how we designed these two experiments. The goal of the study is to evaluate the performance of our proposed method in terms of its precision, recall, and accuracy for generating classification rules.

6.1 Experiment 1: GP Performance

In this research, the prediction of credit-card defaulters will be evaluated as an evolutionary problem with the real-world dataset. We use the GP to generate classification rules. In fact, GP allows us to generate randomly, from a given dataset, a combination of credit cardholders' characteristics for each class type. The final goal of our approach thus is to generate the best classification rules among all possible rules that maximize the accuracy, precision, and recall of generated rules.

Since search algorithms are stochastic, they may generate various results for the same problem instance in multiple simulations. That's why our experimental study is performed throughout 31 independent runs for each problem instance and the obtained results are statistically analyzed by using the Wilcoxon rank sum test with a 99% confidence level ($\alpha = 1\%$). This guarantees that the obtained results of GP algorithm used in this experiment are samples from continuous distributions with equal medians.

Table 3. The parameter setting of GP.

Parameter	Number of objective	Population size	Number of generation	Crossover rate	Mutation rate
Value	1	100	5000	0.9	0.1

The following Table shows the tuning configuration for the algorithm used in our experiments (Table 3).

Before building the GP, we apply the information gain feature selection algorithm. Among 24 attributes, it is found that a total of 12 variables which includes Pay_0 (X7), Pay_2 (X8), Pay_3 (X9), Pay_4 (X10), Pay_5 (X11), Pay_6 (X12), PAY_AMT1 (X19), Limit_Bal (X2), Pay_Amt2 (X20), Pay_Amt3 (X21), Pay_Amt4 (X22), Pay_Amt6 (X24) have higher ranking derived from the integrated model.

The classification rules were generated with an average of more than 86% of precision, recall, and accuracy on the used dataset. As shown in Fig. 7, the precision of generated rules is trusted with 90% for the testing dataset and 97% for training dataset. This is can confirm that the set of returned rules did not contain a high number of false positives and so our reported classification result can be trusted by the manually collected instance. We found similar observation when analyzing the recall and accuracy scores where an average of 86% and 93%, respectively of classification rules were detected. This result confirms the efficiency of our result comparing with the manual inspection process.

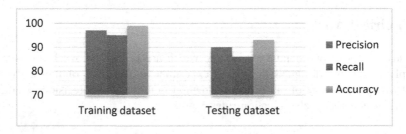

Fig. 7. The performance of the GP

6.2   Experiment 2: Comparative Study

To address the problem of customers default payments, several data mining techniques such as logistic regression (LR), Naïve Bayes, Random Tree, K-nearest neighbor, Multilayer Perceptron (MLP) and Fisher linear discriminant analysis (FLDA) have been successfully applied to predict the default payments of credit card customers. Therefore, to estimate the efficacy, and the performance of the GP algorithm, we compare its precision, recall and accuracy with the precision, the recall, and the accuracy of similar works used others classifiers.

Table 4 compares the precision, recall and accuracy results of our proposed GP algorithm with other existing techniques used Taiwan dataset. We conclude that GP has the highest performance compared to these 5 previous works. In fact, we obtained the highest precision, recall, and accuracy value, respectively with 90%, 86%, and 93%. It is followed by Random Tree with 79.7% precision value, 81.6% recall value, and

Table 4. Comparative study of classification algorithms using customers' default payments dataset of Taiwan

	Precision	Recall	Accuracy	IF-THEN Rules
GP	90%	86%	93%	Yes
FLDA [2]	76.9%	72.4%	72.4%	No
Logistic Regression [2]	79.5%	81%	81%	No
Naïve Bayes [14]	78.6%	80.5%	69.4%	No
K-Nearest Neighbor [2]	73%	72.9%	72.9%	No
Random Tree [14]	79.7%	81.6%	81.5%	No

81.5% accuracy value. Furthermore, the GP can provide interpretable results (IF-THEN rule). Additionally, using classification rules yields a predictive model that is easy to understand for a human. However, the other authors have not use IF-THEN rule to classify credit card defaulters because of our classification method based on the discriminate equation (function-based approach).

For this reason, we conclude that the GP algorithm is an efficient technique for detecting classification rules and outperform all other techniques. As a result, we can suggest that the proposed GP technique is a feasible solution to improve the accuracy and comprehensibility in predicting the default credit card payments.

7 Conclusion

Because credit card default payments cost billions of dollars each year, one major goal of banks is to minimize these credit card losses. To this objective, numerous classification techniques have been applied to detect default payments. However, many classification methods are black box models. It produces results that are difficult for a human to interpret and understand. In this paper, we build an accurate and interpretable credit card default prediction model which proposes a set of classification rules. The performance of our proposed method is assessed using the Taiwan customers' default payments dataset and compared with similar works used others classifiers. The results of the conducted experiments show that our proposal outperforms the other competitor's techniques with an average of more than 86% of precision, recall, and accuracy. However, we plan to continue our research for improving these numbers by using the multi-objective algorithm.

References

1. Li, J.-P.: Applied neural network model to search for target credit card customers. In: Berry, M.W., Hj. Mohamed, A., Yap, B.W. (eds.) SCDS 2016. CCIS, vol. 652, pp. 13–24. Springer, Singapore (2016). https://doi.org/10.1007/978-981-10-2777-2_2
2. Pasha, M., Fatima, M., Dogar, A.M., Shahzad, F.: Performance comparison of data mining algorithms for the predictive accuracy of credit card defaulters. Int. J. Comput. Sci. Netw. Secur. **17**(3), 178–183 (2017)
3. William, H.G.: A Statistical Model for Credit Scoring. Department of Economics, New York University, New York (1992)
4. Sahin, Y., Duman, E.: Detecting credit card fraud by decision trees and support vector machines. In: International Multi Conference of Engineers and Computer Scientists (2011)
5. Setiono, R., Baesens, B., Mues, C.: A note on knowledge discovery using neural networks and its application to credit card screening. Eur. J. Oper. Res. **192**, 326 (2009)
6. Koklu, M., Sabanci, K.: Estimation of credit card customers' payment status by using KNN and MLP. Int. J. Intell. Syst. Appl. Eng. **4**, 249–251 (2016). ISSN: 2147-6799
7. Sahin, Y., Duman, E.: Detecting credit card fraud by ANN and logistic regression (2011)
8. Lee, T.S., Chiu, C.C., Lu, C.J., Chen, I.-F.: Credit scoring using the hybrid neural discriminant technique. Expert Syst. Appl. **23**(3), 245–254 (2002)
9. Cinko, M.: Comparison of credit scoring techniques. Istanbul Commer. Univ. Soc. Sci. J. **9**, 143–153 (2006)
10. Akkoc, S.: An empirical comparison of conventional techniques, neural networks and the three stage hybrid Adaptive Neuro Fuzzy Inference System (ANFIS) model for credit scoring analysis: the case of Turkish credit card data. Eur. J. Oper. Res. **222**, 168–178 (2012)
11. Chou, T.N.: A Novel Prediction Model for Credit Card Risk Management. Chaoyang University of Technology, Taichung (2017)
12. Yeh, I.C., Lien, C.H.: The comparisons of data mining techniques for the predictive accuracy of probability of default of credit card clients. Expert Syst. Appl. **36**, 2473–2480 (2009)
13. Ajay, A., Venkatesh, A.: Jacob, S.G: Prediction of credit-card defaulters: a comparative study on performance of classifiers. Int. J. Comput. Appl. **145**(7), 36–41 (2016). (0975-8887)
14. Napierala, K., Stefanowski, J.: BRACID: a comprehensive approach to learning rules from imbalanced data. J. Intell. Inf. Syst. **39**(2), 335–373 (2012)
15. Machine Learning Repository. www.ics.uci.edu/mlearn/MLRepository.html

Interactive Discovery of Statistically Significant Itemsets

Philippe Fournier-Viger[1(✉)], Xiang Li[2], Jie Yao[1], and Jerry Chun-Wei Lin[2]

[1] School of Humanities and Social Sciences, Harbin Institute of Technology
(Shenzhen), Shenzhen, Guangdong, China
`philfv8@yahoo.com, julie_j_yao@163.com`
[2] School of Computer Science and Technology, Harbin Institute of Technology
(Shenzhen), Shenzhen, Guangdong, China
`leeideal93@gmail.com, jerrylin@ieee.org`

Abstract. Frequent Itemset Mining (FIM) is a fundamental data mining task, which consists of finding frequent sets of items in transaction databases. However, traditional FIM algorithms can find lot of spurious patterns. To address this issue, the OPUS-Miner algorithm was proposed to find statistically significant patterns, called productive itemsets. Though, this algorithm is useful, it cannot be used for interactive data mining, that is the user cannot guide the search toward items of interest using queries, and the database is assumed to be static. This paper addresses this issue by proposing a novel approach to process targeted queries to check if some itemsets of interest to the user are non redundant and productive. The approach relies on a novel structure called Query-Tree to efficiently process queries. An experimental evaluation on several datasets of various types shows that thousands of queries are processed per second on a desktop computer, making it suitable for interactive data mining, and that it is up to 22 times faster than a baseline approach.

Keywords: Itemset mining · Productive itemsets · Query-Tree
Pattern

1 Introduction

Frequent Itemset Mining (FIM) [6], consists of finding frequently occurring patterns in databases to understand the data, and support decision-making. The input of FIM is a customer transaction database, where each transaction is a set of items purchased by a customer. An itemset (set of items) is said to be frequent if its support (number of transactions where it appears) is no less than a predefined *minsup* threshold, set by the user. The task of FIM is to enumerate all frequent itemsets in a transaction database. Although FIM is useful in many domains [8], it can find a large number of patterns, depending on how the *minsup* threshold is set. If the *minsup* threshold is set too high, no patterns are found. But if it is set too low, millions of patterns are found, and algorithms may become

© Springer International Publishing AG, part of Springer Nature 2018
M. Mouhoub et al. (Eds.): IEA/AIE 2018, LNAI 10868, pp. 101–113, 2018.
https://doi.org/10.1007/978-3-319-92058-0_10

very slow and consume a large amount of memory. To set the *minsup* threshold, a user typically run a FIM algorithm several times with different parameter values to find enough but not too many patterns. It was shown that traditional FIM algorithms can find a lot of spurious patterns that are frequent but are uninteresting to the user because their support (frequency) can be explained by the support of their subsets [2,7]. In other words, a pattern can be frequent just because the items that it contains are frequent, while items in that pattern may not be correlated. Analyzing a set of patterns containing many spurious patterns is both inconvenient and time-consuming for the user. To address this problem, an emerging topic is to find patterns that are statistically significant [2,7]. One of the most popular algorithms to find statistically significant frequent itemsets is OPUS-Miner [2]. It discovers a set of patterns called *non-redundant productive itemsets* by applying the Fisher test to determine if the bipartitions of each pattern are significantly correlated. In recent years, the concept of productive itemsets has been adapted for several applications such as discovering periodic patterns [9] and sequential patterns [10]. Although mining productive itemsets is useful as it only shows itemsets that are significant to the user, it has several limitations. First, OPUS-Miner outputs the k patterns that are productive and have the highest lift or leverage, where k is a user-specified parameter. But if k is set to a small value, patterns that are not top-k patterns will not be found, and if k is set to a very large value, the algorithm may find these patterns but become very slow and consume a huge amount of memory. Second, OPUS-Miner is not designed for interactive data mining, as the user cannot guide the search of patterns. If the user wants to know if a specific itemset is productive, he may have to run OPUS-Miner with a large k value, hoping to find this itemset among the top-k patterns. If it is not a top-k pattern, the user may then have to run the algorithm againwith a different value of k, which is inconvenient and time consuming. In fact, OPUS-Miner is unable to process queries to determine if some specific itemsets are non-redundant and productive.

Supporting targeted queries is key to the development of interactive data mining systems as it allows the user to perform queries to search for specific patterns, look at the results, and then send refined queries to search for more interesting patterns [1]. For example, targeted queries can let users quickly search for patterns containing only some items, instead of considering all items [3–5]. To efficiently process targeted queries for FIM in the context of static or incremental databases, the Itemset Tree (IT) data structure was proposed [3], as well as improved versions such as the Min-Max Itemset-Tree [4] and Memory Efficient Itemset-Tree [5]. The IT is a tree structure, which can be incrementally updated and efficiently queried. The IT structure allows processing several types of targeted queries such as (1) calculating the frequency of a given itemset, and (2) finding all frequent itemsets subsuming a set of items and their support. The IT structure has various applications such as predicting missing items in shopping carts in real-time [9]. However, it is not designed to find significant patterns, and thus can also find many spurious patterns.

This paper addresses these limitations of previous work by proposing a novel approach called IDPI (Interactive Discovery of Productive Itemsets) to support targeted queries about non redundant productive itemsets in dynamic databases. An efficient algorithm is proposed to answer queries to check if some itemsets are non redundant and productive in a database. This algorithm relies on a novel structure called Query-Tree. To evaluate the proposed approach, experiments have been carried on multiple real-life datasets used in the FIM litterature.

The rest of this paper is organized as follows. Section 2 introduces preliminaries and defines the problem. Section 3 presents the proposed approach. Section 4 presents the experimental evaluation. Section 5 draws the conclusion.

2   Preliminaries and Problem Statement

The problem of frequent itemset mining is defined as follows [6,8]. Let $I = \{i_1, i_2, \ldots, i_n\}$ be a set of items (symbols). A *transaction database* is a set of transactions $D = \{T_1, T_2, \ldots, T_m\}$, where each transaction T_z ($1 \leq z \leq m$) is a subset of items purchased by a customer ($T \subseteq I$), and z is a unique Transaction IDentifier (TID). An unordered set of items $X \subseteq I$ is said to be an *itemset*. An itemset X is said to be of length r or a r-itemset if it contains r items. The cover of an itemset X in a database D is the set of transaction containing the itemset X, that is $cov(X, D) = \{T | T \in D \wedge X \subseteq T\}$. The *support* of an itemset X in a database D is the number of transactions that contain X, that is $sup(X, D) = |cov(X, D)|$, denoted as $sup(X)$ when the context is clear. For example, consider the transaction database D of Fig. 1, which contains five items (a, b, c, d, e) and five transactions ($T_1, T_2, \ldots, T_5$). The first transaction represents the set of items a and d. The cover of the itemset $\{a, b\}$ is $cov(\{a, b\}, D) = \{T_3, T_4\}$, and the support of $\{a, b\}$ is $sup(\{a, b\}) = \{T_3, T_4\}$.

TID	Items
T_1	$\{a, d\}$
T_2	$\{b, e\}$
T_3	$\{a, b, c\}$
T_4	$\{a, b, d\}$
T_5	$\{b, e\}$

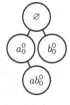

Fig. 1. A transaction database   **Fig. 2.** The query tree of $\{a, b\}$

The traditional problem of frequent itemset mining [6,8] is to find all frequent itemsets in a transaction database, that is all itemsets having a support that is no less than a user-defined *minsup* threshold. To find patterns that are not spurious, an emerging problem in data mining is to find patterns that are statistically significant. For this purpose, Webb et al. proposed to discover the set of *productive itemsets* in a database, defined as follows [2].

Definition 1 (productive itemset). *Let there be an itemset X. Two itemsets $\{Y, Z\}$ are said to be a bipartition of X if $Y \cup Z = X \wedge Y \cap Z = \emptyset \wedge Y \neq \emptyset \wedge Z \neq \emptyset$. Let bipart$(X)$ be the set of all bipartitions of X. Let $P(X \subseteq R)$ be the probability that an itemset X is drawn from the same distribution as the database D. An itemset X of length $k \geq 2$ is said to be productive if $P(X \subseteq R) > \max_{\{Y,Z\} \in bipart(X)} P(Y \subseteq R) \times P(Z \subseteq R)$.*

The constraint of productivity is useful as it ensures that all items within a productive itemset contribute to the support of the itemset. For example, the itemset $\{alchool, liver\_cancer\}$ is productive as the probability (support) of drinking alchool and having liver cancer is higher than what would be expected if those items were not correlated. On the other hand, the itemset $\{alchool, liver\_cancer, black\_hair\}$ is not productive because although this itemset may be frequent the bipartition $\{\{alchool, liver\_cancer\}, \{black\_hair\}\}$ is not correlated (the support of that bipartition can explain the support of the itemset). Thus, mining productive itemsets can filter many spurious patterns. To ensure that productive itemsets are also statistically significant, Opus-Miner applies the Fisher exact test [2]. Besides, OPUS-Miner filters redundant itemsets to show a small set of non redundant productive patterns to the user [2].

Definition 2. *An itemset X is said to be non redundant if there does not exists a proper subset Y of X having the same support, i.e. $\nexists Y \subset X | sup(X) = sup(Y)$.*

The concept of non redundant patterns (also called *generators* or *key patterns*) [11] is interesting according to the Minimum Description Length principle since it represents the smallest sets of items that are common to sets of transactions. For example, in market basket analysis, generator itemsets represent the smallest sets of items common to group of customers.

Discovering non redundant productive itemsets in a database is a very time-consuming task. The reason is that to determine if an itemset X is non redundant and productive, it is necessary to compute the support of all its bipartitions, that is the support of all its non empty subsets. Generally, an itemset X has $2^{|X|} - 1$ non empty subsets. Thus, to determine if a 6-itemset is productive, it is necessary to compute the support of $2^{|6|} - 1 = 63$ itemsets. Besides, as mentioned in the introduction, another important issue is that the state-of-the-art OPUS-miner algorithm is a batch algorithm, which can only be applied to find the top-k productive itemsets in a static database. Thus, if one wants to determine if an itemset X is productive, the user must run the algorithm with a value of k that is large enough to ensure that the itemset X will be among the top-k itemsets, which is very inconvenient as it may require to run the algorithm multiple times and can cause the algorithm to have long execution times. To address this problem, this paper defines the problem of processing queries to determine if an itemset is non-redundant and productive.

Definition 3 (Problem statement). *Given a database D, the problem of interactive discovery of non-redundant productive itemsets is to efficiently answer queries of the form "Is an itemset X productive and non redundant?".*

3   The Proposed IDPI Approach

To efficiently process queries, this paper proposes the IDPI approach. It consists of three components: (1) a variation of the Itemset-Tree structure [3] to compress the database, (2) a novel structure called Query Tree to accumulate information about the support of itemsets to answer queries, and (3) an algorithm that efficiently answer queries by comparing the two aforementioned structure.

3.1   Compressing the Database Using the Itemset-Tree Structure

The proposed approach compresses the database using a variation of the Itemset-Tree structure called Memory Efficient Itemset-Tree (MEIT) [5]. The Itemset-Tree structure was designed for interactive frequent itemset mining an can be updated incrementally to support dynamic databases.

The Itemset-Tree structure. An IT is built for a database D by inserting each transaction T of D into the IT. An IT node g has three fields: (1) $g.itemset$ stores an itemset, (2) $g.sup$ stores its support and (3) $g.childs$ stores pointers to the node's childs (if it is not a leaf). Each itemset stored in an IT node is a transaction or the intersection of one or more transactions. An IT initially only contains a root node denoted as $IT.root$, which stores the empty set, i.e. $IT.root.itemset = \emptyset$. Each itemset stored in an IT node is sorted according to a total order such as the lexicographical order. Based on that order, an itemset $X = \{a_1, a_2, \ldots a_k\}$ is said to share the leading items with an itemset $Y = \{b_1, b_2, \ldots b_l\}$ if there exists an integer $1 \le v \le argmin(\{k, l\})$ such that $a_1 = b_1, a_2 = b_2, \ldots a_v = b_v$.

Constructing an Itemset-Tree. Initially, an IT only contains the root node. The algorithm *Insert-Transaction* is applied for inserting each transaction of D in the IT (Algorithm 1). It was shown that the expected cost of this algorithm is approximately O(1) [3]. As example, Fig. 3 illustrates the construction of an IT by successively inserting each transaction of the database of Fig. 1. Figure 3 (A) shows the tree after the insertion of transaction $\{a, d\}$. A child node has been added to the root to store the itemset $\{a, d\}$ with a support of 1. Figure 3 (B) shows the tree after the insertion of transaction $\{b, e\}$. A child node has been added to the root, representing itemset $\{b, e\}$, with a support of 1. Figure 3 (C) shows the tree after the insertion of transaction $\{a, b, c\}$. Since the itemset $\{a, b, c\}$ shares the leading item $\{a\}$ with the node $\{a, d\}$, a new node $\{a\}$ has been inserted with a support of 2, having $\{a, d\}$ and $\{a, b, c\}$ as childs. The same process is repeated for the other transactions. Figure 3(D), (E) and (F) show the tree after the insertion of transactions $\{a, b, d\}$, $\{b, e\}$ and $\{b, d\}$, respectively.

In the proposed IDPI approach, a variation of the IT called MEIT [5] is used. This data structure is designed to reduce the memory usage of the IT. The difference between the MEIT and IT is that in a MEIT node, items from the parent node are not stored. For example, Fig. 3(F) shows the MEIT corresponding to the IT of Fig. 3(E). It was shown that using a MEIT instead of an IT can reduce memory usage by up to 50% [5]. A reason for using a MEIT in the proposed approach is that once it is constructed, it can be used to efficiently

---

Algorithm 1: Insert-Transaction

---

input: T: a transaction, IT: an itemset-tree

1   $IT.root.sup \leftarrow IT.root.sup + 1$;
2   **if** $T = IT.root.it$ **then** exit;
3   Let ITT be a sub-tree of $IT.root$ such that $ITT.root.it$ and T share some leading items;
4   **if** ITT *does not exist* **then** Add a child node g to $IT.root$ such that $g.itemset = T$ and $g.sup = 1$;
5   **else if** $ITT.root \subset T$ **then** $Construct(T, ITT)$;
6   **else if** $T \subset ITT.root.it$ **then** Create a new node g as a son of $IT.root$ and a father of $ITT.root$ where $g.itemset = T$ and $g.sup = ITT.root.sup + 1$;
7   **else** Create a node g as a father of $ITT.root$ such that $g.itemset = T \cap ITT.root$, $g.sup = ITT.root.sup + 1$. Moreover, create a node h as a son of g, such that $h.itemset = T$ and $h.sup = 1$;

---

find the support of any itemset X, which is required to determine if an itemset is productive and non-redundant. Moreover, a MEIT can be updated in real-time by inserting new transactions if needed, thus to support interactive data mining. Due to space limitation, the reader is referred to [5] for the algorithm for calculating the support of an itemset using a MEIT. Another reason for using a MEIT instead of an IT is that the MEIT facilitates query answering using the proposed Query Tree structure, described in the next subsection.

3.2   Representing Queries Using the Query-Tree Structure

The second component of the proposed IDPI approach is a novel structure called *Query Tree (QT)*. It is designed to increase the performance of support counting using a MEIT. Let there be a query to check if an itemset X is productive and non redundant. To answer this query, it is necessary to compute the support of all its non empty subsets. Using the traditional approach to count support using a MEIT, a query for support counting would need to be performed for each of those itemsets, that is the MEIT would need to be traversed multiple times, which is inefficient. A better approach proposed in this paper is to store X and all its subsets in a Query Tree. Then, this structure is used to quickly calculate the support of all these itemsets by traversing the MEIT only once using a novel query processing algorithm (described in the next sub-section).

The Query Tree structure. A QT is a tree where each node g has four fields: (1) $g.itemset$ stores an itemset, (2) $g.sup$ stores its support, (3) $g.pos$ stores a position (an integer initialized to zero), and (4) $g.childs$ stores a list of pointers to child nodes of g (if g is not a leaf node). It is to be noted that $g.child$ is sorted according to a total $\succ$ order such as the lexicographical order. Initially, a Query-Tree contains a single node, which is the empty set.

Constructing a Query Tree. The QT of an itemset X is built by inserting X and each non-empty subset of X in a QT. This is done by applying a modified version of Algorithm 1 for each non empty subset of X. The modified algorithm does not update the support field of each node (it remains equal to 0). Moreover, the algorithm sorts the child nodes of each node according to the $\succ$ order. The structure of a QT is similar to that of an IT. The differences are that (1) a QT stores itemsets instead of transactions, (2) the *childs* field is sorted, (3) the *sup* field is used differently, and (4) the *pos* field is introduced for matching a query to an MEIT to answer queries (described in the next subsection). For example, the QT, constructed to determine if the itemset $X = \{a, b\}$ is productive and non redundant, is shown in Fig. 2. In that figure, each node g contains an item, where its subscript and superscript indicate $g.sup$ and $g.pos$, respectively.

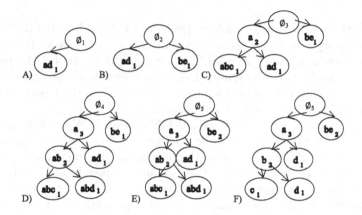

Fig. 3. Construction of the Itemset-Tree for the database of Fig. 1.

3.3 Processing Queries Efficiently Using a Query-Tree

The third component of the proposed approach is a novel algorithm to process queries (Algorithm 2), which takes as input a transaction database D and a set of queries to be processed. Let there be a query to check if an itemset X is productive and non redundant. To process the query, the first step is to build the Query Tree, as described in the previous subsection (a QT can store multiple queries) (line 2). This process creates a list QL initially containing the root of the Query Tree. Then, the MEIT is compared with the Query Tree to calculate the support of X and its subsets (line 3) by calling the $GetSupportUsingQueryTree$ procedure. This procedure stores these support values in the Query Tree nodes. After collecting all the support values, the Fisher test is applied to each bipartition of X to determine if the support of X is significantly different from the expected support of its bipartitions, and the support of X is compared with that of its subsets to determine if X is non redundant (line 5). For each application of the Fisher test, a p value is generated. The algorithm then shows the p values of the itemset X to the user, and indicates if the itemset is non redundant and productive for $p \leq 0.05$ (line 6).

Algorithm 2: IDPI

---

input: D: a transaction database, QD: a set of queries

1 rootMEIT = buildMEIT(D);   // Build MEIT (if not previously built)
2 QL = buildQueryTree(QD);   // Build the Query Tree
3 GetSupportUsingQueryTree(QL,rootMEIT);   // Get support of itemsets
4 **foreach** *query tree node* $QTN \in QL$ **do**
5 | Check if $QTN.itemset$ is productive and non redundant using QT;
6 | Output the result for QTN;   // Output itemset
7 | Insert all child nodes of QTN in QL;
8 **end**

The *GetSupportUsingQueryTree* procedure (Algorithm 3) takes as input
(1) a list of query tree nodes QL sorted according to the $\succ$ order (initially containing the root node), and (2) a MEIT node (initially the root). The procedure
compares the MEIT with the Query Tree by performing a depth-first search on
the MEIT to update the support values of all itemsets in the Query Tree. Each
node in the MEIT is traversed at most once.

To compare a QT node QTN with a MEIT node ITN, a challenge is that
an itemset stored in a MEIT node is not completely stored (for example, the
leftmost node of Fig. 3(F) represents the itemset $\{a, b, c\}$ but only $\{c\}$ is stored
in that node), while itemsets in QT nodes are completely stored. To be able
to compare these two representations of itemsets, we introduce the concept of
suffix of an itemset $X = \{a_1, a_2, \ldots a_k\}$ w.r.t a position pos, which is defined
as $suf(X, pos) = \{a_{pos}, a_{pos+1}, \ldots a_k\}$. For a node QTN, the pos field stored
in QTN indicates that only the items $suf(QTN.itemset, QTN.pos)$ should be
compared with the items in ITN. For example, if $QTN.itemset = \{a, b, c\}$
and $QTN.pos = 2$, and $ITN = \{b\}$, it indicates that only the items $\{b, c\}$
of $QTN.itemset$ should be compared with ITN. For the sake of brevity, let
$QTNsuffix$ denotes $suf(QTN.itemset, QTN.pos)$. When comparing a QT
node QTN and a MEIT node ITN, five distinct cases are encountered:

Case 1. If $suf(QTN.itemset, QTN.pos) \subseteq ITN.itemset$, then it means that
$QTN.itemset$ is included in the itemset represented by ITN. In that case, the
support of QTN is incremented by the support of ITN. Moreover, each child
node $QTNC$ of QTN is added to the list QL (while preserving the $\succ$ order)
with pos equal to the number of items in QTN, so that it will be processed
later. Moreover, QTN is removed from QL.

Case 2. If $QTNSuffix$ has some items in common with $ITN.itemset$,
and all other items of $QTNSuffix$ are greater than the largest item in
$ITN.itemset$ according to the $\succ$ order, it means that $QTN.itemset$ is not
included in the itemset represented by ITN but that it may be included in
those represented by ITN's childs. In this case, the pos value of QTN is saved
in a map, and then pos is incremented by the number of items that QT and
ITN have in common.

Case 3. If there exists an item i in $QTNsuffix$ that is not in $ITN.itemset$ and i is smaller than the last item in $ITN.itemset$ according to the $\succ$ order, it means that QTN is not included in the itemset represented by ITN and those represented by its childs. Hence, QTN is removed from the QL list.

Case 4. If the first item in $QTN.itemset$ is greater than the last item in ITN according to the $\succ$ order, it means that the itemsets represented by QTN and its siblings in QL may be included those represented by ITN and its childs. In that case, QTN and its siblings must remain in QL to be processed next when considering ITN's childs.

Case 5. Otherwise, it is necessary to compare the siblings that succeed QTN according to the $\succ$ order with ITN.

It can be proven that the $GetSupportUsingQueryTree$ procedure is correct to calculate the support of itemsets stored in a Query Tree, although the proof is omitted due to space limitation.

Algorithm 3: GetSupportUsingQueryTree

---

input: QL: a QT node list (initially containing only the QT root node) ITN: a MEIT node (initially the root node)

1 **if** QL *is empty* **then** exit;
2 $QTNsuffix = suf(QTN.itemset, QTN.pos)$;
3 **foreach** $QTN \in QL$ **do**
4   **if** $QTNsuffix \subseteq ITN.itemset$ // Case 1
5   **then**
6          $QTN.sup += ITN.sup$; **foreach** *child* $QTNC$ *of* QTN **do**
7              $QL.add(QTNC)$;   // while preserving the $\succ$ order in QL
8              $tjmap[QTNC] = QTNC.pos$;
9              $QTNC.pos = |QTN.itemset|$;
10   **end**
11         $QL.delete(QTN)$;
12   **end**
13   **else if**
    $QTNsuffix \cap ITN.itemset \neq \emptyset \wedge \forall i \in QTNsuffix \setminus ITN.itemset, i > ITN.itemset.last$
    // Case 2
14   **then**
15         $tjmap[QTNC.itemset] = QTNC.pos$;
16         $QTN.pos += |QTNsuffix \cap ITN.itemset|$;
17   **end**
18   **else if** $\exists i \in QTNsuffix \setminus ITN.itemset \wedge i < ITN.itemset.last$ **then**
19         $QL.delete(QTN)$;   // Case 3
20   **end**
21   **else if** $QTN.itemset.first > ITN.itemset.last$ **then** *break*;   // Case 4
22   **else** *continue*;   // Case 5
23 **end**
24 **foreach** $ITNC \in ITN$ **do** $GetSupportUsingQueryTree(QL, ITNC)$;
25 **foreach** $QTN \in tjmap$ **do** $QTN.pos = tjmap[QTN]$;

The process of calculating the support of itemsets using a Query Tree is illustrated with an example. Consider Fig. 4. It shows how the Query Tree of $\{a, b\}$ is updated by traversing the MEIT using a depth-first search. Five steps ((A), (B), (C), (D), (E)) are illustrated corresponding to the comparison of the QT with the five nodes of the MEIT, respectively. The first and second lines show the content of the QL and Query Tree before the comparison, respectively. The third line shows the MEIT, where the node marked in light gray is the current node ITN used for the comparison. Initially (Fig. 4(A)), all values in the QT are equal to zero. The list QL contains only the root of the QT, representing the empty itemset. This current node, called QTN, is compared with the root of the MEIT, called ITN. Since $QTN.itemset \subseteq ITN.itemset$ ($\varnothing \subseteq \varnothing$), case 1 is applied. Thus, the support of ITN is added to the support of QTN, the childs of QTN are inserted in QL with pos equal to the number of items in QTN, and QTN is removed from QL. After this, QL contains two nodes: a_0^0 and b_0^0. The next node from QL to be considered as QTN is a_0^0. Because the first item of $\{a\}$ is greater than the last item of ITN, case 4 is applied (the main loop is stopped). The current state of QL and the QT are shown in Fig. 4(B). Next, the $GetSupportUsingQueryTree$ is recursively called to compare nodes in QL with the first child of ITN. Thus, the node a_3 becomes the node ITN. This current node of QL, $QTN = a_0^0$, is compared with ITN. Because $QTN.itemset \subseteq ITN.itemset$ ($\{a\} \subseteq \{a\}$), case 1 is applied. Thus, the support of ITN is added to the support of QTN, the childs of QTN are inserted in QL with pos equal to the number of items in QTN, and QTN is removed from QL. After this, QL contains two nodes: ab_0^1 and b_0^0. The next node from QL to be considered as QTN is ab_0^1. Case 5 is applied, and thus the next node in QL is processed, that is b_0^0. Because the first item of $\{b\}$ is greater than the last item of $ITN = \{a\}$, case 4 is applied (the main loop is stopped). The current state of QL and the QT are shown in Fig. 4(C). The same process is repeated for the other nodes of the MEIT following the depth-first search. The final QT is shown in Fig. 4(F). From this tree, it is found that the support of itemsets $\{a\}$, $\{b\}$ and $\{a, b\}$ are 3, 2, and 4, respectively. Thus, $\{a, b\}$ is non redundant, and the Fisher test can be applied using these support values to check if $\{a, b\}$ is productive. Note that in this example, the database is too small to determine if an itemset is productive.

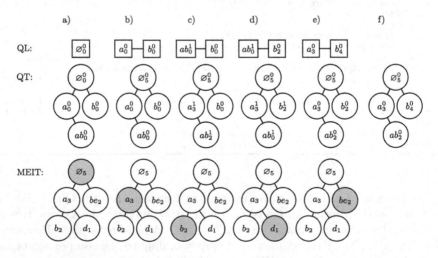

Fig. 4. Updating the query tree of $\{a, b\}$ by traversing the MEIT

4   Experimental Evaluation

To evaluate the proposed IDPI approach, an experiment was performed to compare its performance with that of a baseline approach using an IT to count the support of itemsets (as presented in Sect. 3.1). The goal is to check if the novel QT structure reduces the time to process queries, and generally how many queries may be processed per second on a desktop computer on benchmark datasets. Both approaches were implemented in C++. The experiment was performed on a computer equipped with a Xeon E3-1270 processor running Windows 10 and 64 GB of free RAM. The experiment was carried on real-life and synthetic datasets commonly used in the frequent itemset mining literature, namely Accidents, Chess, Connect, Mushrooms, Pumsb and Retail. In the experiment, n random queries were generated for each dataset, where n was varied from 1000 to 3000, and the length of itemsets in queries was varied from 2 to 10. IDPI and the baseline approach were applied on each set of random queries and the total execution time was measured in seconds. Results are shown in Table 1.

Table 1. Time for processing n queries using IDPI and the baseline approach

Dataset	Itemset length	Time for processing n queries (s)					
		IDPI			Baseline (IT)		
		1000	2000	3000	1000	2000	3000
Mushroom	2–4	1	2	3	9	17	36
	5–7	4	8	14	33	66	121
	8–10	15	35	57	86	194	260
Connect	2–4	11	19	30	77	162	247
	5–7	56	107	150	374	743	1192
	8–10	297	698	926	1501	3361	5503
Accident	2–4	13	18	23	184	358	525
	5–7	35	59	82	511	1063	1507
	8–10	83	160	230	1007	2240	3345
Pumsb	2–4	11	23	35	111	220	328
	5–7	35	86	139	262	522	777
	8–10	168	448	782	461	922	1398
Retail	2–4	27	58	110	72	162	248
	5–7	71	217	434	213	451	704
	8–10	244	861	1402	435	968	1214
Chess	2–4	1	2	2	4	9	48
	5–7	7	15	20	29	56	86
	8–10	50	93	132	159	307	450

It can be observed that the proposed IDPI approach is up to 22 times faster than the baseline approach. IDPI is faster in all cases except on Retail when $n = 3000$ and the itemset length is between 8 to 10. The reason is that in that case the QT becomes very large since for example, a 10-itemset has $2^{10} = 1024$ subsets. However, it can be argued that itemsets of length 8 to 10 are unlikely to be productive (since all their bipartitions must be positively correlated), and long itemsets are rarely useful in practice as they represent very specific cases. It was also found that the proposed approach can process up to 1000 queries per second, which makes it suitable for interactive pattern mining. Generally, the speed of processing queries is influenced by the length of itemsets, whether they share subsets, and the nature of the database. Note that if a QT is reused multiple times on the same database (e.g. on different days), the time for query processing is reduced because the QT is not rebuilt. Overall, the performance of the proposed approach is found to be very satisfying.

5   Conclusion

This paper has defined the problem of interactively discovering non redundant and productive itemsets in transaction databases. To efficiently process targeted queries performed by users to check if some patterns are non redundant and productive, an approach called IDPI was proposed. The approach relies on the MEIT and a novel Query Tree structure to efficiently process queries. Experimental results show that the IDPI approach is up to 22 times faster than a baseline approach and can process up to 1000 queries per second on a desktop computer, making it suitable for interactive pattern mining. In future work, the IDPI approach will be improved to support additional query types.

References

1. Han, J., Pei, J., Kamber, M.: Data Mining: Concepts and Techniques. Elsevier, Waltham (2011)
2. Webb, G.I., Vreeken, J.: Efficient discovery of the most interesting associations. ACM Trans. Knowl. Discov. Data 8(3), 15 (2014)
3. Kubat, M., Hafez, A., Raghavan, V.V., Lekkala, J.R., Chen, W.K.: Itemset trees for targeted association querying. IEEE Trans. Knowl. Data Eng. 15(6), 1522–1534 (2003)
4. Lavergne, J., Benton, R., Raghavan, V.V.: Min-max itemset trees for dense and categorical datasets. In: Chen, L., Felfernig, A., Liu, J., Raś, Z.W. (eds.) ISMIS 2012. LNCS (LNAI), vol. 7661, pp. 51–60. Springer, Heidelberg (2012). https://doi.org/10.1007/978-3-642-34624-8_6
5. Fournier-Viger, P., Mwamikazi, E., Gueniche, T., Faghihi, U.: MEIT: memory efficient itemset tree for targeted association rule mining. In: Motoda, H., Wu, Z., Cao, L., Zaiane, O., Yao, M., Wang, W. (eds.) ADMA 2013, Part II. LNCS (LNAI), vol. 8347, pp. 95–106. Springer, Heidelberg (2013). https://doi.org/10.1007/978-3-642-53917-6_9

6. Agrawal, R., Srikant, R.: Fast algorithms for mining association rules in large databases. In: Proceedings of 20th International Conference on Very Large Databases, pp. 487–499. Morgan Kaufmann, Santiago de Chile (1994)

7. Llinares-López, F., Sugiyama, M., Papaxanthos, L., Borgwardt, K.: Fast and memory-efficient significant pattern mining via permutation testing. In: Proceedings of 21th ACM International Conference on Knowledgs Discovery and Data Mining, pp. 725–734. ACM (2015)

8. Fournier-Viger, P., Lin, J.C.-W., Vo, B., Chi, T.T., Zhang, J., Le, H.B.: A survey of itemset mining. WIREs Data Mining Knowl. Discov. **7**(4), e1207 (2017). https://doi.org/10.1002/widm

9. Nofong, V.M.: Discovering productive periodic frequent patterns in transactional databases. Ann. Data Sci. **3**(3), 235–249 (2016)

10. Petitjean, F., Li, T., Tatti, N., Webb, G.I.: Skopus: mining top-k sequential patterns under leverage. Data Mining Knowl. Discov. **30**(5), 1086–1111 (2016)

11. Fournier-Viger, P., Wu, C.-W., Tseng, V.S.: Novel concise representations of high utility itemsets using generator patterns. In: Luo, X., Yu, J.X., Li, Z. (eds.) ADMA 2014. LNCS (LNAI), vol. 8933, pp. 30–43. Springer, Cham (2014). https://doi.org/10.1007/978-3-319-14717-8_3

Sampling Community Structure in Dynamic Social Networks

Humphrey Mensah[✉] and Sucheta Soundarajan

Department of Electrical Engineering and Computer Science,
Syracuse University, Syracuse, NY, USA
{hamensah,susounda}@syr.edu

Abstract. When studying dynamic networks, it is often of interest to understand how the community structure of the network changes. However, before studying the community structure of dynamic social networks, one must first collect appropriate network data. In this paper we present a network sampling technique to crawl the community structure of dynamic networks when there is a limitation on the number of nodes that can be queried. The process begins by obtaining a sample for the first time step. In subsequent time steps, the crawling process is guided by community structure discoveries made in the past. Experiments conducted on the proposed approach and certain baseline techniques reveal the proposed approach has at least 35% performance increase in cases when the total query budget is fixed over the entire period and at least 8% increase in cases when the query budget is fixed per time step.

1 Introduction

Researchers are interested in a wide variety of problems related to communities in dynamic social networks, including understanding their growth, dissolution, and merging behaviors [10,16,17]. However, before studying such questions, a researcher must first obtain an appropriate dataset. Because typical social networks may contain millions or billions of nodes, it can be a challenge to collect adequate data within a reasonable amount of time, due to both the computational efforts required to collect such data as well as API rate limits imposed by the companies owning the data. For example, when crawling the Twitter friendship or follower network, the Twitter API allows only 15 queries per 15 min [1]. Given such a scenario, a data collector must make the most of a limited query budget: which areas of the graph should be explored in order to obtain information that is most useful for the analysis task at hand? This is a challenge even in static networks; and the challenge is compounded in dynamic networks, where individual nodes or edges may appear or disappear, and the structure of entire regions of the graph may change in a moment.

In this paper, we focus on the problem of crawling a dynamic social network with the goal of obtaining a sample with community structure that is as representative as possible of the true community structure. Here, a community in a

© Springer International Publishing AG, part of Springer Nature 2018
M. Mouhoub et al. (Eds.): IEA/AIE 2018, LNAI 10868, pp. 114–126, 2018.
https://doi.org/10.1007/978-3-319-92058-0_11

network refers to a group of nodes that are densely connected to each other. In online social networks, a community can represent a group of likeminded users. Identifying such users could be used for marketing and recommendations [3]. Identifying the dynamic community structure in online social networks provides insights into questions such as: which group is migrating to what group, how long does it take for a particular group to collapse, when was a particular group formed, etc.

This paper presents Dynamic Sampler (DYNSAMP) which samples the dynamic community structure of online social networks over a period of time when there are resource constraints. Two resource constraint cases are considered: (1) The case where there is a limitation on the number of times one can request information over the entire period considered (e.g., one has a total amount of money to spend on data collection across the timeline), and (2) The case when there is a limitation at each time step on the number of times one can request information about a node (e.g., there is a daily limit on the number of queries that can be made). DYNSAMP works on the notion that the current community structure of a graph might be partially or wholly similar to previously discovered community structures. Experiments show that DYNSAMP has a performance improvement ranging from 35% to 53% when compared to baseline methods when the query limitation is considered over the entire period and 8%–56% in cases when there is a limitation at each time step.

The rest of the paper is organized as follows. First, we discuss some related work. In Sect. 3, we present the problem of sampling in dynamic networks. In Sect. 4, we discuss the proposed approach. Section 5 presents the experiments performed and its set up. Finally, Sect. 6 presents the conclusion to the paper and some future directions.

2   Related Work

There has been little work focused on sampling community structure in networks, and most existing work has focused on static networks.

Maiya and Berger-Wolf [12] proposed an expander graph based sampling approach for static networks. This method begins with a seed node and increasingly grows the sample by selecting a node from the neighborhood of the current sample that maximizes a quality function. Also, in the selection of the next node, there is an assumption that the neighborhood of all nodes are known which is not generalizable to most online social networks.

In [5], the authors proposed a link tracing approach for sampling the community structure of static networks. It begins with a seed node and grows the sample by selecting the node with the highest reference score, defined as the ratio of the number of already discovered connections pointing to a node so far in the crawling process to the degree of the node.

A PageRank-based sampling approach (PRS) proposed by Salehi et al. [14] obtains samples from a static network with high community structures. From the simulation results, authors argue PRS has significantly higher performance.

However, PRS assumes it knows the number of communities in the network which is not realistic with online social networks.

Another link tracing approach (QCA) proposed for dynamic networks is described in [13]. This begins with an initial community structure. It computes each of the existing communities' "force" of accepting the node. The community membership is selected based on the "force". QCA is able to compute community membership of discovered nodes. Even though QCA is one of the few techniques proposed for dynamic networks, it assumes it has an initial community structure which is not practical in most online social networks.

In [11], Lu et al. proposed two incremental sampling algorithms for dynamic graphs that preserves some property of interest. Even though it was demonstrated to be performing well, this approach (1) Makes a similar assumption to [12] by assuming it knows the entire graph and (2) does not sample for communities in the network.

In this paper, we propose a crawling based approach to sample the community structure of dynamic networks with a constraint on the number of times one can request information about a node without any knowledge of the community structure.

3   Preliminaries

3.1   Notations

- $G_t = (V_t, E_t)$ is a true, unobserved graph at time step t, where V_t and $E_t \subset V_t \times V_t$ are the set of nodes and edges, respectively, at time step t.
- $G_t^s = (V_t^s, E_t^s)$ is a sampled graph at time step t, where V_t^s and $E_t^s \subset V_t^s \times V_t^s$ are the sampled set of nodes and edges respectively at time step t.
- $G = \{G_1, G_2, ..., G_n\}$ is the true graph sequence and $G^s = \{G_1^s, G_2^s, ..., G_n^s\}$ represents a sampled graph sequence, where $G_i^s \subset G_i$.
- ω_t represents the community structure similarity metric between G_t and G_t^s at time step t.
- q^t represents the number of queries used at time step t to obtain G_t^s.
- q_v represents a vector of the number of queries made to obtain G^s. The ith vector entry is the number of queries made on time step i.
- q represents the total number of queries made to obtain G^s.
- q_{max}^t represents the maximum number of queries allowed at time step t.
- q_{max} is a the total number of queries allowed over the entire timeline.
- The dynamic community similarity $\aleph$ of a sampled graph G^s and a ground truth graph G is defined as:

$$\aleph(G, G^s) = \frac{1}{n} \sum_{t=1}^{n} \omega_t$$

- τ is a dissimilarity threshold for which we declare two communities to be different.

3.2   Problem Formulation

In this work, we assume the true graph sequence G is not known. We also assume that we can determine whether a node is present in a given timestep at no cost, as in many online social networks. Example, the Twitter API allows up to 900 queries per 15 min when searching for a user. In each step, a node can be queried, and all of its neighbors learned. Assuming the process begins with a query on v_1, the next query can only be made on discovered neighbors of previously queried nodes (either from the current or previous time steps). For dynamic networks, we assume there is a storage limitation on how many graphs can be stored for a period considered. Our goal is to generate a sampled graph sequence G^s such that $\aleph(G, G^s)$ is maximized.

We consider two different problem settings: (1) The query budget limits the total number of queries that can be made over the entire timeline (e.g., queries cost money, and we have a fixed amount of money for the entire sampling process). (2) There is a query limit for each timestep (e.g., queries take time, and each time step has a limited amount of time).

4   Proposed Approach

This work proposes a novel algorithm (DYNSAMP) for sampling a dynamic network such that the community similarity between the true and sampled networks is maximized. The intuition behind DYNSAMP is that the current snapshot of a graph may be similar to an earlier snapshot; or if not, portions may be similar.

DYNSAMP begins by obtaining a sample for the first time step of the sampling process with an allocated number of queries. For subsequent time steps, a fraction of the budget allocated for that time is used to obtain a graph called the *startup graph*. The startup graph is then compared to previously discovered graphs to determine if they are similar. If similar, a portion of the budget allocated for that time step is saved for future use. If not similar, the entire allocated budget for the time step is used. If there is saved budget, it is used to perform extra queries to grow the graph. Figure 1 shows a high-level view of the proposed approach to sampling dynamic social networks. A detailed description of the steps involved is described below.

4.1   Initialization

The sampling process requires as input either a total budget q or vector of daily budgets q_v, depending on the problem setting, the number of time steps n considered, and a dissimilarity threshold τ above which we declare two communities to be different. If the budget constraint applies to the entire period, for each time step t, we allocate a basic budget $\varphi_t = \varrho_t / n_t$ where ϱ_t and n_t is the budget and number of time steps respectively left as at time step t. However, if there is a limitation for each time step, a basic budget of $\varphi_t = q_{max}^t$ is defined for each time step t.

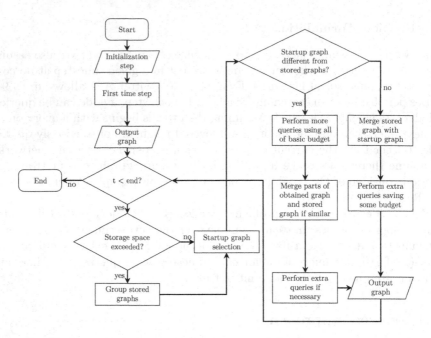

Fig. 1. A high level description of the steps involved in the proposed dynamic network sampling.

4.2 First Time Step

For the first time step of sampling, a *budget* φ_0 is used to generate a sample by beginning with a random node, and in each step, with probability p, querying the node with the maximum observed degree, or with probability $1 - p$, jumping to a random node, and storing the observed graph. Our experimental results suggested that this technique works well in comparison to methods such as random node selection and random walk.

4.3 Startup Graph Selection

In subsequent time steps after the first time step, a fraction of the basic budget η_t is used to obtain a startup graph for the time step under consideration. In this work, a budget of $0.50 * \varphi_t$ is used to obtain the startup graph. The nodes queried are noted and the amount of change in their neighborhood of all previously stored graphs over the period is computed using Jaccard similarity.

In generating the startup graph, DYNSAMP selects the top η_t queried nodes with the highest change in neighborhood as at the time under consideration. This selection process ensures that nodes whose neighborhood have not changed over a period are not selected often. The selected nodes are queried to obtain the startup graph. In cases where the number of queried nodes present in the current time step is less than η_t, a random number of nodes are selected from the current nodes to add up to η_t.

4.4   Comparing Startup Graph to Previous Graphs

Next, the startup graph is compared to all previously obtained graphs to identify any similarities. In this work, the dissimilarity between two graphs $G_1 = (V_1, E_1)$ and $G_2 = (V_2, E_2)$ is defined as $1 - |E_1 \cap E_2|/|E_1 \cup E_2|$.

In comparing a startup graph and a previously discovered graph, if all nodes queried in the startup graph are present in the stored graph, only such nodes and their neighbors are considered. However, if all nodes queried in the startup graph are not present, a random set of queried nodes in the stored graph are selected and their neighbors are considered for comparison between the two graphs. The selection is done such that the number of nodes queried in both graphs are equal. DYNSAMP selects the stored graph most similar to the startup graph.

4.5   Performing Extra Queries

If the startup graph is within τ of the closest graph, the connections in the stored graph that are between nodes present in the current sample are added to the initial graph obtained. In this work, an assumption is made that a check can be made to determine if a node is present or not. The remaining budget is used to perform some extra queries to grow the graph. If budget is allocated for the entire duration, a fraction is saved for future use. By performing extra queries in cases when the graphs are similar, it provides a means of growing the graph that was previously stored.

In cases where the startup graph is identified to be entirely different from all previously obtained graphs, the remaining budget is used to grow the network. A further check is made if some parts of the startup graph are similar to the closest stored graph. Each community is merged with its closest community in the stored graph based on the defined threshold. Communities in this work were obtained using the Louvain method [6]. In the cases where a budget could be saved, the saved budget is used to perform additional queries, since the discovered community structure is deemed wholly new.

4.6   Handling Storage Limitations

Due to space limitations, it may not be possible to store all previous graphs especially when sampling for a larger number of time steps. To address this, for all time steps after the first time step, DYNSAMP checks if the entire storage is used before the sampling for that particular time begins. The stored graphs are clustered into groups.

When the storage limit is exceeded, a check is made to determine the number of unique graphs among all stored graphs. A stored graph is said to be unique when it is not similar to any of the stored graphs. If among all the stored graphs there is only one unique stored graph, this means that the graphs stored are all similar to each other and hence grouped into a single graph. As an example, assuming $G_1^s = (V_1^s, E_1^s), G_2^s = (V_2^s, E_2^s), ..., G_m^s = (V_m^s, E_m^s)$ are the currently stored graphs with a single unique stored graph. A new graph

---

Algorithm 1. DYNSAMP for sampling the community structure of dynamic networks when queries can be saved

---

1 function DYNSAMP $(G, budget, \tau, n)$;
    Input : G, $budget, \tau, n$
    Output: G^s
2 $snaps = n, \varphi_1 = budget/snaps, G_0^s \leftarrow getFirstTimeSample(G_0, \varphi_1)$;
3 Decrement $budget$, Decrement $snaps$;
4 Store graph at $t = 0$;
5 **for** $t = 1$ to n **do**
6   **if** $storage$ $exceeded$ **then**
7 | $groupGraphs()$
8      $\varphi_t = budget/snaps, startup = 0.50 * \varphi_t$;
9      $G_t^s \leftarrow getStartUp(G_t, startup)$;
10      $G_{sel} \leftarrow$ Find closest stored graph;
11      $\delta \leftarrow graphDissim(G_t^s, G_{sel})$;
12   **if** $\delta > \tau$ **then**
13   use all of base size;
14         $G_t^s \leftarrow mergeComPart(G_t^s, G_{sel})$;
15   **if** $\delta > \tau$ **then**
16            $extra = savedqueries$;
17            $G_i^s \leftarrow performExtraQ(G_t, G_t^s, extra)$;
18   **else**
19         $extra = (0.90 * \varphi_t) - startup$;
20         $G_t^s \leftarrow merge(G_t^s, G_{sel})$;
21         $performExtraQ(G_t, G_t^s, extra)$;
22   update saved queries;
23   update queried neighbors;
24   Decrement $budget$, Decrement $snaps$;

$G_\alpha^s = (V_\alpha^s, E_\alpha^s)$ such that $V_\alpha^s = \bigcup_{i=1}^{m} V_i$ and $E_\alpha^s = \bigcup_{i=1}^{m} E_i$ is obtained after the merging process. If there are k unique stored graphs, where $k > 1$, an initial attempt is made to group the graph into k groups. After the grouping into k, if storage is still exceeded, graphs with the least assessed time are repeatedly considered for eviction until the storage criteria is met. Algorithm 1 provides a step by step description of the proposed technique when queries can be saved while Algorithm 2 gives the description of the technique when queries can not be saved.

5   Experiments

This section begins with a description of various real and synthetic datasets used for the experiment. It is followed with how the experiments were set up and the main objectives in the various experiments. The section ends with a discussion of the results of each dataset.

Algorithm 2. DYNSAMP for sampling the community structure of dynamic networks when queries can not be saved

---

1 <u>function DYNSAMP</u> (G, q, τ, n);
   Input : G, q, τ, n
   Output: G^s
2   $G_0^s \leftarrow getFirstTimeSample(G_0, q_{max}^0)$;
3   Store graph at $t = 0$;
4   **for** $t = 1$ *to* n **do**
5   **if** *storage exceeded* **then**
6 | $groupGraphs()$
7      $startup = 0.50 * q_{max}^t$;
8      $G_t^s \leftarrow getStartUp(G_t, startup)$;
9      $G_{sel} \leftarrow$ Find closest stored graph;
10     $\delta \leftarrow graphDissim(G_t^s, G_{sel})$;
11     $extra = q_{max}^t - startup$;
12   **if** $\delta > \tau$ **then**
13       $performExtraQ(G_t, G_t^s, extra)$;
14       $G_t^s \leftarrow mergeComPart(G_t^s, G_{sel})$;
15   **else**
16       $G_t^s \leftarrow merge(G_t^s, G_{sel})$;
17       $performExtraQ(G_t, G_t^s, extra)$;
18   update queried neighbors;
19   updated stored graphs;

5.1 Datasets

We consider five datasets. These include three real world datasets: Autonomous Systems (AS-733) [9], Reality Mining (MIT contact)[8] and Enron email (Enron) [15]. We also include two synthetic datasets (Syn1 and Syn2), generated using Dancer [4]. Dancer generates evolving graphs with embedded community structure.

AS-733 is a communication network constructed from Border Gateway Protocol logs. It contains 733 daily instances, the largest of which has 6474 nodes and 12572 edges. Reality Mining is a human contact network among 100 MIT students. This dataset contains 229 daily instances describing contacts between users, each of which has up to 76 nodes and 418 edges. We aggregate these daily instances using window sizes of 10 days, with a step of 3, to generate a total of 77 snapshots. Enron is an email network. We use a dataset containing daily snapshots during the year 2001, again aggregated as above, for a total of 122 snapshots. These graphs contain up to 7225 nodes and 15938 edges. All networks exhibit the addition and deletion of both nodes and edges. Some snapshots are aggregated to ensure all the different community structure behavior are considered in the experiment.

The synthetic networks both have an initial node count of 2000 initially grouped into 20 and 24 communities for Syn1 and Syn2 respectively. These go through different community evolution phases such as splitting and merging.[1]

The largest time step of Syn1 has 2293 nodes with 17813 edges. Syn1 over the period considered shows an addition and deletion of edges. However, it only demonstrates the addition of nodes over the period. In Syn2, the largest number of nodes over the period is 2859 and the largest number of edges over the period is 21459. Syn2 tends to have communities splitting or migrating more often than communities in Syn1.

5.2 Experimental Setup

In our experiments, we set $\tau = 0.4$ and $p = 0.80$. The budget size in the experiments with a strict budget limitation for each time step is defined to 20% of the number of nodes at each time step. Budgets for the setting in which we have a total number of queries for the entire timeline are stated later in this section.

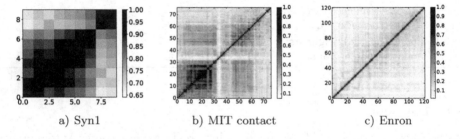

a) Syn1   b) MIT contact   c) Enron

Fig. 2. A plot of the similarity between community structures over time for three different group of networks. 2(a) is a network with totally stable community structure, 2(b) has a partially stable community structure and 2(c) is network with a completely unstable community structure. Black indicates two graphs are equal and white indicates they are completely different. These examples demonstrate stable (Syn1), mixed (MIT), and unstable (Enron) structures.

To the best of our knowledge, there is no sampling method that explicitly focuses on the community structure of dynamic networks without assuming knowledge of the entire network. The proposed method is therefore compared with random walk and breadth-first search baselines.

---

[1] This model requires a number of parameters. We set $k = 20, nBVertices = 2000, nbTimestamps = 10, prMicro = 0.2, prMerge = 0.4, removeVertices = 0.4, prSplit = 0.4, prChange = 0.4, addBetweenEdges = 0.2, addVertices = 0.1, removeBetweenEdges = 0.4, removeWithinEdges = 0.1, updateAttributes = 0.1$. For Syn2, the same settings were maintained with modification to the following: $prMicro = 0.5$, $addBetweenEdges = 0.5$, $removeBetweenEdges = 0.9$, and $k = 24$.

5.3   Evaluation Metrics

We use two metrics to evaluate DYNSAMP and the baselines above. The first metric is based on a Jaccard-based metric proposed in [18], modified for evaluating dynamic samples. Given a sampled set of communities C_i^s and a true set of communities C_i, this metric finds the closest true community to each sampled community, and vice versa, and averages these similarities. We also use the popular Normalized Mutual Information (NMI) metric, described in [2,7].

5.4   Results and Discussion

For each of the datasets, we run DYNSAMP and the baselines 10 times to generate a dynamic sample with specific budget. We compare to communities detected on the complete network by the Louvain method [6]. Results for both evaluation metrics were similar, so we present results for NMI only in Fig. 3.

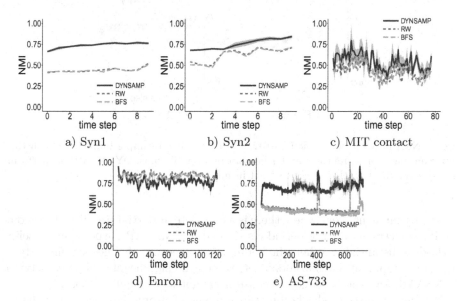

a) Syn1   b) Syn2   c) MIT contact

d) Enron   e) AS-733

Fig. 3. A plot of the NMI between a sampled graph and its corresponding true graph over time. Shading represents the standard deviation over 10 trials. DYNSAMP outperforms the other methods with respect to NMI in most cases. When graph changes at each time step like 3(d), it performs just as baseline methods.

In our experiments, we use budgets of 199000, 850, 13000, 2500 and 2500 respectively for AS-733, MIT-contact, Enron, Syn1 and Syn2. Figure 3 shows a similar plot of the NMI with respect to time (results were similar for the Jaccard-based evaluation metric). In these experiments, the setting where a budget is given over the entire period is used. Similarly, Fig. 4 shows a similarity plot of the NMI with respect to time when there is a budget limitation per timestep.

Dynamic social networks can be categorized into three groups based on the stability of the community structure over the period considered (see Fig. 2 for examples): those that are stable over the entire period (e.g., Syn1), those that are unstable (e.g., Enron), and those that are mixed (e.g., Reality Mining).

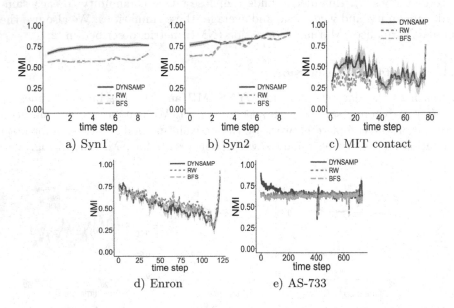

a) Syn1   b) Syn2   c) MIT contact

d) Enron   e) AS-733

Fig. 4. NMI between a sampled and true graphs, with a sample budget for each time step. Shading represents the standard deviation over 10 trials. DYNSAMP outperforms the other methods with respect to NMI in most cases.

In a dynamic network where there is a complete or partial stability of the community structures over the period considered, DYNSAMP outperforms baseline methods substantially. When the community structure changes significantly at each time step, like the Enron dataset, there is no significant difference between DYNSAMP and the baselines, because it cannot learn from the past.

We next investigated whether the number of graph samples stored had a significant impact on the performance of DYNSAMP. The investigation was divided into two: graphs that have some stability over time (Syn1) and graphs with no stability over time (Enron). We observe that, in general, the performance of DYNSAMP is not dependent on the number of graphs being stored. If there is some stability, it will be merged over time and hence keeping several copies of them will neither improve or worsen the performance. In cases where there is no stability, the number of stored graphs has no impact on the learning process.

Overall, we observe that DYNSAMP performs better than baseline methods in most cases. With the Jaccard based measure, it outperforms RW by 42% and BFS by 46% on average, and by 35% and 53% as measured by NMI.

6   Conclusion

Sampling provides a means of selecting some parts of the graph such that certain features of the original graph are preserved. In this paper, we addressed the problem of sampling a dynamic social network when there is a limitation on the number of nodes that could be asked for information. We performed experiments on several real world and synthetic networks. We showed that in most cases the proposed approach outperforms baseline methods. However, in cases where the community structure for each time step changes significantly, the algorithm performs as well as the baseline methods.

References

1. Twitter developer documentation. https://dev.twitter.com/rest/reference/get/followers/ids. Accessed 16 Aug 2017
2. Alvari, H., Hajibagheri, A., Sukthankar, G., Lakkaraju, K.: Identifying community structures in dynamic networks. Soc. Netw. Anal. Min. **6**(1), 77 (2016)
3. Bedi, P., Sharma, C.: Community detection in social networks. Wiley Interdisc. Rev.: Data Min. Knowl. Discov. **6**(3), 115–135 (2016)
4. Benyahia, O., Largeron, C., Jeudy, B., Zaïane, O.R.: DANCer: dynamic attributed network with community structure generator. In: Berendt, B., Bringmann, B., Fromont, É., Garriga, G., Miettinen, P., Tatti, N., Tresp, V. (eds.) ECML PKDD 2016, Part III. LNCS (LNAI), vol. 9853, pp. 41–44. Springer, Cham (2016). https://doi.org/10.1007/978-3-319-46131-1_9
5. Blenn, N., Doerr, C., Van Kester, B., Van Mieghem, P.: Crawling and detecting community structure in online social networks using local information. In: Bestak, R., Kencl, L., Li, L.E., Widmer, J., Yin, H. (eds.) NETWORKING 2012. LNCS, vol. 7289, pp. 56–67. Springer, Heidelberg (2012). https://doi.org/10.1007/978-3-642-30045-5_5
6. Blondel, V.D., Guillaume, J.-L., Lambiotte, R., Lefebvre, E.: Fast unfolding of communities in large networks. J. Stat. Mech.: Theor. Exp. **2008**(10), P10008 (2008)
7. Chen, Y., Qiu, X.: Detecting community structures in social networks with particle swarm optimization. In: Su, J., Zhao, B., Sun, Z., Wang, X., Wang, F., Xu, K. (eds.) Frontiers in Internet Technologies. CCIS, vol. 401, pp. 266–275. Springer, Heidelberg (2013). https://doi.org/10.1007/978-3-642-53959-6_24
8. Eagle, N., Pentland, A.: Reality mining: sensing complex social systems. Pers. Ubiquit. Comput. **10**(4), 255–268 (2006)
9. Leskovec, J., Kleinberg, J., Faloutsos, C.: Graphs over time: densification laws, shrinking diameters and possible explanations. In: Proceedings of the Eleventh ACM SIGKDD International Conference on Knowledge Discovery in Data Mining, pp. 177–187. ACM (2005)
10. Lin, Y.-R., Chi, Y., Zhu, S., Sundaram, H., Tseng, B.L.: Facetnet: a framework for analyzing communities and their evolutions in dynamic networks. In: Proceedings of the 17th International Conference on World Wide Web, pp. 685–694. ACM (2008)
11. Lu, X., Phan, T.Q., Bressan, S.: Incremental algorithms for sampling dynamic graphs. In: Decker, H., Lhotská, L., Link, S., Basl, J., Tjoa, A.M. (eds.) DEXA 2013, Part I. LNCS, vol. 8055, pp. 327–341. Springer, Heidelberg (2013). https://doi.org/10.1007/978-3-642-40285-2_29

12. Maiya, A.S., Berger-Wolf, T.Y.: Sampling community structure. In: Proceedings of the 19th International Conference on World Wide Web, pp. 701–710. ACM (2010)

13. Nguyen, N.P., Dinh, T.N., Xuan, Y., Thai, M.T.: Adaptive algorithms for detecting community structure in dynamic social networks. In: Proceedings of the 2011 IEEE International Conference on Computer Communications, pp. 2282–2290. IEEE (2011)

14. Salehi, M., Rabiee, H.R., Rajabi, A.: Sampling from complex networks with high community structures. Chaos: Interdisc. J. Nonlinear Sci. **22**(2), 023126 (2012)

15. Sun, J., Faloutsos, C., Papadimitriou, S., Yu, P.S.: Graphscope: parameter-free mining of large time-evolving graphs. In: Proceedings of the 13th ACM SIGKDD International Conference on Knowledge Discovery and Data Mining, pp. 687–696. ACM (2007)

16. Thakur, G.S., Tiwari, R., Thai, M.T., Chen, S.-S., Dress, A.W.M.: Detection of local community structures in complex dynamic networks with random walks. IET Syst. Biol. **3**(4), 266–278 (2009)

17. Wang, C.-D., Lai, J.-H., Philip, S.Y.: Neiwalk: community discovery in dynamic content-based networks. IEEE Trans. Knowl. Data Eng. **26**(7), 1734–1748 (2014)

18. Yang, J., McAuley, J., Leskovec, J.: Community detection in networks with node attributes. In: 2013 IEEE 13th International Conference on Data Mining (ICDM), pp. 1151–1156. IEEE (2013)

Predicting Success of a Mobile Game:
A Proposed Data Analytics-Based Prediction
Model

Khaled Mohammad Alomari[1][(✉)] [iD], Cornelius Ncube[2] [iD],
and Khaled Shaalan[2] [iD]

[1] Faculty of Computer Science, Abu Dhabi University, Abu Dhabi, UAE
khaled.alomari@adu.ac.ae
[2] Faculty of Engineering and IT, The British University in Dubai, Dubai, UAE
{cornelius.ncube, khaled.shaalan}@buid.ac.ae

Abstract. Even though billions of dollars in revenue have been generated from mobile game apps, there is still a knowledge gap with regard to mobile game user behavior and methodologies for predicting the likely success of mobile game apps during the development phase. This paper analyses game features and (Acquisition, Retention and Monetization) ARM strategies as primary drivers of mobile game application success. This study addresses these challenges through data driven research of the mobile gaming application market, mobile gaming application features, user acquisition and retention trends, and monetization strategies using the CRISP-DM model for data mining in order to prove a successful method for predictions of mobile game application success. A prediction model is developed then applied to 50 games. The prediction of successful mobile game application from a sample of 50 games is achieved by running a batch prediction for the game features dataset and a separate batch prediction for the user behavior dataset. The model produced a total of 9 titles from the sample with the highest probability of success. The significant outcomes for the comparisons included the predominance of the Social Networking Features, Offers, and (In App Purchase) IAP 90% to 100% of the sample. A model of mobile game app success prediction based upon the game features values that are created is proposed.

Keywords: Mobile games · Prediction model · Data analytics

1 Introduction

The billion-dollar mobile gaming app market began with the miniaturization of traditional video games into functionalities for handheld devices and the advent of "time waster" games [1]. The union of arcade gaming, television gaming consoles, digital computing and modern art produced the likes of Snake, Tetris, and a diversity of Wireless Application Protocol (WAP) games [2–4]. Since the onset of the new markets for e-sports, and other mobile gaming application genres, the rate of growth in mobile gaming software development, digital native downloading and usage trends, and mobile game app revenues has been exponential [1, 5]. Research of these increases has

© Springer International Publishing AG, part of Springer Nature 2018
M. Mouhoub et al. (Eds.): IEA/AIE 2018, LNAI 10868, pp. 127–134, 2018.
https://doi.org/10.1007/978-3-319-92058-0_12

been analyzed in some disciplines using data mining approaches to statistical analytics in order to create snapshots of user data leveraging, automation, and relevant insights. However, as a relatively new market, a limited number of guides, innovative software development models, and analytics for effective acquisition, retention and monetization strategies pertaining to the mobile gaming app market have been published. This paper addresses these challenges through data driven research of the mobile gaming application market, mobile gaming application features, user acquisition and retention trends, and monetization strategies using the CRISP-DM model for data mining in order to develop a successful method and model for predicting mobile game application success. Success in this study indicates that user accepts the game and enable the game to monetize, through finding what most important features in the game.

2   Predicting the Success of a Mobile Game App

Currently, the success of mobile game apps is, measured differently according to the perspectives of different stakeholders. In order for mobile game app to be deemed successful from an economic or accounting perspective, the Life Time Value (LTV) or Customer Lifetime Value (CLV) of the product must be higher for the game than the User Acquisition Cost (UAC) [6]. However, from the perspective of the mobile device producers, [7] the mobile device is more personal to the user than the desktop computer or game console; therefore, sensitivity to user personalization is a critical part of mobile application development and design. From the perspective of the software developer, [8] the mobile app user retention is dependent upon the relevance and utility of the application features and the frequency of use is determined by considerations of leverage, stickiness, and feedback. Collectively, Gualtieri, [9] points that the mobile application contexts of immediacy, location, device, locomotion, and intimacy are the most critical to the user experience. Constantino [10] argues that the mobile app economy revenues have begun to polarize and that the iOS holds the premium mobile game app market while. The Android market consumes most other segments; the Windows and browser platforms are left to fight for the remaining market share. A Deloitte [11] study of mobile game app success predicted that the average revenues per mobile game app, varies according to the size of the installation base, barriers to entry and the scope of the business models. As the mobile device base increases, the mobile game app revenue will increases. However, the success of the mobile game apps will be distributed across a small number of developers. The required capital for mobile game app developers is expected to maintain the current market stratification.

3   Methodology

The methodology for this study is based on the assumptions and structures of the ARM Funnel [5] and CRISP-DM models [12] for data analysis in an approach that is twofold, to include the utilization of two prediction models for game features and for user perspective as shown in Fig. 1. The dual method is designed to utilize statistics in as unique approach to presenting the correlations between the game features and user behavior. The initial data was collected from large datasets of freemium iOS mobile game titles published in the mobileaction Top Charts [13]. The data was prepared, modeled and evaluated based on the CRISP-DM general tasks. The game app data was extracted, segmented and decision trees were created in order to develop the game success prediction model. The user behavior data was mined in order to identify relationships between features such as cost and user retention and classified in order to construct the user behavior prediction model. The final output equations for the two datasets was used to construct an algorithm for future game app performance prediction. The most prominent game and user features were then combined to create an overall measure for mobile game success prediction. The twofold data analysis methodology is presented in Fig. 1:

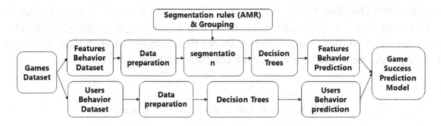

Fig. 1. Twofold data analysis methodology

3.1 Dataset Preparation, Configuration and Analysis

The study used a total of 50 Apple App Store mobile game app titles which were selected from a listing of 500 Freemium top game apps based on generated revenues in US. The method of selection was to extract 50 freemium games from the highest, lowest, and average revenue performances from mobileaction.com [13]. A total of 29 game features were used for the analysis along with the number of downloads, revenues, and daily average usage statistics generated for each game. The outputs are then used to predict features behavior, user behavior and the relationships between outputs for the two prediction models.

4 Data Analysis

The data analysis is based on a dual approach that integrates data mining for the mobile game's features with an analysis of user behavior variables. The sample of game titles consisted of a combination of 19 mobile game app genres.

4.1 Mobile Games Features

The analysis of the 29 sample game features consisted of statistical measurements for the leading game features based on frequency, distribution across the sample, associations, and the outputs of the decision tree. A total of 29 features were divided into 6 categories:

- Social Network/Social Interaction: Facebook, Invite Friends, Request Friend Help, Line Chat, Single Play, Versus, Competitive Play, Leaderboard, Cooperative Play.
- Offers: Unique Offer, Event Offer, Daily Offer.
- Virtual Currency: Soft Currency, Hard Currency, IAP.
- Play Alterations: Time Skip, Time Boost.
- Reward Retention/Punish Absence: Gambling Reward Retention, Cumulative Reward, Non-Cumulative Reward, Achievement.
- Game Features: Customizable, Power-ups, Skill Tree, Unlock Content, Item Upgrade, Status Upgrade, Random Elements, Levels.

The new classifications will provide industry outlooks in future studies of the mobile game app prediction.

Game Feature Decision Tree. The analysis of the game features produced a decision tree from the training data with predictions and accompanying purity, or levels of confidence for 15 of 29 features. Table 1 shows the 15 features which held significance in the decision tree prediction model for the game features dataset:

Table 1. Game feature decision tree outcomes

Results for game features dataset		
Game feature	Confidence level	% of data
Levels	51.31%	100%
Unlock content	34.24%	66%
Item upgrade	30.06%	74%
Unique offer	20.77%	82%
Power up	60.66%	83.67%
Random elements	60.78%	86%
Time skips	25.05%	66%
Customizable	30.06%	93.49%
Request friend help	71.94%	55.10%
Noncumulative	66.49%	66.39%
Daily offer	25.05%	89.29%
Cooperative play	70.18%	76%
Skill tree	23.07%	46%
Competitive play	66.65%	76%
IAP	9.45%	100%

Game Features Prediction Model Evaluation. The Recall for the Actual versus Predicted is 33.33% for Binary 0, and 87.50% for Binary 1, with an Average Recall of 60.42% and Precision is 50.00% for Binary 0, and 77.78% for Binary 1, with an Average Precision of 63.89% and Accuracy are 72.73%. The Average F-score is 0.61 and Average Phi is 0.24.

4.2   Users Behavior Dataset

The variables that were used to measure the user behavior are the Daily Active User, Average Revenue, Average Downloads, and Monthly Average Users.

User Behavior Decision Tree. The decision tree that was created for the user behavior dataset produced outcomes in a different form from the game features as the user behavior data was not binary. The prediction path for user behaviors is furthered through the Daily Average Users node, Revenue Average and Download Averages which each one splits on to 2 instances, with a third path that is initiated based upon Game Name. Unlike the game feature prediction model, a prediction is given for the root node of Unlock Content, which also repeats as the first step down the prediction path. Table 2 shows the decision tree prediction model for the User Behavior Dataset:

Table 2. User behavior decision tree outcomes

Results for user behavior dataset	
Daily average users	Confidence level
Download averages	57.64%
Revenue average	39.87%
Game title	2.49%
Download averages	Confidence level
Daily average users	53.86%
Revenue average	37.10%
Game title	9.04%
Revenue average	Confidence level
Daily average users	48.09%
Download averages	31.04%
Game title	20.87%

5   Results and Discussion

The prediction model generated using by BigML [14] was applied to predict the probability of success or failure of data classifications that have been fed from a data training set.

5.1   Final Prediction Outcomes

The attainment of the prediction of one mobile game app from a sample of 50 was accomplished by running a batch prediction for the game features dataset, and a separate batch prediction for the user behavior dataset. The lists were then integrated, a final list of games which appeared in both lists was generated for further comparison. The batch prediction in BigML [14] computes predictions for each instance in the dataset in one request based upon a Boolean argument for all_fields. According to the prediction model results for the dual datasets, the most successful mobile game app from the 50 game sample was Game of War-Fire Age; the most successful genre was Puzzles, and the most successful developer was EA Sports.

Game Feature Batch Prediction. The batch prediction is created asynchronously in BigML by using the model, logistic regression, or topic model_id and a dataset_id [15]. The status object properties for the batch prediction consist of the code, elapsed time, status messaging, and a progress float between 0 and 1. The predictions for both the game features and the user behaviors may be adjusted through the parameter settings. The mobile game app predictions for this study were created using the model id and dataset_id. The batch prediction for the game features dataset yielded a total of 25 or 50% of the dataset.

User Behavior Batch Prediction. The most successful game predictions were also extracted and compared to the predominating user behaviors for further analysis and to develop a visualization of the future market implications. A total of 24 titles, or 49% of the sample, were produced with the highest probability of success based upon the user behavior data.

5.2 Prediction from Integration of Dual Datasets

Figure 2 illustrate the dual analysis that produced a list of the most successful games based upon features, and a list based upon the most successful user behavior indications. By selecting only the titles which appeared on both lists, the model produced a total of 9 titles from the sample with the highest probability of success. From the 9 title sample, the most successful game was generated by a comparison of user behavior outcomes for the final sample.

The highest performing game features from Sect. 4 were compared with the batch prediction sample of 9 mobile game apps. Where significant outcomes for the comparisons included the predominance of the Social Networking features, Offers, and IAP 90% to 100% of the sample

5.3 Proposed Actionable Model Validation

The success prediction model accurately selects the mobile game app with the highest probability of success from a representative sample of games from several developers based upon a dual analysis. This section will present the code designed for a robust model to predict mobile game app success in Python. The anomaly detection was applied to the game feature and user behavior datasets during the data cleaning process in the development mode. The actionable model was then created by retraining the dataset. The model provides an interpretation of the data and the associations between features and also user behaviors[1].

---

[1] Proposed Actionable Model https://github.com/komari6/MobileGame.

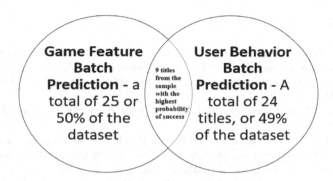

Fig. 2. Integration of dual datasets

6 Conclusion

This study presented a dual methodology which produced success prediction outcomes that are more reliable, in that the model provides for more sources of input for similar analyses. Based upon the outcomes of the dual analysis, the major factors that drive mobile game app success include the extent of advertisement investments and approaches; the presence of violent and sexual content; the opportunity to gamble; the opportunity to compete, and the illusions of fantasy. The successful free-to-play game will require the player to invest substantial amounts of time, as well as currency. Further, irrespective of the genre, the game has to have an addictive element, as opposed to 'just for fun'.

Pioneering mobile game apps were significantly limited in visual and function capacities, which limited the degree to which mobile game apps could compete with video game consoles and pc games [2, 3]. The digitalization of the gaming space has transitioned significantly [16]. As the technological capabilities of smartphones rapidly increases, the market for mobile game apps may be expected to continue to expand with the addition of innovative features and offerings. The game plays have become more complex with larger source codes and incorporate resources that are more complex, to include 2D and 3D graphics, sound, and artificial intelligence [17].

The reliability of the success prediction outcomes that were presented in this study, and that are presented by the proposed model may be further enhanced by the removal of variables that are found in more than 90% of the sample population; by increasing the number of mobile game apps in the sample, and by adding new variables to the model, a more efficient scoring system is enabled that includes the developers. Features such as Facebook and IAPs were represented in 100% of the population; and therefore, had no identifiable impact in contrast to the remaining features. Also, future studies which include comparisons of the performance of paid games and free-to-play games may also add valuable insight.

References

1. Mäyrä, F.: Mobile games. In: Mansell, R., Ang, P.H. (eds.) The International Encyclopedia of Digital Communication and Society. Wiley, Chichester (2015)
2. Lowood, H.: Videogames in computer space: the complex history of Pong. IEEE Ann. Hist. Comput. **31**, 5–19 (2009)
3. Wright, C.: A Brief History of Mobile Games: In the beginning, there was Snake, Pocket Gamer, UK (2016)
4. MADAB: The Art of Automation. Mobile App Developers' Advisory Board (2016)
5. Alomari, K.M., Soomro, T.R., Shaalan, K.: Mobile gaming trends and revenue models. In: Fujita, H., Ali, M., Selamat, A., Sasaki, J., Kurematsu, M. (eds.) IEA/AIE 2016. LNCS (LNAI), vol. 9799, pp. 671–683. Springer, Cham (2016). https://doi.org/10.1007/978-3-319-42007-3_58
6. Sifa, R., Hadiji, F., Runge, J., Drachen, A., Kersting, K., Bauckhage, C.: Predicting purchase decisions in mobile free-to-play games. In: The Eleventh AAAI Conference on Artificia Intelligence and Interactive Digital Entertainment (AIIDE-15) (2015)
7. Unhelkar, B., Murugesan, S.: The enterprise mobile applications development framework. IT Prof. **12**, 33–39 (2010)
8. Law, F.L., Kasirun, Z.M., Gan, C.K.: Gamification towards sustainable mobile application. In: Harun, M.F. (ed.) 5th Malaysian Conference in Software Engineering (MySEC), 13–14 December 2011, Johor Bahru, Malaysia, pp. 349–353. IEEE, Piscataway, NJ (2011)
9. Gualtieri, M.: Forrester's mobile app design context. location, locomotion, immediacy, intimacy, and device. Forrester. http://blogs.forrester.com/mike_gualtieri/11-04-13-forres ters_mobile_app_design_context_location_locomotion_immediacy_intimacy_and_device
10. Constantino, A.: Developer Economics. The State of the Developer Nation, Q1 2015 (2015)
11. Deloitte: Mobile games: leading, but less lucrative. https://www2.deloitte.com/content/dam/ Deloitte/global/Documents/Technology-Media-Telecommunications/gx-tmt-prediction-mob ile-games.pdf
12. Chapman, P., Clinton, J., Kerber, R., Khabaza, T., Reinartz, T., Shearer, C., Wirth, R.: CRISP-DM 1.0 Step-by-step data mining guide (2000)
13. Mobileaction: Top charts for iPhone. ASO Intelligence. https://insights.mobileaction.co/ appreport/?trackId=1095254858&store=ios
14. BigML: Building Your Models. Support. https://support.bigml.com/hc/en-us/articles/ 206616219-How-is-the-confidence-being-estimated-in-a-decision-tree-model-
15. BigML: Classification and Regression with the BigML Dashboard. https://static.bigml.com/ pdf/BigML_Classification_and_Regression.pdf
16. Rogers, A.: How did electronic arts perform in Fiscal 2Q17? Market Realist. http:// marketrealist.com/2016/11/mobile-gaming-key-driver-electronic-arts/
17. Barus, A.C., Tobing, R.D.H., Pratiwi, D.N., Damanik, S.A., Pasaribu, J. (eds.): Mobile game testing. Case study of a puzzle game genre. In: 2015 International Conference on Automation, Cognitive Science, Optics, Micro Electro-Mechanical System, and Information Technology (ICACOMIT) (2015)

Online Anomaly Detection Using Random Forest

Zhiruo Zhao$^{(\boxtimes)}$, Kishan G. Mehrotra, and Chilukuri K. Mohan

Syracuse University, Syracuse, NY, USA
{zzhao11,mehrotra,mohan}@syr.edu

Abstract. In this paper, we focus on how to use random forests based methods to improve the anomaly detection rate for streaming datasets.

The key concept in a current work [12] is to build a random forest where in any tree, at any internal node, a feature is randomly selected and the associated data space is partitioned in half. However, the model parameters were pre-defined and the efficiency on applying this model for various conditions is not discussed. In this paper, we first give mathematical justification of required tree height and number of trees by casting the problem as a classical coupon collector problem. Then we design a majority voting score combination strategy to combine the results from different anomaly detection trees. Finally, we apply feature clustering to group the correlated features together in order to find the anomalies jointly determined by subsets of features.

1 Introduction

Anomaly detection, also known as outlier detection, is one of the most widely studied among different research and application areas. In fact, the discussion of outlier detection in data sets can be traced back to the 18th century when Bernoulli questioned the practice of deleting the outliers [2]. The problem of finding anomalies is often described as the problem of finding patterns in data that do not conform to expected behavior or of finding data objects with behaviors that are very different from expectation [3,8]. Anomalies are usually associated with security threats, financial fraud, medical failure, system failures, etc. One of the most widely applicable areas for anomaly detection is detecting intrusions which requires online detection.

In past decade many online anomaly detection techniques have been proposed. A recent survey for anomaly detection on temporal data can be found in [7]. Proposed techniques include statistics-based methods [13] (which incrementally learn a probabilistic model and determine whether an observation is an anomaly compared to the learned model); the incremental LOF [11] (the online version of LOF in which the neighborhood of an observation is computed incrementally), and a regression method [1] that compares the observed values with expected values for anomaly detection. A bio-inspired detection algorithm can be found in [4]. More recently, Tan *et al.* [12] have proposed a random forest based approach. This approach has good performance in accuracy and time

© Springer International Publishing AG, part of Springer Nature 2018
M. Mouhoub et al. (Eds.): IEA/AIE 2018, LNAI 10868, pp. 135–147, 2018.
https://doi.org/10.1007/978-3-319-92058-0_13

complexity. In this approach, at any node of a balanced binary tree, a feature is randomly selected and the associated data space is partitioned in half; the number of trees and their heights are chosen in an ad-hoc manner.

We analyze the impact of parameters used in random trees both empirically and theoretically, and propose new algorithms that can work well with high-dimensional data.

2   Anomaly Detection for Streaming Data

Consider a data stream arriving at time stamps $t_1, t_2, \ldots, t_n, \ldots$, where each data $\mathbf{X_t}$ is a high-dimensional data point containing d features, $i.e.$ $\mathbf{X_t} = (x_t^1, x_t^2, \ldots, x_t^d)$. In supervised learning a label is also attached with each data point; in anomaly detection context $label \in \{normal, abnormal\}$. In unsupervised anomaly detection, labels are unknown, and the task is to find a set of rules to separate anomalous observations from normal observations. We use F to denote the set of features, namely, $F = \{f_i | i = 1, \ldots, d\}$.

Tan $et\ al.$ [12]'s method combines anomaly scores from a set of T full binary trees. To build a full binary tree, a feature from F is randomly selected at each node and the existing space, associated with the selected feature, is partitioned in two equal parts. A feature can be selected multiple times. An illustration can be found in Fig. 1. The idea is that a point in a (leaf) node's region with more observations should be less anomalous than a point in the region of a leaf with fewer observations.

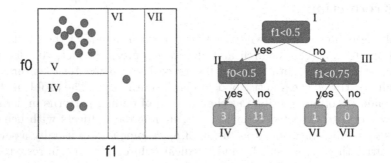

Fig. 1. An illustration of data-space partition by a half-space tree. Left figure shows the data space and partitions whereas the right side shows the associated full binary tree. Leaf node IV corresponds to $f1 < 0.5$ and $f0 < 0.5$ and contains 3 data-points.

The basic idea of this method is to partition the data-space into half-spaces and the points belonging to sparse partitions are possible anomalies. This method has three main phases: tree building, training and testing.

– **Tree Building:** In this phase, T full binary trees of height h are built. To build a tree, features are randomly selected at each node and associated space is partitioned in two equal parts. This phase does not use any data.

- **Training Phase:**   In this phase, the first ϕ data-points are used to construct the trees. For each tree:
    - Using the first ϕ data-points, the *reference* mass profile for each node are obtained, representing the number of data-points (out of ϕ points) that correspond to the node).
    - The *latest* mass profile is set to 0 for each node.
- **Testing:**   For each new observation x, the mass profile at each node for all T trees is evaluated as below:
    - x is fed into the ith tree. Along the path followed by x, each node's *latest* mass profile and *node.latest* are updated by increasing by 1. At the leaf *node* the anomaly score for x, associated with the ith tree is evaluated as:

$$score_i(x) = node.reference * 2^{node.height}. \tag{1}$$

The overall anomaly score for x is the average score over the T trees:

$$Score(x) = \frac{1}{T} \sum_{i=1}^{T} score_i(x).$$

These values are reset for each set of ϕ data points. For each *node*, the *node.reference* and *node.latest* are swapped, *node.latest* is set to 0. When a new observation arrives, the testing procedure continues as described earlier.

This method has shown its advantage in detecting anomalies compared to other state-of-the-art detection algorithms, and is competitive with supervised learning methods. However, the authors confine the evaluations to low-dimensional data streams [12]; and this method has the following deficiencies:

- the tree height and the number of trees are selected without any mathematical justification;
- final score combination is simple averaging although the detection power of each tree is different;
- if the number of noisy features is large, more tree nodes are needed for detecting anomalies; and
- in our view, some anomalies can only be jointly determined by a subset of features, consequently, building random trees over entire feature space might be wasteful.

To improve the efficiency of this random forest approach, this paper makes the following contributions:

- In Sect. 4.1 we give mathematical justification for desired tree height and number of trees by casting the problem as the coupon collector problem.
- In Sect. 4.2 we propose an improved combination strategy to evaluate anomalousness of an observation weighted by importance of a tree.
- We apply feature clustering to group the correlated features together in order to find the anomalies jointly determined by subsets of features in Sect. 4.3).

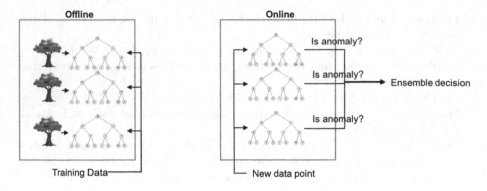

Fig. 2. A framework for streaming anomaly detection

3   Datasets and Evaluation Metrics

In this section, we describe the data sets and metrics we used for evaluating proposed methods.

3.1   Datasets

1. **Synthetic Dataset.** We first construct a synthetic dataset with 5000 obser-vations and one anomaly introducted. In this dataset, 6 features are con-structed such that three of them are highly correlated and the other three features are highly correlated, but the two subsets are not. We construct this dataset to simulate the situations that certain anomalies can only be detected by subsets of features. As shown in Fig. 3, the anomaly (red triangle) can only be detected with respect to feature 0, 1, and 2.
2. **Polish Companies Bankruptcy Dataset** [15]. This data set is collected from the Emerging Markets Information Service (EMIS), which collects the information about emerging markets. The data set contains financial infor-mation about the Polish companies from 2000–2013. We use the 5th year data set which contains companies that are bankrupted after one year. This data set has 64 financial features about 5910 total companies, of which, 410 companies were bankrupt during the predicting period.

3.2   Evaluation Metrics

We mainly use the Area Under Curve (AUC) as the evaluation metric. The area under the ROC curve (AUC) is used to reduce the ROC curve to a single-valued number [5,9]. For a perfect detection algorithm AUC score = 1.0, while for a two class problem for a random guess AUC score = 0.5.

In machine learning, the positive class is often considered to be the class of inter-est; in our work, the positive class is the anomaly class (outliers), denoted as $\mathcal{O}$, and

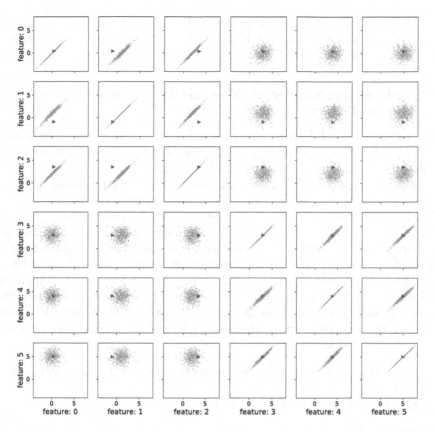

Fig. 3. A synthetic dataset whose attributes must be considered together to find anomalies (Color figure online)

the negative class is the normal class (inliers), denoted as $\mathcal{I}$. Let the set of predicted outliers be denoted by $\hat{\mathcal{O}}$, predicted inlier set be denoted as $\hat{\mathcal{I}}$; then the True Positive Rate (TPR) and the False Positive Rate (FPR) are calculated using:

$$TPR = \frac{|\hat{\mathcal{O}} \cap \mathcal{O}|}{|\mathcal{O}|} \quad \text{and} \quad FPR = \frac{|\hat{\mathcal{O}} \cap \mathcal{I}|}{|\mathcal{I}|}.$$

4   Analysis of Random Trees

In this section, we derive the expected number of trees and height of trees using the results from the coupon collector problem. Next, we design two score combination methods for the final decision making process which alleviate a problem of using score averaging. Finally, we propose to apply feature clustering to group the correlated features and propose to build random trees with features within each feature-cluster. Evaluations on synthetic and real-world data sets show improvement if random trees are built using the later approach compared to using the entire feature set.

4.1   Deriving the Number of Trees and Height of Trees Using Theory of Coupon Collector Problem

Given a fixed forest of T trees, each tree of height h, if the number of features increases, the detection performance will decrease; naturally we need more trees and perhaps taller trees to maintain the level of performance. It is also obvious that to achieve 'good' performance each feature must be represented. Since the feature selection is random, we need to know how many times features must be selected such that all features are represented in the random forest.

In the coupon collector's problem [10], given d types of coupons, a coupon is randomly drawn, with replacement and with equal probability, from a collection of d distinct coupons. The random variable of interest is Y_d, the number of trials such that all coupons are selected at least once. In a generalization of the problem, the random variable of interest is, $Y_{m,d}$; the number of trials such that all coupons are selected at least m times. The goal of the coupon collector's problem is to study the relationship between Y_d and d. A few important results are summarized below [10]:

1. $E(Y_d) = dH_d \approx d \ln d + 0.5772d$, where H_d denotes the dth Harmonic number.
2. $P(Y_d \geq cdH_d) \leq d^{-c+1}$
3. $P(Y_d < d \ln d + cd) \to exp(-e^{-c})$ as $d \to \infty$

Similar results hold for $Y_{m,d}$:

1. $E(Y_{m,d}) = d \ln d + (m-1)d \ln \ln d + O(d)$
2. $P(Y_{m,d} < d \ln d + (m-1)d \ln \ln d + cd) \to exp(-e^{-\frac{c}{(m-1)!}})$ as $d \to \infty$

For example, for $d = 10$, $E(Y_d)$ is approximately 30; if we require that all 10 coupons are picked with probability 0.999 we need approximately 70 trials. For $m = 3$, on average 40 trials will be required; but if we require that all 10 coupons are picked at least 3 times with probability 0.999, we need to perform 93 trials. These numbers increase to 72, and 152 for T_d when $d = 20$; and to 104 and 185 for $Y_{m,d}$ for $m = 3, d = 20$. For example, for $d = 20$ and $m = 3$ we need to build 10 binary trees of height 5 each to meet desired condition.

4.2   Discussion on Score Combination

Each tree provides the mass profile of the leaf nodes, which in turn is used to calculate the anomaly scores; an observation falling in a leaf with smaller mass profile is considered to be more anomalous.

In [12], the final anomaly score for each object is obtained by averaging over all the random trees. However, as we argue below, the anomaly detection power of each tree is different and simple averaging dilutes the final result. To illustrate this, we consider a simple example. Consider three trees each of height 2. The mass profile of the leaf nodes for each trees can be represented by a vector of length 4. Suppose that the score outputs for a data set with 100 objects, for three tree, are: (33, 33, 33, **1**), (**60**, 20, 15, 5), (25, 50, 20, **5**), where the bold font represents the leaf node that contains the test data point. If we consider the simple arithmetic average $((1 + 60 + 5)/3 = 22)$, then the data point does not appear to be anomalous. Although two out of three trees indicate that the data point is an anomaly, the leaf with a high score of 60 significantly affects the final result.

In the following, we discuss two combination methods to alleviate the above concern.

The Minimum Method. Zhao *et al.* [14] evaluate several approaches to combine results from multiple anomaly detection algorithms and observe that using a minimum ranking method results in good performance.

The idea is very simple – an object will be detected as an anomaly if one of the random trees detects it as anomalous. That is, the final score for an object x over T random trees is:

$$\text{FinalScore}(x) = \min_{i=1}^{T} \text{score}_i(x)$$

where $\text{score}_i(x)$ is the anomaly score for x on the ith random tree as defined in Eq. (1).

Majority Voting Approach Using Score Discretization. This is also a straightforward approach – if a majority of the trees indicate that the data point is an anomaly, then the data point is declared anomalous. The main goal is to decide if a data point is an anomaly using the integer score (mass profile). Towards this goal we convert the score for data point x as:

$$b(x) = \begin{cases} 1, & \text{if } score(x) < q_\eta; \\ 0, & \text{otherwise.} \end{cases}$$

where 1 implies that the data point is an anomaly; here q_η is the ηth-quantile of the data set. Typically, η is assigned a small value, such as 0.05 or 0.01. An example illustrates the choice of η and q_η.

If data is uniformly distributed, without any anomalies, then the number of objects at each level would be uniform and result in uniform distribution at the leaf nodes of the tree. For example, if the data set contains 100 points and the tree has 4 leaves, the expected score vector would be (25,25,25,25). On the other hand, in case the data set contains one or more anomalies, then the leaf nodes will have uneven distribution, such as (50,44,2,4). If we use 5% quantile as a cutoff point, then the vector (50,44,2,4) will be converted to (0, 0, 1, 1), implying that a data point is an anomaly if it falls in the cells corresponding to the third or the fourth leaf.

The result obtained by applying majority voting to each object x is denoted by Majority(x), and can be calculated as below:

$$\text{Majority}(x) = \begin{cases} 1, & \text{if } \sum_{i=1}^{T} b_i(x) > \frac{T}{2} \\ 0, & \text{otherwise,} \end{cases}$$

where $b_i(x)$ is the converted binary output for x in the ith tree.

To test the performance of above suggested combination approaches we generated a synthetic data set with 5000 observations which also contained one anomaly. We used 5 random trees, each of height $= 5$; with $\eta = 5\%$. Results are summarized in Table 1.

Table 1. Rank of anomaly for different combination approaches

	Avg.	Minimum	Majority
Rank	508	321	**240**

Based on this experiment we conclude that the majority rule gives the best result.

4.3   Building Detection Trees Using Feature Clustering

There are several situations where some anomalies can only be detected by one subset of features, and other anomalies are better detected by other subsets of features. In these cases, the use of all features dilutes the power of anomaly detection; in particular, this worsens the performance of a random forest where features are randomly selected. To find anomalies which can only be captured using the dependent features, we propose a two step approach in which we first group the dependent features together, then apply the random trees detection algorithm using features in clusters separately. This will maximize intra-tree dependency for trees built on a partition.

Given m features, we partition the feature spaces such that each subset contains features that are highly dependent with each other. The problem of partitioning the feature set in k subsets can be cast as an optimization problem:

$$arg \max_{FS} \sum_{i=1}^{k} \sum_{X \in FS_i} I(X; \lambda_i)$$

where λ_i is the representative feature from the ith feature set FS_i. Here $I(X,Y)$ is the information theoretic measure of dependence between two variables X and Y given by the formula:

$$I(X,Y) = H(X) + H(Y) - H(X,Y),$$

where $H's$ denotes the information content. The problem of partitioning the feature spaces is similar to the classical clustering problem; the only difference is that instead of using the classical Euclidean distance, we use the feature dependency as a similarity metric.

To group the dependent features together for partitioning the feature space, we apply a clustering algorithm. In theory, any clustering algorithm might work but we choose Affinity Propagation (AP) [6] algorithm. This algorithm identifies exemplars among features and forms clusters of features around these exemplars. It operates by simultaneously considering all features as potential exemplars and by exchanging messages between features until a good set of exemplars and clusters emerges. This algorithm has the following advantages compared to k-means clustering:

- AP accepts similarity matrix instead of distance matrix, so that no conversion is needed.
- AP finds actual feature exemplar while k-means finds the 'mean' in a cluster which may not be a data point.
- AP does not require initial set of exemplars and users do not need to explicitly specify the number of clusters.

By applying feature clustering, we decrease the number of features in each cluster. Thus, we expect to decrease the number of trees and their height, without scarifying the detection performance. Results, reported in the following section, support this claim.

4.4   Experimental Results

We evaluate the effect of feature clustering on the synthetic data set. For streaming configuration, we choose $\phi = 2000$, which means that the first 2000 data points are used for feature clustering construction and tree building. The batch size is also 2000 for the following data stream. Each point is evaluated at arrival, and the final AUC score is calculated with respect to the streaming data, e.g., if we have 5000 data points, the first 2000 data points are used for training, AUC score is calculated with respect to the rest 3000 data points, and trees are updated every 2000 data points.

To evaluate the relative performance of algorithms we compare the ranks of the anomalies and also the AUC score.

We apply the algorithm of Tan *et al.* building 10 trees that use all 6 features. To apply our proposed cluster-based algorithm we use 5 trees for the first set of features and another 5 trees for the second set. Results are shown in Fig. 4, in which the results obtained from feature clustering are indicated with "clus". For the same number of trees and the same height of trees, feature clustering results in better solutions than purely random trees. For AUC score, we observe that when given very 'tall' trees (height equals 10), pure random trees produce way better averaged AUC score than height equals 6, however, the variance of AUC score is still way larger than our clustered algorithm and the memory space is exponentially grown for growing height since each tree is a full binary tree. While for our clustered algorithm, we achieve similar averaged AUC score for lower tree budges at tree height of 6 and much lower variance than pure random trees.

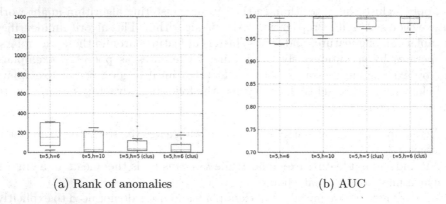

(a) Rank of anomalies   (b) AUC

Fig. 4. Performance comparison for our feature clustering method and random trees method on a synthetic dataset

In addition, we design two sets of experiments to compare the performance of the random tree algorithm with our proposed clustering-based algorithm:

1. Fix the height of each tree, vary the number of trees used for our method and random trees method. Results, shown in Fig. 5(a), indicate that our method outperforms random trees on all values of T, *i.e.* number of trees used.
2. Fix the number of trees, vary the height of each tree. Results shown in Fig. 5(b) indicate that our method outperforms random trees method and becomes very stable when the tree is 'taller', *i.e.*, $h = 7$.

In a third experiment, we apply our clustering based algorithm on the Polish Bankruptcy dataset. This data set has many missing values; we replace missing values by three different methods: column mean, column median and replace by the nearest neighbor by sorting based on gross profit. To compare the performance with Tan *et al.*'s work, we perform two sets of experiments:

– Use 50 trees, each tree of height 10 for Tan *et al.*'s algorithm. For our method, 50 trees are equally distributed among clusters.
– Use 100 trees, each tree of height 15 for Tan *et al.*'s algorithm; for our method, 100 trees are equally distributed among clusters.

These experiments are repeated 30 times for each of the different methods to fill in the missing value. Results in Table 2 show an increase in AUC by at least around 20% for all the three datasets, after missing values are replaced. We observe from the results that:

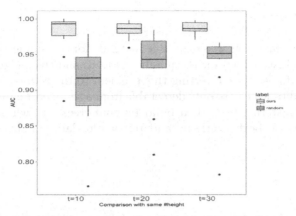

(a) AUC comparison when height of trees is fixed

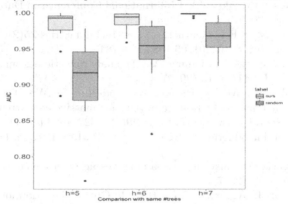

(b) AUC comparison when number of trees is fixed

Fig. 5. Performance comparison for our feature clustering method and random trees method for number of trees and height of trees on a synthetic dataset

Table 2. Averaged AUC for Bankruptcy dataset over 30 trials

	Mean		Median		Sorted	
	Random	Clus	Random	Clus	Random	Clus
$t = 50$, $h = 10$	0.436	**0.602**	0.452	**0.689**	0.527	**0.564**
$t = 100$, $h = 15$	0.556	**0.709**	0.554	**0.709**	0.581	**0.656**

- Our method achieves better results when using the same cost of building trees.
- The clustering cost is less than 5% of the overall time.

5   Conclusion

In this paper, we first reviewed ensemble methods for streaming anomaly detection. We give a justification for the number of trees and tree heights one should use for random forest, by converting this problem to the coupon collector problem. For anomalies which are only detectable from a set of correlated features, we apply feature clustering first, then build random trees on each of the clusters. Our evaluations on both synthetic and real-world datasets show performance improvements.

References

1. Aggarwal, C.C.: On abnormality detection in spuriously populated data streams. In: Proceedings of the 2005 SIAM International Conference on Data Mining, SIAM 2005, pp. 80–91 (2005)
2. Beckman, R.J., Cook, R.D.: Outlier.......... s. Technometrics **25**(2), 119–149 (1983). https://doi.org/10.1080/00401706.1983.10487840
3. Chandola, V., Banerjee, A., Kumar, V.: Anomaly detection: a survey. ACM Comput. Surv. (CSUR) **41**(3), 15 (2009)
4. Chen, Q., Luley, R., Wu, Q., Bishop, M., Linderman, R.W., Qiu, Q.: AnRAD: a neuromorphic anomaly detection framework for massive concurrent data streams. IEEE Trans. Neural Netw. Learn. Syst. **29**(5), 1622–1636 (2017)
5. Fawcett, T.: An introduction to ROC analysis. Pattern Recogn. Lett. **27**(8), 861–874 (2006)
6. Frey, B.J., Dueck, D.: Clustering by passing messages between data points. Science **315**(5814), 972–976 (2007)
7. Gupta, M., Gao, J., Aggarwal, C.C., Han, J.: Outlier detection for temporal data: a survey. IEEE Trans. Knowl. Data Eng. **26**(9), 2250–2267 (2014)
8. Han, J., Pei, J., Kamber, M.: Data Mining: Concepts and Techniques. Elsevier, New York (2011)
9. Hanley, J.A., McNeil, B.J.: The meaning and use of the area under a receiver operating characteristic (ROC) curve. Radiology **143**(1), 29–36 (1982)
10. Motwani, R., Raghavan, P.: Randomized Algorithms. Chapman & Hall/CRC, London (2010)
11. Pokrajac, D., Lazarevic, A., Latecki, L.J.: Incremental local outlier detection for data streams. In: IEEE Symposium on Computational Intelligence and Data Mining, CIDM 2007, pp. 504–515. IEEE (2007)
12. Tan, S.C., Ting, K.M., Liu, T.F.: Fast anomaly detection for streaming data. In: IJCAI Proceedings-International Joint Conference on Artificial Intelligence, vol. 22, no. 1, p. 1511 (2011)
13. Yamanishi, K., Takeuchi, J.-I.: A unifying framework for detecting outliers and change points from non-stationary time series data. In: Proceedings of the Eighth ACM SIGKDD International Conference on Knowledge Discovery and Data Mining, pp. 676–681. ACM (2002)

14. Zhao, Z., Mehrotra, K.G., Mohan, C.K.: Ensemble algorithms for unsupervised anomaly detection. In: Ali, M., Kwon, Y.S., Lee, C.-H., Kim, J., Kim, Y. (eds.) IEA/AIE 2015. LNCS (LNAI), vol. 9101, pp. 514–525. Springer, Cham (2015). https://doi.org/10.1007/978-3-319-19066-2_50
15. Zikeba, M., Tomczak, S.K., Tomczak, J.M.: Ensemble boosted trees with synthetic features generation in application to bankruptcy prediction. Expert Syst. Appl. **58**, 93–101 (2016)

Investigating Effectiveness of Linguistic Features Based on Speech Recognition for Storytelling Skill Assessment

Shogo Okada[1(✉)] and Kazunori Komatani[2]

[1] Japan Advanced Institute of Science and Technology, Nomi, Japan
okada-s@jaist.ac.jp
[2] Osaka University, Suita, Japan

Abstract. This paper investigates the effectiveness of linguistic features based on speech recognition for storytelling skill assessment in group conversations. A multimodal data corpus, including the skill scores of storytellers, is used for this study. Three kinds of automatic speech recognition (ASR) results are compared from the viewpoint of the contribution to the skill assessment task. A regression model to predict the skill is trained by fusing the linguistic features and nonverbal features including utterance length, prosody, gaze, head and hand gestures. Experimental results show that the mean regression accuracy ($R^2 = 0.24$) for the storytelling skills with the linguistic features based on ASR rate 49% is improved from $R^2 = 0.17$ of the non-verbal model by 0.07 points. We summarize that the features extracted from text contribute to the skill assessment task although the ASR results contained not a few errors.

Keywords: Storytelling skill assessment · Multimodal interaction
Automatic linguistic analysis

1 Introduction

Assessment of communication skill is nowadays the focus of attention in studies of computational multimodal analysis. The common approach in these studies depends mainly on automatic nonverbal analysis. Linguistic features are also important in improving the assessment accuracy of the model. Although linguistic features were extracted in some studies [1,2], they used manual transcriptions of spoken dialogue, and the process was not automatic. The main reason is that robust speech recognition on natural and spontaneous conversation is still difficult.

This study investigates the relationship between several types of ASR results and the contribution of linguistic features which are extracted from the ASR results with many errors for communication skill assessment. Two linguistic feature sets (a bag of words (BoW) and parts of speech (PoS)) based on (1) automatic speech recognition (ASR) with an open-domain language model,

© Springer International Publishing AG, part of Springer Nature 2018
M. Mouhoub et al. (Eds.): IEA/AIE 2018, LNAI 10868, pp. 148–157, 2018.
https://doi.org/10.1007/978-3-319-92058-0_14

(2) ASR with a language model trained with manual transcription of the target storytelling corpus and (3) commercial ASR engine. These are compared with feature set extracted directly from the manual transcription (ideal case). For the investigation, a storytelling corpus collected in [3,4] is used for the study. The corpus includes manual transcription of spoken dialogue, various nonverbal features, and multiple indices of the storytelling skill. The assessment model of storytelling skill is trained by fusing the linguistic features and nonverbal features. In regression prediction, we investigate whether the linguistic features extracted by speech recognition improve assessment accuracy.

The main contribution is investigation of the relationship between speech recognition error and the effectiveness of the linguistic features including the error for storytelling assessment. To apply the skill assessment model for applications such as a skill training systems, not only nonverbal features but verbal (linguistic) features are required to extract automatically. The investigation in this study is a first important step and opens a new challenge toward automatic linguistic feature analysis.

2   Related Work

The target variables of communicative skill vary widely, such as public speaking skills [5], speaking assessment [6] for non-native speaker, persuasiveness in social media [1], communication skill in job interviews [7], leadership [8] and communication skills [2] in group discussion.

In most researches, nonverbal features were used to predict the skill variable. Verbal features were used in [1,9]. In [1,10,11], words and their parts of speech (PoS) were extracted from manual transcriptions as linguistic features. In [9], PoS, number of words with more than six characters, ratio of the word vocabulary to the total vocabulary of the corpus and so on were extracted as linguistic features using the ASR system with open domain corpus. However the impact of ASR errors for target corpus was not discussed. In this paper, BoW and PoS features were extracted automatically from ASR results with two different language models. We investigate how the speech recognition error influences the skill assessment using a feature selection strategy using linguistic features including speech recognition error.

3   Multimodal Storytelling Interaction Dataset

The storytelling dataset called the "Multimodal Storytelling Interaction Dataset (MSI Dataset)" was collected in [3,4] and was shared from authors of [4] for this study. According to [3], in this task, two participants were asked to narrate a simple animated (cartoon) story from memory to another participant. A snapshot of the conversation is shown in the left picture of Fig. 1. 24 female participants aged 20 to 25 years were recruited. An eight-group conversation dataset was collected in cooperation with these participants. All storytellers began to explain each episode after the prologue (i.e., introduction of main characters and overview of a story). In total, group conversation data included a maximum of nine episodes (prologue + eight episodes). The dataset was segmented manually into subsequence datasets with nine episodes. We collected a total of 67 subsequences (episodes) as data samples.

The skills of storytelling were evaluated through questionnaires for external observers, who had not watched the video or listened to the story. Third-party participants (evaluators) watched both the contents of the video "Canary Row," the target of the storytelling, and the video that captures group conversations and storytelling. The eight indices are composed of "Eloquence", "Enthusiasm", "Fluentness", "Wittiness", "Preciseness", "Compactness", "Summarization", and "Liveliness". The eight indices were evaluated on a ten-point scale and total point of eight indices was defined as storytelling skill. Three evaluators scored all of the episode data (67 episodes). The agreement among the three evaluators for each skill index is sufficient, because all values of intraclass correlation were greater than 0.7 according to [4].

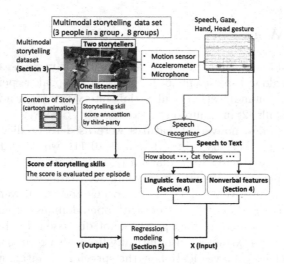

Fig. 1. Overview of storytelling assessment modeling

4   Multimodal Features

We extracted features from storytellers. For storytellers, we calculated the features based on the sum of values of the features extracted from the two storytellers. The reason is that we want to compare feature vectors observed from each group because the skill scores were assigned not to each storyteller separately but to each episode described in the group. Multimodal features are summarized in Table 1. Nonverbal features of storytellers that are extracted in an automatic manner were also used, which were shared with authors [3,4]. The feature set used in this study is composed of prosody, gaze, head and hand gesture. Procedure for feature extraction is described in [3,4].

Linguistic features are extracted from text data, which are results of automatic speech recognition (ASR) for the recorded audio data. In this study, We used (1) open-source ASR engines: Julius [12] with different language models and (2) commercial ASR system: Google Speech API to obtain ASR results with different ASR accuracies. Two language models ($LM_{1,2}$) were used to analyze the effectiveness of the language model trained from manual transcription and the language model trained from an open corpus. Language model LM_1 is publicly available, which was trained with the Corpus of Spontaneous Japanese (CSJ) [13] that contains a large collection of Japanese spoken language data. Language model LM_2 was trained with the manual transcriptions of all sessions in MSI dataset (Sect. 3)[1]. Total three ASR results including Julius ASR engines with two language models and Google Speech API are prepared to extract linguistic features.

Table 1. Multimodal features

Feature description
Time length of each episode

Linguistic
Count of words in utterance by storytellers
Count of words per PoS label

Nonverbal features
Speech
Time length of utterance by storytellers
Count of utterance by storytellers
Count of turn taking
Energy features of storytellers (min, max, mean, var)
Pitch features of storytellers (min, max, mean, var)

Gaze
Time length while storytellers are focused
Time length while listener is focused
Time length of mutual gaze: between tellers
Time length of mutual gaze: between teller - listener
Count of change of gaze state

Hand and head gesture
Time length of gesture segment by storytellers
Count of gesture segment by storytellers

---

[1] This means the model was trained in a closed manner. We used the model to obtain ASR results with different accuracies and to analyze any effects of the accuracies.

Preliminary experiments were done to evaluate the ASR accuracies of the three results. The all utterances spoken by the all participants in MSI dataset was used for test dataset. The ASR accuracies were 25.7%, 48.9% with LM_1 and LM_2 on Julius, and 54.1% on Google Speech API, respectively. The order of results with LM_1 and LM_2 was reasonable because LM_2 was trained with the same corpus with the test data and was adapted to recognize the spoken words on the MSI dataset. Though best accuracy was obtained by Google Speech API, 54% is not sufficient accuracy for ASR. The result also shows that ASR is not easy because the spoken utterances in storytelling include many types of filler and short incomplete word fragments.

Linguistic features were extracted from the text data. The frequency of words (denoted as bag-of-word (BoW)) and part of speech (PoS) of the words was calculated after a Japanese morphological analysis tool MeCab [14] was used to segment texts into words. The tag set of PoS was composed of five types: "noun", "verb", "adjective", "adverb", and "interjection and filler". The text processing was applied to (1) manual transcription, (2) transcription obtained by ASR with LM_1, (3) that by ASR with LM_2 and (4) that by ASR on Google Speech API, and then four linguistic feature sets were obtained. For (1) (4), the frequency of word or PoS category (noun, verbs, etc.) was counted in spoken utterances in an episode. For (2) and (3), the output probability of words, called the confidence measure given by the ASR engine, was also used.

5   Experiments

5.1   Experimental Setting

We performed a regression prediction to investigate the effectiveness of linguistic feature extracted based on speech recognition. The pairs of multimodal features and the storytelling skill index of the 67 episodes were used for the experiments. Evaluation was done with cross validation testing by leaving one episode out. The testing was conducted by omitting one episode from the 67 episodes. We used the coefficient of determination: R^2 and the root mean square error ($RMSE$) as criteria of the regression prediction. The R^2 becomes negative when the difference between predicted score and true score is more than the variance of true scores. Such a case means that the prediction with the trained regression model is difficult.

We used the ridge regression model for the prediction. The ridge parameter in ridge regression model was optimized using a cross validation scheme, with values in the range of [50–200]. We compared the accuracy with the following nine feature sets to analyze the contribution of each feature set to the prediction accuracy.

[(1): L_{ideal}] Linguistic features (PoS and BoW) based on manual transcription (ideal case)

[(2): L_{ASR1}] Linguistic features based on ASR results with general language model: LM_1

Table 2. Comparison of storytelling skill assessment accuracy of uni-modal models with linguistic features. When the R^2 was less than 0, the value is described as 0.

	(1) L_{ideal}		(2) L_{ASR1}		(3) L_{ASR2}		(4) L_{ASR3}	
ASR Accuracy	100 %		25.7% (LM_1)		48.9% (LM_2)		54.1%	
	PoS	BoW	PoS	BoW	PoS	BoW	PoS	BoW
Coeff. of det. R^2	0.099	0.210	0.000	0.013	0.087	0.056	0.061	0.000
RMSE	1.045	0.976	1.108	1.094	1.052	1.070	1.067	1.129

Table 3. Comparison of storytelling skill assessment accuracy of multimodal models with linguistic and nonverbal features

	Nonverbal	Multimodal (PoS + BoW + NV)			
	(5) NV	(6) MM_{ideal}	(7) MM_{ASR1}	(8) MM_{ASR2}	(9) MM_{ASR3}
Coeff. of det. R^2	0.175	0.266	0.144	0.242	0.168
RMSE	1.001	0.943	1.020	0.958	1.003

[(3): L_{ASR2}] Linguistic features based on ASR results with domain-specific language model: LM_2
[(4): L_{ASR3}] Linguistic features based on ASR results using Google Speech API
[(5): NV] Only nonverbal features extracted in an automatic manner
[(6): MM_{ideal}] Multimodal features combining L_{ideal} and nonverbal features
[(7): MM_{ASR1}/(8): MM_{ASR2}/(9): MM_{ASR3}] Multimodal features combining nonverbal features and $L_{ASR1}/L_{ASR2}/L_{ASR3}$.

BoW feature sets were composed of a large number of features (1164 words) so that feature selection is conducted with spearman's rank-order correlation score for the BoW feature set and the multimodal set including the BoW feature set. The feature selection was performed only in the training phase. Variables having significant correlations with storytelling skill indices. The significance level was optimized using a cross validation scheme with values in [0.01, 0.005, 0.001].

5.2 Experimental Results

First, we report the comparison of storytelling skill assessment accuracy of uni-modal models with various linguistic features in Table 2. The objective is to investigate any impact when features automatically extracted from lower ASR results were used and to compare them with the ideal case. The second column in Table 2 denotes the speech recognition accuracy with ASR results ($ASR1, ASR2, ASR3$).

In Table 2, the best performance was obtained with (1) L_{ideal} and is as high as $R^2 = 0.21, RMSE = 0.97$. On the model with PoS features, (3) L_{ASR2} obtained sufficient accuracy because (3) L_{ASR2} obtained almost equal accuracy ($R^2 = 0.08, RMSE = 1.05$) to that of (1) L_{ideal} ($R^2 = 0.09, RMSE = 1.04$). On the models with BoW features, the accuracies of L_{ASR1} and L_{ASR2} were

$R^2 = 0.01$ and 0.05, which were worse than R^2 of (1) L_{ideal}. The result shows the ASR error degrades the accuracy. For the PoS model with (2) L_{ASR1} and the BoW model with (4) L_{ASR3}, regression models could not be trained to predict the skill because R^2 was negative.

Second, we report the accuracy of storytelling skill assessment accuracy of multimodal models with fusing linguistic features and nonverbal features in Table 3. In Table 3, second row denotes the accuracy of model with nonverbal features. Mean coefficient of determination R^2 of nonverbal features ((5) NV) was as high as $R^2 = 0.17, RMSE = 1.00$. The accuracy of (1) L_{ideal} (BoW) was better than the accuracy of (5) NV by about 0.04 points in R^2. This result means that the linguistic features are more effective than nonverbal features when the linguistic features are extracted from manual transcription. The best accuracy was obtained with (6) MM_{ideal} and was as high as $R^2 = 0.26, RMSE = 0.94$. (6) MM_{ideal} improved the accuracy of (5) NV by 0.09 points in R^2. This result means that the linguistic features improve the accuracy of model with nonverbal features.

However it is difficult to recognize the spoken words completely in the real situation. Multimodal features MM_{ASR1}, MM_{ASR2} and MM_{ASR3} were extracted in automatically. The accuracy of MM_{ASR1}, MM_{ASR2} and MM_{ASR3} were $R^2 = 0.14, 0.24, 0.16$, respectively. In multimodal modeling, the feature set in MM_{ASR2} achieved higher accuracy of skill assessment than those in MM_{ASR1} and MM_{ASR3}. This result indicates that the MM_{ASR2} with LM_2 which is trained from manual transcription improved the skill assessment. The accuracy of MM_{ASR2} outperformed that of NV by 0.07 points in R^2.

6 Discussion

6.1 Analysis of the Contributions of Each Linguistic Feature

The objective of the analysis is to clarify the effective linguistic features in the assessment task and the reason why accuracy of L_{ASR3} that achieved higher ASR accuracy was worse than that of L_{ASR2} with lower ASR accuracy. The regression models (L_{ideal}, L_{ASR2}, L_{ASR3}) were trained by removing linguistic features of specific PoS type in the same manner as Sect. 5.2. The contributions of specific linguistic features are identified by comparing the mean accuracy (R^2) of the model with all linguistic features features. If the accuracy degraded, the removed feature set was effective, whereas if the accuracy improved, then the removed feature set was unnecessary.

Table 4 shows the assessment accuracies of the model using linguistic feature sets without a features of specific PoS type of T_1: "noun", T_2: "verb", T_3: "adjective", T_4: "adverb", and T_5: "interjection and filler" for the mean scores of the storytelling skills[2]. In the table, Acc. denotes the accuracy of the test data, and Diff. denotes the difference of accuracy for cases in which the features of specific

---

[2] BoW and PoS features are calculated from word set which were removed words with a specific PoS type.

PoS type were removed. Bolded values indicate that the difference was more than 0.1. From the result of L_{ideal} in Table 4, the most effective PoS features were T_1: noun (Diff. is -0.17) and the second effective one was T_5: interjection and filler (Diff. is -0.02). The other features were not effective for the assessment task in this case.

From the result of L_{ASR2} in Table 4, the most effective PoS features were T_5: interjection and filler (Diff. is -0.10). When features of T_5 were removed from all linguistic features for training L_{ASR2}, the accuracy of L_{ASR2} decreased from 0.12 to 0.02. From the assessment accuracy obtained by removing features of T_5, the "interjection and filler" was effective to predict the true score of skills in L_{ideal} and L_{ASR2}.

On the other hand, when features of T_5 were removed for training L_{ASR3}, the accuracy of L_{ASR3} improved to 0.06 from 0.02. The result also showed that commercial ASR engine (ASR3) which was used for this study did not detect the interjection and filler or reject it. As a result of analysis of ASR results by ASR3, it tends to reject short filler or short utterance.

Table 4. Assessment accuracies of the model using linguistic feature sets that exclude features of specific PoS type

	L_{ideal}		L_{ASR2}		L_{ASR3}	
Baseline Acc.	0.241		0.127		0.029	
PoS of removed features	Acc.	Diff.	Acc.	Diff.	Acc.	Diff.
T_1: noun	0.064	**−0.176**	0.177	+0.050	0.014	−0.015
T_2: verb	0.257	+0.016	0.133	+0.006	0.000	−0.029
T_3: adjective	0.247	+0.006	0.118	−0.009	0.036	+0.007
T_4: adverb	0.255	+0.015	0.154	+0.026	0.016	−0.013
T_5: interjection and filler	0.216	−0.025	0.026	**−0.101**	0.068	+0.039

6.2 Limitation and Future Work

The technical limitations in the study are summarized. In this research, the multimodal features over the two storytellers were averaged to capture the group-level and collaborative storytelling skill. However, the averaging the features from two story tellers sometimes failed on capturing the interaction between them. It might be the case that the nature of the interaction between the two storytellers (e.g. turn taking, dialog) is informative with respect to some skills (e.g. liveliness). The effective features to capture the interaction will be investigated as future work.

The linguistic features provide aggregate language descriptors over an entire talk turn in this research. Taking into account the characteristics of temporal linguistic features in storytelling, it might worth including temporal linguistic features to capture the structure of a sentence. Investigating automatic feature extraction of temporal linguistic features is also important future work.

In evaluation of the proposed multimodal model, we have conducted leave a episode out testing. However, communication skills largely depend on group. We have to evaluate our task by group independent validations. In this stage, we have checked the regression accuracy in the group out testing was not sufficient. The problem is due to a small amount of data set (67 episodes in eight groups) for training the model. Solving the problem by collecting a large scale dataset is also future work.

7   Conclusions

We investigated the relationship between speech recognition errors and contribution of linguistic features. It was verified by using storytelling skill assessment task. Linguistic feature sets were automatically derived from ASR results with the trained language model. Experimental results for evaluating the assessment accuracy show that the ASR results (ASR_2) with language model which was trained from manual transcription resulted in better skill assessment. Another finding was that the linguistic features improved the accuracy of nonverbal features with 0.07 points in R^2, although the ASR accuracy was about 50%, which was not high at all. Such ASR results will be helpful for the skill assessment when manual transcriptions are unavailable that require very high human labor to construct it. Our result is a first step towards it and gives an encouraging result because imperfect ASR results are helpful for the skill assessment. In addition, interjection and filler were effective features to predict the true score of skills. This result was not expected beforehand and is an important finding to construct ASR language models for this purpose.

Acknowledgment. This work was performed under the Research Program of "Dynamic Alliance for Open Innovation Bridging Human, Environment and Materials" in "Network Joint Research Center for Materials and Devices" and Japan Society for the Promotion of Science (JSPS) KAKENHI (15K00300, 15H02746).

References

1. Park, S., Shim, H.S., Chatterjee, M., Sagae, K., Morency, L.P.: Computational analysis of persuasiveness in social multimedia: a novel dataset and multimodal prediction approach. In: Proceedings of ACM ICMI, pp. 50–57 (2014)
2. Okada, S., Ohtake, Y., Nakano, Y.I., Hayashi, Y., Huang, H.H., Takase, Y., Nitta, K.: Estimating communication skills using dialogue acts and nonverbal features in multiple discussion datasets. In: Proceedings of ACM ICMI, pp. 169–176 (2016)
3. Okada, S., Bono, M., Takanashi, K., Sumi, Y., Nitta, K.: Context-based conversational hand gesture classification in narrative interaction. In: Proceedings of ACM ICMI, pp. 303–310 (2013)
4. Okada, S., Hang, M., Nitta, K.: Predicting performance of collaborative storytelling using multimodal analysis. IEICE Trans. **99-D**(6), 1462–1473 (2016)

5. Ramanarayanan, V., Leong, C.W., Chen, L., Feng, G., Suendermann-Oeft, D.: Evaluating speech, face, emotion and body movement time-series features for automated multimodal presentation scoring. In: Proceedings of ACM ICMI, pp. 23–30 (2015)
6. Chollet, M., Prendinger, H., Scherer, S.: Native vs. non-native language fluency implications on multimodal interaction for interpersonal skills training. In: Proceedings of ACM ICMI, pp. 386–393 (2016)
7. Nguyen, L.S., Frauendorfer, D., Mast, M.S., Gatica-Perez, D.: Hire me: computational inference of hirability in employment interviews based on nonverbal behavior. IEEE Trans. Multimedia 16(4), 1018–1031 (2014)
8. Sanchez-Cortes, D., Aran, O., Mast, M.S., Gatica-Perez, D.: A nonverbal behavior approach to identify emergent leaders in small groups. IEEE Trans. Multimedia 14(3), 816–832 (2012)
9. Rasipuram, S.B., Jayagopi, D.B.: Asynchronous video interviews vs. face-to-face interviews for communication skill measurement: a systematic study. In: Proceedings of ACM ICMI, pp. 370–377 (2016)
10. Chatterjee, M., Park, S., Morency, L.P., Scherer, S.: Combining two perspectives on classifying multimodal data for recognizing speaker traits. In: Proceedings of ACM ICMI, pp. 7–14 (2015)
11. Nojavanasghari, B., Gopinath, D., Koushik, J., Baltrušaitis, T., Morency, L.P.: Deep multimodal fusion for persuasiveness prediction. In: Proceedings of ACM ICMI, pp. 284–288 (2016)
12. Lee, A., Kawahara, T.: Recent development of open-source speech recognition engine Julius. In: Proceedings of APSIPA ASC, pp. 131–137 (2009)
13. Furui, S., Maekawa, K., Isahara, H.: A Japanese national project on spontaneous speech corpus and processing technology. In: Proceedings of ISCA Workshop on Automatic Speech Recognition, pp. 244–248 (2000)
14. Kudo, T., Yamamoto, K., Matsumoto, Y.: Applying conditional random fields to japanese morphological analysis. Proc. EMNLP 4, 230–237 (2004)

Visual Analytics Based Authorship Discrimination Using Gaussian Mixture Models and Self Organising Maps: Application on Quran and Hadith

Halim Sayoud$^{(\boxtimes)}$

USTHB University, Algiers, Algeria
halim.sayoud@uni.de, halim.sayoud@gmail.com

Abstract. An interesting way to analyse the authorship authenticity of a document, is the use of stylometry. However, the use of conventional features and classifiers has some disadvantages such as the automatic authorship decision, which usually gives us a speechless authorship classification without (often) any way to measure or interpret the consistency of the results.

In this paper, we present a visual analytics based approach for the task of authorship discrimination. A specific application is dedicated to the authorship comparison between two ancient religious books: the Quran and Hadith. In fact, an important raising question is: could these ancient books be written by the same Author?

Thus, seven types of features are combined and normalized by PCA reduction and three visual analytical clustering methods are employed and commented on, namely: Principal Component Analysis, Gaussian Mixture Models and Self Organizing Maps.

The new visual analytical approach appears interesting, since it does not only show the distinction between the author styles, but also sheds light on how consistent was that distinction (i.e. visually).

Concerning the discrimination application on the ancient religious books, the results have shown the appearance of two separated clusters: namely a Quran cluster and Hadith cluster. The clusters distinction corresponds to a clear authorship difference between the two investigated documents, which implies that the two books (i.e. Quran and Hadith) come from two different Authors.

Keywords: Artificial intelligence · Data mining · Visual analytics
Natural language processing · Authorship attribution · Quran authorship

1 Introduction

Visual Analytics (VA) is defined as the graphical visualisation of the information resulting from an Analytical Modelling (AM). This graphical visualisation represents a bridge between the human and the mathematical results, and helps the experts extracting the important information for taking a decision [1]. It is impossible to dissociate the VA from AM, but in the contrary the two entities have to be associated to help the experts getting clear information from the analysed data.

© Springer International Publishing AG, part of Springer Nature 2018
M. Mouhoub et al. (Eds.): IEA/AIE 2018, LNAI 10868, pp. 158–164, 2018.
https://doi.org/10.1007/978-3-319-92058-0_15

Authorship Discrimination (AD) [2], which represents a sub-field of stylometry, consists in checking whether two text documents belong to the same author or not. This research field can efficiently respond to some literary disputes with regards to the authentic writer of a document [3]. Mostly, stylometry (or authorship attribution) uses AM computations to evaluate the probability that a specific author could have written a given piece of text. This manner, the user or expert can difficultly manage to make a decision with regards to the real author supposed to be the writer of that document.

The originality of this research work is that we propose a new way of authorship analysis by using the VA approach. Furthermore we propose a new set of linguistic features that are also original in stylometry. The principal application of our work is the analysis of the authorship authenticity of the Quran. This task is made by applying an authorship discrimination between the Quran, claimed to be from God [4], and the Hadith (i.e. statements of the Prophet). Our corpus consists of the two ancient books, which are segmented into text segments of the same size: 14 different text segments for the Quran and 11 different text segments for the Hadith. The segments have a medium size of about 2076 words per text.

2 Stylometric Features

Several linguistic features are proposed in the field of authorship attribution. We can quote four main types: Vocabulary based Features, Syntax based Features, Orthographic based features and Characters based features.

In our investigation, a mixture of different features is proposed: Author Related Pronouns (ARP), Father Based Surname (FBS), Discriminative Words (DisW), COST value, Word Length Frequency (WLF), Coordination Conjunction (CC) and Starting Coordination conjunction (SCC). All those features are original and some of them are used for the first time in stylometry (*during the preparation of this work*). Those features are described as follows:

2.1 Author's Pronoun Based Feature

In Arabic, the pronoun I (إني - أنا) is the most used one for representing the speaker person (i.e. myself). In fact, most speakers use the pronoun "I", which is normal, when speaking or writing, like in the following sentence: "انا سعيد لرؤيتك", meaning «I am happy to see you». However, in some few cases, the author's pronouns He (هو) and We (نحن - إنا) are also employed, instead of I, at least in special circumstances. This great variety of speaker's pronoun in Arabic makes a great challenge in trying using them in stylometry.

2.2 On the Use of "أبا" (*Father of*) for Naming People

In the Arabic language, it is usual to call a person using the name of his oldest child. That is, if somebody has a son called Youssof for instance, then it is possible to call him *Aba*-Youssof, which can be translated into *Father-of*-Youssof. This fact is often noticed in verbal communications, when somebody talks with his companions.

2.3   Frequency of Some Discriminative Words

The key idea is to investigate the use of some words that are very discriminative. In practice, we remarked that such words, for instance: الذين (in English: THOSE or WHO in a plural form), are very commonly used by certain speakers. As other example, one can cite the word الأرض (in English: EARTH), which is frequently used in several Arabic religious books.

2.4   COST Parameter Based Feature

Usually, when poets write a series of poems, they make a termination similarity between the neighboring sentences of the poem, such as a same final syllable or letter. To evaluate that termination similarity, a new parameter estimating the degree of text chain (in a text of several sentences) has been proposed: the COST parameter [5].

2.5   Word Length Frequency

The fifth feature is the word length frequency, which is the number of letters composing that word. The word length frequency $F(n)$ for a specific length 'n', represents the number (in percent) of words composed of n letters each, present in the text (In practice we choose $n < 11$).

2.6   Frequency of the Coordination Conjunction «و» (Meaning AND)

The coordination conjunctions represent an interesting type of features, which are widely used in the Arabic literature. In this study, we have limited our investigation to one of the most interesting conjunction, it is the conjunction "و", which corresponds to the coordination conjunction AND (in English).

2.7   Frequency of the Conjunction «و» at the Beginning of Sentence

Herein we are still interested in the frequency of the conjunction "و". However, in this case we only keep the conjunctions that are localized at the beginning of sentences, such as in the following sentence: "And now, what should we do?".

3   Visual Analytics Based Clustering Methods

In pattern recognition, cluster analysis or clustering is the task of grouping a set of objects in such a way that objects in the same group (i.e. cluster) are more similar to each other than to those in other groups [6]. On the other hand, visual analytics [1, 7], which is a combination of several fields (i.e. computer science, information visualization and graphic design) is often used in cluster analysis to make the analyst's judgment easier to develop and more objective. That is, the combination of those two research fields can lead to a strong and efficient analysis tool for handling some classification tasks that could be extremely difficult to perform with conventional analytic tools. Consequently, it appears that the association of visual analytics with clustering analysis may be interesting for solving some stylometric problems, for which we do not possess any training possibility or information to make a supervised classification task. So, it should be extremely motivating to apply them in our application of authorship discrimination (*i.e. Quran vs Hadith*). In our survey, we propose to use the Gaussian Mixtures Models and Self Organizing Maps, separately in order to find out the possible clusters related to the different investigated text segments. Our corpus consists of the two ancient books: Quran and Hadith. However, since the sizes of the two books are different, we segmented them into segments of the same size: there are 14 different text segments for the Quran and 11 different text segments for the Hadith. The segments have the same size and the medium size is about 2076 words per text.

3.1 Principal Components Analysis

A PCA representation of the data, using the 3 most important eigenvectors, is given in Fig. 1. We can notice that all the Quran documents are grouped together in the right side, while all the Hadith ones are separately grouped in the left side.

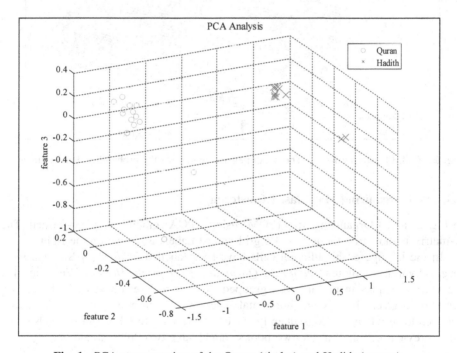

Fig. 1. PCA representation of the Quran (circles) and Hadith (crosses).

3.2 Gaussian Mixture Model Based Clustering

A GMM based clustering is performed after PCA reduction into the 2 most important components. We notice that the different text samples have been clustered into 2 main groups: Quran cluster, at the bottom left side, gathering all the Quran texts and a Hadith cluster at top right, gathering all Hadith texts. The Gaussian mixtures are represented by different 3D gaussians surrounding the two clusters (Fig. 2). This fact confirms, once again, that the writing styles of the 2 books are probably different.

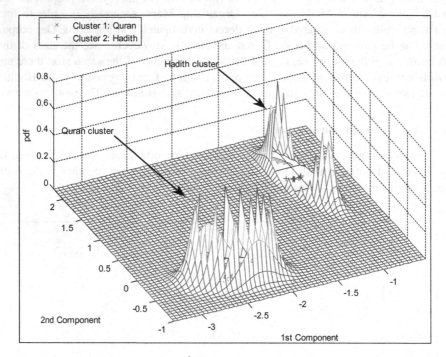

Fig. 2. GMM clustering in 3D. The 3rd dimension represents the probability density function.

3.3   Self-Organizing Map Based Clustering

In Fig. 3, a Self-Organizing Map (SOM) using 3 PCA components is performed. The U-matrix is shown on the left, and a grid named Labels is shown on the right.

In the left figure, the different cells have been labelled (*with regards to the book origin*) by using 2 colours (*red for the Quran and green for the Hadith*). We notice that the Quran samples in red are well grouped together and separated from the Hadith samples in green, by a sharp horizontal black (*dark*) line representing a boundary between the two classes. Consequently, we can see that the SOM clustering leads to the same previous conclusion: the two books should have two different authors.

4   Discussion

In this investigation, we have proposed a new set of linguistic features that are original and not used previously. Furthermore, we have proposed a new graphical way to analyse the authorship authenticity of a document by using three approaches: PCA, GMM and SOM techniques. The different results led to the following conclusions:

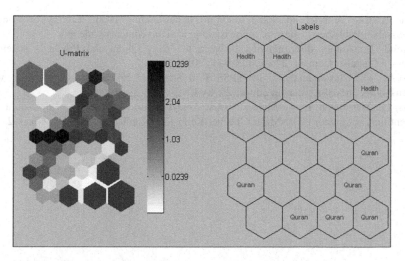

Fig. 3. 2D Self-Organizing Map (*SOM*). We can see 2 main clusters: one cluster is visible at the right bottom and another one at the left top. The different cells have been labelled by using 2 colours (*green for the Hadith and red for the Quran*). The dark lines represents boundaries. (Color figure online)

- Visual Analytics is interesting and promising in the field of authorship attribution.
- Although the first approach (*i.e. PCA*) is not a clustering method, the resulting 3D representation suggests that the two books have two different author styles.
- The second approach, namely GMM, is a clustering technique based on gaussian mixture models. According to the 3D representation, the two books appear to have two different author styles, too.
- The third approach (*i.e. SOM*) is a self organizing neural network, which makes a 2D representation of the different possible clusters. The resulting mapping shows that there are also two different author styles: one for the Quran and one for the Hadith.

Consequently, it appears that the two investigated books (*Quran and Hadith*) have 2 different writing styles, which suggests the hypothesis of 2 different authors.

References

1. Blascheck, T., John, M., Kurzhals, K., Koch, S., Ertl, T.: VA2: a visual analytics approach for evaluating visual analytics applications. IEEE Trans. Vis. Comput. Graph. **22**(1), 61–70 (2016)
2. Sayoud, H.: Segmental analysis based authorship discrimination between the Holy Quran and Prophet's statements. Digital Stud. J. 2014–2015 (2015)
3. Sayoud, H.: A visual analytics based investigation on the authorship of the Holy Quran. In: International Conference on Information Visualization Theory and Applications (IVAPP'2015), 11–14 March 2015, pp. 177–181 (2015)

4. Ibrahim, I.A.: A brief illustrated guide to understanding Islam. Library of Congress, Darussalam Publishers, Houston. www.islam-guide.com/contents-wide.htm
5. Sayoud, H.: Author discrimination between the Holy Quran and Prophet's statements. Literary Linguist. Comput. **27**(4), 427–444 (2012)
6. Norusis, M.: Cluster analysis. In: SPSS 17.0 Statistical Procedures Companion, Marija Norusis, pp. 361–391. Pearson editor (2008). Chap. 16
7. Ellis, G., Mansmann, F.: VisMaster, Visual Analytics. In: Mastering the Information Age. Scientific Coordinator of VisMaster. Daniel Keim Jörn Kohlhammer (2010). Chap. 2

An Optimization Approach Based on Collective Correlation Coefficient for Biomarker Extraction in the Classification of Alzheimer's Disease

Dan Pan[1], An Zeng[2,3(✉)], Jian-Zhong Li[2], Xiao-Wei Song[4],
and Shu-Xia Wang[5]
and for the Alzheimer's Disease Neuroimaging Initiative

[1] Guangdong Construction Polytechnic, Guangzhou 510440, China
[2] Guangdong University of Technology, Guangzhou 510006, China
zengan2010@126.com
[3] Guangdong Key Laboratory of Big Data Analysis and Processing,
Guangzhou 510006, China
[4] Simon Fraser University, Vancouver V6B 5K3, Canada
[5] Guangdong General Hospital, Guangzhou 510080, China

Abstract. In this paper, based on Magnetic Resonance Imaging (MRI), the effective biomarkers were efficiently extracted for the classification of Alzheimer's Disease (AD), mild cognitive impairment (MCI) and health control (HC) with the help of the improved Genetic Algorithm based on the Collective Correlation Coefficient (GA-CCC). Firstly, 544 related features from 68 regions of left and right brain hemispheres were extracted. Secondly, aiming at optimizing Gaussian Process Classifier (GPC) performance, the CCC was employed to help extract the biomarkers for the AD classification and to improve the optimization efficiency of the conventional GA. Finally, experiments showed that the proposed GA-CCC significantly improved the classifications of AD vs. MCI and MCI vs. HC in an efficient way. Plus, many acquired brain regions are known to be strongly involved in the pathophysiological mechanisms of AD.

Keywords: Magnetic Resonance Imaging · Alzheimer's Disease
Collective Correlation Coefficient · Biomarker

Alzheimer's Disease Neuroimaging Initiative—Data used in preparation of this article were obtained from the Alzheimer's Disease Neuroimaging Initiative (ADNI) database (adni.loni.usc. edu). As such, the investigators within the ADNI contributed to the design and implementation of ADNI and/or provided data but did not participate in analysis or writing of this report. A complete listing of ADNI investigators can be found at: http://adni.loni.usc.edu/wp-content/uploads/how_to_apply/ADNI_Acknowledgement_List.pdf.

© Springer International Publishing AG, part of Springer Nature 2018
M. Mouhoub et al. (Eds.): IEA/AIE 2018, LNAI 10868, pp. 165–171, 2018.
https://doi.org/10.1007/978-3-319-92058-0_16

1   Introduction

AD is an irreversible degenerative disorder of the nervous system, and is a persistent neurological dysfunction [1]. Existing AD drug treatments are very rare, but early accurate detection and intervention could slow down the disease progression. MCI is a transitional stage between HC and AD. Current studies have shown that important pathologic signs and biomarkers of AD can be measured by MRI [2]. In recent years, different classification models have been utilized in the classification of the field, and the classifications are almost equivalently effective [3]. However, Gaussian Process Classifier (GPC) [4] has significant advantages among these classification models.

One of characteristics of MRI is "high dimension" and "highly informative". NOT every feature extracted from MR images plays a key role in the classification of AD. However, to find out key features, trying out all combinations of all features is an NP-hard problem. Thus, more efficient feature selection method is necessary.

GA is an optimization algorithm based on genetic theory [5]. Aiming at NP-hard problems, the researchers have put forward a lot of optimization methods to improve the efficiency of GA. As heuristic knowledge employed in knowledge acquisition method (KA-RSPCA), the Collective Correlation Coefficient (CCC) was advocated to select condition attributes in rule induction [6].

In this paper, we proposed an optimization method for feature extraction based on CCC and GA, and applied it in Gaussian process classifiers (GPC) to find out the key biomarkers of the classifications of MCI vs. HC and AD vs. MCI, efficiently.

2   Related Works

In current clinical practice, many computer-aided diagnosis methods for AD or MCI were advocated. In order to understand the morphological changes on MRI images, a number of quantitative features based on MRI image have been employed [7]. In 2016, Jongkreangkrai combined hippocampus and amygdala volumes and entorhinal cortex thickness to improve the classification performance of AD vs. HC [8]. Again, De Schouten et al. combined multiple anatomical MRI measures to enhance the classification of AD vs. HC in the same year [9]. Their experimental results exhibited that the combination of all six measures, i.e. cortical thickness, cortical area, cortical curvature, grey matter density, subcortical volumes, and hippocampal shape, resulted in an AUC of 0.98.

3   Methodology

The proposed Genetic Algorithm based on Collective Correlation Coefficient (GA-CCC) is shown in Fig. 1. Compared with the optimization process of a conventional GA, the GA-CCC mainly enhances the population initialization, crossover and mutation operations. Owing to the limited pages, the detailed descriptions are omitted.

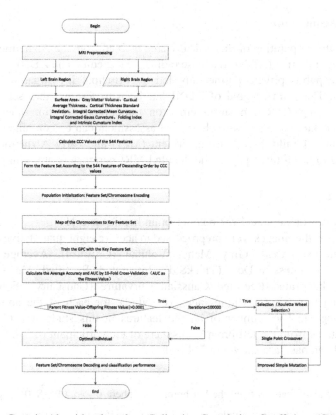

Fig. 1. Genetic Algorithm based on Collective Correlation Coefficient (GA-CCC).

Preprocess. Cerebral cortical remodeling is employed, including motion correction, automatic topology correction, and so on [10] to acquire the 544 features from 68 regions of the left and right brain hemispheres with Freesurfer v5.3.0.

Calculation of the CCC. The CCCs of 544 features are calculated respectively, and the feature set is constructed according to the rank of the CCC values.

Encoding. Population size is 100 and 544 features are binary encoded. A chromosome is a 0/1 string with the length of 544. The features corresponding to the genes appearing to be "1" are set as key ones, and the rest features are set as non-key ones.

Mutation Operator. The feature with lower CCC has the lower mutation probability P_m. The principle of mutation operator is to ascertain P_m according to a CCC value.

4 Materials and Methods

Fifty AD subjects, fifty MCI subjects and fifty demographically matched healthy control subjects were selected. Owing to the limited pages, the details are omitted.

4.1   Data Acquisition

Data used in the preparation of this article were obtained from the Alzheimer's Disease Neuroimaging Initiative (ADNI) database (adni.loni.usc.edu). The ADNI was launched in 2003 as a public-private partnership, led by Principal Investigator Michael W. Weiner, MD. The primary goal of ADNI has been to test whether serial magnetic resonance imaging (MRI), positron emission tomography (PET), other biological markers, and clinical and neuropsychological assessment can be combined to measure the progression of mild cognitive impairment (MCI) and early Alzheimer's disease (AD). Owing to the limited pages, the detailed MRI parameters are omitted.

4.2   Features

There are 34 neuroanatomical regions per brain hemisphere [11].

In this study, the images were preprocessed to acquire eight quantitative indices, i.e. Surface Area (SurfArea), Gray Matter Volume (GrayVol), Average Thickness (ThickAvg), Thickness StDev (ThickStd), Integrated Rectified Mean Curvature (MeanCurv), Integrated Rectified Gaussian Curvature (GausCurv), Folding Index (FoldInd), and Intrinsic Curvature Index (CurvInd), for each of the above 68 neuroanatomic region. The number of all the features in this study was $68 * 8 = 544$ A part of features from the left brain hemisphere of the participant of No. 002_S_0413 in the ADNI database are shown in Table 1.

Table 1. A part of features from the left brain hemisphere of No. 002_S_0413 participant.

Region	Caudal middle frontal	Cuneus	Fusiform	Inferior parietal
SurfArea	2254	1599	3570	4123
GrayVol	5729	3094	11029	11176
ThickAvg	2.361	1.785	2.715	2.381
FoldInd	35	36	99	103
CurvInd	5.3	5.2	11.9	12.5

4.3   The Models

Gaussian Process Classifier (GPC). Here, the classifications of MCI vs. HC and AD vs. MCI were accomplished. The validity of the model is measured by a 10-fold stratified sampling cross-validation test method. Average of multiple AUC values was obtained on test sets. The inputs of GPC model include: covariance matrices K, training set labels Y and likelihood functions $p(y|f)$. Here, the training set labels $Y \in \{0,1\}$. The likelihood function $p(y|f)$ is a Gaussian function with mean 0 and standard deviation of 1. The covariance matrix K is a symmetric positive definite matrix, where the element K_{ij} located at the i-th row and the j-th column is the functional distance between the training data i and j. The covariance function is the square exponential covariance function. Owing to the limited pages, the detailed parameters of the GPC model are omitted.

5   Experimental Results

For the classification of AD vs. MCI, the number of acquired key features was 29 while the AUC reached the peak value of 0.751 after 23,385 iteration times (i.e. 2.19 h running time on a Dell PowerEdge server) with the help of the GA-CCC. These key features are: Gray Matter Volume in bankssts (R, i.e. right hemisphere), superior temporal (R), middle temporal (R), inferior temporal (R), temporal pole (R), and so on. Among the 29 features, the number of those related to the right hemisphere was 23 (occupied 79.3%), which meant that the right hemisphere might be more related to the development from MCI to AD, at least among these subjects. At the same time, the number of those related to the Gray Matter Volume and Surface Area were 13 (occupied 44.8%) and 8 (occupied 27.6%), respectively. Meanwhile, the conventional GA was employed to help distinguish AD from MCI. The number of acquired key features was 31 while the AUC reached the peak value of 0.752 after 37,051 iteration times (i.e. 3.28 h running time). The acquired key features are almost the same as GA-CCC except that two key features, i.e. Gray Matter Volume in temporal pole (L) and Average Thickness in caudal middle frontal (L), were added.

For the classification of MCI vs. HC, the number of acquired key features was 33 while the AUC reached the peak value of 0.765 after 27,449 iteration times (i.e. 2.70 h running time) with the help of the GA-CCC. These key features are: Gray Matter Volume in precuneus (R), precuneus (L), cuneus (R), bankssts (R), superior temporal (R), middle temporal (R), and so on. Among the 33 features, the number of those related to the right hemisphere was 24 (occupied 72.7%), which meant that the right hemisphere might be more related to the MCI development, at least among these subjects. Also, the number of those related to the Gray Matter Volume were 23 (occupied 69.7%). Meanwhile, the conventional GA was utilized to help distinguish MCI from HC. The number of acquired key features was 34 while the AUC reached the peak value of 0.767 after 45,716 iteration times (i.e. 3.87 h running time). The acquired key features are almost the same as those obtained with GA-CCC.

6   Conclusion

In fact, some features in 544 features could result in a decrease in classification performance. Thus, the key to improving the classification effectiveness and efficiency is feature selection. Aiming at this goal, GA-CCC was advocated to enhance the quality of selected features efficiently. Experimental results exhibited that it was feasible and effective for the CCC to be heuristic knowledge of the conventional GA to raise the classification performance. For the classification of AD vs. MCI and MCI vs. HC, the GA-CCC selected the key features within substantially shorter time period than the conventional GA did. Among these key features, more than 70% features were from right hemisphere and more than 40% features were related with Gray Matter Volume. In a word, the GA-CCC is an effective method to efficiently acquire the key biomarkers from MRI images for the classifications of AD vs. MCI and MCI vs. HC.

Acknowledgments. This study was supported by NSF of China (grant No. 61772143, 61300107 and 61672168), NSF of Guangdong (grant No. S2012010010212), NSF of Guangzhou (grant No. 201601010034 and 201804010278) and the Opening Project of Guangdong Key Laboratory of Big Data Analysis and Processing (grant No. 201801). Data collection and sharing for this project was funded by the Alzheimer's Disease Neuroimaging Initiative (ADNI) (National Institutes of Health Grant U01 AG024904) and DOD ADNI (Department of Defense award number W81XWH-12-2-0012). ADNI is funded by the National Institute on Aging, the National Institute of Biomedical Imaging and Bioengineering, and through generous contributions from the following: AbbVie, Alzheimer's Association; Alzheimer's Drug Discovery Foundation; Araclon Biotech; BioClinica, Inc.; Biogen; Bristol-Myers Squibb Company; Cere-Spir, Inc.; Cogstate; Eisai Inc.; Elan Pharmaceuticals, Inc.; Eli Lilly and Company; EuroImmun; F. Hoffmann-La Roche Ltd and its affiliated company Genentech, Inc.; Fujire-bio; GE Healthcare; IXICO Ltd.; Janssen Alzheimer Immunotherapy Research & Development, LLC.; Johnson & Johnson Pharmaceutical Research & Development LLC.; Lumosity; Lund-beck; Merck & Co., Inc.; Meso Scale Diagnostics, LLC.; NeuroRx Research; Neurotrack Technologies; Novartis Pharmaceuticals Corporation; Pfizer Inc.; Piramal Imaging; Servier; Takeda Pharmaceutical Company; and Transition Therapeutics. The Canadian Institutes of Health Research is providing funds to support ADNI clinical sites in Canada. Private sector contributions are facilitated by the Foundation for the National Institutes of Health (www.fnih. org). The grantee organization is the Northern California Institute for Research and Education, and the study is coordinated by the Alzheimer's Therapeutic Research Institute at the University of Southern California. ADNI data are disseminated by the Laboratory for Neuro Imaging at the University of Southern California.

References

1. Chen, B., Zhang, D.Q.: Predicting clinical variables in Alzheimer's disease based on multimodal relevance vector regression. J. Nanjing Univ. (Nat. Sci.) **48**(2), 140–146 (2012)
2. Rathore, S., Habes, M., Iftikhar, M.A., Shacklett, A., Davatzikos, C.: A review on neuroimaging-based classification studies and associated feature extraction methods for Alzheimer's disease and its prodromal stages. NeuroImage **155**, 530–548 (2017)
3. Young, J.M.: Probabilistic Prediction of Alzheimer's Disease from Multimodal Image Data with Gaussian Processes. Doctoral dissertation, University of London (2015)
4. Kitayama, S., Yamazaki, K.: Simple estimate of the width in Gaussian kernel with adaptive scaling technique. Appl. Soft Comput. **11**(8), 4726–4737 (2011)
5. Zheng, L.P., Hao, Z.X.: A review on the theory for the genetic algorithm. Comput. Eng. Appl. **39**(21), 50–53 (2003)
6. Zeng, A., Pan, D., Zheng, Q.L., et al.: Knowledge acquisition based on rough set theory and principal component analysis. IEEE Intell. Syst. **21**(2), 78–85 (2006)
7. Lama, R.K., et al.: Diagnosis of Alzheimer's disease based on structural MRI images using a regularized extreme learning machine and PCA features. J. Healthc. Eng. (2017)
8. Jongkreangkrai, C., Vichianin, Y., Tocharoenchai, C., Arimura, H.: Computer-aided classification of Alzheimer's disease based on support vector machine with combination of cerebral image features in MRI. J. Phys. Conf. Ser. **694**(1), 012036 (2016)
9. De Schouten, V.F., Hafkemeijer, T.M., Dopper, A., van Swieten, E.G., et al.: Combining multiple anatomical MRI measures improves Alzheimer's disease classification. Hum. Brain Mapp. **37**(5), 1920–1929 (2016)

10. Reuter, M., Rosas, M., et al.: Highly accurate inverse consistent registration: a robust approach. Neuroimage **53**(4), 1181–1196 (2010)
11. Jack, C.R., Knopman, D.S., et al.: Tracking pathophysiological processes in Alzheimer's disease: an updated hypothetical model of dynamic biomarkers. Lancet Neurol. **12**(2), 207–216 (2013)

Evolutionary Computation

Lazy Conflict Detection with Genetic Algorithms

Christoph Uran[1,2($\boxtimes$)] and Alexander Felfernig[1]

[1] Institute for Software Technology, Graz University of Technology,
Inffeldgasse 16b, 8010 Graz, Austria
{christoph.uran,alexander.felfernig}@ist.tugraz.at
[2] Faculty of Engineering and IT, Carinthia University of Applied Sciences,
Primoschgasse 8, 9020 Klagenfurt, Austria
c.uran@cuas.at

Abstract. The customization of complex products and services requires configurators with often large and complex knowledge bases. In the case that configuration-related user requirements are inconsistent with the knowledge base, immediate feedback is desired. However, due to the domain's complexity, efficient feedback generation is often not possible. In this paper we show how to use genetic algorithms to pre-generate minimal conflict sets. Their integration into the configurator allows response times required for interactive settings. Our evaluations, based on knowledge bases from the air pollution monitoring domain, show significant performance improvements.

1 Introduction

Configuration is one of the most successful application areas of Artificial Intelligence (AI) [13]. The configuration of highly-variant products and services is a non-trivial task that requires (1) large and complex knowledge bases that describe available components and their possible combinations [5], as well as (2) smart user interfaces that are applicable for domain experts with no (computer) science background [11].

Configurator users want immediate feedback on their actions, i.e., they want to know about possible alternatives to their potentially conflicting requirements [10]. However, near-instantaneous feedback on inconsistencies is often not possible with existing "on-demand" diagnosis approaches. Therefore, we present a method to pre-determine minimal conflict sets for as many conflicting user requirements as possible. We denote this approach *lazy conflict detection*.

One approach to pre-determine potential minimal conflict sets in user requirements is to systematically check all possible combinations of requirements and

The work presented in this paper was partially funded by the European Commission via the Horizon 2020 project AGILE (https://agile-iot.eu/).

analyze whether individual combinations induce a conflict. Due to the exponential number of possible combinations, this approach is infeasible when dealing with large knowledge bases. Therefore, we developed an alternative approach. This approach is based on the observation that, in real world scenarios, for many conflicting sets of user requirements there exists a similar set of user requirements that is also conflicting. This is illustrated by the following example. The user's requirements are a *four-wheel drive* and an *average fuel consumption* of *3 L per 100 km*. However, the configuration knowledge base states, that a four-wheel drive implies a fuel consumption of at least 6 L per 100 km. Therefore, even if the user changes the fuel consumption limit to a higher value, such as 4 L per 100 km, there will be no valid configuration.

Due to this observation, we decided to use *genetic algorithms* [7,9,15] to generate as many conflicting user requirements as possible without having to systematically check all possible combinations of user requirements (since this is infeasible in the general case). The basic approach of genetic algorithms is to randomly initialize a set of individuals (i.e., a *population*), select a desired portion of the population (using a so-called *fitness function*), and then use the genetic operators for *crossover* (also called recombination) and *mutation* to create a new generation of individuals [9]. In this paper, we show how this approach can be used for detecting possible conflicting user requirements. Genetic algorithms have been used for conflict resolution by Carneiro et al. in [1]. However, our approach is focused on conflicts in the sense of constraint satisfaction problems. To the best of our knowledge, no research has yet been conducted on *lazy conflict detection* in general or its combination with genetic algorithms in that area.

The remainder of this paper is structured as follows: Sect. 2 introduces a working example that will be used throughout the paper. Section 3 describes the approach of using genetic algorithms to generate a priori knowledge of conflicts, so called *lazy conflict detection*. Section 4 presents the results of a performance evaluation. Section 5 provides an overview of future work that will be conducted. The paper is concluded with Sect. 6.

2   Working Example

Air pollution monitoring will serve as a working example throughout the paper. The main component is the *monitoring station* (MS), which can have different connectivity modes, different data storage modes, and either a rugged or standard enclosure. A monitoring station can be configured for multiple *deployment environments* (DE), which specify the general properties of the surroundings. Furthermore, each deployment environment consists of multiple *areas* (A), which specify the surroundings in more detail. Finally, each area can have multiple *wall types* (WT), where the monitoring stations can be mounted, and multiple *environmental conditions* (EC), which describe conditions such as humidity, temperature, and pressure. In addition to the components described for this working example, there is a large number of further components available in the configuration environment, cf. [3]. However, these components are not configurable by the user, which is why they are omitted here.

Our simplified configuration knowledge base can be represented as a *configuration task* which is defined as a *constraint satisfaction problem* (CSP). For further details on CSPs and their solutions we refer to [4]. A configuration task is defined as follows [4]:

Definition 1. *A configuration task can be defined as a CSP (V, D, C) where $V = \{v_1, v_2, \ldots, v_n\}$ is a set of finite domain variables, $D = \{dom(v_1), dom(v_2), \ldots, dom(v_n)\}$ and $C = C_{KB} \cup REQ$ is a set of constraints. C_{KB} represents the configuration knowledge base (the configuration model) and REQ represents a set of user (customer) requirements.*

A solution to a given configuration task is called a *configuration* and is defined as follows [4]:

Definition 2. *A configuration (solution) S for a given configuration task $(V, D, C_{KB} \cup REQ)$ is represented by an assignment $S = \{ins(v_1), ins(v_2), \ldots, ins(v_k)\}$ where $ins(v_i) \in dom(v_i)$ and S is complete and consistent with the constraints in $C_{KB} \cup REQ$.*

The variables V in our working example, the air pollution monitoring domain, are the following:

$$V = \{Communication_{MS}, Storage_{MS}, Enclosure_{MS}, Type_{DE}, Context_{DE},$$
$$Location_{DE}, Type_A, Category_A, Traffic_A, Type_{WT},$$
$$AvgTemp_{EC}, AvgWind_{EC}, AvgPressure_{EC}\}$$

The variable domains D are the following:

$$D = \{dom(Communication_{MS}) = \{wired, wireless\},$$
$$dom(Storage_{MS}) = \{local, cloud\},$$
$$dom(Enclosure_{MS}) = \{rugged, standard\},$$
$$dom(Type_{DE}) = \{indoor, outdoor\},$$
$$dom(Context_{DE}) = \{country, tropical, \},$$
$$dom(Location_{DE}) = \{urban, countryside, industrial, \},$$
$$dom(Type_A) = \{indoor, outdoor\},$$
$$dom(Category_A) = \{industry, shop, library, field, \},$$
$$dom(Traffic_A) = \{light, medium, heavy\},$$
$$dom(Type_{WT}) = \{wood, tiles, plaster, \},$$
$$dom(AvgTemp_{EC}) = [-50, 50], dom(AvgWind_{EC}) = [0, 17],$$
$$dom(AvgPressure_{EC} = [1, 10], \}$$

Finally, an example of C_{KB} is the following:

$$C_{KB} = \{Cat_A = field \rightarrow Type_{DE} = outdoor,$$
$$Type_{DE} = outdoor \rightarrow Communication_{MS} \neq wired,$$
$$Cat_A = library \rightarrow Type_{DE} = indoor,$$
$$Type_{DE} = indoor \leftrightarrow Type_A = indoor,$$
$$Category_A = field \rightarrow Traffic_A = light,$$
$$Type_{DE} = outdoor \leftrightarrow AvgWind_{EC} \neq 0\}$$

User requirements (REQ, also represented as constraints) can induce conflicts in the configuration knowledge base (C_{KB}). In such cases, simply informing the user that no solution can be found is not enough. The user also expects assistance in resolving *conflicts* and thereby finding a way out of this so called *no solution found dilemma* [2]. This can be done by determining the *minimal conflict set(s)* in the given user requirements. The definition of a minimal conflict set is the following [4]:

Definition 3. *A conflict set $CS = \{c_a, c_b, \ldots, c_z\}$ is a subset of REQ such that inconsistent($C_{KB} \cup CS$). $C = C_{KB} \cup REQ$ represents the set of all constraints $\{c_1, c_2, \ldots, c_n\}$, C_{KB} represents the set of constraints in the knowledge base (no conflict elements are assumed to be included in C_{KB}), and REQ represents the set of constraints that are user requirements and subject to conflict search. A conflict set CS is* minimal *if there does not exist a $CS' \subset CS$ that has the conflict property.*

There exist two established approaches to determine a minimal conflict set in a set of user requirements. For a detailed discussion we refer to [4,6,12]. For the purpose of identifying conflict sets, we apply QUICKXPLAIN in our implementation [6].

A (minimal) diagnosis for a given set of conflicts needs to be determined in order to know the (minimal) set of constraints that needs to be adapted or deleted from the given conflict sets such that a valid configuration can be found. A *diagnosis task* can be defined as follows [4]:

Definition 4. *A diagnosis task can be defined by the tuple (REQ, C) where $C = C_{KB} \cup REQ$, C_{KB} is the background knowledge, and REQ is the set of constraints to be analyzed (the user requirements).*

A *diagnosis* represents the solution to a given diagnosis task (REQ, C) and is defined as follows [4]:

Definition 5. *A diagnosis for a given diagnosis task (REQ, C) is a set of constraints $\Delta \subseteq REQ$ such that $C_{KB} \cup REQ - \Delta$ is consistent. A diagnosis Δ is* minimal *if there does not exist a diagnosis $\Delta' \subset \Delta$ with the diagnosis property. Finally, a minimal diagnosis Δ is denoted a* minimal cardinality diagnosis *if there does not exist a minimal diagnosis Δ' with $|\Delta'| < |\Delta|$.*

In our working example, we assume the following user requirements which are inconsistent with C_{KB}, i.e., $inconsistent(REQ \cup C_{KB})$:

$$REQ = \{Communication_{MS} = wired, Storage_{MS} = cloud,$$
$$Type_{DE} = outdoor, Category_A = library\}$$

REQ includes the two minimal conflict sets CS_1 and CS_2, i.e., $inconsistent(CS_1 \cup C_{KB})$ and $inconsistent(CS_2 \cup C_{KB})$.

$$CS_1 = \{Communication_{MS} = wired, Type_{DE} = outdoor\}$$
$$CS_2 = \{Type_{DE} = outdoor, Category_A = library\}$$

From CS_1 and CS_2, we can derive the minimal diagnosis Δ_1 [12], i.e., $REQ - \Delta_1 \cup C_{KB}$ is consistent.

$$\Delta_1 = \{Type_{DE} = outdoor\}$$

Different methods of determining minimal diagnoses can be applied. For further details we refer to [2,12]. In our implementation, we use FASTDIAG, which returns a single minimal diagnosis at a time. Similar to QUICKXPLAIN, it relies on the concept of *divide and conquer*. Furthermore, it outperforms other methods of determining diagnoses under most circumstances [2]. For further details on FASTDIAG, refer to [2]. A comparison of different diagnosis methods can be found, for example, in [14].

3   Lazy Conflict Detection Using Genetic Algorithms

We use genetic algorithms in order to pre-generate minimal conflict sets (i.e. sets of user requirements conflicting with the knowledge base) without having to systematically check all possible combinations of user requirements. This leads to less data that has to be stored and makes checking a given set of user requirements for minimal conflict sets more efficient.

The advantage of having a priori knowledge about potential conflicts contained in user requirements is that these conflicts can already be detected at an earlier stage of the configuration process, i.e., before even running the solver. Because a simple lookup in a list of known minimal conflict sets is more efficient than the whole CSP solving process, the user gets feedback much quicker concerning arising conflicts. We denote the a priori generation of minimal conflict sets as *lazy conflict detection*. Algorithm 1 illustrates the basic approach. The individual phases of the algorithm are the following. During the *initialization*, various variables are read from a configuration file. These are, for example, different paths (to further configuration files, the CSP solver, and more) and parameters for the genetic algorithm, such as *mutation probability* and *population size*. Already identified minimal conflict sets from previous sessions are taken into account.

Algorithm 1. Genetic algorithm for local conflict search.

1: $Population \leftarrow \emptyset$
2: **for** $i \leftarrow 1 \ldots n$ **do**
3:     $Population = Population \cup randomize(P_\emptyset, \{dom(c_1), dom(c_2), \ldots, dom(c_m)\})$
4: **end for**
5: **while** $time_{current} \leq time_{max}$ **do**
6:     $Parents \leftarrow \emptyset$
7:     **for all** $REQ \in Population$ **do**
8:         **if** $inconsistent(C_{KB} \cup REQ)$ **then**
9:             $CS \leftarrow QuickXPlain(C_{KB} \cup REQ)$
10:             $store(CS)$
11:             $Parents \leftarrow Parents \cup resolve(REQ, CS)$
12:         **end if**
13:     **end for**
14:     $NewGen \leftarrow \emptyset$
15:     **for** $i \leftarrow 1 \ldots n$ **do**
16:         $NewGen \leftarrow NewGen \cup crossover(pick(Parents), pick(Parents))$
17:     **end for**
18:     $Population \leftarrow mutate(P_m, NewGen)$
19: **end while**

The first step in Algorithm 1 is to create (line 1) and randomize (line 3) an initial population. The randomization has two parameters, which are (1) the probability that a given variable should have no value ($P_\emptyset$) and (2) the user requirement's domain definition, which specifies the values that the user requirement can have ($\{dom(c_1), dom(c_2), \ldots, dom(c_m)\}$). Both parameters were set during the initialization. The probability $P_\emptyset$ means that if there are 10 user requirements and $P_\emptyset$ is 50%, on average 5 of the 10 user requirements will not be set. This means that they can be assigned any allowed value during the solving process and can therefore not be part of a minimal conflict set, thus effectively reducing the number of minimal conflict sets in the user requirements. One reason, why this option should be utilized is, that it is desirable to limit the number of minimal conflicts in a set of user requirements, as will be shown in Sect. 4. Those user requirements that should not be left blank, are randomized using the domain definition that was read during the initialization phase.

Upon generating a population of the desired size n, the list of parents for the future generation is initialized in line 6 and each individual REQ of the population is checked for conflicts (line 8). If the user requirements stored in REQ are inconsistent with the knowledge base C_{KB}, one minimal conflict set CS for the given set of user requirements is determined (line 9) and stored (line 10). Furthermore, a set of user requirements, based on REQ but with a resolved CS, is added to the set of parents (line 11). The return value of *resolve* is a set of sets of user requirements derived from REQ, as described in Formula 1.

$$C_{res} = \bigcup_{c \in CS} \{REQ \setminus \{c\}\} \tag{1}$$

In other words, the set of user requirements REQ that contains the minimal conflict set CS of the size n is cloned n times. Of each of these cloned individuals, one user requirement c of the respective minimal conflict set is removed. This results in n variants of REQ, each without exactly one user requirement c out of CS.

After this has been done, an empty set is created (line 14), which is used to store the new individuals (sets of user requirements), generated via *genetic crossover*. This set therefore holds the new generation, i.e., the population of the next iteration. As long as the desired number of individuals in the population is not reached, two different resolved user requirements (see Formula 1), also called *ancestors* are paired to generate a new individual (i.e. set of user requirements; *child*; line 16). If both ancestors have the same value for a given user requirement, also the child will have this value. If they differ, the child randomly takes the value of one of the ancestors. Furthermore, if the genetic crossover results in an individual with a known minimal conflict set, the individual is not added to the set representing the new generation and a new one is generated.

The last step is to mutate the new generation. For this, each user requirement of each individual is mutated with a given probability P_m. After that, a new iteration begins. In Algorithm 1, all detected minimal conflict sets are written to a file after each iteration. Furthermore, the algorithm terminates after a specified time because we can never be absolutely sure that all possible minimal conflict sets have been detected in real world scenarios.

Three examples for the generated minimal conflict sets are shown below.

$$CS_1 = \{Context_{DE} = country, Location_{DE} = industrial\}$$
$$CS_2 = \{Type_{DE} = indoor, Traffic_A - heavy\}$$
$$CS_3 = \{Type_A = indoor, AvgWind_{EC} = 15\}$$

4   Evaluation

The algorithm described in Sect. 3 has been implemented based on Java and the `clingo`[1] solver. `clingo` is an *answer set programming* (ASP) solver, whose grounding can be interpreted as a CSP. Although a HSDAG-based diagnosis algorithm [12] would find all minimal conflict sets in a set of user requirements, the determination of minimal conflict sets has been accomplished using the QUICK-XPLAIN algorithm [6] here. This is due to the approach of Algorithm 1, where every set of user requirements, that contains at least one minimal conflict set, is freed of exactly one of these minimal conflict sets in every possible way (see Formula 1). This means that the other potentially existing minimal conflict sets are still present in the parent generation and it is therefore highly probable that they are also passed on to at least one of the descendants.

The following configuration has been used when executing the algorithm:

---

[1] https://potassco.org/clingo/.

init_no_preference = 0.7 the probability, that a given user requirement of an
   individual of the randomized staring population is *not* set is **0.7** (symbolized
   by $P_\emptyset$)
population_size = 100 the number of individuals in each generation's population is **100** (symbolized by N)
mutation_probability = 0.1 the probability that a given user requirement of
   an individual is mutated is **0.1**[2] (symbolized by P_m)
num_of_populations = 1 the number of simultaneously existing populations
   is **1**[3]

In order to prevent redundant determinations of minimal conflict sets, the
program reconciles the set of conflicting user requirements with the already
known minimal conflict sets. As a result, only those minimal conflict sets are
calculated that have not been calculated already in a previous generation. As
empirical measurements have shown, this results in significantly less calculations
of minimal conflict sets, i.e., less executions of QUICKXPLAIN.

Figure 1 shows the progression of the following values, averaged over 18 runs,
during the course of 101 generations (the randomized starting population plus
the 100 subsequent generations):

– *generated minimal conflict sets per generation* (triangles)
– *generated globally new minimal conflict sets per generation* (squares)
– *accumulated unique minimal conflict sets* (dots)

As could be expected, the number of additional globally new minimal conflict
sets tends to decrease in later generations.

The program ran 18 times with 101 generations (the randomized starting
population plus the 100 subsequent generations) of 100 individuals (sets of user
requirements) each. This results in 181,800 consistency checks. In comparison,
checking every possible combination of user requirements for consistency systematically would result in $3.65e^{17}$ solver calls. Obviously, a genetic approach can
not guarantee an optimal solution [8,9,15], i.e., it can not be guaranteed that
all possible minimal conflict sets have been found. However, after 18 runs using
the above mentioned configuration, 183 unique minimal conflict sets were found.
Upon integrating these minimal conflict sets into the configurator, it could be
found that, in the case of inconsistent user requirements, the time from starting
the request until getting a response could be reduced by the factor 13 from 2 s
to 155 ms. Furthermore, the time from starting a diagnosis to getting a result
could be reduced by the factor 6 from 15 s to 2.5 s. This results in a significant
improvement concerning the usability of the configurator.

---

[2] A mutation means that the user requirement will either not be set with a probability
   of $P_\emptyset$ or that it will randomly be given a value out of the possible values.
[3] The current implementation does not support multiple populations. See Sect. 5 for
   further details.

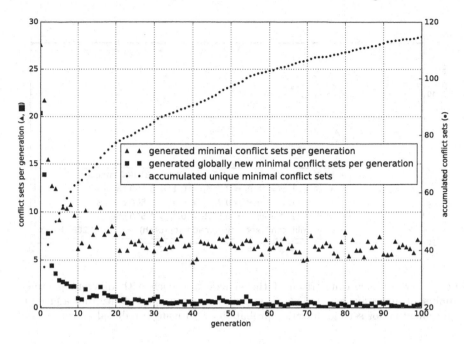

Fig. 1. Average number of conflicts detected by the genetic algorithm per randomized starting population after 18 runs.

As can be seen from Fig. 1, there are few globally new minimal conflict sets after generation 30. Therefore, it would be advisable to limit the number of generations per run to this number and randomize a new starting generation at this point.

Furthermore, a second evaluation has been conducted to determine, how many of all the potentially existing minimal conflict sets can be found with the approach described in this paper. For this, we used a reduced knowledge base so that all potentially existing minimal conflict sets can be found in a reasonable time by systematically checking all possible combinations of user requirements. The systematical approach showed that there are 47 possible minimal conflict sets. 23,147,208 consistency checks were necessary to get all of these minimal conflict sets. Afterwards, the genetic approach has been evaluated with different numbers of successive generations (G) and different variations of the parameters N (the population size), $P_\emptyset$ (the probability that a given user requirement is not set) and P_m (the mutation probability). The results can be seen in Fig. 2.

Figure 2 shows that the genetic approach is, in most test cases, able to deliver all potentially existing minimal conflict sets with a fraction of needed consistency checks. The first test (squares) has been conducted using 31 generations (G), each with an N of 100, a $P_\emptyset$ of 0.7 and a P_m of 0.1. After three runs with this setting, and thus after 9,300 consistency checks, all minimal conflict sets have been detected. This is about 0.04% of the consistency checks needed for

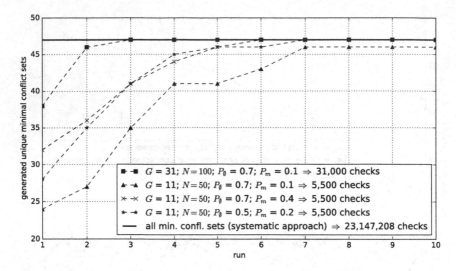

Fig. 2. Performance comparison of the genetic approach with different parameters (number of successive generations G, population size N, probability that a given user requirement is not set $P_\emptyset$, mutation probability P_m) using a reduced knowledge base.

the systematic approach. When reducing G and N, while leaving $P_\emptyset$ and P_m the same (triangles), it can be seen that after 10 runs (5,500 consistency checks) 46 of 47 minimal conflict sets could be found. However, it is possible to get better detection rates by changing P_m and $P_\emptyset$. Figure 2 shows the best empirically found values for P_m (x-symbols) and $P_\emptyset$ (stars). By setting P_m to 0.4, all potentially existing minimal conflict sets could be found after 3,300 consistency checks (6 runs), which is about 0.014% of the systematic approach. A similar effect could be observed when setting $P_\emptyset$ to 0.5, which resulted in 3,850 (7 runs), which is about 0.017% of the systematic approach.

5   Future Work

Issues for future work are the following:

Multiple simultaneous colonies: As has been mentioned in the previous section, there are hardly any globally new minimal conflict sets generated after generation 30 any more. This leads to the conclusion that it would make sense to create multiple randomized starting populations – called *colonies* – and let them run simultaneously. Furthermore, it would make sense to enable migration between the colonies to a certain degree in order to avoid local optima. A colony could also be discarded (*extinction*) if it doesn't generate globally new minimal conflict sets any more. In this case, a new colony could be randomly generated to replace the extinct one.

Handle changing knowledge bases: Currently, the only way to handle a changing knowledge base is to discard the already known minimal conflict sets and to restart the algorithm described in this paper. However, this could be optimized in future by updating the known minimal conflict sets with only the differences between the old and the new knowledge bases.

Adapt grounded program according to minimal conflict sets: The sizes of grounded answer set programs tend to become very large with the higher complexity of knowledge bases. By reducing the grounded program with the help of the generated list of minimal conflict sets, the memory and CPU time consumption can therefore be reduced.

Give live feedback to the user: The minimal conflict sets generated by the approach described in this paper are currently used only when the user decides to send the currently entered requirements to the configurator. However, an improved user interface could also asynchronously check the currently entered user requirements for known minimal conflict sets and warn the user as soon as a conflict is present. This would avoid frustration of the user by displaying arising inconsistencies as early as possible.

6   Conclusion

In this paper, we have introduced a new way of proactively finding minimal conflict sets based on different combinations of user requirements and a given knowledge base using a genetic algorithm. This approach has shown to generate a large number of minimal conflict sets using a fraction of the consistency checks that would have been necessary when systematically checking all possible combinations of user requirements. Furthermore, minimal conflict sets integrated into the configurator led to a 13 times faster detection of inconsistent user requirements. A diagnosis is delivered 6 times faster than before. This paper has also shown that, with the correct parameterization of the algorithm, all potentially existing minimal conflict sets can be found using a fraction of the consistency checks that would have been needed when systematically searching for minimal conflict sets. As future work, among other performance improvements, we will extend the system to simulate multiple concurrent colonies. Furthermore, we will conduct research related to handling changing knowledge bases, optimizing the grounded program with the generated minimal conflict sets, and how to give the user of the configurator live feedback in the case of inconsistencies.

References

1. Carneiro, D., Novais, P., Neves, J.: Using genetic algorithms to create solutions for conflict resolution. Neurocomputing **109**, 16–26 (2013). http://www.sciencedirect. com/science/article/pii/S0925231212006741. New trends on Soft Computing Models in Industrial and Environmental Applications
2. Felfernig, A., Schubert, M., Zehentner, C.: An efficient diagnosis algorithm for inconsistent constraint sets. Artif. Intell. Eng. Des. Anal. Manuf. **26**(1), 53–62 (2012)

3. Felfernig, A., Falkner, A., Atas, M., Polat-Erdeniz, S., Uran, C., Azzoni, P.: ASP-based knowledge representations for IoT configuration scenarios. In: 19th International Configuration Workshop, p. 62 (2017)
4. Felfernig, A., Hotz, L., Bagley, C., Tiihonen, J.: Knowledge-Based Configuration: From Research to Business Cases, 1st edn. Morgan Kaufmann Publishers Inc., San Francisco (2014)
5. Fleischanderl, G., Friedrich, G.E., Haselbock, A., Schreiner, H., Stumptner, M.: Configuring large systems using generative constraint satisfaction. IEEE Intell. Syst. Appl. **13**(4), 59–68 (1998)
6. Junker, U.: QUICKXPLAIN: preferred explanations and relaxations for over-constrained problems. In: Proceedings of the 19th National Conference on Artificial Intelligence, AAAI 2004, pp. 167–172. AAAI Press (2004). http://dl.acm.org/citation.cfm?id=1597148.1597177
7. Man, K.F., Tang, K.S., Kwong, S.: Genetic algorithms: concepts and applications. IEEE Trans. Industr. Electron. **43**(5), 519–534 (1996)
8. Marra, M.A., Walcott, B.L.: Stability and optimality in genetic algorithm controllers. In: Proceedings of the 1996 IEEE International Symposium on Intelligent Control, pp. 492–496, September 1996
9. Mitchell, M.: An Introduction to Genetic Algorithms. MIT Press, Cambridge (1998)
10. Nielsen, J.: Usability Engineering. Morgan Kaufmann Publishers Inc., San Francisco (1993)
11. Pu, P., Chen, L.: Trust building with explanation interfaces. In: Proceedings of the 11th International Conference on Intelligent User Interfaces, IUI 2006, pp. 93–100. ACM, New York (2006). https://doi.org/10.1145/1111449.1111475
12. Reiter, R.: A theory of diagnosis from first principles. Artif. Intell. **32**(1), 57–95 (1987). https://doi.org/10.1016/0004-3702(87)90062-2
13. Stumptner, M.: An overview of knowledge-based configuration. AI Commun. **10**(2), 111–125 (1997). http://dl.acm.org/citation.cfm?id=1216064.1216069
14. Walter, R., Felfernig, A., Küchlin, W.: Constraint-based and SAT-based diagnosis of automotive configuration problems. J. Intell. Inf. Syst. (JIIS), 1–32 (2016)
15. Whitley, D.: A genetic algorithm tutorial. Stat. Comput. **4**(2), 65–85 (1994)

An Algorithm for Combinatorial Double Auctions Based on Cooperative Coevolution of Particle Swarms

Fu-Shiung Hsieh$^{(\boxtimes)}$ (iD) and Yi-Hong Guo

Chaoyang University of Technology, Taichung 41349, Taiwan
fshsieh@cyut.edu.tw, s10527613@gm.cyut.edu.tw

Abstract. A combinatorial double auction is a type of double-side auction which makes buyers and sellers trade goods more conveniently than multiple combinatorial auctions. However, the winner determination problem (WDP) in combinatorial double auctions poses a challenge due to computation complexity. Particle swarm optimization (PSO) is one of the well-known meta-heuristic approaches to deal with complex optimization problems. Although there are many studies on combinatorial auctions, there is little study on application of PSO approach in combinatorial double auctions. In this paper, we consider combinatorial double auction problem in which there are transaction costs, supply constraints and non-negative surplus constraints. We formulate the WDP of combinatorial double auction problem as an integer programming problem formulation. As standard discrete PSO algorithm suffers from the premature convergence problem, we adopt a cooperative coevolution approach to develop a discrete cooperative coevolving particle swarm optimization (DCCPSO) algorithm that can scale with the problem better. The effectiveness of the proposed algorithm is illustrated by several numerical examples by comparing the results with standard DPSO algorithm.

Keywords: Meta-heuristics · Particle swarm · Coevolution
Combinatorial double auction · Integer programming

1 Introduction

Auctions are a popular business model for buying and selling goods or services efficiently. One of the recent trends in the development of auction mechanisms is combinatorial double auctions, which makes it possible for buyers and sellers to trade goods conveniently by placing bids on a combination of goods according to personal preferences rather than just individual items. Combinatorial double auctions are beneficial if complementarities exist between the items to be auctioned. The problem to determine winners in combinatorial double auctions is called the winner determination problem (WDP), which is one of the most challenging research topics on combinatorial double auctions. An excellent survey on combinatorial auctions can be found in the works of de Vries and Vohra [1] and Pekeč and Rothkopf [2]. Combinatorial auctions are notoriously difficult to solve from a computational point of view (Rothkopf et al. [3], Xia et al.[4] due to the exponential growth of the number of combinations in

© Springer International Publishing AG, part of Springer Nature 2018
M. Mouhoub et al. (Eds.): IEA/AIE 2018, LNAI 10868, pp. 187–199, 2018.
https://doi.org/10.1007/978-3-319-92058-0_18

solving the WDP. The WDP can be modeled as a set packing problem (SPP) (Vemuganti [5], Andersson et al. [6], Fujishima et al. [7], Hoos and Boutilier [8]). Sandholm et al. mentions that WDP for combinatorial auction is NP-complete (Sandholm [9–11]). Many centralized algorithms have been developed for WDP.

In this paper, we will propose a meta-heuristic method to solve the above mentioned problem based on swarm intelligence. Particle swarm optimization (PSO), proposed by Kennedy and Eberhart [12], is one of the well-known evolutionary meta-heuristics. PSO is a population based optimization method. Its development was based on observations of the social behavior of animals such as bird flocking, fish schooling and swarm theory. PSO has been applied successfully to nonlinear constrained optimization problems (El-Galland et al. [13]), neural networks (Van den Bergh and Engelbrecht [14], scheduling problems (Tasgetiren et al. [15]), etc. Previous versions of the particle swarm have operated in continuous space, where trajectories are defined as changes in position on some number of dimensions. In [16], Kennedy and Eberhart also proposed a reworking of the algorithm to operate on discrete binary variables. In [16], trajectories of particles are changes in the probability that a decision variable will take on a zero or one value. In the existing literature, many studies indicate that PSO was shown to perform very poorly as problems grow. For example, differential evolution (DE), EA, and PSO were compared in [17], PSO is unable to handle high-dimensional problems [18]. Many efforts have been made to tackle high-dimensional optimization problems. One approach is to adopt a divide-and-conquer strategy. Potter and De Jong [19] provides an approach called cooperative coevolution to decompose a high-dimensional problem into subproblems first and then tackle its subproblems individually. Multiple subpopulations coevolve cooperatively, each dealing with a subproblem of a lower dimensionality. An overall solution is derived from combinations of subsolutions evolved from individual subpopulations. The original cooperative coevolution performed poorly on nonseparable problems due to the interdependencies among different variables [19]. Van den Bergh and Engelbrecht developed two cooperative PSO models, CPSO-Sk and CPSO-Hk, by applying Potter's cooperative coevolution model to PSO [18]. Yang et al. suggested a new decomposition strategy based on random grouping [20]. Li and Yao [21] demonstrates that combining cooperative coevolution PSO and random grouping is an effective divide-and-conquer strategy that can be utilized to help scaling up PSO's performance for solving problems with a large number of variables. However, the above studies focus on optimization problem with real-valued decision variables. As combinatorial double auctions can be formulated as a discrete optimization problem with binary decision variables, further studies are required to test the applicability of these methods in discrete optimization problems.

In this paper, we will propose a discrete cooperative coevolving particle swarm optimization (DCCPSO) algorithm to solve combinatorial double auction problems based on the concept of cooperative coevolving particle swarms. This paper is different from the work [22] in two aspects. First, it focuses on combinatorial double auction problems instead of single-side combinatorial auctions. Second, the proposed DCCPSO algorithm is based on the cooperative coevolving particle swarms to improve performance. To study the performance of the proposed DCCPSO algorithm in solving the combinatorial double auction problem, we also implement a discrete PSO algorithm

(DPSO) for combinatorial double auction problems based on the method proposed by Kennedy and Eberhart [16]. We compare the performance of DCCPSO algorithm and DPSO algorithm in solving combinatorial double auction problems. We present the proposed method by numerical examples. To illustrate the effectiveness of the proposed method, we also compare the results obtained by our DCCPSO algorithm with those of DPSO algorithm.

The remainder of this paper is organized as follows. In Sect. 2, we first we formulate the WDP for combinatorial double auctions. We briefly introduce the way to handle constraints and the fitness function in Sect. 3 and present the DCCPSO algorithm in Sect. 4, respectively. We present our numerical results in Sect. 5 and conclude this paper in Sect. 6.

2 Problem Formulation for Combinatorial Double Auctions

In this paper, we first formulate the combinatorial double auction problem as an integer programming problem. We then develop a meta-heuristic algorithm for it. In a combinatorial double auction, there are a set of buyers, a set of sellers and a mediator for trading goods between the buyers and sellers. Buyers and sellers submit bids to the mediator. The surplus of a combinatorial double auction is the difference between winning buyers' total bid price and winning sellers' total bid price. A combinatorial double auction problem can be modeled as an optimization problem that maximizes the surplus. To formulate the problem, the following notations are defined.

Notations

K :   the number of different types of items in the combinatorial double auction.

I :   the number of potential sellers in a combinatorial double auction. Each $i \in \{1, 2, 3, \ldots, I\}$ represents a seller.

N :   the number of potential buyers in a combinatorial double auction. Each $n \in \{1, 2, 3, \ldots, N\}$ represents a buyer.

J_i :   the number of bids placed by seller $i \in \{1, 2, 3, \ldots, I\}$.

H_n :   the number of bids placed by buyer $n \in \{1, 2, 3, \ldots, N\}$.

d_{nhk} :   the buyer-n's desired units of the $k - th$ items in the $h - th$ bid, where $k \in \{1, 2, 3, \ldots, K\}$.

j :   the $j - th$ bid submitted by a seller in a combinatorial double auction.

h :   the $h - th$ bid created by a buyer in a combinatorial double auction.

p_{sij} :   the price of the $j - th$ bid submitted by seller i.

q_{ijk} :
a nonnegative integer that denotes the quantity of the $k-th$ items in the $j-th$ bid submitted by seller i.

$SB_{ij} = (q_{ij1}, q_{ij2}, q_{ij3}, \ldots, q_{ijK}, p_{sij})$:
a vector to represent the $j-th$ bid submitted by seller i. The $j-th$ bid SB_{ij} is actually an offer to deliver q_{ijk} units of items for each $k \in \{1, 2, 3, \ldots., K\}$ with a total price of p_{sij}.

x_{ij} :
the variable to indicate the $j-th$ bid placed by seller i is a winning bid ($x_{ij} = 1$) or not ($x_{ij} = 0$).

p_{bnh} :
the price of the $h-th$ bid submitted by buyer n

$BB_{nh} = (d_{nh1}, d_{nh2}, d_{nh3}, \ldots, d_{nhK}, p_{bnh})$:
a vector to represent the $h-th$ bid submitted by buyer n. The $h-th$ bid BB_{nh} is actually an offer to deliver d_{nhk} units of items for each $k \in \{1, 2, 3, \ldots., K\}$ with a total price of p_{bnh}.

y_{nh} :
the variable to indicate the $h-th$ bid placed by buyer n is a winning bid ($y_{nh} = 1$) or not ($y_{nh} = 0$).

T_s :
the transaction cost coefficient for a seller to the mediator

T_b :
the transaction cost coefficient for a buyer to the mediator.

The winner determination problem is formulated as follows. There are several constraints for the WDP in combinatorial double auctions, including the supply/demand constraints in (1), non-negative surplus constraints in (2) and the constraints on available items in (3). Note that (1) means that, for each type of item, the total amount of goods supplied by the sellers' winning bids must be greater than or equal to the demands of the buyers' winning bids.

Winner Determination Problem (WDP):

$$\max F(x,y) = \sum_{n=1}^{N} \sum_{h=1}^{H} y_{nh} p_{bnh} - \sum_{i=1}^{I} \sum_{j=1}^{J} x_{ij} p_{sij} + \sum_{n=1}^{N} \sum_{h=1}^{H} y_{nh} T_b p_{bnh} + \sum_{i=1}^{I} \sum_{j=1}^{J} x_{ij} T_s p_{sij}$$

s.t.

$$\sum_{i=1}^{I} \sum_{j=1}^{J} x_{ij} q_{ijk} \geq \sum_{n=1}^{N} \sum_{h=1}^{H} y_{nh} d_{nhk} \quad \forall k \in \{1, 2, \ldots, K\} \tag{1}$$

$$\sum_{n=1}^{N} \sum_{h=1}^{H} y_{nh} p_{bnh} \geq \sum_{i=1}^{I} \sum_{j=1}^{J} x_{ij} p_{sij} \qquad (2)$$

$$\sum_{j=1}^{J} x_{ij} q_{ijk} \leq s_{ik} \quad \forall i \in \{1, \ldots, I\}, k \in \{1, \ldots, K\}$$

$$(3)$$

$$x_{ij} \in \{0, 1\} \, \forall i, j$$

$$y_{nh} \in \{0, 1\} \, \forall n, h$$

3 Fitness Function

Note that the combinatorial double auction problem formulated previously is an optimization problem with binary decision variables and constraints. These constraints must be handled properly in the proposed algorithm. In existing literature, several methods to handle constraints have been proposed, including methods based on preserving feasibility of solutions, methods based on penalty functions and methods based on biasing feasible over infeasible solutions. Two popular constraint handling methods are the methods of penalty function [23, 24] and the methods based on biasing feasible over infeasible solutions [25]. In this paper, we adopt a method based on biasing feasible over infeasible solutions [25].

Let $S_f : S_f = \{(x, y) | (x, y) \text{ is a solution in the current population, } (x, y) \text{ satisfies}$ constraints$\}$ is the set of all feasible solutions in the current population.

$S_{fmin} : S_{fmin} = \min\limits_{(x,y) \in S_f} F(x, y)$, the object function value of the worst feasible solution in the current population.

The fitness function $F_1(x, y)$ is defined as follows:

$$F_1(x, y) = \begin{cases} F(x, y) & if \quad (x, y) \text{ satisfies constraints} \\ U_1(x, y) & otherwise \end{cases} \text{ , where}$$

$$U_1(x, y) = S_{fmin} + \sum_{k=1}^{K} ((\min(\sum_{i=1}^{I} \sum_{j=1}^{J} x_{ij} q_{ijk} - \sum_{n=1}^{N} \sum_{h=1}^{H} y_{nh} d_{nhk}), 0.0))$$

$$+ \min(\sum_{n=1}^{N} \sum_{h=1}^{H} y_{nh} p_{nh} - \sum_{i=1}^{I} \sum_{j=1}^{J} x_{ij} p_{ij}, 0.0)$$

$$+ \sum_{i=1}^{I} \sum_{k=1}^{K} \min(s_{ik} - \sum_{j=1}^{J} x_{ij} q_{ijk}, 0.0)$$

4 Discrete Cooperative Coevolving Particle Swarm Optimization (DCCPSO) Algorithm

This paper focuses on the development of an algorithm for combinatorial double auctions based on a particle swarm approaches. It is well-known that PSO performs very poorly as the size of a problem increases. To tackle this dimensionality issue, we adopt a divide-and-conquer strategy and the idea of cooperative coevolution PSO to dynamically decompose a higher dimensional problem into subproblems of a lower dimensionality, solve subproblems individually and cooperatively evolve solutions. An overall solution is derived from combinations of subsolutions for subproblems, where subsolutions are cooperatively evolved from individual subpopulations. The dynamic decomposition strategy is based on random grouping to increase the probability of allocating two interacting variables to the same subproblems (subcomponents). The dynamic decomposition strategy makes it possible to optimize these interacting variables in the same subproblem (subcomponent).

To describe the DCCPSO Algorithm, we define the following notations.

NS :	The number of swarms
DS :	A set of integers that represent the dimension of each swarm
ds :	An integer that represents the dimension of each swarm; ds is selected from DS
N :	The dimension of a solution; $N = NS \times ds$
s :	The index of a swarm, where $s \in \{1, 2, \ldots, NS\}$
π :	A permutation of the elements of set $\{1, 2, \ldots, N\}$
pop :	The number of particles in a swarm
π_s :	A subsequence of π, where $s \in \{1, 2, \ldots, NS\}$
SW_s :	The s-th swarm.
$SW_s \cdot x_i$:	The x component of the i-th particle in the s-th swarm SW_s
$SW_s \cdot y_i$:	The y component of the i-th particle in the s-th swarm SW_s
$SW_s \cdot x_i^p$:	The personal best of the x component of the i-th particle in the s-th swarm
$SW_s \cdot y_i^p$:	The personal best of the y component of the i-th particle in the s-th swarm
$SW_s \cdot \hat{x}$:	The global best of the x component of the s-th swarm
$SW_s \cdot \hat{y}$:	The global best of the y component of the s-th swarm
$SW_s \cdot vx_{id}$:	The velocity of x component of the i-th particle in the s-th swarm SW_s
$SW_s \cdot vy_{id}$:	The velocity of y component of the i-th particle in the s-th swarm SW_s
V_{max} :	The maximum value of velocity
$sigmoid$:	The sigmoid function

$\hat{x}$: The context vector of the x component constructed by a concatenation of the x component of all global best particles from all NS swarms

$\hat{y}$: The context vector of the y component constructed by a concatenation of the y component of all global best particles from all NS swarms

$\Gamma(s, SW_s \cdot x_i, SW_s \cdot y_i)$: A function that returns a N dimensional vector consisting of $\hat{x}$ and $\hat{y}$ with its s-th component replaced by $SW_s \cdot x_i$ and $SW_s \cdot y_i$, respectively

The proposed DCCPSO algorithm which employs random grouping with dynamically changing group size is outlined below. Suppose the dimension of a solution is N. A solution represented by a N dimensional vector can be split into NS subcomponents, each corresponding to a swarm of ds-dimensions (where $N = NS \times ds$), where ds is chosen uniformly at random from a set DS of integers that represent the dimension of each swarm. The proposed DCCPSO algorithm solves the problem by creating NS swarms, SW_s for each $s \in \{1, 2, \ldots, NS\}$ in Step 1. In order to evaluate the fitness of a particle in a swarm, a context vector $(\hat{x}, \hat{y})$ is constructed, which is a concatenation of all global best particles from all NS swarms. The two nested loops in Step 2 iterate through each swarm and each particle in that swarm to check the personal best $(SW_s \cdot x_i^p, SW_s \cdot y_i^p)$ and the swarm best $(SW_s \cdot \hat{x}, SW_s \cdot \hat{y})$ s of the s-th swarm SW_s for update. The s-th swarm best $(SW_s \cdot \hat{x}, SW_s \cdot \hat{y})$ is used to update the context vector $(\hat{x}, \hat{y})$ if it is better. In the second nested loop, each particle's personal best, neighborhood best, and its corresponding swarm best are used to calculate the particle's next position.

Discrete Cooperatively Coevolving Particle Swarms Optimization (CCPSO) Algorithm

While termination criterion is not met

{

Step 0: Select ds from DS

Step 1:

Randomly generate a permutation π of the set $\{1,2,...,N\}$ of numbers.

Partition π into NS subsequence π_s, where $s \in \{1,2,...,NS\}$.

For each $s \in \{1,2,...,NS\}$

    Assign π_s to construct the indices for the s-th swarm SW_s

End For

For each $s \in \{1,2,...,NS\}$

    Initialize swarm SW_s

End For

Step 2:

For each $s \in \{1,2,...,NS\}$

    For each particle $i \in SW_s$

        If $F_1(\Gamma(s,SW_s.x_i,SW_s.y_i)) > F_1(\Gamma(s,SW_s.x_i^p,SW_s.y_i^p))$

            $SW_s.x_i^p \leftarrow SW_s.x_i$

            $SW_s.y_i^p \leftarrow SW_s.y_i$

        End If

        If $F_1(\Gamma(s,SW_s.x_i^p,SW_s.y_i^p)) > F_1(\Gamma(s,SW_s.\hat{x},SW_s.\hat{y}))$

            $SW_s.\hat{x} \leftarrow SW_s.x_i^p$

            $SW_s.\hat{y} \leftarrow SW_s.y_i^p$

        End If

        If $F_1(\Gamma(s,SW_s.\hat{x},SW_s.\hat{y})) > f(\hat{x},\hat{y})$

            The elements of $\hat{x}$ corresponding to the s-th swarm SW_s is replaced by $SW_s.\hat{x}$

            The elements of $\hat{y}$ corresponding to the s-th swarm SW_s is replaced by $SW_s.\hat{y}$

        End If

    End For

End For

For each $s \in \{1,2,...,NS\}$

For each particle $i \in SW_s$

Perform velocity update for the i-th particle in SW_s

For each $d \in \{1,2,...,ds\}$

Generate a Gaussian random variable

$$rx = \eta(\frac{(SW_s.x_i^P + SW_s.\hat{x})}{2}, |SW_s.x_i^P - SW_s.\hat{x}|)$$

Update velocity $SW_s.vx_{id} = rx$

$$ry = \eta(\frac{(SW_s.y_i^P + SW_s.\hat{y})}{2}, |SW_s.y_i^P - SW_s.\hat{y}|)$$

Update velocity $SW_s.vy_{id} = ry$

End For

End For

End For

}

In updating velocity, a constant V_{max} is used to limit the range of $SW_s \cdot vx_{id}$ and $SW_s \cdot vy_{id}$ to $[-V_{max}, +V_{max}]$. In calculating the values of the fitness function, the following procedure is performed by each particle to transform the velocity $SW_s \cdot vx_{id}$ and $SW_s \cdot vy_{id}$ of a particle by applying a sigmoid function to 1 or 0 as follows.

Procedure to Transform Velocity $(SW_s \cdot vx_{id}, SW_s \cdot vy_{id})$ to $(SW_s \cdot x_i, SW_s \cdot y_i)$

Calculate the velocity of particle i as follows

If $SW_s.vx_{id} > V_{max}$

$SW_s.vx_{id} \leftarrow V_{max}$

End If

If $SW_s.vx_{id} < -V_{max}$

$SW_s.vx_{id} \leftarrow -V_{max}$

End If $vy_{id}^t = vy_{id}^{t-1} + c_1 r_1 (Py_{id}^t - y_{id}^t) + c_2 r_2 (Gy_{id}^t - y_{id}^t)$

If $SW_s.vy_{id} > V_{max}$

$SW_s.vy_{id} \leftarrow V_{max}$

End If

If $SW_s.vy_{id} < -V_{max}$

$SW_s.vy_{id} \leftarrow -V_{max}$

End If

$$sigmoid(SW_s \cdot vx_{id}) = \frac{1}{1 + \exp^{-SW_s \cdot vx_{id}}}$$

$$sigmoid(SW_s \cdot vy_{id}) = \frac{1}{1 + \exp^{-SW_s \cdot vy_{id}}}$$

Update position of particle i as follows
Generate $rsid$, a random variable with uniform distribution $U(0,1)$

$$x_{id}^t = \begin{cases} 1 & rsid < sigmoid(SW_s \cdot vx_{id}) \\ 0 & otherwise \end{cases}$$

Generate $rsid$, a random variable with uniform distribution $U(0,1)$

$$y_{id}^t = \begin{cases} 1 & rsid < sigmoid(SW_s \cdot vy_{id}) \\ 0 & otherwise \end{cases}$$

5 Numerical Results

Although there are benchmarks for testing algorithms for combinatorial auctions, there still lacks a benchmark for combinatorial double auctions. For this reason, we develop a simulation environment to generate test cases for combinatorial double auctions. Our simulation environment generates test cases for combinatorial double auctions based on the number of buyers, the number of sellers, the number of different types of goods to be traded and the upper bound on the number of available quantity for each item. We conduct several numerical experiments to illustrate the effectiveness of the proposed meta-heuristic algorithm for combinatorial double auctions.

Example: Suppose there are five sellers and five buyers that will trade goods in a combinatorial double auction. There are ten types of items (goods). The bids placed by the sellers and buyers are shown in Tables 1 and 2, respectively.

Table 1. The bids placed by five buyers.

Buyer	$k = 1$	$k = 2$	$k = 3$	$k = 4$	$k = 5$	$k = 6$	$k = 7$	$k = 8$	$k = 9$	$k = 10$	Price
$n = 1$	0	1	2	0	1	0	2	2	1	1	650
$n = 2$	0	2	1	0	3	4	0	0	0	0	540
$n = 3$	6	0	0	4	0	7	4	0	1	0	828
$n = 4$	0	0	3	0	0	1	0	0	2	1	475
$n = 5$	3	0	1	4	3	5	4	1	0	0	762

For this example, the parameter of the DCCPSO algorithm is set as follows: $DS = \{2, 5, 10\}$, $V_{max} = 4$ and $pop = 10$. By applying the proposed DCCPSO algorithm, the solution found is $x_{11} = 1$, $x_{21} = 1$, $x_{31} = 1$, $x_{41} = 1$, $x_{51} = 1$, $y_{11} = 1$, $y_{21} = 0$, $y_{31} = 1$, $y_{41} = 0$, $y_{51} = 0$. The value of objective function for this solution is 2142.4 and the number of iterations (generations) is 3.

Table 2. The bids placed by five sellers.

Seller	$k = 1$	$k = 2$	$k = 3$	$k = 4$	$k = 5$	$k = 6$	$k = 7$	$k = 8$	$k = 9$	$k = 10$	Price
$i = 1$	2	3	0	2	0	1	1	0	0	0	168
$i = 2$	2	0	1	0	1	4	1	2	1	0	240
$i = 3$	0	0	1	2	0	0	3	0	0	0	120
$i = 4$	2	0	1	0	2	4	1	0	1	0	270
$i = 5$	2	1	0	0	0	3	0	0	0	2	238

In addition to the example above, we also compare the performance of our proposed algorithm with other approach by conducting several experiments for several test cases. For each test case, the averaged results of 20 independent runs were recorded. For each run, the parameter of the DCCPSO algorithm is set as follows: $DS = \{2, 5, 10\}$, $V_{max} = 4$. The results for pop = 10 is shown in Table 3. These results indicate that the performance of DCCPSO algorithm is similar to that of DPSO algorithm for small examples such as test Case 1 and test Case 2 in Table 3. But DCCPSO algorithm outperforms DPSO algorithm as the problem size increases. DPSO algorithm even cannot generate good fitness function value for bigger examples due to premature convergence. The convergence speed for Case 6 is shown in Fig. 1.

Table 3. The bids placed by five sellers.

Case	N	I	K	PSO	Generation	DCCPSO	Generation
1	5	5	5	544.4	74.4	544.4	22.6
2	5	5	10	871	31.7	871	60.1
3	10	10	5	4274.76	5103.2	4342.2	2855.9
4	10	10	10	4720.25	4633.27	4726.8	1327.18
5	10	10	15	1132.42	3778.4	1314	697.7
6	15	15	5	916.1	5992.6	1227.25	2403.8
7	20	20	5	3856.49	27343.7	6371.73	16173.2

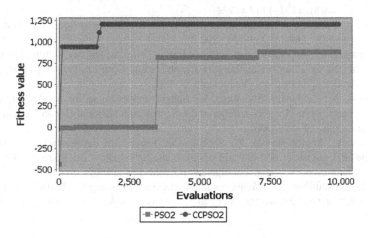

Fig. 1. Fitness values for Case 6.

6 Conclusions

In this paper, we develop a solution algorithm for combinatorial double auctions based on particle swarms. In addition, the proposed DCCPSO algorithm is based on the concept of cooperative coevolving particle swarms, which is also different from the standard discrete particle swarm optimization algorithm for single side combinatorial auctions. We formulate the WDP of combinatorial double auctions as an integer programming problem. The problem is to determine the winners to maximize the surplus of combinatorial double auctions. Due to computational complexity, it is hard to develop a computationally efficient method to find an exact optimal solution for the WDP of combinatorial double auctions. To reduce computational complexity, we adopt a meta-heuristic approach and develop a solution algorithm based on a discrete Particle swarm optimization approach. We conduct experiments to study the performance and computational efficiency of our proposed algorithm. To study the computational efficiency of our proposed algorithm, we conduct the experiments to compare the computational time of our algorithm with discrete PSO algorithm. Although our algorithm does not guarantee generation of optimal solutions, the numerical results indicate that our proposed DCCPSO algorithm is significantly more effective in comparison with discrete PSO algorithm.

Acknowledgment. This paper was supported in part by Ministry of Science and Technology, Taiwan, under Grant MOST-106-2410-H-324-002-MY2.

References

1. de Vries, S., Vohra, R.V.: Combinatorial auctions: a survey. INFORMS J. Comput. **15**(3), 284–309 (2003)
2. Pekeč, A., Rothkopf, M.H.: Combinatorial auction design. Manag. Sci. **49**(11), 1485–1503 (2003)
3. Rothkopf, M., Pekeč, A., Harstad, R.: Computationally manageable combinational auctions. Manag. Sci. **44**(8), 1131–1147 (1998)
4. Xia, M., Stallaert, J., Whinston, A.B.: Solving the combinatorial double auction problem. Eur. J. Oper. Res. **164**(1), 239–251 (2005)
5. Vemuganti, R.R.: Applications of set covering, set packing and set partitioning models: a survey. In: Du, D.-Z. (ed.) Handbook of Combinatorial Optimization, vol. 1, pp. 573–746. Kluwer Academic Publishers, Netherlands (1998)
6. Andersson, A., Tenhunen, M., Ygge, F.: Integer programming for combinatorial auction winner determination. In: Proceedings of the Seventeenth National Conference on Artificial Intelligence, pp. 39–46 (2000)
7. Fujishima, Y., Leyton-Brown, K., Shoham, Y.: Taming the computational complexity of combinatorial auctions: optimal and approximate approaches. In: Sixteenth International Joint Conference on Artificial Intelligence, pp. 548–553 (1999)
8. Hoos, H.H., Boutilier, C.: Solving combinatorial auctions using stochastic local search. In: Proceedings of the Seventeenth National Conference on Artificial Intelligence, pp. 22–29 (2000)

9. Sandholm, T.: An algorithm for optimal winner determination in combinatorial auctions. In: Proceedings of IJCAI 1999, Stockholm, pp. 542–547 (1999)
10. Sandholm, T.: Approaches to winner determination in combinatorial auctions. Decis. Support Syst. **28**(1–2), 165–176 (2000)
11. Sandholm, T.: Algorithm for optimal winner determination in combinatorial auctions. Artif. Intell. **135**(1–2), 1–54 (2002)
12. Kennedy, J., Eberhart, R.C.: Particle swarm optimization. In: Proceedings of IEEE International Conference on Neural Networks, Piscataway, NJ, pp. 1942–1948 (1995)
13. El-Galland, A.I., El-Hawary, M.E., Sallam, A.A.: Swarming of intelligent particles for solving the nonlinear constrained optimization problem. Eng. Intell. Syst. Electr. Eng. Commun. **9**(3), 155–163 (2001)
14. Van den Bergh, F., Engelbrecht, A.P.: Cooperative learning in neural network using particle swarm optimizers. S. Afr. Comput. J. **26**, 84–90 (2000)
15. Tasgetiren, M.F., Sevkli, M., Liang, Y.C., Gencyilmaz, G.: Particle swarm optimization algorithm for single machine total weighted tardiness problem. In: Proceedings of the IEEE congress on evolutionary computation, Oregon, Portland, vol. 2, pp. 1412–1419 (2004)
16. Kennedy, J., Eberhart, R.C., A discrete binary version of the particle swarm algorithm. In: 1997 IEEE International Conference on Systems, Man, and Cybernetics: Computational Cybernetics and Simulation, vol. 5, pp. 4104–4108 (1997)
17. Vesterstrom, J., Thomsen, R.: A comparative study of differential evolution, particle swarm optimization, and evolutionary algorithms on numerical benchmark problems. In: Proceedings of the 2004 Congress on Evolutionary Computation, vol. 2, pp. 1980–1987 (2004)
18. van den Bergh, F., Engelbrecht, A.P.: A cooperative approach to particle swarm optimization. IEEE Trans. Evol. Comput. **8**(3), 225–239 (2004)
19. Potter, M.A., De Jong, K.A.: A cooperative coevolutionary approach to function optimization. In: Davidor, Y., Schwefel, H.-P., Männer, R. (eds.) PPSN 1994. LNCS, vol. 866, pp. 249–257. Springer, Heidelberg (1994). https://doi.org/10.1007/3-540-58484-6_269
20. Yang, Z., Tang, K., Yao, X.: Large scale evolutionary optimization using cooperative coevolution. Inf. Sci. **178**(15), 2985–2999 (2008)
21. Li, X., Yao, X.: Cooperatively coevolving particle swarms for large scale optimization. IEEE Trans. Evol. Comput. **16**(2), 210–224 (2012)
22. Hsieh, F.-S.: A discrete particle swarm algorithm for combinatorial auctions. In: Tan, Y., Takagi, H., Shi, Y. (eds.) ICSI 2017. LNCS, vol. 10385, pp. 201–208. Springer, Cham (2017). https://doi.org/10.1007/978-3-319-61824-1_22
23. Ravindran, A., Ragsdell, K.M., Reklaitis, G.V.: Engineering Optimization: Methods and Applications, 2nd edn. Wiley, Hoboken (2007)
24. Deb, K.: Optimization for Engineering Design: Algorithms and Examples. Prentice-Hall, New Delhi (2004)
25. Deb, K.: An efficient constraint handling method for genetic algorithms. Comput. Methods Appl. Mech. Eng. **186**(2–4), 311–338 (2000)

Partition Crossover Evolutionary Algorithm for the Team Orienteering Problem with Time Windows

Ibtihel Ghobber[✉], Takwa Tlili, and Saoussen Krichen

LARODEC Laboratory, Institut Supérieur de Gestion Tunis,
Université de Tunis, Tunis, Tunisia
takwa.tlili@gmail.com

Abstract. The rapid evolution in tourism domain and new technologies make the search for the destination and site information for the tourists very difficult. In operations research field, this problem is modeled as Tourist Trip Design Problem (TTDP) which is about finding an optimal path-planning solution for tourists in order to visit multiple Points Of Interests (POIs). This paper addresses the team orienteering problem with time windows (TOPTW) that is an extension of TTDP. We apply for the first time the evolutionary algorithm based on partition crossover (EAPX) for solving the TOPTW. This approach is tested using a set of benchmarks then is compared to state-of-the-art algorithms to evaluate its performance. The results indicate the effectiveness of this method in solving the TOPTW.

Keywords: Team orienteering problem with time windows
Tourist Trip Design Problem · Partition crossover
Evolutionary algorithm · Meta-heuristics

1 Introduction

Tourists are often confused about selecting the interesting places to visit during their tour. Since there is a limitation in time and budget, tourists will select those destinations that have the more attractive Points of Interest (POIs). After discovering the interesting POIs, tourists decide to determine how many of them they can visit which path to follow, that fit their visiting time and travel budget limitations. In operations research, seeking for POIs and proposing a tour plan for tourists is modeled as Tourist Trip Design Problem (TTDP) that have been studied by numerous researchers. The main objective of this problem is finding the most interesting POIs that maximize tourist satisfaction, by incorporating visiting time limitations, and opening and closing days/hours of each POI. Gavalas et al. (2014) classified TTDP into two variants. The first is the single tour TTDP variants that aim to find a single path between nodes that maximizes the profit and minimizes the travel cost while the second variants

© Springer International Publishing AG, part of Springer Nature 2018
M. Mouhoub et al. (Eds.): IEA/AIE 2018, LNAI 10868, pp. 200–211, 2018.
https://doi.org/10.1007/978-3-319-92058-0_19

are the multiple tour TTDP which are characterized by determining a multiple POIs that the tourists need to visit with taking into account their visiting time. We focus on an extension of multiple tour TTDP which is the Team Orienteering Problem with Time Windows (TOPTW). This problem aims to find the optimal trip that respects tourists travel time and POIs' time windows and maximize their satisfaction which corresponds to maximize the total collected profit from each POI. Since the TOPTW is demonstrated as an NP-hard problem Vansteenwegen et al. (2009a) many meta-heuristic approaches are proposed in the literature to tackle it. Montemanni and Gambardella (2009) develop ant colony optimization (ACO) for solving TOPTW. This approach integrates ant colony system (ACS) algorithms which are based on a computational paradigm inspired by real ant colonies. It has two elements as follows. The construction phase in which feasible solutions are produced. The local search algorithm used to take down each solution generated in the construction phase to a local optimum. A very fast iterated local search (ILS) meta-heuristic is introduced by Vansteenwegen et al. (2009a) to deal with the TOPTW instances where it based on two steps as follows. The first is the insertion step attempts to add new visits to a tour. The second is the shake step is used to liberate local optima. The total average gap is only 1.8% compared to the ACS.

The main contribution of this paper is to present an evolutionary algorithm based on the partition crossover technique for solving the TOPTW. As noted that this algorithm has proved its performance in solving routing optimization problem. Herein, we detail its different steps and give its pseudo code. To validate the proposed model, we test a set of TOPTW benchmark instances. A comparative study is held to show the competitiveness of the proposed approach.

This paper is structured as follows. In Sect. 2, we define the TOPTW statement and propose its mathematical formulation. The proposed evolutionary algorithm based on partition crossover (EAPX) for TOPTW is explained in Sect. 3. In Sect. 4, computational experiments are provided. Section 5 summarizes the paper.

2 Problem Description

In e-tourism, the TOPTW is characterized by a set of POIs, where each point is associated with a profit which denotes its importance value for the tourist, a visit duration and a time window, as well as a travel time between each pair of POIs. The main goal this problem is to find a fixed number of disjoint routes from the starting node to the ending POI that respect a set of constraints.

Summarizing, the objective function of the TOPTW (1) seeks to maximize the total collected profit from each visited POI which corresponds to the maximization of tourist's ratings, depends on their preferences and considers the following constraints.

- The trip starts and ends at the hotel.
- Every POI is visited at most once.
- The total trip time is limited by $Tmax$.
- Each visit starts with a POI's time windows $[O_i, C_i]$.

2.1   Mathematical Formulation

The TOPTW involves a set of POIs, where each POI is associated with a score S_i a service time T_i and a time window $[O_i, C_i]$. For the depot vertex, which corresponds to the hotel e0 represents O_0 represents the the starting time to depart from the hotel and C_0 the arrival to it, as shown in the Fig. 1. This problem can be modeled as a graph $G = (V, A)$, where $V = \{1, \ldots, n\}$ is the set of POIs and $A = \{(i, j) | i, j \in V, i \neq j\}$ is the set of arcs that connect the POIs. Given m the number of tours. The starting location POI 1 and the end destination POI n of every tour are fixed. The travel time from POI i to POI j is denoted by t_{ij}. In this problem, not all locations can be visited since the total travel time is limited by a given time budget $Tmax$ and each POI can be visited at most once.

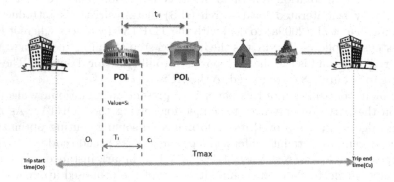

Fig. 1. The TOPTW illustration

Furthermore, the TOPTW uses the following parameters and decision variables.

The TOPTW objective function aims to determine m routes of maximum total collected scores (1).

$$Max\ Z(X) = \sum_{d=1}^{m} \sum_{i=2}^{n-1} S_i\, y_{id} \tag{1}$$

A number of constraints to be respected in the TOPTW can be as stated by (Vansteenwegen et al. 2009b; Cura 2014). These constraints are either (1) Routing constraints or (2) Time constraints detailed as follow.

Sets and parameters	
V	The total number of POIs
m	The number of tours
S_i	The score of POI i
T_i	The service time of POI i
$[O_i, C_i]$	The time window of POI i: The visit of POI i can only start during this time window
t_{ij}	The travel time from POI i to POI j
u_{id}	The position of location i in tour d
α_{ir}	The departure time from the location, which is at position r of tour d
$Tmax$	The maximum total travel time

Decision variables	
$x_{ijd} = \begin{cases} 1 & \text{if in path } d, \text{a visit to vertex } i \text{ is followed by a visit to vertex } j \\ 0 & \text{otherwise} \end{cases}$	
$y_{id} = \begin{cases} 1 & \text{if vertex } i \text{ is visited in path } d \\ 0 & \text{otherwise} \end{cases}$	

1. Routing constraints

$$\sum_{d=1}^{m}\sum_{j=2}^{n-1} x_{1jd} = \sum_{d=1}^{m}\sum_{i=2}^{n-1} x_{ind} = m \tag{2}$$

$$\sum_{d=1}^{m} y_{dk} \leq 1, k = 2, \ldots, n-1 \tag{3}$$

$$\sum_{i=1}^{n-1} x_{ikd} = \sum_{j=2}^{n-1} x_{kjd} = y_{kd}, k = 2, \ldots, n-1, d = 1, \ldots, m \tag{4}$$

$$2 \leq u_{id} \leq n, i = 2, \ldots, n; d = 1, \ldots, m \tag{5}$$

$$u_{id} - u_{jd} + 1 \leq (n-1)(1 - x_{ijd}), i = 2, \ldots, n; d = 1, \ldots, m \tag{6}$$

While the TOPTW can be considered as a vehicle routing problem, a set of routing requirements are taken into account. The constraints (2) guarantee that each tour starts from location 1 and ends at location n. Each POI is visited only once, ensured by Eq. (3). The continuity in a tour is needed in constraints (4) which guarantee that if a POI is visited in a given tour, it is preceded and followed by exactly one other POI in the same tour. The last routing constraints (5) and (6) are about preventing subtours.

2. Time constraints

$$\sum_{i=1}^{n-1}\left(T_i y_{id} + \sum_{j=2}^{n} t_{ij} x_{ijd}\right) \leq Tmax, d = 1, \ldots, m \alpha_{1d} = T_1 \tag{7}$$

$$\alpha_{1d} = T_1, d = 1, \ldots, m \tag{8}$$

$$\alpha_{rd} = max\left[\left(\alpha_{(r-1)d} + \sum_{i=2}^{n}\sum_{j=1}^{n-1}\begin{cases} t_{ij} x_{jid} y_{id} & \text{if } u_{id} = r \\ 0 & \text{otherwise}\end{cases}\right)\sum_{i=1}^{n}\begin{cases} O_i y_{id} & \text{if } u_{id} = r \\ 0 & \text{otherwise}\end{cases}\right. \tag{9}$$

$$\left. + \sum_{i=1}^{n}\begin{cases} T_i y_{id} & \text{if } u_{id} = r \\ 0 & \text{otherwise}\end{cases}\right., r = 2, \ldots, n; d = 1, \ldots, m \tag{10}$$

$$C_i \geq \sum_{d=1}^{m}\sum_{r=2}^{n}\begin{cases} y_{id}(\alpha_{rd} - T_i) & \text{if } u_{id} = r \\ 0 & \text{otherwise}\end{cases}, i = 1, \ldots, n \tag{11}$$

The TOPTW's time restrictions are described as the constraints (7) which guarantee that each tour is completed within a given time limit. The departure time from the first POI is calculated as shown in the constraint (8), moreover, the departure time from the POI r of tour d is given by the Eq. (10). Finally, the time window is defined by Eq. (11).

3   Evolutionary Algorithm Based on Partition Crossover (EAPX)

To solve the TOPTW we propose a new approach named EAPX. It includes the following three main steps. The first phase is the initial population used for the construction the initial solution while the second phase is a local search method used for the improvement of the solutions found in the first phase and partition crossover method for the production of the new generation. All these phases are more detailed in the following subsections. A flowchart depicting the proposed meta-heuristic is given in the Fig. 2.

3.1   Initial Population

The algorithm starts with generating the initial solution Sol_0 using of the both the petal algorithm (PA) and diversity. The petal is designed for building the first half of the initial population. Its description is presented by Ryan et al. (1993), where the nodes are radially numbered about the depot and each petal is formed by a list of radially successive nodes. A feasibility of the petal is proved only if the total travel time does not exceed the imposed time limit T_{max}, which corresponds to latest arrival time to the depot and the nodes' time windows not violated. In this case, we propose a random order of node for each petal. Moreover, the second half of the initial solution is produced by diversity. Another solution is built from each individual of the initial solution with considering a random number of nodes swaps in each sub-route. Our population is formed

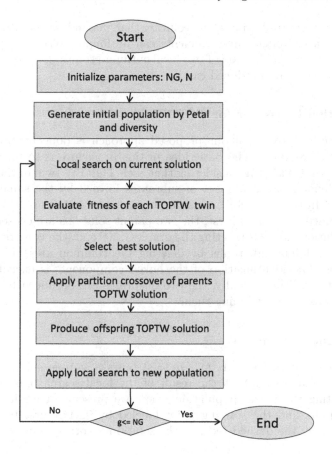

Fig. 2. A flowchart for the proposed EAPX meta-heuristic.

by two TOPTW solutions, constitute the twins. Therefore, each twin includes different sub-routes, which integrates a number of homogeneous petals. In order to find locally optimal solutions, we implement the 2-OPT operator method, used for decreasing the tour travel cost. This technique works on tour crossing over itself and reordered to find local optima tour.

3.2   Local Search

Given the initial population generated by the petal and diversity, a local search algorithm is proposed to improve the performance of the solution S. In this method, we implement many operations which, are detailed as follows. It starts with an arbitrary solution to the TOPTW then attempts to find a better solution by incrementally replacing two scheduled nodes within a route this process is done by the Swap operator. In this case, different combinations are processed for selecting the best nodes. The fitness value is calculated by the total profit. If the change produces a better solution, an incremental change is made to the new solution, repeating until finding the solution that maximizes the fitness of each individual with no further improvements can be found. According to Whitley et al. (2009), the recombination of two local optimum solutions by the PX results usually in local optima produced child.

3.3 Partition Crossover for TOPTW

The reproductive process of our proposed approach is done by the partition crossover (PX) operator. The basic idea of this procedure is to recombine the local optima solutions with considering that each TOPTW twin of the produced solution is divided into a number of subroutes formed by the same nodes for each subtour. In this case, for each subtour, the order of the applied procedure can be explained as follows. First, the two parent solutions are chosen from the TOPTW solutions for constructing the graph G. Second, the constructed graph G is partitioned into subgraphs by deleting the common arcs between these two solutions. The identification of the linked components is executed by the Breadth first algorithm. Finally, the two offsprings are produced from the two parent solutions by recombining them.

3.4 Illustrative Example

For the problem with 23 POIs and $m = 3$ tours a sample solution is shown in the Fig. 3. This example is the result of the local search operator applied after generating the initial population where we present an undirected graph G with 23 POIs and the starting point labeled by 0. The first twin presents the solution 1 by the dashed red line the solution 2 corresponds to the second

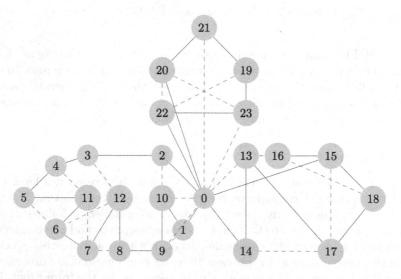

Fig. 3. An illustrative example including 23 POIs and 3 tours (Color figure online)

solution is shown by the solid blue line. In this case, the routes for the solution 1 in each tour are respectively $m1 = \{0, 1, 9, 8, 7, 11, 4, 5, 6, 12, 3, 2, 10, 0\}$, $m2 = \{0, 14, 17, 15, 18, 16, 13, 0\}$, and $m3 = \{0, 23, 20, 22, 19, 21, 0\}$ while for the solution 2 are presented as follows: $m1 = \{0, 1, 10, 9, 8, 12, 7, 6, 11, 5, 4, 3, 2, 0\}$, $m2 = \{0, 14, 13, 17, 18, 15, 0\}$, and $m3 = \{0, 22, 23, 19, 21, 20, 0\}$. After applying the partition crossover method the new generated offspring are showed in the Fig. 4 where the new routes of the first constructed offspring are respectively $m1 = \{0, 1, 10, 9, 8, 7, 11, 4, 5, 6, 12, 3, 2, 0\}$, $m2 = \{0, 14, 17, 15, 18, 16, 13, 0\}$, and $m3 = \{0, 23, 20, 22, 19, 21, 0\}$. The routes of each tour for the second offspring are detailed as follows: $m1 = \{0, 1, 10, 9, 8, 7, 11, 4, 55, 6, 12, 3, 2, 0\}$, $m2 = \{0, 14, 13, 17, 18, 15, 0\}$, and $m3 = \{0, 22, 23, 19, 21, 20, 0\}$.

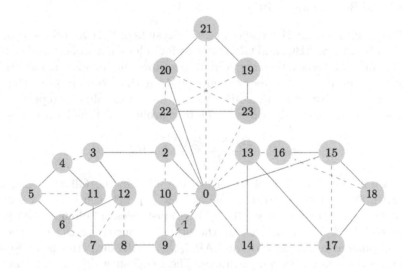

Fig. 4. A TOPTW solution presentation after applying PX (Color figure online)

4 Computational Experiments

The experimentation is designed to evaluate the performance of the EAPX in solving the TOPTW, using the benchmark instances. We first describe the TOPTW benchmark dataset. Then, we detail the results obtained from the experimentation and assess the effectiveness of the algorithm using a comparative study.

4.1 Experimental Setup

The EAPX was coded in Java language and running Windows 10. The experiments were run on a personal computer Hp equipped with Intel Pentium, 1,90 GHz CPU and 4 GB of RAM. In this case, for each instance of the benchmark, the EAPX is executed for 30 runs where its execution ends with best

TOPTW solutions and there is no improvement to be added. The parameters of the proposed algorithm are the number of generation NG = 50 and the number of individuals in half of the population N = 50.

4.2 Results and Discussion

In order to evaluate the performance of the EAPX approach in solving TOPTW, the obtained results are compared to the following methods.

(1) Iterated Local Search (ILS) (Vansteenwegen et al. 2009a) and
(2) Granular Variable Neighborhood Search Based on Linear Programming (GVNS) (Labadie et al. 2012).
(3) Artificial Bee Colony (ABC) (Cura 2014).

Tables 1 and 2 summarize respectively the results of EAPX and the comparison with ILS, GVNS, ABC, and GRASP-ELS for Solomon instances and Cordeau instances. In these tables, the first column describes the instance name, the second column contains the number of tours, and the third column gives the best-known solution (BKS) for the TOPTW. The following columns report respectively for each algorithm the value of the best profit, and the Gap (Sect. 4.2).

$$Gap = \frac{BKS - EAPX}{BKS} * 100\%$$

As seen in the Table 1 EAPX reaches the BKS in the following instances: c-100, r101, r102, r105 and rc107. The average gap between EAPX result and the best-known solution is only 1.39%. For 13 instances of Solomon the optimal solution of EAPX is known and for the other instances are close to the best known. Compared to ILS, GVNS, and ABC, the EAPX outperforms in Solomon instances better than Cordeau instances. The Fig. 5 shows the results noted in Table 1 where the curve shows the obtainment results of the BKS and EAPX for Solomon instances.

As reported in Table 2, EAPX reaches the best-known solution only in two instances are pr06, pr10. It appears that EAPX under performs in Cordeau instances compared to ILS, GVNS, and ABC while the total average gap is 2.54%. Then, based on the obtained results, we can conclude that the performance of EAPX in solving TOPTW instances and the quality of the solution is proved. Our proposed approach is able to produce a good solution to the TOPTW.

Table 1. EAPX vs state-of-the art algorithms (Solomon instances)

Instance	m	BKS	EAPX		ILS		GVNS		ABC	
			Cost	Gap (%)	Cost	Gap (%)	Cost	Gap (%)	Cost	Gap (%)
c101	10	1810	1810	0.0	1720	5.0	1754	3.1	1786	1.3
c102	10	1810	1810	0.0	1790	1.1	1794	0.9	1810	0.0
c103	10	1810	1810	0.0	1810	0.0	1810	0.0	1810	0.0
c104	10	1810	1810	0.0	1810	0.0	1810	0.0	1810	0.0
c105	10	1810	1810	0.0	1770	2.2	1810	0.0	1782	1.5
c106	10	1810	1810	0.0	1750	3.3	1806	0.2	1786	1.3
c107	10	1810	1810	0.0	1790	1.1	1810	0.0	1784	1.4
c108	10	1810	1810	0.0	1810	0.0	1810	0.0	1792	1.0
c109	10	1810	1810	0.0	1810	0.0	1810	0.0	1810	0.0
r101	19	1458	1458	0.0	1441	1.2	1432.2	1.8	1457.4	0.0
r102	17	1458	1458	0.0	1450	0.5	1441.2	1.2	1455.4	0.2
r103	13	1458	1430	1.9	1450	0.5	1446.6	0.8	1455	0.2
r104	9	1458	1410	3.3	1402	3.8	1418.2	2.7	1437.8	1.4
r105	14	1458	1458	0.0	1435	1.6	1441.6	1.1	1458	0.0
r106	12	1458	1433	1.7	1411	1.2	1437.6	1.4	1458	0.0
r107	10	1458	1440	1.2	1431	1.9	1435	1.6	1452	0.4
r108	9	1458	1440	1.0	1430	1.9	1441.8	1.1	1451.8	0.4
r109	11	1458	1410	3.3	1432	1.8	1433.4	1.7	1449.4	0.6
r110	10	1458	1432	1.8	1419	2.7	1433.4	1.7	1449	0.6
r111	10	1458	1410	3.3	1410	3.3	1430.2	1.9	1449.8	0.6
r112	9	1458	1430	1.92	1418	2.7	1434.4	1.6	1448	0.7
rc101	14	1724	1632	5.3	1724	0.0	1690.2	2.0	1705.2	1.1
rc102	12	1724	1689	2.0	1718	0.3	1685	2.3	1705.2	1.1
rc103	11	1724	1686	2.2	1724	0.0	1709	0.9	1721	0.2
rc104	10	1724	1689	2.0	1724	0.0	1718	0.3	1723.4	0.2
rc105	13	1724	1640	4.9	1719	0.3	1689.8	2.0	1716	0.5
rc106	11	1724	1689	2.0	1716	0.5	1690.6	1.9	1706	1.0
rc107	11	1724	1724	0.0	1724	0.0	1718.4	0.3	1724	0.0
rc108	10	1724	1684	2.3	1719	0.3	1713	0.6	1720.6	0.2

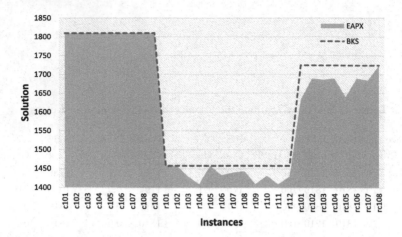

Fig. 5. Analysis of computational results for Solomon instances

Table 2. EAPX vs state-of the art algorithms (Cordeau instances)

Instance	m	BKS	EAPX		ILS		GVNS		ABC	
			Cost	Gap (%)	Cost	Gap (%)	Cost	Gap(%)	Cost	Gap (%)
pr01	3	657	603	8.2	608	7.5	608.4	7.4	617.4	6.0
pr02	6	1220	1192	2.3	1180	0.3	1198.8	1.7	1203.8	1.3
pr03	9	1788	1663	4.9	1738	2.8	1760.8	1.5	1764.6	1.3
pr04	12	2477	2400	3.1	2428	2.0	2467.4	0.4	2474.2	0.1
pr05	15	3351	3347	0.1	3297	1.6	3351	0.0	3351	0.0
pr06	18	3671	3671	0.0	3650	0.6	3670.6	0.0	3670.6	0.0
pr07	5	948	903	4.7	909	4.1	935	1.4	931.4	1.8
pr08	10	2006	1974	1.6	1984	1.1	2004.6	0.1	2006	0.0
pr09	15	2736	2724	0.4	2729	0.3	2736	0.0	2736	0.0
pr10	20	3850	3850	0.0	3850	0.0	3850	0.0	3850	0.0

5   Conclusion

In this paper, we have proposed a new solution for the team orienteering problem with time windows using the EAPX method. This algorithm employs the generation of the initial population, the local search operator, and the partition crossover method. Besides, we have investigated the performance of the EAPX using a comparative study with state of the art methods. The experimental results have shown the effectiveness of this meta-heuristic in solving TOPTW benchmark instances. The proposed approach performs, on good average compared to state-of-the-art algorithms and it reached the best known solutions.

References

Cura, T.: An artificial bee colony algorithm approach for the team orienteering problem with time windows. Comput. Ind. Eng. **74**, 270–290 (2014)

Gavalas, D., Konstantopoulos, C., Mastakas, K., Pantziou, G.: A survey on algorithmic approaches for solving tourist trip design problems. J. Heuristics **20**(3), 291–328 (2014)

Labadie, N., Mansini, R., Melechovskỳ, J., Calvo, R.W.: The team orienteering problem with time windows: an LP-based granular variable neighborhood search. Eur. J. Oper. Res. **220**(1), 15–27 (2012)

Montemanni, R., Gambardella, L.M.: An ant colony system for team orienteering problems with time windows. Found. Comput. Decis. Sci. **34**(4), 287 (2009)

Ryan, D.M., Hjorring, C., Glover, F.: Extensions of the petal method for vehicle routing. J. Oper. Res. Soc. **44**(3), 289–296 (1993)

Vansteenwegen, P., Souffriau, W., Berghe, G.V., Van Oudheusden, D.: Iterated local search for the team orienteering problem with time windows. Comput. Oper. Res. **36**(12), 3281–3290 (2009a)

Vansteenwege, P., Souffriau, W., Berghe, G.V., Van Oudheusden, D.: Metaheuristics for tourist trip planning. In: Sörensen, K., Sevaux, M., Habenicht, W., Geiger, M. (eds.) Metaheuristics in the Service Industry, vol. 624, pp. 15–31. Springer, Heidelberg (2009). https://doi.org/10.1007/978-3-642-00939-6_2

Whitley, D., Hains, D., Howe, A.: Tunneling between optima: partition crossover for the traveling salesman problem. In: Proceedings of the 11th Annual Conference on Genetic and Evolutionary Computation, pp. 915–922. ACM (2009)

A High Winning Opportunities Intraday Volatility Trading Method Using Artificial Immune Systems

Theo Raymond Chan[✉], Kwun-wing Chan, Steve Luk,
and Chun-ho Lee

Chan's Research Company Limited, Hong Kong, China
theo.chan@cnfe.com

Abstract. This paper introduces a quantitative forecasting trading mechanism which captures intraday volatility and at the same time enjoying the Index directional trading profit. The method applies Artificial Immune Network (AIN) to adjust the Index Equilibrium Point Forecasting (IEPF) and Mean Reversion Grid Trading (MRGT) method to maximize its winning opportunity. In practice, a system has been developed over the Hang Seng China Enterprises Index (HSCEI) Futures market. We have applied 9-years real market historical data, approximately 160 Terabytes Bid-Ask and Done Trade full book records, to training up the AIN to enhance the index forecasting result. The performance of the proposed method in backward test appear to be promising, and therefore, a real-time intraday trading system is currently under deployment for a further pilot experiment with the real market trading test.

Keywords: AIS · Artificial immune system · Financial forecasting
Stock future market · Optimization · FinTech

1 Introduction

For the past three decades, many researchers and scientists have adopted the concept of immunology as metaphors and engineering paradigms to solve problems in variety applications, those system are known as Artificial Immune Systems (AIS) [1, 2]. Famous AIS based approaches include negative selection [3], clonal selection theory [4] and immune network theory [2]. This paper introduce anther real world AIS application, a high winning opportunity intraday volatility trading method, which using real market trading data and immune network for index forecasting.

2 Artificial Immune Intraday Volatility Trading Method

2.1 Intraday Volatility Mean Reversion Grid Trading

The proposed method generates profit from intraday volatility [5–7], which we apply a forecasted index equilibrium points [8] as the "mean", then "Buy Low Sell High" with a fixed trading spread. As shown in Fig. 1, the method is to buy every trading spread

© Springer International Publishing AG, part of Springer Nature 2018
M. Mouhoub et al. (Eds.): IEA/AIE 2018, LNAI 10868, pp. 212–218, 2018.
https://doi.org/10.1007/978-3-319-92058-0_20

lower than the nominal market price and sell every trading spread higher than the nominal market price. All execution order is 'Limit Order', also known as the passive order. Since prices tend to oscillate for mid or high-frequency trading within a medium or short time interval, if there are enough oscillations before prices move in a direction, there exists arbitrage.

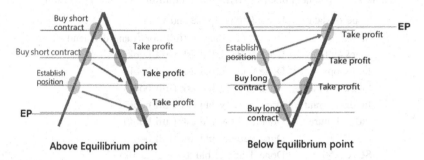

Fig. 1. Arbitrage exists when buy short when above the Equilibrium Points or buy long while below Equilibrium Points with a fixed trading spread

2.2 Index Equilibrium Point Forecasting

The Index Equilibrium Point (EP) is forecasted by calculating the value of each transaction impact in the whole market based on the works in [7–11]. The method proposed in this paper has adopted the Artificial Immune Network [12] to learn and optimize the weight between the correlations and the relative values, as Artificial Immune Network is found more efficient than Artificial Neural Network in trend predicting [13]. Historical market data is applied to train the immune network and weekly forecast of EP is calculated with the market data feed of previous 15 trading days for index directional intraday trading. When week closing, the final market EP feedbacks into the learning network (Fig. 2).

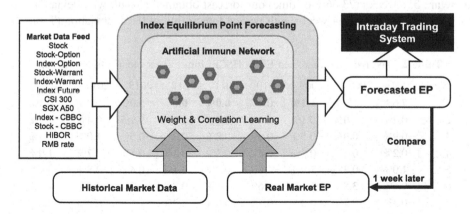

Fig. 2. The proposed design of AIS based Index Equilibrium Point Forecasting

Table 1 shows the related transaction items defined in market data feed of IEPF for Hang Seng China Enterprises Index (HSCEI) Futures market – HHIF [14], where the impact and weight of each transaction are based on the affinity level [15–18] between the antibodies of the immune network from week to week.

Table 1. The data applied in HHIF Index Equilibrium Point Forecasting.

Type of data	Records type (price and QTY)
Stock	Done trade, bid ask (full book) and dividends
Stock-option	Done trade & bid ask (full book)
Index-option	Done trade & bid ask (full book)
Stock-warrant	Done trade & bid ask (full book)
Index-warrant	Done trade & bid ask (full book)
Index Future	Done trade & bid ask (full book)
CSI 300	Done trade & bid ask (full book)
SGX A50	Done Trade & bid ask (full book)
Index - CBBC	Open-high-low-close (OHLC) & volume
Stock - CBBC	Open-high-low-close (OHLC) & volume
HIBOR	Daily interbank offered rate
CNH RMB rate	Exchange rate CNHHKD

3 Simulation and Performance

3.1 Index Forecasting Test

We fed the immune network with all the Bid-ask book record and Done Trade data from 2007 to 2015, which consists of quintillions of records and about 160 Terabytes in size. A backward testing simulation on the index forecasting is then performed based on the trained network. The comparative weekly forecasts are listed in Table 3 as below showing a high accuracy result, where within the 486 weeks from 2007 to 2015, there are 358 weeks (73.66% of time) our forecast obtained a result with deviation less than 1% deviation and 34 weeks with perfect forecasting of 0.0% deviation (Table 2).

Table 2. The monday forecasted EP vs HSCEI future (near month) friday closing.

Week	2007	2008	2009	2010	2011	2012	2013	2014	2015
1	7.6%	−1.3%	1.1%	**0.0%**	**0.0%**	**0.0%**	5.0%	−0.2%	0.3%
2	−0.2%	**0.0%**	0.1%	0.6%	0.5%	−1.1%	0.7%	0.4%	−1.2%
3	−0.9%	**0.0%**	−0.5%	0.6%	0.8%	0.2%	−0.5%	−1.0%	−0.3%
4	−0.2%	−0.3%	0.3%	−0.6%	0.3%	−0.4%	−0.1%	−0.7%	1.0%
5	−1.0%	−0.3%	7.9%	−4.0%	0.2%	2.1%	−0.4%	−2.8%	−3.6%
6	−0.6%	−3.5%	−1.1%	−0.6%	1.5%	−0.7%	−0.3%	−4.6%	−4.7%
7	−0.3%	−0.7%	−0.3%	0.7%	**0.0%**	−0.7%	1.6%	0.3%	2.3%

(continued)

Table 2. (*continued*)

Week	2007	2008	2009	2010	2011	2012	2013	2014	2015
8	**0.0%**	**0.0%**	1.4%	−2.2%	−0.2%	−0.4%	−0.8%	−0.5%	0.9%
9	−1.1%	3.5%	−0.8%	0.1%	0.7%	0.5%	−0.2%	−0.8%	1.6%
10	−0.5%	0.1%	1.2%	0.7%	5.7%	0.1%	0.4%	−0.7%	0.7%
11	0.8%	0.1%	0.3%	0.2%	0.5%	0.7%	0.3%	0.5%	−0.5%
12	0.1%	−9.8%	−0.4%	**0.0%**	0.4%	−0.1%	0.1%	0.7%	0.6%
13	1.3%	3.0%	0.4%	0.3%	−0.4%	−0.4%	−0.2%	−0.4%	0.7%
14	3.7%	11.2%	0.4%	5.0%	0.5%	−0.6%	−4.4%	0.6%	−4.1%
15	6.6%	−0.4%	2.9%	8.7%	**0.0%**	0.3%	−0.1%	0.4%	2.2%
16	0.7%	−0.8%	6.4%	0.7%	−0.4%	2.6%	−0.1%	−1.3%	0.1%
17	−0.1%	−0.7%	0.1%	**0.0%**	0.8%	0.7%	−0.6%	−4.0%	**0.0%**
18	2.4%	−0.3%	0.1%	−0.9%	−3.0%	−0.6%	−0.8%	−0.5%	−0.6%
19	0.6%	−0.3%	−0.2%	0.5%	−5.6%	−2.1%	−0.1%	−0.6%	1.5%
20	0.7%	4.5%	0.2%	0.5%	0.6%	−0.8%	−2.9%	−0.7%	2.7%
21	−0.3%	−0.3%	−0.4%	−3.6%	0.4%	0.1%	0.5%	−0.9%	−0.9%
22	−0.4%	0.6%	5.3%	−0.5%	0.4%	0.8%	−3.1%	−1.0%	−0.9%
23	0.8%	−0.1%	−0.2%	−1.3%	−0.3%	0.7%	0.1%	**0.0%**	−2.5%
24	1.6%	−10.5%	0.3%	0.4%	−3.6%	−0.4%	0.3%	0.8%	1.7%
25	−0.5%	0.6%	0.6%	0.3%	−0.1%	−0.2%	−0.4%	0.4%	−1.3%
26	−2.1%	−0.7%	−0.5%	−0.5%	−0.8%	−0.8%	0.1%	−0.2%	−4.8%
27	3.8%	−5.2%	−0.9%	0.7%	0.3%	−0.5%	−0.9%	1.6%	0.9%
28	**0.0%**	−0.3%	0.1%	−0.5%	−0.3%	0.9%	−0.7%	−0.7%	3.0%
29	−0.1%	−0.7%	−0.2%	−0.1%	−0.1%	−0.6%	−0.7%	−0.6%	6.1%
30	0.5%	0.7%	−0.8%	0.2%	−0.8%	0.4%	0.5%	0.8%	3.7%
31	0.5%	0.7%	−0.5%	−0.7%	−2.9%	0.8%	1.0%	0.8%	−1.1%
32	1.8%	−0.8%	0.4%	0.5%	0.4%	−0.5%	0.2%	−0.6%	**0.0%**
33	−0.7%	−0.9%	−0.2%	0.8%	0.5%	−0.7%	0.7%	0.4%	−1.1%
34	0.5%	−2.8%	**0.0%**	0.7%	−0.9%	0.4%	−0.4%	−0.6%	−1.9%
35	8.5%	4.2%	0.5%	0.1%	−0.8%	0.2%	−0.6%	−1.5%	−3.2%
36	−0.3%	−0.1%	3.1%	−0.6%	0.2%	−4.5%	1.0%	0.9%	−10.9%
37	0.2%	−0.7%	−0.3%	−0.2%	0.5%	−0.8%	−0.9%	−0.7%	−5.3%
38	0.6%	−0.4%	0.6%	0.4%	−0.3%	−1.0%	1.7%	−0.6%	−1.0%
39	10.4%	−0.8%	0.2%	0.1%	−0.4%	−0.6%	0.4%	0.8%	−8.2%
40	13.0%	0.4%	0.2%	1.0%	−3.2%	0.2%	0.6%	0.7%	−6.7%
41	0.1%	0.8%	−0.5%	**0.0%**	−1.0%	1.3%	0.9%	0.9%	−0.7%
42	3.2%	−1.4%	−0.6%	−0.7%	0.7%	0.4%	1.5%	−0.1%	1.3%
43	−1.3%	−7.8%	−0.3%	−0.1%	−0.8%	0.2%	**0.0%**	−0.4%	0.2%
44	−0.3%	7.5%	−5.0%	-2.7%	0.2%	0.5%	0.5%	2.6%	0.3%
45	0.2%	−1.3%	−0.3%	0.7%	**0.0%**	0.7%	−0.1%	−0.8%	0.5%
46	0.2%	−0.4%	−0.6%	0.4%	0.7%	−0.5%	−0.9%	−0.8%	−4.5%

(*continued*)

Table 2. (*continued*)

Week	2007	2008	2009	2010	2011	2012	2013	2014	2015
47	−0.5%	0.7%	**0.0%**	−0.1%	0.4%	0.6%	0.6%	−0.1%	1.3%
48	9.3%	14.9%	−0.3%	**0.0%**	1.1%	−0.8%	0.5%	6.7%	−5.6%
49	−0.3%	−1.2%	5.7%	**0.0%**	−0.7%	−0.4%	−0.7%	**0.0%**	−1.7%
50	0.1%	−0.6%	0.1%	−0.2%	0.5%	−0.2%	−0.3%	−0.6%	−7.8%
51	−0.5%	−1.0%	−0.4%	**0.0%**	0.1%	0.6%	0.7%	−0.7%	3.2%
52	−0.5%	−8.9%	2.4%	0.7%	−0.1%	−0.9%	**0.0%**	0.4%	2.0%
53	**0.0%**	−3.9%	3.1%	2.5%	−1.6%	0.2%	3.6%	−2.1%	−4.7%
54	**0.0%**	**0.0%**	**0.0%**	**0.0%**	**0.0%**	1.0%	**0.0%**	**0.0%**	**0.0%**

3.2   Intraday Volatility Mean Reversion Grid Trading Test

With the EP forecasted previously, another simulation was run on the full trading mechanism based on the following assumptions.

- The market is not affected by our trading more than 3%
- The market cannot be manipulated
- There is a high correlation between Index futures and indices (greater than 95%)
- There is a high correlation between the stock price and derivatives
- There is a difference between the nominal index and the perfect equilibrium market
- Derivatives issuer and market maker need to hedge positions
- Only transactions in the exchange can affect the index
- The market tends to Equilibrium status.

Profit being generated whenever there is a correct prediction of index direction, the number of weeks with correct direction forecast and the percentages of Return On Investment (ROI) for the past 5 years are summarized in Table 3 as below, which shows the trading system gaining profit for 79.1% of the time and the method shows its capability in providing a reasonably good average monthly return of 7.51%.

Table 3. Average accuracy and ROI for five years in backward testing

Year	2011	2012	2013	2014	2015	Overall
Average of accuracy	86.5%	82.7%	83.0%	80.8%	62.5%	**79.1%**
ROI	77.2%	67.5%	68.8%	39.1%	54.6%	**57.68%**
Maximum daily drawdown	−8.02%	−2.25%	−4.38%	−8.12%	−11.73%	**−11.73%**
Average monthly return	7.22%	9.88%	11.90%	3.80%	3.80%	**7.51%**

4 Conclusion and Future Works

The simulation results show that the proposed intraday volatility trading method using Artificial Immune System is feasible to provide high winning opportunity in the future stock market, through learning and predicting the index equilibrium point. The performance of the proposed method in backward simulation appears to be promising and reasonably attractive. To further evaluate the method, the next step would be forward testing. A real-time intraday trading system is, therefore, working in progress for a pilot experiment with the real market trading test.

References

1. Dasgupta, D. (ed.): Artificial Immune Systems and Their Applications. Springer, Heidelberg (1999). https://doi.org/10.1007/978-3-642-59901-9
2. Farmer, J.D., Packard, N.H., Perelson, A.S.: The immune system, adaptation, and machine learning. Phys. D **2**(1–3), 187–204 (1986)
3. Forrest, S., et al.: Self-nonself discrimination in a computer. In: Proceedings of 1994 IEEE Computer Society Symposium on Research in Security and Privacy. IEEE (1994)
4. Burnet, F.M.: The Clonal Selection Theory of Acquired Immunity. Cambridge Univeristy Press, Cambridge (1959)
5. Pastukhov, S.V.: On some probabilistic-statistical methods in technical analysis. Theor. Probab. Appl. **49**(2), 245–260 (2005)
6. Harris, L., Sofianos, G., Shapiro, J.E.: Program trading and intraday volatility. Rev. Financ. Stud. **7**(4), 653–685 (1994)
7. Brock, W.A., Kleidon, A.W.: Periodic market closure and trading volume: a model of intraday bids and asks. J. Econ. Dyn. Control **16**(3), 451–489 (1992)
8. Bailey, W., Stulz, R.M.: The pricing of stock index options in a general equilibrium model. J. Financ. Quant. Anal. **24**(1), 1–12 (2009)
9. Foster, F.D., Viswanathan, S.: Variations in trading volume, return volatility, and trading costs: evidence on recent price formation models. J. Finan. **48**(1), 187–211 (1993)
10. Day, T.E., Lewis, C.M.: The behavior of the volatility implicit in the prices of stock index options. J. Finan. Econ. **22**(1), 103–122 (1988)
11. Manaster, S., Rendleman, R.J.: Option prices as predictors of equilibrium stock prices. J. Finan. **37**(4), 1043–1057 (1982)
12. Butler, M., Kazakov, D.: Modeling the behavior of the stock market with an Artificial Immune System. In: IEEE Congress on Evolutionary Computation (2010)
13. Gunasekaran, M., Ramaswami, K.S.: Evaluation of artificial immune system with artificial neural network for predicting Bombay stock exchange trends. J. Comput. Sci. **7**(7), 967–972 (2011)
14. Hang Seng Indexes Company Limited: Index Methodology for Managing the Hang Seng China Enterprises Index, Hong Kong (2016)
15. Hart, E., Bersini, H., Santos, F.: Tolerance vs intolerance: how affinity defines topology in an idiotypic network. In: Bersini, H., Carneiro, J. (eds.) ICARIS 2006. LNCS, vol. 4163, pp. 109–121. Springer, Heidelberg (2006). https://doi.org/10.1007/11823940_9
16. Castro, L.N.d., Timmis, J.: An artificial immune network for multimodal function optimization. In: Proceedings of the Congress on Evolutionary Computation, CEC (2002)

17. Chen, J., Mahfouf, M.: A population adaptive based immune algorithm for solving multi-objective optimization problems. In: Bersini, H., Carneiro, J. (eds.) ICARIS 2006. LNCS, vol. 4163, pp. 280–293. Springer, Heidelberg (2006). https://doi.org/10.1007/11823940_22
18. Coelho, G.P., Von Zuben, F.J.: omni-aiNet: an immune-inspired approach for omni optimization. In: Bersini, H., Carneiro, J. (eds.) ICARIS 2006. LNCS, vol. 4163, pp. 294–308. Springer, Heidelberg (2006). https://doi.org/10.1007/11823940_23

Expert Systems and Robotics

Joint Angle Error Reduction for Humanoid Robots Using Dynamics Learning Tree

Ryo Hirai[1], Manabu Gouko[2], and Chyon Hae Kim[1(✉)]

[1] Department of System Innovation Engineering, Faculty of Science
and Engineering, Iwate University, Morioka, Japan
tenkai@iwate-u.ac.jp
[2] Department of Mechanical Engineering and Intelligent Systems,
Faculty of Engineering, Tohoku Gakuin University, Sendai, Japan

Abstract. In this paper, we discuss two problems with joints of low-cost humanoid robots.

The first problem is communication errors occurring in angle sensors. We propose a method of compensating for the sensor values by using estimated sensor values by learning the corresponding relationships between the command and sensor values.

Second, there are errors between the command and sensor values. The degree of such errors in a robot arm is affected by both gravity and joint-motion directions. By learning the corresponding relationships between these two factors and the errors, we can estimate these errors and use this estimation to reduce motion error. One of the distinguishing points of the proposed methods is that these two problems are solved by adaptive learning that works under the background system of a moving robot. Another distinguishing point is that the proposed method adapts to the specifications of a robot's joints regardless of intensive a priori knowledge about the specifications.

From experimental results, we found that it is possible to infer the necessary value to compensate the sensor values that occur in the event of communication error. Moreover, by estimating the error between the command and sensor values and using this estimation to reduce the error, we succeeded in reducing the error in joint angle.

1 Introduction

Backlash between gears result in position errors and distortion of dynamics in robots. To overcome these problems, non-backlash structures have been developed. (e.g. Harmonic Drive [1]) Robots have recently become more accessible to ordinary users. However, robots cannot be composed of such high-performance elements due to high cost. Low-cost robots have several hardware limitations, such as motion inaccuracies, errors with the sensor errors, and physical deterioration and failure including backlash.

However, these low-cost robots may perform with high accuracy by compensating for these issues via software. Therefore, they are expected to respond to tasks that requires fine control.

© Springer International Publishing AG, part of Springer Nature 2018
M. Mouhoub et al. (Eds.): IEA/AIE 2018, LNAI 10868, pp. 221–232, 2018.
https://doi.org/10.1007/978-3-319-92058-0_21

Figure 1 shows an example of a typical joint. In a typical servomotor, a motor shaft is adjusted to a command value by using angle-sensor 1 directly connected to it. However, if the gear is placed between the motor and arm member, the arm member deviates from the intended angle due to the backlash between the gears. Angle-sensor 2 can measure true joint angles because the sensor is directly connected to the arm member. However, angle-sensor 1 cannot measure them. Therefore, we use the joint angle of the angle-sensor 2 as information of the joint angle. In this paper, we discuss the following two problems with the joints of humanoid robots.

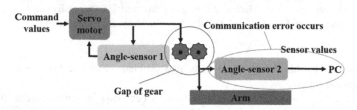

Fig. 1. Schematic of joint structure. The servo motor sets the angle of the left gear through the feedback of angle-sensor 1 according to the command value. However, there is backlash between the gears. Thus, the true joint angle that is measured by angle sensor 2 is not equal to the command value. Also, there are errors in communication between the angle-sensor 2 and a PC. Therefore, we propose a learning method to solve these problems.

1.1   Communication Error of Angle Sensor

In the case that the command values and the sensor values show significantly different values, sensor-communication error will likely occurs. Figure 2 is an example of such an error occurring in an arm joint of the humanoid robot NAO [2]. Sometimes the angle-sensor values significantly differ from the command values. At this time, it is confirmed that the joints move according to the command values. In this case, the angle-sensor value is temporarily lost, and the previous sensor value continually repeats itself. In such an event, it is unclear if movement occurs in accordance with the command values when this sensor-communication error occurs. We believed that if the sensor values can be complemented by estimated sensor values through learning, data close to the sensor values can be obtained even if communication-error occurs.

Several methods have been proposed to detect sensor failure using a Kalman filter [3] or neural network [4, 5]. However, these methods have disadvantages, such as the complexity of setting parameters, and difficulty in incremental learning. By using dynamics learning trees (DLTs), we can avoid such disadvantages. Our proposed learning method use DLTs [10] to learn the correspondence between command and sensor values.

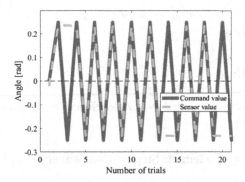

Fig. 2. Example of communication error. Sometimes the angle-sensor values of a joint significantly differ from the command values. If this is caused by communication error, we may obtain the same sensor value as that in step 1 because the 1-step-before value remains on the buffer.

1.2   Error Between Command and Sensor Values

The error caused by the backlash between the command and sensor values occurs as shown in Fig. 1. This is an obstacle in the path to high precision controls. Figure 3 displays the error occurring during the back and forth movement of NAO's arm joint.

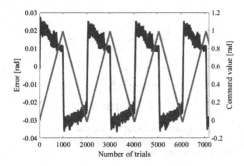

Fig. 3. Example of error between command and sensor values. This figure shows an example of the error between the command and sensor values during the back and forth movement of NAO's arm joint. The features of the error differ according to the moving direction of the joint.

To solve this problem, methods of nullify the backlash by using neural networks have been proposed [6, 7, 8, 9]. To avoid several disadvantages of neural networks, we use a DLT. By learning the characteristics of errors between the command and sensor values and using those characteristics to estimate an error, we can generate the command values that take into account the error, which provide accurate controls.

Our proposed learning method involves two steps. Step 1 involves learning the corresponding relationships between the command and sensor values and mitigating the communication error of the angle sensor. Step 2 involves reducing the error by learning its characteristics.

2   Learning Method

We used a humanoid robot called NAO developed by SoftBank Robotics as the experimental machine.

2.1   Proposed Learning Method: Step 1: Complementation for Angle Sensor Values

Figure 4 shows the proposed method learning the corresponding relationships between the command and sensor values and estimate the sensor values from the command values. During learning, the proposed method determines the command values and move joints of the robot, then determines if the sensor values were obtained correctly. A learning machine learns the corresponding relationships only if the sensor values were obtained correctly and does not learn them if they were not obtained correctly. During estimation the proposed method determines the command values and move joints then determines if the sensor values were obtained correctly. If the sensor values were not obtained correctly, it compensates the sensor values using the estimation, and if they were obtained correctly, it uses the sensor values.

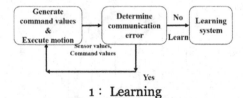

1：Learning

The proposed method learns the
corresponding relationships between
the command and sensor values.

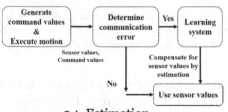

2：Estimation

The proposed method estimates the sensor
values from the command values.

Fig. 4. Proposed method: step 1

2.2 Proposed Learning Method: Step 2: Estimation of Error between Command and Sensor Values

Assuming actual joint angles θ' can be obtained for the input of command values input θ,

$$f(\theta) = \theta' \tag{1}$$

θ: command values
θ':   actual joint angles

It is ideal that $\theta = \theta'$. However, there is an error α between θ and θ'.

$$f(\theta + a) = \theta' \tag{2}$$

θ: command values
θ':   actual joint angles
α: error between command and actual values

It is difficult to calculate α. Therefore, before giving the command values and moving joints, the command values taking the error into account are generated by adding corrections of the error to the command values. Therefore, a learning system learns the characteristics of α and estimates α.

To learn the error characteristics, we specified the error factors. Figure 3 shows the effect of motion direction on the error in an arm potion of NAO. When exercising joints to move back and forth, such as like the command values in the Fig. 3, the features of the error are different between when the joint moves in a positive direction and when it moves in a negative direction. Next, Fig. 5 shows the effect of gravity direction on the degree of error. This figure compares the errors when the same motion is performed in two states. The two states are the gravity direction is perpendicular to the motion direction of arm joints and the gravity direction is parallel to it. The errors also differ between them. It is considered that the gravity and motion directions of joints affect the degree of error from Figs. 3 and 5.

Two learning trees are prepared for use when the motion direction of a joint is in the positive direction and negative direction, moreover all joint angles are input because the direction of gravity on joints is determined by each joint angle of the arm.

For an arm with n joints, as shown in the Fig. 6, the estimated error between the command and sensor values of the ith joint is

$$a_i = \Delta\theta_i(\theta_1, \theta_2, \cdots, \theta_n) \tag{3}$$

θ: joint angles
α_i: error between command and sensor values of ith joint

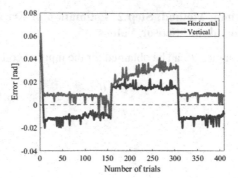

Fig. 5. Effect of gravity direction on degree of error. The errors differ between different gravity directions. The errors in the state in which the gravity direction is perpendicular to the motion direction of arm joints and that in which the gravity direction is parallel to it were compared.

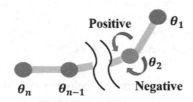

Fig. 6. Example of focusing on second joint of arm with n joints. When focusing on the second joint, the proposed method switches two DLTs according to the moving direction of the second joint. The proposed method makes inputs of the DLTs using the angles of n joints.

Figure 7 shows learning the corresponding relationships between the movement/gravity direction and errors of a joint.

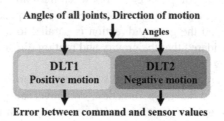

Fig. 7. Proposed method: step 2. Learning the corresponding relationships between the movement/gravity direction and errors of the joint. When a targeted joint is moving in the positive/negative direction, the proposed method applies DLT 1/DLT 2.

2.3   Dynamics Learning Tree

To estimate using steps 1 and 2 of the proposed methods, we use DLTs [10–12] developed by Numakura et al. A DLT learns the mapping from the state vector of a system to the state transition vector of the system. It is hierarchical learning system implemented in a tree structure. Its root node represents an n-dimensional input space. Every main layer of a DLT is composed of n dimensions (sub-layers) with a d-ary tree. At the first main layer, the leaf nodes represent the subspace of the input space of the root node. The size of the subspace is $1/d^n$ of the input space. A DLT with an N-layer n-dimensional (sub-layer) d-ary tree is obtained by constructing an N times n-dimensional d-ary tree from every leaf node of the main layer. Figure 8 shows an example of a DLT with an N-layer 2-dimensional 2-ary tree.

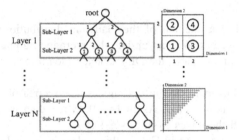

Fig. 8. Dynamics learning tree with N-layer 2-dimensional (sub-layer) 2-ary tree. The tree structure of a DLT (left) and the regions of the input space correspond to the nodes at every layer (right). The number of leaf nodes at the first layer corresponds to the number of the regions of the input space. This figure shows the tree structure of a DLT when all the branches are created, although the branches can be created individually in an online-incremental learning process.

Figure 9 shows an example of the learning process. A DLT with an N-layer n-dimensional d-ary tree divides the input space according to the input data when it obtains a pair of input and output data. The figure also shows an example of a 2-layer 2-dimensional 3-ary tree, which maps the input data to the input space. When the input data illustrated with a circle in Fig. 9 (right) is obtained, all the cells that include the input data are divided. As a result, the DLT obtains the tree structure in Fig. 9 (left). Cell 1 of Fig. 9 (right), which is the smallest cell that includes the input data, is represented by Node 1 of Fig. 9 (left). Every node of the DLT has an averaged output vector that was calculated from the output data. The DLT updates that vector using the following equations when a new pair of input and output data is given.

$$\hat{O}_{Cell\,n} \leftarrow (N_{Cell\,n} \times \hat{O}_{Cell\,n} + O)/(N_{Cell\,n} + 1) \tag{4}$$

$$N_{cell\,n} \leftarrow (N_{cell\,n} + 1) \tag{5}$$

where $N_{Cell\,n}$ is the amount of output data that is learned by Cell n, $\hat{O}_{Cell\,n}$ is the averaged vector learned by Cell n, where O is the given output vector. The DLT hypothesizes the noise with a Gaussian distribution for the set of output data vectors

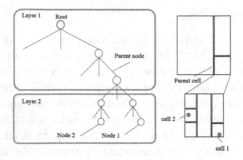

Fig. 9. Input space and DLT. The input space of the learning system is represented by a tree. The tree structure is incrementally constructed when new training I/O data is given. According to the density of data, DLT tunes the discretization of the input space.

obtained inside a cell. The median of the Gaussian distribution is estimated by the averaged output data vectors. We can update the averaged output data vectors when a single output vector is given. Thus, the DLT is able to learn in a online and incremental process.

The DLT applies this update to multiple nodes when a pair of input and output data that should be learned is obtained. As in Fig. 9, when data is given in Cell 1, this update is applied to all the nodes from Node 1 to Root.

Similarly, when data is given in Cell 2, this update is applied to all the nodes from Node 2 to Root.

When the DLT predicts the corresponding output vector from an input vector of a continuous system, it searches on the tree from Root using the input vector as the key to find the bottom node that represents the sub-input-space that includes the input vector. The DLT returns the averaged output vector $\hat{O}_{Cell\,n}$ of this bottom node. Using this search process, the DLT precisely predicts the output of a system around the sub-input space, where the density of learned data is large. Around the sub-input-space, where the density of learned data is small, the DLT generalizes the input-output pairs and predicts the output using the generalization.

The response of the prediction process of the DLT is quite high because it requires only the calculation cost for the tree search of a d-ary tree. The DLT realizes robust prediction for noisy data by using the nodes in the upper layer instead of those in the bottom layer.

3   Experiments

We used joints of a left arm of the humanoid robot NAO (Fig. 10) in our experiments. The joints are labeled as Left shoulder pitch (LSP), left shoulder roll (LSR), left elbow roll (LER), left elbow yaw (LEY), and left wrist yaw (LWY).

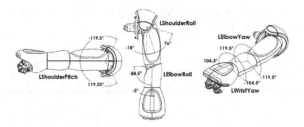

Fig. 10. Joints of NAO. Humanoid robot NAO has 5 joints with the above configurations.

3.1 Method

Experiment 1: Complementation for Sensor Values

We conducted an experiment to confirm that step 1 of the proposed method can complement sensor values using LSR, LEY and LER. We prepared 1000 pieces of learning data and 1000 pieces of verification data consisting of command values of three joints randomly generated and corresponding sensor values. First, the DLT learned the corresponding relationships between the command and sensor values from the learning data. Next, it estimated the sensor values corresponding the command values of the verification data, calculated the average errors by comparing the estimated sensor values and those of the verification data.

Experiment 2: Reducing Error between Command and Sensor Values

We conducted another experiment on the error between the command and sensor values when using step 2 of the proposed method. We used LSR and LER in this experiment. We prepared 1000 pieces of learning data and 1000 pieces of verification data consisting of command values of two joints randomly generated and corresponding sensor values, and the DLTs corresponding to each of 5 joints. The DLT learned the corresponding relationships between "the movement/gravity direction" and "the error between the command and sensor values" using in step 2 of the proposed method. Every time 100 pieces of learning data were learned, a verification was conducted using the verification data. In the verification, the command values of the verification data were added corrections, the robot moved the joints and the average error was calculated each time verification of the 1000 pieces of data was executed. The sensor values were compensated using the DLT used in Experiment 1 when the sensor values were not obtained correctly.

3.2 Results

Figure 11 (a) shows the error between the sensor values and estimated sensor values of Experiment 1. It is evident from the data that the error converges through the learning of 1000 pieces of data. Figure 11 (b) shows the estimated sensor values of the sensor values in Fig. 2 as an example of compensation in case of communication error. The sensor values were estimated to mitigate the communication error. The learning time of

1000 pieces of data was 25.855 s using Windows 8.1 Enterprise, Intel (R) Core (TM) i5-6600 CPU 3.30 GHz and 8 GB memory.

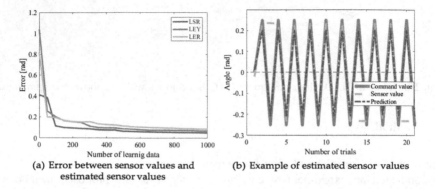

(a) Error between sensor values and estimated sensor values

(b) Example of estimated sensor values

Fig. 11. Results of Experiment 1. Graph (a) shows the estimation errors while the proposed learning method was being trained. The errors monotonically decreased according to the amount of data. Streaming data were acquired from the robot to train the DLTs. Graph (b) shows the complement the sensor values in case of communication error. The sensor values were estimated to complement the communication error.

Figures 12 (a) and (b) show the results of Experiment 2. In step 2 of the proposed method, by adding correction to the command values, the average error became smaller at an early stage. The error decreased compared with the case without compensation. Finally, the error decreased 19.6% at LSR and 19.0% at LER. The learning time of 1000 pieces of data was 149.623 s using the same PC as Experiment 1.

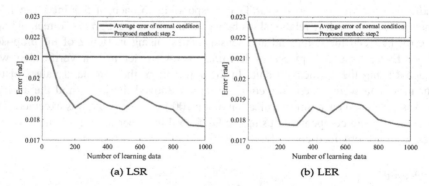

(a) LSR

(b) LER

Fig. 12. Results of Experiment 2. The lines labeled "Average error of normal condition" show the average errors when step 2 of the proposed method was not used (base lines). Step 2 of the proposed method decreased the errors to be lower than the base lines.

4 Consideration

In this paper, we considered the direction of motion and that of gravity as input elements of in step 2 of the proposed method. The experimental results show that the two input elements are effective. Learning efficiency and accuracy can be further improved according to selection of input elements. The reason the direction of movement is effective as an input element in step 2 of the proposed method is that there is a gap in transmission of motion between gears caused by backlash when the direction of motion changes, which is one of the causes of error. Moreover, this step not only improves the performance of gears, but is also expected to be effective against errors caused by deterioration.

We conducted experiments using NAO, however, we will confirm if the method is effective with other robots. In the experiments of this study, angular velocity was always constant. However, robots do not necessarily move at a constant angular velocity. We plan to conduct experiments using angular velocity as a learning objective.

5 Conclusion

We discussed two problems with the joints of humanoid robots. The first problem is the communication error in angle sensors. We proposed a method of learning the corresponding relationships between the command and sensor values to complement the sensor values using the estimated sensor values when communication error occurs as the first step. The second problem is the error between the command and sensor values. From verification, we found that the motion direction of joints and the gravity direction affect the degree of error. Therefore, step 2 of the proposed method corrects the command values through learning the corresponding relationships between the motion/gravity direction and error to reduce the error. We used the humanoid robot NAO in the experiments and DLTs for learning.

In Experiment 1, by learning the data of 1000 command values and corresponding sensor values, the sensor values when communication error occurred were complemented by the estimated sensor values. In Experiment 2, by learning 1000 pieces of data consisting of the motion/gravity directions and error between the command and sensor values, the errors in LSR and LER reduced by a little less than 20%.

References

1. Harmonic Drive. https://www.hds.co.jp/products/lineup/hd/
2. NAO. https://www.ald.softbankrobotics.com/en/cool-robots/nao/find-out-more-about-nao
3. Roumeliotis, S.I., Sukhatme, G., Bekey, G.A.: Fault detection and identification in a mobile robot using multiple-model estimation. In: Proceedings IEEE International Conference Robotics and Automation, Lueven, Belgium, pp. 2223–2228 (1998)

4. Napolitano, M.R., Neppach, C., Casdorph, V., Naylor, S., Innocenti, M., Silvestri, G.: Neural-network-based scheme for sensor failure detection, identification, and accommodation. J. Guid. Control Dyn. **18**(6), 1280–1286 (1995)

5. Naidu, S.R., Zafiriou, E., McAvoy, T.J.: Use of neural networks for sensor failure detection in a control system. IEEE Contr. Syst. Mag. **10**, 44–55 (1990)

6. Seidl, D.R., Lam, S.-L., Putman, J.A., Lorenz, R.D.: Neural network compensation of gear backlash hysteresis in position-controlled mechanisms. IEEE Trans. Ind. Appl. **31**(6), 1475–1483 (1995)

7. He, C., Zhang, Y., Meng, M.: Backlash compensation by neural network online learning. In: Proceedings IEEE International Symposium on Computational Intelligence in Robotics and Automation, pp. 161–165 (2001)

8. Baruch, I.S., Beltran, R.L., Nenkova, B.: A mechanical system backlash compensation by means of a recurrent neural multi-model. In: Second IEEE International Conference on Intelligent Systems, pp. 514–519 (2004)

9. Shibata, T., Fukuda, T., Tanie, K.: Nonlinear backlash compensation using recurrent neural network. Unsupervised learning by genetic algorithm. In: Proceedings of 1993 International Conference on Neural Networks, IJCNN-93-Nagoya, Japan, vol. 1, pp. 742–745 (1993)

10. Numakura, A., Kato, S., Sato, K., Tomisawa, T., Miyoshi, T., Akashi, T., Kim, C.H.: FAD learning: separate learning for three accelerations-learning for dynamics of boat through motor babbling. In: Proceedings of IEEE International Conference on Robotics and Automation, pp. 5609–5614 (2016)

11. Watanabe, K., Nishide, S., Gouko, M., Kim, C.H.: Fully automated learning for position and contact force of manipulated object with wired flexible finger joints. In: Fujita, H., Ali, M., Selamat, A., Sasaki, J., Kurematsu, M. (eds.) IEA/AIE 2016. LNCS (LNAI), vol. 9799, pp. 753–767. Springer, Cham (2016). https://doi.org/10.1007/978-3-319-42007-3_64

12. Eto, K., Kobayashi, Y., Kim, C.H.: Vehicle dynamics modeling using FAD learning. In: Fujita, H., Ali, M., Selamat, A., Sasaki, J., Kurematsu, M. (eds.) IEA/AIE 2016. LNCS (LNAI), vol. 9799, pp. 768–781. Springer, Cham (2016). https://doi.org/10.1007/978-3-319-42007-3_65

Closed-Loop Push Recovery
for an Inexpensive Humanoid Robot

Amirhossein Hosseinmemar[1], Jacky Baltes[2], John Anderson[1($\boxtimes$)],
Meng Cheng Lau[1], Chi Fung Lun[1], and Ziang Wang[1]

[1] Autonomous Agents Laboratory, Department of Computer Science,
University of Manitoba, Winnipeg, Manitoba R3T 2N2, Canada
memar@cs.umanitoba.ca, andersj@cs.umanitoba.ca
[2] Department of Electrical Engineering, National Taiwan Normal University,
Taipei, Taiwan
http://aalab.cs.umanitoba.ca/

Abstract. Active balancing in autonomous humanoid robots is a challenging task due to the complexity of combining a walking gait with dynamic balancing, vision and high-level behaviors. Humans not only walk successfully over even and uneven terrain, but can recover from the interaction of external forces such as impacts with obstacles and active pushes. While push recovery has been demonstrated successfully in expensive robots, it is more challenging with robots that are inexpensive, with limited power in actuators and less accurate sensing. This work describes a closed-loop control method that uses an accelerometer and gyroscope to allow an inexpensive humanoid robot to actively balance while walking and recover from pushes. An experiment is performed to test three hand-tuned closed-loop control configurations; using only a the gyroscope, only the accelerometer, and a combination of both sensors to recover from pushes. Experimental results show that the combination of gyroscope and accelerometer outperforms the other methods with 100% recovery from a light push and 70% recovery from a strong push.

Keywords: Push recovery · Humanoid robot · Autonomous active balancing · Centroidal moment pivot

1 Introduction

Robots have been used for decades, but moving from factory floors to the everyday lives of humans is a challenging task. Traditional wheeled robots are more stable and balanced than humanoid robots [1]. However, humanoid robots are closer to a human's body shape, and as a result they can potentially function better in environments structured for humans, such as offices and homes. One of the main difficulties with humanoid robots is balancing: falls occur easily, even when walking on flat surfaces. Most adult humans not only walk well on both flat and uneven surfaces, they also recover successfully from external forces

© Springer International Publishing AG, part of Springer Nature 2018
M. Mouhoub et al. (Eds.): IEA/AIE 2018, LNAI 10868, pp. 233–244, 2018.
https://doi.org/10.1007/978-3-319-92058-0_22

introduced while walking, such as low-impact obstacle collisions or small pushes in any dimension. Push recovery in robotics involves dealing with these external forces: negotiating and recovering from an abnormal status to a normal situation when either walking or standing [2, 3].

The majority of basic walking algorithms are designed to walk on flat surfaces at a predefined static angle to the ground and with feet parallel to it, and do not account for external forces [4]. While a number of push recovery approaches have been implemented in humanoid robots, these are generally intended to operate on platforms that are currently very expensive: in the hundreds of thousands or even millions of dollars (e.g. Atlas [5]). Such platforms have very powerful servos, allowing significant force to be used to correct aberrations, strong power supplies (e.g. hydraulic), highly precise machining, and very refined, rich sensors. In our work, we deal with sophisticated problems in artificial intelligence and robotics using much less expensive equipment. Working with less expensive equipment means that all elements of software, from vision to control, must be much more robust. For example, push recovery on an inexpensive robot must be achieved with lower torque servos, less precise machining, and limited sensing and computation. Limb and servo damage are also much more likely with inexpensive robots and must be taken into account.

This paper describes work on push recovery implemented on an autonomous humanoid robot meeting adult-size standards for the FIRA HuroCup robotics competition [6]: *Polaris*, a 95 cm tall humanoid based on readily-available Robotis Dynamixel servos. Polaris uses an inertial measurement unit (IMU) as an input sensor for balancing, incorporating both a gyroscope and accelerometer. We present a closed-loop control method that allows Polaris to actively balance while walking as well as to recover from pushes. To evaluate this approach, we isolate the means of perception to examine the effect on this control method. We tested this approach using three sensor configurations for feedback: using only the gyroscope, using only the accelerometer, and finally using a combination of both sensors. These mechanisms were all used to recover from pushes in the form of a suspended 2 kg mass released from varying distances. This approach has also been demonstrated successfully in the field, resulting in several competition awards including a first place award in the RoboCup 2016 humanoid technical challenge for push recovery. It has also been embedded as a part of our robotics code in award-winning FIRA Hurocup entries in 2016 and 2017.

The remainder of this paper is as follows: Sect. 2 describes background on push recovery and related work. Section 3 describes the hardware employed and the closed-loop control method for push recovery. Section 4 describes the evaluation of this work through experimental testing. We then discuss the results and directions for future research.

2 Related Work

There are two common models that are used for walking in humanoid robots, either on their own or in combination with other methods. One of these is the

Linear Inverted Pendulum model [7,8], used in robots such as [9]. The other is Zero Moment Point (ZMP) [10,11]. Humanoid robots such as ASIMO [12], HRP-2 [13], HUBO [14] generate their trajectory based on the ZMP method, and they are indeed the leading humanoid robots in walking. These humanoids walk very stably, and their walk is reliable on predefined or flat surfaces. However, this method is not practical when it comes to collisions or any other type of disturbance and would lead to a fall in almost all such cases [15].

Balancing in a humanoid robot involves maintaining the robot's center of mass (COM) within the support polygon provided by the robot's feet in its current pose. This is illustrated for Polaris in Fig. 1. Any push or other external force moving the COM outside this support polygon will cause a fall.

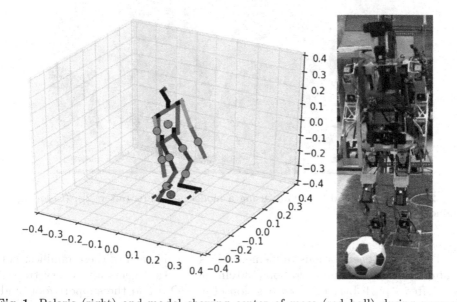

Fig. 1. Polaris (right) and model showing center of mass (red ball) during normal walking gait. (Color figure online)

There have been a number of solutions proposed to solve problem of restoring balance in humanoid robots when they are subjected to external forces such as pushes. These fall into three families:

Center of Pressure Balancing: The Center of pressure (COP) approach [16] is usually based on adjusting the robot's ankles, which in turn can shift the COM back within the support polygon [17,18]. Because of this it is also known as the *ankle strategy*. This method is often used when there is only a small disturbance.

Centroidal Moment Pivoting: Centroidal Moment Pivoting (CMP) [2] adjusts both ankle and hip servos in response to external forces, and is also known as the *hip strategy*. This in turn allows the body to change position and create an angular momentum by swinging the torso. The greater range of movement allows it to recover from both small and medium disturbances.

Step Out: The alternative to adjusting hips and/or ankles when receiving a push is to actively take one or more steps to absorb the external force, thus relocating the COM in the support polygon area [19]. This is also known as the *capture steps* strategy.

Figure 2 illustrates these three families, with the COM shown as a light blue circle, the COP shown as a red circle, and a brown arrow indicating the external force. The yellow arrow indicates one dimension of the support polygon.

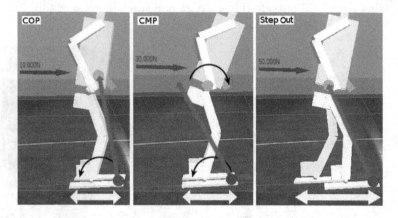

Fig. 2. COP, CMP, and Step Out, using a model of Polaris (after [2]). (Color figure online)

There have been various implementations within each of these families. For example, Toyota's running robot (130 cm high, 50 kg) generates a new trajectory after a push based on the position of its COM and the support foot, and successfully recovers from pushes against the chest during hopping and running [20]. MABEL [21] also demonstrated the ability to stabilise the walk after a push by generating a new trajectory. However, the former is a highly expensive robot that would not compare to the comparatively low-torque servos in Polaris, and the latter is a planar bipedal robot mounted on a boom of radius 2.25 m, and so can only walk around a circle.

Yun et al. [22] introduced a momentum-based stepping controller that tested an adult-sized humanoid robot in a simulation called Locomote, a software package based on Webots. In their solution, the simulator checks the maximum threshold of the angles as well as the torque for each joint of the two legs. If one of its joints passed their threshold, its step trigger function will be called and it will take a step for fall prevention.

Lee et al. [23] presented another stepping approach that was specially for non-stationary and non-continuous grounds, also in a simulation. Their solution was very costly because of calculating COP, COM, and the linear and angular momentum of the robot in real time. Since this approach is non-continuous, it cannot be applied to a normal walking gait.

Hofmann [24] studied humanoid robot balance control. He argued that taking a step for recovering from an external push is the solution for recovering from a large disturbances by moving the COP. Missura et al. [15] also studied push recovery for a simulated humanoid robot that uses capture steps for recovering. In their approach, the simulated robot calculates a desired ZMP location for every step with respect to the COM.

Many of these and other related works are examined only in simulation, or in restricted settings such as walking in a circle while suspended from a pivoting boom. Those that are physically implemented tend to require highly expensive platforms. Our approach is intended to function for small and medium size pushes on an inexpensive platform, which can only rely on lower-torque servos, less precise body machining, and less accurate sensors.

3   Approach

Our approach consists of a closed-loop control mechanism implemented on an autonomous humanoid robot. We begin with an overview of the hardware, and then describe the control design and implementation.

3.1   Hardware

Polaris (Fig. 1) is a 95 cm humanoid robot with 20 degrees of freedom (DOF), weighing 7.5 kg. Polaris makes use of comparatively inexpensive (\$200–\$500) Dynamixel servos from Robotis. All the servos use the TTL serial communication protocol with three pins that share one line for sending and receiving data. Each hip can rotate in the sagittal, frontal and transversal planes. There are 6 MX-106 servos in each leg (Hip transversal, Hip sagittal, Hip frontal, Knee sagittal, Ankle frontal, and Ankle sagittal). The two arms rotate in the sagittal and frontal planes, and each arm has 3 MX-64 servos (Shoulder sagittal, Shoulder frontal, and Elbow sagittal). The neck is made up of 2 MX-28 servos and rotates in the sagittal and transversal planes, moving an attached webcam.

These servos are controlled through a *QutePC-3000* mini-PC, with a 1.1 Ghz Celeron dual core processors. Sensors for balance consist of a single-chip *InvenSense MPU-6050* IMU containing a 3-axis (x, y, z) accelerometer and a 3-axis (x, y, z) gyroscope. The MPU-6050 is connected to the mini-PC using an Arduino Nano micro-controller board.

3.2   Closed-Loop Control

A closed-loop control system is a control system that employs one or more feedback loops. A humanoid robot using a closed-loop control system can receive feedback from its sensors (vision, inertia) describing changes to the environment (pushes, uneven terrain) and correct its trajectory to adapt to these changes. A closed-loop control system is more computationally expensive compared to an

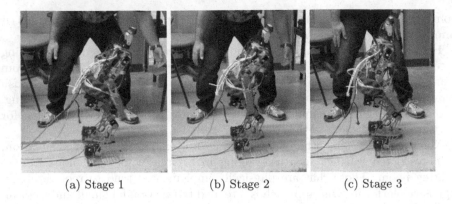

(a) Stage 1   (b) Stage 2   (c) Stage 3

Fig. 3. Push, Reaction, and Recovery (using CMP).

open-loop control system due to the enormous amount of sensory data being processed by the controller. However, it is a more robust control system because of this sensory feedback.

Polaris employs a walking engine based on the linear inverted pendulum model [7,8], which generates appropriate robot motions based on a description provided by the inverse kinematics of the robot, i.e. sets motion vectors for all servos over time. Our closed-loop control mechanism sets inputs to the walking engine, allowing it in turn to adjust the robot's COM, dynamically altering this as the environment changes. As stated in Sect. 3.1, we use the sensory feedback from the MPU-6050's gyroscope and accelerometer as the inputs to measure the control output. The walking engine will adapt the robot's trajectory (control output) as necessary to deal with changes in the environment, from varying terrain to external forces.

We describe our control approach through three phases illustrated in Fig. 3, showing a sample push recovery using this approach. In Stage 1 of the figure, the robot is pushed by hand at a point in its walking gait on a concrete floor, and must recognize that it is in a falling state. Stage 2 represents a brief window in which the robot can calculate a reaction to the push by calculating control changes based on the angular velocity and the linear velocity of the robot's torso. Stage 3 illustrates recovery, where these control changes alter parameters in the robot's walking engine, and these in turn adjust servos accordingly to prevent the robot from falling.

In Stage 1, the closed-loop controller takes as input values from the gyroscope and/or accelerometer, and from these must detect a falling state. In practice this can be computationally expensive because of the range of potential values. To allow a fast response, we discretize values. The control methodology categorizes angular velocity in 50°/s intervals, allowing a definition of constant values for light, medium and strong pushes. This interval was chosen based on three, 5-min robot walk tests to find the maximum angular velocity that Polaris encounters while using different walking parameters for each test. We similarly experimented with linear velocity thresholds by hitting the robot with a weight approximately a quarter of its body weight, and defined light, medium, and strong pushes as linear velocities of 0.9 m/s, 1.2 m/s and 1.4 m/s, respectively.

Our closed-loop control collects 1000 gyroscope and accelerometer readings per second from the IMU, and uses these to continually check if the robot is in a falling state. Based on the three thresholds for linear and angular velocities, the robot can very quickly determine whether it is in a stable state (0 m/s > linear velocity $\leq$ 0.2 m/s, with this range necessary to deal with sensor noise), or when it is in a falling state by exceeding angular velocities or linear velocity thresholds for light, medium, or strong pushes.

In the brief window between when a falling state is recognized and when the fall would be irreversible (Stage 2), the robot must make appropriate response. Knowing which threshold (light, medium, or strong push) has been exceeded allows for a quick response look-up. Our control approach implements CMP active balancing (Sect. 2), which incorporates COM if only the ankles are moved, and similarly discretizes potential responses to support a fast reaction.

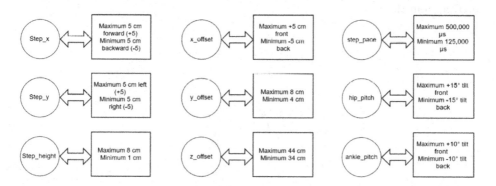

Fig. 4. Walking engine parameters and value ranges.

Our closed-loop controller produces nine outputs that are used to alter parameters in the robot's walking engine through modifying hip and/or ankle positions, and are illustrated in Fig. 4. *Step-x* is the step length on the x-axis of the robot frame (forward-backward). *Step-y* is the step length on the y-axis of the robot frame (left-right). *Step-height* is the foot height from the ground of each step. The *x-offset* is the offset distance of the feet from the origin/centre of the robot (centre point of the torso) on x-axis. *y-offset* is the offset distance on the y-axis from the centre of the torso to each foot. *z-offset* is related to the height of the robot, i.e. standing fully vs. at a crouch. *Step-pace* is the robot's speed in terms of the time it takes to take a single step (not a full walking cycle). The final two parameters are *hip-pitch* and *ankle-pitch* for the lateral motion at the hip and ankles respectively.

Each of these walking engine parameters has minimum and maximum values, also indicated in Fig. 4. Any setting acts as an offset value for the current robot pose. For example, if the robot's torso is leaning too much to the front, the robot will fall over. To encounter this problem, *hip-pitch* can be tuned to adjust the torso's lateral motion which to prevent the robot from falling.

All nine of these responses have particular values based on the strength and direction of the push that has been recognized. Values can be zero, indicating no change. For example, a light push on the right side results in detecting a fall to the left, and modifies the *step-y* value by 2 cm and the *step-pace* value by 0.5 per second, leaving all other values unchanged. These values and their mapping to discretized angular and linear velocities (fall states) have been tuned over several years of robotics competitions as well as testing the robot specifically under push recovery conditions. These have proven themselves in the field to be a very fast method of adapting control to changing conditions (e.g. carpet vs. solid surfaces) in addition to push recovery.

Once the appropriate response has been mapped, the parameters to the walking engine are changed (Stage 3), and servos are collectively altered in the time window that remains to correct for the disturbance. Central to all of this is making Stage 2 as short as possible, leaving time for the servos to be adjusted to recover from the fall.

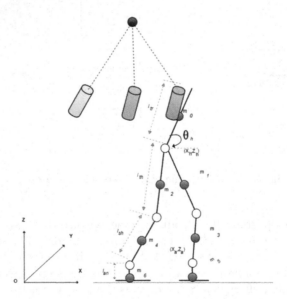

Fig. 5. Humanoid robot with double support contact. The green circles show masses for each individual link. The red gradient cylinder represents a 2 kg mass that is swinging toward the robot, which will create a disturbance upon impact.

4   Evaluation

To evaluate our approach quantitatively, we set up an experiment to control the push force applied to the robot, based on the 2015 RoboCup push recovery technical challenge [25]. This is illustrated abstractly in Fig. 5, showing the robot in the double support phase of a walking gait (i.e., both feet on the ground). The red cylinder represents a 2 kg mass (more than a quarter of Polaris' body weight) that is connected to a 1 m rope. The container is pulled back to a given distance and released naturally, resulting in the mass hitting the robot at torso height, introducing a fixed external force that can be varied depending on the distance at which the mass is released.

For this experiment, the robot was positioned on artificial turf for all trials, with a piece of foam mounted on the robot to protect the electronics from impact. The experiment tested the closed-loop control method using 90 trials divided into three subsets: 30 trials using only the gyroscope as input to the control mechanism, 30 trials using only the accelerometer, and 30 trials using both of these sensors. In each of these divisions, the 2 kg mass was released from a 30 cm distance from the robot (light push) in 10 trials, from a 40 cm distance (medium push) in 10 trials, and from a 50 cm distance (strong push) in 10 trials. Figure 6 illustrates Polaris during the course of one of these trials.

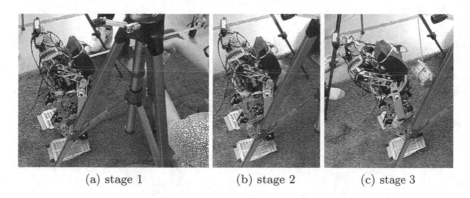

(a) stage 1   (b) stage 2   (c) stage 3

Fig. 6. Polaris recovering from a push on artificial turf.

4.1 Results

The results of all trials are shown in Table 1. Each case in which the robot successfully recovered from the impact is labeled with a 1, and each case in which the robot did not successfully recover is labeled with a 0.

These results are summarized in Fig. 7. Our closed-loop (with threshold) control mechanism is able to recover from majority of pushes (>70%) at the low impact level (30 cm swing) irrespective of the sensor type employed. At the medium impact level (40 cm swing) there is a more distinct difference between use of a gyroscope vs. use of an accelerometer: with an accelerometer, only 40% of the impacts are recoverable compared to the gyroscope. At the strong impact level (50 cm swing), the gyroscope is of no help, but a small number of pushes can be recovered using the accelerometer. The strongest success by far is using both

Table 1. Results of trials for gyroscope-only (Gyro), accelerometer-only (Acc) and both of these sensors together (Gyro+Acc).

MPU-6050 sensors	Gyro			Acc			Gyro+Acc		
Distance, cm	**30**	**40**	**50**	**30**	**40**	**50**	**30**	**40**	**50**
Trials	1	1	0	0	1	0	1	1	0
	1	1	0	1	0	1	1	1	1
	0	1	0	1	0	0	1	0	1
	1	0	0	1	0	0	1	1	1
	1	1	0	0	0	0	1	1	1
	1	0	0	1	0	0	1	1	1
	1	1	0	1	1	0	1	1	0
	1	1	0	1	1	0	1	1	1
	1	1	0	1	1	0	1	1	0
	1	0	0	0	0	0	1	1	1
Successful attempts	**9**	**7**	**0**	**7**	**4**	**1**	**10**	**9**	**7**

sensors together, resulting in the strongest push recovery at all impact levels (30 cm = 100%, 40 cm = 90%, 50 cm = 70%). As pushes become stronger, there is a shorter window for the robot to respond and greater servo alterations to be made. Ultimately neither sensor on its own can recognize a fall early enough to allow a response to a strong push, while fusing both sensors allows this in most cases.

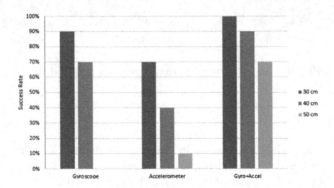

Fig. 7. Summary of successful recovery by distance of mass and type of sensor.

5   Discussion

We have described the design, implementation, and evaluation of a closed-loop control approach for push recovery on an inexpensive 20-DOF humanoid robot.

In addition to the results shown here, this work has also been demonstrated in the field with strong success. This mechanism for push recovery was our mechanism for entering the RoboCup Humanoid league technical challenge push recovery event (this event varies by year and normally has more than one challenge with scores totalled). We won this challenge in 2016, came second in 2015, and had the highest results in the push recovery component in 2017. Recovery from unexpected impacts is an important part of many activities, and this approach also forms a core within our entries to other robotic sporting events such as the 2016 and 2017 FIRA HuroCup. These field evaluations are very important, since each of these events requires robots to work in novel locations with limited set-up time and very limited time for developers to recover from anything unexpected. Such conditions can be expected to be much more challenging than laboratory environments [26]. These events must also go hand in hand with quantitative evaluations however, since while challenging, it is difficult to isolate the performance of one feature in a competitive setting (e.g. how much a push recovery methodology on its own affects playing soccer).

We are currently working on a capture steps method of push recovery, using reinforcement learning and deep reinforcement learning to automatically generate sensor and reaction discretizations like those used in this work. This will allow the robot to recover from even stronger pushes while minimizing the set of servo motions, to both react quickly and limit wear on servos. We will be using the results described here as one baseline comparison for that work.

References

1. Huang, Q., Yokoi, K., Kajita, S., Kaneko, K., Aral, H., Koyachi, N., Tanie, K.: Planning walking patterns for a biped robot. IEEE Trans. Robot. Autom. **17**(3), 280–289 (2001)
2. Stephens, B.: Humanoid push recovery. In: Proceedings of Humanoids-2007, Pittsburgh, PA, pp. 589–595. IEEE (2007)
3. Stephens, B.J., Atkeson, C.G.: Push recovery by stepping for humanoid robots with force controlled joints. In: Proceedings of Humanoids-2010, Nashville, TN, pp. 52–59 (2010)
4. Kim, J.Y., Park, I.W., Oh, J.H.: Walking control algorithm of biped humanoid robot on uneven and inclined floor. J. Intell. Robot. Syst. **48**, 457–484 (2007)
5. Kuindersma, S., Deits, R., Fallon, M., Valenzuela, A., Dai, H., Permenter, F., Koolen, T., Marion, P., Tedrake, R.: Optimization-based locomotion planning, estimation, and control design for Atlas. Auton. Robots **40**(3), 429–455 (2016)
6. Baltes, J., Tu, K.Y., Sadeghnejad, S., Anderson, J.: HuroCup: competition for multi-event humanoid robot athletes. Knowl. Eng. Rev. **32**, 1–14 (2017)
7. Pratt, J., Carff, J., Drakunov, S., Goswami, A.: Capture point: a step toward humanoid push recovery. In: Proceedings of Humanoids-2006, Genoa, Italy (2006)
8. Lee, S.H., Goswami, A.: Reaction Mass Pendulum (RMP): an explicit model for centroidal angular momentum of humanoid robots. In: Proceedings of ICRA-2007, Rome, Italy, pp. 4667–4672 (2007)
9. Kajita, S., Morisawa, M., Miura, K., Nakaoka, S., Harada, K., Kaneko, K., Kanehiro, F., Yokoi, K.: Biped walking stabilization based on linear inverted pendulum tracking. In: Proceedings of IROS 2010, pp. 4489–4496. IEEE, Taipei (2010)

10. Vukobratović, M.: How to control artificial anthropomorphic systems. IEEE Trans. Syst. Man Cybern. **5**, 497–507 (1973)
11. Yi, S.J., Zhang, B.T., Hong, D., Lee, D.D.: Learning full body push recovery control for small humanoid robots. In: Proceedings of the 2011 IEEE International Conference on Robotics and Automation, Shanghai, China (2011)
12. Hirai, K., Hirose, M., Haikawa, Y., Takenaka, T.: The development of Honda humanoid robot. In: Proceedings of ICRA-98, pp. 1321–1326 (1998)
13. Morisawa, M., Kanehiro, F., Kaneko, K., Mansard, N., Sola, J., Yoshida, E., Yokoi, K., Laumond, J.P.: Combining suppression of the disturbance and reactive stepping for recovering balance. In: Proceedings of IROS 2010, Taipei, pp. 3150–3156 (2010)
14. Cho, B.K., Park, S.S., Oh, J.H.: Stabilization of a hopping humanoid robot for a push. In: Proceedings of IROS 2010, Taipei, pp. 60–65 (2010)
15. Missura, M., Behnke, S.: Omnidirectional capture steps for bipedal walking. In: Proceedings of Humanoids-2013, Atlanta, GA, pp. 401–408 (2013)
16. Assman, T., Nijmeijer, H., Takanishi, A., Hashimoto, K.: Biomechanically motivated lateral biped balancing using momentum control. Technical report DC 2011.035, Eindhoven University of Technology (2012)
17. Graf, C., Röfer, T.: A center of mass observing 3D-LIPM gait for the RoboCup standard platform league humanoid. In: Röfer, T., Mayer, N.M., Savage, J., Saranlı, U. (eds.) RoboCup 2011. LNCS (LNAI), vol. 7416, pp. 102–113. Springer, Heidelberg (2012). https://doi.org/10.1007/978-3-642-32060-6_9
18. Stephens, B.: Push recovery control for force-controlled humanoid robots. Ph.D. thesis, Carnegie Mellon University Pittsburgh, Pennsylvania, USA (2011)
19. Missura, M., Behnke, S.: Online learning of foot placement for balanced bipedal walking. In: Proceedings of Humanoids-2014, Madrid, Spain, pp. 322–328 (2014)
20. Tajima, R., Honda, D., Suga, K.: Fast running experiments involving a humanoid robot. In: Proceedings of ICRA-2009, pp. 1571–1576 (2009)
21. Sreenath, K., Park, H.W., Poulakakis, I., Grizzle, J.W.: A compliant hybrid zero dynamics controller for stable, efficient and fast bipedal walking on MABEL. Int. J. Robot. Res. **30**(9), 1170–1193 (2011)
22. Yun, S.K., Goswami, A.: Momentum-based reactive stepping controller on level and non-level ground for humanoid robot push recovery. In: Proceedings of IROS-2011, San Francisco, CA (2011)
23. Lee, S.H., Goswami, A.: Ground reaction force control at each foot: a momentum-based humanoid balance controller for non-level and non-stationary ground. In: Proceedings of IROS-2010, Taipei, pp. 3157–3162 (2010)
24. Hofmann, A.: Robust execution of bipedal walking tasks from biomechanical principles. Ph.D. thesis, Massachusetts Institute of Technology (2006)
25. RoboCup: Humanoid league technical challenge. http://www.robocuphumanoid.org/wp-content/uploads/HumanoidLeagueRules2015-06-29.pdf
26. Anderson, J., Baltes, J., Tu, K.Y.: Improving robotics competitions for real-world evaluation of AI. In: Proceedings of the AAAI Spring Symposium on Experimental Design for Real-World Systems, Stanford, CA, March 2009

Robot Magic: A Robust Interactive Humanoid Entertainment Robot

Kyle J. Morris[1], Vladyslav Samonin[1], John Anderson[1(✉)], Meng Cheng Lau[1], and Jacky Baltes[2]

[1] Autonomous Agents Laboratory, Department of Computer Science, University of Manitoba, Winnipeg, MB R3T 2N2, Canada
andersj@cs.umanitoba.ca
[2] Department of Electrical Engineering, National Taiwan Normal University, Taipei, Taiwan
http://aalab.cs.umanitoba.ca/

Abstract. In recent years, there have been a number of popular robotics competitions whose intent is to advance the state of research by comparing embodied entries against one another in real time. The IEEE Humanoid application challenge is intended to broaden these by allowing more open-ended entries, with a general theme within which entrants are challenged to create the most effective application involving a humanoid robot. This year's theme was Robot Magic, and this paper describes our first-place winning entry in the 2017 competition, running on a ROBO-TIS OP2 humanoid robot. We describe the overall agent design and contributions to perception, learning, control, and representation, which together support a robust live robot magic performance.

1 Introduction

There are many ways of advancing robot technology and artificial intelligence, from studying component elements (mechatronics, kinematics, vision, learning) to building fully-functional agents for particular domains. The history of artificial intelligence research has generally shown the latter to be especially important, since studying components in isolation removes the effects of interaction with other components, and excludes factors that only embodiment brings. This is one of the main motivations for the evaluation of intelligent robotics in competition settings [1], and such competitions have become both an important part of evaluating robotics research and as well as a driver for public interest in robotics and artificial intelligence.

A broad range of robotics competitions exist today, differing by intended audience and goal. The most well known of these are robot soccer competitions such as RoboCup, as well as more specialized competitions (e.g. RoboCup@Home for service robotics) and those emphasizing a broad range of skills (e.g. the FIRA HuroCup, a multi-event robot athletic competition intended to encourage breath in humanoid performance [2]).

© Springer International Publishing AG, part of Springer Nature 2018
M. Mouhoub et al. (Eds.): IEA/AIE 2018, LNAI 10868, pp. 245–256, 2018.
https://doi.org/10.1007/978-3-319-92058-0_23

The IEEE Humanoid Application Challenge is a humanoid competition designed to be more open-ended, and incorporate potential avenues of research not well represented in other competitions, from dexterity and complex motion planning to believability and human-robot interaction. In the last two years, this event has involved the area of entertainment robots as a common ground between entries, with a theme of robot magic - where a humanoid robot can take on any role in a magic show.

Magic is well-known form of entertainment and deception, with tricks for amusement and as a illusion of power possessed by a magician having been recorded from the ancient world through to modern times [3]. It is a cross-cultural activity, and in that sense is something that is accessible to a broad audience, similar to soccer. Magic employs a range of techniques, from slight of hand to physical devices to create these illusions. A key part of any magic act is also distracting or changing the focus of an audience to disguise the mechanisms behind a given trick, a form of disinformation provided through the principles of stagecraft [4].

All of this provides much opportunity for improving work in robotics and artificial intelligence. A plausible robot magic act also has strong connections to other real-world domains: perceiving an error-prone world, goal directed reasoning, adaptation in the face of failure, and successful interaction - all performed in real time under challenging conditions.

We have been successful in our efforts in the Humanoid Application Challenge over a long period of time, having taken first or second place in each year this competition has been run. We most recently placed first in the 2017 Robot Magic Competition, and this paper describes the agent design of this winning entry and its implementation on a ROBOTIS OP2 Humanoid Robot.

2   Related Work

There are a broad range of applications of artificial intelligence that can be considered entertainment-related. There is work on producing art and composing music (e.g. [5]), but these are distinct from live interactive works in that it is the artifact produced by the system - the completed music or art - that is intended to be entertaining to humans, rather than the process (though there are real-time efforts as well, such as Google's *AI Duet* and *Quick, Draw!* [6]). There are also intelligent systems built for playing many games against humans, such as traditional board games such as checkers [7], chess, and a broad range of video games.

While these may be considered live performances, they are distinct from working with robots in a real time setting, since interaction is generally virtual, through a computational user interface rather than a face to face interaction. The challenges are much greater when working with physical robots - sensors are erroneous, items being moved can be dropped, robots trip and fall, batteries run out of power, and all manner of real-world interaction can occur that does not need to be considered in virtual environments. Any physical interaction requires significant systems to be engineered (e.g. vision that is robust to lighting changes).

Because of this, instances of viable physical entertainment robots are less numerous than their software counterparts, and working with humanoid robots in particular introduces many challenges. Balancing is much more difficult than using wheeled robots, for example, not just because of a bipedal walk but because of the complex poses the body can achieve. Beyond balancing, the more complex motion model of a humanoid (and sensors mounted on head that move independently) greatly complicates fundamental robot applications such as simultaneous localization and mapping (SLAM) [8,9]. Such applications are necessary, for example, for a humanoid robot to position itself on a stage during a performance, or manage objects within its space. For that reason, human-like robots intended for interaction with humans (including entertainment) are frequently only partially humanoid in form, with a more rigid body structure and substituting a wheeled platform for legs (e.g. Pepper [10]).

There are some entertainment-related examples of humanoid robots that are not simply toys. For example, Kuroki [11] presented a bipedal robot intended for entertainment purposes, but the core of the work involved complex motion planning so that the robot could perform motions interacting with music, as opposed to interacting with humans directly.

In terms of work directly with magic, there are few directly comparable published works. Koretake [12] presented a robot intended to be used for card magic, but this work focused only on card manipulation through a device without anthropomorphic hands, and with no humanoid body. Even within the context of card magic, the work involved only manipulating cards directly (e.g. second card dealing), as opposed to any means of timing or interaction in an overall magic performance, nor anything beyond card magic. There has been growing discussion of the need for timing and human-robot interaction for effective live performance [13,14], but this discussion has been largely theoretical.

The previous (2016) IEEE Humanoid Application Challenge was also themed on robot magic, and our entry was a humanoid that could autonomously act as an assistant to a human magician [15]. The primary contribution in that work was on machine learning to recognize cards during real time interaction, as opposed to prior work where cards were expected to be reviewed from a fixed distance and angle and required latency that would be unacceptable in a live performance, and an engine for live scripted performance. Our work here furthers this significantly: making the robot central as the magician, focusing on a representation that allows multiple magic tricks of different types to be performed, and improving interaction mechanisms and robustness in the performance. The result is an approach that, while demonstrated as a live magic act, can function broadly in domains that require scripted entertainment and interaction with an audience.

3 Agent Design

In this section we present an architecture that allows for developing robust and extendable live entertainment - while we focus on magic in this particular competition, there is nothing restricting this approach to that one application.

Our architecture is implemented on a ROBOTIS OP2 with 22 degrees of freedom (DOF) and an on-board Atom-based PC. Sensing is provided by an accelerometer and gyroscope for balancing, and a camera, speaker, and microphone for interaction. The robot in performance is depicted in Fig. 1.

Fig. 1. The robot at a live show at IROS 2017, Vancouver.

Our agent architecture (Fig. 2) is centered around live performance, and allows for exploring the notion of a fully embodied agent that perceives, plans, and acts in an entertainment environment. The entertainment, in this case a magic performance, is developed as a series of behaviors structured in a tree. Behaviors can be linked to one another, and are internally structured as finite state machines (FSMs). These collectively represent a show consisting of a series of episodes (magic tricks). Each FSM state may contain various submodules which utilize perception, learning, and robot control. The state transitions may be adjusted dynamically according to high level goals, allowing for reaction to unexpected conditions. Through these, the robot is taken through all the necessary motions and interactions with the audience to present the show. The following subsections describe the major components in this approach.

3.1 Perception Module: Supporting Recognition and Interaction

The perception module receives incoming sensory information and acts as an interface to the planning and learning modules. We extended previous work [15] to create an API for playing card classification, speech recognition, and raw capturing of video and audio input. Perception in terms of the particular objects of interest and methods of interaction is domain specific, and here we cover the work done for a magic performance.

Much of the specific image processing in our work is recognizing cards in real time, so that they can be chosen or shown to an audience. Raw frames are received and stored in an OpenCV Mat after applying gray scaling, blur, and binary thresholding. Front-of-Card recognition is acquired by detecting contours on the input image, and doing a polygon approximation to gather estimated

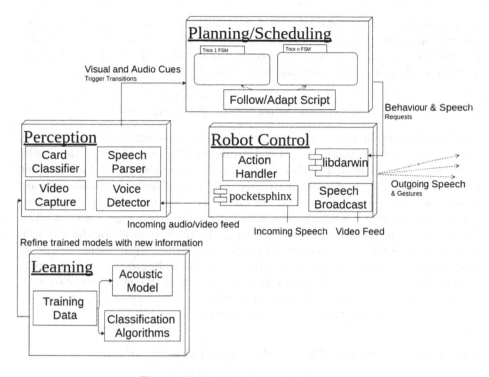

Fig. 2. High Level Agent Architecture

card corners. After applying feature checks and performing an affine transformation, the card suit and rank regions of interest are extracted and sent to the learning module for classification. Working with the rear images of cards is also important for many games, such as when dealing cards. Back-of-card detection undergoes the same preprocessing phase. However, blob detection is instead used to recognize the dotted pattern of the cards back. Each "dot" represents a blob on the back of the card. Among these blobs, the centroid is calculated, and if the cluster of blobs surpasses the minimum density threshold, we deem the card as found.

For speech, raw audio is sampled at 16 mhz and hypothesis strings are then created using the PocketSphinx engine. After a hypothesis is formed, it is mined for keywords in the learning module, and encoded information (detected objects/keywords in speech) that provoke state transitions in the performance. Latency in this component is reduced by performing a window-based sampling of the input speech, instead of waiting for a given speech instance to terminate. In the traditional approach, speech is sampled until there is a lack of speech input. At this point a hypothesis string will be formed. The challenge with this is that in the presence of a loud environment (e.g. audience noise), the speech sample may continue indefinitely as there is no well defined gap in audio input. Waiting for the entire utterance also introduces a significant lag in response in a live performance. We adapt this by forcing a sample window to cut the speech apart in fixed intervals, where mining for keywords may be performed on multiple windows separately. This guarantees key information will be detected within a given window, and promotes timely response in a live performance.

3.2 Learning Module: Adapting to the Environment

The learning module extracts features and performance-critical information from preprocessed perceptual input. Offline learning utilizes vision and speech samples taken from the perception module to train on an ensemble of machine learning models. Training data for playing cards is created using the robot's onboard camera and stored in CSV format. In our system we use CMUSphinx to create a trained acoustic model for the assistant's voice, that will then be used by PocketSphinx for speech recognition during the performance (for the assistant as well as the audience members). Training for playing card recognition uses an ensemble of K-Nearest Neighbours [16] and Logistic Regression. The learning module furthermore acts as a working-memory during the performance by storing run-time information such as card values and audience responses that are required for provoking transitions between behaviors.

3.3 Control Module: The Hardware-Software Interface

The control component provides drivers and lower level primitives for interacting with the robotic hardware. This allows for interfacing the perceptual module with various devices and acts as a middleware in our system to address robot components abstractly. This was necessary as major robotic development tools such as ROS do not yet support the ROBOTIS OP2. We developed an Action Handler built on-top of the libdarwin Framework (the basic action framework built into the ROBOTIS OP2) that allows for simultaneous motion and speech. Audio input is recorded through a NESSIE Adaptive USB Condenser Microphone and the PulseAudio sound server. OpenCV is used to read in video feed from the ROBOTIS OP2's Logitech camera. Sensory input is then passed to the perceptual module where it is preprocessed and encoded for the learning module.

3.4 Planning Module: Magic Tricks as Finite State Machines

The Planning/Scheduling module causes the robot to achieve goal directed behavior and adapts this as necessary during the show. Like any performance, this involves having a representation of the performance and adapting this as the performance unfolds.

Most sophisticated applications intended to run on a robot must consider high level goal-directed reasoning (e.g. planning to pick up an object or move to a location). At the same time, the actions manipulated by a planner are not usually directly executable on a robot as a single instruction (for example, in a humanoid a basic action such as moving forward a discrete amount requires adjusting many servos with careful timing and integrating this with sensors for balance). In our approach, the lowest level of this is handled by the Control Module's Action Handler. Above this we employ a behavior-based approach [17], where behaviors are interconnected and form a context and influence related or lower-level behaviors. Behaviors are constructed as finite state machines, which are in turn connected into larger behavior tree structures, analogous to their use in other types of dynamic activities, such as robot soccer [18].

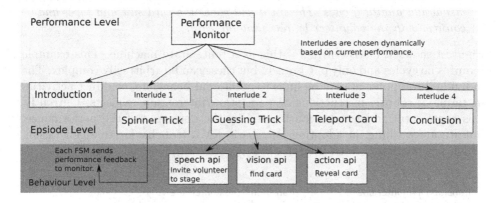

Fig. 3. Structure of a performance

These trees form a three-level hierarchy in our approach, shown in Fig. 3. At the *Performance* level, the objective is to complete a performance within a given time constraint, and maintain audience involvement. A performance consists of an introduction, a number episodes (in our domain, magic tricks or illusions), and a conclusion. This top level acts as a supervisory monitor that overviews the progress in the live show. Below the Performance level is the *Episode* level. Here we focus on an individual portion of the performance, and the objective in our demonstration domain is to successfully complete a single magic trick. Below the episode level, the *Behavior* level interfaces with the control module for performing actions, and interfaces with the perception module to gather information at run time. At a high level, a magic performance can be seen as a finite state machine with transitions between all of the tricks, and connecting interludes in the show. The performance layer adds robustness by supplying a context to the behaviors below it. For example, it can allow transitions between states to change dynamically given the progress in a performance. These may be high-level modifications such as skipping a magic trick in the event that time is running short, or low-level adjustments such as changing a dialog to account for the transition between two potentially unrelated tricks. For example, if trick A was related to trick B, but B is cancelled, a new interlude from A to C is required). This handles a range of dynamic alterations, similar to altering a planned walking path when a new obstacle is discovered.

Performance episodes are domain dependent, and require representing the trick (or other element of performance in a different domain) in terms of one or more behaviours (finite state machines). A verbal description of a magic trick might be:

> *The robot selects a volunteer from the audience and picks up the magic deck. The volunteer picks a card from magic deck. The robot asks the volunteer to show the playing card to the audience. The robot waits for the assistant to provide a cue. The robot will determine card suit and type from visual and auditory cues. The robot will guess the card suit and type, and confirm with the volunteer by revealing the card.*

Figure 4 shows the structuring of this as a finite state machine. This example requires no cycles and only one branch, but these can be arbitrarily complex. The individual components may be links to additional behaviors, or direct activities in terms of robotic instructions or perception/interaction requests. Currently, this representation must be constructed by the developer of the performance, but we are working on adopting automatic XML to behavior tree generation, which has previously been used in other domains [19].

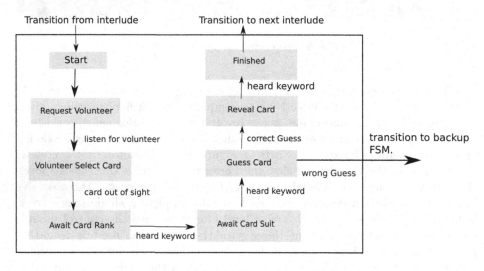

Fig. 4. Example FSM for a magic trick/performance episode.

3.5   Fault Tolerance and Robustness

Like any other robotics domain, a large range of potential problems can occur during a live entertainment performance. The fact that this is carried out in front of an audience, and the unfolding events affect their expectations, makes this even more challenging. Ultimately, no matter what happens, the show must go on. Part of any robust performance involves ensuring the representation of activities is as detailed as possible so that potential problems can be anticipated and planned for. However, there is still always the opportunity for mistakes on behalf of the magician, functionality problems with props, or unexpected behavior from the audience or a volunteer.

In our implementation, we limit the scope of uncertainty in the environment to two types of common mishaps that may occur during a magic show. The first is an error on behalf of a human magician, assistant or volunteer (e.g. script lines are forgotten, or a non-useful response is provided). The second type of error involves hardware or unexpected internal behavior in the robot (e.g. microphone disconnects, battery is low). For the first type of error, the planning component can be used to create a dynamic link to a FSM consisting of backup states, which support recovery to unexpected audience or volunteer responses from a range of tricks. For example, if a volunteer is asked to pick a number within some range, and they select a value outside that range, the robot can react accordingly and return to the trick. These backup states provide additional dialog which acts as a natural bridge from a hiccup in a performance to a reasonable checkpoint.

Some instances of the second type of error can be handled similarly. For example, a backup state is used if lighting is too poor for object recognition, causing the robot to say "My vision isn't working, could someone check the lights?", alerting to the problem and buying time to raise the lights. Beyond these, we also monitor components on the robot from the control module and save checkpoints throughout the show. In the event of an unexpected microphone disconnection, vision crash, or unexpected termination of the main process, the performance may be resumed from the most recent checkpoint by transitioning into a recovery state where the robot will explain that "mistakes happen, we are all humans here" before returning to the checkpoint state using multiple ε-transitions (transitions that do not require a specific trigger for each) through the performance FSM. This recovery process can be seen in Fig. 5.

If there is no known recovery possibility, the planning component can still dynamically alter links between behaviors to allow the show to proceed based on knowledge of what is wrong and what facilities tricks require. For example, if the vision system crashes at a given point in the first trick, this may not be an immediate problem if vision is not needed, but would strongly affect future tricks. If this cannot be recovered from, a dynamic transition can be placed by

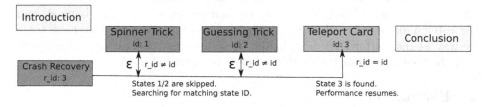

Fig. 5. An outline of the checkpoint recovery system. Upon a run-time crash, we may do multiple ε transitions searching for a recent checkpoint.

the planning module to skip upcoming tricks requiring vision if the vision module has not been detected as working by that point the performance. This supports maintaining what is possible in the show, while also allowing time for problems on the robot to be fixed.

4 A Full Magic Act

As an example of the breath that this approach can support, we created a magic performance for the 2017 IEEE Humanoid Application Challenge. Our performance involves four magic tricks, each focused on a different aspect of robotics for entertainment.

Trick 1: Card Spinning: The first trick requires an audience member to choose a playing card, which is shown to the audience but not the robot. This card is placed face down on a fidget spinner toy and provided to the robot, which is tasked with guessing the card's suit and rank. The robot uses back-of-card detection to transition through the trick. The robot determines the suit and rank of the card through visual and vocal cues from the magician (which are apparent to the audience). When the audience member reveals the card, they find that the pattern on the card has been altered, and changed into a swirled pattern to imply that the fidget spinner rotated the cards face. This breaks the ice with the audience by appearing to not perform very good magic (because the robot is told the card) while surprising with a different manipulation.

Trick 2: Guessing Trick: The second trick creates the illusion that the audience actually expected from the first: the robot determines the card rank and suit without appearing to be explicitly told. This is a common human magic trick, and is done by the assistant using coded key words recognized by the robot to convey the particular suit. At this point, the robot fakes stumbling on the performance. The assistant then claims that this mistake shouldn't be happening, as they've been rehearsing this performance since $*MONTH*$, providing a second recognized code that allows a range of 1..12 to be recognized (for cards Ace...Queen). An alternative special keyword is used for the case of a King. The audience does not notice that the dialog provides card information to the robot subtly.

Trick 3: Card Vanishing: This trick utilizes the kinematics of our robot, by using a magic-box prop for making a playing card disappear. The robot must navigate the box in such a way to flip the contents and hide the card.

Trick 4: Finale: The finale builds the stage experience by appearing to come after the show is finished. The audience member from trick 3 is thanked, and the robot prompts the volunteer to select a chocolate bar from the snack table by way of thanks for their help in the performance. Upon picking a chocolate bar, the volunteer finds their vanished card from trick 3 inside the wrapper.

5 Evaluation

There are many ways of evaluating a work such as this, where a large number of components come together into a functional agent. The individual components can certainly be tested under controlled conditions, either individually or in subsets. In our work, for example, we have tested our vision and learning together. Under dynamic lighting, and with the learning mechanisms described above, we achieve 89% card rank accuracy in dynamic lighting conditions, and 90% suit accuracy. Similarly, there is a noticeable performance increase in reduced speech sampling latency resulting from the window-based approach to sampling speech as opposed to waiting for a speech pause.

This is not as easy to do when looking at the complete agent in its domain: it is difficult to come up with a numerical representation of how good a robot is at magic. Evaluating robots in their intended environment is a strong philosophy of most robotics competitions. In robotic soccer, for example, there are a definite set of rules and a team stands or falls by its performance - presumably the winner of a robotic soccer competition is the strongest team. Magic, however, has no hard and fast rules. The qualities that make a strong performance are in many ways inherently qualitative, and this is similar to many human competitions from sporting events such as gymnastics to entertainment-based performances such as music or drama. In the Humanoid Application Challenge, similar issues have always been an issue in terms of judging the most effective application, even before it began using robot magic as a theme. Like many analogous human contests, dispassionate human judges are used to rank entries in terms of metrics suitable to the domain. For robot magic, entrants are judged based on a live performance and a technical presentation, using metrics such as effectiveness, functionality, technical complexity, and audience involvement, and these are combined from all judges. By this standard the approach described in this paper came out very well, winning first place (a ROBOTIS OP3 robot).

6   Discussion and Future Work

In this paper we have described our approach to robust live performance for a humanoid robot. This involves a number of interacting components for perceiving, learning, and carrying out and altering plans for activity. Central to this is a representation for a performance in terms of behavior structures, and the ability to follow these in spite of problems at run time.

This work has been implemented and demonstrated for a magic performance, but magic is not dissimilar to many other applications, such as comedy or drama. This approach can be used for any application relying on a scripted performance by a humanoid that must deal with technical and interaction-based problems during performances. For example, actors can miss cues, and heckling can interrupt a comedy act, but both of these can be anticipated to some degree.

There is much potential for future work in terms of better learning and interaction mechanisms, improvements in motion control, and the dynamic construction of behaviours to simplify the description of performances. We also intend to explore dynamic performance construction, choosing elements from a known library and altering choices based on what pleases the audience most.

References

1. Baltes, J., Anderson, J.: Advancing artificial intelligence through minimalist humanoid robotics. In: Liu, D., Wang, L., Tan, K.C. (eds.) Design and Control of Intelligent Robotic Systems, pp. 355–376. Springer, Heidelberg (2009). https://doi.org/10.1007/978-3-540-89933-4_17
2. Baltes, J., Tu, K.Y., Sadeghnejad, S., Anderson, J.: Hurocup: competition for multi-event humanoid robot athletes. Knowl. Eng. Rev., 1–14 (2016)
3. Randi, J.: Conjuring. St. Martin's Press, New York (1993)
4. Tufte, E., Swiss, J.I.: Explaining magic: pictorial instructions and disinformation design. In: Tufte, E. (ed.) Visual Explanations. Graphics Press, Cheshire (1997)
5. Liang, F., Gotham, M., Johnson, M., Shotton, J.: Automatic stylistic composition of bach chorales with deep LSTM. In: Proceedings of the 18th International Society for Music Information Retrieval Conference (ISMIR-17), Suzhou, China, October 2017
6. Google: Experiments with Google. https://experiments.withgoogle.com/ai
7. Schaeffer, J., Burch, N., Björnsson, Y., Kishimoto, A., Müller, M., Lake, R., Lu, P., Sutphen, S.: Checkers is solved. Science **317**, 1518–1521 (2007)
8. Bagot, J., Anderson, J., Baltes, J.: Vision-based multi-agent slam for humanoid robots. In: Proceedings of CIRAS-2008), pp. 171–176, June 2008
9. Baltes, J., Cheng, C.T., Bagot, J., Anderson, J.: Vision-based obstacle run for teams of humanoid robots (demonstrated system). In: Proceedings of AAMAS-2011, Taipei, Taiwan, pp. 1319–1320, May 2011
10. Softbank Robotics: Pepper. http://www.softbankrobotics.com
11. Kuroki, Y.: A small biped entertainment robot. In: Proceedings of 2001 International Symposium on Micromechatronics and Human Science, MHS 2001, pp. 3–4 (2001)
12. Koretake, R., Kaneko, M., Higashimori, M.: The robot that can achieve card magic. ROBOMECH J. **2**(1) (2015)
13. Nuñez, D., Tempest, M., Viola, E., Breazeal, C.: An initial discussion of timing considerations raised during development of a magician-robot interaction. In: Proceedings ACM/IEEE Workshop on Timing in Human-Robot Interaction HRI (2014)
14. Tamura, Y., Yano, S., Osumi, H.: Modeling of human attention based on analysis of magic. In: Proceedings of HRI 2014, New York, NY, USA, pp. 302–303. ACM (2014)
15. Morris, K., Anderson, J., Lau, M.C., Baltes, J.: Interaction and learning in a humanoid robot magic performance. In: Proceedings of the AAAI Spring Symposium on Integrated Representation, Reasoning, and Learning in Robotics, March 2018
16. Kotsiantis, S.B., Zaharakis, I., Pintelas, P.: Supervised machine learning: a review of classification techniques (2007)
17. Arkin, R.C.: Behavior-Based Robotics. MIT Press, Cambridge (1998)
18. Anderson, J., Baltes, J.: An agent-based approach to introductory robotics using robotic soccer. Int. J. Rob. Autom. **21**(2), 141–152 (2006)
19. Liu, T., Baltes, J., Anderson, J.: Archangel, a flexible and intuitive architecture for intelligent mobile robots. In: Proceedings of CIRAS-2005, Singapore, December 2005

A Probabilistic Model for Automobile Diagnosis System: Combining Bayesian Estimator and Expert Knowledge

Mustakim Al Helal and Malek Mouhoub[✉]

Department of Computer Science, University of Regina, Regina, Canada
{mhx049,mouhoubm}@uregina.ca

Abstract. Recent trends in Artificial Intelligence based softwares have a strong link up with learning. Probabilistic graphical models have been used over the years for solving problems under uncertainty. In this paper, an automobile diagnosis system is proposed to predict the root reason for a faulty part inside a car engine. The system combines Conditional Probabilistic Distributions (CPDs) from the expert as well as those learnt from the user using a Bayesian estimator. In this regard, a learning function is incorporated to combine the CPDs in terms of weighted mean. These combined CPDs are then modeled by a Bayesian Network that is traversed to return a probabilistic solution according to the symptoms given by the user. The Variable elimination algorithm is used for inference. In this regard, several variable ordering heuristics have been evaluated and compared in terms of time efficiency.

Keywords: Bayesian Network · Uncertainty reasoning
Conditional Probability Distribution · Sigmoid function
Decision learning

1 Introduction

Probabilistic diagnosis applications are among the classical Bayesian Network (BN) problems that have been applied in diverse real life applications. One well known example is medical diagnosis that has been used to assist doctors during their daily tasks. A vehicle engine combines different parts, connected internally to work as a complete system. These parts can have issues that can result in a faulty engine system. This implicitly involves some uncertainty regarding the decision making as to which part of the engine is actually faulty. This has motivated us to propose a car engine diagnosis system for detecting faulty parts in automobiles. Our system has been developed using a Bayesian approach, modeled as a Directed Acyclic Graph (DAG), for detecting the root cause of the problem based on user's input as well as expert's knowledge. More precisely, and using a sigmoid function, our system combines expert's knowledge and user's feedback into Conditional Probabilistic Distribution (CPDs). The goal of the

© Springer International Publishing AG, part of Springer Nature 2018
M. Mouhoub et al. (Eds.): IEA/AIE 2018, LNAI 10868, pp. 257–264, 2018.
https://doi.org/10.1007/978-3-319-92058-0_24

sigmoid function is to learn the combined CPD values and to return the final probabilistic results. The user's provided evidence goes through the system back end and then the Variable Elimination (VE) algorithm is applied to prune out unnecessary nodes from the DAG. While VE suffers from an exponential time complexity in theory, its efficiency in practice can be improved using a variable ordering heuristic. In this regard, we conducted an experimental comparative study of the well known variable ordering heuristics in order to identify the one that best improves the time performance of the VE method. The results of these experiments favor the Min Neighbor heuristic.

2   Related Work

Several works have been reported in the past about expert knowledge with data. Expert knowledge was applied when no historical data were available [1]. Occurs in [2], a method was proposed where statistical data was combined with prior knowledge. However, this method was used to learn a BN but not the CPDs as it is the case in our proposed system. Another fault detection system has also been proposed in [3]. In this latter work, a BN was proposed to detect the faulty feeder's location on a distribution feeder. The BN was developed on the basis of expert knowledge and historical data. On one hand, substantial historical data were used to estimate the prior probability on the target hypothesis and, on the other hand, structured interviews were performed to elicit knowledge from domain experts. The expert knowledge and historical results were compared using the Pearson correlation coefficient [4]. The BN has also been used to detect performance fault in gas turbines [5]. In this regard, a Bayesian Belief Network (BBN) based fault detection system is proposed. This latter does not, however, depend on flight data on different faulty operations which is difficult to find. Rather, the information can be extracted from a deterministic model proposed in their paper.

3   Proposed Model

Artificial Intelligence diagnosis applications often deal with uncertain knowledge and input data, through a probabilistic or a possibilistic approach. We adopt a probabilistic model using a Bayesian approach represented with a DAG. Constructing a DAG that is complete and consistent is important for reasoning about uncertainty and the challenge here is to define the dependencies. The vehicle diagnostic system is a typical problem that can be represented as a BN. This latter can model uncertainty over a given node that is dependent on other nodes. The BN is also very useful to regulate the probability values when there are many possible outcomes. In a vehicle diagnosis system, there could be many reasons for a particular evidence provided by the user. Among those, we need to find out the most likely one. The BN CPD values are useful to reason about the nodes in an efficient way.

Our proposed model can predict the root reason for a faulty car problem. It is implemented using Python for back end development. Flask framework was used to integrate user interface with the back end. For a given problem, we first construct the DAG and then apply the Variable Elimination (VE) algorithm for inference. This latter algorithm is improved using variable ordering heuristics. The equation, combining user's data and expert's knowledge, generates a sigmoid curve. From this equation, we can compute the weights for the user's and the expert's data. The BN corresponding to a given car diagnosis problem is illustrated in Fig. 1. The BN is created first before the expert's CPDs added. To calculate the final CPDs, user's data are saved and the weighted mean function is applied to combine both the CPDs learnt from the user as well as those from the expert. Once the combined CPDs are formed, the VE algorithm is applied and the query results are returned. The DAG, illustrated in Fig. 1, consists of 41 nodes in total. Among them, 17 are root nodes indicating the symptoms, 2 are intermediate nodes and 22 are child nodes indicating the reasons.

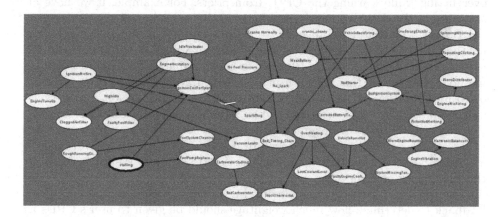

Fig. 1. Bayesian Network representation (DAG) of the diagnosis problem.

To construct the DAG in Fig. 1, we went through the following steps. First, we conducted a study on car engines, the common problems that might occur and their causes[1]. We then identified a list of symptoms and their possible causes. These have been translated into a total of 41 nodes. Root nodes indicate initial symptoms. The 2 intermediate nodes are not directly causing the problem but are involved in the failure of certain parts of the engine. The 22 leaf nodes represent the reasons of the faults.

---

[1] In this regard, we have used the following website: https://auto.howstuffworks.com/ engine.htm. We also relied on the expertise of a car engine mechanic who has been working at Canadian Tire for over 2 years and is experienced about car engine troubleshooting.

3.1 Learning Process

Learning is one of the main contributions in this paper. We designed a learning function which combines user's CPDs and expert's CPD. There are not much work that have been done specifically with learning functions in the case of automobile diagnosis with BNs. A Sigmoid function was designed in this work to combine data. Sigmoid functions were used in early 90s in [6] in mean field theory to achieve a tractable approximation of the true probability distribution. PGMPy [7] can help in building CPDs using user's data. Our model can be extended to get user's feedback about system predictions. This feedback can be accumulated over a long term to improve our results. PGMPy takes data as input in a single file and converts them into CPDs. It provides a *BayesianEstimator* class for learning these CPDs. The Bayesian parameter estimator uses already existing prior CPDs that can be considered as already existing pseudo state counts. The Bayesian estimator gives a more conservative values to the CPDs. One of the advantages of the Bayesian estimator is that it effectively avoids over fitting while learning the CPDs from priors. For example, if we have an attribute in the database which has about 10 tuples having all the values as 1, the Bayesian estimator would not give a value of 1.00. That is what expected for the CPDs since it is not a good practice to put values as 1 or 0 in them. We used *equivalent_sample_size = 10* as a parameter value in *BayesianEstimator()* method. This means that for each parent configuration, we add the equivalent of 10 uniform samples. We consider that expert opinion is of some importance and should be given some weightage when learning from data. Unfortunately the PGMPy [7] does not provide a method which can help in taking into account the expert's CPDs as well as those learned from user's feedback. Our goal is to give a weight to the user feedback as well as the expert's opinion. We can accomplish this using a sigmoid function.

The process of learning is depicted in Fig. 2. The sigmoid function uses user's feedback to determine how much weightage should be given to user's CPDs as well as expert's CPDs. The basic idea behind this is that the significance of learning should depend upon how much data is available. In the next section we will explain the learning function in details.

3.2 Learning Function

User's feedback data is randomly generated using a Python function for testing purposes. The learning function takes the number of rows of an observation as input. For each CPD, the number of rows for a given combination of evidences is saved in a dictionary object. Each CPD is enumerated, the row count for given evidences is looked up and feeded to the learning function. Once the weight for the expert's data, W_{Expert} and the weight for the user's data, W_{Data} are calculated, we multiply them with the corresponding probability of the expert's CPD and user data's CPD respectively. These are added to get the new CPD which would be now used to run inferences. The learning function uses user's feedback data to calculate weightage. We used a sigmoid function for this purpose

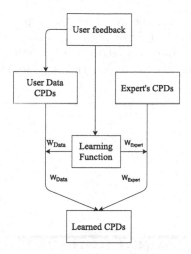

Fig. 2. Learning process diagram

and modified it to provide flexibility in learning from data. The sigmoid function also helps in determining how much importance should be given to user's data. The learning function equation is as follows. $x = d/(1 + e \wedge (n/M - 6))$. Here x is the generic weight value, n is the number of data present for a given observation, M is a learning constant which could regulate the learning rate. A higher value means a slower learning rate. The constant d is helpful if more weight should be provided to either user's data or expert's knowledge. A greater d value will give more weight to user's data in comparison to expert's knowledge. The weight for expert's knowledge can be computed using the following equation: $W_{experts} = 1/(1 + x)$. The weight for user's data can be computed using the following equation: $W_{data} = x/(1 + x)$.

4   Experimentation

In this section, a comparative evaluation of different variable ordering heuristics has been conducted in order to assess the best one in practice to be used with the VE algorithm. In addition, we present in the following how do expert's and user's data converge, in practice, using the sigmoid function we presented previously.

4.1   Sigmoid function

Learning rates are illustrated through graphical representations in Fig. 3 and vary by changing the values of m and d. In Fig. 3 (top chart), as the data increase W_{Data} increases meanwhile W_{expert} keeps decreasing. They both converge to a weight equal to 0.5. In the middle chart of Fig. 3, the visible difference is that the expert curve becomes stable at weight value 0.2 and the data curve becomes stable at a weight value of 0.8. Therefore, it can be realized that we are able to regulate the final weight value at which the expert and the data curve to get stabilized. In the bottom chart of Fig. 3, we note that the only difference in comparison to the middle chart, is that the convergence rate is slower due to the increased learning rate m. Hence, we can also regulate the learning rate.

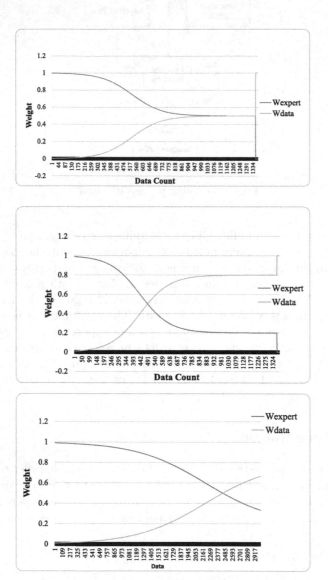

Fig. 3. Combining weights when d = 1 and m = 100 (top), d = 4 and m = 100 (middle) and d = 4 and m = 500 (bottom)

4.2 Heuristics

As we mentioned in Sect. 3, the Variable Elimination algorithm performance depends upon the variable ordering. A good variable ordering can help in reducing the number of multiplication and addition operations which in turn improves the time performance of the algorithm. Various heuristic cost functions can be employed to attain an optimal variable ordering. The most widely used Heuristics cost functions for Variable Elimination are as follows [8].

- *Min-neighbors*: The cost of a variable corresponds to the degree of its node in the DAG (number of neighbors).
- *Min-weight*: The cost of a variable is the product of the domain sizes of its neighbors in the DAG.
- *Min-fill*: The cost of a variable is the number of edges that need to be added to the DAG due to the elimination of its corresponding node.
- *Weighted-min-fill*: Instead of calculating the number of edges (that need to be added) as done in the previous heuristic, we compute the sum of weights of these edges. A weight of an edge is the product of weights of the nodes connected to it.

We applied the above heuristic cost functions on VE and experimentally compared their performances. We ran each algorithm for 5 times and then calculate the mean performance time for each. The results are depicted in Table 1 (the mean time is highlighted in yellow). The Min Neighbor provided the most optimal variable ordering by giving performance with an average execution time of 0.2856 s. The average execution time for Min Fill, Min Weight and Weighted Min Fill were 0.3442s, 0.3788s, 0.4722s respectively. The average execution time without any variable ordering is 0.5322s. As we can see, the Min Neighbor is the best heuristic cost function for our implementation.

Table 1. Comparative results for the variable ordering heuristics

No Heuristic	Min Weight	Min Neighbor	Min Fill	Weighted Min Fill
0.573	0.391	0.308	0.322	0.494
0.526	0.391	0.291	0.333	0.473
0.511	0.359	0.268	0.36	0.474
0.52	0.368	0.274	0.34	0.463
0.531	0.385	0.272	0.366	0.457
0.5322	0.3788	0.2826	0.3442	0.4722

5 Conclusion and Future Work

We have proposed a system for car diagnosis based on BNs. In this regard, we have studied how CPDs can incorporate, through learning, values from expert's and user's data. This application demonstrates how powerful is BN for diagnosis systems. The learning idea, based on a sigmoid function that we propose, can be extended to different diagnosis applications. Our proposed model has the ability to improve its prediction accuracy with time. The more data we feed into the model, the better will be the prediction. Currently, the model is restricted to binary domains only. However, in reality, a car engine part may have many levels of symptoms. For example, a battery condition can be "normal", "replace soon" "replace now" or "service battery". We therefore plan to extend our model in order to include more levels of uncertainty. Another extension that we are planning for our system is to add a Natural Language Processing (NLP) interface. In this regard, we will incorporate a chatbot so that the user can express the problem in an intuitive way. One limitation of our system is that it does not take user's feedback after showing the diagnosis results. We will add this feature in our system in the near future. The user can, for example, select if the given result by the system is right or wrong. In case the user thinks the result is incorrect then he can provide the answer that he thinks is the most likely to be the reason for the fault. This feedback will be stored in a database and used later by the system as additional data.

References

1. Constantinou, A.C., Fenton, N., Neil, M.: Integrating expert knowledge with data in bayesian networks: preserving data-driven expectations when the expert variables remain unobserved. Expert Syst. Appl. **56**(Supplement C), 197–208 (2016)
2. Heckerman, D., Geiger, D., Chickering, D.M.: Learning bayesian networks: the combination of knowledge and statistical data. Mach. Learn. **20**(3), 197–243 (1995)
3. Chien, C.F., Chen, S.L., Lin, Y.S.: Using Bayesian network for fault location on distribution feeder. IEEE Trans. Power Delivery **17**(3), 785–793 (2002)
4. Box, G.E., Hunter, W.G., Hunter, J.S.: Statistics for experimenters: an introduction to design, data analysis, and model building, vol. 1. JSTOR (1978)
5. Romessis, C., Mathioudakis, K.: Bayesian network approach for gas path fault diagnosis. J. Eng. Gas Turbines Power **128**(1), 64–72 (2006)
6. Saul, L.K., Jaakkola, T., Jordan, M.I.: Mean field theory for sigmoid belief networks. J. Artif. Intell. Res. **4**, 61–76 (1996)
7. Ankan, A., Panda, A.: pgmpy: probabilistic graphical models using python. In: Proceedings of the 14th Python in Science Conference, SCIPY 2015 (2015)
8. Koller, D., Friedman, N.: Probabilistic Graphical Models: Principles and Techniques. MIT press, Cambridge (2009)

Knowledge Representation

Socially-Aware Recommendation for Over-Constrained Problems

Muesluem Atas[✉], Thi Ngoc Trang Tran, Alexander Felfernig,
and Ralph Samer

Institute of Software Technology, Graz University of Technology,
Inffeldgasse 16b/II, 8010 Graz, Austria
{muesluem.atas,ttrang,alexander.felfernig,rsamer}@ist.tugraz.at
http://ase.ist.tugraz.at/

Abstract. Group recommender systems support the identification of items that best fit the individual preferences of all group members. A group recommendation can be determined on the basis of aggregation functions. However, to some extent it is still unclear which aggregation function is most suitable for predicting an item to a group. In this paper, we analyze different preference aggregation functions with regard to their prediction quality. We found out that consensus-based aggregation functions (e.g., *Average, Minimal Group Distance, Multiplicative, Ensemble Voting*) which consider all group members' preferences lead to a better prediction quality compared to borderline aggregation functions, such as *Least Misery* and *Most Pleasure* which solely focus on preferences of some individual group members.

Keywords: Group recommender systems · Decision making
Group aggregation functions · Similarity metrics

1 Introduction

Recommender systems are decision support systems that support users in identifying a set of items fitting their wishes and needs [7]. These systems help users to identify useful objects/services (often referred to as *items*) such as movies, books, songs, web sites, financial services, travel destinations, and restaurants [4]. Nowadays, most recommender systems are designed for single users [5]. However, there are many scenarios where items are supposed to be consumed by groups [9]. Examples thereof are deciding about a *restaurant* to visit for a dinner with colleagues, deciding about a *movie* to watch with the family, or deciding about a *travel destination* to visit with friends next year.

Group (i.e., socially-aware) recommender systems support the identification of items that to some extent fit the individual preferences of group members. Examples of such systems are the following. O'Connor et al. [11] present a collaborative filtering movie recommender system for groups named POLYLENS which is based on the *Least Misery* aggregation function. Masthoff [8] introduces concepts to recommend television items to user groups (e.g., choosing

© Springer International Publishing AG, part of Springer Nature 2018
M. Mouhoub et al. (Eds.): IEA/AIE 2018, LNAI 10868, pp. 267–278, 2018.
https://doi.org/10.1007/978-3-319-92058-0_25

a list of television programs to watch together with the family). Moreover, Masthoff found out that group members use some of the aggregation functions (e.g., *Average, Average-Without-Misery,* and *Least Misery*) in television domain and take the fairness aspect into account. Jameson [6] introduces the TRAVEL DECISION FORUM which is used to elicit and aggregate group members' preferences using *Average* aggregation function for selecting tourist destinations. Ardissono et al. [1] introduce INTRIGUE which aggregates group members' preferences using *Average* aggregation function and recommends sightseeing destinations to groups. Furthermore, McCarthy et al. [10] propose a critiquing-based travel recommender system named COLLABORATIVE TRAVEL ADVISORY SYSTEM (CATS) which allows to jointly plan skiing vacations. CATS *averages* the preferences of all group members and recommends a skiing vacation to the group. Ninaus et al. [3] introduce a requirement engineering tool named INTELLIREQ, which is tailored to groups of stakeholders designing release plans. INTELLIREQ is based on the *Majority* aggregation function. Stettinger et al. [12] introduce a domain-independent decision support environment for groups named CHOICLA which is based on multi-attribute utility theory [13].

In this paper, we present a constrained-based socially-aware recommender system which recommends digital SLR (Single-Lens Reflex) cameras to groups by applying different aggregation functions.[1] In this context, we focused on comparing aggregation functions with regard to their capability to predict relevant items in situations where no solutions could be found for a given set of preferences. The result of our study indicates that borderline aggregation functions such as *Least Misery* and *Most Pleasure* have a low prediction quality. They only focus on the lowest and highest values from all individual preferences, i.e., borderline aggregation functions do not consider all existing preferences. On the other hand, consensus-based aggregation functions such as *Average, Ensemble voting, Multiplicative,* and *Minimal Group Distance* consider the preferences of all group members and are more suitable for predicting a product for groups (see Sect. 4).

The remainder of this paper is structured as follows. In Sect. 2, we present a working example from the digital camera domain and explain properties and variables of the used dataset. Section 3 introduces the clustering approach used to synthesize groups. In Sect. 4, we introduce different group aggregation functions and apply these on the synthesized groups. Subsequently, Sect. 5 presents the results of our evaluation. We discuss issues for future work and conclude the paper in Sect. 6.

[1] The work presented in this paper has been partially conducted within the scope of the research projects *WeWant* (basic research project funded by the Austrian Research Promotion Agency) and *OpenReq* (Horizon 2020 project funded by the European Union).

2 Working Example

For demonstration purposes, we introduce a group recommendation scenario from the domain of digital cameras. The work presented in this paper has been conducted in *two phases*: *First*, we conducted a user study where each participant had to declare his/her preferences with regard to a digital camera. *Second*, we synthesized the collected data in order to form groups which were then used to evaluate different preference aggregation functions with regard to their prediction quality.[2] Each participant of the user study had to declare preferences (i.e., constraints) regarding 10 different camera variables and then select three out of these 10 variables which are most important for him/her. Finally, if the defined preferences were inconsistent with the underlying product catalog, participants had to select an alternative camera from the product catalog. For simplicity, we reduce our product catalog from 20 to 5 entries (see Table 1).

Table 1. An example product catalog. In this context, *eff-res* = effective resolution in mega-pixel, *display* = display size in inch, *touch* = touch screen functionality (yes/no), *wifi* = wireless communication functionality (yes/no), *nfc* = near field communication support (yes/no), *gps* = global positioning system functionality (yes/no), *video-res* = video resolution, *zoom* = zoom factor of the camera, *weight* = weight in grams, and *price* = price in Euro.

Product ID	Eff-res	Display	Touch	Wifi	nfc	gps	Video-res	Zoom	Weight	Price
P1	20.9	3.5	yes	yes	no	yes	4K-UHD/3840x2160	3.0	1405	5219
P2	6.1	2.5	yes	yes	no	no	No-Video-Function	3.0	475	659
P3	6.1	2.2	no	no	no	no	No-Video-Function	7.8	700	189
P4	6.2	1.8	yes	yes	yes	no	4K-UHD/3840x2160	5.8	860	2329
P5	6.2	1.8	no	no	no	yes	Full-HD/1920x1080	3.0	560	469

All sessions where user requirements were inconsistent (i.e., over-constrained) with the product catalog (i.e., no solution could be found) were stored. In the following, these sessions were used to synthesize user groups that form the basis for our evaluation of different preference aggregation functions. Our approach to group synthesis is introduced in Sect. 3.

3 Building Synthetic Homogeneous Groups

Since the dataset from our user study is collected from individual participants, dataset for groups has to be synthesized. Synthesizing a dataset by clustering individual participants (i.e., forming groups) is a common approach in recommender systems [2]. The metrics in Formulae 1–3 are used to determine preference similarity $sim(p, c)$ between a reference participant p who currently declared his/her preferences and a candidate participant c from a set of candidates. In this

---

[2] This approach follows group synthesis approaches as introduced in [2].

context, $s(p_i, c_i)$ denotes the similarity of the preference i between a reference participant p and a candidate participant c. In addition, $w(i)$ indicates the importance (weight) of a preference i for a participant, $val(i)$ represents the *value* of preference i, and $minval(p_i)/maxval(p_i)$ are minimum/maximum values of a preference i taken from the product catalog.

Formula 2, *Near-Is-Better* (NIB) is used if the preferences of the candidate participant have to be as near as possible to the preferences of the reference participant. For instance, the recommended camera should be the one which its price is as near as possible to the price specified by the customer. Formula 3, *Equal-Is-Better* (EIB) is applied in situations where the preferences of two participants have to be equal. For a complete overview of related attribute-level similarity functions we refer to [7].

$$sim(p, c) = \frac{\sum_{i \in variables} s(p_i, c_i) * w(i)}{\sum_{i \in variables} w(i)} \tag{1}$$

$$NIB : s(p_i, c_i) = 1 - \frac{|val(p_i) - val(c_i)|}{maxval(p_i) - minval(p_i)} \tag{2}$$

$$EIB : s(p_i, c_i) = \begin{cases} 1 & \text{if } p_i = c_i \\ 0 & \text{otherwise} \end{cases} \tag{3}$$

The following part of this section presents the clustering of participants in order to form groups of similar participants (i.e., homogeneous groups). In order to calculate the similarity between two participants (i.e., potential group members), Formula 2 (NIB) is applied to the variables *effective resolution, display size, zoom, weight,* and *price.* Furthermore, Formula 3 (EIB) is applied to the variables *touch-screen, wifi, nfc, gps,* and *video resolution.* For the purpose of clustering homogeneous group members, the similarity among participants has to be calculated first. Then, the n most similar group members (e.g., cluster size = 4) are selected as group members. This process is repeated for the remaining participants until all groups have been determined. An example of a synthesized group is depicted in Table 2.

Table 2. A synthesized homogeneous group with cluster size of 4. Participants with similar preferences are considered as group members.

Participant	Eff-res	Display	Touch	Wifi	nfc	gps	Video-res	Zoom	Weight	Price
1st participant	20.8	2.5	yes	yes	no	yes	4K-UHD/3840x2160	5.0	700	1649
2nd participant	20.9	2.5	yes	yes	no	yes	4K-UHD/3840x2160	5.0	475	2149
3rd participant	20.9	2.7	yes	yes	no	yes	4K-UHD/3840x2160	7.8	560	2749
4th participant	14.2	2.7	yes	yes	no	no	4K-UHD/3840x2160	5.0	475	659

In order to provide a better understanding for the application of similarity metrics, we will show how the similarity between the 1st group member and the 2nd group member can be calculated (see Table 2). For simplicity, we assume

Table 3. The chosen products and three most important camera variables selected by the participants from Table 2.

Participant	1st imp. variable	2nd imp. variable	3rd imp. variable	Chosen product
1st participant	eff-res	Weight	Price	P1
2nd participant	eff-res	Price	Video-res	P1
3rd participant	eff-res	Display	Price	P3
4th participant	eff-res	Weight	Price	P2

equal weights of all the camera variables for both group members ($w(i) = 1$). Formula 4 shows the similarity calculation between the 1st group member and the 2nd group member on *effective resolution*. In order to apply Formula 2 (NIB) on the *effective resolution* variable, *maximum* and *minimum* effective resolution values are required. The *maxval* and *minval* values are taken from the maximum and minimum effective resolution values of the product catalog (see Table 1).

$$s(1^{st}participant_{eff-res}, 2^{nd}participant_{eff-res})$$

$$= 1 - \frac{|val(1^{st}participant_{eff-res}) - val(2^{nd}participant_{eff-res})|}{maxval(eff-res) - minval(eff-res)} \quad (4)$$

$$= 1 - \frac{|20.8 - 20.9|}{20.9 - 6.1} = 0.9932$$

$$sim(1^{st}participant, 2^{nd}participant)$$

$$= \frac{\sum_{i\in variables} s(1^{st}participant_i, 2^{nd}participant_i) * w(i)}{\sum_{i\in variables} w(i)}$$

$$= \frac{0,9932 + 1 + 1 + 1 + 1 + 1 + 1 + 0,7581 + 0,9006}{1 * 10} \quad (5)$$

$$= 0.9652$$

By applying Formula 2 and Formula 3 to all the remaining variables, the similarity between two group members regarding their preferences can be calculated as presented in Formula 5.

The task is now to predict a product for the whole group using aggregation functions (see Sect. 4). The similarities between the group member's preferences and products from the product catalog are presented in Table 4.

4   Applying Group Aggregation Functions and Recommending Products to Groups

For aggregating individual group member's preferences to a group preference, group aggregation functions have to be used. In collaborative filtering scenarios, group aggregation functions are often applied to the ratings predicted for group members first and then a recommendation for the group can be proposed.

However, in our evaluation, we first calculated similarities between group member preferences and products from the product catalog and then applied different aggregation functions on all of these similarities. This intermediate step is needed for determining the attribute similarity. Our approach can be demonstrated based on the group members' preferences in Table 2. The group has to decide about the *gps* feature of the camera and group members articulated the following preferences: *eval(1st participant, gps)* = *yes; eval(2nd participant, gps)* = *yes; eval(3rd participant, gps)* = *yes; eval(4th participant, gps)* = *no*. In such a setting, one has first calculate similarities between group member's preferences and products from the product catalog and then apply an aggregation function to derive a group recommendation.

In order to predict products to groups, the following aggregation functions have been applied (see Formulae 6–11). We differentiate between consensus-based (*Average, Minimal Group Distance, Multiplicative,* and *Ensemble voting*) and borderline (*Least Misery and Most Pleasure*) aggregation functions. Formula 6 (AVG) returns the *average* value of all individual values for an item i as a recommendation, whereby *eval(p,i)* denotes the *evaluation* of item i by the participant p. Formula 7 (*Least Misery*) returns the item with the highest of all lowest individual values and Formula 8 (*Most Pleasure*) returns the highest value of all individual values for an item i as a recommendation. *Minimum Group Distance* (MGD) in Formula 9 returns a value d which has the minimum distance to all individual values. *Multiplicative* (MUL) in Formula 10 returns the product of all individual values for an item i as a recommendation. *Ensemble Voting* (ENS) in Formula 11 returns the majority item from the items predicted by individual aggregation functions which are defined in Formula 6–10.

$$AVG(i) = \frac{\Sigma_{p \in Participants} eval(p, i)}{|Participants|} \tag{6}$$

$$LMIS(i) = min(\bigcup_{p \in Participants} eval(p, i)) \tag{7}$$

$$MPLS(i) = max(\bigcup_{p \in Participants} eval(p, i)) \tag{8}$$

$$MGD(i) = arg \min_{d \in \{1..5\}} (\Sigma_{p \in Participants} |eval(p, i) - d|) \tag{9}$$

$$MUL(i) = \prod_{p \in Participants} eval(p, i) \tag{10}$$

$$ENS(i) = maxarg_{(d \in \{1..5\})} (\#(\bigcup_{p \in Participants} eval(p, i) = d)) \tag{11}$$

Table 4 depicts the recommended items chosen by aggregation functions based on the similarity values between group member preferences and products from the product catalog. For instance, *AVG* determines *Product 1* (P1) for the whole group. After predicting products for a group, the precision (i.e., prediction quality) of each aggregation function can be calculated (see Table 5).

Table 4. Similarities between group member's preferences (see Tables 2 and 3) and products from the product catalog (see Table 1). Weights ($w(i)$) of Table 3 have been taken into account. The weight sequence $\{4, 3, 2, 1\}$ is used here, whereby the first value refers to the 1st, the next value to the 2nd, and the third value to the 3rd most important variable, and the last one refers to the remaining variables. Different aggregation functions are applied on these similarity values, then the product with the highest similarity is recommended to the group.

Participant	P1	P2	P3	P4	P5	
1st participant	0.7046	0.5307	0.4179	0.5431	0.4566	
2nd participant	0.7603	0.4809	0.3018	0.5580	0.3816	
3rd participant	0.7311	0.4828	0.3718	0.4708	0.3458	
4th participant	0.4681	0.7673	0.5638	0.6397	0.5339	
Aggregation function						Predicted product
AVG	**0.6660**	0.5654	0.4138	0.5529	0.4294	**P1**
LMIS	0.4681	**0.4809**	0.3018	0.4708	0.3458	**P2**
MPLS	0.7603	**0.7673**	0.5638	0.6397	0.5339	**P2**
MGD	**0.7046**	0.5307	0.4179	0.5431	0.4566	**P1**
MUL	**0.1833**	0.0945	0.0264	0.0913	0.0322	**P1**
ENS						**P1**

The precision of an aggregation function is *the ratio between the number of correctly predicted products and the total number of predictions (chosen products).*

In the following section we present the evaluation of results based on the data collected from our user study.

Table 5. Calculated prediction quality (precision) of each aggregation function. The value "1" refers to a correct prediction (i.e., the product chosen by a group member and predicted product by the aggregation function are identical) and "0" refers to an incorrect prediction. Consensus-based aggregation functions *AVG, MGD, MUL,* and *ENS* predict P1 as the most suitable product for the group with a precision of 50% ($\frac{2}{4}$). Borderline aggregation functions *LMIS* and *MPLS* predict P2 as the most suitable product for the group and achieve a precision of 25% ($\frac{1}{4}$).

Participant	Chosen product	AVG (P1)	LMIS (P2)	MPLS (P2)	MGD (P1)	MUL (P1)	ENS (P1)
1st participant	P1	1	0	0	1	1	1
2nd participant	P1	1	0	0	1	1	1
3rd participant	P3	0	0	0	0	0	0
4th participant	P2	0	1	1	0	0	0
Precision		50%	25%	25%	50%	50%	50%

5   Evaluation

The evaluation of the over-constrained camera dataset collected from our user study will be presented here. We conducted a user study with 263 computer science students ($\sim$85% male and $\sim$15% female) from two universities in Austria.[3] Each user study participants articulated 14 different preferences (10 out of 14 preferences refer to different camera variable values, three refer to the three most important camera variables, and a reference value refers to the selected product from the product list). All the 20 products from our product catalog were digital SLR cameras which were manually collected from the NIKON company's website.[4] The acquired data about the importance of the camera variables was essential for our analysis. For instance, a participant who defines the *price* as his/her most important variable is most probably focused on the price and wants get the best digital camera for a specific price. In contrast to a different participant who defined, for example, the *effective resolution* and some other technical properties as the most important ones. Such fine-grained information about the preferences of group members helps to improve the prediction quality of group recommendation.

For determining the aggregation function with the highest precision, we varied different parameters such as *group size* and *importance of the camera variables (weights)*. We analyzed the precision of each aggregation function with 210 different weight sequences and 5 different group sizes (ranging from 2 to 6) and generated 1050 (210 * 5) combinations thereof. Groups could be formed with different group sizes, for example, for group size of 4, there are 65 groups (263 participants/group size of $4 = 65.75 \Rightarrow 65$ groups). After groups were formed, similarities between group member's preferences and products from product catalog (n = 20) were calculated. Then, aggregation functions were applied on these similarities in order to predict a product for a group. We analyzed our dataset with all the combinations and found out that group size of 4 leads to the highest precision. Consequently, the 4-member groups achieve the highest similarity results for our camera dataset and for group sizes higher and lower than 4, the group gets diverse. In order to confirm this statement, we calculated the average precision of aggregation functions for each group size which is depicted in Fig. 1. Here we can clearly see, that the precision of aggregation functions increases with group sizes ranging from 2 to 4 and decreases starting with group size 5. We can conclude that there exists a correlation between the degree of group homogeneity and prediction quality of the group recommendation algorithm.

After the optimal group size was found, we focused on finding the optimal weight sequence (weight sequence which achieves the highest precision). As already mentioned before, 210 different weight sequences were used. Each sequence consisted of 4 different values: the first value refers to the 1st, the next

---

[3] Graz University of Technology (www.tugraz.at) and Alpen-Adria Universität Klagenfurt (www.aau.at).

[4] All the products from the product catalog were manually collected from www.nikonusa.com and www.nikon.de.

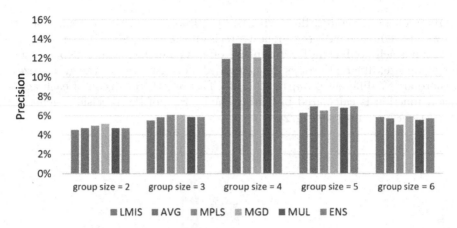

Fig. 1. Average precision of aggregation functions for each group size. The highest precision of each aggregation function is achieved for group size of 4.

value to the 2nd, and the third value to the 3rd most important variable, and the last one refers to the remaining variables. In our user study, weight sequences were generated by using the following rules:

(1) All the values in the weight sequence should be ranked in the descending order whereby the first value represents the 1st most important variable and the last value represents the less important camera variables.
(2) All values in the weight sequence lie in the range of 1 to 10. Formula 12 shows the number of all the used weight sequences (=210).

$$Number\ Of\ Weights = \binom{n}{k} = \binom{10}{4} = \frac{10!}{4! * (10 - 4)!} = 210 \qquad (12)$$

In order to determine the weight sequence with the highest precision, we first calculated the average precision of all aggregation functions for each weight sequence and then selected the weight sequence with the highest precision. We figured out that the weight sequence {10, 8, 4, 1} achieves the highest precision (see Fig. 2). Furthermore, we analyzed the top five weight sequences which achieve the highest precisions in order to find the pattern behind the optimal weight sequences (i.e., weight sequences with the highest precision). One main finding was that the first 2 values which represent the weights of the two most important camera variables are close to each other and the two last values which represent the weight of the 3rd most important variable and the weights of the remaining camera variables are close to each other. In addition to that, regarding the optimal weight sequences, we figured out that the weight of the most important variable is always as high as possible (i.e., 10) and the weights of the remaining of camera variables are as low as possible (i.e., 1). Therefrom we learn that the domain values of the weight sequences are not equally distributed, rather extreme values are used for the most and least important variables in the weight sequence. Figure 2 illustrates the precision of aggregation functions for the weight sequence with the highest precision (i.e., {10, 8, 4, 1}) - the highest precision is achieved again for group size of 4. As aforementioned, depending on the group size, different groups are generated. For instance, for the group size of 3, there are 87 different groups (=263/3). Thereby, the precision of each aggregation function is calculated by taking the average of the precisions generated for all the 87 groups (see Fig. 2).

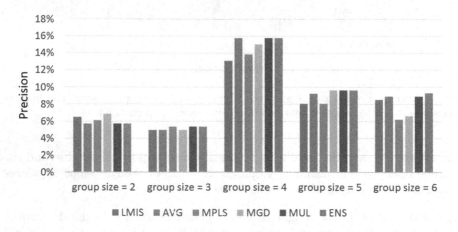

Fig. 2. Precision of aggregation functions for the weight {10, 8, 4, 1}. Group size of four leads again to the highest precision for each used aggregation function and aggregation functions *AVG, MUL,* and *ENS* achieve the highest precision.

Once the optimal weight and optimal group size were obtained, we moved our focus towards finding the optimal aggregation function which represents the main task of this paper. In order to determine the most optimal aggregation function, we took the highest of the average precisions calculated for each aggregation function. The precision of each aggregation function were calculated by taking the average of precisions generated for 1050 combinations (1050 combination is tailored by combining six different group sizes and 210 weight sequences). The final result includes the following precisions of the aggregation functions: $AVG = 7.34\%$, $ENS = 7.32\%$, $MUL = 7.26\%$, $MGD = 7.22\%$, $MPLS = 7.21\%$, and $LMIS = 6.80\%$.[5] These results are also clearly displayed in Figs. 1, 2, and Table 5. They show that *LMIS* and *MPLS* always lead to a low precision since they focus only on the lowest and highest values of all individual preferences and do not consider other group member preferences. Furthermore, *AVG, ENS, MUL,* and *MGD* which take all of group members' preferences into account lead to better precisions.

---

[5] The precision of each aggregation function is not high, because these are the average precisions calculated for all different combinations of weight sequences and group sizes (we varied 210 different weight sequences and six different group sizes).

6   Conclusion and Future Work

In this paper, we analyzed the applicability of preference aggregation functions for groups in situations where the preferences of group members become inconsistent (i.e., over-constrained). Our socially-aware constrained-based recommender system shows that borderline aggregation functions like *LMIS* and *MPLS* lead to a low precision because these functions take the minimum/maximum values from all the individual group member preferences and don't consider the preferences of other group members. Besides, consensus-based aggregation functions (such as *AVG*, *ENS*, *MUL*, and *MGD*) which consider all group members' preferences are more suitable to predict a product for the groups. Furthermore, we also demonstrated that modifications of the group size and the usage of different weight sequences have a potential to achieve better precision. Moreover, we tested the dataset with 210 different weight sequences and different group sizes (2–5). We found out that the domain values of the weight sequences are not equally distributed, rather extreme values are used for the most and least important variables in the weight sequence. In addition, the 4-member groups achieve the highest similarity results for our camera dataset and for group sizes higher and lower than 4, the group gets diverse. The chosen group aggregation functions are representatives of consensus-based and borderline functions. The analysis of further related aggregation functions is within the scope of our future work. Socially-aware decisions are usually made in groups consisting of similar group members (e.g. taking vacation with friends or watching a movie with the family). Thus, we clustered similar participants in order to form homogeneous groups. Finally, we plan for the future to build diverse/randomized groups instead of homogeneous groups and try to find the most suitable aggregation function for such groups.

References

1. Ardissono, L., Goy, A., Petrone, G., Segnan, M., Torasso, P.: Intrigue: personalized recommendation of tourist attractions for desktop and hand held devices. Appl. Artif. Intell. **17**(8–9), 687–714 (2003)
2. Baltrunas, L., Makcinskas, T., Ricci, F.: Group recommendations with rank aggregation and collaborative filtering. In: Proceedings of the Fourth ACM Conference on Recommender Systems, RecSys 2010, pp. 119–126, New York, NY, USA. ACM (2010)
3. Felfernig, A., Ninaus, G., Grabner, H., Reinfrank, F., Weninger, L., Pagano, D., Maalej, W.: An overview of recommender systems in requirements engineering. In: Maalej, W., Thurimella, A. (eds.) Managing Requirements Knowledge, pp. 315–332. Springer, Heidelberg (2013). https://doi.org/10.1007/978-3-642-34419-0_14
4. Felfernig, A., Atas, M., Tran, T.N.T., Stettinger, M., Erdeniz, S.P., Leitner, G.: An analysis of group recommendation heuristics for high- and low-involvement items. In: Benferhat, S., Tabia, K., Ali, M. (eds.) IEA/AIE 2017. LNCS (LNAI), vol. 10350, pp. 335–344. Springer, Cham (2017). https://doi.org/10.1007/978-3-319-60042-0_39

5. Herlocker, J.L., Konstan, J.A., Terveen, L.G., Riedl, J.T.: Evaluating collaborative filtering recommender systems. ACM Trans. Inf. Syst. **22**(1), 5–53 (2004)
6. Jameson, A.: More than the sum of its members: challenges for group recommender systems. In: Proceedings of the Working Conference on Advanced Visual Interfaces, AVI 2004, pp. 48–54, New York, NY, USA. ACM (2004)
7. Jannach, D., Zanker, M., Felfernig, A., Friedrich, G.: Recommender Systems: An Introduction, 1st edn. Cambridge University Press, New York (2010)
8. Masthoff, J.: Group modeling: selecting a sequence of television items to suit a group of viewers. User Model. User-Adap. Inter. **14**(1), 37–85 (2004)
9. Masthoff, J.: Group recommender systems: combining individual models. In: Ricci, F., Rokach, L., Shapira, B., Kantor, P. (eds.) Recommender Systems Handbook, pp. 677–702. Springer, Boston (2011). https://doi.org/10.1007/978-0-387-85820-3_21
10. McCarthy, K., Salamó, M., Coyle, L., McGinty, L., Smyth, B., Nixon, P.: Group recommender systems: a critiquing based approach. In: Proceedings of the 11th International Conference on Intelligent User Interfaces, IUI 2006, pp. 267–269, New York, NY, USA. ACM (2006)
11. O'Connor, M., Cosley, D., Konstan, J.A., Riedl, J.: Polylens: a recommender system for groups of users. In: Proceedings of the Seventh Conference on European Conference on Computer Supported Cooperative Work, ECSCW 2001, pp. 199–218, Norwell, MA, USA. Kluwer Academic Publishers (2001)
12. Stettinger, M., Felfernig, A., Leitner, G., Reiterer, S., Jeran, M.: Counteracting serial position effects in the choicla group decision support environment. In: Proceedings of the 20th International Conference on Intelligent User Interfaces, IUI 2015, pp. 148–157, New York, NY, USA. ACM (2015)
13. von Winterfeldt, D., Edwards, W.: Decision Analysis and Behavioral Research. Cambridge University Press, Cambridge (1986)

Formalizing Arguments
From Cause-Effect Rules

Karima Sedki[1,2]([✉])

[1] LIMICS (INSERM UMRS 1142), Université Paris 13, Sorbonne Paris Cité,
93017 Paris, Bobigny, France
karima.sedki@univ-paris13.fr
[2] UPMC Université Paris 6, Sorbonne Universités, Paris, France

Abstract. This paper proposes a method allowing the formalisation of
cause-effect rules that are reported by expert's knowledge as argumentation framework. The rules represent causal relation between two given
concepts. Such rules have the advantage to be easily elicited by domain
experts, however the inference mechanism is rather ad hoc and there is
no good theoretical foundation. The objective of the proposition is to
overcome the major limit of the reported cause-effect rules, that is the
need of efficient reasoning.

1 Introduction

In this paper, we consider two techniques for knowledge representation which are
cause-effect rules and weighted argumentation framework (WAF). Cause-effect
rules represent causal relation between two given concepts. They are widely
used in causal maps [1]. There is a causal relation between two given concepts
whenever a change in one of those concepts affects the other one. According to
[6], causal relations are the major way in which understanding about the world
is organized. They are easier to grasp, however the reasoning has some limits
because they do not model uncertainty within the variables and they allow only
limited forms of inferences. WAF [4] is an extension of Dung argumentation
framework [3]. It is defined on a set of arguments and a set of attacks between
them. Weights are assigned to each attack. Our proposition consists in transforming cause-effect rules into its corresponding WAF. The aim of our proposition is
to overcome the major limit of the reported cause-effect rules, that is the need
of efficient reasoning. In fact, WAF is an interesting formalism for reasoning. In
addition it allows dealing with dynamics through the consideration of a varying
set of observations which is not the case with cause-effect rules.

2 Cause-Effect Rules

There is a causal relation between two given concepts whenever a change in
one of those concepts affects the other one. Formally, by a cause-effect rule

© Springer International Publishing AG, part of Springer Nature 2018
M. Mouhoub et al. (Eds.): IEA/AIE 2018, LNAI 10868, pp. 279–285, 2018.
https://doi.org/10.1007/978-3-319-92058-0_26

we mean an expression of the form {*Increasing/Decreasing*} *in* concept x leads to *Str* {*Increasing/Decreasing*} *in* concept y where x is a causal concept and y is an effect concept. Increasing and Decreasing are states of each concept. *Str* = {*Low/Medium/Strong/VeryStrong*} is the strength of the cause-effect relation. For easy elicitation, natural numbers are often used to represent the strength of each rule. The value 1 is used to represent the strength *low*, 2 for *medium*, 3 for *Strong*, 4 for *verystrong*. We distinguish two types of rules:

- **Positive rules:** They are of the form: *Increasing in x* leads to *Str Increasing in y*, or *Decreasing in x* leads to *Str Decreasing in y*. For example, *Increasing in Stress leads to strong increasing in Food Intake*, is a positive rule. Here, *Stress* is a causal concept at the state *Increasing* while *Foodintake* is an effect concept, *Strong* represents the strength of the relation.
- **Negative rules:** They are of the form: *Increasing in x* leads to *Str Decreasing in y*, or *Decreasing in x* leads to *Str Increasing in y*. For example, *Increasing in Stress causes strong decreasing in Physical Health*, is a negative rule.

Formally, the state increasing (resp. decreasing) of a given concept c_1 is represented by c_1^+ (resp. c_1^-). The notation $State(c_1) = \{c_1^-, c_1^+\}$ is used to represent the possible states of c_1. Let us consider some rules that are taken from [5] and given in Table 1.

Table 1. Examples of cause-effect rules in obesity diagnosis.

r_i	Rules	Str
r_1	Increasing in Stress leads to strong Increasing in Food Intake	3
r_2	Decreasing in Stress leads to strong Decreasing in Food Intake	3
r_3	Increasing in Food Intake leads to medium Increasing in Obesity	2
r_4	Decreasing in Food Intake leads to medium Decreasing in Obesity	2
r_5	Increasing in Stress leads to medium Increasing in Depression	2
r_6	Decreasing in Stress leads to medium Decreasing in Depression	2
r_7	Decreasing in Depression leads to medium Decreasing in Obesity	2
r_8	Increasing in Depression leads to medium Increasing in Obesity	2
r_9	Increasing in Exercice leads to very strong Decreasing in Obesity	4
r_{10}	Decreasing in Exercice leads to very strong Increasing in Obesity	4

3   Dung's Argumentation Framework and Weighted Argumentation Framework

Definition 1. *An argumentation framework is a pair* $AF = \langle \mathcal{A}, \mathcal{R} \rangle$ *where* $\mathcal{A}$ *is a finite set of arguments and* $\mathcal{R}$ *is a binary attack relation defined on* $\mathcal{A} \times \mathcal{A}$. *Given two arguments* σ *and* $\gamma, \sigma \mathcal{R} \gamma$ *(or* $(\sigma, \gamma) \in \mathcal{R}$) *means* σ *attacks* γ.

There can exist several extensions to AFs: preferred, stable, grounded, etc. They are also called acceptability semantics.

Definition 2. *Let $AF = \langle \mathcal{A}, \mathcal{R} \rangle$ be an argumentation framework and $\mathcal{S}$ be a subset of arguments (i.e., $\mathcal{S} \subseteq \mathcal{A}$):*

- *$\mathcal{S}$ is a conflict-free of AF iff there are no arguments $\sigma, \gamma \in \mathcal{S}$ such that $\sigma \, \mathcal{R} \, \gamma$.*
- *$\sigma \in \mathcal{A}$ is acceptable with respect to $\mathcal{S}$ iff $\forall \gamma \in \mathcal{A}$ such that $\gamma \, \mathcal{R} \, \sigma, \exists \theta \in \mathcal{S}$ such that $\theta \, \mathcal{R} \, \gamma$.*
- *$\mathcal{S}$ is an admissible extension iff it is conflict-free and each argument in $\mathcal{S}$ is acceptable with respect to $\mathcal{S}$.*
- *$\mathcal{S}$ is a preferred extension iff it is maximal (for set inclusion) among admissible extensions.*

Definition 3. *A Weighted Argumentation Framework is a triple $WAF = \langle \mathcal{A}, \mathcal{R}, w \rangle$ where $\langle \mathcal{A}, \mathcal{R} \rangle$ is a Dung abstract argumentation framework, and $w\colon \mathcal{A} \to \Re$ is a function that assigns a real number to each attack. We let $\Re$ denote the real numbers greater than or equal to zero.*

We focus on the method developed in [2] where the authors defined some aggregation functions allowing to evaluate each extension for a given semantics.

Definition 4 (Σ-most attacking extensions). *Let $WAF = \langle \mathcal{A}, \mathcal{R}, w \rangle$ be a weighted argumentation framework. Let $\mathbb{E}$ be the set of extensions of $WAF = \langle \mathcal{A}, \mathcal{R} \rangle$ for a given semantics. Let Σ be an aggregation function. For any extension E of $\mathbb{E}$, one defines $Out_\Sigma(E) = \Sigma_{\sigma \in E, \gamma \in \mathcal{A} \setminus E, s.t. (\sigma, \gamma) \in \mathcal{R}} w(\sigma, \gamma)$. The Σ-most attacking extensions of $\mathbb{E}$ are given by: $Ma_\Sigma(\mathbb{E}) = argmax_{E \in \mathbb{E}}(Out_\Sigma(E))$.*

Definition 4 states that the Σ-most attacking extensions are those for which the sum of weights of outgoing attacks is maximal.

Definition 5 (Σ-least attacked extensions). *Let $WAF = \langle \mathcal{A}, \mathcal{R}, w \rangle$ be a weighted argumentation framework. Let $\mathbb{E}$ be the set of extensions of $WAF = \langle \mathcal{A}, \mathcal{R} \rangle$ for a given semantics. Let Σ be an aggregation function. For any extension E of $\mathbb{E}$, we define $In_\Sigma(E) = \Sigma_{\sigma \in E, \gamma \in \mathcal{A} \setminus E, s.t. (\gamma, \sigma) \in \mathcal{R}} w(\gamma, \sigma)$. The Σ-least attacked extensions of $\mathbb{E}$ are given by: $La_\Sigma(\mathbb{E}) = argmin_{E \in \mathbb{E}}(In_\Sigma(E))$.*

Definition 5 states that the Σ-least attacked extensions are those having the smallest sum of weights of attacks towards them.

Definition 6 (Globally Σ-best defended extensions). *Let $WAF = \langle \mathcal{A}, \mathcal{R}, w \rangle$ be a weighted argumentation framework. Let $\mathbb{E}$ be the set of extensions of $WAF = \langle \mathcal{A}, \mathcal{R} \rangle$ for a given semantics. Let Σ be an aggregation function. For any extension E of $\mathbb{E}$, the degree of its global defense is defined by: $Def_\Sigma^g(E) = Out_\Sigma(E) - In_\Sigma(E)$. The globally Σ-best defended extensions of $\mathbb{E}$ are given by: $Gdb_\Sigma(\mathbb{E}) = argmax_{E \in \mathbb{E}}(Def_\Sigma^g(\mathbb{E}))$.*

4 Formalisation of Cause-Effect Rules as WAF

We define an argument as a pair where the first element is a set of premises, the second element is a claim, and from the premises a claim is inferred. Given a cause-effect rule, the premise of an argument of the corresponding WAF corresponds to the state of the causal concept and its claim corresponds to the state of the effect concept. We use $pr(\sigma)$ (resp. $cl(\sigma)$) to denote the premise (resp. claim) of the argument σ.

Definition 7. *Let $r_{i=1...n}$ be the set of cause-effect rules, C be a set of concepts, c_1, c_2 be two concepts in C such that $State(c_1) = \{c_1^-, c_1^+\}, State(c_2) = \{c_2^-, c_2^+\}$ and r_1 be a cause-effect rule between c_1 and c_2. An argument is defined over r_1 denoted by $\sigma: State(c_1) \rightarrow State(c_2)$ such that $State(c_1)$ is either c_1^- or c_1^+ and $State(c_2)$ is either c_2^- or c_2^+.*

Assume that we have an argument σ such that $\sigma: State(c_1) \rightarrow State(c_2)$. Let $State(c_1) = c_1^-$ and $State(c_2) = c_2^+$ then $\sigma: c_1^- \rightarrow c_2^+$ can be read as "c_1^- entails c_2^+" or "c_1^- causes c_2^+". $pr(\sigma) = c_1^-, cl(\sigma) = c_2^+$. Note that an argument has one premise and one claim in the obtained WAF.

Example 1. From the cause-effect rules of Table 1, the following arguments are constructed:

$\sigma_1: Stress^+ \rightarrow FoodIntake^+$	$\sigma_2: Stress^- \rightarrow FoodIntake-$
$\sigma_3: FoodIntake^+ \rightarrow Obesity^+$	$\sigma_4: FoodIntake^- \rightarrow Obesity^-$
$\sigma_5: Stress^+ \rightarrow Depression^+$	$\sigma_6: Stress^- \rightarrow Depression^-$
$\sigma_7: Depression^+ \rightarrow Obesity^+$	$\sigma_8: Depression^- \rightarrow Obesity^-$
$\sigma_9: Exercice^+ \rightarrow Obesity^-$	$\sigma_{10}: Exercice^- \rightarrow Obesity^+$

The argument σ_1 is defined from the rule r_1 (see Table 1). $pr(\sigma_1) = Stress^+$ and $cl(\sigma_1) = FoodIntake^+$. It means that an increase of Stress will cause (or entails) an increase of Food Intake.

In the constructed WAF, we distinguish two types of attack relations between arguments. The first one occurs between two arguments contradicting each other because their claims are mutually exclusive. The second one occurs when some arguments challenge the inference of another argument. The former are called *rebuttal attacks* while the later are called *undercut attacks*. Let us use the complement notation to express contradictory or inconsistent elements such as $cl(\sigma) = \overline{cl(\sigma')}$ that expresses the claims of the arguments σ and σ' are contradictory. t.

Definition 8. *Given two arguments σ and σ', we say that σ attacks σ' and the attack is said to be rebuttal iff $cl(\sigma) = \overline{cl(\sigma')}$. The set of rebuttal attacks is denoted by $\mathcal{R}_r$.*

Definition 9. *Given an argument $\sigma \in \mathcal{A}$, if $\exists \sigma' \in \mathcal{A}$ such that $pr(\sigma') = \overline{cl(\sigma)}$ then σ undercuts σ'. The undercut attack is denoted by $\mathcal{R}_u$ and $\mathcal{R}_u = \{(\sigma, \sigma')\}$.*

Example 2. In Example 1, 10 arguments are defined from the rules given in Table 1. $\mathcal{R}_r = \{(\sigma_1,\sigma_2),(\sigma_2,\sigma_1),(\sigma_3,\sigma_4),\ (\sigma_4,\sigma_3),(\sigma_5,\sigma_6),(\sigma_6,\sigma_5),(\sigma_7,\sigma_8),\ (\sigma_8,\sigma_7),(\sigma_9,\sigma_{10}),(\sigma_{10},\sigma_9),(\sigma_3,\sigma_8),(\sigma_8,\sigma_3),(\sigma_4,\sigma_7),(\sigma_7,\sigma_4),(\sigma_3,\sigma_9),\ (\sigma_9,\sigma_3),\ (\sigma_4,\sigma_{10}),(\sigma_{10},\sigma_4),(\sigma_7,\sigma_9),(\sigma_9,\sigma_7),(\sigma_8,\sigma_{10}),(\sigma_{10},\sigma_8)\}.$ $\mathcal{R}_u = \{(\sigma_1,\sigma_4),\ (\sigma_2,\sigma_3),\ (\sigma_6,\sigma_7),(\sigma_5,\sigma_8)\}.$

In WAF, each attack is associated with a weight, indicating the relative strength of that attack. In the WAF obtained from a given rules, the weights correspond to the strengths associated to each cause-effect rule.

Definition 10 (Attack weight). *Let $r_{i=1,\dots,n}$ be a set of cause-effect rules such that $str(r_{1,\dots,n})$ be the corresponding strengths and $WAF = \langle \mathcal{A}, \mathcal{R}, w \rangle$ be the obtained WAF where $\mathcal{A}$ is the set of arguments, $\mathcal{R}$ is the set of attacks and w is a function that maps a natural number to each attack. Then: If $(\sigma, \sigma') \in \mathcal{R}$ and σ is defined from $r_{i=1,\dots,n}$ then $w(\sigma, \sigma') = str(r_{1,\dots,n})$.*

5   Reasoning in the Obtained WAF

We must define what we call active arguments and active attacks. An argument is active because its premise belongs to the set of observations as stated by Item 1 of Definition 13 given below. However, an argument can be indirectly activated by other active arguments, even if its premise does not belong to the set of observations. Namely, an argument can also be activated by what we call (i) its supporting argument (defined in Definition 11 given below) which may be also active or by (ii) its undercutting argument (defined in Definition 12 given below) which may be also active.

Definition 11 (Supporting argument). *Let $r_{i=1,\dots,n}$ be the set of cause-effect rules and $WAF = \langle \mathcal{A}, \mathcal{R}, w \rangle$ be the corresponding weighted argumentation framework. Let σ, σ' be two arguments in $\mathcal{A}$. σ is a supporting argument of σ' iff $pr(\sigma') = cl(\sigma)$.*

Definition 12 (Undercutting argument). *Let $r_{i=1,\dots,n}$ be the set of cause-effect rules and $WAF = \langle \mathcal{A}, \mathcal{R}, w \rangle$ be the corresponding weighted argumentation framework. Let σ, σ' be two arguments in $\mathcal{A}$. σ is an undercutting argument of σ' iff $pr(\sigma') = \overline{cl(\sigma)}$.*

Definition 13 (Active argument). *Let $r_{i=1,\dots,n}$ be the set of cause-effect rules and $WAF = \langle \mathcal{A}, \mathcal{R}, w \rangle$ be the corresponding weighted argumentation framework. Let $\mathcal{O}$ be a set of observations. An argument $\sigma \in \mathcal{A}$ is active with respect to $\mathcal{O}$ iff:*

- *$pr(\sigma) \in \mathcal{O}$, or*
- *$\exists \sigma' \in \mathcal{A}$ which is an active and supporting argument of σ, or*
- *$\exists \sigma' \in \mathcal{A}$ which is an active and undercutting argument of σ.*

$\mathcal{A}_{Act} \subseteq \mathcal{A}$ *denotes the set of active arguments.*

Example 3. Let us consider the arguments of Example 2 and assume that the set of observations $\mathcal{O} = \{Stress^+\}$ then $\mathcal{A}_{Act} = \{\sigma_1, \sigma_3, \sigma_4, \sigma_5, \sigma_7, \sigma_8\}$. σ_1 and σ_5 are active directly from $\mathcal{O}$ since we have $pr(\sigma_1) \in \mathcal{O}$ and $pr(\sigma_5) \in \mathcal{O}$. σ_3 is activated by σ_1 since we have $pr(\sigma_3) = cl(\sigma_1)$ (from Definition 11, σ_1 is active and it is a supporting argument of σ_3). σ_7 is activated by σ_5 since we have $pr(\sigma_7) = cl(\sigma_5)$ (from Definition 11, σ_5 is active and it is a supporting argument of σ_7). σ_8 is activated by σ_5 (σ_5 is active and it is an undercutting argument of σ_8). σ_4 is activated by σ_1 (σ_1 is active and it is an undercutting argument of σ_4).

Definition 14 (Active rebuttal attacks). *The set of active rebuttal attacks is a subset $\mathcal{R}_r^{Act} \subseteq \mathcal{R}$ such that $(\sigma, \sigma') \in \mathcal{R}_r^{Act}$ iff $\sigma, \sigma' \in \mathcal{A}_{Act}$.*

Definition 14 states that a rebuttal attack is active if and only if both the attacker and the attacked arguments are in the set of active arguments.

Definition 15 (Active undercut attacks). *The set of active undercuts attacks is a subset $\mathcal{R}_u^{Act} \subseteq \mathcal{R}$ such that $(\sigma, \sigma') \in \mathcal{R}_u^{Act}$ iff $\sigma \in \mathcal{A}_{Act}$.*

An undercut attack is active if and only if the attacker argument is active.

Definition 16 (Active weights). *Let σ, σ' be two arguments in $\mathcal{A}_{Act}$, $w(\sigma, \sigma')$ is active iff $(\sigma, \sigma') \in \mathcal{R}_r^{Act}$ or $(\sigma, \sigma') \in \mathcal{R}_u^{Act}$. We use w_{Act} to denote a function that assigns to each active attack its associated weight.*

Once the WAF is built, we have to define acceptability semantics.

Example 4. Let us consider the cause-effect rules given in Table 1. Assume that we have the set of observations $\mathcal{O}_1 = \{Depression^+, Exercice^+\}$. From Definitions 13, $\mathcal{A}_{Act} = \{\sigma_7, \sigma_9\}$. From Definition 14, $\mathcal{R}_r^{Act} = \{(\sigma_7, \sigma_9), (\sigma_9, \sigma_7)\}$. From Definition 15, $\mathcal{R}_u^{Act} = \{\emptyset\}$. From Definition 16, each active rebuttal attack is associated with its weight. The WAF obtained from $\mathcal{O}_1$ is a sub-WAF $= \langle \mathcal{A}_{Act}, \mathcal{R}_r^{Act} \cup \mathcal{R}_u^{Act}, w_{Act} \rangle$. The standard sub-$W\hat{A}F$ has two preferred extensions: $E_1 = \{\sigma_7\}, E_2 = \{\sigma_9\}$. Using Definition 4, $Out_\Sigma(E_1) = 2$. $Out_\Sigma(E_2) = 4$. Thus, Σ-most attacking extension is E_2. Using Definition 5, $In_\Sigma(E_1) = 4$. $In_\Sigma(E_2) = 2$. Thus, Σ-least attacked extension is E_2. Using Definition 6, the degree of the defense of E_1 (resp. E_2) is given as follows: $Def_\Sigma^g(E_1) = Out_\Sigma(E_1) - In_\Sigma(E_1) = -2$. $Def_\Sigma^g(E_2) = Out_\Sigma(E_2) - In_\Sigma(E_2) = 2$. Thus the globally Σ-best defended extension is E_2. This means that the most plausible situation regarding the judgments represented in the above cause-effect rules and the given observations concerns decreasing of obesity ($Obesity^-$) which is the claim of σ_9 since it belongs to the Σ-best defended extension.

6   Conclusion

Our proposition consists in transforming cause-effect rules into the corresponding WAF. Reasoning with WAF is very interesting, especially in situations of inconsistency induced in case when there are many cause-effect rules. In addition, our method allows us to deal with dynamics through the consideration of a varying set of observations in the obtained WAF. For example, having an observation about an increase in food intake in obesity problem, only some arguments and attacks can be active.

References

1. Chaib-Draa, B.: Causal maps: theory, implementation and practical applications in multiagent environments. IEEE Trans. Knowl. Data Eng. (2001)
2. Coste-Marquis, S., Konieczny, S., Marquis, P., Ouali, M.A.: Selecting extensions in weighted argumentation frameworks. In: Computational Models of Argument, pp. 342–349 (2012)
3. Dung, P.M.: On the acceptability of arguments and its fundamental role in non-monotonic reasoning, logic programming and n-person games. Artif. Intell. **77**(2), 321–358 (1995)
4. Dunne, P.E., Hunter, A., McBurney, P., Parsons, S., Wooldridge, M.: Weighted argument systems: basic definitions, algorithms, and complexity results. Artif. Intell. **175**(2), 457–486 (2011)
5. Giabbanelli, P.J., Torsney-Weir, T., Mago, V.K.: A fuzzy cognitive map of the psychosocial determinants of obesity. Appl. Soft Comput. **12**(12), 3711–3724 (2012)
6. Huff, A.: Mapping Strategic Thought (1990)

Merging Guaranteed Possibilistic Bases to Rank IDS Alerts

Lydia Bouzar-Benlabiod[(✉)], Lila Meziani, Nacer-Eddine Rim,
and Zakaria Mellal

Laboratoire de la Communication dans les Systèmes Informatiques,
Ecole nationale Supérieure d'Informatique, BP 68M, 16309 Oued-Smar, Alger, Algeria
{l_bouzar,l_meziani,bn_rim,bz_mellal}@esi.dz

Abstract. Intrusion Detection Systems (IDS) are security tools that generate alerts when detecting a malicious activity. The main drawback of IDS is the high number of generated alerts. We propose an approach that integrates the preferences of several security experts to rank IDS results. The experts' preferences are expressed either in IFO-BCF (Instantiated First Order) logic or in IFO-guaranteed possibilistic one. A new logical preferences merging algorithm is given, it takes in input the different experts' preferences and produces a unique preferences base. The resulted preferences base is used to rank the IDS alerts.

Keywords: IDS alerts · Preferences merging
Guaranteed possibilistic logic · IFO formulas

1 Introduction

In AI, merging multisources data is a real challenge. The fusion result must match the agents' expectations and be as coherent as possible.

The possibilistic logic [5,7,8] is an extension of classical logic which allows to deal with prioritized information. When all the formula's weights ($\alpha'_i s$) are equal to 1 then propositional logic is recovered. Possibilistic logic handles inconsistent pieces of information (e.g., [1,9,10]).

There is a specific syntactic representation of the possibilistic logic that is called the guaranteed possibilistic logic. It is based on the notion of guaranteed possibility measures [6]. A weighted formula (ϕ, α) means that the guaranteed possibility degree of ϕ is at least equal to α, i.e., $\Delta_i \geq \alpha$.

Intrusion Detection Systems (IDS) generates a huge number of alerts. In [3] authors proposed an algorithm that ranks IDS alerts using knowledge and preferences of one security expert using IFO QCL logic. In this paper we gather each experts' preferences into one IFO-guaranteed possibilistic base (which is a new syntactic representation in possibilistic logic). We merge all the experts bases into one. Finally we rank the IDS alerts according to their satisfaction degrees to the merging resulted base. The ranked list of alerts is then presented to the security administrator.

M. Mouhoub et al. (Eds.): IEA/AIE 2018, LNAI 10868, pp. 286–291, 2018.
https://doi.org/10.1007/978-3-319-92058-0_27

2 Instantiated First Order (IFO) Formulas [3,4]

Let P be a set of predicate symbols. The following defines the language composed of instantiated first order formulas [3]

1. (1) if P is a predicate symbol of arity m and $\{c_1, c_2, \ldots, c_m\}$ is a set of constants then $P(c_1, c_2, \ldots, c_m)$ is an IFO formulas.
2. (2) if ϕ and φ are IFO formulas then $(\phi \wedge \varphi)$, $(\phi \vee \varphi)$, $(\neg \phi)$ are IFO formulas.

IFO formulas are only obtained by applying items (1) and (2) a finite number of times.

IFO language is composed of instantiated first order formulas where all terms are constants.

3 IFO Guaranteed Possibilistic Base

An IFO guaranteed possibilistic base (*IFO-Δ-base*) is composed of a set of weighted IFO formulas (φ_i, α_i). Each interpretation ω that satisfies φ_i has a satisfaction degree at least equal to α_i, formally :

$$\forall \omega, \omega \models \varphi_i, \pi_\Delta(\omega) \geq \alpha_i. \tag{1}$$

Each Δ-base has a unique *possibility distribution* π_Δ, such that:

$$\pi_\Delta(\omega) = \begin{cases} 0 \text{ if } \omega \text{ falsifies all the formulas of } \Delta, \\ max\{\alpha_i : (\varphi_i, \alpha_i) \in \Delta, \omega \models \varphi_i\} \text{ otherwise} \end{cases} \tag{2}$$

When dealing with a classical possibilistic base, we are interested in the falsified formulas having greatest weight while with a Δ base, we are interested in the satisfied formulas having the greatest weight.

It has been shown in [2] that we can transform any possibilistic base to a guaranteed possibilistic base and vice versa

4 Guaranteed Possibilistic Merging

Let $\Delta_1 = \{[\phi_i, \alpha_i] : i = 1, ..., n\}$ and $\Delta_2 = \{[\psi_j, \beta_j] : j = 1, ..., m\}$ be two IFO-Δ bases. Let $\pi_1(\omega)$, $\pi_2(\omega)$ be their corresponding guaranteed possibilty distributions. $\oplus$ is a merging operatoe. $\Delta_\oplus$ is the synctactic form of $\pi_\oplus(\omega) = \oplus(\pi_1(\omega), \pi_2(\omega))$ and it is formally defined as follows:

$$\Delta_\oplus = \{[\phi_i, \oplus(\alpha_1, 0)] : (\phi_i, \alpha_i) \in \Delta_1\} \cup \{[\psi_j, \oplus(0, \beta_j)] : (\psi_j, \beta_j) \in \Delta_2\} \cup$$
$$\{[\phi_i \wedge \psi_j, \oplus(\alpha_i, \beta_j)] : (\phi_i, \alpha_i) \in \Delta_1, (\psi_j, \beta_j) \in \Delta_2\} \cup \{[\top, \oplus(0, 0)]\} \tag{3}$$

$\Delta_\oplus$ contains all the formulas of Δ_1 and Δ_2 plus their conjunctions. It also contains a tautologie with a degree equal to $\oplus(0, 0)$.

Let $\Delta_1 = \{[\phi_1, \alpha_1]\}$ and $\Delta_2 = \{[\phi_2, \alpha_2]\}$ two IFOΔ-bases, each one contains one preference. Let $\oplus$ be a merging operator. For a given interpretation ω we have one of the following cases:

1. If $\omega \models \phi_1$ and $\omega \models \phi_2$ then $\pi_\oplus(\omega) = \oplus(\pi_1(\omega), \pi_2(\omega)) = \oplus(\alpha_1, \alpha_2)$.
2. If $\omega \models \phi_1$ and $\omega \not\models \phi_2$ then $\pi_\oplus(\omega) = \oplus(\pi_1(\omega), \pi_2(\omega)) = \oplus(\alpha_1, 0)$ (if $\omega \not\models \phi_1$ and $\omega \models \phi_2$ then $\pi_\oplus(\omega) = \oplus(\pi_1(\omega), \pi_2(\omega)) = \oplus(0, \alpha_2)$).
3. if $\omega \not\models \phi_1$ and $\omega \not\models \phi_2$ then $\pi_\oplus(\omega) = \oplus(\pi_1(\omega), \pi_2(\omega)) = \oplus(0, 0)$.

The fusion of $\Delta_1, ..., \Delta_n$ [2] (n IFO-guranteed possibilistic bases (Δ-bases)) is done incrementally:

$$\Delta_\oplus = \oplus(\oplus(... \oplus (\oplus(\Delta_1, \Delta_2), \Delta_3)..., \Delta_{n-1}), \Delta_n). \qquad (4)$$

The most used merging operators in preference merging are the arithmetic average and the weighted average.

Example 1. Let Mod be a predicate symbol representing a module, and $\{DB, NT, ES, AI\}$ be the set of its possible values (DB: Data base, NT: Networks, ES: Embedded Systems and AI for Artificial Intelligence). Let A and B be two students expressing their choices over the modules using IFOΔ-bases: $\Delta_A = \{(Mod(DB) \wedge Mod(AI), 0.9), (Mod(AI), 0.7)\}$ and $\Delta_B = \{(Mod(DB) \wedge Mod(ES), 0.8), (Mod(ES), 0.6), (Mod(DB) \vee Mod(NT), 0.35)\}$. These two students are in the same class and we have to choose only two modules trying to satisfy both of them. Using the arithmetic average merging operator: $\oplus(a, b) = (a+b)/2$, we obtain: $\Delta_\oplus = \{(Mod(DB) \wedge Mod(AI) \wedge Mod(ES), 0.85)), (Mod(DB) \wedge Mod(AI), 0.625)), (Mod(AI) \wedge Mod(ES), 0.65), (Mod(AI) \wedge (Mod(DB) \vee Mod(NT)), 0.525), (Mod(AI), 0.35), (Mod(DB) \wedge Mod(ES), 0.4), (Mod(ES), 0.3), (Mod(DB) \vee Mod(NT), \oplus(0, 0.175))\}$.
Let us compute the preference degree of all possible interpretations (solutions), according to $\Delta_\oplus$. We only consider interpretations with two modules.
Then the selected interpretation is ω_1 and the preferred modules are Data bases and Artificial Intelligence.

$\omega(Mod(DB), Mod(ES), Mod(AI), Mod(NT))$	Guaranteed possibility degree
(1,1,0,0)	0.4
(1,0,1,0)	0.625
(1,0,0,1)	0.175
(0,1,1,0)	0.65
(0,1,0,1)	0.3
(0,0,1,1)	0.525

5   Guaranteed Possibilistic Fusion to Rank IDS Alerts

5.1   Merging Experts Preferences

Each expert expresses his preferences using IFO formulas. Experts' formulas are transformed in an IFO-Δ base. The IFO-Δ bases are then merged according to Algorithm 1.

Algorithm 1. Merging IFO-Δ-bases

---

1. **Inputs :** $\Delta_1,...,\Delta_n$ such that the IFOΔ-base Δ_i represents the prefereces of the ith expert.
   Variables
   Output={}; /* The merging $\Delta_\oplus$*/
2. **For** i from 1 to n **Do**
   (a) Find all the combinations having i formulas $C_1,...,C_m$ such that each combination C_j does not have more than one formula from each Δ base.
   (b) $C_j = \{(\phi_{j,1},\alpha_{j,1}),...,(\phi_{j,i},\alpha_{j,i})\}$.
   (c) **For** each combination C_j of size i **Do**
       i. Output= Output $\cup\{(\phi_{j,1} \wedge ... \wedge \phi_{j,i},(\alpha_{j,1} + ... + \alpha_{j,i})/n)\}$
3. **Return** Output;

$\Delta_\oplus$ is composed of the conjunctions of formulas taken from each expert preferences base. The preference degree of these conjunction is the arithmetic average of their initial degrees. We use this merging operator only because we consider that all the experts have the same experience. Else the weithed average can be used.

The proposed algorithm has a polynomial computational complexity.

5.2   Ranking IDS Alerts Using Security Experts' Preferences

The aim is to reduce and classify the IDS alerts thanks to the experts' preferences. We will present to the security administrator a ranked list of alerts. We use IDS alerts collected from the $PLACID^1$ project. Alerts were collected from a french university network. Different Intrusion Detection Systems (IDS) were deployed on different network points and the issued alerts were saved in XML files using IDMEF (Intrusion Detection Message Exchange Format) format. During three months of monitoring, 1099302 alerts have been produced by different intrusion detection systems. In our model, an alert is considered as an interpretation where the domain of each attribute is the list of different attribute values. Each alert contains a set of facts representing its attributes in a predicate form. The ranking process is as following:

---

[1] https://sites.google.com/site/anrplacid/.

- Construct from each expert's IFO formulas an IFOΔ-base.
- Merge the Δ_i's into one $\Delta_\oplus$ using Algorithm 1.
- Rank the IDS alerts according to their satisfaction degree to $\Delta_\oplus$.

Expert 1: P_1: $Ids(snort - interne) \wedge (Severity(high) \vee Severity(medium))$.
P_2: $Ids(snort - public) \wedge Severity(high)$.
P_3 $Severity(meduim)$. Expert 1 prefers *snort-intern* alerts having a *high* or a *medium* severity, then those coming from *snort-public* IDS with a *high* severity. At last alerts having a *medium* severity.

Expert 2: P_1: $Severity(medium) \wedge Ids(Snort - public) \vee Severity(high)$. P_2: $Severity(high) \wedge Ids(Snort - interne)$. P_3: $Severity(medium)$. Expert 2 wants to see first the "high" severity alerts or those coming from *snort-public* IDS with *medium* severity. As second preferences "high" severity alerts of *snort-intern* IDS or those with a *medium* severity.

Expert 3: P_1: $Severity(high)$. P_2: $Severity(meduim)$. P_3: $Severity(low)$. Expert 3 prefers rank alerts according to their Severity degree. Table 1 summarizes the obtained results.

Table 1. Alerts number befor and after processing the ranking algorithm

Input alert number	Removed alert number	Removed alert rate	Preferred alert number	Preferred alert rate	Max pre-ferred alert number	Max pre-ferred alert rate	Execution time (ms)
695269	490457	70%	204812	29%	44085	6%	99056

Table 1 shows the efficiency of the proposed solution. Only 6% of initial alerts match the expressed preferences, and will be presented to the security administrator at the top of IDS alerts. The rest of the alerts are presented in the

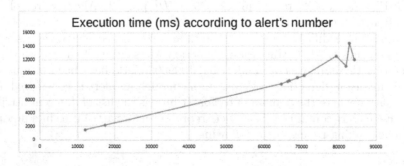

Fig. 1. Running time (ms)

decreasing order of their satisfaction degree. Figure 1 shows that the execution time increases linearly according to the alerts' number.

Number of alert handled per second $\approx \frac{\text{initial alerts number}}{\text{total execution time}} \approx \frac{695269}{99.056} \approx 7019$

6   Conclusion

In this paper, a specific syntactic form of the possibilistic logic witch is the IFO guaranteed possibilistic logic is defined, this logic encodes only preferences and each formula of the IFO guaranteed possibilistic base is assigned a weight that represent it preference degree. We propose a merging solution to fusion different security experts' preferences. Each security expert expresses his preferences describing alerts that he thinks are the most dangerous. The resulted base is used to rank a set of real IDS alerts.

As future work, we think to implement an on-line merging and ranking algorithm.

References

1. Benferhat, S., Dubois, D., Prade, H.: How to infer from inconsistent beliefs without revising ? In: Proceedings of the International Joint Conference on Artificial Intelligence, IJCAI 1995, pp. 1449–1455, Montreal Canada, August 1995
2. Benferhat, S., Kaci, S.: Logical representation and fusion of prioritized information based on guaranteed possibility measures: application to the distance-based merging of classical bases. Artif. Intell. **148**(1), 291–333 (2003)
3. Bouzar-Benlabiod, L., Benferhat, S., Bouabana-Tebibel, T.: Instantiated first order qualitative choice logic for an efficient handling of alerts correlation. Intell. Data Anal. **19**(1), 3–27 (2015)
4. Brewka, G., Benferhat, S., Le Berre, D.: Qualitative choice logic. Artif. Intell. **157**(1), 203–237 (2004)
5. Dubois, D., Lang, J., Prade, H.: Possibilistic logic. In: Gabbay, D., Hogger, C., Robinson, J. (eds.) Handbook of Logic in Artificial Intelligence and Logic Programming, vol. 3. Oxford University Press, New York (1994)
6. Dubois, D., Prade, H.: Possibility theory as a basis for preference propagation in automated reasoning. In: IEEE International Conference on Fuzzy Systems, pp. 821–832 (1992)
7. Kraus, S., Lehmann, D., Magidor, M.: Nonmonotonic reasoning, preferential models and cumulative logics. Artif. Intell. **44**(12), 167–207 (1990)
8. Lang, J.: Possibilistic logic: complexity and algorithms. In: Kohlas, J., Moral, S. (eds.) Algorithms for Uncertainty and Defeasible Reasoning, volume 5 of Handbook of Defeasible Reasoning and Uncertainty Management Systems (Gabbay D., Smets P. Eds.), vol. 5, pp. 179–220. Kluwer Academic Publishers, Dordrecht (2001)
9. Mu, K., Liu, W., Jin, Z., Bell, D.A.: A syntax-based approach to measuring the degree of inconsistency for belief bases. Int. J. Approx. Reason. **52**(7), 978–999 (2011)
10. Qi, G., Liu, W., Bell, D.A.: Measuring conflict and agreement between two prioritized knowledge bases in possibilistic logic. Fuzzy Sets Syst. **161**(14), 1906–1925 (2010)

Transformation Between CP-net
and CPC-net

Sultan Ahmed and Malek Mouhoub$^{(\boxtimes)}$

Department of Computer Science, University of Regina, Regina, Canada
{ahmed28s,mouhoubm}@uregina.ca

Abstract. A *Conditional Preference Network* (CP-net) graphically represents user's preferences, while a *CP-net with Comfort* (CPC-net) represents both preferences and comfort. Preference indicates user's habitual behavior and comfort indicates user's genuine decisions. In this paper, firstly, we show how to obtain the corresponding CPC-net given a CP-net and the comfort on each value of the problem variables. Secondly, we describe a method to find the corresponding CP-net for a given CPC-net.

1 Introduction

Human choices involve habitual behavior and genuine decisions [5]. Habitual behavior is user's expressed desire and is represented using preferences. A CP-net [2] is a graphical tool for representing and reasoning about user's qualitative and conditional preferences. A CP-net consists of a directed graph on the problem variables, which defines the preferential dependencies. For each variable in a CP-net, there is a CPT that captures the preference order on the values of the variable for each of its parent combination. On the other hand, genuine decisions [5] require to perceive and reason about a given situation, and to obtain a solution of the problem raised by the situation. This type of choices is environmentally motivated and is represented using user's comfort [1]. To capture both preference and comfort, a *Preference-Comfort* (PC) relation is used [1]. A PC relation is generalized for two or more values using a PC order. A *CP-net with Comfort* (CPC-net) [1] is an extension of the CP-net, which is used to represent and reason about preference and comfort. A CP-net and a CPC-net share a common directed graph to represent the preferential dependencies, while for each variable in a CPC-net, there is a *CPT with Comfort* (CPTC) that defines the PC orders on the values of the variable for each of its parent combination.

In this paper, we study the transformation process between CP-net and CPC-net. Firstly, we propose an algorithm that we call *Build-PC-Orders*. Build-PC-Orders finds the PC orders on the values of a variable given the preference order and the comfort on the values. This algorithm checks every permutation on the values. To generate the permutations, the Heap's algorithm [3] is used. We consider that there is a PC order corresponding to a permutation if, for every two consecutive values in the permutation, there is a PC relation. Given the parent combination for each variable in a CP-net, the algorithm is used to obtain

© Springer International Publishing AG, part of Springer Nature 2018
M. Mouhoub et al. (Eds.): IEA/AIE 2018, LNAI 10868, pp. 292–300, 2018.
https://doi.org/10.1007/978-3-319-92058-0_28

the PC orders that define the CPTC of the variable. That is how we find the corresponding CPC-net. Secondly, we propose the algorithm *Build-Preference-Order* that finds the corresponding preference order for a set of PC orders of a variable. The algorithm works in two steps. (1) It finds the preference relations induced in the PC orders. This is done by checking every consecutive pair in every PC order. If a consecutive pair induces a PC relation, then this latter will be saved. (2) Given the preference relations, the preference order can then be obtained using a topological sort. This is done using the Kahn's algorithm [4]. By finding the preference order for each variable of a CPC-net given the parents' instantiation, we construct the corresponding CP-net.

2   Background

We assume a set $V = \{X_1, X_2, \cdots, X_n\}$ of variables with corresponding domains $D(X_1), D(X_2), \cdots, D(X_n)$. The set of possible complete assignments is then $O = D(V) = D(X_1) \times D(X_2) \times \cdots \times D(X_n)$, where we use $D(\cdot)$ to denote the domain of a set of variables. A preference relation is a binary relation over two assignments. Given two assignments $x_1, x_2 \in D(X)$ where $X \subseteq V$, we write $x_1 \succ x_2$ to denote that x_1 is strictly preferred to x_2. A preference relation is anti-reflexive, anti-symmetric and transitive. A preference order over $D(X)$ for a variable X is an ordering of the values in $D(X)$ according to the preference relations over $D(X)$ given that, for every $x_1, x_2 \in D(X)$, there is a preference relation. A CP-net [2] graphically represents user's conditional preferences under the *ceteris paribus* assumption. A CP-net consists of a directed graph, in which preferential dependencies over the set V of variables are represented using directed arcs. For each variable $X \in V$, there is a CPT that gives the preference orders over $D(X)$ for each $p \in D(Pa(X))$, where $Pa(X)$ is the set of X's parents.

User's genuine decision is represented using comfort [1]. Given the cost of an option s, the comfort $c(s)$ is calculated as: $c(s) = 1/cost(s)$. It indicates that, the more cost the option has, the less comfortable the user feels. Given $x_1 \in D(X_1)$ and $x_2 \in D(X_2)$, we naturally get: $cost(x_1, x_2) = cost(x_1) + cost(x_2)$ that implies $c(x_1, x_2) = c(x_1)c(x_2)/(c(x_1) + c(x_2))$. Generally, for a complete assignment $x_1, x_2, \cdots, x_n$ on V, we get $c(x_1, x_2, \cdots, x_n) = \prod_{i=1}^{n} c(x_i) / \sum_{i=1}^{n} (\prod_{j=1, j \neq i}^{n} c(x_j))$. An outcome $o \in D(V)$ and its comfort $c(o)$ are denoted using the pair $(o, c(o))$. To represent preference with comfort, a PC relation is used.

Definition 1 ([1]). *Let $X \subseteq V$ and $x_1, x_2 \in D(X)$. We say that there is a PC relation ${}_c\!\succ$ on x_1 and x_2, iff $x_1 \succ x_2$ or $c(x_1) > c(x_2)$ holds. It is denoted as $(x_1, c(x_1))\ {}_c\!\succ (x_2, c(x_2))$ (interchangeably $x_1\ {}_c\!\succ x_2$). If both $x_1 \succ x_2$ and $c(x_1) > c(x_2)$ hold, the PC relation is harmonic and is denoted as $x_1\ {}_h\!\succ x_2$. If $x_1 \succ x_2$ holds and $c(x_1) > c(x_2)$ does not hold, the PC relation is preference-harmonic and is denoted as $x_1\ {}_{ph}\!\succ x_2$. If $x_1 \succ x_2$ does not hold and $c(x_1) > c(x_2)$ holds, the PC relation is comfort-harmonic and is denoted as $x_1\ {}_{ch}\!\succ x_2$.*

Definition 2 *([1]). Let $X \subseteq V$. A PC order $\overset{i}{\underset{c}{\succ}}{}^{X}$ for X is an ordering on $D(X)$, such that for every consecutive $x_1, x_2 \in D(X)$ in $\overset{i}{\underset{c}{\succ}}{}^{X}$, there is a PC rela-tion $x_1 \overset{}{\underset{c}{\succ}} x_2$. If every PC relation in $\overset{i}{\underset{c}{\succ}}{}^{X}$ is harmonic, $\overset{i}{\underset{c}{\succ}}{}^{X}$ is harmonic. If every PC relation in $\overset{i}{\underset{c}{\succ}}{}^{X}$ is preference-harmonic, $\overset{i}{\underset{c}{\succ}}{}^{X}$ is preference-harmonic. If every PC relation in $\overset{i}{\underset{c}{\succ}}{}^{X}$ is comfort-harmonic, $\overset{i}{\underset{c}{\succ}}{}^{X}$ is comfort-harmonic. If $\overset{i}{\underset{c}{\succ}}{}^{X}$ is not harmonic, preference-harmonic and comfort-harmonic, it is hybrid.*

CP-net with Comfort (CPC-net) [1] represents conditional preferences and absolute comforts. CP-net and CPC-net have a common directed graph. In both cases, the *conditional preferential independence* is used to obtain the graph. However, in a CPC-net, for each variable $X \in V$, there is a *CPT with Comfort* (CPTC) that gives the PC orders over $D(X)$ for each $p \in D(Pa(X))$.

Example 1. A CP-net with variables A and B is shown in Figs. 1(a) and (b), where $D(A) = \{a_1, a_2, a_3\}$ and $D(B) = \{b_1, b_2\}$. Figures 1(a) and (c) depict a CPC-net on A and B with the comforts $c(a_1) = 0.9$, $c(a_2) = 0.2$, $c(a_3) = 0.5$, $c(b_1) = 0.3$ and $c(b_3) = 0.4$. The PC orders over $D(A)$ are: $(a_1, 0.9) \ {}_{h}{\succ} (a_2, 0.2) \ {}_{ph}{\succ} (a_3, 0.5)$ and $(a_1, 0.9) \ {}_{h}{\succ} (a_3, 0.5) \ {}_{ch}{\succ} (a_2, 0.2)$. The first one indicates that the user chooses a_1 over a_2 in terms of preference and comfort, i.e., a_1 has more preference and comfort over a_2; and the user chooses a_2 over a_3 in terms of preference, i.e., a_2 has more preference over a_3. In Fig. 1(a), B preferentially depends on A. Given $A = a_1$ or a_3, the PC orders over $D(B)$ are: $(b_1, 0.3) \ {}_{ph}{\succ} (b_2, 0.4)$ and $(b_2, 0.4) \ {}_{ch}{\succ} (b_1, 0.3)$. $\qquad\square$

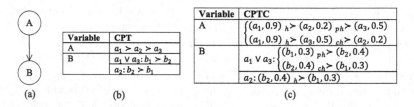

Variable	CPT
A	$a_1 > a_2 > a_3$
B	$a_1 \vee a_3 : b_1 > b_2$
	$a_2 : b_2 > b_1$

Variable	CPTC
A	$\begin{cases}(a_1, 0.9) \ {}_{h}{\succ} (a_2, 0.2) \ {}_{ph}{\succ} (a_3, 0.5)\\ (a_1, 0.9) \ {}_{h}{\succ} (a_3, 0.5) \ {}_{ch}{\succ} (a_2, 0.2)\end{cases}$
B	$a_1 \vee a_3: \begin{cases}(b_1, 0.3) \ {}_{ph}{\succ} (b_2, 0.4)\\ (b_2, 0.4) \ {}_{ch}{\succ} (b_1, 0.3)\end{cases}$
	$a_2: (b_2, 0.4) \ {}_{h}{\succ} (b_1, 0.3)$

(a)   (b)   (c)

Fig. 1. A CP-net (a) & (b) and a CPC-net (a) & (c).

3   Constructing the CPC-net from a Given CP-net

Given the preference order and the comforts over $D(X)$ for a variable X, we describe to obtain the PC orders by checking every permutation over $D(X)$. To generate the permutations, we apply the Heap's algorithm [3]. For any two consecutive elements x_1 and x_2 in a permutation, we can determine whether $x_1 \succ x_2$ holds or not, using the transitivity and anti-symmetry principles of preference order. For example, given a preference order $y_1 \succ y_2 \succ y_3 \succ y_4$ over y_1, y_2, y_3 and y_4, we have that $y_1 \succ y_3$ holds and $y_4 \succ y_2$ does not hold. On the other hand, the comforts $c(x_1)$ and $c(x_2)$ are directly comparable as they are numerical values. From the preference relation and comforts of x_1 and x_2, we can determine if $x_1 \, {}_h\!\succ x_2$, $x_1 \, {}_{ph}\!\succ x_2$, $x_1 \, {}_{ch}\!\succ x_2$ or neither of them holds. For a permutation, if there is a PC relation for every pair of the consecutive elements, there is a corresponding PC order which can be obtained by assigning the corresponding PC relation in every pair of the consecutive elements.

Example 2. Let X be a variable with its domain $\{x_1, x_2, x_3\}$. The preference order is $x_1 \succ x_2 \succ x_3$ and the set of comforts is $c(X) = \{c(x_1), c(x_2), c(x_3)\}$, where $c(x_1) = 0.3$, $c(x_2) = 0.5$ and $c(x_3) = 0.2$. To find the PC orders, we first find all possible permutations $x_1x_2x_3$, $x_1x_3x_2$, $x_2x_1x_3$, $x_2x_3x_1$, $x_3x_1x_2$ and $x_3x_2x_1$. For the first permutation $x_1x_2x_3$, we need to check if a PC order exists or not. For the first pair of consecutive elements x_1 and x_2, we have that $x_1 \succ x_2$ and not $c(x_1) > c(x_2)$. These give us $x_1 \, {}_{ph}\!\succ x_2$. For the second pair of consecutive elements x_2 and x_3, we get $x_2 \, {}_h\!\succ x_3$. Therefore, a PC order corresponding to the permutation exists, which is $x_1 \, {}_{ph}\!\succ x_2 \, {}_h\!\succ x_3$. $\square$

To find all PC orders from the preference order and the set of comforts of a variable X, we propose an algorithm that we call *Build-PC-Orders*. Build-PC-Orders (a variant of the Heap's algorithm [3]) is a recursive algorithm that has five inputs. The first input l is an integer that is initially equal to the number of the values in X. Only this input is passed as parameter in the recursive calls of the algorithm. The second input $DomX$ is an array that initially contains an arbitrary sequence (permutation) of the values in X. The third and fourth inputs, $\succ$ and $c(X)$, are the preference order and the set of comforts on $D(X)$ correspondingly. The fifth input m indicates the number of values in X. The latter three inputs do not change during the execution of the algorithm. $\succ$ and $c(X)$ are needed to determine if there is a PC relation between two values. m is needed to check if there is a PC relation for every pair of the consecutive elements for a permutation. Build-PC-Orders returns the all PC orders on $D(X)$ in an array S indexed by k. k indicates the number of PC orders which is initially 0.

In lines 1 and 15–25, Build-PC-Orders follows the Heap's algorithm [3] and traverses through every permutation of the values in variable X. When Build-PC-Orders finds a new permutation stored in the array $DomX$, it checks if there is a corresponding PC order to the permutation and the PC order (if it exists) is stored in the array S using lines 2–14. The range of index for S is 0 to $k-1$. When there is a new permutation, $S[k]$ is initialized with *null* in line 2. Using lines 3–13, every pair of consecutive elements in the permutation is checked. When a PC relation is found, it is merged with $S[k]$. For example, if $S[k] = x_1 \, {}_{ph}\!\succ x_2 \, {}_h\!\succ x_3$ and the PC relation $x_3 \, {}_{ch}\!\succ x_4$ is found, after merging the PC relation with $S[k]$, $S[k]$ would be $x_1 \, {}_{ph}\!\succ x_2 \, {}_h\!\succ x_3 \, {}_{ch}\!\succ x_4$. There would be two options. (1) There exists a PC relation for every pair of consecutive elements. In this case, after merging the PC relations with $S[k]$, we will have the PC order in $S[k]$. Then, k is increased by 1 in line 14. (2) There does not exist a PC relation for at least a pair of consecutive elements. In this case, the loop will break in line 10 and Build-PC-Orders will be returned using line 11. k is not increased.

Example 3. Let us apply Build-PC-Orders algorithm to find the PC orders for a variable X, having its domain $\{x_1, x_2, x_3\}$. We initially have $l = 3$. Consider

---

Algorithm 1. Build-PC-Orders

Input: An integer l that is initially equal to the number of values in variable X; an array $DomX$ that initially contains an arbitrary sequence of values in X; the preference order $\succ$ on $D(X)$; the set of comforts $c(X)$ on $D(X)$; the number of values m in X

Output: The PC orders on $D(X)$ are stored in array S indexed by k

---

```
1: if l = 1 then
2:     Set S[k] = null
3:     for i = 0; i < m − 1; i = i + 1 do
4:         if DomX[i] ₕ≻ DomX[i + 1] then
5:             Merge (DomX[i] ₕ≻ DomX[i + 1]) with S[k]
6:         else if DomX[i] ₚₕ≻ DomX[i + 1] then
7:             Merge (DomX[i] ₚₕ≻ DomX[i + 1]) with S[k]
8:         else if DomX[i] ₆ₕ≻ DomX[i + 1] then
9:             Merge (DomX[i] ₆ₕ≻ DomX[i + 1]) with S[k]
10:        else
11:            return
12:        end if
13:    end for
14:    Set k = k + 1
15: else
16:    for i = 0; i < l − 1; i = i + 1 do
17:        Build-PC-Orders(l − 1)
18:        if l is even then
19:            Swap DomX[i] and DomX[l − 1]
20:        else
21:            Swap DomX[0] and DomX[l − 1]
22:        end if
23:    end for
24:    Build-PC-Orders(l − 1)
25: end if
```

---

that $DomX$ is initially $[x_1, x_2, x_3]$. The preference order $\succ$ is $x_1 \succ x_2 \succ x_3$. The comforts are $c(x_1) = 0.3$, $c(x_2) = 0.5$ and $c(x_3) = 0.2$. The value m is 3. For the first call (call 0), lines 17–22 will continue twice, one for $i = 0$ and another for $i = 1$. Then, in line 24, Build-PC-Orders will be called. Let us assume lines 17–22 for $i = 0$. In line 17, Build-PC-Orders is called with $l = 2$ (call 1). For call 1, lines 17–22 will continue for $i = 0$. In line 24, Build-PC-Orders will be called.

Let us assume lines 17–22 for $i = 0$ in call 1. In line 17, Build-PC-Orders is called with $l = 1$ (call 2). In line 2 of call 2, $S[0]$ is set as $null$. For the first pair of consecutive elements x_1 and x_2 in $DomX$, we have $x_1 {}_{ph}\succ x_2$ in line 6. In line 7, after merging $x_1 {}_{ph}\succ x_2$ with $S[0]$, we have $S[0]$ is $x_1 {}_{ph}\succ x_2$. For the second pair of consecutive elements x_2 and x_3 in $DomX$, we have $x_2 {}_h\succ x_3$ in line 4. In line 5, after merging $x_2 {}_h\succ x_3$ with $S[0]$, we have $S[0]$ is $x_1 {}_{ph}\succ x_2 {}_h\succ x_3$. At this stage, we have a PC order in $S[0]$. In line 14, k is increased by 1 and the call 2 is ended. In call 1, because l is 2 and i is 0, $DomX[0]$ and $DomX[1]$ are swapped in lines 18–19. Now, $DomX$ is $[x_2, x_1, x_3]$.

In line 24 (call 1), Build-PC-Orders is called with $l = 1$ (call 3). For this call, we find the second PC order $x_2\ _{ch}\succ x_1\ _h\succ x_3$ in $S[1]$. In line 14, k is increased by 1 and the call is ended. At this stage, call 1 is also ended. In line 21 of call 0, $DomX[0]$ and $DomX[2]$ are swapped; and $DomX$ is $[x_3, x_1, x_2]$.

Now, let us assume lines 17–22 for $i = 1$ in call 0. In line 17, Build-PC-Orders is called with $l = 2$ (call 4). For call 4, lines 17–22 will continue for $i = 0$ and, in line 24, Build-PC-Orders will be called. In line 17, Build-PC-Orders is called with $l = 1$ (call 5). For this call in line 2, $S[2]$ is set as *null*. For the first pair of consecutive elements x_3 and x_1 in $DomX$, $x_3\ _c\succ x_1$ does not hold. Therefore, in line 11, call 5 is returned. $DomX[0]$ and $DomX[1]$ are swapped in lines 18–19 of call 4; and $DomX$ is $[x_1, x_3, x_2]$. In line 24, Build-PC-Orders is called with $l = 1$ (call 6). In this call, the permutation $x_1x_3x_2$ is checked and no PC order is obtained. At this stage, calls 6 and 4 are ended. In line 21 of call 0, $DomX[0]$ and $DomX[2]$ are swapped; and $DomX$ is $[x_2, x_3, x_1]$.

In line 24 (call 0), Build-PC-Orders is called with $l = 2$ (call 7). In line 17, Build-PC-Orders is called with $l = 1$ (call 8) in which no PC order is found for $x_2x_3x_1$. $DomX[0]$ and $DomX[1]$ are swapped in lines 18–19 of call 7. Now, $DomX$ is $[x_3, x_2, x_1]$. In line 24, Build-PC-Orders is called with $l = 1$ (call 9). For this call, the permutation $x_3x_2x_1$ is checked and no PC order is obtained. At this stage, calls 7 and 1 are ended. The algorithm is terminated. It stores two PC orders $x_1\ _{ph}\succ x_2\ _h\succ x_3$ and $x_2\ _{ch}\succ x_1\ _h\succ x_3$ in the array S.   □

Boutilier et al. [2] described how to construct a CP-net from user's conditional preferences. Given the CP-net and the set of comforts $c(X)$ on $D(X)$ for every variable X, we describe in the following how to construct the corresponding CPC-net. Note that both the CP-net and the CPC-net share a common directed graph. In contrast, each variable has a CPT in a CP-net, while each variable has a CPTC in a CPC-net. Constructing the CPC-net from a CP-net is straightforward. We need to traverse through each variable in the CP-net. For each variable X in the CP-net, given $CPT(X)$ and $c(X)$, we need to obtain the $CPTC(X)$. This can be done by applying the Build-PC-Orders algorithm. For each $p \in D(Pa(X))$, $CPT(X)$ defines a preference order over $D(X)$. Given the preference order and $c(X)$, the Build-PC-Orders can find the all PC orders over $D(X)$ for $p \in D(Pa(X))$. The PC orders on $D(X)$ for each $p \in D(Pa(X))$ give the $CPTC(X)$. The directed graph of the CP-net and the CPTCs on each variable define the CPC-net.

4 Constructing the CP-net from a Given CPC-net

We describe how to find the preference order from the PC orders over $D(X)$ for a variable X. In a PC order, only a harmonic or preference harmonic PC relation induces a preference relation [1]. Therefore, firstly, we find all the preference relations by iterating every PC relation for every PC order. Secondly, we apply Kahn's algorithm [4] for topological sorting of the preference relations to obtain the preference order. To perform the task, we propose the algorithm *Build-Preference-Order* that takes the PC orders in an array S (indexed by k) as input and produces the preference order in Q. Q is initially *null*. An array P is declared in line 1 to store the preference relations. In lines 2–9, every PC relation for every PC order in S is traversed. If a PC relation induces a preference relation that is already not in P, then the preference relation is inserted in P.

Lines 10–21 of Build-Preference-Order follow the Kahn's algorithm [4] for topological sorting of the preference relations in P. In lines 10–11, an array T is declared and every element, that no other element has more preference over it, is inserted in T. Lines 13–20 continue till T is *empty*. In lines 13–14, an element is removed from T and is "preferentially" merged with Q. For example, merging x_1 with $Q = null$ will result $Q = x_1$; merging x_2 with $Q = x_1$ will result $Q = x_1 \succ x_2$; merging x_3 with $Q = x_1 \succ x_2$ will result $Q = x_1 \succ x_2 \succ x_3$; and so on. In lines 15–20, every preference relation in P in which the removed element in line 13 precedes is deleted; and if no other element has more preference over the proceeding element, then the proceeding element is inserted in T.

Algorithm 2. Build-Preference-Order

Input: The array S that contains the PC orders over $D(X)$ for a variable X; and the number of elements k in S

Output: The preference order Q that is initially set to *null*

1: Let P be an empty array that can contain preference relations
2: **for** $i = 0; i < k; i = i + 1$ **do**
3:　　Let $S[i]$ be $x_1 \ {}_c{\succ}\ x_2 \ {}_c{\succ}\ \cdots \ {}_c{\succ}\ x_m$
4:　　**for** $j = 1; j < m; j = j + 1$ **do**
5:　　　　**if** $(x_j \ {}_h{\succ}\ x_{j+1}$ or $x_j \ {}_{ph}{\succ}\ x_{j+1})$ and $x_j \succ x_{j+1}$ is not in P **then**
6:　　　　　　Insert $x_j \succ x_{j+1}$ in P
7:　　　　**end if**
8:　　**end for**
9: **end for**
10: Let T be an empty array that can contain values of X
11: Insert every x_i in T such that $x_j \succ x_i$ is not in P
12: **while** T is not empty **do**
13:　　Remove an element x_i from T
14:　　Merge x_i with Q
15:　　**for each** $x_i \succ x_j$ in P **do**
16:　　　　Delete $x_i \succ x_j$ from P
17:　　　　**if** there is no element $x \succ x_j$ for $x \in D(X)$ in P **then**
18:　　　　　　Insert x_j in T
19:　　　　**end if**
20:　　**end for**
21: **end while**

Example 4. We are given the PC orders $x_1 \ {}_{ph}{\succ}\ x_2 \ {}_h{\succ}\ x_3$ and $x_2 \ {}_{ch}{\succ}\ x_1 \ {}_h{\succ}\ x_3$ stored in $S[0]$ and $S[1]$ correspondingly, and $k = 2$. We obtain the corresponding preference order using Build-Preference-Order algorithm. Initially, we have that $Q = null$. In line 1, the array P is declared, which has no element. Lines 3–8 continue for $i = 0$ and $i = 1$. For the first iteration ($i = 0$), in line 3, we have that $S[0] = x_1 \;_{ph}\succ x_2 \;_{h}\succ x_3$. For the nested loop, lines 5–7 continue twice. Firstly, $x_1 \;_{ph}\succ x_2$ is checked in line 5. It induces the preference relation $x_1 \succ x_2$ that is already not in P. Therefore, $x_1 \succ x_2$ is inserted in P in line 6. Secondly, $x_2 \;_{h}\succ x_3$ induces the preference relation $x_2 \succ x_3$ that is also not in P. $x_2 \succ x_3$ is also inserted in P. At this point, we have that $P = [x_1 \succ x_2, x_2 \succ x_3]$. Similarly, after completing lines 1–9, we have that $P = [x_1 \succ x_2, x_2 \succ x_3, x_1 \succ x_3]$.

In line 10, the array T is declared. In line 11, we have that $T = [x_1]$. Lines 13–20 continue, since T is not *empty*. In line 13, x_1 is removed from T and T is *empty*. In line 14, we have that $Q = x_1$. Lines 16–19 repeat for $x_1 \succ x_2$ and $x_1 \succ x_3$. Firstly, for $x_1 \succ x_2$, in line 16, $x_1 \succ x_2$ is deleted from P and we have that $P = [x_2 \succ x_3, x_1 \succ x_3]$. In lines 17–19, since there is no element in P such that $x \succ x_2$, x_2 is inserted in T and we have that $T = [x_2]$. Secondly, for $x_1 \succ x_3$, in line 16, $x_1 \succ x_3$ is deleted from P and we have that $P = [x_2 \succ x_3]$. Since we have $x_2 \succ x_3$ in P, in lines 17–19, no element is inserted in T.

Again, lines 13–20 continue, since T is not *empty*. In line 13, x_2 is removed from T and T is empty. In line 14, we get that $Q = x_1 \succ x_2$. Lines 16–19 continue for $x_2 \succ x_3$. In line 16, $x_2 \succ x_3$ is deleted from P and P is empty. In lines 17–19, x_3 is inserted in T and we have that $T = [x_3]$. Since T is not *empty*, lines 13–20 continue again. In line 13, x_3 is removed from T and T is empty. In line 14, we get that $Q = x_1 \succ x_2 \succ x_3$. Since there is no element in P, the loop for lines 15–20 is not continued. Since there is no element in T, the loop for lines 12–21 is not continued and the algorithm is terminated. We have the preference order $x_1 \succ x_2 \succ x_3$ in Q, which has been produced by the algorithm. $\square$

Obtaining the corresponding CP-net of a given CPC-net is often a necessary task, especially for evaluating the comparison queries in CPC-nets as discussed in [1]. It can be done in a straightforward manner. We need to traverse through each variable in the CPC-net. For each variable X in the CPC-net, given $CPTC(X)$, we need to obtain the $CPT(X)$. This can be done by applying the Build-Preference-Order algorithm. For each $p \in D(Pa(X))$, $CPTC(X)$ defines a set of PC orders over $D(X)$. Given the PC orders, the Build-Preference-Order can find the preference order over $D(X)$ for $p \in D(Pa(X))$. The preference orders on $D(X)$ for each $p \in D(Pa(X))$ give the $CPT(X)$.

5   Conclusions

We have proposed the methods to transform a CP-net to the corresponding CPC-net and vice-versa. A CP-net and a CPC-net differ in the fact that: there is a CPT for every variable in a CP-net, while there is a CPTC for every variable in a CPC-net. Therefore, we have basically illustrated the transformation methods between CPT and CPTC given the comfort information. The work is useful in constructing CPC-nets and evaluating comparison queries in CPC-nets.

References

1. Ahmed, S., Mouhoub, M.: On graphical modeling of preference and comfort. Technical report (2017). http://hdl.handle.net/10294/7834
2. Boutilier, C., Brafman, R.I., Domshlak, C., Hoos, H.H., Poole, D.: CP-nets: a tool for representing and reasoning with conditional ceteris paribus preference statements. J. Artif. Intell. Res. (JAIR) **21**, 135–191 (2004)
3. Heap, B.: Permutations by interchanges. Comput. J. **6**(3), 293–298 (1963)
4. Kahn, A.B.: Topological sorting of large networks. Commun. ACM **5**(11), 558–562 (1962)
5. Katona, G.: Psychological Analysis of Economic Behavior. McGraw-Hill, New York (1951)

Machine Learning

Online Detection of Shill Bidding Fraud Based on Machine Learning Techniques

Swati Ganguly and Samira Sadaoui$^{(\boxtimes)}$

University of Regina, Regina, SK, Canada
{gangulys, sadaouis}@uregina.ca

Abstract. E-auctions have attracted serious fraud, such as Shill Bidding (SB), due to the large amount of money involved and anonymity of users. SB is difficult to detect given its similarity to normal bidding behavior. To this end, we develop an efficient SVM-based fraud classifier that enables auction companies to distinguish between legitimate and shill bidders. We introduce a robust approach to build offline the optimal SB classifier. To produce SB training data, we combine the hierarchical clustering and our own labelling strategy, and then utilize a hybrid data sampling method to solve the issue of highly imbalanced SB datasets. To avert financial loss in new auctions, the SB classifier is to be launched at the end of the bidding period and before auction finalization. Based on commercial auction data, we conduct experiments for offline and online SB detection. The classification results exhibit good detection accuracy and misclassification rate of shill bidders.

Keywords: Data clustering · Data labeling · Data sampling
Supervised learning · SVM · In-auction fraud · Shill bidding · Fraud detection

1 Introduction

E-auctions have greatly facilitated the selling and acquisition of goods and services. However, this industry, which involves millions of dollars, makes it attractive to fraudsters. Auctions are vulnerable to crimes committed by malicious moneymakers due to reasons like anonymity of users, flexibility of bidding, reduced legal policies against auction fraud and low costs of auction services. As per the Internet Crime Complaint Center (IC3), auction fraud is one of the most reported cybercrimes. In the IC3 report of 2015, a loss of 18 million USD has been recorded through 9,847 auction complaints. It is challenging to detect fraud occurring during the bidding process, called In-Auction Fraud (IAF), such as shill bidding, bid shielding and bid shading. In this study, we concentrate on Shill Bidding (SB) because it has been recognized as the most prevalent IAF and also the most difficult to detect due to its similarity to usual bidding behavior [6, 7, 22]. To improve his revenue, a seller may perform SB by creating fake accounts and/or colluding with other auction users. By considering the empirical studies of detecting shills, which experimented with data from different auction sites, this type of IAF occurred frequently [7, 19, 22]. Moreover, for many years, users complained about SB in various blogs and articles [14]. Contrary to eBay claim that only less than 0.1% of transactions are SB, it is estimated that the percentage

© Springer International Publishing AG, part of Springer Nature 2018
M. Mouhoub et al. (Eds.): IEA/AIE 2018, LNAI 10868, pp. 303–314, 2018.
https://doi.org/10.1007/978-3-319-92058-0_29

is actually 15%, 18% and 28% respectively for the three top selling categories: computer and networking, health and beauty, and eBay motors [13]. According to [5, 23], SB could lead to market failure. When caught, the guilty seller may be prosecuted. In 2001, three sellers were charged of SB worth a pay-off of $300,000 through 1100 auctions of art paintings [23]. The fraud was conducted on eBay with more than 40 fake accounts. In 2012, an auto-auction company was fined $70,000 for conducting SB fraud[1], and in 2014, a lawsuit was carried out against an auction company of real estate for committing SB[2].

The complexity of SB strategies makes their detection a difficult problem to solve. Additionally, to be successful, any SB detection model should address two important aspects: (1) dealing with the tremendous amount of auction data, including detailed information about bidders, sellers and auctions; and (2) learning from the characteristics of SB behavior to be able to detect SB accurately in new auctions. These requirements can be handled by Machine Learning Techniques (MLTs). Each MLT has its own pros and cons depending on the problem it is applied to. Numerous publications have showed the effectiveness of SVM across several classification and fraud detection applications. We select SVM to build our SB classifier because it possesses strong theoretical foundations, generalization capabilities, very good performance when learning with imbalanced training data (like SB data), and very fast execution when classifying new data (time is a critical requirement of e-auctions).

In this paper, we propose an approach to build offline the optimal SVM-based SB detection model, which comprises of several steps: measurement, clustering, labeling and sampling of SB data, and SVM parameter tuning. Unlike other fraud datasets, SB data are lacking because they are difficult to obtain. To produce SB data, we first define metrics to measure the SB patterns, and then compute the metrics from raw auction data. To generate SB training data, we apply the Hierarchical Clustering and then our own labelling strategy. Fraud data are highly imbalanced in nature, and this class imbalance has been shown to decrease the performance of MLTs [8, 10]. Also, imbalanced data results in misclassifying the minority class because MLTs are often biased towards the majority class [12]. This is inappropriate in fraud detection applications since fraudulent instances tend to be classified as normal. To be effective in solving the imbalanced learning problem, we utilize a hybrid method of data over-sampling and under-sampling. The learned SVM model once online is to be launched at the end of the bidding period of each auction to detect suspicious bidders before processing payment. First for each participant, the SB features are calculated based on the bidding transactions. Subsequently, the fraud classifier is fed with the new SB instances in order to deduce their labels: normal or suspicious. We use "suspicious" as the finding requires confirmation. Indeed, further investigation is conducted to confirm or reject the suspicion. When suspected bidders are found to be actual shills, necessary actions are then taken by the auction admin, such as cancelling the infected auction to avert money loss for honest bidders, especially for high-priced products. To assess the performance of our SB classifier in both training and testing, we conduct

---

[1] https://www.trademe.co.nz/trust-safety/2012/9/29/shill-bidding.

[2] https://nypost.com/2014/12/25/lawsuit-targets-googles-auction-com.

several experiments based on the most adequate classification metrics for fraud data and imbalanced data.

Our work improves previous SB studies in several aspects, such as the offline process to build the fraud detection model. To train accurately the SB classifier, we utilize a collection of the most relevant strategies practised by shills rather than uncertain features (like feedback ratings) or general auction features (like transaction records). In spite of SB datasets being highly imbalanced, none of the past research on SB classification proposed a pre-processing phase to address this problem. Moreover, a SB classifier should be able to operate in real-life scenarios. Still, existing SB detection approaches did not implement any online detection strategy. In our work, thanks to the auction-wise classification features, we are able to cancel any auction infected by SB in order to avert money loss for the winners.

2 Related Works

SB detection studies are limited contrary to other fraud detection applications. There is only one study [15] where SVM has been deployed to classify SB. However, this work employed general auction features, like item price (11), user profiles (3) and transaction frequencies (15), and also uncertain features, like reputation feedback (12). These features are inappropriate to train accurately a SB classifier. Furthermore, this paper did not disclose any information about the preprocessing and learning steps. Another work [25] utilized 1-class SVM to determine outliers (abnormal behavior) according to the bidder history and feedback ratings, and then applied Decision Trees to find shills. Our approach is different from these two SB classifiers with respect to the classification features. For instance, as pointed out by [17], feedback ratings may not be fully trusted because they are not always honest and can bias the fraud classifier. At times, fake accounts can be created to accumulate positive ratings, and also users do not always provide feedback, which leads to insufficient information for assessing the behaviour of sellers and buyers. Moreover, the two previous systems focus only on learning SB behaviour. Nowadays, it is also important to develop an online SB detection approach, like ours, that is able to suspend an auction if it is infected by SB. There is another research on SB detection [7] but it differs from our work in the following aspects. This study developed an incremental Back-propagation ANN. But it is often found that ANN suffers from local minima and high computational cost, and also there are many ANN parameters to control. These are not issues for SVM. Feedback rating is used as one of the classification attributes but as mentioned earlier ratings are not reliable to assess shills. The classifier in [7] deals with bidder-wise classification features resulting in actions taken against fraudsters only. Actions if not taken against each infected auction cannot stop the financial loss from happening. More recently, in [9], the authors proposed prevention and detection methods of shill bidders. The prevention method regulates the creation of unauthorized user profiles by verifying certain legal parameters against an existing database. The detection method implements a 2-layered hybrid model. First, the authors applied the K-means clustering based on two features to partition bidders for the learning purpose. For the online phase, the authors employed Hidden Markov Model to compare each new bid with the learned bidding behaviour to determine if a bidder is a shill or not. Processing each bid negatively impacts the system performance. Moreover, using only two attributes does not provide sufficient information to classify shill bidders.

3   Construction of Shill Bidding Dataset

3.1   Raw Auction Data

For our study, we utilize actual auction data that have been made public in the following link: www.modelingonlineauctions.com/datasets. The link displays auctions of three popular products extracted over a period of two months from eBay: Cartier wristwatches, Palm Pilot PDAs and Xbox game consoles. We select the PDA product because it attracted a large number of bidders, and according to eBay, today PDA belongs to the top 12 most sold item among 34 categories. Moreover, this product has a good price range and its auctions have a long duration (7 days). In fact, the higher the price, more a possibility of SB activities [6]. Also, shills have a better chance to imitate normal behavior in auctions with a long duration [5]. So based on these factors that encourage SB, our auction dataset is appropriate for SB learning. In Table 1, we conduct a statistical analysis of the PDA auction dataset.

Raw auction data are not always in a favourable condition, and thus require some cleansing. From the PDA set, we remove incomplete data, like records with a blank bidder ID, and noisy data, like auctions with less than three bids because they may bias the classification results. So, we delete 2.6% of auctions as shown in Table 1, and consequently we are left with 145 auctions.

3.2   SB Patterns and Weights

We choose eight SB patterns that have been found to be dominant across infected auctions [7, 19, 22]. These patterns represent the classification features that will decide whether a bidder is behaving suspiciously or normally (Table 2).

Afterwards, we assign weights (low, medium and high) to the SB patterns (Table 2). A weight denotes the relative importance of a pattern on the bidder's label, and the combination of all the weighted patterns influences the classification decision. Some of the patterns are similar to normal bidding behavior, thus making it difficult to differentiate between a normal and suspicious activity. E.g. we know that shills usually participate in auctions of some particular sellers. But there are situations where a normal bidder competes a lot for a certain seller due to reasons like the seller has an excellent reputation or he is the only one selling the item [22]. That is why we attach a medium weight to the 'Buyer Tendency' pattern. Furthermore, both 'Nibble Bidding' and 'Winning Ratio' indicate that some bidders, in spite of competing rigorously, hardly win. Both highly suggest shilling, and thus are assigned with a high weight. In fact, eBay has proclaimed in its buying guides that there are high chances that a bidder is performing SB when he nibbles with consecutive low increments but without winning the auction. For the experiments, we assign a value of 0.3 to the low weight, 0.5 to the medium weight, and 0.7 to the high weight [19].

Table 1. Statistics of source data

	PDA dataset
Total auctions	149
Total bidders (with unique ID)	1024
Total bids	3166
Average number of bidders per auction	7
Average number of bids per auction	21
Average winning price	$229.04
1-Bid auctions	NIL
2-Bid auctions	4

Table 2. Typical shill bidding strategies

Name	Description	Motive	Source	Weight
Starting price	Seller sets an unusually low starting price when compared to concurrent auctions (selling the same product)	To attract people to the auction	Auction	Low
Early bidding	Bidder submits a bid very early in the auction	To allure legitimate bidders to participate in that auction	Bid	Low
Bidding ratio	Bidder participates aggressively in the middle stage of the auction	To raise the auction price and attract higher bids from other participants	Bid	Medium
Nibble bidding	Bidder outbids oneself with consecutive small bids	To raise the auction price gradually	Bid	High
Last bidding	Bidder becomes inactive at the final stage of an auction	To prevent oneself from winning the auction	Bid	Medium
Winning ratio	Bidder competes aggressively in many auctions but hardy wins any auctions	The target is not to win the auction but to raise the price of the product	Bidder	High
Buyer tendency	Bidder participates exclusively in auctions of few sellers rather than a diversified lot	Collusive act involving the fraudulent seller and an accomplice who acts as a normal bidder to raise the price	Bidder	Medium
Auction bids	The number of bids in an auction with shilling is much more than that of concurrent auctions without shilling	To make the product appear more popular	Auction	Low

3.3   SB Measurement

To produce SB data, the eight SB patterns are measured for all the bidders of the 145 auctions. Based on the auction data source (organized with a total of 25 attributes), the patterns are computed against each bidder in each auction. As a result, we produce a SB dataset with a tally of 1639 instances. An instance, which represents the misbehavior of a bidder in an auction, is a vector of 10 fields: Auction ID, Bidder ID, and the eight fraud features. We measure most of these patterns based on the algorithms presented in [19] except for 'Nibble Bidding' and 'Starting Price' that we introduce in this paper. Each pattern is formulated in a way that the higher the value (normalized to [0, 1]), more the chances of fraud by the bidder. Next, we divide the SB dataset into two parts according to the start date of auctions: (1) 90% of data will be used for training the SVM classifier (offline SB detection). The resulting training set has a total of 1488 instances (130 auctions and 922 bidders); (2) 10% of more recent data will be used to test the SB classifier. The testing dataset contains 151 instances (15 auctions and 102 bidders).

4   Clustering Shill Bidding Data

The most challenging task of constructing any training set is to label its data. To this end, we need first to cluster the SB training data. We choose Hierarchical Clustering since researchers have successfully utilized this clustering method for partitioning fraud data [16, 18]. This method is found to produce better quality of the generated clusters when compared to other clustering techniques. It does not require the number of clusters to be defined in advance by the user. Determining this number shouldn't be done randomly. In our case, instead of hard clustering the data directly into two groups, we want the clusters to be created systematically. We can then label the clusters as 'Normal' or 'Suspicious' according to their general behavioural property as explained in the next section. The computational complexity is high for Hierarchical Clustering [7]. Still given the fact that our training set is of average size, this clustering type will work fast. In addition, since the training phase is an offline and one-time operation, the time-efficiency is not an issue. More precisely, we utilize the centroid linkage as the similarity measure to partition our training dataset since it is less affected by outliers unlike single-link or complete-link [7]. After applying Hierarchical Clustering on our training dataset, we obtain eight clusters exposed in Table 3.

Table 3. Data clustering and labelling results

Cluster ID	Size (approx.)	Label
Cluster 1	78%	Normal
Cluster 3	14%	
Cluster 5	<1%	
Cluster 7	2%	
Cluster 2	2%	Suspicious
Cluster 4	1%	
Cluster 6	<1%	
Cluster 8	1%	

5   Labelling Shill Bidding Data

In each cluster, we categorize each fraud pattern into 'low' or 'high' behavioral property according to the average value of all the bidders in that particular cluster. Here, a cluster denotes the most prominent SB patterns. Table 4 provides two examples of cluster analysis and labelling. In 'Cluster 1', we found that except for 'Starting Price' (low weight), all the other shill patterns are low in property. This means the bidders in this cluster are behaving normally as most of the SB patterns are low in property. In 'Cluster 2', bidders have dominant shill patterns with high and medium weights. Among these, the presence of high-weight patterns, 'Nibble Bidding' and 'Winning Ratio', indicates that bidders in this cluster are most probably shills. This way, based on which fraud pattern of what weight falls in the high or low property category, we label the cluster as 'Normal' or 'Suspicious'.

In Table 3, among the 8 generated clusters, 4 clusters with around 5% of instances show strong implication of SB because of the patterns dominating these clusters. In these 4 clusters, patterns with high weights mostly belong to the high property category, which implies that the values of these patterns are higher than average. Thus, we label them as suspicious. The remaining clusters with 95% of instances are labelled as normal because the patterns in the high property category are of low weight, and most of the patterns with high weights are in the low property category. In summary, we obtain a labelled training set with 95% of normal instances and 5% of suspicious instances. This set is a highly imbalanced dataset that requires sampling before the learning process can take place in order to build an efficient SB detection model.

Table 4. Clustering analysis

Cluster ID	Behavioural property	Label
Cluster 1	**Low Value:** Early Bidding (low weight) Auction Bids (low weight) Bidding Ratio (medium weight) Buying Tendency (medium weight) Last Bidding (medium weight) Winning Ratio (high weight) Nibble Bidding (high weight) **High Value:** Starting Price (low weight)	Normal
Cluster 2	**Low Value:** Auction Bids (low weight) Starting Price (low weight) **High Value:** Early Bidding (low weight) Bidding Ratio (medium weight) Buying Tendency (medium weight) Last Bidding (medium weight) Nibble Bidding (high weight) Winning Ratio (high weight)	Suspicious

6   Sampling Shill Bidding Data

Handling screwed class distribution is a constant area of study in machine learning. A training dataset is imbalanced if the occurrence of positive instances (the minority class) is much less than the occurrence of negative instances (the majority class). In this situation, the classifiers are biased towards the negative class, which means that positive instances tend to be classified as negatives ones. This is inappropriate in fraud detection problems because once fraudulent transactions are labelled as normal and authenticated as legitimate, they can never be tracked thereafter. Moreover, as demonstrated in [8], classifiers suffer from low performance when dealing with highly imbalanced data. There are two ways for addressing the imbalanced learning problem: data sampling or cost-sensitive learning. We choose data sampling because it performs with similar effectiveness, if not better than that of cost-sensitive learning, and for moderate size of training sets, like ours, cost-sensitive learning algorithms do not work well [24]. In our study, we apply two intelligent over-sampling and under-sampling schemes: (1) SMOTE [3], which generates new positive instances and randomly places them between positive instances and their neighbors. When compared to other over-sampling techniques, SMOTE is more useful in creating a generalized decision region [2], and relatively achieves better results than any other random sampling and probabilistic estimation methods [4]; (2) SpreadSubsample [11], which produces a random subsample of the negative class based on the spread frequency (user defined) between the positive and negative class. For example, a spread frequency of 10 implies that for 10 positive instances, this method keeps 1 negative instance. Our labelled SB training set is highly imbalanced with a ratio equal to 19:1. Since SVM is efficient with moderately screwed class imbalance, therefore we need to perform data sampling by achieving the balancing ratio of 2:1. We try three methods, SMOTE only, SpreadSubsample only, and hybrid of both, to determine which one works the best for our particular SB training set. The experimental results showed that the hybrid method is more efficient. Indeed, we have achieved an AUC value of 86% for hybrid, 80% with SMOTE only, and 71% with SpreadSubsample only.

7   SVM Classification of Shill Bidding

SVM has been proved to be an efficient classifier in several fraud application problems [20], such as telecommunication, credit card, insurance and power utility. We chose SVM for the SB classification task for the following important facts:

- It is almost impossible to linearly separate auction data because of the evolving nature of the bidding process on one hand, and the distinctive features of SB fraud on the other hand [7]. This is where the kernel functions of SVM come into play to deal with no linearly separable auction data.
- According to a well-cited research [2] (cited 950 times), SVM is very efficient with moderately imbalanced data. Another work [21] showed that once sampling is performed on the training set, SVM outperforms major classifiers, like K-Nearest Neighbour, Decision Tree and Logistic Regression. In terms of the minority class,

SVM has been found to be superior to Naive Bayes and Decision Tree on several imbalanced benchmark datasets [26].

To build the optimal SB classifier, we need to select the best kernel and tune efficiently the SVM parameters. Since auction data are non-linearly separable, we need to use the non-linear kernel RBF shown to be effective in many classification and fraud detection problems [26]. Also, when the number of features is small and the number of instances is comparatively much higher, like our training set, RBF is the most suitable for classification. Next, we search for the best values of the cost parameter C and the free kernel parameter γ. This is accomplished with the help of the K-fold Cross-Validation (CV) process that tries various pairs of C and γ until the best performance is attained. The range that we define for C is [0.01, 10.0] and for γ is [0.01, 0.9] as done in many past studies. Table 5 exposes the performance results for 5-fold and 10-fold CV. We can see that when the value of K is 10, the SVM model performs better since it achieves an AUC of 86% contrary to 82% when K is 5. There are several classification metrics but not all are suitable to assess the performance of fraud data and imbalanced data. In fraud detection problems, we are more concerned about suspicious bidders rather than normal bidders. So, here we focus on the detection accuracy and misclassification rate of the positive class. In Table 5, the Recall rate of 0.77 and Precision rate of 0.72 indicate that the SVM classifier does a good justice to the fraud class with acceptable detection rates. The SB classifier exhibits a very good overall performance of 0.86.

Table 5. Cross-validation

K = 5					
C	γ	Precision	Recall	F-measure	AUC
1.5	0.1	0.692	0.310	0.429	0.654
1.5	0.9	0.708	0.586	0.642	0.791
2.3	0.1	0.760	0.655	0.704	0.826
2.3	0.9	0.680	0.586	0.630	0.791
2.5	0.1	0.760	0.655	0.704	0.826
3.0	0.1	0.731	0.655	0.691	0.825
K = 10					
C	γ	Precision	Recall	F-measure	AUC
1.5	0.1	0.778	0.483	0.596	0.740
1.5	0.9	0.773	0.586	0.667	0.791
2.3	0.1	0.792	0.665	0.717	0.826
2.3	0.9	0.696	0.552	0.615	0.774
2.5	**0.1**	**0.778**	**0.724**	**0.750**	**0.860**
3.0	0.1	0.769	0.690	0.727	0.843

8   Simulation

This phase consists of applying the SB classifier to the unlabelled testing dataset (15 PDA auctions) to detect potential fraudsters. We represent the classification results with the confusion matrix (Table 6). The actual numbers of normal and suspicious instances are found to be 139 and 12 respect. We can see that out of 139 normal instances, 132 have been correctly classified but 7 incorrectly classified. On the other hand, out of the 12 suspicious instances, 8 are correctly predicted but 4 remained undetected. Since we are dealing with fraud data, it is far more important to minimize the number of False Negatives (suspicious bidders incorrectly classified as normal) than that of False Positives (normal bidders incorrectly classified as suspicious). Indeed, bidders belonging to the False Positive category can be further investigated and then cleared of the accusation [17]. However, instances in the False Negative category, once labelled as normal and authenticated as legitimate transactions, can never be tracked thereafter.

Table 6. Testing results – confusion matrix

		Predicted class	
		Normal	Suspicious
Actual class	Normal	132 (TN)	7 (FP)
	Suspicious	4 (FN)	8 (TP)

In this study, we focus on the detection accuracy (Recall) and misclassification rate (False Negative Rate) of fraudulent bidders. The second metric denotes the percentage of fraudulent instances incorrectly identified as normal.

- Recall = TP/(TP + FN) = 8/(8 + 4) = 0.66
- False Negative Rate = FN/(FN + TP) = 4/(8 + 4) = 0.34

As per the Recall value, we can state that our model has detected 66% of shill bidders correctly. The remaining 34% of bidders have been incorrectly labelled as normal, which is the False Negative Rate. The graphical representation of AUC is depicted in the left-hand graph of Fig. 1 whereas the ideal ROC curve (when AUC = 1) is seen in the right hand. An AUC of 80% is achieved during testing, which is very good.

It is critical for any fraud detection model to return the classification results of new data as fast as possible. In e-auctions, the response time is a critical requirement. The time report for SB training is 294 s (1488 instances) and testing is 4 (151 instances). Time is not an issue when training the SVM model since it is done offline and conducted only once. In real-life situations, we launch our classifier at each auction where the number of instances (bidders) hardly exceeds 50. Thus, we can claim that the fraud classifier has no time-efficiency issue when testing unseen bidding data.

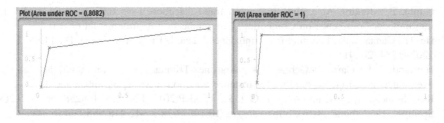

Fig. 1. Testing results – area under ROC

9 Conclusion

Detecting SB before finalizing the auction deal is necessary to avoid money loss for the winners. For this purpose, we have devised an online SVM-based SB detection system. There is a lack in SB classification studies because SB data are difficult to obtain. We have applied clustering and labelling techniques to label SB data and sampling to solve the imbalanced learning issue. Once the bidding transactions of an auction are available, we analyze them all at once to detect more accurately fraud in each auction, and take actions if the auction is infected. The SB classifier has exhibited a very good performance in both training and testing. Since time is a critical requirement of e-auctions, we can fully automate the verification of suspicious bidders by using the trust management framework defined in [1].

References

1. Abedinzadeh, S., Sadaoui, S.: A rough sets-based agent trust management framework. Int. J. Intell. Syst. Appl. **5**(4), 1–9 (2013)
2. Akbani, R., Kwek, S., Japkowicz, N.: Applying support vector machines to imbalanced datasets. In: Boulicaut, J.-F., Esposito, F., Giannotti, F., Pedreschi, D. (eds.) ECML 2004. LNCS (LNAI), vol. 3201, pp. 39–50. Springer, Heidelberg (2004). https://doi.org/10.1007/978-3-540-30115-8_7
3. Chawla, N.V., et al.: SMOTE: synthetic minority over-sampling technique. J. Artif. Intell. Res. **16**, 321–357 (2002)
4. Chawla, N.V.: C4.5 and imbalanced data sets: investigating the effect of sampling method, probabilistic estimate, and decision tree structure. In: International Conference on Machine Learning (2003)
5. Dong, F., Shatz, S., Xu, H.: Combating online in-auction frauds: clues, techniques and challenges. Comput. Sci. Rev. **3**(4), 245–258 (2009)
6. Dong, F., Shatz, S.M., Xu, H., Majumdar, D.: Price comparison: a reliable approach to identifying SB in online auctions? Electron. Commer. Res. Appl. **11**(2), 171–179 (2012)
7. Ford, B.J., Haiping, X., Valova, I.: A real-time self-adaptive classifier for identifying suspicious bidders in online auctions. Comput. J. **56**(5), 646–663 (2013)
8. Ganguly, S., Sadaoui, S.: Classification of imbalanced auction fraud data. In: Mouhoub, M., Langlais, P. (eds.) AI 2017. LNCS (LNAI), vol. 10233, pp. 84–89. Springer, Cham (2017). https://doi.org/10.1007/978-3-319-57351-9_11

9. Gupta, P., Mundra, A.: Online in-auction fraud detection using online hybrid model. In: International Conference on Computing, Communication & Automation (2015)
10. He, H., Garcia, E.A.: Learning from imbalanced data. IEEE Trans. Knowl. Data Eng. **21**(9), 1263–1284 (2009)
11. Hernandez, J., Carrasco-Ochoa, J.A., Martínez-Trinidad, J.F.: An empirical study of oversampling and undersampling for instance selection methods on imbalance datasets. In: Ruiz-Shulcloper, J., Sanniti di Baja, G. (eds.) CIARP 2013. LNCS, vol. 8258, pp. 262–269. Springer, Heidelberg (2013). https://doi.org/10.1007/978-3-642-41822-8_33
12. Köknar-Tezel, S., Latecki, L.J.: Improving SVM classification on imbalanced data sets in distance spaces. In: IEEE International Conference on Data Mining, pp. 259–269 (2009)
13. Nikitkov, A., Bay, D.: Online auction fraud: ethical perspective. J. Bus. Ethics **79**(3), 235–244 (2008)
14. Nikitkov, A., Bay, D.: SB: empirical evidence of its effectiveness and likelihood of detection in online auction systems. Int. J. Account. Inf. Syst. **16**, 42–54 (2015)
15. Ochaeta, K.: Fraud Detection for Internet Auctions. "A Data Mining Approach", Master's Thesis, College of Technology Management, National Tsing-Hua University, Hsinchu, Taiwan (2008)
16. Phua, C., et al.: A comprehensive survey of data mining-based fraud detection research. arXiv preprint arXiv:1009.6119 (2010)
17. Resnick, P., et al.: Reputation systems. Commun. ACM **43**(12), 45–48 (2000)
18. Sabau, A.S.: Survey of clustering based financial fraud detection research. Informatica Economica **16**(1), 110 (2012)
19. Sadaoui, S., Wang, X.: A dynamic stage-based fraud monitoring framework of multiple live auctions. Appl. Intell. (2016). https://doi.org/10.1007/s10489-016-0818-7
20. Sallehuddin, R., Ibrahim, S., Elmi, A.H.: Classification of SIM box fraud detection using support vector machine and artificial neural network. Int. J. Innov. Comput. **4**(2), 19–27 (2014)
21. Seiffert, C., et al.: An empirical study of the classification performance of learners on imbalanced and noisy software quality data. Inf. Sci. **259**, 571–595 (2014)
22. Trevathan, J., Read, W.: Detecting SB in online English auctions. In: Handbook of Research on Social and Organizational Liabilities in Information Security, p. 446 (2008)
23. Trevathan, J.: Getting into the mind of an "in-auction" fraud perpetrator. Comput. Sci. Rev. **27**, 1–15 (2018)
24. Weiss, G.M., McCarthy, K., Zabar, B.: Cost-sensitive learning vs. sampling: which is best for handling unbalanced classes with unequal error costs? In: International Conference on Data Mining, pp. 35–41 (2007)
25. Yoshida, T., Ohwada, H.: Shill bidder detection for online auctions. In: Zhang, B.-T., Orgun, M.A. (eds.) PRICAI 2010. LNCS (LNAI), vol. 6230, pp. 351–358. Springer, Heidelberg (2010). https://doi.org/10.1007/978-3-642-15246-7_33
26. Zhang, S., Sadaoui, S., Mouhoub, M.: An empirical analysis of imbalanced data classification. Comput. Inf. Sci. **8**(1), 151 (2015)

Efficient Examination of Soil Bacteria Using Probabilistic Graphical Models

Cory J. Butz[1]([⊠]), André E. dos Santos[1], Jhonatan S. Oliveira[1],
and John Stavrinides[2]

[1] Department of Computer Science, University of Regina, Regina, Canada
{butz,dossantos,oliveira}@cs.uregina.ca
[2] Department of Biology, University of Regina, Regina, Canada
john.stavrinides@uregina.ca

Abstract. This paper describes a novel approach to study bacterial relationships in soil datasets using probabilistic graphical models. We demonstrate how to access and reformat publicly available datasets in order to apply machine learning techniques. We first learn a Bayesian network in order to read independencies in linear time between bacterial community characteristics. These independencies are useful in understanding the semantic relationships between bacteria within communities. Next, we learn a Sum-Product network in order to perform inference in linear time. Here, inference can be conducted to answer traditional queries, involving posterior probabilities, or MPE queries, requesting the most likely values of the non-evidence variables given evidence. Our results extend the literature by showing that known relationships between soil bacteria holding in one or a few datasets in fact hold across at least 3500 diverse datasets. This study paves the way for future large-scale studies of agricultural, health, and environmental applications, for which data are publicly available.

Keywords: Probabilistic graphical models · Deep learning · Soil Bacteria

1 Introduction

There are currently terabytes of data that hold important information on how bacteria interact with humans and their environment. However, there is presently no way to identify important patterns and extract relevant information from across all of these datasets. The development of culture-independent metagenomic methods has enabled in-depth surveys of microbes across many host and non-host environments, providing new insight into microbial diversity, metabolism, community dynamics, and host interactions [23]. This research has been enabled by the development of algorithms to handle, parse, and analyse metagenomic data for analysis and comparison at small scales. There are now tens of thousands of publicly available datasets; yet, existing software packages,

© Springer International Publishing AG, part of Springer Nature 2018
M. Mouhoub et al. (Eds.): IEA/AIE 2018, LNAI 10868, pp. 315–326, 2018.
https://doi.org/10.1007/978-3-319-92058-0_30

including powerful applications like METAGENAssist [2], do not provide the means for large-scale comparative metagenomics studies across these datasets. The ability to conduct such analyses across the terabytes of data will enable researchers to begin unravelling the complex global relationships between microbial consortia, gene complements, and environmental conditions. This capability can be harnessed for a variety of applications, ranging from epidemiology to agricultural land use. Understanding the conditions that lead to spikes in *E. coli* and *Salmonella* populations in the general environment, for example, and whether these depend on the presence of specific microbial consortia can be used to identify key bioindicators of pending disease outbreaks. Similarly, there is enormous utility in comparative metagenomics for understanding human health. For example, gut microbiota are critical to human health, modulating cholesterol and insulin levels, as well as immune responses [3]. Comparative metagenomics methods can not only assist in predicting specific microbial communities that lead to bowel disease, but would be instrumental for identifying the optimal microbial consortia that can be used for the development of fecal transplantation therapeutics for disease treatment [5]. Are there other human-associated microbial consortia elsewhere in and on the human body that may be linked to a propensity for specific diseases, or be predictive of patient responsiveness to particular treatments? By also considering genetic information, large-scale comparative metagenomics can help identify virulence factors that may contribute to specific diseases, or even examine the dynamics of polymicrobial infections. Our current inability to carry out such large-scale comparative metagenomic analyses is presently limiting our ability to extract valuable information from the wealth of data that are currently available. Developing this capability would inherently alter the depth and scope of biodiversity and epidemiological research, propelling it from smaller-scale local analyses to broader, global comparisons that can highlight novel dependencies between genes, microbes, environment, and health.

This paper describes a novel approach to study bacterial relationships in soil datasets using *probabilistic graphical models* [11,18]. Soil datasets describing bacterial communities based on 165 rRNA amplicons are publicly available at the Metagenomics Analysis Server [19]. Download restrictions imposed by the website resulted in 35 sets of 100 projects (rows) each. The combined dataset, consisting of 922 attributes and 3500 rows, suffers from underfitting as the ratio of attributes to rows is far too high. The attributes were classified based on the representation of bacterial genera across datasets, which allowed us to select those bacterial genera that were represented in the 99th percentile of all datasets. This yielded a useful dataset with 10 genera and 3500 rows classified into 5 categories on which two probabilistic networks can be learned; one for semantics and another for inference.

We first learned a *Bayesian network* (BN) [21] in order to read independencies in linear time between community characteristics. These independencies are useful in studying the semantic relationships between community properties. The *Genie* [12] software was used to learn conditional relationships that succinctly describe the BN. Next, we learn a *Sum-Product network* [22] in order to perform exact inference in linear time. Here, inference can be conducted to answer traditional queries involving posterior probabilities or MPE queries, which ask for the most likely values of the non-evidence variables given evidence. For example, the SPN can be queried using conditional probability queries (e.g. what is the probability of a particular species being present given the presence of a given nutrient), and most probable explanation queries (e.g. what is the most probable set of environmental conditions given the presence of a particular microbe). Our results extend the literature by showing that known relationships between soil bacteria holding in one or a few datasets in fact hold across at least 3500 diverse datasets.

This paper represents an innovative and progressive first step in the advancement of metagenomics research through the creation of probabilistic graphical models to capture and connect large-scale datasets. These models can provide insight into the interdependencies between microbes, environment, and health. We will enhance our ability to identify important links between variables across terabytes of data, which is presently not possible. Our methodology will advance current metagenomics research, making it a transformative idea that will stimulate the development of additional next-generation tools for interdisciplinary metagenomic analyses. In addition, it will provide the means for broadening the scope of research questions that can be addressed at the interfaces of microbial diversity and community and ecosystem structure, agricultural practices, industrial processes, water quality monitoring, and human health.

2   Data Preprocessing

Several steps of data preprocessing are required before the data can be analyzed.

Amplicon [19] projects examining soil communities were identified using the search function at MG-RAST, filtered by selecting soil as the material, 16s as the target gene, and amplicon as the sequence type. This search produced approximately 4000 projects. Perl scripts were used to download abundance data at the genus level in sets of 100 using the MG-RAST API as follows. The query used the RDP database, an e-value of $1 \times 10-5$ and an identity of 97% over 100 bp. This step resulted in 35 tables of 100 projects each, yielding 3500 projects. The resulting BIOM files were converted into tab-delimited files using Perl scripts.

The 35 tables were combined into one dataset, involving 922 bacterial genera as attributes and 3500 projects as rows, by assigning value 0 whenever a project did not identify a particular bacterium. As the bacterial concentration values are discrete real numbers, the values to be subsequently used in our study were categorized as follows for simplicity.

It is important to realize that bacterial abundances vary wildly from project to project not only due to differing bacterial communities but also because of differences in sampling (sequencing) depth. Hence, categorization based upon one fixed threshold may not be a reliable representation of the values. Instead, we elected to use the notion of percentiles. Statistically speaking, a percentile is the value below which a given percentage of a group of data values fall. All bacterial concentration values 0 (non-existent) are categorized as value 0. Bacterial concentration values below the 25th percentile are categorized as value 1; those below the 50th percentile are value 2; the 75th, value 3; and the remaining bacterial concentration values are categorized as 4. Thus, values 1 to 4 indicate low concentrations to high concentrations, respectively.

Learning a probabilistic model from a dataset with 922 attributes and 3500 rows will lead to *underfitting* [15]. We verified that this was empirically the case. To overcome underfitting, we propose the following technique in order to reduce the number of attributes. For each bacterium, count the number of non-zero values. From this ordered list of 992 count values, the 97th percentile gives 28 bacteria; the 98th percentile yields 19 bacteria; and the 99th percentile yields 10 bacteria. We use the three datasets on the 97th, 98th, and 99th percentiles when learning two kinds of probabilistic graphical models as described in the remainder of this paper.

3   A Soil Bacteria Bayesian Network

In this section, we describe how Bayesian networks are used to study relationships between soil bacteria.

A *Bayesian network* (BN) [21] is a DAG with associated conditional probability distributions. The multiplication of the conditional probability distributions of a BN over a finite set of variables U is a joint probability distribution $p(U)$. A BN is an efficient tool for knowledge representation, since all independences holding on the DAG also hold in the defined distribution.

There are many approaches to learning BNs from data [20]. One objective is to minimize the Kullback-Leibler $I(p,p')$ cross-entropy (Kullback and Leibler 1951), a measure of closeness between a true distribution p and an approximate distribution p'. The cross entropy is defined by:

$$I(p,p') = \sum_x p(x) \log \frac{p(x)}{p'(x)},$$

where x is a configuration of a set of attributes (variables) U. With a fixed p, we can choose, from the set of all possible distributions $\{p'\}$, the distribution p_0 that minimizes $I(p,p')$.

We use the *Genie* [12] software for learning a BN. The structure algorithm used is *Bayesian search* [8]. The parameters used are as follows. Maximum parent count is 8, iterations 20, sample size 50, link probability 0.1, and prior link probability 0.001. Experiments are run on a MacBook Pro with 2.9 GHz Intel Core i7 processor and 16 GB of RAM.

The BN learned from the 99th percentile soil bacteria dataset is depicted in Fig. 1. Recall that independency information can be read from BNs in linear time [18]. The BN in Fig. 1 encodes, for instance, the following 3 probabilistic independencies: $I(Arthrobacter, Streptomyces, *)$, $I(Clostridium, Bacillus, *)$, $I(Burkholderia, \{Bacillus, Mycobacterium\}, *)$, where $*$ in $I(X, Y, *)$ means

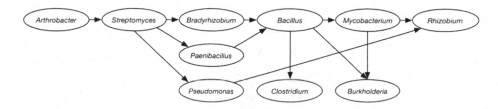

Fig. 1. BN learned from data with percentile 99.

$U - XY$. These independencies have never before been reported in the literature and suggest directions of future work.

As inference in BNs is NP-hard [7,10], we turn our attention to another kind of probabilistic graphical model.

4   A Soil Bacteria Sum-Product Network

In this section, we learn a Sum-Product network from a soil bacteria dataset in order to conduct exact inference in linear time.

Sum-Product networks (SPNs) [22] are a class of deep learning model with tractable probabilistic inference. This is an attractive feature when compared to probabilistic graphical models in general. The *scope* [14] of an SPN is the set of variables that appear in it. A univariate distribution is tractable if its partition function and its mode can be computed in O(1) time [14].

Definition 1. [14] *An SPN is defined as follows:*

- *A tractable univariate distribution is an SPN.*
- *A product of SPNs with disjoint scopes is an SPN.*
- *A weighted sum of SPNs with the same scope is an SPN, provided all weights are positive.*
- *Nothing else is an SPN.*

An SPN can be graphically understood as a rooted directed acyclic graph. Each internal node is either a sum or product operation. Each leaf node is a univariate distribution over its variable. Each edge from a sum node to a child has a positive weight.

The value of an SPN S is the value of its root. The value of a product node v_i is the product of the values of its children. The value of a sum node v_i is

$$\sum_{v_j \in Ch(v_i)} w_{ij} val(v_j), \tag{1}$$

where $Ch(v_i)$ are the children of v_i, $val(v_j)$ is the value of node v_j, and w_{ij} is the positive weight of the edge from v_i to v_j. The value of a leaf node is the value of its univariate distribution. SPNs will be depicted with univariate distributions and sum node edge weights understood.

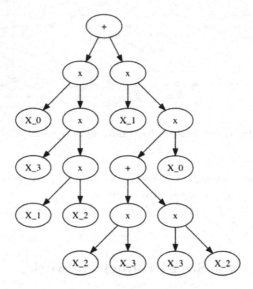

Fig. 2. An SPN over four attributes X_0, X_1, X_2, and X_3.

Example 1. An SPN over four attributes X_0, X_1, X_2, and X_3 is illustrated in Fig. 2.

Gens and Domingos [14] introduced LEARNSPN, given as Algorithm 1, which has become the standard unsupervised learning algorithm for SPNs. LEARNSPN applies two general steps, namely, a "chop" operation in line 4 for splitting attributes (columns) in the dataset and a "slice" operation in line 8 for clustering instances (rows) in the dataset.

The chopping method of LEARNSPN splits a dataset vertically. Two chopping methods, *g-test* [26] and *mutual information* [9], are often applied. Although the scoring metric is different, both methods adhere to the following scoring procedure.

One attribute $X_i \in V$ is chosen at random. Then the score $s(X_i, X_j)$ is computed, for all other attributes X_j. If $s(X_i, X_j)$ is greater than a threshold, then X_j is considered to be similar to X_i and they are grouped together. Next, $s(X_j, X_k)$ is computed, for all X_k not previously grouped with X_i. Again, if $s(X_j, X_k)$ is greater than a threshold, then X_k is considered similar to X_j, which means X_k is similar to X_i, and X_k is grouped with X_i and X_j. This process repeats until no more variables can be grouped with X_i.

G-test tests pairwise independence of attributes as follows:

$$G(X_i, X_j) = 2 \sum_{x_i} \sum_{x_j} c(x_i, x_j) log \frac{c(x_i, x_j)|T|}{c(x_i)c(x_j)}, \tag{2}$$

where $c(\cdot)$ counts the occurrences of a setting of a variable pair or singleton [26], and *log* is the natural logarithm. One of the threshold values used in [25] is 2. We will not review mutual information, since we used g-test in our experiments.

Algorithm 1. LEARNSPN(T, V)

Input: a set of instances T over attributes V
Output: an SPN S
Main:
1: **if** $|V| == 1$ **then**
2:     $S \leftarrow$ LEAF(T, V) ▷ Univariate distribution
3: **else**
4:     $V_1, \ldots, V_k \leftarrow chop_m(T, V_i)$ ▷ Chop using method m
5:     **if** $k > 1$ **then**
6:         $S \leftarrow \prod_{i=1,\ldots,k}$ LEARNSPN(T, V_i)
7:     **else**
8:         $T_1, \ldots, T_k \leftarrow slice_n(T_i, V)$ ▷ Slice using method n
9:         $S \leftarrow \sum_{i=1,\ldots,k} \frac{|T_i|}{|T|}$ LEARNSPN(T_i, V)

10: **return** S

The slicing method of LEARNSPN splits a dataset horizontally. *K-means* [17] and expectation-maximization for fitting *Gaussian mixture models* [13] are two slicing methods commonly used.

Consider using *Gaussian mixture models* (GMM) for the slicing operation in Algorithm 1. The process is nearly identical to that for k-means, except that the representation of each cluster and the assignment of instantiation to cluster are more involved. As in [25], we assume there are two clusters. Each cluster is a Gaussian distribution represented by its mean and co-variance matrix. These can be randomly assigned initially without disturbing the end result. Next, the probability of each instantiation I_i being in each cluster is computed. I_i is assigned to the cluster with the higher probability. Do this for every instantiation. The mean and covariance matrix are recalculated for each cluster by following the expectation-maximization algorithm. This process repeats 100 times or until the clusters do not change. More formally, each cluster k_j is represented by a Gaussian distribution, denoted $\mathcal{N}(I|\mu_j, \Sigma_j)$, where μ_j is its vector mean and Σ_j is its covariance matrix. The scoring of each instantiation I_i being in each cluster is the probability $p(k_j|I_i)$, which can be computed as:

$$p(k_j|I_i) = \frac{w_j \, \mathcal{N}(I|\mu_j, \Sigma_j)}{c},$$

where w_j is a cluster weight and c is a normalization function. As we applied GMM in our experiments, we refer the reader to [6] for a comparison of the various combinations of chopping and slicing methods.

For learning an SPN, we selected the best parameter configurations based on the average validation log-likelihood scores, then evaluated such models on the test sets. We select the best SPN model based upon an exhaustive grid search for possible hyper-parameters. For g-test, we consider the values $\{5, 10, 15, 20\}$. For the minimum amount of rows considered when chopping, we use the values $\{10, 50, 100, 500\}$. For the Laplace smoothing values on the leaves, we consider

$\{0.1, 0.2, 0.5, 1, 2\}$. With respect to the EM algorithm, we leave all the default parameters for *scikit-learn*'s EM unchanged.

We learn the best SPN for each of the 97th, 98th, and 99th percentile datasets. Table 1 shows the log-likelihood and other characteristics of each learned SPN.

Table 1. Best results for each percentile.

Percentile	Vars	Edges	Levels	Weights	Leaves	Alpha	Min-slice	g-test	Train	Valid	Test
97th	28	116	9	16	95	2	10	10	-32.86	-36.45	-35.60
98th	19	74	5	13	57	2	10	10	-24.35	-27.00	-26.99
99th	10	85	9	21	56	2	10	5	-13.46	-14.63	-14.56

The SPN can be queried using conditional probability queries (e.g. what is the probability of a particular species being present given the presence of a given nutrient), and most probable explanation queries (e.g. what is the most probable set of environmental conditions given the presence of a particular microbe).

We can infer possible relationships among bacterial by running *most probable explanation* (MPE) queries. More specifically, given that a specific bacterium has high concentration, we want to know what is the highest probability concentration of all other bacteria. For each bacterial group, we observe in the SPN its concentration being high. Here, we only use the dataset for 99th percentile. Then, we query MPE for all other bacteria, yielding its most probable state. These results are shown in Table 2. The cases with (4,4) are graphically depicted in Fig. 3. Low concentration results for the 99th percentile are given in Table 3.

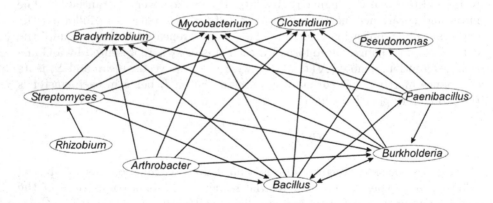

Fig. 3. Graphically illustrating the (4,4) relationship in Table 2.

Let us analyze Fig. 3. Bacteria that associate with plants at the root interface can enhance plant growth by delivering or enhancing plant uptake of specific nutrients like nitrogen and phosphorus, helping to outcompete non-beneficial bacteria, and by producing various plant hormones that can directly stimulate

Table 2. For the 99th percentile, MPE for each bacteria in the first column being high, where 0 means not considered and 1 to 4 means low to high concentrations, respectively.

	Streptomyces	*Rhizobium*	*Arthrobacter*	*Bacillus*	*Mycobacterium*	*Bradyrhizobium*	*Burkholderia*	*Clostridium*	*Paenibacillus*	*Pseudomonas*
Streptomyces		0	0	4	4	4	4	4	3	3
Rhizobium	4		0	0	0	1	1	0	1	0
Arthrobacter	0	0		4	4	4	4	4	3	3
Bacillus	0	0	0		4	4	4	4	4	4
Mycobacterium	0	0	0	0		1	1	0	1	0
Bradyrhizobium	0	0	0	0	0		1	0	1	0
Burkholderia	0	0	0	4	4	4		4	3	3
Clostridium	0	0	0	0	0	0	0		0	0
Paenibacillus	0	0	0	4	4	4	4	4		4
Pseudomonas	0	3	0	0	0	1	1	0	1	

Table 3. For the 99th percentile, MPE for each bacteria in the first column being low, where 0 means not considered and 1 to 4 means low to high concentrations, respectively.

	Streptomyces	*Rhizobium*	*Arthrobacter*	*Bacillus*	*Mycobacterium*	*Bradyrhizobium*	*Burkholderia*	*Clostridium*	*Paenibacillus*	*Pseudomonas*
Streptomyces		0	0	0	0	1	1	0	1	0
Rhizobium	0		0	0	0	1	1	0	1	0
Arthrobacter	0	0		0	0	1	1	0	1	0
Bacillus	0	0	0		0	1	1	0	1	0
Mycobacterium	0	0	0	0		1	1	0	1	0
Bradyrhizobium	0	0	0	0	0		1	0	1	0
Burkholderia	0	0	0	0	0	1		0	1	0
Clostridium	0	0	0	0	0	1	1		1	0
Paenibacillus	0	0	0	0	0	1	1	0		0
Pseudomonas	1	0	0	0	0	1	1	0	1	

plant growth [16]. Current research has demonstrated that these plant-growth promoting bacteria form communities with other bacteria that can encourage plant-microbe associations to further enhance plant growth. An understanding of soil bacterial communities therefore has significant implications for agriculture.

To highlight a few examples of the interactions revealed by the network in Fig. 3, a high abundance of *Bacillus* is correlated with a high abundance of the nitrogen-fixing bacterium, *Bradyrhizobium*. The co-inoculation of *Bacillus* and

Bradyrhizobium has been shown to increase the formation of nitrogen-fixing nodules in the roots of soybean [4]. Also implied by the network is that a high *Paenibacillus* abundance is associated with a high *Bradyrhizobium* abundance. Cowpea plants co-inoculated with *Bradyrhizobium* and both *Paenibacillus polymyxa Loutit* strain L and *Bacillus* strain LBF-410 resulted in increased nitrogen-fixing nodules and increased root biomass [1]. *Bacillus* and *Paenibacillus* have been reported to have phosphorus-mobilizing capabilities, and may therefore enhance the plant-growth promoting properties of *Bradyrhizobium* through provisioning of an additional important nutrient [16].

A different association inferred by the network is the relationship between *Streptomyces* and the nitrogen-fixing *Rhizobium*. Unlike in the associations above where the abundance of the other bacteria infer the abundance of the nitrogen-fixer, in this association a high abundance of the nitrogen-fixing *Rhizobium* infers that *Streptomyces* abundance will also be high. *Streptomyces* lydicus WYEC108 develops a beneficial relationship with nodules that have been formed by *Rhizobium* on pea plants. Vegetative hyphae of *S.* lydicus WYEC108 colonize the surface of the nitrogen-fixing nodules, allowing them to reproduce within root surface cell layers [24]. In this circumstance, the establishment of *Rhizobium* in a relationship with the pea plant further enhances colonization of *Streptomyces*, thereby increasing its abundance.

The network we have generated in Fig. 3 describes general pairwise bacterial interactions predicted from 3500 diverse soil environments. Although only a select few examples were provided to demonstrate the accuracy of the predicted associations, many of the relationships described by the MPE network have been validated experimentally in individual studies that focused on a few select bacterial strains; however, because our MPE network was generated using data from 3500 diverse soil environments, the bacterial associations predicted by the network describe microbial interactions that are global, and occur across very different soil environments. There are many additional dependencies and codependencies inferred by the network. The next steps will be to deconstruct the species groups within each genus to determine whether there are more specific dependencies that can be defined. Having an understanding of these relationships can enable us to manipulate soil communities to increase and enhance crop growth and yields for agriculture. The utility and robustness of the graph in Fig. 3 illustrates that these bacteria relationships holds across 3500 diverse datasets rather than just a few. Thus, our results extend the literature in insightful ways.

5   Conclusion

There is presently no tool available for conducting large-scale comparative analyses across all available metagenomic datasets. As such, studies are localized and focus on one or a few projects. For instance, the co-inoculation of *Bacillus* and *Bradyrhizobium* has been shown to increase the formation of nitrogen-fixing nodules in the roots of soybean [4]; Cowpea plants co-inoculated with

Bradyrhizobium and both *Paenibacillus polymyxa Loutit* strain L and *Bacillus* strain LBF-410 resulted in increased nitrogen-fixing nodules and increased root biomass [1]; and *Bacillus* and *Paenibacillus* have been reported to have phosphorus-mobilizing capabilities, and may therefore enhance the plant-growth promoting properties of *Bradyrhizobium* through provisioning of an additional important nutrient [16].

These 3 studies together are included in Fig. 3, a graph illustrating high correlations between 10 soil bacteria that hold on 3500 diverse datasets. In this way, our research extends the literature and suggests exciting avenues of future work. Independency relationships between these 10 bacterial genera are suggested by the BN in Fig. 1.

References

1. de Araújo, F., de Araújo, A., Figueiredo, M.: Role of plant growth-promoting bacteria in sustainable agriculture. In: Sustainable Agriculture: Technology, Planning and Management. Nova Science Publishers, New York (2011)
2. Arndt, D., Xia, J., Liu, Y., Zhou, Y., Guo, A., Cruz, J., Sinelnikov, I., Budwill, K., Nesbø, C., Wishart, D.: Metagenassist: a comprehensive web server for comparative metagenomics. Nucleic Acids Res. **40**(W1), W88–W95 (2012)
3. Bäckhed, F., Ley, R., Sonnenburg, J., Peterson, D., Gordon, J.: Long-term follow-up of colonoscopic fecal microbiota transplant for recurrent Clostridium difficile infection. Science **307**(5717), 1915–1920 (2005)
4. Bai, Y., Zhou, X., Smith, D.: Enhanced soybean plant growth resulting from coinoculation of bacillus strains with Bradyrhizobium japonicum. Crop Sci. **43**(5), 1774–1781 (2003)
5. Brandt, L., Aroniadis, O., Mellow, M., Kanatzar, A., Kelly, C., Park, T., Stollman, N., Rohlke, F., Surawicz, C.: Long-term follow-up of colonoscopic fecal microbiota transplant for recurrent Clostridium difficile infection. Am. J. Gastroenterol. **107**, 1079–1087(2012)
6. Butz, C., Oliveira, J., dos Santos, A.: On learning the structure of sum-product networks. In: 2017 IEEE Symposium Series on Computational Intelligence (SSCI), pp. 2997–3004 (2017)
7. Cooper, G.: The computational complexity of probabilistic inference using Bayesian belief networks. Artif. Intell. **42**(2–3), 393–405 (1990)
8. Cooper, G., Herskovits, E.: A Bayesian method for the induction of probabilistic networks from data. Mach. Learn. **9**(4), 309–347 (1992)
9. Cover, T., Thomas, J.: Elements of Information Theory, 2nd edn. Wiley (2012)
10. Dagum, P., Luby, M.: Approximating probabilistic inference in Bayesian belief networks is NP-hard. Artif. Intell. **60**(1), 141–153 (1993)
11. Darwiche, A.: Modeling and Reasoning with Bayesian Networks. Cambridge University Press, Cambridge (2009)
12. Druzdzel, M.: SMILE: Structural modeling, inference, and learning engine and genie: a development environment for graphical decision-theoretic models (1999)
13. Duda, R., Hart, P., Stork, D.: Pattern Classification. Wiley (2012)
14. Gens, R., Domingos, P.: Learning the structure of sum-product networks. In: Proceedings of the Thirtieth International Conference on Machine Learning, pp. 873–880 (2013)

15. Goodfellow, I., Bengio, Y., Courville, A.: Deep Learning. MIT Press (2016)
16. Gouda, S., Kerry, R., Das, G., Paramithiotis, S., Shin, H.S., Patra, J.: Revitalization of plant growth promoting rhizobacteria for sustainable development in agriculture. Microbiol. Res. **206**, 131–140 (2017)
17. Hastie, T., Tibshirani, R., Friedman, J.: Overview of supervised learning. In: The Elements of Statistical Learning. Springer Series in Statistics, pp. 9–41. Springer, New York (2009). https://doi.org/10.1007/978-0-387-21606-5_2
18. Koller, D., Friedman, N.: Probabilistic Graphical Models: Principles and Techniques. MIT Press (2009)
19. Meyer, F., Paarmann, D., D'Souza, M., Olson, R., Glass, E., Kubal, M., Paczian, T., Rodriguez, A., Stevens, R., Wilke, A., Wilkening, J., Edwards, R.: The metagenomics rast server - a public resource for the automatic phylogenetic and functional analysis of metagenomes. BMC Bioinform. **9**(1), 386 (2008)
20. Neapolitan, R.: Learning Bayesian Networks. Pearson Prentice Hall, Upper Saddle River (2004)
21. Pearl, J.: Probabilistic Reasoning in Intelligent Systems: Networks of Plausible Inference. Morgan Kaufmann (1988)
22. Poon, H., Domingos, P.: Sum-product networks: a new deep architecture. In: Proceedings of the Twenty-Seventh Conference on Uncertainty in Artificial Intelligence, pp. 337–346 (2011)
23. Riesenfeld, C., Schloss, P., Handelsman, J.: Metagenomics: Genomic analysis of microbial communities. Annu. Rev. Genet. **38**(1), 525–552 (2004)
24. Tokala, R., Strap, J., Jung, C., Crawford, D., Salove, M., Deobald, L., Bailey, J., Morra, M.: Novel plant-microbe rhizosphere interaction involving Streptomyces lydicus wyec108 and the pea plant (Pisum sativum). Appl. Environ. Microbiol. **68**(5), 2161–2171 (2002)
25. Vergari, A., Di Mauro, N., Esposito, F.: Simplifying, regularizing and strengthening sum-product network structure learning. In: Proceedings of the Joint European Conference on Machine Learning and Knowledge Discovery in Databases, pp. 343–358 (2015)
26. Woolf, B.: The log likelihood ratio test (the G-test). Ann. Hum. Genet. **21**(4), 397–409 (1957)

Object Detection in Images Based on Homogeneous Region Segmentation

Abdesalam Amrane[1,2]([✉]), Abdelkrim Meziane[1],
and Nour El Houda Boulkrinat[1]

[1] Research Center on Scientific and Technical Information (CERIST),
16030 Ben Aknoun, Algiers, Algeria
`amrane@mail.cerist.dz`
[2] Université Abderrahmane Mira Béjaia,
Rue Targa Ouzemour, 06000 Béjaia, Algeria

Abstract. Image segmentation for object detection is one of the most fundamental problems in computer vision, especially in object-region extraction task. Most popular approaches in the segmentation/object detection tasks use sliding-window or super-pixel labeling methods. The first method suffers from the number of window proposals, whereas the second suffers from the over-segmentation problem. To overcome these limitations, we present two strategies: the first one is a fast algorithm based on the region growing method for segmenting images into homogeneous regions. In the second one, we present a new technique for similar region merging, based on a three similarity measures, and computed using the region adjacency matrix. All of these methods are evaluated and compared to other state-of-the-art approaches that were applied on the Berkeley image database. The experimentations yielded promising results and would be used for future directions in our work.

Keywords: Region proposal · Region growing · Region merging
Image segmentation

1 Introduction

Object detection is the process of finding instances of semantic objects such as persons, animals and vehicle in images or videos. One way to address the object detection problem is to use image segmentation methods. Currently, many applications require an automatic segmentation step in very different fields, with specificities related to the processed images [1]. Image segmentation is an essential process for many applications, such as object recognition, target tracking, content-based image retrieval [2]. Image segmentation methods are mainly grouped into three categories: Threshold-based techniques, Edge-based techniques and Region-based techniques [3].

© Springer International Publishing AG, part of Springer Nature 2018
M. Mouhoub et al. (Eds.): IEA/AIE 2018, LNAI 10868, pp. 327–333, 2018.
https://doi.org/10.1007/978-3-319-92058-0_31

More recently, hybrid models, which incorporate both edge and region information in their segmentation algorithms, have been introduced [4]. Image segmentation can be classified into supervised and unsupervised segmentation methods [5]. In this work, we are interested in unsupervised methods (automated
segmentation methods).

The unsupervised segmentation algorithms divides the image into homogeneous regions (a set of neighboring pixels) but without considering the significance of these regions. While human segmentation tends to divide the image
into objects that have a meaning (called semantic segmentation). For this reason,
researchers try to bring automatic segmentation as close as possible to human
segmentation.

In this paper, we propose a fully automated approach to region segmentation
in images, that combines region growing and edge preservation methods. We also
give a brief description of our implementation and evaluation results obtained
using the Berkeley Segmentation Dataset[1] (BSD).

2   Related Works

Object detection can be treated in two phases. The first phase uses the region
proposals method to segment an image into candidate objects. The second phase
classifies every proposal region into different classes of objects using trained
classifiers such as SVM [6] or Neural Network [7]. In object detection, some of the
efficient techniques exploit sliding window and boosting [8]. The main drawback
of the sliding window is that the number of proposals can have a complexity of
$O(10^6)$ for a 640×480 image [9], which increases the computational time and
cost. To solve these problems, the authors of [9] proposed to use the superpixel
labeling method to effectively detect objects. Superpixel represents a set of pixels
which have similar colors and spatial relationships. Unfortunately, the use of
superpixels also suffers from the problem of choosing the number of clusters K
(maximal number of objects present in an image). A small value will generate a
sub-segmentation and a great value will generate an over-segmentation.

There are several image segmentation techniques that were proposed in the
literature. They are classified in three categories: Threshold Technique Segmentation, Region Based Segmentation and Edge Based Segmentation. Each one of
these approaches has advantages and disadvantages depending on the application domains [10,11]. Recently, the authors of [1] proposed an interested work
based on region merging strategies that start by an over-segmentation process.
Unfortunately, the author does not quote the execution time of the segmentation
process.

We present in this work, an unsupervised image segmentation method for
object detection. The proposed approach uses the region growing method combined with edge detection and some filters like bilateral filter, which serves to
smooth images.

---

[1] http://www.eecs.berkeley.edu/Research/Projects/CS/vision/grouping/resources.
html.

3   Proposed Method

In this work, we propose a new hybrid segmentation method that combines two techniques: edge based region growing and region merging method for object detection. For this reason, we use our algorithm which is based on region growing method (pixel aggregation) reinforced using canny edge to preserve the boundaries of objects. The generic algorithm is composed of three steps. we present the steps of our method Fig. 1 which are detailed in the following subsections.

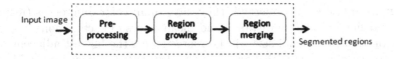

Fig. 1. Architecture of proposed method

3.1   Image Pre-processing

– Denoise image using median filter,
– Compute canny edge for original image I,
– Smooth original image I (using bilateral filter),
– Convert smoothed image to LAB color space,
– Normalize color values between 0 and 1.

3.2   Region Growing Segmentation

– Select initial seed point located in position (1,1) from image I,
– Define a similarity measure S(p,q) based on two criteria:
    • Euclidean distance between the LAB color of pixels p and q,
    • Verify non-edge pixels for pixel p and q.
– Evaluate the neighbors of seed point (seed$_p$) as above:
    • If the neighboring pixels of seed point satisfies the defined criteria, they will be grown (add pixel q to seed$_p$). The 3 neighbors of pixel q are added into the neighbors list of p according to the moving direction between pixels p and q,
    • Else consider pixel q as a new seed point (seed$_q$).
– Repeat the process until all pixels in the image are treated.

We use 8-connected neighborhood to grow the neighboring pixels to the current seed. The formula of Euclidian distance used is:

$$D_{Lab}(x,y) = \sqrt{(L_x - L_y)^2 + (a_x - a_y)^2 + (b_x - b_y)^2} \qquad (1)$$

We grow each pixel that has distance value D_{Lab} less than or equal to the best threshold; I choose value 0.10 (that is perceptually acceptable). To examine the neighboring pixels, we enumerate each neighboring pixels of a given pixel p in a clockwise direction {0,1,..,7} which corresponds to the orientation degree of pixels. This technique improves the processing time and allows a fast scan of the whole image.

3.3 Region Merging

For an initial-segmented image:

- Define a criterion for merging two adjacent regions,
- Compute features for each region and construct a region adjacency matrix,
- Iteratively merge all adjacent regions satisfying the merging criterion,
- Repeat process until all regions are merged.

The merging criterions that we propose are the following:

- Regions are allowed to merge if they have small color differences (using previous defined Euclidian distance and mean colors of each region),
- Region that have small size will be merged with the biggest adjacent region,
- All adjacent regions with Lambda value less than a given threshold will be merged.

We use Full Lambda Schedule method introduced by Robinson [12], described as follow:

$$L\left(v_i, v_j\right) = \frac{\frac{|O_i| \cdot |O_j|}{|O_i| + |O_j|} \cdot ||u_i - u_j||^2}{l(v_i, v_j)} \qquad (2)$$

where:

$|O_i|$ and $|O_j|$ are the areas of regions i and j,
$||u_i - u_j||^2$ is the euclidean distance between the mean color values of regions i and j,
$l(v_j, v_t)$ is the length of the common boundary of regions i and j.

4   Experimental Evaluation

In order to make an objective comparison between different segmentation methods, we use some evaluation criteria wich have already been defined in literature. Briefly stated, there are two main approaches [13]: supervised evaluation criteria and unsupervised evaluation criteria. Supervised evaluation use a ground truth, whereas unsupervised evaluation enable the quantification quality of a segmentation result without any prior knowledge [14]. The evaluation of a segmentation result makes sense at a given level of precision.

In our work, we choose to use a supervised evaluation. Our evaluation is based on the Berkeley Segmentation Dataset and for each of these algorithms, we examine two metrics:

1. Probabilistic Rand Index: measures the probability that the pair of samples have consistent labels in the two segmentations. The range of PRI is between [0,1], with larger value indicating greater similarity between two segmentations [15];
2. Variation of Information: measures how much we can know of one segmentation given another segmentation [15]. The range of VoI is between $[0, \infty]$, smaller value indicating better results.

Table 1. Quantitative comparison of different algorithms

Algorithms	PRI	VoI
Efficient graph-based image segmentation	0.770	2.188
Texture and boundary encoding-based segmentation	0.785	2.002
Weighted modularity segmentation	0.752	2.103
Mean-shift	0.772	2.004
Marker controlled watershed	0.753	2.203
Multiscale normalized cut	0.742	2.651
Our's	0.764	2.191

Table 2. Best results of segmentation process

Original images	Segmentation results	Measures
		PRI = 0.91 VoI = 1.12 Regions = 10
		PRI = 0.93 VoI = 1.68 Regions = 21
		PRI = 0.97 VoI = 0.66 Regions = 7
		PRI = 0.95 VoI = 0.85 Regions = 24

Our experiments were performed on a machine with an intel core i7-2630QM. We compare our method with other segmentation algorithms, including: Efficient Graph-Based Image Segmentation [16], Texture and Boundary Encoding-based Segmentation [17], Weighted Modularity Segmentation [18], Mean-Shift

[19], Marker Controlled Watershed [20], Multiscale Normalized Cut [21]. The segmentation results are presented in Table 1.

Our method for unsupervised image segmentation gives acceptable results especially we have used only color feature for similarity measure. We observe that the average time execution is less than 25 s. As a result, we can say that our method gives a high quality segmentation result with minimum time consumption. Table 2 shows some examples:

5 Conclusions

In this paper, we have proposed a hybrid method for unsupervised image segmentation. We have taken advantage of the fast edge based region growing algorithm and region merging techniques to overcome the problems of over-segmentation and sub-segmentation encountered in the super-pixel and sliding window for object detection.

Our algorithms have been tested on the publicly available Berkeley Segmentation Dataset as well as on the Semantic Segmentation Dataset. Then, they have been compared with other popular algorithms. Experimental results have demonstrated that our algorithms have produced acceptable results. However, the obtained regions do not exactly match the shapes of the objects contained in the images. Other treatment would be required to make the correspondence between regions and objects. Thereby, we can confirm the complexity of the segmentation domain and then we will explore other approaches to improve the object detection process by using machine learning in our future works.

References

1. Krahenbuhl, A.: Segmentation et analyse géométrique: application aux images tomodensitométriques de bois. Thesis, Université de Lorraine (2014)
2. Peng, B., Zhang, L., Zhang, D.: Automatic image segmentation by dynamic region merging. IEEE Trans. Image Process. **20**(12), 3592–3605 (2011)
3. Hedberg, H.: A survey of various image segmentation techniques. Department of Electroscience, Box 118 (2010)
4. Fox, V., Milanova, M., Al-Ali, S.: A hybrid morphological active contour for natural images. Int. J. Comput. Sci. Eng. Appl. **3**(4), 1–13 (2013)
5. Niyas, S., Reshma, P., Thampi, S.M.: A color image segmentation scheme for extracting foreground from images with unconstrained lighting conditions. Intelligent Systems Technologies and Applications 2016. AISC, vol. 530, pp. 3–19. Springer, Cham (2016). https://doi.org/10.1007/978-3-319-47952-1_1
6. Heisele, B.: Visual object recognition with supervised learning. IEEE Intell. Syst. **18**(3), 38–42 (2003)
7. Erhan, D., Szegedy, C., Toshev A., Anguelov D.: Scalable object detection using deep neural networks. In: CVPR (2014)
8. Bappy, J.H., Roy-Chowdhury, A.: CNN based region proposals for efficient object detection. In: IEEE International Conference on Image Processing (ICIP) (2016)
9. Yan, J., Yu, Y., Zhu, X., Lei, Z., Li, S.Z.: Object detection by labeling superpixels. In: CVPR (2015)

10. Blasiak, A.: A Comparison of image segmentation methods. Thesis in Computer Science (2007)
11. Pantofaru, C., Hebert, M.: A comparison of image segmentation algorithms. Carnegie Mellon University (2005)
12. Robinson, D.J., Redding, N.J., Crisp, D.J.: Implementation of a fast algorithm for segmenting SAR imagery. Scientific and Technical report, Defense Science and Technology Organization, Australia (2002)
13. Rosenberger, C., Chabrier, S., Laurent, H., Emile, B.: Unsupervised and supervised image segmentation evaluation. Adv. Image Video Segm. **29**(1), 365–393 (2006)
14. Zhang, Y.J.: A survey on evaluation methods for image segmentation. Pattern Recognit. **29**, 1335–1346 (1996)
15. Li, S., Wu, D.O.: Modularity-based image segmentation. IEEE Trans. Circ. Syst. Video Technol. **25**(4), 570–581 (2015)
16. Felzenszwalb, P., Huttenlocher, D.: Efficient graph-based image segmentation. Int. J. Comput. Vis. **59**(2), 167–181 (2004)
17. Rao, S.R., Mobahi, H., Yang, A.Y., Sastry, S.S., Ma, Y.: Natural image segmentation with adaptive texture and boundary encoding. In: Zha, H., Taniguchi, R., Maybank, S. (eds.) ACCV 2009. LNCS, vol. 5994, pp. 135–146. Springer, Heidelberg (2010). https://doi.org/10.1007/978-3-642-12307-8_13
18. Browet, A., Absil, P.-A., Van Dooren, P.: Community detection for hierarchical image segmentation. In: Aggarwal, J.K., Barneva, R.P., Brimkov, V.E., Koroutchev, K.N., Korutcheva, E.R. (eds.) IWCIA 2011. LNCS, vol. 6636, pp. 358–371. Springer, Heidelberg (2011). https://doi.org/10.1007/978-3-642-21073-0_32
19. Comaniciu, D., Meer, P.: Mean shift: a robust approach toward feature space analysis. IEEE Trans. Pattern Anal. Mach. Intell. **32**(7), 1271–1283 (2010)
20. Soille, P.: Morphological Image Analysis: Principles and Applications. Springer, Berlin (2004). https://doi.org/10.1007/978-3-662-05088-0
21. Cour, T., Benezit, F., Shi, J.: Spectral segmentation with multiscale graph decomposition. In: IEEE Conference on Computer Vision and Pattern Recognition, CVPR, vol. 2, pp. 1124–1131. IEEE (2005)

Optimization of Just-in-Time Adaptive Interventions Using Reinforcement Learning

Suat Gonul[1,2]([✉]), Tuncay Namli[2], Mert Baskaya[1,2], Ali Anil Sinaci[2], Ahmet Cosar[1], and Ismail Hakki Toroslu[1]

[1] Department of Computer Engineering, Middle East Technical University, 06800 Ankara, Turkey
suat@srdc.com.tr
[2] SRDC Software Research and Development and Consultancy Ltd., 06800 Ankara, Turkey

Abstract. Momentary context data is an important source for intelligent decision making towards personalization of mobile phone notifications. We propose a reinforcement learning based personalized notification delivery algorithm, reasoning over momentary context data. Beyond the state of the art, we propose new approaches for faster convergence of the algorithm and jump start of learning performance at the beginning of the learning process. We test our approach in both simulated and real settings trying to optimize the timing of the notifications. Our eventual, practical aim is to make office workers more physically active during the work time. We compare the results obtained for standard and improved algorithms in both testbeds where improved versions yield better results.

1 Introduction

Our research is motivated by the need of guiding people to adopt behaviors towards a healthier life with personalized support [1]. The literature provides overwhelming evidence on better outcomes driven by personalized support throughout the care programs addressing chronic diseases, obesity, sedentary lifestyle and many other prevalent health problems [2,3]. Our aim is to introduce a smart algorithm providing personalized support by analysing people's momentary context data. Such support can be provided via mobile-app notifications called just-in-time adaptive interventions (JITAI). JITAIs are widely used in behavior change therapies coping the aforementioned health problems [4].

Thanks to the advances in mobile and sensing technologies, it is now possible to deliver JITAIs wherever and whenever needed, by assessing various contextual data about environment, mental/physical states of users. We utilize reinforcement learning (RL) to find out optimal, *personalized* JITAI delivery policies. The proposed learning algorithm assesses the momentary changes in user context variables in real-time to determine the best timing to deliver interventions. It constantly improves its internal policy based on the reactions of users to the delivered JITAIs.

© Springer International Publishing AG, part of Springer Nature 2018
M. Mouhoub et al. (Eds.): IEA/AIE 2018, LNAI 10868, pp. 334–341, 2018.
https://doi.org/10.1007/978-3-319-92058-0_32

The challenge is to find out a near-optimal policy quickly *(fast conver-gence)*, which works relatively good even at the beginning of the learning pro-cess *(jump start)*. The standard RL algorithms e.g. SARSA [5] cannot meet these objectives, both of which are required to maximize the engagement with the mobile app while keeping the burden on users minimal [6]. The novelty of the study lies first in modelling the JITAI delivery problem with RL elements for providing personalized support in an automated manner. Furthermore, we advance standard RL methods to tackle with these two challenges. We validate the proposed methods in both real-life and simulated settings, where the aim is to increase physical activity levels of office workers during the working hours.

2   Related Work

Studies claiming to be providing personalized, automated interventions to help people coping with their health problems, are mostly rule-based systems. Such systems execute the same set of rules on the available (real-time) data to decide on the intervention to be sent [7]. Machine learning approaches are recommended as a solution for dynamic, personalized delivery policies [8]. For instance, [9] uses Bayesian modeling for predicting lapse status based on recovery progress and lapse history parameters; and provide personalized interventions based on the prediction. [10] introduces a model-based approach maintaining a parameterized model of individuals' aerobic capability that predicts performance to be able to guide users with adaptive goal setting interventions. Control systems engineering based dynamic modelling is also used to adapt both the intervention content and associated delivery policy [11].

From a domain-independent perspective, studies utilize machine learning classifiers to identify people's most interruptable moments for notification deliv-ery [12,13]. For instance, [12] builds a classifier using features including commu-nication activity, context, phone state and so on. To our knowledge, no other study utilized RL for building an easily generalizable, personalized intervention delivery algorithm as ours and used it in a real-life setting.

3   Drawing on RL for JITAI Optimization

Using RL for JITAI optimization is convenient as the elements of RL methodol-ogy and the problem of interest match perfectly as depicted in Fig. 1. A person and associated context data correspond to the environment entity. The context data at a certain point in time represents the state that the environment is in. Changing context of the person is modeled as a series of state transitions of the environment. JITAIs delivered to the person correspond to the actions performed by the learning agent. The reaction of the person to the JITAIs is emitted as a reward signal reflecting the acceptance of the JITAI by the person.

We propose two main improvements on this base RL setup, addressing the fast convergence and jump start challenges introduced before, respectively:

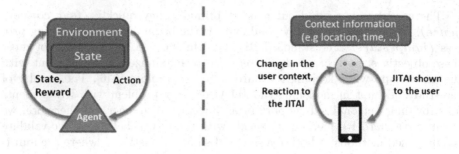

Fig. 1. Analogy between a traditional RL setup and JITAI delivery problem

(1) better rewarding mechanism of past actions and (2) learning transfer [14] to use the common knowledge acquired in other environments i.e. persons.

Better retrospective rewarding of actions is realized by assessing whether JITAIs are reacted or discarded once seen by the user and rewarding only the reacted ones. Traditionally, we would have rewarded all the past actions in the same way in proportion to their temporal proximity to the current state. However, the discarded JITAIs do not contribute to the action leading to a positive result as they were never engaged by the user. As a complementary adaptation, we treat a previous JITAI delivering action as if it was taken in the current state when the person checks the phone screen and engages with the JITAI. Both adaptations provide updating the states that are more suitable to deliver a JITAI with more rewards compared to the traditional approach.

To identify common states suitable for intervention delivery across individuals, we propose a learning transfer approach to utilize the learnt knowledge for one person in the learning process of another person. For example, people are usually less likely to engage with JITAIs while they are driving. Although learning such information for each person separately is an inefficient approach, a standard RL agent follows this way. It develops a personalized JITAI delivery policy by utilizing the data associated to a single person for whom the policy is developed. In this case, each time the agent is in an unknown state, its only option is to take a random action. Thanks to the learning transfer, though, it can make an educated guess considering the actions those were taken by other agents in the same or similar states.

To achieve the learning transfer between environments, we first decided to have policies as the knowledge to be transferred between environments. This enables utilization of same/similar state-action pairs across environments and helps achieving a jump start in terms of the effectiveness of the algorithm at the beginning phase of the learning process by reducing the number of actions taken randomly. We keep a common policy that aggregates state-action pairs generated by all of the agents. This common policy is then used to train a supervised learning based classifier to predict the action to be taken in an unknown state. For example, assume that two agents have learnt that sending JITAIs while the person is driving and when the phone screen is off would yield negative rewards in the mornings and in the evenings respectively. Then, a third agent comes across with an unknown state where the person is driving, the phone screen is off and the time is around noon. In this case, the third agent utilizes the classifier, which classifies the new unknown state into the class of states that are not suitable to deliver a JITAI. As a result, the agent would not take a random action and prefer not to deliver a JITAI.

4   Testbeds and Results

Simulated Experiment: We perform two types of simulation activity. First, daily activities of people are simulated by selecting type, occurrence and duration of activities randomly from pre-defined persona templates. A template includes a set of activities placed on a timeline. For each simulated day, a new set of activities are generated such that each activity contains information regarding the time, location, physical activity, phone screen status and emotional status of the person. Second, persons' reactions to JITAIs are simulated using a rule-based mechanism. For example, there must be at least 2 h between two subsequent JITAI engagement, JITAIs cannot be reacted while driving and so on. The aim of the simulated experiment is to show that the proposed contributions are effective compared to the standard approaches on capturing even such hard-coded rules.

We compare three cases in Figs. 2 and 3, reflecting how the contributions we propose effect the learning results. In each figure, SARSA (red line), SARSA-IRR (blue line) and SARSA-IRR-LT (green line) depict respectively the performances of the standard RL SARSA algorithm, SARSA with improved retrospective rewarding and SARSA with both improved retrospective rewarding and learning transfer approaches.

Figure 2 shows the average rewards collected at each simulated day during the experiment. While rewards collected through the entire process are shown on the left, performance of the algorithms at the beginning from a closer perspective are on the right. The blue line laying over the red one on the left part, indicates faster

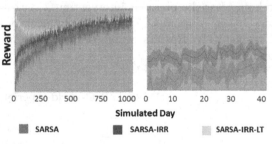

Fig. 2. Average rewards per simulated day (Color figure online)

convergence achieved by the improved retrospective rewarding. On the right, the green line outperforms the others indicating a jump start at the beginning of the learning process. The figure also shows that SARSA-IRR-LT collects more reward (the area under the lines) than the others throughout the experiment, showing that it is more effective considering the ratio of number of engaged JITAIs to the total of number JITAIs sent.

Figure 3 shows the aver-
age number of interventions
reacted by the participants.
According to the figure,
SARSA-IRR yields the highest number of engagement,
which seems as a contradic-
tion with Fig. 2, where it got
less rewards than SARSA-
IRR-LT. However, SARSA-
IRR-LT was in fact more
conservative considering the

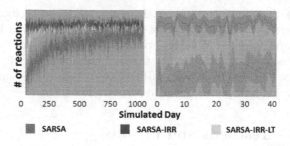

Fig. 3. Average number of interventions engaged
(Color figure online)

number of delivered JITAIs. As a result, it created less negative rewards thanks
to the learning transfer approach, which was trained in previous simulations.

Real-World Experiment: We recruited 17 office workers to make them more
physically active during their work life. Our aim was to motivate them to take a
break via JITAIs in the form of mobile app notifications. The app collects their
contextual data (wi-fi, activity and phone screen status) during the day. Upon
an update on one of these variables, the algorithm decides in real time to deliver
a JITAI or not. It updates its internal policy by processing the user reactions
that could be: discarding a JITAI, seeing the JITAI details or clicking one of
the two buttons (positive/negative) located in the JITAI detail page indicating
their willingness to perform the suggested activity.

The participants are divided into three groups namely; control-fix, control-
sarsa and focus. Control-fix group receives interventions 4 times a day such that:
at least one hour after starting to work (morning and afternoon) and at least
one hour after the previous intervention. Control-sarsa and focus groups receive
interventions dynamically based on the decisions of SARSA and SARSA-IET-
LT respectively. Results obtained from an almost 2 weeks of experiment are
presented in Table 1.

Table 1. Real-world experiment results

	Control-fix	Control-sarsa	Focus
Average reaction time in seconds	2252	500	712
Total number of engaged JITAIs	10	67	72
Ratio of engaged JITAIs to total JITAIs	3%	23%	38%
Average number of daily JITAIs (per user)	4	7	2

As we have expected, even for this small, initial experiment we have obtained
significantly better results for our proposed solution. Both, SARSA and SARSA-
IRR-LT yield better results than the fixed schedule considering the number of
engaged JITAIs and its ratio to the total number of JITAIs sent. Reaction times

for the fixed schedule is also quite high compared to the dynamic delivery mechanisms indicating that dynamic algorithms were better in adjusting the timing of JITAIs. Comparing the base SARSA and SARSA-IRR-LT, the latter outperforms on the ratio of engaged JITAIs, validating the proposed improvements on the base algorithms. The reaction time is higher for SARSA-IRR-LT, as if it performed worse in terms of timing of JITAIs. However, the SARSA algorithm sends much more JITAIs than SARSA-IRR-LT, that are probably seen by users earlier. This assumption is consistent with the lower engagement ratios of SARSA. It is also consistent with the lower rewards but higher number of engagements observed in the simulated experiment for the base SARSA algorithm.

5   Discussion and Future Work

We have already argued the superiority of the proposed approach in simulated and real-life settings in the previous section. However, there were a set of limitations while reaching the presented results. First of all, the validation of the approach in real life could be performed on bigger data produced through a longer experiment. Furthermore, the learning transfer mechanism could be improved with a more realistic dataset. In this study, we have trained the state classifier with the data produced in the simulation testbed, which only reflects the few hardcoded rules such as JITAI can only be reacted when the user is sedentary, users would not react to JITAIs too frequently, etc. Using a real-life dataset with many other features, covering a longer time; like the one constructed in [12] would better reflect the variances of real-life.

A technical limitation related to the real-time experiment was delayed retrieval of context change updates, reducing the accuracy of real-time assessment of dynamically chaning user context. As a future work, we plan to improve the sensing part of the mobile app for more accurate data collection, which would also include additional metrics related to phone status and phone usage patterns.

Although our aim was to break sedentary lifestyles of office workers, the proposed approach can be generalized to provide personalized guidance in various chronic health related problems. In fact, in a broader ongoing work, we introduce a JITAI definition framework to calibrate JITAI parameters like content, rules for delivery and so on targeting a specific problem. This preliminary study allows us to see the limitations of the proposed approach to be able to apply it in a broader experiment where diabetic patients will be guided to gain habits for blood glucose monitoring and physical exercising. We aim using the proposed approach in that broader experiment to fine-tune the timing of JITAIs by just re-defining the list of actions i.e. JITAIs.

6   Conclusion

In this study, we adapt standard RL methods for learning over people's momentary context data to optimize the timing of the interventions for each individual. We incorporate knowledge from behavior psychology field to represent this optimization problem in computer science with RL elements.

After problem formulation, we introduce two improvements on the base methods to accelerate the learning process towards convergence; and to achieve a jump start of learning performance at the beginning. We apply a retrospective rewarding approach, which would not reward past useless actions. Furthermore, we propse a learning transfer method to learn the common patterns across individuals and use that knowledge to achieve a jump start of learning performance for new environments i.e. individuals.

We evaluate the proposed approach in both simulated and real-life settings. The simulated experiment clearly shows that our approach advances the state of the art towards utilization of an RL-based learning algorithm for obtaining personalized intervention delivery mechanisms to cope with health problems. The proposed methods yield better results also in the real-world experiment considering the total number engagement with JITAIs, ratio of number of engaged JITAIs to total number of JITAIs and reaction times to JITAIs metrics.

Acknowledgement. The research leading to these results has received funding partially from the European Community's H2020 Programme under grant agreement no H2020-PHC-689444, POWER2DM project (Predictive Model-Based Decision Support for Diabetes Patient Empowerment) and partially from The Scientific and Technological Research Council of Turkey (TÜBİTAK).

References

1. Yardley, L., Morrison, L., Bradbury, K., Muller, I.: The person-based approach to intervention development: application to digital health-related behavior change interventions. J. Med. Internet Res. **17**(1), 30 (2015)
2. Ramachandran, A., Snehalatha, C., Ram, J., Selvam, S., Simon, M., Nanditha, A., Oliver, N., Shetty, A.S., Godsland, I.F., Chaturvedi, N., Majeed, A., Toumazou, C., Alberti, K.G., Johnston, D.G.: Effectiveness of mobile phone messaging in prevention of type 2 diabetes by lifestyle modification in men in India: a prospective, parallel-group, randomised controlled trial. Lancet Diabetes Endocrinol. **1**(3), 191–198 (2013)
3. Eaton, C.B., Hartman, S.J., Perzanowski, E., Pan, G., Roberts, M.B., Risica, P.M., Gans, K.M., Jakicic, J.M., Marcus, B.H.: A randomized clinical trial of a tailored lifestyle intervention for obese, sedentary, primary care patients. Ann. Fam. Med. **14**(4), 311–319 (2016)
4. Nahum-Shani, I., Smith, S.N., Tewari, A., Witkiewitz, K., Collins, L.M., Spring, B., Murphy, S.: Just in time adaptive interventions (JITAIs): an organizing framework for ongoing health behavior support. Methodology Center Technical report (14-126) (2014)
5. Rummery, G.A., Niranjan, M.: On-line Q-learning using connectionist systems, vol. 37. University of Cambridge, Department of Engineering (1994)

6. Pellegrini, C.A., Pfammatter, A.F., Conroy, D.E., Spring, B.: Smartphone applications to support weight loss: current perspectives. Adv. Health Care Technol. **1**, 13 (2015)
7. Dantzig, S., Geleijnse, G., Halteren, A.T.: Toward a persuasive mobile application to reduce sedentary behavior. Pers. Ubiquit. Comput. **17**(6), 1237–1246 (2013)
8. Kelly, J., Gooding, P., Pratt, D., Ainsworth, J., Welford, M., Tarrier, N.: Intelligent real-time therapy: harnessing the power of machine learning to optimise the delivery of momentary cognitive-behavioural interventions. J. Ment. Health **21**(4), 404–414 (2012)
9. Hammond, R.A., Ornstein, J.T., Fellows, L.K., Dubé, L., Levitan, R., Dagher, A.: A model of food reward learning with dynamic reward exposure. Front. Comput. Neurosci. **6**, 82 (2012). https://doi.org/10.3389/fncom.2012.00082
10. Mohan, S., Venkatakrishnan, A., Silva, M., Pirolli, P.: On designing a social coach to promote regular aerobic exercise. In: AAAI, pp. 4721–4727 (2017)
11. Navarro-Barrientos, J.E., Rivera, D.E., Collins, L.M.: A dynamical model for describing behavioural interventions for weight loss and body composition change. Math. Comput. Model. Dyn. Syst. **17**(2), 183–203 (2011)
12. Pielot, M., Cardoso, B., Katevas, K., Serrà, J., Matic, A., Oliver, N.: Beyond interruptibility: predicting opportune moments to engage mobile phone users. Proc. ACM Interact. Mob. Wearable Ubiquit. Technol. **1**(3), 91 (2017)
13. Oh, H., Jalali, L., Jain, R.: An intelligent notification system using context from real-time personal activity monitoring. In: IEEE International Conference on 2015 Multimedia and Expo (ICME), pp. 1–6. IEEE (2015)
14. Taylor, M.E., Stone, P.: Transfer learning for reinforcement learning domains: a survey. J. Mach. Learn. Res. **10**, 1633–1685 (2009)

EP-Based Infinite Inverted Dirichlet Mixture Learning: Application to Image Spam Detection

Wentao Fan[1], Sami Bourouis[2], Nizar Bouguila[3(✉)], Fahd Aldosari[4],
Hassen Sallay[4], and K. M. Jamil Khayyat[4]

[1] Huaqiao University, Xiamen, China
fwt@hqu.edu.cn
[2] Taif university, Taif, Kingdom of Saudi Arabia
s.bourouis@tu.edu.sa
[3] Concordia University, Montreal, QC, Canada
nizar.bouguila@concordia.ca
[4] Umm Al-Qura University, Makkah, Saudi Arabia
{fmdosari,hmsallay,kmkhayyat}@uqu.edu.sa

Abstract. We propose in this paper a new fully unsupervised model based on a Dirichlet process prior and the inverted Dirichlet distribution that allows the automatic inferring of clusters from data. The main idea is to let the number of mixture components increases as new vectors arrive. This allows answering the model selection problem in a elegant way since the resulting model can be viewed as an infinite inverted Dirichlet mixture. An expectation propagation (EP) inference methodology is developed to learn this model by obtaining a full posterior distribution on its parameters. We validate the model on a challenging application namely image spam filtering to show the merits of the framework.

1 Introduction

Contemporary times have witnessed an exponential increase in the volume of data generated everyday. These data can be textual or visual (in the form of images and videos). The organization, analysis, and modeling of these data is a crucial problem that has been growing in importance. One of the challenging data analysis tasks is clustering. Finite mixture models have been widely used for clustering since they offer a formal approach for unsupervised learning [1]. Many statistical frameworks based on finite mixture models have been proposed in the past. Despite the fact that the majority of these frameworks assume that the per-components densities are Gaussian, some recent works have considered other densities by taking the nature of the data into account. Examples of these research works includes inverted Dirichlet-based models, which we will consider in this paper, for semi-bounded data (i.e. positive vectors) [2]. An important problem when deploying mixture models is the automatic selection of the number of components. This problem has been tackled in [2] using the minimum

© Springer International Publishing AG, part of Springer Nature 2018
M. Mouhoub et al. (Eds.): IEA/AIE 2018, LNAI 10868, pp. 342–354, 2018.
https://doi.org/10.1007/978-3-319-92058-0_33

message length approach that has been shown in [3] to be a generalization of several other well known model's selection criteria. The main problem with this approach is that it needs running the estimation algorithm for different number of components and then selecting the optimal one according to the resulting message length which is actually time consuming. In this paper we go a step further by considering an infinite number of mixture components components [4] via a nonparametric Bayesian approach [5].

Nonparametric Bayesian approaches, which are statistically well based, have received a lot of attention recently and are now well-understood and accepted. These approaches are generally based on considering Dirichlet processes (DPs) [6]. DPs allows a technically sound approach for unsupervised Bayesian clustering and have been deployed in a variety of domains and applications such as computer vision, pattern recognition, data mining, and information retrieval [7–9]. In this paper, we rely on DPs to develop our nonparametric Bayesian model. Indeed, the proposed work can be viewed as an extension of the finite mixture framework developed in [10], based on the inverted Dirichlet [2], to the infinite case. The main idea is to allow the complexity and accuracy of the model to increase as the data size increases [11–13]. Having the infinite inverted Dirichlet mixture model in hand, a challenging problem that we will tackle in this paper is the learning of its parameters. Markov Chain Monte Carlo (MCMC) techniques have dominated the literature in the case of infinite mixture models learning. Unfortunately MCMC approaches have been shown to be computationally extensive. Thus, we consider here, a deterministic approximation technique to MCMC, known as expectation propagation (EP), has been introduced and has been shown to be a good learning alternative [14 16]. EP is an extension to assumed-density filtering (ADF) [17] which is a one pass, sequential approximation method. In contrast to the ADF, the order of the input data points is not crucial in the EP inference and its inference accuracy is improved by re-using the data points many times. This allows the simultaneous estimation of the parameters and selection of the number of clusters. The resulting statistical framework is applied to tackle the challenging problem of image spam detection where visual content of emails is considered for the filtering task.

The remainder of this paper is organized as follows. Section 2 presents our statistical framework. Section 3 develops in details the model's expectation propagation learning approach. The experimental evaluation is given in Sect. 4. Finally, Sect. 5 draws the conclusion.

2   Model Specification

In this work, we focus on the Dirichlet process mixture of inverted Dirichlet distributions, which can also be considered as an infinite inverted Dirichlet mixture model since it is composed of an infinite number of mixture components.

2.1   Finite Inverted Dirichlet Mixture Model

If a D-dimensional random positive vector $\boldsymbol{X} = (X_1, \ldots, X_D)$ is distributed according to the inverted Dirichlet mixture model with J components, then the probability density function of $\boldsymbol{X}$ is given by

$$p(\boldsymbol{X}|\boldsymbol{\pi}, \boldsymbol{\alpha}) = \sum_{j=1}^{J} \pi_j \mathcal{ID}(\boldsymbol{X}|\boldsymbol{\alpha}_j),\tag{1}$$

where $\boldsymbol{\pi} = \{\pi_j\}$ are the mixing proportions that have to be positive and sum to unity. $\mathcal{ID}(\boldsymbol{X}|\boldsymbol{\alpha}_j)$ is the inverted Dirichlet distribution associated with the jth component and is parameterized by $\boldsymbol{\alpha}_j = (\alpha_{j1}, \ldots, \alpha_{jD})$ as

$$\mathcal{ID}(\boldsymbol{X}_i|\boldsymbol{\alpha}_j) = \frac{\Gamma(\sum_{l=1}^{D+1} \alpha_{jl})}{\prod_{l=1}^{D+1} \Gamma(\alpha_{jl})} \prod_{l=1}^{D} X_{il}^{\alpha_{jl}-1} \Big(1 + \sum_{l=1}^{D} X_{il}\Big)^{-\sum_{l=1}^{D+1} \alpha_{jl}}\tag{2}$$

where $0 < X_{il} < \infty$ for $l = 1, \ldots, D$, $\alpha_{jl} > 0$ for $l = 1, \ldots, D+1$. The mean, variance and covariance of the inverted Dirichlet distribution are given by

$$E(X_l) = \frac{\alpha_l}{(\alpha_{D+1} - 1)}\tag{3}$$

$$var(X_l) = \frac{\alpha_l(\alpha_l + \alpha_{D+1} - 1)}{(\alpha_{D+1} - 1)^2(\alpha_{D+1} - 2)}\tag{4}$$

$$cov(X_a, X_b) = \frac{\alpha_a \alpha_b}{(\alpha_{D+1} - 1)^2(\alpha_{D+1} - 2)}\tag{5}$$

2.2   Stick-Breaking Representation

In this section, we extend the finite inverted Dirichlet mixture model to the infinite counterpart using Dirichlet process prior with stick-breaking construction [18]. Assume that a random distribution G is distributed according to a Dirichlet process $G \sim \mathrm{DP}(b, H)$ with the base distribution H and concentration parameter b, its stick-breaking representation can be described as

$$\lambda_j \sim \mathrm{Beta}(1, b), \qquad \theta_j \sim H, \qquad \pi_j = \lambda_j \prod_{s=1}^{j-1}(1 - \lambda_s), \qquad G = \sum_{j=1}^{\infty} \pi_j \delta_{\theta_j}\tag{6}$$

where δ_{θ_j} is the Dirac delta measure centered at θ_j, π_j are the mixing proportions with the constraint that $\sum_{j=1}^{\infty} \pi_j = 1$. If a set of N i.i.d observations $\mathcal{X} = (\boldsymbol{X}_1, \ldots, \boldsymbol{X}_N)$ follows an inverted Dirichlet mixture model with an infinite number of components, then the probability of $\mathcal{X}$ is defined as

$$p(\mathcal{X}|\boldsymbol{\pi}, \boldsymbol{\alpha}) = \prod_{i=1}^{N} \Big[\sum_{j=1}^{\infty} \pi_j \mathcal{ID}(\boldsymbol{X}_i|\boldsymbol{\alpha}_j)\Big]\tag{7}$$

3   EP-Based Learning

3.1   Expectation Propagation

In this subsection, a brief introduction to the EP approximation scheme is presented. Consider an observed data set of N i.i.d vectors $\mathcal{X} = (\boldsymbol{X}_1, \ldots, \boldsymbol{X}_N)$ which follow a model with unknown parameter Θ, then the joint distribution of $\mathcal{X}$ and Θ can be represented in the form of a product of factors as in [14]:

$$p(\mathcal{X}, \Theta) = \prod_i f_i(\Theta) \tag{8}$$

One possible factorization is to consider $N + 1$ terms (the prior term + the data terms) as: $f_0(\Theta) = p(\Theta)$ and $f_i(\Theta) = p(\boldsymbol{X}_i|\Theta)$, $i = 1, \ldots, N$. The main idea of the EP algorithm is to approximate the posterior distribution $p(\Theta|\mathcal{X})$ by a product of factors:

$$q(\Theta) = \frac{\prod_i \tilde{f}_i(\Theta)}{\int \prod_i \tilde{f}_i(\Theta) d\Theta} \tag{9}$$

where each factor $\tilde{f}_i(\Theta)$ is an appropriate approximation to $f_i(\Theta)$. In the EP learning framework, we first initialize all the factors $\tilde{f}_i(\Theta)$, then each factor is optimized sequentially in the context of the remaining factors. In order to estimate a specific factor $\tilde{f}_j(\Theta)$, we first remove it from the current approximation to the posterior as

$$q^{\backslash j}(\Theta) - \frac{q(\Theta)}{\tilde{f}_j(\Theta)} \tag{10}$$

We then obtain a new distribution by combining Eq. (10) with the true factor $f_j(\Theta)$ as

$$\widehat{p}(\Theta) = \frac{f_j(\Theta) q^{\backslash j}(\Theta)}{\int f_j(\Theta) q^{\backslash j}(\Theta) d\Theta} \tag{11}$$

Consequently, we can update the approximated posterior $q(\Theta)$ by minimizing the KL divergence: $\mathrm{KL}\big(\widehat{p}(\Theta) \parallel q(\Theta)\big)$. This is achieved by matching the sufficient statistics of $q(\Theta)$ to the corresponding moments of $\widehat{p}(\Theta)$. Then, we can update the approximating factor $\tilde{f}_j(\Theta)$ as

$$\tilde{f}_j(\Theta) = Z_j \frac{q(\Theta)}{q^{\backslash j}(\Theta)} \tag{12}$$

where $Z_j = \int f_j(\Theta) q^{\backslash j}(\Theta) d\Theta$ is a normalization constant. Therefore, each factor can be updated iteratively in the context of remaining factors as described in the above steps until convergence.

3.2   EP Model Learning

In this section, we adopt Expectation Propagation (EP) to learn the infinite inverted Dirichlet mixture model. Since our model is fully Bayesian, we need to introduce priors for parameters λ and α. Based on the stick-breaking representation of the Dirichlet process as defined in Eq.(6), the prior of λ is a particular Beta distribution parameterized by $a_j = 1$ and b_j in the form of

$$p(\lambda) = \prod_{j=1}^{\infty} \text{Beta}(\lambda_j | a_j, b_j) = \prod_{j=1}^{\infty} b_j (1 - \lambda_j)^{b_j - 1} \tag{13}$$

For the parameter α_j of the jth component of the inverted Dirichlet mixture model, inspired by [19] in which a Gaussian assumption is adopted as the priors for the parameters of Beta distribution, we adopt a $D+1$ dimensional Gaussian with mean vector μ_j and the precision matrix A_j (the inverse covariance matrix) as the prior for α_j as:

$$p(\alpha_j) = \mathcal{N}(\alpha_j | \mu_j, A_j) = \frac{|A_j|^{1/2}}{(2\pi)^{(D+1)/2}} \exp\left(-\frac{1}{2}(\alpha_j - \mu_j)^T A_j (\alpha_j - \mu_j) \right) \tag{14}$$

The first step of EP learning is to initialize all of the approximating factors $\widetilde{f}_i(\Theta)$, where $\Theta = \{\alpha, \lambda\}$, by initializing all the involved hyperparameters: $\{a_j, b_j, \mu_j, A_j\}$. We also truncate the stick-breaking representation for the infinite inverted Dirichlet mixture model at a value of J as:

$$\lambda_J = 1, \qquad \pi_j = 0 \text{ when } j > J, \qquad \sum_{j=1}^{J} \pi_j = 1 \tag{15}$$

where the truncation level J is infered automatically during the EP learning process. Next, the posterior approximation $q(\Theta)$ is initialized by setting $q(\Theta) \propto \prod_i \widetilde{f}_i(\Theta)$, where the corresponding hyperparameters of $q(\Theta)$ are denoted as $\{a_j^*, b_j^*, \mu_j^*, A_j^*\}$. Since each approximated term $\widetilde{f}_i(\Theta)$ is in exponential form, we can easily compute the hyperparameters of $q(\Theta)$ according to [14, 16],

$$a_j^* = \sum_i a_{i,j} - N, \qquad\qquad b_j^* = \sum_i b_{i,j} - N \tag{16}$$

$$\mu_j^* = \Big(\sum_i A_{i,j}^{-1}\Big)\Big(\sum_i A_{i,j}\mu_{i,j}\Big), \qquad\qquad A_j^* = \sum_i A_{i,j} \tag{17}$$

In order to update the factor $\widetilde{f}_i(\Theta)$, we have to remove it from the posterior $q(\Theta)$. Then, the corresponding hyperparameters can be computed analytically as

$$a_j^{\backslash i} = a_j^* - a_{i,j} + 1, \qquad\qquad b_j^{\backslash i} = b_j^* - b_{i,j} + 1 \tag{18}$$

$$\mu_j^{\backslash i} = (A_j^{\backslash i})^{-1}(A_j^* \mu_j^* - A_{i,j}\mu_{i,j}), \qquad\qquad A_j^{\backslash i} = A_j^* - A_{i,j} \tag{19}$$

Next, the updated posterior $\widehat{p}(\Theta)$ can be calculated as

$$\widehat{p}(\Theta) = \frac{1}{Z_i} f_i(\Theta) q^{\backslash i}(\Theta) \tag{20}$$

where the normalization constant Z_i is evaluated by

$$Z_i = \int f_i(\Theta) q^{\backslash i}(\Theta) \tag{21}$$

It is noteworthy that the normalization constant Z_i in Eq. (20) is analytically intractable, since it involves an integration over the product of an inverted Dirichlet and a Gaussian distribution. To tackle this problem, we apply the Laplace approximation to approximate the integrand with a Gaussian distribution as suggested in [19] (details can be viewed in Appendix A). After obtaining Z_i and $\widehat{p}(\Theta)$, we can revise the posterior $q(\Theta)$ by matching its sufficient statistics to the corresponding moments of $\widehat{p}(\Theta)$. This is achieved by calculating the partial derivative of $\ln Z_i$ with respect to the corresponding model hyperparameters. For $a_j^{\backslash i}$, we can calculate the partial derivative as

$$\nabla_{a_j}^{\backslash i} \ln Z_i = \frac{1}{Z_i} \int f_i(\Theta) \frac{q^{\backslash i}(\Theta)}{q^{\backslash i}(\lambda_j^{\backslash i})} \frac{\partial}{\partial a_j^{\backslash i}} q^{\backslash i}(\lambda_j^{\backslash i}) d\Theta$$
$$= E_{\widehat{p}}[\ln \lambda_j] + \Psi(a_j^{\backslash i} + b_j^{\backslash i}) - \Psi(a_j^{\backslash i}) \tag{22}$$

By applying moment matching, we obtain

$$E_{\widehat{p}}[\ln \lambda_j] = E_q[\ln \lambda_j] = \Psi(a_j^*) - \Psi(a_j^* + b_j^*) \tag{23}$$

Similarly, we can compute the partial derivatives of $\ln Z_i$ with respect to the other model hyperparameters:

$$\nabla_{b_j}^{\backslash i} \ln Z_i = E_{\widehat{p}}[1 - \ln \lambda_j] + \Psi(a_j^{\backslash i} + b_j^{\backslash i}) - \Psi(b_j^{\backslash i}) \tag{24}$$

$$\nabla_{\mu_j}^{\backslash i} \ln Z_i = A_j^{\backslash i} E_{\widehat{p}}[\alpha_j] - A_j^{\backslash i} \mu_j^{\backslash i} \tag{25}$$

$$\nabla_{A_j}^{\backslash i} \ln Z_i = \frac{1}{2} \left\{ |(A_j^{\backslash i})^{-1}| - \left[\sum_{l=1}^{D+1} E_{\widehat{p}}[\alpha_{jl}^2] - 2 E_{\widehat{p}}[\alpha_{jl}] \mu_{jl}^{\backslash i} + (\mu_{jl}^{\backslash i})^2 \right] \right\} \tag{26}$$

The right hand sides in the above equations can be computed analytically by using Eq. (39) in the Appendix. Furthermore, the expectations in the above equations can be acquired by applying the moment matching technique as

$$E_{\widehat{p}}[\alpha_j] = E_q[\alpha_j] = \mu_j^*, \qquad E_{\widehat{p}}[\alpha_j^2] = E_q[\alpha_j^2] = (\mu_j^*)^2 \tag{27}$$

By substituting the above expectations into the corresponding partial derivative equations, we can update the hyperparameters of $q(\Theta)$. After obtaining $q(\Theta)$ and $q^{\backslash i}(\Theta)$, we can update the revised hyperparameters for the approximating factor f_i as

$$a_{i,j} = a_j^* - a_j^{\backslash i} + 1, \qquad b_{i,j} = b_j^* - b_j^{\backslash i} + 1 \tag{28}$$

$$\boldsymbol{\mu}_{i,j} = A_{i,j}^{-1}(A_j^* \boldsymbol{\mu}_j^* - A_j^{\backslash i} \boldsymbol{\mu}_j^{\backslash i}), \qquad A_{i,j} = A_j^* - A_j^{\backslash i} \tag{29}$$

The above procedure is repeated until the hyperparameters of the approximating factor converge. The same procedure is applied sequentially for the remaining factors. The complete learning process is summarized in Algorithm 1.

Algorithm 1. EP learning of infinite inverted Dirichlet mixture

---

1: Choose the initial truncation level J.
2: Initialize the approximating factors $\tilde{f}_i(\Theta)$ by initializing all the involved hyperparameters $\{a_j, b_j, \boldsymbol{\mu}_j, A_j\}$.
3: Initialize the posterior approximation by setting $q(\Theta) \propto \prod_i \tilde{f}_i(\Theta)$. The hyperparameters of $q(\Theta)$ are calculated by Eqs. (16) and (17).
4: **repeat**
5:    Select a factor $\tilde{f}_i(\Theta)$ to refine.
6:    Remove $\tilde{f}_i(\Theta)$ from the posterior $q(\Theta)$ by division $q^{\backslash i}(\Theta) = q(\Theta)/\tilde{f}_i(\Theta)$.
7:    Evaluate the new posterior by setting the sufficient statistics (moments) of $q(\Theta)$ to the corresponding moments of $\hat{p}(\Theta)$.
8:    Update the factor $\tilde{f}_i(\Theta)$ by updating the corresponding hyperparameters as in Eqs. (28) and (29).
9: **until** Convergence criterion is reached.
10: Calculate the expected value of λ_j as $E[\lambda_j] = \frac{a_j^*}{a_j^* + b_j^*}$, and submit it into Eq. (6) to obtain the estimated values of the mixing coefficients π_j.
11: Detect the optimal number of components J by eliminating the components with small mixing coefficients close to 0.

---

4   Experimental Results: Image Spam Detection

Exchanging emails play an important role in our daily activities. Spam filtering has been one of the most challenging problems in digital communication in the last couple of decades [20]. Spams do not only compromise ressources, but also cause security problems. Various techniques and approaches have been proposed in the past to deal with this problem. Many of the proposed solutions are based on machine learning techniques. These techniques are able to detect and extract hidden patterns that could discriminate between legitimates and spam emails. Two major challenges in the spam filtering problem are its dynamic nature and dealing with the non-textual content. Thus, a good filtering approach should be adaptive [21,22] and should be able to deal with the presence in images in emails. Contrary to textual data, images pose several significant challenges. Indeed, it is important to choose an appropriate representation that can describe well the content of the image present in a given email. And the resulting representation should provide a semantically meaningful output which is very difficult taking into account the fact that an image possesses a rich structure. Embedding spam images into emails is a successful trick that is widely used now by spammers. This trick is generally referred to as image-based spam and has drawn some attention recently [23–26]. In this section, we validate our proposed model in the challenging task of image spam detection. Our model is considered simultaneously with the probabilistic Latent Semantic Analysis (pLSA) model [27] with bag-of-words representation [28]. We have considered three challenging spam data sets of images extracted from real spam in our experiments: the personal spam emails collected by Dredze et al. [29], a subset of the publicly available SpamArchive corpus used by [24,29] and the Princeton spam image benchmark[1]. We have used one common ham data set of images which was collected and used by Dredze et al. [29]. In total, there are 2,550 images in the Dredze ham data set, 3,210 images in the Dredze spam data set, 3,550 images in the SpamArchive and 1,071 images in Princeton spam image benchmark. Sample spam images are shown in Fig. 1. We have downsampled all images to the spatial resolution of 100×100 pixels as a preprocessing step. In our experiments, we have randomly divided each data set (both ham and spam) into two halves: one for constructing the visual vocabulary and another for testing.

Fig. 1. Sample spam images from Dredze spam data set.

We have proceeded as following in order to construct the visual vocabulary, First, the key points of each image were detected using the Difference-of-Gaussian (DoG) interest point detector and described using Scale-Invariant Feature Transform (SIFT) resulting in a 128-dimensional vector for each key point [30]. Then, the K-Means algorithm was used to cluster all the SIFT vectors into a visual vocabulary. We have constructed the visual vocabulary by setting the number of clusters (i.e. number of visual words) to 800, 1000 and 850, respectively for each data set. The pLSA model was applied by considering 45 aspects for all data sets and each image in the data set was then represented

---

[1] http://www.cs.jhu.edu/~mdredze/datasets/image_spam.

by a 45-dimensional vector. Finally, the resulting vectors were clustered by our mixture model. The entire procedure was repeated 10 times for evaluating the performance of our approach. Tables 1, 2 and 3 represent the average confusion matrices for detecting spam images of each data set using our mixture model. In these tables, SI stands for spam images while HI denotes ham images. Moreover, we compared the performances of our expectation propagation infinite inverted Dirichlet mixture (EPInInDM), infinite inverted Dirichlet mixture (InInDM) learned via MCMC technique as proposed in [31], variational infinite inverted Dirichlet mixture model (varInInDM) as proposed in [32], and variatioanl infinite Gaussian mixture model (varInGM) model in terms of the average classification accuracy rate and the average false positive rate. The corresponding results as well as the number of correct detected images (both spam and ham) are illustrated in Table 4. Based on this table, the proposed EPInInDM model obtains the highest average accuracy rate and lowest false positive rate.

Table 1. Dredze.

	SI	HI
SI	1250	355
HI	60	1215

Table 2. SpamArchive.

	SI	HI
SI	1351	424
HI	93	1182

Table 3. Princeton.

	SI	HI
SI	378	158
HI	61	1214

Table 4. The number of correct detected images (both spam and ham) $\hat{N}$, and the average classification accuracy rate (Acc.) of image spam detection computed using different algorithms over 10 random runs.

	Dredze		SpamArchive		Princeton	
	$\hat{N}$	Acc. (%)	$\hat{N}$	Acc. (%)	$\hat{N}$	Acc. (%)
EPInInDM	2465	85.59	2533	83.04	1592	87.90
InInDM	2401	83.36	2488	81.49	1530	84.39
varInInDM	2290	79.51	2426	79.53	1441	79.50
varInGM	2263	78.58	2360	77.39	1435	79.25

5   Conclusion

We proposed an infinite mixture model based on inverted Dirichlet distribution to model positive vectors. We developed and evaluated an expectation propagation algorithm to learn the parameters of the proposed infinite model. The experiments confirm the power of the proposed approach in tackling a very challenging problem namely image spam filtering. The presented statistical framework is of general applicability, as it can work in any situation where positive feature vectors are extracted.

Acknowledgements. The authors would like to thank the Deanship of Scientific Research at umm Al-Qura University for the continuous support. This work was supported financially by the Deanship of Scientific Research at Umm Al-Qura University under the grant number 15-COM-3-1-0006. The first author was supported by the National Natural Science Foundation of China (61502183).

A   The calculation of Z_i in Eq. (21)

The normalized constant Z_i in Eq. (21) can be calculated as

$$Z_i = \int f_i(\Theta)q^{\backslash i}(\Theta)d\Theta = \sum_{j=1}^{J} \bar{\lambda}_j \prod_{s=1}^{j-1}(1-\bar{\lambda}_s) \int \mathcal{ID}(\boldsymbol{X}_i|\boldsymbol{\alpha}_j)N(\boldsymbol{\alpha}_j|\boldsymbol{\mu}_j^{\backslash i}, A_j^{\backslash i})d\boldsymbol{\alpha}_j$$

(30)

where $\bar{\lambda}_j$ is the expected value of λ_j. Since the integration involved in Eq. (30) is analytically intractable, we tackle this problem by adopting the Laplace approximation to approximate the integrand with a Gaussian distribution [19]. First, we define $h(\boldsymbol{\alpha}_j)$ as the integrand in Eq. (30):

$$h(\boldsymbol{\alpha}_j) = \mathcal{ID}(\boldsymbol{X}_i|\boldsymbol{\alpha}_j)\mathcal{N}(\boldsymbol{\alpha}_j|\boldsymbol{\mu}_j^{\backslash i}, A_j^{\backslash i})$$

(31)

Then, the normalized distribution for this integrand which is indeed a product of a Dirichlet distribution and a Gaussian distribution is given by

$$\mathcal{H}(\boldsymbol{\alpha}_j) = \frac{h(\boldsymbol{\alpha}_j)}{\int h(\boldsymbol{\alpha}_j)d\boldsymbol{\alpha}_j}$$

(32)

Our goal for the Laplace method is to find a Gaussian approximation which is centered on the mode of the distribution $\mathcal{H}(\boldsymbol{\alpha}_j)$. We may obtain the mode $\boldsymbol{\alpha}_j^*$ numerically by setting the first derivative of $\ln h(\boldsymbol{\alpha}_j)$ to 0, where

$$\ln h(\boldsymbol{\alpha}_j) = \ln \frac{\Gamma(\sum_{l=1}^{D+1} \alpha_{jl})}{\prod_{l=1}^{D+1} \Gamma(\alpha_{jl})} + \sum_{l=1}^{D}(\alpha_{jl}-1)\ln X_{il} - \sum_{l=1}^{D+1} \alpha_{jl}$$

$$\ln(1+\sum_{l=1}^{D} X_{il}) - \frac{1}{2}(\boldsymbol{\alpha}_j - \boldsymbol{\mu}_j^{\backslash i})^T A_j^{\backslash i}(\boldsymbol{\alpha}_j - \boldsymbol{\mu}_j^{\backslash i}) + \text{const.}$$

(33)

We can calculate the first and second derivatives with respect to $\boldsymbol{\alpha}_j$ as

$$\frac{\partial \ln h(\boldsymbol{\alpha}_j)}{\partial \boldsymbol{\alpha}_j} = \begin{bmatrix} \Psi(\sum_{l=1}^{D+1} \alpha_{jl}) - \Psi(\alpha_{j1}) + \ln X_{i1} - \ln(1+\sum_{l=1}^{D} X_{il}) \\ \vdots \\ \Psi(\sum_{l=1}^{D+1} \alpha_{jl}) - \Psi(\alpha_{jD}) + \ln X_{iD} - \ln(1+\sum_{l=1}^{D} X_{il}) \end{bmatrix} - A_j^{\backslash i}(\boldsymbol{\alpha}_j - \boldsymbol{\mu}_j^{\backslash i})$$

(34)

$$\frac{\partial^2 \ln h(\boldsymbol{\alpha}_j)}{\partial \boldsymbol{\alpha}_j^2} = \begin{bmatrix} \Psi'(\sum_{l=1}^{D} \alpha_{jl}) - \Psi'(\alpha_{j1}) & \cdots & \Psi'(\sum_{l=1}^{D} \alpha_{jl}) \\ \vdots & \ddots & \vdots \\ \Psi'(\sum_{l=1}^{D} \alpha_{jl}) & \cdots & \Psi'(\sum_{l=1}^{D} \alpha_{jl}) - \Psi'(\alpha_{jD}) \end{bmatrix} - A_j^{\backslash i}$$

(35)

where $\Psi(\cdot)$ is the digamma function. Then, we can approximate $h(\boldsymbol{\alpha}_j)$

$$h(\boldsymbol{\alpha}_j) \simeq h(\boldsymbol{\alpha}_j^*) \exp\left(-\frac{1}{2}(\boldsymbol{\alpha}_j - \boldsymbol{\alpha}_j^*)\widehat{A}_j(\boldsymbol{\alpha}_j - \boldsymbol{\alpha}_j^*)\right) \tag{36}$$

where the precision matrix $\widehat{A}_j$ is given by

$$\widehat{A}_j = -\left.\frac{\partial^2 \ln h(\boldsymbol{\alpha}_j)}{\partial \boldsymbol{\alpha}_j^2}\right|_{\boldsymbol{\alpha}_j = \boldsymbol{\alpha}_j^*} \tag{37}$$

Therefore, the integration of $h(\boldsymbol{\alpha}_j)$ can be approximated by using Eq. (36) as

$$\int h(\boldsymbol{\alpha}_j)d\boldsymbol{\alpha}_j \simeq h(\boldsymbol{\alpha}_j^*)\int \exp(-\frac{1}{2}(\boldsymbol{\alpha}_j-\boldsymbol{\alpha}_j^*)\widehat{A}_j(\boldsymbol{\alpha}_j-\boldsymbol{\alpha}_j^*))d\boldsymbol{\alpha}_j = h(\boldsymbol{\alpha}_j^*)\frac{(2\pi)^{(D+1)/2}}{|\widehat{A}_j|^{1/2}} \tag{38}$$

Finally, we can rewrite Eq. (30) as following:

$$Z_i = \sum_{j=1}^{J} \bar{\lambda}_j \prod_{s=1}^{j-1}(1-\bar{\lambda}_s)h(\boldsymbol{\alpha}_j^*)\frac{(2\pi)^{(D+1)/2}}{|\widehat{A}_j|^{1/2}} \tag{39}$$

References

1. McLachlan, G., Peel, D.: Finite Mixture Models. Wiley, New York (2000)
2. Bdiri, T., Bouguila, N.: Positive vectors clustering using inverted dirichlet finite mixture models. Expert Syst. Appl. **39**(2), 1869–1882 (2012)
3. Bouguila, N., Ziou, D.: High-dimensional unsupervised selection and estimation of a finite generalized dirichlet mixture model based on minimum message length. IEEE Trans. Pattern Anal. Mach. Intell. **29**(10), 1716–1731 (2007)
4. Rasmussen, C.E.: The infinite Gaussian mixture model. In: Proceedings of Advances in Neural Information Processing Systems (NIPS), pp. 554–560. MIT Press (2000)
5. Blackwell, D., MacQueen, J.: Ferguson distributions via pólya urn schemes. Ann. Stat. **1**(2), 353–355 (1973)
6. Korwar, R.M., Hollander, M.: Contributions to the theory of Dirichlet processes. Ann. Prob. **1**, 705–711 (1973)
7. Blei, D.M., Jordan, M.I.: Variational inference for Dirichlet process mixtures. Bayesian Anal. **1**, 121–144 (2005)
8. Bouguila, N., Ziou, D.: A Dirichlet process mixture of Dirichlet distributions for classification and prediction. In: Proceedings of the IEEE Workshop on Machine Learning for Signal Processing (MLSP), pp. 297–302 (2008)
9. Zhang, X., Chen, B., Liu, H., Zuo, L., Feng, B.: Infinite max-margin factor analysis via data augmentation. Pattern Recogn. **52**(Suppl. C), 17–32 (2016)
10. Bertrand, A., Al-Osaimi, F.R., Bouguila, N.: View-based 3D objects recognition with expectation propagation learning. In: Bebis, G., Boyle, R., Parvin, B., Koracin, D., Porikli, F., Skaff, S., Entezari, A., Min, J., Iwai, D., Sadagic, A., Scheidegger, C., Isenberg, T. (eds.) ISVC 2016. LNCS, vol. 10073, pp. 359–369. Springer, Cham (2016). https://doi.org/10.1007/978-3-319-50832-0_35

11. Minka, T., Ghahramani, Z.: Expectation propagation for infinite mixtures. In: NIPS 2003 Workshop on Nonparametric Bayesian Methods and Infinite Models (2003)
12. Bouguila, N.: Infinite Liouville mixture models with application to text and texture categorization. Pattern Recogn. Lett. **33**(2), 103–110 (2012)
13. Bouguila, N., Ziou, D.: A Dirichlet process mixture of generalized Dirichlet distributions for proportional data modeling. IEEE Trans. Neural Netw. **21**(1), 107–122 (2010)
14. Minka, T.: Expectation propagation for approximate Bayesian inference. In: Proceedings of the Conference on Uncertainty in Artificial Intelligence (UAI), pp. 362–369 (2001)
15. Minka, T., Lafferty, J.: Expectation-propagation for the generative aspect model. In: Proceedings of the Conference on Uncertainty in Artificial Intelligence (UAI), pp. 352–359 (2002)
16. Chang, S., Dasgupta, N., Carin, L.: A Bayesian approach to unsupervised feature selection and density estimation using expectation propagation. In: Proceedings of the IEEE Computer Society Conference on Computer Vision and Pattern Recognition (CVPR), pp. 1043–1050 (2005)
17. Maybeck, P.S.: Stochastic Models, Estimation and Control. Academic Press, New York (1982)
18. Ishwaran, H., James, L.F.: Gibbs sampling methods for stick-breaking priors. J. Am. Stat. Assoc. **96**, 161–173 (2001)
19. Ma, Z., Leijon, A.: Expectation propagation for estimating the parameters of the beta distribution. In: Proceedings of the IEEE International Conference on Acoustics, Speech, and Signal Processing (ICASSP), pp. 2082–2085 (2010)
20. Zhang, Y., Wang, S., Phillips, P., Ji, G.: Binary PSO with mutation operator for feature selection using decision tree applied to spam detection. Knowl. Based Syst. **64**, 22–31 (2014)
21. Amayri, O., Bouguila, N.: Improved online support vector machines spam filtering using string kernels. In: Bayro-Corrochano, E., Eklundh, J.-O. (eds.) CIARP 2009. LNCS, vol. 5856, pp. 621–628. Springer, Heidelberg (2009). https://doi.org/10.1007/978-3-642-10268-4_73
22. Amayri, O., Bouguila, N.: Online spam filtering using support vector machines. In: Proceedings of the 14th IEEE Symposium on Computers and Communications (ISCC 2009), 5–8 July Sousse, Tunisia, pp. 337–340. IEEE Computer Society (2009)
23. Biggio, B., Fumera, G., Pillai, I., Roli, F.: A survey and experimental evaluation of image spam filtering techniques. Pattern Recogn. Lett. **32**, 1436–1446 (2011)
24. Fumera, G., Pillai, I., Roli, F.: Spam filtering based on the analysis of text information embedded into images. J. Mach. Learn. Res. **7**, 2699–2720 (2006)
25. Biggio, B., Fumera, G., Pillai, I., Roli, F.: Image spam filtering using visual information. In: Proceedings of the 14th International Conference on Image Analysis and Processing (ICIAP), pp. 105–110 (2007)
26. Mehta, B., Nangia, S., Gupta, M., Nejdl, W.: Detecting image spam using visual features and near duplicate detection. In: Proceedings of the 17th International Conference on World Wide Web, pp. 497–506 (2008)
27. Hofmann, T.: Unsupervised learning by probabilistic latent semantic analysis. Mach. Learn. **42**(1/2), 177–196 (2001)
28. Csurka, G., Dance, C.R., Fan, L., Willamowski, J., Bray, C.: Visual categorization with bags of keypoints. In: Workshop on Statistical Learning in Computer Vision, 8th European Conference on Computer Vision (ECCV), pp. 1–22 (2004)

29. Dredze, M., Gevaryahu, R., Elias-Bachrach, A.: Learning fast classifiers for image spam. In: Proceedings of the Conference on Email and Anti-Spam (CEAS), pp. 487–493 (2007)
30. Lowe, D.G.: Distinctive image features from scale-invariant keypoints. Int. J. Comput. Vis. **60**(2), 91–110 (2004)
31. Bdiri, T., Bouguila, N.: An infinite mixture of inverted Dirichlet distributions. In: Lu, B.-L., Zhang, L., Kwok, J. (eds.) ICONIP 2011. LNCS, vol. 7063, pp. 71–78. Springer, Heidelberg (2011). https://doi.org/10.1007/978-3-642-24958-7_9
32. Fan, W., Bouguila, N.: Topic novelty detection using infinite variational inverted Dirichlet mixture models. In: 14th IEEE International Conference on Machine Learning and Applications, ICMLA 2015, Miami, FL, USA, 9–11 December 2015, pp. 70–75 (2015)

Bayesian Learning of Finite Asymmetric Gaussian Mixtures

Shuai Fu[✉] and Nizar Bouguila[✉]

Concordia University, Montreal, Canada
f_shuai@encs.concordia.ca, bouguila@ciise.concordia.ca

Abstract. Asymmetric Gaussian mixture (AGM) model has been proven to be more flexible than the classic Gaussian mixture model from many aspects. In contrast with previous efforts that have focused on maximum likelihood estimation, this paper introduces a fully Bayesian learning approach using Metropolis-Hastings (MH) within Gibbs sampling method to learn AGM model. We show the merits of the proposed model using synthetic data and a challenging intrusion detection application.

Keywords: Asymmetric Gaussian mixture · Metropolis-Hastings
Gibbs sampling · MCMC · Intrusion detection

1 Introduction

A large volume of data is generated everyday. A crucial task is the analysis and modeling of these data. Many statistical and data mining approaches have been proposed in the past. Among these approaches, finite mixture models [1–4] have received a lot of attention because they are flexible and powerful probabilistic tools for modeling data [5]. In recent years, there has been an increasing trend of applying finite mixtures into unsupervised learning domains involving statistical modeling of data, such as astronomy, ecology, bioinformatics, pattern recognition, computer vision and machine learning [6]. As an improvement of naive Bayes methodologies, mixture modeling can be viewed as the superimposition of a finite number of component densities which respects the dependency between data groups, bringing more generality and robustness.

As an efficient approach, Gaussian mixture model (GMM) [7] is widely deployed because of its outstanding suitability in several domains such as computer vision, pattern recognition and data mining. In this paper, we choose asymmetric Gaussian mixture (AGM) model [8] for modeling because it uses two variance parameters for left and right parts of each distribution in the mixture which allows to accurately model non-Gaussian datasets [9,10] including asymmetric ones.

A challenging issue when deploying mixture models is the learning of the model's parameters. The estimation of the parameters of mixture distributions

© Springer International Publishing AG, part of Springer Nature 2018
M. Mouhoub et al. (Eds.): IEA/AIE 2018, LNAI 10868, pp. 355–365, 2018.
https://doi.org/10.1007/978-3-319-92058-0_34

can be accomplished by using maximum-likelihood-based expectation maximization (EM) [11] algorithm. However, EM has some drawbacks such as overfitting and dependency on initialization [12–14]. Therefore, an alternative is the
fully Bayesian approach, based for instance on Markov Chain Monte Carlo
(MCMC) methods [15], which has been found to be useful in many applications by considering parameters priors which can avoid overfitting problems. As
a sampling-based learning approach, the main difficulty of MCMC method is
that, under some circumstances, direct sampling is not always straightforward.
As widely deployed implementations of MCMC method, Metropolis-Hastings
[15] and Gibbs sampling [16] methods can be introduced to solve this problem
through applying proposal priors and posteriors and sampling one parameter
by giving the others. By combining the advantages of both sampling techniques
together, the Metopolis-Hastings within Gibbs method [13,17] is selected as the
learning algorithm for AGM model.

The rest of this paper is organized as follows. Section 2 illustrates the AGM
model and its Bayesian learning process. Section 3 is devoted to experimental results using both synthetic data and a real application (network intrusion
detection). Finally, Sect. 4 concludes the paper.

2   Bayesian Model

2.1   Asymmetric Gaussian Mixture Model

Assuming that the AGM model has M components then the likelihood function
[8] is defined as follows:

$$p(\mathcal{X}|\Theta) = \prod_{i=1}^{N} \sum_{j=1}^{M} p_j p(X_i|\xi_j) \tag{1}$$

where $\mathcal{X} = (X_1, ..., X_N)$ is the set of N observations, $\Theta = \{p_1, ..., p_M, \xi_1, ..., \xi_M\}$
represents the parameters set, p_j ($0 < p_j \leq 1$ and $\sum_{j=1}^{M} p_j = 1$) is the weight for
each component in the mixture model and ξ_j is the AGD parameters of mixture
component j. Giving $X = (x_1, ..., x_d)$, the probability density function [8] can
be defined as follows:

$$p(X|\xi_j) \propto \prod_{k=1}^{d} \frac{1}{(\sigma_{l_{jk}} + \sigma_{r_{jk}})} \times \begin{cases} \exp\left[-\frac{(x_k - \mu_{jk})^2}{2(\sigma_{l_{jk}})^2}\right] & if\ x_k < \mu_{jk} \\ \exp\left[-\frac{(x_k - \mu_{jk})^2}{2(\sigma_{r_{jk}})^2}\right] & if\ x_k \geq \mu_{jk} \end{cases} \tag{2}$$

where $\xi_j = (\mu_j, \sigma_{lj}, \sigma_{rj})$ is the set of parameters of component j and $\mu_j = (\mu_{j1}, ..., \mu_{jd})$ is the mean, $\sigma_{lj} = (\sigma_{lj1}, ..., \sigma_{ljd})$ and $\sigma_{rj} = (\sigma_{rj1}, ..., \sigma_{rjd})$ are
the left and right standard deviations for AGD. To be more specific, $x_k \sim N(\mu_{jk}, \sigma_{ljk})$ ($x_k < \mu_{jk}$) and $x_k \sim N(\mu_{jk}, \sigma_{rjk})$ ($x_k \geq \mu_{jk}$) for each dimension.

In order to simplify the Bayesian learning process, we introduce a M-dimensional membership vector Z for each observation $X_i, 1 < i < N, Z_i = (Z_{i1}, ..., Z_{iM})$ which indicates to which specific component X_i belongs [6], such that:

$$Z_{ij} = \begin{cases} 1 & \text{if } X_i \text{ belongs to component } j \\ 0 & \text{otherwise} \end{cases} \tag{3}$$

in other words, $Z_{ij} = 1$ only if observation X_i has the highest probability of belonging to component j and accordingly, for other components, $Z_{ij} = 0$.

By combining Eqs. (1) and (3) together we derive the complete likelihood function:

$$p(\mathcal{X}, Z|\Theta) = \prod_{i=1}^{N} \prod_{j=1}^{M} (p_j p(X_i|\xi_j))^{Z_{ij}} \tag{4}$$

2.2   Learning Algorithm

Before describing MH-within-Gibbs learning steps, the priors and posteriors need to be specified. First, we denote the posterior probability of membership vector Z as $\pi(Z|\Theta, \mathcal{X})$ [18]:

$$Z^{(t)} \sim \pi(Z|\Theta^{(t-1)}, \mathcal{X}) \tag{5}$$

the number of observations belonging to a specific component j can be calculated using $Z^{(t)}$ as follows:

$$n_j^{(t)} = \sum_{i=1}^{N} Z_{ij} \ (j = 1, ..., M) \tag{6}$$

thus $n^{(t)} = (n_i^{(t)}, ..., n_M^{(t)})$ represents the number of observations belonging to each mixture component.

Since the mixture weight p_j satisfies the following conditions ($0 < p_j \leq 1$ and $\sum_{j=1}^{M} p_j = 1$), a natural choice of the prior is Dirichlet distribution as follows [19,20]

$$\pi(p_j^{(t)}) \sim \mathcal{D}(\gamma_1, ..., \gamma_M) \tag{7}$$

where γ_j is known hyperparameter. Consequently, the posterior of the mixture weight p_j is:

$$p(p_j^{(t)}|Z^{(t)}) \sim \mathcal{D}(\gamma_1 + n_1^{(t)}, ..., \gamma_M + n_M^{(t)}) \tag{8}$$

Direct sampling of mixture parameters $\xi \sim p(\xi|Z, \mathcal{X})$ could be difficult so Metropolis-Hastings method should be deployed using proposal distributions for

$\xi^{(t)} \sim q(\xi | \xi^{(t-1)})$. To be more specific, for parameters of AGM model which are μ, σ_l and σ_r, we choose proposal distributions as follows:

$$\mu_j^{(t)} \sim \mathcal{N}_d(\mu_j^{(t-1)}, \Sigma) \tag{9}$$

$$\sigma_{lj}^{(t)} \sim \mathcal{N}_d(\sigma_{lj}^{(t-1)}, \Sigma) \tag{10}$$

$$\sigma_{rj}^{(t)} \sim \mathcal{N}_d(\sigma_{rj}^{(t-1)}, \Sigma) \tag{11}$$

the proposal distributions are d-dimensional Gaussian distributions with Σ as $d \times d$ identity matrix which makes the sampling a random walk MCMC process.

As the most important part of Metropolis-Hastings method, at the end of each iteration, for new generated mixture parameter set $\Theta^{(t)}$, an acceptance ratio r needs to be calculated in order to make a decision whether they should be accepted or discarded for the next iteration. The acceptance ratio r is given by:

$$r = \frac{p(\mathcal{X} | \Theta^{(t)}) \pi(\Theta^{(t)}) q(\Theta^{(t-1)} | \Theta^{(t)})}{p(\mathcal{X} | \Theta^{(t-1)}) \pi(\Theta^{(t-1)}) q(\Theta^{(t)} | \Theta^{(t-1)})} \tag{12}$$

where $\pi(\Theta)$ is the proposed prior distribution which can be decomposed to d-dimensional Gaussian distributions such that $\mu \sim \mathcal{N}_d(\eta, \Sigma)$ and $\sigma_l, \sigma_r \sim \mathcal{N}_d(\tau, \Sigma)$ given known hyperparameters η and τ. Since mixture weight p has been computed previously during the Gibbs sampling part, it should not be included in Eq. (12). Further information about the calculation of acceptance ratio r is explained in Appendix A.

Once acceptance ratio r is derived by Eq. (15), we compute acceptance probability $\alpha = min[1, r]$ [21]. Then $u \sim U_{[0,1]}$ is supposed to be generated randomly. If $\alpha < u$, the proposed move should be accepted and parameters should be updated by $p^{(t)}$ and $\xi^{(t)}$ for next iteration. Otherwise, we discard $p^{(t)}$, $\xi^{(t)}$ and set $p^{(t)} = p^{(t-1)}$, $\xi^{(t)} = \xi^{(t-1)}$.

We summarize the MH-within-Gibbs learning process for AGM model in the following steps:

Input: Data observations $\mathcal{X}$ and components number M
Output: AGM mixture parameter set Θ

1. Initialization
2. Step t: For $t = 1, \ldots$
      Gibbs sampling part
   (a) Generate $Z^{(t)}$ from Eq. (5)
   (b) Compute $n_j^{(t)}$ from Eq. (6)
   (c) Generate $p_j^{(t)}$ from Eq. (8)
      Metropolis-Hastings part
   (d) Sample $\xi_j^{(t)}$ ($\mu_j^{(t)}, \sigma_{lj}^{(t)}, \sigma_{rj}^{(t)}$) from Eqs. (9) (10) (11)
   (e) Compute acceptance ratio r from Eq. (15)
   (f) Generate $\alpha = min[1, r]$ and $u \sim U_{[0,1]}$
   (g) If $\alpha \geq u$ then $\xi^{(t)} = \xi^{(t-1)}$

3   Experimental Results

3.1   Design of Experiments

We apply the AGM model to both synthetic data and intrusion detection. For synthetic data validation, testing observations will be generated from AGM with known components number M and experimental results will be evaluated by comparing the estimated and actual mixture parameters. In intrusion detection application, we select NSL-KDD dataset [22] as testing database. K-means algorithm is used for initialization and the results analysis will be based on statistics derived from confusion matrix.

3.2   Synthetic Data

The main goals of this section are feasibility analysis and efficiency evaluation of the AGM learning algorithm. The number of observations is set to 300 grouped into two clusters $(M = 2)$. Hyperparameters are set to $\gamma_j = 1$ [23] for sampling mixture weight p_j from Eq. (8). η and τ are considered as d-dimensional zero vectors in prior distributions of mixture parameter ξ.

Different proposed component numbers $(M' = 1, \ldots, 5)$ are tested during the AGM learning process and the statistics are summarized in Table 1. In order to select the best number of components, we consider marginal likelihood as described in [13]. The probability density functions are plotted for both original and estimated AGM components and the polylines show the trace of accepted moves for each component.

In terms of the best fit result, the accuracy is evaluated by calculating the Euclidean distance between original and estimated mixture parameter sets ξ and $\hat{\xi}$ (Table 2). In summary, the estimation of mean is accurate because the Euclidean distance between μ_j and $\hat{\mu}_j$ is small but the distance between standard deviation σ_{lj}, σ_{rj} and $\hat{\sigma}_{lj}, \hat{\sigma}_{rj}$ is slightly significant. However, this difference has not affected the clustering result.

Table 1. AGM Learning Statistics

Component number M'	Moves accepted	Acceptance ratio	Marginal likelihood
1	22	7.33%	-1596.143
2	11	3.67%	-1500.370
3	14	4.67%	-1684.518
4	63	21.00%	-1522.148
5	39	13.00%	-1517.533

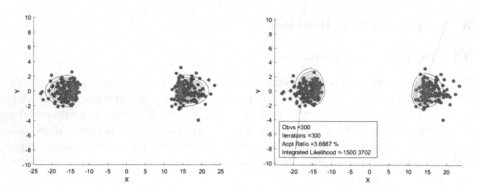

Fig. 1. Original synthetic observations and learning result $(M' = M = 2)$

Table 2. Accuracy analysis $(M' = M = 2)$

Component number $j = 1$	Mean (μ_j)	Left standard deviation (σ_{lj})	Right standard deviation (σ_{rj})
ξ	$[-15.00, 0.00]$	$[10.00, 1.00]$	$[1.00, 1.00]$
$\hat{\xi}$	$[-14.99, 0.25]$	$[4.77, 1.13]$	$[2.31, 1.88]$
Euclidean distance	0.246	5.236	1.581
Component number $j = 2$	Mean (μ_j)	Left standard deviation (σ_{lj})	Right standard deviation (σ_{rj})
ξ	$[15.00, 0.00]$	$[1.00, 1.00]$	$[10.00, 1.00]$
$\hat{\xi}$	$[14.02, -0.24]$	$[2.04, 1.04]$	$[5.70, 1.59]$
Euclidean distance	1.010	1.036	4.338

3.3   Intrusion Detection

Along with the development of information-based industries, network security problems are becoming increasingly important today. In order to address this challenge, many data mining methodologies were proposed including both classification-based [24] and clustering-based [25,26] ones. However, classification-based solutions generally perform ineffectively for dynamic and variate attacking methods because changes of the intrusion patterns cannot be automatically adapted by supervised learning algorithms. Consequently, unsupervised approach such as AGM model is more favorable for modern intrusion-detection.

We select NSL-KDD [22], an improved KDDCUP'99 intrusion-detection data-set, as the testing target since redundant records have been removed from original dataset to avoid potential learning bias. Before applying the testing models onto the dataset, the data pre-processing is needed since discrete enumerated values must be translated to numerical ones and be normalized properly to lead an accurate result. Therefore, we substitute enumerated values with their numbers of occurrences which could reflect the density distribution of discrete values. Having all numerical data in hand, we apply feature scaling method to normalize numerical values between 0 to 1 as follows:

$$x' = \frac{x - min(x)}{max(x) - min(x)} \tag{13}$$

where x and x' denote original and normalized values. In this way we could use unified proposal distribution for every dimension with the same value of hyperparameter Σ during random walk MCMC sampling step (Table 3).

Table 3. Translation and normalization of internet protocols (enumerated values)

Internet protocols	Number of occurrences	Normalized values
ICMP	1655	0
UDP	3011	0.071867
TCP	20526	1

K-means clustering algorithm [27] is chosen for the comparison of accuracy. Testing data records with total amount of 25192 (20% of NSL-KDD dataset) are clustered into two groups with 11743 intrusions and 13449 normal behaviors indicating components number $M' = 2$. In order to better evaluate the pros and cons of models, results derived from Gaussian mixture model (GMM) will also be taken into consideration. The comparison based on confusion matrices resulted from K-means, GMM and AGM model (Table 4) reveals the fact that based on a less accurate initialization given by K-means (60.85%), GMM performs almost the same way as K-means and the difference between these two models is trivial. In contrast, AGM model makes a significant improvement with much higher accuracy rate (80.47%) and precision percentage (96.86%), while much lower false positive rate (4.26%) illustrating AGM model is capable of effectively detecting intrusions from background noises. Compared with K-means and GMM, AGM model has a higher false negative rate (28.58%) which means it tends to strictly identify normal behaviors as intrusions which could be mitigated by reducing dimensions of dataset using feature selection methodologies.

Table 4. Confusion matrices and statistics of K-means, GMM and AGM models

K-means	NF [a]	F [b]	GMM	NF	F	AGM	NF	F
NF	2445	9298	NF	2464	9279	NF	11484	259
F	565	12884	F	584	12865	F	5621	7828

	K-means	GMM	AGM
Accuracy	60.85%	60.85%	76.66%
Precision	20.82%	20.98%	97.79%
False Positive Rate	41.92%	41.90%	3.20%
False Negative Rate	18.77%	19.16%	32.86%

[a]Non fault-prone, [b]Fault-prone.

4   Conclusion and Future Work

This paper illustrated a new intrusion detection approach by applying asymmetric Gaussian mixtures with a fully Bayesian learning process which is achieved by applying a hybrid sampling-based MH-within-Gibbs learning algorithm. According to the experiment results, the AGM model is proved as an effective approach for clustering. In spite of the advantages of AGM we mentioned above, some improvements are still needed to promote the accuracy and flexibility and mitigate the drawbacks. Therefore, we plan to extend the Bayesian learning process and introduce model selection and feature selection methodologies to improve the performance in the case of high-dimensional datasets. The proposed work could be applied to other applications such as content-based images summarization [28], retrieval [29], and suggestion [30].

Acknowledgment. The completion of this research work was made possible thanks to Concordia University via a Concordia University Research Chair Tier II.

Appendix A

A.1 Derivation of Acceptance Ratio r by Eq. (12)

The derivation of acceptance ratio r is based on the assumption that mixture parameters are independent from each other which means that:

$$
\begin{aligned}
\pi(\Theta) &= \pi(p, \xi) = \pi(\xi) \\
&= \prod_{j=1}^{M} \pi(\mu_j)\pi(\sigma_{lj})\pi(\sigma_{rj}) \\
&= \prod_{j=1}^{M} \mathcal{N}_d(\mu_j|\eta, \Sigma)\mathcal{N}_d(\sigma_{lj}|\tau, \Sigma)\mathcal{N}_d(\sigma_{rj}|\tau, \Sigma)
\end{aligned}
\tag{14}
$$

in Eq. (14), since the mixture weigh p is generated following Gibbs sampling method whose acceptance ratio is always 1, it should be excluded from Metropolis-Hastings estimation step. Accordingly, apply the same rule to the proposal distribution as well:

$$
\begin{aligned}
q(\Theta^{(t)}|\Theta^{(t-1)}) &= q(\xi^{(t)}|\xi^{(t-1)}) \\
&= \prod_{j=1}^{M} \mathcal{N}_d(\mu_j^{(t)}|\mu_j^{(t-1)}, \Sigma)\mathcal{N}_d(\sigma_{lj}^{(t)}|\sigma_{lj}^{(t-1)}, \Sigma)\mathcal{N}_d(\sigma_{rj}^{(t)}|\sigma_{rj}^{(t-1)}, \Sigma)
\end{aligned}
\tag{15}
$$

by combining Eqs. (2), (4), (9), (10), (11), (14) and (15), Eq. (12) can be written as follows:

$$
\begin{aligned}
r &= \frac{p(\mathcal{X}|\Theta^{(t)})\pi(\Theta^{(t)})q(\Theta^{(t-1)}|\Theta^{(t)})}{p(\mathcal{X}|\Theta^{(t-1)})\pi(\Theta^{(t-1)})q(\Theta^{(t)}|\Theta^{(t-1)})} \\
&= \prod_{i=i}^{N}\prod_{j=1}^{M}\left(\frac{p(X_i|\mu_j^{(t)},\sigma_{lj}^{(t)},\sigma_{rj}^{(t)})}{p(X_i|\mu_j^{(t-1)},\sigma_{lj}^{(t-1)},\sigma_{rj}^{(t-1)})}\right) \\
&\times \frac{\mathcal{N}_d(\mu_j^{(t)}|\eta,\Sigma)\mathcal{N}_d(\sigma_{lj}^{(t)}|\tau,\Sigma)\mathcal{N}_d(\sigma_{rj}^{(t)}|\tau,\Sigma)}{\mathcal{N}_d(\mu_j^{(t-1)}|\eta,\Sigma)\mathcal{N}_d(\sigma_{lj}^{(t-1)}|\tau,\Sigma)\mathcal{N}_d(\sigma_{rj}^{(t-1)}|\tau,\Sigma)} \\
&\times \frac{\mathcal{N}_d(\mu_j^{(t-1)}|\mu_j^{(t)},\Sigma)\mathcal{N}_d(\sigma_{lj}^{(t-1)}|\sigma_{lj}^{(t)},\Sigma)\mathcal{N}_d(\sigma_{rj}^{(t-1)}|\sigma_{rj}^{(t)},\Sigma)}{\mathcal{N}_d(\mu_j^{(t)}|\mu_j^{(t-1)},\Sigma)\mathcal{N}_d(\sigma_{lj}^{(t)}|\sigma_{lj}^{(t-1)},\Sigma)\mathcal{N}_d(\sigma_{rj}^{(t)}|\sigma_{rj}^{(t-1)},\Sigma)}
\end{aligned}
\tag{16}
$$

References

1. Bouguila, N., Ziou, D.: MML-based approach for finite dirichlet mixture estimation and selection. In: Perner, P., Imiya, A. (eds.) MLDM 2005. LNCS (LNAI), vol. 3587, pp. 42–51. Springer, Heidelberg (2005). https://doi.org/10.1007/11510888_5
2. Bouguila, N., Ziou, D., Hammoud, R.I.: A Bayesian non-Gaussian mixture analysis: application to eye modeling. In: IEEE Computer Society Conference on Computer Vision and Pattern Recognition (CVPR 2007), 18–23 June 2007, Minneapolis, Minnesota, USA (2007)
3. Sefidpour, A., Bouguila, N.: Spatial color image segmentation based on finite non-Gaussian mixture models. Expert Syst. Appl. **39**(10), 8993–9001 (2012)
4. Bouguila, N., Amayri, O.: A discrete mixture-based kernel for SVMs: application to spam and image categorization. Inf. Process. Manag. **45**(6), 631–642 (2009)
5. McLachlan, G.J., Peel, D.: Finite Mixture Models. Wiley, Hoboken (2000)
6. Bouguila, N., Ziou, D., Monga, E.: Practical Bayesian estimation of a finite beta mixture through Gibbs sampling and its applications. Stat. Comput. **16**(2), 215–225 (2006)
7. Elguebaly, T., Bouguila, N.: Bayesian learning of generalized Gaussian mixture models on biomedical images. In: Schwenker, F., El Gayar, N. (eds.) ANNPR 2010. LNCS (LNAI), vol. 5998, pp. 207–218. Springer, Heidelberg (2010). https://doi.org/10.1007/978-3-642-12159-3_19
8. Elguebaly, T., Bouguila, N.: Background subtraction using finite mixtures of asymmetric Gaussian distributions and shadow detection. Mach. Vis. Appl. **25**(5), 1145–1162 (2014)
9. Bouguila, N., Almakadmeh, K., Boutemedjet, S.: A finite mixture model for simultaneous high-dimensional clustering, localized feature selection and outlier rejection. Expert Syst. Appl. **39**(7), 6641–6656 (2012)
10. Boutemedjet, S., Ziou, D., Bouguila, N.: Model-based subspace clustering of non-Gaussian data. Neurocomputing **73**(10–12), 1730–1739 (2010)
11. Dempster, A.P., Laird, N.M., Rubin, D.B.: Maximum likelihood from incomplete data via the EM algorithm. J. R. Stat. Soc. Ser. B (Methodol.) **39**(1), 1–38 (1977)
12. Bouguila, N., Ziou, D.: On fitting finite Dirichlet mixture using ECM and MML. In: Singh, S., Singh, M., Apte, C., Perner, P. (eds.) ICAPR 2005. LNCS, vol. 3686, pp. 172–182. Springer, Heidelberg (2005). https://doi.org/10.1007/11551188_19

13. Bouguila, N., Ziou, D., Hammoud, R.I.: On Bayesian analysis of a finite generalized Dirichlet mixture via a metropolis-within-Gibbs sampling. Pattern Anal. Appl. **12**(2), 151–166 (2009)
14. Bouguila, N., Elguebaly, T.: A fully Bayesian model based on reversible jump MCMC and finite beta mixtures for clustering. Expert Syst. Appl. **39**(5), 5946–5959 (2012)
15. Hastings, W.K.: Monte Carlo sampling methods using Markov chains and their applications. Biometrika **57**(1), 97–109 (1970)
16. Bouguila, N.: Bayesian hybrid generative discriminative learning based on finite Liouville mixture models. Pattern Recogn. **44**(6), 1183–1200 (2011)
17. Bourouis, S., Mashrgy, M.A., Bouguila, N.: Bayesian learning of finite generalized inverted Dirichlet mixtures: application to object classification and forgery detection. Expert Syst. Appl. **41**(5), 2329–2336 (2014)
18. Elguebaly, T., Bouguila, N.: Bayesian learning of finite generalized Gaussian mixture models on images. Sig. Process. **91**(4), 801–820 (2011)
19. Bouguila, N., Ziou, D.: A powreful finite mixture model based on the generalized Dirichlet distribution: unsupervised learning and applications. In: 17th International Conference on Pattern Recognition, ICPR 2004, Cambridge, UK, 23–26 August 2004, pp. 280–283. IEEE Computer Society (2004)
20. Bouguila, N., Ziou, D.: Dirichlet-based probability model applied to human skin detection [image skin detection]. In: 2004 IEEE International Conference on Acoustics, Speech, and Signal Processing, ICASSP 2004, 17–21 May 2004, Montreal, Quebec, Canada, pp. 521–524. IEEE (2004)
21. Luengo, D., Martino, L.: Fully adaptive Gaussian mixture metropolis-hastings algorithm. In: IEEE International Conference on Acoustics, Speech and Signal Processing, ICASSP 2013, 26–31 May 2013, Vancouver, BC, Canada, pp. 6148–6152. IEEE (2013)
22. Tavallaee, M., Bagheri, E., Lu, W., Ghorbani, A.A.: A detailed analysis of the KDD CUP 99 data set. In: IEEE Symposium on Computational Intelligence for Security and Defense Applications, CISDA 2009, 8–10 July 2009, Ottawa, Canada, pp. 1–6. IEEE (2009)
23. Stephens, M.: Bayesian analysis of mixture models with an unknown number of components - an alternative to reversible jump methods. Ann. Stat. 40–74 (2000)
24. Puttini, R.S., Marrakchi, Z., Mé, L.: A Bayesian classification model for real-time intrusion detection. In: AIP Conference Proceedings, vol. 659, pp. 150–162 (2003)
25. Zhong, S., Khoshgoftaar, T.M., Seliya, N.: Clustering-based network intrusion detection. Int. J. Reliab. Qual. Saf. Eng. **14**(02), 169–187 (2007)
26. Fan, W., Bouguila, N., Ziou, D.: Unsupervised anomaly intrusion detection via localized Bayesian feature selection. In: Cook, D.J., Pei, J., Wang, W., Zaïane, O.R., Wu, X. eds.: 11th IEEE International Conference on Data Mining, ICDM 2011, 11–14 December, Vancouver, BC, Canada, pp. 1032–1037. IEEE Computer Society (2011)
27. Hartigan, J.A., Wong, M.A.: Algorithm as 136: a k-means clustering algorithm. J. Roy. Stat. Soc. Ser. C (Appl. Stat.) **28**(1), 100–108 (1979)
28. Bouguila, N.: Spatial color image databases summarization. In: Proceedings of the IEEE International Conference on Acoustics, Speech, and Signal Processing, ICASSP 2007, 15–20 April 2007, Honolulu, Hawaii, USA, pp. 953–956. IEEE (2007)

29. Bouguila, N., Ziou, D.: Improving content based image retrieval systems using finite multinomial Dirichlet mixture. In: Proceedings of the 2004 14th IEEE Signal Processing Society Workshop Machine Learning for Signal Processing, pp. 23–32. IEEE (2004)
30. Boutemedjet, S., Ziou, D., Bouguila, N.: Unsupervised feature selection for accurate recommendation of high-dimensional image data. In: Platt, J.C., Koller, D., Singer, Y., Roweis, S.T. (eds.) Advances in Neural Information Processing Systems 20, Proceedings of the Twenty-First Annual Conference on Neural Information Processing Systems, 3–6 December 2007, Vancouver, British Columbia, Canada, pp. 177–184. Curran Associates, Inc. (2007)

Multiple Water-Level Seawater Temperature Prediction Method for Marine Aquaculture

Takanobu Otsuka[1]([⊠]), Yuji Kitazawa[2], and Takayuki Ito[1]

[1] Nagoya Institute of Technology, Nagoya, Japan
otsuka.takanobu@nitech.ac.jp
[2] Nichiyu Giken Kogyo Co. Ltd., Tokyo, Japan

Abstract. The importance of aquaculture continues to grow due to the decrease in natural marine resources and an increase in worldwide demand. To avoid losses from aging and abnormal weather, we must predict multiple water levels of seawater temperature to maintain a more stable supply of marine resources, particularly for high-value added products, such as pearls and scallops. In this paper, we propose an algorithm that estimates seawater temperature in marine aquaculture by combining seawater temperature data and actual weather data.

1 Introduction

In discussions of aquaculture, understanding its environment is critical. Unlike wild fish and shellfish, farmed fish and shellfish in an aquaculture environment are restricted by tanks and rafts and cannot swim freely. As a result, fish and shellfish in restricted fishing grounds are threatened when fluctuations in red tides and seawater temperatures occur. In this paper, we propose an algorithm that predicts seawater temperature in a marine aquaculture field by combining sea temperature data and actual weather data.

The second section of this paper demonstrates the importance of water temperature management in pearl farming and the problems resolved by this research. In Sect. 3, we describe our proposed prediction algorithm. The results of our evaluation experiments are explained in Sect. 4, Sect. 5 introduces previous research. And, finally, we summarize this paper in Sect. 6 and describe our future work.

2 Issues and Current Status of Pearl Farming

Pearls have been valued worldwide for centuries and their use in jewelry dates back to the early 2nd century BC [Yamada 1980]. Prior to the establishment of pearl culture technology, only a few pearls were produced out of 10,000 natural shells, and such scarcity greatly contributed to their value. In 1893 (Meiji 26), pearls were first artificially cultivated in Aki Bay in Mie Prefecture, and in the

© Springer International Publishing AG, part of Springer Nature 2018
M. Mouhoub et al. (Eds.): IEA/AIE 2018, LNAI 10868, pp. 366–371, 2018.
https://doi.org/10.1007/978-3-319-92058-0_35

1920s, the development of artificial cultured pearls stabilized and began to be supplied around the world.

Seawater temperature collection and prediction are widely performed, but seawater temperature measurement using satellites for remote sensing can only obtain the temperatures a few millimeters below the surface [Lobitz 2000]. Another service's [HYCOM 2016] model predicts seawater temperature on a global scale by integrating ocean currents and meteorological data. However, both methods only target seawater temperatures at the surface, but water temperatures between 2 to 10 meters is important for seafood cultivation for both fish and shellfish. Such shellfish as pearls, scallops, and shellfish are farmed in nets. To install nets vertically, the water temperature at each level between 2–10 m must be collected and predicted.

3   Seawater Temperature Prediction Using Actual Data

3.1   Seawater Temperature Prediction Algorithm

In this section, we describe our random forest algorithm that we use for seawater temperature predictions. Random forest is a machine learning method that can efficiently learn decision trees created in large quantities by exploiting randomness. When compared with a representative supervised learning Support Vector Machine (SVM), random forest gives more importance to feature quantity that can be calculated by learning, resulting in less overlearning [Breiman 2007]. In addition, we collected data from the Ise Bay meteorological observatory nearest Ago Bay, which is the observation point for 2007 to 2017 [JMA2 2017], from a database provided by the meteorological agency. We conducted multiple regression analysis by random forest at each of the following locations and constructed and tested our prediction model.

A satellite photograph of the actual data acquisition site is shown in Fig. 1.

In this study, we model the seawater temperature changes at each point by the temperature and wind speed data as a weather condition and construct a water temperature prediction algorithm.

3.2   Data Prediction Flow

We constructed our prediction model based on the actual data of each site. Random forest was used for the prediction algorithm and modeling. All calculations were done on Python, and direct access to the server's database was possible. We constructed this prediction model to use large-scale data. After modeling each point, we input each day's weather forecast after it was announced by the Japan Meteorological Agency (JMA) at 15:00. In other words, by inputting the forecast values of hourly temperatures and wind speeds from the meteorological forecast data provided by JMA, we can predict seawater temperatures at depths of 0.5, 2, 5, and 8 m at each site in one-hour units. The data prediction flow is shown in Fig. 2.

We describe the prediction results of the actual prediction model in the next section.

Fig. 1. Overview of data collection location

4 Experimental Result

The differences in the amount of data reflect the maintenance and the loss of land data erased by typhoons. We describe our preliminary verification for verifying the depth, the model size, and the prediction accuracy of the decision tree in the random forest method in the next section.

In this section, we describe the prediction results using actual data. For prediction accuracy verification, we used the forecast data released by the JMA in Ise city as the input to the prediction model for each site using the data listed below. JMA's forecast data are announced at 15:00 every day and include the forecast value of the temperature and wind speed at every hour from 0:00 to 23:00 on the following day. By inputting the forecast data into the prediction model for each location, we can obtain the forecast data of water temperatures at depths of 0.5, 2, 5, and 8 m every hour from 0:00 to 23:00 on the following day and compare them with the actual measured value of the water temperature at each depth of each site during the same period. The missing data in each data string are complemented by generating an intermediate data value before and after the time series. We set the maximum depth of the random forest decision tree in this accuracy verification to 30 based on the findings obtained in the preliminary verification in the previous section. The data sequence used to verify the accuracy prediction is shown below.

Data string used for prediction accuracy verification

– Meteorological measured data of South Ise meteorological observatory (temperature, wind speed per hour) from 01/05/2016 to 01/05/2017: 8,688 cases;

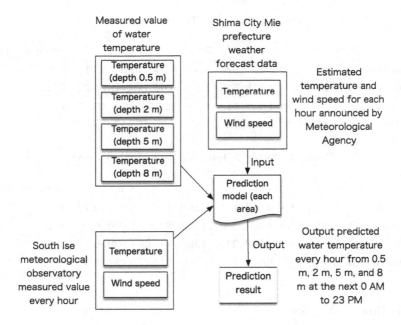

Fig. 2. Data prediction flow

- Actual water temperature measurement in Gokasho Bay (every hour): 8,751 cases;
- Actual water temperature measurement in Matoya Bay (every hour): 8,748 cases;
- Actual water temperature measurement in the inner front of Ago Bay (every hour): 8,751 cases;
- Actual water temperature measurement for the center of Ago Bay (every hour): 8,710 cases.

We made our predictions in two steps to show which parameters are most effective for prediction. Prediction 1 was made using only the water temperature and the weather data, and prediction 2 was made by learning with the temperature and wind speed for all of the water temperature and meteorological data. The prediction 1 result is shown in Table 1, and the prediction 2 result is shown in Table 2. Regarding the error in the prediction result, we compared the predicted value of the water temperature at each water depth/point for January 6, 2016 to January 7, 2017 output by the prediction model with the actual measured value at each point. We averaged the differences after comparing them. The maximum error is the one with the largest error during the comparison.

Numerical values after the comma at each water temperature indicate the maximum error at each depth. The maximum error at each point is also shown in the table.

Table 1. Result 1: Temperature only

Area	0.5 m	2 m	5 m	8 m	Maximum error
Gokasho	1.175, 7.10	1.113, 6.46	1.083, 6.25	1.095, 6.14	6.46
Matoya	1.157, 6.10	1.171, 5.68	1.158, 6.62	1.141, 7.37	7.37
Inner of Ago	1.121, 11.9	1.188, 11.6	1.136, 12.24	1.079, 10.47	12.24
Center of Ago	1.157, 6.39	1.109, 7.01	1.070, 6.25	0.969, 5.68	7.01

Table 2. Result 2: Temperature and wind speed

Area	0.5 m	2 m	5 m	8 m	Maximum error
Gokasho	1.008, 5.99	0.978, 6.06	0.951, 5.46	0.971, 6.49	6.49
Matoya	1.029, 5.60	1.051, 5.76	1.042, 5.80	1.030, 6.16	6.16
Inner of Ago	1.042, 12.9	1.060, 11.6	1.006, 11.76	1.030, 6.16	12.91
Center of Ago	0.994, 6.56	0.971, 6.52	0.938, 6.32	0.853, 5.57	6.57

5   Related Works

Modeling and forecasting tidal currents and seawater temperatures have long been conducted in oceanography [Kumar 1981]. Recently, in addition to aircraft, marine environmental information is obtained and predicted based on various sensors mounted on artificial satellites. Research that predicts atmospheric and oceanic conditions using a relatively small 2- to 20-km mesh range [Hodur 1997] has improved the sensing accuracy of sea surface temperatures using infrared and microwave sensors mounted on artificial satellites [Lobitz 2000]. Particularly in the summer and winter, the sea surface temperature is often approximated to the atmospheric temperature due to the influence of solar radiation and temperature change, but these factors have less impact on the middle sea water temperature. Therefore, we must forecast not only sea surface temperatures by remote sensing but also the seawater temperatures of the water depth that is actually used for farming.

6   Conclusion

We proposed an algorithm that predicts seawater temperature at the water depths used for aquaculture. Such prediction of the water depths that are actually used for farming (as proposed in this research) has not been previously carried out, despite its importance for successful aquaculture. We proposed an algorithm using a prediction model based on both actual weather data and seawater temperature data with a high prediction accuracy of about 1°C. We will continue our research by reducing outliers and coping with overlearning and long-term seawater temperature prediction on a monthly basis. Future work will support seawater temperature and chlorophyll a and salinity concentrations to further promote sustainable aquaculture.

Acknowledgment. The part of this research was supported by collaborative with Nichiyu Giken Kogyo Co., Ltd.

References

[HYCOM 2016] Chassignet, E.P., Hurlburt, H.E., Smedstad, O.M., Halliwell, G.R., Hogan, P.J., Wallcraft, A.J., Bleck, R.: Ocean prediction with the hybrid coordinate ocean model (HYCOM). In: Chassignet, E.P., Verron, J. (eds.) Ocean Weather Forecasting, pp. 413–426. Springer, Netherlands (2006). https://doi.org/10.1007/1-4020-4028-8_16

[Shriver 2007] Shriver, J.F., et al.: 1/32° real-time global ocean prediction and value-added over 1/16° resolution. J. Mar. Syst. **65**(1), 3–26 (2007)

[Hodur 1997] Hodur, R.M.: The Naval Research Laboratory's coupled ocean/atmosphere mesoscale prediction system (COAMPS). Monthly Weather Rev. **125**(7), 1414–1430 (1997)

[Breiman 2007] Breiman, L.: Random forests. Mach. Learn. **45**(1), 5–32 (2007)

[tenki.jp 2017] tenki.jp: Weather Data. http://www.tenki.jp/past/2016/12/26/. Accessed 26 Dec 2016

[JMA1 2017] Japan Meterological Agency: Result of accuracy verification of weather forecast. http://www.data.jma.go.jp/fcd/yoho/kensho/yohohyoka_top.html

[Lobitz 2000] Lobitz, B., et al.: Climate and infectious disease: use of remote sensing for detection of Vibrio cholerae by indirect measurement. Proc. Nat. Acad. Sci. **97**(4), 1438–1443 (2000)

[Cox 1995] Cox, C.: Some problems in optical oceanography. J. Mar. Res. **14**, 63–78 (1955)

[Hosoda 2011] Hosoda, K., Kawamura, H., Lan, K.-W, Shimada, T., Futoki, S.: Temporal scale of sea surface temperature fronts revealed by microwave observations. IEEE Geosci. Rem. Sens. **9** (2011)

[FPO 2017] Tategami area pearl farming reconstruction project, NPO corporation fishery industry, fishing village activation promotion organization. http://www.fpo.jf-net.ne.jp/. 04/02/3027

[Yamada 1980] Yamada, A.: World History of Pearls. ISBN 978-4-12-102229-5

[LAW 2016] Act on promotion of pearl (Act No. 74 of June 7, 2016): Japan Law database. http://law.e-gov.go.jp/htmldata/H28/H28HO074.html

[MIE1 2017] Fishing season situation: Mie Prefectural Fisheries Research Institute. http://www.pref.mie.lg.jp/suigi/hp/000200511.htm

[MIE2 2017] Mie Prefecture pearl farming related fishing ground water temperature monitoring system: Mie Prefecture Pearl Farming Liaison Council. http://www.ohyamanet.info/m-shinkyo/index.php

[JMA2 2017] Japan Meteorological Agency: Past weather data search. http://www.data.jma.go.jp/obd/stats/etrn/index.html

[Kumar 1981] Kumar, M., Monteith, J.L.: Remote sensing of crop growth. In: Smith, H. (ed.) Plants and the Daylight Spectrum, pp. 133–144. Academic Press, London (1981)

Substation Signal Matching
with a Bagged Token Classifier

Qin Wang[1], Sandro Schönborn[2]([✉]), Yvonne-Anne Pignolet[2], Theo Widmer[3],
and Carsten Franke[2]

[1] ETH Zürich, Zürich, Switzerland
qwang@student.ethz.ch
[2] ABB Corporate Research, Baden, Switzerland
{sandro.schoenborn,yvonne-anne.pignolet,carsten.franke}@ch.abb.com
[3] ABB Power Grid - Grid Automation, Baden, Switzerland
theo.widmer@ch.abb.com

Abstract. Currently, engineers at substation service providers match customer data with the corresponding internally used signal names manually. This paper proposes a machine learning method to automate this process based on substation signal mapping data from a repository of executed projects. To this end, a bagged token classifier is proposed, letting words (tokens) in the customer signal name vote for provider signal names. In our evaluation, the proposed method exhibits better performance in terms of both accuracy and efficiency over standard classifiers.

1 Introduction

Matching utility customer-specified signal names for protection, control and monitoring functions with signal names used by a system provider is a common task in substation automation engineering. To ensure consistency, the system providers maintain an internal library that contains the names to be used for function signals for all projects. This helps the system provider to standardize and streamline its processes and ensures that signal names of important substation automation functions are used in the same manner. On the other hand, the naming schemes used by customers usually differ, both among different customers and compared to provider libraries. Consequently, when starting to work on a new substation automation project, an engineer at the system provider must assign the correct library signal names to customer signal names, a cumbersome, error-prone, and time-consuming process. The matching quality is extremely important to ensure the substation automation systems can work correctly and fits in the customer's environment once deployed and the customer's tools can interoperate with it seamlessly. Hence, in current practice this task is typically carried out by experienced engineers.

© Springer International Publishing AG, part of Springer Nature 2018
M. Mouhoub et al. (Eds.): IEA/AIE 2018, LNAI 10868, pp. 372–380, 2018.
https://doi.org/10.1007/978-3-319-92058-0_36

The objective of our paper is to find a way to automate this process and thus to improve the engineers' efficiency. More precisely, we present how we devised and evaluated a machine learning-based system that suggest matching library signal names for customer-specified signal names. The system extracts its internal knowledge from past projects that were carried out with a manual signal name assignment. In other words, a repository of past projects is used to build training and testing data sets for our system. Signal name matching is difficult as customer signal names can be arbitrary and typically contain abbreviations, ambiguity and misspellings. Different naming schemes for lines, e.g., L1, L2, L3 or R, Y, B are both used. In contrast, the provider library consists of a restricted set of known unique and clean signal names. In past project data, the engineers that carried out the matching sometimes made mistakes or ignored the library signal names, in other words the learning data is noisy.

Formal Problem Definition: Since the signal names in the provider library are fixed, this matching problem can be modeled as a text classification task predicting library signal names for customer signal names. Thus, each possible provider signal forms its own class and the problem is an instance of multi-class classification. In our case, we use 3745 possible classes in the provider signal library. The formal task is to *predict* the correct signal class c for a given customer input name $\tilde{x}$, encoded as a string. A model for the prediction is learned from past project data. To support the engineer with multiple possibilities to choose from, the system is to suggest k candidates of matching provider names $c_1, c_2, \ldots, c_k$, sorted by their relevance.

We do not expect the various substation setups to adhere to similar structures and thus consider each name individually. By choosing simple text classification, solely based on customer signal name, we neither require textual similarity between customer and library names nor a common structure among signal names.

Data Set: The data set that is used for this work consists of totally 8969 unique pairs of customer signal names with corresponding provider signal names from 170 past projects. Projects have a varying degree of similarity. The overlap across customer signal names is rather low between different projects, indicating the need to standardize names using library signal names.

Method: We propose to use an efficient and accurate token dictionary as a name classifier. In the token dictionary, each word of the customer signal name can vote for possible library names. It is similar to a Naïve Bayes classifier but aggregates and normalizes votes differently. We also explore and adapt a range of existing text classification methods and compare their classification performance as well as their computational efficiency. For this evaluation, we consider standard text classification methods, such as Naïve Bayes, Random Forest and Support Vector Machine and additionally construct a sequence-aware recurrent neural network.

A full version of this paper can be found on https://arxiv.org/abs/1802.04734.

2 System Overview

We setup and evaluate a machine learning pipeline with different classification algorithms to identify library signals from input customer signal names. The pipeline consists of methods for data pre-processing, classification and post-processing. Pre-processing prepares the raw input so it can be processed by the classification algorithms applied afterwards. In particular, they require tokenized text or numerical vectors as input. In post-processing, we ensure constraints, such as respecting known antonyms in the final signal name, are satisfied.

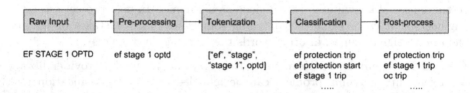

| Raw Input | Pre-processing | Tokenization | Classification | Post-process |

| EF STAGE 1 OPTD | ef stage 1 optd | ["ef", "stage", "stage 1", optd] | ef protection trip
ef protection start
ef stage 1 trip
..... | ef protection trip
ef stage 1 trip
oc trip
..... |

Fig. 1. Proposed pipeline to identify library signals from input customer signal names

Pre-processing. Pre-processing consists of normalization, data cleaning and tokenization. Data cleaning is mainly relevant to build a good training set while normalization and tokenization are always applied, also in test scenarios.

Normalization: Signal names are normalized to lower case. This avoids mismatches due to different capitalization methods.

Cleaning: Signal name pairs where the provider name does not occur in the library are removed. These cases exist because either special naming schemes were required by the customer, or the project was implemented before the library was created. Furthermore, we remove all examples that have identical customer and internal signal name. Theses examples can easily be recognized and predicted, and are thus not our main interest and would not help to discriminate between different methods in the evaluation. After all the normalization and cleaning steps, we have a dataset appropriate for learning and testing.

Tokenization: Most classification methods rely on tokens extracted from signal names. A token is typically a single word in a multi-word signal name. We split between words using a set of separator characters, except numbers nouns. In this case, we tokenize Noun N into Noun and Noun N to capture the context of the number. Empty tokens are discarded. Customer signal names are represented as vectors of token counts, similar to the bag-of-words model [1].

Classification. Classification algorithms take the tokenized signal as an input and identify the best matching library signal classes. We evaluate Naïve Bayes, Random Forest, and linear Support Vector Machines (SVM). Furthermore, we present a Neural Network approach and devise a token dictionary algorithm, which turns out to be well suited for this problem in terms of performance and hardware demands. A basic lookup table serves as a comparison baseline.

Post-processing. For substation signal mapping, there are antonym token pairs that should not appear simultaneously on customer and internal signal names. For example, if "underfreq" is a token in the customer signal name, then the prediction should never contain "overfreq". In addition, there are also keywords which must appear on both customer and internal sides. For example, if "interlocked" is a token in the customer signal name, then the prediction should also contain this key token. In order to make our predictions more accurate, a post-processing pipeline is implemented to penalize predictions which contain an antonymous token and reward those with the same keywords as customer signal. This processing step basically reorders our list of predictions to make sure that better predictions are shown on top.

3   Classification Methods

In this section we present the core classification methods we evaluate later. We implement them using the Scikit-Learn [2] and Tensorflow [3] libraries.

Standard Classification Methods
Lookup Table: We use a simple lookup table as our baseline. For each customer signal in the training set, we maintain a list of corresponding library signals. The list is sorted by appearance frequency in the training set. Given a test customer signal, the table returns a sorted list of up to k library signals.

Naïve Bayes: This method assumes conditional independence among multinomial token occurrence probabilities for each class. Despite the simplifying assumption, it often performs well, even with small training sets. The resulting model typically provides fast classification with a moderate memory footprint.

Random Forest: Random forests are ensemble learning methods that counteract single decision tree's shortcomings by taking many trees into account [4]. Contrary to Naïve Bayes classifiers, they can also represent (non-sequential) dependencies among tokens. Random Forests are efficient to train and classify but can require a lot of memory to store all the trees.

Support Vector Machine: Most text classification problems are linearly separable [5] and Random forests are not optimal for very high dimensional sparse feature vectors. Hence linear Support Vector Machine (SVM) classifiers that maximize error margins are widely used for text classification. SVM training is typically memory-inefficient for large datasets and sparse features. We thus resort to the stochastic linear Hinge loss SVM described in [6] to reduce computation time and memory footprint. Splitting part of the training set for probability calibration enables us to suggest k candidate signal names.

Recurrent Neural Network
All methods based on bag-of-words tokens ignore the order of words in a signal name. To capture the sequence of tokens in a signal name, we implement a recurrent neural network of the LSTM-type to classify a sequence of "GloVe" [9] embedding vectors of individual tokens.

Such a setup has been successfully applied to large text classification problems but requires a lot of resources [8].

Vectorization and Embedding: Unlike the above models that use bag-of-word counts as input features, we use pre-trained GloVe word embeddings.

Classification Network: Bidirectional Long Short-Term Memory (BLSTM) networks have been shown to outperform unidirectional LSTMs, standard Recurrent

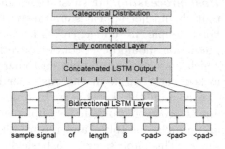

Fig. 2. BLSTM signal classification.

Neural networks, and Multilayer Perceptrons on text tasks due to their stronger ability to capture contextual information [10]. In our model, one BLSTM layer processes the sequence of token vectors as input and generates output vectors. In the cell, we use the standard sigmoid activation function. All output vectors are concatenated and fed to a fully connected classification layer with a softmax output providing the predicted class probabilities.

Optimization. We train the network by minimizing the cross-entropy loss of softmax logits using the Adam Optimizer [11] and a learning rate of 10^{-3}.

Token Dictionary

A lookup of the complete signal name, as with the lookup table, is too specific and does not generalize well. But typical customer names still contain specific words which indicate the appropriate library name, almost like keywords. We thus introduce a token dictionary which looks up each token individually and lets it vote for library names it appeared with in the past. Voting allows for ambiguity where the same keyword appears in many classes. Each token votes for all possible hypotheses that could have generated it.

The test signal $\tilde{x}$, to be classified, is treated as a set of its N tokens $\tilde{x} = [t_1, t_2, \ldots, t_N]$. Each token t_i votes for all classes according to the frequency of co-occurrence. The vote of a token t_i for class c is its number of occurrences in examples for said class $n(t_i, c)$. The weight of a vote for class c given token t_i is computed from $n(t_i, c)$, the frequency the token appeared in samples of class c.

$$v(c \mid t_i) = \frac{n(t_i, c)}{\sum_{c'} n(t_i, c')} = \frac{n(t_i, c)}{n(t_i)}. \tag{1}$$

By normalization, the total vote of a single token is split among all possible classes. Common tokens will only contribute weak votes compared to more discriminative tokens. This effect is similar to the one achieved by inverse document frequency normalization. All token votes are summed to form the total vote for for the complete customer name.

$$v(c \mid \tilde{x}) = \sum_{i=1}^{N} v(c \mid t_i). \tag{2}$$

The normalized votes form a probability distribution over all possible K classes.

$$P(c \mid \tilde{x}) = \frac{v(c \mid \tilde{x})}{\sum_{c'=1}^{K} v(c' \mid \tilde{x})}. \tag{3}$$

Formally, such a classifier is a bagged collection of discriminative, weak, single-token classifiers. The token dictionary classifier works as a bag-of-words model. The resulting vote aggregation adds individual contributions and is thus different from multiplying token likelihoods $P(t_i \mid c)$ in the Naïve Bayes classifier. Also, consider the different normalization of token likelihoods and single-token posterior (3). Aggregation of additive votes typically leads to broader prediction distributions than in the Naïve Bayes case. Also, adding votes ensures that a single token can "activate" a library name while all other typical words are absent. To ensure such behavior, the Naïve Bayes method needs explicit prior initialization, e.g. with Laplace smoothing [7].

By choosing the top k classes with maximal $P(c \mid \tilde{x})$, the algorithm can be easily extended for multiple predictions. It is based on standard Python hashtables, uses little memory and is extremely fast at learning and predicting.

4   Evaluation

All evaluation experiments are run on a workstation with a 4.4.0 Linux kernel, an Intel(R) Core(TM) i5-4570 CPU @ 3.20 GHz processor (four cores), and 8 GB of RAM memory. Scikit-learn and Tensorflow are the main libraries we used. For the comparison, results of Lookup Table, Naïve Bayes, Random Forest, SVM, LSTM, and our proposed token dictionary are shown here. The models are evaluated on the dataset described in Sect. 1, including all tokens appearing in the library. 34 (20%) of the projects are used as a (randomly chosen) test set.

Classification Performance. All testing models outperform our baseline look-up table by a considerable margin. For single-prediction results, random forest outperforms all the other models in term of accuracy, F1, and Recall [7]. In addition, **Top 10 accuracy**, where the top 10 entries of a prediction list for a single query is considered as a match if the true label appears, is provided. Here, the proposed token dictionary and Naïve bayes outperform other models by at least 5% and achieve 91% accuracy. LSTM performs worse than other classifiers despite its large model size, indicating that temporal token dependencies are not crucial in our problem.

In addition to standard evaluation methods, the influence of the amount of training data on accuracy is measured. As shown in Fig. 3, in terms of accuracy, most methods continuously improve when more data are fed. However, this improvement is not significant: less than 5% difference is achieved when when using 100% instead of 50% training data.

Run Time. Table 1 presents the runtime measurements of the training and testing phase, using the whole training set for all models. In terms of training time, LSTM is significantly slower than the others because of its large number

Method	Accuracy	Top 10 Accuracy	F1	Recall
Lookup Table	0.66	0.74	0.67	0.66
Naïve Bayes	0.70	**0.91**	0.69	0.70
Linear SVM	0.69	0.90	0.69	0.69
LSTM	0.68	0.85	0.68	0.68
Random Forest	**0.78**	0.88	**0.79**	**0.78**
Token Dict	0.73	**0.91**	0.73	0.73

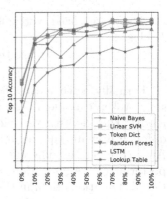

Fig. 3. *Left:* evaluation results on full training set. The best values are printed in bold font. *Right:* top 10 accuracy against amount of training data.

of parameters to train. SVM can be trained within ten minutes. The other three models, Naïve Bayes, Random Forest, and Token Dictionary execute the training within less than one minute. In terms of prediction time, all models except SVM respond to each query within 0.1 s on average, indicating that these models can be directly used by engineers on a standard workstation without inflicting a bad user-experience. The fastest model, Token Dictionary, processes more than 70 queries within a second, making it the ideal choice in terms of user-experience.

Table 1. Runtime and memory consumption.

Method	Training time (s)	Mean prediction time (ms)	Peak memory usage (MB)	Model size (MB)
Naïve Bayes	21	17.7	1061	1.2
Linear SVM	361	147.7	1250	1.9
LSTM	12083	34.9	3232	294.1
Random Forest	41	71.9	4583	20.8
Token Dict	16	12.8	143	0.7

Memory Consumption. The last evaluation concerns memory. Although all models currently fit on the 8 GB machine, it is important that the algorithms still work when more data are available in the future. As shown in Fig. 1, token dictionary is memory-friendly and consumes less than 150 MB even for the largest training set we have. In comparison, random forest and LSTM model requires 4583 MB and 3232 MB. These results indicate that random forest and LSTM models might need additional memory on a workstation if more training data are available, while token dictionary is able to capture the mapping relationship between tokens and classes using a rather small amount of memory. Note that the models are compressed.

Discussion. In the evaluation of the classifiers under scrutiny we haven seen that the token dictionary features very good classification results combined with favourable running time and memory consumption. A considerable part of the latter is probably also due to the fact that it has been implemented outside the scikit-learn framework. For example one notices a seven-fold difference in the peak memory usage of Naïve Bayes compared to the token dictionary, which cannot be explained by the complexity of the method. Since the classification performance of the token dictionary exceeded the performance of the other methods we did not re-implement the other methods for a more accurate resource consumption comparison. Among further experiments we ran on this data set we evaluated the classification results when expanding abbreviations and observed that it does not bring a significant improvement. On the other hand, including 2-grams and 3-grams (sequences of 2 and 3 tokens) in the token dictionary does improve the classification as inter-token dependencies can be captured with little additional effort. Thanks to the evaluation of the accuracy compared to the number of training files used, we have seen that our approach (regardless of the classification method) can produce good results already for relatively small data sets. More precisely, even if only 35 past projects are used for training, the predictions offer a high enough accuracy to reduce the engineers' workload.

5 Conclusion

We modeled the substation signal name matching task as a classification problem and evaluated a set of common machine learning methods as well as a bespoke LSTM and token-based dictionary classifier on a data set built from past substation engineering project. Our proposed token dictionary method offers the fastest and most memory-efficient solution for the given task. Moreover, it gives the most accurate list of suggestions and competitive single-prediction results. A potential direction of future work concerns unseen tokens. Due to the nature of bag-of-word models, when encountering new tokens, it is impossible for these classifiers to convert these tokens into features, thus they will fail to capture the information in them, leading to lower-quality predictions. One way to address this is to use a distance measure finding close known tokens to replace it.

References

1. Hotho, A., Nürnberger, A., Paaß, G.: A brief survey of text mining. In: Ldv Forum, vol. 20 (2005)
2. Pedregosa, F., Varoquaux, G., Gramfort, A., Michel, V., Thirion, B., Grisel, O., Blondel, M., Prettenhofer, P., Weiss, R., Dubourg, V., et al.: Scikit-learn: machine learning in Python. J. Mach. Learn. Res. **12**, 2825–2830 (2011)
3. Abadi, M., Agarwal, A., Barham, P., Brevdo, E., Chen, Z., Citro, C., Corrado, G.S., Davis, A., Dean, J., Devin, M., et al.: Tensorflow: large-scale machine learning on heterogeneous distributed systems. arXiv preprint arXiv:1603.04467 (2016)
4. Liaw, A., Wiener, M., et al.: Classification and regression by randomforest. R News **2**(3), 18–22 (2002)

5. Joachims, T.: Text categorization with support vector machines: Learning with many relevant features. In: Machine learning: ECML-98 (1998)
6. Bottou, L.: Large-scale machine learning with stochastic gradient descent. In: Lechevallier, Y., Saporta, G. (eds.) Proceedings of COMPSTAT 2010. Springer, Heidelberg (2010). https://doi.org/10.1007/978-3-7908-2604-3_16
7. Manning, C.D., Raghavan, P., Schütze, H., et al.: Introduction to Information Retrieval. Cambridge University Press, Cambridge (2008)
8. Tang, D., Qin, B., Liu, T.: Document modeling with gated recurrent neural network for sentiment classification. In: Proceedings of the 2014 Conference on Empirical Methods in Natural Language Processing (EMNLP) (2015)
9. Pennington, J., Socher, R., Manning, C.: Glove: global vectors for word representation. In: Proceedings of the 2014 Conference on Empirical Methods in Natural Language Processing (EMNLP) (2014)
10. Graves, A., Schmidhuber, J.: Framewise phoneme classification with bidirectional LSTM and other neural network architectures. Neural Netw. **18**(5), 602–610 (2005)
11. Kingma, D., Ba, J.: Adam: a method for stochastic optimization. arXiv preprint arXiv:1412.6980 (2014)

Meta-Heuristics

Cuckoo Search via Lévy Flight Applied to Optimal Water Supply System Design

Ricardo Soto[1](✉), Broderick Crawford[1](✉), Rodrigo Olivares[1,2](✉),
Carlos Castro[3](✉), Pía Escárate[1], and Steve Calderón[1]

[1] Pontificia Universidad Católica de Valparaíso, Valparaíso, Chile
{ricardo.soto,broderick.crawford}@ucv.cl
{pia.scarate,steve.calderon}@mail.pucv.cl
[2] Universidad de Valparaíso, Valparaíso, Chile
rodrigo.olivares@uv.cl
[3] Universidad Técnica Federico Santa María, Valparaíso, Chile
Carlos.Castro@inf.utfsm.cl

Abstract. Designing optimal water supply systems is an important purpose of any urban system that involves relevant installation, operation and maintenance costs. However, achieving the optimal design is known to be a complex task, indeed the corresponding mathematical model for this problem leads to a non-linear and non-convex problem classified as NP-hard. In this paper, we propose using the cuckoo search algorithm which a modern bio-inspired metaheuristic based on the obligate brood parasitic behavior of cuckoo birds. This behavior is combined with the interesting Lévy flight, which mimic the exploration of some birds and flies, that move by combining straight flights and ninety degrees turns. The proposed approach results in a fast convergence algorithm able to noticeably reduce the number of objective function evaluations needed to solve this problem.

Keywords: Optimal water supply system design
Cuckoo search algorithm · Metaheuristics

1 Introduction

A water supply network is a vital component of any urban infrastructure and its optimal design may clearly reduce installation, operation, and as a consequence maintenance costs. Several methods have been proposed to design efficient water distribution networks, but the presence of inherently interrelated design parameters such as the water demand, minimum pressure requirements, network layout, energy uses, as well as pipe types make the problem complex and tedious to solve. Indeed, the corresponding mathematical modeling of a water supply network leads to a non-linear and non-convex problem classified as NP-hard [34].

The research work devoted to this problem can be seen as a long story from the 1960's. Preliminary reports were based on complete search and considered models involving some assumptions such as the use of continuous

© Springer International Publishing AG, part of Springer Nature 2018
M. Mouhoub et al. (Eds.): IEA/AIE 2018, LNAI 10868, pp. 383–395, 2018.
https://doi.org/10.1007/978-3-319-92058-0_37

diameters [10,19] and split pipes [21,25]. It is known that conversion of continuous diameter to the nearest commercial size cannot guarantee the real optimal solution, while split pipes are not commonly employed. During the last two decades, various metaheuristics have been used to solve this problem, some examples are differential evolution [30], memetic algorithms [2], ant colony optimization [17,35], simulated annealing [4], and genetic algorithms [5,8,9,11,20,22,28,32]. Genetic algorithms is clearly the most present metaheuristic in this context exhibiting good results, but generally achieving slow convergence rates requiring a big amount of iterations to reach an optimal value. Some works based on particle swarm optimization have focused on this concern, illustrating better convergence rates [15,16,24,31], diminishing the number of function evaluations to reach a result.

In this paper, we propose a new cuckoo search algorithm for the optimal design of water distribution networks. Cuckoo search is a modern nature-inspired metaheuristic [33] based on the obligate brood parasitic behavior of cuckoo birds. Brood parasitism involves the manipulation and use of host individuals either of the same or different species for incubation. Particularly, cuckoos are known for laying their eggs in nests from other bird species, and also for removing the other bird eggs to increase incubation probability. In practice, an egg represents a solution and cuckoo eggs represent potentially better solutions than the current ones in nests. In this work, this aggressive behavior is combined with Lévy flight as proposed in [33]. A Lévy flight can be seen as the search pattern observed on some birds and fruit flies, that explore by interleaving straight flights and ninety degrees turns. This search pattern can analogously be used for the efficient exploration of potential solutions [1,18,26,27]. The proposed approach results in a fast convergence algorithm able to noticeably reduce the number of objective function evaluations needed to reach the best known optimums for three case studies widely employed in the literature: two-loop network and New York City tunnels network.

This paper is organized as follows. In Sect. 2, we describe the model for the optimal design of water supply networks. Section 3 describes the classic cuckoo search algorithm. The experimental results of the three case studies are presented in Sect. 4. Finally, in Sect. 5, we conclude and give some directions for future work.

2   Problem Statement

A water supply system consists in a collection of components namely valves, reservoirs, and pipes adequately linked to each other in order to supply water to a given city. The optimal design of such a system implies to determine the values of all the decision variables involved in such a way the investment is minimized and a set constraints related to network layout, hydraulic laws, and energy are satisfied. For facilitating comparison, we employ the mathematical model traditionally used in the literature [6,22,24,35] where decision variables correspond to pipe sizes of the network, while head requirements, layout, water demand, and connectivity are given by the case study.

Objective Function

$$\text{minimize} \sum_{i \in NP} c(D_i)L_i \tag{1}$$

where NP is the number of pipes, $c(D_i)$ is the cost per unit length of the ith link with diameter D_i, and L_i is the length of the ith link. This objective function is subjected to the following constraints.

Constraints

The problem is subjected to several system constraint related to mass conservation, energy conservation, pressure, and water demand. For instance, for each linked node the mass conservation law must be guaranteed as follows.

$$\sum_{j \in NP_{in,n}} Q_j - \sum_{k \in NP_{out,n}} Q_k = Q_n, \quad \forall n \in NN \tag{2}$$

where $NP_{in,n}$ and $NP_{out,n}$ correspond to the set of pipes entering and leaving node n, respectively. Q_n is the demand at node n and NN is the node set. Next, the energy conservation must be assured, that is, the total head loss around a loop should be zero as shown below.

$$\sum_{i \in Loop\ p} \Delta H_i = 0, \quad \forall p \in NL \tag{3}$$

where ΔH_i is the head loss due to friction in pipe i, NL correspond to the loop set in the network, and ΔH_i is computed by the Hanzen-Williams equation as stated in Eq. 4

$$\Delta H_i = \frac{\alpha L_i Q_i^{1,852}}{C_{HW_i}^{1,852} D_i^{4,871}}, \quad \forall i \in NP \tag{4}$$

where L_i is the length of the pipe i, Q_i is the pipe flow, C_{HW_i} is the roughness coefficient of pipe i, D_i the diameter of the pipe i, and α is the conversion factor which depends on the unit used for computation ($\alpha = 10.667$ for the present work). Then, the minimum pressure constraint must assure that pressure head for all nodes must be greater than the given minimum as shown below.

$$H_n \geqslant H_n^{min}, \quad \forall n \in NN \tag{5}$$

where H_n^{min} is the minimum required pressure head at each node. Finally, the pipe diameters must be taken from a set commercial sizes as follows.

$$D_i \in \{D\}, \quad \forall i \in NP \tag{6}$$

where D_i denotes the diameter of pipe i and $\{D\}$ the set of available commercial pipe sizes.

3   Cuckoo Search

Cuckoos belong to a class of birds that follows the obligate brood parasitic behavior. Brood parasitism involves the manipulation and use of host individuals either of the same or different species for incubation. Particularly, cuckoos are known for laying their eggs in nests from other bird species, and also for removing the other bird eggs to increase incubation probability. The external cuckoo eggs are eventually discovered by the host bird, which may take off the foreign eggs or abandoning its nest to then building a new one. This phenomena is mimicked by the cuckoo search approach, where an egg represents a solution and cuckoo eggs represent potentially better solutions than the current ones in nests. In the simplest form as in the current work each nest has only one egg.

Algorithm 1. Cuckoo Search

Require: $Nest_n$, α, λ
Ensure: Egg_{best}
 1: $Nests \leftarrow generateInitialPopulation(Nest_n)$
 2: **while** ¬stopCondition **do**
 3:    $Egg_i \leftarrow getCuckooByLevyFlight(Nest, \alpha, \lambda)$
 4:    $Egg_j \leftarrow chooseRamdomlyFrom(Nests)$
 5:    **if** $cost(Egg_i) \leq cost(Egg_j)$ **then**
 6:       $Egg_j \leftarrow Egg_i$
 7:    **end if**
 8:    $Egg_{best} \leftarrow findCurrentBest(Nests)$
 9:    $Nests \leftarrow abandonWorseNests(p_\alpha)$
10:    $Nests \leftarrow buildNewSolcution(Egg_{best})$
11: **end while**

Algorithm 1 depicts the cuckoo search procedure for minimization. Firstly, an initial population of host nest in randomly produced. Then, between lines 2 and 11, a loop iterates until a stop criteria is reached, which is usually an optimal value bound or a maximum number of iterations. Next, a new solution is produced by employing Lévy flights, which is computed by Eqs. 7 and 8, where x_i^{t+1} corresponds to the new solution, t is the iteration number, and the product $\oplus$ means entry-wise multiplications. α corresponds to the step size, where $\alpha > 0$, and determines how far the process can go for a fixed number of iterations. At line 4, an Egg_j is selected by random, which at line 5 is compared with the one selected via Lévy flights. The egg having the best cost is maintained and the other one discarded. Finally, the worse nests are abandoned depending on the probability p_a and new solutions are produced.

$$x_i^{t+1} = x_i^t + \alpha \oplus Lévy(\lambda) \tag{7}$$

$$Lévy \sim u = t^{-\lambda}, (1 < \lambda \leq 3) \tag{8}$$

The first phase is to initialize the algorithm by setting up the indicators and the set S of strategies to be interleaved during the solving process. Then, the

CSP is solved until a given cutoff and the best performing strategy s_j is selected by using the choice function. Once the best s_j is selected, the CSP is solved and at each time a variable is fixed by enumeration the score of indicators is gathered. The strategies are evaluated via the choice function and the best scored one is activated next during the exploration of the search tree.

4   Case Studies and Experimental Results

In this section we present the case studies with the corresponding experimental results. We consider three well-known problems widely employed in the literature: the two-loop network and the New York City tunnel expansion problem. The algorithms have been implemented in Matlab 2013 interfaced with EPANET 2.0 for the computation of nodal pressure heads. The experiments have been performed on a 3.3 GHz Intel Core i3 with 4Gb RAM running Windows 7. A probability $p_a = 0.25$ is used for the configuration of the cuckoo algorithm, which is suggested in [33] as a suitable value for most optimization problems.

4.1   Two-Loop Network

The two-loop network introduced by [25] is composed of 6 demand nodes, 8 pipes, and a reservoir which supply the network by gravity (see Fig. 1). Every pipe of the network has a length of 1000 m and the value 130 is assumed as the Hanzen-Williams coefficient for all pipes. The network is limited to the use of 14 commercial diameter sizes (see Table 1) and it must guarantee a minimum pressure head of 30 m for all nodes. Demand and elevation for nodes are depicted in Table 2.

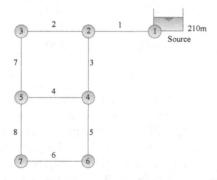

Fig. 1. Two-loop network.

Table 3 presents the results previously published in terms of average number of function evaluations. As commonly reported for this problem, 10 runs are performed to compute the average. The proposed cuckoo search (CS) algorithm noticeably outperforms the best results.

Table 1. Pipe cost data of two-loop network.

Pipe	Diameter (mm)	Cost ($/m)
1	25.4	2
2	50.8	5
3	76.2	8
4	101.6	11
5	152.4	16
6	203.2	23
7	254.0	32
8	304.8	50
9	355.6	60
10	406.4	90
11	457.2	130
12	508.0	170
13	558.8	300
14	609.6	550

Table 2. Demand and elevation for nodes of two-loop network.

Node	Demand (m^3/h)	Elevation (m)
1(Reservoir)	−1120	210
2	100	180
3	100	190
4	120	185
5	270	180
6	330	195
7	200	190

It is able to reach the global optimum of $419,000 with an average of only 398.4 objective function (Z) evaluations favorably compared to 250,000 for the genetic algorithm (GA) [22], 25,000 for simulated annealing (SA) [4], 11,323 for shuffled frog leaping algorithm (SFLA) [6], 5,138 for particle swarm optimization (PSO) [31], 5,000 for harmony search (HS) [7], 4,750 for differential evolution (DE) [30], 3,215 for scatter search (SS) [12], 3,120 for particle swarm optimization (PSO) [24], and 3,080 for the hybrid particle swarm optimization and differential evolution (PSO-DE) [24].

In Table 4, we provide additional results in order to illustrate the robustness of the approach when the population size (number of nests) vary. We employ a set of values (20, 25, 30, 35, and 40) belonging to the interval of nests ($Nest_n$) tested in [33]. We report the lowest, highest, and average number of objective

Table 3. Different results obtained for the two-loop network.

Technique	Cost ($)	$\bar{x}$ number of Z evaluations
GA	419,000	250,000
SA	419,000	25,000
SFLA	419,000	11,323
PSO	419,000	5,138
HS	419,000	5,000
DE	419,000	4,750
SS	419,000	3,215
PSO	419,000	3,120
PSO-DE	419,000	3,080
CS	419,000	**398.4**

function evaluations to reach the optimum as well as the corresponding standard deviation. The results demonstrate that the approach is quite stable when its population size is moderately modified.

Indeed, it is able to reach the optimum in all nest configurations by needing a reduced number of Z evaluations.

Table 4. Z evaluations required to reach the optimum by varying the number of nests.

$Nest_n$	Lowest number of Z evaluations	$\bar{x}$ number of Z evaluations	Highest number of Z evaluations	σ
20	208	469.5	950	261.7
25	174	**398.4**	646	178.1
30	224	517.8	1766	456.1
35	292	433.4	816	141.8
40	**156**	444	842	199.6

4.2 New York City Tunnels Network

The third case study corresponds to the New York City tunnel expansion problem firstly presented by [23]. This network consists of 20 nodes linked trough 21 tunnels and one reservoir that feeds the network by gravity (see Fig. 2). The goal of this problem is not building the network from scratch, but rather to expand it as nodes 16, 17, 18, 19, and 20 are unable to satisfy pressure requirements. The expansion must be carried out by duplicating some tunnels for which it is also necessary to decide their diameters from 15 commercial available sizes. Pipe cost, nodal demand and pipe length of this network are depicted in Tables 5, 6, and 7, respectively. The Hanzen-Williams coefficient for this problem is set to 100 for the whole network.

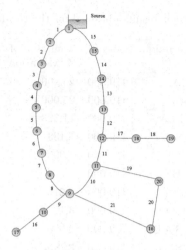

Fig. 2. New York City tunnels network.

Table 5. Pipe cost data of New York network.

Pipe	Diameter (mm)	Cost ($/m)
1	0	0
2	36	93.5
3	48	134
4	60	176
5	72	221
6	84	267
7	96	316
8	108	365
9	120	417
10	132	469
11	144	522
12	156	577
13	168	632
14	180	689
15	192	746
16	204	804

Table 6. Nodal demand of the New York network.

Node	Demand (m_3/hr)	Min. head (ft)
1	−22,017.5	300
2	92.4	255.5
3	92.4	255.5
4	88.2	255.5
5	88.2	255.5
6	88.2	255.5
7	88.2	255.5
8	88.2	255.5
9	170.0	255.5
10	1.0	255.5
11	170.0	255.5
12	117.1	255.5
13	117.1	255.5
14	92.4	255.5
15	92.4	255.5
16	170.0	260
17	57.5	272.8
18	117.1	255.0
19	117.1	255.0
20	170.0	255.0

Table 7. Pipe length of the New York network.

Pipe	Length (ft)	Diameter (ft)
1	11,600	180
2	19,800	180
3	7,300	180
4	8,300	180
5	8,600	180
6	19,100	180
7	9,600	132
8	12,500	132
9	9,600	180
10	11,200	204
11	14,500	204
12	12,200	204
13	24,100	204
14	21,100	204
15	15,500	204
16	26,400	72
17	31,200	72
18	24,000	60
19	14,400	60
20	38,400	60
21	26,400	72

The reported results for the New York network are depicted in Table 8. The best feasible solution corresponds to 38.52×10^6, which is reached by two approaches, being CS clearly faster than PSO-DE [24] with an average of 1,368.4 evaluations in contrast to 3,540. Remaining approaches are unable to reach the best solution: PSO [24], DE [30], and ACO [13] stays at 38.64×10^6 as the best optimum with 3,570; 5,494; and 13,928 iterations, respectively. Finally, the work of [6] on SFLA reaches 38.80×10^6, as best optimum, by needing between 21,569 and 24,817 iterations.

Equally to previous case studies, the performance of the CS algorithm remains stable for this problem when the nest configuration vary (see Table 9). The CS reaches the optimum in all nest configurations while demanding a reasonable effort.

4.3 Convergence

Figure 3 illustrates convergence charts for the best run of each studied problem.

This allows one to observe how CS converges through the iterations to a better solution. All charts demonstrates the rapid convergence of the proposed

Table 8. Different results obtained for the New York network.

Technique	Cost (10^6 $)	$\bar{x}$ number of Z evaluations
SFL	38.80	between 21,569 and 24,817
ACO	38.64	13,928
DE	38.64	5,494
PSO	38.64	3,570
PSO-DE	38.52	3,540
CS	38.52	**1,368.4**

Table 9. Z evaluations required to reach the optimum by varying the number of nests.

$Nest_n$	Lowest number of Z evaluations	$\bar{x}$ number of Z evaluations	Highest number of Z evaluations	σ
20	836	1,967.3	2324	515.7
25	**794**	1,812.6	2582	648.8
30	1,342	1,673.6	2198	269.3
35	1,284	1,743.8	2186	266.2
40	1,150	**1,368.4**	1972	254.8

approach, which exhibit a good balance between solution quality and computational effort needed. In all cases, CS speedily converges from the beginning reaching a final stable progress.

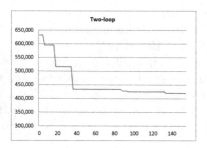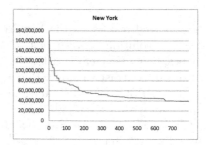

Fig. 3. Convergence charts (x-axis: iteration number, y-axis: design cost).

5   Conclusions and Future Work

In this paper, we have presented a new cuckoo search algorithm for the optimal design of water supply systems. This approach is effectively combined with Lévy flights resulting in a fast convergence algorithm. We have performed a set of experiments in order to compare our approach with the best-performing approximate methods reported in the literature. We considered three widely used case studies: two-loop and New York networks. The results illustrate that cuckoo search requires a considerable minor number of objective function evaluations to reach the best known optimums: 398.4 vs. 3,080 (PSO-DE) for the two-loop network; 1,540 vs. 3,540 (DE) for the New York network.

The promising results of the experiments open up opportunities for further research. We suggest different directions for future work. Perhaps the most straightforward one is about the use of cuckoo search for solving other combinatorial problems, given the CS algorithm is relatively easy and fast to implement. Another future research direction is related to the use of pre-filtering phases as illustrated in [29]. A pre-filtering phase allows to reduce the potential space of solutions alleviating the work of the metaheuristic. Finally, the use of autonomous search [3,14] for the self tuning of the cuckoo configuration would be another interesting trend to pursue.

Acknowledgment. Ricardo Soto is supported by Grant CONICYT/FONDECYT/ REGULAR/1160455. Broderick Crawford is supported by Grant CONICYT/FONDECYT/REGULAR/1171243. Rodrigo Olivares is supported by CONICYT/FONDEF/IDeA/ID16I10449, FONDECYT/STIC-AMSU/17STIC-03, FONDECYT/MEC/MEC80170097, and Postgraduate Grant Pontificia Universidad Católica de Valparaíso (INF - PUCV 2015–2018).

References

1. Reynolds, A.M., Frye, M.A.: Free-flight odor tracking in drosophila is consistent with an optimal intermittent scale-free search. PLoS ONE **2**(4), e354 (2007)
2. Baños, R., Gil, C., Reca, J., Montoya, F.G.: A memetic algorithm applied to the design of water distribution networks. Appl. Soft Comput. **10**(1), 261–266 (2010)
3. Crawford, B., Soto, R., Monfroy, E., Palma, W., Castro, C., Paredes, F.: Parameter tuning of a choice-function based hyperheuristic using particle swarm optimization. Expert Syst. Appl. **40**(5), 1690–1695 (2013)
4. Cunha, M., Sousa, J.: Water distribution network design optimization: simulated annealing approach. J. Water Resour. Plann. Manage. **125**(4), 215–221 (1999)
5. Dandy, G., Simpson, A., Murphy, L.: An improved genetic algorithm for pipe network optimization. Water Resour. Res. **32**(2), 449–458 (1996)
6. Eusuff, M., Lansey, K.: Optimization of water distribution network design using the shuffled frog leaping algorithm. J. Water Resour. Plan. Manage. ASCE **129**(3), 210–225 (2003)
7. Geem, Z.W.: Optimal cost design of water distribution networks using harmony search. Eng. Optim. **38**(3), 259–277 (2006)
8. Gupta, I., Gupta, A., Khanna, P.: Genetic algorithm for optimization of water distribution systems. Environ. Modell. Softw. **14**(5), 437–446 (1999)
9. Halhal, D., Walters, G., Ouazar, D., Savic, D.: Water network rehabilitation with structured messy genetic algorithms. J. Water Resour. Plan. Manage. **123**(3), 137–146 (1997)
10. Jacoby, S.L.S.: Design of optimal hydraulic networks. J. Hydraul. Div. **94**(3), 641–661 (1968)

11. Keedwell, E., Khu, S.-T.: A hybrid genetic algorithm for the design of water distribution networks. Eng. Appl. AI **18**(4), 461–472 (2005)
12. Lin, M., Liu, Y., Liu, G., Chu, C.: Scatter search heuristic for least-cost design of water distribution networks. Eng. Optim. **39**(7), 857–876 (2007)
13. Maier, H., Simpsom, A., Zecchin, A., Foong, W., Phang, K., Seah, H., Tan, C.: Ant colony optimization for the design of water distribution systems. J. Water Resour. Plan. Manage. ASCE **129**(3), 200–209 (2003)
14. Monfroy, E., Castro, C., Crawford, B., Soto, R., Paredes, F., Figueroa, C.: A reactive and hybrid constraint solver. J. Exp. Theoret. Artif. Intell. **25**(1), 1–22 (2013)
15. Montalvo, I., Izquierdo, J., Pérez, R., Tung, M.M.: Particle swarm optimization applied to the design of water supply systems. Comput. Math. Appl. **56**(3), 769–776 (2008)
16. Montalvo, I., Izquierdo, J., Pérez-García, R., Herrera, M.: Improved performance of PSO with self-adaptive parameters for computing the optimal design of water supply systems. Eng. Appl. AI **23**(5), 727–735 (2010)
17. Ostfeld, A., Tubaltzev, A.: Ant colony optimization for least cost design and operation of pumping and operation of pumping water distribution systems. J. Water Resour. Plann. Manage. **134**(2), 107–118 (2008)
18. Pavlyukevich, I.: Lévy flights, non-local search and simulated annealing. J. Comput. Phys. **226**, 1830–1844 (2007)
19. Pitchai, R.: A model for designing water distribution pipe networks. Ph.D. thesis, Harvard University (1966)
20. Prasad, D., Park, N.: Multiobjective genetic algorithms for design of water distribution networks. J. Water Resour. Plan. Manage. **130**(1), 73–82 (2004)
21. Quindry, G., Brill, E., Lienman, J.: Water distribution system design criteria. Technical report, Department of Civil Engineering, University of Illinois at Urbana-Champaign, Urbana, IL (1979)
22. Savic, D., Walters, G.: Genetic algorithms for least-cost design of water distribution networks. J. Water Resour. Plan. Manage. ASCE **123**(2), 67–77 (1997)
23. Schaake, J., Lai, D.: Linear programming and dynamic programming applications to water distribution network design. Technical report 116, Hydrodynamics Laboratory, MIT, Cambridge, MA (1969)
24. Sedki, A., Ouazar, D.: Hybrid particle swarm optimization and differential evolution for optimal design of water distribution systems. Adv. Eng. Inf. **26**(3), 582–591 (2012)
25. Shamir, U., Alperovits, E.: Design of optimal water distribution systems. Water Resour. Res. **13**(6), 885–900 (1977)
26. Shlesinger, M.F.: Search research. Nature **443**, 281–282 (2006)
27. Shlesinger, M.F., Zaslavsky, G.M., Frisch, U. (eds.): Lévy Flights and Related Topics in Phyics. Springer, Heidelberg (2007)
28. Simpson, A., Murphy, L., Dandy, G.: Genetic algorithms compared to other techniques for pipe optimisation. J. Water Resour. Plan. Manage. ASCE **120**(4), 423–443 (1994)
29. Soto, R., Crawford, B., Galleguillos, C., Monfroy, E., Paredes, F.: A pre-filtered cuckoo search algorithm with geometric operators for solving sudoku problems. Sci. World J. **2014**, 12 (2014). Article ID 465359
30. Suribabu, C.R.: Differential evolution algorithm for optimal design of water distribution networks. J. Hydroinf. **12**(1), 66–82 (2010)
31. Suribabu, C.R., Neelakantan, T.R.: Design of water distribution networks using particle swarm optimization. J. Urban Water **3**(2), 111–120 (2006)

32. Vairavamoorthy, K., Ali, M.: Water network rehabilitation with structured messy genetic algorithms. Comput. Aided Civil Infrastruct. Eng. **15**(5), 374–382 (2000)
33. Yang, X.-S., Deb, S.: Cuckoo search via lévy flights. In: World Congress on Nature & Biologically Inspired Computing (NaBIC), pp. 210–214. IEEE (2009)
34. Yates, D.F., Templeman, A.B., Boffey, T.B.: The computational complexity of the problem of determining least capital cost designs for water supply networks. Eng. Optim. **7**(2), 143–155 (1984)
35. Zecchin, A.C., Simpson, A.R., Maier, H.R., Leonard, M., Roberts, A.J., Berrisford, M.J.: Application of two ant colony optimisation algorithms to water distribution system optimisation. Math. Comput. Modell. **44**(5–6), 451–468 (2006)

Performance Evaluation of Particles Coding in Particle Swarm Optimization with Self-adaptive Parameters for Flexible Job Shop Scheduling Problem

Rim Zarrouk[1,2]([envelope]) and Abderrazak Jemai[3]

[1] Polytechnic School, University of Carthage, 2078 La Marsa, Tunisia
`rima.zarrouk@gmail.com`
[2] LR-NOCCS, National Engineering School of Sousse,
University of Sousse, 4023 Sousse, Tunisia
[3] Faculty of Sciences of Tunis, University of Tunis El Manar, Tunis, Tunisia

Abstract. The metaheuristic Particle Swarm Optimization (PSO) is well suited to solve the Flexible Job Shop Scheduling Problem (FJSP), and a suitable particle representation should importantly impact the optimization results and performance of this algorithm. The chosen representation has a direct impact on the dimension and content of the solution space. In this paper, we intend to evaluate and compare the performance of two different variants of PSO with different particle representations (PSO with Job-Machine coding Scheme (PSO-JMS) and PSO with Only-Machine coding Scheme (PSO-OMS)) for solving FJSP. These procedures have been tested on thirteen benchmark problems, where the objective function is to minimize the makespan and total workload and to compare the run time of the different PSO variants. Based on the experimental results, it is clear that PSO-OMS gives the best performance in solving all benchmark problems.

Keywords: Flexible Job Shop Problem
Particle swarm optimization · Scheduling · Particle coding
PSO performance

1 Introduction

The Flexible Job Shop Scheduling Problem (FJSP) is an extension of the classical job shop scheduling problem, where each operation could be processed on more than one machine and each machine can process several operations. Metaheuristics such as the Genetic Algorithm (GA), the Ant Colony (ACO), the Tabu Search (TS) and the Particle Swarm Optimization (PSO) are widely recognized as efficient approaches for many hard optimization problems. Extended research surveys on the use of these metaheuristics to solve FJSP can be found in [4,7]. Even though all metaheuristics have a probabilistic behavior, the PSO is much

© Springer International Publishing AG, part of Springer Nature 2018
M. Mouhoub et al. (Eds.): IEA/AIE 2018, LNAI 10868, pp. 396–407, 2018.
https://doi.org/10.1007/978-3-319-92058-0_38

simpler to implement and is more controllable due to its fewer parameters. In this work, we are interested in the improvement of the PSO performance in terms of solution optimality.

As a metaheuristic, the PSO has been the subject of much theoretical research [2] to improve its convergence through the action on its parameters (i.e. cognitive-factor, social-factor and inertia-weight) [17,18], and to modify the position and velocity Eqs. (1) and (2) [1,6] through the special clustering of particles [8,13] and PSO hybridization [15].

Before we can apply the PSO to solve the FJSP, one common and important issue to be addressed is how we can represent each PSO particle as a schedule in FJSP in order to improve the makespan. The data structures and the algorithm are combined together to make efficient programs. A bad coding representation can increase the size of the search space or slow down the algorithm. In the literature, a lot of particle representation schemes have been used to bridge the PSO particle with FJSP, such as the disjunctive graph-based, operation-machine-based, priority-rule-based or matrix-based ones. In [13], the solution was a graph where each node represented one operation to which was assigned a unique number based on the job and the use of the machine. In [5,8,9,15], the particle position was always represented as a vector or a string (operation-machine-based) that had a size equal to twice the number of total operations. In [8], the particles were presented like in the operation-machine-based schema with the integration of operation priorities. The choice of the particles coding in FJSP has been important and all these works are done for the resolution of this problem.

To sum up, the most used particle position schema is followed by the operation-machine-based method with a length equal to $2|Op|$. In this paper, two improvement levels of PSO-FJSP are proposed. The first improvement level deals with the change of PSO parameters. We choose to work with dynamic parameters. The second improvement level deals with the PSO particle coding schema and the parameters change. We propose two different variants of PSO with various types of particle representation procedures such as PSO with Job-Machine coding scheme (PSO-JMS) and PSO with Only-Machine coding scheme (PSO-OMS) with a special scheduling function.

This paper is organized as follows: Sects. 2 and 3 define respectively FJSP and PSO. Section 4 presents the proposed approach. The simulation results is set in Sect. 5. The conclusion is drawn in Sect. 6.

2   Problem Description

The FJS problem is defined by the n-uplet (J, O, M, a, d):

- $J = J_1, J_2, \ldots, J_n$ a set of n independent jobs;
- $J_n = (o_{n1}, o_{n2}, \ldots, o_{nf})$ a set of f operations.
- $O = (O_{11}, O_{12}, \ldots), (O_{21}, O_{22}, \ldots), \ldots, (O_{n1}, O_{n2}, \ldots)$ the set of operations, where O_{ji} is operation i of job j;
- $M = \{m_1, m_2, \ldots, m_k\}$ a set of machines;

- $a : O \times M \rightarrow \{0,1\}$, $a(o_{ji}, m_k) = 1$ if o_{ji} can be processed by m_k;
- $d : O \times M \rightarrow N$, $d(o_{ji}, m_k)$ defines the duration of o_{ji} on m_k.

The goal is to find a schedule of operations that minimizes the completion times of all jobs (MakeSpan (MS) of the schedule and the total machine workload (W_T)), where, C_j is the completion time of job J:

$$MS = Max(C_1, C_2, \ldots, C_j) \tag{1}$$

The total machine workload is as follows:

$$W_T = \sum_{j=1}^{n} \sum_{i=1}^{n_i} d(o_{ji}, m_k) \tag{2}$$

The following assumptions are made:

- All machines are available at time 0;
- All jobs are released at time 0 independently from each other (there is no precedence relationship between jobs);
- Setting up times of machines and transportation times between operations are negligible;
- Maintenance activities and machine breakdowns are neglected; preemption is not allowed.

Let $M(O_{i,j})$ be the set of machines which supports the operation $O_{i,j}$. Two categories of FJSP are dealt with: $FJSP^T$ (total) and $FJSP^P$ (partial).

$$FJSP = \begin{cases} FJSP^T, & if \;\; a(o_{ji}, m_k) = 1; \;\; \forall i, j \\ FJSP^P, & otherwise \end{cases} \tag{3}$$

Table 1 describes the processing time of different operations on their corresponding machines. It can be seen from this that the two leftmost columns display jobs and operations. This instance is composed of 4 jobs and 4 machines. Jobs 1, 2, 3 and 4 have respectively 3, 3, 4 and 1 operations. Table 1 shows an $FJSP^T$ instance that will be used throughout this section to illustrate the varied coding.

3   PSO for FJSP

PSO works by having a population of candidate solutions, which are moving around in the search space in order to improve their current solutions [14]. The movements of particles are guided by their own best-known position in the search-space as well as the entire swarm's best-known position. At each instant, each particle p takes a new position vector noted $X_p(t)$ and a new velocity vector noted $V_p(t)$. This is computed using:

$$V_{p,d}(t+1) = w.V_{p,d}(t) + K_1.r_1(Xbest_{p,d}(t) - X_{p,d}(t)) + K_2.r_2(Xgbest_d(t) - X_{p,d}(t)) \tag{4}$$

$$X_{p,d}(t+1) = X_{p,d}(t) + V_{p,d}(t+1) \tag{5}$$

Table 1. $FJSP^T$ benchmark

Job	Operation	Processing time			
		M1	M2	M3	M4
1	1	1	2	3	1
1	2	1	2	3	5
1	3	3	2	2	1
2	1	3	4	1	4
2	2	3	1	3	2
2	3	2	1	3	4
3	1	4	1	2	2
3	2	1	3	3	4
3	3	2	4	1	3
3	4	1	2	1	2
4	1	1	3	6	1

where d is the dimension of vectors, $Xbest_{p,d}(t)$ is the best position reached by the particle up to time, and $Xgbest(t)$ is the best position ever found by the whole swarm. The inertia weight W is used to balance the global and local search abilities of PSO. A large inertia weight improves the global search ability while a small inertia weight facilitates local search. K_1 and K_2 are positive constants called respectively the coefficient of the self-recognition component and the coefficient of the social component. The personal learning factor K_1 change the velocity of a particle towards its personal best position. The social learning factor K_2 changes the velocity of a particle towards the global best position. r_1 and r_2 are the key factors that affect the convergence performance of PSO. However, r_1 and r_2 in standard PSO are random numbers in the interval $[0,1]$, which cannot ensure that the whole problem space can be completely traversed.

The complexity of the problem is as follows:

– The dimension of the solutions space: $2|Op|$
– The size of the solutions space: $|Op|!|M|^{|Op|}$
– The size of the search space: $|Op|!|M|^{|Op|}$
– Maximum number of visited solutions: Swarm_size * Max_iteration (if no solution is either revisited by a particle or visited by more than one particle)

4 Proposed Approach

4.1 Self-adaptive Parameters

In [17], the authors developed a self-adaptive weight w particle swarm optimization to improve the search ability of the PSO (Eq. 6). However, every particle calculated its own inertia coefficient according to its fitness value. And according to [9], the learning factors ($K_1(t)$ and $K_2(t)$) were dynamically calculated as a function of w value (Eqs. 7 and 8). In the two cited papers, the authors improved the efficiently of these dynamic parameters to solve the traditional functions (sphere, Griewank, Schaffer, etc.), but in our paper, we apply these equations to solve FJSP and we prove that the dynamic and self adaptive w, $K_1(t)$ and $K_2(t)$, are more efficient than the static ones.

$$W = \begin{cases} w_{\max} & , \; if \; pBest > Best_{avg,current\_iter} \\ w_{\min} + \frac{(w_{\max}-w_{\min})(pBest-Best_{\min,current\_iter})}{Best_{avg,current\_iter}-Best_{\min,current\_iter}} & , otherwise \end{cases} \tag{6}$$

where w_{max} is the maximum of the inertia coefficient, w_{min} is the minimum of the inertia coefficient, $current_{iter}$ is the current iteration number, $Best_{avg,current\_iter}$ is the fitness value average of all particles in the current iteration, and $Best_{min,current\_iter}$ is the minimum fitness value of all particles in the current iteration of all particles. w_{max} should be set as 0.9 and w_{min} should be set as 0.4.

$$K_1(t) = 0.5 * (w + 1)^2 \tag{7}$$

$$K_2(t) = \min(4.2 * (w_{\min} + 1)) + K_1(t) + 0.000001 \tag{8}$$

4.2   Proposed Technique

Particle coding procedures refer to the mapping between the particle position in PSO and the scheduling solution in FJSP. It is an important step to be carried out so that each particle in PSO can represent a schedule in FJSP. In the particle representation, the mapping between the particle and the scheduling solution is established through the connection of the operation sequence of all the jobs with the particle position sequence. According to the processing constraints of the problem, each operation in the operation sequence of all the jobs is assigned to each machine in turn to form a scheduling solution. The particle representation can ensure that the decoded scheduling solutions are feasible and can follow the particle swarm optimization algorithm model. In this paper, at any iteration t, the position vector $X_p(t)$ of a particle p models a feasible schedule of the FJSP instance. The length of this vector is varied according to the coding type. The particle coding is done by two forms: operation-machine-based (job-machine schema) or only machine-based (only-machine schema).

Basic Job-Machine Schemas. In the Job-Machine Schema (JMS), $X_p(t)$ has $2|Op|$ elements. The first $|Op|$ elements, noted $X_{p_o}(t)$, represents a partial order of operations, the second $|Op|$ elements, noted $X_{p_m}(t)$, represents the allocated numbers of machines. Figure 1 represents a $X_p(t)$ vector for a FSJP instance represented in Table 1. This figure shows the two parts $X_{p_o}(t)$ and $X_{p_m}(t)$. In this example, the operations assigned to machine 3 are: the first operations of job 2 and the third and fourth operations of job 3. The operations of job 1 are presented by number 1 and the green color, and operations of job 2 are presented by number 2 and the blue color. Job 3 and 4 operations are presented by numbers 3 and 4 respectively and by the red and purple colors respectively.

The operating procedure of the scheduling function in basic PSO-JMS is as follows:

Fig. 1. 1 JMS - example of a schedule for three jobs, nine operations on four machines (Color figure online)

Each particle operation is scheduled according to their order in the vector $X_{p_o}(t)$; i.e, the operation coded by $X_{p_o}(t)[l]$ is scheduled before the one coded by $X_{p_o}(t)[l+1]$.

Improved Job-Machine Schema with Reduced Search Space. The improved PSO-JMS has a special scheduling function that helps the population to follow a well-defined research trajectory, thus a reduced solution space. The operating procedure of the scheduling function is as follows:

The ith operations of all jobs are scheduled before the $i+1^{th}$ operations (i.e. all O_{ij} are scheduled before any $O_{i+1,j}$) and the operations are handled according to the order of elements in the vector $X_{p_o}(t)$. The dimension of the solution space is $2.|Op|$, the size of the solutions space: $|O|!.|M|^{|Op|}$. The size of the search space: $|M|^{|Op|}$. The number of visited solutions: Swarm_size $*$ Max_iteration.

Only-Machine Schema. In the Only-Machine Schema (OMS), the $X_p(t)$ vector has $|Op|$ elements. This vector represents the Ids of the allocated machines. Figure 2 shows an example of a result schedule of the benchmark represented in Table 1. Based on OMS and Algorithm_1, we develop a PSO variant (PSO-OMS) for FJSP. The new approach PSO-OMS has two main advantages. First, there is a the reduction in the solution space, and second, there is a reduction in the search space.

– Reduction in the solution space: The simple particle coding helps to reduce the solution space automatically:
  • Dimension of solution space: $|Op|$.
  • Size of solution space: $|M|^{|Op|}$.
  • Size of search space: $|M|^{|Op|}$.
– Reduction in search space: PSO-OMS has the same special scheduling function as the improved version of PSO-JMS. The order of execution of the operations is illustrated in Fig. 3.

This method helps the particles to follow a well-defined path during scheduling, i.e. avoiding particles to move to a bad position and forcing it to move to another that is well close to the best position.

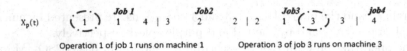

Fig. 2. OMS- example of a schedule for 4 jobs, 11 operations on 4 machines

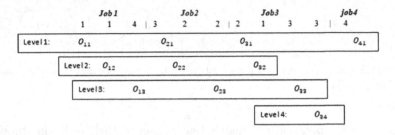

Fig. 3. Scheduling function for PSO-OMS

5   Experimental Results

5.1   Experimental Procedure

In this paper, 50% of the populations are using the localization approach, [10] and the other 50% are using a random method to initialize the particles positions $X_p(t)$. For the initial velocity vector $V_p(t)$, all particles have random values between 0 and 1. We work with asynchronous PSO where every particle computes its fitness, then immediately updates $Xgbest$. The asynchronous update process may give, depending on the optimization problem, better results and better convergence.

The PSO variants developed and tested in this work are:

- PSO with job-machine coding: PSO-JMR.
- PSO with only-machine coding: PSO-OMR.

The parameters of PSO-JMR and PSO-OMR are: the number of particles, number of iterations, the optimization problem and the size of the problem.

We have worked with 10 benchmarks (MK01MK10) of [3] and three benchmarks (4 * 5, 8 * 8 and 10 * 10) of [10]. The parameters of the instances are set in Table 2.

The following experiments are carried out:

Experiment 1: For comparative measurements of the makespan (MS) defined in Eq. 1, the workload total WL (Eq. 2), the CPU time and the percentage of the particles converge to the best position over all iterations (%conv) with PSO-JMR and PSO-OMR. Simulations are done for 4 * 5, 8 * 8, 10 * 10 and for the 10 benchmarks of Brandimarte using 500 particles and 500 iterations. All results are obtained after 30 runs.

Experiment 2: To compare our solution to the others ones.

Table 2. FJSP instances

Instance	n	m	|O|	FJSP categories
MK01	10	6	55	$FJSP^P$
MK02	10	6	58	$FJSP^P$
MK03	15	8	150	$FJSP^P$
MK04	15	8	90	$FJSP^P$
MK05	15	4	106	$FJSP^P$
MK06	10	15	150	$FJSP^P$
MK07	20	5	100	$FJSP^P$
MK08	20	10	225	$FJSP^P$
MK09	20	10	240	$FJSP^P$
MK10	20	15	240	$FJSP^P$
4 * 5	4	5	12	$FJSP^T$
8 * 8	8	8	27	$FJSP^P$
10 * 10	10	10	30	$FJSP^T$

Experiment 3: To evaluate the impact of the number of iterations on the final MS, we fix the swarm size (500 particles), vary the number of iterations (from 10 to 5000) for the benchmark MK01 and visualize the evolution of the standard deviation.

Experiment 4: To evaluate the impact of the number of particles on the final MS, we fixe the Max_iteration (500 iterations), vary the number of particles (from 10 to 5000) for the benchmark MK01 and visualize the evolution of the standard deviation.

For experiences 3 and 4, we study the standard deviations of the results found during 30 runs in Eqs. 9, 10 and 11, to better prove the fitness results of PSO-OMS.

The standard deviation regarding the mean position is as follows:

$$\sigma 1 = \sqrt{\frac{1}{N} \cdot \sum_{i=1}^{N} (Gbest_i - Mean)^2} \qquad (9)$$

The standard deviation regarding the best position is as follows:

$$\sigma 2 = \sqrt{\frac{1}{N} \cdot \sum_{i=1}^{N} (Gbest_i - Best)^2} \qquad (10)$$

The standard deviation regarding the worst position is as follows:

$$\sigma 3 = \sqrt{\frac{1}{N} \cdot \sum_{i=1}^{N} (Gbest_i - worst)^2} \qquad (11)$$

where $Best = Min(Gbest_i)$ is the best value of the found makespan, $worst = Max(Gbest_i)$ is the worst value of makespan, and $Mean = \sum_{i=1}^{N} \frac{Gbest_i}{N}$ is the average value of all the makespan found during the N runs (N = 30).

5.2 Simulation Results

The experiments are performed on a dual core machine at 2,8 GHz and 8 GB of RAM. All results are obtained after 30 trials, the scheduler is implemented in C language and all run times are given in seconds.

Experiment 1: Table 3 presents for each benchmark and for each PSO variant the best obtained fitness, the CPU time, the total workload and the number of particles, with have reached the best position. We notice that PSO-OMS gives the best fitness, a minimum workload and a maximum %conv (Greater than 2 to 10 times). Since our main goal is the minimization of the makespan and the total workload, the best choice is the PSO with OMS.

Experiment 2: Tables 4 and 5 compare the best fitness obtained by the PSO-OMS (blue columns) to the other ones. The blue columns are our results. We notice that PSO-OMS gives the best fitness in 70% of the benchmarks compared to [5] and 100% better than the other references.

Experiment 3: Fig. 4 shows the curves of the three standard derivations ($\sigma 1, \sigma 2, \sigma 3$) of PSO-JMS and PSO-OMS, for the benchmark MK01 when we vary the iteration number from 10 to 5000, while the population size is set to 500.

When we fixe the swarm size at 500 particles and we change the iterations number, we note that:

- When the number of iteration is less than 50, the percentage of MS values close to the worst value is high compared to good and mean values.
- When the number of iteration is between 50 and 1000 iterations, the percentage of worst and mean values is close to the best values.
- When the number of iteration exceeds 1000 particles, the behavior of the algorithms is improved and the percentage of best fitness values increases.

Experiment 4: Fig. 5 shows the curves of the three standard derivations ($\sigma 1, \sigma 2, \sigma 3$) of PSO-JMS and PSO-OMS, for the benchmark MK01 when we varied the population size from 10 to 5000, whereas the iteration number is set to 500. Each simulation is repeated 10 times.

When we fixe the number of iterations numbers at 500 and we change the swarm size, we note that:

- When the number of particles is less than 500, the percentage of MS values close to the worst value is high compared to good and mean values.
- When the number of particles is between 500 and 1000 iterations, the percentage of worst and means values is close to the best values.
- When the number of particles exceeds 1000 particles, the behavior of the algorithms is improved and the percentage of best fitness values rises.

Table 3. Comparisons between different coding presentations

	Basic PSO				PSO-JMS				PSO-OMS			
	MS	WL	%conv	CPU time	MS	WL	%conv	CPU time	MS	WL	%conv	CPU time
4 * 5	11	32	10	1.79	11	37	20	1.65	11	32	39	0.93
8 * 8	19	81	5	6.21	16	76	16	5.33	15	75	18	2.01
10 * 10	12	56	2	7.86	10	56	5	6.69	8	46	27	2.61
MK01	42	171	<1	15.87	40	148	2	15.09	39	146	23	7.91
MK02	29	155	<1	19.56	27	154	2	16.77	26	151	19	9.36
MK03	204	855	<1	84.03	204	852	1	85.98	204	852	7	42.30
MK04	67	466	<1	39.55	62	352	1	36.02	62	345	34	19.30
MK05	177	702	<1	58.54	173	687	1	52.21	173	683	14	27.61
MK06	78	424	<1	96.18	63	403	1	92.05	63	398	19	50.17
MK07	150	717	<1	47.12	139	693	<1	42.73	139	693	14	22.22
MK08	523	2524	<1	198.96	523	2524	<1	190.279	523	2524	11	101.36
MK09	341	2514	<1	245.16	307	2290	1	221.14	307	2275	10	125.80
MK10	252	2053	<1	219.63	205	1989	<1	203.29	205	1957	7	117.60

Table 4. PSO-OMS vs Other algorithms (1)

	[5]		[8]		[15]		[16]		[11]		[9]	
Max_iteration	50		100 * |O|		1000		Varied[a]		1000		100	
Swarm size	100		10		500				400		300	
MK01	40	40	40	40	40	39	40	39	40	39	40	39
MK02	26	26	27	27	26	26	26	26	26	26	26	26
MK03	204	204	204	204	204	204	204	204	204	204	204	204
MK04	60	60	62	60	60	60	60	60	60	60	61	60
MK05	173	173	178	171	173	171	172	171	172	171	173	173
MK06	58	60	78	62	60	60	60	60	57	60	62	60
MK07	144	140	147	140	140	139	139	139	139	139	139	139
MK08	523	523	523	523	523	523	523	523	523	523	523	523
MK09	307	307	341	307	307	307	307	307	307	307	310	307
MK10	201	205	252	205	205	205	197	205	197	205	214	205

[a]Varied according to Benchmark size.

Table 5. PSO-OMS vs Other algorithms (2)

	[12]		[15]		[11]	
Max_iteration	Varied[a]		1000		1000	
Swarm size			500		400	
4 * 5	11	11	11	–	11	11
8 * 8	16	15	14	14	14	14
10 * 10	8	8	7	7	7	7

[a]Varied according to Benchmark size.

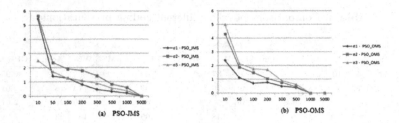

Fig. 4. The standard deviations values for 30 runs with 500 particles

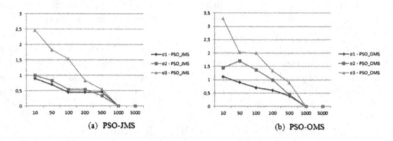

Fig. 5. The standard deviations values for 30 runs with 500 iterations

6   Conclusion

In this paper, an improved version of PSO is provided to solve FJSP. Firstly, we analyze and improve PSO with PSO-JMS for FJSP. Second, we define and improve PSO with only machine schema PSO-OMS for FJSP. We analyze and reduce the solution and search spaces. In the above description, the PSO-OMS for FJSP has proved to be the best variant for solving FJSP benchmarks. The experimental results have confirmed that this variant gives the best makespan and total workload in a minimum run time with a guarantee of particles convergence.

In the future, we will be interested in some more realistic features, e.g., maintenance and breakdowns of machines, which can also be incorporated in the FJSP and solved with the Two-phase PSO. Moreover, we will test the new PSO variant for FJSP with fuzzy processing times.

References

1. Bonyadi, M.R., Michalewicz, Z.: A locally convergent rotationally invariant particle swarm optimization algorithm. Swarm Intell. **8**(3), 159–198 (2014)
2. Bonyadi, M.R., Michalewicz, Z.: Particle swarm optimization for single objective continuous space problems: a review (2017)
3. Brandimarte, P.: Routing and scheduling in a flexible job shop by tabu search. Ann. Oper. Res. **41**(3), 157–183 (1993)
4. Chaudhry, I.A., Khan, A.A.: A research survey: review of flexible job shop scheduling techniques. Int. Trans. Oper. Res. **23**(3), 551–591 (2016)

5. Gao, L., Peng, C.Y., Zhou, C., Li, P.G.: Solving flexible job shop scheduling problem using general particle swarm optimization. In: Proceedings of the 36th CIE Conference on Computers & Industrial Engineering, pp. 3018–3027 (2006)
6. Gao, Y., Du, W., Yan, G.: Selectively-informed particle swarm optimization. Sci. Rep. **5** (2015)
7. Genova, K., Kirilov, L., Guliashki, V.: A survey of solving approaches for multiple objective flexible job shop scheduling problems. Cybern. Inf. Technol. **15**(2), 3–22 (2015)
8. Girish, B.S., Jawahar, N.: A particle swarm optimization algorithm for flexible job shop scheduling problem. In: IEEE International Conference on Automation Science and Engineering, CASE 2009, pp. 298–303. IEEE (2009)
9. Huang, S., Tian, N., Wang, Y., Ji, Z.: Multi-objective flexible job-shop scheduling problem using modified discrete particle swarm optimization. SpringerPlus **5**(1), 1432 (2016)
10. Kacem, I., Hammadi, S., Borne, P.: Approach by localization and multiobjective evolutionary optimization for flexible job-shop scheduling problems. IEEE Trans. Syst. Man Cybern. Part C (Applications and Reviews), **32**(1), 1–13 (2002)
11. Li, X., Gao, L.: An effective hybrid genetic algorithm and tabu search for flexible job shop scheduling problem. Int. J. Prod. Econ. **174**, 93–110 (2016)
12. Moslehi, G., Mahnam, M.: A pareto approach to multi-objective flexible job-shop scheduling problem using particle swarm optimization and local search. Int. J. Prod. Econ. **129**(1), 14–22 (2011)
13. Singh, M.R., Mahapatra, S.S.: A quantum behaved particle swarm optimization for flexible job shop scheduling. Comput. Industr. Eng. **93**, 36–44 (2016)
14. Singh, M.R., Mahapatra, S.S., Mishra, R.: Robust scheduling for flexible job shop problems with random machine breakdowns using a quantum behaved particle swarm optimisation. Int. J. Serv. Oper. Manage. **20**(1), 1–20 (2014)
15. Tang, J., Zhang, G., Lin, B., Zhang, B.: A hybrid algorithm for flexible job-shop scheduling problem. Procedia Eng. **15**, 3678–3683 (2011)
16. Wang, Y.M., Yin, H.L., Qin, K.D.: A novel genetic algorithm for flexible job shop scheduling problems with machine disruptions. Int. J. Adv. Manuf. Technol. **68**, 1317–1326 (2013)
17. Yang, Q., Tian, J., Si, W.: An improved particle swarm optimization based on difference equation analysis. J. Differ. Equ. Appl. **23**(1–2), 135–152 (2017)
18. Zhang, L., Tang, Y., Hua, C., Guan, X.: A new particle swarm optimization algorithm with adaptive inertia weight based on Bayesian techniques. Appl. Soft Comput. **28**, 138–149 (2015)

Simulation-Based Comparison of P-Metaheuristics for FJSP with and Without Fuzzy Processing Time

Zarrouk Rim[1,2]([⊠]), Bennour Imed[2], and Jemai Abderrazek[3]

[1] Polytechnic School, University of Carthage, 2078 La Marsa, Tunisia
rima.zarrouk@gmail.com
[2] LR-NOCCS, National Engineering School of Sousse,
University of Sousse, 4023 Sousse, Tunisia
[3] Faculty of Sciences of Tunis, University of Tunis El Manar, Tunis, Tunisia

Abstract. The population based metaheuristic (P-metaheuristic) is a stochastic algorithm for optimization. This paper presents five different P-metaheuristics (BAT, Firefly, Cuckoo search, basic Particle swarm optimization (BPSO) and a modified PSO (M-PSO)) for solving Flexible Job Shop Problem with and without fuzzy processing time (FJSP/fFJSP). We intend to evaluate and compare the performance of these different algorithms by using thirteen benchmarks for FJSP and four benchmarks for fFJSP. The results demonstrate the superiority of the M-PSO algorithm over the other techniques to solve both FJSP and fFJSP.

Keywords: Flexible job shop scheduling problem
Particle swarm optimization · Population based metaheuristics
Fuzzy processing time

1 Introduction

The population-based metaheuristics (P-metaheuristics) are stochastics algorithms for optimization, which are based on social psychological principles. Among these algorithms, we can find Particle Swarm Optimization (PSO), BAT, Cuckoo Search (CS) and FireFly (FF). In this paper, we are interested in the P-metaheuristics for solving the Flexible Job Shop scheduling Problem (FJSP) and the fuzzy FJSP (fFJSP). FJSP consists in scheduling a set of jobs, composed from atomic operations, on target machines so that the completion time (makespan) of all jobs is minimal. To make the problem much closer to the real applications, the processing time becomes fuzzy variables, so a new problem is introduced: fFJSP.

© Springer International Publishing AG, part of Springer Nature 2018
M. Mouhoub et al. (Eds.): IEA/AIE 2018, LNAI 10868, pp. 408–413, 2018.
https://doi.org/10.1007/978-3-319-92058-0_39

To solve this problem, it is necessary to show which algorithm is better. For this reason, we choose to work under four P-metaheuristics (PSO, FF, CS, and BAT) to solve FJSP and fFJSP. In the literature, some work has been done for the resolution of FJSP with the FF algorithm, like in [5]. There, a hybrid discrete FF was presented to solve the multi-objective FJSP. Some other work has used the BAT algorithm like in [10]. The authors utilized Bat to solve the dual flexible job shop scheduling problem. Only in 2016 with [1], the authors used the CS algorithm to solve the FJSP. Some other work has utilized PSO for the resolution of FJSP, with or without hybridization with other algorithms. However, there has been some work that used PSO for fFJSP. In [8], PSO combined with genetic operators was used for FJSP with fuzzy processing time. The authors in [3] designed an improved version of discrete PSO to solve fFJSP. All BAT, CS and FF work in the literature review, has been used to solve FJSP and not to solve fFJSP.

In this paper, we intend to evaluate and compare the performance of these different P-metaheuristics. These procedures are tested on thirteen references problems, for FJSP, and are tested on a single problem for fFJSP, where the objective function is to minimize the makespan and total machines' workload and compare the run time of the different algorithms.

This paper is organized as follows: Sect. 2 defines FJSP and fFJSP. Section 3 presents the four P-metaheuristics algorithms. Section 4 presents the proposed approach. Section 4 is for the experimental results. The conclusion is in Sect. 5.

2 FJSP with and Without Fuzzy Processing Time

FJSP is defined by the n-uplet (J, O, M, a, d):

- $J = J_1, J_2, \ldots, J_n$ a set of n independent jobs;
- $J_n = (o_{n1}, o_{n2}, \ldots, o_{nf})$ a set of f operations;
- $O = (O_{11}, O_{12}, \ldots), (O_{21}, O_{22}, \ldots), \ldots, (O_{n1}, O_{n2}, \ldots)$ the set of operations, where O_{ji} is operation i of job j;
- $M = \{m_1, m_2, \ldots, m_k\}$ a set of machines;
- $d : O \times M \rightarrow N$, $d(o_{ji}, m_k)$ defines the duration of o_{ji} on m_k.

One or more optimization criteria can be used for FJSP such as: the MakeSpan (MS) and the total machine workload (W_T).

$$MS = Max(C_1, C_2, \ldots, C_j) \tag{1}$$

where C_j is the completion time of job J in a given schedule.

$$W_T = \sum_{j=1}^{n} \sum_{i=1}^{n_i} d(o_{ji}, m_k) \tag{2}$$

In the fFJSP, the processing time of o_{ji} on machine m_k is represented as a triangular fuzzy number (TFN): $t_{i,j,k} = (t_{i,j,k}^1, t_{i,j,k}^2, t_{i,j,k}^3)$ where $t_{i,j,k}^1$ is the best processing time, $t_{i,j,k}^2$ is the most probable processing time and $t_{i,j,k}^3$ is the worst processing time. The fuzzy completion time or the total fuzzy machine workload is computed according to $t_{i,j,k}$ in TFN form [6].

3   Modified PSO

The operating procedure of the scheduling function in BPSO is as follows: Each particle operation is scheduled according to their order in the vector X_{p_o}; i.e. the operation coded by $X_{p_o}[l]$ is scheduled before the one coded by $X_{p_o}[l+1]$. M-PSO, with a reduced search space, has a special scheduling function that helps the population to follow a well-defined research trajectory, thus a reduced solution space. The operating procedure of the scheduling function is as shown in Fig. 1. The ith operations of all jobs are scheduled before the $i+1^{th}$ operations (i.e. all o_{ji} are scheduled before any $o_{j+1,i}$ and the operations are handled according to the order of elements in the vector X_{p_o}. For more explanation, the operations executed in level 1 are: o_{11}, o_{21}, o_{31} and o_{41} respectively, that means that only the first operation of every job is scheduled. In level 2, the second operation of every job is executed. The same scenario is repeated in level 3 and 4. The choice of this strategy is due firstly to the dependence constraint of the operations of the same job required in FJSP and fFJSP. Secondly, this method helps the particles to follow a well-defined path during scheduling, which means avoiding particles to move to a bad position and forcing them to move to another well close to the best.

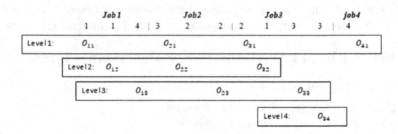

Fig. 1. Scheduling function for M-PSO

4   Experimental Results

The experiments are performed on a dual core machine at 2.8 GHz and 8 GB of RAM. All results are obtained after 10 trials; the scheduler is implemented in C language and all run times are given in seconds.

Experiment-1 P-Metaheuristics for FJSP
The simulations are done with 10 benchmarks of Brandimarte (MK01–MK10) [2] and three benchmarks (4 * 5, 8 * 8 and 10 * 10) of [4] using 500 particles and 500 iterations. Tables 1 and 2 present for each benchmark and for each optimization algorithm the best obtained makespan (MS), the CPU time (Ct), the total workload (W_T) and the number of particles that has reached the best position (R_p). We notice that M-PSO gives the best fitness, a minimum workload and a maximum R_p (Greater than 3 times the R_p of the other algorithms) and it has a CPU time comparable to the others. Compared to BPSO, our approach reduces

a 50% CPU time in all benchmarks and a minimum MS for 80 % of benchmarks. For the small instances, FF has the best results in all the objective functions, but not in the Brandimarte instances. Since our main goal is the minimization of the makespan and the total workload, the best population based metaheuristic is M-PSO.

Table 1. Different population-based metaheuristic algorithms for FJSP instances (1)

	BAT				CS				FF			
	MS	w_T	R_p	Ct	MS	w_T	R_p	Ct	MS	w_T	R_p	Ct
4*5	11	32	21	6.01	11	32	18	2.33	11	32	30	3.6
8*8	16	77	11	12.51	16	75	12	6.01	14	77	21	6.75
10*10	8	49	10	14.2	10	46	12	7.41	7	42	15	9.2
MK01	40	148	12	24.6	40	146	7	18.09	57	148	6	20
MK02	27	154	19	21.08	29	151	10	17	45	154	17	18.36
MK03	204	852	1	101.9	204	852	1	90.98	268	852	6	91.03
MK04	66	364	5	41.77	66	345	1	38.31	89	403	10	39.23
MK05	173	686	5	70.40	173	683	1	57.18	206	687	10	61.8
MK06	63	403	7	150.65	63	424	6	112.7	142	424	8	100.65
MK07	139	693	1	98.71	139	693	<1	43.64	223	693	5	40.9
MK08	523	2524	1	279.54	523	2524	<1	213.02	589	2524	2	205.36
MK09	307	2294	1	359.13	307	2275	<1	311.37	485	2514	1	298.68
MK10	205	2053	1	341.25	205	1989	<1	299.6	406	1989	1	265.7

Table 2. Different population-based metaheuristic algorithms for FJSP instances (2)

	BPSO				M-PSO			
	MS	w_T	R_p	Ct	MS	w_T	R_p	Ct
4*5	11	32	10	2.33	11	32	20	1.65
8*8	16	75	9	10.25	14	73	16	5.33
10*10	10	49	8	13.01	7	46	11	6.69
MK01	40	146	5	30.24	39	146	9	15.09
MK02	27	154	1	32.98	26	151	10	16.77
MK03	204	852	1	169.65	204	852	1	85.98
MK04	62	345	1	84.21	60	345	3	36.02
MK05	173	686	1	111.03	170	683	3	52.21
MK06	63	424	1	190.58	60	398	9	92.05
MK07	139	693	1	95.66	139	693	1	42.73
MK08	523	2524	1	190.2	523	2524	1	190.27
MK09	307	2275	1	221.14	307	2275	1	221.14
MK10	205	1989	1	203.29	201	1957	2	203.29

Table 3. MS results for the 5 P-Metaheuristics - fFJSP

		BAT	CS	FF	BPSO	M-PSO
I1	AV	(20.1; 29.4; 40.3)	(21.4; 32; 43.6)	(26.2; 36.9; 47.7)	(21.1; 37.4, 48.2)	(19.9; 29.6; 40.6)
	BV	(19; 28; 39)	(19; 30; 43)	(25; 32; 40)	(20, 30, 40)	(17; 29; 39)
	WV	(22; 30; 42)	(23; 33; 46)	(27; 41; 54)	(23, 41, 55)	(19; 31; 44)
I2	AV	(33.2; 48.3; 62.7)	(35.1; 51.4; 65.5)	(37.9; 53.3; 66.9)	(37.4; 48.6; 63.1)	(31.7; 46.8; 60.3)
	BV	(32; 47; 59)	(34; 47; 60)	(38; 49; 61)	(34; 49; 60)	(30; 47; 59)
	WV	(38; 50; 64)	(38; 54; 66)	(43; 60; 66)	(40; 50; 64)	(35; 47; 57)
I3	AV	(38.4; 51.9; 70.1)	(39.1; 52.5; 74.4)	(39.9; 55.4; 73.0)	(35.4; 48.6; 63.1)	(32.9; 46.2; 60.8)
	BV	(36; 51; 65)	(37; 49; 65)	(38; 51; 66)	(34; 47;64)	(33; 44; 60)
	WV	(40; 53; 73)	(40; 55; 77)	(40; 59; 75)	(40; 50; 73)	(35; 49; 64)
I4	AV	(25.7; 37.3; 55.0)	(29.2; 40.3; 57.5)	(35.2; 43.9; 61.3)	(28.8; 45.9; 65.3)	(24.8; 36.6; 50.3)
	BV	(23; 36; 50)	(26; 37; 52)	(29; 41; 64)	(26; 36; 52)	(21; 35; 49)
	WV	(25; 44; 59)	(29; 46; 60)	(39; 52; 63)	(29; 52; 72)	(24; 38; 51)

Experiment-2 P-Metaheuristics for fFJSP

The simulations in Tables 3 and 4 are done with the four fFJSP instances (I1, I2, I3 and I4) introduced by [6], using 500 particles and 500 iterations. Table 4 compares the results of M-PSO with previous work [3,6,7,9] in terms of MS for a more measured effectiveness of our proposed approach.

From Table 3, it can be seen that M-PSO is the best P-metaheuristic among all the algorithms in solving the instances. Compared with other algorithms, M-PSO gives the best values in terms of average value (AV), best value (BV) and worst value (WV), which implies that M-PSO is the most effective one.

Table 4. M-PSO VS others algorithms for fFJSP

		M-PSO	ID-PSO [3]	DIGA [6]	CGA [7]
PS[a]		100	100	100	150
MG[b]		1000	1000	1000	1000
I1	AV	(19.9; 29.6; 40.6)	(20.6, 29.87, 40.17)	(22.8, 33.4, 44.6)	(23.1,33.1,43.4)
	BV	(17; 29; 39)	(19, 28, 40)	(20, 31, 40)	(21,29,41)
	WV	(19; 31; 44)	(21, 31, 41)	(25, 37, 49)	(25,37,47)
I2	AV	(31.7; 46.8; 60.3)	(32.47, 46.17, 57.53)	(35.4, 48.4, 62.3)	(35.0,47.1,60.6)
	BV	(30; 47; 59)	(30, 46, 58)	(33, 48, 57)	(32,47,57)
	WV	(35; 47; 57)	(35, 47, 57)	(37, 50, 65)	(38,49,64)
I3	AV	(32.9; 46.2; 60.8)	(32.47, 46.20, 60.90)	(37.3, 53.0, 66.9)	(36.4,50.8,66.0)
	BV	(33; 44; 60)	(33, 45, 60)	(37, 49, 64)	(34,47,63)
	WV	(35; 49; 64)	(35, 49, 64)	(41, 58, 75)	(38,53,71)
I4	AV	(24.8; 36.6; 50.3)	(24.90, 36.67, 51.00)	(29.2, 42.9, 57.5)	(27.4,40.4,55.0)
	BV	(21; 35; 49)	(23, 35, 49)	(29, 41, 56)	(26,37,51)
	WV	(24; 38; 51)	(27, 38, 51)	(29, 46, 60)	(29,42,59)

[a] Population size.
[b] Maximum generation.

From Table 4, is noted that M-PSO has the best results among all other work [6,7,9] in terms of AV, BV and WV. Therefore, we can say that our approach is outperform compared to other metaheuristics.

5 Conclusion

Many population-based metaheuristics have been applied to FJSP and fFJSP. In this paper, these algorithms are used to solve both FJSP and fFJSP and try to prove their efficient. The main contribution of this study is to provide an effective solution to the problem using P-metaheuristics and compare these algorithms to finally realize that the modified version of basic PSO (M-PSO) is the best way to solve problems.

In future work, we will pay more attention to fFJSP with other fuzzy constraints other than the fuzzy processing time and suggest some effective scheduling algorithms for fFJSP under machine breakdown cases.

References

1. Al-Obaidi, A.T.S., Hussein, S.A.: Two improved cuckoo search algorithms for solving the flexible job-shop scheduling problem. Int. J. Perceptive Cogn. Comput. **2**(2), 25–31 (2016)
2. Brandimarte, P.: Routing and scheduling in a flexible job shop by tabu search. Ann. Oper. Res. **41**(3), 157–183 (1993). https://doi.org/10.1007/BF02023073
3. Huang, S., Tian, N., Wang, Y., Ji, Z.: An improved version of discrete particle swarm optimization for flexible job shop scheduling problem with fuzzy processing time. Math. Probl. Eng. **2016** (2016)
4. Kacem, I., Hammadi, S., Borne, P.: Approach by localization and multiobjective evolutionary optimization for flexible job-shop scheduling problems. IEEE Trans. Syst. Man Cybern. Part C Appl. Rev. **32**(1), 1–13 (2002)
5. Karthikeyan, S., Asokan, P., Nickolas, S., Page, T.: A hybrid discrete firefly algorithm for solving multi-objective flexible job shop scheduling problems. Int. J. Bio-Inspired Comput. **7**(6), 386–401 (2015)
6. Lei, D.: A genetic algorithm for flexible job shop scheduling with fuzzy processing time. Int. J. Prod. Res. **48**(10), 2995–3013 (2010)
7. Lei, D.: Co-evolutionary genetic algorithm for fuzzy flexible job shop scheduling. Appl. Soft Comput. **12**(8), 2237–2245 (2012)
8. Niu, Q., Jiao, B., Xingsheng, G.: Particle swarm optimization combined with genetic operators for job shop scheduling problem with fuzzy processing time. Appl. Math. Comput. **205**(1), 148–158 (2008)
9. Xia, W., Zhiming, W.: An effective hybrid optimization approach for multi-objective flexible job-shop scheduling problems. Comput. Ind. Eng. **48**(2), 409–425 (2005)
10. Xu, H., Bao, Z.R., Zhang, T.: Solving dual flexible job-shop scheduling problem using a bat algorithm. Adv. Prod. Eng. Manag. **12**(1), 5 (2017)

Resolving the Manufacturing Cell Design Problem via Hunting Search

Ricardo Soto[1](✉), Broderick Crawford[1](✉), Rodrigo Olivares[1,2](✉),
and Nicolás Pacheco[1](✉)

[1] Pontificia Universidad Católica de Valparaíso, Valparaíso, Chile
{ricardo.soto,broderick.crawford}@pucv.cl, nicolas.pacheco.s@mail.pucv.cl
[2] Universidad de Valparaíso, Valparaíso, Chile
rodrigo.olivares@uv.cl

Abstract. The Manufacturing Cell Design Problems consists in divide a production plant into cells, through which the machines and their processed parts are grouped. The main goal is to build an optimal design that reduces the movements of parts among cells. In this paper, we resolve this problem using a recent population-based metaheuristic called Hunting Search. This technique is inspired by the behavior of a herd of animals working together to hunt a prey. The experimental results demonstrate the efficiency of the proposed approach, which reach all global optimums for a set of 27 well-known instances.

Keywords: Manufacturing cell design problem · Optimization
Metaheuristic · Hunting search

1 Introduction

One of the most recurring problems in factories is designing manufacturing cells to optimize at best the production with the existent resources, due to a bad design will impact negatively. Manufacturing Cell Design Problem (MCDP) is a strategy that proposes an approach based on the use of matrices which represents machines and cells in a production plant. In the last few years, many researches can be found for solving MCDP, such as a production flow analysis for planning group technology [2], the part families problem in flexible manufacturing systems [3], an evaluation of search algorithms and clustering efficiency measures for machine-part matrix clustering [10], and a linear formulation of the machine-part cell formation problem [1].

Several researchers consider applying approximation methods as metaheuristics to resolve MCDP: solving the MCDP via invasive weed optimization [8], a migrating birds optimization algorithm for machine-part cell formation problems [6], solving MCDP by using a dolphin echolocation algorithm [7], solving MCDP using a shuffled frog leaping algorithm [9], among others. In this paper, we resolve

M. Mouhoub et al. (Eds.): IEA/AIE 2018, LNAI 10868, pp. 414–420, 2018.
https://doi.org/10.1007/978-3-319-92058-0_40

it using a recent population-based metaheuristic called Hunting Search (HuS) [4,5] inspired by the behavior of a herd of animals working together to hunt a prey such as lions, wolves, and dolphins.

We perform computational experiments by using a set of 90 well-known MCDP instances, which were resolved beforehand using exact optimization methods [1]. The results were promising, reaching the global optimum in all instances.

The outline of this paper is as follows. Section 2 describes the MCDP. Section 3 presents the approach used. Then, in Sect. 4 we conduce a discussion of the computational experimental. Finally, conclusions and future works are presented in Sect. 5.

2 Manufacturing Cell Design Problem

Group Technology is a technique based on a general principle that could be understood as "a single solution can be found to a set of similar problems". Manufacturing Cell Design applies this principle, dividing production plants into cells and each one them has machines that process and produce a set of similar parts; similarities could be geometrical, materials, weight, necessary operations, and others.

The principal idea of the MCDP is to identify an ideal cell design that minimizes inter-cell movements, where each movement means that a part must visit another cell. An optimal organization implies benefits such as increase productivity, reduce of production costs and time.

To reorganize, routes of each part must be known, allowing to determine which machines were visited by the part. In this approach, a binary matrix will be used to represent machines (rows) that are needed to manufacture a part (columns). The binary machine-part matrix is denoted as $A = a_{ij}$.

After identify our Machine-Part matrix using a constant number of cells, we proceed to get the machine-cell matrix and part-cell matrix. Those three are used to get a new distribution for machines and parts in cells.

Boctor gave a mathematical formulation to resolve MCDP [1]. The objective function of this problem is represented by the following mathematical model:

$$\text{minimize} \sum_{k=1}^{C} \sum_{i=1}^{M} \sum_{j=1}^{C} a_{ij} z_{jk} (1 - y_{ik}) \tag{1}$$

subject to

$$\sum_{k=1}^{C} y_{ik} = 1 \tag{2}$$

$$\sum_{k=1}^{C} z_{jk} = 1 \tag{3}$$

$$\sum_{i=1}^{M} y_{ik} \leq M_{max} \tag{4}$$

where M : number of machines, P : number of parts, C : number of cells, i : index of machines (i = 1,..., M), j : index of parts (j = 1,..., P), k : index of cells (k = 1,..., C), M_{max} : max number of machines per cell, $A = a_{ij}$: binary machine-part incidence matrix, with $a_{ij} = 1$ if machine i is visited by part j to be processed, or $a_{ij} = 1$ otherwise. $Y = y_{ik}$: binary machine-cell matrix, where $y_{ik} = 1$ if machine i belongs to the cell k, or $y_{ik} = 0$ otherwise. Finally, $Z = z_{jk}$: binary part-cell matrix, where $y_{jk} = 1$ if part j belongs to the cell k, or $y_{jk} = 0$ otherwise.

3   Hunting Search

Hunting Search (HuS) is based on the natural behavior of a herd of animals working together to encircle and hunt a prey. It was created by R. Oftadeh and M.J. Mahjoob [5] and later revised by themselves [4]. The distance between each hunter and the prey determine the chance of a successful hunt.

3.1   Hunting Search Steps

A hunter represents a solution, the hunter leader is the best solution at the moment and the prey is the optimum.

1. Initialize an optimization problem and algorithm parameters: In this step the parameters of the MCDP and Hunting Search (HuS) are specified. The HuS ones are:
2. Initialize hunting group: Using the parameter HGS, feasible random solutions are generated to fill the hunting group. After that, a leader is chosen.
3. Moving toward the leader: Each hunter reach a new position after moving toward the leader as follows:

$$x_i' = x_i + Rand \times MML \times (x_i^{leader} - x_i) \tag{5}$$

where x_i' is the new position to be calculated, x_i is the actual position, $Rand$ is a uniform random number which varies between 0 and 1, MML is defined in step 1, and x_i^{leader} is the current leader position.

4. Position correction: To conduct an efficient hunt, each hunter except the leader cooperate and choose a new position to find better solutions. This is determined as follows:

$$x_i' = \begin{cases} x_i' \in \{x_i^1, ..., x_i^{HGS}\} \text{ with probability HGCR} \\ x_i \in x_i \text{ with probability (1 - HGCR)} \end{cases} \tag{6}$$

With probability HGCR, the new position will be selected randomly from the hunting group. With probability 1-HGCR, the new position will be selected randomly without being limited to the values stored in the hunting group. It must be feasible. Each position chosen from the HG is examined to determine if it should be corrected or not. PCR parameter defined in step 1 sets the rate of position correction, if it falls into PCR then the hunter needs a position correction, if it falls into 1-PCR then its new position doesn't require correction. Therefore, position correction is performed as follows:

$$x_i' \leftarrow x_i' - Ra(it) \tag{7}$$

where: $Ra(it)$ is equals to:

$$Ra(it) = Ra_{min}(max(x_i) - min(x_i))exp\left(\frac{Ln\left(\frac{Ra_{min}}{Ra_{max}}\right) \times it}{IE}\right) \tag{8}$$

where: it : Actual iteration value, $max(x_i)$, : Maximum possible value of the hunter position, $min(x_i)$: Minimum possible value of the hunter position, $Ra_{max})$: Maximum value of relative search radius of the hunter, $Ra_{min})$: Minimum value of relative search radius of the hunter, and IE : Maximum number of iterations defined in step 1. The new position must be feasible and better than the last one, if not then the hunter will return.

5. Reorganizing the hunting group: As the search progress, there's a chance that the HG get trapped in a local minimum or maximum. If this happens, the hunters must reorganize themselves to keep finding the optimum. Hunters know when they got trapped calculating the difference between the leader and worse hunter, if this is lesser than REORG (defined in step one), then a new position for each hunter must be calculated as follows:

$$x_i' = x_i + \frac{rand \times [r(max(x_i), min(x_i)) - x_i]}{\alpha \times EN^\beta} \tag{9}$$

where $r(max(x_i), min(x_i))$ is a random value between the maximum and minimum possible value of the hunter position (x_i). EN represent the number of times that HG get trapped in a minimum or maximum local. The values of α and β determine the global convergence rate of the algorithm, small values cause a slow convergence, this is recommended for large optimization problems, and large values cause the algorithm to converge faster, this is recommended for small optimization problems [5].

6. Repeat steps 3, 4 and 5 until termination criterion is satisfied: Each time we reach step 6, the termination criterion must be examined to determine if this is satisfied or not. If not, then steps 3, 4 and 5 are repeated.

4   Experimental Results

The MCDP and HuS were encoded in Java and executed on Windows 7 professional with an Intel Core i3-2120CPU @ 3.30 ghz (4CPUs) processor, 16 GB

RAM, and 120 GB SSD. The algorithm performance was evaluated in an experimental way, executing and resolving each of the 90 boctor instances 31 times. The parameters used after a sampling were:

- REORG = 15, MML = 0.09, HGCR = 0.9, PCR = 0.3, α = 1, β = 0.5, IE = 15000, maxRad = 0.9, minRad = 0.5

A total of 3 experiments were performed, each one resolved the 27 instances 31 times. The difference is that the value of HGS varies by 40, starting with HGS = 20 (first experiment), and finishing with HGS = 100 (last experiment).

Tables 1, 2 and 3 show the results of HuS; where: ID is the instance number, IT is the average iteration number where the optimum was found, RT is the average time (milliseconds), and OP is the median of optimums reached by HuS. The last row of each table shows the average for IT and RT, in addition, the times that HuS optimums equals to Boctor's one.

The experimental results exhibit that the proposed approach is able to reach the global optimum for all 27 instances with HGS = 100, that's because a larger group of hunters were working together to find the optimum.

Table 1. HuS results for Boctor's problem 1

	Boctor	HGS = 20			HGS = 60			HGS = 100		
ID	OP	IT	RT	OP	IT	RT	OP	IT	RT	OP
1	11	13128	19271	11	2751	14840	11	9493	72222	11
2	11	12498	9383	11	61	185	11	913	3283	11
3	11	6323	4232	11	257	542	11	281	1004	11
4	11	11480	7561	11	286	570	11	111	369	11
5	11	12425	8076	11	432	851	11	1537	4958	11
6	27	10505	25022	28	4051	29170	27	3911	49235	27
7	18	12606	19257	20	6656	59842	20	4513	55680	18
8	11	10389	12305	11	8348	38623	11	1224	11383	11
9	11	9816	9393	11	611	2091	11	312	1796	11
		11019	12722	7	2606	16302	8	2477	22214	9

Table 2. HuS results for Boctor's problem 2

	Boctor	HGS = 20			HGS = 60			HGS = 100		
ID	OP	IT	RT	OP	IT	RT	OP	IT	RT	OP
10	7	10481	14462	7	7284	34939	7	6916	55260	7
11	6	12256	9890	6	3833	9030	6	1361	5616	6
12	4	14108	10698	4	3106	6978	4	905	5285	4
13	3	10242	7410	3	152	325	3	1030	5214	3
14	3	9673	6522	3	440	885	3	205	683	3
15	7	6672	14393	7	1015	6378	7	113	1280	7
16	6	9040	12659	6	2818	17077	6	2911	21920	6
17	6	9429	11314	7	3494	15673	7	2471	15926	6
18	6	10239	10376	7	2223	7670	6	579	3065	6
		10238	**10858**	**7**	**2707**	**10995**	**8**	**1832**	**12694**	**9**

Table 3. HuS results for Boctor's problem 3

	Boctor	HGS = 20			HGS = 60			HGS = 100		
ID	OP	IT	RT	OP	IT	RT	OP	IT	RT	OP
19	4	14854	21994	4	9190	43760	5	8627	72305	4
20	4	14998	12257	4	9328	22250	4	4072	18978	4
21	4	13769	9675	4	3184	6587	4	1398	4645	4
22	3	11386	7797	3	2408	5249	3	1294	4404	3
23	1	14007	9467	1	1255	2510	1	481	1595	1
24	9	9952	22099	9	1518	14088	9	3973	50883	9
25	4	10434	14147	6	1700	9558	4	1860	15237	4
26	4	10490	12516	5	3169	11373	4	2028	16730	4
27	4	12978	12858	4	326	1006	4	1561	7528	4
		12541	**13646**	**7**	**3564**	**12931**	**8**	**2810**	**21367**	**9**

5 Conclusions

In this paper, we have presented an approach to resolve MCDP via Hunting
Search. This algorithm is an approximate method that is inspired by the behavior of a herd of animals working together to hunt a prey. On the other hand,
we present and resolve the MCDP. MCDP is a strategy to divide production
plants into cells and each one them has machines that process and produce a
set of similar parts. Experimental results illustrated a good performance and
robustness by the algorithm, reaching the global optimum in all 90 well-known
instances of Boctor. As future work, we plan to integrate autonomous search
to the presented approach, helping to dynamically select the best parameters

setting during the search process by analyzing the performance indicators, such as fitness, distances and variability of solutions, among others.

Acknowledgment. Ricardo Soto is supported by Grant CONICYT/FONDECYT/ REGULAR/1160455. Broderick Crawford is supported by Grant CONICYT/ FONDECYT/REGULAR/1171243. Rodrigo Olivares is supported by CONICYT/ FONDEF/IDeA/ID16I10449, FONDECYT/STIC-AMSUD/17STIC-03, FONDE-CYT/MEC/MEC80170097, and Postgraduate Grant Pontificia Universidad Católica de Valparaíso (INF - PUCV 2015-2018).

References

1. Boctor, F.F.: A linear formulation of the machine-part cell formation problem. Int. J. Prod. Res. **29**(2), 343–356 (1991)
2. Burbidge, J.L.: Production flow analysis for planning group technology. J. Oper. Manag. **10**(1), 5–27 (1991). Special Issue on Group Technology and Cellular Manufacturing
3. Kusiak, A.: The part families problem in flexible manufacturing systems. Ann. Oper. Res. **3**(6), 277–300 (1985)
4. Oftadeh, R., Mahjoob, M., Shariatpanahi, M.: A novel meta-heuristic optimization algorithm inspired by group hunting of animals: hunting search. Comput. Math. Appl. **60**(7), 2087–2098 (2010)
5. Oftadeh, R., Mahjoob, M.J.: A new meta-heuristic optimization algorithm: Hunting search. In: 2009 Fifth International Conference on Soft Computing, Computing with Words and Perceptions in System Analysis, Decision and Control. IEEE, September 2009
6. Soto, R., Crawford, B., Almonacid, B., Paredes, F.: A migrating birds optimization algorithm for machine-part cell formation problems. In: Sidorov, G., Galicia-Haro, S.N. (eds.) MICAI 2015. LNCS (LNAI), vol. 9413, pp. 270–281. Springer, Cham (2015). https://doi.org/10.1007/978-3-319-27060-9_22
7. Soto, R., et al.: Solving manufacturing cell design problems by using a dolphin echolocation algorithm. In: Gervasi, O., et al. (eds.) ICCSA 2016. LNCS, vol. 9790, pp. 77–86. Springer, Cham (2016). https://doi.org/10.1007/978-3-319-42092-9_7
8. Soto, R., Crawford, B., Castillo, C., Paredes, F.: Solving the manufacturing cell design problem via invasive weed optimization. In: Silhavy, R., Senkerik, R., Oplatkova, Z.K., Silhavy, P., Prokopova, Z. (eds.) Artificial Intelligence Perspectives in Intelligent Systems. AISC, vol. 464, pp. 115–126. Springer, Cham (2016). https://doi.org/10.1007/978-3-319-33625-1_11
9. Soto, R., Crawford, B., Vega, E., Johnson, F., Paredes, F.: Solving manufacturing cell design problems using a shuffled frog leaping algorithm. In: Gaber, T., Hassanien, A.E., El-Bendary, N., Dey, N. (eds.) The 1st International Conference on Advanced Intelligent System and Informatics (AISI2015), November 28-30, 2015, Beni Suef, Egypt. AISC, vol. 407, pp. 253–261. Springer, Cham (2016). https://doi.org/10.1007/978-3-319-26690-9_23
10. Venugopal, V., Narendran, T.: A genetic algorithm approach to the machine-component grouping problem with multiple objectives. Comput. Ind. Eng. **22**(4), 469–480 (1992)

Improved Exploration and Exploitation in Particle Swarm Optimization

Dania Tamayo-Vera[1], Stephen Chen[2(✉)], Antonio Bolufé-Röhler[1],
James Montgomery[3], and Tim Hendtlass[4]

[1] School of Mathematics and Computer Science,
University of Havana, Havana, Cuba
{d.tamayo,bolufe}@matcom.uh.cu
[2] School of Information Technology, York University, Toronto, Canada
sychen@yorku.ca
[3] School of Technology, Environments and Design,
University of Tasmania, Hobart, Australia
james.montgomery@utas.edu.au
[4] Department of Computer Science and Software Engineering,
Swinburne University of Technology, Melbourne, Australia
thendtlass@swin.edu.au

Abstract. Exploration and exploitation are analyzed in Particle Swarm Optimization (PSO) through a set of experiments that make new measurements of these key features. Compared to analyses on diversity and particle trajectories, which focus on particle motions and their potential to achieve exploration and exploitation, our analysis also focuses on the *pbest* positions that reflect the actual levels of exploration and exploitation that have been achieved by PSO. A key contribution of this paper is a clear criterion for when restarting particles can be expected to be a useful strategy in PSO.

Keywords: Exploration · Exploitation
Particle Swarm Optimization · Multi-modal search spaces

1 Introduction

To improve "exploration" and "exploitation", we must first have clear measurements on existing levels of these features, and these measurements require precise definitions. We begin by dividing a multi-modal search space into attraction basins which each have a single local optimum. Each point in an attraction basin has a monotonic path of increasing (for maxima) or decreasing (for minima) fitness to its local optima. A search point (e.g. the current position of a particle) is then defined to be performing "exploration" if it is in a different attraction basin than its reference solution (e.g. the particle's *pbest* position), and it is defined to be performing "exploitation" if it is in the same attraction basin as its reference solution.

© Springer International Publishing AG, part of Springer Nature 2018
M. Mouhoub et al. (Eds.): IEA/AIE 2018, LNAI 10868, pp. 421–433, 2018.
https://doi.org/10.1007/978-3-319-92058-0_41

Optimization in a multi-modal search space involves exploration to find the best attraction basin and exploitation to find the local optimum within this attraction basin. The performance of a search technique in multi-modal search spaces thus depends on its ability to perform both exploration and exploitation, and it is noted that Particle Swarm Optimization (PSO) [1] has several weaknesses in its ability to perform each of these two critical tasks. A large number of modifications have been proposed to address these weaknesses [2], but most of these modifications do not have consensus acceptance (e.g. by becoming part of a standard implementation such as [3]).

We believe the lack of precise definitions for the concepts of "exploration" and "exploitation" [4] have interfered with the ability to specifically identify PSOs weaknesses in these critical tasks, and thus to subsequently measure if any of the proposed modifications have had the intended effect. The improved precision of the above definitions for exploration and exploitation allow us to conduct quantitative experiments in which the effects of modifications can be measured at both the operational level (e.g. more exploitation has been observed) and at the performance level (e.g. average results on benchmark functions has improved).

Our research begins with an analysis on the operational characteristics of a standard implementation of PSO [3]. The first key observation we make is that many *pbest* positions in the final swarm do not represent local optima. This result exposes a weakness in the ability of PSO to perform exploitation. If PSO was able to fully exploit all of the attraction basins represented by its *pbest* positions, its performance could improve. Additional measurements also indicate that a very small number of attraction basins are fully exploited/have their local optimum reached, and this observation raises concerns about the effectiveness of exploration in PSO.

Based on the above analysis, we make several modifications to PSO. The effects of these modifications are measured using an experimental procedure that is presented as part of the Background Section. Baseline measurements of exploration and exploitation in standard PSO are then presented in Sect. 3. In Sect. 4, we introduce a modification to improve exploitation in PSO, and we present both operational and performance data to support the usefulness of this modification. We then add another modification to improve exploration in Sect. 5, and we again present both operational and performance data to verify its benefits. We then provide a Discussion of our experiments and results before some brief Conclusions close the paper.

2   Background

"Exploration" and "exploitation" are highly discussed topics in metaheuristics and evolutionary computation. However, these concepts often lack precise definitions. A broad survey of over 100 papers led Crepinšek, Liu, and Mernik to the unexpected conclusion that "The fact that until now exploration and exploitation have only been implicitly defined in EAs comes as a big surprise" [4]. We believe the lack of precise definitions hinders the ability to specify and collect quantitative data for in-depth analysis. A subsequent complaint of contemporary research is that a large amount of it has "only presented experimental results [on benchmark problem sets] and did not provide adequate discussion (neither from theoretical perspective, nor general discussions) on merits of the proposed approach" [2].

The theoretical perspective that we will provide in this paper is based on quantitative data collected on the Rastrigin function. The basic experimental procedure was first presented as part of the development of Leaders and Followers? [5], and it leverages the known structure of the search space for the Rastrigin function. Specifically, every point in the search space with an integer value in each dimension is a local optimum, and the nearest local optimum for every other point can be found by rounding that point's coordinate values to their nearest integer. These features allow us to divide the search space into non-overlapping attraction basins, know the fitness of (the local optimum of) an attraction basin, and calculate the difference in fitness between an existing solution and its nearest local optimum. We believe that an analysis based on these types of quantitative data can provide a more "adequate discussion" as requested in [2].

Our analysis will also focus specifically on the achievement of exploration and exploitation as opposed to "inputs" such as diversity and particle trajectories. For example, it has been said that "Diversity is related to the notions of exploration and exploitation: the more diverse a swarm is, the more its particles are dispersed over the search space, and the more the swarm is exploring" [6]. However, it should be noted that even though a diverse swarm has the potential for more exploration, there is nothing that prevents a diverse swarm from performing exploitation instead (according to our definitions). In fact, studies which analyze the oscillatory nature of particle trajectories [7] clearly demonstrate that even particles which travel far away from their reference solutions (e.g. a *pbest* attractor) often spend significant time near these reference solutions as well. By focusing on the effects to *pbest* positions, our experiments measure what has happened in terms of exploration and exploitation as opposed to what was hoped to happen.

3 An Analysis of Standard PSO

We base our experiments on a version of standard particle swarm optimization [3] with a ring topology and the key parameter values of $\chi = 0.72984$ and $c_1 = c_2 = 2.05$. Additional implementation details are the use of $p = 50$ particles [3], zero initial velocities [8], and Reflect-Z for particles that exceed the boundaries of the search space (i.e. reflecting the position back into the search space and setting the velocity to zero) [9]. The source code for this implementation is available online [10].

All of our experiments with Rastrigin are based on averages for 30 independent trials in $n = 30$ dimensions using a termination condition of $10,000 \cdot n$

total function evaluations (FEs). As shown in (1), Rastrigin develops a globally convex, multi-modal search space by superimposing a sinusoid over a parabolic base function. The standard parameters are $A = 10$ and $x_i \in [-5.12; 5.12]$. Rastrigin is an n-dimensional minimization problem with a single global optimum of zero when all $x_i = 0$, and it contains a high number of local optima evenly distributed across the entire search space. These optima are located at the integer coordinates of a regular grid of size one, which means that the function has 11^n optima within the search boundaries defined above. Given a solution in this well-structured search space, the nearest (local) optimum for any solution x can be easily determined by rounding each component x_i to its nearest integer.

$$f(x) = An + \sum_{i=1}^{n} [x_i^2 - A \cos (2\pi x_i)] \tag{1}$$

Knowing the location of every local optima and the boundaries of their attraction basins allows us to easily and directly measure aspects of exploration and exploitation according to our previous definitions. We can also measure what we call the "fitness of an attraction basin" — i.e. the fitness of the local optimum of an attraction basin. For our implementation of standard PSO, we have recorded the fittest solution (i.e. the solution that would be $gbest$ when using a star topology), the fittest attraction basin represented by the $pbest$ positions, and the fittest attraction basin visited by any particle (see Fig. 1). It should be noted that the three curves plateau after about 50% of the allocated function evaluations. This premature convergence happens despite PSO's inability to fully exploit all of the attraction basins represented by $pbest$ positions, and in particular the fittest of these attraction basins. It should be noted that the fittest attraction basin is not necessarily associated with the fittest overall solution, and this situation is the likely cause of the gap between the curves for the fittest solution and the fittest attraction basin represented by a $pbest$ position.

It is also worthwhile to note the large gap between the fittest attraction basin visited by a particle and the fittest attraction basin retained by a $pbest$ position. This gap indicates a large divergence between what is happening at the particle level (e.g. their diversity and trajectories) and with their $pbest$ positions (i.e. what updates are actually being stored). We thus focus our attention on $pbest$ positions by recording the fitness of each $pbest$ and its associated attraction basin. The difference between these two values is a measure of the amount of exploitation that has occurred in that attraction basin. For the Rastrigin function in 30 dimensions, we define a difference of less than 10 between these two values to indicate that the represented attraction basin has been "fully exploited". The total height of each attraction basin is at least 600, so a gap of less than 10 represents significant exploitation.

Table 1 shows the average number of $pbest$ positions that represent fully exploited attraction basins at the end of the 30 independent trials. We also report the total number of distinct attraction basins that have been fully exploited, the number of times a $pbest$ which is within 10 of the local optimum of its current attraction basin moves into another attraction basin (i.e. that its particle has

Table 1. Analysis of standard PSO

Algorithm	Fully exploited final *pbests*	Fully exploited attraction basins	Fully exploited *pbests* moved	Function fitness
PSO	38.2	13.1	0.0	66.8

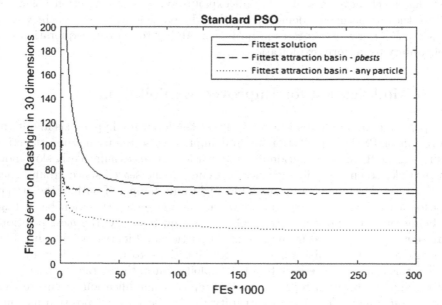

Fig. 1. Analysis of Standard PSO. The gap between the fittest solution and the fittest attraction basin represented by a *pbest* position shows a weakness in the ability of PSO to perform exploitation.

performed successful exploration after full exploitation), and the fitness of the best overall solution at the end of the allocated 300,000 FEs.

Two key observations can be made from the collected data. First, a large number of *pbest* positions (i.e. 11.8/50 or 23.6%) are still a large distance away from their nearest local optimum (i.e. they have a fitness difference of at least 10). This indicates a weakness in the ability of PSO to perform exploitation in the vicinity of these *pbest* positions. Second, no particles (i.e. 0.0) that achieve "full exploitation" of an attraction basin ever move their *pbest* position into a different attraction basin (i.e. perform exploration according to our definitions). At the end of the allocated FEs, the *pbest* positions represent an average of 13.1 distinct attraction basins that have been fully exploited.

These observations contradict a common narrative on the operation of PSO. The goal of a ring topology (compared to a star topology) is to slow down, not stop, communication amongst the particles. However, our results indicate that all of the particles and their *pbest* positions have not converged to a single optimum, and that at least 13 distinct attraction basins remain on average. The communication chain in PSO is broken by the inability of a particle which has achieved full exploitation of one attraction basin to ever successfully explore (i.e. move its *pbest* to) another attraction basin – this includes known attraction basins such as the (fitter) attraction basins represented by the *pbest* positions for other particles in the swarm. In combination with the observation of (11.8) particles which never achieve the full exploitation of any attraction basin, we believe these experiments demonstrate that the particle trajectories achieved by standard PSO have weaknesses in both their ability to perform exploration and their ability to perform exploitation.

4   A Modification for Improved Exploitation

The preceding observations lead us to make the following hypothesis about the operation of PSO. Exploitation to find improving solutions in the attraction basins for the Rastrigin function in 30 dimensions requires sufficiently slow moving particles to ensure a fine-grained sampling of the search space around each *pbest* attractor/reference solution. This might only happen if both of the attractors for a particle (i.e. *pbest* and *lbest*) are in the same attraction basin (e.g. by being the same position). In PSO with a ring topology, the *lbest* positions represent the fittest *pbest* from the current particle and its two neighbours. This strategy makes it possible for some *pbest* positions to never be *lbest*, and we believe this could be necessary to allow exploitation in the attraction basin that the given *pbest* position represents. We propose a modification to ensure that every *pbest* position has the opportunity to also be an *lbest* position at some time so as to increase the probability of fully exploiting its represented attraction basin.

Our modification will select the *lbest* position for a given particle by rotating through the usual *pbest* positions from which it normally selects its *lbest* position. This rotation involves four steps in each cycle which repeat until allocated function evaluations are exhausted. In the first step, *lbest* is selected as usual, i.e. the *lbest* of particle i is the fittest of $\{pbest_{i-1}, pbest_i, pbest_{i+1}\}$. In the next three steps, the *lbest* of particle i is selected as $pbest_{i-1}$ first, then $pbest_i$, and finally $pbest_{i+1}$. A simple parameter tuning revealed that, for Rastrigin, a suitable frequency for the rotation cycle is to move to the next step every 40 iterations (i.e. 2000 function evaluations if the population size is 50).

The goal of this modification is to promote the exploitation of more attraction basins. As it is shown in Table 2, this goal has been achieved as the number of particles which can fully exploit an attraction basin as evidenced by the location of its final *pbest* position increases to an average of 44.6 per trial. As these particles perform exploitation, they are less likely to abandon their attraction basins, and this leads in an increase in the number of distinct attraction basins that are fully exploited – which now averages 42.9 per trial. Another positive outcome, as Fig. 2 shows, is that premature convergence of the fittest solution no longer occurs, and this helps the swarm achieve a better overall performance on Rastrigin. However, the number of *pbest* positions that are in fully exploited attraction

basins which move to another attraction basin remains at 0.0, and this limits
the ability of this modification to reduce the gap between the fittest attraction
basin visited by any particle and the fittest attraction basin represented by a
pbest position.

Table 2. Analysis of rotate PSO

Algorithm	Fully exploited final *pbests*	Fully exploited attraction basins	Fully exploited *pbests* Moved	Function fitness
Rotation PSO	44.6	42.9	0.0	46.5

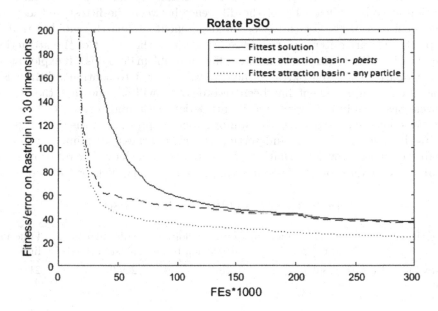

Fig. 2. Analysis of Rotate PSO. The gap between the fittest solution and the fittest
attraction basin represented by a *pbest* position has been reduced.

5   A Modification for Improved Exploration

The previous modification was able to improve the number of fully exploited
attraction basins, but it is still a very small number. A key weakness in PSO
appears to be the inability of a particle which has performed exploitation in
one attraction basin to ever achieve successful exploration in another attraction
basin. Based on our hypothesis that exploitation to find a better solution around
a *pbest* position requires sufficiently slow particle speeds, the ability of a particle

to find a highly fit solution (e.g. one that has experienced a large amount of exploitation) in another attraction basin will be extremely unlikely due to the relatively high speeds caused by the large attraction vectors that result from having attractors at least as far apart as the size of an attraction basin. If particle speeds which allow the visiting of different attraction basins (i.e. our definition of exploration) make finding highly fit solutions in these attraction basins next to impossible, then modifications that alter more than particle trajectories (e.g. increasing diversity) will be necessary to achieve "successful" exploration (i.e. exploration which leads to a moved/updated *pbest* position).

Our next modification aims to restart particles that have fully exploited their current attraction basin without improving the best overall fitness of the swarm. During the normal operation of PSO, we cannot measure the fitness of an attraction basin, so we instead predict that a particle has fully exploited its attraction basin if the fitness of its *pbest* position has not improved during a rotation cycle by at least 1% of the difference between the fittest and least fit *pbest* positions in the swarm. A secondary benefit of this threshold is that it adapts the restart criteria to the search space (e.g. the height of the attraction basins which will of course vary across different problem domains). If exploitation is continuing for a given particle, then we will allow it to continue. Otherwise, if insufficient improvement has been recorded, we will assume that the stalled particle has already fully exploited its attraction basin and restart it. A restart involves relocating the particle to a uniform random position in the search space, setting its velocity to zero, and setting the *pbest* fitness to infinity. A simple parameter tuning revealed that good results can be achieved if rotation steps occur every 40 iterations and restarts are performed every cycle or 160 iterations.

Table 3. Analysis of Rotate + Restart PSO

Algorithm	Fully exploited final *pbests*	Fully exploited attraction basins	Fully exploited *pbests* moved	Function fitness
Rotation + Restart PSO	38.0	218.2	209.9	21.5

Table 3 shows that the most distinctive feature of adding restarts to PSO is the large number of *pbests* from fully exploited attraction basins that are now moved/updated (through being restarted). This measurement is based on the actual fitness difference between the *pbest* position and its attraction basin being less than 10 as opposed to the predictive estimate used to restart the particle. The ability to restart particles once they have fully exploited their attraction basins improves exploration as indicated by the increase in the number of attraction basins that are fully exploited. As Fig. 3 shows, this improved exploration greatly reduces the gap between the curves for the fittest attraction basin represented by a *pbest* position and the fittest attraction basin visited by any particle. The effect on performance is also observed with a large improvement for PSO on the Rastrigin function.

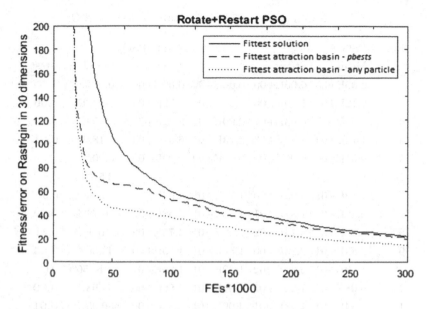

Fig. 3. Analysis of Rotate + Restart PSO. The gap between the fittest attraction basin represented by a *pbest* position and the fittest attraction basin visited by any particle has been reduced.

To further study the proposed modifications, we tested them on the CEC 2013 benchmark [11] (see Table 3). This benchmark consists of 28 unimodal and multi-modal functions divided into three sets: unimodal functions (1 to 5), basic multi-modal functions (6 to 20), and composite multi-modal functions (21 to 28). The experimental setup follows the directions given in [11]: a total of 51 randomized trials with a maximum allocation of 300,000 function evaluations were performed on each function.

We report the mean and standard deviation of the fitness errors and the relative differences of the mean errors (%-diff). The %-diff of the mean error m_1 of standard PSO with respect to the mean m_2 of the modified PSO is given by $100 \cdot (m_1 - m_2)/\max(m_1, m_2)$. Hence, positive %-diff values indicate that the modified PSO outperforms standard PSO. A t-test between the two results is also reported in order to make a comparison on the basis of statistically significant differences at the 5% level. However, we are unable to report additional insights for *pbest* positions since these previous experiments leveraged a unique feature from Rastrigin which allowed precise measurements of exploration and exploitation.

6   Discussion

An unexpected observation in the operation of standard PSO is that we never detected a *pbest* position from a "fully exploited" attraction basin being replaced

Table 4. Comparison PSO and Rotate + Restart PSO.

No.	PSO		Rotate + Restart PSO			
	Mean	Stdev	Mean	Stdev	%-diff	t-test
1	0.00E+00	0.00E+00	0.00E+00	0.00E+00	0.00%	-
2	2.12E+06	1.06E+06	3.21E+06	1.72E+06	−34.07%	**0.00**
3	7.09E+07	6.03E+07	2.09E+07	2.22E+07	70.59%	**0.00**
4	1.73E+04	3.83E+03	2.13E+04	6.61E+03	−18.69%	**0.01**
5	0.00E+00	0.00E+00	0.00E+00	0.00E+00	0.00%	-
1–5					3.57%	
6	1.62E+01	8.98E+00	1.72E+01	8.94E+00	−5.88%	0.07
7	6.46E+01	1.81E+01	1.50E+01	5.58E+00	76.72%	**0.00**
8	2.09E+01	5.74E−02	2.09E+01	4.75E−02	−0.05%	0.22
9	2.89E+01	2.26E+00	1.54E+01	1.89E+00	46.56%	**0.04**
10	1.19E−01	5.31E−02	1.39E−01	1.80E−01	−14.56%	0.05
11	6.08E+01	1.20E+01	2.06E+01	5.66E+00	66.08%	**0.00**
12	8.34E+01	1.78E+01	4.09E+01	8.32E+00	50.95%	**0.01**
13	1.36E+02	2.34E+01	9.01E+01	1.56E+01	33.63%	**0.03**
14	2.59E+03	4.09E+02	1.11E+03	2.74E+02	57.33%	**0.00**
15	3.98E+03	6.36E+02	3.42E+03	6.19E+02	14.02%	**0.04**
16	1.65E+00	3.73E−01	2.11E+00	2.83E−01	−21.78%	**0.04**
17	1.04E+02	1.63E+01	8.02E+01	7.86E+00	22.81%	**0.00**
18	1.68E+02	2.84E+01	2.11E+02	1.89E+01	−20.42%	**0.00**
19	5.89E+00	1.60E+00	3.32E+00	6.02E−01	43.70%	**0.00**
20	1.17E+01	4.93E−01	1.10E+01	4.15E−01	5.61%	0.15
6–20					23.65%	
21	2.24E+02	5.81E+01	2.16E+02	4.12E+01	3.85%	0.05
22	3.09E+03	4.80E+02	1.05E+03	2.68E+02	66.04%	**0.00**
23	4.57E+03	6.42E+02	3.48E+03	5.13E+02	24.01%	**0.00**
24	2.76E+02	6.26E+00	2.48E+02	8.31E+00	10.06%	**0.00**
25	2.92E+02	7.16E+00	2.65E+02	6.27E+00	9.20%	0.13
26	2.30E+02	6.57E+01	2.03E+02	2.16E−01	11.80%	**0.03**
27	1.04E+03	4.86E+01	7.53E+02	5.64E+01	27.68%	**0.00**
28	3.00E+02	2.80E+01	2.94E+02	6.50E+01	2.00%	0.74
21–28					19.33%	
1–28					18.83%	

by a new *pbest* position in a different attraction basin. This implies that once exploitation of an attraction basin occurs, no further exploration for new attraction basins is ever successful. This statement only applies directly to the Rastrigin function and the current experiments (and specifically the current implementation of PSO), so it is useful to study this function more closely to see how the current results might extend to other functions and other modified versions of PSO.

The study on Rastrigin presented in [5] shows how the potential for successful exploration drops from over 50% to near zero as the reference solution experiences more and more exploitation. In PSO, the reference solutions are *pbest* positions, and for *pbest* positions that have a fitness within 10 of their nearest local optimum, the experiments in [5] suggest that a vanishingly small proportion of the (fitter) attraction basins in Rastrigin will have solutions that are fitter than this (fully exploited) reference solution. Essentially, the operational characteristics of PSO turn any multi-modal search space (like Rastrigin) with a large number of relatively steep attraction basins into a "needle in the haystack" type search space. High speed particles which are necessary to travel between attraction basins cannot perform the fine-grained search in these newly explored attraction basins to find a solution in them that is fitter than their current *pbest*. Across the CEC benchmark (see Table 4), the modified version of PSO tends to perform significantly better than standard PSO on the functions that (like Rastrigin) have many steep attraction basins. Conversely, in accordance with "No Free Lunch" [12], the current modifications can perform significantly worse on fitness landscapes such as $f18$ that appear to have larger and shallower attraction basins.

Many other modified versions of PSO have also led to significant improvements on benchmark functions. However, a large amount of them have "only presented experimental results [on benchmark problem sets] and did not provide adequate discussion (neither from theoretical perspective, nor general discussions) on merits of the proposed approach" [2]. The modifications in this paper are supported by measurements of actually achieved exploration and exploitation. In particular, an analysis of particle positions (e.g. diversity [6] or particle trajectories [7]) can still miss the limited effect that their associated modifications can have on the movement of *pbest* positions. We believe that any (modified) form of PSO that has 0.0 *pbest* positions which move from a fully exploited attraction basin to a different attraction basin can benefit from the restarting of these stalled particles.

A large amount of research on restart methods for PSO has been conducted (e.g. [13,14]), and the restart methods used in the current modifications are highly rudimentary in comparison. Nonetheless, we believe the presented experimental methods which can accurately measure the number of distinct attraction basins that achieve full exploitation can be useful for on-going research in this area. One consideration for future research is to ensure that stalled particles which are to be restarted do not represent fitter attraction basins than those that have been more fully exploited by the swarm. Our *lbest* rotation strategy which attempts to support the full exploitation of all attraction basins represented by a *pbest* position seems to work well in combination with our simple restart strategy to achieve good initial results.

7 Conclusions

The presented analysis of exploration and exploitation in Particle Swarm Optimization has benefited from the ability to make direct measurements on aspects of these important concepts. Unexpected weaknesses in the ability of PSO to perform exploration and to perform exploitation have been observed through specific measurements on *pbest* positions. The presented modifications represent only the first step in a line of research that will focus on increasing the number of attraction basins that PSO can fully exploit in a multi-modal search space. Targeted restarts are expected to be a key component of this future research.

References

1. Kennedy, J., Eberhart, R.: Particle swarm optimization. In: 1995 Proceedings of IEEE International Conference on Neural Networks, vol. 4, pp. 1942–1948. IEEE (1995)
2. Bonyadi, M.R., Michalewicz, Z.: Particle swarm optimization for single objective continuous space problems: a review (2017)
3. Bratton, D., Kennedy, J.: Defining a standard for particle swarm optimization. In: 2007 Swarm Intelligence Symposium, pp. 120–127. IEEE (2007)
4. Črepinšek, M., Liu, S.H., Mernik, M.: Exploration and exploitation in evolutionary algorithms: a survey. ACM Comput. Surv. (CSUR) **45**(3), 35 (2013)
5. Gonzalez-Fernandez, Y., Chen, S.: Leaders and followers – a new metaheuristic to avoid the bias of accumulated information. In: 2015 IEEE Congress on Evolutionary Computation (CEC), pp. 776–783. IEEE (2015)
6. Bosman, P., Engelbrecht, A.P.: Diversity rate of change measurement for particle swarm optimisers. In: Dorigo, M., Birattari, M., Garnier, S., Hamann, H., Montes de Oca, M., Solnon, C., Stützle, T. (eds.) ANTS 2014. LNCS, vol. 8667, pp. 86–97. Springer, Cham (2014). https://doi.org/10.1007/978-3-319-09952-1_8
7. Bonyadi, M.R., Michalewicz, Z.: Impacts of coefficients on movement patterns in the particle swarm optimization algorithm. IEEE Trans. Evol. Comput. **21**(3), 378–390 (2017)
8. Engelbrecht, A.: Particle swarm optimization: velocity initialization. In: 2012 IEEE Congress on Evolutionary Computation (CEC), pp. 1–8. IEEE (2012)
9. Helwig, S., Branke, J., Mostaghim, S.: Experimental analysis of bound handling techniques in particle swarm optimization. IEEE Trans. Evol. Comput. **17**(2), 259–271 (2013)
10. https://www.researchgate.net/publication/259643342_source_code_for_an_implementation_of_standard_particle_swarm_optimization_-_revised?ev=prf_pub (June 2017)
11. Liang, J., Qu, B., Suganthan, P., Hernández-Díaz, A.G.: Problem definitions and evaluation criteria for the CEC, special session on real-parameter optimization. Computational Intelligence Laboratory, Zhengzhou University, Zhengzhou, China and Nanyang Technological University, Singapore, Technical report 201212, pp. 3–18 (2013)

12. Wolpert, D.H., Macready, W.G.: No free lunch theorems for optimization. IEEE Trans. Evol. Comput. **1**(1), 67–82 (1997)
13. Venter, G., Sobieszczanski-Sobieski, J.: Particle swarm optimization. AIAA J. **41**(8), 1583–1589 (2003)
14. Kaucic, M.: A multi-start opposition-based particle swarm optimization algorithm with adaptive velocity for bound constrained global optimization. J. Glob. Optim. 1–24 (2013)

Optimizing Scale-Free Network Robustness with the Great Deluge Algorithm

James Paterson$^{(\boxtimes)}$ and Beatrice Ombuki-Berman

Department of Computer Science, Brock University,
500 Glenridge Ave., St. Catharines, ON L2S 3A1, Canada
{jp11cy,bombuki}@brocku.ca

Abstract. This paper examines the robustness of scale-free networks against degree-based attacks on their nodes. Having a robust network means the network is less likely to suffer catastrophic failure if some parts of its structure are destroyed. Many critical real world systems such as the Internet and power grids can be modeled as networks, so finding a way to reduce the chance of failure in these systems is very important.

The robustness of these networks is increased using an optimization procedure based on edge swaps. In previous work, the optimization has been done with a simple hill climbing algorithm. The hill climber is prone to getting stuck in local optima, so Buesser et al. proposed using simulated annealing as a metaheuristic to get better solutions, getting good results.

This paper introduces a great deluge metaheuristic approach for this problem. To the author's knowledge, this algorithm has never been used for network robustness optimization before, and shows promising results. Testing indicates that the great deluge-based optimization results in larger improvements to network robustness than the simulated annealing optimization, and is considerably faster for small networks.

1 Introduction

Many different real world systems can be modeled as networks [1–3], and many of these networks have to contend with the failure of some of their components. These failures may be random, such as a server in a computer network having a hardware failure, or may be part of a malicious attack on the network, such as a hacker shutting down that server [1,4]. These failures can be disastrous for the network. In the example of the computer network, having too many components fail may mean that some computers on the network are no longer able to connect to some other computers.

Many real world networks such as the Internet and electrical power grids are critical pieces of infrastructure. If these networks are attacked, or have components fail for some other reason, it could have disastrous consequences. Networks

© Springer International Publishing AG, part of Springer Nature 2018
M. Mouhoub et al. (Eds.): IEA/AIE 2018, LNAI 10868, pp. 434–446, 2018.
https://doi.org/10.1007/978-3-319-92058-0_42

that are very robust to damage are less likely to suffer catastrophic failure. Keeping this in mind when creating or modifying networks will help to improve the stability of these systems.

In order to create robust networks, some measure of robustness is needed. Many such measures exist, but a common one used in previous work is the R value [1]. R value measures the average size of the network's largest connected component as the network is attacked.

Using this R value, a given network can be improved using any number of optimization techniques. The most basic of these is a hill climbing algorithm, as used in [1]. In this algorithm, a series of small random changes are made to the network. The random change is implemented using an "edge swap" [1], an operation that swaps the endpoints of two randomly selected edges in the network graph. At each iteration, a change is only kept if it strictly improves the network's robustness. This will lead to improvements in robustness, but the algorithm has a tendency to get stuck in local optima.

To combat this issue, a metaheuristic can be used in the optimization process. Buesser et al. [4] and Louzada et al. [5] used simulated annealing to get better optimization results than the basic hill climber. In each iteration of the simulated annealing algorithm, inferior networks have a chance to be accepted based on the difference in robustness with the network from the previous iteration and a temperature parameter that decreases over time. Other approaches, such as a memetic-algorithm-based optimizer, have also been explored [6].

In this paper, an algorithm called great deluge [7] is used as a metaheuristic for the robustness optimization. In each iteration of the great deluge algorithm, networks are accepted if their robustness is greater than some threshold value, which rises over time.

The great deluge algorithm was compared to the simulated annealing algorithm through a series of experiments. In these tests, the run time and the level of improvement in robustness were measured. Tests were performed on networks of varying sizes from 100 nodes up to 500 nodes. The great deluge optimizer is shown to outperform the simulated annealing optimizer in terms of robustness improvement, though with larger networks it takes longer to run.

2 Background Information

2.1 Complex Networks

Complex networks [3,8] are networks that have non-trivial topological features. These networks may be highly clustered, or have some hierarchical structure. These types of structures can arise out of the properties of the real world system. For example, a social network is likely to be highly clustered since there will be social groups formed through shared interests, schools, workplaces, etc. People will be more likely to have connections with others in the social groups they belong to than a random person on the opposite side of the world.

One common type of complex network is the scale-free network [3]. In a scale-free network, the degree distribution follows a power law distribution. This means that the network will contain a small number of "hub" vertices with large degrees, and many vertices of low degree. The hub vertices follow a sort of hierarchy, with the larger hubs being more rare and the smaller hubs being more common. Many real world networks are scale-free or approximately scale-free, such as the Internet [2].

Generating Scale-Free Networks. A common algorithm for generating scale-free networks is the Barabási-Albert (BA) model [3]. This algorithm uses a preferential attachment mechanism to create the network. The network grows, starting from an initial population of m_0 nodes. New nodes are added one at a time until the graph has n nodes. Each new node is connected to $m \leq m_0$ nodes in the current network; the probability of a particular node having this connection is proportional to its degree. This means that new nodes are more likely to connect to nodes that already have many connections. The probability p_i that the new node will be connected to node i is:

$$p_i = \frac{k_i}{\sum_j k_j} \tag{1}$$

where k_i is the degree of node i and $\sum_j k_j$ is the total degree of all nodes currently in the network.

2.2 Attacking Networks

Many real world systems rely on networks of various kinds in order to maintain operations. If these networks were to fail, it could have disastrous consequences. In order to design networks that are unlikely to fail, it is important to study potential causes for network failure. These causes include both random failures of network components as well as intentional sabotage of the network. These are collectively referred to as "attacks" against networks.

This initial study looks only at degree-based attacks on nodes. In this attack, a list of network nodes is sorted in descending order according to their degrees. The node with the highest degree is removed first, then the node with the second highest degree, and so on. The sorted list of nodes is recalculated after each removal, since the degrees of the nodes may have changed.

Scale-free networks are particularly vulnerable to degree based attacks [4]. This type of attack causes scale-free networks to quickly lose all of their hub nodes and break apart. Other types of networks, such as random networks, are much more robust to this type of attack. These networks are not reliant on high degree nodes in the same way that scale-free networks are, so their removal has less of an impact.

2.3 Optimization Procedures

An optimization procedure is an algorithm which explores a search space to find a state with an optimal value. This section describes two such algorithms. These descriptions all assume that a maximum value is desired, though they can be applied equally well to finding minimum values.

Simulated Annealing. Simulated annealing (SA) [4] is a metaheuristic that helps find approximations of the global optimum in a search space. It is inspired by the process of annealing in metallurgy, which is a method to improve the strength of a material by heating it and allowing it to gradually cool down.

The algorithm begins with an initial problem state S and a "temperature" parameter T. A small random change is made to the state, resulting in a new state S'. The fitness of these states is compared using a fitness function f. If $f(S') > f(S)$, then the change is kept. Otherwise, the change is kept with a probability dependent on the difference in fitness scores and the temperature parameter. A smaller difference in fitness scores will mean the inferior state is more likely to be kept, as will a higher temperature value. This process repeats until a certain number of iterations have passed, or some other stopping criteria is met.

The temperature parameter T starts out high at the beginning of the search, and is gradually lowered according to some "cooling schedule". This cooling process is what allows simulated annealing to give better results than a simple hill climbing algorithm. The high temperature at the beginning of the search allows the algorithm to avoid getting trapped in local optima by moving through "valleys" in the search space. The lower temperature towards the end of the procedure then allows the search to settle into a solution.

Great Deluge Algorithm. The great deluge algorithm (GD) [7] is a meta-heuristic with similar uses to simulated annealing. The idea of GD comes from imagining a person in a flood caused by a torrential downpour, trying to stay on dry land.

The algorithm begins with an initial problem state S and a "water level" parameter L. In each step of the GD search, a small random change is made to the state, creating state S'. This state is then evaluated according to a fitness function f. If $f(S') > L$, then the change is accepted. L is then increased by some small value called the "rain rate", and the process is repeated until stopping criteria are met.

This algorithm helps to avoid local optima by allowing the search to move through inferior states, so long as they have fitness scores above the current threshold. As the search proceeds, the threshold is gradually increased so the algorithm settles into a solution.

2.4 Previous Work

In [9], Schneider et al. introduced the R measure, a useful way of quantifying a network's robustness to attacks. This measure is described in detail in Subsect. 3.1. In their paper, Schneider et al. used a hill climbing algorithm to improve the robustness of generated scale-free and random networks, as well as two real world networks. They found that this approach works well, with all networks becoming significantly more robust after the optimization.

They also discovered that optimizing networks in this manner produces "onion-like" structures, where a core group of highly connected nodes is surrounded by several shells of smaller degree nodes. Each of these shells contains nodes mostly of the same degree, with the degree decreasing with distance from the center. In these networks, almost any pair of nodes with the same degree will have a path between them that does not pass through any nodes with higher degree. This is a useful property for a graph in danger of degree-based attacks. As the high degree nodes in the center shells are removed, the rest of the nodes are more likely to stay connected through the lower degree nodes in the outer shells.

Buesser et al. expanded on the work of Schneider et al. in [4]. Instead of using a simple hill climbing algorithm, they instead used simulated annealing to help with the robustness optimization. Tests performed on scale-free networks generated with the BA model showed that the SA-based optimization outperformed that of the hill climber.

3   Optimizing Robustness

3.1   R Value

In order to perform a robustness optimization on a network, it is necessary to quantify "robustness". Schneider et al.'s [1, 9] R measure uses the average size of the largest connected component over the attack procedure to define the network robustness.

$$R = \frac{1}{N-1} \sum_{Q=0}^{N} s(Q), \qquad (2)$$

where N is the number of nodes in the graph and $s(Q)$ is the fraction of nodes remaining in the largest connected component (LCC) after Q nodes are removed.

This measure provides a good indication of network robustness, since networks that are vulnerable to failure will see a rapid drop in LCC size as the attack breaks up the network. On the other hand, networks that are less vulnerable to these attacks will retain a larger portion of their nodes in the LCC, since they do not break up as quickly. The R value can be anywhere between 0 (a network that starts off fully disconnected) and 0.5 (a network that starts off fully connected).

3.2   Optimization Algorithms

The main goal of this paper is to modify the structure of a given scale-free network to improve its robustness to degree-based attacks. This optimization procedure should preserve the scale-free properties of the network. In other words, the degree distribution should not change after optimization. The optimization is done through a series of edge swaps. This edge swap operation was used by Schneider et al. in [1,9], by Buesser et al. in [4], and Louzada et al. in [5]. It is described in detail below. The great-deluge-based optimizer and the simulated-annealing-based optimizer from [4] are also described below.

Edge Swap Operation. The edge swap operation, as described in [1], involves selecting two edges at random from the graph. If the first edge is (v_1, v_2) and the second edge is (v_3, v_4), the edge swap operation consists of removing the original edges and adding two new edges: (v_1, v_4) and (v_2, v_3). Swapping the edges like this means that each vertex will have the same degree after the swap as it did before, so the degree distribution will not change. This ensures that the graph will still be scale free after the swap is performed. The edges are selected so that the swap operation does not create any loops or add an edge where one already exists.

Simulated Annealing. The simulated annealing optimizer performs a series of edge swaps with a chance of accepting edge swaps that do not lead to an immediate increase in robustness. The probability that an inferior swap is accepted is based on the difference in robustness values before and after the swap, and the temperature parameter, T:

$$p = e^{\frac{R_{new} - R_{old}}{T}} \tag{3}$$

The temperature is lowered over time, allowing the optimizer to eventually converge to a robust network.

Great Deluge. In the great deluge optimizer, edge swaps are accepted if the graph's robustness is greater than a threshold value L, also called the water level. This water level is gradually increased by the given rain rate R. These two parameters are initialized as a percentage of the initial robustness value of the graph.

4   Experiments

Experiments were performed using an application written in Python 2.7, using the igraph library [10] for access to common graph functions. An initial runs of tests were performed on each of the two optimizers to determine good values for their parameters. Once good parameters were established, the performance of the two optimizers were compared on graphs of varying sizes.

All tests were performed on graphs generated with the Barabási-Albert model. The graphs used for the parameter tests were generated with $n = 50$ nodes, initial graph size of $m_0 = 3$, and $m = 3$ edges added for each new node.

In all of these tests, the optimizers were tested on how well they improved the robustness of the graphs and how long they took to do so. Optimization time was measured in seconds, and robustness improvement was measured as the percent increase in R value after optimization.

4.1   Simulated Annealing Parameters

For the simulated annealing optimizer, all 100 combinations of the parameters in Table 1 were tested with 20 runs each.

Table 1. Parameters used for testing the SA optimizer

Starting T	Stopping T	T decay rate
.3	0.01	0.05
0.6	0.05	0.1
1	0.1	0.15
1.5	0.15	0.2
2		0.25

For all of the tests, the SA optimizer would decrease the temperature once 10 iterations had passed without finding a solution with an improved R value.

Starting Temperature. The first parameter examined was the starting temperature for the simulated annealing optimizer. Five different values were tested for this parameter. The run times for these 5 sets did not follow normal distributions, so a Kruskal-Wallis test was performed to check if there was a significant difference in the medians of the sets. This test resulted in a p-value < 0.01, indicating there was some significantly different set, and pairwise Wilcoxon rank-sum tests indicated a significant difference between all sets. This means that higher starting temperatures led to a longer run time, which is to be expected (Table 2).

Table 2. Median runtime and change in R value from SA optimizer under different starting temperatures

Starting temperature	Median runtime	Median change in R
0.3	2.83 s	−2.36%
0.6	4.00 s	−2.91%
1.0	4.86 s	−2.18%
1.5	5.79 s	−2.13%
2.0	6.63 s	−2.56%

The change in R value was also examined for different values of starting temperature. For these results, all sets were normal except for the set with a starting temperature of 0.6, which had a p-value of 0.02819. A Kruskal-Wallis test resulted in a p-value of 0.9547, indicating there was no significant difference in change in R value between different starting temperatures.

Stopping Temperature. The next parameter tested was the stopping temperature for the SA optimizer. All 4 different parameter values resulted in run times which were not normally distributed. A Kruskal-Wallis test resulted in a p-value < 0.01, indicating a significant difference in the median run times. Pairwise Wilcoxon rank-sum tests showed significant differences between all 4 sets, indicating that higher stopping temperatures resulted in lower run times, which is to be expected (Table 3).

Table 3. Median runtime and change in R value from SA optimizer under different stopping temperatures

Stopping temperature	Median runtime	Median change in R
0.01	7.57 s	−0.61%
0.05	4.88 s	−2.61%
0.10	3.78 s	−2.88%
0.15	3.16 s	−3.32%

Normality tests on the R value change for the different stopping temperature values showed that 3 of the 4 sets were normally distributed, with one set (stopping temperature of 0.1) being not normally distributed. A Kruskal-Wallis test performed on these sets showed significance with a p-value < 0.01. A series of Wilcoxon rank-sum tests on these sets showed that the only significantly different results came from the set with a stopping temperature of 0.01, which resulted in the highest change to R value.

Temperature Decay Rate. Finally, the temperature decay rate of the SA optimizer was examined. The distributions of the run times for the 5 different parameter values tested were all not normal, so a Krusal-Wallis test was performed to determine if there was a significant difference in the median run times. This test resulted in a p-value < 0.01, and pairwise Wilcoxon rank-sum tests confirmed that all sets were significantly different from each other. A lower decay rate makes the run time longer (Table 4).

For the change in R value, 4 out of the 5 decay rates had a normal distribution, but the 0.15 decay rate had a non-normal distribution, with a p-value of 0.03262. A Kruskal-Wallis test resulted in a p-value of 0.9639, indicating no significant difference in mean R value change.

Table 4. Median runtime and change in R value from SA optimizer under different temperature decay rates

Temperature decay rate	Median runtime	Median change in R
0.05	15.02 s	−2.50%
0.10	7.12 s	−2.39%
0.15	4.61 s	−2.29%
0.20	3.53 s	−2.42%
0.25	2.68 s	−2.37%

Discussion. Most of the parameters did not have much of an effect on how well the optimizer improved the graph. The only parameter which had any effect was the stopping temperature, where the lowest tested value performed best. It should also be noted that the SA optimizer performed very poorly on these small graphs. The median change in R for all tests ended up being negative. This is not the case when moving up to larger graphs.

4.2   Great Deluge Parameters

For the great deluge optimizer, all 64 combinations of the parameters in Table 5 were tested with 20 runs each.

Table 5. Parameters used for testing the GD optimizer

Initial water level	Rain rate	Max steps without improvement
0.5	0.001	20
0.7	0.005	40
0.9	0.01	60
1	0.02	80

Starting Water Level. For the great deluge optimizer, the run times for different values for the starting water level were examined. Of the four tested parameter values, all resulted in non-normally distributed run times. A Kruskal-Wallis test showed significance (p-value 0.002082). Pairwise Wilcoxon rank-sum tests showed that, in general, lower starting water levels resulted in longer run times (Table 6).

For the R value changes, all four parameter values had non-normally distributed results. A Kruskal-Wallis test resulted in a p-value of 0.9942, so starting water level did not have a significant effect on change in R value.

Table 6. Median runtime and change in R value from GD optimizer under different starting water levels

Starting water level	Median runtime	Median change in R
0.5	1.73 s	17.42%
0.7	1.58 s	17.57%
0.9	1.43 s	16.65%
1.0	1.24 s	17.53%

Rain Rate. For the rain rate, all 5 different parameters had non-normally distributed run times. A Kruskal-Wallis test resulted in a p-value < 0.01, indicating a significant difference in the median run times. A series of pair-wise Wilcoxon rank-sum tests showed that all sets had significantly different results, with lower rain rates taking a longer time to run (Table 7).

Table 7. Median runtime and change in R value from GD optimizer under different rain rates

Rain rate	Median runtime	Median change in R
0.001	9.37 s	30.51%
0.005	2.42 s	24.34%
0.010	1.60 s	19.28%
0.020	0.83 s	10.13%
0.050	0.48 s	1.55%

Out of the 5 different rain rates tested, all but one set had non-normally distributed changes in R value. A Kruskal-Wallis test resulted in a p-value < 0.01, indicating a significant difference in median R value change. Pairwise Wilcoxon rank-sum tests showed significant differences between all parameter values, indicating that lower rain rates resulted in better R improvement.

Number of Iterations Without Improvement. The final parameter tested for the great deluge optimizer was the number of iterations without improvement allowed before the algorithm would terminate. Of the four values tested for this parameter, all had non-normally distributed run times. A Kruskal-Wallis test showed that there was a significant difference in medians for at least one of these values. Wilcoxon rank-sum tests showed that all 4 values had significantly different medians. Predictably, the more iterations allowed, the longer the algorithm took to run (Table 8).

The change to R values also had non-normal distributions for all four values of this parameter. A Kruskal-Wallis test indicated a significant difference in

Table 8. Median runtime and change in R value from GD optimizer under different maximum numbers of iterations without improvement to R

Max iterations with no improvement	Median runtime	Median change in R
20	0.69 s	11.55%
40	1.28 s	16.73%
60	1.93 s	20.62%
80	2.45 s	23.02%

median, and pairwise Wilcoxon rank-sum tests showed significant differences between all tested parameter values. It seems that increasing the number of iterations without improvement results in a larger increase in R value.

Discussion. For the great deluge optimizer, both the rain rate and the maximum number of steps without an improvement in R value had significant effects on the performance of the algorithm. Smaller rain rates and larger number of max iterations both led to a larger increase in R value. This makes sense since both of these parameters mean that the algorithm takes a slower approach to a good solution, and is less likely to get trapped early on in a local optimum. The starting water level, however, had little effect on performance.

4.3   Simulated Annealing vs. Great Deluge

Once good values were established for the parameters, tests were performed to compare the performance of the two optimizers. Four sets of tests were performed, using $n = 100$, $n = 200$, $n = 300$, and $n = 500$ nodes. All four sets used an initial graph size of $m_0 = 4$ nodes, and add $m = 4$ edges for each new node. For each of these sets, 30 runs were performed using each optimizer.

Table 9. Results of tests between SA and GD optimizers

Network size	Optimizer	Average runtime (s)	Average change in R
100	Simulated annealing	90.37	12.2%
	Great deluge	66.53	69.3%
200	Simulated annealing	380.4	24.5%
	Great deluge	335.8	106.5%
300	Simulated annealing	769.2	31.7%
	Great deluge	805.0	127.0%
500	Simulated annealing	2122	40.9%
	Great deluge	2453	142.3%

Table 9 shows the results of these tests and Table 10 shows information about the statistical tests performed on these results. In Table 10, The columns "Runtime normal" and "R change normal" show if the network run time and change in R value follow normal distributions for both optimizers. In cases where the data are normally distributed, t-tests were used to check for statistical significance. For non-normally distributed data, Wilcoxon rank-sum tests were performed instead. The "p-value" columns show the results of these statistical tests between the results of the GD optimizer and the SA optimizer.

Of all the tests, only the run time on $n = 200$ and $n = 300$ node networks were not significantly different between the two optimizers. For $n = 100$ node networks, the run times were significantly different, with the GD optimizer being faster (as shown in Table 9). For $n = 500$ node networks, the SA optimizer was faster than the GD optimizer. It seems that as the size of the graph increases, great deluge starts to take longer than simulated annealing to converge to a solution. If this trend continues for graphs of larger sizes than those tested here, it may prove problematic.

Despite the run time problems with the larger graphs, the GD optimizer leads to considerably larger increases in network R value than the SA optimizer. For all network sizes, the GD optimizer resulted in a statistically larger increase in network R value. In three of the four network sizes tested, the GD optimizer more than doubled the R value of the network, while the SA optimizer's best result only improved R by 41%.

Table 10. Results of statistical tests on SA and GD optimizer performance

Network size	Runtime normal	Runtime p-value	R change normal	R change p-value
100	Yes	<0.01*	Yes	<0.01*
200	No	0.5250	No	<0.01*
300	No	0.0837	Yes	<0.01*
500	No	0.0024*	Yes	<0.01*

*Statistically significant

Overall, the GD optimizer seems to be the better choice. Fast runtime is not as important as a large R improvement, as long as the optimization does not take an unfeasibly long time to run. A few extra minutes of optimization time for the GD optimizer is worth the larger improvement to network robustness.

5   Conclusion and Future Work

Previous work in the literature indicated that simulated annealing can be used to optimize network robustness. The main objective of this paper was to apply another metaheuristic—the great deluge algorithm—to the problem, and compare its performance with that of SA. We found that the GD optimizer led to greater increases to network R value than the SA optimizer in every test. The

GD optimizer did take a longer time to run on the largest network, and likely will take even longer for even larger networks.

One potential avenue of future work is to examine a wider range of parameters for the GD optimizer to improve optimization speed and for SA to get greater increases in R. Other future work on this topic may focus on different optimization heuristics (such as genetic algorithms), different robustness measures, and attack procedures based on centrality measures other than node degree. These other attack procedures may be more effective against different types of networks, and the different robustness measures may more accurately represent a networks vulnerability to different attacks.

Acknowledgements. The support provided by the Natural Sciences and Engineering Research Council (NSERC) of Canada is gratefully acknowledged.

References

1. Herrmann, H.J., Schneider, C.M., Moreira, A.A., Andrade Jr., J.S., Havlin, S.: Onion-like network topology enhances robustness against malicious attacks. J. Stat. Mech. Theor. Exp. **2011**(01), P01027 (2011)
2. Cohen, R., Erez, K., Ben-Avraham, D., Havlin, S.: Breakdown of the internet under intentional attack. Phys. Rev. Lett. **86**(16), 3682 (2001)
3. Albert, R., Barabási, A.L.: Statistical mechanics of complex networks. Rev. Mod. Phys. **74**(1), 47 (2002)
4. Buesser, P., Daolio, F., Tomassini, M.: Optimizing the robustness of scale-free networks with simulated annealing. In: Dobnikar, A., Lotrič, U., Šter, B. (eds.) ICANNGA 2011. LNCS, vol. 6594, pp. 167–176. Springer, Heidelberg (2011). https://doi.org/10.1007/978-3-642-20267-4_18
5. Louzada, V.H., Daolio, F., Herrmann, H.J., Tomassini, M.: Generating robust and efficient networks under targeted attacks. In: Król, D., Fay, D., Gabryś, B. (eds.) Propagation Phenomena in Real World Networks, pp. 215–224. Springer, Cham (2015). https://doi.org/10.1007/978-3-319-15916-4
6. Zhou, M., Liu, J.: A memetic algorithm for enhancing the robustness of scale-free networks against malicious attacks. Phys. A Stat. Mech. Appl. **410**, 131–143 (2014)
7. Dueck, G.: New optimization heuristics: the great deluge algorithm and the record-to-record travel. J. Comput. Phys. **104**(1), 86–92 (1993)
8. Lü, J., Chen, G., Ogorzalek, M.J., Trajković, L.: Theory and applications of complex networks: advances and challenges. In: 2013 IEEE International Symposium on Circuits and Systems (ISCAS), pp. 2291–2294. IEEE (2013)
9. Schneider, C.M., Moreira, A.A., Andrade, J.S., Havlin, S., Herrmann, H.J.: Mitigation of malicious attacks on networks. Proc. Natl. Acad. Sci. **108**(10), 3838–3841 (2011)
10. Csárdi, G., Nepusz, T. http://igraph.org/python/

Solving the MCDP Using a League Championship Algorithm

Ricardo Soto[1](✉), Broderick Crawford[1](✉), Rodrigo Olivares[1,2](✉),
and Jaime Romero Fernández[1](✉)

[1] Pontificia Universidad Católica de Valparaíso, Valparaíso, Chile
{ricardo.soto,broderick.crawford}@pucv.cl, jaime.romero.f@mail.pucv.cl
[2] Universidad de Valparaíso, Valparaíso, Chile
rodrigo.olivares@uv.cl

Abstract. This paper focuses on modeling and solving the Manufacturing Cell Design Problem (MCDP) through a Algorithm (LCA). This problem considers the grouping of machines and parts into sets called cells. Each cell contains machines that process parts with the goal of minimizing the movements between cells. LCA represents problem solutions as teams, simulating their regular championship environment. During each week the teams generate new formations from an environment analysis both internal and external, in order to improve the performance of teams. We illustrate experimental results on well-known 90 benchmarks, where the global optimum is reached in almost all instances.

Keywords: League Championship Algorithm
Manufacturing Cell Design Problem · Metaheuristics
Combinatorial optimization

1 Introduction

This paper focuses in solving the Manufacturing Cell Design Problem (MCDP). This problem considers in finding an allocation of machines and parts to minimize the movement of these among machine groups (families), or also called cells. We have chosen an incomplete search technique; that is, this technique does not explore 100% of the search space. The technique aforementioned is based on the regular championship environment called League Championship Algorithm (LCA) [3], where each team represents MCDP solution, the new solutions generated are symbolized as the team's formation.

The MCDP has been implemented and investigated in different platforms with different metaheuristics. thus we can compare results of different metaheuristics, against our metaheuristic in the same way we can compare against the optimal result for each MCDP problem.

© Springer International Publishing AG, part of Springer Nature 2018
M. Mouhoub et al. (Eds.): IEA/AIE 2018, LNAI 10868, pp. 447–453, 2018.
https://doi.org/10.1007/978-3-319-92058-0_43

The results are based on well-known 90 benchmark which are shown by sets of tables, with the goal to analyze the results to verify the behavior of LCA solving MCDP. Where the optimum is obtained for the entire set of problems.

2 State of the Art

The study of MCDP is traced to decades behind, as a new shape in the manufacture strategy or manufacture of parts, where the goal is to minimized the movement between machines that produces parts, when are grouped in cells. This procedure works with a matrix of machine per parts, where are structured a Block Diagonal Form (BDF) [11].

Different metaheuristics have been used solve the MCDP. For example, Aljaber et al. (1997) [1], and Lozano et al. (1999) [4], used Tabu Search; solving MCDP using a Invasive Weed Optimization [7], solving MCDP via Firefly Algorithm [8] and using an artificial Fish Swarm Algorithm [9]. Therefore, is generated the concept of gather the parts and group together according to their characteristics; also appeared the idea to group together machines in family or cells. Actually, are established what allocation are represented through a matrix.

Because of the above, they continue the research and experimentation with new techniques and behaviors, as are LCA.

3 Manufacturing Cell Design Problem

The Manufacturing Cells Design (MCDP) is defined as a production strategy where it is realized a separation of an organization in production units, that are part of groups or families of components, also called as production cells [6]. Where the goal is to minimize movements parts between cells, to minimize time, production costs and used machines [12]. MCDP are understand under the concept *"similar parts must be manufactured in the same way"* [5], the similar parts with properties such as weight, manufacturing materials and necessary operation, they must belong in the same production unit.

In first time, the MCDP requires the organization of elements involved in its modelling. For that, is build incidence matrix to summarize the information. The first matrix is called as Machine-Part matrix; it determinate through zeros and ones, the machines necessary to parts production [10]. The machines are represented as matrix rows; the parts as matrix cols.

The MCDP goal is minimize the production costs. MCDP model has parameters, variables and domains that are represented as:

$$\text{minimize} \sum_{k=1}^{C} \sum_{i=1}^{M} \sum_{j=1}^{C} a_{ij} z_{jk}(1 - y_{ik}) \tag{1}$$

subject to

$$\sum_{k=1}^{C} y_{ik} = 1 \quad (2) \qquad \sum_{k=1}^{C} z_{jk} = 1 \quad (3) \qquad \sum_{i=1}^{M} y_{ik} \le M_{max} \quad (4)$$

where M: number of machines, P: number of parts, C: number of cells, i: index of machines (i = 1,..., M), j: index of parts (j = 1,..., P), k: index of cells (k = 1,..., C), M_{max}: max number of machines per cell, $A = a_{ij}$: binary machine-part incidence matrix, with $a_{ij} = 1$ if machine i is visited by part j to be processed, or $a_{ij} = 1$ otherwise. $Y = y_{ik}$: binary machine-cell matrix, where $y_{ik} = 1$ if machine i belongs to the cell k, or $y_{ik} = 0$ otherwise. Finally, $Z = z_{jk}$: binary part-cell matrix, where $y_{jk} = 1$ if part j belongs to the cell k, or $y_{jk} = 0$ otherwise.

4   League Championship Algorithm (LCA)

The League Championship Algorithm is a technique based on a regular championship environment and it consists in to compete the solutions in matches. In this way based on the performance of each team (metaheuristic agent) and the opponent, a new formation is generated to improve the team performance and have a best MCDP problem solution [4]. In this context, each MCDP solution is represented as team [1], for this paper, this team is represented as a vector with the formation, where in terms of MCDP this vector is similar to a machine-part matrix.

Initially is generated the initials formations for all teams, it is played the first week of the championship, where the match result depends the each fitness team, for the next week new formations are generated from these results.

The championship ends when all teams playing vs all teams and one team is the champion. The champion is the team with best fitness, and the best solution for the MCDP problem.

In LCA are chosen a set of L solutions in the search space, these solutions will be gradually transformed during the weeks of the championship. Each solution have a fitness calculated from the objective function, this value represents how strong is the team. Then, a team with best fitness, will play better [3].

During each week new formations are generated, these are used for playing against its next team in the next week. The way in that a formation changes in one week to other, is the result of a match analysis of one team and of the opponents searching a design of the best formation in the next match [3]. Algorithm follows these instructions can be seen in 1.

5 Experimental Results

Experiments were generated with the next configuration: Number of Teams (L) 60, Number of Sessions (S) = 500, $p_c = 0.5$, $\psi 1 = 0.2$ and $\psi 2 = 1$. The matrix with size 16×30 used in test, were obtained from problem sets studied F. Boctor. A linear formulation of the machine-part Cell formation problem [2]. The optimal values obtained from Boctor research are represented in the next tables in the col "Boctor", the "LCA" represents the best optimal obtained and "LCA-A" represents the average from all results in each instance, all for 2 and 3 cells.

Algorithm 1. LCA algorithm

```
 1: Teams = InicializateFormations();
 2: for (j = 1 : S) do
 3:     Scheduled =GenerateScheduled(L);
 4:     for (t = 1 : T) do
 5:         if j!= 0 and t!= 0 then
 6:             GenerateNewFormations(Results[t-1],p_c,ψ2,ψ1);
 7:         end if
 8:         BestFormations[t]=getBestFormations(Scheduled[t]);
 9:         Scheduled=DetermineWinners(BestFormations,Scheduled);
10:     end for
11: end for
12: return Best Formation Championship(BestFormations);
```

Table 1. Results MCDP 2 Cells, MMax 8 and 9

	Cells = 2							
	MMax = 8				MMax = 9			
	Boctor	LCA	RPD	LCA-A	Boctor	LCA	RPD	LCA-A
Problem 1	11	11	0%	11	11	11	0%	11
Problem 2	7	7	0%	7,4	6	6	0%	6
Problem 3	4	4	0%	4,8	4	4	0%	4
Problem 4	14	14	0%	17,4	13	13	0%	17,2
Problem 5	9	9	0%	9	6	6	0%	7
Problem 6	5	5	0%	5	3	3	0%	3
Problem 7	7	7	0%	7	4	4	0%	4
Problem 8	13	13	0%	13	10	10	0%	10
Problem 9	8	8	0%	9	8	8	0%	8
Problem 10	8	8	0%	8	5	5	0%	5

Table 2. Results MCDP 2 Cells, MMax 10 and 11

| | Cells = 2 | | | | | | | | | | | |
| | MMax =10 | | | | MMax = 11 | | | | MMax = 12 | | | |
	Boctor	LCA	RPD	LCA-A	Boctor	LCA	RPD	LCA-A	Boctor	LCA	RPD	LCA-A
Problem 1	11	11	0%	11	11	11	0%	11	11	11	0%	11
Problem 2	4	4	0%	6,8	3	3	0%	5,8	3	3	0%	5,2
Problem 3	4	4	0%	4	3	3	0%	4,8	1	1	0%	5
Problem 4	13	13	0%	15,3	13	13	0%	16,2	13	13	0%	15,8
Problem 5	6	6	0%	8	5	5	0%	6,8	4	4	0%	5,4
Problem 6	3	3	0%	3,8	3	3	0%	6	2	2	0%	5,4
Problem 7	4	4	0%	6	4	4	0%	4	4	4	0%	4
Problem 8	8	8	0%	11	5	5	0%	6,8	5	5	0%	5
Problem 9	8	8	0%	10	5	5	00%	9	5	5	0%	7,4
Problem 10	5	5	0%	5	5	5	0%	5,4	5	5	0%	6,2

Tables 1, 2, 3 and 4 show that LCA was capable to reach 100% of known optimal, it is a promising beginning for this metaheuristic solving MCDP, which can be tested in others instances more difficulty in future work, it can be seen that the algorithm has a considerable robustness, because there is no great variation between the optimum of each instance and its average.

Table 3. Results MCDP 3 Cells, MMax 6 and 7

| | Cells = 3 | | | | | | | |
| | MMax = 6 | | | | MMax = 7 | | | |
	Boctor	LCA	RPD	LCA-A	Boctor	LCA	RPD	LCA-A
Problem 1	27	27	0%	28,2	18	18	0%	20,2
Problem 2	7	7	0%	7,6	6	6	0%	6,4
Problem 3	9	9	0%	9	4	4	0%	7
Problem 4	27	27	0%	28,4	18	18	0%	19,2
Problem 5	11	11	0%	11,8	8	8	0%	10,4
Problem 6	6	6	0%	6	4	4	0%	4,4
Problem 7	11	11	0%	11,4	5	5	0%	5
Problem 8	14	14	0%	14,2	11	11	0%	12,6
Problem 9	12	12	0%	12	12	12	0%	12,8
Problem 10	10	10	0%	10,8	8	8	0%	8,6

Table 4. Results MCDP 3 Cells, MMax 8 and 9

| | Cells = 3 | | | | | | | |
| | MMax = 8 | | | | MMax = 9 | | | |
	Boctor	LCA	RPD	LCA-A	Boctor	LCA	RPD	LCA-A
Problem 1	11	11	0%	13,6	11	11	0%	11
Problem 2	6	6	0%	7,2	6	6	0%	6
Problem 3	4	4	0%	4,2	4	4	0%	4
Problem 4	14	14	0%	17,8	13	13	0%	17
Problem 5	8	9	0%	9,4	6	6	0%	7,8
Problem 6	4	4	0%	5,4	3	3	0%	3,2
Problem 7	5	5	0%	6,2	4	4	0%	4,6
Problem 8	11	11	0%	12,2	10	10	0%	10
Problem 9	8	8	0%	9,4	8	8	0%	8
Problem 10	8	8	0%	8	5	5	0%	5

6 Conclusion

In this paper, we present the resolution of the MCDP problem through optimization algorithm based on the behavior of a sports championship: LCA. It is used a vector in the model of MCDP that represents the machine-part matrix and in the algorithm optimization a team to approach the nature binary of MCDP. We tested 90 instances with optimum known, the results are quite promising, the algorithm is able to get about 100% of global optimum, with a significant robustness, where it is able to obtain optimum values with the same parameter settings. As future work, we try to experiment with new instances more difficult, to test how LCA behaves in other contexts.

Acknowledgment. Ricardo Soto is supported by Grant CONICYT/FONDECYT/ REGULAR/1160455. Broderick Crawford is supported by Grant CONICYT/ FONDECYT/REGULAR/1171243. Rodrigo Olivares is supported by CONICYT/ FONDEF/IDeA/ID16I10449, FONDECYT/STIC-AMSUD/17STIC-03, FONDE-CYT/MEC/MEC80170097, and Postgraduate Grant Pontificia Universidad Católica de Valparaíso (INF - PUCV 2015–2018).

References

1. Aljaber, N., Baek, W., Chen, C.: A tabu search approach to the cell formation problem. Comput. Ind. Eng. **32**(1), 169–185 (1997)
2. Boctor, F.F.: A linear formulation of the machine-part cell formation problem. Int. J. Prod. Res. **29**(2), 343–356 (1991)
3. Kashan, A.H.: League championship algorithm (LCA): an algorithm for global optimization inspired by sport championships. Appl. Soft Comput. **16**, 171–200 (2014)

4. Lozano, S., Díaz, A., Eguía, I., Onieva, L.: A one-step tabu search algorithm for manufacturing cell design. J. Oper. Res. Soc. **50** (1999)
5. Medina, P.D., Cruz, E.A., Pinzon, M.: Generacion de celdas de manufactura usando el algoritmo de ordenamiento binario (AOB). Scientia Et Technica **16**(44), 106–110 (2010)
6. Mururgan, M., Selladurai, V.: Manufacturing cell design with reduction in setup time through genetic algorithm. Asian Research Publication Network (2007)
7. Soto, R., Crawford, B., Castillo, C., Paredes, F.: Solving the manufacturing cell design problem via invasive weed optimization. In: Silhavy, R., Senkerik, R., Oplatkova, Z.K., Silhavy, P., Prokopova, Z. (eds.) Artificial Intelligence Perspectives in Intelligent Systems. AISC, vol. 464, pp. 115–126. Springer, Cham (2016). https://doi.org/10.1007/978-3-319-33625-1_11
8. Soto, R., Crawford, B., Lama, J., Paredes, F.: A firefly algorithm to solve the manufacturing cell design problem. In: Silhavy, R., Senkerik, R., Oplatkova, Z.K., Silhavy, P., Prokopova, Z. (eds.) Artificial Intelligence Perspectives in Intelligent Systems. AISC, vol. 464, pp. 103–114. Springer, Cham (2016). https://doi.org/10.1007/978-3-319-33625-1_10
9. Soto, R., Crawford, B., Vega, E., Paredes, F.: Solving manufacturing cell design problems using an artificial fish swarm algorithm. In: Sidorov, G., Galicia-Haro, S.N. (eds.) MICAI 2015. LNCS (LNAI), vol. 9413, pp. 282–290. Springer, Cham (2015). https://doi.org/10.1007/978-3-319-27060-9_23
10. Soto, R., Kjellerstrand, H., Durán, O., Crawford, B., Monfroy, E., Paredes, F.: Cell formation in group technology using constraint programming and boolean satisfiability. Expert Syst. Appl. **39**(13), 11423–11427 (2012)
11. Xambre, A.R., Vilarinho, P.M.: A simulated annealing approach for manufacturing cell formation with multiple identical machines. Eur. J. Oper. Res. **151**(2), 434–446 (2003)
12. Yin, Y., Yasuda, K.: Manufacturing cells' design in consideration of various production. Int. J. Prod. Res. **40**(4), 885–906 (2002)

ACO-Based Measure for SYN Flooding Over Mobile Data Connectivity

Joseph C. Mushi$^{(\boxtimes)}$, Mussa Kissaka, and Kosmas Kapis

College of Information and Communication Technologies,
University of Dar es Salaam, Dar es Salaam, Tanzania
joseph.cosmas@udsm.ac.tz

Abstract. Dynamics in IP-based SYN-flooding, whereby attacker can create slave daemon generators and distribute attacks, have frightened integration of mobile services over mobile data connectivity. This study proposes unsupervised learning model inspired by three ingredients of ants foraging behaviour to improve accuracy in detection of SYN dynamics and reduces the number of falsified alarms. The evaluation establishes simulation environment and analyse collected data using Mean Value Analysis (MVA) method, whereby results prove the model to dynamically classify, detect and wedge-out SYN-flooding at 58.4% utilization of GGSN gateway.

Keywords: Synchronize sequence numbers · SYN · Network flood
Mobile services · Internet Protocol · Ants Colony Optimization

1 Introduction

Every tunnel from Internet Protocol (IP) networks along mobile data connectivity is usually served by one or more Radio Access Bearer (RAB) assigned by Radio Network Controller (RNC) in mobile networks. When the tunnel is closed, assigned RABs are normally released to allow re-usability due to their scarcity [1]. However, if IP traffic generates SYN-flood attacks, numerous RABs will be assigned and held to exhaustion that can subsequently overwhelm RNC. Currently, the diameter protocol has been mandated to provide Authentication, Authorization and Accounting (AAA) measures along IP traffic to Gateway GPRS Support Node (GGSN) gateway. The protocol use conventional Additive Increase Multiplicative Decrease (AIMD) to detect and control SYN-flood at GGSN [2].

The AIMD deploys static contention window (Cwnd) and round-trip time (RTT) to control SYN-flooding by wedging out interface whose respective Cwnd value decrease to zero. The static nature of AIMD algorithm increases risks of RABs exhaustion if SYN-flooding attacker uses multiple slave-daemons to replicate sources of floods that establish parallel sessions before values of pre-assigned Cwnds decrease to zero. Thus, the 3rd Generation Partnership Project (3GPP) consortium has recommended on strict intelligent measures to mitigate risks of SYN-flood in case mobile-network operators (MNOs) want to integrate mobile services into IP networks [2, 3].

This study has designed an intelligent model to classify, detects and control SYN flood attacks through learning of traffic flow from IP networks to cellular networks to

© Springer International Publishing AG, part of Springer Nature 2018
M. Mouhoub et al. (Eds.): IEA/AIE 2018, LNAI 10868, pp. 454–461, 2018.
https://doi.org/10.1007/978-3-319-92058-0_44

increase accuracy of flood detection in control of SYN-flood along mobile data connectivity. Solving the accuracy in detection of SYN-flood has attracted several research studies. Majority of these studies have focused on detection measures that set threshold value on utilization above which the measure raised flood alarm [4]. Others studies have focused on detecting anomalies on traffic flow and use cumulative sum algorithm (CUSUM) to validate attacking traffic [5]. On gateway perspective, some studies have proposed stateful measures to the gateway of victim node that consume much resources [6].

2 Enhancement for SYN-Flood Over Mobile Data Connectivity

The designed model is enhanced using Ants Colony Optimization (ACO) technique to increase accuracy in detection and control of SYN flooding along mobile data connectivity. It establishes a digital nest of Ants colony at GGSN node that generates two kinds of agents namely patroller-agent and forward-agent. The structure of the agents is composed of java object-class characterised with semi-static and dynamic motion. The motion enables agents to move in attached IP-networks along layer-3 nodes, in which the patroller-agents embed themselves for classification and early detection of SYN-flood. Once patrollers detect flood, they will raise flood-alarm to attract forward-agents to visit for verification of the source.

2.1 Packet Classification

The model begins by commanding GGSN to generate patroller-agents in a volume equivalent to numbers of layer-3 nodes recorded in GGSN's routing-table.

As depicted in Fig. 1, each patroller is sent to layer-3 nodes to perform classification, which begins by examining the type of every packet originating from subnets of respective layer-3 node destined to mobile networks through GGSN and vice versa. If

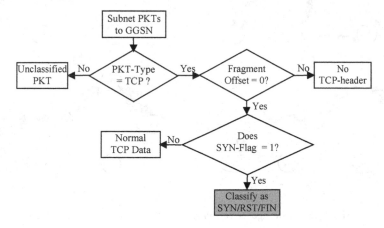

Fig. 1. Classification of SYN-flagged packet by agents

the packet type is TCP, the classification computes 6-bits control offset to determine presence of TCP header before examining its offset for a raised SYN, RST, FIN or ACK flag. If the packet is comprised of examined flag, the classification records its occurrence and proceed with observation over a period of time τ. If recorded occurrence over time τ goes beyond threshold value, it creates layer-2 Explicit Congestion Notification (ECN) packet that signal SYN flood then converts ECN into a layer three ECN-Echo (ECE) and broadcast to GGSN.

2.2   Flood Detection and Alarm Verification

Detection is initiated when broadcasted ECE reaches GGSN, which in-turn poured number of forward-agents into connected IP networks to traverse along layer-3 nodes. As depicted in Fig. 2(a), the agents are initially move randomly without any lead. This is because the exact source of ECE-broadcast that brought about unverified SYN-alarm to GGSN is yet to be known as it was received with intermediate-router's address. As depicted by Fig. 2(b), while forward-agent moves along intermediate router, it performs fresh classification to confirm whether unverified alarm was truly originating from respective router. If the alarm was proven to originate from current visited router, the forward-agent will send another strong ECE-broadcast for other forward-agent to attract to verified source and return to GGSN to report the last-mile source of SYN flood.

Each forward-agent that attracted to S_8 will broadcast ECE, and as depicted by Fig. 2(c) and (d), more agent will converge to S_8 then return to GGSN to verify it as truly SYN source.

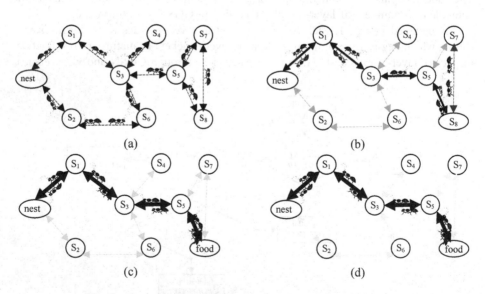

Fig. 2.   Forward-agents verifying truly source and positive alarm

2.3   Verification of Positive Alarm

To verify the status of SYN alarm, the model at GGSN depends on the volume of forward-agents, which returns after record SYN-classification of subnet j attached to router k. Based on the classification, let a ratio between arrival rate of SYN packets over acknowledged FIN+RST packets denoted as λ_{jk}. If v_{jk} denotes expected visiting ratio of SYN packets from subnet j on duration T (τ_1, τ_2,... τ_h), then corresponding density of SYN-flood over unit discrete time series τ_1, τ_2,... τ_h is derived from Little theorem such that:

$$D_T = \frac{\sum_{k \in N} \lambda_k v_k}{T} \; ; \quad T = (\tau_1, \tau_2, \cdots, \tau_h) \tag{1}$$

Basically, SYN-flood results from traffic inequality between generated SYN-flagged packets as compared to corresponding RST+FIN-flagged packets. Assume $\alpha(0 < \alpha < 1)$ denotes proportion mean value indication of traffic behaviour, and $\beta(0 \leq \beta \leq 1)$ denotes exponential weighted moving average factor of traffic-change due to SYN flow, based on Chernoff's inequality on upper bounds for lower tail distribution (Tropp 2012), the function of SYN-flood density on taffic-change can be deduced from Eq. (1) such that

$$f_k = D_T \geq \frac{(1 - \alpha) \exp(\beta)}{T} \sum_{\forall k \in N} \lambda_k v_k \tag{2}$$

The traffic behaviour of SYN flow can be foretold at GGSN by learning three parameters namely throughput of returned forward agents, round-trip time (RTT) of acknowledged FIN/RST, and possible packet-loss of acknowledge packet (ACK). From inspiration of three ingredients of ants foraging behaviour, the model considers throughput of returning forward-agents as positive reaction that could lead to SYN-flood, RTT as parameter that induce negative reaction and packet-loss rate as amplification for fluctuation. The three ingredients are used to deduce probabilistic learning model that verify whether classified SYN-flood results from positive attack or result from normal traffic of SYN versus RST+FIN pairs.

2.3.1   Positive Reaction

Misbehaving of SYN-flow from subnet j may lead to convergence of forward-agents to router k. and therefore an increase through of returned forward-agents to GGSN gateway. Let the function of throughput of returned forward-agents recorded by GGSN from subnet j denoted by f_{jk}. Let N denotes total number of routers on attached IP networks as recorded onto GGSN's routing table. The probability that any increase in throughput due to forward-agents at GGSN is contributed by classification of SYN from subnet j in respect to other routers is deduced such that

$$P_k = \frac{f_k}{\sum_{k \in N} f_k} \tag{3}$$

Replacing f_k in Eq. (3) with corresponding value in Eq. (2) to reflect last-mile detection of SYN flood into observed throughput at GGSN lead to Eq. (4) such that

$$P_k = \frac{(1 - \alpha) \exp(\beta)}{T} \sum_{\forall k \in N} \frac{\lambda_k v_k}{f_k} \tag{4}$$

2.3.2 Negative Reaction

In normal SYN flow, every SYN packets ends with acknowledged RST or FIN packet. Due to network condition, acknowledged RST/FIN can get lost and lead to false SYN-flood classification. Thus, negative reaction is ingredient that counterbalance false classification. As depicted in Fig. 3, when forward-agent observes SYN packet from subnet j to GGSN at time T_1, it expects acknowledged ACK/RST/FIN at T_4 otherwise it treats delay as signs of SYN flood. This means any positive deviation of acknowledged ACK/RST/FIN from the weighted mean value of RTT increase probability of flood alarm.

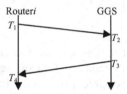

Fig. 3. Consideration on estimating round-trip time (RTT)

Let forward-agent observes SYN packet from subnet j to GGSN at time T_1. If ACK/RST/FIN arrives at router k around T_4, the weighted mean value of RTT denoted as α is derived in Eq. (5) such that

$$\alpha_k = \frac{(T_4 - T_1) - (T_3 - T_2)}{(T_4 - T_1)} \tag{5}$$

Assuming $(T_4 - T_1)$ is direct proportion to $(T_3 - T_2)$, the forward-agent will observe high waiting-delay as $\alpha \rightarrow 0$ to reflects true sign of SYN-flood while minimal waiting-delay as $\alpha \rightarrow 1$ to reflect otherwise. Consequently, to reinforce RTT on network environment that reflect true-positive alarm then a negative reaction that counterbalance positive reaction should set $\alpha \rightarrow 0$, which deduce Eqs. (4) to (6) such that

$$P_k = \frac{\exp(\beta)}{T} \sum_{\forall k \in N} \frac{\lambda_k v_k}{f_k} \tag{6}$$

2.3.3   Amplification of Fluctuation

Forward-agents that traces source of ECE-broadcast may classify SYN-flood on intermediate router that was not original source of the traced ECE. In ACO, this phenomenon is called amplification of fluctuation such it may help lost forward-agents to discover optimal source of SYN-flood and return to add value on verification at GGSN. Assuming $\delta(0 \leq \delta \leq 1)$ denotes weighted average of percentage difference between flux-in of lost forward-agents to router k and flux-out of forward-agents that trace router k only to classify SYN-flood on different router. The impact of such fluctuation on the function of forward-agents that returned to GGSN to verify subnet j as true source of SYN-flood is derived such that

$$f_k = (1 - \delta)f_k(t_0) \tag{7}$$

To induce amplification of fluctuation into general model, replace Eq. (7) in Eq. (6) such that

$$P_k = \frac{\exp(\beta)}{T(1 - \delta)} \sum_{\forall k \in N} \frac{\lambda_k v_k}{f_k} \tag{8}$$

Equation (8) represent mathematical model that probabilistic verify true-positive SYN alarm detected on last-mile router k, whose subnet j is a source of SYN attacks to GGSN gateway.

3   Evaluation and Result Discussion

3.1   Evaluation Method

The model was evaluated using Omnet++ simulation tool which establishes simulation environment on INET framework. The simulation sets agent-generator at GGSN node with ability to initiates patroller-agents and forward-agents. The simulation also sets six routers ($N = 6$) over IP networks, in which three slave daemons were attached on three different routers. As stipulated in Table 1, the daemons were configured with Tribe Floodnet 2k (TFN2K) that generates SYN-flood at an average rate of 35, 85 and 550 packets per seconds.

The simulation customized GGSN to deploy verification model in Eq. (8) and Mean Value Analysis (MVA) algorithm that helps to analyse and inference data generated from verification model, and furthermore adopts parameters IETF and 3GPP standards.

Table 1. Parameters for simulation and MVA analysis

Parameter	Description	Value
N	Number of possible routing-paths	6
β	Exponential weighted moving average factor	0.98
δ	Initial weighted average factor	0.99
L	Rate of SYN packets generated by simulated attackers	35, 85, 550

3.2   Evaluation Results

3.2.1   Recorded Utilization on Simulated SYN Floods

The study analysed increase of utilization due to returned forward-agents from three routers whose subnets host attacker1, attacker2 and attacker3 that respectively generate attacks at a rate of 35, 85, and 550 SYN-packets per second. Figure 4(a) shows utilization recorded when the attackers activated while classification and detection model deactivated. The Figure shows TotalUtils parameter that sums up utilizations observed by GGSN from three interfaces. The TotalUtils graph depicted that the total utilization reaches 100% at only 31% of simulation time.

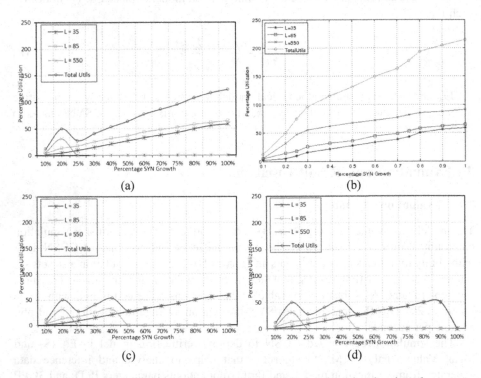

Fig. 4. Utilization measured while the model is deactivated and activated

But, when the classification and detection model was activated the TotalUtils parameter becames under control. As depicted in Fig. 4(b), (c) and (d), everytime TotalUtils parameters reaches 58.4% the subnet that generates SYN-packets at higher rates was wedged-out. At first the attacker that generates 550 SYN-packets per second was wedged out at 21%, followed by the one generated at 85 SYN-packets per second that wedged out at 39%, and last comes the attacker generates at 35 SYN-packets per second which wedged out at 87%.

3.3 Discussion of Results

The simulation was focusing on showcasing efficiency that classification and detection model is rewarding to the GGSN node by examining three parameters of utilization, response-time and mean-density during SYN-flood attacks. According to Fig. 4(b), (c) and (d), close observation revealed that the model manages to wedge-out traffic to GGSN that originate from subnet j of router k whenever increase of utilization reaches 58.4%, which outperform several research studies whose detection measure scored threshold of 60% and above.

4 Conclusion

This study devices a quality of service (QoS) measure to enhance GGSN accuracy on classification, detection and thereafter control of SYN-flood attacks from IP networks along mobile data connectivity. The study designed a model that learns network environment from inspiration of Ants Colony Optimization (ACO) technique to classify and detect truly positive SYN-flood alarm. Using Ants foraging behaviour, the model *positively* verifies a subnet that generates SYN-packets at higher rate to facilitate last-mile detection of source of SYN flood. The model uses weighted mean of RTT to *negatively* reward forward-agents about classified SYN-packets of reported subnet in a manner that counterbalance falsified signs of SYN-flood. Further, the model *amplifies* lost forward-agents to add-value on truly positive SYN-alarm.

References

1. Lee, P.P.C., Bu, T., Woo, T.: On the detection of signaling DoS attacks on 3G/WiMax wireless networks. Comput. Netw. **53**(15), 2601–2616 (2010)
2. Stallings, W.: Cryptography and Network Security: Principles and Practices, 4th edn. Pearson Education Inc, Upper Saddle River (2005)
3. Gurtov, A.: Host Identity Protocol (HIP): Towards the Secure Mobile Internet. Wiley, West Sussex (2008)
4. Zou, C.C., Duffield, N., Towsley, D., Gong, W.: Adaptive defense against various network attacks. IEEE J. Sel. Areas Commun. **24**(10), 1877–1887 (2006)
5. Siris, V.A., Papagalou, F.: Application of anomaly detection algorithms for detecting SYN flooding attacks. Comput. Commun. **29**, 1433–1442 (2006)
6. Ohsita, Y., Ata, S., Murata, M.: Detecting distributed denial-of-service attacks by analysing TCP SYN packets statistically. IEICE Trans. Commun. **89**(10), 2868–2877 (2006)

Multi-Agent Systems

On Commitments Creation, Compliance and Violation

Asma Mobaiddin[1] and Nadim Obeid[2,3(✉)]

[1] School of Foreign Languages, The University of Jordan, Amman, Jordan
[2] King Hussein School of Computing Sciences, Princess Sumaya University
for Technology, Amman, Jordan
[3] King Abdullah II School for Information Technology,
The University of Jordan, Amman, Jordan
obein@ju.edu.jo

Abstract. The importance of specifying a standard framework for agent communication languages (ACL) with a clear semantics has been widely recognized. The semantics should be verifiable, clear and practical. We aim, in this paper, to present a clear way of detecting whether or not a commitment is violated. We will define a violation/compliance criterion based on the existence of arguments/proofs for the induced commitment(s). The logic which we shall employ is temporal modal defeasible logic which formalizes *commitments* that agents undertake as a consequence of communicative actions. A clear meaning in terms of the commitments it induces is associated with each speech. Commitments are represented as modal sentences.

Keywords: Agent communication languages · Defeasible logic
Modal logic · Commitments · Proof

1 Introduction

1.1 A Subsection Sample

Agents, in Multi-Agents Systems (MAS) need to communicate using an Agent Communication Language (ACL). It is easy to define the different syntactic features of *speech acts* that agents can perform during a dialogue. However, this is not easy when semantics is taken into consideration. Given that agents in an MAS may be heterogeneous, a clear comprehension of the semantics of each utterance is essential. Two important issues must be carefully considered: (1) the interpretation of each speech act which should be unique and (2) the verifiability that the messages exchange between agents conform to such a semantic of that particular ACL [35]. Providing a suitable formal semantics for ACLs which properly addresses the above issues remains an important challenge of multi-agent theory.

The research effort in MAS communication has produced two main computational interpretations of speech acts: the mentalistic approach and the social semantic approach. The mentalistic approach [7] involves attributing *beliefs* and *intentions* to artificial agents.

© Springer International Publishing AG, part of Springer Nature 2018
M. Mouhoub et al. (Eds.): IEA/AIE 2018, LNAI 10868, pp. 465–476, 2018.
https://doi.org/10.1007/978-3-319-92058-0_45

The social semantics approach [13, 18, 19, 26] made an effort to model commitments that agents undertake as a consequence of communicative actions. Many approaches were presented to represent and reason about commitments. The approach in [5], considered the semantic issues and developed a unified framework for pragmatic and semantic issues. Their approach extends the temporal system CTL with modalities for commitments and their actions, argument modality, and a dynamic logic (DL) to define a logical semantics for agent communication. It introduced an accessibility relation to define the semantics of commitments. However, the proposal was criticized in [6] because the semantics *is defined in a recursive manner, which makes its verification extremely hard. In addition, the satisfaction semantics focuses on checking the truth condition of the content of commitment, which is a part of the semantics of commitment itself.* In [13], an approach is proposed that aimed to distinguish between dialogue game-based and commitment-based protocols. The game-based approach considers that protocols may be represented using suitable arrangements which allow them to be joined in diverse ways to develop the overall structure of a dialogue (cf. [14–18, 22]. It was observed in [13] that commitment-based approaches to ACL semantics are "essentially motivated by the requirement of verifiability": an observer cannot usually verify whether a computer system is in states that can properly be called "beliefs" or "intentions", but adherence to public commitments is more easily monitored [8, 27].

In this paper, we employ the social semantics approach [18, 19] which attempts to model *commitments* that agents undertake as a consequence of communicative actions. A social commitment is an obligation that an agent (participant in an interaction, the debtor) makes to another agent/participant (the creditor), in which the debtor indicates its willingness to accept some proposition(s) or to perform some action that causes some proposition(s) to hold and to support it if challenged. When making a commitment, an agent has to follow, and behave in accordance with, this commitment.

To illustrate the idea, we shall consider a simple purchase scenario that involves a Customer (Cust) and a Retailer (Ret). Ret wants to be paid for goods which she/he can provide. Cust wants to buy goods and is willing to pay. For instance, if Cust knows that the price of a piece of Product 1 (P1) is 10 US dollars and puts an order for 100 pieces of P1 then a commitment, say $C_{cust\text{-}Ret}$, representing Cust's readiness to buy 100 pieces of P1 at 10 US dollar a piece is created. If Ret replies with Ok and reconfirms the price then $C_{cust\text{-}Ret}$ is activated and a commitment $C_{Ret\text{-}Cust}$, indicating the Ret's readiness to deliver the items is created. If the Cust agrees, then $C_{Ret\text{-}Cust}$ is activated. The agents could carry on further negotiating aspects related to modes of delivery and payment. In this example, we shall only present a few moves to elaborate how commitments could be created, activated, withdrawn, fulfilled and violated.

In the context of an on-going dialogue between Cust and Ret, suppose that Ret decides at $t_f = 10.30$ AM to make a promise to Cust that it will deliver a free sample of P1 as in M_{k1}.

M_{k1} (Ret):   A free sample of P1 will be delivered at $t_f \oplus 1$ h.

Cust replies by agreeing at $t_f \oplus 3$ min sec in M_{k2}.
M_{k2} (Cust):   Ok.

Suppose that at $t_f \oplus 1$ h, Cust makes M_{k3}.

M_{k3} (Cust):   A free sample of P1 is delivered.

Our aim is to present a clear way of detecting whether or not a commitment is violated. We will define a violation/compliance criterion based on the existence of arguments/proofs for the induced commitment(s). The logic which we shall employ is temporal modal defeasible logic which formalizes *commitments* that agents undertake as a consequence of communicative actions. That is, it associates with each speech act a clear meaning in terms of a commitment induced by that speech act. Commitments are represented as modal sentences.

The rest of the paper is organized as follows. In Sect. 2, we give a brief presentation of Temporal Deontic Defeasible Logic (TDDL). In Sect. 3, we give a formal account of speech acts, dialogue moves. In Sect. 4 we discuss commitments and operations on them. In Sect. 5, we present some concluding remarks.

2   Temporal Deontic Defeasible Logic (TDDL)

In TDDL [19], commitments are represented as modal sentences such as Committed$_{G1, G2}$ B which states that agent G1 is committed to agent G2 to bring about B. TDDL is an extension on the Temporal Defeasible Logic (TDL) system, presented in [25], that enables us to represent explicitly time and temporal events/actions. Regarding time, It employs a temporal system called PI which takes equally points and intervals as primitives [20, 23]. PI has (1) a precedence relation $\leq_p$ between time units (e.g., point and/or interval), (2) a predicate **Meets** on intervals, (3) a predicate **In** which determines whether or not a time point is within an interval and (4) a next operator $\oplus$. Depending on the granularity of time used, $t_0 \oplus 1$ s refers to one second after t_0, $t_0 \oplus 5$ s refers to 5 s after t_0 and $t_0 \oplus 1$ h refers to one hour after t_0.

The language of TDDL, L$_{TDDL}$, is defined as follows. Let P$_{TDDL}$ stand for a set of propositional atoms, Agt for a set of agents. (Committed$_{G1,G2}$ B) where G1,G2 $\in$ Agt and G1 $\neq$ G2, is the modality that represents the commitment of agent G1 to agent G2 to bring about B.

Let Lit = P$_{TDDL}$ $\cup$ {$\neg p |$ $p \in$ P$_{TDDL}$} and TLit = Lit $\cup$ {p[t]| $p \in$ Lit}
We shall employ Exempted as the dual of committed, i.e.,
Exempted $\equiv \neg$Committed$\neg$
We define, ModLit, modal literals as
ModLit = {($?_{G1,G2}$ p), ($\neg?_{G1,G2}$ p)}| $p \in$ TLit and
    ? $\in$ {Committed, $\neg$Committed$\neg$}}.

The language of L$_{TDDL}$ has connectives $\wedge$, $\vee$, $\rightarrow$, $\Rightarrow$ and $\neg$. $\vdash$ (resp. $\vdash \sim$) denotes classical inference (resp. defeasible inference), $\rightarrow$ (resp. $\Rightarrow$) denotes the implication of classical (resp. defeasible) logic and $\rightsquigarrow$ denotes a defeater. L$_{TDDL}$ has a preference relation $\geq$ that defines priorities among rules. R1 $\geq$ R2 means that R1 is preferred over R2.

Let A, B, ... be propositions, t, t_1, t_2 ... are time units (points or intervals), G, G1, G2, ... be agents/users, R, R1, R2, ... be rules, and α, α_1, α_2, ... be actions/events. A $\Rightarrow$ B represents a defeasible implication, akin to a default rule [1, 9, 19, 21, 23, 24].

A $\rightsquigarrow$ B represents a defeater. Defeaters do not directly sanction drawing conclusions but they can block the application of some defeasible rules.

We employ the following notations/predicates:

(1) A[t] to express a temporal expression. A[t] can be read as A holds at/during t.
(2) Occurs (G1, α)[t] to express that the action α was/is/will be performed during/at the time t by the agent/user G1.

2.1   Definite and Defeasible Proofs

Let R be a rule and B $\in$ L_{TDDL}. We employ Ant(R) to represent the set of literals that occur in the antecedent of R and Conseq(R) for its consequent. Let K be a set of rules. We partition K into three subsets: K_s to designate strict rules, K_d to designate defeasible rules and K_{dft} to denote defeaters in K. Let $K_{sd} = K_s \cup K_d$. Let K[B] refers to the set of rules in K where B occurs in its consequent. $K^{Committed}$[B] refers to the set of rules in K which introduce the operator Committed and B occurs in its consequent.

Definition 2.1 We define a defeasible theory DT as a tuple (KB, $\geq$) where KB = $\langle$Fact, K$\rangle$ such that Fact refers to a finite set of facts, K refers to a finite set of rules, and $\geq$ is a preference relation on K. $\geq$ is used for conflicting rules, i.e., rules whose conclusions are contradictory and they are applicable at the same time.

We employ D-Provable to mean definite provable (i.e., using facts and strict rules) and Def-Provable to mean defeasibly provable where propositions with defeasible implication $\Rightarrow$ could be used.

An inference from KB is a labelled literal that takes one of the following forms:

(1) $+\Delta$(B)[t] (B[t] is D-Provable),
(2) $-\Delta$(B)[t] (B[t] is not D-Provable),
(3) $+\delta$(B)[t] (B[t] is Def-Provable) and
(4) $-\delta$(B)[t] (B[t] is not Def-Provable).

Due to the lack of space, we give an informal presentation of the notions $+\Delta$(B)[t], $-\Delta$(B)[t], $+\delta$(B)[t] and $-\delta$(B)[t]. For a formal presentation, please cf. [18, 19].

B is D-Provable ($+\Delta B$) iff B is a fact or there is an $R_1 \in K_s$ such that Conseq (R_1) = B and every member of Ant(R1) is D-Provable. The negative proof $-\Delta$(B) can easily be defined by negating every clause in $+\Delta B$.

To show that a non-modal sentence B is Def-Provable ($+\delta$(B)), there are two choices: either (1) we show that B is D-Provable or (2) make use of K_d. This requires us to perform one of the following three steps: (2.1) find an applicable rule in K_{sd} that has B as a consequent, (2.2) show that ¬B is not D-Provable or (2.3) counterattack each rule that attacks the conclusion B by stronger rule that supports B.

A Def-proof of a (possibly temporal) modal literal/proposition B, $+\delta$(B), is a finite sequence $P_n = (P(1), ..., P(n))$ of labelled literals of the form A, $+\delta$(Committed A), $-\delta$ (Committed A), $+\delta$(Exempted A) and $-\delta$(Exempted A) such that P(1), ..., P(n) satisfy the proof conditions presented in the other definitions.

A rule is applicable for a literal B if B occurs in the head of the rule, all non-modal literals in the antecedent are given as facts and all the modal literals have been defeasibly proved. Conversely, a rule is not applicable if at least one of the modal literals in the antecedent has not been proved or is not a fact if it is a non-modal literal.

To prove $+\delta$(Committed B), we have two possibilities: (1) the commitment B is a member of Fact or (2) B is derivable using rules. This case requires the following conditions to hold: (2.1) none of (Committed $\neg$B), ($\neg$Committed B) and (Exempted $\neg$B) is a member of Fact; (2.2) there must be a rule R1 that introduces B as a commitment and the rule is applicable on B; (2.3) every rule R2 for $\neg$B is defeated by a rule that is preferred over it by a rule for B. If R2 is a Commitment rule, then it can be counterattacked by any type of rule; if R2 is a defeater or an Exempted rule, then only a commitment rule can counterattack it.

The negation of the definition of defeasible provability gives us the proof condition of defeasible refutability for Commitment. To show that B is defeasibly refutable as a commitment, it must be the case that (1) (Committed B $\notin$ Fact) and (2.1) one of the following three statements (Committed $\neg$B), ($\neg$Committed B) and (Exempted $\neg$B) is a member of Fact and (2.2) there must not be a rule for (Committed B) or (2.3) if there is a rule R2 for $\neg$B then (2.3.1) R2 is not a rule for (Committed $\neg$B) or any rule R3 for B, R3 is not preferred over R2 and (2.3.1) R2 is neither a defeater nor an Exempted rule or any rule R3 for (Committed B), R3 is not preferred over R2.

3   Speech Acts and Dialogue Moves

We consider the following set, Sp-Acts, of basic speech acts [19]:

(1) Assert: G can make a move ("Assert" A) if A is not inconsistent with its KB and G is committed to support A if challenged.
(2) Retract: G1 can only make the move "Retract" A as a reply to an ("Assert" A) move made earlier by G.
(3) Accept: G can make the move "Accept" A to signal that it accepts A. It has to be a reply to a previous ("Assert" A, "Request" A or "Promise" A) made by G1. The conditions which apply to "Assert" A applies here.
(4) Reject: ("Reject" A) a countermove to ("Accept" A).
(5) Justify: G can make the move "Justify" A to G1 to explicitly state that G1 has to provide a proof (e.g., an argument) that supports A. This move is usually a reply to an ("Assert" A) move made by G1. A reply to this move will be something like ("Assert" P) where P is a proof of A.
(6) Request/Order(A): G can make the move "request" A to G1 which if accepted by G1, G1 is obliged to cause A to hold. Question can be a request for information.
(7) Promise(A): If G makes the move "Promise A", then G is obliged to cause A to hold.

Definition 3.1 (Dialogue Move): A Dialogue Move can be defined as follows:
M = (k, G1, λ, B, G2, r) where

1. k is the identifier of the move M. (i.e., the kth element of the sequence in a dialogue).
2. G1 is the participant that made the move.
3. $\lambda \in$ Sp-Acts.
4. B is the content of the message which G wants to pass on to G1.
5. G2 is the agent to whom the message is addressed.
6. $r \leq k$ is the identifier of a previous move to which M is a reply.

Let M be a move, we define the following functions: Id(M) = k, Sender(M) = G, Receiver(M) = G1, Content(M) = B, speechAct(M) = λ and reply-to(M) = r.

4 Commitments

Associated with each agent is an ordered set of commitments which are accessible to all agents. With each speech act we associate a meaning in terms of the commitment induced by it. Furthermore, for each speech act, we define a criterion pointing out when the corresponding commitment is violated. These criteria could all be dealt with using the proof theory of the proposed logic.

Following [18, 19], we make a distinction between propositional commitments and action commitments. The emphasis in this paper is on propositional commitment. In this type of commitment, the debtor indicates that it accepts some proposition and will support it if challenged. In the second type, the debtor makes an undertaking that it will carry out some action in order to cause some propositions to hold. Propositional commitments can be further classified into basic propositional commitments and conditional propositional commitment.

Let C = Committed$_{G1,G2}$ B be a modal proposition representing a commitment made by G1 to G2 to bring about B. We shall employ the following predicates:

1. Created(C)   C is created.
2. Activated(C)   C is activated.
3. Fulfilled(C)   C is fulfilled.
4. Withdrawn(C)   C is withdrawn.
5. Violated(C)   C is violated.

We may use functions such as Time-Created(C), Time-Activated(C), Time-Active(C), Time-Fulfilled(C) and Time-Withdrawn(C).

The use of these predicates and functions is essential to define the state(s) of the commitment(s) made by an agent, to another agent, during a certain period of time. Using these predicates we can easily compute which commitments made by an agent G1 to G2 are created, activated/active, violated, withdrawn or violated at a particular time or during a specific period and vice versa.

It is important to note that Created(C) at t does not necessarily give us the ability to infer that C holds at t $\oplus$ 1 s. Indeed, only Activated(C)[t] enables us to infer that C holds at t. Furthermore, the fact that a commitment is a modal sentence allows us to clearly distinguish between the commitment C where C = (Committed$_{G1,G2}$ B) and the proposition B which is the subject of the commitment. In addition, the use of a modal operator to represent commitments allows us to determine when a commitment is fulfilled or violated without the complexity of having to deal with a recursive definition [cf. 18].

We shall divide the speech acts into three classes:

S-Committer   = {Assert, Argue, Promise},
R-Committer   = {Justify, Request} and
N-Committer   = {Retract, Reject}

A speech act that The S-Committer commits the sender, the R-Committer commits the receiver and N-Commiter does not commit any participants or releases one of the participants of one of its commitments. A dialogue evolves from one step to another as soon as a move is uttered.

Definition 3.2: A Propositional Commitment (PC) is usually created following a move M_k that occurs at t_k where $M_k = (k, G1, \lambda, B, G2, r)[t_{Mk}]$ and $\lambda \in \{$Assert, Accept, Justify, Request, Promise$\}$. As mentioned above, $Id(M_k) = k$, $Sender(M_k) = G1$, $Receiver(M) = G2$, $Content(M_k) = B$, $speechAct(M_k) = \lambda$ and reply-to$(M_k) = r$.

The commitment which results is either

$C_{1,2} =$ (Committed$_{G1,G2}$ B) if SpeechAct$(M_k) \in$ S-Committer or
$C_{2,1} =$ (Committed$_{G2,G1}$ B) if SpeechAct$(M_k) \in$ R-Committer

Notice that Content$(M_k) = B$ may have an (implicit or explicit) temporal reference t_A associated with it. $C_{1,2}$ (resp. $C_{2,1}$) does not depend for its fulfillment on any particular condition.

A PC could be in one of the following states:

State1: Commitment Creation

If SpeechAct$(M_k) \in \{$Accept$\}$, then the creation and the activation of $C_{1,2}$ could be represented by the following formula:

$$Occurs\text{-}Sp\text{-}Act(M_k)[t_k] \Rightarrow Created(C_{1,2})[t_k \oplus 1] \wedge Activated(C_{1,2})[t_k \oplus 1]$$

$$(CR - Act)$$

Therefore, at $t_k \oplus 1$, we have $-\delta(Content(C_{1,2}))$, $+\delta(Created(C_{1,2}))$ and $+\delta(C_{1,2})$.

If SpeechAct$(M_k) \in \{$Assert, Promise$\}$, then the creation of $C_{1,2}$ could be represented by the following formula:

$$Occurs\text{-}Sp\text{-}Act(M_k)[t_k] \Rightarrow Created(C_{1,2})[t_k \oplus 1] \qquad (CR1)$$

Therefore, at $t_k \oplus 1$, we have $-\delta(Content(C_{1,2}))$, $+\delta(Created(C_{1,2}))$ and $-\delta(C_{1,2})$.

If SpeechAct$(M_k) \in$ S-Committer = {Justify, Request}, then the creation of $C_{2,1}$ could be represented by the following formula:

$$\text{Occurs-Sp-Act}(M_k)[t_{Mk}] \Rightarrow \text{Created}(C_{2,1})[t_k \oplus 1] \qquad (CR2)$$

Therefore, at $t_{Mk} \oplus 1$, we have $-\delta(\text{Content}(C_{2,1}))$, $+\delta(\text{Created}(C_{2,1}))$ and $-\delta(C_{2,1})$.

Example 3.1. If $M_{k1} = $ (k1, Ret, "Promise", $B[t_f \oplus 1\ h]$, Cust, 0)$[t_f]$ is uttered, where B = "A free sample of P1 will be delivered", then The commitment $C_{Ret\text{-}Cust} = (\text{Committed}_{Ret,Cust}\ B[t_f \oplus 1\ h])$ is created at $t_f \oplus 1$. Formally,

$$\text{Occurs-Sp-Act}(M_{k1})[t_f] \Rightarrow \text{Created}(C_{Ret-Cust})[t_f \oplus 1].$$

Therefore, at $[t_f \oplus 1\ s]$, we can neither prove $B[t_f \oplus 1\ h]$ nor prove $C_{Ret\text{-}Cust}$, i.e., we have $-\delta B[t_f \oplus 1\ h]$, $+\delta(\text{Created}(C_{Ret\text{-}Cust}))$, $-\delta(C_{Ret\text{-}Cust})$.

State2: Commitment Activation

As mentioned above, If SpeechAct$(M_k) \in \{\text{Accept}\}$, then the creation and the activation of $C_{1,2}$ take place at the same time.

If Speech$(M_k) \in \{\text{Assert, Promise}\}$, then $C_{1,2}$ is created following M_k. However, it will not be activated until Receiver(M_k) makes a move $M_j = $ (j, G2, λ, A, G1, k)$[t_j]$ where $\lambda \in \{\text{Accept}\}$. If such a move is made at t_j such that (1) Before(t_k, t_j) and Before (t_j, t_A) where A = Content(M_k), and (2) $C_{1,2}$ is not withdrawn then Time-Activated $(C_{1,2}) = t_j \oplus 1$. This can formally be represented as:

$$\text{Occurs-Sp-Act}(M_k)[t_M] \wedge \text{Occurs-Sp-Act}(M_j)[t_j] \Rightarrow \text{Activated}(C_{1,2})[t_j \oplus 1]) \quad (ACT1)$$

$$\text{Activated}(C_{1,2})[t_j \oplus 1] \Rightarrow C_{1,2})[t_j \oplus 1] \qquad (ACT2)$$

Therefore, at $t_j \oplus 1$, we have $-\delta\text{Content}(M_k)$, $+\delta\text{Created}(C_{1,2})[t_k])$, $+\delta(C_{1,2})$.

Similarly, $C_{2,1}$ will not be activated until Receiver(M_k) makes a move M_j ("Accept" A). If such a move is made at t_j such that Before(t_k, t_j) and Before(t_j, T_A) and $C_{2,1}$ is not withdrawn, then Time-Activated$(C_{2,1}) = t_j \oplus 1$.

Example 3.2. If Cust replies, at $t_f \oplus 3\ s$, to M_{k1} made by Ret with M_{k2}:

$$M_{k2} = (k2,\ \text{Cust, "Accept",}\ B[t_f \oplus 1h],\ \text{Ret, k1})$$

then $C_{Ret\text{-}Cust}$ will be activated. This can be expressed formally as:

$$\text{Occurs-Sp-Act}(M_{k1})[t_f] \wedge \text{Occurs-Sp-Act}(M_{k2})[t_f \oplus 4s] \Rightarrow$$

$$\text{Activated}(C_{Ret-Cust})[t_f \oplus 4s]$$

$$\text{Activated}(C_{Ret-Cust})[t_f \oplus 4s] \Rightarrow C_{Ret-Cust}[t_f \oplus 4s]$$

Thus, at $t_f \oplus 4\ s$, we have $-\delta\text{Content}(M_{k1})$, $+\delta(\text{Created}(C_{Ret\text{-}Cust}))$, $+\delta(C_{Ret\text{-}Cust}).)$

S3. Commitment Withdrawal

The withdrawal of a commitment $C_{1,2}$ which resulted from a move M_k, made at t_k and was activated at t_j where t_k is before t_j, can only take place if a move M_{wdraw}

(countermove to M_k where if M_k asserts B, M_{wdraw} will assert $\neg$B) is made at t_{wdraw} where t_j is before t_{wdraw} and t_{wiraw} is before $t_{Fulfill}$.

$$C_{1,2}[t_{wdraw}] \wedge \text{Occurs-Sp-Act}(M_{wdraw})[t_{wdraw}] \Rightarrow \text{Withdrawn}(C_{1,2})[t_{wdraw\oplus 1}]$$
$$(W - DW)$$

$$\text{Withdrawn}(C_{1,2})[t_{wdraw\oplus 1}] \Rightarrow \neg C_{1,2}[t_{wdraw} \oplus 1] \qquad (W - DW1)$$

Therefore, at $t_{wdraw} \oplus 1$ we have: $-\delta\text{Content}(C_{1,2})A$, and $\delta(\neg C_{1,2})$.

Example 3.3. If Cust, at $t_f \oplus 10$ min makes move $M_{k3} = \text{Occurs-Sp-Act}(k3, \text{Cust},$ "Assert", $\neg$B, Ret, k1)$[t_f \oplus 1$ h$]$

$$\text{Occurs-Sp-Act}(M_{k3})[t_f \oplus 10\text{min}] \Rightarrow \text{Withdrawn}(C_{Ret,Cust})[t_f \oplus 10\text{min} \oplus 1s]$$

$$\text{Withdrawn}(C_{Ret,Cust})[t_f \oplus 10\text{min} \oplus 1s] \Rightarrow \neg C_{Ret,Cust}[t_f \oplus 10\text{min} \oplus 1s]$$

S4: Commitment Fulfillment
Let $t_k \oplus 1$ be the time when $C_{1,2}$ is activated, t_{Ful} be the time when the content of move M_k should be fulfilled such that $t_k \oplus 1$ is before t_{Ful}. Let t' be a point in time just before t_{Ful}, i.e., $t' \oplus 1 = t_{Ful}$. If we have $+\delta(C_{1,2})[t_k \oplus 1]$, $-\delta\text{Content}(M_k)[t_k \oplus 1, t']$ and $+\delta\text{Content}(M_k)[t_{Ful}]$ then $C_{1,2}$ is fulfilled at $[t_{Ful}]$.

$$C_{1,2}[t_k \oplus 1] \wedge \neg\text{Content}(M_k)[t_k \oplus 1, t'] \wedge \text{Content}(M_k)[t_{Ful}] \Rightarrow \text{Fulfilled}(C_{1,2})[t_{Ful}]$$
$$(F1)$$

$$\text{Fulfilled}(C_{1,2})[t_{Ful}] \Rightarrow \neg C_{1,2}[t_{Ful} \oplus 1] \qquad (F2)$$

Therefore, at $t_{Ful} \oplus 1$ we have: $+\delta\text{Content}(M_k)$, $+\delta(\text{Fulfilled}(C_{1,2})$ and $\delta(\neg C_{1,2})$.

Example 3.4. If Cust, at $t_f \oplus 1$ h makes move $M_{k3} = (k3, \text{Cust}, \text{"Assert"}, B, \text{Ret}, k1)$ $[t_f \oplus 1$ h$]$ then $B[t_f \oplus 1$ h$]$ becomes true. Hence, $(C_{Ret,Cus})$ will be fulfilled.
Occurs-Sp-Act$(M_{k3})[t_f \oplus 1$ h$] \Rightarrow \text{Content}(M_{k1})[t_f \oplus 1$ h $\oplus 1$ s$]$
$B[t_f \oplus 1$ h$] \wedge C_{Ret,Cust}[t_f \oplus 3$ s$] \Rightarrow \text{Fulfilled}(C_{Ret,Cust})[t_f \oplus 1$ h$]$
Fulfilled$(C_{Ret,Cust})[t_f \oplus 1$ h$] \Rightarrow \neg C_{Ret,Cust}[t_f \oplus 1$ h$])$

S5. Commitment Violation
Let $t_k \oplus 1$ be the time when $C_{1,2}$ is activated, t_{Ful} be the time when the content of move M_k should be fulfilled such that $t_k \oplus 1$ is before t_{Ful}. Let ϑ a threshold period of time. That is, if Content(M_k) is expected to hold at t_{Ful} and if Content(M_k) still does not hold at $t_{Ful} \oplus \vartheta$ then we want to say that $C_{1,2}$ is violated. That is, If we have $+\delta(C_{1,2})$ $[t_k \oplus 1]$, $-\delta\text{Content}(M_k)[t_k \oplus 1, t_{Ful} \oplus \vartheta]$ then $C_{1,2}$ is violated at $[t_{Ful} \oplus \vartheta]$.

$$C_{1,2}[t_k \oplus 1] \wedge \neg\text{Content}(M_k)[t_k \oplus 1, t_{Ful} \oplus \vartheta] \Rightarrow \text{Violated}(C_{1,2})[t_{Ful} \oplus \vartheta] \quad (\text{Violated1})$$

Therefore, at $t_{Ful} \oplus 1$ we have: $-\delta\text{Content}(M_k)[t_k \oplus 1, t_{Ful} \oplus \vartheta]$, $+\delta(\text{Violated}(C_{1,2})$ and $+\delta(C_{1,2})$.

Example 3.4. $C_{Ret,Cust}$ is violated if at $t_f \oplus 1$ h + 2 h a delivery of P1 is not made.

$C_{Ret\text{-}Cust})[t_f \oplus 4 \text{ s}] \wedge \neg Content(M_{k1})[t_f \oplus 4 \text{ s},t_f \oplus 1 \text{ h} + \vartheta] \Rightarrow Violated(C_{Ret\text{-}Cust})$
$[t_{Ful} \oplus \vartheta]$

5 Conclusions and Future Work

We have, in this paper, presented a way to detect whether or not a commitment is violated. We have defined a violation/compliance criterion based on the existence of arguments/proofs for the induced commitment(s). The logic which we have employed is temporal modal defeasible logic which formalizes *commitments* that agents undertake as a consequence of communicative actions. That is, we have associated with each speech act a clear meaning in terms of a commitment induced by that speech act. Commitments are represented as modal sentences. For a commitment/modalized sentence C, we have employed the predicates Created(C), Activated(C), Fulfilled(C), Withdrawn(C) and Violated(C) to define the state(s) of the commitment(s) made by an agent to another agent during a certain period of time. The use of a modal operator allowed us to determine when a commitment is fulfilled, violated or withdrawn without the complexity of having to deal with a recursive definition.

Regarding the implementation of TDDL, we have already started the task of developing a TDDL reasoner. We are inspired and make use of the approaches proposed in [2–4, 10]. The basic idea of the TDDL reasoner, which we are developing, is to translate a TDDL theory D into a logic program P, and then use a logic meta-program that simulates the proof theory of TDDL. We will show that the time complexity of the algorithm remains computationally feasible. We shall employ the algorithm proposed in [12] to show that TDDL has linear complexity and the work proposed in [11] to include the notion of inferiorly defeated rules to manage the superiority relation. This will be elaborated on in a forthcoming publication where we intend to provide an experimental evaluation and develop a realistic application which is a supply chain management of a pharmaceutical company.

It is worthwhile investigating more refined notions of violation criteria and violation types, and the possibility of associating some penalty to be paid by the debtor if the commitment is violated, depending on the type of violation.

References

1. Al-Shaikh, A., Khattab, H., Moubaiddin, A., Obeid, N.: A defeasible description logic for representing bibliographic data. In: Taha, N., Al-Sayyed, R., Alqatawna, J., Rodan, A. (eds.) Social Media Shaping e-Publishing and Academia, pp. 95–105. Springer, Cham (2017). https://doi.org/10.1007/978-3-319-55354-2_8
2. Antoniou, G., Billington, D., Governatori, G., Maher, M.J.: Embedding defeasible logic into logic programming. Theor. Pract. Log. Program. **6**(6), 703–735 (2006)
3. Antoniou, G., Dimaresis, N., Governatori, G.: A modal and deontic defeasible reasoning system for modelling policies and multi-agent systems. Expert Syst. Appl. **36**(2), 4125–4134 (2009)

4. Bassiliades, N., Antoniou, G., Vlahavas, I.: A defeasible logic reasoner for the semantic web. Int. J. Semant. Web Inf. Syst. (IJSWIS) **2**(1), 1–41 (2006)

5. Bentahar, J., Moulin, B., Meyer, John-Jules Ch., Lespérance, Y.: A New Logical Semantics for Agent Communication. In: Inoue, K., Satoh, K., Toni, F. (eds.) CLIMA 2006. LNCS (LNAI), vol. 4371, pp. 151–170. Springer, Heidelberg (2007). https://doi.org/10.1007/978-3-540-69619-3_9

6. Bentahar, J., El-Menshawy, M., Qu, H., Dssouli, R.: Communicative commitments: model checking and complexity analysis. Knowl. Based Syst. **35**, 21–34 (2012)

7. Cohen, P., Levesque, H.: Communicative actions for artificial agents. In: Proceedings of the International Conference on Multi-Agent Systems. AAAI Press, San Francisco (1995)

8. Guerin, F., Pitt, J.: Denotational semantics for agent communication language. In: Proceedings of the Fifth International Conference on Autonomous Agents, pp. 497–504. ACM (2001)

9. Hijazi, S., Jabri, R., Obeid, N.: On drug dosage control using description defeasible logic. In: International Conference on Computational Science and Computational Intelligence (CSCI). IEEE (2017)

10. Kontopoulos, E., Bassiliades, N., Governatori, G., Antoniou, G.: Extending a defeasible reasoner with modal and deontic logic operators. In: IEEE/WIC/ACM International Conference on Web Intelligence and Intelligent Agent Technology, vol. 3, pp. 626–629 (2008)

11. Lam, H.-P., Governatori, G.: What are the necessity rules in defeasible reasoning? In: Delgrande, J.P., Faber, W. (eds.) LPNMR 2011. LNCS (LNAI), vol. 6645, pp. 187–192. Springer, Heidelberg (2011). https://doi.org/10.1007/978-3-642-20895-9_17

12. Maher, M.J., Rock, A., Antoniou, G., Billington, D., Miller, T.: Efficient defeasible reasoning systems. Int. J. Artif. Intell. Tools **10**(4), 483–501 (2001)

13. Maudet, N., Chaib-Draa, B.: Commitment-based and dialogue-game-based protocols: new trends in agent communication languages. Knowl. Eng. Rev. **17**(02), 157–179 (2002)

14. Moubaiddin, A., Obeid, N.: Towards a formal model of knowledge acquisition via cooperative dialogue. ICEIS **5**, 182–189 (2007)

15. Moubaiddin, A., Obeid, N.: The role of dialogue in remote diagnostics. In: Proceedings of the 20th International Conference on Condition Monitoring & Diagnostic Engineering Management, pp. 677–686 (2007)

16. Moubaiddin, A., Obeid, N.: Dialogue and argumentation in multi-agent diagnosis. In: Nguyen, N.T., Katarzyniak, R. (eds.) New Challenges in Applied Intelligence Technologies, Studies in Computational Intelligence, vol. 134, pp. 13–22. Springer, Heidelberg (2008). https://doi.org/10.1007/978-3-540-79355-7_2

17. Moubaiddin, A., Obeid, N.: Partial information basis for agent-based collaborative dialogue. Appl. Intell. **30**(2), 142–167 (2009)

18. Moubaiddin, A., Obeid, N.: On formalizing social commitments in dialogue and argumentation models using temporal defeasible logic. Knowl. Inf. Syst. **37**(2), 417–452 (2013)

19. Moubaiddin, A., Salah, I., Obeid, N.: A temporal modal defeasible logic for formalizing social commitments in dialogue and argumentation models. Appl. Intell. **48**, 1–20 (2017)

20. Obeid, N.: Towards a model of learning through communication. Knowl. Inf. Syst. **2**(4), 498–508 (2000)

21. Obeid, N.: A formalism for representing and reasoning with temporal information, event and change. Appl. Intell. **23**(2), 109–119 (2005)

22. Obeid, N., Moubaiddin, A.: Towards a formal model of knowledge sharing in complex systems. In: Szczerbicki, E., Nguyen, N.T. (eds.) Smart Information and Knowledge Management, Studies in Computational Intelligence Series, pp. 53–82. Springer, Heidelberg (2010)
23. Obeid, N., Rao, R.B.: On integrating event definition and event detection. Knowl. Inf. Syst. **22**(2), 129–158 (2010)
24. Obeid, N., Rawashdeh, E., Alduweib, E., Moubaiddin, A.: On ontology-based diagnosis and defeasibility. In: International Conference on Computational Science and Computational Intelligence (CSCI), pp. 57–62. IEEE (2016)
25. Sabri, K.E., Obeid, N.: A temporal defeasible logic for handling access control policies. Appl. Intell. **44**(1), 30–42 (2016)
26. Singh, M.: Synthesizing coordination requirements for heterogeneous autonomous agents. Auton. Agent. Multi-Agent Syst. **3**(2), 107–132 (2000)
27. Wooldridge, M.: Semantic issues in the verification of agent communication languages. Auton. Agent. Multi-Agent Syst. **3**(1), 9–31 (2000)

Online Learning for Patrolling Robots Against Active Adversarial Attackers

Mahmuda Rahman[✉] and Jae C. Oh

Department of Electrical Engineering and Computer Science,
Syracuse University, Syracuse, NY 13210, USA
mrahma01@syr.edu, jcoh@ecs.syr.edu

Abstract. We study the online route planning problem for patrolling robots, to assign them to optimal routes to patrol in a large crime-prone area. To model the actively engaging, intelligent, and adversarial opponents, we use the Stackelberg Security Game between the patrolling robots and the attackers. We leverage a graph-based bandit algorithm [16] with adaptive adjustment of the reward for the robots in this game to perplex the best response attackers and gradually succeed over them. Our graph bandits can outperform other stochastic bandit algorithms [10] when a simulated annealing-based scheduling mechanism is incorporated to adjust the balance between exploration and exploitation. Hence our method can successfully assign a small group of patrolling robots to cover a large number of routes.

Keywords: UCB1 Bandits · Stackelberg Game · Mixed strategy

1 Introduction

We develop a model for Dynamic Patrol Assignment Problem (DPAP) to address the increasing need for protecting major public facilities in response to global threats. Patrolling robots are equipped with necessary defensive tools for this purpose, but they are expensive to build. Therefore, we need to consider the constraint that only a limited number of such robots can be deployed for patrolling a selected number of routes.

Patrol activities should ideally exhibit unpredictability against adversarial observers who might plan an attack. We consider DPAP as an online learning problem and introduce an algorithm that selects routes for patrolling robots to address threats posed by different attack patterns in each time step. The idea is to maximize the coverage of available routes based on their sensitivity and vulnerability to attacks. The objective is to increase the team payoff of patrolling defenders (i.e., patrolling robots) and decrease that of the attackers over time. We model this as a game between attackers and defenders where the defenders use online reinforcement learning mechanism to predict the next attack pattern.

© Springer International Publishing AG, part of Springer Nature 2018
M. Mouhoub et al. (Eds.): IEA/AIE 2018, LNAI 10868, pp. 477–488, 2018.
https://doi.org/10.1007/978-3-319-92058-0_46

As the game proceeds, both attackers and defenders learn from the response of their respective actions to the other. The correlation between different attack patterns observed by the defenders facilitates their appropriate assignment to critical routes dynamically. We enhance the UCB1 algorithms using a graph-based memory model for this purpose. We consider the attackers as a group always plays their best response strategy.

At each round of patrolling, a Patrolling Robot (PR) is assigned to a route out of a predefined number of routes. For the sake of simplicity, we assume each such routes takes equal amount of time for assigned robot to patrol. Observing the history of the assignments of PRs, the attacking team selects an attack pattern as their best response. Each attack pattern enables the attackers to pose attacks on a certain number of routes at the same time. If an attacker attacks a route which is being patrolled by a PR, the attack is defended. The reward of a PR comes from patrolling a route at the time when that route is under attack. However, absence of any PR on a route which is under attack, penalize the entire team of robots. Under this circumstance, reward of defending a route is stochastic as vulnerability of a route can rise and fall over time by the opportunistic attackers. This situation can be modeled as a zero-sum repeated game between a PR and an attacker.

However, observing the earlier deployments of the PRs, attackers can change its attack pattern in an adversarial manner. Therefore, a PR cannot keep choosing same routes in too many consecutive rounds in the game. Patrolling schedule must balance exploitation (minimizing violations of offenders) with exploration (maximizing the omnipresence of PRs) to make the next assignments of routes for PRs hard to be predicted by the best response attacker and increase the chance of their encounters. We can model this trade-off by solving a bi-objective optimization problem using bandits algorithm [11]. Like [12], we also consider this problem based on the dynamic interaction through a game between the PRs and attackers. But instead of modeling it as a planning problem and solved it using Monte Carlo Tree Search [9] which can result in high branching factor, we formulate it as an online reinforcement learning problem.

Our contributions in this paper are the following:

- we formulate a zero-sum repeated Sackelberg Security Game between PRs and the attacking team with a utility function that facilitates the online learning of PRs from the attack dynamics.
- we develop a graph bandit based centralized algorithm to compute the online route selection strategy for PRs balancing the exploration and exploitation of different routes.
- we simulate the performance of our algorithm under different synthetic attack environments to show its efficacy.

2   Patrolling Robots as UCB1 Bandits

We consider each PR in DPAP running a multi-armed bandit algorithm and all the available routes to be its arms. We assume the number of routes is fixed for this problem. Therefore, selecting a route by a PR is same as choosing an arm to pull from the available arms in a Multi-Armed Bandit problem. The most popular stochastic bandit algorithm, UCB1 [1] has been used for that purpose where each PR runs a UCB1 bandit instance to select a route i from n available routes to maximizes the UCB value: $x_i + \sqrt{\frac{2\log(f)}{f_i}}$ where x_i denotes the current average reward of the route i and f_i denotes the number of times route i has been picked so far in total t rounds. Here f denotes the total count of all items picked so far as $f = \Sigma_{i=1}^{t}(f_i)$. With the assumption that one robot is sufficient to handle criminal activities along with a route, to make sure that robots are assigned to mutually exclusive routes, we used Independent Bandits (IBA) [10]. IBA assumed independence between bandits and used Probability Ranking Principle (PRP) [17] to select routes for the team of cooperating PRs.

The UCB values corresponding to each route can be normalized to the probability for that route to be selected by a PR. This probability changes over time according to strategy selected by the PR and the attackers. In each round, the best response attack pattern is chosen by the attacking team to attack routes which are least defended by the PRs. As the adversarial attack patterns (i.e., attackers' selection of routes) changes in a stochastic manner, PR bandits try to learn the best assignment of routes for the next round by adjusting their probabilities based on the updated UCB value of the routes (arms of the corresponding bandits) based on their reward feedback.

Most works including of [2] considered the similar problem as a finite-horizon MDP [4] where the learning process ends after T steps and the objective is to maximize the accumulated total reward. They applied a variant of MCTS [9], where UCB1 is used as a tree policy leveraging UCT algorithm [9]. They extensively used repeated SSG where an attacker is drawn from a distribution. Their work is based on [12] in which a defender's mixed strategy is discretized to ensure finite state and action space to formalize a Bayesian Stackelberg Game; otherwise, the branching factor for the tree will be too large to come up with a practical solution.

3 Stackelberg Game for Route Selection

The problem of optimal online assignment for PRs is hard as the corresponding bandits are required to coordinate their decision-making with the ultimate goal of achieving maximum team performance [13]. This is aimed at foiling attacks to increase the reward, which involves frequent visits to every route based on the crime intensity and frequency. To this extent, this online learning problem requires optimization of team reward which can be formulated as a Stackelberg Security Game.

In Stackelberg Security Game (SSG) [13], the attacker has a perfect model of how the defender (i.e., PR) moves. [5] developed an offline model using Integer Linear Programming using backward induction where the leader considers what the best response of the follower would be before committing. The leader then picks its move to maximizes its payoff anticipating the predicted response from the follower. For the online problem, we consider defending a team of PRs to be the leader who is continuously learning whereas attacking team changes its strategy in an adversarial manner.

In SSG, each player has a set of pure strategies: for our problem the strategy space is the set of all routes. A mixed strategy of the defender is a probability distribution over pure strategies and is represented by a probability vector. As mentioned earlier, we compute the strategy of a PR by normalizing the UCB values of the corresponding routes for the associated bandit. Therefore, each normalized value indicates the probability of a route to be selected by that specific PR.

We formalize a zero sum repeated SSG between attackers and defenders similar to [2]. Our SSG model has the following components:

- Time Horizon T: the number of rounds.
- Set S of total n number of routes: $S = \{S_1, S_2, S_3, ...S_n\}$.
- A set D of k: Defenders (i.e. PR): $D = \{d_1, d_2, d_3, ...d_k\}$ where $k << n$. Each of them running a UCB bandit to compute its strategy against the attacking team and selects non identical routes to patrol.
- A set A of m independent and mutually exclusive attack patterns: $A = \{a_1, a_2, a_3, ...a_m\}$. Each of these attack patterns can have multiple attacker posing attacks at the same time to different routes. In each round, an attack pattern is selected by the attacking team to pose attacks on the routes that specific attack pattern covers.
- A set of Strategy:
  • Attacking team knows the history of deployments of PRs and selects an attack pattern capable of attacking multiple routes (one by each attacker instance) at the same time. So each attack pattern is defined by a zero-one vector of $n \times 1$ where an entry with value 1 marks the route an to be attacked according to the attack pattern.
  • Every PR bandit runs a defender bandit d to play a strategy based on the probability derived from the UCB values. It is an $n \times 1$ probability vector P_d proportional to the UCB1 values such that with $p_d^i \in P_d$ denotes the probabilities of a route i among n available routes to be selected for patrolling by the PR d.
- Utilities: Payoff for both the PRs and attackers are defined in the following manner when an attack is posed:
  • For a PR d, let $u_d^c(i)$ and $u_d^{\bar{c}}(i)$ be its payoff when the route i is attacked and covered and not covered by d respectively. Therefore under the probability p_d^i, the expected utility of the PR when route i is attacked is given by

$$U_d(i, p_d^i) = u_d^c(i)p_d^i + u_d^{\bar{c}}(i)(1 - p_d^i) \tag{1}$$

  • For an Attacker a, let $u_a^c(i)$ and $u_a^{\bar{c}}(i)$ be its payoff by attacking the route i which is covered and not covered by the a PR respectively. Therefore under the probability p_d^i, the expected utility of the Attacker when route i is attacked is given by

$$U_a(i, p_d^i) = u_a^c(i)p_d^i + u_a^{\bar{c}}(i)(1 - p_d^i) \tag{2}$$

The challenge in this game theoretic formulation is to maximize the expected payoff of the PRs as a team of bandits. As mentioned before, we want to leverage UCB1 algorithm for this purpose where the utility of every arm of each PR is proportional to its associated UCB value. If $P_b(t)$ is this probability vector at time t for all the routes by a PR d, then in a pure strategy game, the next PR b' will ignore the highest UCB valued route of b to let b select that and adjust its probability vector $P_{b'}$ for the remaining routes. In this way, the team of k PRs choices of routes is set against the best attack pattern For a mixed strategy game, we further impose a probability distribution over all the routes available to a PR using the annotation of routes as nodes of the graph of the graph based bandit we leverage. The vector $P(t)$ is the probability computed from normalizing the UCB values of all candidate routes to be selected by the group of PRs according to the above process for a certain round t. Then a single attack pattern a is selected which can attack the route given all such vectors $P'(t)$ till the round t.

$$b_a(t) = argmax_{i \in n} U_a(i, P'(t)) \tag{3}$$

Upon receiving the feedback from the choices made by the attackers at round t the PRs subsequently adjusts their strategies by updating the UCB values as bandits to maximize their expected payoff as they confront the attackers and gets rewarded according to the game we defined. We intend to maximize the expected payoff of the PR d which is:

$$E\left[\Sigma_{t=1}^{T} U_d(b_a(t), P'(t)) \right] \tag{4}$$

The overall payoffs of both teams are measured by summing up their individual utilities as the members of the corresponding team. When normalized, for a bandit $d \in D$, its UCB values corresponds to the probability $p_d^i \in P_d$. Without the loss of generality, P_d preserves the relative ranking of all the routes to be chosen by bandit d. As the team of PRs plays more rounds against different attack patterns, it learns to minimize its regret [2] and maximize the expected team utility.

4   Balancing Exploration and Exploitation

Normalized UCB value, which is used as coverage probability for SSG in our approach reflects the exploitation-exploration trade-off for a PR bandit. As we are using Graph-Based UCB1 [16] instances, routes are represented as nodes. Routes found to be attacked and get defended by PRs at a round of patrolling are connected with edges according to our graph-based approach. However, in SSG game the feedback is coming from opponents who want to foil the strategy taken by the bandits. Therefore we enhance our algorithm to handle the presence of an adversary. We relaxed the node-weight sharing mechanism between neighboring nodes and gave each node equal reward like IBA. This is because we assume that the attackers observe all the deployments history of defender PR bandits before selecting an attack strategy. Node-weight imposes obvious bias towards some routes over the others which facilitates the selection of a representative node for graph coverage which motivated the graph based bandit originally. However, in the presence of adversaries, this method suffers from the weakness of compromising the next defense strategy from the part of the PRs, exposing the most promising route to be selected next by a PR to confront best response opponent. To avoid the danger of getting the next action from the PR predicted by the opponents, bandits need to randomize its strategy and entice the attackers to attack a seemingly less defended route to capture them.

4.1   Active and Dormant Routes

[16] introduced adaptive annotation of graph bandit nodes as active and dormant. It was inspired by the need for a selection policy for graph-based bandits to reduce the search space by finding active arms faster. In this section, we discuss how we use this method to annotating the routes and find the solution to DPAP which can result in a better coverage of routes under adversarial setting. As described in DPAP, each route is considered as an arm in our bandit algorithm and hence a node in our graph. On a certain round, a route can be in one of the following two states:

Definition 1. *A route is **active** for a time step if it is currently selected by our bandit algorithm. Such an arm as route (node) has most outgoing edges in our graph.*

In the beginning, all routes are active because each of them is equally likely to be selected.

Definition 2. *A route is **dormant** if it is selected by the bandit but found one of k routes which for which an active route is identified by another bandit at the same time.*

These arms are dormant in a sense that they equally qualify to represent a specific attack pattern.

Routes selected by bandits with no match in the attack pattern receive a reward of 0 but stays active. Because even though those arms indicates its failure to cover that specific attack at certain iteration, our algorithm does not rule out its potential for covering a new attack pattern from the attackers.

Similar to [16], we also define transition of a route as an arm from one state to the other occurs in the following situations:

- A route gradually becomes dormant from active with its repeated failure to be the route to match with the attack pattern
- A route gradually becomes active from dormant if it frequently matches with the route from the incoming attack patterns

The transition of an arm from the dormant state to an active state potentially results in covering more attack patterns. While selecting an arm for each iteration, every bandit needs to update the value of a counter r initialized to 0. We update the counter in the following manner:

- If a dormant arm from the previous iteration becomes active in the current iteration, then r is set to 0.
- If (1) an active arm from the previous iteration becomes dormant in the current iteration, or (2) a dormant arm selected by the bandit fails to get a reward in the current iteration and goes back to active state then r is incremented by one.
- If an arm stays in the same state then the value of r will be unchanged.

If an arm is found to be in a dormant state, UCB value for that arm is smoothed by the parameter θ in the following manner:

$$\theta = 1 + \log(1 + r_n) \tag{5}$$

Therefore, UCB value for every dormant arm i for a bandit is:

$$x_i + (1 - \exp^{-1/\theta}) \sqrt{\frac{2 \log(f)}{f_i}} \tag{6}$$

This gives our algorithm enough opportunity to balance between exploration and exploitation adaptively instead of using a parameter set to a fixed value to scale it. Instead of trying with different parameters, by increasing the value of r for a previously active arm which transformed as dormant in the current iteration, we scale down the UCB value for the arms selected by the subsequent bandits by $(1 - \exp^{-1/\theta})$. So that for such a route, less exploration will take place, and it gets biased towards exploring that route to give it a fair chance of getting selected without being exposed to the attacker.

4.2   Comparison Between Different Randomization

We propose a randomized algorithm as a solution to DPAP. It is rooted in the updated selection policy for graph bandits proposed in [16]. Graph-based bandit solved for set coverage problem by choosing a representative node to cover for its neighborhood. For DPAP, that solution introduces bias to certain specific routes for PRs and hence easy to predict for attackers. Therefore, we modified their reward mechanism for each node (route as an arm) in the graph so that each node is independent of its neighbors. We also propose adaptive simulated annealing policy for node selection to control the transition of the arms' states and helps PRs select the ones which are active and rewarding without imposing too much reward bias to certain specific route choices. This apparent randomization is achieved by tuning the value of counter r and the temperature parameter $theta$ for the annealing is adjusted accordingly.

We compare this mechanism with several other randomized bandit approaches; namely, uniform-random, ϵ-greedy and α-exploitation.

- With **uniform random** approach, we select a random route from all available routes for a PR to patrol

- In ϵ-**greedy** approach, with a very small fixed *epsilon* probability a random route is assigned to a PR; otherwise, it selects the route with highest UCB value
- According to α-**exploitation** method, exploitation term (average reward) of a route is scaled with a fixed small value of α exploitation; whereas, the exploration term is adjusted with a scaling factor of $(1 - \alpha)$

We conducted several sets of experiments on the synthetic data to show the result of the game we defined. In all our experiments, we considered a certain amount of overlap between the strategies of different attackers so that the problem is suitable to model using the graph as edges are created by the routes attacked together by the same attack pattern. Our online learning algorithm helps the defending team to learn these attack patterns in terms of UCB values and compute the attack probabilities to deploying a set of PRs to withstand the attacks.

We allowed a 25% overlap between different attack-strategies. Our generated dataset has more than half a dozen different attack strategies, each consisting of 25 different attack routes targeted simultaneously by attackers over total 100 routes. A successful attack or defense gives a unit of reward and negative reward to corresponding attacker or bandit respectively. To view it as a zero-sum game, we keep 25 PRs playing as bandits against 25 attackers.

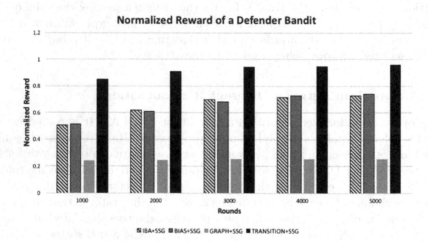

Fig. 1. Comparison of different learning method of 25 defenders for 100 routes against 25 attackers

Figure 1 shows the normalized reward between 0 and 1; each PR is getting by being a member of the defending team. The histogram is plotted by taking the average of every 1000 iteration up to 5000 rounds. We show how different strategy taken by the defending team changes the reward dynamics. We run our experiment with IBA based SSG, Reward Bias based SSG, Node weight based graph bandits without and with the state transition. We observed that Graph-based PR bandit instances playing SSG as a defender with state transition against attackers are receiving the highest amount of reward within 1000 rounds. A graph with no state transition is worst performing one as it exposes the rewarding pattern to the attackers through weight biased for nodes which give ample scope to the best response attackers to change their attack-strategy successfully against the defenders.

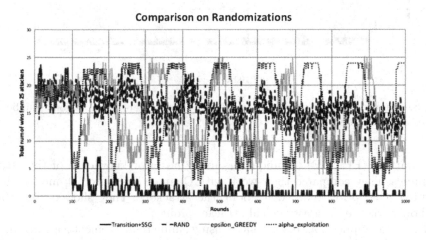

Fig. 2. Total number of successful attacks by 25 attackers compared under different randomized defender deployment scenario

We observed that even though the experiment shows the result of the game played for 1000 to 5000 rounds, within 100 rounds our proposed method is a clear winner over the other methods. We compare the performance of our proposed method with other randomized strategies as well. Figure 2 shows the outcome of the game played under the same environment using bandits who randomize their decision of selecting routes using graph-based bandits but used uniform-random, ϵ-greedy and α-exploitation as well as that of our proposed state transition mechanism for randomization.

We also change the configuration of the problem environment, where the number of routes is changed to 200 from 100 and attackers, and PRs doubled as well. It is found that the problem gets harder with scaling up the number of routes even with the same ratio of PRs and attackers as we can see in Fig. 3 that convergence took almost 2000 rounds of play instead of 1000.

5 Related Work

[19] also investigated repeated security games with unknown pay off and attacker behavior. In their work, they used "Follow the Perturbed Leader with Uniform

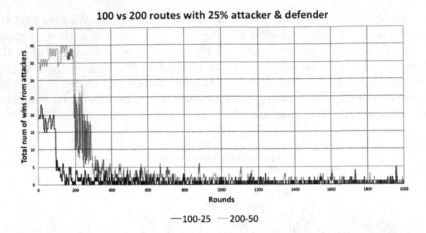

Fig. 3. Total number of successful attacks by 25 attackers when various number of routes are considered

Exploration" (FPL-UE) technique assuming no prior knowledge of the attack dynamics. They compared their work with Quantal Response [20] model which requires some prior knowledge about the attackers. They showed that their method works well against typical attacker profiles.

Practical implications of such game using online reinforcement learning methods have been depicted in the work of [15,18,21]. In [22], they used an iterative learning and planning mechanism that keeps updating the adversary model periodically. They used EM [7] algorithm with dynamic planning against adaptive attackers. In that work, instead of using SSG, they used Dynamic Bayesian Network [6] for modeling the problem.

[14] introduced Rolling Down Randomization (RDR), a technique to generate randomized policies where the similar problem has been modeled using POMDP [8]. Above a given expected reward threshold, their defenders need to generate a randomized policy. To make it hard for an opponent to anticipate the defender's action, their method increased the policy entropy. Their work leveraged both linear and nonlinear optimization methods for a single defender.

6   Conclusion

In this paper, we introduced an online learning algorithm for patrolling robots against adversarial attackers. Our algorithm schedules the route to patrol for each robot in every round by treating the PRs as UCB1 bandits. We show the effectiveness of our algorithm to deal with different attack patterns across different rounds over some routes. Instead of choosing the best-response attack pattern, an attacking team may choose best response routes by the individual attackers independently. Therefore, the team of PRs needs to learn the complex nature of heterogeneous attack patterns within a single round of play.

An attacker can only maximize its utility by performing a successful attack (avoiding a PR). We are interested to see how the learning mechanism of bandits gets affected by the attacking team if attackers also employ learning against the PRs. For future work, we intend to extend the SSG using MAB settings for both the teams where each of them can select its routes by online implicit opponent modeling [3].

References

1. Auer, P., Cesa-Bianchi, N., Fischer, P.: Finite-time analysis of the multiarmed bandit problem. Mach. Learn. **47**(2–3), 235–256 (2002). https://doi.org/10.1023/A:1013689704352
2. Balcan, M.F., Blum, A., Haghtalab, N., Procaccia, A.D.: Commitment without regrets: online learning in stackelberg security games. In: Proceedings of the Sixteenth ACM Conference on Economics and Computation, EC 2015, pp. 61–78. ACM, New York (2015). https://doi.org/10.1145/2764468.2764478
3. Bard, N., Johanson, M., Burch, N., Bowling, M.: Online implicit agent modelling. In: Proceedings of the 2013 International Conference on Autonomous Agents and Multi-agent Systems, AAMAS 2013, pp. 255–262. International Foundation for Autonomous Agents and Multiagent Systems, Richland (2013). http://dl.acm.org/citation.cfm?id=2484920.2484963
4. Bellman, R.: A markovian decision process. Indiana Univ. Math. J. **6**, 679–684 (1957)
5. Brown, G., Carlyle, M., Salmerón, J., Wood, K.: Defending critical infrastructure. Interfaces **36**(6), 530–544 (2006). https://doi.org/10.1287/inte.1060.0252
6. Dagum, P., Galper, A., Horvitz, E.: Dynamic network models for forecasting. In: Proceedings of the Eighth Conference on Uncertainty in Artificial Intelligence, UAI 1992, pp. 41–48. Morgan Kaufmann Publishers Inc., San Francisco (1992). http://dl.acm.org/citation.cfm?id=143802.143815
7. Gupta, M.R., Chen, Y.: Theory and use of the EM algorithm. Found. Trends Signal Process. **4**(3), 223–296 (2011). https://doi.org/10.1561/2000000034
8. Kaelbling, L.P., Littman, M.L., Cassandra, A.R.: Planning and acting in partially observable stochastic domains. Artif. Intell. **101**(1–2), 99–134 (1998). https://doi.org/10.1016/S0004-3702(98)00023-X
9. Kocsis, L., Szepesvári, C.: Bandit based Monte-Carlo planning. In: Fürnkranz, J., Scheffer, T., Spiliopoulou, M. (eds.) ECML 2006. LNCS (LNAI), vol. 4212, pp. 282–293. Springer, Heidelberg (2006). https://doi.org/10.1007/11871842_29
10. Kohli, P., Salek, M., Stoddard, G.: A fast bandit algorithm for recommendation to users with heterogenous tastes. In: desJardins, M., Littman, M.L. (eds.) AAAI. AAAI Press (2013). http://dblp.uni-trier.de/db/conf/aaai/aaai2013.html#KohliSS13
11. Lai, T.L., Robbins, H.: Asymptotically efficient adaptive allocation rules. Adv. Appl. Math. **6**(1), 4–22 (1985)
12. Marecki, J., Tesauro, G., Segal, R.: Playing repeated stackelberg games with unknown opponents. In: Proceedings of the 11th International Conference on Autonomous Agents and Multiagent Systems, AAMAS 2012, vol. 2, pp. 821–828. International Foundation for Autonomous Agents and Multiagent Systems, Richland (2012). http://dl.acm.org/citation.cfm?id=2343776.2343814

13. Nittis, G.D., Trovò, F.: Machine learning techniques for stackelberg security games: a survey. CoRR abs/1609.09341 (2016). http://arxiv.org/abs/1609.09341
14. Paruchuri, P., Tambe, M., Ordóñez, F., Kraus, S.: Security in multiagent systems by policy randomization. In: Proceedings of the Fifth International Joint Conference on Autonomous Agents and Multiagent Systems, AAMAS 2006, pp. 273–280. ACM, New York (2006). https://doi.org/10.1145/1160633.1160681
15. Pita, J., Jain, M., Marecki, J., Ordóñez, F., Portway, C., Tambe, M., Western, C., Paruchuri, P., Kraus, S.: Deployed armor protection: the application of a game theoretic model for security at the Los Angeles International Airport. In: Proceedings of the 7th International Joint Conference on Autonomous Agents and Multiagent Systems: Industrial Track, pp. 125–132. International Foundation for Autonomous Agents and Multiagent Systems (2008)
16. Rahman, M., Oh, J.C.: Graph bandit for diverse user coverage in online recommendation. Appl. Intell. (2017). https://doi.org/10.1007/s10489-017-0977-1
17. Robertson, S.E.: Readings in information retrieval. In: The Probability Ranking Principle in IR, pp. 281–286. Morgan Kaufmann Publishers Inc., San Francisco, (1997). http://dl.acm.org/citation.cfm?id=275537.275701
18. Tsai, J., Kiekintveld, C., Ordonez, F., Tambe, M., Rathi, S.: Iris-a tool for strategic security allocation in transportation networks (2009)
19. Xu, H., Tran-Thanh, L., Jennings, N.R.: Playing repeated security games with no prior knowledge. In: Proceedings of the 2016 International Conference on Autonomous Agents & Multiagent Systems, AAMAS 2016, pp. 104–112. International Foundation for Autonomous Agents and Multiagent Systems, Richland (2016). http://dl.acm.org/citation.cfm?id=2936924.2936944
20. Yang, R., Ordonez, F., Tambe, M.: Computing optimal strategy against quantal response in security games. In: Proceedings of the 11th International Conference on Autonomous Agents and Multiagent Systems, AAMAS 2012, vol. 2, pp. 847–854. International Foundation for Autonomous Agents and Multiagent Systems, Richland (2012). http://dl.acm.org/citation.cfm?id=2343776.2343818
21. Yin, Z., Jiang, A.X., Johnson, M.P., Kiekintveld, C., Leyton-Brown, K., Sandholm, T., Tambe, M., Sullivan, J.P.: Trusts: scheduling randomized patrols for fare inspection in transit systems. In: IAAI (2012)
22. Zhang, C., Sinha, A., Tambe, M.: Keeping pace with criminals: designing patrol allocation against adaptive opportunistic criminals. In: Proceedings of the 2015 International Conference on Autonomous Agents and Multiagent Systems, AAMAS 2015, pp. 1351–1359. International Foundation for Autonomous Agents and Multiagent Systems, Richland (2015). http://dl.acm.org/citation.cfm?id=2772879.2773326

Perception of Fairness in Culturally Dependent Behavior: Comparison of Social Communication in Simulated Crowds Between Thai and Japanese Cultures

Sutasinee Thovuttikul[1,2(✉)], Yoshimasa Ohmoto[1],
and Toyoaki Nishida[1,2]

[1] Department of Intelligence Science and Technology,
Graduate School of Informatics, Kyoto University, Kyoto, Japan
thovutti@ii.ist.i.kyoto-u.ac.jp,
{ohmoto,nishida}@i.kyoto-u.ac.jp
[2] RIKEN Center for Advanced Intelligence Project, Kyoto, Japan

Abstract. Living in unfamiliar cultures is difficult because of the differences in thinking patterns, viewpoints, and greeting styles involving physical contact. Cultural misunderstanding may cause major problems. The solutions for solving such problems may differ depending on the cultural backgrounds of the concerned individuals. In this paper, we present our findings about the cultural understanding of learners during interactions based on experiments involving simulated crowds pertaining to perceived communication differences between Thai and Japanese participants. The participants are asked to live in a shared virtual space to obtain multiple tickets available at two service counters. A virtual service person provides a ticket upon request at each counter. In our experiment, the waiting style (line and group waiting) and the service person's fairness (fair and unfair service) are varied. Participants from Thai and Japanese cultures focus on different features while waiting. Thai participants tend to focus on queue jumpers and emotional feeling, whereas Japanese participants emphasize on speed as their reason for selecting a counter.

Keywords: Cultural learning system · Human perception of different cultures
Fairness and culture · Waiting behavior · Simulated crowd

1 Introduction

With the advances in technology, the world seems smaller now than in the past. Traveling to different parts of the world is becoming increasingly faster and easier [1]. However, different countries have different lifestyles and customs, which are still not well understood by foreigners. For example [2], an American, while greeting an Asian (e.g., a Vietnamese woman) for the first time, makes the mistake of hugging and kissing her in public, thereby insulting her. Even though hugs and kisses are very simple greeting behaviors in western culture, it is considered rude in Asian culture. Intercultural tourism is superficial [3] because travelers visit the other culture/country

© Springer International Publishing AG, part of Springer Nature 2018
M. Mouhoub et al. (Eds.): IEA/AIE 2018, LNAI 10868, pp. 489–495, 2018.
https://doi.org/10.1007/978-3-319-92058-0_47

for a very short time. They might not understand complex situations but might at least learn good behavior that would help them avoid misunderstandings and communication mistakes. A simple unavoidable activity for a tourist is waiting in queues among a crowd. Waiting is related to the idea of fairness [4]. Although fairness is a simple word, it is complicated by many factors. We emphasize certain factors such a learner's cultural background or role/position of communication. Here, we hypothesize that participants with different cultural backgrounds may have different perceptions of the same activity. Hall [5] discusses about territoriality and personal space. Each person is surrounded by an invisible bubble that depends on many things: relationships with nearby people, emotions, activities, and culture. Hall [6] states that culture shields people from attention while at the same time causing them to ignore certain things. Therefore, we aim to understand concepts regarding attention and ignoring certain actions in a public space in different cultures.

Communication is "the exchange of information between a sender, a receiver and the inference (perception) of meaning between the individuals involved" [7]. If the sender and receiver are from different cultures, both must learn from each other to understand encoding and decoding patterns. A crowded place is suitable for practicing cultural communication because similar behavior can be easily observed in a large crowd. Some unique behaviors may be difficult to observe in a small group because there would be many different behaviors, with each being represented by only a few people. However, in a large crowd, most would behave similarly, so we can easily observe unique behavior. Many virtual simulation systems have been developed to represent different cultural behaviors and communication styles, e.g., cultural agent behavior models [8–11], useful scenarios [9–11], and powerful interactive tools [9] are developed. In these studies, participants gain only one-to-one conversation experience and may understand cultural behaviors (e.g., greetings) from the interaction but may not understand the cultural background, for example, why and when they should act freely or act carefully. In this paper, we focus on the perceptual processes involved in learning about different cultures, i.e., awareness and interpretation processes. As a case study, we select an international traveler to help us understand cultural communication. In Sect. 2, we discuss our hypothesis and explain how our solution is used to confirm our hypothesis. In Sect. 3, we describe our experimental settings and present concrete results. Finally, in Sect. 4, we summarize our findings and present our future plan based on the present results to achieve the main goal of our research.

2   System Architecture

In this study, we investigate the concrete effects of different cultural backgrounds while learning cultural communication behavior. We apply the perception of cultural learning using a "simulated crowd" [12, 13] to create a virtual ticket counter (VTC), in which each participant uses a terminal to participate in social activities in a shared virtual space. A shared virtual environment is set up on a network so that participants can converse (Fig. 1(A)). We use the Wizard of Oz system (WOZ) technology to capture the human body and thereby create a natural interaction environment for the participant

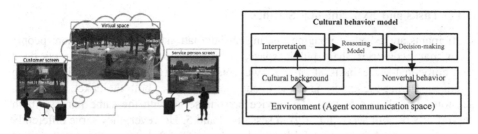

Fig. 1. System setting (A) experiment setting and (B) cultural behavior model

[14]. A simple model is designed to control the agent's behavior: walking, collision avoidance, and waiting.

To learn culture-dependent behavior for communication, the participant should be aware of differences to be considered while learning about a new culture (Fig. 1(B)). Generally, fairness is an importance condition for waiting [4] in all cultures. Service persons serve customers on a first-come-first-serve basis in all sessions. When a queue-jumping customer who is a friend of the service person arrives at the counter, the service person will either accept (femininity) or reject (masculinity) the request. We will compare the different interpretations of this action between Thai and Japanese participants. Another condition for waiting is the waiting style. Thai culture prefers group waiting, whereas Japanese culture prefers line waiting. Hofstede's [3] cultural dimensions are used to categorize thinking, belief, and behavior from more than 40 countries. From the six available dimensions, we select two dimensions that are relevant to waiting. (1) Individualism versus collectivism: This dimension represents people-based differences. In individualism, waiting is an instruments and everyone has equal rights to receive services/goods. In collectivism, waiting is a social activity. Groups are formed based on relationships with family or friends or other salient social functions (Thai 20, Japanese 46 [3]). (2) Masculinity versus femininity: This dimension describes how gender influences roles. In masculine culture, the strong are serviced first. Competitiveness is considered appropriate for the waiting process. In feminine culture, force or urgency is not stressed upon. People relax and enjoy the waiting time (Thai 34, Japanese 95 [3]). Generally, if the main choices made in an activity are clearly different, selection can be easily made visually. However, if they are similar, other priorities should be carefully considered. Here, we hypothesize that culture influences people's choices or ability to ignore a condition.

3   Experiment

We aim to reveal the factors affecting participants' learning. Perception plays a key role in deducing the meaning of events to understand cultural communication styles.

3.1   Tasks and Experimental Settings

Participants are asked to imagine visiting an international theme park, where people from many countries share public space. Participants wait for getting tickets on a first-come-first-serve basis at one of two counters: A (line waiting) and B (group waiting). During the experiment, the queue jumper reaches both the ticket counters in sessions 2, 3, 4, and 5. Both the service persons serve with the same fairness (both serve fairly or both serve unfairly) in sessions 2 and 5. However, they serve differently in sessions 3 and 4 (one serves fairly and the other unfairly). Japanese students (average age = 21, age range = 18–24, n = 16) were recruited from Kyoto University, Japan, and Thai students (average age = 22, age range = 19–30, n = 16) were recruited from Chiang Mai University, Thailand. To find differences in perception between the two participant groups, we taught them about the activities and conversation between the customer agents and service person avatars. We started each session by asking the participant to observe a video of the activities in the virtual space. Then, the participant was asked to practice getting a ticket once at both the line- and group-waiting counters. Next, we asked the participant to select a counter and wait for a ticket thrice. Finally, at the end of each session, we asked participants to state their reason for each choice.

3.2   Experimental Results

Participants had three chances to select a counter (A or B). They were free to select the same or different counters. The counter selection and its reasons were noted as the "counter selection result" and "reasoning result," which are key experimental results.

Counter Selection Results. Analysis of variance (ANOVA) was applied to our results to calculate the selection frequency. A significant difference was found for the line waiting selection (F (1, 30) = 7.059, p = 0.0125), which indicated that using different waiting styles and service person's fairness levels affected participants' counter selection differently according to their nationalities. The average frequency of the line waiting selection at counter A is shown in Fig. 2. The counter selection analysis showed that more Thai participants went to counter A than Japanese participants in almost all sessions. However, in the questionnaire analysis, they did not write the same reason for all the selections. Therefore, the participants could not confirm their perceptions and interpretations by only their counter selection. Then, we continued analyzing the counter selection result because the reasoning results were more clearly defined with regard to the participants' thoughts during selection.

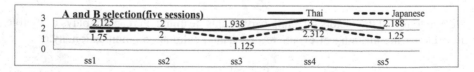

Fig. 2.   Counter selection result

Reasoning Results. As previously mentioned, we control two factors—customer waiting style and service person's fairness—to study the cultural influence on communication. The agents always wait in line at counter A and in random positions at counter B. The service person's fairness behavior is different in each session. We group all five sessions into two categories: same conditions of fairness (both service persons are fair or unfair in session 1, 2, and 5) and different conditions of fairness (one service person is fair and the other is unfair in sessions 3 and 4). The number of answers for the reasoning result in the questionnaire was counted without considering the counter selection because we intended to consider only the stimulus perceived by the participant from our system during the counter selection. The counter selection reasoning was dependent on the following parameters: (1) queue jumper/fair or unfair service, (2) waiting style/waiting position, (3) speed (waiting and service speeds), (4) interaction with service person, and (5) emotional feeling (like, do not like, worried, happy, or angry). We compared the cultural influence on waiting style conditions between Thai and Japanese participants. The main influence originated from significant differences in emotional feeling when comparing the same and different conditions of fairness $(F (1, 30) = 6.919, p = 0.0133)$. When the service had the same fairness, Thai participants used their emotional feeling as the reason to select the counter more times than Japanese participants. In contrast, when one service person was unfair and the other was fair, only small number of Thai participants use emotion feeling as their reason; however, the number of Japanese participants who use emotion feeling was lower (Fig. 3(A)). The significant difference in fairness was $(F (1, 30) = 5.565, p = 0.0210)$. This implied that Thai participants focused more on fairness and queue jumping than Japanese participants under both the conditions (Fig. 3(B)). Another significant difference was found in the speed of activities $(F (1, 30) = 3.008, p = 0.0931)$. Speed was used as the reasoning more by Japanese participants than Thai participants under both the conditions (Fig. 3(C)). No significant difference was observed for the interaction and waiting position, but most Thai participants paid more attention to the service person's interaction than the Japanese participants.

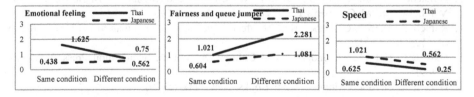

Fig. 3. Reasoning results: (A) emotional feeling, (B) fairness and queue jumper and (C) speed

4 Discussion and Conclusion

In this paper, we presented an experiment to compare the effect of cultural perception on fairness in waiting behavior between Thai and Japanese cultures. A novel contribution of this paper is that we determine the effect of the cultural background on the perception of different fairness levels in the waiting behavior. Participants should generally prefer fair service, but some Thai participants ignore the queue jumper and wait at their preferred counter because they think that the person might be in a hurry. Out of the total Thai participants who accepted the queue jumper (9 of 16), seven found one queue jumper in a line to be acceptable under any conditions and two found one queue jumper to be acceptable only when they were relaxing while waiting with a random group. This result confirmed that Thai participants were relaxed and did not stress upon force or urgency waiting; this Thai culture reflects femininity (score 34). In contrast, most Japanese participants worried about speed (14 of 16), which was more than the corresponding number of Thai participants; this fact indicated masculinity (score 95), which involves competitiveness and desire to protect their rights.

The relationship between collectivism and proxemics (distance) is difficult to derive and measure by the physical settings in a virtual simulation [9]. Thai culture is based on collectivism (score 20). We found that Thai participants forgive the queue jumper because they believe that the jumper is a friend of the service person. Therefore, collectivism may affect the physical position as well as the work status and relationships with friends or family. Japanese participants with a medium score of 46 in the individualism culture desire to reach the counter faster by any means such as queue jumpers or familiarizing themselves with waiting. They believe that everyone has equal rights to be serviced based on a first-come-first-serve basis. Hence, collectivism is said to be related to groups and relationships. In the future, we will perform experiments with participants from different cultures to check whether more factors affect participant behavior.

References

1. Samovar, L.A., Porter, R.E., McDaniel, E.R., Roy, C.S.: Communication Between Cultures. Cengage Learning, Boston (2016)
2. Dresser, N.: Multicultural Manners: Essential Rules of Etiquette for the 21st Century. Wiley, Hoboken (2011)
3. Hofstede, G., Hofstede, J.G., Minkov, M.: Cultures and Organizations: Software of the Mind, 3rd edn. McGraw Hill Professional, New York (2010)
4. Rafaeli, A., Barron, G., Haber, K.: The effects of queue structure on attitudes. J. Serv. Res. **5** (2), 125–139 (2002)
5. Hall, E.T., Hall, M.R.: Understanding Cultural Differences. Intercultural Press, Yarmouth (1989)
6. Hall, E.T.: Beyond Culture. Anchor Books, New York (1989)
7. Mullins, L.J.: Essentials of Organizational Behaviour. Pearson Education, New York (2008)
8. Degens, N., Endrass, B., Hofstede, G.J., Beulens, A., André, E.: 'What I see is not what you get': why culture-specific behaviours for virtual characters should be user-tested across cultures. AI Soc. **32**(1), 37–49 (2017)
9. Kistler, F., Endrass, B., Damian, I., Dang, C.T., André, E.: Natural interaction with culturally adaptive virtual characters. J. Multimodal User Interfaces **6**(1–2), 39–47 (2012)

10. Hall, L., Tazzyman, S., Hume, C., Endrass, B., Lim, M.Y., Hofstede, G., Paiva, A., Andre, E., Kappas, A., Aylett, R.: Learning to overcome cultural conflict through engaging with intelligent agents in synthetic cultures. Int. J. Artif. Intell. Educ. **25**(2), 291–317 (2015)
11. Endrass, B., Degens, N., Hofstede, G.J., André, E., Mascarenhas, S., Mehlmann, G., Paiva, A.: Integration and evaluation of prototypical culture-related differences. In: Workshop on Culturally Motivated Virtual Characters, 11th Conf. on IVAs, pp. 1–9. Springer (2011)
12. Thovuttikul, S., Lala, D., Ohashi, H., Okada, S., Ohmoto, Y. Nishida, T.: Simulated crowd: towards a synthetic culture for engaging a learner in culture-dependent nonverbal interaction. In: Workshop on Eye Gaze in Intelligent Human Machine Interaction, Conference on Intelligent User Interfaces, California (2011)
13. Thovuttikul, S., Lala, D., Kleef, V.N., Ohmoto, Y. Nishida, T.: Comparing people's preference on culture-dependent queuing behaviors in a simulated crowd. In: Proceedings of the 11th International Conference on Cognitive Informatics and Cognitive Computing, pp. 153–162. IEEE Press, Japan (2012)
14. Lala, D., Thovuttikul, S., Nishida, T.: Towards a virtual environment for capturing behavior in cultural crowds. In: 6th International Conference on Digital Information Management, pp. 310–315. IEEE Press, Melbourne (2011)

Simultaneous Exploration and Harvesting in Multi-robot Foraging

Zilong Jiao$^{(\boxtimes)}$ and Jae Oh$^{(\boxtimes)}$

Department of Electrical Engineering and Computer Science,
Syracuse University, Syracuse, NY 13244, USA
{zijiao,jcoh}@syr.edu

Abstract. We study the multi-robot foraging problem in an unknown environment with risks. Robots have to explore entire unknown environment without stepping into risk areas and simultaneously collect all discovered targets. We present a novel algorithm that integrates the frontier-based exploration algorithm with auction-based task-allocation. Extensive simulation studies demonstrate that our algorithm can balance the tasks of environment exploration and target collection efficiently.

Keywords: Multi-robot foraging · Auction methods · Target delivery

1 Introduction

The multi-robot foraging task is for deploying a group of robots to explore unknown environment and transport discovered targets back to their home base. In this paper, we extend the frontier-based exploration algorithm proposed in [1] to simultaneously explore the unknown environment and collect discovered targets with a team of homogeneous mobile robots.

Multi-robot exploration is essential in multi-robot foraging task, and it has many applications in practice, including planetary exploration, cleaning, harvesting and environmental data collecting. During exploration, targets may be discovered and require immediate harvesting [5]. In this case, robots should be allocated efficiently, so that the tasks of environment exploration and target collection can be well balanced in real-time. There are many existing work [6,9] proposed for task allocation in multi-robot exploration. However, among those work, balancing the performance of target collection and environment exploration has not received enough attention. Our contribution includes introducing a new algorithm that integrates exploration of the environment and harvesting; extensively evaluating the performance of the multi-robot exploration with a various number of deployed robots and different task allocation methods.

We provide insights on how multi-robot exploration strategy can get benefit from robot target-collection behavior. In extensive simulation studies, our work is evaluated based on three criteria: the total exploration time and the total length of trajectories traveled by robots and exploration redundancy.

© Springer International Publishing AG, part of Springer Nature 2018
M. Mouhoub et al. (Eds.): IEA/AIE 2018, LNAI 10868, pp. 496–502, 2018.
https://doi.org/10.1007/978-3-319-92058-0_48

We also compare our work with the frontier-based exploration algorithm proposed in [1]. The experiment results demonstrate that our proposed algorithm can effectively balance the tasks of environment exploration and target collection.

In the next section, we define our multi-robot foraging problem. In Sect. 2, we discuss the related literature. Section 3 presents the details of our proposed algorithm, followed by the simulation results in Sect. 4. Finally, we conclude the paper in Sect. 5.

2   Related Work

Frontier-based algorithms are widely applied to coordinated multi-robot exploration in practice. In [1], during exploration robots keep expanding explored areas by moving toward their assigned frontiers. When assigned frontiers are reached, new frontiers are assigned to the robots based on decision theory. Their proposed work is considered as a centralized approach since the authors assume that robots have unlimited communication. To overcome the limited communication during exploration, Fox et al. [2] proposed a distributed algorithm for environment mapping by having robots exchange frontier information at waypoints. Visser et al. [8] investigated the effects of balancing robots movement cost and information gain while assigning frontiers to the robots. Among all the frontier-based exploration algorithm cited above, the impact of target collection on environment exploration is not addressed. In [3], the auction process is divided into five steps: task announcement, metric evaluation, bid submission, close of auction and progress monitoring/contract renewal. The effectiveness of the auction algorithm proposed in the paper was demonstrated in their MURDOCH system. In [7], a bidding algorithm is proposed for the limited communication, and it enables distributed frontier assignments among robots.

In our proposed algorithm, the performance of frontier-based exploration is further improved when robots are strategically allocated for target collection. We use auction-based task allocation to balance the tasks of environment exploration and target collection, which makes our work fundamentally different from the others [3,7].

3   Proposed Algorithm

In our exploration task, robots need to simultaneously explore the entire environment while continuously collecting all discovered targets. To effectively fulfill the task, we extended the multi-robot exploration algorithm proposed in [1]. In contrast to the original algorithm, the proposed algorithm is integrated with an auction-based task-allocation method, which can balance tasks of environment exploration and target collection. Interested readers may refer to [1] for the details of the frontier-based exploration algorithm used in this paper.

During exploration, robots need to deliver items from targets as they are discovered. By using Algorithm 1, we ensure that each target will be served by at least one robot. In the proposed algorithm, robots have two types: Explorers and Workers, and they can switch their roles appropriately. Let R_t^E be the set of Explorers at time t. Once a target is discovered by a robot, the robot will become an auctioneer and start auction among all the robots in R_t^E. A centralized scheduler ensures that only one auction can be triggered at any time. The auction in Algorithm 1 is based on single-item first-price sealed-bid auction and closely follows the general steps proposed in [3].

Algorithm 1. Allocate a robot for a discovered target (executed by each robot)

1: **function** ROBOTATAUCTION()
2:    **while** auction is not closed **do**
3:       listen to all the other robots
4:       **if** discovered a target T **then**
5:          become auctioneer
6:          broadcast T's location (x_T, y_T) // announce the task
7:       **if** received a target location (x_T, y_T) **then**
8:          store (x_T, y_T) in r's local memory
9:          **if** r is an Explorer **then**
10:             $bid \leftarrow (1 - d_{r,T}/d_{max}) + \alpha \cdot (1 - n_{\Delta t}/N)$
11:             broadcast bid // submit the bid for T
12:       **if** r is the auctioneer **and**
13:          received the set of $bids$, B, from all robots in $R_t^E \setminus \{r\}$ **then**
14:             $best\_bid = \max(B)$
15:             $winner \leftarrow$ the bidder of the $best\_bid$ in B; // determine the winner
16:             broadcast $winner$
17:       **if** received $winner$ **and** $r = winner$ **then**
18:          become Worker
19:          close the auction

In the proposed algorithm, a robot r bids a target T based on two factors: the distance $d_{r,T}$ from r to T and $n_{\Delta t}$, the number of unknown cells explored by r within the last Δt time units. Let N be the number of cells in the global occupancy map and d_{max} be the maximum possible distance between any robot and any target. The bidding function of a robot is a linear combination of *task valuation* $(1 - d_{r,T}/d_{max})$ and *robot fitness* $\alpha \cdot (1 - n_{\Delta t}/N)$, where α is a constant ranging over $[0, 1]$. Because of the bidding function, a robot which is closer to the target and covers fewer cells recently will bid higher for the announced target. The robots explored more unknown cells tend to have better chance to explore more unknown cells in future; these robots should not become Workers easily. Once the auctioneer receives all the bids, it will set the Explorer which bids the highest value to be the winner of the auction. Then the winner will become a Worker and move directly back and forth between the discovered target and the base. If the auctioneer does not win, it will become a regular Explorer.

When exploration is completed, remaining Explorers, $\overline{R^E}$, will all be allocated to transport discovered targets. Considering the limited computing power of a robot, we have the robot with lowest ID in $\overline{R^E}$ randomly assign each of the robots in $\overline{R^E}$ to one of the discovered targets.

4   Simulation Results

We implemented our simulation with C++ in Gazebo [4], and our simulation was run on a server with an 8-core CPU and 128 GB memory. For 100 robots, one instance of simulation takes about two days. For each experiment, we report the average performance of 12 simulation instances with standard deviation. The frontier-based exploration algorithm with no auction is evaluated by a fewer simulation runs for each experiment instance, since the algorithm shows similar performance in each simulation given the same number of robots.

Given a number of robots, the performance of their exploration is evaluated based on three criteria: (1) *total length of trajectories traveled by all robots during their exploration*; (2) *total number of simulation iterations for robots to explore entire environment*; (3) *the end of exploration, extra number of times that the cells, in the global occupancy map, are updated*. In terms of the third criteria, we assume that each cell in the global occupancy map only needs to be updated once by exactly one robot.

The frontier-based exploration algorithm was tested with different numbers of robots, including groups with sizes of 1, 5, 10, 20, 40, 60, 80 and 100. The resulting performance, which is presented in the left column of Fig. 1, shows that the time for finishing exploration does not change significantly when the number of deployed robot exceeds 20. In addition, as more robots are deployed both trajectory length and exploration redundancy increase. Figure 2 illustrates an example of the frontier-based exploration, given 20 robots.

In contrast to the stand-alone frontier-based exploration, in the proposed algorithm the robot which discovers a target directly becomes a Worker to collect the target. The performance of the algorithm, as the number of robots changes, is presented in the right column of Fig. 1. As for the auction-based task allocation, task valuation and robot fitness are linearly combined in robots' bidding functions. Because of robot fitness, robots which contribute less to the exploration will be allocated to collect targets. The effect of auction with both task valuation and robot fitness is shown in the right column of Fig. 1. In those experiments, the constant α is empirically set as 0.5, and fitness of a robot is evaluated based on the number of cells covered by the robot in the global occupancy map within the last 100 simulation iterations.

In Figs. 1b and d, both exploration time and trajectory length are reduced, because of auction. With the bidding function, a robot at a better exploratory position can keep exploring environment rather than being allocated for target collection. Instead, a robot which is left behind has a higher probability of becoming a Worker, because the areas close to its assigned frontiers are often explored by the robots moving in front of it. Figure 1f shows that exploration

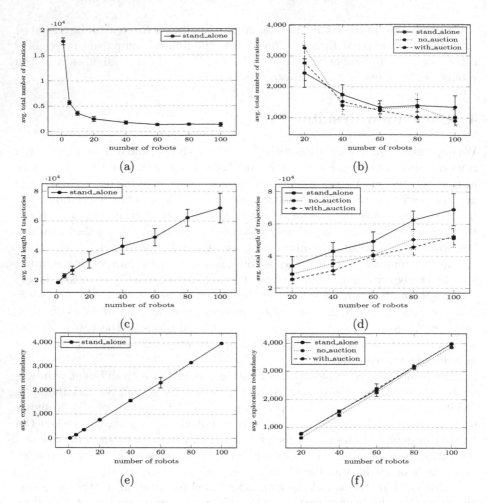

Fig. 1. Left column: performance of stand-alone frontier-based exploration. Right column: performance of stand-alone frontier-based exploration and frontier-based exploration with target delivery. Standard deviation is presented for the result of each given number of robots.

redundancy in this series of experiments is almost identical to the one in the stand-alone frontier-based exploration. This is an indication that the proposed auction-based task-allocation method performs well on minimizing the impact of target collection on environment exploration.

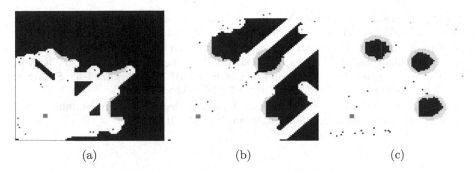

(a)   (b)   (c)

Fig. 2. Image (a) to (c) show the frontier-based exploration done by 20 robots (the small black squares). The black areas are unexplored, and the small grey squares are the targets. Image (c) shows the final state of the exploration. Since the robots can not enter the risk areas, the internal parts of risk areas will not be explored.

5 Conclusion

In this paper, we presented a novel method for integration of exploration and task allocation in multi-robot foraging task. With the carefully designed bidding function, we showed that the auction-based task allocation could be well integrated with the frontier-based exploration to balance the tasks of environment exploration and target collection. However, our method is based on the assumptions that robots have unlimited energy and accurate sensing and motion measurement. Realizing those assumptions can be difficult in a real-world scenario. In our future work, we will consider the energy consumption issue and the uncertainty introduced by robots' sensing and motion. Also, we will study distributed coordination methods for multi-robot exploration.

References

1. Burgard, W., Moors, M., Stachniss, C., Schneider, F.E.: Coordinated multi-robot exploration. IEEE Trans. Rob. **21**(3), 376–386 (2005)
2. Fox, D., Ko, J., Konolige, K., Limketkai, B., Schulz, D., Stewart, B.: Distributed multirobot exploration and mapping. Proc. IEEE **94**(7), 1325–1339 (2006)
3. Gerkey, B.P., Mataric, M.J.: Sold!: Auction methods for multirobot coordination. IEEE Trans. Robot. Autom. **18**(5), 758–768 (2002)
4. Koenig, N., Howard, A.: Design and use paradigms for Gazebo, an open-source multi-robot simulator. In Proceedings of 2004 IEEE/RSJ International Conference on Intelligent Robots and Systems, IROS 2004, vol. 3, pp. 2149–2154. IEEE (2004)
5. Lee, U., Magistretti, E., Gerla, M., Bellavista, P., Lió, P., Lee, K.-W.: Bio-inspired multi-agent data harvesting in a proactive urban monitoring environment. Ad Hoc Netw. **7**(4), 725–741 (2009)
6. Pini, G., Brutschy, A., Pinciroli, C., Dorigo, M., Birattari, M.: Autonomous task partitioning in robot foraging: an approach based on cost estimation. Adapt. Behav. **21**(2), 118–136 (2013)

7. Sheng, W., Yang, Q., Tan, J., Xi, N.: Distributed multi-robot coordination in area exploration. Robot. Auton. Syst. **54**(12), 945–955 (2006)
8. Visser, A., Slamet, B.A.: Balancing the information gain against the movement cost for multi-robot frontier exploration. In: Bruyninckx, H., Přeučil, L., Kulich, M. (eds.) European Robotics Symposium 2008. STAR, vol. 44, pp. 43–52. Springer, Heidelberg (2008). https://doi.org/10.1007/978-3-540-78317-6_5
9. Wei, C., Hindriks, K.V., Jonker, C.M.: Dynamic task allocation for multi-robot search and retrieval tasks. Appl. Intell. **45**(2), 383–401 (2016)

Natural Language Processing

Auto-detection of Safety Issues
in Baby Products

Graham Bleaney[1]($\boxtimes$), Matthew Kuzyk[1], Julian Man[1], Hossein Mayanloo[1],
and H. R. Tizhoosh[2]

[1] Systems Design Engineering, University of Waterloo, Waterloo, ON, Canada
gbleaney@gmail.com, matthew.kuzyk@gmail.com, julianglman@gmail.com,
mhossein2005@gmail.com
[2] KIMIA Lab, University of Waterloo, Waterloo, ON, Canada

Abstract. Every year, thousands of people receive consumer product related injuries. Research indicates that online customer reviews can be processed to autonomously identify product safety issues. Early identification of safety issues can lead to earlier recalls, and thus fewer injuries and deaths. A dataset of product reviews from Amazon.com was compiled, along with *SaferProducts.gov* complaints and recall descriptions from the Consumer Product Safety Commission (CPSC) and European Commission Rapid Alert system. A system was built to clean the collected text and to extract relevant features. Dimensionality reduction was performed by computing feature relevance through a Random Forest and discarding features with low information gain. Various classifiers were analyzed, including Logistic Regression, SVMs, Naïve-Bayes, Random Forests, and an Ensemble classifier. Experimentation with various features and classifier combinations resulted in a logistic regression model with 66% precision in the top 50 reviews surfaced. This classifier outperforms all benchmarks set by related literature and consumer product safety professionals.

Keywords: Online reviews · Product safety · Text mining
Machine learning

1 Introduction

Thousands of people are injured or killed from consumer product related injuries every year. Between October 1, 2011 and September 30, 2012, the United States Consumer Product Safety Commission (CPSC) recorded over 3,800 deaths that involved consumer products [1]. In order to minimize damage to the public, governmental regulatory agencies such as the CPSC are mandated to ensure the safety of consumer products by enforcing product recalls [2]. These organizations

The original version of this chapter was revised: Table 4 and Fig. 2 were corrected. The erratum to this chapter is available at https://doi.org/10.1007/978-3-319-92058-0_87

© Springer International Publishing AG, part of Springer Nature 2018
M. Mouhoub et al. (Eds.): IEA/AIE 2018, LNAI 10868, pp. 505–516, 2018.
https://doi.org/10.1007/978-3-319-92058-0_49

particularly target products that are designed for vulnerable populations in their investigations, such as consumer products designed for young children and the elderly [3].

Despite the efforts of these agencies, product safety issues still occur. One prominent example is the Samsung Galaxy Note7 phone, which was recalled for catching fire [4]. When consumers encounter issues like these, they sometimes voice their concerns about a product in online reviews. In some cases, the complaints are serious enough to warrant an investigation, and possibly a recall. For example, customers were complaining about their Galaxy Note7 phones catching fire as early as August 24th, 2016 [5], but Samsung only started working with the CPSC on September 9th, 2016 [6], and the product was not recalled until September 15th, 2016 [4]. Consumers are exposed to preventable risk in the time between the first customer complaint and the first regulatory action. Earlier detection of product safety issues, using a system such as the one presented in this paper, could reduce consumer exposure to risk and help organizations like the CPSC fulfill their mandate.

Currently, the CPSC detects product safety issues through consumer and manufacturer reports. Consumer reports are collected from a phone hotline and through their online "SaferProducts.gov" website [7]. The CPSC also monitors product-related hospital visits through the National Electronic Injury Surveillance System (NEISS) [1]. Finally, the CPSC also has a small internet surveillance team that does manual surveillance [8]. The manual nature of their work means that many of these customer complaints go unnoticed. A solution that automatically parses reviews and identifies those that mention a safety issue could lead to earlier investigations for dangerous products. Conversations with the Director of Field Investigations at the CPSC, and an Internet Investigative Analyst at the CPSC, validated the need for such a solution; such a solution would be "immediately useful" [3], especially due to their limited manpower. This limited manpower meant that such a solution would also have to be very precise, with one investigator stating they could not tolerate more than 50% of the safety issues identified being false positives [9].

Domain literature suggests that it is possible to build a system to automatically identify product safety issues in online reviews, using machine learning and natural language processing. A project by the University of Washington data science team was able to predict food recalls with 45% precision by classifying AmazonFresh reviews using Term Frequency-Inverse Document Frequency (TF-IDF) features and a Support Vector Machine (SVM) classifier [10]. Another study was able to predict 50% of Toyota Recalls from posts in the online Toyota-Nation forums by using a "Smoke Word" list and the k-Nearest Neighbor (kNN) classifier [11]. In the consumer product space, one study was able to achieve 39% precision in the top 400 reviews when classifying safety issues in online toy reviews [12] using a "Smoke Word" list technique developed by Abrahams et al. [13]. However, the precision of this solution does not meet the 50% precision benchmark set by the CPSC agents.

A major limitation of much of the current literature is the use of "Smoke Words" to identify safety issues. Using the presence of single words as features removes the broader context of sentences, which could aid in safety issue detection. For example, the word "screaming" might appear in a review describing a child "screaming in pain" or "screaming with delight".

The work presented in this paper is both novel and necessary for the following reasons. First, the study explores a new application area, baby products, which has not been addressed by any previous works. Second, this paper utilizes many machine learning and data collection techniques that have not been previously used to classify product safety issues. Finally, this study establishes the requirements for a practical solution that could be used by product safety organizations such as the CPSC, and surveys machine learning techniques to identify those that can best meet the organizations' requirements.

The objective of this study was to build a system that automatically detects consumer product safety issues from online reviews and meets the benchmarks outlined by the CPSC. As a starting point, consumer reviews in the baby product category were targeted, due to their status as a vulnerable population. Various machine learning tools and techniques were tested in order to achieve this objective.

2   Materials

The primary dataset used for review classification was the Amazon review corpus of 142 million reviews provided by Dr. McAuley of UCSD [14]. From this corpus, approximately 7,000,000 reviews in the "Baby" product category were available for experimentation. From these reviews, the data needed to be labelled for use in supervised machine learning. In cases where it was not clear whether a review counted as mentioning a "safety issue", the rules in Table 1 were used.

Table 1. Rules for manual labelling

Issue Mentioned in Review	Safety Issue?
Person harmed during correct use of the product	**Yes**
Person harmed during incorrect use of the product	**Yes**[1]
Harm could have occurred, but was avoided through an action by the user	**Yes**
Different product (i.e., not the product the review is associated with) has a safety issue	**Yes**[2]
Potential harm is suggested, with no evidence (e.g., "This is made in China, so it's probably full of toxic chemicals")	**No**

[1]CPSC suggests firms test for and correct issues arising from foreseeable misuse [15]
[2]It is important to highlight potential safety issues, even if tied to a wrong product causing more follow up

Given the rarity of reviews mentioning product safety issues relative to the size of the whole review corpus, the search space for reviews mentioning safety issues had to be reduced. This was done by combining the CPSC's list of recalled products with the Amazon review dataset, using Universal Product Codes (UPCs). These reviews were filtered to ensure that they were written before the official recall date, to imitate the data that would be available to the system in real-world usage. In total, 2,285 reviews were labeled.

Throughout the testing process, classifiers were tested on unlabelled Amazon reviews (discussed in Sect. 3.4), and the results were labeled. Combining these reviews with the previous labelling, led to a total of 3,773 labelled reviews available for the final training run presented in this paper, 424 of which mentioned product safety issues.

Manual analysis showed that the labelled reviews mentioned only a subset of known safety issues, and skewed toward low severity ones. For these reasons, the labelled data was augmented with other datasets, including SaferProducts.gov complaints, CPSC recall descriptions, and European Commission Rapid Alert data. All of the datasets used are shown in Table 2. Since the reports from these additional datasets explicitly mention harm, they were considered labelled as "Mentions Safety Issue". Each dataset was downsampled to 3,333 complaints due to computational constraints of the hardware available. These were sampled randomly to avoid bias.

Table 2. Explanation of datasets used in final evaluation

Name	Number of Complaints	Description
Amazon Reviews	3,773 labelled/used, 7,155,102 unlabelled	Reviews of products on Amazon
SaferProducts.gov	30,386 labelled, 3,333 used	Reports submitted to the CPSC indicating harm caused by a consumer product
CPSC Hazard Descriptions	14,835 labelled, 3,333 used	Descriptions that accompany CPSC recalls
European Commission Rapid Alert	51,272 labelled, 3,333 used	Descriptions that accompany EU recalls

Additional materials included "Smoke Word" lists: lists of words that could indicate danger if used in a review. The "Smoke Word" list used was compiled by combining a "Smoke Word" list provided by analysts at the CPSC [8], a "Smoke Word" list generated by Abrahams et al. in their analysis of children's toy safety issues [12], and a custom "Smoke Word" list generated from the labelled reviews dataset by computing TF-IDF (see Sect. 3.2) feature importance. This generated "Smoke Word" list was reviewed, and any words that did not seem to indicate an issue were removed.

3   Methods

A system diagram for the product safety issue detection system is shown in Fig. 1. The system includes a data collection (scraping and downloading) component, a machine learning component, and a user interface component; this paper focuses mainly on the machine learning component. The machine learning system was comprised of three sub-components: a text preprocessing component, a feature extraction component, and a classification component. These components can be run with no human interaction, allowing near-instantaneous identification of reviews mentioning product safety issues, reducing the time it takes organizations like the CPSC to identify product safety issues.

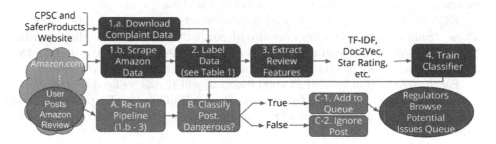

Fig. 1. System diagram for the product safety issue detection system.

3.1   Text Preprocessing

Prior to extracting features, the review text was cleaned by removing non-English words, converting to lower case, and stemming. Non-English word removal was important for removing proper nouns, such as product brand names. While brand names may sometimes provide context for product quality, not removing brand names was found to bias the classifier against large brands that previously had one particularly public recall. Stemming is a heuristic process to convert words to a base form. For example, stemming might convert "safer" and "safely" to the same base stem "safe", to help classifiers treat similar words identically. The snowball stemmer in the NLTK library was used for stemming.

3.2   Feature Extraction

Following the text cleaning process, feature vectors were generated from each review. The results of each feature extraction technique were concatenated to form a single feature vector per review. TF-IDF, Doc2Vec, star rating, and "Smoke Word" count features were all used.

TF-IDF converts text to a vector of word counts weighted by word rarity. This representation helps classifiers identify words that only appear in a small number of documents. Bigram (pairs of words) counts, in addition to unigrams, were computed because they help handle negation [16].

Doc2Vec is an unsupervised neural network model, based on the word2vec model, for converting text into a vector representation that retains semantic information [17]. A custom Doc2Vec model was trained on a subset of the Amazon review corpus, and used to extract Doc2Vec features from text. The subset consisted of 500,000 reviews randomly sampled from the corpus.

Star ratings are Amazon's user generated numerical product ratings. They were included as a feature to proxy the user's sentiment. For the non-Amazon datasets (e.g. recalls and consumer complaints), the star rating was assumed to be one star, due to the negative sentiment of the data.

"Smoke Word" lists are curated lists of words indicative of safety issues. These "Smoke Word" lists were acquired from multiple sources, as discussed in Sect. 2. "Smoke Word" count was computed from these "Smoke Word" lists by counting total occurrences of all smoke words that appeared in a review.

Feature extraction yielded 256,000 features, which was reduced to 2,400 features using a Random Forest to compute feature importance. Feature information gain was calculated as part of the Random Forest training process, with low gain features being discarded.

3.3   Classification

Several commonly used classifiers were tested: SVM, Logistic Regression, Naïve-Bayes, Random Forest, k-Nearest Neighbor (kNN), and an Ensemble classifier.

SVM, Logistic Regression, and Naïve-Bayes classifiers were used because they were effective for text classification in literature [18]. SVMs find the linear separating hyperplane with maximum distance from the closest points of each class. When the data is not linearly separable, kernels are used to project data to a higher dimension where the data is linearly separable [19]. In this study, linear kernels were used. Logistic Regression fits the data to a logistic distribution and results in a linear separating hyperplane [20]. L2 regularization with parameter $\lambda = 0.001$ was used. Naïve-Bayes classifiers use Bayes' conditional probability formula to predict the most probable class for a given data point [20]. The classifier makes the naïve assumption that features are conditionally independent.

Random Forests combine the predictions of a large number of small decision trees, which are trained on separate subsets of features and training examples [21]. Each random forest had 10 trees, each trained with the square root of the total number of features. kNN is a simple classifier in which the k closest training examples vote on the class of a new data point. kNN has been used in literature for text classification [11]. The $k = 5$ nearest neighbors were used in this study. Ensemble classifiers aggregate the results of several other classifiers [22]. In this study, the Ensemble classifier aggregated the results of the other classifiers by averaging their model scores.

Classifiers output a model score for each review, between zero and one. A high model score indicated a high probability that the review "Mentions Safety Issue". The threshold for this classification was chosen by finding the threshold with the maximum F1 score in the training dataset. F1 score is a measure of classifier performance, which is outlined in Sect. 3.4.

3.4 Validation

Classifier performance was compared using peak F1 score, and classifier output on the 50 lowest model score and 50 highest model score reviews.

F1 score is the harmonic average between the precision (percentage of reviews classified as "Mentions Safety Issue" that actually mentioned safety issues) and recall (percentage of reviews mentioning safety issues that the classifier was able to correctly identify). F1 score is a common measure of classifier performance [23]. F1 score was measured for only reviews from the Amazon dataset. Performance was validated using 5-fold cross validation, a technique commonly used in literature [24,25]. This involved dividing the data into five partitions (or folds), running five training cycles while holding out a different partition each time for validation, and training on the other partitions.

Classifier behavior on the 50 lowest model score and 50 highest model score Amazon reviews was examined using a confusion matrix, showing occurrences of their predicted class versus their actual class. In this case, confusion matrices show true positive, false positive, true negative, and false negative counts, where a "positive" example is a review indicating a safety issue. Examining the confusion matrix of the highest and lowest model score reviews is a technique used in literature [12]. Measuring precision on the top 50 reviews, simulated the real world usage of the classifier; investigators are likely to only examine very high model score reviews, given the volume of reviews on the internet [9].

In this study, the classifiers were run on 100,000 previously unseen reviews. The top and bottom reviews were manually labelled (see Sect. 2 for rules). Reviews were labelled by two raters, in order to validate the labels by calculating inter-rater agreement. Fleiss' kappa statistic was found to be $\kappa = 0.713$, which indicated "substantial agreement" [26].

4   Results

The classifiers outlined in Subsect. 3.3 were trained on the combination of labelled baby product reviews, recall descriptions, and consumer complaints that were described in Sect. 2. The results are presented in Table 3, with the best results highlighted in bold. Each row contains confusion matrix data on true positives (TP), false positives (FP), true negatives (TN), and false negatives (FN). The Ensemble classifier had the highest F1 at 0.491, SVM had the highest precision at 53.4%, and Logistic Regression had the highest recall at 70.8%.

Table 3. Classifier results for training on Amazon reviews, recall descriptions, and consumer complaints, and tested on only Amazon reviews. Best results are highlighted in **boldface**

Classifier	F1	Precision	Recall	TP	FP	TN	FN
kNN	0.430	0.347	0.590	191	372	2220	133
Logistic Regression	0.457	0.339	**0.708**	229	452	2140	95
Naïve-Bayes	0.387	0.469	0.334	108	129	2463	216
Random Forest	0.442	0.387	0.527	171	279	2313	153
SVM	0.451	**0.524**	0.398	129	117	2475	195
Ensemble	**0.491**	0.491	0.491	159	166	2426	165

A random sample of 100,000 unlabeled Amazon reviews were classified by each trained classifier, and the reviews with the highest and lowest scores were considered to be labelled as "Mentions Safety Issue" and "Does Not Mention Safety Issue" respectively. The computation time taken to classify the reviews was negligible. These reviews were then manually labelled to validate the classifier-assigned labels.

Table 4 shows classifier precision, calculated in terms of the positive — "Mentions Safety Issue"— class. Recall was not calculated, because there was no data on the total number of safety issues in the 100,000 unlabelled reviews. A few reviews in the random sample were not in English, and were removed from the analysis as a result.

The best performing classifier was the Logistic Regression classifier, with 66% precision. This result surpassed all of the benchmarks defined, which will be discussed further in Sect. 5. To determine the significance of these results, 50 randomly sampled 1-star reviews for baby products were manually labelled. 16% of these 1-star reviews mentioned a safety issue. A chi-squared test demonstrated with $p < 0.0001$ that the Logistic Regression classifier results were a statistically significant improvement over randomly selecting 1-star reviews.

Table 4. Evaluation of classifiers based on reviews that they assigned the highest and lowest scores. Best results are highlighted in **boldface**

Classifier	Precision	TP	FP	TN	FN
kNN	0.163	8	41	50	0
Logistic Regression	**0.660**	33	17	50	0
Naïve-Bayes	0.478	22	24	48	2
Random Forest	0.260	13	37	50	0
SVM	0.560	28	22	49	1
Ensemble	0.490	24	25	50	0

Below are some examples of reviews that were identified by the Logistic Regression classifier:

- "... my 3 year old opened the window anyways and **fell out of the second story window**..."
- "...**YOUR CHILD CAN CHOKE ON THIS TOY!** My 5-month old daughter was playing when one of the legs became **lodged in her throat**..."

The reviews causing false positives and negatives were investigated, and two main reasons were identified: negation and lack of severity. Negation caused reviews such as this one to be mistakenly classified as "Mentions Safety Issue": "We hand washed them and air dried them, but *never had mold*". Some false positive reviews only mentioned low severity issues: "I am really concerned this *odor is toxic*", which did not meat the criteria of being a safety issue (Table 1)

Classifier Performance and Precision Benchmarks

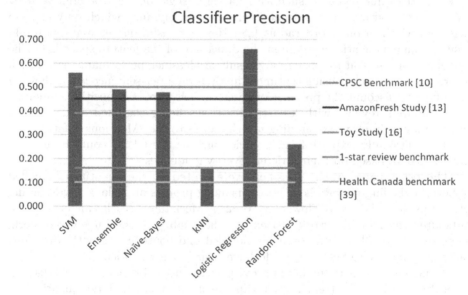

Fig. 2. Classifier precision and benchmarks set by similar studies, and investigators from government agencies.

5   Discussion and Conclusions

Different classifiers were trained to identify product safety issues mentioned in online baby product reviews. SVMs, Logistic Regression, and Naïve-Bayes classifiers performed well, an observation which agrees with reports in literature [18]. Precision benchmarks and classifier precision on the top 50 reviews are summarized in Fig. 2. The Logistic Regression classifier had 66% precision, with the next highest being SVM at 56% precision. These classifiers outperformed the precision benchmarks set in literature. Winkler et al. used a "Smoke Word" list and achieved 39% precision when identifying product safety issues in Amazon reviews of toys [12]. Winkler et al. used a different subset of the same review corpus, and a similar evaluation methodology as this study (measuring precision on the top reviews output by the classifier), and so is most closely comparable to the results found here. Another study predicted food product recalls with 45% precision on AmazonFresh review data, using an SVM classifier [10]. A key difference with that study is it evaluated results against the entire dataset scored by the classifier, rather than just reviews with the top model scores. The Logistic Regression and Naïve-Bayes classifiers also exceeded the performance benchmarks set by users: the CPSC required a minimum precision of 50% [8], and a former Health Canada investigator required a precision of 10% [27]. Finally, the performance exceeded the 16% precision which was achieved in Sect. 4 by assuming all one star reviews mention product safety issues.

While the results outperformed all benchmarks set, there were still many false positives due to issues such as negation. "Negation" can be addressed by using larger n-grams. The current approach uses bigrams, which only capture negation within a one word radius [28]. However, using larger n-grams would result in an exponential increase in the dimension of the feature space [28]. The extremely sparse feature space may result in classifier performance issues. An alternative approach is using sentiment analysis on a per-sentence level, allowing classifiers to discount the presence of danger words in overall positive sentences.

To address reviews with low severity issues being classified as dangerous, results may be improved by adding severity levels to the "Mentions Safety Issue" label. Additionally, experts from agencies such as the CPSC could be used to label the data based on their stricter severity guidelines.

The performance of the classifiers were limited by the quantity of labelled reviews. Labelling reviews is a time consuming process at scale. Crowdsourcing platforms such as CrowdFlower or Amazon Mechanical Turk can be used to outsource the labelling work. To ensure the quality of the outsourced work, some expert labelled data could be included and contributors with low inter-rater agreement (see Sect. 3.4) could have their labels excluded.

It may be possible to further improve performance using neural networks [29]. Neural networks are extremely powerful classifiers, requiring large quantities of labelled data. Future work may explore the application of neural networks to safety issue detection in online reviews.

The implemented solution was limited to English baby product reviews. There is reason to believe that it is possible to apply this approach to all product categories. Every dataset used has data across all product categories, so expanding the scope of the system is as simple as repeating the process described in this paper. Other languages can be supported by following the same process with analogous datasets. For example, Health Canada reports all Canadian recalls in French [30], which is a good analog for CPSC recall data. Additionally, Amazon operates non-English domains, which could be used for non-English review data.

The system described in this paper is almost ready for practical use. It continuously scrapes Amazon reviews throughout the day, and classifies them. In a real world setting, users of the system would be providing feedback on the reviews the system highlights (i.e., true vs false positive), which could be used to continuously retrain and improve the classifiers.

The system can help reduce consumer product related deaths and injuries by reducing issue detection time, and thus remediation time. The classifier was developed alongside a user interface, which was tested with CPSC and Health Canada investigators, and met their requirements. This work also has applications in industry: companies can monitor online reviews for their products, and quickly identify and rectify safety issues. It is the authors' hope that this work will be used to improve consumer product safety where possible.

Acknowledgments. The authors would like to thank Dr. Olga Vechtomova (University of Waterloo, Canada) for her guidance. The authors appreciate the insights on product safety agencies provided by Christine Simpson (former Health Canada Product Safety Officer), Dennis Blasius (CPSC, Director of Field Investigations Division), Michelle Mach and Renee Morelli-Linen (both CPSC Internet Investigative Analysts). The authors would also like to thank Dr. Alan Abrahams for his advice and for providing his smoke word list. Finally, the authors would like to thank Dr. Julian McCauley for providing his corpus of Amazon reviews.

References

1. United States Consumer Product Safety Commission 2015 Annual Report to the President and Congress (2015). https://www.cpsc.gov/s3fs-public/FY15 AnnualReport.pdf. Accessed 14 Mar 2017
2. About CPSC. https://www.cpsc.gov/About-CPSC/Contact-Information. Accessed 16 Mar 2017
3. CPSC Director Interview. In collab. with Dennis Blasius, 9 January (2017)
4. 15 September 2016. https://www.cpsc.gov/Recalls/2016/samsung-recalls-galaxy-note7-smartphones. Accessed 14 Mar 2017
5. The world's first fried Note 7. 24 August 2016. http://tieba.baidu.com/p/4747843017. Accessed 14 Mar 2017
6. Samsung is finally working with the U.S. government on a formal recall of the Galaxy Note 7, September 9 2016. https://www.recode.net/2016/9/9/12866952/samsung-cpsc-galaxy-note-7. Accessed 14 Apr 2017
7. CPSC Hotline. https://www.cpsc.gov/s3fs-public/178.pdf. Accessed 14 Mar 2017
8. CPSC User Test #1. In collab. with Michelle Mach and Renee Morelli-Linen, 14 February (2017)
9. CPSC User Test #2. In collab. with Michelle Mach and co, 9 March (2017)
10. Preliminary Classification. Mining Online Data for Early Identification of Unsafe Food Products. https://uwescience.github.io/DSSG2016-UnsafeFoods/preliminary-classification-models/
11. Zhang, X., Niu, S., Zhang, D., Wang, G.A., Fan, W.: Predicting vehicle recalls with user-generated contents: a text mining approach. In: Chau, M., Wang, G.A., Chen, H. (eds.) PAISI 2015. LNCS, vol. 9074, pp. 41–50. Springer, Cham (2015). https://doi.org/10.1007/978-3-319-18455-5_3

12. Winkler, M., et al.: Toy safety surveillance from online reviews. Decis. Support Syst. **90**, 23–32 (2016)
13. Abrahams, A.S., et al.: Vehicle defect discovery from social media. Decis. Support Syst. **54**(1), 87–97 (2012)
14. Amazon product data. http://jmcauley.ucsd.edu/data/amazon/
15. Step 6: Best Practices. CPSC.gov. https://www.cpsc.gov/Business-Manufactur ing/Business-Education/Safety-Academy/Step-6
16. Pang, B., Lee, L., Vaithyanathan, S.: Thumbs up?: sentiment classification using machine learning techniques. In: Proceedings of the ACL-2002 Conference on Empirical Methods in Natural Language Processing, EMNLP 2002, vol. 10, Stroudsburg, PA, USA, p. 79 (2002)
17. Lau, J.H., Baldwin, T.: An empirical evaluation of doc2vec with practical insights into document embedding generation. In: arXiv:1607.05368 [cs], July 2016. Accessed 16 Mar 2017
18. Khorsheed, M.S., Al-Thubaity, A.O.: Comparative evaluation of text classification techniques using a large diverse Arabic dataset. In: Lang. Resour. Eval. **47**(2), 513–538 (2013). Accessed 16 Mar 2017
19. Suykens, J.A.K., Vandewalle, J.: Least squares support vector machine classifiers. In: Neural Process. Lett. **9**(3), 293–300 (1999). ISSN: 1370–4621. http://journals. scholarsportal.info/detailsundefined. Accessed 16 Mar 2017
20. Ng, A.Y., Jordan, M.I.: On discriminative vs. generative classifiers: a comparison of logistic regression and naive Bayes. Adv. Neural Inf. Process. Syst. **2**, 841–848 (2002)
21. Liaw, A., Wiener, M.: Classification and regression by random forest. R News **2**(3), 18–22 (2002)
22. Ruta, D., Gabrys, B.: Classifier selection for majority voting. Inf. Fusion **6**(1), 63–81 (2005)
23. Van Rijsbergen, C.J.: Information Retrieval, 2nd edn. Butterworth-Heinemann, Newton (1979). ISBN 978-0-408-70929-3
24. Law, D., Gruss, R., Abrahams, A.S.: Automated defect discovery for dishwasher appliances from online consumer reviews. In: Exp. Syst. Appl. **67**, 84–94 (2017)
25. Wang, S., Manning, C.D.: Baselines and bigrams: simple, good sentiment and topic classification. In: The 50th Annual Meeting of the Association for Computational Linguistics: Short Papers, vol. 2. Stroudsburg, PA, USA, pp. 90–94 (2012)
26. Richard Landis, J., Koch, G.G.: The measurement of observer agreement for categorical data. Biometrics, 159–174 (1977)
27. Christine User Test #1. In collab. with Christine Simpson, 8 February 2017
28. Qu, L., Ifrim, G., Weikum, G.: The bag-of-opinions method for review rating prediction from sparse text patterns. In: Proceedings of the 23rd International Conference on Computational Linguistics. Association for Computational Linguistics, pp. 913–921 (2010)
29. Collobert, R., Weston, J.: A unified architecture for natural language processing: deep neural networks with multitask learning. In: Proceedings of the 25th International Conference on Machine Learning, ICML 2008, pp. 160–167. ACM, New York (2008). ISBN 978-1- 60558-205-4
30. Health Canada French Language Recall Alerts. Health Canada. http://www. canadiensensante.gc.ca/recall-alert-rappel-avis/index-fra.php. Accessed 28 Oct 2017

Conversation Envisioning Framework
for Situated Conversation

Maryam Sadat Mirzaei[1,2](✉)(iD), Qiang Zhang[2], Stef van der Struijk[2],
and Toyoaki Nishida[1,2]

[1] RIKEN Center for Advanced Intelligence Project (AIP), Kyoto, Japan
maryam.mirzaei@riken.jp, nishida@i.kyoto-u.ac.jp
[2] Graduate School of Informatics, Kyoto University,
Yoshida-Honmachi, Kyoto 606–8501, Japan
{qiang.zhang,stefstruijk}@ii.ist.i.kyoto-u.ac.jp

Abstract. This paper introduces virtual reality conversation envisioning (VRCE) framework as an effective approach for analyzing situated conversations. The goal of VRCE is to raise understanding of shared information, facilitate common ground formation and promote smooth communication, especially in cross-cultural interactions. In this method, a situated conversational scenario is reconstructed in a VR environment to enable detailed analysis from first and third person view, empowered by flexible traverse in the time dimension. This framework allows participants and meta-participants (observers) to actively engage in the envisioning process in VR. A conversation description language (CDL) is introduced for encoding the obtained interpretations and developing a conversation envisioner. We focused on a bargaining scenario as a situated conversation with rich cultural practices. Preliminary experiments with this scenario indicated the effectiveness of VRCE to achieve better reasoning about the situation and received positive participant feedback.

Keywords: Conversation envisioning · Virtual reality
Situated conversation · Conversation description language

1   Introduction

Conversation involves using of words, prosody, facial expressions, gestures, and actions all seamlessly combined to convey meaning [1] and human manage to decode all these signals to perceive the messages. Conversation analysis has long been of interest to researchers across different domains of linguistics, sociology, anthropology, communication and computer sciences [2] as it holds great promise as arenas for understanding the essence of human interaction. Conversation informatics (CI) builds on conversation analysis and integrates scientific and engineering principles with utility considerations. CI analyzes conversational interactions and thought-sharing using social signals to design conversational artifacts that can smoothly interact with people [3].

© Springer International Publishing AG, part of Springer Nature 2018
M. Mouhoub et al. (Eds.): IEA/AIE 2018, LNAI 10868, pp. 517–529, 2018.
https://doi.org/10.1007/978-3-319-92058-0_50

We propose conversation envisioning (CE) as an approach to bridge the scientific and engineering aspect of conversation informatics. In line with the explicit aspects of conversation, analyzing tacit information is of paramount importance. In this view, CE aims to unveil tacit thoughts and mental states of people who interact during the conversation (Fig. 1). Conversation Envisioning tries to scratch the surface of the interaction and discover tacit information by focusing on how common ground (CG) is formed and updated during the conversation. We emphasize on the dynamic nature of the CG by considering conversation as a continuous process of updating the shared space during the discourse of the interaction.

Fig. 1. (a) The interpretation of own's thoughts, mental states, intentions; both verbals and non-verbals (b) the perception of the listener, possible interpretations, mental states, and tacit thoughts (c) the update of the common ground.

This notion has been investigated as "grounding" in the studies by Traum [4] and Nakano et al. [5], who analyzed the process of building and repairing the CG. A practical example can be found in the study by Visser et al. [6] who proposed a computational model of grounding to provide overlapping verbal and non-verbal behavior by a virtual agent for efficient conversation.

In the case of conversation 'in-the-wild', however, the interaction goes beyond the limited incremental process of grounding and includes more active and dynamic aspects. For instance, in case of negotiations over price, participants combine strategic actions and improvisations to achieve multiple goals such as maintaining a friendly relationship (long-term connection) rather than merely following negotiation protocols to gain the best price. These goals are not always explicit but sometimes hidden or contradictory. Thus, for an agent to converse smoothly with humans, it is crucial to understand the underlying messages exchanged through (non-)verbal interactions. As there is no straightforward solution, a longitudinal effort involving (meta-)participants such as instructors, scientists, and engineers is needed to understand and augment conversations.

This paper proposes conversation envisioner as a computational platform that is designed to support a continuous collaboration and longitudinal effort by (meta-)participants, including data collection, analysis, modeling, building AI (meta-)participants, evaluating hypotheses and applications such as training and real-time assistance. We leverage VR technology and use it as a platform to facilitate uncovering taϲit thoughts in situated conversation. Furthermore, we propose conversation description language (CDL) to systematically describe the conversation and realize envisioning by including the hypothesis brought by (meta-)participants. The goal of virtual reality conversation envisioning (VRCE) is to realize smoother communication and common ground building. We take bargaining as a situated interaction with rich socio-cultural aspects and show how VRCE can be effective by providing timely assistance in cross-cultural communications with limited or no shared background.

The present research has, therefore, three contributions: (1) proposing CE as a new computational framework for analyzing tacit dimensions of conversation, (2) introducing VRCE as a platform for augmenting conversation with CE, and (3) presenting CDL as a language for describing conversational components.

2 Situated Conversation Envisioning: Bargaining Scenario

A lot of communicative actions rely on what is present in a given situation. In this view, the situation gives meaning to the verbal and non-verbal interactions and influence shared knowledge and common ground building [7]. According to the situated cognition theory, *"every human thought and action is adapted to the environment that is situated because what people perceive, how they conceive of their activity and what they physically do develop together"* [8]. Therefore, this study puts particular emphasis on situated conversations, where conversational interactions involve frequent references to a specific situation comprising not just physical, but social entities and relations.

We select bargaining topic as it represents a cardinal illustration of a social interaction that provides useful information for analyzing broad and various forms of complex social relationships between people. Bargaining relationship is a microcosm within which many of the causes and consequences of social interaction and interdependence may be fruitfully examined [9]. It is an instance of negotiation, which is an essential part of everyday life, thus demands a thorough understanding of the situation for reaching an agreement.

Some studies have viewed bargaining as a dynamic decision-making process resembling the ultimatum bargaining game. They started from basic bidding problem and moved toward more complex situations [10,11]. Others tried to generate agents that are believable negotiators [12]. However, bargaining can be viewed as a more complex social interaction, which is influenced by multiple factors such as culture or emotion and may involve multiple goals such as building trust and friendship rather than merely negotiating over price.

2.1 Cultural Aspects of Bargaining

Culture plays a significant role in bargaining. Hence, a unified bargaining practice or model may not be valid across different cultures. For instance, while in some cultures bargaining may be viewed as a simple trade-off, other cultures may consider bargaining as a chance to socialize and build relationships. Such interaction itself may be formed on the basis of gaining some benefits like making a long-term relationship with the customer in order to guarantee future purchases or building trust with the shopkeeper to facilitate future transactions by reducing the cost and saving the time. The influence of culture on negotiation is modeled by Hofstede et al. [12]. According to this model, masculine cultures are interested in fast profitable trades without considering past trustworthiness in subsequent deals, whereas feminine cultures value building trust and relationship as it might pay off in future negotiations. Similarly, in collectivist societies, negotiation builds on the established relationship. Individualist societies, however, focus on personal interest and explicitness, which sometimes offend collectivists.

Fig. 2. Analysis and interpretations rubric

2.2   Emotional Aspect of Bargaining

Almost every human interaction involves emotion, therefore we cannot leave this out when analyzing the conversation between shopkeeper and customer. In fact, negotiation is a complex emotional decision-making process with an aim to reach an agreement for goods or service exchange [13]. In an attempt to reach a deal, people exchange a lot of verbals and non-verbals, each having a specific emotional effect. These can shape the course of the conversation so that parties are directed toward the deal or distracted to a subsidiary goal. For instance, what may be started as bargaining over the price, can turn into a heated conversation to protect one's pride when it is interpreted as an attack on self-image.

2.3   Envisioning of the Bargaining Scenario

The complicated interactions underlying the bargaining situation is essential to investigate for designing cognitive agents that are capable of interpreting such situations and interacting with people, given the bewildering complexity of the situation and in-depth knowledge involved.

To begin the analysis, the conversation is divided into several quanta as packages including the most relevant information to the meaning and expressions of a significant segment of the conversation [3]. Next, the observers annotate each quantum, based on *(i)* the interpretation of what is said by each side (for every single utterance accompanied by non-verbals, if any), *(ii)* the expectations of each side (i.e. what they expect from the other person as a reaction/response in the given situation) and *(iii)* the mental process and reasoning, which induce those expectations and interpretations. Figure 2 shows the analysis rubric.

The annotation of reasoning process behind the actions/reactions is based on a model inspired by the theory of mind's belief-desire reasoning [14] as illustrated in Fig. 3. It is important to note that one's action can have multiple interpretations, each may induce different reactions, which can lead the conversation into different branches. Moreover, cultural and emotional aspects directly or indirectly affect one's action.

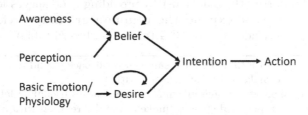

Fig. 3. Simplified scheme of belief-desire reasoning

The following is an extract of a successful scenario, in which the goal of both parties are realized and the deal is successfully formed. In this scenario, the customer and the shopkeeper, two strangers, but from the same cultural background, are interacting to successfully make a deal. The extract shows how other goals may be pursued (building trust and relationship, here) preceding to or in conjunction with the main goal i.e. negotiating to maximize the benefit. The customer opens up using pre-expansion *"You know what?"* (line 1) as a

```
1 C: [Look at the item] You know what? [Moving hand vertically up down]
2 S: [nods]
3 C: I am about to marry,
4 S: [Wide eyes + nodding]
5 C: and I am looking for something very nice to decorate my table [use
       hands to show the size of the table]. Its color is brown. So, what
       do you suggest? [extending arm toward partner]
6 S: Oh! Congratulations on your marriage! [cheerful voice]
7 C: Thank you. [smiles]
```

preliminary signal to an announcement, which is followed by the shopkeeper's nod showing that he is attentively listening. With this, they made a minimal **joint project** [15, p. 86] in which the customer seeks the shopkeeper's consent to make her announcement. Upon receiving the signal, the customer proceeds and announces about her upcoming marriage. In case she did not receive any signal of interest, she would consider it inappropriate to make her announcement and would choose to close the project by saying *"Never mind"* or get to the point directly by saying *"I'm looking for a table cloth"*. However, the customer presupposes that the shopkeeper would be engaged into her story, thus she prefers the **risk** of being ignored to the benefit of being able to make a relationship while having a strategy against being ignored. The shopkeeper (whether real or out of politeness) shows that he is engaged in her story (nodding with wide eyes, line 4). Through sharing personal information with the shopkeeper, both partners of the conversation get closer as a result of the grounding. This initiates building trust and prospective relationship. This type of interaction can be seen in feminine and collectivist **cultures**, where building trust and making relationship comes before the trade. The customer explains her purpose of shopping and **expects** the shopkeeper to fortify the built-trust by providing good suggestions. She also expects the shopkeeper to **expand the common ground** by referring to the topics she has already added to the CG (marriage, brown table).

Awareness: C is *aware* that S shares same cultural background
Desire: C *wants* to make a friendly relation with S
Belief: C *thinks* sharing personal information can lead to friendly relations with S
Intention: C *uses* a personal story to make a friendly relation with S
Action: C *shares* marriage story

During the rest of the interaction, both participants tried to maintain the positive mood and friendly atmosphere, which resulted in a successful deal and a long-term relationship. As mentioned earlier, however, in case the shopkeeper chose to ignore the customer's joint project, the conversation could have led to a different path. We refer to this notion as **branching** and we have collected and classified a number of such branches for analysis in the present study.

3   Virtual Reality Conversation Envisioning Framework

Many verbal and nonverbal clues are included in a small piece of conversation. Yet, it is not easy to trace all these signals. Speech is transient, likewise, gestures are fleeting and quickly disappear. In this view, we need an effective framework that allows for recording, making traces, performing investigations, and extracting tacit information of the conversation by involving (meta-)participants.

The proposed framework, VRCE, provides (meta-)participants with a deft tool that grants multiple features such as abilities to traverse through different time points in the conversation, to experience first and third person view, to add details, analysis and annotations on-the-fly and to trace the changes. For

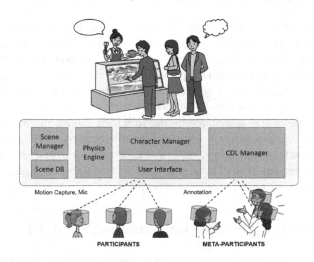

Fig. 4. VRCE framework

instance, it allows for creating branches in the conversation when necessary, indicating possibilities or alternative interpretations.

To this end, the conversation is reconstructed in the Unity3D environment. The procedure starts by recording participants' speech and capturing their gestures using Perception Neuron motion capture system, followed by constructing 3D scene and avatars of the participants. Finally, the transformed speech is synchronized with the gestures so that the full scenario is regenerated in VR to enable (meta-)participants actively participate in CE (Fig. 4).

VRCE can serve as a tool for *Annotation, Training* and *Assistance*. The first mode aims to facilitate the interpretation of the conversation for (meta-) participants by providing necessary functions. It can take client as annotator and record annotations from the 1st person view using HMD or take researchers as annotators to capture structured annotation from the 3rd person view via a user-friendly interface. As a training tool, it can be used for educational purposes to teach discrete educational points such as the cultural differences. It can also serve as an assistive tool for trainees (especially from different cultures) to use the system for learning purposes by playing the role of the characters or benefiting from the 1st person view and learning from interpretations. Such system can be helpful for understanding other cultures or even one's own culture, especially for children and elder people. It has a potential for game-playing situation, augmented by live interpretation to detect miscommunications. It also allows the learners to try different alternatives of conversation (branches) by which participants can experience how small modifications can lead the conversation to a totally different direction. In this view, it allows the participants to find *why* a certain situation happened by letting them go back and forth through the conversation and find the reasons. Furthermore, by providing the ability to switch and converse through different branches, VRCE exposes them to *what if* questions to explore different alternatives. It also stimulates the participants to think of *what else* could happen in that situation hence provide an option to add branches in the run-time. Finally, it allows the researchers to investigate learners' behavior and the distribution of learners' choices by recording their interactions. This allows investigators to make a root-cause analysis of an action and analyzing the probabilities of its occurrence.

The last mode is the assistance mode, in which the agent can act the role of the (meta-)participants and converse with people or serve as an assistant by providing interpretations and revealing important tacit information to smooth the conversation, to expand the common ground, and to advocate empathy (allowing for viewing things from partner's perspective).

4   Conversation Description Language (CDL)

We aim to obtain and estimate the causal relationships of the events and the mental process of the participants either from observations or interpretations rather than statistical computations. This highlights the importance of a conversation manager as an automated annotation system that can convert and transfer the expert knowledge into the system. It is anticipated that using such annotation tool as a scientist workbench would allow us to understand and predict the behaviors that can be exploited to produce embodied conversational agents that are acceptable both perceptually and behaviorally.

The first step toward this goal is to have a method for capturing and encoding the logical structure of the conversation and transferring meta-participants' interpretations in natural language into a simulator. This paper introduces CDL as a language for describing the structure of various components underlying the conversation. As a conceptual framework, it encompasses identities that point to objects in the environments and referred to in the conversation, actions/events identified in the verbal/non-verbal behaviors of participants, and the estimation of abstract mental processes of the participants. It also allows a large degree of ontological promiscuity, required by the analysts until reaching a conclusion.

CDL employs an entity-attribute-value representation consisting of statements in the theme-rheme form, where the theme shows a reference to a value represented by the rheme, e.g. `object1.color=red`. Alternatively, a functional notation can also be used as: `color(object1)=red`. When more than one entities are involved as referent, an (ordered) set representation is used, such as: `{John,Mary}.children={Judy, Peter}`   or   `children ({John, Mary})={Judy, Peter}` or `{father:John, mother:Mary}.children={Judy, Peter}`.

Unlike classic modal logic that requires a consistent set of propositions for a possible world, we define situation to be a series of compatible events that may result in a consistent representation of the local world. For example, the two statements `object1.color=red` and `object1.weight=100g` can be embedded into the same situation, while `object1.price=100$` and `object1.price=20$` cannot, as the latter may cause inconsistency in the commonsense world. As such, the analyst is requested to embed these statements into two different discourses.

A generic form of CDL expressions is: `discourse-id [theme-rheme pair(s)]`. For example, a CDL expression for a conversation segment: 'The table cloth's price is 500.' might be:

```
[S.expresses=proposal-1] @discourse-1
[table-cloth-3.price=500] @proposal-1
```

if the utterance is interpreted as "in the given discourse [`discourse-1`], S expressed `proposal-1` in which the price of a table-cloth [`table-cloth-3`] is 500."

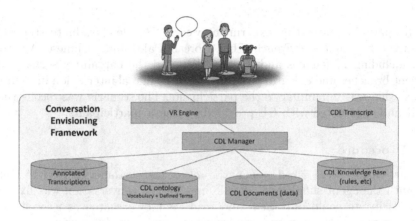

Fig. 5. CDL as an integral part of the conversation envisioner

Finally, in cases that the ontological analysis is difficult to resolve at current state (e.g. C: 'How much is that?'), the analyzer should proceed, assuming that the ontological promiscuity will be resolved later (e.g., S: 'The red one?').

The role of CDL in conversation envisioner is illustrated in Fig. 5. The main idea is to move from annotation to structural representation of CDL, in order to understand/predict the conversation. Given the annotation rubric (Fig. 2), meta-participants augment the raw transcription of the scenario into annotated transcripts. To this end, they consult the CDL knowledge-base to find relevant rules or worked examples that transform an abstract idea into a CDL expression by using existing entity-attribute pairs in CDL ontology or introducing new ones. The generated entity-attribute-value expressions are then stored in the CDL documents and indexed by the knowledge-base for future uses. The whole process is governed by CDL manager that consists of: *(i)* **annotated transcripts** including interpretations to abstract annotated events into CDL expressions, by unveiling latent information not appearing on the surface, *(ii)* **ontology** including basic vocabulary and the relations that can be extended on-demand, *(iii)* weakly structured **documents** that record sessions to be used as the background for new conversations or as a source to induce conversation knowledge, and *(iv)* **knowledge-base** for interpreting/predicting conversations and including hypotheses proposed by meta-participants, which can also be used to implement AI-participants and AI-interpreters.

5   Experimental Evaluation

A preliminary experiment was conducted to investigate the following questions:

Q1. Does VRCE help selecting better choices during conversation to make a deal?

Q2. Does VRCE raise the participants' awareness of the situation in order to refine their choices for successful interaction?

Q3. Do the participants find VRCE useful for perceiving the situation in cross-cultural interaction?

The participants of this experiment were 20 (under-)graduate students of our university (Japanese, French, Thai, Korean, Palestinian, Chinese, American, etc.), including 11 females and 9 males. We used the bargaining scenario with different branches and cultural points obtained from real interaction in a cultural context that was unfamiliar to the participants. The scenario was reconstructed in VR and augmented with CE provided by (meta-)participants.

5.1   Procedure

The participants were asked to play the role of the customer and try to make a deal with the agent shopkeeper. While most of the conversation was fixed and the participants could only hear and read their own sentences as well as the agent's sentences, there were some branching points in the conversation where the participants were asked to choose their next utterance to the shopkeeper from the given options (16 branches at 2 levels, 4 choices at each level). There were an equal number of successful (closing the deal successfully) and failure branches. For instance, in the case of a failure, participants' attitude or offer made the shopkeeper very angry and reluctant to sell anything to them. Even in such a situation, participants were still provided with a chance to repair the conversation and revive the deal. Each branch was given a specific score as all branches were distinct from each other in terms of mood, outcome and final price. The experiment consisted of three parts as follows:

Part I: The participants were randomly divided into two groups (CE and control). The CE group received the interpretations during the conversation especially before selecting the branches, whereas the control group did not receive anything. The CE was provided by the *assistant agent* and was taken from the meta-participants' analysis, which included a summary of the interaction (verbal and non-verbal), mood analysis, and description of the situation from the shopkeeper point-of-view without giving any suggestions on choice selection (Q1).

Part II: The participants in the control group were given a second chance to redo the conversation, this time augmented by CE and select the choices again. This was done in an attempt to evaluate the effect of CE in building common ground and raising awareness of the participant to review their choices (Q2).

Part III: To address the third research questions (Q3), we conducted another experiment in which all participants received CE. The participants evaluated the usefulness of interpretations for understanding the situation, given the different cultural background. This part was followed by a questionnaire to elicit participants' feedback on VRCE.

5.2   Analysis of the Results

Table 1 compares the results of CE versus the control group (Part I) and suggests that participants' average score in CE group ($M = 64.40$) were statistically higher than those in the control group ($M = 26.20$). Therefore, it can be inferred that providing interpretation has significantly affected the participants' scores as it helped them understand the situation better, hence choose the options that lead to a successful deal [$t(18) = 2.32, p = .03$]. The result can provide a positive answer for the Q1 in the usefulness of CE for selecting better choices and realizing the goal of the task i.e., closing a deal.

Table 1. T-test analysis of CE vs. control groups

Group Statistics: Independent Sample Test (95% Confidence)							
	Group	N	Mean	SDMean	t	df	Sig. (2-tailed)
Scores	Control	10	26.20	11.50	2.33	18	0.03
	CE	10	64.40	11.71			

The results in Table 2 shows the effect of the VRCE in helping the participants gain a better understanding of the situation, and revising their choices in the second run (Part II). The results provide a positive response for Q2, indicating that participants' average scores had a significant (41%) increase after they received CE [$t(4) = 2.83, p = .04$]. While these results might be influenced by repetition effect, participants commented that the assistant agent substantially helped them to revise their choices.

Table 2. Paired-sample t-test

Group Statistics: Paired Sample Test (95% Confidence)							
	Group	N	Mean	SDMean	t	df	Sig. (2-tailed)
Scores	Before CE	10	26.20	11.50	2.83	4	0.04
	After CE	10	67.66	14.08			

In Part III, the participants evaluated the interpretations as useful for 85.71% of the instances on average. This result was fortified by participants' feedback on a Likert-scale questionnaire (1: strongly disagree ∼ 5: strongly agree) as shown in Table 3. As the results suggest the majority of the participants believed that the

Table 3. Participants' feedback on VRCE using a Liket-scale questionnaire

I think ...	
The design of VR environment was acceptable	3.73
The intonation and gestures of the avatars were expressive	3.63
I could concentrate enough on the conversation in the VR environment	4.26
The VR environment helped me see things from customer's view (1st person view)	3.78
The system helps me to consider what situations I may face during bargaining situation	4.15
It is enjoyable to explore other cultures with this system	4.63
It is enjoyable to explore other people's personality with this system	4.63
The scenario was an interesting social interaction	4.31
The idea of selecting a choice to lead the conversation was interesting	4.37
The choice boxes given during the conversation were interesting	3.87
The points given by the Assistant Agent(AA) during the conversation were interesting	4.31
Points given by the AA help me understand the situation better	4.50
Having an AA to interpret important points during conversation is a good idea	4.25
The interpretation was good enough to clarify the situation	4.12
The AA showed most of the points that I did not know/realize	4.06
Most of the interpretations were important to help to understand the situation	4.00
Including cultural interpretations were very helpful	4.43
The AA helped me understand cultural points better	4.31
Including mood interpretations were very helpful	4.43
Including other person's behavior analysis was very helpful	4.43
The points given by AA helped me select the choice in conversation	4.27
The AA helped me understand why the conversation went to a particular path	4.18
Using AA's interpretation can lead to smoother communication	4.00
This method is an effective way to understand other cultures or people	4.42

interpretations were useful for perceiving the situation in cross-cultural interaction (Q3). Moreover, the idea of VRCE, the setting of the VR environment, and game-like nature of the experiment received positive feedback.

6   Conclusion

This paper introduces CE as a computational framework to highlight the tacit information of the conversation. Using VR platform, we tried to envision a bargaining scenario as a situated interaction with multiple goals, cultural implications, and emotional affect. VRCE is a platform that allows (meta-)participants to engage in a story and learn it from different perspectives. It aims to provide the (meta-)participants with the maximum degree of freedom with respect to space and time and to support multiple tasks ranging from the end-user service (learning and online assistance) to the meta-user service (analysis and synthesis). In this study, we also introduced CDL as a language to describe the structure of the conversation, and CDL manager as a means to encode (meta-)participants' interpretations. While there is still room for lots of improvements, preliminary experiments showed that VRCE could facilitate common ground building in situated interactions especially when the cultural backgrounds are different. Future directions include using VRCE as an educational tool to facilitate cross-cultural interactions and as a scientist workbench for envisioning tacit dimensions of the conversation in order to design agents that are aware of these dimensions.

References

1. Tomasello, M.: Origins of Human Communication. MIT Press, Cambridge (2010)
2. Kasper, G., Wagner, J.: Conversation analysis in applied linguistics. Annu. Rev. Appl. Linguist. **34**, 171–212 (2014)
3. Nishida, T., Nakazawa, A., Ohmoto, Y., Mohammad, Y.: Conversational Informatics. Springer, Tokyo (2014). https://doi.org/10.1007/978-4-431-55040-2
4. Traum, D.R.: A computational theory of grounding in natural language conversation. Technical report, Rochester University, NY, Department of Computer Science (1994)
5. Nakano, Y.I., Reinstein, G., Stocky, T., Cassell, J.: Towards a model of face-to-face grounding. In: Proceedings of the 41st Annual Meeting on ACL, pp. 553–561 (2003)
6. Visser, T., Traum, D., DeVault, D., et al.: A model for incremental grounding in spoken dialogue systems (2012)
7. Rickheit, G., Wachsmuth, I.: Situated Communication. Walter de Gruyter, Berlin (2006)
8. Clancey, W.J.: Situated Cognition: On Human Knowledge and Computer Representations. Cambridge University Press, Cambridge (1997)
9. Rubin, J.Z., Brown, B.R.: The Social Psychology of Bargaining and Negotiation. Academic Press, San Diego (1975)
10. Güth, W.: On ultimatum bargaining experimentsa personal review. J. Econ. Behav. Organ. **27**(3), 329–344 (1995)
11. Nouri, E., Georgila, K., Traum, D.: Culture-specific models of negotiation for virtual characters: multi-attribute decision-making based on culture-specific values. AI Soc. **32**(1), 51–63 (2017)
12. Hofstede, G.J., Jonker, C.M., Verwaart, T.: An agent model for the influence of culture on bargaining. In: Proceedings of the 1st International Working Conference on Human Factors and Computational Models in Negotiation. ACM (2008)
13. Thompson, L.: Mind and Heart of the Negotiator. Prentice Hall Press, Upper Saddle River (2000)
14. Wellman, H.M.: Making Minds: How Theory of Mind Develops. Oxford University Press, New York (2014)
15. Clark, H.H.: Using Language. Cambridge University Press, Cambridge (1996)

A Graph Based Approach to Sentiment Lexicon Expansion

Adam Westgate and Iren Valova[✉]

Computer and Information Science Department, University of Massachusetts,
Dartmouth, MA 02747, USA
{awestgate1,ivalova}@umassd.edu

Abstract. Lexicons are a crucial aspect of any method that aims analyze textual sentiment. In this paper we aim to provide an algorithm in which we can obtain meaningful polarity values for words using a graph constructed from their synonyms. We show that this polarity graph can provide polarity values within a lexicon where needed (i.e. where another method such as a classifier left gaps). We then assess the value of this algorithm against other recent methods of sentiment lexicon expansion. We conclude that this method supplies significant, yet highly nuanced utility in terms of supplying necessary semantic orientation for words without.

Keywords: Natural language processing · Lexicon expansion
Sentiment analysis · Graph traversal

1 Introduction

Sentiment analysis is a method of using natural language processing, computational linguistics and text analysis to determine subjective information and emotion within a body of text.

One of the most prevalent uses for sentiment analysis is opinion mining (Pang and Lee 2008). Through understanding the sentiment of different texts it is possible to understand if a review is positive or negative without needing to evaluate any score. If social media posts were mined and evaluated, public opinion on a topic could be determined by evaluating the individual emotion of the posts and comparing them to others (Agarwal et al. 2011). An example of this could be posts on popular social media platforms being used to evaluate approval of political candidates during an election cycle.

The process of obtaining meaningful sentiments from bodies of text is centered around the polarity of the words comprising it. Polarity is the emotional reactivity of a word in terms of how positive or negative it is. Much of the work in sentiment analysis is done by evaluating the polarity on the document. In recent years, sentence and phrase levels have become more prevalent. In these cases, context often plays a significant role in evaluation.

© Springer International Publishing AG, part of Springer Nature 2018
M. Mouhoub et al. (Eds.): IEA/AIE 2018, LNAI 10868, pp. 530–541, 2018.
https://doi.org/10.1007/978-3-319-92058-0_51

A word's polarity is often obtained from a pre-existing lexicon as available in the Natural Language Toolkit (NLTK). They contain polarities for individual words that are ordinarily derived from training classifiers on certain corpora (typically bodies of text like movie reviews or social media posts). There are often many words within these lexicons that are missing polarity values entirely, which may present an issue when attempting to obtain any sort of sentiment from a grouping of text such as a sentence, phrase or paragraph. This issue is specifically what the proposed polarity graph attempts to solve. The polarity graph attempts to provide a way for the user to assign polarity to words where needed based on a pre-existing lexicon without the need for excess classifier training or similar processes.

The polarity graph algorithm works by assembling a graph of synonyms and deriving a polarity from a user-designated word that would not otherwise be available in an existing lexicon. Synonyms that contain a polarity value can often prove useful in assigning polarity to a word because by definition synonyms are words of similar meaning. This allows for effective assignment of polarity values to words in a lexicon without a need for context.

2   Methodology

The central purpose of the algorithm is to assign a meaningful polarity value to a target word chosen by the user. This behavior can be broken into three major steps: graph generation, path generation, and polarity assignment. The first step involves recursively "laying out" synonyms of the target word and linking them to other synonymous words. Next, paths are generated through the linkages and analyzed until a set of optimal paths are found. Finally, a polarity value is assigned to the target word using the most significant of the optimal paths.

2.1   Graph Generation

A graph is an abstract data type consisting of vertices (also known as nodes) that are interconnected through linkages referred to as edges. Edges indicate some form of relational bond between the data represented by the vertices. Ordered pairs are often used to indicate the edges between two vertices. Following this, a graph can be formally defined as such:

Definition 1.1. *(Graph Data Type) A graph G can be defined as a pair (V,E), where V is a set of vertices, and E is a set of edges between the vertices $E \subseteq \{(u,v)|u,v \in V\}$.*

The graph is generated by recursively obtaining synonyms of words in the current layer and repeatedly adding them to the graph. The "origin" of the graph is the target word and in its first iteration all of its synonyms are obtained from Thesaurus.com and WordNet using the library PyDictionary. Through each iteration, a layer of synonyms is generated from the nodes in the previous layer.

For efficiency, a hard cap of eight was put on the number of generated synonyms. This is empirically derived and further elaborated upon in Sect. 3.

In the beginning stages, the antonyms of the target word are stored and the generation function of the graph is terminated when any antonym of the target word is found. Since an antonym is a word of opposite meaning to the target word, it presents a necessary stopping point in the graph generation process and is the destination point for path generation. The graph generation is arranged in this way because the algorithm is centered on obtaining the most meaningful words related to the target word while avoiding jumping too far into words that possess a meaning far removed from it.

When the word generation is complete, edges are formed between the word nodes. Synonyms of each node, barring the target word and antonym, are checked against the graph. If the synonyms are within the graph, a link is formed. Simply put, this changes the structure of the graph from a tree to a layout resembling a web.

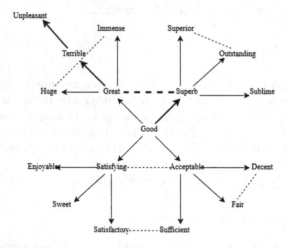

Fig. 1. A graph generated with the algorithm with target word "Good". The bold arrows/dotted lines represent the optimal path. Some words have been omitted for convenience.

Figure 1 represents a graph generated by the algorithm. "Good" is our target word and therefore portrayed in the center of the graph. The arrows represent a link from the "parent" word to its child synonyms. To clarify, this means the synonyms pointed to were spawned from the parent's list of synonyms. The dashed lines represent words that are "siblings" – synonymous yet not spawned from one-another. Stemming from "good" and terminating at "unpleasant" is a series of bold lines that represent the most optimal pathway. This is used in the final polarity calculation and will be expanded upon in the following sections.

2.2 Path Generation and Utilization Rules

A path is defined as a list of nodes from a given source node (in this case the target word) to any other node that is sequentially and incrementally traversable. The primary focus of this algorithm lies on the paths between the target word and its antonym on the graph. Therefore, it is necessary to extract these paths from a set of all potential paths within the graph that begin with the target word. These extracted paths that begin with the target word and end with the antonym are referred to as potential paths and can be obtained utilizing the Potential Path Rule.

Definition 1.2 *(Potential Path Rule). Let Q be some path in the graph and Q_i be the ith node in path Q. Let R be some potential path in the graph. Allow w_t to be a node containing the target word and w_a to be a node containing its antonym. Under these conditions, the following must always be true:*

$$(Q \equiv R) \leftrightarrow Q_0 = w_t \wedge Q_n = w_a \text{ where } n = |Q|, n > 0 \qquad (1)$$

Path reduction is centered around pulling near-optimal paths from a set of all potential paths from the target word to the antonym. Near-optimal paths are paths that adhere to the Potential Path Rule.

The usability of a path is heavily dependent on the sign of the polarity values for each node in the path. If the polarity values are consistently alternating throughout the path then the sentiment of each word is in a sense "contradictory" to each other – meaning, due to their polarities, the connotations of the words will be vastly different and thus no useful polarity for the target word can be derived from them.

Definition 1.3 *(Near-Optimal Path Rule). Let R be some potential path in the graph, and O represent a set of near-optimal paths. Let S_n represent the nth node of path R, and P_n represent the polarity of node S_n. Assume that the number of path nodes t4. The sign of P_n is given by the standard function $sgn(P_n)$. Assume $n \geq k$. Under these conditions the following must always be true:*

$$R \in O \to \forall S_n \in R, sgn(P_n) = sgn(P_{n-1})... = sgn(P_{n-k}) \text{ where } k = \lfloor t/2 \rfloor \ (2)$$

Definition 1.4 *(Optimality Rule). Let O be the set of near-optimal pathways, and I represent some optimal pathway. Under these conditions the following must always be true:*

$$|O| \geq 1 \to \exists I \in O \qquad (3)$$

Furthermore, assume O_n is the nth path of the set of near-optimal pathways O. I once more represents some optimal pathway. The following must always be true:

$$O_n \equiv I \leftrightarrow |O_n| = max\{|O_1|, ..., |O_m|\} \text{ where } m = |O|, |O| \geq 1 \qquad (4)$$

From this, optimal pathways (assuming there is more than one) must be ranked for the sake of polarity assignment. This is done by ranking in order of the distance of the polarity of the optimal pathway's distance from 0 using absolute value. Mathematically this would arrange the values in a descending order in terms of $|Pol(I_x)|$ where I_x is an element of the set of optimal pathways I. For the sake of the calculating the polarity of the target word, the first pathway in this ranked list (with average polarity furthest from 0) is used.

2.3   Polarity Assignment

The end result of the polarity assignment step is to assign a meaningful polarity to the target word. This often disregards the intensity of the polarity for a couple of reasons. The first being that the intensity simply isn't important when the word itself presumably had no polarity to begin with in whichever lexicon is being utilized by the user. The second reason is that when weighting the polarities of the words in the path the intensity of their polarity values can often be diminished, leading to a sum that is smaller than the polarity values of even the synonyms nearest to the target word. This weighting is necessary and will be elaborated upon throughout the section.

The polarity of the target word is determined using a form of weighted average on the polarity values of the words in the optimal path. Assuming X_i is the ith node of some optimal path, n is the length of X, w_t is the node of the target word and Pol() is a function used to return the polarity of a word corresponding to a node, then the formula can be expressed as such:

$$Pol(w_t) = \frac{\sum_i^n i^{-1} * Pol(X_i)}{\sum_i^n i^{-1}} \ where \ n > 1 \tag{5}$$

The significance of using a weighted average throughout the path is simply to limit the polarity value of the words that are farther from the target word. The paths are generated beginning with the target word as a source and then by traversing synonyms until the antonym is reached – meaning the words closest to the antonym will be towards the end of the path and the words closest to the target word will be towards to the start of the path. Linguistically synonyms have similar meanings to each other and therefore those words closest to the target word in the graph will have a more similar meaning to the target word than those closer to the antonym. It is for this reason that the weighting of the polarities in the average progressively decrease. Those in the beginning of the path will have more relevance when calculating the polarity of the target word as opposed to those at the end of the path.

A prime example of this pattern can be observed in the optimal path generated for the word "good". The path concludes with the antonym "unpleasant" and is ordered as follows:

$$good \rightarrow superb \rightarrow great \rightarrow terrible \rightarrow unpleasant$$

The five words within this path are commonly used and their definitions are well known, however for the sake of drawing an important comparison the definition of a word close to the target, like "superb" should be compared to the definition of "good" as well as a word close to the antonym like "terrible". "Good" is an adjective defined as "of a favorable character or tendency", and "superb" is defined as "extremely good: excellent or brilliant in a very noticeable way" (Merriam-Webster's Dictionary). These are both similar descriptive words of varying connotative intensity as indicated by their definitions. Conversely, the word "terrible" is defined as "extremely or distressingly bad or serious" (CN). This meaning is clearly of substantial difference to the meaning of the target word, "good".

3   Results and Experimentation

The two most important criteria to observe when testing the polarity graph are (in order of importance): what the final polarity values are for the target word, and what optimal pathways were selected within the target word's associated graph. Polarity assignment is the purpose of the algorithm, so it is imperative to test the returned values. As for the pathways, it is important to track and understand how the parameters affect which pathways are deemed optimal by the algorithm because they are crucial for the final polarity assignment. It also offers a great insight into the behavior of the algorithm under different testing conditions.

It is nearly impossible to run tests with this algorithm on every word absent in the lexicon, however testing can still be useful when practiced on words that are exemplary of a wide range of polarity values. In the first section we test for accuracy of the polarity values assigned to some very different words. In the second section we analyze the pathways generated and selected as optimal for a few different words under different conditions.

3.1   Polarity Assignment Results

In order to accurately assess the quality of this algorithm's ability to autonomously determine the polarity of words, a set of useful test cases must be used as input. Due to the fact that this algorithm is by no means intended to replace a typical polarity assignment method like a bayes classifier, the accuracy and utility of the polarity web can be exacted when compared to words from an existing lexicon of words from a trained classifier. When the polarities of the algorithm is consistently similar to the polarities obtained from a classifier, it can be said that the algorithm is accurately averaging and interpreting the polarities of the words and their synonyms within that lexicon. Table 1 is an example from a lexicon trained on the NLTK default movie reviews corpus.

Within the algorithm, there is an important parameter used to define the num_syns that are generated for each level of the graph.

Table 1. Polarity values obtained from the algorithm and their accuracy relative to the pre-existing lexicon values.

Word	Graph polarity	Lexicon polarity	Accuracy
Good	0.58	0.7	82.85%
Bad	−0.69	−0.7	98.57%
Great	0.67	0.8	83.75%
Terrible	−0.66	−1.0	66.0%
Okay	0.39	0.5	78.0%
Average	−0.03	−0.15	20.0%
Perfect	0.8	1	80.0%
Poor	−0.59	−0.4	52.5%
Adequate	−0.013	0	–%
Uninspired	−0.23	−0.4	57.5%

The time of the algorithm is highly dependent on three factors: graph generation, path formation and the num_syns constant. Graph generation terminates at the first obtained antonym, meaning the number of jumps required from the target word to the antonym drastically affects the performance of the algorithm. Path formation can be a more lengthy process depending on the size of the graph and the time to find optimal paths can increase based on the number of conflicting near-optimals. Finally, the num_syns constant can affect these two factors on its own. Reducing the number of synonyms per generated graph layer can result in the omission of certain synonyms that may or may not be important to an optimal path. Additionally, reducing or increasing the number of synonyms per layer could affect how long the algorithm should run until the antonym is found.

For these reasons, it would be of no use to state the variances in runtime for the different values of num_syns in testing. The polarity however remains ever-so relevant. Table 2 contains a few examples of polarity variations when num_syns is adjusted. The words "great", "adequate" and "terrible" were picked from the original list because they are, respectively, examples of positive, neutral, and negative polarity words.

As exemplified in Table 2, the ideal number of synonyms generated per word lies at eight. Beyond eight, at ten, the polarity score drops due to the fact that many synonyms generated from PyDictionary's synonym lists, which are from Thesaurus.com (Bora 2014), contain their synonyms in descending order of meaning. The addition of these synonyms that are later in the list incentivizes the formation of optimal pathways that have significantly less of a relation to the target word which in turn creates a meaningless polarity value. To further expand upon the effect of the num_syns parameter, Table 3 shows the polarities for the word "great" at a wider range of num_syns values.

The values below eight typically have a less accurate polarity value that trend towards an optimal value at around eight. Some words have their most accurate

Table 2. Polarities for different num_syns values over three different words.

Word	Num synonyms	Polarity	Lexicon polarity	Accuracy
Great	6	0.51	0.8	63.75%
Great	8	0.67	0.8	83.75%
Great	10	−0.699	0.8	−99.85%
Terrible	6	−0.5	−1.0	50.00%
Terrible	8	−0.66	−1.0	66.00%
Terrible	10	−0.03	−1.0	3.00%
Adequate	6	0.08	0	-%
Adequate	8	−0.013	0	-%
Adequate	10	0.24	0	-%

Table 3. Polarities for the word "great" at different num_syns values.

Num synonyms	Polarity	Lexicon polarity	Accuracy
4	0.23	0.8	28.75%
5	0.51	0.8	63.75%
6	0.51	0.8	63.75%
7	0.51	0.8	63.75%
8	0.67	0.8	83.75%
9	0.60	0.8	75.00%
10	−0.699	0.8	−99.85%

polarity at seven, nine or in rare cases another number. This is a fundamental problem with using a constant for a parameter such as this and will be discussed in the next section.

3.2   Optimal Pathway Results

The selection and construction of optimal pathways within the algorithm is crucial to its polarity calculation. For this reason it is necessary to present and discuss some examples of optimal pathways generated by the algorithm and how the num_syns constant affects them.

The num_syns constant can have an extremely significant effect on the result of the algorithm. To better illustrate this juxtaposition, Fig. 2 gives an example of two pathways for the word "good", at two different values for num_syns.

Though the two pathways are almost entirely different, their polarities were calculated at 0.51 and 0.68 respectively with a lexicon polarity of 0.7. This placed them both at highly accurate percentages of 72.85% and 97.14%. The main issue here being, of course, the vast difference of length between the two. A path like the one presented at num_syns of 6 does not only sum to a less-accurate polarity

| num_syns = 6 | good → great → high → big → hefty → tremendous → colossal → enormous → humongous → immense → huge → monstrous → atrocious → rotten |
| num_syns = 8 | good → superb → great → terrible → unpleasant |

Fig. 2. Pathways at different values for num_syns.

value, but it is also much more complex and with such complexity is a significant bottleneck in efficiency. This reinforces the importance of the constant being set at a value of eight, because not only was the polarity accuracy typically low in testing, the length of the pathways were typically too long or too short.

In order to give further insight into the pathways obtained by the algorithm, below an example of some of the pathways that correspond some of the words that were used as test cases in the previous section (at num_syns = 8) (Fig. 3):

Terrible	terrible → atrocious → awful → ghastly → horrendous → awesome → wonderful
Great	great → tremendous → amazing → magnificent → terrific → terrible → unfortunate → poor
Adequate	adequate → tolerable → unexceptional → insignificant → lesser → minor → inferior

Fig. 3. Pathways for a few different test cases.

Two of these test cases produced paths consisting of seven words, while one produced a path of eight. We found through testing that the number of words in each pathway was often somewhat related to the number of "layers" in the graph (each time child synonyms of a parent word were generated a "layer" is added). In the case of the word "Adequate" for example, there were seven layers until the first antonym was reached and likewise, there were seven layers. As for "Great" there were seven layers and eight words in the optimal path.

4   Discussion

The uses and behavior of the polarity graph is specialized and is designed to be used on a smaller scale than most methods of lexicon expansion. Many methods of lexicon expansion use a form of supervised learning or classification to assign polarity to words. While these methods are often effective, it is important to evaluate their uses and performance against this algorithm with the purpose of defining its strengths and weaknesses.

4.1 Analysis of Results

Num_syns is a constant that determines how many synonyms are generated per word for each iteration of the graph generation. The constant is typically hard-set at eight based on results from testing, however this is not always the optimal value for obtaining the most meaningful polarity of a word. In an ideal scenario, num_syns would have a corresponding function that autonomously determines its value for each unique word. However, at the time of writing this function has not been created and may be too difficult to develop.

The method of optimal path selection is not ordinarily an issue, though it can create problems in specific situations based on two conflicting optimal paths. As of now, the path selection allocates optimality by finding the largest path with the most consistently signed polarity values for the words in the path. If the paths have identical lengths and identically signed values, then the polarity with the greatest distance from 0 is selected. This works effectively to eliminate paths that may be meaningless (e.g. a path that consistently alternates between positive and negative words), but can also create situations where the less meaningful optimal path is selected from two equally sized, equally proportioned optimal paths. Extra logic possibly could be included to determine the magnitude of the polarities in the words of conflicting optimal paths to determine which one is more worthy of entering the final polarity calculation. This could be done by analyzing the meanings of the words within the paths, however, interpreting the meaning of words is a complex task that likely moves into topics largely beyond those covered in this paper. The reward of implementing such logic could also prove meaningless or even detrimental to the algorithm and the potential benefit is a solution to a problem that occurs in situations that are so rare that it doesn't justify the endeavor at the time of writing. That being said, if further development of this algorithm were to occur, this would still be an improvement worth exploring.

The dictionary library used for convenience in the development of this algorithm is PyDictionary which is a thesaurus and dictionary library for Python. It obtains its synonym and antonym lists from Thesaurus.com and these synonyms are listed in order of similarity to the word in question. Due to the hard cap on how many synonyms are added to the graph per iteration, some of the words in this list will inevitably be cut off and never used. The arrangement of synonyms in the graph generation process is dependent on the order they are listed in the given Thesaurus. If words with meanings far removed from the target word are placed earlier in the graph generation process, then the pathways could easily be structured to have words with less-relevant meanings earlier in the path which would cause them to be weighted more highly than words with more relevant meanings. This situation could also omit words with more relevant meanings entirely from the generation process; which would result in otherwise relevant words being left out of optimal pathways therefore trivializing their resultant polarity values. Despite all of this, these potential problems can be remedied simply by selecting the right thesaurus, so this is a somewhat negligible flaw.

4.2   Related Works

Some of the earliest methods on determining the polarity of missing words within a lexicon were performed by Hatzivassiloglou and McKeown (1997). The central idea of their method was to expand the lexicon of a corresponding corpora based on groupings of adjectives. Some of the more prominent ideas discovered in this work was the use of "and" to conjoin to words of similar polarities and "but" to conjoin words of opposite meaning. This provided an effective way to retrieve a viable polarity for a word from other words with known polarities. The purpose of the work done in this paper is to find the polarity of words beyond context – in situations where methods such as conjoined adjectives are otherwise unavailable. Therefore, the methods are different in both purpose and execution.

The concept of using word synonyms in order to determine semantic orientations is not necessarily unique. Godbole et al. (2011) proposed a method within their work that expands a lexicon using a tree of synonyms. Their method, while similar, is also notably different in key areas. The method utilized a tree of synonyms for a given word and weighs them based on their level in the tree. The final polarity for each word is calculated as a summation of all of its paths within the tree. The primary difference between the polarity graph and their work is the behavior of the graph. When the optimal path is selected, the synonyms that best summarize the polarity of the target word are used in the summation and the other paths are omitted. Additionally, the weighting within the polarity graph method is based on order of the path not the tree. The weighting of the words is done in a descending order from the beginning of the path, so the polarity value of the contained words are not entirely dependent on the order in which they are generated.

Wiebe (2000) devised a method for assigning subjectivity to adjectives based on a small seed corpus and analysis of the distribution of the adjectives in question. The practicality of this method lies in its ability to provide meaningful sentiment beyond context, so subjectivity is something that has been largely ignored. Though it could be argued that is a major fault, this method is not intended to be used in contexts where subjectivity is important to the lexicon. Additionally, Wiebe's method does not provide any sort of sentimental information regarding the words.

Turney (2002) proposed unsupervised learning to determine the semantic orientation of reviews and classify them as recommendations or not. The algorithm handled this by analyzing the associations of phrases within reviews with the words "poor" and "excellent". The final semantic calculation was used to determine whether the algorithm would view the review as a recommendation or not. This differs greatly from the algorithm proposed in this paper, as the polarity graph is focused on assigning polarity on the token-level, not the phrase level or above.

Kim and Hovy (2004) used a heuristic dictionary-based approach method similar to the one presented by Turney. They used WordNet to construct a network of synonymous words (much like what was done with the polarity graph) and then determined their paths to seed words "good" and "bad" (as Turney did with "poor" and "excellent"). This method used those paths to assign polarities to the words in question. In the sense of the network construction, this method is similar to the polarity graph proposed in this paper. However, the path generation is much different as those within the polarity graph do not utilize seed words.

5 Conclusion

In this paper we propose a way to obtain polarity values for words within a given lexicon. Each run of the algorithm is focused on obtaining the polarity for a single input word referred to as the target word.

The results of the algorithm are promising when compared to those within the same lexicon. The accuracy is high on average for the tested cases (assuming those chosen by a classifier were ideal) and those without a high accuracy still maintain the same sign (positivity or negativity) as the polarity in the lexicon.

While the present proof of concept is challenged in situations where corpora that must be analyzed are exceedingly context-dependent, the polarity graph is very useful in the field of sentiment analysis. Its context-free nature has a highly nuanced purpose; however the results of testing are promising and it therefore maintains practical utility.

References

Pang, B., Lee, L.: Opinion mining and sentiment analysis. Found. Trends Inf. Retrieval **2**(1–2), 1–135 (2008). https://doi.org/10.1561/1500000011

Agarwal, A., Xie, B., Vovsha, I., Rambow, O., Passonneau, R.: Sentiment analysis of Twitter data. In: Proceedings of the Workshop on Languages in Social Media, pp. 30–38. Association for Computational Linguistics, June 2011

Good: (n.d.). https://www.merriam-webster.com/dictionary/good. Accessed 30 June 2017

Terrible: (n.d.). https://www.merriam-webster.com/dictionary/terrible. Accessed 30 June 2017

Godbole, N., Skiena, S., Srinivasaiah, M.: U.S. Patent No. 7,996,210. U.S. Patent and Trademark Office, Washington, DC (2011)

Bora, P.: PyDictionary: A "Real" Dictionary Module for Python (2014). https://pypi.python.org/pypi/PyDictionary/1.3.4. Accessed 06 July 2017

Hatzivassiloglou, V., Mckeown, K.R.: Predicting the semantic orientation of adjectives. In: Proceedings of the Eighth Conference on European Chapter of the Association for Computational Linguistics (1997). https://doi.org/10.3115/979617.979640

Wiebe, J.: Learning subjective adjectives from corpora. AAAI/IAAI **20**(0), 0 (2000)

Turney, P.D.: Thumbs up or thumbs down?: semantic orientation applied to unsupervised classification of reviews. In: Proceedings of the 40th Annual Meeting on Association for Computational Linguistics, pp. 417–424. Association for Computational Linguistics, July 2002

Kim, S.M., Hovy, E.: Determining the sentiment of opinions. In: Proceedings of the 20th International Conference on Computational Linguistics, p. 1367. Association for Computational Linguistics, August 2004

Solving Simple Arithmetic Word Problems Precisely with Schemas

Sowmya S. Sundaram$^{(\boxtimes)}$ and Savitha Sam Abraham

IIT Madras, Chennai, India
sowmyassundaram@gmail.com

Abstract. A question answering system has been presented for solving simple arithmetic word problems. It focusses on achieving high precision such that interested students can use it as a tool for checking their work. This is possible because of the representation of schemas that sets up expectations for solving word problems. There are some unique advantages it presents, such as robustness to the type of question and generation of interpretable solutions.

Keywords: Question answering · Knowledge representation

1 Introduction

Solving natural language word problems is an interesting problem solving exercise in artificial intelligence because it involves transforming the input problem into a mathematical language. The meaning of the word problem is tied with the underlying mathematical domain. Hence, the intermediate representation is of significance. It brings out the significant challenges in natural language processing as well as knowledge representation. Given a word problem such as "John has three mangoes. He ate 1 mango. How many mangoes does he have now?", our system will try to identify the type of word problem, transform it into our intermediate representation and derive the answer "2". The system proposed can be used to develop an interactive word problem solver. The student can see the solution as well as the steps that led to it instead of a number alone and would not get confused by a faulty answer presented by the system as is possible in a purely statistically driven system.

The contributions of our work are (a) an intermediate representation for simple arithmetic word problems, (b) a process of identifying the type of word problem and (c) an end-to-end question answering system.

2 Related Work

The body of works that try to solve this problem can be broadly classified into two types - knowledge based and empirical. [5] gives a comprehensive review of

© Springer International Publishing AG, part of Springer Nature 2018
M. Mouhoub et al. (Eds.): IEA/AIE 2018, LNAI 10868, pp. 542–547, 2018.
https://doi.org/10.1007/978-3-319-92058-0_52

knowledge based systems used to solve both math and physics word problems. The interest in such problems died down due to the enormous human effort required for crafting rules to convert natural language to an intermediate representation and the lack of standard datasets to compare systems. Of particular interest to this work are a set of systems that were developed for solving addition/subtraction word problems. These systems used schemas for representing word problems. Schemas set up expectations for what is required in a word problem. [6–8] are some of the works that used this approach. However, we do not know about the range of word problems they could solve as they show a few examples which suggest that the effort in the natural language processing part is negligible.

There has been a resurgence of interest in these problems from [1] which matched the numbers in the word problem to coefficients in equation templates. It posed it as a learning problem which took a word problem, its associated equations and the answer for training and posed a model. Many works that follow a similar vein have been proposed such as [2,9,10]. A somewhat similar work is [11] which does not use the term schema but nevertheless builds a model to identify the type of word problem and then solve the associated equations.

In this context, we place this work at the intersection of both styles. We have a flavour of statistical analysis in the identification of schemas and the use of trained parsers as well as the precision of knowledge based systems with the use of an intermediate representation.

3   Description of the System

The question answering system has several modules. Broadly they deal with handling natural language, identifying a schema, reasoning and presenting the answer.

Algorithm 1. The Problem Solving Process

Input: Word Problem: p
　　　Trained Schema Identifier Model: m
　　　Domain Knowledge: d
Output: Number: ans
1　WordProblem p_1 = simplify(p)
2　Schema s = m.identifySchema(p_1)
3　List<Predicates> program = represent(p_1, s)
4　ans = solve(program, d)
5　Print ans

---

4   Schemas

Schemas are templates that organize similar experiences and provide a mechanism to find the characteristic components of these experiences and reason with them. [14] gives a detailed description on schemas. The book also describes a word-problem solving system in detail. The aim of the work was interdisciplinary - to model student behaviour and to come up with a computational model. Hence many steps required manual intervention (Table 1).

Table 1. Schemas used

Schema	Example word problem
Group	John has 5 apples. Mary has 3 apples. How many apples do they have altogether?
Compare	John has 5 apples. Mary has 2 apples less than John. How many apples does Mary have?
Change	John has 5 apples. He gave 1 apple to Mary. How many does he have now?

4.1   Representation of Schemas

We use Prolog [15] to help us reason with the predicates generated from the natural language. We convert the word problem into a set of predicates and combine it with rules defined for the domain. Then, we execute the query on this combined program. To illustrate, we show how we represent the compare schema below in Table 2. For clarity, we have not specified every rule that is in our knowledge base. These rules capture the equations associated with a particular schema.

Table 2. Representation of schemas

Keyword Check:
cType(C, comparePlus) :- keyword(C, longer).
cType(C, comparePlus) :- keyword(C, taller).
cType(C, comparePlus) :- keyword(C, more).
cType(C, compareMinus) :- keyword(C, shorter).
cType(C, compareMinus) :- keyword(C, less).
Rules:
cValue(C, Num) :- compare(C), entity(K1, X), type(X, Ent), entity(K2, Y), type(Y, Ent), X <> Y, value(X, V1), value(Y, V2), not(var(V1)), not(var(V2)), V1 > V2, Num is V1 - V2, !.
cValue(C, Num) :- compare(C), entity(K1, X), type(X, Ent), entity(K2, Y), type(Y, Ent), X <> Y, value(X, V1), value(Y, V2), not(var(V1)), not(var(V2)), V1 < V2, Num is V2 - V1, !.

4.2   Identification of Schemas

Identification of a schema is a non-trivial task [14]. Traditional knowledge-based systems that used schemas depended completely on keywords. A keyword may be present but the associated schema may not be relevant. Consider, "John has 7 apples altogether. He gave 3 apples to Mary. How many does he have now?". This is an example of change, not group. Hence, we define a pattern recognition task to identify the type of schema. The features are inspired by [14]. The resources for extracting these features are the Stanford NLP Suite [12], WordNet [16] and Concept Net 5 [17]. A word problem is converted into a vector and fed to a multilayer perceptron. The features are described below.

- Whether there is a permanent alteration - if the lemma of the verb is not 'be', there is a permanent alteration.
- Change in tense - can be extracted from the POS tags of the verb.
- Presence of Multiple Agents - if there are multiple proper nouns that act as subjects.
- Presence of Multiple Objects - if there are multiple numbered entities.
- Presence of keywords like altogether, in all etc.
- Presence of unit - if a word from a pre-defined file of units is present in the word problem.
- Presence of "if... then".
- Presence of "left".
- Presence of "than, more, less".
- Set completion - if there is a relation between two entities or if there are antonyms or if there is a sense of requirement.

5   Natural Language Processing

From the natural language description of the word problem, predicates are extracted using a procedural approach based on the relations extracted by the dependency parser. Using a combination of the Part-Of-Speech (POS) tags and the relations identified by the dependency parser, predicates are generated as illustrated below.

Ruth put 2 apples in a basket.
happens(ev1,10).
agent(ev1, ruth).
entity(ev1, ent1).
type(ent1, apple).
value(ent1, 2).
loc(ev1, basket).

6 Experiments

The system was implemented in Java. The multilayer perceptron was coded using WEKA [18] and Prolog [15] was used for reasoning. The rules were designed on a set of 60 word problems - 20 for each schema. Three datasets from [9] was used for experimental purposes. The first dataset has 134 word problems which are quite straightforward. The second dataset has 140 word problems which have extraneous information, long sentences and involve the use of decimals. The third dataset has 121 word problems and has short sentences but extra information. We perform comparison with other rule-based systems. We have implemented [8] (System 1) for this purpose. We also use [13] (System 2) for comparison, using the values stated in the paper as is. Similarly, we use a rule-based version of [9] (System 3).

The Table 3 shows values of precision for each dataset. The contribution of our work lies in its precision. This is because our system reports that it cannot solve a problem if there are no rules that could be applied by the Prolog reasoner. All the other systems have 100% recall. Hence, their accuracy reflects their precision.

Table 3. Experimental analysis with precision

System	DS1	DS2	DS3
Our system	**98.3**	**97.7**	**92.3**
System 1	12.7	0.7	0
System 2	96.3	80.0	90.1
System 3	94.0	77.1	81.0

A dataset of 134 unseen word problems was taken from [9] and annotated with the relevant schema. The schema identifier was tested on this dataset. Out of these 134 word problems, 124 were identified correctly. The baseline method is a purely keyword-driven approach. The statistics are presented in Table 4.

Table 4. Performance of schema identification

System	Accuracy (%)
Schema identifier	92.50
Baseline	66.41

7 Discussion and Conclusion

The work presented is most suited for building automatic word problem solvers for students. It has high precision and hence will not confuse the student. Further avenues such as semantic parsing can be explored. A hybrid system of question answering has been presented. It discusses the advantages of representation. A method of identifying word problems has also been presented. We hope that this system helps in building scalable software for the interested student in future.

References

1. Kushman, N., Artzi, Y., Zettlemoyer, L., Barzilay, R.: Learning to automatically solve algebra word problems. In: ACL, vol. 1, pp. 271–281 (2014)
2. Koncel-Kedziorski, R., Hajishirzi, H., Sabharwal, A., Etzioni, O., Ang, S.D.: Parsing algebraic word problems into equations. Trans. Assoc. Comput. Linguist. **3**, 585–597 (2015)
3. Ling, W., Yogatama, D., Dyer, C., Blunsom, P.: Program induction by rationale generation: learning to solve and explain algebraic word problems. arXiv preprint arXiv:1705.04146 (2017)
4. Bobrow, D.G.: A question-answering system for high school algebra word problems. In: Proceedings of the Fall Joint Computer Conference, Part I, 27–29 October 1964, pp. 591–614. ACM (1964)
5. Mukherjee, A., Garain, U.: A review of methods for automatic understanding of natural language mathematical problems. Artif. Intell. Rev. **29**(2), 93–122 (2008)
6. Dellarosa, D.: A computer simulation of childrens arithmetic word-problem solving. Behav. Res. Methods Instrum. Comput. **18**(2), 147–154 (1986)
7. Fletcher, C.R.: Understanding and solving arithmetic word problems: a computer simulation. Behav. Res. Methods Instrum. Comput. **17**(5), 565–571 (1985)
8. Bakman, Y.: Robust understanding of word problems with extraneous information. arXiv preprint math/0701393 (2007)
9. Hosseini, M.J., Hajishirzi, H., Etzioni, O., Kushman, N.: Learning to solve arithmetic word problems with verb categorization. In: Proceedings of the 2014 Conference on Empirical Methods in Natural Language Processing (EMNLP), pp. 523–533 (2014)
10. Zhou, L., Dai, S., Chen, L.: Learn to solve algebra word problems using quadratic programming. In: EMNLP, pp. 817–822 (2015)
11. Mitra, A., Baral, C.: Learning to use formulas to solve simple arithmetic problems. In: ACL (2016)
12. Manning, C.D., Surdeanu, M., Bauer, J., Finkel, J., Bethard, S.J., McClosky, D.: The stanford corenlp natural language processing toolkit. In: Proceedings of 52nd Annual Meeting of the Association for Computational Linguistics: System Demonstrations, pp. 55–60 (2014)
13. Sundaram, S.S., Khemani, D.: Natural language processing for solving simple word problems. In: 12th International Conference on Natural Language Processing, p. 390 (2015)
14. Marshall, S.P.: Schemas in Problem Solving. Cambridge University Press, Cambridge (1996)
15. Wielemaker, J., Schrijvers, T., Triska, M., Lager, T.: SWI-Prolog. Theor. Pract. Logic Programm. **12**(1–2), 67–96 (2012)
16. Princeton university "about wordnet." Princeton University (2010). http://wordnet.princeton.edu
17. Concept net 5. http://conceptnet5.media.mit.edu
18. Eibe Frank, M.A.H., Witten, I.H.: The weka workbench. online appendix for "data mining: Practical machine learning tools and techniques" (2016)

Neural Networks

The Effect of Sentiment on Stock Price Prediction

Bruce James Vanstone⑩, Adrian Gepp(✉)⑩, and Geoff Harris⑩

Bond Business School, Bond University, Gold Coast, Australia
{bvanston,adgepp,gharris}@bond.edu.au

Abstract. Accurately predicting stock prices is of great interest to both academics and practitioners. However, despite considerable efforts over the last few decades, it still remains an elusive challenge. For each of Australia's 20 largest stocks, we build two neural network autoregressive (NNAR) models: one a basic NNAR model, and the other an NNAR model extended with sentiment inputs. By comparing the prediction accuracy of the two models, we find evidence that the inclusion of sentiment variables based on news articles and twitter sentiment can enhance the accuracy of the stock price prediction process.

Keywords: Stock prices · Sentiment
Auto Regressive Neural Networks · Prediction

1 Introduction

Accurately predicting stock prices is of great interest to both academics and practitioners. However, despite considerable efforts over the last few decades, it still remains an elusive challenge. Much of the difficulty is related to the fact that prices are inherently noisy observations of random variables, which in turn represent the sum of investors' future expectations around company value. Much of the academic work to date has focused on either econometric modelling [1], or on supplementing machine learning models with either technical or fundamental variables [2], or both.

The majority of technical variables are different mathematical derivations of the same underlying price or volume data, and as such, may offer little or no new information to the prediction process. Fundamental variables may have the potential to offer additional information, however, their disclosure is usually annually or semi-annually, and as such, they are not available in the required frequency for shorter term prediction.

The Efficient Market Hypothesis (EMH) [3] is the primary theory in finance relevant to price prediction. This hypothesis asserts that a stock price instantaneously reflects all available information implying that prices react instantaneously to news and it should not be possible to outperform the market. It should be noted that the extent to which markets are considered efficient is somewhat controversial [4].

© Springer International Publishing AG, part of Springer Nature 2018
M. Mouhoub et al. (Eds.): IEA/AIE 2018, LNAI 10868, pp. 551–559, 2018.
https://doi.org/10.1007/978-3-319-92058-0_53

As market prices represent the combined views of investors' expectations of a company's future value, there is every reason to expect that news articles and twitter opinions may represent exogenous variables which may be useful in shorter-term price prediction. Theoretical models of the effect of investor sentiment usually posit the existence of two types of traders: 'noise traders', who hold random beliefs about future dividends, and 'rational arbitrageurs', who hold Bayesian beliefs [5]. It is reasonable to assume that noise traders may be influenced by negative news stories, which would lead them to sell investments to rational arbitrageurs, creating temporary downward pressure on prices.

In 2007, using text from the Wall Street Journal's *Abreast of the Market* column, Tetlock [6] finds that high media pessimism predicts short-term downward pressure on market prices followed by a reversion to fundamentals, and further that unusually high or low pessimism predicts high market trading volume. These results are consistent with the theoretical finance models and are inconsistent with the theory of media content as a proxy for new information about fundamental asset values. This is because if media content was a proxy for new information, then there would be no expectation that market prices would revert back to prior fundamental values, instead, the new information should establish a new fundamental value.

It appears then, that noise traders may well sell stock to rational arbitrageurs after periods of negative news. Rational arbitrageurs exploit the temporary drop in stock prices to acquire stock with the expectation that it quickly returns to fundamental value, thus obtaining a profit. As the primary drivers of this approach are the rational arbitrageurs, we source our news and sentiment scores from Bloomberg, which ensures we use a source applicable to sophisticated investors.

In this paper, for each of Australia's 20 largest stocks, we build two Neural Network Autoregressive (NNAR) models: one a basic NNAR model, and the other an NNAR model extended with sentiment inputs. By comparing the prediction accuracy of the two models, we aim to assess whether the inclusion of sentiment variables based on news articles and twitter sentiment can enhance the accuracy of the stock price prediction process.

2   Methodology

2.1   Sentiment Scores

This paper sources sentiment scores from Bloomberg that are based on both news articles and Twitter. Sentiment scores and closing price data are obtained for all stocks in the S&P ASX20 for the period 1st January 2015 to 30th June 2017. The starting date is the date that Bloomberg first began publishing the sentiment scores.

Bloomberg publish six sentiment scores on a daily basis. Table 1 shows the Bloomberg field names and brief description of the six sentiment score variables.

As the scores are part of Bloomberg's proprietary offering to customers, the exact method Bloomberg uses to derive the scores is not disclosed in detail. However, this is not an issue for this work, as we are specifically interested in

Table 1. Bloomberg sentiment data

Bloomberg field name	Brief description	Name used in this paper
NW043	News publication count	NEWS_COUNT
NW044	News positive sentiment count	NEWS_POS
NW045	News negative sentiment count	NEWS_NEG
NW039	Twitter publication count	TWITTER_COUNT
NW040	Twitter positive sentiment count	TWITTER_POS
NW041	Twitter negative sentiment count	TWITTER_NEG

how future prices are influenced by the reactions of professional investors to the published scores.

In Bloomberg's methodology, a human expert initially reads each article and assigns a positive, negative, or neutral label, based on their judgement of how the news story would affect an existing holder of that security. These manually created cases are then provided to a machine learning model which, when trained, is capable of taking a news story and providing a probability of whether the story could be expected to have a positive, negative, or neutral effect on a pre-existing holder.

In practice, news is released in continuous time. For each news article, Bloomberg determines article-level sentiment, consisting of both a score and confidence. The score value is 1, 0, or -1, representing positive, neutral, or negative sentiment predictions from the model. The confidence ranges from 0 to 100, representing a likelihood probability. Bloomberg then produce company-level daily sentiment scores, which are a confidence-weighted average of the past 24 h of story-level sentiments. These company-level scores are published every morning approximately ten minutes before the market opens.

2.2 Neural Network Autoregressive Models

In this paper, we fit Neural Network Autoregressive $\text{NNAR}(p, P, k)$ models. These are feed-forward, single hidden layer neural networks that use lagged inputs, and are well suited to forecasting non-linear univariate time series data.

For non-seasonal time series, the fitted model is denoted $\text{NNAR}(p, k)$, where p is the optimal number of lags (according to AIC) for a linear $\text{AR}(p)$ model, and k is the number of hidden nodes. This is analogous to an $\text{AR}(p)$ model but with nonlinear functions. For seasonal time series, the fitted model is denoted $\text{NNAR}(p, P, k)m$, which is analogous to an ARIMA $(p, 0, 0)(P, 0, 0)m$ model, but with nonlinear functions (where k is still the number of hidden nodes). In the case of seasonal time series, the defaults are $P = 1$ and p is chosen from the optimal linear model fitted to the seasonally adjusted data [7].

Two NNAR models are created for each stock. For each model built, a total of 20 networks are fitted, each with random starting weights. These are then averaged when computing forecasts. The networks are trained for one-step fore-casting, and multi-step forecasts are computed recursively. The number of hidden nodes in each network follows the popular heuristic of half of the number of input nodes (including external regressors) plus 1.

2.3   Neural Network Autoregressive Models

Initially, the data is split into two parts: all the data except the last month is used to train the NNAR models and the final month is used for out-of-sample testing. To assess the predictive value of the sentiment scores, two NNAR models are built for each stock using the in-sample data. The first model (BASIC) uses only lagged values of price to predict future prices. The second model (SENTIMENT) extends the first model by supplying the six sentiment scores shown in Table 1, as additional predictors. Rolling daily predictions for each stock are then made using both models for every day of the out-of-sample period. The future (out-of-sample) predictions from each of the models is then compared to the actual future prices, and an RMSE (Root Mean Square Error) is calculated for each model. We then compare the two RMSEs for each stock to determine which model, BASIC or SENTIMENT, was closest to the actual future prices.

Figure 1 shows the workflow applied to each stock in the S&P ASX20. All code was developed in R, version 3.3.2.

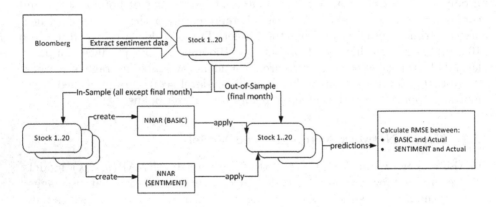

Fig. 1. Workflow

3   Results

Table 2 shows the summary statistics for the downloaded stock data. For each stock, there are three rows showing the number of observations and the mean of each of the six sentiment metrics. There is one row each for showing these values for all data, training data, and test data. It is clear that the positive and negative metrics do not sum to the total metric for either the news or twitter

Table 2. Daily summary statistics

Stock code	Dataset	Obs.	Daily summary statistics by stock (All data)					
			NEWS_ COUNT	NEWS_ POS	NEWS_ NEG	TWITTER_ COUNT	TWITTER_ POS	TWITTER_ NEG
AMP	All	631	21.75	2.24	1.15	4.36	0.79	0.39
AMP	Train	610	21.86	2.24	1.19	4.45	0.83	0.40
AMP	Test	21	21.86	2.81	0.38	2.43	0.10	0
ANZ	All	630	125.63	6.40	4.65	18.70	1.21	1.10
ANZ	Train	609	126.68	6.53	4.70	18.62	1.23	1.12
ANZ	Test	21	113.14	2.81	4.67	20.67	0.90	0.81
BHP	All	631	473.74	33.70	31.15	131.11	14.82	39.28
BHP	Train	610	478.70	34.07	32.17	134.22	15.03	40.87
BHP	Test	21	402.33	27.38	11.48	79.19	8.95	9.43
BXB	All	631	16.67	1.75	0.76	0.32	0.02	0.02
BXB	Train	610	16.65	1.82	0.78	0.33	0.02	0.02
BXB	Test	21	16.38	0.29	0.29	0.10	0	0
CBA	All	627	131.15	6.76	5.42	31.24	1.32	0.78
CBA	Train	606	130.90	6.86	5.45	31.54	1.37	0.80
CBA	Test	21	146.81	4.24	5.90	26.52	0.29	0.33
CSL	All	631	14.85	2.06	0.54	0.68	0.10	0.01
CSL	Train	610	14.54	2.57	0.54	0.63	0.10	0.01
CSL	Test	21	21.33	3.48	0.43	1.14	0.10	0
IAG	All	631	18.38	1.57	0.77	2.44	0.28	0.21
IAG	Train	610	18.23	1.55	0.79	2.45	0.27	0.21
IAG	Test	21	25.90	2.52	0.48	2.14	0.71	0.05
MQG	All	629	42.23	5.12	2.34	17.21	4.86	1.68
MQG	Train	608	42.61	5.20	2.24	17.26	4.80	1.70
MQG	Test	21	38.62	4.29	5.90	19.00	7.29	1.57
NAB	All	627	53.97	5.80	3.90	36.21	2.46	1.81
NAB	Train	606	53.95	5.95	3.93	36.86	2.54	1.87
NAB	Test	21	61.43	3.05	4.38	24.24	0.86	0.57
ORG	All	626	30.70	2.63	1.91	3.59	0.47	0.68
ORG	Train	605	30.78	2.71	1.99	3.60	0.49	0.71
ORG	Test	21	32.19	1.00	0.19	3.95	0.24	0.10
QBE	All	631	24.88	2.20	1.30	3.35	0.32	0.29
QBE	Train	610	24.63	2.20	1.27	3.29	0.32	0.28
QBE	Test	21	35.19	2.86	2.38	5.76	0.33	0.81
SUN	All	631	24.46	1.03	0.55	1.41	0.12	0.10
SUN	Train	610	24.22	1.04	0.57	1.41	0.12	0.10
SUN	Test	21	34.05	1.10	0.19	1.57	0.14	0.05
TLS	All	631	43.86	6.90	2.55	208.38	1.52	1.98
TLS	Train	610	44.10	7.02	2.53	204.57	1.52	1.94
TLS	Test	21	43.14	4.62	3.95	297.62	1.71	3.52
WBC	All	628	123.29	7.65	3.90	39.08	3.71	3.61
WBC	Train	607	122.58	7.72	3.86	37.71	3.54	3.43
WBC	Test	21	151.71	6.67	5.71	74.48	7.81	9.52
WES	All	631	31.99	3.38	1.42	1.77	0.20	0.12
WES	Train	610	31.98	3.48	1.37	1.80	0.20	0.12
WES	Test	21	37.90	1.67	3.19	1.19	0	0.05
WOW	All	630	28.10	3.12	1.90	20.92	0.23	0.18
WOW	Train	609	28.18	3.21	1.97	19.39	0.22	0.19
WOW	Test	21	28.38	0.90	0.76	31.95	0.38	0.10
WPL	All	631	85.83	4.34	3.30	9.74	1.18	1.67
WPL	Train	610	86.57	4.48	3.39	9.79	1.21	1.72
WPL	Test	21	78.81	1.95	1.57	9.71	0.52	0.67

categories. This is because the Bloomberg process described earlier explains that each article or tweet is classified as either positive, neutral or negative.

Table 2 shows the variability in the sentiment metrics by stock. Some stocks clearly generate a lot of news media attention (such as BHP and ANZ), whilst others generate relatively little (such as CSL and IAG). This suggests it is appropriate to model each stock using a separate NNAR model. It is also interesting that the company which generates the largest amount of twitter sentiment (TLS) has only a medium amount of news coverage. Therefore, it is reasonable to assume that the news sentiment metrics and the twitter sentiment metrics are measuring different things. The expectation would be that news sentiment typically captures the effects of well researched, newspaper style stories, often focused around specific business events. Twitter sentiment is a proxy for the

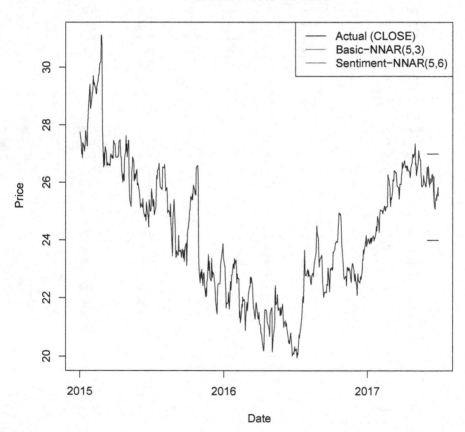

Fig. 2. Time series of WOW showing both in-sample and out-of-sample prediction periods

mood of the crowd, and more likely conveys collective consumer satisfaction with the company or its products.

Three stocks had to be removed due to having very few or no sentiment observations in Bloomberg during the test period, leaving a total of 17 stocks on which to perform modelling. As the sentiment scores are count data, the square root transformation was applied before the scores were submitted as inputs to the NNAR (SENTIMENT) model. Additionally, all inputs to both models were standardized by subtracting the column means and dividing by their respective standard deviations.

The NNAR (BASIC) and NNAR (SENTIMENT) models were trained against the in-sample data, and predictions were made on the out-of-sample data. Figure 2 depicts WOW (Woolworths Ltd.) showing the time series of prices used for training, as well as the out-of-sample predictions in context. Figure 3 focuses

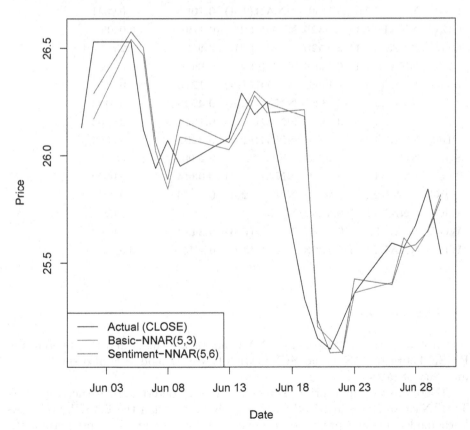

Fig. 3. WOW out-of-sample prediction

on the out-of-sample prediction period for WOW, allowing a visual inspection of the quality of both the BASIC and the SENTIMENT model forecasts.

Table 3 shows the overall prediction accuracy results for each stock and model combination. It also shows the RMSE for both models on the out-of-sample data, and indicates where the SENTIMENT model achieved a better accuracy than the BASIC model.

Table 3. Prediction results. Boldface indicates the more accurate model.

Stock code	Out-of-sample prediction accuracy				RMSE (SENTIMENT) − RMSE (BASIC)
	BASIC model	BASIC RMSE	SENTIMENT model	SENTIMENT RMSE	
AMP	NNAR(3,2)	0.0585	**NNAR(3,5)**	**0.0568**	−0.0018
ANZ	NNAR(3,2)	0.3964	**NNAR(3,5)**	**0.3938**	−0.0026
BHP	NNAR(1,1)	0.3439	**NNAR(1,4)**	**0.3124**	−0.0314
BXB	NNAR(1,1)	0.1130	**NNAR(1,4)**	**0.1099**	−0.0031
CBA	**NNAR(1,1)**	**0.9325**	NNAR(1,4)	0.9530	0.0205
CSL	**NNAR(1,1)**	**2.1520**	NNAR(1,4)	2.4021	0.2501
IAG	**NNAR(1,1)**	**0.1208**	NNAR(1,4)	0.1306	0.0098
MQG	NNAR(1,1)	1.1366	**NNAR(1,4)**	**1.1216**	−0.0150
NAB	NNAR(2,2)	0.4329	**NNAR(2,4)**	**0.4225**	−0.0103
ORG	NNAR(1,1)	0.1383	**NNAR(1,4)**	**0.1351**	−0.0033
QBE	NNAR(1,1)	0.3303	**NNAR(1,4)**	**0.3205**	−0.0097
SUN	**NNAR(2,2)**	**0.2047**	NNAR(2,4)	0.2090	0.0043
TLS	NNAR(1,1)	0.0352	**NNAR(1,4)**	**0.0344**	−0.0009
WBC	NNAR(2,2)	0.4620	**NNAR(2,4)**	**0.4598**	−0.0022
WES	**NNAR(1,1)**	**0.4432**	NNAR(1,4)	0.4485	0.0053
WOW	NNAR(5,3)	0.2586	**NNAR(5,6)**	**0.2483**	−0.0102
WPL	**NNAR(4,2)**	**0.4203**	NNAR(4,6)	0.5015	0.0811

4   Discussion

As Table 3 shows, RMSEs using NNAR models are small, and the difference in RMSE between BASIC and SENTIMENT NNAR models is also small in the majority of cases.

There are two appropriate statistical tests to determine whether the SENTIMENT model is statistically significantly better than the BASIC model. As both models make a prediction on every day of the out-of-sample period, the average RMSEs of each model can be compared with a paired samples t-test. The paired samples t-test null hypothesis is that the true difference in means between the average RMSEs of the SENTIMENT and the BASIC model is zero.

An alternative approach is to use the non-parametric sign test, which treats the data to be tested as a Binomial experiment. In this case, the hypothesis is that the true probability of either outcome is 0.5, or, in other words, either model being the best is equally likely.

A paired-samples t-test was conducted to compare the average RMSEs in the BASIC and SENTIMENT models. There was no significant difference in the scores for the BASIC model and the SENTIMENT model; t(16 degrees of freedom) $= -1.0541$ and a one-sided p-value $= 0.1537$.

A similar result was achieved using the signs test. The test was unable to reject the null hypothesis that the true probability of the SENTIMENT model being better is 50%. The signs test with 11 positive results out of a possible 17 yields a one-sided p-value of 0.1662. The number of times the SENTIMENT model would need to beat the BASIC model to achieve statistical significance at the 5% level with the signs test would be 13 out of 17 experiments.

Overall, the sentiment model outperformed the basic model 65% of the time. Although this result is clearly not definitive, it provides some tantalizing evidence that sentiment metrics may have a part to play in stock market price prediction.

It is known that prediction of prices is a difficult problem, and better success has been found with predicting stock returns, or stock price direction (the sign of stock returns). The results of this study suggest that sentiment metrics could be used to incrementally improve existing models that attempt to predict stock returns or direction. In finance, prediction of volatility is also of major importance to investors, and sentiment may well have a role to play there also.

The results of this preliminary study motivate future work that involves modelling and predicting stock returns, direction and volatility using sentiment metrics and a wide variety of machine learning techniques. It is our goal to determine the extent to which sentiment metrics provide additional insight into stock performance.

In an environment where prediction accuracy is of paramount importance, the search for suitable exogenous variables to use as predictors in formal models is a relentless one.

References

1. Rapach, D.E., Zhou, G.: Forecasting stock returns. In: Handbook of Economic Forecasting, vol. 2(Part A), pp. 328–383 (2013)
2. Atsalakis, G.S., Valavanis, K.P.: Surveying stock market forecasting techniques - part II: soft computing methods. Expert Syst. Appl. **36**(3), 5932–5941 (2009)
3. Fama, E.: The behaviour of stock market prices. J. Bus. **38**, 34–105 (1965)
4. Yen, G., Lee, C.F.: Efficient market hypothesis (EMH): past, present and future. Rev. Pac. Basin Financ. Markets Policies **11**(02), 305–329 (2008)
5. Long, J.B.D., Shleifer, A., Summers, L.H., Waldmann, R.J.: Noise trader risk in financial markets. J. Polit. Econ. **98**(4), 703–738 (1990)
6. Tetlock, P.C.: Giving content to investor sentiment: the role of media in the stock market. J. Financ. **LXII**(3), 1139–1168 (2007)
7. Hyndman, R., Athanasopoulos, G.: Forecasting: Principles and Practice. OTexts, Melbourne (2013)

RFedRNN: An End-to-End Recurrent Neural Network for Radio Frequency Path Fingerprinting

Siqi Bai[✉], Mingjiang Yan, Yongjie Luo, and Qun Wan

University of Electronic Science and Technology of China, Chengdu, China
baisiqi530@163.com

Abstract. Radio frequency (RF) fingerprinting is a commonly used indoor positioning method. However, the random fluctuation of radio signals is a major challenge for RF positioning. Traditional methods only match the signal patterns at a single time or space point without regard to the spatial or temporal pattern of the signal. Inspired by the application of neural networks in the field of natural language processing, we presents an end-to-end RF fingerprint positioning model, named RFedRNN. The model consists of two Recurrent Neural Networks (RNNs). The first RNN encodes the RF sequence into a vector from which the second RNN decodes the corresponding target path. Training this neural network is to learn a mapping from a sequence of RF fingerprints to a path, called path fingerprinting. This method has low labor cost and the parameters do not increase with the expansion of data set, which is suitable for mobile devices. Simulation and the real-world dataset experiments show that the proposed method is superior to the existing methods in positioning accuracy and robustness.

Keywords: Recurrent Neural Network · Encoder-decoder
Path fingerprinting · Positioning

1 Introduction

Location information plays an important role in context awareness. Many applications rely on precise and robust positioning techniques such as providing navigation for the visually impaired, tracking special personnel or supplies, implementing smart buildings, augmenting reality, and more. Many positioning scenarios occur where satellite signals are obscured, such as indoors, and the global positioning system does not achieve the desired results in these scenarios, so other positioning techniques are required as a supplement [1].

The radio frequency (RF) fingerprint location method learns the position model through the position fingerprint information in the environment, which avoids directly modeling the signal in a complex environment and is therefore widely used in practical applications. Fingerprint information can be position

© Springer International Publishing AG, part of Springer Nature 2018
M. Mouhoub et al. (Eds.): IEA/AIE 2018, LNAI 10868, pp. 560–571, 2018.
https://doi.org/10.1007/978-3-319-92058-0_54

related observations, such as time of arrival (TOA), angel of arrival, received signal strength (RSS), etc., or signal characteristics such as power delay profile, channel impulse response, channel frequency response, and the like. Machine learning methods that have been used in fingerprinting include kth nearest neighbor (KNN), decision tree, support vector machine, radial basis function (RBF), (deep) neural networks and so on [2]. Most of the existing methods assume that the samples are independent of each other. The fingerprint signals at each grid point are collected, and the observed signals are matched or fitted to the most similar fingerprints to estimate the target position. These methods do not consider the spatial or temporal patterns of signals, and we call them point matching methods. Measurement noise, multipath effects [3], and the movement of wireless devices cause the signal to fluctuate randomly in time and space. Signals at two locations that are far apart may have similar signal measurement vectors, resulting in large location mismatch errors.

In this paper, the spatial or temporal patterns of RF signals in the positioning environment are used to improve the accuracy and robustness of mobile positioning. The spatial pattern is related to the geographical distribution of the signal, which constrains the location of the target's movement. The temporal pattern is the signal sequence pattern as the target moves through the environment and can be used to infer where the target is located. Compared to a single signal measurement at a fixed location, the time information carried by the pattern can be used to constrain and correct positioning results.

There are already some positioning methods that take advantage of the signal's spatial or temporal pattern. For example, the peak-based WiFi fingerprinting method [4] determines that a target is near an access point (AP) by detecting pre-defined peaks in the signal sequence. This method corrects errors well, but if the target moves faster, the peak of the measurement may not be accurate due to the missed scan. In a noisy environment, considering the entire signal sequence is more robust than considering only the peak. The Walkie-Markie method [5] uses the entire signal sequence to construct a given path pattern and obtains the target position estimate by matching the path pattern. These methods are more suitable for narrow positioning areas with significant path patterns, such as corridors. HyungJune Lee et al. [6] trained a Radial Basis Function (RBF) network by combining historical signals to estimate the current position of the moving target. However, the RBF network is not a model that specializes in sequence signals and can not learn the context dependencies between adjacent points in a signal sequence. In addition, state-space models, such as Kalman Filter (KF) [7], are often used to calibrate mobile positioning but require rough positioning results or learning observational and state models, not end-to-end methods.

Recurrent Neural Network (RNN) has been widely used in the field of natural language processing. Among them, encoder-decoder Recurrent Neural Network (edRNN) is a great machine translation model [8]. We propose an end-to-end RF path fingerprinting method based on edRNN model, referred to as RFedRNN for the purpose of using the RF signal sequence to learn the spatial or temporal pattern of the path, so as to improve the positioning accuracy and robustness of the moving target. The model consists of two RNNs: the signal encoder RNN extracts the features of the historical signal sequence and encodes them into a fixed-length RF context vector representation; then, the path decoder RNN decodes the corresponding path position sequence. In addition, we use a low labor cost data collection method and a special data construction method. Finally, we compared the performance of the proposed method with the existing methods through simulation and a real-world WiFi dataset respectively. The results show that the proposed method is superior to existing methods in positioning accuracy and robustness, especially for the real-world dataset.

2   RFedRNN: Sequence Learning Model for Mobile Positioning

2.1   Problem Statement

We consider the problem of the mobile device estimating the current location by matching historical path information. This problem can be viewed as a supervised sequence learning problem [9]. Let S denote the training sample set extracted from a fixed distribution $\mathcal{D}_{\mathcal{X} \times \mathcal{Y}}$. The input space $\mathcal{X} = (\mathbb{R}^m)^*$ is a set of all m-dimensional real signal vectors whose sampling length is T. In this paper, the input signal vector is formed by RSS or (and) TOA measurements between the mobile device and the AP. Alternatively, the input signal vector may be formed by other position parameters or features. The target space $\mathcal{Y} = (\mathbb{R}^d)^*$ is a set of all path vectors with a sampling length T in the positioning space, and d represents the dimension of the position space. Each sample in S is a sequence pair $(\mathbf{x}, \mathbf{y})$, where $\mathbf{x} = (x_1, x_2, ..., x_T)$ represents the RF signal sequence input, $\mathbf{y} = (y_1, y_2, ..., y_T)$ represents the sequence of target positions corresponding to the input, and the length of the sequence is both T. This article considers the case of $d = 2$, that is, the target to be located is in a two-dimensional plane. The purpose of the localization problem is to train a mapping function, $f : \mathcal{X} \mapsto \mathcal{Y}$, with the training data set S by minimizing the measurement error L, and the function f can map the signal sequence to a position sequence and generalize to a sequence pair that does not appear in the training set.

2.2   RNN Model

RNN is a neural network used to process sequence data [10]. Unlike feedforward neural networks, RNNs share model parameters at each time step. This mechanism allows the model to extend and generalize to samples of different lengths, share statistical strengths of different lengths and locations over time, and estimate models require far fewer training samples than models without parameter sharing. A typical RNN model is shown in Fig. 1. At each time step, the state of the hidden unit h_t is related not only to the input x_t, but also to the state of the hidden unit at the last moment, and the network parameters between the hidden units are shared.

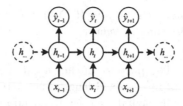

Fig. 1. Computation graph of a basic RNN model.

The RNNs have a strong ability of representation, any function that is computable by Turing can be calculated by an RNN of finite dimension cycle. According to the different attributes of the sequences, RNNs with different structures can be designed in practice, such as bidirectional RNNs, deep RNNs, encoder-decoder RNNs, etc. [10]. In view of the design of the structure of parameter sharing unit, gated RNN can effectively mitigate the problem of gradient disappearance and gradient explosion. Commonly used gated RNNs include Long Short Term Memory (LSTM) and Gated Recurrent Unit (GRU) networks [11]. In this paper, LSTM is used as an implementation of RNN.

2.3 Sequence Learning Mobile Positioning Model: RFedRNN

The parameter sharing mechanism of RNNs allows the network can be extended to a very long sequence. When the RNN model is used in positioning, it can learn the signal dependence of adjacent locations or moments in the entire positioning area, that is the spatial or temporal pattern, so as to reduce the positioning error caused by the signal uncertainty. We propose a model named RFedRNN for use in RF mobile positioning, as shown in Fig. 2. The model consists of two RNNs. The signal encoder RNN encodes the radio frequency signal sequence into a fixed

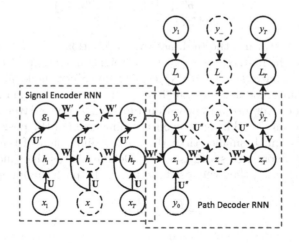

Fig. 2. Computation graph of the RFedRNN model.

length context vector. The path decoder RNN decodes the corresponding path position sequence from the context vector.

Signal Encoder RNN. The purpose of the signal encoder RNN is to encode the input signal sequence $\mathbf{x}$ into a fixed-length vector representation. As shown on the left side of Fig. 2, the signal encoder RNN adopts a bidirectional RNN structure. The information of the hidden layer unit of a bidirectional RNN can propagate along two directions of time. Use h_t and g_t to represent hidden layer units propagating forward and backward along time respectively. The update formula of the calculation graph is:

$$h_t = \tanh(b + Wh_{t-1} + Ux_t)$$
$$g_t = \tanh(b' + W'g_{t-1} + U'x_t)' \tag{1}$$

where $\tanh(\cdot)$ denotes the activation function of hyperbolic tangent. W, U, b and W', U', b' denote the hidden layer weight matrix, the input layer weight matrix, and the hidden layer bias vector propagating forward and backward along time respectively. The hidden layer state (h_T, g_T) of the last moment is taken as the encoding vector of the signal sequence, that is, the RF context vector, which contains the input information and the hidden information at all times. It is then entered into the path decoder RNN.

Path Decoder RNN. The purpose of the path decoder RNN is to decode the corresponding path vector $\mathbf{y}$ from the RF context vector (h_T, g_T). The path decoder RNN is shown on the right of Fig. 2, using a basic RNN structure. The RF context vector (h_T, g_T) is taken as the initial state of the hidden layer, in addition, the output of the network fed back to the next moment of input. Use z_t to indicate the hidden unit state, update the formula as:

$$z_t = \tanh(b'' + W''h_{t-1} + U''y_{t-1})$$
$$\hat{y}_t = c + Vz_t . \tag{2}$$

Hidden layers still use the tanh activation function. W'', U'', b'' denote the hidden layer weight matrix, the input layer weight matrix, and the hidden layer bias vector of the path decoder RNN, respectively. Since the location is continuous, the regression model is more realistic than the classification model. So the output layer does not use an activation function, a linear layer is replaced to regress the position. In addition, the output dimension of the position regression model is usually much smaller than the output dimension of the classification model, so the convergence speed is faster. Defining L_t as the squared loss of y_t after a given $x_1, ..., x_t$, then the loss function of the path mapping is:

$$L(\Theta) = \sum_t L_t = -\frac{1}{2}\sum_t \|\hat{y}_t - y_t\|^2 . \tag{3}$$

The gradient descent method can learn the network parameter set of RFe-dRNN, Θ, including weight matrix $U, U', U'', V, V', V'', W, W', W''$ and bias vector b, b', b'', c. The gradient of the model can be calculated by back propagation algorithm [10]. According to the scale of the problem in the experimental part of this paper, the number of neurons in hidden layer units is chosen as 100, that is, the dimensions of h_t and g_t.

Data Collection and Construction Methods. Fingerprint location method based on point matching needs to obtain the signal fingerprint of each grid point in the locating environment in the data collection phase, which is called point collection. Point collection of traditional fingerprint database needs to collect data on each grid point separately and mark the position. It takes dozens of hours to complete point collection in a normal building. In order to reduce labor costs, researchers have proposed some new data collection methods, such as automated robotic collection [12] and crowdsourcing [13]. The data obtained by these methods are generally the sequence of location fingerprints on multiple paths. In order to locate using traditional location methods, it is usually necessary to convert these path data into grid data again [14]. The method proposed in this paper can directly take the collected radio frequency signal path data as the input of the neural network without the need of converting into grid data first, thus simplifying the data collection mode and saving the labor cost.

After getting the path data, the value of the input sequence length T of need to be determined. T represents the length of time or length of historical information that the model can take advantage of. If T is too short, the historical information that can be used by the model is not sufficient. If T is too long, redundant information will be added, which is equivalent to introducing extra noise, resulting in degraded positioning performance. A appropriate value of T can be selected by experiments.

Finally, the radio frequency signal data including the latest T moments including the current time is taken as the input sequence, and the corresponding target position is used as the output sequence to form a data set. The data set is divided into training set, calibration set and test set, and normalized.

3   Experimental Evaluation

We have used both a simulation tool and a real-world dataset to evaluate and compare the performance of the proposed method and the existing method. The algorithms used for comparison are typical point matching methods: KNN [15], deep neural networks (DNN) [16] and support vector regression (SVR), as well as the method of using the path information: RBF [6] and KF [7]. KF method usually needs a preliminary target position as input. We use KNN and SVR positioning results as the initial position of KF, which are respectively denoted as KNN+KF and SVR+KF methods. In addition, similar to the idea of RBF method [6], we use historical measurement to regress the current position through the above three point matching methods, which are respectively denoted as KNN Path, DNN Path and SVR Path.

3.1   Simulation

Pylayers [17] was used to simulate the human environment walking trajectory and radio signals. It is a fixed-point radio propagation simulation platform that evaluates indoor location algorithms using radio signals, including indoor human motion, whose signal parameters of location can be calculated using multi-wall models or ray tracing. The simulation environment is seted to 40 m long and 15 m wide. There are 4 APs in total, as shown in Fig. 3, in which the blue trajectory is a simulated trajectory, and the departure and destination rooms of the agent are randomly selected. We spliced the acquired RSSs and TOAs of all APs as input signals, so the signal dimension m is 8.

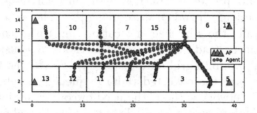

Fig. 3. Simulation environment floor plan (Color figure online).

A total of 20 random simulated paths were generated as data sets. Each path took 5 min and consisted of 301 sample points with a signal sampling rate of 1 Hz. Gaussian noise is added to the signal. According to the data construction method described in Sect. 2.3, $301 - T + 1$ path samples can be obtained for each path. If we take $T = 10$, that is 292 samples. Then the total number of 20 paths is 5840. The simulation experiments used three sizes of datasets: 20 paths ($dataset1$), 10 paths ($dataset2$) and 5 paths ($dataset3$). According to a ratio of 6 : 2 : 2, the data set is divided into training set, calibration set and test set. Table 1 compares the root mean square error (RMSE) estimates obtained from the models under the three data sets. All experimental results were averaged over 5 experiments with a signal to noise ratio (SNR) setting of 20 dB and a T of 10. As can be seen from Table 1, using a larger data set results in a smaller RMSE, but collecting a large amount of data requires more labor costs, which is often counterbalanced in positioning accuracy and labor costs.

Table 1. RMSE comparison of different data sets ($SNR = 20$ dB, $T = 10$)

Dataset	$dataset1$	$dataset2$	$dataset3$
RMSE(m)	1.08	1.16	1.67

The $dataset2$ is selected for the experiment below. Figure 4 shows the loss function of the model against training, validation and test set, with SNR equal

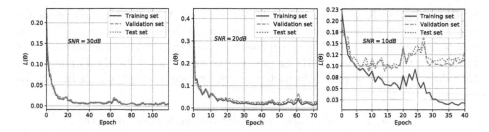

Fig. 4. Loss function of simulation data set.

to 30 dB, 20 dB, and 10 dB, respectively. Epoch indicates the number of training iterations. We use mini-batches learning method, the batchsize is set to 100, and the learning rate is set to 0.01. In addition, we use techniques such as dropout [18] and early stop to prevent overfitting. The optimization algorithm adopted is Adam [10]. Figure 4 shows that the model is easier over-fitted when the SNR is small.

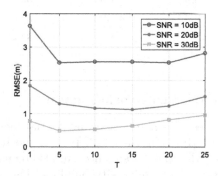

Fig. 5. Effect of sequence length T on RMSE at different SNRs.

The size of the input sequence length T and the sampling rate together determine the length of the historical information utilized by the model. Figure 5 plots the impact of T value on the positioning error under different SNR. Where, $T = 1$ means that no historical path information is utilized. It is observed from the figure that the use of historical path information is too long or too short will lead to larger errors. When SNR is high, the best T value is relatively small; when SNR is low, the best T value increases. The experimental results are consistent with our intuition. When the SNR is high, the single point shorter path pattern matching has been able to get better results. However, when the SNR is low, the signal pattern is contaminated by noise and the longer time pattern needs to be utilized to obtain better results.

Table 2 compares the RMSE for RFedRNN and other methods at different SNRs. It can be seen that RFedRNN can achieve a lower RMSE at both high

SNR and low SNR. In contrast, RBF can get close to RFedRNN performance, but in the next section of we will see that the performance of the RBF on the real-world dataset is poor. Other approaches that exploit path information either perform better at higher SNRs or perform better at lower SNRs. For methods that do not utilize the path information, performance is better only at high SNR.

Table 2. RMSE comparison of different algorithms (unit: m)

Algorithms	SNR = 30 dB	SNR = 20 dB	SNR = 10 dB
RFedRNN	0.52	1.16	2.55
RBF	0.73	1.33	2.53
KNN Path	0.69	1.29	3.08
DNN Path	0.79	1.9	2.87
SVR Path	0.62	1.35	2.61
KNN+KF	0.56	1.69	3.15
SVR+KF	0.6	1.55	2.95
KNN	0.57	1.99	3.94
DNN	0.92	1.92	3.55
SVR	0.69	1.87	3.65

3.2   Experiment on the Real-World Dataset

In this section we will test the model learning spatial model with a published real-world WiFi dataset [19]. For the RNN model, the input sequence is not necessarily a time series, the spatial sequence can also be used as a model input. The dataset was measured in a university building. The total number of APs scanned is 136, that is, the input signal dimension m equals to 136. Data collection was carried out in 13 floors in total, and we used layer 4 as the experimental data set. The data points and floor plans are shown in Fig. 6, which contains a total of about 130 sampling points with a sampling interval of about 2 m and 50 samples at each sampling point. The distribution of datasets is identified in Fig. 6 (blue dot indicates training set, green dot indicates calibration set and red dot indicates test set). The dataset is constructed as described in Sect. 2.3, noting that T here represents the length of the path, not the time.

First, we examine the effect of different T values on the RMSE of position estimation, as shown in Fig. 7. It can be observed that the curves are similar to the curves in Fig. 5, but they are not exactly the same. This may be due to the difference in sampling interval between the two experiments. More importantly, the signal model and noise distribution of the measured environment are different from the simulation environment. The measured environment is often more complex than the simulated environment, so longer historical information can be utilized to improve positioning performance.

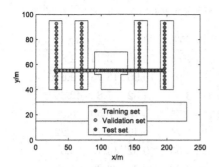

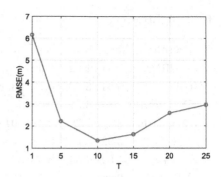

Fig. 6. Floor plan of real-world dataset. (Color figure online)

Fig. 7. The effect of T on the RMSE.

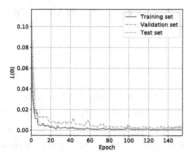

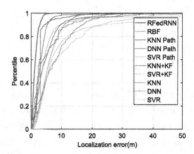

(a) Loss function curve of the real-world dataset.

(b) Comparison of positioning error CDF.

Fig. 8. The results of real dataset test.

Figure 8(a) shows the loss function of the RFedRNN model respected to training, validation and test set. In Fig. 8(b) and Table 3, the cumulative distribution function (CDF) of the localization error and test time between different algorithms is compared. As can be seen, the performance of RFedRNN is significantly better than the other algorithms. The positioning error of KNN Path is the second lowest, but its running time is about 20 times that of RFedRNN. In the previous simulation, RBF performed fairly well, but it did not perform as well in the real-world dataset. The difference between the experimental results of real data and simulation data shows again that the signal model and noise distribution in the real environment are very different from the simulation environment. In real environment, the signal model and the noise distribution are more complex. The model needs better generalization ability to show good performance in real environment. Experiments exhibit that RFedRNN model shows better generalization ability.

Table 3. Error(unit: m) and test time(unit: s) comparison of different algorithms

Algorithms	Mean	Std	Min	Max	50%	75%	90%	95%	Test time
RFedRNN	1.34	1.02	0.02	7.73	1.08	1.86	2.85	3.44	2.83
RBF	5.94	3.79	0.17	23.99	5.19	7.99	10.96	13.26	0.02
KNN Path	2.85	3.51	0.00	48	2.4	3	4.32	7.8	42.66
DNN Path	3.5	5.79	0.07	104.08	2.76	4.05	5.28	6.50	0.02
SVR Path	6.92	15.47	0.05	106.51	3.59	5.71	9.49	16.41	23.22
KNN+KF	5.02	4.84	0.01	34.89	3.52	6.55	9.62	14.16	5.09
SVR+KF	9.29	11	0.14	115.47	5.73	9.82	22.71	33.09	1.87
KNN	5.87	6.85	0.00	45.73	3	7.8	12.28	16.98	4.98
DNN	7.95	6.4	0.42	35.03	5.92	11.2	16.68	20.48	0.01
SVR	10.73	13.98	0.26	139.06	5.73	13.44	24.77	37.73	1.76

4   Summary

In recent years, RNN has been successfully applied in sequence learning problems such as speech, language and image. In a wireless positioning environment, the RF signal received by the moving target is also in the form of a sequence. This paper makes an exploratory research on the application of RNN model in wireless location, and proposes a location model named RFedRNN and the corresponding data collection and construction methods. Both simulation and real-world data experiments show that the proposed model shows good performance in mobile localization. As one of the deep learning architectures, RNN is expected to be applied to larger and more complex real-world positioning. The research content of this paper can be used as a reference to study the application of RNN in wireless location in the future.

Acknowledgments. This work was supported in part by the National Natural Science Foundation of China (NSFC) under Grant U1533125 and 61771108.

References

1. Zafari, F., Gkelias, A., Leung, K.: A survey of indoor localization systems and technologies (2017)
2. Khalajmehrabadi, A., Gatsis, N., Akopian, D.: Modern WLAN fingerprinting indoor positioning methods and deployment challenges. IEEE Commun. Surv. Tutorials **19**, 1974–2002 (2017)
3. Xiao, Z., Wen, H., Markham, A., Trigoni, N., Blunsom, P., Frolik, J.: Non-line-of-sight identification and mitigation using received signal strength. IEEE Trans. Wirel. Commun. **14**(3), 1689–1702 (2015)
4. Kim, Y., Shin, H., Cha, H.: Smartphone-based Wi-Fi pedestrian-tracking system tolerating the RSS variance problem. In: IEEE International Conference on Pervasive Computing and Communications, pp. 11–19 (2012)

5. Shen, G., Chen, Z., Zhang, P., Moscibroda, T., Zhang, Y.: Walkie-Markie: indoor pathway mapping made easy. In: Usenix Conference on Networked Systems Design and Implementation, pp. 85–98 (2013)
6. Lee, H.J., Wicke, M., Kusy, B., Guibas, L.: Localization of mobile users using trajectory matching. In: ACM International Workshop on Mobile Entity Localization and Tracking in GPS-Less Environments, Melt 2008, San Francisco, California, USA, pp. 123–128, September 2008
7. Paul, A.S., Wan, E.A.: Rssi-based indoor localization and tracking using sigma-point kalman smoothers. IEEE J. Sel. Top. Sig. Process. **3**(5), 860–873 (2009)
8. Cho, K., Van Merrienboer, B., Gulcehre, C., Bahdanau, D., Bougares, F., Schwenk, H., Bengio, Y.: Learning phrase representations using RNN encoder-decoder for statistical machine translation. In: Computer Science (2014)
9. Dieterich, T.G.: Machine learning for sequential data: a review. In: Caelli, T., Amin, A., Duin, R.P.W., de Ridder, D., Kamel, M. (eds.) SSPR /SPR 2002. LNCS, vol. 2396, pp. 15–30. Springer, Heidelberg (2002). https://doi.org/10.1007/3-540-70659-3_2
10. org.cambridge.ebooks.online.book.Author@ea: Deep Learning
11. Chung, J., Gulcehre, C., Cho, K.H., Bengio, Y.: Empirical evaluation of gated recurrent neural networks on sequence modeling. Eprint Arxiv (2014)
12. Mirowski, P., Milioris, D., Whiting, P., Ho, T.K.: Probabilistic radio-frequency fingerprinting and localization on the run. Bell Labs Tech. J. **18**(4), 111133 (2014)
13. Wang, B., Chen, Q., Yang, L.T., Chao, H.C.: Indoor smartphone localization via fingerprint crowdsourcing: challenges and approaches. IEEE Wirel. Commun. **23**(3), 82–89 (2016)
14. Mirowski, P., Ho, T.K., Whiting, P.: Building optimal radio-frequency signal maps. In: International Conference on Pattern Recognition, pp. 978–983 (2014)
15. Tran, Q., Tantra, J.W., Foh, C.H., Tan, A., Yow, K.C., Qiu, D.: Wireless indoor positioning system with enhanced nearest neighbors in signal space algorithm. In: Vehicular Technology Conference, VTC-2006 Fall, pp. 1–5. IEEE (2006)
16. Zhang, W., Liu, K., Zhang, W., Zhang, Y., Gu, J.: Deep neural networks for wireless localization in indoor and outdoor environments. Neurocomputing **194**(C), 279–287 (2016)
17. Amiot, N., Laaraiedh, M., Uguen, B.: PyLayers: an open source dynamic simulator for indoor propagation and localization. In: IEEE International Conference on Communications Workshops, pp. 84–88 (2013)
18. Zaremba, W., Sutskever, I., Vinyals, O.: Recurrent neural network regularization. Eprint Arxiv (2014)
19. http://www.artechhouse.com/static/Downloads/campos.zip

A Quantitative Analysis Decision System Based on Deep Learning and NSGA-II for FX Portfolio Prediction

Hua Shen$^{(\boxtimes)}$ and Xun Liang

RenMin University of China, Beijing 100872, China
sarah_h_shen@yahoo.com, xliang@ruc.edu.cn

Abstract. Forecasting foreign exchange (FX) rate and optimizing FX portfolio with the help of Artificial Intelligence has aroused wide interest among global capital market. As far as we know, this is the first paper which, from the perspective of institutional and individual investors, proposes a complete quantitative analysis decision system based on Deep Learning and NSGA-II to forecast FX rate and select FX portfolio successively. To be specific, we provide a whole procedure from data collection to FX forecasting with Stacked Autoencoders and further to optimal FX portfolio selection with NSGA-II. Furthermore, an empirical analysis has been conducted with 28 FX currency pairs, in which our algorithm has been compared with two other machine learning algorithms. Ultimately, our system provides optimized FX portfolio solutions for investors with diverse preference.

Keywords: Deep learning · Stacked autoencoders · NSGA-II

1 Introduction

Recent decades have witnessed an ascending number of governments, institutions and individuals paying much attention to foreign exchange (FX) rate prediction concerning its significant role in world economy. Increasingly, researches start to utilize machine learning methods to forecast FX rate [1]. Although there are a rising number of researchers who use the state-of-the-art deep learning methods for FX rate forecasting, few researches have been explored in providing a complete decision support for FX investments in capital market [2, 3]. Under this circumstance, we propose a practical quantitative decision analysis system based on deep learning and NSGA-II for FX rate forecasting and portfolio selecting. It involves the whole procedure of data collection—foreign exchange rate forecasting—FX portfolio selection, which is conducive to FX investment decision making from the perspective of investors. Furthermore, for the first time, we propose a FX forecasting model based on deep learning with SAE-SVR (Stacked Autoencoders and Support Vector Regression), and an FX portfolio Dual-Object optimization algorithm based on NSGA-II. The following sections will give the detailed descriptions.

© Springer International Publishing AG, part of Springer Nature 2018
M. Mouhoub et al. (Eds.): IEA/AIE 2018, LNAI 10868, pp. 572–579, 2018.
https://doi.org/10.1007/978-3-319-92058-0_55

2   The Quantitative Analysis Decision System

2.1   An Overview of the Quantitative Analysis Decision System

In general, the architecture of the Quantitative Analysis Decision System for FX portfolio prediction can be illustrated as Fig. 1. Historical raw data from existing FX transaction platform (MetaTrader4 of FXCM) would be put into the system. After being preprocessed for normalization and vectorization, the vectorized time series data would be sent into the SAE-SVR model, in which a forecasted vector dataset will be produced. In order to maximize the returns and to minimum the risks at the same time, the system utilizes a FX Dual-Objective Optimization Algorithm based on NSGA-II to select portfolio from the forecasted dataset. Finally we obtain the top 6 optimal portfolio solutions from the system. In practice, investors can choose the solutions in terms of different preferences, furthermore, these solutions could be combined with various derivatives such as FX Forward, FX Future, FX Swap, Currency Swap, FX Options, etc.

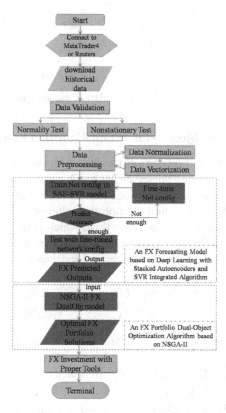

Fig. 1. The foreign exchange forecasting-portfolio quantitative decision analysis system

2.2   An FX Forecasting Model Based on SAE-SVR Algorithm

The Deep Learning forecasting model we proposed innovatively combines the merit of Stacked Autoencoders (SAE) to deeply learn features of datasets with the advantage of SVR's superior predicting capacity. The brief process is demonstrated in Fig. 2. Overall, the SAE-SVR model consists of one Input Layer, K Hidden Layers and one SVR Output Layer. Each hidden layer represents a Sparse Autoencoder, which can learn part-whole features of the dataset. The result of the Kth feature layer will be sent into SVR model for final prediction. For more details, please refer to author's existing publication [4].

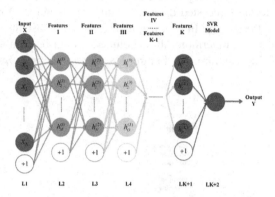

Fig. 2. Deep learning with SAE-SVR integrated algorithm structure

2.3   FX Portfolio Dual-Object Optimization Algorithm Based on NSGA-II

In order to select optimal FX portfolio solutions using results generated by the SAE-SVR model, considering diverse Multi-Objective Evolutionary Algorithms (MOEAs) [5], we take use of an improved version of Elitist Non-dominated Sorting Genetic Algorithm- NSGA-II to find the optimal solution with maximized return rate and minimized investment risk at the same time, which is in converging near the true Pareto-optimal set [6]. In this paper, concerning an FX portfolio pool with N currency pairs, we propose an FX Portfolio Dual-Object Model as below.

$$\begin{cases} \max ER(x) = \sum_{i=1}^{N} x_i R_i \\ \min SD(x) = \sum_{i=1}^{N} x_i std(R_i) \end{cases}$$
$$s.t. \sum_{i=1}^{N} x_i = 1, x_i \geq 0, i = 1, 2, \ldots N \tag{1}$$

ra ID="Par6">Where $X = (x_1, x_2 \ldots, x_N)$ indicates the target portfolio solution, we set $0 \leq x_i \leq 1, \sum_{i=1}^{N} x_i = 1$. $R = (R_1, R_2 \ldots, R_N) \in R$ indicates the return vector for all the N currency pairs. Besides, ER(x), SD(x), std(R_i) means the Expected Return, the Investment Risk, and the Standard Deviation for a specific portfolio respectively.

Furthermore, we take use of the Elitist Non-Dominated Sorting Genetic Algorithm II (NSGA-II) to optimize the FX Portfolio Dual-Object Model and finally obtain the optimal portfolio solutions. To be concrete, the main procedure of our FX Portfolio Dual-Object Optimization Algorithm based on NSGA-II can be illustrated in Fig. 3.

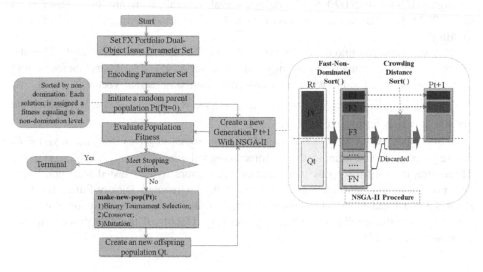

Fig. 3. The FX portfolio dual-object optimization algorithm flow chart

First of all, the parameter set should be determined according to the practical issues. Secondly, the parameter set will be encoded for the sake of following implementation. Thereafter, a random parent population P0 is created, and the population is sorted based on the non-domination. Next, the first offspring population Q_0 is created in usual GA method involving binary tournament selection, crossover and mutation operators. Then the following generations will be generated step-by-step. Table 1 gives a creation procedure description of the tth generation. For NSGA-II details, readers are encouraged to refer to the original studies.

Table 1. The tth generation created procedure of NSGA-II

$R_t = P_t \cup Q_t$	Combine parent and offspring population
$F = fast - non - dominated - sort(R_t)$	$F = (F_1, F_2, \ldots, F_N)$, all non-dominated fronts of R_t
$P_{t+1} = \emptyset, i = 1$ until $|P_{t+1}| + |F_i| \leq N$	Until the parent population is filled
Crowding-distance-assignment (F_i)	Calculate crowding-distance in F_i
$P_{t+1} = P_{t+1} \cup F_i$	Include the ith non-dominated front in the parent pop
i = i + 1	Check the next front for inclusion
Sort $(F_i, \prec_n)$	Sort in descending order using $\prec_n$
$P_{t+1} = P_{t+1} \cup F_i[1 : (N - |P_{t+1}|)]$	Choose the first $(N - |P_{t+1}|)$ elements of F_i
$Q_{t+1} = make - new - pop(P_{t+1})$	Use make-new-pop to create a new population Q_{t+1}
t = t + 1	Increment the generation counter

3 Data Processing

We collect G7 currencies (USD, GBP, EUR, JPY, AUD, CAD, CHF) from Meta-Trader4, and CNY from SAFE (State Administration of Foreign Exchange) website during 5/21/2009 to 2/1/2016 with daily interval. Overall, there are 28 currency pairs and 52223 records, which are divided into 38703 as TrainingSet and 13520 as TestingSet.

Before being sent into the system, the data will be normalized between [0, 1] scale. Then we get the normalized currency pair time series $Z = (z_1, \ldots, z_T)$ before being transformed into an L-lag-window multi-dimension time series vector $X = [X_1, \ldots, X_M] = (x_{ij})_{i,j=1}^{L,M}$, where $X_i = (z_i, \ldots, z_{i+L-1})' \in R^L$, $M = T - L + 1$, and the lag-window L is an integer meeting $2 \leq L \leq T/2$.

The output vector is a one-dimensional time series vector $Y = (y_1, \ldots, y_M) \in R$, where $y_n = z_{n+L}$, and y_n indicates the forecasting value of $X_n = (z_n, \ldots, z_{n+L-1})' \in R^L$. Thereafter, the 28 time series input and output vectors will be tested with non-linear and non-stationary attributes successively, with Augmented Dickey-Fuller for Unit Root Test to validate the non-stationary attribute and Jarque-Bera test for Normality Test to verify the nonlinear attribute respectively. Details of the data processing can also be found in [4].

4 Empirical Analysis

We benchmark our SAE-SVR model with Artificial Neural Network and Support Vector Regression. In summary, the SAE-SVR model has higher predicting accuracy with 610.92% (MSE) and 240.61% (MAE) compared with ANN and SVR. The detailed forecasting results of 28 currency pairs in comparison with ANN and SVR are illustrated in [4]. Moreover, they will act as the input of the FX Portfolio Dual-Object Optimization Algorithm in the following part after being transformed into general scale by $s_i = s_{max} - z_i(s_{max} - s_{min})$.

The expiration date of our dataset is 02/01/2016, therefore, we set it as benchmark date and select the data during 50 days before it to compute the return rate and standard deviation of each currency pair. Table 2 illustrates the output results.

Afterwards, the return rates and standard deviations are sent into the NSGA-II Algorithm. For the sake of more rapid computation, lower time complexity and better precision, we get rid of negative return rate currency pair before implementing NSGA-II simulation. During the empirical test, we test different generation settings of NSGA-II, and the corresponding Pareto Front diagrams are represented in Fig. 4.

It turns out the Optimization Algorithm with 150 generations obtains the highest expected return rates and lowest risks. So we select top 6 portfolio solutions based on the FX Portfolio Dual-Object Optimization Algorithm with 150 generations, the results are shown in Table 3. From the perspective of investors, risk preference investors can focus on 1–3 solutions for a higher expected return rate as well as higher risk, while risk aversion investors could focus on 4–6 solutions for a lower investment risk but also relative lower expected return rate. In summary, investors with diverse return rate and risk preferences could select a couple of solutions provided by our quantitative analysis decision system in practical FX investment.

Table 2. Return rate and standard deviation of each currency results

Currency pair	EURUSD	GBPUSD	AUDUSD	EURGBP	USDCAD	EURCAD	GBPCAD
RETURN(R)	−0.00814	−0.0056	0.001469	−0.0013	−0.00575	−0.01595	−0.01027
STD(R)	0.005413	0.004716	0.006188	0.00568	0.005477	0.009524	0.005852
Currency pair	AUDCAD	EURAUD	GBPAUD	USDJPY	EURJPY	GBPJPY	CADJPY
RETURN(R)	−0.00439	−0.00867	−0.00767	0.017073	0.009015	0.012546	0.018132
STD(R)	0.004703	0.010337	0.006284	0.006031	0.005936	0.006993	0.009869
Currency pair	AUDJPY	USDCHF	EURCHF	GBPCHF	CADCHF	AUDCHF	CHFJPY
RETURN(R)	0.016961	0.009572	−0.00091	0.001333	0.011588	0.008666	0.00939
STD(R)	0.010665	0.006277	0.002692	0.006398	0.008022	0.008963	0.005946
Currency pair	USDCNY	EURCNY	GBPCNY	CADCNY	AUDCNY	JPYCNY	CHFCNY
RETURN(R)	−0.00018	0.003119	0.006087	0.003512	0.00825	−0.00346	−0.0002
STD(R)	0.001119	0.005538	0.004578	0.004342	0.005868	0.004348	0.009266

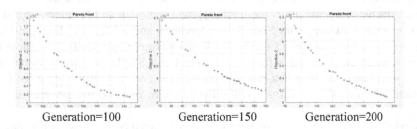

| Generation=100 | Generation=150 | Generation=200 |

Fig. 4. Pareto front diagram of the FX portfolio dual-object optimization algorithm

Table 3. Top 6 portfolio solutions of the optimization algorithm (Descending Order of ER)

NO.	USD CNY	JPY CNY	CHF CNY	USD JPY	EUR JPY	GBP JPY	CAD JPY	AUD JPY	USD CHF	GBP USD
1	0	0	0	5.15%	0.01%	0.28%	78.50%	0.52%	3.63%	3.75%
2	0	0	0	5.15%	0.01%	0.28%	78.50%	0.52%	3.63%	3.75%
3	0	0	0	6.32%	0.07%	0.28%	69.01%	0.73%	3.77%	3.59%
4	0	0	0	7.66%	0.18%	0.25%	54.07%	4.75%	3.93%	3.36%
5	0	0	0	7.82%	0.19%	0.25%	52.90%	4.68%	3.95%	3.34%
6	0	0	0	7.31%	0.21%	0.27%	49.77%	0.97%	4.05%	3.25%
NO.	GBP CHF	CAD CHF	AUD CHF	CHF JPY	EUR CNY	GBP CNY	CAD CNY	AUD CNY	ER(x)	SD(x)
1	0.87%	1.85%	0.20%	0.16%	2.23%	1.85%	0.53%	0.57%	0.016146	0.009088
2	0.87%	1.85%	0.20%	0.16%	2.23%	1.85%	0.53%	0.57%	0.016146	0.009088
3	1.26%	1.65%	0.25%	0.24%	2.26%	2.62%	7.35%	0.70%	0.014967	0.008605
4	1.87%	1.34%	0.32%	0.43%	2.37%	3.45%	15.21%	0.90%	0.013532	0.008071
5	1.92%	1.31%	0.33%	0.44%	2.37%	3.55%	16.12%	0.92%	0.013375	0.008005
6	2.08%	1.22%	0.33%	0.40%	2.32%	3.84%	23.09%	0.97%	0.012356	0.00759

5   Conclusion

In general, we innovatively propose the Quantitative Analysis Decision System based on Deep Learning and NSGA-II for FX forecasting and portfolio selection, which gives a complete procedure of FX investment. It involves FX trading platform selection—data collection—foreign exchange rate analysis—portfolio optimal selections. To be specific, the most important modules in this system consist of an FX Forecasting Model based on Deep Learning with SAE-SVR Algorithm, and a FX Portfolio Dual-Object Optimization Algorithm based on NSGA-II. Furthermore, we verify the whole procedure with 28 currency pairs from MetaTrader4 and SAFE website, and implement the empirical analysis with self-programming codes, and finally provide a list of FX investment solutions for investors with different return rate and risk preference.

Acknowledgements. The work was supported by the National Natural Science Foundation of China (No. 71531012), and the Natural Science Foundation of Beijing (No. 4172032).

References

1. Deng, S., Yoshiyama, K., Mitsubuchi, T., Sakurai, A.: Hybrid method of multiple kernel learning and genetic algorithm for forecasting short-term foreign exchange rates. Comput. Econ. **45**, 49–89 (2015)
2. Shen, F., Chao, J., Zhao, J.: Forecasting exchange rate using deep belief networks and conjugate gradient method. Neurocomputing **167**, 243–253 (2015)
3. Zhang, R., Shen, F., Zhao, J.: A model with fuzzy granulation and deep belief networks for exchange rate forecasting. In: International Joint Conference on Neural Networks, pp. 366–373 (2014)

4. Shen, H., Liang, X.: A time series forecasting model based on deep learning integrated algorithm with stacked autoencoders and SVR for FX prediction. In: Villa, A.E.P., Masulli, P. (eds.) ICANN 2016. LNCS, vol. 9887, pp. 326–335. Springer, Cham (2016). https://doi.org/10.1007/978-3-319-44781-0_39
5. Li, H., Zhang, Q.: Multiobjective optimization problems with complicated Pareto sets, MOEA/D and NSGA-II. IEEE Trans. Evol. Comput. **13**, 284–302 (2009)
6. Kannan, S., Baskar, S., Mccalley, J.D., Murugan, P.: Application of NSGA-II algorithm to generation expansion planning. IEEE Trans. Power Syst. **24**, 454–461 (2009)

Towards Machine Learning Based IoT Intrusion Detection Service

TagyAldeen Mohamed$^{(\boxtimes)}$, Takanobu Otsuka$^{(\boxtimes)}$, and Takayuki Ito$^{(\boxtimes)}$

Department of Computer Science, Nagoya Institute of Technology,
Gokiso, Showa-ku, Nagoya, Japan
tagy.mohamed@itolab.nitech.ac.jp,
{otsuka.takanobu,ito.takayuki}@nitech.ac.jp
http://itolab.nitech.ac.jp

Abstract. IoT Security is one of the most critical issues when developing, implementing and deploying IoT platforms. IoT refers to the ability of communication, monitoring and remote control of automated devices through the internet. Due to low computational capabilities, less power, and constrained technologies, IoT is vulnerable to various cyber attacks. Security mechanisms such as cryptography and authentication are hard to apply due to the aforementioned constraints on IoT devices. To overcome this issue Intrusion Detection Systems (IDSs) play main role as a high-security solution. This paper shows a proposed IDS based on machine learning techniques to be implemented into IoT platforms as a service. We used Random forest as a classifier to detect intrusions, then we applied neural network classifier to detect the categorization of the detected intrusion. The experimental results showed the proposed model can effectively detect intrusions, yet categorization of the intrusion suffers from low accuracy and high bias.

Keywords: Anomaly detection · Neural network · IoT security · IDS

1 Introduction

With the recent revolution of low-cost computing devices along with technological advancement in communication, the next generation of internet services, which touch every aspect of our life has been developed. Internet-of-Things (IoT) concept is used as a multitude of objects interconnected to each other and to the internet allowing people and objects to interact and create smart environments for transportation systems, cities, health, energy and any other possible objects.

Since Internet Of Things operate in completely isolated environments and was never designed to handle security threats, (IoT) is vulnerable to malicious attacks, furthermore because of it's opening development, deployment and limited resources. Its heterogeneous and distributed character make it difficult to apply standard security mechanism [2], causing systems to take wrong and dangerous actions.

© Springer International Publishing AG, part of Springer Nature 2018
M. Mouhoub et al. (Eds.): IEA/AIE 2018, LNAI 10868, pp. 580–585, 2018.
https://doi.org/10.1007/978-3-319-92058-0_56

Intrusion Detection System is one of the techniques which helps to determine network security, by alarming when an intrusion is detected. Security vulnerabilities are both technically difficult and economically costly. Hence, the role of Intrusion Detection System (IDS), as special-purpose devices to detect anomalies and attacks in the network, is important.

We propose using cloud computing for anomaly detection, to use it as a robust and scalable security solution for IoT platforms. Our proposed solution is based on neural network and random forest. We perform all the analysis in the cloud, so that, IoT performance isn't affected.

The remaining of the paper is organized as follows, in Sect. 2 we present the IoT structure and it's security issues, the used machine learning algorithms, and the IDS detection methods. In Sect. 3, we show the detailed design of our proposed solution, In Sect. 4, we present results discussion and Future work.

1.1   IoT Security Challenges

IoT traditional network security solutions may not be directly applicable due to the differences in IoT structure and behavior. We consider the following issues as the main reasons for that lack [3]. (1) IoT design focuses mainly on functionality with tradeoff to security. Manufacture companies seek new functions working at lowest cost. (2) Low operating energy and minimal computational capabilities. Therefore security mechanism such as encryption protocols and authentication can not be directly applied. (3) The lack of a single standard for IoT architecture. IoT may have different policies, and connectivity domains. Therefore, security law and regulations are not applied yet [6]. These Given challenges along with the use of hacking software, vulnerabilities can be easily discovered. Penetration testing tools, which are able to automate attacks against IoT systems, are easily accessible. Such tools [4] are convenient enough to enable even low-skilled exploiters to cause huge damage to IoT platforms in several ways. According to [5] IoT testing guidance issues can be described with 10 different security domains.

1.2   Intrusion Detection System

Intrusion detection systems are strategically placed on a network in order to detect threats and monitor network traffic. The IDS take either network or host based approachs for recognizing attacks. The IDS achieves this mission by collecting data from systems and network sources and perform analysis on it for possible [6] threats. The IDS main functions are offering information on threats, perform actions when threat is detected and record important events within the network [6].

Detection techniques fall into several classes:

1. **Signature based Detection** are based on set of rules used to match patterns in the network traffic. It has the advantage of detecting well known attacks, but it fails to detect novel attacks that aren't known to the database.

2. **Anomaly based** is a behavior based detection. It observes changes in normal activity through profiling the objects which are being monitored. This technique is efficient in identifying new malicious activities, but sometimes it fails to identify popular attacks or provides false positive alarms.
3. **Hybrid IDS** is a hybrid of signature-based and anomaly-based techniques. This technique consumes energy and resources, but is efficient in terms of detection and for identifying attacks and threats. With this mixed technique IDS is able to identify well known attacks along with novel attacks.

1.3   Artificial Neural Network

Neural networks are a set of tools that can automatically detect patterns to classify new data [10]. While there is a large number of machine learning algorithms, the main performance of all of them relies on optimal features selection An artificial neural network consists of a collection layered of processing elements that are interconnected and transform a set of inputs into a set of outputs [11]. In all anomaly detection approaches learning and testing phases are used in order to differentiate data generated from IoT systems are anomalous or not. The main challenge is in disputing whether are all anomalies in IoT datasets are considered as intrusions. However, the most important advantage of neural networks is the ability to "learn" the characteristics of novel attacks, and to identify instances that are unlike any of which has been observed.

1.4   Random Forest

A random forest is a meta estimator that fits a number of decision tree classifiers on various sub-samples of the dataset and use averaging to improve the predictive accuracy and control over-fitting. It is a supervised classification algorithm which creates forest with a number of decision trees [7]. Random forests are a way of averaging multiple deep decision trees, trained on different parts of the same training set, with the goal of reducing the variance. A tree classification algorithm is used to construct a tree with a different bootstrap sample from the original data. When the formation of a forest is completed, a new object which is to be classified is taken from each of the trees in the forest.

1.5   Network Features

We propose using dataset UNSW-NB15 [1] to employ a customized machine learning algorithm for learning general behaviors in the dataset in order to differentiate between normal and malicious activities. Dataset UNSW-NB15 is a modren labeled dataset for evaluating NIDSs, created by cyber security research group at ACCS. The dataset contains over 2.5 million records as CSV format along with 49 features. Categories are 9 types of modern attacks and 1 normal traffic patterns. The features type are different: Integer, Float, Binary, Nominal and Timestamp. We think this dataset has different attack families which may reflect real world and modern attacks.

2   Intrusion Detection Service

Our solution is divided into two parts. A device collects end nodes traffic and sends it to the cloud analyzer. In this solution, we propose using Raspberry Pi 3 as the main device for all the implementations of our proposed solution. The device acts as an interface between the application layer in the top level and the end nodes layer. Since sensors usually have low (or no) computational power, this service is a more suitable approach to secure the end nodes in IoT network by watch and monitor abnormal behaviors.

The second part is a cloud-based intrusion detector based on Random Forests and Neural Network. It receives IoT traffic from the aforementioned device, performs features extraction, and classification on the extracted features. Random Forest is used to detect if the data point is classified as intrusion or not. The Neural Network is used to categorize the detected intrusion

Our solution is divided into three modules: (1) Data collection Module, (2) Data processing and (3) Detection module and alerting.

2.1   Traffic Gathering Module

We propose using Tshark. Tshark is a network protocol analyzer. It is capable of capturing packet data from a live network connection, for a particular time window or read packets from a previously saved capture file. Our idea is to capture IoT network traffic and save it as pcap files. Then we upload these files to the cloud analyzer. Our proposed traffic capture algorithm is based on traffic capture time and the size of pcap file. Tshark configuration allow capture specific features of the network traffic along with of deep inspection. Since the proposed model handles only numerical features, pcap files are processed by Bro-IDS and other scripts to mine the features, Bro-IDS is an open-source traffic analyzer, considered as a security monitor and malicious activities inspector. MySQL technology is used to store the extracted features. The extracted features are then passed to the processing module to be analyzed.

2.2   Detection Module

Random Forest Classifier: Scikit-Learn' ExtraTreesClassifier are used to classify intrusions with 31 estimators (decision trees). Measurement of decision tree's quality was done with Information gain ratio. Other settings were left default, Number of estimators and criterion were selected by hand.

Neural Network architecture was selected by trial and error. The input layer has the same number as the dataset features. Sigmoid activation function $h_\theta(x) = \frac{1}{1+e^{-\theta^T x}}$ gave better results than ReLU and tanh. Dense layers are fully connected. The output layer has softmax as activation function, $\text{softmax}(\mathbf{x})_i = \frac{e^{x_i}}{\sum_{j=1} e^{x_j}}$ output dimensions are dataset data categories: 9 are attacks and 1 is normal. Dropout regularization is used to prevent overfitting.

3 Simulation Results

Normal or Intrusion Classification: In order to evaluate the aforementioned algorithms, we used UNSW-NB15 [1] as a simulation to real IoT traffic. The results show that Random Forest works fine with UNSW-NB15 [1].

Confusion matrix is used to evaluate performance. It also helped to identify which classes the algorithm didn't classify correctly. Precision, recall, and F1-score were calculated. Table 1 shows the results of metrics performance, 0 means the sample is classified as a normal data point, 1 represents an intrusion. Table 1 shows the classification result.

Table 1. Random forest classification results

Class	Precision	IRecall	F1-score
0	1.00	0.98	0.99
1	0.88	1.00	0.93
Avg/total	0.99	0.98	0.98

Intrusion Categorization: Intrusion classes represented with numbers 0–9 corresponding to the dataset labels. For example, the precision of the normal class which is represented by number 6 is approximately 1 and recall is 0.98. The results showed that mostly classes 2,4 and 6 were classified, Class 6 always classified correctly, which suggest differentiating features present in class 6. Predictions mostly fall under class 2 and 4. Therefore instances of the classes 2 and 4 have high recall score. Class 5 and 2 are similar, most data point predicted to be class 2, so the precision is low as Table 2 shows.

Table 2. Neural network categorization results

Class	Precision	IRecall	F1-score
0	0.00	0.00	0.00
1	0.00	0.00	0.00
2	0.04	0.81	0.07
3	0.02	0.00	0.00
4	0.16	0.60	0.25
5	0.06	0.00	0.00
6	1.00	0.98	0.99
7	0.00	0.00	0.00
8	0.00	0.00	0.00
9	0.00	0.00	0.00
Avg/total	0.89	0.87	0.88

We tried changing neural network architecture in order to get better performance, it made an impact on which classes the data points were classified to, but the overall classification accuracy stayed almost the same. Different residual layer techniques, bypasses between layers and other techniques were used but no positive impact on the accuracy.

4 Conclusion and Future Work

IoT's heterogeneous and distributed characters make traditional intrusion detection methodologies hard to deploy. To overcome this issue, we proposed Cloud computing service as an efficient mechanism to process data from different resources of IoT platforms. Effectivness in time and intrusion detection is a must for critical IoT applications. Towards verifying our hypothesis, we test the proposed model on UNSW-NB15 [1].

Algorithms and techniques [8] will be improved in future. Now we are working on IoT environment to test and deploy our proposed solution. In the future work, IoT network traffic features will be studied closely to provide high accuracy. Data collection and pre-processing along with detection algorithms will be presented from IoT test environment. We plan to extend this proposal in three manners. (1) IoT traffic Features selection regarding anomaly detection, (2) IPv6 and it's feature extraction, and (3) Performance of the proposed methods regards detecting anomalies as intrusions.

References

1. Moustafa, N., Slay, J.: UNSW-NB15: a comprehensive data set for network intrusion detection systems (UNSW-NB15 network data set). In: 2015 Military Communications and Information Systems Conference (MilCIS). IEEE (2015)
2. Suo, H., Wan, J., Zou, C., Liu, J.: Security in the Internet of Things: a review. In: International Conference on Computer Science and Electronics Engineering (ICCSEE), vol. 3 (2012)
3. Pacheco, J., Hariri, S.: IoT security framework for smart cyber infrastructures. In: 1st International Workshops on Foundations and Applications of Self Systems (2016)
4. Aircrack-ng tools for Wifi network security. https://www.aircrack-ng.org/
5. OWASP IoT Testing Guidance. https://owasp.org
6. Hodo, E., Bellekens, X., Hamilton, A., Tachtatzis, C., Atkinson, R.: Shallow and deep networks intrusion detection system: a taxonomy and survey (2017)
7. Breiman, L.: Random forests. Mach. Learn. 45(1), 5–32 (2001)
8. ITKST42: information security technology course. https://github.com/Moskari/ITKST42-network-data-classifier
9. Matthew, V., Philip, K.: PHAD: packet header anomaly detection for identifying hostile network traffic. Department of Computer Sciences Florida Institute of Technology Technical report CS-2001-04 (2001)
10. Witten, I.H., Frank, E.: Data Mining: Practical Machine Learning Tools and Techniques. Morgan Kaufmann, San Francisco (2005)
11. de Lima, I.V.M., Degaspari, J.A., Sobral, J.B.M.: Intrusion detection through artificial neural networks. In: Network Operations and Management Symposium NOMS 2008, pp. 867–870. IEEE, 7–11 April 2008

Planning, Scheduling and Spatial Reasoning

A Spatio-Semantic Model for Agricultural Environments and Machines

Henning Deeken[1,2,3], Thomas Wiemann[1(✉)], and Joachim Hertzberg[1,3]

[1] Knowledge-Based Systems Group, University of Osnabrück, Osnabrück, Germany
{henning.deeken,thomas.wiemann,joachim.hertzberg}@uni-osnabrueck.de
[2] CLAAS E-Systems KGaA mbH & Co KG, Dissen a.T.W, Germany
henning.deeken@claas.de
[3] DFKI Robotics Innovation Center, Osnabrück Branch, Osnabrück, Germany
{henning.deeken,joachim.hertzberg}@dfki.de

Abstract. Digitization of agricultural processes is advancing fast as telemetry data from the involved machines becomes more and more available. Current approaches commonly have a machine-centric view that does not account for machine-machine or machine-environment relations. In this paper we demonstrate how to model such relations in the generic semantic mapping framework SEMAP. We describe how SEMAP's core ontology is extended to represent knowledge about the involved machines and facilities in a typical agricultural domain. In the framework we combine different information layers – semantically annotated spatial data, semantic background knowledge and incoming sensor data – to derive qualitative spatial facts about the involved actors and objects within a harvesting campaign, which add to an increased process understanding.

Keywords: Semantic mapping · Environment modeling · Ontologies
Agriculture

1 Introduction

Digitization of agricultural processes currently concentrates on recording and processing telemetry data from individual machines to support precision farming. This implicitly leads to a machine-centric view on the ongoing processes. But many agricultural processes are complex, cooperative orchestrations of multiple machines. Automatic decision support in harvesting campaigns is still limited in assistance systems, as representations of cooperative agricultural processes and tools to analyze inter-machine relations are mostly missing.

Information on the whole process can not be derived from a single machine's telemetry data, but is covert in the combined telemetry of multiple machines. To embed this abstract data from different machines in the context of the ongoing process, machine data has to be fused with additional knowledge and information about the environment and the process itself. Most importantly, symbolic representations of the spatial relations between agricultural machines and their

© Springer International Publishing AG, part of Springer Nature 2018
M. Mouhoub et al. (Eds.): IEA/AIE 2018, LNAI 10868, pp. 589–600, 2018.
https://doi.org/10.1007/978-3-319-92058-0_57

environment are needed to identify and monitor process states and associated events. Analyzing the geo location of individual machines and processing of spatial relations between them is therefore a valuable contribution to automated process managing in agriculture. Modern agricultural machines already provide a geo-referenced stream of telemetry data, based on RTK-GPS. The positional data is often used to inspect the containment of machines in polygonal boundaries representing fields and farms, to spatially locate machines at those facilities. Such a quantitative, geometric analysis already extracts a lot of relevant information, but does not account for qualitative relations between the machines and facilities nor for knowledge representation and reasoning on a semantic level.

Representing such spatial relations in terms of a well-defined semantic terminology allows to infer complex facts, built up from basic spatial relations to take a process-centric view on harvesting campaigns. This requires a machine-readable environment model that can be paired with geo-referenced telemetry-data from agricultural machines to geolocalize individual machines and derive spatial relations between machines and their environment, respectively. To meet these requirements, we use the semantic mapping framework SEMAP [1] to represent an agricultural domain. We show how to create a semantic environment model for agricultural environments and machines and how to connect it to the underlying geometric model. We illustrate how to ground qualitative spatial relations between a static environment and a set of dynamic vehicles with SEMAP.

In an application example, we replay telemetry of a harvesting campaign to continuously update the spatio-semantic environment model to derive symbolic facts about the ongoing process. Via rule-based inference we analyze the domain-specific spatial relations of a maize harvesting campaign to detect events such as the correct positioning of a transport vehicle next to the harvester for overloading.

2   Related Work

State of the art solutions in digital agriculture allow to record and process telemetry data of agricultural machines like position, velocity, and internal parameters like fuel consumption or mass throughput [2]. This data is used in precision farming to optimize the application of fertilizers or herbicides, and collected in farm management information systems to aggregate telemetry data to analyze the performance of agricultural machines [3,4]. They also help to plan agricultural operations by maintaining information about crop rotations [5] or by creating field boundaries and sub-plots based on GPS data [6] to support the application of fertilizers and herbicides tillage strategies [7]. Automated scheduling of entire harvesting campaigns is also possible [8]. Usually, these solutions operate on centralized systems with web-based front ends [9]. This often causes severe latencies due to connectivity issues in remote or rural areas [10].

Fleet overview applications inform the operators about an on-going harvest operation by exchanging telemetry information between machines in real time and display vehicle positions on a static 2D map. Process-related decision making is still completely in the operator's hands, as these assistance systems do not provide a context-dependent and process-oriented analysis. To automatically detect relevant situations that give insight into the agricultural process – e.g., an empty transport vehicle arriving at the field ready for overloading – is a key feature to increase process transparency, which is necessary for improving agricultural efficiency through more process-oriented decision support systems.

To solve these problems, existing approaches from semantic mapping in robotics can be transferred to this application domain. Semantic maps are representations that in addition to spatial data provide assignments to known concepts for the mapped entities, such that semantic background knowledge can be used to reason about the environment [11]. Recent advances in semantic mapping are concerned with constructing general models of multi-modal environment data that can be flexibly queried for task-specific data in individual applications, see [12] for an overview.

Being able to analyze spatial relations in terms of qualitative predicates is important in data retrieval and reasoning. To fully utilize qualitative spatial reasoning, it is necessary to derive qualitative symbolic data from quantitative metric information. In [13], Wolter and Wallgrün pointed out that this process of qualification is essential for qualitative spatial reasoning in practical applications, but still rarely seen. The lack of qualification is also apparent when working with semantic maps. Tools for performing spatial analysis on quantitative metric data are also seldom used in semantic mapping. In our previous work [1], we showed the advantages of maintaining environment data in form of a generalized and persistent model, from which task-specific semantic maps can be extracted, rather than maintaining and aligning several different layers of semantic, geometric and topological information in parallel. We proposed to pair spatial databases and declarative knowledge bases to combine ontological and logical rule-based inference with spatial querying and analysis capabilities and called it the semantic mapping framework SEMAP.

In this paper, we integrate an ontology for agricultural processes into SEMAP to make knowledge about harvesting campaigns accessible for automatic analysis. We use this knowledge together with SEMAP's spatial reasoning capabilities to recognize relevant events in an maize harvesting process. In the presented experiment we were able to detect the correct positioning of an overloading vehicle based on recorded telemetry in an real life harvesting campaign.

3   The SEMAP Framework

The SEMAP framework is designed to represent and manage spatio-semantic environment data. Its purpose is to provide information about the objects and the environment in a specific application domain. It connects conceptual knowledge about the environment and factual knowledge about present object instances with their geometric representations to hold a combined spatio-semantic model that allows spatial analysis as well as semantic inference.

To manage the fundamentally different structure of semantic and spatial information, SEMAP internally separates environment data into two dedicated databases to ensure optimized performance for each data modality especially in terms of data storage and retrieval. An outline of SEMAP's internal structure is given in Fig. 1. The semantic part is represented by a knowledge base system component (KB) that is based on description logics with the obligatory separation into terminological and asserted knowledge. The environment's conceptual model and facts about the environment are represented in the Web Ontology Language (OWL) [14] and maintained in Apache JENA, which provides inference for ontological and rule-based reasoning as well as the capability to query the stored knowledge. The spatial part is a dedicated spatial database system (DB) that stores geometric primitives, and provides operators for quantitative spatial analysis and spatial querying. It is implemented as an extension to Post-GIS using the SFCGAL plugin to create custom spatial operators, especially for detecting 3D spatial relations.

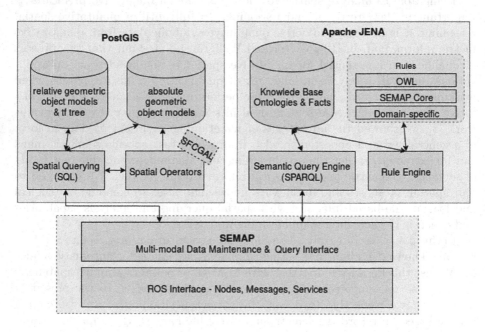

Fig. 1. SEMAP's architecture features a spatial database and a knowledge base system, which are combined by a multi-modal querying interface.

The framework's strength lies in combining both query systems to support combined queries with semantic and spatial aspects. In such queries, SEMAP utilizes the DB's spatial operators to ground qualitative spatial relations that are only stored implicitly in the geometric environment representation. Such relations are automatically inserted into the KB as facts for further inference. This approach enables rule-based reasoning and to construct complex spatial queries based on simpler deductions. This multi-modal query interface is advantageous in real-world applications, as it allows to answer complex questions about the positions, relations and roles of the stored objects in a natural way. The framework's core components are designed to be domain-independent, yet extensible with domain-specific semantic models, rule-sets and geometries. A more detailed description of the SEMAP framework and its spatial querying capabilities is given in [1].

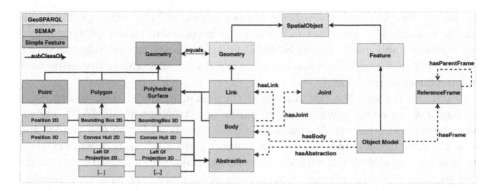

Fig. 2. An excerpt of the ontology that implements the semantics of SEMAP's environment model.

Figure 2 sketches SEMAP's core ontology. It uses standards from the Open Geospatial Consortium (OGC), because these well-defined models of geo-spatial data are in alignment with PostGIS's data types, which were also defined by the OGC. GeoSPARQL's `SpatialObject` and the fundamental distinction between geometries and features are integrated in SEMAP's upper ontology.

Here, the concept `Geometry` describes any kind of spatial primitive and provides a semantic wrapper for all OGC data types and serves as a bridge to the well known Simple Feature Ontology. SEMAP's KB contains a corresponding `Geometry` sub-concept, for every geometric primitives stored in SEMAP's DB. The property `semap:hasDbId` is used to create an associative link between the geometric primitive and its semantic wrapper. SEMAP internally uses these associations to join spatial and semantic data.

The super-concept `Feature` is used for all things that can be described spatially like SEMAP's `ObjectModel`, which aggregates sets of semantically wrapped geometries to represent an object. For this, it uses the `geo:hasGeometry` property and its two specializations: `semap:hasBody` composes a set of geometries that constitute the object's actual body. In case of articulated objects, the `Link` and `Joint` concepts are used to describe the object's kinematics. `semap:hasAbstraction` provides a set of coarser representations, like oriented and axis-aligned bounding boxes and convex hulls. These abstractions are used for accelerated spatial processing and enable the analysis of directional relations like `left-of` or `above-of`, based on projection and half space geometries described in [15].

To create a spatio-semantic environment model for a particular application, domain-specific ontologies, knowledge bases and rule-sets can be imported into SEMAP. To describe domain-specific concepts spatially and reason about them as part of SEMAP's environment model, the respective entities can be associated with an `ObjectModel` via the `semap:hasObjectModel` relation, cf. Fig. 4(b).

4   Applying SEMAP in Agriculture

In this section, we detail the process of customizing SEMAP for a specific application domain. Our goal is to create a spatio-semantic model of agricultural environments and machinery in SEMAP for spatial analysis and rule-based reasoning to derive more information about ongoing agricultural processes that involve multiple machines.

First, we present the description of the semantic model used to represent agricultural concepts, such as fields, farms and tractors in SEMAP's knowledge base. After that we discuss how spatial data is added to this model and how to continuously update the environment model by using telemetry data from actual agricultural machines. Finally, we make use of SEMAP's capabilities to ground spatial predicates to answer both spatial and semantic queries. We demonstrate how to analyze basic spatial predicates between agricultural machines and their environment and how rule-based reasoning is used to identify complex and domain-specific spatial relations. The demonstration scenario is the detection of the correct positions of multiple machines in the planned process, especially the correct positioning of a transport vehicle ready for overloading in a maize harvesting campaign.

4.1   The AgriCo Ontology

Our semantic model extends the logistics core ontology (LogiCo) by Daniele et al. [16]. This semantic model describes environments and resources in logistics. Since this domain is very similar to the general process of harvesting, we extended LogiCo with additional concepts needed to represent agricultural processes. We call this extended ontology AgriCo as depicted in Fig. 3.

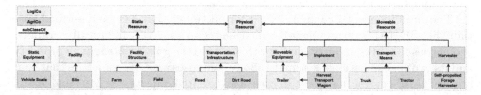

Fig. 3. Excerpts of the domain-specific model added to SEMAP. The LogiCo ontology (yellow) provides a model of static and movable resources, to which the AgriCo ontology (green) adds agricultural concepts like farms and tractors. (Color figure online)

All components of our model are based on Physical Resources in the real world, which can be Static or Movable Resources. Three sub-classes are used to describe static locations of interest: The Facility concept defines areas and structures designated for a specific purpose in the given domain and the Facility Structure defines aggregates of different facilities. In AgriCo, for example, Farm serves as an aggregate of agricultural facilities like Silos. Additionally, the Static Equipment concept describes utilities available at a facility, e.g., a Vehicle Scale for weighing transport vehicles. Another important sub-class of static resources are the different kinds of Transportation Infrastructure to represent connections between locations. Since this important concept was missing in the LogiCo ontology, we added this concept and suitable sub-classes like Roads and Dirt Roads.

For movable resources, LogiCo gives concepts for Transport Means, i.e., trucks, and Movable Equipment such as trailers. AgriCo defines Tractors as another kind of transportation and the Implement concept to account for various kinds of machinery that can be connected to a tractor for example plows, sowers or specialized Harvest Transport Wagons. The latter inherit properties from the trailer and implement concept, e.g., to denote the volumetric capacity vie the logico:hasCapacity attribute or describe the interfaces use to control the active pickup systems and scraper floor via agrico:hasISOBUSInterface. Furthermore, we added the Harvester to represent combine and forage harvesters, which are directly derived from the Movable Resource concept, as they can not be used for transporting goods in a supply chain.

4.2 Instantiating the Environment Model

The semantic model presented so far provides the conceptual basis from which instances of agricultural facilities and machinery can be created and described. To link them to a spatio-semantic data sets in SEMAP, we proceeded as follows:

First, we imported the AgriCo ontology into SEMAP's KB component. Next, we allowed that the hasObjectModel property can map from instances of LogiCo's Physical Resource to SEMAP's ObjectModels. This way, the domain-specific concepts and instances thereof can have a spatial representation in SEMAP. Finally, we instantiated the agricultural concepts and their spatio-semantic representation with an appropriate data set.

To setup static resources in our environment model, we used a set of polygonal boundaries to represent farms and fields and other facilities. Figure 4(a) shows an excerpt of the environment. It consists of the farm's grounds (blue), three silos (orange) and a vehicle scale (violet), as well as two fields (green). The data was modeled in Google Earth and automatically read into SEMAP's KB and DB components using a KML file importer. In Fig. 4(b), the underlying semantic representation is depicted with three instances of AgriCo concepts related to their object representation using the hasObjectModel relation. Here farm1 connects to farm1_obj. The polygonal boundary farm1_boundary is connected via the hasConvexHull2D property, which is a sub-property of hasAbstraction.

To add movable resources to the static environment, we created three dimensional and articulated object models of a tractor-trailer combination and a forage harvester as displayed in Fig. 6(b). These objects are modeled in the Unified Robot Description Format, since SEMAP supports this format natively. The underlying semantic representation is a straight forward extension to the example in Fig. 4(b), yet more complex due to the individual links and joints.

To introduce dynamics to our spatio-semantic model of farms and fields, we used telemetry data recorded on real agricultural machines to continuously update the position and articulation of the machines within it. We replayed the machine's GPS signals and joint states in the Robot Operating System (ROS) and connected a bridge node to SEMAP, such that the environment model was updated accordingly.

(a) The spatial data used to represent a farm (incl. silos) and two fields.

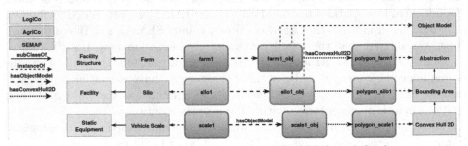

(b) The semantic representation within SEMAP's knowledge base.

Fig. 4. To represent a farm's facilities in SEMAP, we used the 2D polygonal boundaries, shown in (a), stored in the DB component. These spatial model are connected to instances of the domain-specific concepts of AgriCo via SEMAP's `ObjectModel` concept, as illustrated in (b).

5 Application Example

By moving the agricultural machines through the static environment in our experimental setup, the spatial relations between environment and machines and the machines themselves are changed continuously. SEMAP's spatial and semantic reasoning capabilities can be used to detect these spatial relations, which gives insight into the agricultural process underlying the machine activities.

For example, to detect where a movable resource is located topologically, we check whether its 2D position is spatially in a facility's boundary. The derived spatial predicate semap:isIn2D is used to infer that the topological relation logico:isAt holds, too. The reasoning takes place in two steps: First, we make use of SEMAP's qualification capabilities to ground spatial relations between agricultural machines and the environment or between pairs of agricultural machines. To perform such a quantitative spatial analysis, a suitable query is posed to SEMAP's DB backend. Figure 5(a) gives an example how to query for object pairs for whose 2D convex hulls a containment relation holds. The derived results are then inserted into SEMAP's knowledge base as qualitative semantic knowledge about the spatial relations. In case of our example, the objects pairs found by the query are inserted as facts over the isIn2D relation.

Second, we use the derived knowledge in order to reason about more complex spatial relations or to derive domain-specific information. An example for such rule-based inference is given in Fig. 5(b). This rule identifies the topological relation of a movable resources being at a facility, by using the 2D spatial containment relation for grounding the isAt predicate.

```
rosservice call /containment_query
"reference_object_types: ['Facility'] reference_object_geometry_type: 'ConvexHull2D'
target_object_types: ['MovableResource'] target_object_geometry_type: 'ConvexHull2D'
fully_within: false insert_kb: true"
```

(a) SEMAP query to extract containment relations.

```
?machine rdf:type logico:MovableResource
?machine semap:hasObjectModel ?machine_obj
?machine_obj semap:hasPosition2D ?machine_abstr_pos2D
?facility rdf:type logico:Facility
?facility semap:hasObjectModel ?facility_obj
?facility_obj semap:hasConvexHull2D ?facility_abstr_ch2D
?machine_abstr_pos2D semap:isIn2D ?facility_abstr_ch2D
⟹
?machine logico:isAt ?facility
```

(b) Rule to ground topological relations based on spatial relations.

Fig. 5. To geometrically ground spatial containment relations, we used the query shown in (a). The query results where extracted into SEMAP's KB as facts over the isIn2D relation and then used the rule (b) to derive that the topological relation isAt holds between machines and facilities.

While this seems a simple transition, it is important to note that this rule infers from a *spatial* predicate to a *topological* relation and that based on a grounding in the quantitative *geometric* data. Furthermore, the rule is generic for all instances of `Movable Resource` at any instance of `Facility` and its sub-concepts, which makes it applicable in a wide range of applications. The underlying spatial querying is also done automatically in SEMAP's multi-modal query interfaces, such that further queries to the environment model can be posed using the high-level relation `isAt`, without having to deal with the data transfer from DB to KB explicitly. This is convenient during application development.

(a) Overloading in reality.   (b) Overloading in RViz.

```
?sfh   rdf:type  agrico:Harvester
?sfh   semap:hasObjectModel  ?sfh_obj
?sfh_obj  semap:hasLeftOfProjection2D  ?sfh_proj_l2D
?tv   rdf:type  agrico:TransportVehicle
?tv   semap:hasObjectModel  ?tv_obj
?tv   semap:hasConvexHull2D  ?tv_abstr_ch2D
?tv_abstr_ch2D  semap:isIn2D  ?sfh_proj_l2D
⟹
?tv   agrico:positionedForOverloading  ?sfh
```

(c) The rule for grounding the `positionedForOverloading` relation in SEMAP.

Fig. 6. We used telemetry data from an actual overloading procedure (a), to move and articulate the machines in ROS and visualize them in RViz (b). We also synchronized the telemetry with our SEMAP model and used the rule (c) to identify the correct spatial positioning of two machines for overloading harvested goods from a forage harvester onto a transport vehicle.

Figure 6 exemplifies how to combine several basic spatial relations with domain-dependent knowledge to construct complex domain-specific relations.

For example, we used SEMAP to detect that a transport vehicle (TV) is correctly positioned for an overloading procedure, due to the directional relations of the self-propelled forage harvester (SFH). Figure 6(a) depicts such a situation in real life, whereas (b) shows visualization of a similar scene represented in SEMAP. It shows the object models subject of the rule shown in (c). To identify that the transport vehicle is properly positioned for overloading, the rule checks the trailer's 2D convex hull for containment in the harvester's `left-of` projection, to verify that the transport vehicle is left-of the harvester. If so, the relation `positionedForOverloading` is inferred to hold between the transport vehicle and the harvester. This is valuable information about the underlying agricultural process, which was previously covert in the telemetry data of both machines, but due to SEMAP's spatio-semantic processing is now explicitly available within SEMAP's KB, where it can be used for further processing.

6 Conclusion and Future Work

In this paper we used the SEMAP framework for combined spatial and semantic reasoning about machine-environment and machine-machine relations in an agricultural domain. To create a semantic model of agricultural environments and machines, we extended an ontological model from the logistics domain resulting in the agricultural core ontology AgriCo. Based on this semantic model, we instantiated a data set that combined factual knowledge with spatial data in our framework. Using recorded telemetry data, we moved and articulated several agricultural machines to replay a forage maize harvesting campaign. We used SEMAP's spatial operators for quantitative spatial analysis to classify containment relations between fields and machines. Using rule-based reasoning over the identified relations, we were able to detect process states relevant to analyze the harvesting process, namely that a transport vehicle is ready for overloading due to its position relative to the harvester.

Our approach demonstrated that the use of semantic mapping technology in agriculture is beneficial, as we were able to extract valuable information about the agricultural process out of the geo-referenced stream of telemetry data. The derived knowledge about machine-machine and machine-environment relations is validated in the geometric state of the environment and also available as machine-readable facts that adhere to a formal ontological model, which opens up possibilities for the further development of decision support systems.

To further improve SEMAP's spatio-semantic querying, temporal information must be included, too. Currently, the data model is updated continuously to represent the environment's current state, but provides neither a history of past states, nor methods to query about temporal change. This denies the possibility to detect events by querying the temporal sequence of certain relations and states. Adding a temporal information layer to SEMAP will be a necessary next step to realize temporal analysis. For this, stream reasoning approaches like the Continuous SPARQL framework (CSPARQL) [17] could be used.

Acknowledgment. Work by Deeken is supported by the German Federal Ministry of Education and Research in the SOFiA project (Grant No. 01FJ15028). The DFKI Osnabrück branch is supported by the state of Niedersachsen (VW-Vorab). The support is gratefully acknowledged.

References

1. Deeken, H., Wiemann, T., Lingemann, K., Hertzberg, J.: SEMAP-a semantic environment mapping framework. In: 2015 European Conference on Mobile Robots (ECMR), pp. 1–6. IEEE (2015)
2. Steinberger, G., Rothmund, M., Auernhammer, H.: Mobile farm equipment as a data source in an agricultural service architecture. Comput. Electron. Agric. **65**(2), 238–246 (2009)
3. Pfeiffer, D., Blank, S.: Real-time operator performance analysis in agricultural equipment. In: 73rd International Conference on Agricultural Engineering (AgEng), pp. 6–7 (2015)
4. Steckel, T., Bernardi, A., Gu, Y., Windmann, S., Maier, A., Niggemann, O.: Anomaly detection and performance evaluation of mobile agricultural machines by analysis of big data. In: 73rd International Conference on Agricultural Engineering (AgEng), pp. 6–7 (2015)
5. Dury, J., Garcia, F., Reynaud, A., Bergez, J.E.: Cropping-plan decision-making on irrigated crop farms: a spatio-temporal analysis. Eur. J. Agron. **50**, 1–10 (2013)
6. Lauer, J., Richter, L., Ellersiek, T., Zipf, A.: TeleAgro+: analysis framework for agricultural telematics data. In: 7th ACM SIGSPATIAL International Workshop on Computational Transportation Science, IWCTS 2014, pp. 47–53. ACM (2014)
7. Sørensen, C.G., Nielsen, V.: Operational analyses and model comparison of machinery systems for reduced tillage. Biosyst. Eng. **92**(2), 143–155 (2005)
8. Amiama, C., Pereira, J.M., Castro, A., Bueno, J.: Modelling corn silage harvest logistics for a cost optimization approach. Comput. Electron. Agric. **118**, 56–65 (2015)
9. Kaloxylos, A., Groumas, A., Sarris, V., Katsikas, L., Magdalinos, P., Antoniou, E., Politopoulou, Z., Wolfert, S., Brewster, C., Eigenmann, R., et al.: A cloud-based farm management system: architecture and implementation. Comput. Electron. Agric. **100**, 168–179 (2014)
10. Mark, T.B., Whitacre, B., Griffin, T., et al.: Assessing the value of broadband connectivity for big data and telematics: technical efficiency. In: 2015 Annual Meeting, 31 January–3 February 2015, Atlanta, Georgia. Southern Agricultural Economics Association (2015)
11. Nüchter, A., Hertzberg, J.: Towards semantic maps for mobile robots. Rob. Auton. Syst. **56**, 915–926 (2008)
12. Kostavelis, I., Gasteratos, A.: Semantic mapping for mobile robotics tasks: a survey. Rob. Auton. Syst. **66**, 86–103 (2015)
13. Wolter, D., Wallgrün, J.O.: Qualitative spatial reasoning for applications: new challenges and the SparQ toolbox. IGI Global (2010)
14. Bechhofer, S.: Owl: web ontology language. In: Liu, L., Özsu, M.T. (eds.) Encyclopedia of Database Systems, pp. 2008–2009. Springer, Boston (2009). https://doi.org/10.1007/978-0-387-39940-9
15. Borrmann, A., Rank, E.: Topological operators in a 3D spatial query language for building information models. In. Proceedings of the 12th International Conference on Computing in Civil and Building Engineering (ICCCBE) (2008)
16. Daniele, L., Ferreira Pires, L.: An ontological approach to logistics. In: Enterprise Interoperability, Research and Applications in the Service-Oriented Ecosystem, IWEI 2013, ISTE Ltd., Wiley (2013)
17. Barbieri, D.F., Braga, D., Ceri, S., Della Valle, E., Grossniklaus, M.: C-SPARQL: SPARQL for continuous querying. In: Proceedings of the 18th International Conference on World Wide Web, pp. 1061–1062. ACM (2009)

Chromosome Mutation vs. Gene Mutation in Evolutive Approaches for Solving the Resource-Constrained Project Scheduling Problem (RCPSP)

Daniel Morillo[1], Federico Barber[2(✉)], and Miguel A. Salido[2]

[1] Departamento de Ingeniería Civil e Industrial,
Pontificia Universidad Javeriana Cali, Cali, Colombia
daniel.morillo@javerianacali.edu.co
[2] Instituto de Automática e Informática Industrial,
Universitat Politècnica de València, València, Spain
{fbarber,msalido}@dsic.upv.es

Abstract. Resource-Constrained Project Scheduling Problems (RC-PSP) are some of the most important scheduling problems due to their applicability to real problems and their combinatorial complexity (NP-hard). In the literature, it has been shown that metaheuristic algorithms are the main option to deal with real-size problems. Among them, population-based algorithms, especially genetic algorithms, stand out for being able to achieve the best near-optimal solutions in reasonable computational time. One of the main components of metaheuristic algorithms is the solution representation (codification) since all search strategies are implemented based on it. However, most codings are affected by generating redundant solutions, which obstruct incorporating new information. In this paper, we focus on the study of the mutation operator (responsible for diversity in the population), in order to determine how to implement this operator to reduce the obtaining of redundant solutions. The computational assessment was done on the well-known PSPLIB library and shows that the proposed algorithm reaches competitive solutions compared with the best-proposed algorithms in the literature.

Keywords: RCPSP · Redundant solutions · Mutation operator

1 Introduction

The Resource-Constrained Project Scheduling Problem (RCPSP) is a widely studied problem due to its inherent complexity and that main scheduling problems can be modeled as a variation of RCPSP. There is a great amount of research, from both academic and enterprise areas, that addresses this problem through both exact and metaheuristic approaches. The RCPSP is an NP-hard problem [1] and only small-sized instances can be solved exactly in a reasonable

© Springer International Publishing AG, part of Springer Nature 2018
M. Mouhoub et al. (Eds.): IEA/AIE 2018, LNAI 10868, pp. 601–612, 2018.
https://doi.org/10.1007/978-3-319-92058-0_58

time. Metaheuristic methods appear to be the main option for the resolution of large-scale instances of RCPSP, obtaining near-optimal solutions in affordable computational effort.

Based on the results of the numerous metaheuristic algorithms assessed on the well-known benchmark for the RCPSP -the PSPLIB library [14]- it can be concluded that population algorithms (especially genetic algorithms) are considered to be the best option to solve the RCPSP. The main lists of results and comparisons can be found in [13,18]. These algorithms are mainly composed of three components: first, the coding which allows transforming a real solution into a representation that will be used by the search strategy; second, the decoder, it is a constructive procedure that allows obtaining a real solution using a coding; and third, the search strategy, it is a metaheuristic methodology as such, which establishes the movement rules for exploring the solution space.

Main encodings used by metaheuristic approaches are affected by generating redundant solutions. The latter are different solution representations that correspond to a single real solution. This issue is a serious disadvantage for a search procedure as the computational effort can be wasted in redundant solutions that do not contribute new information to the search. In this paper, we addressed this problem from the perspective of the operator responsible for introducing diversity to the population in a genetic algorithm: the mutation operator. Currently, the Boctor's insertion is the operator most used because it has experimentally achieved the best results. Although several mutation operators in a genetic algorithm for solving the RCPSP has been proposed, very few papers have been devoted to the study of how to implement it. For this reason, first, we compared the main implementations of this operator, called here as Chromosome Mutation and Gene Mutation. Then, we estimated how to implement this operator to reduce the generation of redundant solutions. Finally, we compared the proposed GA (with the newly proposed mutation) with the most successful algorithms reported in the literature. The purpose of this assessment is to show that the proposed mutation operator is highly competitive, and it can be adapted easily to other algorithms.

The remaining of this paper is organized as follows. Section 2 presents a detailed problem description. Section 3 provides an overview of methods proposed in the literature for solving the RCPSP. Section 4 introduces the genetic algorithm, definitions of the mutation and the new operator. Section 5 presents the computational results using the PSPLIB instances. Finally, Sect. 6 presents the conclusions of this research.

2   Problem Description

Formally, the RCPSP can be defined as follows: a project consists of a set of n non-preemptive activities $X = \{1, ..., i, ..., n\}$ and a set of m shared resources $R = \{1, ..., k, ..., m\}$, and there is a maximum amount b_k of each available resource. Each activity i has a duration d_i and requires a total of r_{ik} resource of each type k for its realization. Generally, activities 1 and n are dummy activities and their duration and consumption are equal to zero, representing the start and end of the project. The objective is to determine the start time of each activity X in order to minimize the completion time of the project (*makespan*), taking into account both the precedence and resource constraints.

An RCPSP example is shown in Fig. 1. It consists of a project with eleven activities. The first and last are dummy activities, which represent the start and the end of the whole project. There are three types of resources, all of them with a maximum amount available of four unit resources. The path depicted in bold is the critical path for the relaxed problem without resource constraints.

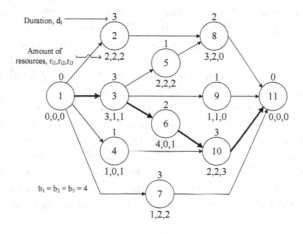

Fig. 1. An RCPSP example.

3 Literature Review

In the literature, the RCPSP has shown to be an NP-hard combinatorial problem [1], so it is not possible to find a global optimal solution for real-size problems in a reasonable time. Mainly two types of approaches have been studied and developed in the literature to solve the RCPSP: exact and approximate methods (the latter includes heuristics and metaheuristics).

3.1 Exact Methods

The branch and bound ($B\&B$) schemes are mainly those who stand out within exact methods. Basically, they are an exhaustive search yet efficient, that enumerates partial solutions of the solution space in branches of a tree graph, cutting those branches that do not contain the optimal solutions. There are several $B\&B$ algorithms to solve the RCPSP [10], they can find the optimal solution for small instances, but become impractical for large instances. Currently, metaheuristic methods produce the best results, finding good approximations to the optimal solution with relatively small computational effort.

3.2   Approximate Methods

Metaheuristic methodologies consist of iterative methods that incorporate an escape strategy from local optima. Most metaheuristic that tackle the RCPSP can generally be classified into four groups: schedule generation schemes and priority rules, x-pass methods, metaheuristic algorithms, and local improvement methodologies.

Schedule Generation Schemes and Priority Rules. The first group includes the heuristic methodologies that allow building a complete solution (a schedule). To achieve this goal, two elements are needed: a Sequence Generator Scheme (SGS) and a Priority rule (PR). There are two types of SGSs: the serial scheme and the parallel scheme. It has not been determined in the literature which scheme is better. The search space of the parallel scheme is smaller than the serial scheme, but it does not always contain the optimal solution, while the serial scheme always contains the optimum solution.

A PR is a mathematical expression that allows different feasible subsets of activities to be chosen during the execution of SGS in order to build a complete schedule. There are many priority rules in the literature and are classified in four sets: network-based rules, critical path-based rules, resource-based rules, and composite rules. There is no priority rule that can be considered to be the best in all cases. However, the latest starting time (LST) is a priority rule that is widely used and that provides successful results in many problems [11].

x-Pass Methods. The second group, includes priority-rules-based heuristics, also known as x-pass methods. Essentially, they use one or both SGS and select one or more PR to build a solution. They can be single pass or multi-pass, depending on how many schedules are generated. In single pass methods, an activity is selected at each stage according to a PR. In multi-pass methods, there are many possibilities for combining a SGS and priority rules, but each generated schedule is independent of the previous ones. Sampling methods can also be included in this group. They randomly select the activities for scheduling. One of the best sampling methods is the regret-based biased random sampling (RBBRS), which assigns a PR-based probability to each activity.

Metaheuristic Algorithms. The third group includes metaheuristic algorithms, which use both SGS and priority rules to build initial solutions. However, they have movement rules that allow them to explore, improve the initial solutions and escape of local optima. The metaheuristics are considered algorithms that achieve the best results to solve the RCPSP. Thus, there are many proposed algorithms in the literature, such as Genetic Algorithms (GA) [16,19], Tabu Search (TS) [12], Simulated Annealing (SA) [2,3], Scatter Search (SS) [15,18], Particle Swarm Optimization (PSO)[4,8], and Ant Colony Optimization (ACO) [5,21]. The population-based methods and the hybrid algorithms produce the best results to solve the RCPSP.

Local Improvement Methodologies. The fourth group includes local improvement methodologies, which are usually applied to the best solutions found by other algorithms in order to improve a given solution. Thus, these methods cannot build a solution by themselves. The most well-known method is the Forward-Backward Improvement (FBI) [20].

4   A Genetic Algorithm with a New Mutation Operator

In this section, we briefly described the problem of redundant solutions, then the proposed genetic algorithm (GA) with the new mutation operator to solve the RCPSP is presented. For this purpose, first, we depict the general elements of GA and then we focus on describing in detail the new mutation operator.

4.1   Redundant Solutions

An essential component of all metaheuristic algorithms is the coding (solution representation), which stands for how to code a complete solution (the start time of each activity). Each search strategy is implemented over this representation. In this way, the metaheuristic procedures apply their movement rules to make a search in the neighborhood given by such codification.

The activity list representation (AL) is one of the most used coding in the literature. It consists of an array of n elements that represents activities. The position of each activity in the array represents the priority of the activity to be scheduled by using an SGS. This list is feasible with respect to precedence constraints. Most procedures make a search by modifying the activity list. However, it can be easily deduced that different ALs can obtain equal solutions when they are decoded, which are called redundant solutions. For example, Fig. 2 shows two different ALs of feasible solutions for the instance presented in Fig. 1. The two Als were decoded by using the serial SGS. Although the two ALs are different (see the underlined activities in Fig. 2), the solutions obtained are exactly the same. It is worth noting that the differences between the ALs are not just a simple activity swap.

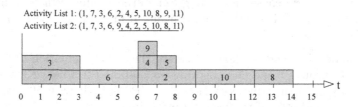

Fig. 2. Example of redundant solutions using the activity list representation.

Redundancy in solutions can occur in any search procedure when permutations are generated over the activity list. This phenomenon may cause that part of the computational effort is wasted on individuals that do not have new information. As the mutation operator is responsible for introducing new information, we focus the study on it.

4.2   General Operators

Solutions Encoding and Fitness Function. The activity list plus two genes are used as the codification of solutions for the RCPSP. The two additional genes are the SGS gene and the direction gene. The SGS gene represents the method to be used to decode a solution: its value will be 0 when the serial scheme is used or 1 when the parallel scheme is used. The direction gene can be forward or backward (with a value equal to 0 or 1, respectively). The fitness function is to minimize the *makspan*.

Initial Population. To generate the initial population, the Regret Based Biased Random Sampling (RBBRS) with the Latest Start Time (LST) as a priority rule is applied. The values of the SGS gene, direction gene and execute mode are randomly chosen.

Population Size. There is not a standard method to estimate the best population size in the RCPSP. Most authors carry out computational experiments to estimate this parameter. Based on our experiments, it was found that the population size should be related to the number of activities and to the number of available iterations. Let Pop be the population size, NoI be the number of iterations and NoG be the number of generations. Such parameters are defined in Expression 1.

$$Pop = \left(\frac{1}{n} * NoI\right) + 15 \quad \text{and} \quad NoG = \frac{NoI}{Pop} \tag{1}$$

Selection. Stochastic sampling with replacement is used, depending on the fitness value of the solutions. Therefore, every individual in the population has a probability of being chosen according to its fitness value. When an individual is chosen, a replica of that individual is included in the next selection.

Replacement. It refers to how to create the next population $P3$ from the parents population $P1$ and the offspring population $P2$. First, $P1$ and $P2$ are sorted according to their fitness value. Then, $P3$ is built with 50% of the best $P1$ individuals and 50% of the best $P2$ individuals.

Local Improvement. The well-known forward-backward improvement (FBI) was implemented in the proposed GA.

Crossover. A modified two-point crossover is used over the AL. Thus, two random integers q_1 and q_2 with $0 < q_1 < q_2 < n$ are generated. The first genes from 0 to q_1 are taken from parent 1, next genes from q_1 to q_2 must be searched from the beginning of the AL of parent 2, and then the first activities that are not repeated in the child are inherited. In the same way, the remaining ones (q_2 to n) are taken from parent 1. For SGS and direction genes, the gene values are inherited when they are the same in both parents. Otherwise, the gene values are randomly generated.

4.3 Mutation

To solve the RCPSP, the Boctor's insertion [2] is the most widespread operator in the literature, since this achieves the best results in the benchmark instances. It can be defined as follows: initially, an activity i is randomly selected in an AL $L = (a_1, ..., a_i, ..., a_n)$, then the $maxPred$ and $minSuc$ position (the maximum position of the last predecessor and the minimum position of the first successor, respectively) are calculated; finally, a random value $Pos \in [minSuc, maxPred]$ are randomly generated and the activity i is inserted in Pos position.

Here, we define two ways to implement the mutation operator: the Chromosome Mutation (CM) and the Gene Mutation (GM), which are described below.

Chromosome Mutation. In this mutation, the operator is implemented over a coded solution (a complete individual), i.e. over a complete chromosome (an AL). In this case, a mutation probability of 0.05 implies that on average only the five percent of individuals in the population suffered a mutation, which consists of the insertion of a single activity.

Gene Mutation. This mutation implements the operator on each activity, i.e. on each gene without differentiating individuals (solutions), therefore the operator runs through each gene generating a random number to determine whether it mutates or not. It is the standard mutation used in the literature. We can define this mutation as a Bernoulli experiment, where each mutation can be classified as success or failure. With this in view, assuming the usual mutation probability ($P_M = 0.05$) and that the mutations are independent events, the probability that a solution will be affected by the mutation (PS) and the number of average insertions per solution (N_I) can be estimated as follows (2):

$$P_S = 1 - (0.95^n) \quad \text{and} \quad N_I = n * P_M \tag{2}$$

P_S and N_I are increasing functions that depend on the number of activities. Specifically, P_S grows faster than N_I function. For instances with 45 activities the probability that a solution mutes goes up to 45% and from 100 activities this probability is almost 100%. For its part, N_I is a linear function, the more activities, the more mutations (insertions) are done.

In the literature, the mutation commonly used is the Gene Mutation. In contrast, we proposed to implement the Chromosome Mutation. The main advantage is that the mutation parameters (number of insertions and the probability that a solution mutes) can be precisely controlled, because in the Chromosome Mutation these parameters are independent of the number of activities. Based on the computational results (Sect. 5), we fixed the number of insertions as 3 and the probability mutation as 90%.

5   Computational Results

This section is split into two parts: the first one is dedicated to the comparison between the Chromosome Mutation and the Gene Mutation, and in the second one a comparison with the best metaheuristic algorithms reported in the literature. Both parts of this assessment were done by using the well-known PSPLIB library [14]. It consists of four instance sets ($j30$, $j60$, $j90$ and $j120$), with 30, 60, 90 and 120 activities, respectively. The first 3 sets have 480 instances, and the last set has 600 instances. For $j60$, $j90$ and $j120$ not all optimum values are known; so, the comparison was made regarding the critical path (LB0); while for the j30 instances, all optimum values are known, so the comparison was made regarding the optimum *makespan*. The experiments were performed on a personal computer with Intel(R) Core(TM) $i7$ CPU to 3.30 GHz.

5.1   Chromosome Mutation vs. Gene Mutation

To compare between the Chromosome Mutation (CM) and Gene Mutation (GM) and to establish the proper number of insertions and the value of mutation probability, first, we found an equivalence between these mutations assuming the usual GM probability (0.05) and then we compared the performance of the GM and CM by using the PSPLIB library. To carry out this mutation study, the local improvement FBI was not used to avoid biases in the results. Table 1 shows a resume of this equivalences, e.g. a GM over a 120 activities instance is equivalent to CM with a mutation probability of 0.998% and 6 insertions per mutation.

Table 1. Equivalences between Gene Mutation and Chromosome Mutation.

Gene Mutation with probability of 0.05.			
	n	Mutation probability	Number of insertions
Chromosome Mutation	$j30$	0.785	1.5
	$j60$	0.953	3
	$j120$	0.998	6

Figures 3, 4 and 5 show the surfaces of the average deviations with respect to the optimum *makespan* (set $j30$) or respect to the critical path (sets $j60$

and $j120$), depending on the number of insertions and the probability of CM, respectively. In general, it can be seen that the *makespan* and the number of insertions appear to be independent of the number of activities.

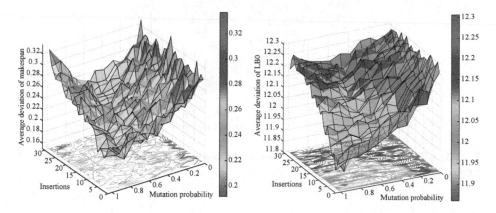

Fig. 3. Average deviations regarding optimum *makespan* based on the number of insertions and the CM probability for set $j30$.

Fig. 4. LB0-based average deviations based on the number of insertions and the CM probability for set $j60$.

Figure 3 is the most irregular figure, this is because it has the smallest amplitude in the deviations with respect to *makespan*, with a value of 0.16, since these instances have the least number of activities and the GA can found solutions close to the optimum, reaching it in some cases, shortening this amplitude. Figures 4 and 5 show a more defined behavior, with a higher amplitude (0.5 and 0.9, respectively). Despite this, the values of the parameters converge to a probability of 90% with 3 insertions per mutation. Based on the results, it can be concluded that the GM is not the best way to implement the mutation operator since the GM depends on the number of activities. On the other hand, we counted the average number of redundant solutions generated by the Gene Mutation and the Chromosome Mutation for set $j30$. In all iterations, the Chromosome Mutation generated approximately 20% less redundant solutions than the Gene Mutation.

There are two main reasons for which the results suggest that the probability of mutation per solution and the number of insertions are independent of the number of activities. The first is that the redundant solutions are not directly dependent on the number of activities in a project, so 3 insertions are enough to reduce the number of redundant solutions generated. The second is that a greater number of insertions could obstruct the performance of the other operators in their goal of converging (exploiting) the search space. For this same reason, a probability close to 90% is enough to introduce new information to the search.

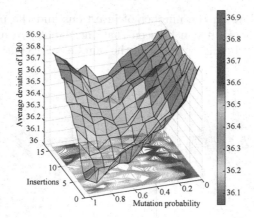

Fig. 5. LB0-based average deviations based on the number of insertions and the CM probability for set $j120$.

5.2 Comparative Assessment

Kolisch and Hartmann [13] present a detailed survey on the best metaheuristics for solving the RCPSP. They proposed to use iterations as the comparison criterion instead of execution time. Following the Kolisch and Hartmann's classification, Paraskevopoulos et al. [18] updated such comparisons by considering the newest algorithms. The top methodologies of this latest survey were compared with the proposed GA, we distinguish two variants of the proposed algorithm depending on a number of iterations counted by the FBI: first, the **GA-AMGS** considers that the FBI uses three iterations: the current, the forward and the

Table 2. Computational comparisons among the main competitive metaheuristics for solving the RCPSP on set $j30$ (left), set $j60$ (mid) and set $j120$ (right).

j30 set algorithm	%dev			j60 set algorithm	%dev			j120 set algorithm	%dev		
	1.000	5.000	50.000		1.000	5.000	50.000		1.000	5.000	50.000
SAILS [18]	0.03	0.01	0.00	SAILS [18]	11.05	10.72	10.54	ACOSS [5]	35.19	32.48	30.56
GA-AMES *	**0.06**	**0.01**	**0.00**	**GA-AMES ***	**11.11**	**10.78**	**10.56**	**GA-AMES ***	**32.98**	**32.01**	**30.65**
GA, TS-PR [12]	0.10	0.04	0.00	SS-PR [15]	11.12	10.74	10.57	SAILS [18]	33.32	32.12	30.78
SS-PR [15]	0.05	0.02	0.01	GAPS [16]	11.72	11.04	10.67	GA [7]	34.19	32.34	30.82
GAPS [16]	0.06	0.02	0.01	ACOSS [5]	11.72	10.98	10.67	GA-hybrid FBI [22]	34.07	32.54	31.24
GA-AMGS *	**0.13**	**0.05**	**0.01**	GA [7]	11.45	10.95	10.68	GAPS [16]	35.87	33.03	31.44
ACOSS [5]	0.14	0.06	0.01	SS-FBI [6]	11.73	11.10	10.71	SS-PR [15]	34.51	32.61	31.37
SS-FBI [6]	0.27	0.11	0.01	GA-hybrid FBI [22]	11.56	11.10	10.73	SS-FBI [6]	35.22	33.10	31.57
GA [7]	0.15	0.04	0.02	GA, TS-PR [12]	11.71	11.17	10.74	**GA-AMGS ***	**34.09**	**32.82**	**31.86**
GA-hybrid FBI [22]	0.27	0.06	0.02	**GA-AMGS ***	**11.49**	**11.04**	**10.78**	GA, TS-PR [12]	34.74	33.36	32.06
TS [17]	0.46	0.16	0.05	GA [9]	12.21	11.70	11.21	GA [9]	37.19	35.39	33.21
GA [9]	0.38	0.22	0.08	ANGEL [21]	11.94	11.27	-	ANGEL [21]	36.39	34.49	-

backward schedule. The second, **GA-AMES** considers that the FBI uses a single iteration since a decoding function is not needed. Table 2 shows a summary of the results.

This results indicate that the proposed algorithm leads to highly competitive solutions between state-of-the-art algorithms for solving the RCPSP. As expected, the **GA-AMES** leads to better solutions than the **GA-AMGS**; and, despite being a basic genetic algorithm, it also outperformed other population algorithms, indicating the significant effect of the new mutation operator.

6   Conclusions

This paper proposes an efficient genetic algorithm with a new mutation operator for solving the RCPSP. Its codification is based on the activity list with both types of SGS and also both schemes direction. The main contribution is to compare the different ways of implementing the mutation and to determine which is the most appropriate to provide new information to the search and decrease the generation of redundant solutions.

The experimental analyses carried out to assess the mutation impact on the population diversity showed that most of the used mutation operators can lead to redundant solutions without introducing diversity in the population. To address this issue, we proposed a multiple insertion mutation over the chromosomes. The proposed GA algorithm has been evaluated on the well know PSPLIB instances [14]. These computational experiments show that the proposed GA achieves high-quality solutions regarding the best state-of-the-art algorithms for solving the RCPSP. Also, the high impact of the number of mutation operator insertions on the *makespan* is demonstrated. Besides, as a general contribution from these results, this operator can be easily incorporated or adapted to other metaheuristics approaches for generating perturbation in the solution population and improving their performance.

Acknowledgements. This paper has been partially supported by the Spanish research projects TIN-2013-46511-C2-1-P and TIN2016-80856-R.

References

1. Blazewicz, J., Lenstra, J., Kan, A.: Scheduling subject to resource constraints: classification and complexity. Discrete Appl. Math. **5**(1), 11–24 (1983)
2. Boctor, F.F.: Resource-constrained project scheduling by simulated annealing. Int. J. Prod. Res. **34**(8), 2335–2351 (1996)
3. Bouleimen, K., Lecocq, H.: A new efficient simulated annealing algorithm for the resource-constrained project scheduling problem and its multiple mode version. Eur. J. Oper. Res. **149**(2), 268–281 (2003)
4. Chen, R.M.: Particle swarm optimization with justification and designed mechanisms for resource-constrained project scheduling problem. Expert Syst. Appl. **38**(6), 7102–7111 (2011)

5. Chen, W., Shi, Y.J., Teng, H.F., Lan, X.P., Hu, L.C.: An efficient hybrid algorithm for resource-constrained project scheduling. Inf. Sci. **180**(6), 1031–1039 (2010)
6. Debels, D., De Reyck, B., Leus, R., Vanhoucke, M.: A hybrid scatter search/electromagnetism meta-heuristic for project scheduling. Eur. J. Oper. Res. **169**(2), 638–653 (2006)
7. Debels, D., Vanhoucke, M.: A decomposition-based genetic algorithm for the resource-constrained project-scheduling problem. Oper. Res. **55**(3), 457–469 (2007)
8. Fahmy, A., Hassan, T.M., Bassioni, H.: Improving RCPSP solutions quality with stacking justification - application with particle swarm optimization. Expert Syst. Appl. **41**(13), 5870–5881 (2014)
9. Hartmann, S.: A self-adapting genetic algorithm for project scheduling under resource constraints. Naval Res. Logist. **49**(5), 433–448 (2002)
10. Herroelen, W., De Reyck, B., Demeulemeester, E.: Resource-constrained project scheduling: a survey of recent developments. Comput. Oper. Res. **25**(4), 279–302 (1998)
11. Klein, R.: Bidirectional planning: improving priority rule-based heuristics for scheduling resource-constrained projects. Eur. J. Oper. Res. **127**(3), 619–638 (2000)
12. Kochetov, Y.A., Stolyar, A.A.: Evolutionary local search with variable neighborhood for the resource constrained project scheduling problem. In: Workshop on Computer Science and Information Technologies CSIT 2003, Ufa, Russia (2003)
13. Kolisch, R., Hartmann, S.: Experimental investigation of heuristics for resource-constrained project scheduling: an update. Eur. J. Oper. Res. **174**(1), 23–37 (2006)
14. Kolisch, R., Sprecher, A.: PSPLIB - a project scheduling library. Eur. J. Oper. Res. **96**, 205–216 (1996)
15. Mahdi Mobini, M.D., Rabbani, M., Amalnik, M.S., Razmi, J., Rahimi-Vahed, A.R.: Using an enhanced scatter search algorithm for a resource-constrained project scheduling problem. Soft. Comput. **13**(6), 597–610 (2008)
16. Mendes, J., Gonçalves, J., Resende, M.: A random key based genetic algorithm for the resource constrained project scheduling problem. Comput. Oper. Res. **36**(1), 92–109 (2009)
17. Nonobe, K., Baraki, T.: Formulation and Tabu search algorithm for the resource constrained project scheduling problem. In: Essays and Surveys in Metaheuristics, pp. 557–588. Springer, Boston (2002). https://doi.org/10.1007/978-1-4615-1507-4_25
18. Paraskevopoulos, D., Tarantilis, C., Ioannou, G.: Solving project scheduling problems with resource constraints via an event list-based evolutionary algorithm. Expert Syst. Appl. **39**(4), 3983–3994 (2012)
19. Peteghem, V.V., Vanhoucke, M.: A genetic algorithm for the preemptive and non-preemptive multi-mode resource-constrained project scheduling problem. Eur. J. Oper. Res. **201**(2), 409–418 (2010)
20. Tormos, P., Lova, A.: A competitive heuristic solution technique for resource-constrained project scheduling. Ann. Oper. Res. **102**(1–4), 65–81 (2001)
21. Tseng, L.Y., Chen, S.C.: A hybrid metaheuristic for the resource-constrained project scheduling problem. Eur. J. Oper. Res. **175**(2), 707–721 (2006)
22. Valls, V., Ballestin, F., Quintanilla, S.: A hybrid genetic algorithm for the resource-constrained project scheduling problem. Eur. J. Oper. Res. **185**(2), 495–508 (2008)

Energy-Conserving Risk-Aware Data Collection Using Ensemble Navigation Network

Zhi Xing[(✉)] and Jae C. Oh

EECS, College of Engineering and Computer Science, Syracuse University,
Syracuse, NY 13244, USA
{zxing01,jcoh}@syr.edu

Abstract. The *Data-collection Problem* (DCP) models robotic agents collecting digital data in a risky environment under energy constraints. A good solution for DCP needs a balance between safety and energy use. We develop an *Ensemble Navigation Network* (ENN) that consists of a Convolutional Neural Network and several heuristics to learn the priorities. Experiments show ENN has superior performance than heuristic algorithms in all environmental settings. In particular, ENN has better performance in environments with higher risks and when robots have low energy capacity.

Keywords: Deep reinforcement learning · Ensemble methods

1 Introduction

With the advances in areas such as computer vision, machine perception, and control theory, robot's capabilities and potentials have been greatly increased. As a result, humans are gradually replaced by robots in complex tasks as driving, delivery, and surveillance. For example, scientists may need to collect data in a rainforest that could be dangerous for human. They can set the locations of interests and let cheap Unmanned Aerial Vehicles (UAVs) collect data autonomously. Threats in the environment, such as animals and bad weather, can destroy the UAVs and must be addressed by UAVs' state-of-art navigation algorithms. As a UAV reaches a location of interest, it collects and sends data to the base station via satellite. Occasionally, UAVs may be destroyed, but the algorithms anticipate such situations. Scenarios like this motivate the proposed *Data-collection Problem* (DCP).

The Data-collecting Robot Problem (DRP) [15] assumes a uniform risk distribution and unlimited energy. DRP is formulated as a planning problem on a complete graph; the objective is to decide which locations of interests should be visited, in what order, and by how many robots. Heuristic algorithms that consist of clustering and tour-building steps are proposed. However, in a real world, the distribution of risk is not uniform, and the robot may run out of energy. In

© Springer International Publishing AG, part of Springer Nature 2018
M. Mouhoub et al. (Eds.): IEA/AIE 2018, LNAI 10868, pp. 613–625, 2018.
https://doi.org/10.1007/978-3-319-92058-0_59

such cases, a more elaborate formulation is necessary. Inspired by [7,8], where graph-based algorithms are employed to solve a Markov Decision Problem, we formulate DCP in a grid world, which enables us to model non-uniform risks. Also, our formulation considers energy consumption of robots. Therefore, the solution should consider recharging at the base.

The energy constraint greatly increases the problem complexity, especially in an environment of non-uniform risk. When there is a shorter path to higher risk, decisions need to be made based on various factors, such as the risk, energy level, distance to the recharging station, and locations of interests. A good solution will find a good balance between *safety and energy* (S&E). Due to this difficulty, the objective in this formulation is to collect as much data as possible using all UAVs, i.e., the solution does not consider whether a location should be visited or how many robots should be used, unlike the previous work [5,15].

This paper proposes the *Data-collection Problem* (DCP) that models autonomous data-collection in risky environment under energy constraints. Good solution of DCP needs to find good balance between *safety and energy* (S&E). We design four navigation algorithms with different priorities between S&E and develop the *Ensemble Navigation Network* (ENN) that learns new heuristic from the four navigation algorithms and other heuristic information. ENN is able to find better balance between S&E from the given heuristics.

2   Related Work

Markov Decision Processes (MDPs) with mean payoff objectives (total reward collected) have been heavily studied since the 60s. See [12] for a comprehensive survey. Moreover, MDPs with energy constraints are studied quite extensively [6]. However, the combination of the two has just started to attract attention. The most recent and related work is [2], where the Energy Markov Decision Process (EMDP) is proposed. Given an EMDP and its initial state, the task is to compute a safe strategy that maximizes the expected mean payoff, where safe means the energy never drops to 0. The focus of their work is to construct approximations of optimal strategies, using linear programming methods, with different assumptions about the problem structure. In contrast, our work focuses on providing a practical end-to-end solution using deep reinforcement learning.

Lane and Kaelbling model a robotic package delivery problem as MDP [7,8]. To deal with the intractable number of states, they create action *macros* that treats an entire policy of the MDP as an action, and then the original problem is reduced to subproblems with much smaller state spaces and a problem of selecting the order in which the packages should be delivered. The grid-based MDP is partially transformed to a graph-based optimization problem, and off-the-shelf combinatorial optimization routines for the Traveling Salesman Problem is employed to achieve an exponential speedup. Their work considers the stochasticity of robot movement, but it does not have any energy constraint.

One may also argue that the problem is studied by the Vehicle Routing Problem (VRP) community, such as the Green VRP [4], by modeling the risk

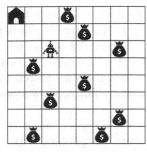

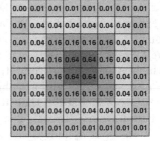

(a) Base, agent and items.   (b) Risk distribution.

Fig. 1. An example of DCP environment. (a) shows the locations of the base, agent and items. The robot represents the agent. The money bags represent items. The house represents the base. (b) shows a color-coded risk distribution, where the numbers are the risk values.

as a non-linear cost function. However, the differences between our work and the VRPs include: (1) our optimization goal is to maximize the reward collected instead of minimizing the distance traveled and using the cost as a constraint, because in our case the cost of an agent is relatively small, and (2) our formulation makes it much easier and intuitive to model non-uniform risk distribution.

Deep Reinforcement Learning (DRL) achieves impressive performance on various tasks [10,11,13,14]. As shown later in this paper, the number of states in DCP can easily become intractable, and the reward distribution may contain higher-level features such as clusters. Due to these factors, we leverage DRL to find a good balance between S&E in DCP.

3   Problem and Approach

Imagine the scientists mentioned in Sect. 1 can obtain satellite images of an area of interest. From these images, they can select a set of locations to probe in detail. Note that some locations may be more important than others. The area of interest may not change much over time, but the locations of interests within the area may frequently change with the needs of the scientific research. Based on these assumptions, we formulate DCP as follows.

DCP is a Markov Decision Problem (MDP) on a $N \times N$ grid of cells. Each cell (x, y) has a risk value $\rho_{x,y}$, which is visible to the agent and indicates the probability of the agent being disabled when visiting the cell. In a real-world scenario where the risk values are unknown, we can use low-cost UAVs to estimate the distribution using Monte Carlo sampling. Let Cell $(0, 0)$ be the base, whose risk $\rho_{0,0} = 0$. Each item, which models a location of interest, or the agent, which models a UAV, occupy a cell. Item locations are randomly generated, and therefore they may form clusters that can be considered as features by the convolutional neural network (Fig. 1). The figure does not show the current energy level and a maximum energy level of the agent.

The Markov Decision Process of DCP proceeds in discrete time. The initial state s_0 is randomly generated. At each step t, the agent receives the state of the environment s_t, and selects an action a_t from the action set $\mathcal{A} = \{stay,$ $up,\ down,\ left,\ right,\ up\text{-}left,\ up\text{-}right,\ down\text{-}left,\ down\text{-}right\}$ according to some policy π, which is a mapping from states s_t to actions a_t. In return, the agent receives the next state s_{t+1} and a scalar reward r_t. The process repeats until the agent reaches a terminal state, then it restarts.

The transition from s_t to s_{t+1} is as follows. The agent moves to an adjacent cell according to a_t. If a_t moves the agent out of a boundary, the agent stays along the axis perpendicular to that boundary. The agent then collects an item if any, after which the agent may be disabled with a probability equals to the risk of the cell. In the end, the energy level of the agent is reduced by one, regardless of the action taken, unless it is in the base, in which case the energy level is restored to the maximum. If the energy level drops to 0, the agent is disabled.

Items contain non-uniform positive rewards known the agent. These rewards reflect the scientists' *estimated values of data* at the locations of interests. The agent obtains a reward immediately after it collects an item, which is returned to the agent as r_t. There is *no* negative reward when the agent is disabled. The terminal state is reached when the agent is disabled, or all the items are collected. The objective is to maximize the total reward collected in an *episode* at the end.

Reinforcement Learning (RL) is a common method for MDPs. In RL, the discounted accumulated return, *return* for short, is defined as $R_t = \sum_{k=0}^{\infty} \gamma^k r_{t+k}$, where the discounting factor $\gamma \in [0,1]$ signifies the importance of immediate rewards. The goal of learning agent is to maximize the expected return for every state s_t, in other words, to find the optimal policy π^*. The state-action value function $Q^\pi(s,a) = \mathbb{E}[R_t | s_t = s, a]$ is the expected return for selecting action a in state s and following policy π afterwards. The optimal value function $Q^*(s,a) = \max_\pi Q^\pi(s,a)$ is the maximum value achievable for state s and action a by any policy. Similarly, the state-only value function $V^\pi(s) = \mathbb{E}[R_t | s_t = s]$ gives the expected return of state s for following policy π. The advantage function $A^\pi(s,a) = Q^\pi(s,a) - V^\pi(s)$ indicates the advantage of a in s.

Deep Reinforcement Learning uses deep neural networks to approximate either $Q^*(s,a)$ or π^*. The Asynchronous Advantage Actor-Critic (A3C) algorithm [9] uses a CNN to learn both the policy $\pi(a|s;\theta)$ and the $V(s;\theta_v)$ function. This is an actor-critic method, where the policy $\pi(a|s;\theta)$ is the actor and an estimate of $A^\pi(s,a)$ using $V(s;\theta_v)$ is the critic. The CNN used takes pixel images from console and game scores as input; it has better performance than the Deep Q Network in [10,11].

4   Algorithm

We choose a planning algorithm from previous work [15] for navigation without energy constraint, which is then used in designing four navigation algorithms that have different priorities between S&E during navigation with energy constraint. With these four navigation algorithms as heuristic inputs, a deep neural network is eventually developed for finding the balance between S&E in DCP.

Algorithm 1. Loss-Per-Gain (LPG)

Input: Current state s, action set $\mathcal{A}$, the safest paths $\mathcal{P}._,.$ calculated by Dijkstra's
Algorithm, see Section 4.1 for more details
Output: Agent's action a and the target item i^*
  Initialize minimum loss-per-gain $v^* \leftarrow +\infty$
  Get agent location (x_z, y_z) from s
  for all item i in current state s **do**
    Initialize loss-per-gain $v \leftarrow +\infty$
    Get location (x_i, y_i) and reward r_i of item i from s
    for all item $j \neq i$ in current state s **do**
      Get location (x_j, y_j) and reward r_j of item j from s
      Compute the difference in success probabilities
$$\Delta = \mathcal{P}_{x_z,y_z}(x_j, y_j) - \mathcal{P}_{x_z,y_z}(x_i, y_i) \times \mathcal{P}_{x_i,y_i}(x_j, y_j)$$
$$v \leftarrow v + \Delta \times r_j$$
    $v \leftarrow v/(\mathcal{P}_{x_z,y_z}(x_i, y_i) \times r_i)$
    if $v < v^*$ **then**
      $v^* \leftarrow v, i^* \leftarrow i$
  Select the $a \in \mathcal{A}$ that follows the safest path from (x_z, y_z) to (x_{i^*}, y_{i^*}) according to
  $\mathcal{P}_{x_z,y_z}$
  return a, i^*

4.1 Maximizing Reward Without Energy Constraint

As a first step, we ignore the energy constraint and focus on finding the path
that maximizes the expected reward from collecting items. This reduces the
problem to the one similar to the one in [15], where six heuristics were proposed
to maximize expected reward from a graph-based world. Out of the six, five
heuristics are shown to solve the DCP without incurring high time complexity.

To adopt the heuristics, Dijkstra's algorithm [3] is used to compute the *safest
path* from any cell to any other cell on the grid. Given agent's and items' locations, a complete undirected graph can be built from the grid, where a node
represents a *key cell* in the grid that contains the agent or an item, and the edge
weight represents *success probability* of traveling from one key cell to another
alone the safest path. Details are omitted due to space limitation.

The tour-building heuristics from [15] can then be applied to find paths
that have a high expected reward. Our experiments show Loss-Per-Gain (LPG)
algorithm gives the highest reward on average. Algorithm 1 presents the LPG
algorithm that is adapted to DCP. In the algorithm, $\mathcal{P}_{x,y}(x', y')$ stands for the
success probability of following the safest path from (x, y) to (x', y').

4.2 Navigation Under Energy Constraint

With the energy constraint, a *navigation algorithm* needs to consider both collecting items and returning for recharge. There are two extreme routes to take
for navigating to the base. One is to follow the shortest path by going directly
towards the base, which uses the least amount of energy but can be risky. The

---

Algorithm 2. Closest-First (CF)

Input: Current state s, action set $\mathcal{A}$
Output: Agent's action a and the target item i^*
  Initialize minimum distance $d^* \leftarrow +\infty$
  Get agent location (x_z, y_z) from s
  for all item i in current state s **do**
    Get location (x_i, y_i) of item i from s
    $d \leftarrow \mathbf{max}(|x_z - x_i|, |y_z - y_i|)$
    if $d < d^*$ **then**
      $d^* \leftarrow d,\ i^* \leftarrow i$
  Select the $a \in \mathcal{A}$ that minimizes $\mathbf{max}(|x_z - x_{i^*}|, |y_z - y_{i^*}|)$
  return a, i^*

Algorithm 3. Structure of the navigation algorithms discussed in Sect. 4.2

Input: Current state s, planning algorithms $\mathcal{N}_0$ for navigation to base, $\mathcal{N}_1$ for navigation to items // assume $\mathcal{N}_0$ and $\mathcal{N}_1$ take a location (x, y) as input and return an action that follows the safest path from (x, y) to a target, the target (an item or the base), and the length of the safest path
Output: Agent's action a
  Get energy level e of agent from s
  Get location (x_z, y_z) of agent from s
  $a_0, {\scriptstyle -}, {\scriptstyle -} \leftarrow \mathcal{N}_0(x_z, y_z)$ // "_" means the value is not useful
  $a_1, i^*, l_1 \leftarrow \mathcal{N}_1(x_z, y_z)$
  Get location (x_{i^*}, y_{i^*}) of item i^* from s
  ${\scriptstyle -}, {\scriptstyle -}, l'_0 \leftarrow \mathcal{N}_0(x_{i^*}, y_{i^*})$
  if $e < l_1 + l'_0$ **then**
    $a \leftarrow a_0$ // Go to the base
  else
    $a \leftarrow a_1$ // Go to the item
  return a

---

other is to follow the safest path calculated by Dijkstra's algorithm, which is the least risky but may be longer and therefore cost more energy.

Similarly, there are two extremes for collecting items, but intractable to compute; we use the LPG algorithm to approximate the safety-conservative extreme and the Closest-First (CF) algorithm (Algorithm 2), which always navigates towards the item that has the minimal Manhattan distance regardless of the reward and risk, as an approximate to the energy-conservative extreme.

From the above methods, or *planning algorithms* hereafter, four navigation algorithms are designed:

- **Safe-Reward** follows LPG path to items and shortest path to the base.
- **Safe-Recharge** follows CF path to items and safest path to the base.
- **Safe-Both** follows LPG path to items and safest path to the base.
- **Safe-Neither** follows CF path to items and shortest path to the base.

Algorithm 3 shows the navigation algorithms. With pre-calculated safest path information, their time complexities are of the same order as the given planning algorithms. This makes them ideal for the deep learning method discussed in the following. More effective algorithms can be crafted by considering every step during the navigation. However, that would increase the time complexity by a factor linear to the number of steps from the current location to the target.

4.3 Finding the Balance

Finding a good balance between S&E *manually* requires creating elaborate rules, which easily becomes intractable for large and diverse environments. Therefore, we proposed an *Ensemble Navigation Network* (ENN) to learn good balance using a linear combination of the above navigation algorithms and the information discussed in the following. Figure 2 shows the structure of ENN.

Structure of ENN. The ENN is a Convolutional Neural Network (CNN) with a number of heuristics. The heuristics, H_i for $i \in [1, n]$ and $n \in \mathbb{N}^+$, take state s as input and generate an action vector $H_i(s)$ which gives each action $a \in \mathcal{A}$ a *score*. The CNN takes state s as input and generates one weight $w_i(s; \theta)$ vector for each action vector of the heuristics, a bias $b(s; \theta)$ and a state value estimation $V(s; \theta_v)$, where θ and θ_v represent the network parameters. The final policy $\pi(s; \theta)$ is a softmax function σ of a linear combination of all the outputs:

$$\pi(s; \theta) = \sigma(\sum_{i=1}^{n} w_i(s; \theta) \times H_i(s) + b(s; \theta))$$

where $\times$ denotes *element-wise* multiplication, or the *Hadamard product*.

The CNN in ENN. In ENN, two $N \times N$ matrices M^{item} and M^{agent} represent a state s. M^{item} encodes the locations of items, the value at x-th row y-th column, $m_{x,y}^{\text{item}}$, is the reward of the item at (x, y). If there is no item, $m_{x,y}^{\text{item}} = 0$. M^{agent} encodes the agent's location and energy level. $m_{x,y}^{\text{agent}} = e$ where e is the energy level when agent is at coordinate (x, y), $m_{x,y}^{\text{agent}} = 0$ otherwise.

The CNN takes M^{item} and M^{agent} as input. Following the input layer is a number of convolutional layers, after which is a fully connected layer that summarizes features from the last convolutional layer. The final layer is the output layer, which gives the aforementioned weights $w_i(s; \theta)$, bias $b(s; \theta)$ and state value estimation $V(s; \theta_v)$ linear outputs. Although the network parameters θ and θ_v are shown differently for generality, they share all the parameters except for those in the output layer in our experiments.

The Heuristics in ENN. There are ten heuristics in ENN, each of which gives an action vector for the actions in $\mathcal{A}$. The four navigation algorithms proposed in Sect. 4.2 are included. Their outputs are one-hot vectors that indicate the chosen actions. Other than these four, the followings are also included:

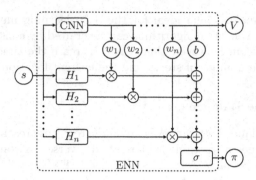

Fig. 2. Structure of ENN. ENN is composed of a Convolutional Neural Network (CNN) and a number of heuristics H_i, all of which take game state s as input. The heuristics output action vectors $H_i(s)$ and the CNN outputs one weight $w_i(s; \theta)$ for each action vector, a bias $b(s; \theta)$, and a state value estimation $V(s; \theta_v)$, where θ and θ_v represent network parameters. The final policy $\pi(s; \theta)$ is a softmax function σ of a linear combination of all the outputs.

- **Loss-Per-Gain** one-hot vector for the action chosen by LPG algorithm.
- **Closest-First** one-hot vector for the action chosen by CF algorithm.
- **Safe-Trip-Home** one-hot vector for the action that follows the safest path to the base.
- **Fast-Trip-Home** one-hot vector for the action that follows the shortest path to the base.
- **Distance-To-Home** score vector for each action that is the shortest-distance-to-base after the actions are taken.
- **Risk** score vector for each action that is the risk of taking action.

5   Evaluation

This section compares ENN with the navigation algorithms proposed in Sect. 4.2. In all the following experiments, ENN has two convolutional layers, all of which have filters of size 3×3 and strides of size 1 with same paddings[1]. The filter counts are 32 and 16 in that order. The fully connected layer has 256 hidden units. All the hidden layers are followed by rectifier nonlinearity. The network is implemented using TensorFlow [1].

We use the Asynchronous Advantage Actor-Critic (A3C) training algorithm from [9]. Training takes 1 million steps by 16 threads. The maximum batch size is 32. The reward discount factor $\gamma = 0.99$. We use Adam optimizer with an initial learning rate of 1×10^{-4} that is linearly annealed to 0 during training.

The output of ENN is considered a stochastic policy in our experiments, i.e., the agent randomly draws an action according to the probability distribution

---

[1] Input is padded with 0s so that the input and output are of the same size.

defined by the output. This helps break symmetries in navigation when the agent is trapped in infinite loops.

As discussed in the following, there are two metrics for performance, the total rewards collected and the reward collected per energy spent. Since the goal is to maximize the total reward, the former is primary, and the later is secondary.

Table 1. Risk values of three different risk distributions in Sect. 5.1. Each distribution has four layers of risk values, as shown in Fig. 1b for high risk. From outer to inner, layers are denoted as $\rho^{(0)}$, $\rho^{(1)}$, $\rho^{(2)}$ and $\rho^{(3)}$.

Risk distribution	$\rho^{(0)}$	$\rho^{(1)}$	$\rho^{(2)}$	$\rho^{(3)}$
Low risk	0.01	0.02	0.04	0.08
Medium risk	0.01	0.03	0.09	0.27
High risk	0.01	0.04	0.16	0.64

Table 2. Experiments on the high-risk distribution specified in Table 1 (Average of 10,000 runs). For each run, the max reward is 30, and an agent's initial and max energy is 8 and 16, respectively. For each game, **Reward** is the total reward collected, **Energy** is the total energy consumed, **Reward/Energy** is the reward collected per energy consumed. **Avg.** means the average over 10,000 runs. **SD.** is the standard deviation. **Incr.%** is ENN's increment as a percentage of an algorithm's corresponding average. For example, Safe-Reward's reward incr.% is the difference between ENN's reward and Safe-Reward's reward as a percentage of Safe-Reward's.

Algorithm	Reward			Energy			Reward/Energy		
	Avg.	SD.	Incr.%	Avg.	SD.	Incr.%	Avg.	SD.	Incr.%
Safe-Reward	11.55	6.38	**13.99**	29.65	19.75	−19.49	0.495	0.301	**38.18**
Safe-Recharge	7.39	5.33	**78.26**	12.03	9.42	98.46	0.691	0.339	**−0.95**
Safe-Both	8.51	5.16	**54.73**	24.35	18.27	−1.99	0.429	0.241	**59.52**
Safe-Neither	8.05	6.08	**63.45**	11.05	9.85	116.07	0.854	0.341	**−19.87**
ENN	13.16	7.17	—	23.87	16.88	—	0.685	0.314	—

5.1 Different Risk Distributions

We first consider environments of 8×8 cells. The initial state of an environment contains a random number of *items* with a total *reward* of 30. The initialization of items is a random process that repeatedly puts a reward of 1 to a random cell in the environment, which follows a multinomial distribution of 30 repeats over 64 choices. Therefore, the count of *items* is random and is determined by the initialization process. With this setting, the number of states is of the order of $64^{30} + 64^{29} + \ldots + 64^0$ due to the arrangement of rewards. Note that this calculation assumes random locations and values of *rewards* for each episode, and it is an overestimation. The initial energy level of agent is 8, and the maximum energy level is 16, which is large enough for a round trip from the base station to any other cell with some leeway.

Table 3. Results of experiments on the medium-risk distribution specified in Table 1. Terms used in the table and other experimental settings are the same as Table 2.

Algorithm	Reward			Energy			Reward/Energy		
	Avg.	SD.	Incr.%	Avg.	SD.	Incr.%	Avg.	SD.	Incr.%
Safe-Reward	13.43	6.62	**9.66**	33.14	19.88	−25.94	0.495	0.266	**44.31**
Safe-Recharge	9.51	6.95	**54.84**	17.56	15.36	39.77	0.625	0.311	**14.33**
Safe-Both	9.08	5.45	**62.21**	25.05	18.58	−2.03	0.439	0.241	**62.80**
Safe-Neither	12.04	8.17	**22.34**	19.16	16.80	28.09	0.771	0.312	**−7.34**
ENN	14.73	7.51	—	24.54	16.46	—	0.715	0.302	—

Table 4. Results of experiments on the low-risk distribution specified in Table 1. Terms used in the table and other experimental settings are the same as Table 2.

Algorithm	Reward			Energy			Reward/Energy		
	Avg.	SD.	Incr.%	Avg.	SD.	Incr.%	Avg.	SD.	Incr.%
Safe-Reward	18.08	8.37	**7.10**	39.55	23.23	−14.09	0.546	0.238	**17.37**
Safe-Recharge	13.41	8.42	**44.34**	27.58	21.54	23.21	0.578	0.269	**11.00**
Safe-Both	11.78	6.82	**64.38**	29.90	21.64	13.64	0.478	0.245	**34.07**
Safe-Neither	17.88	9.60	**8.29**	34.30	24.83	−0.93	0.655	0.265	**−2.08**
ENN	19.36	8.87	—	33.98	18.68	—	0.641	0.250	—

Three different risk distributions are considered. Each distribution has four risk values $\rho^{(0)}$, $\rho^{(1)}$, $\rho^{(2)}$ and $\rho^{(3)}$ that form four layers in the environment. In Fig. 1b, the distribution, denoted as *high risk*, has $\rho^{(0)} = 0.01$, $\rho^{(1)} = 0.04$, $\rho^{(2)} = 0.16$ and $\rho^{(3)} = 0.64$. Table 1 shows the risk values for all three distributions: *high risk*, *medium risk* and *low risk*. The terms high, medium and low describe both the risk values and the differences between risk values.

The results of experiments on the high-risks, medium-risk, and low-risk environments are shown in Tables 2, 3 and 4 respectively. ENN performs the best in all risk distributions, followed by the Safe-Reward navigation algorithm. The others' performance varies with the risk distribution. In the tables, the difference in measurement between ENN and a navigation algorithm is shown as a percentage of the navigation algorithm's measurement, highlighted in bold.

In high-risk environments, as shown in Table 2, Safe-Reward collects 11.55 rewards and consumes 29.65 energy per episode on average. This gives it a 0.495

reward per energy (RPE)[2]. In comparison, ENN can collect 13.16 rewards and consumes 23.87 energy per episode on average. With 0.685 RPE, ENN achieves a 13.99% increase in rewards and a 38.18% increase in RPE over Safe-Reward.

As the risk distribution varies from high to low, ENN's advantage in reward collection decreases, this is possibly because as the variance in risk values decreases, the difference between expected rewards of different routes become smaller. The only exception is the Safe-Both navigation algorithm, for which ENN's advantage increases. This is because Safe-Both follows the safest paths both towards the items and towards the base, this makes the route too long to be finished, and the agent stays on base most of the time. Therefore for this algorithm, energy is a much more limiting factor than risk, and reducing the risk does not improve its reward collection as much as for the others.

The situation for RPE is more interesting. As the risk distribution goes from high to low, ENN's advantage goes up then down. There are two ways for ENN to improve upon the navigation algorithms, (a) is via saving energy by taking a shorter path of higher risk, and (b) is via improving safety by following a safer yet longer path and thus consuming more energy. (a) increases RPE and (b) decreases it. In a medium-risk environment, (a) has the better effect compared to that in a high-risk environment; therefore the improvement in RPE is better. In a low-risk environment, (a) should have even better effect. However, since the risk is too low, the agent can collect most of the items, and as the items are collected, the reward density decreases and the distances between items increase regardless of what route is taken. This undermines the effect of (a) and decreases ENN's advantage in RPE. However, there is an exception in this RPE trend for the Safe-Neither algorithm, for which ENN's advantage is negative and monotonically increases. This is because Safe-Neither completely disregards the risk by always following the shortest path, which provides high RPE. However, as the risk decreases, the agent survives for longer, so the density of reward decreases and so does Safe-Neither's RPE.

Another interesting observation is that Safe-Both performs better compared to Safe-Recharge and Safe-Neither regarding reward collected in high-risk environments, but becomes worse in medium-risk and low-risk environments because shortest paths are more beneficial in safer environments.

5.2   Effect of Energy Capacity

To study the effect of energy capacity, we run additional experiments with initial and maximum energy set to 16 and 32 respectively. The risk distribution is fixed to high risk shown in Fig. 1b. Moreover, the other experimental settings are the same as those in Sect. 5.1. A new ENN is trained with the new energy capacity because the network used in Sect. 5.1 has never experienced states with energy level higher than 16 during training.

As shown in Table 5, with more energy at disposal, the algorithms that take advantage of safest paths shine. Specifically, Safe-Both and Safe-Reward become

---

[2] Reward per energy is also an average over 10,000 runs.

Table 5. Results of experiments where the initial and maximum energy levels are set to 16 and 32 respectively. Terms used in the table and other experimental settings are the same as Table 2.

Algorithm	Reward			Energy			Reward/Energy		
	Avg.	SD.	Incr.%	Avg.	SD.	Incr.%	Avg.	SD.	Incr.%
Safe-Reward	17.66	9.10	**12.01**	34.18	21.14	14.30	0.598	0.235	−**5.44**
Safe-Recharge	10.46	7.71	**89.04**	12.66	10.61	208.71	0.948	0.312	−**40.35**
Safe-Both	19.43	8.71	**1.82**	41.10	21.87	−4.92	0.536	0.218	**5.49**
Safe-Neither	9.73	7.17	**103.34**	10.87	9.31	259.36	1.001	0.298	−**43.50**
ENN	19.78	8.54	—	39.07	20.29	—	0.566	0.229	—

dominantly better than Safe-Recharge and Safe-Neither, with Safe-Both being the best. ENN's advantage over Safe-Both is trivial because of the need to change Safe-Both's choices is too small to make a difference.

6 Conclusion

This paper proposes the *Data-collection Problem* (DCP). The problem models a situation where a robotic agent collects digital data in a risky environment under energy constraint. A good solution must find a good balance between *safety and energy* (S&E).

We design four navigation algorithms that have different priorities during the mission. They represent different optimization goals, e.g., safety-first or energy-first. An *Ensemble Navigation Network* (ENN), which consists of a Convolutional Neural Network and several heuristics with navigation algorithms, is developed to automatically find a good balance between S&E.

ENN is trained using deep reinforcement learning and has superior performance in all experiments conducted. From the experiments, we learn that ENN has a better advantage over the four navigation algorithms when the risk is high or the energy is limited.

Acknowledgements. This research was supported in part through computational resources provided by Syracuse University and by NSF award ACI-1541396.

References

1. Abadi, M., Agarwal, A., Barham, P., Brevdo, E., Chen, Z., Citro, C., Corrado, G.S., Davis, A., Dean, J., Devin, M., et al.: Tensorflow: Large-scale machine learning on heterogeneous distributed systems. arXiv preprint arXiv:1603.04467 (2016)
2. Brázdil, T., Kučera, A., Novotný, P.: Optimizing the expected mean payoff in energy markov decision processes. In: Artho, C., Legay, A., Peled, D. (eds.) ATVA 2016. LNCS, vol. 9938, pp. 32–49. Springer, Cham (2016). https://doi.org/10.1007/978-3-319-46520-3_3

3. Dijkstra, E.W.: A note on two problems in connexion with graphs. Numer. Math.
    1(1), 269–271 (1959)
4. Erdoğan, S., Miller-Hooks, E.: A green vehicle routing problem. Transp. Res.
    Part E Logistics Transp. Rev. **48**(1), 100–114 (2012)
5. Hudack, J., Oh, J.: Multi-agent sensor data collection with attrition risk. In: Pro-
    ceedings - The 26th International Conference on Automated Planning and Schedul-
    ing, ICAPS (2016)
6. Kučera, A.: Playing games with counter automata. Reachability Prob., 29–41
    (2012)
7. Lane, T., Kaelbling, L.P.: Approaches to macro decompositions of large markov
    decision process planning problems. In: Intelligent Systems and Advanced Manu-
    facturing, pp. 104–113. International Society for Optics and Photonics (2002)
8. Lane, T., Kaelbling, L.P.: Nearly deterministic abstractions of markov decision
    processes. In: AAAI/IAAI, pp. 260–266 (2002)
9. Mnih, V., Badia, A.P., Mirza, M., Graves, A., Lillicrap, T.P., Harley, T., Silver,
    D., Kavukcuoglu, K.: Asynchronous methods for deep reinforcement learning. In:
    International Conference on Machine Learning (2016)
10. Mnih, V., Kavukcuoglu, K., Silver, D., Graves, A., Antonoglou, I., Wierstra, D.,
    Riedmiller, M.: Playing atari with deep reinforcement learning. arXiv preprint
    arXiv:1312.5602 (2013)
11. Mnih, V., Kavukcuoglu, K., Silver, D., Rusu, A.A., Veness, J., Bellemare, M.G.,
    Graves, A., Riedmiller, M., Fidjeland, A.K., Ostrovski, G., et al.: Human-level
    control through deep reinforcement learning. Nature **518**(7540), 529–533 (2015)
12. Puterman, M.L.: Markov Decision Processes: Discrete Stochastic Dynamic Pro-
    gramming. Wiley, New York (2014)
13. Silver, D., Huang, A., Maddison, C.J., Guez, A., Sifre, L., Van Den Driessche, G.,
    Schrittwieser, J., Antonoglou, I., Panneershelvam, V., Lanctot, M., et al.: Master-
    ing the game of go with deep neural networks and tree search. Nature **529**(7587),
    484–489 (2016)
14. Silver, D., Schrittwieser, J., Simonyan, K., Antonoglou, I., Huang, A., Guez, A.,
    Hubert, T., Baker, L., Lai, M., Bolton, A., et al.: Mastering the game of go without
    human knowledge. Nature **550**(7676), 354–359 (2017)
15. Xing, Z., Oh, J.C.: Heuristics on the data-collecting robot problem with immediate
    rewards. In: Baldoni, M., Chopra, A.K., Son, T.C., Hirayama, K., Torroni, P.
    (eds.) PRIMA 2016. LNCS (LNAI), vol. 9862, pp. 131–148. Springer, Cham (2016).
    https://doi.org/10.1007/978-3-319-44832-9_8

Automatically Generating and Solving Eternity II Style Puzzles

Geoff Harris⬤, Bruce James Vanstone⬤, and Adrian Gepp$^{(\boxtimes)}$⬤

Bond Business School, Bond University, Gold Coast, Australia
{gharris,bvanston,adgepp}@bond.edu.au

Abstract. The Eternity II puzzle is an NP-complete problem. Prior researchers have generated data sets that are similar to the Eternity II problem. These data sets can be created in linear time, but this comes at the cost of easing the problem by introducing exploitable statistical features. The first contribution of this paper is a new method to generate data sets that are truly of Eternity II style. The second contribution is an Eternity II specific implementation of a constraint-satisfaction-problem style algorithm. Unlike most other published algorithms, this one has no form of look-ahead, filtering, forward checking, back jumping or k-consistency checks. Instead, it uses knowledge about the structure of the puzzle and the uniform distribution of edge colours. This approach is up to three orders of magnitude faster than previously published attempts.

Keywords: Eternity II · Edge Matching Puzzle
Constraint satisfaction problem · NP-complete

1   Introduction

Edge Matching Puzzles (EMPs) belong to the NP-complete (NP-C) problem set for their worst-case complexity [1] and, depending on the objective function chosen, optimization of those solutions may result in an NP-hard problem. With the release of two high prize money puzzles, labelled Eternity and Eternity II, EMPs have attracted the attention of academics from a range of disciplines. The first Eternity puzzle was solved by exploiting statistical features (non-uniformities) in the distribution of piece colours. This weakness was corrected in Eternity II, which remains an open problem.

The contribution of this paper is two-fold. First, we develop an efficient algorithm to generate data sets that are truly of Eternity II style puzzle. Second, we present a naïve algorithm for solving such puzzles, which has no look-ahead, no forward checking, no back jumping and no k-consistency checks. Empirical tests reveal that our algorithm outperforms all previously published results.

2   Literature Review

Ansótegui et al. [2] provided a theoretical framework of the generalized EMP, established some terminology with mathematical definitions and provided both

ⓒ Springer International Publishing AG, part of Springer Nature 2018
M. Mouhoub et al. (Eds.): IEA/AIE 2018, LNAI 10868, pp. 626–632, 2018.
https://doi.org/10.1007/978-3-319-92058-0_60

elementary and advanced SAT and CSP solution algorithms. However, to ensure runtimes were feasible the authors only considered puzzles of edge size $n \in \{6, 7, 8\}$. Due to the combinatorial explosion with increasing n, they could not attempt the actual commercial puzzle of size $n = 16$.

The first published result of the commercial $n = 16$ problem used a hybrid approach of Tabu search and local neighbourhood techniques to claim a score of 458/480 [3]. (The standard score is calculated from the number of edges that match.) However, the researchers noted that with their implementation the largest puzzle that they could solve was $n = 8$.

In a more practical CSP approach to the Eternity II puzzle, researchers have considered the constrained enumeration to all solutions of the problem [4]. Their reinforced filtering of the data structures enabled them to efficiently solve some EMP instances of size $n = 10$. However, these EMP puzzles were substantially easier to solve than the Eternity II style $n = 10$ puzzles.

An evolutionary algorithm approach only achieved 396/480 on the $n = 16$ commercial Eternity II puzzle [5]. Despite the poor score, the significance of this work is that three separate evolutionary algorithms were evaluated.

In another attempt of the general problem, a Tabu search algorithm was used as a two-phase divide and conquer technique [6]. They achieved a best score of 418/480 on the $n = 16$ puzzle at the 2010 International Conference on Metaheuristics and Nature Inspired Computing (META'10). Using a conceptually similar guided hyper-heuristic, the winners of the META'10 achieved a substantially higher best score of 461/480. However, both were unable to solve any puzzle of size $n > 8$.

The above quoted results need to be viewed in light of the academically unpublished, publicly available results of Louis Verhaard [7] who obtained a score of 467/480 for the commercial Eternity II puzzle.

3   Generation of Eternity II Style Puzzle Datasets

The frequency distribution of edge colours of the commercial Eternity II puzzle is shown in the left panel of Fig. 1. The distributions of inner and frame colours are uniform (to maximize entropy) In addition, (i) tiles are not permitted to be rotated and (ii) globally symmetric patterns of tiles are not allowed. These conditions ensure unique (non-degenerate) solutions that are a necessary requirement for a puzzle to be classed as an Eternity II style puzzle.

In the puzzle generation algorithm described by Ansótegui et al. [2], a random number generator is used to create the colour distribution on the tile edges. Consequently, their results are for a combination of Eternity II style puzzles and other EMP problems, which they refer to as GEMP (General Edge Matching Puzzles). In stark contrast to the left panel of Fig. 1, consider the colour distribution shown in the right panel for one of the easier $n = 10$ puzzles [4], which has many statistical weaknesses that can be exploited by algorithms with domain trimming heuristics. That is, it is reasonable to expect the use of lookahead, forward checking, back jumping and k-consistency checks should result

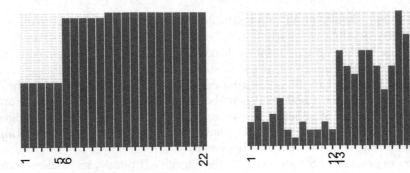

Fig. 1. The distribution of frame and inner-edge colours in the commercial Eternity II puzzle (left) contrasted with a typical 10×10 EMP [4] (right). For Eternity II, the frame colours are numbered 1 to 5 and the inner colours are numbered 6 to 22. For the typical EMP, the frame colours are numbered 1 to 12 and the inner colours are numbered 13 to 25. (Color figure online)

in exploitation by those algorithms to dramatically reduce the size of the search space. Unlike the methods above that can result in EMP problems that do not meet the requirements of an Eternity II style puzzle, we propose an algorithm that always generates an $n \times n$ Eternity II style puzzle with $N = n^2$ tiles consisting of i unique frame colours and j unique inner colours where $f(i) \leq f(j) \div 2$:

```
Generate a list of 4(n-1) colors from a uniform range of [1..i]
          colors
Generate a list of 2(n-1)(n-2) colors from a uniform range of
          [1..j] colors
Generate N blank tiles on an n by n grid
Repeat
   Randomly assign the frame colors to adjacent edges of the
          frame pieces
   Randomly assign the inner colors to adjacent edges of the
          inner pieces
   Validate tiles for rotation and symmetry
Until All N tiles are validated.
```

Any puzzle generated by this algorithm will fulfil the necessary and sufficient conditions to be classed an Eternity II style hard EMP.

4   Our Zero Look-Ahead Algorithm (ZLA)

A brute force algorithm that does not employ look-ahead simply attempts to instantiate the next variable available. However, given the assumption $P \neq NP$ [8], we need a method of variable instantiation which will reasonably trim the branching factor of the implemented search tree that incorporates the specifics of Eternity II style puzzles. The smallest domains from the root node will be those associated with the corners as there are only four elements possible for each domain. Thus, our ZLA begins by instantiating a single corner piece, which is arbitrarily chosen as the top left corner of the puzzle. It is self-evident that all solutions (after removing those with rotational redundancy) to the entire puzzle necessarily have the same corner piece in that position. Ipso facto, our first domain can be created as a single corner piece.

For reasonable sized puzzles, as a potential constituent if this were a look-ahead approach, the next smallest domain will be a tie between the other three corner variables. However, our ZLA works on the application of instantiating the most logically constrained of the neighbouring variables. The next variable to instantiate is thus one of the two frame positions adjacent to the top left corner. As the Eternity II style puzzles have uniform colour distributions, there will be a tie between these two variables. Thus, without any computational loss, we can choose to instantiate the variable to the right of the top left corner. Once that variable has been instantiated, we again utilise knowledge of the puzzle's properties to realize that the shortest path going forward is to work down the rows, using a zigzag pattern across and back pairs of rows.

The elements of each domain are accessed via a global indexing structure which connects domains to rotations of pieces by the top edge of each rotated piece with one of the sides. There are no look-ahead, forward check, back jumping or k-consistency checks performed by the algorithm. Other than using an index to ensure it only considers pieces that could be instantiated into a variable, the only runtime check performed is whether that piece is already in use or not.

5   Results and Discussion

Our ZLA algorithm was implemented in Pascal using bit sets to speed up comparison operations. The source code (and all datasets used for the results) have been uploaded to Bitbucket [9]. The implementation was tested against published benchmarks [4] for correctness and efficacy. The results of running our implementation on the full set of 48 benchmarks is shown in Table 1. Note that we have adjusted our runtimes (by multiplying them by 3.31) to enable a more objective comparison with the prior published results. Specifically, we sourced an i7 laptop from 2014 and determined from a respected online site (CPUBoss) that the difference in single threaded CPU speed of the Athlon used by Ansótegui et al. [2] and the early i7 in the laptop was a factor of 3.31.

In 40 of the 48 benchmarks, the ZLA outperformed all other implementations. This is an interesting result as the benchmarks are for EMP puzzles that have distinctly non-uniform colour distributions that should favour the other implementations that use a various mix of forward checking, look-ahead, back jumping and k-consistency checks. ZLA totally ignores any exploitable structure to the colours or tiles. Nevertheless, overall as judged by the cumulative geometric mean (as suggested in [2]), the ZLA implementation clearly outperforms the other implementations by a substantial margin.

Table 1. Comparison of runtimes (seconds) published by Ansótegui et al. [2] with our ZLA implementation on the datasets provided by Bourreau and Benoist [4]. Boldface indicates the fastest runtime on that particular puzzle.

Puzzle ID	PLA-ONION	Benoist	MAC	SAT(PD)	ZLA
E_7_1.b6i6	30	50	1968	3040	**17**
E_7_2.b6i6	45	**33**	96	602	115
E_7_3.b6i6	184	179	10322	17713	**4.3**
E_7_4.b6i6	**9**	20	1517	250	42
E_8_1.b8i8	**33**	188	13036	4281	145
E_9_1.b9i9	4866	20000	20000	5937	**1540**
E_9_2.b9i9	337	2140	20000	3240	**127**
E_9_3.b11i12	16	5	277	28.5	**0.06**
E_9_4.b9i12	3	3	491	3.7	**0.07**
E_9_5.b10i11	51	160	549	174	**0.5**
E_9_6.b9i10	2657	931	20000	9854	**404**
E_9_7.b9i11	4	69	1251	57	**0.1**
E_9_8.b8i9	20000	15299	20000	6950	**4136**
E_9_9.b9i10	5193	16526	20000	6869	**57**
E_9_10.b10i10	**16**	119	8404	62	73
E_9_11.b9i11	35	21	2849	3	**2**
E_9_12.b10i10	15	70	7278	303	**3**
E_9_13.b10i10	27	14	7568	29	**3**
E_9_14.b9i10	916	1961	15231	3645	**29**
E_9_15.b10i10	592	2298	2436	569	**14**
E_9_16.b9i10	12	2710	15280	876	**4**
E_9_17.b9i10	392	2317	20000	11323	**9**
E_10_1.b11i11	7372	12106	20000	**5904**	14704
E_10_2.b11i11	7641	20000	20000	**3257**	6804
E_10_3.b11i11	8480	11399	20000	6012	**721**
E_10_4.b11i11	1849	4544	20000	6075	**1486**
E_10_5.b14i14	16	8	34	0.7	**0.05**
E_10_6.b11i12	2077	2552	20000	1098	**88**
E_10_7.b12i15	2	18	3	6.7	**0.01**
E_10_8.b13i14	13	34	88	14	**0.08**
E_10_9.b12i14	24	130	70	63.5	**0.1**
E_10_10.b12i12	444	196	20000	611	**34**
E_10_11.b13i13	14	54	321	65	**0.1**
E_10_12.b12i13	9	53	173	36	**0.1**
E_10_13.b12i12	**67**	2222	20000	260	106
E_10_14.b12i13	97	187	6553	253	**0.5**
E_10_15.b11i12	179	224	20000	688	**25**
E_10_16.b13i13	14	29	179	4.5	**0.4**
E_10_17.b13i13	0	18	684	6.6	**0.6**
E_10_18.b12i13	24	87	2647	2	**0.4**
E_10_19.b12i13	58	348	4886	3.5	**1**
E_10_20.b11i14	282	1573	9175	45.6	**3**
E_10_21.b12i13	60	261	5364	21	**2**
E_10_22.b12i13	1	38	3986	7	**2**
E_10_23.b12i12	233	1055	17019	223	**6**
E_10_24.b12i12	414	8913	20000	1094	**18**
E_10_25.b12i12	107	123	20000	202	**8**
E_10_26.b12i12	2000	9950	20000	3526	**80**
Geometric Mean	94.79	310.04	3419.49	234.26	**7.76**

A more meaningful comparison is with harder EMP puzzles, which is shown in Table 2 using datasets provided by Ansótegui et al. [2]. In-line with the previous research, each cell represents the median time, over 100 instances of these puzzles, for a particular implementation. It is interesting to note that ZLA is the fastest implementation across all puzzles. This is in spite of there still being a proportion of harder puzzles that do not meet the conditions for being Eternity II style. That is, some of the puzzles still have exploitable statistical features that should favour the non-ZLA implementations.

Table 2. Comparison of runtimes (seconds) published by Ansótegui et al. [2] for their GEMP problems with our ZLA algorithm for corresponding hard Eternity II style problems. Times for ZLA have been adjusted as specified above to allow direct comparison with the earlier results. Boldface indicates the fastest runtime on that particular puzzle.

Solver	Median time (s)					
Puzzle Size ($n \times n$)	6×6		7×7			8×8
Colours inner:frame	6 : 2	6 : 4	7 : 2	7 : 3	7 : 4	8 : 2
PLA-DOM	15	520	18193	9464	581	8387
PLA-CHESS	0.5	5249	137	4181	6906	510
PLA-ONION	82	382	$> 2 \times 10^4$	$> 2 \times 10^4$	429	$> 2 \times 10^4$
MAC+GAColor	0.94	328	96	646	348	208
MAC+GAColor+Ctadiff	0.73	377	94	727	395	516
SAT(P)	7.45	$> 2 \times 10^4$	4418	$> 2 \times 10^4$	7960	6465
SAT(PD)	0.55	777	125	1785	682	359
MAC_b dom/deg	19	2415	$> 2 \times 10^4$	$> 2 \times 10^4$	3307	$> 2 \times 10^4$
Minion	125	3463	$> 2 \times 10^4$	$> 2 \times 10^4$	4675	$> 2 \times 10^4$
Benoist	133	681	$> 2 \times 10^4$	8535	124	$> 2 \times 10^4$
ZLA-E II style puzzles	**0.026**	**0.017**	**1.152**	**12.111**	**0.801**	**88.069**

6 Conclusion and Future Work

The first contribution of this paper is determining the criteria required for an Edge Matching Puzzle (EMP) to be of Eternity II style, and providing an algorithm to generate puzzles guaranteed to meet these criteria. This provides a valuable way to test algorithms to solve hard Eternity II style puzzles and is an improvement over methods in the existing literature that generate datasets that sometimes do not meet the Eternity II style criteria.

The second main finding from this work is that for the range of Eternity II style puzzles examined, a ZLA implementation was significantly faster (up to many orders of magnitude) than the CSP or SAT implementations published to date. This is an interesting result that reinforces the assertion in prior literature that a good variable ordering heuristic will outperform computationally expensive domain reduction heuristics and back jumping [10]. That is, the computational expense of invoking those heuristics will almost always slow down the search to result in slow implementation runtimes relative to a well-constructed (instance-specific) variable ordering heuristic.

An unexpected result was the complete dominance of the ZLA implementation on the relatively easy EMP puzzles. It was anticipated here that any CSP or SAT implmentation would be able to exploit the statistical features in easy puzzle instances and thus outperform the ZLA implementation.

There are future research opportunities in testing which domain minimization heuristics, when added to the ZLA implementation, result in better runtimes than the raw ZLA implementation presented in this paper. The knowledge gained in the comparison of the trade-off between computational overhead against the search space size reduction should be of great value to the CSP and SAT community.

References

1. Demaine, E.D., Demaine, M.L.: Jigsaw puzzles, edge matching, and polyomino packing: connections and complexity. Graphs Combinatorics **23**, 195–208 (2007)
2. Ansótegui, C., Béjar, R., Fernández, C., Mateu, C.: On the hardness of solving edge matching puzzles as SAT or CSP problems. Constraints **18**, 1–31 (2013)
3. Schaus, P., Deville, Y.: Hybridization of CP and VLNS for eternity II. In: Journées Francophones de Programmation par Contraintes (JFPC 20008) (2008)
4. Bourreau, E., Benoist, T.: Fast global filtering for eternity II. Constraint Program. Lett. (CPL) **3**, 036–049 (2008)
5. Munoz, J., Gutierrez, G., Sanchis, A.: Evolutionary techniques in a constraint satisfaction problem: puzzle eternity II. In: IEEE Congr. Evol. Comput. (CEC 2009), pp. 2985–2991. IEEE (2009)
6. Wang, W.S., Chiang, T.C.: Solving eternity-II puzzles with a tabu search algorithm. In: Proceedings of the 3rd International Conference on Metaheuristics and Nature Inspired Computing (META), vol. 10 (2010)
7. Verhaard, L.: Details of eternity II solver eii (2009). http://www.shortestpath.se/eii/eii_details.html
8. Aaronson, S.: Guest column: NP-complete problems and physical reality. ACM Sigact News **36**(1), 30–52 (2005)
9. Harris, G., Vanstone, B., Gepp, A.: Code and data repository: automatically generating and solving eternity II style puzzles (2018). https://bitbucket.org/bvanston/bag-canadian-conference-2018/src/master/
10. Bessière, C., Régin, J.-C.: MAC and combined heuristics: two reasons to forsake FC (and CBJ?) on hard problems. In: Freuder, E.C. (ed.) CP 1996. LNCS, vol. 1118, pp. 61–75. Springer, Heidelberg (1996). https://doi.org/10.1007/3-540-61551-2_66

Rough Sets

A Game-Theoretic Rough Set Approach for Handling Missing Data in Clustering

Nouman Azam[1]([⊠]), Mohammad Khan Afridi[1], and JingTao Yao[2]

[1] National University of Computer and Emerging Sciences,
Peshawar, Pakistan
nouman.azam@nu.edu.pk
[2] Department of Computer Science, University of Regina,
Regina S4S 0A2, Canada
jtyao@cs.uregina.ca

Abstract. An important issue in clustering is how to deal with data containing missing values. A three-way decision making approach has recently been introduced for this purpose. It includes an added option of deferment which is exercised whenever it is not clear to include or exclude an object from a cluster. A critical issue in the three-way approach is how to decide the thresholds defining the three types of decisions. We examine the role of game-theoretic rough set model (GTRS) to address this issue. The GTRS model induces three-way decisions by implementing a game between multiple cooperative or competitive criteria. In particular, a game in GTRS is proposed which realizes the determination of thresholds from the viewpoint of tradeoff between accuracy and generality of clustering. Experimental results are reported for two datasets from UCI machine learning repository. The comparison of the GTRS results with another three-way model of (1, 0) suggests that the GTRS model significantly improves generality by upto 65% while maintaining similar levels of accuracy. In comparison to the (0.5, 0.5) model, the GTRS improves accuracy by upto 5% at a cost of some decrease in generality.

Keywords: Clustering · Missing data · Three-way
Game-theoretic rough sets

1 Introduction

Clustering is an important data analysis task that aims to form groups of similar objects [13,14]. A key issue in clustering is how to form groups of objects in the presence of data containing missing values [2,7]. Two strategies are commonly used in this regards [13]. The first strategy is to apply some preprocessing on the data before clustering. The second strategy is to incorporate additional mechanisms into the clustering model itself for handling missing values.

The preprocessing strategy includes approaches based on deletion of objects containing missing values and imputing the missing attribute values [11]. Extensions of these basic preprocessing techniques include pairwise deletion [5], mean

© Springer International Publishing AG, part of Springer Nature 2018
M. Mouhoub et al. (Eds.): IEA/AIE 2018, LNAI 10868, pp. 635–647, 2018.
https://doi.org/10.1007/978-3-319-92058-0_61

substitution [4], multiple imputation [11] and expectation-maximization imputation [3]. The second strategy, i.e., handling missing values at the model level includes approaches such as assignment of objects with missing values to clusters having a high number of missing values [12], making a separate cluster of objects having missing values [8] and assignment of objects with missing values to clusters based on their neighborhood [9]. In this article, we consider the model based strategy as it is sometimes preferred over the preprocessing strategy [12].

A model based strategy known as three-way clustering approach was recently being formulated for clustering of objects containing missing values [17]. It generalizes some of the previously related work reported in [18,19]. Speaking more specifically, it makes three-way decisions in the form of accepting an object as belonging to a cluster, rejecting an object as belonging to a cluster or deferring the decision of accepting or rejecting. The deferment decision option is exercised whenever due to high uncertainty it is not conclusive and clear as to whether or not to include an object in a cluster. The three-way approach critically depends on a pair of thresholds that control the three types of decisions. The issue of automatically determining the thresholds has not being sufficiently addressed in the existing studies. The commonly used approaches are either to use fix values for thresholds or use the domain expert intuition [17–19].

In this article, we propose a game-thoeretic rough set (GTRS) based approach for determining the thresholds defining the three-way decisions for clustering [6]. In particular, a game in GTRS is proposed that determines thresholds based on a tradeoff between the properties of accuracy and generality of clustering. Experimental results on two UCI machine learning repository datasets suggest that the GTRS significantly improves the generality by upto 65% when compared to another three-way model defined by thresholds (1, 0). Moreover the GTRS also improves the accuracy by upto 5% at some cost of decrease in generality when compared to another three-way model defined by thresholds of (0.5, 0.5). These results indicate that the proposed approach can effectively cluster the data containing missing values.

2   A Review of Three-way Clustering

In this section, we briefly review the fundamental notions of three-way clustering and then point out a limitation in existing three-way clustering approaches.

2.1   Basic Notions of Three-way Clustering

A general framework of three-way clustering was introduced in [17]. The framework receives its motivation from the theory of three-way decisions [16]. Recently, there is a growing interest in the theory of three-way decisions from theoretical as well as application perspectives [15]. Let $U = \{o_1, o_2, o_3, ...\}$, be the set of objects called universe and $\{c_1, c_2, c_3, ...\}$ be a family of clusters. The three-way framework uses a couple of sets to represent each cluster c_k, i.e.,

$$c_k = \{In(c_k), Pt(c_k)\}, \tag{1}$$

where, $In(c_k)$ and $Pt(c_k)$ are subsets of U. The two sets are used to define three regions corresponding to cluster c_k as follows,

$$Inside(c_k) = In(c_k), \tag{2}$$

$$Partial(c_k) = Pt(c_k), \tag{3}$$

$$Outside(c_k) = U - In(c_k) - Pt(c_k). \tag{4}$$

The $Inside(c_k)$ consists of objects that are contained in c_k, the $Partial(c_k)$ is the set of object that may be contained in c_k and the $Outside(c_k)$ region consists of objects that are not contained in c_k.

An evaluation function and a pair of thresholds may be used to define the inside, partial and outside regions [17]. The evaluation function reflects the association between an object and a cluster, whereas the thresholds define limits on the association for inclusion in different regions. Let $e(c_k, o_i)$ denote an evaluation function that represents the association between a particular cluster c_k and a certain object o_i, with (α, β) being some thresholds. The three regions are defined as follows,

$$Inside(c_k) = \{o_i \in U \mid e(c_k, o_i) \geq \alpha\}, \tag{5}$$

$$Partial(c_k) = \{o_i \in U \mid \beta < e(c_k, o_i) < \alpha\}, \tag{6}$$

$$Outside(c_k) = \{o_i \in U \mid e(c_k, o_i) \leq \beta\}. \tag{7}$$

This means that if the evaluation for an object is above or equal to the threshold α, we will include it in the $Inside(c_k)$. If the evaluation for an objects is below or equal to the thresholds β we will include it in the $Outside(c_k)$. If the evaluation is between the two thresholds, we will include the object in the $Partial(c_k)$.

The inclusion in different regions are controlled by considering different settings of (α, β) thresholds. The determination of suitable values for the thresholds is an important research issue in this context. We further highlights this issue in the next section.

2.2   Issue of Determining Thresholds in Three-way Clustering

In this section, we demonstrate with an example a potential problem arising due to lack of attention towards the determination of thresholds. A three step approach will be used for the application of the three-way framework to handle missing values that is described in [16]. In Step 1, the set of objects U is divided into two sets, i.e., C is the set of objects with complete values and M is the set objects with missing values. A conventional algorithm such as K-means is used to cluster objects in the set C. Since the objects in set C do not have missing values, therefore the level of uncertainty is minimum and conventional approaches for clustering are suitable for clustering such objects. In Step 2, an incomplete dataset is constructed randomly from C according to the missing rate of the whole dataset U. This means that if the original dataset contains 30% of data with missing values, then approximately 30% of objects will be randomly selected from C with induced missing values. This leads to a division of C into two sets, i.e., the constructed dataset consisting of objects with 30% missing values denoted as U_m and the remaining objects in C with no missing values denoted as U_c. The set U_c will be used to compute suitable (α, β) thresholds based on clustering the objects in U_m. The outcome of this step will be the selection of suitable values for (α, β) thresholds that will do a good job of clustering the objects with induced missing values. In Step 3, the objects with missing values, denoted by M are being decided in the three-way framework outlined in Sect. 2.1. In particular, the association of an object with each cluster (determined in Step 1) is checked in a three-way framework. It is sufficient to consider the first two steps of this approach to highlight a limitation in existing studies.

Table 1. Sample dataset with missing data

	A_1	A_2	A_3	A_4		A_1	A_2	A_3	A_4		A_1	A_2	A_3	A_4
o_1	5.9	3.2	4.8	2	o_{11}	5.6*	2.8	4.1*	1.6	o_{21}	6.3	2.7*	4.9	1.8*
o_2	6.1	2.8*	4.2	1.5*	o_{12}	5.5	2.5	4	1.5	o_{22}	6.2	2.8	4.8	1.8
o_3	6.4	2.8	4.6	1.3	o_{13}	5.5	2.6	4.4	1.4	o_{23}	5.9	3	5.1	1.8
o_4	6.4*	2.5	4.3*	1.4	o_{14}	6.1*	2.7	4.6*	1.4	o_{24}	6.4	2.8	5.6	2.1
o_5	6.3	2.3	4.4	1.5	o_{15}	5.8	2.6	4	1.4	o_{25}	6.5	3	5.5	1.8
o_6	6.3	2.8	4.9	1.6	o_{16}	5.8	2.7	5.1	1.9	o_{26}	6.3	2.8	5.1	1.5
o_7	5.5	2.4	3.8	1.3	o_{17}	5.7	2.5	5	2	o_{27}	6.1*	2.8	5.6*	1.4
o_8	5.8	2.7*	4	1.4*	o_{18}	6.1	2.8*	5.6	2.2*	o_{28}	6.4	3.1	5.5	1.8
o_9	5.5	2.4	3.7	1.2	o_{19}	6	2.2	5	1.5	o_{29}	6*	2.9	4.8*	1.5
o_{10}	6	2.8	4.5	1.4	o_{20}	5.6	2.8	4.9	2	o_{30}	5.9	3	5.1	1.8

Consider Table 1 which represents C and contains information about 30 objects. It is sufficient to consider set C only to demonstrate a limitation in existing approaches. The rows of the table correspond to objects denoted as o_i and the columns corresponds to attributes denoted as A_j. The values in the table with a * on top represent missing values. In particular, there are 9 objects with induced missing values which leads to a missing rate of $9/30 = 30\%$. Please note we considered missing rate for objects not for values. For Table 1, the sets $U_c = \{o_1, o_3, o_5, o_6, o_7, o_9, o_{10}, o_{12}, o_{13}, o_{15}, o_{16}, o_{17}, o_{19}, o_{20}, o_{22}, ..., o_{26}, o_{28}, o_{30}\}$ and $U_m = \{o_2, o_4, o_8, o_{11}, o_{14}, o_{18}, o_{21}, o_{27}, o_{29}\}$.

As a first step, let's assume that some conventional clustering is being applied on C and this results in the formation of two clusters, i.e., $c_1 = \{o_1, ..., o_{15}\}$ and $c_2 = \{o_{16}, ..., o_{30}\}$. In the second step, based on the objects with induced missing values, we aim to determine suitable thresholds that will do a good job of clustering these objects. The three-way clustering approach introduced in Sect. 2.1, is used for this purpose.

To apply three-way approach for clustering, we need to compute the evaluation function $e(c_k, o_i)$. We consider the following evaluation function,

$$e_{(c_k, o_i)} = \frac{\text{Number of } o_i \text{ neighbors belonging to } c_k}{\text{Total neighbors of } o_i}. \tag{8}$$

To determine neighbors we need a certain distance metric. We use the following distance metric,

$$d(o_i, o_j) = \sqrt{\sum_{a=1}^{A}(o_i^a - o_j^a)^2}. \tag{9}$$

Moreover, the missing values are ignored in the calculations. For example, the distance between object o_1 and o_2 is determined as,

$$
\begin{aligned}
d_{(2,1)} &= \sqrt{\sum_{a=1}^{A}(o_2^a - o_1^a)^2} \\
&= \sqrt{(6.1 - 5.9)^2 + (* - 3.2)^2 + (4.2 - 4.8)^2 + (* - 2)^2} \\
&= \sqrt{(6.1 - 5.9)^2 + (4.2 - 4.8)^2} = 0.63
\end{aligned} \tag{10}
$$

Using this distance metric, the nearest neighbors, say seven neighbors of o_2 are $o_5, o_{10}, o_{15}, o_3, o_{22}, o_1$ and o_{12}. Using the nearest neighbors, we may compute the evaluation function for a certain object corresponding to a particular cluster. The evaluation function for o_2 corresponding to cluster c_1 is given by,

$$e(c_1, o_2) = \frac{\text{Number of } o_2 \text{ neighbors belong to } c_1}{\text{Total number of } o_2 \text{ neighbors}} = 6/7 = 0.8571. \tag{11}$$

This means that 85.71% neighbors of o_2 belongs to cluster c_1. In the same way, the evaluation function $e(c_2, o_2)$ is given by,

$$e(c_2, o_2) = \frac{\text{Number of } o_2 \text{ neighbors belong to } c_2}{\text{Total number of } o_2 \text{ neighbors}} = 1/7 = 0.1429. \tag{12}$$

The evaluation functions for other objects in U_m can be similarly computed and are given in Table 2. Equations (5)–(7) can now be utilized to decide the inclusion of objects into one of the three regions corresponding to each cluster.

From evaluation functions in Table 2, it may be noted that different threshold settings will lead to different regions. For instance, if we set thresholds $(\alpha, \beta) = (1, 0)$, than only objects o_4, o_8 and o_{18} will be clustered, as their evaluation values are above or equal to the threshold α. In particular, o_4 and o_8 will be in $Inside(c_1)$ and o_{18} will be in $Inside(c_2)$. This means that we will be able to correctly cluster 3 out of 9 objects, at an accuracy of 100%. It should be noted that (during clustering of C) $o_1, ..., o_{15}$ were in c_1 and $o_{16}, ..., o_{30}$ were in c_2. On the other hand, if we set $(\alpha, \beta) = (0.5, 0.5)$, than all the 9 objects will be clustered. This can be seen from the evaluation functions given in Table 2. However, only 6 objects will be clustered correct.

A formal definition of accuracy and generality is,

$$Accuracy(\alpha, \beta) = \frac{\text{Correctly clustered objects}}{\text{Total clustered objects}},\tag{13}$$

$$Generality(\alpha, \beta) = \frac{\text{Total clustered objects}}{\text{Total objects in } U}.\tag{14}$$

Table 2. Evaluation function values for objects in U_m

	o_2	o_4	o_8	o_{11}	o_{14}	o_{18}	o_{21}	o_{27}	o_{29}
c_1	0.8571	1	1	0.4286	0.8571	0	0.4286	0.8571	0.7143
c_2	0.1429	0	0	0.5714	0.1429	1	0.5714	0.1429	0.2857

Accuracy is the measure of how many objects are correctly clustered. On the other hand, generality is the measure of how many objects are being clustered. It should be noted that setting thresholds to increase generality may affect accuracy. Similarly, setting thresholds to increase accuracy may affect generality. Therefore, the determination of thresholds may be approached based on a tradeoff or balance between accuracy and generality of clustering. We consider the use of game-theoretic rough sets for automatically determination of this tradeoff.

3   Game-Theoretic Rough Sets

The game-theoretic rough sets or GTRS provides a game-theoretic mechanism between multiple criteria that are realized as game players for determining thresholds [6]. It formulates strategies for players in the form of changes in thresholds in order to improve the overall quality of three-way decisions. The overall objective of a game in GTRS is to select suitable thresholds of three-way decisions, based on the available criteria.

A typical game in GTRS is of the form {P, S, u}, where,

- P is a finite set of n players,
- $S = S_1 \times \ldots \times S_n$, where S_i is a finite set of strategies available to player i. Each vector $s = (s_1, \ldots, s_n) \in S$ is called a strategy profile where player i plays strategy s_i,
- $u = (u_1, \ldots, u_n)$ where $u_i: S \mapsto \Re$ is a real-valued utility or payoff function for player i.

Let us denote the strategy profile of all the players expect player i as $s_{-i} = (s_1, \ldots, s_{i-1}, s_{i+1}, \ldots, s_n)$. This means that we can write $s = (s_i, s_{-i})$. Thus, all the players expect i are committed to play s_{-i}, when player i chooses s_i.

The Nash equilibrium is generally used to determine game solution or game outcome in GTRS. A strategy profile $(s_1, ..., s_n)$ is a Nash equilibrium, when,

$$u_i(s_i, s_{-i}) \geq u_i(s'_i, s_{-i}), \text{ where } (s'_i \neq s_i) \tag{15}$$

In a typical GTRS game, the players are considered as different criteria that highlight various quality related aspects of three-way decisions such as accuracy, generality, precision recall, uncertainty or cost. Each of these criteria is effected differently when various thresholds are being used. The strategies are therefore formulated as direct changes in the thresholds. Finally, suitable measures are defined for evaluating each criteria.

Table 3. A typical two-player game in GTRS

		P_2		
		s_1	s_2	...
	s_1	$u_1(s_1, s_1), u_2(s_1, s_1)$	$u_1(s_1, s_2), u_2(s_1, s_2)$	...
P_1	s_2	$u_1(s_2, s_1), u_2(s_2, s_1)$	$u_1(s_2, s_2), u_2(s_2, s_2)$	...
	...	...	...	...

Table 3 shows a typical two player game in GTRS. The players in the game are denoted by P_1 and P_2. The cells in the table corresponds to strategy profiles. Each cell contains a pair of payoff functions based on their strategy profile. For example the top right cell corresponds to a strategy profile (s_1, s_2) which contains payoff functions $u_1(s_1, s_2)$ and $u_2(s_1, s_2)$. Playing the game results in the selection of Nash equilibrium which is utilized in determining a possible strategy profile and the associated thresholds.

4   Three-way Clustering with GTRS

In Sect. 2.2 we noted that the determination of thresholds may be approached based on a tradeoff between accuracy and generality of three-way clustering. In this section, we propose a GTRS based game for this purpose.

4.1   Formulating a Game in GTRS for Three-way Clustering

We noted in Sect. 3 that in order to formulate and analyze problems with GTRS we need to first identify the three components, i.e., players, strategies and the payoff functions.

The players are defined to reflect the overall objective or goal of the game. Our objective in this game is to improve the quality of clustering the data with missing values. In Sect. 2.2, we noted that the quality of clustering can be improved by considering a tradeoff between accuracy and generality of clustering. Therefore the properties of accuracy and generality are considered as game players in this game. The player accuracy will be denoted by A and the player generality will be denoted by G. The player set is given by $P = \{A, G\}$.

The strategies in the game represent actions or moves of the players in a game. We also noted in Sect. 2.2 that by changing the thresholds, the measures of accuracy and generality are affected differently. Therefore, we considered modification in thresholds as possible strategies. In particular, three strategies are formulated, i.e., decrease α (denoted as $\alpha\downarrow$), increase β (denoted as $\beta\uparrow$) or simultaneously decrease α and increase β (denoted as $\alpha\downarrow \beta\uparrow$). A player will choose a strategies that maximize its benefit. Please be noted that these strategies are formulated based on the initial thresholds settings of $(\alpha, \beta) = (1, 0)$. The strategies may be formulated in different ways based on different initial threshold settings. This has been discussed in detail in the reference [1].

The payoff functions are used to measure the outcome of selecting a certain strategy. As discussed earlier, the players A and G are affected by changes in threshold values which in this case are represented as different game strategies. For a certain strategy profile, say (s_m, s_n) that leads to thresholds (α, β), the payoffs for the players A and G are given by,

$$u_A(s_m, s_n) = Accuracy(\alpha, \beta), \tag{16}$$

$$u_G(s_m, s_n) = Generality(\alpha, \beta). \tag{17}$$

where $Accuracy(\alpha, \beta)$ and $Generality(\alpha, \beta)$ are defined in Eqs. (13)–(14). Each player choose a strategy to maximize his benefits. For player A, an accuracy value of 1.0 means maximum payoff and a value of 0.0 means a minimum payoff. Similarly, for player G, a generality value of 1.0 means a maximum payoff and generality value of 0.0 means a minimum payoff.

4.2   Realization of Accuracy Versus Generality Tradeoff

We consider the constructed game as a competition between accuracy and generality of clustering. Table 3 is used to highlight this. The rows correspond to strategies for player A and the columns correspond to strategies of player G. Each cell represents a strategy profile of the form (s_m, s_n), where s_m is the strategy of player A and s_n is the strategy of player G. Each player aims to select a strategy which will configure the thresholds in order to improve his respective utility. The payoffs corresponding to a strategy profile (s_m, s_n) are given by $u_A(s_m, s_n)$ and $u_G(s_m, s_n)$ for players A and G, respectively.

Each player in a game will prefer a strategy that will maximize his benefits. For the considered two player game, a strategy profile will be the Nash equilibrium according to Eq. (15) if,

For Accuracy: $\forall s_m \in S_A, u_A(s_m, s_n) \geq u_A(s'_m, s_n), where (s'_m \neq s_m),$ (18)

For Generality: $\forall s_n \in S_G, u_G(s_m, s_n) \geq u_G(s_m, s'_n), where (s'_n \neq s_n).$ (19)

This means that no player will benefit from changing their strategy other than the strategy specified by the profile (s_m, s_n).

We now examine how to determine the changes in the thresholds based on a certain strategy profile. From the game description in Sect. 4.1, we noted that there are four distinct ways for changing the thresholds, namely,

$$\alpha - = \text{single player suggests to decrease } \alpha, \tag{20}$$

$$\alpha -- = \text{both players suggest to decrease } \alpha, \tag{21}$$

$$\beta + = \text{single player suggests to increase } \beta, \tag{22}$$

$$\beta ++ = \text{both players suggest to increase } \beta. \tag{23}$$

Algorithm 1. GTRS based threshold learning algorithm

Input: K, U, $\alpha-$, $\alpha--$, $\beta+$ and $\beta++$.
Output: Three-way clustering of objects.
1: Initialize $\alpha = 1.0$, $\beta = 0.0$.
2: Divide U into C and M.
3: Apply K-mean clustering on C.
4: Randomly remove values in C by following the percentage of missing values in M.
5: Divide C into U_c and U_m.
6: **Repeat**
7:    Calculate the utilities of players by using Eqs. (13) and (14).
8:    Populate the payoff table with calculated values.
9:    Calculate equilibrium in a payoff table by using Eqs. (18) and (19).
10:   Determine selected strategies and corresponding thresholds (α', β').
11:   $(\alpha, \beta) = (\alpha', \beta')$.
12: **Until** $Accuracy(\alpha, \beta) \leq Generality(\alpha, \beta)$ or $\alpha \leq 0.5$ or $\beta \geq 0.5$
                  or Maximum iterations reached.
13: Evaluate objects in M using Eq. (8).
14: Use (α, β) determined in Line 11, with three-way framework of Eqs. (5)–(7).

The above definitions can be used to associate threshold pairs with a strategy profile. For instance, a strategy profile with (s_1, s_1) which equals to $(\alpha\downarrow, \alpha\downarrow)$ is represented as $(\alpha--, \beta)$, since the players suggest a decrease in threshold α as defined in Eq. (21). In the next section, we examine how to obtain the values of the four variables in Eqs. (20)–(23) based on an interactive game.

4.3   Learning with Iterative Games in GTRS

We consider an iterative game that will repeatedly modify the thresholds in the aim of improving the overall clustering quality. The improvement in successive iterations based on thresholds modifications may be realized as a form of learning. In particular, the learning is related to the modification in thresholds and its impact on the payoffs of the two players. We utilize this relationship to define the four variables, i.e., $\alpha-, \alpha--, \beta+$ and $\beta++$.

Let (α, β) be the initial threshold values at a particular iteration. At the end of the iteration, a Nash equilibrium is used to determine the game solution and the corresponding thresholds, say, (α', β'). The initial thresholds (α, β) and determined thresholds (α', β') are used to determine the four variables in Eqs. (20)–(23) as follows,

$$\alpha_- = \alpha - (\alpha \times (Generality(\alpha', \beta') - Generality(\alpha, \beta)), \tag{24}$$

$$\alpha_{--} = \alpha - c(\alpha \times (Generality(\alpha', \beta') - Generality(\alpha, \beta)), \tag{25}$$

$$\beta_+ = \beta - (\beta \times (Generality(\alpha', \beta') - Generality(\alpha, \beta)), \tag{26}$$

$$\beta_{++} = \beta - c(\beta \times (Generality(\alpha', \beta') - Generality(\alpha, \beta)). \tag{27}$$

We used generality in the above equations as we want to see improvements in generality while we repeatedly modify the thresholds. Please note that the initial thresholds have minimum generality. The constant c in Eqs. (25) and (27) is used to control the amount of change in thresholds. When c is set low, the thresholds are fine tuned at the cost of more computational overhead. While a high value of c reduces computational overhead, however, fine tuning of thresholds may not be possible. **Algorithm 1** describes an iterative GTRS based learning mechanism for determining thresholds. A dataset is provided to the algorithm which then computes a threshold pair (α, β) for the three-way clustering. The iterative process stops when either the $Generality(\alpha, \beta) \geq Accuracy(\alpha, \beta)$ or boundary region becomes empty or the algorithm runs a specified number of times or when either $\alpha \leq 0.5$ or $\beta \geq 0.5$.

5   Experimental Results and Discussion

To assess the usefulness of the GTRS based approach, we consider Iris and Pendigit datasets from UCI machine learning repository [10]. In order to simulate a dataset with missing values, we randomly removed attribute values from some of the objects. The objects with missing values make up the set U_m and the remaining objects make up the set U_c. In the reported experiments, we use percentage of missing values of 5%, 10%, 15%, 20%, 25% and 30%. We also compared the results with extreme threshold settings of $(\alpha, \beta) = (1, 0)$ and $(\alpha, \beta) = (0.5, 0.5)$, referred to as $(1, 0)$ model and $(0.5, 0.5)$ model, respectively.

Experimental results on Iris dataset are presented in Table 4. The $(1, 0)$ model has an average accuracy of 98.4% with a generality of 38%. The $(0.5, 0.5)$ model has an accuracy of 89%, with significantly improved generality of 99.3%. The determined thresholds with GTRS model are $(\alpha, \beta) = (0.56 \pm 0.05, 0.24 \pm 0.1)$ with an accuracy of 92.8% and generality of 92.7%. In comparison to $(1, 0)$ model, the GTRS model improved generality by 54.5% at the cost of 5.6% decrease in accuracy. While, in comparison to the $(0.5, 0.5)$ model, accuracy improved by upto 4.8% with an average decrease of 6.5% was observed in generality.

Experimental results on Pendigit dataset are presented in Table 5. For $(1, 0)$ model, an average accuracy of 99% was achieved with a generality of 18%. Similarly, for $(0.5, 0.5)$ model, the accuracy is 90% with a generality of 99%.

Table 4. Iris dataset

Missing	(1, 0) Model		GTRS Model			(0.5, 0.5) Model	
	Accuracy	Generality	(α, β)	Accuracy	Generality	Accuracy	Generality
5%	1.0000	0.3743	(0.55, 0.29)	0.9402	0.9394	0.8991	0.9914
10%	0.9908	0.3453	(0.56, 0.21)	0.9473	0.9360	0.8951	0.9920
15%	0.9831	0.3827	(0.55, 0.25)	0.9407	0.9382	0.8844	0.9941
20%	0.9844	0.3927	(0.57, 0.20)	0.9375	0.9187	0.8865	0.9923
25%	0.9733	0.3903	(0.57, 0.30)	0.9354	0.9151	0.8895	0.9932
30%	0.9746	0.4062	(0.58, 0.25)	0.9280	0.9156	0.8877	0.9933
Average:	0.9844	0.3819	(0.56, 0.24)	0.9382	0.9272	0.8904	0.9927

Table 5. Pendigit dataset

Missing	(1, 0) Model		GTRS Model			(0.5, 0.5) Model	
	Accuracy	Generality	(α, β)	Accuracy	Generality	Accuracy	Generality
5%	0.9888	0.1217	(0.59, 0.23)	0.9574	0.9545	0.8917	0.9943
10%	0.9946	0.1947	(0.58, 0.20)	0.9513	0.9494	0.9001	0.9914
15%	0.9944	0.1892	(0.61, 0.23)	0.9478	0.9455	0.9040	0.9981
20%	0.9955	0.1947	(0.62, 0.23)	0.9455	0.9440	0.9013	0.9843
25%	0.9946	0.1975	(0.62, 0.21)	0.9443	0.9399	0.9060	0.9943
30%	0.9931	0.2013	(0.62, 0.23)	0.9411	0.9414	0.9020	0.9886
Average:	0.9935	0.1832	(0.61, 0.22)	0.9479	0.9458	0.9008	0.9918

The GTRS model set $(\alpha, \beta) = (0.61 \pm 0.05, 0.22 \pm 0.15)$ with an accuracy of 94.8% and a generality of 94.6%. It can be observed that in comparison to $(1, 0)$ model, the GTRS model improved generality by upto 76.3% at a cost of mere 4.6% decrease in accuracy. Similarly, when comparison to $(0.5, 0.5)$ model, GTRS model improved accuracy by upto 4.8% at a cost of 4.6% decrease in generality.

To gain more insights, we also provide comparisons with the three-way approach using fix thresholds reported in [17]. In their experiments they achieved average accuracy of 91.07% for the Iris and 75.13% for Pendigit datasets using different missing rates. The GTRS outperforms this approach by achieving accuracies of 94.2% and 94.8% which are 3.13% and 18.5% higher in comparison to the three-way approach with fixed thresholds. These results indicate that the GTRS model may be a more suitable approach for handling data with missing values in clustering.

6   Conclusion

A three-way decision making approach provides a useful solution to deal with clustering of data containing missing values. A critical issue in the application of three-way decisions is the determination of effective thresholds that define different types of decisions. The existing studies lack in providing explicit mechanisms in determining suitable values of thresholds. We address the determination of effective values of thresholds based on a game in GTRS. In particular, a game based on the tradeoff between accuracy and generality is constructed that automatically determines effective thresholds based on the data itself. The GTRS shows an improvement in results when compared to other two other commonly used three-way models defined by threshold settings of (1, 0) and (0.5,0.5). In comparison to the (1, 0) model the GTRS improves the generality by upto 65% while maintaining similar levels of accuracy while in comparison to (0.5, 0.5) model the GTRS improves the accuracy by upto 5% at a cost of some decrease in generality. The reported results and comparisons strongly advocate for the use of the proposed approach for handling missing values.

Acknowledgements. This work was partially supported by a Discovery Grant from NSERC Canada and Indigenous Student Scholarship from HEC Pakistan.

References

1. Azam, N., Yao, J.T.: Formulating game strategies in game-theoretic rough sets. In: Lingras, P., Wolski, M., Cornelis, C., Mitra, S., Wasilewski, P. (eds.) RSKT 2013. LNCS (LNAI), vol. 8171, pp. 145–153. Springer, Heidelberg (2013). https://doi.org/10.1007/978-3-642-41299-8_14
2. Bugnet, M., Kula, A., Niewczas, M., Botton, G.A.: Segregation and clustering of solutes at grain boundaries in mgrare earth solid solutions. Acta Mater. **79**, 66–73 (2014)
3. Dempster, A.P., Laird, N.M., Rubin, D.B.: Maximum likelihood from incomplete data via the EM algorithm. J. Roy. Stat. Soc.: Ser. B (Methodol.) **39**(1), 1–38 (1977)
4. Eye, A.V.: Statistical Methods in Longitudinal Research: Principles and Structuring Change. Statistical Modeling and Decision Science, vol. 1 (2014)
5. Haitovsky, V.: Missing data in regression analysis. J. Roy. Stat. Soc. **30**, 67–82 (1968)
6. Herbert, J.P., Yao, J.T.: Game-theoretic rough sets. Fundam. Inf. **108**(3–4), 267–286 (2011)
7. Hu, J., Li, T., Wang, H., Fujita, H.: Hierarchical cluster ensemble model based on knowledge granulation. Knowl.-Based Syst. **91**, 179–188 (2016)
8. Iam-On, N., Boongeon, T., Garrett, S., Price, C.: A link-based cluster ensemble approach for categorical data clustering. IEEE Trans. Knowl. Data Eng. **24**(3), 413–425 (2012)
9. Li, J.H., Song, S.J., Zhang, Y.L., Zhou, Z.: Robust k-median and k-means clustering algorithms for incomplete data. Mathe. Probl. Eng. **2016**, 1–8 (2016)
10. Lichman, M.: UCI machine learning repository (2013). http://archive.ics.uci.edu/ml. Accessed 9 Feb 2017
11. Little, T.D., Lang, K.M., Wu, W., Rhemtulla, M.: Missing Data. Wiley, New York (2016)
12. Timm, H., Dring, C., Kruse, R.: Different approaches to fuzzy clustering of incomplete datasets. Int. J. Approximate Reasoning **35**(3), 239–249 (2004)
13. Xu, D., Tian, Y.: A comprehensive survey of clustering algorithms. Ann. Data Sci. **2**(2), 165–193 (2015)
14. Xu, R., Wunsch, D.: Survey of clustering algorithms. IEEE Trans. Neural Netw. **16**(3), 645–678 (2005)

15. Yang, X., Li, T., Fujita, H., Liu, D., Yao, Y.: A unified model of sequential three-way decisions and multilevel incremental processing. Knowl.-Based Syst. **134**, 172–188 (2017)
16. Yao, Y.: Rough sets and three-way decisions. In: Ciucci, D., Wang, G., Mitra, S., Wu, W.-Z. (eds.) RSKT 2015. LNCS (LNAI), vol. 9436, pp. 62–73. Springer, Cham (2015). https://doi.org/10.1007/978-3-319-25754-9_6
17. Yu, H.: A framework of three-way cluster analysis. In: Polkowski, L., Yao, Y., Artiemjew, P., Ciucci, D., Liu, D., Ślęzak, D., Zielosko, B. (eds.) IJCRS 2017. LNCS (LNAI), vol. 10314, pp. 300–312. Springer, Cham (2017). https://doi.org/10.1007/978-3-319-60840-2_22
18. Yu, H., Su, T., Zeng, X.: A three-way decisions clustering algorithm for incomplete data. In: Miao, D., Pedrycz, W., Ślęzak, D., Peters, G., Hu, Q., Wang, R. (eds.) RSKT 2014. LNCS (LNAI), vol. 8818, pp. 765–776. Springer, Cham (2014). https://doi.org/10.1007/978-3-319-11740-9_70
19. Yu, H., Zhang, C., Wang, G.: A tree-based incremental overlapping clustering method using the three-way decision theory. Knowl.-Based Syst. **91**, 189–203 (2016)

Scalable Implementations of Rough Set Algorithms: A Survey

Bing Zhou$^{(\boxtimes)}$, Hyuk Cho, and Xin Zhang

Department of Computer Science, Sam Houston State University,
Huntsville, TX 77341, USA
zhou@shsu.edu

Abstract. With the rapid change of volume, variety, and velocity of data across real-life domains, learning from big data has become a growing challenge. Rough set theory has been successfully applied to knowledge discovery from databases (KDD) for handling data with imperfections. Most traditional rough set algorithms were implemented in a sequential manner and ran on a single machine, becoming computationally expensive and inefficient for handling massive data. Recent computing frameworks, such as MapReduce and Apache Spark, made it possible to realize parallel rough set algorithms on distributed clusters of commodity computers and speed up big data analyses. Although a variety of scalable rough set implementations have been developed, (1) most proposed research compared their work with outdated sequential implementations; (2) certain distributed computing frameworks were used more frequently, overlooking recently developed frameworks; and (3) existing issues and guidance in adapting new computing frameworks are lacking. The main objective of this paper is to provide current state-of-the-art scalable implementations of rough set algorithms. This paper will help researchers catch up with the recent developments in this field and further provide some insights to develop rough set algorithms in up-to-date high performance computing environments for big data analytics.

Keywords: Rough set · Scalable · Parallel · Distributed
Hadoop MapReduce · Apache Spark

1 Introduction

Rough set (RS) theory is a mathematical approach for handling data with imperfections [1]. Compared with other mathematical theories that tackle data related issues, such as probability theory [2], fuzzy set theory [3], possibility theory [4], and evidential belief theory [5], RS theory requires no prior knowledge and represents imprecise data based only on its internal structure; thus, it can effectively represent different aspects of data. RS theory has drawn researchers' attentions and has found numerous interesting applications in the areas of machine learning, knowledge discovery from databases (KDD), expert systems, voice recognition, and image processing, to name a few.

© Springer International Publishing AG, part of Springer Nature 2018
M. Mouhoub et al. (Eds.): IEA/AIE 2018, LNAI 10868, pp. 648–660, 2018.
https://doi.org/10.1007/978-3-319-92058-0_62

Although the traditional sequential RS algorithms have been successfully used for rough approximation, decision rule generation, and attribute reduction, they become computationally challenged in processing very large data. For example, experimental study showed that the RS package in R is not able to process dataset with 30,000 instances and 10 attributes on a single computer with 48 CPU cores and 62 GB of memory [6]. Accordingly, this big data challenge has necessitated the development of scalable RS algorithms using novel computing platforms such as distributed systems. The core idea behind distributed systems is to use a group of networked computers to complete a common task. It is also called parallel systems because the processors in a typical distributed system run concurrently in parallel. The inception of parallel computing can be traced back from the 1970s, and various hardware and software architectures have been used ever since. Individual machines that support multi-cores/CPUs could be used for parallel computation. However, a more reliable and fault-tolerant solution would be realized over a network of computers under a unified communication framework.

There are a few novel paradigms that are capable of processing big data in distributed computing environments. One of these software frameworks is Hadoop MapReduce [7], which can process large amounts of data in parallel on clusters of commodity computers. Typically, the MapReduce framework and the Hadoop Distributed File System (HDFS) are running on the same set of computer nodes. This configuration allows the framework to effectively schedule tasks, monitor them, and re-execute failed tasks. Recently, another cluster-computing framework, called Apache Spark, was developed. Particularly, Spark performs in-memory processing of data; thus, it runs much faster than Hadoop MapReduce [8]. Other recent big data processing frameworks include Apache Flink [9], Apache Storm [10], and Apache Samza [11]. They are distributed real-time computing frameworks for stream processing that can also work for batch data processing, whereas MapReduce and Spark are originally designed to work for static batch data processing.

The followings are observed in RS research. Much work has focused more on expanding RS theory for applications with big data than on developing scalable algorithms, although most algorithms based on the RS theory are particularly suited for parallel processing [12]. Research on enhancing the scalability has been repeatedly proposed without referring to other similar approaches; many proposed scalable algorithms only compared their work with traditional sequential algorithms, excluding other existing parallel methods; recent work on scalable algorithms was implemented on the Hadoop MapReduce framework, while other newly developed distributed platforms were not much explored; a few survey papers [13–15] exist in the literature, but still lacking a comprehensive review of the existing scalable frameworks of RS algorithms. To address these issues, this paper aims at providing researchers with current scalable implementations of fundamental RS tasks on state-of-the-art distributed computing frameworks. It will help uncover existing issues and research directions and also shed light on further development of computing frameworks that can improve big data analyses using scalable RS algorithms.

The rest of the paper is organized as follows. Section 2 briefly discusses fundamental RS concepts and tasks. Section 3 introduces the recently-developed popular big data computing frameworks and their differences. Section 4 summarizes exiting scalable RS implementations. Section 5 gives remarks with the future research directions. Finally, Sect. 6 concludes the paper.

2   Rough Set Based Data Reasoning

RS is a formal approximation of a crisp set (i.e., conventional set) in terms of the lower and the upper approximations of the original set [1]. As shown in Fig. 1, each small square represents a group of objects sharing the same attribute subset, $[x]$, called equivalence class. If $[x]$ is in the lower approximation (the inner grey rectangle area), it is surely in the set, while $[x]$ is in the upper approximation (the outer rectangle area), it is surely not in the set.

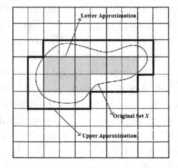

Fig. 1. Lower and upper approximations in a rough set.

Notice that any given set X can be approximated into three regions: the positive region (the union of all objects in the lower approximations), the negative region (the union of all objects in non-empty intersection with X), and the boundary region (the difference between the upper and lower approximation). Accordingly, all objects are categorized into certain exact and possible (approximated) ones with the help of these three regions. RS-based methodology can serve as a useful tool to complement capabilities of other knowledge discovery methods. In what follows, we briefly review the fundamental RS tasks.

2.1   Rough Approximations

The fundamental concept of RS theory is the equivalence relation, which expresses that due to the lack of knowledge in information tables we are unable to discern some objects from others [1].

Instead of dealing with a single object, let us consider a set of indiscernible objects in RS theory. Consider two finite non-empty sets U and A, where U is an approximation space, and A is a set of attributes. Let V_a denote a set of values for each attribute $a \in A$. The equivalence relation $I(A')$, where $A' \subseteq A$, can be defined as: $xI(A')y$ if and only if $a(x) = a(y)$. That is, two objects x and y are indiscernible if they have the same value on every attribute $a \in A$. The family of all equivalence classes of $I(A')$, called the partition determined by A', is donated by $U/I(A')$, or simply U/A'. An equivalence class of $I(A')$, i.e., each small square in Fig. 1, is denoted $[x]_{A'}$.

Now the lower and the upper approximations can be defined respectively as:

$$\underline{apr}_{A'}(X) = \{x \in U \mid [x]_{A'} \subseteq X\} \quad \text{and}$$
$$\overline{apr}_{A'}(X) = \{x \in U \mid [x]_{A'} \cap X \neq \emptyset\}, \tag{1}$$

where every subset of U has a lower approximation as well as a upper approximation. The lower approximation is the union of all equivalence classes that are completely included in the set, and the upper approximation is the union of all equivalence classes that have non-empty intersection with the set.

Additionally, approximation accuracy can be defined as:

$$Accuracy_{A'}(X) = \frac{\mid \underline{apr}_{A'}(X) \mid}{\mid \overline{apr}_{A'}(X) \mid}, \tag{2}$$

where $\mid \cdot \mid$ is the set cardinality. Notice that X is a crispy set with respect to A' when $Accuracy_{A'}(X) = 1$, and X is a rough set when $0 \leq Accuracy_{A'}(X) < 1$.

2.2   Decision Rule Generations

An information table contains two types of attributes, called condition and decision (classification) attributes. Each tuple in an information table determines a decision rule. Decision rules are often interpreted as "if-then" rules. A typical example of decision rule is: if (Weather, sunny) and (Windy, no) then (Play Golf, yes). That is, when the conditions supported by the condition attributes are satisfied, certain decision should be taken.

When two or more decision rules have the same conditions but different decisions, such rules are called *inconsistent* rules, and information tables containing inconsistent rules are called inconsistent table. As a practical method, a set of decision rules generated from information tables is used for learning.

The process of decision rule generation is also called knowledge acquisition in the literature [34,35]. More specifically, there are two types of knowledge acquisition tasks, data regression that is used to predict continuous real values and data classification that is used to predict predefined discrete classes.

2.3   Attribute Reductions

As an important data preprocessing step, feature selection, also known as attribute reduction, refers to the process of removing superfluous condition attributes from the information table. Many reduction criteria are used to choose informative attributes. Attribute reduction relies on the definition of rough approximation and functional dependency between attributes.

For subsets of attributes $B \subseteq A$ and $C \subseteq A$, $B \to C$ is a total dependency if the values of attributes in C are uniquely determined by the values of attributes in B. Partial dependency between attributes can also be considered, that is, attributes in C depend on those in B in a degree d ($0 \le d \le 1$), denoted $B \to_d C$, where d is calculated as the ratio of the number of consistent rules to all rules in a table. When $d = 1$, we say that C totally depends on B.

Attribute reduction is referred to as a minimal subset of attributes that provide the same approximation accuracy and degree of dependencies as in the original table. For a subset of attributes $A' \subseteq A$ and an attribute $a \in A'$ [1]:

- Attribute a is dispensable in A' if $I(A') = I(A' - \{a\})$; otherwise a is indispensable in A'.
- Set A' is independent if all its attributes are indispensable.
- Subset C of A' is a reduct of A' if C is independent and $I(C) = I(A')$.

To be more specific, a reduct is a set of attributes that preserves partition. Therefore, attributes that do not belong to a reduct are superfluous to classification of objects in the information table.

3 Distributed Computing Frameworks

As datasets explored in RS tasks are usually very large, processing large scale data is computationally expensive; thus, researchers seek to make RS algorithms more scalable using high performance computing paradigms. In this section, we summarize recently-developed distributed computing frameworks.

3.1 MapReduce Paradigm

Hadoop is a software framework that realizes parallel processing of large dataset stored in the HDFS, following the MapReduce model. MapReduce introduced by Google [7] is a programming model facilitating computation of vast amounts of datasets on large computer clusters on commodity hardware. Basically, the framework splits the input data and distributes the split data across the cluster, then the Map function is performed on each split in parallel. Finally, the results are aggregated and sent to the Reduce function to produce a single output [54].

As shown in Fig. 2, a complete Hadoop cluster consists of three components: the HDFS master (namenode), the job submission node (jobtracker), and many slave nodes. Each slave node runs a tasktracker for executing Map and Reduce tasks and a datanode daemon for serving HDFS data [52].

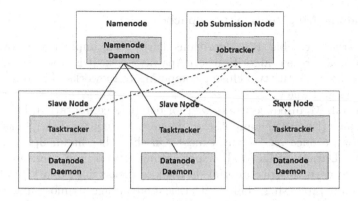

Fig. 2. Hadoop cluster architecture [52].

3.2 Apache Spark

Apache Spark is a distributed computing framework with in-memory data processing engine, developed by AMPLab in UC Berkeley [8] and then donated to Apache Software Foundation (ASF). Because of its multi-stage in-memory computation property, the framework allows user programs to load data into memory and query it repeatedly; thus, it runs learning algorithms up to 100 times faster than Hadoop MapReduce does [36].

Like Hadoop, Apache Spark is a distributed platform that has a master-slave architecture. As shown in Fig. 3, a Spark cluster has a single master/driver node and several slave/worker nodes. The master process executes on the master node, which manages executor processes and can be integrated with resource management modules like Apache Hadoop YARN [37] and Apache Mesos [38]. Each slave process runs on the worker node and performs all the data processing. Each executor stores the computation results in-memory, cache or disk storage.

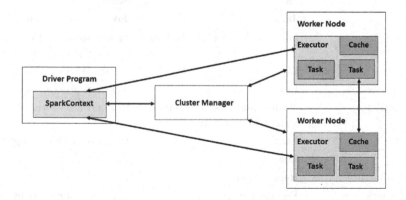

Fig. 3. The Apache Spark framework [53].

3.3 Hadoop MapReduce vs. Apache Spark

Several earlier scalable RS algorithms have been implemented on Hadoop MapReduce and recent algorithms on Apache Spark. It is worth comparing the differences between the two cluster computing frameworks. The differences are summarized in Table 1.

In general, MapReduce works well for one-pass computation, but inefficient for multi-pass (iterative) computation, requesting frequent disk I/O as it follows WORM (write once read many times). On the other hand, Spark's Resilient Distributed Dataset (RDDs) allow performing several map operations in memory, with no need to write interim datasets to disks; thus, Spark fits better for iterative data processing. This is a critical advantage as most machine learning algorithms work iteratively. Furthermore, Spark guarantees fault-tolerance by tracking lost data with RDDs and Directed Acyclic Graph (DAG) of nodes, which also improves RDD reads and writes.

It should be noted that although we do not review other parallel computing frameworks, such as Message Passing Interface (MPI) and Graphics Processing Unit (GPU), they are important and still useful as they are considered vital precursors of the state-of-the-art computing frameworks.

Table 1. Hadoop MapReduce vs. Apache Spark.

Criteria	Hadoop MapReduce	Apache Spark
Installation	Bound to Hadoop	Unbound to Hadoop
Storage	HDFS	HDFS, HBase, etc.
Resource management	YARN	YARN, Mesos, SIMR, standalone
Computation model	Disk-based batch processing	In-memory batch and stream processing
Written in	Java	Scala
API	Java	Java, Python, Scala, R
Library	Separate tools (e.g., Mahout)	Spark Core, Spark Streaming Spark SQL, MLlib, GraphX
OS	Linux	Linux, Windows, Mac OS
Data processing	Linear processing	Iterative processing
Interactivity	No in-build interactive mode except Pig and Hive	In-build interactive mode
Speed	Fast	100x faster than MapReduce
Cost	Low	High
Fault tolerance	Replication	RDD
Bottle neck	Frequent disk I/O	Large memory consumption

4   Scalable Implementations of Rough Set Algorithms

A variety of distributed RS algorithms have been proposed. Table 2 summarizes the existing scalable implementations of RS algorithms.

The effective computation of rough approximations is an essential step in knowledge acquisition and reduction based on RS. Following the initial work of Zhang et al. [19], others [25, 27, 39, 40] provided similar parallel strategies of computing RS approximations on Hadoop MapReduce, each of which used different MapReduce algorithms to compute equivalence class, decision class, indexes, and association. Zhang et al. [18, 35] later extended their work for handling incomplete Information Systems (IS) and continuous attributes. Kawhale et al. [23] provided the Map and Reduce functions based on data cube. Asfoor et al. [6] proposed to calculate fuzzy rough lower and upper approximations based on fuzzy similarity matrix on MPI. Li et al. [17] proposed a method of approximation for the dominance-based RS approach (DRSA). Huang et al. [20] provided a prototype of computing rough approximation using Apache Spark; however, this short paper did not provide details on the parallel methodology.

Similar to rough approximation, most work on parallel attribute reduction made use of the MapReduce framework on the Hadoop platform. Gromniak [21] implemented RS random and dynamic reducts in the MapReduce paradigm and the performance was compared to Monte Carlo feature selection. Cui et al. [24] proposed an algorithm for knowledge reduction using MapReduce, based on information entropy and the results were compared with reduction based on positive regions. Xu et al. [42] examined a parallel attribute reduction algorithm by focusing on fuzzy rough set theory and mutual information, but it does not calculate the fuzzy rough lower and upper approximations explicitly. El-Alfy et al. [28] provided a scalable implementation of a genetic algorithm in Hadoop MapReduce to approximate the minimum reduct. Lv et al. [33] designed two strategies of an incremental attribute reduction algorithm for big data using MapReduce. Yang et al. [31] presented a parallel attribute reduction method for massive data based on MapReduce and their work was extended in [43] to compute attribute core. Xi et al. [32] and Qian et al. [44] presented parallel attribute reduction algorithms similar to Yang et al. [31] based on MapReduce. Zhang et al. [16] proposed a Parallel Large-scale Attribute Reduction (PLAR) algorithm with four representative heuristic feature selection algorithms on Spark. Chen et al. [30] proposed an attribute reduction algorithm for energy data using Spark by taking advantage of in-memory computing, where a heuristic formula was used for measuring the significance of attribute to reduce search space.

Data classification using RS has been actively used for knowledge acquisition. More recently, with emergence of big data, researchers show RS-based classification techniques produce efficient results. Chaudhuri [26] proposed a supervised parallel fuzzy rough Support Vector Machine (SVM) for data classification using MapReduce. Zhang et al. [41] presented parallel RS based methods for knowledge acquisition using MapReduce. Dai et al. [46] developed a Naive Bayes classification algorithm that is combined with RS theory for text classification in MapReduce framework. Kwiatkowski et al. [29] presented a scalable frequent

Table 2. Scalable RS implementations on big data frameworks.

RS task	Approach	BigData framework	Reference
Rough approximation	Parallel method	MapReduce	[19, 25, 27, 39, 40]
	Data cube	MapReduce	[23]
	Fuzzy rough approximation	MPI & Spark	[6]
	Composite RS	GPUs	[35]
	DRSA-based approximation	Multi-core	[17]
	Incomplete IS	MapReduce	[18]
	NA	Spark	[20]
Attribute reduction	PLAR algorithm	Spark	[16]
	Random and dynamic reducts	MapReduce	[21]
	Information entropy	MapReduce	[24]
	Fuzzy rough parallel reduct	NA	[42]
	Parallel genetic algorithm	MapReduce	[28]
	Heuristic formula	Spark	[30]
	Parallel method	MapReduce	[31, 32, 44]
	Attribute core	MapReduce	[43]
	Incremental attribute reduct	MapReduce	[33]
Classification	Fuzzy rough SVM	MapReduce	[26]
	FDP method	NA	[29]
	Parralel method	MapReduce	[41]
	Naive Bayes	MapReduce	[46]
Regression	Fuzzy rough set	Spark	[22]
Association	NIS-Apriori algorithm	Spark	[45]

pattern mining algorithm, called FDP, a modified FP-growth algorithm, and implemented the RS-based lazy classification method.

Vluymans et al. [22] proposed a distributed prototype selection method based on fuzzy rough set theory for big data regression and the experiments were carried in Apache Spark. Wu et al. [45] developed a parallel Apriori association rule learning algorithm for Non-deterministic Information Systems (NIS) in Apache Spark.

5   Remarks and Future Research

This section provides some remarks on current status and desirable potential research directions in the development of scalable RS algorithms.

1. While a variety of distributed methods have been proposed for most RS tasks on big data platforms, some of these methods did not provide enough details for interested readers to implement or reproduce the experiments. For

instance, Nandgaonkar et al. [27], Pradeepa et al. [39], and Patil [40] did not include any experimental studies, and Huang et al. [20] did not provide details on the parallel methodology.

2. Validations of most existing research were performed by comparing performance with traditional sequential algorithms. It can be more useful to compare with recent methodologies and frameworks that can handle big data.

3. Mahout [50] is a software library produces implementations of parallel machine learning algorithms on top of Apache Hadoop. MLlib [51] is part of Apache Spark that implements a variety of machine learning algorithms. It is worth noting that, while RS package has been deployed in some popular data mining tools, such as WEKA [47], R [48], and ROSETTA [49], the RS algorithms for handling large scale datasets are currently not included in Mahout or MLlib libraries. Implementation of distributed RS algorithms in the state-of-the-art computing platforms would encourage wider audience to perform various big data analyses.

4. While many parallel methods aimed to be deployed on Hadoop MapReduce, only a few were implemented on Apache Spark, MPI, and GPU. It is not clear whether a universal implementation can be developed across different platforms, or to say the least, whether these parallel methods can be easily transformed to work on other platforms.

5. Most work focused on the two fundamental RS tasks: computing lower/upper approximations and attribute reductions. Therefore, it is desirable to develop scalable RS algorithms for other important data mining and machine learning tasks.

6   Conclusions

For various big data analyses in very large information systems, the computation of RS tasks becomes a demanding process in terms of both processing time and memory utilization. The traditional sequential RS algorithms are no longer suitable for handling big data. This raises the need for developing scalable implementations of algorithms that can make more efficient use of time and memory. In this paper, we review existing parallel implementations of RS tasks, including computations of rough approximations, attribute reductions, classification, regression, and association rule learning. We highlight the recent developments in this field, and provides some insights on developing scalable algorithms for big data analyses using RS theory. We also identify existing issues and provide potential future research directions to stimulate readers' interest in the field.

References

1. Pawlak, Z.: Rough Sets, Theoretical Aspects of Reasoning About Data. Kluwer Academic Publishers, Dordrecht (1991)
2. Duda, R.O., Hart, P.E.: Pattern Classification and Scene Analysis. Wiley, New York (1973)
3. Zadeh, L.A.: Fuzzy sets. Inf. Control **8**(3), 338–353 (1965)
4. Zadeh, L.: Fuzzy sets as a basis for a theory of possibility. Fuzzy Sets Syst. **1**(1), 3–28 (1978)
5. Shafer, G.: A Mathematical Theory of Evidence. Princeton University Press, Princeton (1976)
6. Hasan, A., Srinivasan, R., Vasudevan, G., Verbiest, N., Cornelis, C., Tolentino, M.E., Teredesai, A., Cock, M.D.: Computing fuzzy rough approximations in large scale information systems. In: BigData Conference, pp. 9–16 (2014)
7. Dean, J., Ghemawat, S.: MapReduce: simplified data processing on large clusters. Commun. ACM **51**(1), 107–113 (2008)
8. Zaharia, M., Xin, R.S., Wendell, P., Das, T., Armbrust, M., Dave, A., Meng, X., Rosen, J., Venkataraman, S., Franklin, M.J.: Apache spark: a unified engine for big data processing. Commun. ACM **59**(11), 56–65 (2016)
9. Apache Flink: Scalable stream and batch data processing. https://flink.apache.org/
10. Apache Storm. http://storm.apache.org/
11. Samza. http://samza.apache.org/
12. Pawlak, Z.: Rough set approach to knowledge-based decision support. Eur. J. Oper. Res. **99**(1), 48–57 (1997)
13. Jadhav, S., Suryawanshi, S.: A survey on parallel rough set based knowledge acquisition using MapReduce from big data (2014)
14. Nandgaonkar, Suruchi, V., Raut, A.B.: A survey on parallel method for rough set using MapReduce technique for data mining. Int. J. Eng. Comput. Sci. (2015)
15. Li, T., Luo, C., Chen, H., Zhang, J.: PICKT: a solution for big data analysis. In: Ciucci, D., Wang, G., Mitra, S., Wu, W.-Z. (eds.) RSKT 2015. LNCS (LNAI), vol. 9436, pp. 15–25. Springer, Cham (2015). https://doi.org/10.1007/978-3-319-25754-9_2
16. Zhang, J., Li, T., Pan, Y.: PLAR: parallel large-scale attribute reduction on cloud systems. In: PDCAT, pp. 184–191 (2013)
17. Li, S.Y., Li, T.R., Zhang, Z.X., Chen, H.M., Zhang, J.B.: Parallel computing of approximations in dominance-based rough sets approach. Knowl. Based Syst. **87**, 102–111 (2015)
18. Zhang, J.B., Wong, J.S., Pan, Y., Li, T.R.: A parallel matrix-based method for computing approximations in incomplete information systems. IEEE Trans. Knowl. Data Eng. **27**(2), 326–229 (2015)
19. Zhang, J.B., Li, T.R., Ruan, D., Gao, Z.Z., Zhao, C.B.: A parallel method for computing rough set approximations. Inf. Sci. **194**, 209–223 (2012)
20. Huang, K.M., Chen, H.Y., Hsiung, K.L.: On realizing rough set algorithms with apache spark. In: Third International Conference on Data Mining, Internet Computing and Big Data, pp. 111–112 (2016)
21. Gromniak, W.: Scalability of attribute selection methods: application of rough sets and MapReduce. Dissertation Institute of Mathematics, University of Warsaw (2015)

22. Sarah, V., Asfoor, H., Saeys, Y., Cornelis, C., Tolentino, M.E., Teredesai, A., Cock, M.D.: Distributed fuzzy rough prototype selection for big data regression. In: NAFIPS/WConSC, pp. 1–6 (2015)
23. Kawhale, R., Patil, S.: Obtaining approximation with data cube using MapReduce. Int. J. Recent Innov. Trends Comput. Commun. **3**(7), 4880–4884 (2015). ISSN: 2321–8169
24. Cui, W.P., Huang, L.: A MapReduce solution for knowledge reduction in big data. IJCSA **13**(1), 17–30 (2016)
25. Dhande, V., Sarkar, B.K.: Obtaining rough set approximation using MapReduce technique in data mining (2016)
26. Chaudhuri, A.: Parallel fuzzy rough support vector machine for data classification in cloud environment. Informatica **39**(4), 397–420 (2015)
27. Nandgaonkar, S.V., Raut, A.B.: Parallel rough set approximation using MapReduce technique in Hadoop (2015)
28. El-Alfy, E., Alshammari, M.: Towards scalable rough set based attribute subset selection for intrusion detection using parallel genetic algorithm in MapReduce. Simul. Model. Pract. Theory **64**, 18–29 (2016)
29. Kwiatkowski, P., Nguyen, S.H., Nguyen, H.S.: On scalability of rough set methods. In: Hüllermeier, E., Kruse, R., Hoffmann, F. (eds.) IPMU 2010. CCIS, vol. 80, pp. 288–297. Springer, Heidelberg (2010). https://doi.org/10.1007/978-3-642-14055-6_30
30. Chen, M., Yuan, J., Li, L., Liu, D., Li, T.: A fast heuristic attribute reduction algorithm using Spark. In: 2017 IEEE 37th International Conference Distributed Computing Systems (ICDCS) (2017)
31. Yang, Y., Chen, Z., Liang, Z., Wang, G.: Attribute reduction for massive data based on rough set theory and MapReduce. In: Yu, J., Greco, S., Lingras, P., Wang, G., Skowron, A. (eds.) RSKT 2010. LNCS (LNAI), vol. 6401, pp. 672–678. Springer, Heidelberg (2010). https://doi.org/10.1007/978-3-642-16248-0_91
32. Xi, D., Wang, G., Zhang, X., Zhang, F.: Parallel attribute reduction based on MapReduce. In: Miao, D., Pedrycz, W., Ślęzak, D., Peters, G., Hu, Q., Wang, R. (eds.) RSKT 2014. LNCS (LNAI), vol. 8818, pp. 631–641. Springer, Cham (2014). https://doi.org/10.1007/978-3-319-11740-9_58
33. Lv, P., Qian, J., Yue, X.: Incremental attribute reduction algorithm for big data using MapReduce. J. Comput. Methods Sci. Eng. **16**(3), 641–652 (2016)
34. Feng, L., Li, T., Ruan, D., Gou, S.: A vague-rough set approach for uncertain knowledge acquisition. Knowl. Based Syst. **24**(6), 837–843 (2011)
35. Zhang, J.B., Wong, J., Li, T., Pan, Y.: A comparison of parallel large-scale knowledge acquisition using rough set theory on different MapReduce runtime systems. Int. J. Approximate Reasoning **55**(3), 896–907 (2014)
36. Xin, R.S., Rosen, J., Zaharia, M., Franklin, M., Shenker, S., Stoic, I.: Shark: SQL and rich analytics at scale. In: 2013 ACM SIGMOD International Conference on Management of Data, pp. 13–24 (2013)
37. Karun, A.K., Chitharanjan, K.: A review on Hadoop–HDFS infrastructure extensions. In: 2013 IEEE Conference on Information & Communication Technologies (ICT), pp. 132–137 (2013)
38. What is Apache Spark? https://databricks.com/spark/about
39. Pradeepa, A., Thanamani, A.: Hadoop file system and fundamental concept of MapReduce Interior and closure rough set approximations. Int. J. Adv. Res. Comput. Commun. Eng. **2**(10), 5865–5868 (2013)
40. Patil, P.: Data mining with rough set using MapReduce. Int. J. Innov. Res. Comput. Commun. Eng. **2**(11), 6980–6986 (2014)

41. Zhang, J.B., Li, T.R., Pan, Y.: Parallel rough set based knowledge acquisition using MapReduce from big data. In: 1st International Workshop on Big Data, Streams and Heterogeneous Source Mining: Algorithms, Systems, Programming Models and Applications, pp. 20–27. ACM (2012)

42. Xu, F., Wei, L., Bi, Z., Zhu, L.: Research on fuzzy rough parallel reduction based on mutual information. J. Comput. Inf. Syst. **10**(12), 5391–5401 (2014)

43. Yang, Y., Chen, Z.: Parallelized computing of attribute core based on rough set theory and MapReduce. In: Li, T., Nguyen, H.S., Wang, G., Grzymala-Busse, J., Janicki, R., Hassanien, A.E., Yu, H. (eds.) RSKT 2012. LNCS (LNAI), vol. 7414, pp. 155–160. Springer, Heidelberg (2012). https://doi.org/10.1007/978-3-642-31900-6_20

44. Qian, J., Miao, D., Zhang, Z., Yue, X.: Parallel attribute reduction algorithms using MapReduce. Inf. Sci. **279**, 671–690 (2014)

45. Wu, M., Sakai, H.: On parallelization of the NIS-apriori algorithm for data mining. Procedia Comput. Sci. **60**, 623–631 (2015)

46. Dai, Y., Sun, H.: The naive Bayes text classification algorithm based on rough set in the cloud platform. J. Chem. Pharm. Res. **6**, 1636–1643 (2014)

47. Weka 3 - Data mining with open source machine learning software in Java. https://www.cs.waikato.ac.nz/ml/weka/

48. R: The R project for statistical computing. https://www.r-project.org/

49. Komorowski, J., Ohrn, A., Skowron, A.: The ROSETTA rough set software system. In: Handbook of Data Mining and Knowledge Discovery, pp. 2–3 (2002)

50. Owen, S.: Mahout in Action. Manning, Shelter Island (2012)

51. Meng, X., Bradley, J., Yavuz, B., Sparks, E., Venkataraman, S., Liu, D., Freeman, J., Tsai, D., Amde, M., Owen, S., Xin, D.: MLlib: machine learning in apache spark. J. Mach. Learn. Res. **17**(1), 1235–1241 (2016)

52. Lin, J., Dyer, C.: Data-Intensive text processing with MapReduce. Synthesis Lectures on Human Language Technologies, vol. 3, pp. 1–177 (2010)

53. https://spark.apache.org/docs/latest/img/cluster-overview.png

54. Garca-Gil, D., Ramrez-Gallego, S., Garca, S., Herrera, F.: A comparison on scalability for batch big data processing on Apache Spark and Apache Flink. Big Data Analytics **2**(1) (2017)

Fuzzy Clustering Ensemble for Prioritized Sampling Based on Average and Rough Patterns

Matt Triff, Ilya Pavlovski, Zhixing Liu, Lori-Anne Morgan,
and Pawan Lingras[(✉)]

Mathematics and Computing Science, Saint Mary's University, Halifax, Canada
{matt.triff,pawan}@cs.smu.ca

Abstract. This paper uses fuzzy clustering to extend a previous prioritized sampling proposal. In many big data problems, modeling an individual object such as a large engineering plant can be a tedious process requiring up to a month of analysis. A solution is to model as many representative objects as possible to represent the entire population. A new object can then use a model (or combination of models) from previously analyzed objects that best matches its characteristics. Since the modeling process can continue indefinitely adding models over time, we prioritize the sampling based on the ability of objects to represent as many characteristics as possible. The approach is demonstrated with a large set of weather stations to create a ranked sample based on hourly and monthly variations of important weather parameters, such as temperature, solar radiation, wind speed, and humidity. The weather patterns are represented using a combination of average and rough patterns to capture the essence of the distribution. The weather stations are grouped using Fuzzy C-Means and the objects with the largest fuzzy memberships are used as the representatives of each cluster. The weather stations representing a combination of different clustering schemes are then ranked based on the number of weather patterns they represent.

Keywords: Clustering · Fuzzy clustering · Rough patterns
Sampling · Weather

1 Introduction

Unsupervised clustering can be used to group a large set of patterns into a more manageable smaller number of groups. If the resulting clusters are compact and well separated enough, we can use the medoid (the object closest to the centroid) as a representative for the entire cluster. This fact can be used for sampling purposes. If we have n objects that can be clustered into k compact clusters, we can only analyze the medoids of the k clusters. The analysis for the medoid for $cluster_i$ can then be used for all the objects that belong to $cluster_i$. This approach can be used to reduce or prioritize tedious modeling processes

© Springer International Publishing AG, part of Springer Nature 2018
M. Mouhoub et al. (Eds.): IEA/AIE 2018, LNAI 10868, pp. 661–669, 2018.
https://doi.org/10.1007/978-3-319-92058-0_63

in engineering analysis. Many engineering models require weeks or months of careful modeling. Ideally, we want to model every engineering plant. However, it is not always possible to wait for the modeling process to be complete for the entire set. In that case, we can use a combination of models that best match the new plant as an interim solution.

In a previous paper [4] we used the conventional crisp clustering to group a set of weather stations from a reasonably large weather dataset, consisting of three years worth of hourly variations in temperature, solar radiation, wind speed and humidity. In order to develop the most meaningful profile descriptions, the weather stations are first represented using average hourly variations for each month of the year. However, a quick analysis of the resulting clustering suggested that the average values do not capture the extreme fluctuations in some of the more severe climates. Therefore, the representations of the weather stations are further enhanced by adding rough hourly patterns for each month of the year. A rough pattern consists of low and high values of a quantity [3]. It is especially relevant in knowledge representations where variation in the values is as important as the average values. For example, two places may have the same average temperature of say 25 °C but one of them may have a low of 10° and high of 30° as opposed to another where the temperature varies only by ±5°.

This paper extends the previous approach by using the Fuzzy C-Means algorithm for clustering [1,2]. Fuzzy clustering allows an object to belong to multiple clusters by assigning membership values. Fuzzy memberships make it easier to pick the most representative member for each cluster and cluster combination by taking the sum of fuzzy memberships of the weather stations for each cluster used in the combination.

2   Study Data and Knowledge Representation

The study data consists of weather data collected from weather stations in North America. For the purposes of this study, 1000 weather stations were randomly selected. The weather stations cover Canada and the United States of America. The weather data was recorded from each weather station at an interval of once per hour, over the course of three years. This resulted in raw data for each weather station having approximately 24 h * 365 days * 3 years = 26280 records.

The data collected from the weather stations includes parameters for temperature, solar radiation, humidity and wind speed. In order to create a more concise knowledge representation for clustering, the values were aggregated. Each weather station has four different knowledge representations. Each knowledge representation corresponds to one of the four parameters. Each month of weather data for each parameter is aggregated into average and rough hourly patterns. For example, the temperature between 00:00 and 01:00 in the month of January is aggregated as the minimum, average, and maximum temperature values that occurred throughout the entire month, during that hour. This means that each parameter measured by a single weather station has three values for every hour of every month for every year collected. A single weather station is therefore represented by 3 values * 24 h * 12 months * 3 years = 2592 values for each parameter.

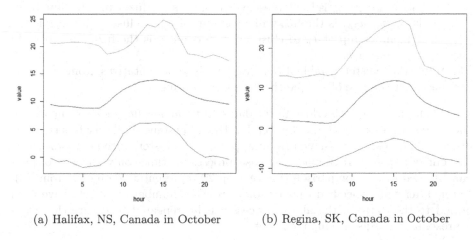

(a) Halifax, NS, Canada in October   (b) Regina, SK, Canada in October

Fig. 1. Plotted knowledge representation of the temperature parameter, for two weather stations

Figures 1a and b show examples of two such weather locations. Both figures show lines plotted for the high, average, and lows for each hour of the day, accumulated over the same hour for the entire month. Between the two figures, we can see distinct behaviours, with the temperature being much lower in Regina. We also see that the temperature is warmer over a shorter period of time, rising and falling quickly.

3   Prioritized Fuzzy Clustering Ensemble

We will describe the proposed fuzzy clustering ensemble based on the weather clustering problem. However, it can be generalized to any similar criterion. Due to space restrictions, we refer the readers to [1,2] for fuzzy clustering and [3] for rough patterns. The steps for the proposed technique are as follows:

F1. Collect a large number of weather files from weather stations spread across the region.

F2. Extract average, min., and max. hourly patterns for all the twelve months for important weather parameters such as temperature, solar radiation, wind speed, and humidity.

F3. For the dataset obtained by F2, determine the appropriate number of clusters for each of the weather parameters. Create clustering schemes such as $T = t_1, t_2, ..., t_5$ for temperature, $S = s_1, s_2, ..., s_{10}$ for solar radiation, $W = w_1, w_2, ..., w_5$ for wind speed, $H = h_1, h_2, ..., h_5$ for humidity.

F4. Find the best representative weather station for each cluster, such as t_i, s_j, w_k, h_m, where $i, j, k, m = 1, ..., 5$ or 10. Find a representative for each cluster combination such as $t_i - s_j - w_k - h_m$ such that the sum $ut_{pi} + us_{pj} + uw_{pk} + uh_{pm}$ is the largest, where ut_{pi} is the fuzzy membership of x_p to cluster t_i, us_{pj} is the fuzzy membership of x_p to cluster s_j, uw_{pk} is the fuzzy membership of x_p to cluster w_k, and uh_{pm} is the fuzzy membership of x_p to cluster h_m.

F5. Rank the cluster combinations (and their representatives from step F4) based on the size of sample they are representing.

When a new object is added to the dataset, it can now be quickly compared to the representive objects found by step F4. Based on some similarity function, the object can quickly be assigned to an approximate cluster, without reprocessing the entire dataset. To further decrease processing time, only the top objects can be used in the comparison (i.e. the top 20 representative objects from F5). Later, after some specified time or some specified number of objects have been added to the dataset, the above process can be repeated to ensure the set of representative objects remain current.

4   Results and Discussions

Once the data has been converted to our specified knowledge representation, it is ready to be clustered. In order to determine the best clustering scheme for the data, we first determine the optimal number of clusters. The optimal number of clusters for a given dataset can be defined as the optimization of within cluster scatter. Within cluster scatter is the average distance between two points within a cluster.

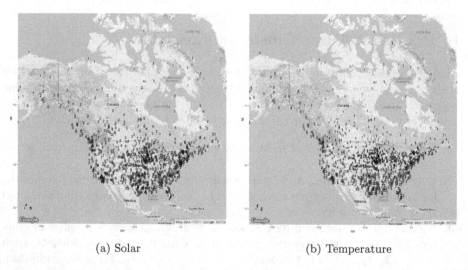

(a) Solar   (b) Temperature

Fig. 2. Weather stations plotted by location, labelled by the cluster they most belong to

Since objects in Fuzzy C-Means clustering belong to many clusters at once, using within cluster scatter does not provide useful results. Instead, the data for each parameter is first clustered separately using the K-means algorithm to determine a reasonable number of clusters. If there are too few clusters and too many objects grouped together, the resulting within cluster scatter will be very large. Too many clusters and the clusters become less useful as each object trends towards receiving it's own cluster. Therefore, to determine the optimal number of clusters we compare the results of clustering with various number of clusters. By plotting the within cluster scatter versus the number of clusters, we can determine where the "knee" of the curve is. This "knee" defines the point where the clusters are relatively compact, but have enough members to still be valuable. The results for each of the parameters were plotted. The plots are not shown due to space restrictions. Based on those plots, the optimal number of clusters was found to be five for all parameters except solar, where the optimal number was ten. This method of determining the optimal number of clusters is admittedly slightly subjective. In general, having an additional one or two clusters would not significantly impact the results. We found that this number of clusters provided reasonable results for Fuzzy C-Means clustering.

Each weather station was plotted by location and labelled based on the cluster it had the greatest affinity to. There are some general patterns that can be observed in the clustering of all the different parameters. First, it is clear that the weather patterns detected by these weather stations is largely regional. In most cases, the clusters are grouped together not only by their similar weather parameter (solar, temperature, humidity, or wind), but also by their physical location.

Some interesting patterns can also be observed from viewing these clusters. For example, all of Canada, except southern Ontario and Quebec, typically have similar weather patterns. Coastal weather stations are the most similar, often belonging to the same cluster on both the East and West coasts. Solar has the most variation, as can be inferred from the higher optimal number of clusters. The solar clusters are also necessarily smaller, with more regional variation in the United States, particularly in the Midwestern and Southern United States. Whereas most clusters appear in large groups and bands across the continent, solar has smaller clusters of regional variation.

Cluster	1	2	3	4	5	6	7	8	9	10
Temperature	141	199	236	345	79					
Solar	44	90	163	60	110	69	107	142	169	46
Wind	329	79	307	45	240					
Humidity	138	297	64	156	345					

Fig. 3. Cluster sizes for each parameter, based on the cluster that a given object has the highest degree of belonging

Figure 3 shows the sizes of the clusters for each of the four parameters. The parameters with five clusters each have a large cluster of approximately 330–345 objects. These clusters typically correspond to the United States Mid-West and East coast, where there is a higher density of weather stations. Each parameter also has one or two comparatively small clusters, with around 45–80 objects. These clusters correspond with a number of different areas, such as Alaska and the Canadian coasts, where a smaller number of weather stations have been sampled. Solar, with a larger number of overall clusters, has the smallest range of all clusters, from 44 to 169 weather stations. This again shows the smaller regional variations that can be observed in solar patterns.

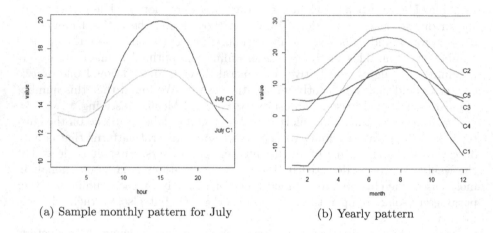

(a) Sample monthly pattern for July   (b) Yearly pattern

Fig. 4. Sample of average temperature patterns, by cluster

The monthly average temperature patterns of two clusters for July can be observed in Fig. 4a. Although the temperature varies throughout the day, and by the month, the patterns of the fluctuation can define our clusters. In Fig. 4a, we see that Cluster 5 has relatively constant temperature throughout the entire day. For Cluster 1, we see that the temperature falls more dramatically overnight. When comparing these results to the map of weather stations labelled by temperature cluster in Fig. 2b it was observed that weather stations in Cluster 1 are predominantly located in Canada, whereas the weather stations in Cluster 2 the Southern band of the United States, closer to the equator, where we would expect more temperature variation throughout the day.

From Fig. 4b, we can see the yearly temperature patterns for each of the five clusters. In this case, we can see that clusters 1–4 have similar weather patterns throughout the year, cold during the winter months of the Northern hemisphere, and steadily rising through Spring, peaking in Summer, and falling in the Fall. The difference between the weather stations in each cluster is where the range of temperatures lie. Additionally, we can see the range is greatest in Cluster 1, where the curve is steepest. Finally, Cluster 5 is the outlier, in that the temperature throughout the entire year remains relatively constant, with only a (relatively) slight increase over the Summer months. As shown in Fig. 2b, Cluster 5 consists mostly of weather stations on the West coast and in Alaska.

The yearly average solar patterns from the ten different clusters are shown in Fig. 5b. Here the patterns are more difficult to discern between clusters. In general, all clusters follow the same pattern of having the most sunlight in the Summer months, and the least in Winter months. Similarly to the temperature clusters, the clusters vary in the range of the amount of light they receive. Weather stations in Cluster 1 will almost always receive the least light. Weather stations in Cluster 1 are mainly located in Northern Canada and the Canadian Arctic, where daylight hours are more limited throughout the year.

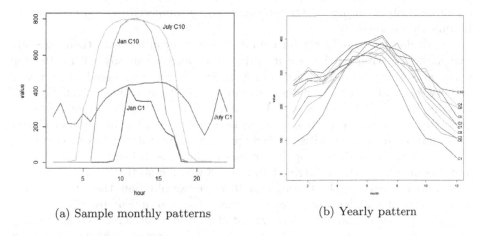

(a) Sample monthly patterns   (b) Yearly pattern

Fig. 5. Sample of average solar patterns, by cluster

The sample of monthly solar patterns shown in Fig. 5a show more pronounced differences betweeen clusters 1 and 10. Cluster 10, situated mostly in the state of Georgia, where although the patterns differ in the length of daylight hours, the curves are very similar between January and July. Cluster 1, consisting of weather stations in Alaska and the Canadian Arctic show very different patterns between the two months, with very limited daylight hours in January, and constant daylight hours throughout July. Throughout, the peak amount of sunlight in cluster 1 is approximately half the peak of cluster 10.

Once the clusters for the individual parameters have been determined, meta-clusters can be created. Meta-clusters are combinations of the parameters clusters. Simply, these cluster combinations are the set of weather stations that have the greatest degree of belonging to a given set of parameter clusters (t_i, s_j, w_k, h_m). For all possible cluster combinations, we rank them by the number of weather stations that belong to the cluster combination i.e. the size. From our data, we show the top 10 cluster combinations in Fig. 6. Out of all 1250 possible cluster combinations, only 197 had at least one weather station. Of the

Weather	o_{w1}	o_{w2}	o_{w3}	o_{w4}	o_{w5}	o_{w6}	o_{w7}	o_{w8}	o_{w9}	o_{w10}
Temperature	t_4	t_3	t_4	t_2	t_3	t_4	t_1	t_3	t_4	t_5
Solar	s_8	s_9	s_3	s_4	s_3	s_7	s_2	s_9	s_3	s_1
Wind	w_1	w_3	w_5	w_3	w_3	w_1	w_1	w_5	w_5	w_4
Humidity	h_2	h_5	h_2	h_5	h_5	h_2	h_2	h_4	h_5	h_1
Size	37	33	33	30	26	25	23	23	22	21

Fig. 6. Cluster sizes for the top 10 cluster combinations for the weather patterns

197 cluster combinations, only 60 had at least five weather stations. All of the valid cluster combinations can serve as our prototypical weather profiles. Based on these clusters, future weather stations can be compared to their centroids to be quickly assigned.

Analyzing the top 10 cluster combinations, we can see that their sizes are reasonably distributed. We see a fairly steep decrease in size within the top seven cluster combinations, decreasing by 38% before more gradual decreases of between zero and two weather stations in all the remaining cluster combinations. The largest decreases, of 11% and 13% occur between combinations 1 and 2, and 4 and 5, respectively. Based on these decreases, the top four cluster combinations may be prioritized when applying the prototypical weather profiles to new data. In total, the top 10 clusters encompass 273 of the 1000 weather stations analyzed. This is larger than the 253 weather stations found in the top 10 via crisp clustering [4]. Through qualtitative examination, the set of weather stations found via the fuzzy clustering ensemble also appear to cover a larger variation in weather patterns. The largest cluster combination consists primarily of a set of weather stations within the Great Lakes region. The second largest cluster combination consists primarily of a set of weather stations within the American South. In analyzing these cluster combinations, we see that the location of their composite weather stations are in physically similar locations. This similarity can occur in proximity or topography.

5   Summary and Conclusions

This paper uses a fuzzy clustering ensemble of objects that are clustered using different criteria to create prioritized sampling. We use a weather stations dataset to illustrate the proposed approach. The weather stations are clustered using four different criteria: temperature, solar radiation, wind speed, and humidity. The representation of a weather station for each criteria uses a combination of average and rough patterns. The patterns reflect daily variations over 12 months. The weather stations sampling is ranked based on the ability of the weather station to represent most real world weather patterns. The proposed approach is a fuzzy extension of a similar approach that used crisp clustering. The fuzzy memberships made it easier to identify the most representative weather stations for a given clustering combination. The top rankings resulting from fuzzy clustering seemed to cover a larger variation in weather patterns than the corresponding results obtained from crisp clustering.

References

1. Bezdek, J.C.: Pattern Recognition with Fuzzy Objective Function Algorithms. Kluwer Academic Publishers, Norwell (1981)
2. Dunn, J.C.: A fuzzy relative of the isodata process and its use in detecting compact well-separated clusters. Cybern. Syst. **3**(3), 32–57 (1973)
3. Lingras, P., Butz, C.J.: Rough support vector regression. Eur. J. Oper. Res. **206**(2), 445–455 (2010)
4. Triff, M., Pavlovski, I., Liu, Z., Morgan, L.A., Lingras, P.: Clustering ensemble for prioritized sampling based on average and rough patterns. In: Proceedings of 23rd International Symposium on Methodologies for Intelligent Systems, Warsaw, Poland p. 530 (2017)

Detecting Overlapping Communities in Social Networks with Voronoi and Tolerance Rough Sets

Kushagra Trivedi and Sheela Ramanna[(⊠)]

Department of Applied Computer Science, University of Winnipeg,
Winnipeg, MB R3B 2E9, Canada
trivedi-k@webmail.uwinnipeg.ca, s.ramanna@uwinnipeg.ca

Abstract. In this work, we propose a novel method based on Voronoi diagrams and tolerance rough set method (TRSM) to detect overlapping communities. In the proposed Voronoi TRSM approach, a social network is represented as a graph. A Voronoi diagram is a partitioning of a plane into regions based on closeness to points in a specific set of sites (seeds). These seeds are used as a core for determining tolerance classes. The upper approximation operator from TRSM is used to obtain overlapping nodes. We have experimented with three well-known real networks and compared with Fuzzy-Rough and a Matrix Factorization-based approach. The results with proposed Voronoi TRSM approach are promising in terms of the extended modularity measure and the dense communities measure.

Keywords: Community detection · Density-based clustering
Social networks · Soft computing · Tolerance rough sets
Voronoi diagram

1   Introduction

Analyzing real-world networks to identify community structures can reveal various useful and interesting information. A community structure in such networks is identified by locating the nodes which are closely linked to each other more than rest of the graph. This concept was theoretically denoted by modularity and local modularity which were proposed as indices of community structure [10]. Soft computing approaches for community detection can be found in [7,20]. Inspired by a Voronoi-based community detection method from [5], tolerance rough sets [13,18], we propose a novel graph-based method (Voronoi TRSM) to detect overlapping communities. Since classical rough set theory relies on an equivalence (binary) relation to approximate a set, it essentially partitions

This research has been supported by the NSERC Discovery grants program and the Queen Elizabeth II Scholarship Program.

the universe (a region) into disjoint (non-overlapping) equivalence classes. However, a tolerance relation uses a non-transitive binary relation that is reflexive and symmetric is necessary. This is particularly useful in dealing with overlapping regions. The motivation for this work is three fold: (i) Voronoi diagrams are well-known for partitioning metric spaces, (ii) Voronoi diagrams provide crisp partition (with no overlaps), whereas a tolerance relation permits overlap, and finally (iii) rough-set methods approximate a space using two operators: lower and upper approximators directly derived from the dataset. It is the upper approximators that is of interest since it encapsulates the uncertain region. Fuzzy rough hybrid approaches permits soft partitioning and hence their suitability for benchmarking. The proposed approach was compared with the Fuzzy-Rough approach [20] and a Matrix Factorization based approach [3] for three small real world networks. These networks are the Dolphin Network [9], Zachary Karate Club Network [8] and American Political Books network [3]. The results with proposed Voronoi TRSM approach are promising in terms of the extended modularity measure and the dense communities measure.

2 Related Works

Detecting community structures in complex networks has a long and rich history [21]. The most common algorithms include modularity-based algorithms [1,11] and local modularity-based algorithms (e.g., local maximum degree algorithm [4]). In general, the merit of using the modularity-based approach with geometric clustering can lead to better formation of communities in the networks [5]. Random walk-based approaches to detecting overlapping communities include [19] and a Voronoi seed detection based algorithm for finding and extracting a community [5]). Rough-fuzzy hybrid approach to detect overlapping protein complexes in protein-protein interaction (PPI) networks was explored in [20]. In [7], a hybrid fuzzy-rough method is used to represent a social network where a vertex (node) can be part of several communities with different memberships of their association with each community.

3 Preliminaries

Here we recall the Voronoi diagram properties [5,14] followed by the tolerance form of rough sets used in this paper.

Voronoi Diagram Properties
We recall the definition of a graph where G is a directed and weighted graph defined as a pair of (V, E) in which V is a set of vertices (nodes), and $E \subseteq V \times V$ is a set of edges [5]. The length (weight) of an edge connecting nodes $p, q \in V$ is denoted by $len(p, q)$ which is obtained by summing up the length of edges that belong to the path. The distance $d(p_i, q_i)$ between two nodes p_i and q_i is the length of the shortest path between the two nodes. Thus, the definition of an edge length assures that the graph can be treated as a metric space where $len(p, q) > 0$.

Here, $len(p,q)$ is 1 if p and q are directly connected and 0 otherwise. Let set $S = \{s_1, s_2, \ldots, s_g\} \subset V$ of generator points or seeds. The Voronoi diagram of graph G with respect to S is the partitioning of V into node sets $V_1, V_2, \ldots, V_g \subset V$, where each point set or Voronoi cell is associated with a generator point and satisfying the following properties [5]: (a) The Voronoi cells cover the original graph with no overlaps defined as $\bigcup_{i=1}^{n} V_i = V$, $V_i \cap V_j = \emptyset$, $i, j = 1, 2, \ldots, n$. (b) Nodes that belong to a Voronoi cell are closest to the generator point associated with the cell defined as $d(p, s_i) \le d(p, s_j)$, for all $p \in V$, $i, j = 1, 2, \ldots, n$.

Calculating Edge Weights

In this work, we have chosen the edge clustering coefficient introduced in [15] for determining the weights for edges. The $ECC_{i,j}$ of an edge connecting node i to node j is defined as $ECC_{i,j} = \frac{n_{i,j}+1}{min[(e_i-1)(e_j-1)]}$ [5] where e_i and e_j are the degrees of the two nodes, $n_{i,j}$ is the number of triangles the edge between i and j, and $min[(e_i - 1)(e_j - 1)]$ is the number of potential triangles it could belong to. If the ECC value is small, then it is more likely that an edge will connect to nodes in different clusters. As a result, the edge length (weight) as the inverse of ECC is used in the Voronoi partitioning or clustering [5].

Calculating Local Density

In addition to an ECC distance measure, a better choice of seed nodes is essential in the partitioning of the Voronoi diagram. Hence the seed selection method based on the relative local density of nodes [5,6], which is calculated as $\rho_i = \frac{e_i}{e_i+e_o}$ where e_i is the number of edges *inside* the sub-graph consisting of the neighbours of node i, and e_o is the number of edges going *out* of the neighborhood. ρ_i is maximum for nodes within the center of the communities. Seed points on a graph will be the seed points with maximum local density in a region within radius r which is measured using the above defined ECC distance between nodes. This approach for choosing the centroid avoids the selection of multiple seed points within one cluster. In this work, we follow the same strategy in partitioning the graph with increasing values of r [5].

3.1   Evaluation Measures and Datasets

In this work, we use two well-known evaluation measures. The choice of these measures were also dictated by the fact that we could replicate the results for two comparative studies with overlapping communities on small networks. (i) Extended Modularity (EQ) [17] $EQ = \frac{1}{2m} \sum_i \sum_{v \in C_i, w \in C_i} \frac{1}{O_v O_w} \left[A_{vw} - \left(\frac{k_v k_w}{2m} \right) \right]$ where A_{vw} is the element of adjacency matrix of the network. In this work, to facilitate comparison with two other methods, we consider unweighted networks since the weights of other methods are unknown. It takes value 1 if there is an edge between vertex v and vertex w and 0 otherwise. And $m = \frac{1}{2} \sum_{vw} A_{vw}$ is the total number of edges in the network. k_v is the degree of v. O_v be the number of communities to which vertex v belongs. EQ measure is indicative of the overlapping nature of the community structure.

(ii) Average Degree (d_{com}) [12]: We use this measure to identify the strength of a community. It is defined as the average of degrees in a community. It is fairly straightforward and useful measure to test the density of a community. This measure is defined in the Clique Percolation Method) (CPM) which is the most prominent algorithm for overlapping community detection [12].

We have used the following three networks in this work: (i) Zachary Karate Club Network which is a well-known real-world network which consists of 34 nodes and 78 edges and shows the relationships between members [8], (ii) Dolphin Network which has of 62 nodes [9] representing bottle nose dolphins and 159 edges showing the relations and interactions between them, (iii) The American political books network representing frequently co-purchased books on Amazon.com. It has 105 nodes and 441 edges [3].

4   Voronoi TRSM Method

In this work, we define a tolerance space [18] for overlapping communities as a quadruple $O = (U, S, I, \nu)$, where U is the set of all nodes in the graph G such that $U = \{n_0, n_1, ..., n_j\}$ and S is a set of seed points of Voronoi cells defined as $S = \{s_0, s_1, ..., s_i\}$. I is the uncertainty function which defines a *neighbourhood* for a seed point and is defined as $I_r(s_i) = \{n_j | f_D(s_i, n_j) \leq r\} \cup \{s_i\}$ where s_i is the seed whose tolerance class is being calculated and n_j are all nodes in the universe, $f_D(s_i, n_j)$ is a function that returns distance between seed s_i and any node n_j and r is the neighbourhood parameter. The *vague inclusion* is a set inclusion function and is defined as $\nu(I(s_i), X) = \frac{|I(s_i) \cap X|}{|I(s_i)|}$. We can now approximate our Voronoi cells in such a way that the upper approximation defined as $\mathcal{U}_O(X) = \{n_j \in U : \nu(I(s_i), X) > 0\}$ will gives us all the nodes that may be part of multiple communities and hence an overlap region is formed. The lower approximation defined as $\mathcal{L}_O(X) = \{n_j \in U : \nu(I(s_i), X) = 1\}$ includes nodes that *definitely* belong to a community. The lower and upper approximations of set X can be defined as

The algorithm of our proposed framework is given as a flowchart in Fig. 1. We start with initializing r = 0.1. We calculate edge weights for all edges, followed by local density of each node. We select those nodes as seeds that have highest local density such that two seeds do not appear in same region (within r of the same region). We then create the Voronoi partition of the space for all seeds. Since the Voronoi partitioning creates *crisp* boundaries, we use the tolerance rough set model to obtain the soft cell boundaries to detect *overlap*. We then calculate the tolerance class of each seed based on $I_r(s_i)$. Next, we calculate the vague inclusion function using $\nu(I(s_i), X)$ of one tolerance class with other tolerance classes in a different Voronoi partition. Since we already the nodes that *definitely* belong to a partition, we do not need to calculate the lower approximation. Hence, we only calculate the upper approximation $\mathcal{U}_O(X)$ to discover additional nodes. These nodes are added to the Voronoi cells of partition X. We repeat these steps for all the partitions and nearby tolerance class of every seed.

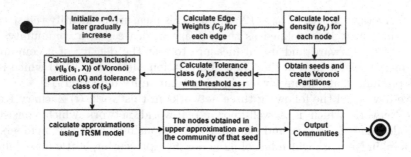

Fig. 1. Flowchart of algorithm

5   Experiments and Results

We have implemented the Voronoi TRSM algorithm in Python with IntelCore i5 CPU 2.7 GHz and 12 GB RAM. We get our best results at $r = 2.5$ and $k = 2$ where k is the number of communities and determined by selecting 2 seeds with the highest local density and r is parameter for the region to be covered. We start by taking r value as 1 and slowly increasing it to obtain noticeable results. Table 1 gives comparative results in terms of EQ and d_{com} for the three networks. The best results are bold-faced.

Table 1. Results

Approach	Communities	EQ	d_{com}
Dolphin Network			
Voronoi TRSM	2	0.3982	**171**
Fuzzy-Rough [20]	2	**0.4036**	167.5
Matrix factorization [3]	2	0.3677	154.5
Zachary Karate Club Network			
Voronoi TRSM	2	**0.2864**	87
Fuzzy-Rough [20]	2	0.2668	75.5
Matrix factorization [3]	2	0.2749	**89.5**
American Political Books Network			
Voronoi TRSM	3	**0.340**	**318**
Matrix factorization [3]	3	0.329	314

We have given the graphical representation of the two datasets by all three methods in Fig. 2. For instance, the nodes (3, 9, 10, 20) are the overlapping nodes found by Voronoi TRSM shown for Zachary in Fig. 2(a). In Fig. 2(b), Matrix factorization method discovers 4 overlapping nodes as well (31, 32, 9, 3). In Fig. 2(c), 5 overlapped nodes are discovered (29, 28, 20, 10, 9). The discovered nodes are similar to the ones found by our proposed method. Also, we have nodes

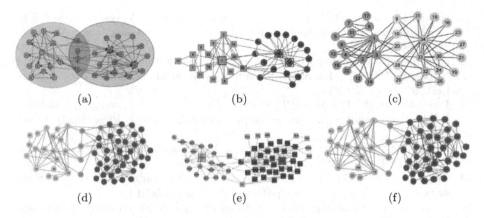

Fig. 2. Obtained community structure for both networks. From left to right: Voronoi TRSM, Matrix factorization, Fuzzy-Rough. Zachary Karate Club Network shown in Fig. 2(a) to (c) and Dolphin Network shown in Fig. 2(d) to (f).

that make community the most dense as per d_{com} and fairly modular as per EQ. It is interesting to note that nodes 9, 10 are typically misclassified by well-known methods: Infomap [16] and Louvian [2] methods in a non-overlapping case.

6   Conclusion and Future Work

In conclusion, we have proposed a novel method based on a geometric approach (Voronoi diagrams) combined with a soft computing method (TRSM) to detect overlapping communities in social networks. We have experimented with three well-known real networks using two measures. We have compared our method with fuzzy-rough and matrix factorization methods. The choice of these measures were dictated by the fact that we could replicate the results from these two methods. As a first attempt, the results based on an extended modularity measure and dense community measure show promise. Future work will include large networks and other standard measures.

References

1. Blondel, V.D., Guillaume, J.L., Lambiotte, R., Lefebvre, E.: Fast unfolding of communities in large networks. J. Stat. Mech. Theor. Exp. **2008**(10), P10008 (2008)
2. Campigotto, R., Céspedes, P.C., Guillaume, J.L.: A generalized and adaptive method for community detection. ArXiv preprint arXiv:1406.2518 (2014)
3. Cao, X., Wang, X., Jin, D., Cao, Y., He, D.: Identifying overlapping communities as well as hubs and outliers via nonnegative matrix factorization. Sci. Rep. **3**, 2993 (2013)
4. Chen, Q., Wu, T.T., Fang, M.: Detecting local community structures in complex networks based on local degree central nodes. Phys. A Stat. Mech. Appl. **392**(3), 529–537 (2013)

5. Deritei, D., Lázár, Z.I., Papp, I., Járai-Szabó, F., Sumi, R., Varga, L., Regan, E.R., Ercsey-Ravasz, M.: Community detection by graph Voronoi diagrams. New J. Phys. **16**(6), 063007 (2014)
6. Fortunato, S.: Community detection in graphs. Phys. Rep. **486**(3), 75–174 (2010)
7. Kundu, S., Pal, S.K.: Fuzzy-rough community in social networks. Pattern Recogn. Lett. **67**, 145–152 (2015)
8. Lancichinetti, A., Fortunato, S., Kertész, J.: Detecting the overlapping and hierarchical community structure in complex networks. New J. Phys. **11**(3), 033015 (2009)
9. Lusseau, D.: The emergent properties of a dolphin social network. Proc. Roy. Soc. Lond. B Biol. Sci. **270**(Suppl 2), S186–S188 (2003)
10. Newman, M.E.J., Girvan, M.: Finding and evaluating community structure in networks (2004). http://arxiv.org/pdf/cond-mat/0308217v1:PDF
11. Newman, M.E.: Fast algorithm for detecting community structure in networks. Phys. Rev. E **69**(6), 066133 (2004)
12. Palla, G., Derényi, I., Farkas, I., Vicsek, T.: Uncovering the overlapping community structure of complex networks in nature and society. Nature **435**(7043), 814–818 (2005)
13. Pawlak, Z.: Rough sets. Int. J. Comput. Inf. Sci. **11**(5), 341–356 (1982)
14. Peters, J., Ramanna, S.: Proximal three-way decisions: theory and applications in social networks. Knowl. Based Syst. Elsevier **91**, 4–15 (2016)
15. Radicchi, F., Castellano, C., Cecconi, F., Loreto, V., Parisi, D.: Defining and identifying communities in networks. Proc. Nat. Acad. Sci. USA **101**(9), 2658–2663 (2004)
16. Rosvall, M., Bergstrom, C.T.: Maps of random walks on complex networks reveal community structure. Proc. Nat. Acad. Sci. **105**(4), 1118–1123 (2008)
17. Shen, H., Cheng, X., Cai, K., Hu, M.B.: Detect overlapping and hierarchical community structure in networks. Phys. A Stat. Mech. Appl. **388**(8), 1706–1712 (2009)
18. Skowron, A., Stepaniuk, J.: Tolerance approximation spaces. Fundamenta Informaticae **27**(2, 3), 245–253 (1996)
19. Whang, J.J., Gleich, D.F., Dhillon, I.S.: Overlapping community detection using seed set expansion. In: Proceedings of ACM International Conference onIinformation & Knowledge Management, pp. 2099–2108 (2013)
20. Wu, H., Gao, L., Dong, J., Yang, X.: Detecting overlapping protein complexes by rough-fuzzy clustering in protein-protein interaction networks. PLoS ONE **9**(3), e91856 (2014)
21. Xie, J., Kelley, S., Szymanski, B.K.: Overlapping community detection in networks: the state-of-the-art and comparative study. ACM Comput. Surv. **45**(4), 43:1–43:35 (2013)

Internet of Things (IoT), Ubiquitous Computing and Big Data

Multi-objective Optimization at the Conceptual Design Phase of an Office Room Through Evolutionary Computation

Ayca Kirimtat and Ondrej Krejcar[✉]

Faculty of Informatics and Management, Center for Basic and Applied Research,
University of Hradec Kralove, Hradec Kralove, Czech Republic
a.kirimtat@gmail.com, ondrej.krejcar@uhk.cz

Abstract. An implementation of multi-objective optimization for design of an office room is presented through maximizing illuminance value and minimizing cooling energy consumption on a summer extreme day in a Mediterranean hot climate region. Existing literature shows different examples of multi-objective optimization problems in the field of performance-based building design. Principally, performance criteria such as energy and daylight should be integrated in the early stage of the conceptual design phase to provide energy-efficient solutions in buildings. Since most of the architectural design problems are difficult to solve, multi-objective optimization methods provide many design solutions to the decision makers. We used Non-Dominated Sorting Genetic Algorithm II namely NSGA-II to present many design alternatives by satisfying two conflicting objectives at the same time in the presented office room problem.

Keywords: Office room · Energy · Daylight · Evolutionary computation

1 Introduction

Performance-based optimization is widely-used method in the field of building design since it presents various energy-efficient solutions to decision makers. Thus, the efficient optimization techniques are preferred more than traditional design method namely "trial-and-error" since it is possible to find more than one near-optimal design alternatives. Design process is mainly operated by optimization algorithms, which generate different design alternatives, and simulation engines and it is also based on well-defined objective functions, constraints and design variables. The most preferred and efficient optimization algorithms to solve performance-based design problems in buildings are Evolutionary Algorithms such as NSGA-II [1].

In the context of Energy Performance of Building Directive (EPDB), nearly-zero energy building (nZEB) concept has to be achieved in all new buildings in Europe [2]. Furthermore, nZEB concept requires sustainability measures and it is based on performance assessment such as taking advantage of daylight, providing visual and thermal comfort. These assessments can be achieved by operating simulation engines in the early stage of design process which has already been done for years. However, the

© Springer International Publishing AG, part of Springer Nature 2018
M. Mouhoub et al. (Eds.): IEA/AIE 2018, LNAI 10868, pp. 679–684, 2018.
https://doi.org/10.1007/978-3-319-92058-0_65

idea of presenting many performance-based design alternatives could be done by multi-objective optimization algorithms. This methodology is called Computational Generative Design or Algorithmic Modeling in building design which is a new trend in architecture [3]. With the integration of multi-objective optimization algorithms to simulation provides many design alternatives to the decision makers at the same time making performance assessment [4].

Since the whole building system is both non-linear and complicated, multi-objective optimization methods are highly preferred for building analysis. Delgarm et al. [5] used multi-objective artificial bee colony algorithm together with EnergyPlus simulation tool to present comfort-energy efficient solutions for building envelope. Futrell et al. [6] used four different algorithms to make an optimization for a classroom design according to changing daylight performance. In the study of Horkouss et al. [7], a methodology for the simulation-based multi-criteria optimization of NZEBs was used in various case studies in Lebanon and France. Most of the building design problems correspond to fulfill the requirements of the conflicting objectives, since they are stated as complicated problems. Additionally, calculation of the illumination value and energy consumption value is known as non-linear problems. The DIVA component of Grasshopper Environment with the Radiance and Energy Plus was used as a calculation tool. For the multi-objective optimization, NSGA-II was used to present many design alternatives to the decision-makers.

2 Problem Definition

In the model, we aim minimizing cooling energy consumption and maximizing illuminance value on a summer extreme day based on design variables and two conflicting objective functions. The case study office room is located in a Mediterranean hot climate region, thus climatic data of this region was acquired from the EnergyPlus Weather Data official website.

2.1 Design Variables

In the model, 4 design variables $(x_1 - x_4)$ are considered for the conceptual design of an office room. They are continuous variables as width of building, length of building, height of building, and window size. x_1 is changing reel numbers between 4 m and 10 m and it represents the width of building. x_2 refers to length of the building as reel numbers between 4 m and 10 m. x_3 which is building height and varying between 2.5 m and 5 m as reel numbers. Finally, x_4 describes window size scale to south façade of the office room and it is moving between 0.5 and 0.9 as reel numbers.

2.2 Objective Functions

In the model, there are two objective functions namely maximizing illuminance *(IL)* value and minimizing cooling energy consumption *(CEC)* which are conflictive in the problem. Each of them are separately defined in the generative model through Grasshopper Parametric Design Environment. Illuminance was used as a daylighting metric and according to Mardaljevic et al., a value between 300 lx and 500 lx is generally recommended for the illuminance on the horizontal plane at desk height in offices [8]. Daylight simulation part of the "DIVA plugin" which was developed for Grasshopper Parametric Design Environment was used for the illuminance calculation. Maximization of the illuminance *(IL)* value is the first objective function. In the energy simulation part of the generative model, only cooling energy consumption of the presented office room are counted for energy consumption calculation. Thermal part of the "DIVA plugin" which was again developed for Grasshopper Parametric Design Environment was used as an interface of the EnergyPlus simulation engine. Thermal part of the DIVA plugin reads all of the calculated data for cooling energy consumption *(CEC)* value from Energy Plus simulation engine. Minimization of cooling energy consumption is the second objective.

$$\max(IL), \min(CEC) \tag{1}$$

$$CEC = \sum\nolimits_{n=1}^{24} EC_{cooling_n} \tag{2}$$

where n corresponds each calculated one hour for a summer extreme day in a Mediterranean hot climate region.

3 Non-dominated Sorting Genetic Algorithm II (NSGA-II)

Multi-objective optimization algorithms are frequently used for engineering applications. As multi-objective optimization algorithms (MOEAs), Evolutionary Algorithms (EAs) such as NSGA-II [9] are preferred rather than other algorithms since they are most studied and applied in benchmark problems. Conversely, they are also satisfying for multi-objective architectural problems (MAPs) [10], as they find set of design solutions. In this research, NSGA-II was used to carry out multi-objective optimization at the conceptual design phase of an office room. Deb et al. [9] developed NSGA II, and it is known as very powerful MOEA. NSGA-II mainly focuses on elitism, superior of feasibility, non-dominated sorting, since it homogenously presents Pareto-optimal results. The most important characteristics of NSGA-II is listed as follows:

- In order to reach non-dominated solutions, the algorithm makes O (MN2) sorting,
- It calculates "Crowding Distance" depending upon cuboid volume between neighboring elements, which join the same rank value,
- Throughout binary tournament selection, it uses crowding distance, superior of feasibility, in concurrence with ranking for diversity preserving,
- It uses elitism strategy along with compounding offspring members and elite parents,
- It employs genetic operator, which is "Simulated Binary Crossover (SBX)",
- It makes use of polynomial mutation operator (PM).

4 Parametric Model

The parametric model was developed in the Grasshopper Algorithmic Modeling Environment which is a plug-in for Rhinoceros CAD program [11]. Thermal and daylight parts of the DIVA [12] plug-in were used to run energy and daylight simulations inside of the GH plug-in. Figure 1 explains the flowchart of the generative model, simulation and optimization processes. Firstly, generative model was created parametrically, secondly energy and daylight simulation models were described and operated to see the first results, and finally optimization algorithm namely NSGA-II was run for the simulation-based optimization process.

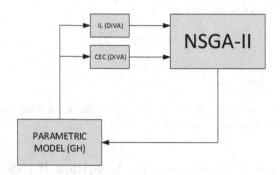

Fig. 1. Flowchart of the study

Radiance [13], which is a physically based rendering system, is used for the daylight simulation in DIVA-for-Rhino Grasshopper plug in. Basically, a light-backwards ray-tracing method with extensions is used in Radiance. While making simulations, Radiance uses deterministic and stochastic ray-tracing methods to provide high accuracy for all illumination methods. However, EnergyPlus [14] simulation engine is used for the energy simulation part of DIVA-for-Rhino Grasshopper.

5 Computational Results

NSGA-II algorithm was operated for the optimization process on an Intel Core-i5 computer, with 4 GB of RAM. Roughly, 3.5 s was the average computation time for each generation of one individual in the 100 population. All individuals were gathered in the first front in 20th generation, and runs were completed in approximately 3 h. Figure 2 presents the Pareto graph of NSGA-II with 100 various design alternatives. The presented NSGA-II showed different design alternatives according to objective functions *CEC* and *IL*. Cooling energy consumption values were obtained between 4.1160 kWh/day and 15.4981 kWh/day which means the dimensions of the office room gets bigger the higher energy consumption occurs. On the other hand, illuminance values varied between 558 lx and 2711 lx that means the energy consumption value gets bigger the daylight amount of the inside gets higher, since dimensions of the office room increases.

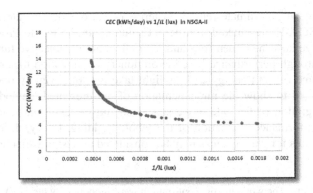

Fig. 2. Pareto graph of NSGA-II and design solutions

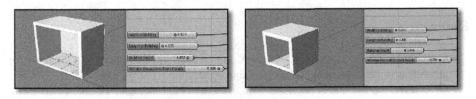

Fig. 3. Design solutions for NSGA-II: *CEC*: 15.4981 kWh/day and *IL*: 2711 lx on the left, *CEC*: 7.1628 kWh/day and *IL*: 1801 lx on the right

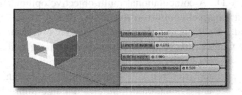

Fig. 4. Design solution for NSGA-II: *CEC*: 4.1160 kWh/day and *IL*: 558 lx

In Figs. 3 and 4, different design alternatives for the office room from top to bottom of the Pareto Front graph are illustrated in perspective views. However, we only focused one office space in the problem, since both the energy and daylight simulations take too long if we focus on more than one office room. Moreover, if the number of office room increases, the ranges of objective functions will also change.

6   Conclusion

Multi-objective optimization problem for the conceptual phase of an office room design is formulated based on two conflicting objective functions namely maximizing illuminance value and minimizing cooling energy consumption on a summer extreme day in a Mediterranean hot climate region. In terms of various design alternatives in the population, NSGA-II presented 100 different solutions in the Pareto Front graph. The aim is to observe how the dimensions and their effect on the objective functions values are changed through performance-based evolutionary computation methods. Since the computation time of both energy and daylight take too long, simply one office room space was studied to show the implementation of the presented method. As a future study, the integration of the side office spaces should be taken into consideration to enhance the performance evaluation of the whole building. Lastly, different types of reflective materials for glazing areas may be considered as design variables of the office room spaces.

Acknowledgement. The work and the contribution were supported by the SPEV project "Smart Solutions in Ubiquitous Computing Environments 2018", University of Hradec Kralove, Faculty of Informatics and Management, Czech Republic.

References

1. Si, B., Tian, Z., Jin, X., Zhou, X., Tang, P., Shi, X.: Performance indices and evaluation of algorithms in building energy efficient design optimization. Energy **114**, 100–112 (2016)
2. Groezinger, J., Boermans, T., John, A., Seehusen, J., Wehringer, F., Scherberich, M.: Overview of Member States information on NZEBs Working version of the progress report - final report (2014)
3. Touloupaki, E., Theodosiou, T.: Energy performance optimization as a generative design tool for nearly zero energy buildings. Procedia Eng. **180**, 1178–1185 (2017)
4. Bre, F., Fachinotti, V.D.: A computational multi-objective optimization method to improve energy efficiency and thermal comfort in dwellings. Energy Build. **154**, 283–294 (2017)
5. Delgarm, N., Sajadi, B., Delgarm, S.: Multi-objective optimization of building energy performance and indoor thermal comfort: a new method using artificial bee colony (ABC). Energy Build. **131**, 42–53 (2016)
6. Futrell, B.J., Ozelkan, E.C., Brentrup, D.: Optimizing complex building design for annual daylighting performance and evaluation of optimization algorithms. Energy Build. **92**, 234–245 (2015)
7. Harkouss, F., Fardoun, F., Biwole, P.H.: Multi-objective optimization methodology for net zero energy buildings. J. Build. Eng. **16**, 57–71 (2017)
8. Mardaljevic, J., Heschong, H., Lee, E.: Daylight metrics and energy savings. Light. Res. Technol. **41**, 261–283 (2009)
9. Deb, K., Pratap, A., Agarwal, S., Meyarivan, T.: A fast and elitist multi objective genetic algorithm NSGA-II. IEEE Trans. Evol. Comput. **6**(2), 182–197 (2002)
10. Chatzikonstantinou, I., Sariyildiz, S., Bittermann, M.S.: Conceptual airport terminal design using evolutionary computation. In: 2015 IEEE Congress on Evolutionary Computation (CEC), pp. 2245–2252 (2015)
11. Grasshopper, Algorithmic Modeling for Rhino. http://www.grasshopper3d.com/
12. DIVA for Rhino. http://www.solemma.net/DIVA-for-Rhino/DIVA-for-Rhino.html
13. Ward, G.J.: The RADIANCE lighting simulation and rendering system. In: Lighting Group Building Technologies Program. Lawrence Berkeley Laboratory (1994)
14. Crawley, D.B., Lawrie, K., Pedersen, C.O., Winkelmann, F.C.: EnergyPlus: energy simulation. Program **42**(4), 49–56 (2000)

Data Analytics and Visualization
for Connected Objects: A Case Study
for Sleep and Physical Activity Trackers

Karim Tabia[1,2]([✉]), Hugues Wattez[1,2], Nicolas Ydée[1,2], and Karima Sedki[3]

[1] Univ Lille Nord de France, 59000 Lille, France
tabia@cril.univ-artois.fr
[2] UArtois, CRIL UMR CNRS 8188, 62300 Lens, France
[3] LIMICS (INSERM UMRS 1142),
Univ. Paris 13, UPMC Univ. Paris 6, Sorbonne Universités, Paris, France

Abstract. In recent years, a large number of connected objects for the monitoring of activities (health and well-being, sleep, fitness, nutrition, etc.) have emerged and are very popular with the general public. No doubt that their price, their ease of use and their interest in their health and well-being contribute to this success around the world. However, many of these consumer-connected objects suffer from several limitations, especially with regard to their high-level or smart functionalities and the added value of the information provided by such objects. In this paper, we first focus on such limitations then provide a real case study in monitoring physical activities and sleep using Fitbit smart watches. We propose some high level functionalities by taking advantage of the large amount of data collected and using data analytics and visualization techniques.

1 Introduction

Wearable connected objects that focus on health and well-being (e.g. connected watches, fitness wristbands, sleep trackers, etc.) are largely being used and are being democratized on a large scale [10]. Reluctance regarding their use still exists for various considerations [2,5,6] such as the lack of security of the data collected, the lack of customization, the lack of functionalities and services "intelligent" and high level, the lack of interoperability, etc.

In the last decade, more and more IoT devices and applications are dedicated to help users monitor and improve their health and well-being [8]. Physical activity trackers (also called activity monitors or sports/fitness monitors or activity trackers) are connected devices (such as wrist bracelets or Smart watches) or Smartphone applications that measure the intensity, duration and amount of the activities performed by the user. They measure features such as walking or running distance, calory consumption and expenditure, and in some cases, heart rate and "quality" of sleep. Such devices are widely used and very popular as

© Springer International Publishing AG, part of Springer Nature 2018
M. Mouhoub et al. (Eds.): IEA/AIE 2018, LNAI 10868, pp. 685–696, 2018.
https://doi.org/10.1007/978-3-319-92058-0_66

they aim at helping users to increase their motivation and improve their performances. Moreover, in addition to improving well-being, the trackers allow user's
awareness about physical activity, they help ensuring regular physical activity
and decreasing the risks of many chronic diseases [3,10].

Wearable activity trackers and more generally most IoT devices still have
many issue regarding interoperability, security, personalization and sensors reliability to name a few [5,6]. The lack of "smart" features and services is due,
among other things, to not taking advantage of the large amounts of data collected and generated to learn and automatically extract information that can
be very useful. For example, with devices such as smart watches and connected
bracelets, we can collect a lot of data of physical activities and sleep (e.g. distance
traveled, number of steps, number of awakenings, duration of deep sleep ...). The
majority of these devices are limited to displaying simple statistics describing
these activities. It is clear that extracting information like correlations between
factors, recurring patterns, trends, etc. from these physical activity and sleep
data and possibly cross-referencing them with other factors (e.g. environmental factors such as temperature, noise, luminosity, pollution, etc.) can provide
interesting elements to explain for example what is strongly correlated with dis-
turbed sleep. This type of information derived from the analysis of activity data
constitutes a very interesting added value [1,9]. Now, even if useful and relevant
information has been extracted, it is necessary to represent the results of the
analytics in an intuitive and efficient way so that the user can directly perceive,
for example, the impact of the different factors on her sleep quality. Visualization will play an important role for the effective retrieval and interpretation of
results by users [4]. Our study confirms that big data and analytics along with
appropriate knowledge visualization techniques can help improve the usefulness
of activity trackers and more generally IoT devices.

In this paper, we first focus on large public IoT limitations and provide a
real case study in monitoring physical activities and sleep using Fitbit smart
watches. Two users are hired in this study for several months and real data
has been collected in real life conditions. We propose then some high level and
smart functionalities by taking advantage of the large amount of data collected
and using data analytics and visualization techniques.

This paper is organized as follows: Sect. 2 recall the main limits and lack of
smart functionalities in activity tracking connected objects. In Sect. 3 we present
our case study and we provide discussions and concluding remarks in Sect. 4.

2   Main Issues with Activity Trackers from a Usefulness Persective

Like many IoT devices, activity and sleep trackers still suffer from many problems
and limits [2,6]. For instance, one can mention the reliability of the sensors, the
lack of security while exchanging and storing the data, lack of interoperability
with other devices (especially those of other manufacturers) and of course lack of
intelligent or smart functionalities. In this paper, we focus only on user-related
aspects in terms of useful functionalities and efficient user interaction.

2.1   Lack of Personalization

One of the challenges facing the use of IoT is personalization, especially in case of general public applications. Personalization aims to provide services tailored specifically for the user needs and preferences. For example, IoT devices aiming at improving sleep quality would provide the user personalized recommendations regarding for instance *when to go to bed, temperature of the room, food/drinks to avoid, physical activity...*, and trigger alerts and warnings in case of sleep deficiency/disorder, physical activity deficiency, food deficiency/excess, etc. In order to learn the factors they may have an impact on the sleep quality of the user, there is need to measure the sleep quality and learn correlations with factors associated with good/bad sleep quality to provide useful recommendations while taking into account user profile, preferences and constraints (for more details on this issue, see [7]).

2.2   Lack of Smart Functionalities

While IoT devices are capable of collecting many types of data with their sensors and potentially acquire complementary data from other sources, the collected data is often neither correlated nor exploited to give relevent information, pieces of knowledge, advices and recommendations to the user for improving his life style. For instance, the quality of sleep is affected by a number of factors such as physical activity, dietary habits (alcohol intake, caffeine containing beverages, smoking, etc.), environmental factors, etc. It is then possible to correlate and analyse all these data in order to highlight which factors have a positive or negative impact on the user's sleep quality. Of course, this needs making use of big data/datamining techniques and data analytics to extract useful knowledge from the large amounts of user-generated and ambient data.

2.3   Lack Intuitive and Interactive Dashboards and User Interfaces

As just mentioned above, in addition to analyzing the data of physical activities and sleep collected by connected objects, we will have to report this data and potentially pieces of knowledge to the user, through user-friendly, intelligent and interactive interfaces. Thanks to visualization techniques, the user can then see for example disorders that he may have during his sleep and the link that this may have with his physical activities or ambient factors. Unfortunately, as shown in the dashboard of Fig. 1, most activity and sleep trackers display only very basic statistics and graphs summarizing the daily activities. There for instance no analysis or interactivity. It is true that the characteristics of the screens used by the users (smartphones or connected watches) impose limits for the display but the very basic nature of the data to display does not lend itself to elaborate visualizations as we will illustrate it in our case study.

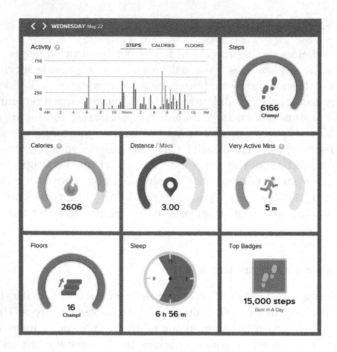

Fig. 1. Example of a Fitbit tracker dashboard

3   Case Study

In order to show what kind of improvements activity and sleep trackers could benefit from using data analytics (and more generally big data techniques) and visualization, we conducted a case study where two volunteers were hired in order to collect real data form an activity and sleep trackers in real life conditions.

In order to learn from the data relevant information (e.g. the factors they may have an impact on the sleep quality of the user), there is need to use as much data as possible and extract such useful knowledge (e.g. learn correlations and patterns with factors associated with good/bad sleep quality). Hence the collected data should include all i) the factors that may describe the sleep quality (e.g. awakenings count, minutes asleep, etc.) and ii) factors that may have an impact or influence on sleep quality (e.g. physical activity, food, temperature, noise, etc.). We distinguish two types of data:

- *User-generated data:* Such data can be sensed by dedicated devices (ex. physical activity) or by the user through a graphical interface on a laptop or mobile phone (ex. food intake). In our study, user-generated data consists only in physical activity and sleep data collected by the used Smart watches.
- *Ambient data:* This refers to factors such as air quality, noise level, temperature, luminosity, etc. Such data could also be provided by some IoT devices or retrieved from special applications and sources (e.g. Web sources). In our

study, we used external sources to acquire weather and air quality data corresponding to the location where the volunteers were living.

3.1 Specifications of the Activity Trackers Used in the Study

The two Fitbit Smart watches that are selected are Fitbit Blaze having the following specifications:

- *Sensors:* An altimeter, ambient light sensor, three-axis accelerometer, optical heart rate monitor. In addition, a connected GPS is used.
- *Data tracked:* As detailed below, the trackers collect activity data (e.g. distance, floors climbed, heart rate...) and sleep (e.g. time in bed, awakening account, etc.). Some data is not sensed but derived from activity data such as the number of calories burned.
- *Operating system:* The devices are connected with smartphones running Apple MacOS X 10.6 or later, Microsoft Windows Vista or later.

For more details on the Fitbit Blaze tracker, please see[1]

3.2 Raw Data

Like most activity and sleep tracking tools, the Fitbit Blaze trackers just collect some data and remotely store it using a Smartphone connection in the form of log records which can be downloaded or displayed in various ways to the user. We collected the raw data on a monthly basis. Each month a .csv file is downloaded and contains only the records of activity and sleep (of course, other information could be downloaded). The following is an example of log records for activity data.

```
Date,CaloriesBurned,Steps,Distance,Floors,MinutesSedentary,MinutesLightlyActive,MinutesFairlyActive,
MinutesVeryActive,ActivityCalories
''15-11-2016'', ''2 184'', ''9 800'', ''6,14'', ''14'', ''662'', ''164'', ''30'', ''23'', ''896''
''16-11-2016'', ''2 202'', ''9 707'', ''5,96'', ''18'', ''656'', ''164'', ''14'', ''39'', ''933''
''17-11-2016'', ''2 126'', ''9 847'', ''6,13'', ''19'', ''726'', ''145'', ''20'', ''29'', ''796''
''18-11-2016'', ''2 250'', ''8 695'', ''5,07'', ''17'', ''642'', ''291'', ''2'', ''7'', ''1 013''
''19-11-2016'', ''2 271'', ''8 744'', ''5,15'', ''2'', ''667'', ''270'', ''6'', ''4'', ''1 009''
''20-11-2016'', ''1 888'', ''4 201'', ''2,34'', ''11'', ''525'', ''165'', ''0'', ''0'', ''533''
''21-11-2016'', ''2 222'', ''10 261'', ''6,26'', ''15'', ''720'', ''184'', ''18'', ''34'', ''971''
''22-11-2016'', ''2 135'', ''8 750'', ''5,52'', ''17'', ''1 260'', ''146'', ''7'', ''27'', ''829''
''23-11-2016'', ''2 209'', ''8 993'', ''5,68'', ''17'', ''713'', ''141'', ''22'', ''42'', ''920''
''24-11-2016'', ''2 029'', ''7 581'', ''4,77'', ''14'', ''731'', ''177'', ''3'', ''8'', ''727''
''25-11-2016'', ''2 079'', ''8 577'', ''5,24'', ''16'', ''705'', ''189'', ''5'', ''24'', ''802''
```

Here is an example of log records for sleep.

```
Date,minutesAsleep,minutesAwake,awakeningsCount,timeInBed
15-07-2016,''516'', ''47'', ''3'', ''574''
16-07-2016,''500'', ''26'', ''0'', ''526''
17-07-2016,''620'', ''59'', ''5'', ''679''
18-07-2016,''366'', ''27'', ''2'', ''393''
```

---

[1] Fitbit Blaze User Manual https://staticcs.fitbit.com/content/assets/help/manuals/manual_blaze_en_US.pdf.

The collected files correspond to the activity tracking of two users wearing Fitbit Blaze trackers during 8 months. In the current work, the date columns are omitted since we do not mine sequential patterns. Of course, this means that we make a strong hypothesis implying that each day data is independant of the previous and following days. This hypothesis is very debatable for assessing for example the quality of sleep and physical activity (for instance, three days of bad sleep but distant from each other should be considered less serious than three days in a row of bad sleep). But with this hypothesis, we lose the dependence and relationship between the activities of successive days.). This issue is discussed in the last section and left for future works.

3.3 Data Preprocessed and Enrichment

As mentioned earlier, in order to provide relevant information, there is need to enrich the tracking data provided by the trackers with other data. For instance, there is no doubt that ambient data (e.g. room temperature, noise level, luminosity, etc.) has an impact on the sleep quality but such data is not provided by the used Fitbit trackers. In our study, we used APIs for getting (i) weather data (e.g. temperature, humidity, wind, etc.) from http://www.meteociel.fr/, (ii) air quality data from http://www.atmo-hdf.fr dedicated to monitoring and assessment of air quality in Hauts-de-France (location where the two volunteers hired in this study live) and from http://www.openhealth.fr/.

Many technologies and techniques are used to process and mine the data and display the results. First, the csv files containing tracking data are organized by day and by user. Each raw contains both activity and sleep data. Then the data is enriched with ambient data for that day. For visualization, data is first put into a relational database such that the visualization scripts needing complex SQL queries could run efficiently in real time to allow user interactivity.

3.4 Analytics and High Level Feature Definition

This is the part where the added value is expected to be mined from the data collected from the trackers and other sources. In this study, we addressed two types of relevant information that can be automatically extracted from data:

- *Correlations among basic features:* The goal here is to extract meaningful correlations among the features of the data. For instance, one could be interested to know *how* and *to which extent* the intensity of physical activity is related the number of awakenings. In this study, we extract different types of statistical correlations such as Pearson, Spearman and Kendall correlations.
- *High level correlations:* Since the correlations among basic features are somewhat limited from a user's point of view, we need to define high level features such that the user finds the provided information really relevant. For instance, in order to learn the factors they may have a negative/positive impact on the sleep quality of the user, there is need to "assess" the sleep quality from the basic features then learn correlations with factors associated with good/bad

sleep quality (what is formally a good or bad sleep?). Sleep quality could automatically be estimated based on sleep tracking data (ex. awakenings count)
or through forms answered each day by the user assessing his sleep quality.
Note that there is to the best of our knowledge no high level sleep measure
in the litterature that could be directly computed from the basic features[2].
In this study, we simply relied on an existing score called *sleep efficiency*
assessing sleep quality as the number of minutes of sleep over the number of
minutes spent in bed which is obviously not satisfactory. The definition of
sleep quality measures should be done by experts or subjectively rated by the
user herself.

3.5   Visualization

Once relevant informations extracted from the data, there remains to display it
for the user. One of the goals here is to display the results in an intuitive and
interactive way while most of the time users monitor their activities through
smartphones or directly on smart watches having very limited display possibilities. The following provides few examples illustrating how relevant information
(e.g. correlations) could be displayed.

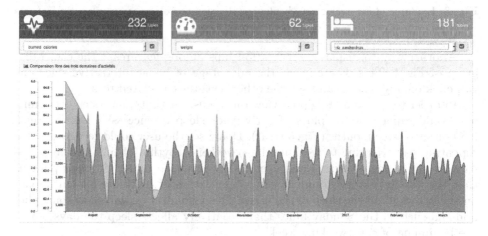

Fig. 2. Example of superposed plots displaying inter-relationships among features of
interest

---

[2] Polysomnography (PSG) is the main method of sleep monitoring used to detect sleep
disorders in a medical context. It is performed during a whole night in a hospital by
placing on the patient different signals (electrodes on the scalp, eyelids, and chin,
etc.). Such a method is efficient but it is obtrusive, costly and cannot be conducted
frequently on a large number people.

In order to display statistical correlations existing among some features of interest, a very easy way is to superpose the graphs of features of interest as illustrated in Fig. 2. The superposed graphs when appropriately scaled visually display some inter-relationships between the chosen features (here, the number of burned calories, the weight and the number of awakenings).

One could also use a simple correlogram (see of Fig. 3) where respectively colors and circle diameters tell about the positive/negative nature of the correlations and the strength of these correlations.

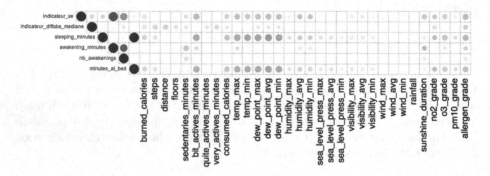

Fig. 3. Example of a correlogram displaying Pearson correlations among some features

Another way to display inter-relationships among features is the chord diagram of Fig. 4. This diagram has the advantage of being interactive since one can click on any feature and see the other features correlated to it.

In order to give a more global view on the user activity and sleep over time, one could superpose the plots of activity or sleep of successive weeks (Fig. 5 left) or successive months (Fig. 5 right). Doing so, the user could recognize some repeating patterns due to working days/weekend rhythm of life, holidays, seasons or any repeated events and cycles. The intuition underlying this point is that the weekly/monthly/annual, etc. organization of daily life has an impact on the activity and the sleep of the users. This visualization will show some phenomena such as the Sunday blues that negatively affects sleep the days before the beginning of each working week.

Many other visualizations could be used and many other forms of knowledge could be extracted and displayed. As for implementation, for the analytics part, we used R packages while we use many Web-based technologies (e.g. D3.js) for the visualization part. Following section focuses on the main issues encountered in our case study.

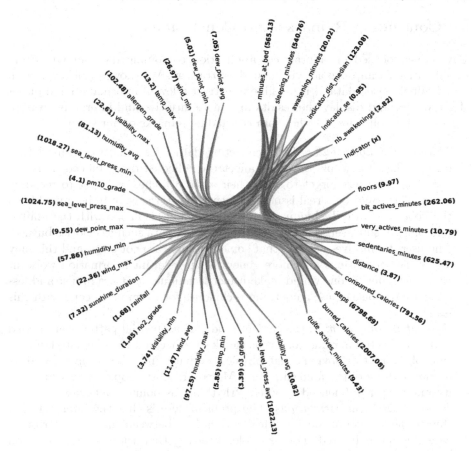

Fig. 4. Example of a chord diagram displaying inter-relationships among some features

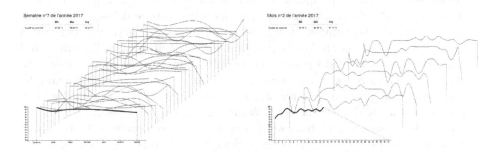

Fig. 5. Example of superposed plots of sleep

4   Concluding Remarks and Conclusions

This paper focused on a practical application combining data analytics and visualization to improve activity and sleep trackers. We showed that even with very limited sensed data, it is possible to extract relevant information and pieces of knowledge and display the results in a more intuitive and interactive way to the user. The following are the main concluding remarks of our study.

- *Missing and noisy data:* While collecting data over time, we realized that missing data for whole days can affect the collected data. Indeed, it is not rare that the users forget to wear their smart watches or forget to recharge them. This could be a real issue if sequential patterns were to be mined from the collected data. Techniques to be used should also cope with the limited reliability of some sensors and also some derived data such as calories burned. The users themselves realized that some measures are not exact and this may affect the correlations and more generally the relevant information we want to extract. Hence, one would make use of techniques that are robust and less sensitive to noise or use smoothing techniques for example to cope with this issue.
- *Sequential dimension:* In the current study, no sequential patterns are mined and no extracted information needs to take into account the sequential dimension of data. It is obvious that physical activity and sleep in last few days influence those of the following ones. Moreover, most people's physical activity and sleep is influenced by weekly rhythm... as pointed out above.
- *Beyond statistical correlations:* The problem here is that the interpretation (hence the utility) of the statistical correlations between the basic attributes which is quite limited. For example, knowing that there is a correlation between the number of minutes spent in bed and the number of active minutes of physical activity is not very meaningful for a user. What would be really useful is to define quality indicators of good sleep and good physical activity. For this latter, for example, an indicator can be defined if the number of steps or the number of minutes of recommended activities per day is exceeded. Same for sleep. We believe that such indicators are still limited and that a good quality of sleep and activities depends on several parameters and its evaluation must take into account the history of activities. For example, the quality of physical activity and sleep over several days should be evaluated instead of days separately. What can also be very useful is to mine cause-effect relationships instead of just statistical correlations. Cause-effect relations could help the user to make changes in his activities to improve his well-being.
- *Beyond user-generated data:* Through our case study it becomes obvious that in order to provide smart functionalities there is need to use the data collected by the sensors but also some other user-generated data (ex. food intake, smoking or user profile can be provided by the user through a graphical interface on a laptop or mobile phone). Other sources of information are ambient data (ex. weather, pollution, ...). The main issues here are the one heterogeneous

data provided by different sources and the one of interoperability between different IoT devices such as connected scales, connected thermometers... that could be used in our case study.

– *Towards more interactivity and smartness:* Many smart functionalities could be added based on the knowledge that can be extracted form the available data. For example, it is possible to design prediction models such supervised classifiers and regression models that could answer some user queries or make recommendations. One could for example predict her sleep quality given her physical activity and other data for a given day. An example of recommendation would be to advice at what time it is best to go sleep, which food to avoid or set the temperature of the room to a given level to have optimal sleep. To increase interactivity along with such functionalities, one could for example want to know what will be her sleep quality if she exercises a given amount of physical activity. Such prediction models could be built using history data of physical activity and sleep of the user. This latter will have a friendly user interface to set any parameter of interest for her and see what will be the impact of the fixed parameters on his sleep quality or any other parameter of interest to her.

To sum up, this preliminary work focused on the high-level functionalities that can be implemented to improve the usefulness of physical activity and sleep trackers. Our approach is to exploit the data collected by the connected objects possibly enriched with other data to extract relevant information and display it to the user in a visual and interactive way. We presented a real case study where we highlighted the problems encountered and built a prototype for demonstration. We finally propose several tracks for future works. This will require relying on big data techniques and analytics as well as exploiting the power of visualization techniques for better interaction with the user.

References

1. Ahmed, E., Yaqoob, I., Hashem, I.A.T., Khan, I., Ahmed, A.I.A., Imran, M., Vasilakos, A.V.: The role of big data analytics in internet of things. Comput. Netw. **129**, 459–471 (2017). Special Issue on 5G Wireless Networks for IoT and Body Sensors
2. Ammar, M., Russello, G., Crispo, B.: Internet of things: a survey on the security of IoT frameworks. J. Inf. Secur. Appl. **38**, 8–27 (2018)
3. Larry Durstine, J., Gordon, B., Wang, Z., Luo, X.: Chronic disease and the link to physical activity. J. Sport Health Sci. **2**(1), 3–11 (2013). Children's Physical Activity and Health: Chronic disease in children and young adults
4. Dongxiao, G., Li, J., Li, X., Liang, C.: Visualizing the knowledge structure and evolution of big data research in healthcare informatics. Int. J. Med. Inf. **98**, 22–32 (2017)
5. Lee, S.-E., Choi, M., Kim, S.: How and what to study about iot: Research trends and future directions from the perspective of social science. Telecommun. Policy **41**(10), 1056–1067 (2017). Celebrating 40 Years of Telecommunications Policy - A Retrospective and Prospective View

6. Macaulay, T.: Chapter 8 - availability and reliability requirements in the IoT. In: Macaulay, T. (ed.) RIoT Control, pp. 141–155. Morgan Kaufmann, Boston (2017)
7. Vallee, T., Sedki, K., Despres, S., Jaulant, M.-C., Tabia, K., Ugon, A.: On personalization in IoT. In: 2016 International Conference on Computational Science and Computational Intelligence (CSCI). IEEE, December 2016
8. Lee, J.W., Park, K.H.: A reliable IoT system for personal healthcare devices. Fut. Gener. Comput. Syst. **78**, 626–640 (2018)
9. Jing, W., Li, H., Liu, L., Zheng, H.: Adoption of big data and analytics in mobile healthcare market: an economic perspective. Electron. Commer. Res. Appl. **22**, 24–41 (2017)
10. Yin, Y., Zeng, Y., Chen, X., Fan, Y.: The internet of things in healthcare: an overview. J. Ind. Inf. Integr. **1**(Suppl. C), 3–13 (2016)

Reliability-Aware Routing of AVB Streams in TSN Networks

Ayman A. Atallah[(⊠)], Ghaith Bany Hamad, and Otmane Ait Mohamed

Department of Electrical and Computer Engineering,
Concordia University, Montreal, Canada
{a_atal,g_banyha,ait}@encs.concordia.ca

Abstract. Modern cars integrate a large number of functionalities with high bandwidth, real-time, and reliability requirements. Time-Sensitive Networking (TSN) standards provide the network specifications to meet the timing requirements for many of these safety-critical functionalities. For instance, TSN standards guarantee maximum jitter of 2 ms for AVB streams over up to 7 hops. In this paper, we investigate the problem of meeting the required transmission reliability of Audio Video Bridging (AVB) streams in TSN networks under transient errors using temporal redundancy approach. An ILP-based routing technique that determines the path and number of replicas for each AVB stream to meet the minimum reliability requirement for each stream as well as maximize the overall network reliability. The Mean Time To Detected Error (MTTDE) is used to measure the transmission reliability. Results show that, the proposed approach is capable of finding feasible routing solutions with up to 50% less bandwidth compared to typical approaches as well as it achieves higher MTTDE by 10-folds comparing to the non-optimized solutions.

1 Introduction

Over the last few years, tremendous progress has been achieved in the electronics systems for automotive industry. For instance, electrical/electronic (E/E) architectures of modern luxury vehicles are built of up to 100 Electronic Control Units (ECUs) [2]. In the automotive systems, some of these ECUs are part of Advance Driver Assistant Systems (ADASs) such as, Adaptive Cruise Control (ACC) and brake-by-wire system. The safety-critical nature of such real-time systems requires communication networks with high transmission reliability and very low latency. Ethernet-based multi-hop networking is one of the interesting solutions for the future in-vehicle communication networks. Several factors support this choice such as the scalability, large bandwidth, and the possibility of achieving more reliable transmission through temporal redundancy [8]. However, typical Ethernet-based networks do not match the real-time requirements of the automotive safety-critical applications [3]. Thus, a new set of Ethernet-based standards to support safety-critical and real-time applications called as the IEEE Time-Sensitive Networking (TSN) standards was developed. TSN-based

© Springer International Publishing AG, part of Springer Nature 2018
M. Mouhoub et al. (Eds.): IEA/AIE 2018, LNAI 10868, pp. 697–708, 2018.
https://doi.org/10.1007/978-3-319-92058-0_67

standards support three categories of traffic according to the timing characteristics: (i) Time-Triggered (TT) traffic; (ii) shaped, or so-called, Audio Video Bridging (AVB) traffic; and (iii) Best-Effort (BE) traffic. TT traffic is scheduled in Time Division Multiple Access (TDMA)-like scheme, i.e., it has a deterministic end-to-end delay. Whereas, AVB traffic is divided into two sub-classes that have a guaranteed Worst Case end-to-end Delay (WCD), In particular, AVB class-A, which has the tightest timing properties, has a guaranteed WCD of 2 ms over seven hops. On the other hand, BE traffic is divided into five strict priority non-preemptive classes. Each class provides different levels of Quality of Service (QoS).

According to the ISO26262 standard, safety-critical applications should receive -at least- one correct message every application-specific interval, namely, Diagnostic Test Interval (DTI) to be considered as properly functioning [4]. However, the reliability of critical traffic is affected by the messages corruption due to the transient errors. Several error mitigation techniques can be used to enhance the transmission reliability such as spatial redundancy (i.e., routing each stream through multiple disjunct paths) or temporal redundancy (i.e., sending multiple copies of each stream through the same path). In this paper we refer to the number of stream replicas as the Redundancy Level (RL) or repetition. The reliability gain using temporal redundancy approach for AVB traffic against transient errors is analyzed in [7]. The introduced analysis conducts the temporal redundancy as a separate step that follows the routing step, i.e., the RL is assigned for streams that already have fixed routing. We will call this strategy as 2-step approach. In fact, 2-step approach neglects the interrelation between the messages routing and the redundancy assignment which limits the design space exploration. For instance, the gain in the transmission reliability depends on the available bandwidth along the selected path. In particular, routing a message through larger bandwidth path allows more redundancy which implies higher reliability. Furthermore, transmission reliability depends on the route itself, i.e., longer paths implies higher transient error rates. Moreover, 2-step approach may result in an infeasible RL assignment due to the bandwidth limitation which implies utilizing more resources, e.g., physical links, as we illustrated in Sect. 4. Therefore, new technique to simultaneously investigate the messages routing and RL assignment in single-step is required to ensure that the whole design space can be explored to identify valid solutions.

In this paper, we are interested in the reliable-aware routing for AVB traffic. In fact, we exploit the temporal redundancy concept to maximize the transmission reliability under transient errors. The problem under consideration is defined by the following inputs: (i) network topology; (ii) available links' bandwidth; (iii) the set of AVB streams to be routed; and (iv) the base-period (DTI) of each stream. The objective of this problem is to attain the maximum transmission reliability. In particular, we adapt the overall Mean Time To Detected Error (MTTDE) as the reliability measure. In order to solve this problem, an ILP formulation is proposed to generate the optimal solution that defines the following: (i) the routing of the AVB streams; and (ii) RL for each AVB stream to achieve the desired reliability.

Results show that the proposed approach is capable of finding feasible solutions for certain routing problem using 50% of the bandwidth required by the 2-step approach. Furthermore, results demonstrate that optimizing the reliability over the whole network generates a routing that enhances the transmission reliability by more than 10-folds compared with the non-optimized solution. To the best of our knowledge, this is the first work proposes a technique that maximizes the overall transmission reliability and guarantees stream-specific reliability bounds for each AVB stream in the TSN network.

The remainder of this paper is structured as follows: the related work for temporal redundancy exploitation in safety-critical applications is presented in Sect. 2. The system model and the utilized method to measure the transmission reliability in Sect. 3. In Sect. 4, a motivational example is presented. Section 5 describes the proposed ILP formulation. The proposed approach is evaluated and results discussed in Sect. 6. Finally, the conclusion is presented in Sect. 7.

2   Related Work

Modern vehicles are being equipped with increasing number of autonomous systems which pushes the reliability requirements for in-vehicle networks. In this context, different schemes of temporal redundancy have been proposed to enhance the transmission reliability. A Constraint Logic Programming (CLP) optimization is presented in [9] for FlexRay networks. The proposed technique generates an optimized schedule that minimizes the bandwidth utilization while meeting a transmission reliability criteria. The required RL for each message is specified, i.e., the required reliability is attained. Then, the valid schedule that optimizes the bandwidth utilization is generated. Li et al. [5] propose an on-demand retransmission approach to enhance the fault resilience in FlexRay network. Given a synthesized schedule, an MILP formulation to minimize the extra bandwidth that is required for the on-demand retransmission. To achieve this goal, in [6], a master node is defined which senses the error occurrence and triggers an on-demand retransmission. Once the master node detects an error, the corrupted frame is retransmitted through the dynamic (best-effort) time slots.

Aforementioned literature handle a single hop networks. On the other hand, switched multi-hops networks implies an additional complexity. This is mainly due to the dependency between traffic routing and RL assignment. For instance, longer paths imply a greater chance of transient error which may require more replicas. On the other hand, routing the traffic in advance may result in a conflict between the required RL and the available bandwidth of the selected paths. This dependency can be resolved by specifying the number of replicas using a pessimistic transient error probability based on the assumption that each stream is routed through the longest possible path. However, this may result in over conservative solutions that consume unnecessary additional bandwidth. Thus, the optimal solution regarding reliability and bandwidth utilization requires handling the reliability requirements and routing constraints jointly. In this regard, Smirnov et al. [7] introduce an analytical evaluation of the transmission reliability attained by applying temporal redundancy to already routed traffic. Authors proposed a method to calculate the MTTDE in the network given a particular RL setup. However, as we mentioned earlier, exploiting the temporal redundancy in a separate phase after routing synthesis does not guarantee the stream-specific reliability bounds. In particular, RL assignment can be rendered infeasible due to a conflict with the available bandwidth.

3   Fundamentals

3.1   System Model

We consider a switched multi-hop network composed of a set of ECUs and switches that are connected by physical links. ECUs exchange periodic messages through the switches according to a static routing table. The network topology is modeled as a directed graph $G(\mathcal{V}, \mathcal{L})$ where every ECU and switch is represented by a vertex $v_i \in \mathcal{V}$. The physical connection between any two vertices v_k and v_l is represented as an edge $l \in \mathcal{L}$. An example of a network topology is shown in Fig. 1. This network is composed of 8 ECUs ($ECU_0 - ECU_7$) and 4 switches ($B_0 - B_3$), whereas, 13 full-duplex links connect them. $\mathbf{M}$ represents the set of AVB messages, where every message is denoted by the source and destination vertices (v_s, v_d). Every message m has a specific DTI and, namely, (Td_m) and minimum MTTDE, (ψ_m). The value of Td_m as well as ψ_m is assumed to be predefined by the design engineers based on the criticality of the application. Whereas, r_m refers to the number of replicas of message m that are sent during Td_m. In the contrast of Td_m, the value of r_m is determined by the proposed algorithm such that ψ_m is satisfied for each message and the MTTDE for the whole network, $MTTDE_N$, is maximized. N_m represents the set of all possible paths p_m^i for the message m. In particular, the path p_m is denoted by an ordered sequence of connected vertices starts by the source ECU and ends by the destination ECU. For instance, message m with ECU_0 and ECU_7 as source and destination, respectively, has three valid paths that composes N_m: $p_m^1 = \langle ECU_0, B_0, B_3, ECU_7 \rangle$, $p_m^2 = \langle ECU_0, B_0, B_2, B_3, ECU_7 \rangle$, and $p_m^3 = \langle ECU_0, B_0, B_1, B_2, B_3, ECU_7 \rangle$. $S_{(m,l)}$ refers to the transmission time of m on link l. Finally, every link l has an available capacity of C_l. In particular, maximum bandwidth that is available for AVB traffic in TSN standard is 75% [1].

3.2   Transmission Reliability

Transmitted messages are vulnerable to transient errors during every transmission through the network's links with certain Bit Error Rate (BER). In this work, the transmission reliability of each AVB stream is measured by its MTTDE

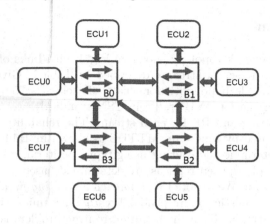

Fig. 1. Example TSN topology model.

where perfect error detection mechanism is assumed. In particular, probability P_{Cm} that a message $m_i \in M$ is delivered to its destination can be computed as Eq. (1).

$$P_{Cm} = (1 - BER)^{Nr_m \cdot S_m} \tag{1}$$

where Nr_m and S_m refer to the path length and the size of message m. Given that temporal redundancy is applied, a transmission failure for message m occurs if the network fails to deliver -at least- one correct replica of this message during Td_m. Hence, the probability of the transmission failure P_{Fm} is obtained as shown in Eq. (2).

$$P_{Fm} = (1 - P_{Cm})^{\gamma_m} \tag{2}$$

where γ_m is the minimum number of replicas which reach the destination within a interval of Td_m according to the maximum jitter which affects the message J_{max}. γ_m is computed as follows:

$$\gamma_m = r_m - \frac{J_{max}}{Td_m} \tag{3}$$

Then, MTTDE for transmission of m can be computed by Eq. (4) which is introduced in [7].

$$MTTDE_m = \int_0^\infty (1 - P_{Fm})^{\frac{t}{Td_m}} dt = -\frac{Td_m}{\ln(1 - P_{Fm})} \tag{4}$$

Then, the failure rate of transmission for message m is computed by Eq. (5).

$$\lambda_m = \frac{1}{MTTDE_m} = -\frac{\ln(1 - P_{Fm})}{Td_m} \tag{5}$$

Finally, $MTTDE_N$, which is the objective function of the proposed routing algorithm, is computed by Eq. (6).

$$MTTDE_N = \frac{1}{\sum_{m \in M} \lambda_m} \tag{6}$$

4   Motivation

Considering the network topology shown in Fig. 1 with links of 12 Mbit transmission rate and the set of streams described in Table 1. Given that BER is 10^{-9} and the available bandwidth for this traffic class is 75% (the maximum bandwidth percentage for AVB traffic in TSN standard), we are interested to determine the routing and RL for each stream. The reliability criteria of these streams are measured by minimum MTTDE as shown in Table 1. One possible approach is to determine the routing using typical criteria, e.g., shortest path. Then the number of required replicas are determined based on the path length of each routed stream. We denote this approach as *routing-first*. Another option is to determine pessimistic failure probability P_{Fm} assuming the longest possible path for each stream. Then the resultant routing problem is solved with the already assigned RL. We denote this approach as *reliability-first*.

Table 1. The streams of the motivational example

Index	(Source, Destination)	Size (KB)	Period (ms)	MTTDE (sec)
M_1	(ECU_0, ECU_3)	1	2	3×10^6
M_2	(ECU_0, ECU_3)	1.5	3	3×10^6
M_3	(ECU_7, ECU_4)	0.5	2	3×10^6

The solution obtained by *routing-first* approach is depicted in Table 2. First, the messages are routed based on shortest path criteria. Thus, M_1 and M_2 are routed through the same 1-hop path. Then, the required repetitions based on the assigned paths are obtained as two replicas for each message according to Eq. (4). However, required bandwidth after the temporal redundancy exceed the available bandwidth of the link (B_0, B_1) by 56%. Hence, *routing-first* is incapable to provide a feasible solution for this problem.

Table 2. Resultant routing and number of replicas obtained by *routing-first* approach.

Index	Path	Repetition	U_{max}
M_1	(ECU_0, B_0, B_1, ECU_3)	2	**156%**
M_2	(ECU_0, B_0, B_1, ECU_3)	2	**156%**
M_3	(ECU_7, B_3, B_2, ECU_4)	2	44.4%

With regard to *reliability-first* approach, the required RL for each message is determined according to Eq. (4) assuming paths of length 3 hops (longest possible path). Then, the messages are routed based on the shortest path criteria. The obtained routing and repetition based on this approach are shown in Table 3. We can see that, M_2 has three replicas which conflicts with the available bandwidth

Table 3. Resultant routing and number of replicas obtained by *reliability-first* approach.

Index	Path	Repetition	U_{max}
M_1	(ECU_0, B_0, B_1, ECU_3)	2	89%
M_2	-	3	-
M_3	(ECU_7, B_3, B_2, ECU_4)	2	44%

Table 4. Resultant routing and number of replicas obtained by the proposed approach.

Index	Path	Repetition	U_{max}
M_1	(ECU_0, B_0, B_1, ECU_3)	2	89%
M_2	$(ECU_0, B_0, B_2, B_1, ECU_3)$	2	89%
M_3	(ECU_7, B_3, B_2, ECU_4)	2	44%

of links along the three possible paths that connect ECU_0 with ECU_3. Thus, *reliability-first* is unable to provide a feasible solution for this problem.

The aforementioned two examples show the limitations of handling the routing and redundancy assignment in two separate steps. On the other hand, the proposed approach handles this two problems jointly to generate routing that guarantee feasible RL assignment. For example, it was able to provide a feasible solution for the illustrative example presented in this section as depicted in Table 4.

5   Proposed Reliability-Aware Routing

This section presents the proposed ILP formulation for a reliability-aware routing of AVB streams. In the following, the formulation for the valid routing constraints, capacity constraints, reliability constraint, and the objective function that represents the network reliability measured by the overall MTTDE of all messages. The ILP is defined by the following constraints:

1. $m \in M$: Message.
2. N_m: The set of possible paths for message m.
3. $L_{(m,n,)}$: The set of links that compose path n for message m.
4. C_l: Available capacity of link $l \in L$.
5. $S_{(m,l)}$: Transmission time for message m on link l.
6. $R_{(m,n)}$: The set of repetitions r_m that satisfy the required MTTDE for message m if it is routed through path n.
7. $F_{(m,n,r)}$: Failure rate for message m at path of length n for repetition r.
8. $H_{(m,n)}$: Length (number of hops) of the path n for message m.

The ILP uses the following decision variables:

1. $X_{(m,n,r)}$: Binary variable indicates whether message m is routed to path n_m with repetition r.
2. $G_{(m,l,r)}$: Binary variable indicates whether message m passes through link l with repetition r.
3. $Xc_{(m,n,r)}$: Auxiliary binary variable represents the complement of $X_{(m,n,r)}$.

The routing is considered valid *iff* there is a particular path $p_m \in P$ is assigned for each message $m \in M$ with particular repetition $r_m \in R_m$. To enforce the algorithm to generate a valid routing, we introduce constraint (7) for every message:

$$\forall m \in M : \sum_{n \in N_m} \sum_{r \in R_{mn}} X_{(m,n,r)} = 1 \tag{7}$$

This constraint ensures valid routing by enforcing one path to be assigned for every message $m \in M$. The variable $X_{(m,n,r)}$ is defined by the following constraints (8) to (10). We introduce constraint (8) to enforce $X_{(m,n,r)}$ to be '1' if the path n is assigned to message m with repetition r.

$$\forall m \in M, \forall n \in N_m, \forall r \in R_{(m,n)} : X_{(m,n,r)} + \left(H_{(m,n)} - \sum_{l \in L_{(m,n)}} G_{(m,l,r)} \right) \geq 1 \tag{8}$$

This constraint states that if a message m is assigned to all links that compose path n with repetition r, then the sum term over links $l \in L_{(m,n)}$ will be equal to the path length $H_{(m,n)}$. Thus, $X_{(m,n,r)}$ is enforced to be '1'. Whereas, constraints (9) and (10) are introduced to ensure that $X_{(m,n,c)}$ cannot be activated unless all links along path n, $L_{(m,n)}$, are allocated for message m.

$$\forall m \in M, \forall n \in N_m, \forall r \in R_m : -N \cdot Xc_{(m,n,r)} + \left(H_{(m,n)} - \sum_{l \in L_{(m,n)}} G_{(m,l,r)} \right) \leq 0 \tag{9}$$

This constraint states that a message m is not assigned to path n with repetition r unless all links $l \in L_{(m,n)}$ are assigned for message m with repetition r. $Xc_{(m,n,r)}$ is the complement of $X_{(m,n,r)}$ as defined in constraint (10).

$$\forall m \in M, \forall n \in N_m, \forall r \in R_m : X_{(m,n,r)} + Xc_{(m,n,r)} = 1 \tag{10}$$

Constraint (11) is introduced to represent the available capacity of physical links.

$$\forall l \in L : \sum_{m \in M} \sum_{r \in R_m} G_{(m,l,r)} \cdot S_{(m,l)} \cdot r \leq C_l \tag{11}$$

This constraint states that a link cannot be loaded by a traffic which exceeds its available capacity. To ensure that every message $m \in M$ has a particular repetition, constraint (12) is introduced.

$$\forall m \in M, \forall n \in N_m, \forall l \in L_{(m,n)} : \sum_{r \in R_{(m,n)}} G_{(m,l,r)} \leq 1 \qquad (12)$$

This constraint states that message m cannot has different repetitions at any link $l \in L_{(m,n)}$. Solving the problem described by this set of constraints generates a solution (routing and repetition) that meets the required $MTTDE_m$ for each m. However, in order to explore the reliability optimal solution for the routing problem, the objective function (13) is introduced. This objective minimizes the total failure rate of all messages which maximizes $MTTDE_N$ as shown in Eq. (6).

$$\min \sum_{m \in M} \sum_{n \in N_m} \sum_{r \in Rm} X_{(m,n,r)} \cdot F_{(m,n,r)} \qquad (13)$$

The inner two sums in Eq. (13) have only one nonzero element corresponds to the failure rate λ_m of the assigned path n and repetition r of the stream m. The outer sum corresponds to the failure rate of the whole network λ_N which maximizes $MTTDE_N$.

6   Experimental Results

In this section, different automotive case studies are presented to evaluate the proposed reliability-aware routing with respect to the performance and the applicability for design space exploration. In this analysis, the trade-off between the reliability and maximum utilization of the network is investigated. MATLAB 2014a is employed to solve the ILP optimization problem. The reported results have been carried out on a workstation with an Intel Core i7 6820IIQ processor running at 3.0 GHz and 16 GB RAM.

6.1   Performance Evaluation

The first analysis investigates the efficiency of the proposed ILP formulation in terms of the runtime. In fact, we present the runtime of 24 synthetic test cases of different sizes and loads. In particular, networks composed of 3, 4, and 5 switches, i.e., have paths length up to 2, 3 and 4 communication hops, respectively, are considered. Different number of messages are considered ranges from 20 to 90 message are routed through each network. The sources and destinations of the messages are randomly assigned from a set of 20 ECUs in each network. All messages have a payload of 1,500 Bytes, a period of 0.01 s, a required MTTDE of 10^6 s for BER of 10^{-9}, and a repetition up to 3 replicas. Messages are transmitted over 100 Mbit Ethernet links. The maximum links utilization is chosen to be 50%. The runtime results for test cases are shown in Fig. 2.

We can see the super-linear growth of the solving time with the number of messages as well as the size of network. However, these values are still reasonable for off-line processing at the design stage.

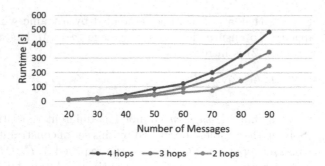

Fig. 2. Runtime for 24 synthetic test cases for different number of hops and messages by the proposed reliability-aware routing.

6.2   Co-optimization Case Study

In this section, we consider a network which consists of 13 ECUs exchanging 70 messages over four switches. Messages are routed through paths of length up to 3 communication hops. Messages have payloads of 1, 2, and 3 KB, a period of 1, 2, 5, 10 and 20 ms, required MTTDE of 10^6 s for BER of 10^{-9}, and a repetition up to 3 replicas. Messages are transmitted over 100 Mbit Ethernet links. We solved the optimization problem for six different utilization constrains ranges from 25% to 75% of the links bandwidth to explore the trade-off between transmission reliability and network utilization. Figure 3 depicts the optimal transmission reliability for different possible values of the maximum links utilization. This co-optimization yields 6 Pareto-optimal solutions. Increasing the available bandwidth implies that messages can be routed through shorter paths and more replicas can be sent for each message. This explains the increase of the transmission reliability depicted in Fig. 3. The distribution of the 70 messages in terms of the number of assigned replicas for different utilization constraints is shown in Fig. 4. It can be noticed that, by allocating more bandwidth, the number of messages with two repetitions is decreasing, while, the number of messages that get the maximum repetitions (3 replicas in this case) is increasing.

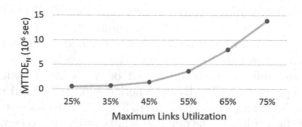

Fig. 3. $MTTDE_N$ for different utilization constraints.

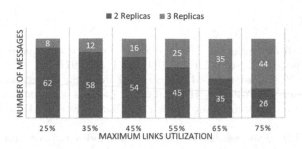

Fig. 4. Messages distribution with respect to the repetitions.

To demonstrate the advantage of the proposed approach over the 2-steps approaches explained in Sect. 4, we tried to solve the same routing problem using *routing-first* and *reliability-first* approaches for different links utilization constraints varies from 25% to 75%. The routing results in terms of whether a feasible solution is found are depicted in Table 5. We can notice that the proposed approach is able to find a solution with a utilization of 25% only. Whereas, *routing-first* and *reliability-first* approaches needed up to 65% and 45% of the link capacities, respectively, to find a solution.

Table 5. Solution feasibility using the proposed approach, *routing-first*, and *reliability-first*.

U_{max}	15%	25%	35%	45%	55%	65%	75%
Proposed approach	✗	✓	✓	✓	✓	✓	✓
Routing-first	✗	✗	✗	✓	✓	✓	✓
Reliability-first	✗	✗	✗	✗	✗	✓	✓

7 Conclusion

In this paper, a new technique to achieve reliability-aware routing for AVB traffic in automotive TSN networks. A new ILP formulation is introduced to investigate the reliability-aware optimal solution for a particular links utilization. The proposed technique jointly determines the routing and the required redundancy level to meet the reliability criteria for each stream and maximize the reliability of the network. The results of different case studies demonstrate the efficiency and co-optimization capabilities of the proposed technique. For instance, large routing problems (up to 90 messages over 5 hops) are solved within a reasonable time (less than 500 s). Furthermore, the results show that the overall network reliability can be improved by 10-folds by adapting the temporal redundancy approach compared to non-optimized solutions.

References

1. IEEE Standard for Local and Metropolitan Area Networks-Audio Video Bridging (AVB) Systems. IEEE Std 802.1BA-2011, pp. 1–45 (2011)
2. Chakraborty, S., Lukasiewycz, M., Buckl, C., Fahmy, S., Chang, N., Park, S., Kim, Y., Leteinturier, P., Adlkofer, H.: Embedded systems and software challenges in electric vehicles. In: Design, Automation and Test in Europe (DATE), pp. 424–429 (2012)
3. Decotignie, J.D.: Ethernet-based real-time and industrial communications. Proc. IEEE **93**(6), 1102–1117 (2005)
4. ISO26262, Road vehicles - Functional Safety – Part 1–9, 1st edition. Standard, International Organization for Standardization (2011)
5. Li, W., Natale, M.D., Zheng, W., Giusto, P., Sangiovanni-Vincentelli, A., Seshia, S.A.: Optimizations of an application-level protocol for enhanced dependability in flexray. In: Design, Automation and Test in Europe (DATE), pp. 1076–1081 (2009)
6. Marques, L., Vasconcelos, V., Pedreiras, P., Silva, V., Almeida, L.: Efficient transient error recovery in flexray using the dynamic segment. In: IEEE International Conference on Emerging Technology and Factory Automation (ETFA), pp. 1–4 (2014)
7. Smirnov, F., Glaß, M., Reimann, F., Teich, J.: Formal reliability analysis of switched ethernet automotive networks under transient transmission errors. In: Design Automation Conference (DAC), pp. 1–6 (2016)
8. Steiner, W., Peón, P.G., Gutiérrez, M., Mehmed, A., Rodriguez-Navas, G., Lisova, E., Pozo, F.: Next generation real-time networks based on it technologies. In: IEEE International Conference on Emerging Technologies and Factory Automation (ETFA), pp. 1–8 (2016)
9. Tanasa, B., Bordoloi, U.D., Eles, P., Peng, Z.: Scheduling for fault-tolerant communication on the static segment of flexray. In: Real-Time Systems Symposium (RTSS), pp. 385–394 (2010)

Data Science, Privacy, and Security

A Comparative Study on Chrominance Based Methods in Dorsal Hand Recognition: Single Image Case

Orcan Alpar and Ondrej Krejcar[(✉)]

Faculty of Informatics and Management, Center for Basic and Applied Research,
University of Hradec Kralove, Rokitanskeho 62,
500 03 Hradec Kralove, Czech Republic
orcanalpar@hotmail.com, ondrej.krejcar@uhk.cz

Abstract. Dorsal hand recognition is a crucial topic in biometrics and human-machine interaction; however most of the identification systems identify and segment the hands from the images consisting of high contrast backgrounds. In other words, capturing and analyzing images of hands on a white or black or any colored background is way too easy to achieve high accuracy. On the contrary, in continuous authentication or in interactive human-machine systems, it can be not possible nor feasible to process high contrast images, like hands on computer keyboards which is not as simple as single color backgrounds even the feature to be extracted is solely the hand color. Therefore we deal with processing of the images consisting of hands on computer keyboards to compare various luminance and chrominance methods by YCbCr color space extraction and to find ways to achieve higher accuracy without any succeeding erosion, dilation or filtering. The methods focused on chromatic intervals could be summarized as: fixed intervals, covariance intervals and fuzzy 2-means. Our main contribution briefly is a necessary accuracy comparison and validation of the common methods on the single images. The highest accuracy is found as 96% by fuzzy 2-means applied to chrominance layers of the image.

Keywords: Dorsal hand recognition · Segmentation · YCbCr color space
Chrominance intervals

1 Introduction

As dorsal hand recognition is important for many fields; accuracy of segmentation however is very crucial for biometrics and related branches, mostly in skin color based recognition. The main issue is not in recognizing hands on a camera to evaluate the interaction nor in identifying the hands on a single color background, which both are so simple. On the contrary, it would be harder if the hands are on very tangled background like the computer keyboards and in motion with a high accuracy. Therefore we focus on the chrominance methods to compare the accuracy of the raw segmented images without any kind of following image processing algorithms.

There are many papers dealing with hand recognition or at least start with it for any various purposes [1–6] while skin color identification is still a very basic approach for

© Springer International Publishing AG, part of Springer Nature 2018
M. Mouhoub et al. (Eds.): IEA/AIE 2018, LNAI 10868, pp. 711–721, 2018.
https://doi.org/10.1007/978-3-319-92058-0_68

the initiation of identification such as in [7, 8]. Among the articles recently published on hand recognition, there are some papers very relevant to our research topic and starting with YCbCr conversion. Just like us, Chitra and Balakrishnan [9] conducted comparative experiments to find out the difference between HSCbCr and YCbCr; while Kaur and Kranthi [10] between YCbCr and CIE-Lab color spaces in skin color identification. Qiu-yu et al. [11] dealt with YCbCr imaging with K-means for segmentation of face and hands; Shen and Wu [12] for segmentation of lips.

Although we had already proposed an adaptive way of segmentation of the hands on the keyboards [13], governed by finding a minimum tissue from the hands of the users to create a confidence interval depending on their chrominance values, the accuracy was the main weakness of this research. We dealt with the hands of seven subjects to find out whether there would be any significant difference in blue difference chroma (Cb) and red difference chroma (Cr) totally omitting the luminance (Y) layer of the images. We figured out that the Cb and Cr levels significantly vary in hands of the users and even in the region of hands under the identical light conditions namely $98.5477 \leq Cb \leq 116.8542$ and $147.6682 \leq Cr \leq 161.1963$. Simple as it seems, accurate segmentation was nearly impossible though, due to non-homogenous distribution of color values on hands.

There are two types of errors could be determined when dealing with segmentation of the dorsal hands from images; which are Type I error (false positive) which corresponds incorrect classification of a non-hand pixel; Type II error (false negative) which corresponds incorrect classification of a hand pixel. Strictly depending on the context of the research indeed, the importance of these error types may vary; yet we will concentrate on both by comparing the segmented binary images by our algorithms with the binary images segmented by Adobe Photoshop. On the other hand, an image closeness algorithm is also presented to find the closeness between these binary images.

Considering the outcomes and the reason of the research since we focus on enhancing the warning system already presented in [14], we only analyzed the left hands on the keyboards to figure out the intervals of Cb and Cr for future research of us and to present a comparative study for the researchers who need to prime a system of color based hand recognition with high accuracy. Therefore we firstly introduce the preliminaries of YCbCr conversion and subsequently we present the major methods for interval determination and hand segmentation. Finally, the results of accuracy comparison are mentioned in detail before the conclusion section. As an important remark: This paper tries to shed light on the strict situations that segmentation of the hands on the keyboard is mandatory from the images not from a video sequence. Therefore any kind of difference algorithms are disabled as well as any kind of preprocessing of the images.

2 Comparative Study

As the preliminaries of the research, we firstly present the YCbCr color space and the results of conversion from RGB images consisting of hands on keyboard.

2.1   YCbCr Conversion

Given an RGB image captured by a camera mounted above a laptop keyboard, any pixel $p_{i,j,k}$ on the image $I_{i,j,k}$ could be mathematically denoted as:

$$p_{i,j,k} \in I_{i,j,k}(i = [1{:}w], j = [1{:}h], k = [1{:}3]) \tag{1}$$

where $w \in \mathbb{Z}^+$ is the width, $h \in \mathbb{Z}^+$ is the height of the image; $i \in \mathbb{Z}^+$ is the row $j \in \mathbb{Z}^+$ is the column number and $k \in \mathbb{Z}^+$ is the layer of color channel: 1 for red, 2 for green and 3 for blue. The conventional conversion between RGB and YCbCr color spaces is mainly identical which originated by a conversion matrix $[C]$ with the scale factors of:

$$[C] = \begin{bmatrix} 65.481 & 128.553 & 24.966 \\ -37.797 & -74.203 & 112 \\ 112 & -93.786 & -18.214 \end{bmatrix} \tag{2}$$

and with the offset of:

$$[O] = \begin{bmatrix} 16 \\ 128 \\ 128 \end{bmatrix} \tag{3}$$

So that each pixel $y_{i,j,m}$ in an YCbCr image $Y_{i,j,k}$ generated from an RBG image $I_{i,j,k}$ is computed as follows:

$$y_{i,j,m} \in Y_{i,j,m}(i = [1{:}w], j = [1{:}h], m = [1{:}3]) = [C]I_{i,j,k} + [O] \tag{4}$$

for each channel separately, where $m \in \mathbb{Z}^+$ represents channel number: 1 for Y, 2 for Cb and 3 for Cr. In other notation:

$$y_{i,j,1} \in Y_{i,j,1} = 16 + \left(65.481\, I_{i,j,1} + 128.553\, I_{i,j,2} + 24.966\, I_{i,j,3}\right) \tag{5}$$

$$y_{i,j,2} \in Y_{i,j,2} = 128 + \left(-37.797\, I_{i,j,1} + -74.203\, I_{i,j,2} + 112\, I_{i,j,3}\right) \tag{6}$$

$$y_{i,j,3} \in Y_{i,j,3} = 128 + \left(112\, I_{i,j,1} + -93.786\, I_{i,j,2} + -18.214\, I_{i,j,3}\right) \tag{7}$$

which transforms the pixel values from [0 255] into [16 235] for Y and [16 240] for Cb and Cr channels. An example of the conversion with the hands we're trying to segment accurately is shown in Fig. 1.

As seen in Fig. 1 bottom row, Cb and Cr layers give adequate information about human skin since the differentiation of the hands and surrounding is clear. In the Cb layer, the hands is explicitly darker than the keyboard while in the Cr layer it is lighter. Therefore, the intersection set of the predetermined intervals would be enough; however erroneous segmentation is the main issue despite what is expected even if the intervals are rational.

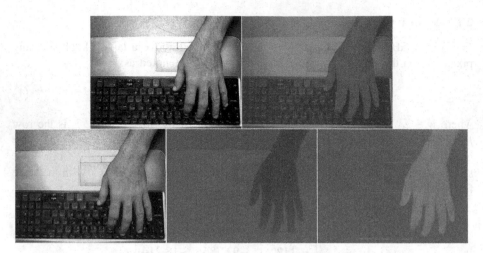

Fig. 1. Original RGB image on the top-left; Converted YCbCr image on the top-right; Y, Cb and Cr channels of the YCbCr image on the bottom in order

2.2　Constant Interval Method

It is commonly expected that $77 \leq Cb \leq 127$ and $133 \leq Cr \leq 173$ intervals include human-skin color; however with a very wide confidence range indeed. Given this assumption, if we manipulate the RGB images and search for the pixels inside of these intervals to get binary pixels $b_{i,j}$ of newly created image $B_{i,j}$,

$$b_{i,j} \in B_{i,j} = \begin{cases} 1, & 77 < y_{i,j,2} < 127 \, \Lambda \, 133 < y_{i,j,3} < 173 \\ 0, & \text{o/w} \end{cases} \tag{8}$$

On the other hand, one more assumption which we also had adopted in our research [14] is $96 \leq Cb \leq 118$ and $142 \leq Cr \leq 164$ intervals. These intervals certainly are narrower than the previous ones which were perfectly fitting to our requirements and are leading to

$$b_{i,j} \in B_{i,j} = \begin{cases} 1, & 96 < y_{i,j,2} < 118 \, \Lambda \, 142 < y_{i,j,3} < 164 \\ 0, & \text{o/w} \end{cases} \tag{9}$$

Depending on the context, each of the fixed intervals give acceptable results with some errors as seen in Fig. 2. Considering the white pixels represent the segmented hand.

It is obvious from the images that both intervals cause some errors, type I or II depending on the wideness of the interval which will be addressed in the section of accuracy evaluation.

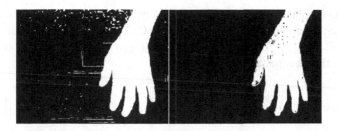

Fig. 2. Segmentation results of first and second fixed intervals

2.3   Covariance Interval Method

Through the emerging new methodologies and excessive number of studies on recognition, it is possible to find public human-skin tissue datasets that will create a confidence interval, like the SFA database [15] providing tissue samples from all across the world. Varying from 1 pixel to 35 × 35 pixels, 3354 samples of skin images could be found in that database for image segmentation purposes. Given the sample variety in the dataset, it is possible to find means and covariance between the Cb and Cr values of the sample images. However, as the sample size change, mean values covariance and related intervals may drastically vary. Among 3354 samples, very small portion of the 25 × 25 images of human skin tissue is presented in Fig. 3.

Fig. 3. Some skin tissue examples from the SFA dataset (25 × 25 resolution)

Given the number of tissue sample t, we computed the average of Cb and Cr values of each sample and covariance of Cb and Cr. For two matrices of Cb: $y_{i,j,2} \in Y_{i,j,2}(i = [1:w], j = [1:h], m = 2)$ and Cr: $y_{i,j,3} \in Y_{i,j,3}(i = [1:w], j = [1:h], m = 3)$ layers of an image, the covariance is defined as:

$$Cov(y_{i,j,2}, y_{i,j,3}) = \frac{1}{wh - 1} \sum_{i=1}^{w} \sum_{j=1}^{h} (y_{i,j,2} - \mu_{y_{i,j,2}})(y_{i,j,3} - \mu_{y_{i,j,3}}) \qquad (10)$$

where μ stands for the mean. As stated above, the covariance matrices may vary as well as the mean values depending on the sample size, therefore results for the various sample sizes are presented below in Fig. 4.

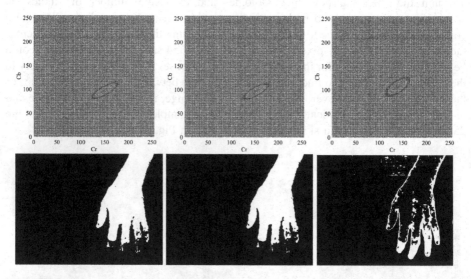

Fig. 4. Covariance intervals on the top, results of identification on the bottom, from left to right: random 10 samples, 100 samples, 3000 samples

It possible seems interesting that while samples size increase and about to reach the maximum number of samples, the segmentation fails and gives terrible results if compared to very simple fixed interval method. On the other hand, random 10 and 100 samples don't give accurate segmentation either; yet more reliable that large sample size.

2.4   Fuzzy 2-Means

Fuzzy C-means is very promising method for binarization and segmentation for hands on white background or more generally if the contrast is incontrovertible. We mostly utilize 2-means for thermal images to segment hands from high contrast images as presented in [16, 17] which are indeed exercises of crisp or hard-2 means by binarization of the color patterns. Despite the process roadmap for RGB images, YCbCr images consist one redundant luminance layer that should be omitted. If we try to segment an image into two clusters, the objective function would be:

$$J = \sum_{a=1}^{2} \sum_{b=1}^{ijk} u_{a,b}^{m} d_{ab},$$

(11)

where $u_{a,b}$ represents memberships and for ijk data on an image consisting of Cb and Cr layers and d_{ab} is the squared Euclidean distance between data points $[X_b] = \bar{p}_{ij}$ and clusters $[C_b]$ therefore $u_{a,b}$ should satisfy:

$$\sum_{b=1}^{2} u_{a,b} = 1$$

(12)

Afterwards $u_{a,b}$ is manipulated by:

$$u_{a,b} = \left((d_{ab})^{1/(m-1)} \sum_{s=1}^{2} \left(\frac{1}{d_{as}} \right)^{1/(m-1)} \right)^{-1}$$

(13)

To calculate the mean values of two clusters by:

$$[C_b] = \sum_{a=1}^{N} u_{ab}^{m} [X_b] / \sum_{a=1}^{N} u_{ab}^{m}$$

(14)

which is also a palette matrix $[C_b]$ with two rows and three columns; however all non-binary values are turned into binary. The final binary image B_{ij} could easily be found by $B_{ij} = \bar{R}_{ij} \cdot [\check{C}_b]$, shown in Fig. 5 below.

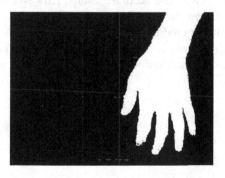

Fig. 5. Result of Fuzzy 2-means segmentation

Although there are some false positive errors, the hand is segmented from the keyboard pretty accurate.

3 Evaluation of Accuracy

Despite the various meanings of accuracy, what we focus on here is the correctness of differentiation between skin and non-skin pixels. As we already processed the image we used throughout the paper by Photoshop for manual segmentation of the hand from the keyboard, the binary imaged reveled by this process is only an estimate of the hand even if the segmentation is carried out very precisely. Let's define the segmented image which could be considered as the very close estimate of correctly identified hand on the keyboard, as

$$z_{i,j} \in Z_{i,j}(i = [1{:}w], j = [1{:}h]) \tag{15}$$

so the main accuracy θ between $Z_{i,j}$ and segmented image $b_{i,j} \in B_{i,j}$ using the image closeness algorithm could be stated as:

$$\theta = \left(\sum_{i=1}^{w} \sum_{j=1}^{h} b_{i,j} . z_{i,j} \middle/ \sum_{i=1}^{w} \sum_{j=1}^{h} z_{i,j} \right) - \left(\sum_{i=1}^{w} \sum_{j=1}^{h} |b_{i,j} - z_{i,j}| / wh \right) \tag{16}$$

where $0 \leq \theta \in \mathbb{R}^+ \leq 1$ disregarding the importance difference between false negative and false positive errors; however the closeness algorithm is totally alterable upon the requirements if type I and II errors are crucial to differentiate. The results are presented in Table 1 in descending results of accuracy order; where the first two columns of the accuracy evaluation consist of reference image and negative of the reference image to validate the closeness algorithm. The reference images indeed are identical achieved by Photoshop; while the compared images are the results of the corresponding algorithms.

As seen from the table that, for the image we were dealing with fuzzy 2-means and narrow interval give very close and accurate results. However fuzzy method has more false positives while narrow interval has more false negative; yet both could be enhanced with a very simple eroding algorithm. On the other hand, dataset gives very misleading results despite many researchers are using public dataset for their papers since any kind of public datasets are very easy to find and to implement without any hard effort.

Table 1. Results of accuracy test

	REFERENCE IMAGE	COMPARED IMAGE	θ
REF IMAGE			1
NEGATIVE IMAGE			0
FUZZY 2-MEANS			0.960
NARROW INTERVAL			0.957
WIDE INTERVAL			0.893
10 RANDOM SAMPLES (SFA database)			0.839
100 RANDOM SAMPLES (SFA database)			0.826
3000 RANDOM SAMPLES (SFA database)			0.295

4 Conclusion and Discussion

The main purpose of this paper is finding more accurate solutions for dorsal hand recognition on a single frame without any video sequence or more importantly without any kind of white or single color background that will utterly ease the segmentation. Although there are way too more methods in the literature concerning YCbCr image conversion and hand recognition, we selected the ones we used or will use in our research, which are constant interval, covariance interval revealed from public datasets and fuzzy 2-means.

Depending on the requirements in hand segmentation with a single image, it is possible to use fuzzy 2-means and narrow interval method; however as the skin color changes it is possible to see more accurate results from fuzzy 2-means. In our biomedical research, we focus only on the wrist section in the images, therefore we neglect false negative errors.

AS future research opportunities, it is also possible to use CNN for segmentation of binary images as well as other relevant techniques. On the other hand, if the background is saved, like the keyboard itself for this case, the double image cases could be applicable by difference algorithms.

Acknowledgement. The work and the contribution were supported by the SPEV project "Smart Solutions in Ubiquitous Computing Environments 2018", University of Hradec Kralove, Faculty of Informatics and Management, Czech Republic. We are also grateful for the support of Ph.D. student Ayca Kirimtat in consultations regarding application aspects.

References

1. Frolova, D., Stern, H., Berman, S.: Most probable longest common subsequence for recognition of gesture character input. IEEE Trans. Cybern. **43**(3), 871–880 (2013)
2. Ghotkar, S., Kharate, G.K.: Vision based real time hand gesture recognition techniques for human computer interaction. Int. J. Comput. Appl. **70**(16), 1–6 (2013)
3. Weber, H., Jung, C.R., Gelb, D.: Hand and object segmentation from RGB-D images for interaction with planar surfaces. In: 2015 IEEE International Conference on Image Processing (ICIP), pp. 2984–2988. IEEE (2015)
4. Feng, K.P., Wan, K., Luo, N.: Natural gesture recognition based on motion detection and skin color. Appl. Mech. Mater. **321**, 974–979 (2013)
5. Plouffe, G., Cretu, A.M., Payeur, P.: Natural human-computer interaction using static and dynamic hand gestures. In: 2015 IEEE International Symposium on Haptic, Audio and Visual Environments and Games (HAVE), pp. 1–6. IEEE (2015)
6. Tu, Y.J., Kao, C.C., Lin, H.Y., Chang, C.C.: Face and gesture based human computer interaction. international journal of signal processing. Image Process. Patt. Recogn. **8**(9), 219–228 (2015)
7. Alpar, O., Krejcar, O.: A new feature extraction in dorsal hand recognition by chromatic imaging. In: Nguyen, N.T., Tojo, S., Nguyen, L.M., Trawiński, B. (eds.) ACIIDS 2017. LNCS (LNAI), vol. 10192, pp. 266–275. Springer, Cham (2017). https://doi.org/10.1007/978-3-319-54430-4_26

8. Jeong, J., Jang, Y.: Max–min hand cropping method for robust hand region extraction in the image-based hand gesture recognition. Soft. Comput. **19**(4), 815–818 (2015)

9. Chitra, S., Balakrishnan, G.: Comparative study for two color spaces HSCbCr and YCbCr in skin color detection. Appl. Math. Sci. **6**(85), 4229–4238 (2012)

10. Kaur, A., Kranthi, B.V.: Comparison between YCbCr color space and CIELab color space for skin color segmentation. IJAIS **3**(4), 30–33 (2012)

11. Qiu-yu, Z., Jun-chi, L., Mo-yi, Z., Hong-xiang, D., Lu, L.: Hand gesture segmentation method based on YCbCr color space and k-means clustering. Int. J. Sig. Process. Image Process. Patt. Recogn. **8**(5), 105–116 (2015)

12. Shen, X.G., Wu, W.: An algorithm of lips secondary positioning and feature extraction based on YCbCr color space. In: International Conference on Advances in Mechanical Engineering and Industrial Informatics, pp. 1472–1478. Atlantis Press (2015)

13. Alpar, O., Krejcar, O.: Dorsal hand recognition through adaptive YCbCr imaging technique. In: Nguyen, N.-T., Manolopoulos, Y., Iliadis, L., Trawiński, B. (eds.) ICCCI 2016. LNCS (LNAI), vol. 9876, pp. 262–270. Springer, Cham (2016). https://doi.org/10.1007/978-3-319-45246-3_25

14. Alpar, O., Krejcar, O.: Fuzzy warning system against ulnar nerve entrapment. In: 2017 IEEE International Conference on Fuzzy Systems (FUZZ-IEEE). IEEE (2017)

15. Casati, J.P.B., Moraes, D.R., Rodrigues, E.L.L.: SFA: a human skin image database based on FERET and AR facial images. In: IX workshop de Visao Computacional, Rio de Janeiro (2013)

16. Alpar, O., Krejcar, O.: Quantization and equalization of pseudocolor images in hand thermography. In: Rojas, I., Ortuño, F. (eds.) IWBBIO 2017. LNCS, vol. 10208, pp. 397–407. Springer, Cham (2017). https://doi.org/10.1007/978-3-319-56148-6_35

17. Alpar, O., Krejcar, O.: Superficial dorsal hand vein estimation. In: Rojas, I., Ortuño, F. (eds.) IWBBIO 2017. LNCS, vol. 10208, pp. 408–418. Springer, Cham (2017). https://doi.org/10.1007/978-3-319-56148-6_36

Frequency and Time Localization
in Biometrics: STFT vs. CWT

Orcan Alpar and Ondrej Krejcar[✉]

Faculty of Informatics and Management, Center for Basic and Applied Research,
University of Hradec Kralove, Rokitanskeho 62,
500 03 Hradec Kralove, Czech Republic
orcanalpar@hotmail.com, ondrej@krejcar.org

Abstract. Biometrics is a science discipline dealing with unique traits of the individuals including habitual characteristics. Once the unique features revealed from these characteristics are extracted as signals instead of raw data, it is possible to search for the new distinguishable traits. One of the traits, if any kind of time based signal is extracted, could be frequency component versus time component of the signal, depending on the content of the feature extraction and yet most of the signals consisting of a magnitude or a value as a dependent variable fit the requirements. The magnitude/value representation may vary indeed; however our previous researches proved that key-codes and key-press signals in biometric keystroke authentication and dislocation and speed signals in online signature verification are very useful of this kind of analysis. Therefore in this paper, we present the methods for extracting distinguishable features and frequency vs. time representation by short time Fourier transform (STFT) and continuous wavelet transformation (CWT) to introduce related research methodologies by comparing the outcomes and future opportunities. While presenting our approach to Biometric keystroke authentication and online signature verification, we also aim to present the differences of these methods with basic roadmaps and graphical results.

Keywords: Biometrics · Short time Fourier transformation
Continuous wavelet transformation · Keystroke authentication
Online signature verification

1 Introduction

In biometrics, the main focus is to find and extract distinguishable features from users for classification or authentication. These features could be biological like DNA; or physical/genetic like fingerprints; or behavioral/habitual like handwriting. Among many more examples of unique characteristics of individuals, what we deal here is biometric signals gathered by extraction of habitual features, which would be signing or keystroke styles. Although to be fair, what we know in signature analysis, no matter online or offline, is comparing geometrical, global or local features. It is very similar indeed in keystroke authentication where mostly key-press and inter-key times are extracted and classified, which are all in time domain [1–6] as we also focused on in [7–10]. However time domain solutions are very limited and sometimes not satisfactory

© Springer International Publishing AG, part of Springer Nature 2018
M. Mouhoub et al. (Eds.): IEA/AIE 2018, LNAI 10868, pp. 722–728, 2018.
https://doi.org/10.1007/978-3-319-92058-0_69

even if some papers deal with not only dislocation but with speed signals [11, 12] or some very novel features.

Given the speed signals are differentiable, it is also possible to state that frequency components may be as well. For instance in keystroke authentication as we previously stated in [13], the keystroke signals could be analyzed to achieve higher frequency regions for a unique biometric trait. In addition, as we presented in [14, 15], frequency feature could be extracted from electronic signatures while a genuine user is signing on a specially designed interface. Frequency component extraction from the signals is rather old concept indeed; however it is rather new in biometrics. The main reason of this drawback is treating the biometric features as data not as signals. For instance, in keystroke authentication, if the key-press and inter-key times are extracted and only the values of them are stored, there will be only a data matrix. However as we recently presented in [16, 17], if the process is continuously tracked and the signal is sampled by a high resolution algorithm, it is possible to analyze the discrete or interpolated or even digitized or binary train signals by particular signal processing techniques. Therefore, we introduce the methodology for turning time-domain signals into frequency domain to achieve frequency vs time representation of biometric signals for guidance of the readers.

In Fig. 1 below, the samples of signals we're analyzing are presented for password "orcan7890*" and a unique signature.

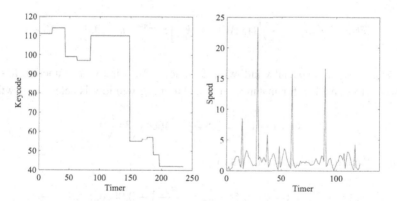

Fig. 1. Signal Samples: keystroke on the left, signature on the right.

In following sections, STFT and CWT are briefly presented as preliminaries and these signals are processed by each method to achieve frequency vs time representation.

2   Short-Time Fourier Transformation

The major method for years to reveal and examine the frequency component of signals is Fourier transformation. If the signal is analog or interpolated from a discrete signal, it refers to a continuous area which is computed by:

$$F(u) = \frac{1}{N} \int_0^{N-1} f(x)e^{-j2\pi ux}dx, \ u = 0, 1, \ldots, N-1 \qquad (1)$$

or when the signal is discrete or digital or even binary, it would be computed by:

$$F(u) = \frac{1}{N} \sum_{x=0}^{N-1} f(x)e^{\frac{-j2\pi ux}{N}}, \ u = 0, 1, \ldots, N-1 \qquad (2)$$

where $f(x)$ is main signal, $F(u)$ is frequency domain representation and u is the frequency component; $u = 0, 1, \ldots N-1$, for every time series signal x; $x = 0, 1, \ldots N-1$, N is the total number of samples and j is the imaginary unit. However, this transformation only leads to find the frequencies regardless of time. Therefore it is obviously necessary to divide the signals into windows by windowing function and analyze these time variant windows instead. Considering this kernel, a method called Short-time transformation is very useful which could be designated for continuous signals by:

$$STFT_f^u(t', u) = \int_0^{N-1} \left[f(x)W\left(\dot{x} - \dot{x}'\right) \right] e^{-j2\pi ux}dx, \ u = 0, 1, \ldots, N-1 \qquad (3)$$

or for discrete signals by:

$$STDFT_f^u(t', u) = \sum_{x=0}^{N-1} \left[f(x)W\left(\dot{x} - \dot{x}'\right) \right] e^{-j2\pi ux}, \ u = 0, 1, \ldots, N-1 \qquad (4)$$

where $W\left(\dot{x} - \dot{x}'\right)$ is a special windowing function. The windowing function has some alternatives to consider; for instance, if the Hamming window is selected, it will be:

$$W_n\left(\dot{x} - \dot{x}'\right) = 0.54 - 0.46\cos\left(2\pi\frac{n}{N}\right), \qquad (5)$$

while Blackman window will lead to

$$W_n\left(\dot{x} - \dot{x}'\right) = 0.42 - 0.5\cos\left(2\pi\frac{n}{N-1}\right) + 0.08\cos\left(4\pi\frac{n}{N-1}\right), \qquad (6)$$

where $0 \leq n \leq N$. Through the STFT, it is possible to create a spectrogram by $\left| STDFT_f^u(t', u) \right|^2$ which actually is three dimensional plane; however and more likely it is represented by a surface colored.

2.1   Experiments of STFT

Since we mainly deal with biometric authentication, we extracted the frequencies from keystrokes and signature signals by STFT as presented in Figs. 2 and 3.

It is seen from the spectrogram of windows size = 0.5 in each windowing function that there are three major frequencies of the signature signal. As a brief conclusion of

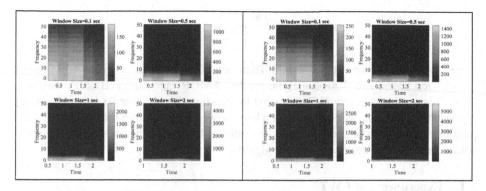

Fig. 2. SFTF of keystroke signal: Blackman in the left square; Hamming in the right square

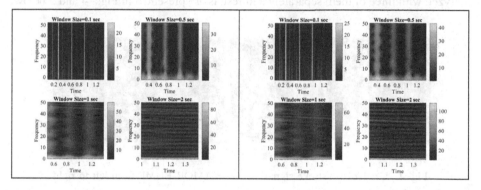

Fig. 3. STFT of signature signal: Blackman in the left square; Hamming in the right square

this part, it is easy to state that according to the signal size of biometric signals, lower window sizes provides good time localization; while higher window sizes gives the information of frequency. For the two samples, Blackman or Hamming windowing function didn't cause significant difference.

3 Continuous Wavelet Transformation

Just like the STFT, CWT is useful for acquiring frequency vs time representation; however the main difference between is that CWT proposed variable and thus flexible window size that doesn't crop the signal. The signal $f(x)$ where x is independent variable corresponding time, is transformed by:

$$W_x(a, b) = \int_{-\infty}^{\infty} f(x) \frac{1}{a} \psi\left(\frac{x - b}{a}\right) dx \tag{7}$$

where a is the scale, b is the time variable. Given $f(x) = e^{i2\pi cx}$ with a frequency component c, the Fourier transformation will give $\delta(\xi - c)$, so we achieve:

$$W_x(\mathrm{a}, \mathrm{b}) = \int_{-\infty}^{\infty} \hat{f}(\xi)\hat{\psi}(a\xi)e^{i2\pi b\xi}d\xi \qquad (8)$$

where $\hat{\psi}(a\xi)$ is the wavelet function. There are three generalized types of wavelets: generalized morse (MORSE), analytic morlet (AMOR) and bump (BUMP) wavelets. AMOR is supposed to provide better time localization; BUMP enables better frequency representation; while MORSE is somewhere between and flexible through altering the parameters. On the contrary, despite the traditional assumptions, it is always better to select wavelet type depending on the signal characteristics.

3.1   Experiments of CWT

As mentioned above, there are three types of wavelets and the keystroke signals are analyzed with three of them separately and results are presented in Figs. 4 and 5 below.

Fig. 4. CWT of keystroke signal: MORSE AMOR BUMP from left to right

It is obvious from the spectrograms that three major frequency components are visible by MORSE and AMOR again; yet there is a slight difference of the power multipliers. BUMP wavelet doesn't give proper but more importantly precise localization of the high frequencies; which could be considered as it is not very suitable for short signals.

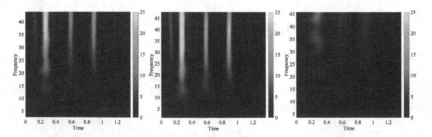

Fig. 5. CWT of signature signal: MORSE AMOR BUMP from left to right

4 Conclusion and Discussion

In this paper, we provide the preliminaries for STFT and CWT revealed by the transformation of biometric signals from time domain into frequency domain. What we focus here is to provide a benchmark of STFT vs. CWT as a guide for shedding light on the researchers who deal with the frequencies of the biometric signals. The main difference of the biometric signal among the others is shortness, therefore for very short signals, it is harder to reveal frequency and time localization together. Moreover, STFT provides valuable information for biometric signals only in case of meaningful amplitude of the signal; while for keystroke signal, CWT could localize the frequency component better. In keystroke case, the amplitude of the signal only formed by key codes so higher number of the code doesn't mean that amplitude is also greater, therefore the power results of STFT is totally meaningless for this case.

Acknowledgement. The work and the contribution were supported by the SPEV project "Smart Solutions in Ubiquitous Computing Environments 2018", University of Hradec Kralove, Faculty of Informatics and Management, Czech Republic. We are also grateful for the support of Ph.D. student Ayca Kirimtat in consultations regarding application aspects.

References

1. Roth, J., Liu, X., Ross, A., Metaxas, D.: Biometric authentication via keystroke sound. In: 2013 International Conference on Biometrics (ICB), pp. 1–8. IEEE (2013)
2. Sarier, N.D.: Multimodal biometric identity based encryption. Future Gener. Comput. Syst. (2017). https://doi.org/10.1016/j.future.2017.09.078
3. Kroeze, C.J., Malan, K.M.: User authentication based on continuous touch biometrics. South Afr. Comput. J. **28**(2), 1–23 (2016)
4. Mondal, S., Bours, P.: A study on continuous authentication using a combination of keystroke and mouse biometrics. Neurocomputing **230**, 1–22 (2017)
5. Alshanketi, F., Traore, I., Ahmed, A.A.: Improving performance and usability in mobile keystroke dynamic biometric authentication. In: Security and Privacy Workshops (SPW). IEEE (2016)
6. Alsultan, A., Warwick, K., Wei, H.: Non-conventional keystroke dynamics for user authentication. Patt. Recogn. Lett. **89**, 53–59 (2017)
7. Alpar, O.: Intelligent biometric pattern password authentication systems for touchscreens. Expert Syst. Appl. **42**(17), 6286–6294 (2015)
8. Alpar, O.: Keystroke recognition in user authentication using ANN based RGB histogram technique. Eng. Appl. Artif. Intell. **32**, 213–217 (2014)
9. Alpar, O., Krejcar, O.: Biometric swiping on Touch screens. In: Saeed, K., Homenda, W. (eds.) CISIM 2015. LNCS, vol. 9339, pp. 193–203. Springer, Cham (2015). https://doi.org/10.1007/978-3-319-24369-6_16
10. Alpar, O., Krejcar, O.: Pattern password authentication based on touching location. In: Jackowski, K., Burduk, R., Walkowiak, K., Woźniak, M., Yin, H. (eds.) IDEAL 2015. LNCS, vol. 9375, pp. 395–403. Springer, Cham (2015). https://doi.org/10.1007/978-3-319-24834-9_46

11. Goel, M., Findlater, L., Wobbrock, J.: WalkType: using accelerometer data to accommodate situational impairments in mobile touch screen text entry. In: Proceedings of the SIGCHI Conference on Human Factors in Computing Systems (2012)

12. Bhateja, A.K., Chaudhury, S., Saxena, P.K.: A robust online signature based cryptosystem. In: 2014 14th International Conference on Frontiers in Handwriting Recognition (ICFHR). IEEE (2014)

13. Alpar, O.: Frequency spectrograms for biometric keystroke authentication using neural network based classifier. Knowl.-Based Syst. **116**, 163–171 (2017)

14. Alpar, O., Krejcar, O.: Online signature verification by spectrogram analysis. Appl. Intell. **48**, 1189–1199 (2017). https://doi.org/10.1007/s10489-017-1009-x

15. Alpar, O., Krejcar, O.: Hidden frequency feature in electronic signatures. In: Fujita, H., Ali, M., Selamat, A., Sasaki, J., Kurematsu, M. (eds.) IEA/AIE 2016. LNCS (LNAI), vol. 9799, pp. 145–156. Springer, Cham (2016). https://doi.org/10.1007/978-3-319-42007-3_13

16. Alpar, O., Krejcar, O.: Biometric keystroke signal preprocessing Part I: signalization, digitization and alteration. In: Benferhat, S., Tabia, K., Ali, M. (eds.) IEA/AIE 2017. LNCS (LNAI), vol. 10350, pp. 267–276. Springer, Cham (2017). https://doi.org/10.1007/978-3-319-60042-0_31

17. Alpar, O., Krejcar, O.: Biometric keystroke signal preprocessing Part II: manipulation. In: Benferhat, S., Tabia, K., Ali, M. (eds.) IEA/AIE 2017. LNCS (LNAI), vol. 10350, pp. 289–294. Springer, Cham (2017). https://doi.org/10.1007/978-3-319-60042-0_34

An Evaluation of User Movement Data

Janelle Mason, Christopher Kelley, Bisoye Olaleye, Albert Esterline,
and Kaushik Roy$^{(\boxtimes)}$

North Carolina Agricultural and Technical State University,
Greensboro, NC 27411, USA
{jcmason, cekelley}@aggies.ncat.edu, kroy@ncat.edu

Abstract. In this paper, an empirical evaluation of different classification techniques is conducted on user movement data. The datasets used here for experiments are composed of accelerometer data collected from various devices, including smartphones and smart watches. The user movement data was processed and fed into five traditional machine learning algorithms. The classification performances were then compared with a deep learning technique, the Long Short Term Memory-Recurrent Neural Network (LSTM-RNN). LSTM-RNN achieved its highest accuracy at 89% as opposed to 97% from a traditional machine learning algorithm, specifically, K-Nearest Neighbors (k-NN), on wrist-worn accelerometer data.

Keywords: User movement · Behavioral biometrics · Deep learning
Long short term memory-recurrent neural network · Accelerometer data

1 Introduction

Biometrics has become extremely popular in the last decade and has propelled our ability to produce meaningful biometric data. Such data allows human characteristics to be used as a valid and accurate basis for identification. Physical attributes, fingerprint, face, and iris, have allowed reasonable accuracy in identifying human users [1]. Previously, this area of research focused on voice recognition, but now it tends to be based on physical movement [1].

According to the Pew Research Center, a global median of 43% of people say they own a smartphone, and nearly 73% of Americans own a smartphone [2]. With this large growth in popularity and availability of mobile devices, behavioral biometrics has proven to be a viable means for user movement acquisition.

User movement can vary from walking patterns to swipe movements on either a phone or a computer mouse, each unique to an individual, making them suitable methods for identification and verification. For gait classification, modern systems are able to extract features such as limps, forward lean, foot placement, and walking patterns.

Researchers are now able to capture much of these user movements through Global Positioning Systems (GPS), accelerometers, and gyroscopic sensory devices. We analyze the accuracies of different classification techniques on different sets of user movement data in this research effort.

© Springer International Publishing AG, part of Springer Nature 2018
M. Mouhoub et al. (Eds.): IEA/AIE 2018, LNAI 10868, pp. 729–735, 2018.
https://doi.org/10.1007/978-3-319-92058-0_70

The rest of this paper is organized as follows. Section 2 discusses related work, and Sect. 3 briefly describes the datasets used for experimentation. Section 4 provides information on the approaches that were used during experimentation, and Sect. 5 shows the results. Section 6 provides our conclusions.

2 Related Work

In [3], the author reports on a comprehensive analysis of different classification methods used on biometric walking data collected from a Nexus One Android smartphone. This dataset is obtained from the UCI Machine Learning Repository [4] and consists of data collected from 22 volunteers with the accelerometer (cellphone) mounted in their chest pocket. The data was processed and fed into traditional classifiers, including K-Nearest Neighbors (k-NN), and various deep learning techniques, including Convolutional Neural Networks (CNNs) and Recurrent Neural Networks (RNNs).

As reported in [5], data was collected to determine usability for smart environments (smart houses, offices, etc.) and surveillance applications. Wrist accelerometers located on volunteers' right wrists were used to collect acceleration data. Activities of daily living (ADL) examples include personal hygiene (e.g., brushing teeth and combing hair) and mobility (e.g., climbing stairs, descending stairs, and walking, etc. [5]. The following three objectives must be fulfilled to allow for easy automated motion recognition: (1) the computational models must adapt to individual body shape, weight, height, etc.; (2) models must be represented in efficient ways; and (3) we must be able to classify run-time acceleration data using available models.

The researchers in [5] used Gaussian Mixture Modeling and Regression to create models that can be used for classification. The authors in [5] break down movements related to the ADL [6] into lower level activities, referred to as "motion primitives". A few motion primitives, as given above in the ADL examples, allow one to determine a volunteer's autonomy in performing each of several ADLs.

In a similar experiment [7], acceleration and gyroscopic data was collected using a waist mounted Samsung Galaxy S II from 30 volunteers aged 19–48 years old. Volunteers performed less specific ADLs than the experiments reported in [5]. These activities include: walking, walking upstairs, walking downstairs, sitting, standing, and laying. Each volunteer performed the ADL twice, once with the Galaxy S on the left side of the belt, and once with the sensor place in whichever spot the volunteer preferred. There were five seconds of rest between each ADL.

Once the sensor signals were collected, they were pre-processed and broken down into samples of "fixed-width sliding windows of 2.56 s and 50% overlap (128 readings per window)" [7]. 561 features were extracted after preprocessing and the dataset was randomly partitioned into a 70% (for training) - 30% (for testing) split. This complete dataset was made available at [8]. The multi-class Support Vector Machine (SVM) was then used for classification. The experiments showed 96% overall accuracy, which indicates that smartphone/smartwatch accelerometers may be a viable resource for collecting motion data.

3 Datasets and Preparation

In this research, we used five different datasets, each from the UCI Machine Learning Repository [4]. These sets vary depending on the data format and collection devices/methods. Each dataset contains accelerometer data collected from multiple volunteers performing different physical activities such as walking, running, standing, climbing stairs, etc. The datasets used in this research are described briefly in the following subsections.

3.1 Activity Recognition Data from a Single Chest Mounted Accelerometer [3]

This dataset consists of data from accelerometers mounted on the chests of 15 different participants performing seven activities: (1) working at a computer, (2) standing up, walking and going up/down stairs, (3) standing, (4) walking, (5) going up/down stairs, (6) walking and talking with someone, and (7) talking while standing. This dataset contains no usable vectors other than X, Y, and Z acceleration values. To prepare this dataset, we gathered the raw values from all activities for each participant and combined them into a single comma-separated-values (csv) file.

3.2 Localization Data for Posture Reconstruction [9]

This dataset was originally collected in 2010 and was used to detect 'falls' in a study about elderly independent living. Volunteers in this collection were required to wear accelerometer tags on the left ankle, right ankle, belt, and chest. Each vector is localization data for the tags in the dataset. The tags can be identified by one of the eight attributes. There were 164,860 instances in this set and eight attributes: (1) sequence name, (2) tag identifier, (3) timestamp, (4) date, (5) X coordinate, (6) Y coordinate, (7) Z coordinate, and (8) activity.

3.3 Smartphone-Based Recognition of Human Activities and Postural Transitions [4, 8]

This dataset contains recordings from a group of 30 volunteers performing a set of ADL and postural transitions while wearing a waist-mounted smartphone with embedded inertial sensors [11]. In [12], a smartphone application was developed based on the Google Android Operating System for Activity Recognition (AR). A Fast Fourier Transform (FFT) was used for finding the signal frequency components. Researchers in [12] conducted an evaluation on 789 test samples with approximately equal number of samples per class. The results show some false predictions, mostly in the dynamic activities.

3.4 ADL Recognition Wrist-Worn Accelerometer Data Set [7]

This dataset is composed of recordings of 14 different ADL, including brushing teeth, climbing stairs, eating meat/soup, pouring water, and using the telephone. The data was collected from 16 volunteers performing these activities, using a tri-axial accelerometer attached to the right wrist of the volunteer. Each file in the dataset contains start time, activity label, and volunteer label, as well as gender, X, Y, and Z acceleration values.

4   User Movement Classification

After processing our datasets, we passed each into five traditional classifiers and then into a deep learning technique, LSTM-RNN, in order to obtain user movement classification accuracies. The machine learning algorithms we used were k-NN, SVM, Naïve Bayes, Classification and Regression Trees (CART) and Logistic Regression (LR) [10]. Each of the classic algorithms came from SciKit-Learn (sklearn), a Python library used for machine learning. It provides pre-made models that allow for parameter customization and yet provide consistent and accurate results.

The LSTM-RNN model used in this research was from [10, 12] and built using Google's Tensorflow [13]. LSTM-RNN, a type of recurrent neural network, was mainly introduced to avoid the long-term dependency problem. Figure 1 depicts modules of a neural network containing four layers, where these layers exist in the form of three gates (the forget, input, and output gates) and one cell unit. The LSTM-RNN has a chain like structure that links multiple repeating modules composed of four separate layers in which copies of the network are passed from one to another in an attempt to keep the contextual value of the last piece of information around. Each module passes information on to the next allowing the LSTM to remember contextual information for an extended period of time. In this research, 100 epochs were used. After the execution of the 100th epoch, the average score was calculated to determine the average LSTM-RNN test accuracy.

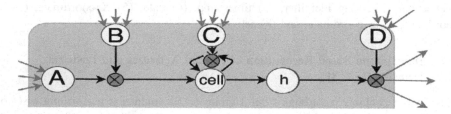

Fig. 1. Repeated cell modules of an LSTM-RNN and internal functions of a single cell.

Each classifier received the input for both training and testing data, but due to inconsistencies between each of the dataset's dimensions, additional steps were taken to get the necessary output. During data preprocessing, some of the datasets had strings as activity labels such as 'walking', 'running', 'standing' and some datasets used integers to represent the activity executed by the subject(s). For consistency, we exported the datasets with string representations of activities into Microsoft Excel and used find/replace functionality to reform the information. Finally, we used sklearn's preprocessing label encoder to make it easier to handle user data. The features were extracted after preprocessing and then the dataset was randomly partitioned into a

70% (training) - 30% (testing) split. In order to gain accurate, well-rounded results, we ran each program five times. Our accuracy scores reported below reflect the averages of the five runs for each dataset.

5   Results and Discussions

The results for each classification technique are shown in Tables 1 through 5. The dataset in Table 1 contains only X, Y, and Z acceleration values. In Table 1, k-NN achieved the best accuracy of 82%. LSTM-RNN obtained a reasonable accuracy of 58% and outperformed other classifiers, except for k-NN, on the activity recognition dataset. Table 2 shows the person activity performances for localization data. CART achieved a highest accuracy of 58% followed by SVM. LSTM-RNN performed poorly on this dataset. In Table 3, SVM outperformed other classifiers, including LSTM-RNN. Most of the classifiers performed relatively well on the human activities and transitions dataset. Table 4 demonstrates ADL Recognition accuracies on the Wrist-worn Accelerometer Data Set [7]. We found that k-NN achieved an accuracy of 97% and it outperformed other classifiers. LSTM-RNN also showed a reasonable accuracy of 89% on wrist-worn accelerometer data.

Table 1. Activity recognition from single chest-mounted accelerometer [3]

Classifier	Average accuracy
k-NN	**82.00%**
SVM	48.00%
Naïve Bayes	41.00%
CART	34.00% (c)
	34.00% (r)
LR	7.00%
LSTM	58.00%

Table 2. Localization data for person activity data set [9]

Classifier	Average accuracy
k-NN	42.00%
SVM	46.00%
Naïve Bayes	38.00%
CART	0.00% (c)
	58.00% (r)
LR	12.00%
LSTM	38%

Table 3. Smartphone-based recognition of human activities and postural transitions data set [8]

Classifier	Average accuracy
k-NN	87.00%
SVM	**92.00%**
Naïve Bayes	75.00%
CART	81.00% (c)
	81.00% (r)
LR	90.00%
LSTM	87.10%

Table 4. ADL recognition with Wrist-worn Accelerometer Data Set [7]

Classifier	Average accuracy
k-NN	**97.00%**
SVM	96.00%
Naïve Bayes	72.00%
CART	78.00%(c)
	78.00% (r)
LR	79.00%
LSTM	89.0%

6   Conclusions

In this paper, we show how effective classical machine learning techniques can be in classifying user movement data as well as the effectiveness of LSTM-RNN on the same sets of data. The purpose of this experiment was to compare the performance of both classical machine learning techniques and LSTM-RNN on these different sets of user movement data. We found that the raw user movement data in the form of X, Y, and Z acceleration values made an excellent data source only when there was a large number of records to train the LSTM-RNN. A dataset with fewer records and preprocessed features allowed each traditional classifier to perform much better. In the end, we found that the LSTM-RNN underperformed in comparison to the some of the classical machine learning techniques with its highest accuracy score reaching 89% in comparison to k-NN with a 97% accuracy score. This seems to be the case because LSTM-RNN requires a large set of training data to be effective while SVM and k-NN perform reasonably well on all the datasets. We conclude that further research on these topics will be necessary.

References

1. Mahfouz, A., Mahmoud, T., Eldin, A.: A survey on behavioral biometric authentication on smartphones. J. Inf. Secur. Appl. **37**, 28–37 (2017). https://doi.org/10.1016/j.jisa.2017.10.002

2. Poushter, J.: Smartphone ownership and internet usage continues to climb in emerging economies. In: Pew Research Center Global Attitudes & Trends (2016). http://www.pewglobal.org/2016/02/22/smartphone-ownership-and-internet-usage-continues-to-climb-in-emerging-economies/. Accessed 29 Sept 2016

3. Arias, B.A.: An analysis of user movement classification. Master's project. North Carolina Agricultural & Technical State University (2016)

4. Lichman, M.: UCI machine learning repository activity recognition from single chest-mounted accelerometer dataset. https://archive.ics.uci.edu/ml/datasets/Activity+Recognition+from+Single+Chest-Mounted+Accelerometer. Accessed 30 Nov 2017

5. Bruno B., Mastrogiovanni, F., Sgorbissa, A., Vernazza, T., Zaccaria, R.: Human motion modelling and recognition: a computational approach. In: 2012 IEEE International Conference Automation Science and Engineering (CASE), 20 August 2012

6. Katz, S., Chinn, A., Cordrey, L.J., et al.: Multidisciplinary studies of illness in aged persons: a new classification of functional status in activities of daily living. J. Chronic Dis. **9**(1), 55–62 (1959). https://doi.org/10.1016/0021-9681(59)90137-7

7. Lichman, M.: UCI machine learning repository dataset for ADL recognition with Wrist-worn Accelerometer Data Set (2013). https://archive.ics.uci.edu/ml/datasets/Dataset+for+ADL+Recognition+with+Wrist-worn+Accelerometer#. Accessed 26 Nov 2017

8. Lichman, M.: UCI machine learning repository smartphone-based recognition of human activities and postural transitions data set (2013). https://archive.ics.uci.edu/ml/datasets/Smartphone-Based+Recognition+of+Human+Activities+and+Postural+Transitions. Accessed 25 Nov 2017

9. Lichman, M.: UCI machine learning repository localization data for person activity data set (2013). https://archive.ics.uci.edu/ml/datasets/Localization+Data+for+Person+Activity. Accessed 25 Nov 2017

10. Hallström, E.: Using the LSTM API in TensorFlow (3/7) (2016). https://medium.com/@erikhallstrm/using-the-tensorflow-lstm-api-3-7-5f2b97ca6b73. Accessed 29 Nov 2017

11. Reyes-Ortiz, J.L., Ghio, A., Anguita, D., Parra, X., Cabestany, J., Català, A.: Human activity and motion disorder recognition: towards smarter interactive cognitive environments. Paper presented at the 21th European Symposium on Artificial Neural Networks, Computational Intelligence and Machine Learning, Bruges, Belgium, 24–26 April 2013 (2013)

12. Anguita, D., Ghio, A., Oneto, L., Parra, X., Reyes-Ortiz, J.L.: Human activity recognition on smartphones using a multiclass hardware-friendly support vector machine. In: Bravo, J., Hervás, R., Rodríguez, M. (eds.) IWAAL 2012. LNCS, vol. 7657, pp. 216–223. Springer, Heidelberg (2012). https://doi.org/10.1007/978-3-642-35395-6_30

13. Google (n.d.): TensorFlow. https://www.tensorflow.org. Accessed 25 Nov 2017

Classifying Political Tweets Using Naïve Bayes and Support Vector Machines

Ahmed Al Hamoud[1], Ali Alwehaibi[1], Kaushik Roy[2(✉)], and Marwan Bikdash[1]

[1] Department of Computational Science and Engineering, North Carolina Agricultural and Technical State University, Greensboro, NC 27401, USA
aalhamou@aggies.ncat.edu
[2] Department of Computer Science, North Carolina Agricultural and Technical State University, Greensboro, NC 27401, USA
kroy@ncat.edu

Abstract. Twitter, which is one of the most popular microblogging platforms and contains a huge amount of meaningful information, can be used in opinion mining and sentiment analysis. Twitter data contains text communication of more than 330 million active users monthly. This research effort applies the machine learning techniques to determine whether the contents of tweets are political or apolitical. Preprocessing involves cleaning-up the texts to obtain meaningful information and accurate opinions. Bag-of-Words (BOW), Term Frequency (TF) and Term Frequency-Inverse Document Frequency (TF-IDF) were used to extract the features from twitter data. We then used Chi-Square technique to select the salient features from a high dimensional feature set. Finally, Support Vector Machines (SVMs) and Naive Bayes (NB) were applied to classify the twitter data. The results suggest that SVMs with BOW provide the highest accuracy and F-measure.

Keywords: Sentiment analysis · Natural language processing
Opinion mining · Feature selection

1 Introduction

Opinion mining or sentiment analysis consists of finding the opinion or emotion (e.g. positive, negative, or neutral) within a given text. Sentiment analysis can be considered as a classification task as it determines the orientation of a text into either positive or negative. The internet is filled with information containing opinions about a multitude of topics; however, many of these information sources are not classified by topics. Sentiment analysis can be used to derive meaningful information from these sources. In this research, we mainly focus on extracting the sentiment from the twitter data to determine whether a tweet is political or apolitical using different machine learning techniques.

Sentiments can be gathered and analyzed from many sources, including text documents such as movie reviews or microblogs such as Twitter [1]. Since its launch in 2006, Twitter has grown more popular as a free microblogging communication

© Springer International Publishing AG, part of Springer Nature 2018
M. Mouhoub et al. (Eds.): IEA/AIE 2018, LNAI 10868, pp. 736–744, 2018.
https://doi.org/10.1007/978-3-319-92058-0_71

platform. Twitter has more than one billion unique visitors to websites which include twitter posts or links every month. It has become a vast source of information, with 330 million of active monthly users as of 2017 [2]. Twitter allows users to post and publish their thoughts and opinions in the form of short messages called tweets. These tweets may contain up to 140 characters. Anyone can read, reply to, and post tweets. These contain user opinions on a vast number of topics, including political news, reviews about products, etc.

Twitter allows researchers to access the tweets on a large scale through a free app, called Twitter API [3], which makes it readily accessible for researchers. For sentiment classification, it is more useful to sort out large amount of unnecessary information by focusing on classifying the user attitudes and opinions toward a specific topic or product. Twitter allows people to express their opinions in bite-sized tweets that are easy to analyze through machine learning. In a consumer-driven economy, knowledge of the opinions of consumers can drive choices of manufacturers and help them meet the user demands. Politicians and other groups can measure the opinions of mass people through sentiment analysis on Twitter and initiate meaningful actions.

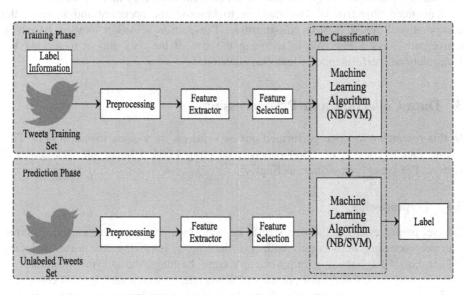

Fig. 1. Supervised classification pipeline.

2 Related Work

Sentiment classification is a field related to Natural Language Processing (NLP), computational linguistics, and text mining [4]. It can be performed at the document level, sentence, aspect and word level [5]. In sentiment classification, machine learning techniques are commonly used to determine whether a document or a sentence expresses a positive or negative sentiment. In supervised machine learning methods, the dataset is trained on labeled documents as shown in Fig. 1. Manual annotation of data is an expensive and time-consuming task; instead, automatic labeling based on a list of words or a machine learning dictionary can be used. A huge amount of labeled training data is usually required in order to train the sentiment classifier [6].

An opinion-oriented information retrieval technique proposed by Pang et al. [7] used Naive Bayes (NB), Support Vector Machines (SVMs), and Maximum Entropy (ME) to classify movie reviews by topics and sentiments. SVMs provided higher accuracy than ME or NB; however, while these methods were reasonably accurate for topic based classification, the accuracy was significantly lower for sentiment classification. A study in [8] collected data containing emoticons from Usenet newsgroups, and used tokenization, NB and SVM to perform sentiment analysis. The authors in [19] were able to obtain up to 70% accuracy on the test set. Go et al. [9] used Twitter to collect training data and then obtained sentiment polarities through the use of NB, SVM, and ME. The authors in [4] considered emoticons as noises and classified the tweets as positive or negative. Another study by Zaman and Brown [10] used latent semantic indexing/latent semantic analysis to analyze a very large dataset from the Los Angeles Times. They tested three different weighting schemes and found that TF-IDF weighting significantly outperformed both raw term frequency and log-entropy.

The main objective of this study is to improve the accuracy and increase the computational speed in text classification. The feature selection method based on Chi-square plays a key role in reducing the size of the data and in increasing the computational performance in text classification.

3   Data Collection and Preprocessing

In this research effort, we performed our experiments on a dataset used in [11]. This twitter dataset consists of 2,004 tweets, containing 1,691 political and 313 apolitical tweets. The tweets are written in English.

3.1   Preprocessing

Dataset preprocessing is the first step to be performed prior to extracting the features. The preprocessing steps begins with text cleaning by removing any noise, including HTML tags, URL links (e.g. http://example.com), hashtags, the @ symbol followed by a username (e.g. @JohnSmith), dates, or Twitter special words such as re-tweets ("rt"). After noise removal, tokenization is used to split the text by spaces and punctuation marks. Stop-words are also removed. The most frequent words such as ("the", "an", "and" "of", etc.) are not useful for our context and often do not carry meaningful information, so they are removed. Uppercase letters are transformed to lowercase letters. This allows the program to consider identical words such as "Great" and "great" as two counts of the same word, not one count for each of two different words. Tokenization also removes any repeated sequences of letters in the words (such as "cooool", "helloooo", etc.) and reverts them back to their original English form. Finally, word stemming is performed by removing the suffixes and/or prefixes; for example, "Retrieval" becomes "retrieve". We used Porter Stemmer algorithms for word stemming [12].

4   Feature Extraction Methods Used

This research effort uses the Bag-of-Words (BOW), Term Frequency (TF) and Term Frequency-Inverse Document Frequency (TF-IDF) to extract the features from twitter data.

4.1   Bag of Words Model

The Bag-of-Words (BOW) model [9] uses the relative frequency of occurrences of a set of keywords as a quantitative measure to convert each text document to a vector. Relative frequencies are used instead of absolute word counts in order to reduce the effect of length difference among documents. In BOW, sentence structure and grammar will be ignored.

4.2   TF-IDF

TF-IDF is a combination of Term Frequency (TF) and Inverse Document Frequency (IDF), and it is often used in information retrieval and text mining [13]. It is computed by combining the product of a function of term frequency $(f_{t,d})$ and a function of the inverse of document frequency $(1 \backslash W_t)$ as follows.

- TF measures how frequently a term t occurs in a document d by dividing it by the maximum number of occurrences of any term t in the same document d [14].

$$TF_{t,d} = \frac{F_{t,d}}{\max\ (F_{t,d})} \tag{2}$$

- IDF measures how important a term t is by computing the logarithm of the number of documents in the corpus divided by the number of documents in which a given term appears [15]. If a word appears many times, the word will be considered of little importance.

$$IDF_{t,d} = \log\left(\frac{N}{df_t}\right) \tag{3}$$

The combination of the Eqs. 3 and 4 is formulated as:

$$TF - IDF_{t,d} = TF_{(t,d)} * IDF_{t,d} \tag{4}$$

Where, N is the total number of tweets in the corpus $N = |D|$. $df(t)$ is the number of tweets in the corpus that contain the term t. $TF(d, t)$ is the term frequency in which the term t appears in a tweet d.

5 Feature Selection Using Chi-Square

Feature selection, also known as variable selection, is a technique widely used in text classification to find the most representative features [16]. For this study, we used the Chi-Square test model [17] to select the most important features from the feature vectors. In statistics, Chi-square test is used to determine whether there is a significant relationship between two events, where the events **A** and **B** are independent if

$$P(AB) = P(A)P(B) \tag{5}$$

Chi-square, x^2, can be computed as follows [12]:

$$x^2(D, t, C) = \sum_{t \in \{0,1\}} \sum_{t \in \{0,1\}} \frac{(N_t, C - E_t, C)}{E_t, C} \tag{6}$$

where N is the observed frequency, E is the expected frequency for each call, and t is a random variable that takes $t = 1$ if the document contains term t and $e_t = 0$ if the document does not contain t, and C is a random variable that takes $c = 1$ if document is in class c and $c = 0$ if the document is not in class c.

6 Classifiers Used for Sentiment Analysis

Our aim in this work is to classify the tweets as political or apolitical using SVM and NB. The process of data classification consists of two phases; the training phase and the prediction phase as demonstrated in Fig. 1.

6.1 Naive Bayes (NB) Classifier

The Naive Bayesian classifier [13] is a probabilistic classification method in which the probability is calculated for each document. It is based on Bayes' theorem and it works well with classification of large quantities of short texts such as tweets from Twitter. There are two models for Naive Bayes: multivariate Bernoulli and the multinomial model. In our experiment, we used the multinomial model [18].

6.2 Support Vector Machines (SVMs)

SVMs are a well-known classification method based on the Structural Risk Minimization principle (SRM) from statistical learning theory [19]. The objective of SRM is to find the maximum margin hyperplane between two classes of data [20]. SVM can classify linear and nonlinear data with a linear or a polynomial kernel or a radial basis kernel [21]. The separating hyperplane of linear data used with SVM can be written as

$$\mathbf{W} * X + b = 0 \tag{1}$$

Where W is weight vector to the hyperplane, $W = \{w_1, w_2, \ldots, w_n\}$; n is the number of attributes, b is a scalar known as bias [22] and X is the point of the object, and $|b|/\|W\|$ is the distance between origin and the hyperplane H [23]. The distance between hyperplanes (margin) H_1 and H_2 is $2/\|W\|$ as illustrated in Fig. 2.

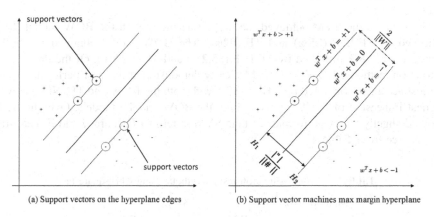

(a) Support vectors on the hyperplane edges   (b) Support vector machines max margin hyperplane

Fig. 2. SVM maximum margin hyperplane [24].

7   Experiment Results

7.1   Evaluation

We evaluated our classifiers by computing the standard performance metrics, including Accuracy, Precision and F-measure [18], and by using 10-fold cross validation. For the experiment, the twitter dataset was divided into two parts: 25% for testing and 75% for training. We used True Positive (TP), True Negative (TN), False Positive (FP) and False Negative (FN) to calculate accuracy, precision and F-measure. A tweet is considered as TP if it is correctly identified as political. A tweet is FN, if, for example, a political tweet is incorrectly identified as apolitical. A tweet is considered to be FP, if a non-political tweet is considered as political. A tweet is TN if an apolitical tweet is correctly labeled as apolitical. The accuracy, precision and F-measures can be calculated as follows:

$$Accuracy = \frac{tp + tn}{tp + tn + fp + fn} \tag{7}$$

$$Precision = \frac{tp}{tp + fp} \tag{8}$$

$$F_1 = 2 * \frac{Precision * Recall}{Precision + Recall} \tag{9}$$

The F1 score (F-measure) is a combination of precision and recall.

7.2 Results and Discussion

In this experiment, an NB classifier and linear SVM classifier were used to classify the test dataset. First, we apply the NB and SVMs on the dataset without using chi-square test and placed the results in Table 1. Next, we applied chi-square test to the feature vectors extracted from the twitter data and obtained the results with SVM and NB (See Table 2).

In Table 1, the SVM achieved the highest accuracy with the BOW model (88%), followed by TF-IDF (85%) and TF (82%). The BOW model obtained the highest F-measure of 88% followed by TF-IDF (85.2%) and TF (81.5%). Of the three feature extraction methods, BOW with SVM clearly demonstrated the best performance. The highest accuracies obtained by NB are 85% with both the BOW and TF. NB achieved a highest F-measure of 84.5% by using both the BOW and TF models. Overall, the NB showed slightly lower performances than SVM in terms of accuracy and F-measure as we can see from Table 1.

Table 1. The classification results without using Chi-Square test.

Method	NB		SVM	
	Accuracy	F-Measure	Accuracy	F-Measure
BOW	85%	84.5%	88%	88%
TF	85%	84.5%	82%	81.5%
TF-IDF	81%	80%	85%	85.2%

Table 2. The classification results using Chi-Square test.

Method	NB		SVM	
	Accuracy	F-Measure	Accuracy	F-Measure
BOW	82%	79.4%	84%	79%
TF	86%	86.5%	86%	86.4%
TF-IDF	83%	82.6%	86%	85%

Table 2 reports the performances after using Chi-Square feature selection method. The accuracy of the TF-IDF model with NB increased to 83%, while its F-measure increased to 82.6%. The accuracy and F-measure of TF using NB increased to 86% and 86.5%, respectively. However, the accuracy and F-measure of BOW using NB decreased to 82% and 79.4%, respectively. Chi-square with SVM showed an increase in performance of the TF and TF-IDF models. TF increased to 86% and its F-measure increased by nearly 5% to 86.4%, while TF-IDF increased to 86% with a small loss of 0.2% in performance for F-measure. BOW with Chi-square showed a decrease in performance from 88% to 84%.

The inclusion of Chi-square, as a feature selector, significantly increased the performance of the SVM for both the TF and TF-IDF models in terms of accuracy and F-measures. However, the BOW performed best without Chi-Square, and it obtained the highest performances using SVM with an accuracy of 88% and an F-measure of 88%. Overall, the results with feature selection based on Chi-square show a significant improvement in the classification; this may be due to the reduction of the domain text and corpus size associated with the use of Chi-square.

8 Conclusions and Future Work

This research effort applies the SVM and NB on twitter data to find if the contents of tweets are political or apolitical. We applied BOW, TF and TF-IDF to extract the features from twitter data. We then applied Chi-Square technique to select the prominent features. The results suggest that SVMs with BOW achieve the highest accuracy and F-measure of 88%. In the future, research may be performed to further develop this technique; goals include increasing the accuracy of the technique has been used in this paper and creating a hybrid approach combining supervised learning with a lexicon-based approach. Future work will also use the techniques developed in the present study to create a corpus of tweets upon which to perform sentiment analysis on selected political topics, individuals, or policies. This entails selecting topics of interest, developing a set of tweets which belong to each category, and performing sentiment analysis on each subcategory.

Acknowledgements. This research is based upon work supported by the Science & Technology Center: Bio/Computational Evolution in Action Consortium (BEACON).

References

1. Twitter. https://www.twitter.com/
2. Twitter by the Numbers: Stats, Demographics and Fun Facts (2018). https://www.omnicoreagency.com/twitter-statistics/
3. Developer Twitter. https://developer.twitter.com/en/docs
4. Karamibekr, M., Ghorbani, A.A.: Verb oriented sentiment classification. In: Proceedings of the 2012 IEEE/WIC/ACM International Joint Conferences on Web Intelligence and Intelligent Agent Technology, vol. 01, pp. 327–331 (2012)
5. Medhat, W., Hassan, A., Korashy, H.: Sentiment analysis algorithms and applications: a survey. Ain Shams Eng. J. **5**, 1093–1113 (2014)
6. Abdel Hady, M.F., Karali, A., Kamal, E., Ibrahim, R.: Unsupervised active learning of CRF model for cross-lingual named entity recognition. In: El Gayar, N., Schwenker, F., Suen, C. (eds.) ANNPR 2014. LNCS (LNAI), vol. 8774, pp. 23–34. Springer, Cham (2014). https://doi.org/10.1007/978-3-319-11656-3_3
7. Pang, B., Lee, L., Vaithyanathan, S.: Thumbs up?: sentiment classification using machine learning techniques. In: Proceedings of the ACL-02 Conference on Empirical Methods in Natural Language Processing, vol. 10, pp. 79–86 (2002)
8. Read, J.: Using emoticons to reduce dependency in machine learning techniques for sentiment classification. In: Proceedings of the ACL Student Research Workshop, pp. 43–48 (2005)
9. Go, A., Bhayani, R., Huang, L.: Twitter sentiment classification using distant supervision. CS224N Project Report, Stanford **1**(12) (2009)

10. Zaman, A.N.K., Brown, C.G.: Latent semantic indexing and large dataset: study of term-weighting schemes. In: 2010 5th International Conference on Digital Information Management, ICDIM 2010, pp. 1–4 (2010)

11. Marchetti-Bowick, M., Chambers, N.: Learning for microblogs with distant supervision: political forecasting with Twitter. In: Proceedings of the 13th Conference of the European Chapter of the Association for Computational Linguistics, pp. 603–612 (2012)

12. Porter, M.F.: An algorithm for suffix stripping. Program **14**, 130–137 (1980)

13. Leskovec, J., Rajaraman, A., Ullman, J.D.: Mining of Massive Datasets. Cambridge University Press (2014)

14. Luhn, H.P.: A statistical approach to mechanized encoding and searching of literary information. IBM J. Res. Dev. **1**, 309–317 (1957)

15. Sparck Jones, K.: A statistical interpretation of term specificity and its application in retrieval. J. Doc. **28**, 11–21 (1972)

16. Rutkowski, L., Tadeusiewicz, R., Zadeh, Lotfi A., Zurada, Jacek M. (eds.): ICAISC 2008. LNCS (LNAI), vol. 5097. Springer, Heidelberg (2008). https://doi.org/10.1007/978-3-540-69731-2

17. Tang, J., Alelyani, S., Liu, H.: Feature selection for classification: a review. In: Data Classification: Algorithms and Applications, p. 37 (2014)

18. Manning, C.D., Schütze, H.: Foundations of statistical natural language processing. MIT Press, Cambridge (1999)

19. Vapnik, V.N.: An overview of statistical learning theory. IEEE Trans. Neural Netw. **10**, 988–999 (1999)

20. Gunn, S.R., et al.: Support vector machines for classification and regression. ISIS Technical Report, vol. 14, pp. 85–86 (1998)

21. Han, J., Pei, J., Kamber, M.: Data Mining: Concepts and Techniques. Elsevier (2011)

22. Ben-Hur, A., Weston, J.: A user's guide to support vector machines. Data Min. Tech. Life Sci. **609**, 223–239 (2010)

23. Fletcher, T.: Support vector machines explained: introductory course. Internal report 1–19 (2009)

24. Cortes, C., Vapnik, V.: Support-vector networks. Mach. Learn. **20**, 273–297 (1995)

Anti-spoofing Approach Using Deep Convolutional Neural Network

Prosenjit Chatterjee and Kaushik Roy[(⊠)]

Department of Computer Science,
North Carolina A&T State University, Greensboro, USA
pchatterjee@aggies.ncat.edu, kroy@ncat.com

Abstract. Our research aims at classifying biometric image samples from well-known spoofing databases that encompass images with different resolution and sizes using a deep Convolutional Neural Network (CNN). In this effort, we optimally use the CNN for biometric image classification to prevent spoofing attack in an extensive range. This work detects the presentation attacks on facial and iris images using our deep CNN, inspired by VGGNet and Alex-Net. We applied the deep neural net techniques on three different biometric image datasets, namely ATVS, CASIA two class, and CASIA cropped. The datasets, used in this research, contain images that are captured both in controlled and uncontrolled environment along with different resolutions and sizes. We obtained the best test accuracy of 97% on ATVS Iris datasets. For CASIA two class and CASIA cropped datasets, we achieved the test accuracies of 96% and 95%, respectively.

Keywords: Biometric · Presentation attack detection
Deep convolutional neural network

1 Introduction

Biometric object classification is inevitable in the prevention of spoofing attacks. Government organizations incorporate biometric scans as a measure of unique identifications of million people. Therefore, it is important that integrity of such a large-scale biometric deployment must also be protected. The biometric recognition technologies are increasingly becoming susceptible to sophisticated sensor level spoofing attacks [1–3]. To mitigate that, we need to classify the biometric objects using a robust method. The latest trend on image recognition of large-scale image repositories became very successful with the introduction of Convolutional Neural Networks (CNNs) [2]. The use of high end GPU-based system makes the application faster than ever before, for image processing and classification.

In this paper, we have explored different CNN architectures and their performances on different spoofing datasets. The main focus of this paper is to use a deep neural network that can mitigate spoofing attacks. This research implements a deep CNN denoted as modified VGGNet hereafter, inspired by VGGNet [4] and Alex-Net [5].

© Springer International Publishing AG, part of Springer Nature 2018
M. Mouhoub et al. (Eds.): IEA/AIE 2018, LNAI 10868, pp. 745–750, 2018.
https://doi.org/10.1007/978-3-319-92058-0_72

The rest of this paper is organized as follows. Section 2 discusses the related work. Section 3 describes the CNN architecture used in this paper. Section 4 discusses the datasets used. Section 5 shows the experimental results, and Sect. 6 provides our conclusions.

2   Related Work

Recently, deep learning techniques have been successfully used for anti-spoofing approaches. Yang et al. [2] reported diverse techniques of spoofing attacks, including texture -based, motion -based, 3D-shape -based, and multi-spectral reflectance -based anti-spoofing. Authors in [2] proposed a face localization, and spatial and temporal augmentation methods to mitigate spoofing attack. Menotti et al. [3] researched on deep representation for detecting spoofing attack in different biometric substances. Krizhevsky et al. [5] applied 2D convolution to facilitate the training of interestingly large CNNs for image classification. Hilton et al. [6] proposed a dimensionality reduction method that used a layer-by-layer pre-training approach in a neural network implemented through deep learning. A key benefit of deep learning is the analysis and learning of massive amount of unsupervised data, making it a valuable tool for mitigating spoofing attack, where raw data is largely unlabeled and uncategorized [7].

3   CNN Architecture Used to Mitigate Spoofing Attacks

We investigated different CNN architectures, including Spoof Net [3], VGGNet [4], Alex Net, and ImageNet [5], and their possible deployment towards anti-spoofing. They show reasonable performances in classifying the real and fake images with high accuracy scores. However, their success rates are limited to ideal image datasets, and relatively high training time. Most of them (i.e. SpoofNet [3], VGGNet [4], AlexNet, and ImageNet [5]) need high-end GPU systems to run, for their complex framework and their convolution layers distributions. VGGNet, with its deep neural network architecture, has potential for Presentation Attack Detection (PAD). However, it has slow processing mechanism and high-end GPU/CPU memory requirements.

This research develops a deep CNN in an attempt to prevent the spoofing attacks. After extensive investigation and analysis, we designed a 'modified VGGNet' based on the VGGNet [4] and AlexNet [5] implementations. We prepared our input image datasets that considered the images captured both in the controlled and uncontrolled environment to mimic the real-world scenario.

Our 'modified VGGNet', has a total of 14 discrete Convolution 2D layers, 5 Max Pooling 2D Layers, 1 Flatten layer, and 2 Dense 2D layers. In this research, we use sigmoid function instead of soft-max approach for the faster 2D binary classification and validation. The CNN architecture used in this paper is shown in Fig. 1.

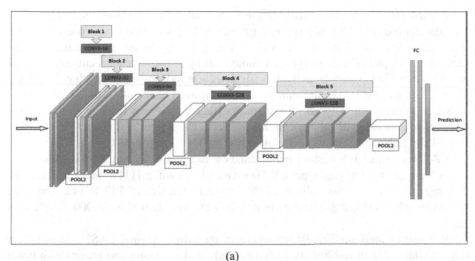

(a)

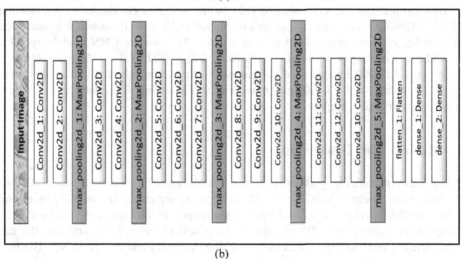

(b)

Fig. 1. (a) Architecture of CNN, (b) Distribution of layers.

4 Datasets Used

Our research was conducted on three biometric image datasets: ATVS [8, 9], CASIA [10], and CASIA-cropped. ATVS [8, 9] is an iris image dataset that consists of periocular images. The periocular region includes iris, eyebrows, eyelids, and eyelashes. The dataset contains 50 subjects and each subject had both eyes photographed four times each of two different sessions. Each image was then gone through grayscale printing and successive scanning for fake image generation. Each subject contains 32 image samples, 800 per class (real and fake), and a total of 1600 with a uniform resolution of 640 × 480.

CASIA [10] dataset contains both the high resolution still images and video clips. This dataset contains 50 subjects and four classes. Every class contains one landscape-style video and one portrait-style video. The four classes are categorized as "real subjects", "cut photo" attacks (printed photo of subject with eyeholes cut out, real user positioned behind photo to fool blinking detection systems), "wrap photo" (printed photo of subject held up to the camera, photo is moved back and forth to fool liveness detection systems), and video replay attacks (tablet or screen held up to the camera while playing a video of subject). In this research, we placed 'real images' in one class and all the 'fake images' in other class.

CASIA-cropped is a custom-built image dataset that was created from the original CASIA images by applying OpenCV Haar cascade classifier [11] in order to detect the face regions. We then normalized all the image to the size of 140 × 140. There are approximately 94,000 color images in this dataset, with 22,000 to 26,000 samples per class.

We also created another dataset where images from original CASIA dataset were resized with different resolutions, including high quality images and images with lower resolutions using image augmentation [12]. In this work, we considered high resolution (720 × 1280) portrait images, standard-resolution (640 × 480) landscape images, and standard-resolution (480 × 640) portrait images. To train the CNN models, we also considered some low-resolution images (e.g., 240 × 320, 225 × 225, etc.). Overall, there were 127,000 images used for our work. Approximately 101,600 images were used for training and 25,400 images were used for testing. This dataset was mainly used for verification purpose.

5 Results and Discussions

To achieve reasonable performance, we ran different implementations of CNNs, including the modified VGGNet, on all the datasets separately for multiple times and observed their performances and minute variations. In this research, we used 80% samples for training and 20% for testing purposes. In Table 1, we compare the test accuracies of our 'modified VGGNet' with the Alex-Net and Inception V3. The best results we achieved using 'modified VGGNet' on different segment of image datasets are shown in the Table 1. The test accuracy reported for the 'modified VGGNet' was significantly higher as compared to the other two popular CNNs i.e. AlexNet and Inception V3.

Table 1. Classification accuracies of different implementations of CNNs.

CNNs architecture	Datasets		
	ATVS Iris	CASIA two class	CASIA cropped
Modified VGG Net	97%	96%	95%
Alex Net	95%	91%	37%
Inception-v3	94%	95%	92.10%

The Receiver Operating Characteristics (ROC) curve shown in Fig. 2, explains the True Positive Rate (TPR) versus the False Positive Rate (FPR) for our modified VGGNet on different image datasets. In the best-case scenario, TPR should be as close as possible to 1.0, meaning that during training and validation none of the images were rejected by mistake. The FPR should be as close to 0.0 as possible, meaning that all presentation attacks were rejected and none were mistakenly accepted as real images. In all cases, the area under the curve remains in the range of 0.96 to 1.00, which is close to the ideal value of 1.0. However, the TPR is generally higher for the ideal grayscale ATVS images as compared to less controlled CASIA color image datasets and to CASIA cropped datasets.

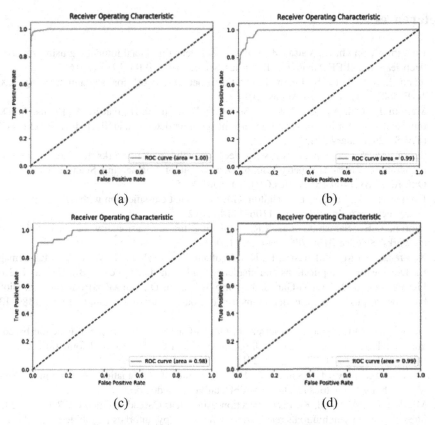

Fig. 2. ROC Curve on: (a) ATVS Iris (real vs. fake) (TPR: 100%), (b) CASIA (real vs. fake) (TPR: 99%), (c) CASIA cropped (real vs. cropped) (TPR: 98%), (d) CASIA custom resized images (real vs. fake) (TPR: 99%).

6   Conclusions and Future Work

In this paper, we performed an extensive analysis of different CNN architectures, including our modified VGGNet, on different spoofing datasets. Our approach achieved encouraging performances in detecting the spoofing attacks in both the ideal and non-ideal situations. For ATVS, CASIA and CASIA cropped datasets, we achieved the highest accuracies of 97%, 96% and 95%, respectively. Our future work will mainly focus on the mitigation of spoofing attack on a mobile platform.

Acknowledgements. This research is based upon work supported by the Science & Technology Center: Bio/Computational Evolution in Action Consortium (BEACON) and the Army Research Office (Contract No. W911NF-15-1-0524).

References

1. Bharati, A., Singh, R., Vatsa, M., Bowyer, K.: Detecting facial retouching using supervised deep learning. IEEE Trans. Inf. Forensics Secur. **11**(9), 1903–1913 (2016)
2. Yang, J., Lei, Z., Li, S.: Learn convolutional neural network for face anti-spoofing. arXiv: 1408.5601v2 [cs.CV], 26 August 2014
3. Menotti, D., Chiachia, G., Pinto, A., Schwartz, W., Pedrini, H., Falcão, A., Rocha, A.: Deep representations for iris, face, and fingerprint spoofing detection. arXiv:1410.1980v3 [cs.CV], (T.IFS), 29 January 2015
4. Simonyan, K., Zisserman, A.: Very deep convolutional networks for large-scale image recognition. Visual Geometry Group, Department of Engineering Science, University of Oxford, arXiv:1409.1556v6 [cs.CV], 10 April 2015
5. Krizhevsky, A., Sutskever, I., Hinton, G.E.: Imagenet classification with deep convolutional neural networks. In: NIPS, pp. 1106–1114 (2012)
6. Hinton, G.E., Salakhutdinov, R.R.: Reducing the dimensionality of data with neural networks. Science **313**(5786), 504–507 (2006)
7. Najafabadi, M.M., Villanustre, F., Khoshgoftaar, T.K., Seliya, N., Wald, R., Muharemagic, E.: Deep learning applications and challenges in big data analytics. J. Big Data **2**, 1 (2015)
8. Fierrez-Aguilar, J., Ortega-Garcia, J., Torre-Toledano, D., Gonzalez-Rodriguez, J.: BioSec baseline corpus: a multimodal biometric database. Pattern Recognit. **40**(4), 1389–1392 (2007)
9. Galbally, J., Ortiz-Lopez, J., Fierrez, J., Ortega-Garcia, J.: Iris liveness detection based on quality related features. In: Proceedings International Conference on Biometrics, ICB, New Delhi, India, pp. 271–276, March 2012
10. Chinese Academy of Sciences (CASIA), Institute of Automation: Antispoofing Dataset (2010). http://biometrics.idealtest.org/dbDetailForUser.do?id=3
11. Mordvintsev, A., Abid, K.: Face Detection using Haar Cascades. Open CV Tutorial (2013). https://opencv-pythontutroals.readthedocs.io/en/latest/py_tutorials/py_objdetect/py_face_detec-tion/py_face_detection.html
12. Dellana, R., Roy, K.: Data augmentation in CNN-based periocular authentication. In: 2016 ICICM

Sentiment Classification of Short Texts

Movie Review Case Study

Jaspinder Kaur[✉], Rozita Dara[✉], and Pascal Matsakis[✉]

University of Guelph, Guelph, Canada
{jaspinde, drozita, pmatsaki}@uoguelph.ca

Abstract. Over the few years, Sentiment analysis has been the heart of social media research due to the huge volume of opinionated data available on the web and its pervasive real life and commercial applications. Sentiment classification of shorter texts such as movie reviews is challenging due to lack of contextual information which often leads to interesting and unexpected results. Historically, this problem has been addressed using machine learning algorithms that usually learn from rule-based approaches or manually defined sparse features. In the recent years, Deep Neural Networks have gained a lot of attention in sentiment analysis due to their ability to effectively capture subtle semantic information from the input. These methods are capable of building dense continuous feature vectors, which is difficult to model in conventional models such as bag-of-words. In this paper, we conduct experiments and compare several machine learning algorithms Support Vector Machine, Naïve Bayes, Random Forest, and a Deep Learning Algorithm. We selected Convolution Neural Network (CNN) trained on top of various pre-trained word vectors for movie review classification. We validate above models on IMDB movie review data-set, experimental results demonstrate that the task of sentiment analysis can benefit more from the CNN rather than the machine learning techniques.

Keywords: Sentiment analysis · Machine learning
Convolution Neural Network

1 Introduction

Movie reviews are the powerful way to measure the performance of a movie. They provide an overall reaction of public to the movie: whether they liked it or no. Movie reviews exist in a variety of different forms on the internet: websites dedicated to only movie reviews (such as IMDB, yahoo Movies), sites that collect all reviews from the top publications and then present the overall average result (like Rotten Tomatoes, Meta Critic), and in personal blogs and sites where personal user or critic often express their opinion on the movie. Movie makers and general public can use these reviews to analyze the strong and weak points in the movie, and can examine whether the movie meets the expectations of the public. But, shifting through large number of reviews is an intimidating task.

Sentiment analysis [19] is the field of Natural Language Processing which uses computational approach to discern the opinionated content and find the overall polarity

© Springer International Publishing AG, part of Springer Nature 2018
M. Mouhoub et al. (Eds.): IEA/AIE 2018, LNAI 10868, pp. 751–761, 2018.
https://doi.org/10.1007/978-3-319-92058-0_73

(Positive or negative) expressed in it. For example: Sentiment analysis of movie review classifies it as a positive or negative review. One of the major challenge with sentiment analysis of short texts (like movie reviews) is to identify whether a particular sentence or word is actually an opinion. Also, sometimes the sentiment or opinion is expressed in a very subtle way and it's hard to identify the polarity of sentiment. For example: "I love the plot but overall it's just boring and uneventful.". They are also very brief in length, and have many slang words, misspellings, short forms and html tags which bring in new challenges to the task of sentiment analysis.

Mostly machine learning approaches [1, 29] have been used in the past for the sentiment analysis [9]. These algorithms typically take input as fixed-length vectors. One of most common and effective fixed length vector representation is "bag-of-words" (BOW) model [13] due to its simplicity and overall accuracy. Most of the past work has been dedicated to engineering effective features [30] in order to achieve higher performance. Another problem with machine learning approaches is that they ignore the semantic information present in the text and consider only the syntactic representation of words. It is therefore advisable to make your classifier less dependent on the extensive task of feature engineering [30, 20]. In recent years, Deep learning models [17, 21, 25] have gained a lot of attention due to their ability to effectively capture the subtle semantic information present in the input text, such as the mutual association between words and negation scopes. It also eliminates the need to manually-defined feature vectors as the model itself learn features during training. These methods are capable of building dense continuous feature vectors, which is difficult to model in conventional models such as bag-of-words. Among Deep learning models, CNN's have shown impressive results on the task of sentence classification across multiple datasets [14, 23, 24]. In this paper, we are using CNN inspired from the work by Kim [22]; trained on top of pre-trained word vectors. The purpose of this paper is twofold (I) to conduct experiments in order the compare several machine learning algorithms; Support Vector Machine(SVM), Naïve Bayes, Random Forest and Deep learning model (CNN) for movie review sentiment classification, and (II) comparing several feature selection measures to enhance the overall accuracy of the supervised machine learning approaches.

This paper is organized as follows. In Sect. 2, we discuss some background information and related work in the field of sentiment analysis. In Sect. 3, we describe our proposed model in detail. In Sect. 4, we describe our experimental setup and Sect. 5, present our results and some discussion. Finally, in Sect. 6, we conclude our work.

2   Related Work

Sentiment classification [4] of short texts has been the area of focus of research for over a decade now. Various machine learning approaches have been used to classify text. Most of these techniques were a slight variation of "Bag of Words" model [13]. Other techniques involve expectation maximization or clustering. For example - In [2, 3] Turney predict the sentiment of the review by the average semantic orientation of phrases in the review. They used "Point Wise mutual information (PMI)" and "Latent

Semantic Analysis (LSA)" to select features and find the semantic orientation of the review. Pang [2] used naïve Bayes, Support Vector Machine and maximum entropy to classify sentiments in text and achieved accuracy close to 84%. A number of other novel techniques [5–7, 12] have been proposed to classify sentiment. Recently, Deep Learning models [17, 25, 22] have gained a lot of attention in sentiment analysis of short texts due to their ability to capture the semantic information in the text. Also, these models can automatically learn feature from the raw text, thus removing the need for the extensive task of feature engineering [30]. Kalchbrenner [28] proposed CNN model with multiple Convolution layers and takes input as low-dimensional dense word vectors. Similar to Kalchbrenner works, Kim [22] introduced a single layer CNN, trained on the top of the pre-trained word vectors and performed comparably.

3 Proposed Approach

3.1 Deep Learning Model

CNN has been used to perform sentiment classification of movie reviews. CNN is a feed-forward neural network made up of several layers. Each neuron receives an input from several neurons in the previous layer and has learnable weights and biases. The single-layer architecture of our model has been inspired from [17, 22]. Our model has only one convolution layer, followed by max- pooling layer and fully connected softmax layer discussed below. The model has been illustrated in Fig. 1.

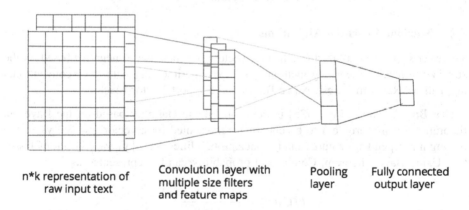

| n*k representation of raw input text | Convolution layer with multiple size filters and feature maps | Pooling layer | Fully connected output layer |

Fig. 1. Architecture of Convolution Neural Network [22]

Convolution Layer. This layer is the building block of CNN and handles all the extensive computations. It performs a convolution operation on the input layer and then transfers the results to the next layers.

Non- Linear Activation Function Layer. This is an activation layer that came right after Convolution Layer. The job of this layer is to introduce non-linearity to System which has been doing all the linear operations (multiplication and summation) in the previous layer. ReLU is preferred over the non-linear functions as the hyperbolic tangent or sigmoid as your model can train faster and it also prevent gradient vanishing problem.

Pooling Layer. The pooling layer is also referred as downsampling layer which drastically reduces the spatial dimension of the input volume, thus helps in minimizing the overall computational cost and also the problem of overfitting. The basic three options for pooling layer are max pooling, average pooling, and Euclidean norm pooling.

Dropout Layer. The dropout layer "drops out" some random activations and set them to zero. This will make sure that network is not that fitted to training data and thus reducing the problem of overfitting.

Fully Connected Layer. Fully connected layer connects each neuron in a layer to every neuron in another layer.

The input to our model is a sentence matrix, rows of which are distributed word vector representation of each word in the input text. These word vectors are the outputs from trained word2vec [25] model. These vectors were trained using conventional bag of words model and have d dimensions. Words that did not belong to pre- trained training set are initialized randomly. The first step is to apply convolution on the sentence matrix (input text) using filters, and a feature map is produced. The height of the filters can be changed and width of the filters is set to d. Weight matrix and bias for each filter are learned. Any number of filters can be applied during the convolution process to learn features from the same region.

3.2   Machine Learning Algorithms

The next step is to classify these feature vectors into positive or negative based on the supervised machine learning methods. We are experimenting with three conventional algorithms: Random Forest, Naïve Bayes and Support Vector Machine.

Naïve Bayes. Naïve Bayes [35] is the probabilistic classifier based on the Bayesian theorem. Given a problem to be classified represented by a vector $g = (y_1, y_2,..... y_n)$ having n independent features and instance probabilities $p(C_m \mid y_1, y_2,..... y_n)$ for Classes C_m. Using Bayes theorem, Conditional probability can be represented as:

$$P(Cm|y) = \frac{p(Cm)p(y|Cm)}{p(y)}$$

Naive Bayes based text classification managed to perform well despite the conditional independence condition which doesn't really hold in real life situations. Also, it has been shown that it can effectively solve certain problems with highly dependent features. We are using multinomial naïve Bayes classifier which is suitable for classification on discrete features (say word counts).

Random Forest. Random forest [18] is an ensemble machine learning approach for classification which makes use of multiple decision trees during training and then outputs the class which is the majority of classes output by the individual decision trees. Random Forest efficiently handles outlier or noise in data and enhance overall performance of classifier. It adds randomness [18] to the data while classification process, such that each tree is highly uncorrelated with other random trees. This results in highly promising classification accuracy, compared to other state-of-art techniques. Researchers have used this classifier in wide range of applications includes medical research [8], text classification [31] and sentiment analysis [33].

Support Vector Machine. Support Vector Machine [34] is a statistical model for outlier detection, text classification or regression. The SVM is a non-probabilistic linear classifier. Suppose the goal is to classify some given data points in one of the two classes. SVM finds hyperplane or set of hyperplanes to separate data points over a high dimensional space such that the best hyperplane represents the large margin between the two classes. We used [15, 16] SVM^{light} package for training as well as testing with all the variables set to default for review classification.

4   Experimental Settings

The dataset used has been taken from IMDB movie reviews that are made available by Andrew Mass (Cornell Computer Science [11]). The dataset has 50K movie reviews split into 25 K for training and 25K for testing. The 25K labeled training reviews doesn't include any of same reviews as testing set. Also, the movie reviews are highly polar (either positive (rating >= 7) or negative (rating <= 4)) and do not include any of the neutral reviews. Also, no more than 30 reviews are allowed for any given movie.

4.1   CNN Experimental Setup

In our experiments, for our baseline model we are using "adam" to train our model on pre-trained words vectors of 300 dimensions [32, 26], Rectified Linear unit (ReLU) activation function [27], 1- max pooling [28], initial learning rate of 0.001, drop-out of 0.4, filter size (3, 4, 5) and feature map of size 100. The model has been built on python version. The model has been trained on 50 epochs without early stopping. The choice of hyperparameters and model parameters often affects the overall performance of CNN. In our experiments, we keep all our baseline model settings constant while changing only the component of our interest. Also, we are using 10-fold Cross Validation to validate the stability of our model.

Effect of Filter Size. Tuning of filter size can have a large impact on the performance of the model. Combining multiple filter around the single best filter usually outperformed single best filter region. From the Table 1, it's clear that best multiple filter size would be (3, 4, 5) while keeping fixed feature space of 100.

Table 1. Effect of single filter region size and multiple filter region size on average training and testing accuracy calculated over 10- fold CV

Filter region size	Training accuracy	Testing accuracy
1	95.8	84.3
2	96.3	85.4
3	96.0	86.9
1, 2	96.9	87.1
1, 2, 3	97.1	87.8
2, 3, 4	97.2	87.9
3, 4, 5	97.5	88.9

Effect of Number of Feature Maps. From the Table 2, it's clear that increasing the number of feature maps often leads to overfitting and thus reduce the overall performance. Another important point is that it takes longer training time when the number of feature has been increased. The best number would be 100 while keeping fixed filter size of (3, 4, 5).

Table 2. Effect of number of feature maps on average training and testing accuracy

Feature map	Training accuracy	Testing accuracy
50	86.2	84.3
100	87.1	87.2
200	95.8	86.8
300	96.9	86.5
400	97.0	85.3

4.2   Machine Learning Model's Experiment Setup

To implement machine learning methods on our movie review dataset, we are using bag of words [13] framework. Bag of Words is the text representation in NLP (Natural Language Processing) and IR (Information Retrieval) which represent the text into a set of words ignoring the grammar and linguistic information that sentences have. Mathematically, let $\{g_1, g_2,...g_n\}$ is the set of n feature that can appear in any document d. $n_i(d)$ is the number of times the feature g_i appears in the document d. Then, the overall document can be represented as a vector $d = \{n_1(d), n_2(d) ... n_i(d)\}$.

In machine learning models, feature engineering [6] is an exhaustive task and can easily affect the overall performance of the model. After preprocessing the dataset, the next step would be to select features which can be used to train the classifier rather than considering the full feature space which is computationally extensive. Since, we have almost 280000 different words in all of the reviews. We are using tf-idf and chi-Square ($\chi2$) to select 4000 features from our dataset and then train our model on them.

Term Frequency/Inverse document frequency. tf-idf takes into account the normalized count of the frequency of words in a corpus rather than the focusing on the raw count of frequency of a word. Table 3 shows the positive and negative words in our dataset with highest tf-idf score.

Table 3. Words with highest tf-idf score for the positive reviews and negative reviews.

Highest tf-idf score positive words	Highest tf-idf score negative words
Excellent	Bad
Great	Worst
Perfect	Life
Love	Stupid
Outstanding	Crap
Wonderful	Lame
Excellent	Horrible
Amazing	Suck
Plot	Boring
Best	Poor

Chi-Square ($\chi 2$). Chi-Square is a statistical feature selection method for feature selection. Chi-square is calculated between each feature and target class label to identify whether the feature is related to the target class label.

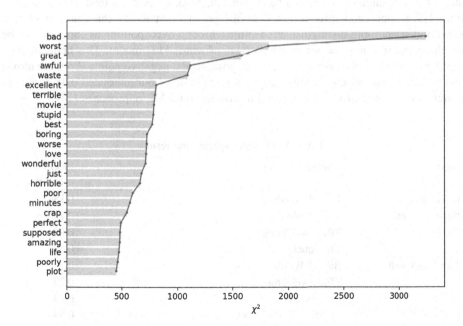

Fig. 2. Bar graph representing the words (positive and negative) with highest Chi-Square Score

The idea is that if the feature is independent of the target label it is not useful for classifying the observation. So, to limit our feature space we can remove words with chi-square less than the chosen threshold. Thus, higher the value the value of chi-Square the more relevant term is for the category. Figure 2 shows the words with highest chi-square for both positive and negative reviews.

After we are done with cleaning and loading the dataset, dataset has been converted into features vectors containing features based on Tf- idf score or Chi-square ($\chi2$) score.

5 Discussion and Results

We have used several machine learning models and a Deep Learning model to do sentiment analysis of movie reviews. By summarizing our major findings in the Table 4, It's clear that sentiment analysis of movie reviews can benefit more from the CNN rather than conventional Machine Learning approaches.

Among the machine learning models, Naïve Bayes performs the worst and Random Forest turns out to be the best, although the differences are not very large. Also, it is very clear from Table 4 that performance of machine learning algorithms heavily depends on choice of data representation and feature extraction techniques [5, 7]. For example, Random forest with features selected using Chi-Square can perform better than the usual bag-of-words model. On the contrary, deep learning models [10] emerge as a powerful tool that can automatically learn features from the text, and optimize them during training phase to have better generalization of the problem. Thus, an extra step of feature engineering would be eliminated. Also, CNN can effectively capture the underlying contextual information [22, 30] present in the text through convolution layer and select more distinguishable features through max- pooling as compared to the machine learning approaches based on bag- of-words [13] model. This helps in classifying ambivalent reviews; such that both positive and negative points about the movie are written in the review. Additionally, Large volume of our annotated dataset aids in better performance of CNN compared to conventional ML approaches [14].

Table 4. Overall experimental results

Model	Feature selection	Model accuracy
Naïve Bayes	Bag of Words	0.78
Support vector machine	Bag of Words	0.79
	Tf/Idf weighting	0.80
	Chi-Square	0.83
Random forest	Bag of Words	0.78
	Tf/Idf weighting	0.83
	Chi-Square	0.84
CNN	Pre-trained word vectors and fine tune them during training	0.88

Tuning of parameters and hyper-parameters in CNN [14] affects the performance of the overall model. For example: Small filter window tends to lose long-distance relationships, whereas large windows may result in data sparsity and can increase the training time. Using trial and error approach, we consider filter sizes between 1 to 9 to train and test our model. Mostly combining multiple filter regions around the single best filter results in a better performance. For example: (3, 4, 5) results in better performance for our dataset. Similarly, drop-out rate between 0.4−0.9 acts as good regularizer.

6 Conclusion

We evaluate CNN and some machine learning models such as Support Vector Machine Random Forest and Naïve Bayes. on IMDB movie review dataset for sentiment classification. We conclude that CNN model can easily outperform other machine learning models in the task of sentiment classification of short- texts such as movie reviews with an accuracy of 88.9%. Additionally, tuning of parameters and hyperparameters (such as drop-out rate, learning rate, filter size and size of feature maps) in CNN plays a vital role.

Among machine learning models, Random forest tends to do the best and Naïve Bayes performs the worst. Also, it has been noticed that choice of feature selection measures affects the performance of machine learning models. The experiments confirm the reliability of CNN for sentiment analysis of short-texts, and we believe that CNN model would make a considerable progress in the field of sentiment classification.

Our future work will focus on comparing several deep learning models including Long short-term memory (LSTM) Recurrent Neural Network for sentiment classification in short texts.

References

1. Pang, B., et al.: Thumbs up?: sentiment classification using machine learning techniques. In: Proceedings of the ACL-2002 Conference on Empirical Methods in Natural Language Processing, vol. 10, pp. 79–86 (2002)
2. Turney, P.D.: Thumbs up or thumbs down? semantic orientation applied to unsupervised classification of reviews. In: Proceedings of the Association for Computational Linguistics (ACL), pp. 417–424 (2002)
3. Turney, P.D., Littman, M.L.: Measuring praise and criticism: inference of semantic orientation from association. ACM Trans. Inf. Syst. TOIS 21(4), 315–346 (2003)
4. Pang, B., Lee, L.: Opinion mining and sentiment analysis. Found. Trends Inf. Retr. 2(1–2), 1–135 (2008)
5. Mudinas, A., et al.: Combining lexicon and learning based approaches for concept-level sentiment analysis. In: Proceedings of the First International Workshop on Issues of Sentiment Discovery and Opinion Mining, Article 5, pp. 1–8. ACM, New York (2012)
6. Joshi, A., et al.: C-feel-it: a sentiment analyzer for micro blogs. In: Proceedings of ACL: Systems Demonstrations, HLT, vol. 11, pp. 127–132 2011

7. Zhai, Z., et al.: Clustering product features for opinion mining. In: WSDM 2011, 9–12 February 2011, Hong Kong, China (2011)
8. Yang, F., Wang, H.Z., Mi, H., Cai, W.W.: Using random forest for reliable classification and cost-sensitive learning for medical diagnosis. BMC Bioinform. **10**(1), S22 (2009)
9. Medhat, W., Hassan, A., Korashy, H.: Sentiment analysis algorithms and applications: a survey. Ain Shams Eng. J. **5**(4), 1093–1113 (2014)
10. Socher, R., Perelygin, A., Wu, J., Chuang, J., Manning, C.D., Ng, A., Potts, C.: Recursive deep models for semantic compositionality over a sentiment treebank. In: Proceedings of the 2013 Conference on Empirical Methods in Natural Language Processing, pp. 1631–1642 (2013)
11. Large Movie Review Dataset, http://ai.stanford.edu/~amaas/data/sentiment/. Accessed 26 Feb 2018
12. Lin, C., He, Y.: Joint sentiment/topic model for sentiment analysis. In: Proceedings of the 18th ACM Conference on Information and Knowledge Management, pp. 375–384. ACM, November 2009
13. Harris, Z.S.: Distributional structure. Word **10**(2–3), 146–162 (1954)
14. Johnson, R., Zhang, T.: Effective use of word order for text categorization with convolutional neural networks. arXiv preprint arXiv:1412.1058 (2014)
15. Joachims, T.: Making large-scale SVM learning practical. In: Schölkopf, B., Smola, A. (eds.) Advances in Kernel Methods - Support Vector Learning, pp. 44–56. MIT Press (1999)
16. Support Vector Machine, http://svmlight.joachims.org/. Accessed 26 Feb 2018
17. LeCun, Y., Bengio, Y., Hinton, G.: Deep learning. Nature **521**(7553), 436 (2015)
18. Breiman, L.: Random forests. Machine learning **45**(1), 5–32 (2001)
19. Pang, B., Lee, L.: Opinion mining and sentiment analysis. Found. Trends® Inf. Retr. **2**(1–2), 1–135 (2008)
20. Abbasi, A., Chen, H., Salem, A.: Sentiment analysis in multiple languages: Feature selection for opinion classification in web forums. ACM Transactions on Information Systems (TOIS) **26**(3), 12 (2008)
21. Bengio, Y.: Deep learning of representations: looking forward. In: Dediu, A.-H., Martín-Vide, C., Mitkov, R., Truthe, B. (eds.) SLSP 2013. LNCS (LNAI), vol. 7978, pp. 1–37. Springer, Heidelberg (2013). https://doi.org/10.1007/978-3-642-39593-2_1
22. Kim, Y.: Convolutional neural networks for sentence classification. arXiv preprint arXiv: 1408.5882 (2014)
23. Mu, Y., et al.: Event-related theta and alpha oscillations mediate empathy for pain. Brain Res. **1234**, 128–136 (2008)
24. Kalchbrenner, N., Grefenstette, E., Blunsom, P.: A convolutional neural network for modelling sentences. arXiv preprint arXiv:1404.2188 (2014)
25. Zhang, Y., Wallace, B.: A sensitivity analysis of (and practitioners' guide to) convolutional neural networks for sentence classification. arXiv preprint arXiv:1510.03820 (2015)
26. Mikolov, T., Sutskever, I., Chen, K., Corrado, G.S., Dean, J.: Distributed representations of words and phrases and their compositionality. In: Advances in Neural Information Processing Systems, pp. 3111–3119 (2013)
27. Maas, A.L., Hannun, A.Y., Ng, A.Y.: Rectifier nonlinearities improve neural network acoustic models. Proc. ICML **30**(1), 3 (2013)
28. Kalchbrenner, N., Grefenstette, E., Blunsom, P.: A convolutional neural network for modelling sentences. In: Proceedings of the 52nd Annual Meeting of the Association for Computational Linguistics, vol. 1 Long Papers, Baltimore, Mary, pp. 655–665 (2014)
29. Kotsiantis, S.B., Zaharakis, I., Pintelas, P.: Supervised machine learning: A review of classification techniques. Emer. Artif. Intell. Appl. Comput. Eng. **160**, 3–24 (2007)

30. Yu, L., Liu, H.: Efficient feature selection via analysis of relevance and redundancy. JMLR **5** (Oct), 1205–1224 (2004)
31. Xu, B., Guo, X., Ye, Y., Cheng, J.: An improved random forest classifier for text categorization. JCP **7**(12), 2913–2920 (2012)
32. Google. https://code.google.com/archive/p/word2vec/. Accessed 26 Feb 2018
33. Gokulakrishnan, B., Priyanthan, P., Ragavan, T., Prasath, N., Perera, A.: Opinion mining and sentiment analysis on a twitter data stream. In: 2012 International Conference on Advances in ICT for Emerging Regions (ICTer), pp. 182–188. IEEE, December 2012
34. Adankon, M.M., Cheriet, M.: Support vector machine. In: Encyclopedia of Biometrics, pp. 1303–1308. Springer, Boston (2009)
35. Rish, I.: An empirical study of the naive Bayes classifier. In: IJCAI 2001 Workshop on Empirical Methods in Artificial Intelligence, vol. 3(22), pp. 41–46. IBM, August 2001

Study on Data Anonymization
for Deep Learning

Ayahiko Niimi[✉]

Future University Hakodate, 2-116 Kamedanakano, Hakodate,
Hokkaido 041-8655, Japan
niimi@fun.ac.jp
http://www.fun.ac.jp/~niimi/

Abstract. In this paper, we propose privacy protection data mining through deep learning. We discuss existing privacy protection data mining, study its features, and examine an anonymizing tool for deep learning. Experiments using anonymization tools (UAT) confirmed that deep learning does not reduce accuracy by making it anonymous.

Keywords: Deep learning · Privacy preserving data mining
Anonymization · Accuracy · Computational cost

1 Introduction

Big data and data mining require large amounts of data. Depending on the target, there are data on personal information and privacy. Thinking about the ways of using such data and the appropriate risk assessment method to be employed is important. Privacy preserving data mining is used for the safe utilization of data, including private information with an emphasis on privacy.

In contrast, deep learning is a machine learning method. It is a recent topic in AlphaGo [1] and image analysis. Deep learning is a new technology that has recently attracted considerable attention in the field of machine learning.

In this paper, we propose privacy preserving data mining through deep learning. We use existing privacy preserving data mining techniques, consider their features, and examine the anonymization tool for deep learning.

2 Privacy Preserving Data Mining

Big data and data mining require large amounts of data. Depending on the target, data includes personal and private information. We must think about the ways of using such data and the required appropriate risk assessment method. Privacy preserving data mining is employed for the safe utilization of data, such as personal and private information, with an emphasis on privacy [2–4]. Privacy preserving data mining is a generic term for technologies that extract useful information from data while protecting privacy.

© Springer International Publishing AG, part of Springer Nature 2018
M. Mouhoub et al. (Eds.): IEA/AIE 2018, LNAI 10868, pp. 762–767, 2018.
https://doi.org/10.1007/978-3-319-92058-0_74

Privacy preserving data mining includes research on input data, research on secret computation, and research on output data. Research on input data involves input data privacy protection technology. This is a technique used when transforming raw data that can data to be analyzed. Input data privacy preserving technology is technology that reduces the risk of privacy infringement by processing or deleting data that may expose to the identification of individuals. Representative methods include "anonymization" and "randomization." A study on secret computation is a technique that enables only the analysis of results while concealing the data. This is a technique that accumulates data in a state that makes no sense on a standalone basis and only analyzes the data by displaying it. This research is based on techniques such as encryption and secret sharing. Through confidential calculations, we can identify between the administrator of anonymized data and data mining performer [5]. Research on output data is a technique to reduce the risk of privacy infringement when outputting analysis results as data. This is a technique for avoiding the risk of exposing the attribute of a specific individual by controlling the response to the query, which is the command for analyzing and adding noise to the analysis result.

2.1   Study on Input Data

Consider the "anonymization" and "randomization" of representative methods of input data privacy protection technology. Anonymization prevents data from returning to a specific individual for raw data. Anonymization includes properties such as attribute deletion, attribute change, and, generalization: (1) attribute deletion means deleting a specific attribute, (2) attribute change is a method of eliminating an individual's identity by replacing information specifying an individual with some other information, and (3) generalization is a technique to lower specificity and discrimination by roughening the granularity of information.

The sole application of these methods is not sufficient to reduce the risk. For example, at instances when the amount of data becomes large, when linking with other information, and when the data are accompanied by time change, the individual can probably be identified.

"k-Anonymity" and "l-diversity" are proposed as indices for evaluating the risk of re-specifying anonymized data and the risk of attribute estimation [6,7].

"k-Anonymity" is a mechanism that reduces the risk of individuals being identified by making k or more pieces of information possibly identifiable individuals exist. For example, at $k = 3$, data are processed such that there are three or more pieces of data having attribute values for identifying the same individual. Hence even if a single attribute value identifying an individual is viewed because there are three or more attributes, identifying an individual becomes impossible.

With "k-Anonymity", individual attributes can be estimated if their attributes are biased even if there are k same data. "l-diversity" can help reduce the risk of privacy infringement through individual attribute estimation.

Randomization is a method of reducing the risk of individual identification by randomizing or adding noise based on rules predefined for raw data. Because data are converted to "nonexistent data," associating data with individuals is difficult. As original data are converted to "nonexistent data" by randomization, the result of data mining is affected.

A method of restoring original data by randomizing the data using Bayesian estimation has been proposed [3].

2.2 Multi Party Computation

Multi party computation is a generic term for a method of outputting only the operation result while hiding the information of each party among plural analysts [5]. It is a method of encrypting an input value and receiving only the calculation result and a method of using a cryptogram having homomorphism. If cryptograms with homomorphism are used, it is possible to perform computations with the confidential information kept secret by encrypting individual information. By decoding only the calculation result, the calculation result can be obtained.

2.3 Study on Output Data

If there is bias in the data, or in the case of a small number, it is conceivable that the individual can be specified by the search. For such risks, techniques such as limiting the output and adding noise to the output result are employed. Such a technique is called query inference control.

3 Deep Learning

Deep learning is a new technology that has recently attracted considerable attention in the field of machine learning [8–10]. Numerous researchers have focused on improving the performance [10].

The basic theory and basic improvement methods of deep learning are described in a previous paper [11, 12].

Apache Spark is also a platform that processes large amounts of data [13]. It has generalized the Map/Reduce processing. It processes data by caching the work memory, and efficient iterative algorithms are executed by maintaining shared data, which is used for repeated processing in the memory. In addition, machine learning and graph algorithm libraries are prepared, and an easily build environment for stream data mining can be easily built.

H2O is a library of deep learning for Spark [14, 15].

SparkR is an R package that provides a light weight frontend for Apache Spark from R [16]. In Spark 1.5.0, SparkR provides distributed data frame implementation that supports operations, such as selection, filtering, and aggregation, similar to R data frames, dplyr, but on large datasets. SparkR also supports distributed machine learning using MLlib.

In this paper, we use R and Spark. An extensive library can be used with R to gain high performance through parallel and distributed processing of Spark.

4   Privacy Preserving Data Mining in Deep Learning

Consider privacy protection data mining in deep learning. Deep learning calculation is intensive and the accuracy drops if randomized. Randomization: Reconstruction calculation is difficult. If it is a secret computation, the calculation is intensive. To deal with a large amount of data, a method for anonymizing input data is suitable.

Many anonymizing tools have been developed. As an open source anonymizing tool, "Cornell Anonymization Toolkit" (CAT) [17] and "UTD Anonymization ToolBox" (UAT) [18] are available.

The CAT is designed for interactively anonymizing published dataset to limit identification disclosure of records under various attacker models.

The UAT was developed by UT Dallas data security and privacy lab. The toolbox currently contains six different anonymization methods over three different privacy definitions:

1. Datafly
2. Mondrian multidimensional k-Anonymity
3. Incognito
4. Incognito with l-diversity
5. Incognito with t-closeness
6. Anatomy

Many anonymization tools have been developed, but they are not specialized for deep learning. Deep learning has the following features.

1. High expressive power of learning model
2. Use of large amounts of input data
3. Performance of iterative calculations

Existing anonymizing tools, such as association rules and decision trees, have been devised for machine learning, where the expressive power of learning models is low. Because deep learning has a high expressive power of models, individuals may be identified even after using input data privacy protection technology. In addition, because it is necessary to be applicable to large amounts of data, emphasis must also be given to the calculation time.

After considering the problems of the existing anonymizing tools, we need to consider an anonymizing tool for deep learning. An anonymization tool for deep learning must have the following attributes: (1) an individual cannot be identified through deep learning and (2) the calculation amount is small. In addition, because we assume that the existing deep learning framework performs parallel distributed processing, the anonymizing tool should preferably perform parallel distributed processing.

5   Data Set

Sample data of UAT was used for the experiments. The task of data set it to predict whether income exceeds \$50K/yr based on census data. The data set is also known as "Census Income" dataset or "Adult" data set.

6   Experiment

To investigate the problem of using an existing anonymizing tool for deep learning, consider an experiment in which deep learning is employed for the anonymization of data using an existing anonymization tool. UAT is employed as the existing anonymizing tool. This tool is an open source anonymization tool, and hence, it is easy to use it in experiments. Apache Spark and Sparking Water are used as a deep learning framework on R.

The experimental environment was constructed on AWS EC 2. The instance type used was m4.large, 2.3 GHz Intel Xeon E5-2686 v4 (Broadwell), the memory was 8 GB.

Sample data of UAT (`census-income_1K.data` and `census-income_ALL.data`) was used. We used `census-income_1K.data` (42 attributes, 463 cases) as the training data and `census-income_ALL.data` (42 attributes, 95130 cases) as the test data. As a parameter of UTA, $k = 10$ was used. Using anonymization using UAT, the number of attributes changed from 42 to 40. The time required for anonymization was 8 s for `census-income_1K.data` and 34 s for `census-income_ALL.data`. The middle layer of deep learning included three layers (100, 100, and 200). The activation functions of deep learning are as follows.

- RectifierWithDropout
- Rectifier
- TanhWithDropout
- Tanh
- MaxoutWithDropout
- Maxout

The error rate of test data of deep learning before anonymization and the error rate of test data of deep learning after anonymization are as follows (Table 1):

Because of anonymization, we did not observe any decline in accuracy.

Table 1. Result of deep learning

Activation function	Error rate before anonymization	Error rate after anonymization
RectifierWithDropout	5.74	5.74
Rectifier	6.19	6.19
TanhWithDropout	7.20	7.20
Tanh	7.73	7.73
MaxoutWithDropout	8.22	8.22
Maxout	9.5	9.5

7 Conclusion

In this paper, privacy protection data mining by deep learning was proposed. We discussed existing privacy protection data mining techniques, examined their features, and examined an anonymizing tool for deep learning. Experiments using anonymization tools confirmed that deep learning does not reduce accuracy because of anonymization. In the future, we will conduct experiments using other data sets and examine the problems encountered while using existing anonymizing tools for deep learning.

References

1. Alphago – deepmind. Accessed 24 Feb 2018
2. Agrawal, R., Srikant, R.: Privacy-preserving data mining. SIGMOD Rec. **29**(2), 439–450 (2000)
3. Aggarwal, C.C., Yu, P.S.: A general survey of privacy-preserving data mining models and algorithms. In: Aggarwal, C.C., Yu, P.S. (eds.) Privacy-Preserving Data Mining. Advances in Database Systems, vol. 34, pp. 11–52. Springer, Boston (2008). https://doi.org/10.1007/978-0-387-70992-5_2
4. Sakuma, J., Kobayashi, S.: Privacy-Preserving Data Mining. Jpn. Soc. Artif. Intell. **24**(2), 283–294 (2009)
5. Cramer, R., Damgård, I., Nielsen, J.B.: Multiparty computation from threshold homomorphic encryption. In: Pfitzmann, B. (ed.) EUROCRYPT 2001. LNCS, vol. 2045, pp. 280–300. Springer, Heidelberg (2001). https://doi.org/10.1007/3-540-44987-6_18
6. Machanavajjhala, A., Gehrke, J., Kifer, D., Venkitasubramaniam, M.: L-diversity: privacy beyond k-anonymity. In: 22nd International Conference on Data Engineering (ICDE 2006), pp. 24–24, April 2006
7. Sweeney, L.: k-anonymity: a model for protecting privacy. Int. J. Uncertainty Fuzziness Knowl. Based Syst. **10**(05), 557–570 (2002)
8. Bengio, Y.: Learning deep architectures for AI. Found. Trends Mach. Learn. **2**(1), 1–127 (2009)
9. Le, Q.: Building high-level features using large scale unsupervised learning. In: 2013 IEEE International Conference on Acoustics, Speech and Signal Processing (ICASSP), pp. 8595–8598, May 2013
10. Goodfellow, I.J., Warde-Farley, D., Mirza, M., Courville, A., Bengio, Y.: Maxout Networks. ArXiv e-prints, February 2013
11. Niimi, A.: Deep learning for credit card data analysis. In: World Congress on Internet Security (WorldCIS-2015), Dublin, Ireland, pp. 73–77, October 2015
12. Niimi, A.: Deep learning with large scale dataset for credit card data analysis. In: Fuzzy Systems and Data Mining II, Proceedings of FSDM 2016, Macau, pp. 149–158, December 2016
13. Apache Spark, lightning-fast cluster computing. Accessed 15 Sept 2015
14. 0xdata - H2O.ai - fast scalable machine learning. Accessed 15 Sept 2015
15. Candel, A., Parmar, V.: Deep Learning with H2O. H2O (2015). Accessed 15 Sept 2015
16. SparkR (R on Spark) - Spark 1.5.0 documentation. Accessed 15 Sept 2015
17. Cornell anonymization toolkit. Accessed 31 Jan 2017
18. UTD anonymization toolbox. Accessed 31 Jan 2017

Information Disclosure, Security, and Data Quality

A. N. K. Zaman$^{(\boxtimes)}$, Charlie Obimbo, and Rozita A. Dara

School of Computer Science, University of Guelph,
50 Stone Road East, Guelph, ON N1G 2W1, Canada
{azaman,cobimbo,drozita}@uoguelph.ca

Abstract. Data sharing is important to interested parties for mining trends and patterns in designing data-driven decision-making systems. However, sharing raw data creates severe problems like identity theft or personal information leakage such as disclosure of illness of a specific person. This study analyzed results from an Adaptive Differential Privacy (ADiffP) algorithm that satisfies ε-differential privacy for publishing sanitized data. The algorithm was tested with two different data sets to measure its robustness by comparing other existing works. The results obtained from the proposed algorithm show that the sanitized data preserves the same pattern as the raw data. Additionally, classification accuracies for sanitized data are also promising.

Keywords: Differential privacy · Data anonymization
Privacy preserving data publishing · Data sanitization

1 Introduction

In this digital era, almost everyone is sharing their personal information while doing online shopping, visiting a doctor's office, and in social networks. According to Statistics Canada,[1] 77% of Canadians are concerned about the privacy and security of their personal data. Despite their concerns, 63% of Canadians do their sensitive transactions over the internet. Additionally, 57% of Canadians keep their private and confidential information in digital form on their computers. Removing personally identifiable information (PII) from a data set is not enough to secure the privacy of a person [1]. As a result, data sanitization algorithms are needed to ensure controlled disclosure of data for interested parties. Ideas of interactive, and non-interactive anonymization techniques are mentioned in [2,3]. In the literature, the differential privacy (DP) paradigm [4] is widely used in the interactive framework [5–7]. In the case of a non-interactive framework, sanitized data set is published by a data custodian for public use. In this research, the non-interactive framework is adopted as this approach has a number of advantages [2,3,8,9] over its counterpart (interactive approach).

---

[1] https://www.statcan.gc.ca/.

© Springer International Publishing AG, part of Springer Nature 2018
M. Mouhoub et al. (Eds.): IEA/AIE 2018, LNAI 10868, pp. 768–779, 2018.
https://doi.org/10.1007/978-3-319-92058-0_75

The rest of the paper is organized as follows: Sect. 2 describes a formal definition of differential privacy, Laplace mechanism and random noise, and anonymization for data masking. Section 3 surveys and presents recent published work related to this work. Section 4 states the Adaptive Differential Privacy (ADiffP) algorithm for data sanitization. Sections 5 and 6 present data sets, results and discussion respectively. Section 7 describes the concluding remarks of this paper.

2   Privacy Constraint

Current privacy preserving models (such as partition based models and interactive models) [2,10,11] are vulnerable to different privacy-breaching attacks. In the proposed system, ε-differential privacy will be used. It is capable of protecting published data sets from different privacy breach attacks.

Differential privacy is a new paradigm that provides a strong privacy guarantee [4]. Partition-based privacy models [10,11] ensure privacy by imposing syntactic constraints on the output. For example, the output may be required to be indistinguishable among k records, or the sensitive value to be well represented in every equivalence group. Instead, differential privacy makes sure that a malicious user will not be able to get any information about a targeted person, whether a data set contains that person's record or not. Informally, a differentially private output is insensitive to any particular record. Thus, while preserving the privacy of an individual, the output of the differential privacy method is computed as if from a data set that does not contain targeted person's record. Current research shows that ε-differential privacy is able to protect from most attacks [8].

Differential Privacy. Let $\mathcal{M}$ be a randomization algorithm over the domain $\mathbb{N}^{|x|}$. Then $\mathcal{M}$ is (ε, δ)-differentially private if ($\forall S \subseteq Range(\mathcal{M}) \wedge \forall DB_1, DB_2 \in \mathbb{N}^{|x|} \ni \|DB_1 - DB_2\|_1 \leq 1$):

$$Pr[\mathcal{M}(DB_1) \in S] \leq \exp(\varepsilon) Pr[\mathcal{M}(DB_2) \in S] + \delta \tag{1}$$

Where, DB_1 and DB_2 are two databases. Now, if $\delta = 0$ then the randomization algorithm $\mathcal{M}$ becomes ε-differentially private

$$\frac{Pr[\mathcal{M}(DB_1) \in S]}{Pr[\mathcal{M}(DB_2) \in S]} \leq exp(\varepsilon) \tag{2}$$

A stronger privacy guarantee may be achieved by choosing a lower value of ε. The values could be 0.01, 0.1, or may be $\ln 2$ or $\ln 3$ [12,13]. In this research, the value of ε is used in the range: $0.01 \geq \varepsilon \leq 1.0$. If it is a very small ε then

$$\exp(\varepsilon) \approx 1 + \varepsilon \tag{3}$$

To process numeric and non-numeric data with the differential privacy model, the following techniques will be needed.

2.1   Laplace Mechanism and Random Noise

Dwork et al., [5] proposed the Laplace mechanism to add noise for numerical values and ensure differential privacy. The Laplace mechanism takes a database DB as input and consists of a function f and the privacy parameter λ. The privacy parameter λ specifies how much noise should be added to produce the privacy preserved output. The mechanism first computes the true output $f(DB)$, and then perturbs the noisy output. A Laplace distribution having a probability density function, π:

$$\pi\left(\frac{x}{\lambda}\right) = \frac{1}{2\lambda}\exp(-(|x|/\lambda)) \tag{4}$$

generates noise, where, x is a random variable; its variance is $2\lambda^2$ and mean is 0. The sensitivity of the noise is defined by the following formula:

$$\hat{f}(DB) = f(DB) + lap(\lambda) \tag{5}$$

where, $lap(\lambda)$ is sampled from Laplace distribution. The expected magnitude of $|lap(\lambda)|$ is approximately $\frac{1}{\lambda}$. In a similar way, the following mechanism

$$\hat{f}(DB) = f(DB) + lap\left(\frac{1}{\varepsilon}\right) \tag{6}$$

ensures ε-differential privacy. For a random variable v, the random noise $N_r = lap\left(\frac{1}{\varepsilon}\right)$ is generated using the following equation [14]:

$$N_r = -sign(v) * \ln(1 - 2 * |v|) \tag{7}$$

For this research, $v = \left(\frac{1}{\varepsilon}\right)$ as the value of $\left(\frac{1}{\varepsilon}\right)$ is always positive and random for every group of data. Finally, the random Laplace noise, N_r, is generated using the following equation:

$$N_r = \left\lceil \left|-sign\left(\frac{1}{\varepsilon}\right)\right| * \ln\left(\left|1 - 2*\left(\frac{1}{\varepsilon}\right)\right|\right)\right\rceil = \left\lceil 1*\ln\left(\left|1 - 2*\left(\frac{1}{\varepsilon}\right)\right|\right)\right\rceil$$
$$= \left\lceil \ln\left(\left|1 - 2*\left(\frac{1}{\varepsilon}\right)\right|\right)\right\rceil \tag{8}$$

Thus:

$$N_r = \left\lceil \ln\left(\left|1 - 2*\left(\frac{1}{\varepsilon}\right)\right|\right)\right\rceil \tag{9}$$

Within the last five years, some recently published works [4,15–17] also prove that adding Laplace noise secures data from the adversary.

Theorem 1.1 ([4]). *The Laplace mechanism satisfies $(\varepsilon, 0)$-differential privacy.*

Proof. Let us consider $DB_1 \in \mathbb{N}^{|\chi|}$, and $DB_2 \in \mathbb{N}^{|\chi|}$ such that $||DB_1 - DB_2||_1 \leq 1$. Let f be some function $f : \mathbb{N}^{|\chi|} \rightarrow \mathbb{R}^k$, and let P_{DB_1} denote the probably density function (π) of $M_L(DB_1, f, \varepsilon)$ and let P_{DB_2} denotes the probably density function of $M_L(DB_2, f, \varepsilon)$. At some arbitrary point $x \in \mathbb{R}^k$, then,

$$
\begin{aligned}
\frac{P_{DB_1}(x)}{P_{DB_2}(x)} &= \prod_{i=1}^{k} \left(\frac{\exp\left(-\frac{\varepsilon|f(DB_1)_i - x_i|}{\Delta f}\right)}{\exp\left(-\frac{\varepsilon|f(DB_2)_i - x_i|}{\Delta f}\right)} \right) \\
&= \prod_{i=1}^{k} \left(\frac{\exp(\varepsilon|f(DB_1)_i - x_i| - |f(DB_2)_i - x_i|)}{\Delta f} \right) \\
&\leq \prod_{i=1}^{k} \exp\left(\frac{\varepsilon|f(DB_1)_i - f(DB_2)_i|}{\Delta f} \right) \\
&= \exp\left(\frac{\varepsilon \cdot ||f(DB_1) - f(DB_2)||_1}{\Delta f} \right) \\
&\leq \exp(\varepsilon)
\end{aligned}
\tag{10}
$$

2.2 Anonymization

Data anonymization is a procedure that converts data to a new form that produces secure data and prevents information leakage from that data set. However, the anonymized data should still be able to be data mined to obtain useful information/pattern. Data anonymization may be achieved in different ways; however, data suppression and generalization are standard methods to perform data anonymization. In this research, generalization and suppression are used to achieve data anonymization.

Generalization. To anonymize a data set DB, the process of generalization takes place by substituting an original value of an attribute with a more general form of a value. The general value is chosen according to the characteristics of an attribute. For example, in this work, profession: **filmmaker** and **singer** are generalized with the **artist**, and the **age 34** is generalized with a range [**30–35**).
Let

$$
DB = r_1, r_2, ..., r_n
\tag{11}
$$

be a set of records, where every record r_i represent the information of an individual with attributes

$$
A = A_1, A_2, ..., A_d
\tag{12}
$$

It is assumed that each attribute A_i has a finite domain, denoted by $\Omega(A_i)$. The domain of DB is defined as

$$
\Omega(DB) = \Omega(A_1) \times \Omega(A_2) \times ... \times \Omega(A_d)
\tag{13}
$$

3   Related Works

There are various algorithms for privacy preserving data mining (PPDM) and privacy preserving data publishing (PPDP), however, not much is found in literature that addresses the privacy preservation to achieve the goal of classification [9,18]. Some of the recent research done on privacy preserving data publishing are reported below:

In [19], Fan and Jin implemented two methods: Hand-picked algorithm (HPA) and Simple random algorithm (SRA) which are variations of l-diversity [10] technique, and use Laplace Mechanism [4] for adding noise to make data secure. The authors also claimed that their methods satisfies ϵ-differential privacy. The authors used four real-world data sets: **Gowalla, Foursquare, Netflix, and Movie-Lens** and performed empirical studies to evaluate their work. The authors reported some data loss while imposing privacy on the raw data.

In [20], Loukides et al., implemented a disassociation algorithm for electronic health record privacy. They used anonymization technique along with horizontal partitioning, vertical partitioning, and refining operations on the data set as needed to impose privacy. The authors used **EHR dataset** for their experiments. The proposed algorithm is called k^m-anonymity, a variation of k-anonymization algorithm and they follow an interactive model for their implementation, both (k-anonymization and interactive model) are limitations [4,9] of their work.

In the paper [21], Al-Hussaeni, Fung, and Cheung implemented Incremental Trajectory Stream Anonymizer (ITSA) algorithm to publish private trajectory data (e.g., GPS data of a moving entity). The authors use anonymization and LKC-privacy (L: a positive integer, K: an anonymity threshold $K \geq 1$, and C: a confidence threshold $0 \leq C \leq 1$) to develop the propose technique. They test their algorithm with two different data sets: *MetroData* and *Oldenburg*. The authors compared their result with k-anonymity algorithm and show that their algorithm works better.

Kisilevich et al., [22] presented a multidimensional hybrid approach called kACTUS-2 which achieves privacy by utilizing suppression and swapping techniques, this method is developed by adopting k-anonymization model. The authors investigated data anonymization for data classification. The authors adopted five data sets: Adult, German Credit, TTT, Glass Identification, and Waveform for their experiments. They claim that their work produces better classification accuracy of anonymized data. As the propose algorithm based on k-anonymization model, it inherits all limitations [9] of k-anonymity model, also as the suppression technique is applied, then one of the major drawbacks is that, sparse data results in high information loss [23].

Li et al., [24] proposed and demonstrated two k-anonymity based algorithms: Information based Anonymization for Classification given k (IACk) and, a variant of IACk for a given distributional constraints (IACc). They utilized global attribute generalization and local value suppression techniques to produce anonymized data for classification. The authors adopted the Adult data set for their experiments. The authors report that IACk algorithm shows better classification performance compared to InfoGain Mondrian [25]. Again, as the proposed algorithm is based on k-anonymization model, it inherits [9] all limitations of k-anonymity model.

4   Adaptive Differential Privacy (ADiffP) Algorithm

This research work uses an Adaptive Differential Privacy (ADiffP) algorithm [8] that satisfies ε-Differential Privacy guarantee. Algorithm 1 represents the ADiffP algorithm.

Algorithm 1. ADiffP Algorithm

---

1 **Inputs** : Raw data set: DB, Predictor attributes: A_{Pr},
      Class attribute: A_{Cl},
      Privacy budget: ε,
      Taxonomy Tree depth (TT d): d

2 **Output**: Generalized data set $\widehat{DB}$

3 Predictor Attribute Generalization: $A_{Pr} \longrightarrow \widehat{A_{Pr}}$, based on the Taxonomy Tree

4 Split the generalized data set, DB_g by traversing the taxonomy tree, and predictor attributes similarities i.e., $DB_g = DB_{g_1} \cup DB_{g_2} \cup ... \cup DB_{g_n}$ [where, $DB_{g_i} \in DB_g$ and $i = 1, 2, 3, ..., n$]

5 Setup initial privacy budget: $\hat{\varepsilon} = \varepsilon/(\left|\widehat{A_{Pr}}\right|)$

   /* ε is a small number like 0.1 or 0.25 or 0.5 etc. initially   */

6 START: for $i = 1$ to n

7   Count the frequency, f_r of the each generalized group

8   Set the adaptive privacy budget for DB_{g_i}: $\varepsilon^i = \hat{\varepsilon}/(|f_r| + d)$

9   Add Laplace noise to the frequency as $f_i + lap(1/\varepsilon^i)$

10 END for

11 Merge subgroups with new frequencies as $\widehat{DB} = \widehat{DB_{g_1}} \cup \widehat{DB_{g_2}} \cup ... \cup \widehat{DB_{g_n}}$

12 The output is differential privacy preserved anonymized data set, $\widehat{DB}$

In line 3, the algorithm generalizes the raw data set to its generalized form to add a layer of privacy to prevent data breaches. Taxonomy tree helps find the hierarchical relations between the actual attribute for its general form. Taxonomy tree will never be published with the sanitized data set. The proposed algorithm (in line 4) then partitions[2] the generalized data set based on the similarities of the predictor attributes and Taxonomy Tree. At this stage, the algorithm also counts the frequency of each group (number of rows in that group). In line 5, the algorithm calculates the initial privacy budget based on the number of predictor attributes in the input data set. The final privacy budget is then calculated for a certain group in line 8. Next, the Laplace noise is generated to add the frequency

---

[2] Non-synthetically.

of that certain group. This process repeats until noise is added to all groups of the generalized data set (line 6 to 10). As the proposed algorithm recalculates the privacy budget depending on the number of predictor attributes and the size of a group, we consider this procedure as an adaptive noise addition. As soon as the algorithm ends the noise addition process, it merges all the sub-groups to form anonymized and differential private sanitized data set (line 12). Finally, this data set is published for interested parties (e.g., data miners).

5 Data Set

Two different data sets are used to evaluate the quality of the sanitized and published data: the Adult Data Set and the Haberman's Survival data set, both are collected from the UCI machine learning repository [26].

The adult data set consists of 45,222 tuples and is 5.4 MB in size. It is a census data set and publicly available for download. It contains real-life data with 6 numeric attributes, 8 categorical/non-numerical attributes, and a class information to classify two different income levels as $>50K$ & $\leq 50K$.

The Haberman's Survival data set consists of 306 tuples and it contains 3 numerical and 1 class attributes.

6 Result and Discussion

The sanitized and published data set is evaluated to measure the usability in the case of data classification. Figure 1 represents the classification accuracies of the Adult and the Haberman's Survival data sets. The classification accuracies are measured with the Naive Bayes Tree (NBTree) [27] classifier. The same experiment ran five times at a particular taxonomy tree (TT) depth, $d = 2, 4, 8$, and 12 that corresponded to different values of the privacy budget ε (i.e., 0.5, 0.25, 0.1, etc.) to generate the sanitized data. Each time, taxonomy tree depth, d and privacy budget, ε were varied while running the experiment to produce the anonymized data. Then, to classify the sanitized data, the classification algorithm was applied. The average (arithmetic mean) of the classification accuracies from five runs is reported in this paper. The classification accuracy for the sanitized data using the proposed algorithm achieved approximately 83% at the lowest privacy budget $\varepsilon = 0.1$ or 0.25 with the higher values of $d = 12$ and 8.

One of the uses of the Receiver Operating Characteristic (ROC) curve is to evaluate the sensitivity/specificity pair corresponding to a particular classification task regarding the input data set. The Area Under Curve (AUC) of a ROC curve demonstrates how well a parameter can distinguish between two classes of a data set. Figures 2 and 3 show the ROC curves for the Adult and Haberman's Survival data sets before and after sanitization.

For the Adult data set, the area under the ROC values are 0.9 and 0.86 and they are pretty much the same, meaning that the controlled addition of noise did not change the patterns of the data set. In the case of the Haberman's Survival data set, the ROC curve is more robust for the sanitized data. The ADiffP

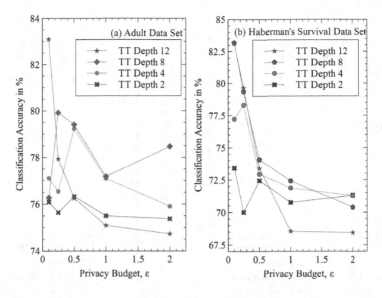

Fig. 1. Classification accuracy for the adult and the Haberman's survival data set

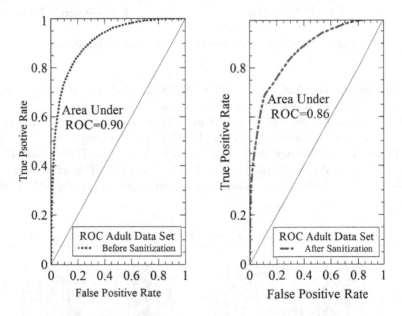

Fig. 2. ROC curves for the adult data set

algorithm added more records as part of the noise addition process to the data set. The additional records make the data set more balanced, and hence, the classifier is able to distinguish two data classes more efficiently. The ROC curves for the sanitized data with the proposed algorithm are close to the Y-axis, and

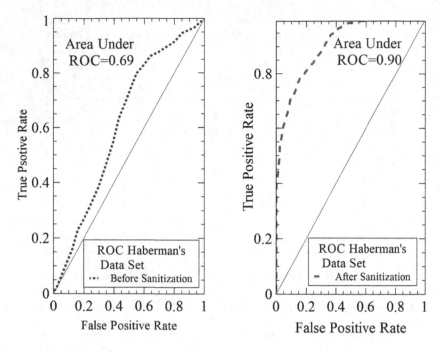

Fig. 3. ROC curves for the Haberman's survival data set

above 0.5 means the NBTree classifier [27,28] is efficiently distinguishing the data items for the sanitized published data set.

The performance of the proposed algorithm, ADiffP, was compared with five other anonymization algorithms: DiffGen [3], k-anonymity ($k = 5$), k-Map ($k = 5$), δ-Presence ($0.5 \leq \delta \leq 1.0$), and (e, d)-Differential Privacy ($e = 2, d = 1e - 6$) algorithms [29,30]. In the case of NBTree classifier, AdiffP algorithm showed better performance compared to five other algorithms, shown

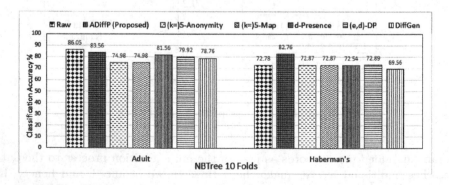

Fig. 4. Comparisons between proposed algorithm and five other algorithms

in Fig. 4. The major reason to drop the classification accuracy of the partitioned based algorithms is the difficulty in choosing quasi-identifiers (QIDs) [2]. In those algorithms, QIDs were suppressed fully, and due to loss of information the usability of sanitized data dropped significantly. The classification accuracy for the Adult data set before sanitization is better than the classification accuracy with the sanitized data using proposed algorithm. However, the accuracy is better in the case of the sanitized data for the Hebermman's Survival data set. Figure 4 describes the comparison between the proposed algorithm with five other existing algorithms.

7 Conclusion

This research evaluates the performance of the ADiffP data sanitization algorithm that utilizes generalization and Laplace noise in an adaptive way for generating and publishing sanitized data sets from a micro or Health Insurance Portability and Accountability Act (HIPAA) [31] compliance data set. Also, ADiffP ensures ϵ-Differential Privacy guarantee. The Adult and the Haberman's Survival data sets are (benchmark) used for testing. Experiments indicate that the proposed ADiffP algorithm is capable of publishing quality sanitized data without changing the actual data patterns in the raw data set. Moreover, the addition of adaptive noise and the data generalization process prevents disclosure of information.

References

1. Zaman, A.N.K., Obimbo, C., Dara, R.A.: An improved differential privacy algorithm to protect re-identification of data. In: IEEE Canada International Humanitarian Technology Conference, IHTC 2017, Toronto, ON, Canada, 21–22 July 2017, pp. 133–138 (2017)
2. Zaman, A.N.K.: Privacy preserving data sanitization and publishing. Ph.D. thesis, School of Computer Science, University of Guelph (2017)
3. Mohammed, N., Chen, R., Fung, B.C., Yu, P.S.: Differentially private data release for data mining. In: Proceedings of the 17th ACM SIGKDD International Conference on Knowledge Discovery and Data Mining, KDD 2011, pp. 493–501. ACM, New York (2011)
4. Dwork, C., Roth, A.: The algorithmic foundations of differential privacy. Found. Trends Theor. Comput. Sci. 9(3–4), 211–407 (2014)
5. Dwork, C., McSherry, F., Nissim, K., Smith, A.: Calibrating noise to sensitivity in private data analysis. In: Halevi, S., Rabin, T. (eds.) TCC 2006. LNCS, vol. 3876, pp. 265–284. Springer, Heidelberg (2006). https://doi.org/10.1007/11681878_14
6. Roth, A., Roughgarden, T.: Interactive privacy via the median mechanism. In: Proceedings of the Forty-Second ACM Symposium on Theory of Computing, STOC 2010, pp. 765–774. ACM, New York (2010)
7. Friedman, A., Schuster, A.: Data mining with differential privacy. In: Proceedings of the 16th ACM SIGKDD International Conference on Knowledge Discovery and Data Mining, KDD 2010, pp. 493–502. ACM, New York (2010)

8. Zaman, A.N.K., Obimbo, C., Dara, R.A.: A novel differential privacy approach that enhances classification accuracy. In: Proceedings of the Ninth International C* Conference on Computer Science and Software Engineering, C3S2E 2016, pp. 79–84. ACM, New York (2016)

9. Fung, B.C.M., Wang, K., Chen, R., Yu, P.S.: Privacy-preserving data publishing: a survey of recent developments. ACM Comput. Surv. **42**(4), 14:1–14:53 (2010)

10. Chen, B.C., Kifer, D., LeFevre, K., Machanavajjhala, A.: Privacy-preserving data publishing. Found. Trends Databases **2**(1–2), 1–167 (2009)

11. Wong, R.C.W., Li, J., Fu, A.W.C., Wang, K.: (α, k)-anonymity: an enhanced K-anonymity model for privacy preserving data publishing. In: Proceedings of the 12th ACM SIGKDD International Conference on Knowledge Discovery and Data Mining, KDD 2006, pp. 754–759. ACM, New York (2006)

12. Zaman, A.N.K., Obimbo, C.: Privacy preserving data publishing: a classification perspective. Int. J. Adv. Comput. Sci. Appl. (IJACSA) **5**(9), 129–134 (2014)

13. Dwork, C.: A firm foundation for private data analysis. Commun. ACM **54**(1), 86–95 (2011)

14. Polansky, A.M.: Introduction to Statistical Limit Theory. Chapman and Hall/CRC Texts in Statistical Science. CRC Press, Hoboken (2011)

15. Zaman, A.N.K., Obimbo, C., Dara, R.A.: An improved data sanitization algorithm for privacy preserving medical data publishing. In: Mouhoub, M., Langlais, P. (eds.) AI 2017. LNCS (LNAI), vol. 10233, pp. 64–70. Springer, Cham (2017). https://doi.org/10.1007/978-3-319-57351-9_8

16. Andrés, M.E., Bordenabe, N.E., Chatzikokolakis, K., Palamidessi, C.: Geo-indistinguishability: differential privacy for location-based systems. In: Proceedings of the 2013 ACM SIGSAC Conference on Computer and Communications Security, CCS 2013, pp. 901–914. ACM, New York (2013)

17. Lee, J., Clifton, C.: Differential identifiability. In: Proceedings of the 18th ACM SIGKDD International Conference on Knowledge Discovery and Data Mining, KDD 2012, pp. 1041–1049. ACM, New York (2012)

18. Boyd, K., Lantz, E., Page, D.: Differential privacy for classifier evaluation. In: Proceedings of the 8th ACM Workshop on Artificial Intelligence and Security, AISec 2015, pp. 15–23. ACM, New York (2015)

19. Fan, L., Jin, H.: A practical framework for privacy-preserving data analytics. In: Proceedings of the 24th International Conference on World Wide Web, WWW 2015, pp. 311–321. International World Wide Web Conferences Steering Committee, Republic and Canton of Geneva (2015)

20. Loukides, G., Liagouris, J., Gkoulalas-Divanis, A., Terrovitis, M.: Disassociation for electronic health record privacy. J. Biomed. Inf. **50**, 46–61 (2014)

21. Al-Hussaeni, K., Fung, B.C.M., Cheung, W.K.: Privacy-preserving trajectory stream publishing. Data Knowl. Eng. **94**, 89–109 (2014)

22. Kisilevich, S., Elovici, Y., Shapira, B., Rokach, L.: Protecting persons while protecting the people. In: Gal, C.S., Kantor, P.B., Lesk, M.E. (eds.) ISIPS 2008. LNCS, vol. 5661, pp. 63–81. Springer, Heidelberg (2009). https://doi.org/10.1007/978-3-642-10233-2_7

23. Liu, J., Wang, K.: Anonymizing transaction data by integrating suppression and generalization. In: Zaki, M.J., Yu, J.X., Ravindran, B., Pudi, V. (eds.) PAKDD 2010. LNCS (LNAI), vol. 6118, pp. 171–180. Springer, Heidelberg (2010). https://doi.org/10.1007/978-3-642-13657-3_20

24. Li, J., Liu, J., Baig, M.M., Wong, R.C.: Information based data anonymization for classification utility. Data Knowl. Eng. **70**(12), 1030–1045 (2011)

25. Kristen, L., DeWitt, D.J., Ramakrishnan, R.: Workload-aware anonymization techniques for large-scale datasets. ACM Trans. Database Syst. **33**(3), 17:1–17:47 (2008)
26. Lichman, M.: UCI Machine Learning Repository (2015). Accessed June 2017
27. Smith, T.C., Frank, E.: Introducing machine learning concepts with WEKA. In: Mathé, E., Davis, S. (eds.) Statistical Genomics: Methods and Protocols. MMB, vol. 1418, pp. 353–378. Springer, New York (2016). https://doi.org/10.1007/978-1-4939-3578-9_17
28. Farid, D.M., Zhang, L., Rahman, C.M., Hossain, M., Strachan, R.: Hybrid decision tree and naïve bayes classifiers for multi-class classification tasks. Expert Syst. Appl. **41**(4, Part 2), 1937–1946 (2014)
29. Fabian, P., Florian, K., Ronald, L., Klaus, A.K.: ARX - a comprehensive tool for anonymizing biomedical data. In: Proceedings of the AMIA 2014 Annual Symposium, Washington D.C., USA, pp. 984–993, November 2014
30. Fabian, P., Florian, K.: Contributors: ARX - Powerful Data Anonymization Tool (2017). http://arx.deidentifier.org/. Accessed April 2017
31. US Government: Health Insurance Portability and Accountability Act (HIPAA) (2016). http://www.hhs.gov/hipaa/. Accessed June 2017

Intelligent Systems Approaches in Information Extraction

Adapting Named Entity Types to New Ontologies in a Microblogging Environment

Elisabetta Fersini[1]([⊠]), Pikakshi Manchanda[2], Enza Messina[1], Debora Nozza[1], and Matteo Palmonari[1]

[1] University of Milano-Bicocca, Milan, Italy
{fersini,messina,debora.nozza,palmonari}@disco.unimib.it
[2] University of Exeter Business School, Exeter, UK
p.manchanda@exeter.ac.uk

Abstract. Given the potential rise in the amount of *user-generated content* on social network, research efforts towards Information Extraction have significantly increased, giving leeway to the emergence of numerous Named Entity Recognition (NER) systems. Based on varying application scenarios and/or requirements, different NER systems use different entity classification schemas/ontologies to classify the discovered entity mentions into entity types. Indeed, comparisons and integrations among NER systems become complex. The situation is further worsened due to varying granularity levels of such ontologies used to train the NER systems. This problem has been approached in the state of the art by developing a deterministic manual mapping between concepts belonging to different ontologies. In this paper, we discuss the limitations of these methods and, inspired by a transfer learning paradigm, we propose a novel approach named *LearningToAdapt* (L2A) to mitigate them. L2A learns to transfer an input probability distribution over a set of ontology types defined in a source domain, into a probability distribution over the types of a new ontology in a target domain. By using the inferred probability distribution, we are able to re-classify the entity mentions using the most probable type in the target domain. Experiments conducted with benchmark data show remarkable performance, suggesting L2A as a promising approach for domain adaptation of NER systems.

1 Introduction and Motivation

The extensive use of social media platforms on a daily basis generates a huge amount of raw data that needs to be processed to extract useful information and discover interesting insights. As a result, Information Extraction (IE) in the form of entities mentions, events and relations is of utmost significance for knowledge discovery from natural language text. Identifying **entity mentions**, which are text phrase(s) denoting real world objects, from unstructured texts and

© Springer International Publishing AG, part of Springer Nature 2018
M. Mouhoub et al. (Eds.): IEA/AIE 2018, LNAI 10868, pp. 783–795, 2018.
https://doi.org/10.1007/978-3-319-92058-0_76

classifying them according to a given domain classification hierarchy/**ontology**[1] is referred to as the task of Named Entity Recognition (NER). In order to identify and classify entity mentions, most of the state of the art models [1,2] leverage different kinds of contextual information available in the analysed text (e.g., the use of articles and/or prepositions before the entity mention), as well as in other corpora (e.g., the distribution of words across different classes of entity mentions represented in a knowledge base). The task of identifying and classifying entities in text has been recognized to be particularly difficult when performed on short and noisy texts like microblog posts. In addition to the intrinsic difficulty of entity classification, it is often the case that different NER systems use different ontologies for entity classification, and a system using one source ontology may need to be adapted to use a different target ontology according to application requirements. For example, in a domain with strong focus on *music*, one may want to use distinct classes for *music artists* and *bands*, while in another domain more centered on *movie*, one may want to distinguish between *persons* and *fictional characters*. In this scenario, performing a mapping from the types in the *source domain* to the types available in the *target domain* is not a trivial task.

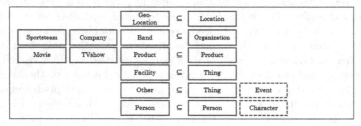

Ritter (Source) Ontology [1]   *Microposts (Target) Ontology [6]*

Fig. 1. Manual mapping between two ontologies

A first investigation aimed at dealing with this issue has been presented in [3], where a manual mapping between ontologies has been defined. Although this study represents a fundamental step towards the definition of cross-domain NER systems, some open problems need to be accurately addressed:

1. **Mention Misclassification:** Entity mentions are often misclassified by a NER system due to two main reasons: (a) the training set is composed of very few instances, and (b) the training set is characterized by an unbalanced distribution over the ontology types. For instance, if the entity mention "Black Sea" is erroneously recognized as *Band* in the *source domain* instead of *Geo-Location*, the deterministic manual mapping would map to the wrong entity type (*Organization*).

---

[1] In this paper we use the term *ontology* interchangeably with the term *classification schema*.

2. **Type Uncertainty:** There are also cases where the type of identified entity mention may be particularly uncertain, since a mention may have subtly different meanings in the real world. In this case the decision of determining its type becomes difficult.

While well-structured texts provide meaningful insights into the contextual usage of a mention, there can still be cases where it is difficult for an entity recognition system to correctly classify a mention. Consider, for instance, the entity mention "Starbucks" in a well-structured document snippet:

```
Millie Bobby Brown showed off her vocal talent in a silly clip
from the Starbucks drive-thru...
```

Here, the mention can either be classified as a *Geo-Location* (a particular Starbucks shop), or as *Organization* (the Starbucks company). The problem of correctly classifying such ambiguous mentions in short textual formats (such as microblog posts) tends to become even more challenging due to the concise nature and lack of context of microblog posts.

3. **Fork Mapping:** There are cases where mentions classified as member of one type in the source ontology could be cast into one of two or more different types in the target ontology, which we refer to as **fork mapping**. In our investigation, we have identified two cases (as seen in Fig. 1):

- when an entity of type *Person* in the source ontology should be mapped to *Person* or *Character* in the target ontology, and
- when an entity of type *Other* in the source ontology should be mapped to *Thing* or *Event* in the target ontology.

In this case, in order to re-classify entity mentions based on a deterministic manual mapping, an expert has to select one target type for each source type involved in a fork mapping.

In order to tackle the above mentioned issues we propose a novel approach called *LearningToAdapt* (L2A), which is intended to adapt a NER system trained on a source ontology to a given target domain. Although our approach has been experimented for microblog posts, it can be applied to a variety of different textual formats. The main motivation underlying the proposed solution is concerned with two main issues:

1. The amount of data available to accurately train a NER system in the target domain can be limited. A major assumption in many NER systems based on machine learning (e.g. Conditional Random Fields [4] and Labelled LDA [5]) is that the training and test data must be in the same feature space and have the same distribution. However, when a NER system needs to be adapted to a new domain ontology, this assumption may not hold.

2. The training of a NER system based on a new complex target ontology can be expensive in terms of time and labour. Many NER systems are grounded on complex ontologies to train a probabilistic model able to recognize and classify entity mentions in a given domain (e.g. in [1] a Labelled LDA is trained using Freebase as the underlying domain ontology, which is composed of more than

39 million real-world entities). Moreover, the dimension of knowledge bases increases rapidly thanks to the new upcoming entities evolving every day. In this case, it could be very expensive to re-train any NER model on either updated or brand new ontologies.

The rest of the paper is organized as follows: Sect. 2 presents the proposed solution, named *LearningToAdapt* (L2A), for addressing the problem of adapting a NER system from a source to a target domain. An overview of the datasets used and the analysis conducted on these datasets are presented in Sect. 3. As main contributions, this section shows three main findings: (1) L2A is able not only to adapt an existing NER system to a new target domain, but it also enables the correction of misclassified entities as well as entities involved in type uncertainty and fork mapping; (2) our approach is able to achieve remarkable accuracy on adaptation by considering only 10% of the data, confirming its ability to deal with scenarios where small number of training instances are available; (3) L2A outperforms not only the state of the art manual mapping approach, but also two additional baselines based on probabilistic sampling and Conditional Random Fields in terms of traditional performance measures and specific capabilities. To conclude, some related works are presented in Sect. 4, followed by some final remarks and future directions in Sect. 5.

2   The Proposed Approach

The problem of adapting the types of entity mentions from a source domain to the types in a target domain can be viewed as a machine learning problem. In particular, given a set of entity mentions identified by a NER model originally trained in a source domain, the main goal is to learn how to map the source type probability distribution to the target one. More precisely, let R_S be a NER model trained on a set $\Omega_S = \{s_1, s_2, ..., s_n\}$ of entity mentions annotated according to a source ontology O_S. Let $\Omega_T = \{t_1, t_2, ..., t_m\}$ be a set of entity mentions that needs to be automatically labelled according to a target ontology O_T, by using a NER model R_S previously trained on Ω_S. Then, the labelling of Ω_T using R_S can be viewed as a transfer learning problem. In particular, the main goal is to learn a target predictive function $f(\cdot)$ in Ω_T using some knowledge both in the source domain S and the target domain T. More formally, let $P(\Omega_T, O_S)$ be the distribution in the source domain used to label an entity mention $t_i \in \Omega_T$ with the most probable type $c_S^* \in O_S$ according to R_S. Let $c_T \in O_T$ be the type in the target domain that we want to discover. Now, the adaption of a source type c_S (of a given entity mention) to a target type c_T can be modeled as a learning problem aimed at seeking a function $\phi : P(\Omega_T, O_S) \to c_T$ over the hypothesis space Φ. In our case, it is convenient to represent ϕ as a function $f : P(\Omega_T, O_S) \times c_T \to \mathbb{R}$ such that:

$$g(P(t_i, c_S)) = \arg \max_{c_T \in O_T} f\left(P(t_i, c_S), c_T\right) \tag{1}$$

In order to tackle this problem, we need to create an input space representing each entity mention t_i that can be used for learning how to map the predicted source type $c_S \in O_S$ to the target type $c_T \in O_T$. As mentioned before, the input space corresponds to $P(\Omega_T, O_S)$, and in particular to the explicit distribution given by R_S for each entity mention. The output space denotes the most probable type $c_t \in O_T$. Using a model that is able to estimate a posterior distribution of c_T, we can therefore estimate the type distribution $P(\Omega_T, O_T)$ in the target domain. Figure 2 reports an example of the input and output space for L2A.

$P(\Omega_l, O_s)$ from R_s $\qquad\qquad\qquad\qquad\qquad g\big(P(\Omega_l, O_s)\big) = c_T \in O_T$

Entity Mention	Source Type	P(Facility)	P(Person)	P(Organization)	P(Band)	P(Movie)	P(TVshow)	Target Type
Paris B.O.	Facility	0.36	0.34	0.05	0.1	0.05	0	Location
Harry Potter	Person	0	0.5	0	0.2	0.1	0	Character
@EF	Organization	0	0.1	0.7	0.2	0	0	Organization
....		...	...	...	...	...	...	...

P(Location)	P(Character)	P(Person)	P(Organization)	P(Event)	P(Product)
0.8	0.05	0.05	0.1	0	0
0	0.6	0.2	0.1	0	0.1
0	0.4	0.5	0.1	0	0
...	...	...	...	...	...

$P(\Omega_l, O_T)$

Fig. 2. Example of input-output space in L2A

In order to solve this adaptation problem, it is necessary to determine the function f that is able to correctly label an entity mention $t_i \in \Omega_T$ according to the prediction $P(t_i, c_S)$ given by a NER model previously trained on Ω_S. To accomplish this task, f can be fitted with any machine learning algorithm.

3   Experiments

In this section, we evaluate the effectiveness of our approach by measuring the performance in terms of accuracy improvement with respect to a Conditional Random Fields trained over the target domain and two baseline adaptation approaches that exploit a deterministic manual mapping and a non-deterministic one between the source and the target domains.

3.1   Experimental Settings

To perform an experimental analysis of the proposed approach, we consider as **Ground Truth (GT)** two benchmark datasets of tweets made available for the NEEL Challenges for #Microposts2015 [6] and #Microposts2016 [7] Workshops. These ground truths are composed of 4016 and 8664 entity mentions. In order to identify entity mentions from these datasets, we use a state of the art NER system called **T-NER** [1]. T-NER is trained using an underlying source ontology O_S (known as Ritter Ontology) to finally derive a NER model R_S. The Ritter Ontology (O_S) is composed by several types: *Band, Company, Facility, Geo-Location, Movie, Other, Person, Product, Sportsteam, TVshow*.

Once the entity types are recognized by R_S and classified according to O_S, they need to be mapped to the entity types available in the target ontology (known as Microposts Ontology) O_T, i.e. *Character, Event, Location, Person, Product, Organization, Thing*.

To finally induce the L2A model, a *training set*, each for #Microposts2015 and #Microposts2016 has been **automatically** created by extracting only the mentions that perfectly match between the ones identified by T-NER and the ones in the Microposts Ground Truth datasets. This is needed because we should discard the mentions that T-NER have wrongly segmented and consider only the ones that permit to obtain a correct correspondence between mentions, probability distributions and target types. For each entity mention t_i *(T-NER)* given by T-NER and for each mention $t_j(GT)$ in the Ground Truth, a couple $<t_i, c_T>$ is added to the training set if and only if there is a perfect match between the entity mentions t_i *(T-NER)* and $t_j(GT)$, where c_T is the correct type for that mention in the target domain (made available from the Ground Truth). This automatic procedure for generation of training sets used as input by the L2A model is applicable and replicable on any labelled benchmark. As a result, the training sets for #Microposts2015 and #Microposts2016 are composed of 1660 and 3003 entity mentions, respectively.

In order to demonstrate the need of adaptation approaches in the context of limited number of data in the target domain, we report the results of the well-known Conditional Random Fields [4] model trained and tested over the target domain. Moreover, the proposed approach have been compared with three adaptation **Baseline** models, defined as:

- Baseline-Deterministic (**BL-D**): we consider the manual mapping between O_S and O_T shown in Fig. 1;
- Baseline-Probabilistic (**BL-P1**): we extended the previous baseline in order to deal with fork mapping in a non-deterministic way. In particular, for those mentions in O_S that can be classified in more than one type in O_T, we sample the target type according to the a-priori distribution of mapping in the training set (e.g. 30% of *Person* entity mentions in O_S are classified as *Character* and 70% as *Person* in O_T).
- Baseline-Probabilistic (**BL-P2**): since the manual mapping directly depends on the T-NER output, it will never be able to correct the target type of the mentions which have been incorrectly classified by T-NER. For this reason, an additional probabilistic baseline (BL-P2) has been introduced. For each mention, given the associated source type $c_S \in O_S$, we sample the target type c_T from the distribution $P(O_T|c_S \in O_S)$ estimated on the training set.

Regarding **L2A**, the input space used for training the models has been derived using the Ritter system [1] (T-NER). In particular, we used Labelled

LDA [5] in T-NER to derive $P(\Omega_T, O_S)$ for the subsequent L2A training phase. Concerning the experimental evaluation, a 10-folds cross validation has been used. To compare L2A with the baseline models, we consider several traditional performance measures, i.e. micro-averaged Precision and Recall, macro-averaged F-Measure and Strong Typed Mention Match (STMM)[2]. Concerning the models used to train L2A, i.e. Naïve Bayes (NB), Support Vector Machine (SVM), Decision Tree (DT), K-Nearest Neighbors (KNN), Bayesian Networks (BN), Multi Layer Perceptron (MLP) and Multinomial Logistic Regression (MLR), no parameter optimization has been performed since the aim of this work was to propose an extensive method that could work well in several problems[3].

3.2   Experimental Evaluation

In this section, we present some computational experiments to show the relevance of the proposed approach for the aforementioned datasets. First of all, the class-wise accuracy contribution for adapting a source type to a target is reported in Tables 1 and 2, where the accuracy contribution for a target type $c_T \in O_T$ represents the number of correctly labelled named entities, classified as c_T over the total number of instances of the ontology type c_T.

From the overall accuracy, it is easy to note that all the L2A configurations are able to achieve good adaptation performance in terms of global accuracy and significantly higher than the baseline models. Lower accuracy contributions by L2A can be observed for the entity types *Character* and *Thing*. This can be caused by the low number of training instances available for *Character* (1.27% in #Microposts2015 and 0.99% in #Microposts2016 dataset) and for *Thing* (2.35% in #Microposts2015 and 2.30% in #Microposts2016 dataset), do not allowing any algorithm to provide remarkable contributions to the total accuracy. As an intuitive consequence, CRF model, that is trained over the target domain, is able to better capture these classes and obtain a slightly performances improvement.

Analysing the adaptation results of L2A from a qualitative point of view, it is interesting to highlight that the model is able to correctly re-classify the target types of entity mentions that were wrongly assigned by T-NER system. For example, "iPhone" was classified as a *Company* by T-NER (which would lead to the type *Organization* using manual mapping), while L2A correctly re-classifies this entity mention as a *Product*. As another example, "Ron Weasley" (a character in Harry Potter) was misclassified as *Band* by T-NER, while L2A correctly re-classifies it as a *Character*. In the latter case, L2A was able to assign the correct type among the two possible types defined according to fork mapping. Although there are very few instances in the training sets for the target types *Character* and *Event* and the performance of our approach is not very high in terms of accuracy contribution, the proposed approach seems to be promising.

As expected, in Table 3 the deterministic baseline (BL-D) achieves good performance in terms of Precision, but low performance of Recall. In fact, BL-D is

---

[2] https://github.com/wikilinks/neleval.
[3] The experiment have been conducted using default parameters of models implemented in WEKA: www.cs.waikato.ac.nz/ml/weka/.

Table 1. Class-wise accuracy contribution for #Microposts2015 (%): baselines vs L2A.

Entity type	Baselines				L2A						
	BL-D	BL-P1	BL-P2	CRF	BN	NB	MLR	MLP	SVM	DT	KNN
Character	0.00	0.03	**0.04**	**0.04**	0.00	0.00	0.00	0.00	0.00	0.00	0.00
Event	0.00	0.49	0.12	1.04	**1.20**	**1.20**	0.00	0.00	0.00	0.06	0.54
Location	24.76	24.76	22.27	5.41	26.45	26.45	26.20	**27.71**	26.27	27.59	27.41
Organization	11.63	11.63	12.53	2.89	15.24	15.30	**17.71**	17.59	17.65	17.47	17.11
Person	27.29	26.23	21.59	19.16	25.30	25.30	**27.47**	27.05	26.99	26.99	26.75
Product	2.35	2.35	1.29	1.26	1.02	1.02	2.05	**2.71**	1.99	2.11	2.35
Thing	0.66	0.42	0.09	**0.71**	0.00	0.00	0.00	0.00	0.00	0.00	0.00
Overall	66.69	65.91	57.93	30.51	69.22	69.28	73.43	**75.06**	72.89	74.22	74.16

Table 2. Class-wise accuracy contribution for #Microposts2016 (%): Baselines vs L2A.

Entity type	Baselines				L2A						
	BL-D	BL-P1	BL-P2	CRF	BN	NB	MLR	MLP	SVM	DT	KNN
Character	0.00	0.02	0.02	**0.16**	0.00	0.00	0.00	0.00	0.00	0.03	0.00
Event	0.00	1.62	0.69	0.24	2.26	0.20	0.67	1.53	0.63	2.26	**2.30**
Location	29.77	29.77	28.44	1.62	32.93	**34.43**	32.13	33.97	31.90	33.63	33.83
Organization	8.72	8.72	8.88	2.36	11.92	11.29	13.22	11.92	**13.55**	13.32	13.39
Person	25.31	24.48	19.32	9.10	23.34	25.94	25.34	**26.04**	24.98	25.37	24.94
Product	2.00	2.00	1.05	**8.85**	1.47	0.13	1.80	1.67	1.96	1.90	1.96
Thing	0.50	0.24	0.09	**0.89**	0.10	0.13	0.00	0.03	0.00	0.13	0.30
Overall	66.30	66.86	58.48	23.23	72.03	72.13	73.16	75.16	73.03	76.66	**76.72**

accurate when labelling mentions thanks to the deterministic mapping, at the expenses of Recall. Also in this case, it can be easily noted that L2A (in all the learning settings) significantly outperforms the Baselines both for the #Microposts2015 and #Microposts2016 datasets. These results show that the proposed approach provides significant results with respect to every performance measure and obtains a balanced contribution of Precision and Recall. L2A, learning on distributions as input space, is able to highly improve the Recall. This is likely due to its ability to learn how to map the initial hypothesis given by T-NER to a new target type, adapting type mentions that where previously misclassified.

Moreover, we measured the capabilities of our approach with respect to the three issues stated in Sect. 1, i.e. mention misclassification, type uncertainty and fork mapping. To this purpose, we provide some results according to the following measures:

1. **Mention Misclassifications Correctly Mapped (MMCM)**: percentage of entity mentions that T-NER has wrongly classified and L2A is able to correctly map according to the target ontology. In our case, in the

#Micropost2015 and #Micropost2016 datasets, T-NER has wrongly classified 524 and 921 entity mentions respectively.

2. **Type Uncertainty Correctly Mapped (TUCM)**: percentage of uncertain entity mentions that L2A correctly maps in the target ontology. To compute this measure, we consider an *uncertain mention* as a mention t_i that has a low gap between probability distribution over different types.

   More formally, t_i is considered as *uncertain* if:

   $$P(t_i, c_{T_j}) - P(t_i, c_{T_k}) \leq \alpha \quad \forall j \neq k \qquad (2)$$

   where α is a parameter that has been experimentally determined as equal to 0.2. The number of mentions that have been recognized as *uncertain* in the datasets are 59 for #Micropost2015 and 109 for #Micropost2016.

3. **Fork Mapping Correctly Resolved (FMCR)**: percentage of mentions of a type defined as fork mapping (i.e. *Event* and *Character*) that have been correctly classified by L2A. The number of mentions that fall under this category are 50 for #Micropost2015 and 145 for #Micropost2016 datasets.

Table 3. Precision, Recall, F-Measure and STMM (%): Baselines *vs* L2A

		Baselines				L2A						
		BL-D	BL-P1	BL-P2	CRF	BN	NB	MLR	MLP	SVM	DT	KNN
#Microposts2015	Precision	0.73	0.73	0.58	0.48	**0.75**	**0.75**	0.69	0.70	0.69	0.71	0.71
	Recall	0.67	0.66	0.58	0.31	0.69	0.69	0.73	**0.75**	0.73	0.74	0.74
	F-Measure	0.38	0.40	0.32	0.27	0.38	0.39	0.38	0.40	0.38	0.42	**0.43**
	STMM	0.68	0.68	0.58	0.34	0.70	0.70	0.71	**0.73**	0.70	0.72	0.72
#Microposts2016	Precision	0.72	0.73	0.58	0.05	0.73	0.72	0.71	0.72	**0.72**	**0.75**	**0.75**
	Recall	0.66	0.60	0.53	0.23	0.72	0.72	0.73	0.75	0.73	**0.77**	**0.77**
	F-Measure	0.37	0.36	0.30	0.08	0.44	0.44	0.42	0.45	0.42	0.50	**0.51**
	STMM	0.68	0.62	0.65	0.09	0.72	0.72	0.71	0.73	0.71	**0.75**	**0.75**

The results are shown in Table 4, where L2A is compared only with the probabilistic baselines (BL-P1 and BL-P2). Since we are measuring the adaptation abilities, we do not report the performances of CRF and the deterministic baseline (BL-D) because the measures always amount to zero scores. While CRF is not performing any adaptation, BL-D mimics a fixed manual mapping a priori defined. This means that if an entity mention is incorrectly classified in the source ontology, it will always be mapped to the corresponding (incorrect) class in the target ontology. For instance, if the mention "Paris" is incorrectly classified by T-NER as *Movie* (whereas its correct type is *Location*), BL-D will map Paris to *Product*, thus providing no improvement for the MMCM capability. The same reasoning is applicable also for TUCM and FMCR capabilities.

The first consideration that can be derived from Table 4 is that almost all the learning models are performing considerably well for the considered measures. In particular, we can observe that the best performances of our approach are obtained (on average) when using **Decision Tree** as model for L2A. Secondly, it can also be observed that in most cases, the results on #Microposts2015 set are worse than the ones on #Microposts2016. This is due to the fact that the number of entity mentions available for training L2A in the #Microposts2016 are about twice as much in #Microposts2015 (as stated in Sect. 3.1). In other words, the higher the number of mentions that L2A can use to learn the correct mapping, the better would be our approach's capabilities.

Table 4. L2A capabilities (%)

Learning models	#Microposts2015			#Microposts2016		
	MMCM	TUCM	FMCR	MMCM	TUCM	FMCR
BN	22.71	27.12	**40.00**	27.14	38.53	46.90
DT	**36.07**	45.76	2.00	**40.50**	**56.88**	47.59
KNN	34.92	45.76	18.00	39.52	52.29	**47.59**
MLR	25.95	45.76	0.00	25.73	43.12	13.79
MLP	35.88	**57.63**	0.00	32.03	53.21	31.72
NB	22.90	27.12	**40.00**	33.98	44.04	4.14
SVM	25.57	42.37	0.00	24.00	31.19	0.00
BL-P1	2.67	15.25	17.42	4.67	14.68	33.92
BL-P2	19.03	27.15	5.44	18.17	24.37	14.63

Furthermore, in order to better understand the poor results of FMCR, we conducted a detailed investigation on the predictions obtained by each model. For #Microposts2015, the number of mentions involved in a fork mapping is 50 (21 for the entity type *Character* and 29 for the entity type *Event*). Given the low frequency of these entity types in the dataset (note that the entity types *Location*, *Person* and *Organization* are composed of more than 400 instances each), it is very difficult for a machine learning algorithm to learn how to recognize their presence. On the other hand, in #Microposts2016, there are 145 entities involved in a fork mapping: 30 entities are *Character* and 115 *Event*. The results in terms of FMCR are promising but, following the previous intuition, the increase is mainly due to correctly classified instances for the entity type *Event*, while only few instances of the type *Character* have been correctly identified. For #Microposts2016, BL-P1 is able (on average) to correctly map 79 out of 115 instances of type *Event*. However, it should be noted that BL-P1 wrongly maps 262 instances that correspond to 9% of the total number of instances.

In order to show the ability of L2A to work with a limited number of training instances, learning curves[4] have been estimated for all the models. A graphical representation in terms of overall Accuracy both for #Microposts2015 and #Microposts2016 has been reported in Fig. 3. An important observation is concerned with the ability of the proposed approach to learn mapping from a source

---

[4] The accuracy reported at 100% could be different from Tables 1 and 2 due to a random seed selection during 10-folds cross-validation.

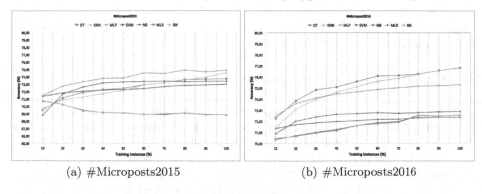

(a) #Microposts2015   (b) #Microposts2016

Fig. 3. Learning curves

to target domain, even when a small number of training instances are available. In fact, L2A is able to adapt an entity type with only 10% of the training data, ensuring an average accuracy of 71%. The only exception is represented by NB in #Microposts2015, where the high variance of the training data implies a model characterized by overfitting.

4   Related Work

Building upon [8], this is the first work aimed at addressing the problem of automatically adapting entity mention types given by a NER system, trained on a source ontology, to comply to a new domain. Manual mapping has been used to bridge the gap between NER systems using different ontologies [3]. When many-to-one mapping is used, which means that one source type is mapped to at most one target type, and when the source classification is reasonably accurate, manual mapping may achieve a good performance. However, in contexts such as microblogging platforms, where gross-grained ontologies are used for classification and pre-trained NER systems are affected by the dynamics of new upcoming entities, these mappings have several limitations (as discussed in Sect. 2).

Domain adaptation has been investigated in the context of NER for formal texts [9]. In [10], the authors presented a NER rule-based language which is further used for building domain-specific rule-based NER systems. A recent transfer learning based method has been proposed in [11] for adapting a NER system in medical context by using a linear chain CRF model which learns domain-specific patterns based on the correlations between source and target entity types.

Although these approaches deal with the problem of domain adaptation of NER systems, they do not tackle the problem in a microblogging context where the language used by the users can significantly vary and new entities can frequently emerge. Finally, marginally related to our investigation, we can find machine learning methods applied to Ontology Matching [12,13]. Textual annotation and re-classification statistics have been also proposed in [14] in order to semantically interpret class-to-class ontology mapping. However, these approaches have been based on collecting feedback on class-to-class mapping in order to improve ontology alignments.

5   Conclusions and Future Work

In this paper, we presented an approach to learn mapping between classes of different ontologies using an input probability distribution over source ontology types so as to infer a probability distribution over target ontology types. In the experimental evaluation, the proposed L2A model demonstrated good capabilities to deal with open problems for NER systems, mention misclassification, type uncertainty and fork mapping. The comparison of L2A with the state of the art approaches and probabilistic baselines proved the importance of having a specific method for dealing with the adaptation of ontologies. As future works, we aim at investigating an extended feature space exploiting Neural Network Language Models for including the distributional representations of each entity. We also plan to perform additional experimental evaluations including the proposed model in an information extraction pipeline.

References

1. Ritter, A., Clark, S., Etzioni, O.: Named entity recognition in tweets: an experimental study. In: Proceedings of the Conference on Empirical Methods in Natural Language Processing, pp. 1524–1534 (2011)
2. Liu, X., Zhang, S., Wei, F., Zhou, M.: Recognizing named entities in tweets. In: Proceedings of the 49th Annual Meeting of the Association for Computational Linguistics: Human Language Technologies, vol. 1, pp. 359–367 (2011)
3. Rizzo, G., Troncy, R.: NERD: a framework for unifying named entity recognition and disambiguation extraction tools. In: Proceedings of the 13th Conference of the European Chapter of the Association for Computational Linguistics, pp. 73–76 (2012)
4. Lafferty, J.D., McCallum, A., Pereira, F.C.N.: Conditional random fields: probabilistic models for segmenting and labeling sequence data. In: Proceedings of the 18th International Conference on Machine Learning, pp. 282–289 (2001)
5. Ramage, D., Hall, D., Nallapati, R., Manning, C.D.: Labeled LDA: a supervised topic model for credit attribution in multi-labeled corpora. In: Proceedings of the Conference on Empirical Methods in Natural Language Processing, pp. 248–256 (2009)
6. Rizzo, G., Cano, A.E., Pereira, B., Varga, A.: Making sense of microposts (#Microposts2015) named entity recognition and linking challenge. In: Proceedings of the 5th Workshop on Making Sense of Microposts Co-located with the 24th International World Wide Web Conference, pp. 44–53 (2015)
7. Rizzo, G., van Erp, M., Plu, J., Troncy, R.: Making sense of microposts (#Microposts2016) named entity recognition and linking challenge. In: Proceedings of the 6th Workshop on Making Sense of Microposts Co-located with the 25th International World Wide Web Conference, pp. 50–59 (2016)
8. Manchanda, P., Fersini, E., Palmonari, M., Nozza, D., Messina, E.: Towards adaptation of named entity classification. In: Proceedings of the Symposium on Applied Computing, pp. 155–157. ACM (2017)

9. Daumé III, H.: Frustratingly easy domain adaptation. In: Proceedings of the 45th Annual Meeting of the Association for Computational Linguistics, pp. 256–263 (2007)
10. Chiticariu, L., Krishnamurthy, R., Li, Y., Reiss, F., Vaithyanathan, S.: Domain adaptation of rule-based annotators for named-entity recognition tasks. In: Proceedings of the Conference on Empirical Methods in Natural Language Processing, pp. 1002–1012 (2010)
11. Qu, L., Ferraro, G., Zhou, L., Hou, W., Baldwin, T.: Named entity recognition for novel types by transfer learning. In: Proceedings of the Conference on Empirical Methods in Natural Language Processing, pp. 899–905 (2016)
12. Eckert, K., Meilicke, C., Stuckenschmidt, H.: Improving ontology matching using meta-level learning. In: Aroyo, L., et al. (eds.) ESWC 2009. LNCS, vol. 5554, pp. 158–172. Springer, Heidelberg (2009). https://doi.org/10.1007/978-3-642-02121-3_15
13. Shi, F., Li, J., Tang, J., Xie, G., Li, H.: Actively learning ontology matching via user interaction. In: Bernstein, A., Karger, D.R., Heath, T., Feigenbaum, L., Maynard, D., Motta, E., Thirunarayan, K. (eds.) ISWC 2009. LNCS, vol. 5823, pp. 585–600. Springer, Heidelberg (2009). https://doi.org/10.1007/978-3-642-04930-9_37
14. Atencia, M., Borgida, A., Euzenat, J., Ghidini, C., Serafini, L.: A formal semantics for weighted ontology mappings. In: Cudré-Mauroux, P., et al. (eds.) ISWC 2012. LNCS, vol. 7649, pp. 17–33. Springer, Heidelberg (2012). https://doi.org/10.1007/978-3-642-35176-1_2

A Rough Set Approach to Events Prediction in Multiple Time Series

Fatma Ezzahra Gmati[1], Salem Chakhar[2(✉)], Wided Lejouad Chaari[1], and Huijing Chen[2]

[1] COSMOS, National School of Computer Science, University of Manouba, Manouba, Tunisia
fatma.ezzahra.gmati@gmail.com, wided.chaari@ensi-uma.tn
[2] Portsmouth Business School and Centre for Operational Research and Logistics, University of Portsmouth, Portsmouth, UK
{salem.chakhar,huijing.chen1}@port.ac.uk

Abstract. This paper introduces and illustrates a rough-set based approach to event prediction in multiple time series. The proposed approach uses two different versions of rough set theory to predict events occurrences and intensities. First, classical Indiscernibility relation-based Rough Set Approach (IRSA) is used to predict event classes and occurrences. Then, the Dominance-based Rough Set Approach (DRSA) is employed to predict the intensity of events. This paper presents the fundamental of the proposed approach and the conceptual architecture of a framework implementing this approach.

Keywords: Event prediction · Multiple time series · Rough sets
Dominance-based Rough Set Approach

1 Introduction

Event prediction problem is encountered in different research and practical domains. There are several event prediction approaches that have been proposed in the literature. Among these approaches, we may identify the following ones, which are the oldest and also the most used: (i) dynamic systems modeling; (ii) event frequency analysis; (iii) classification based approaches; (iv) events' sequences identification based approaches; and (v) temporal pattern identification based approaches. These approaches are characterized by at least one of the following shortcomings: (1) consider univariate time series only; (2) ignore the temporal dimension; (3) leading to information loss through 'artificial' aggregation of time-varying data; (4) require the use of numerical data only and fail to consider qualitative ones; and (5) ignore the preference that may be associated with the considered variables.

In this paper, a special attention is given to temporal pattern identification based approaches. In this type of approaches, events are predicted based on

---

The original version of this chapter was revised: The middle name of the third author was corrected. The erratum to this chapter is available at https://doi.org/10.1007/978-3-319-92058-0_87

© Springer International Publishing AG, part of Springer Nature 2018
M. Mouhoub et al. (Eds.): IEA/AIE 2018, LNAI 10868, pp. 796–807, 2018.
https://doi.org/10.1007/978-3-319-92058-0_77

some characterizing patterns that precede the occurrences of events. This contrasts with the events' sequences identification based approaches where only the sequences of preceding events are considered. The temporal pattern identification approaches have been applied in several event prediction problems such as flooding [2,4], earthquakes [11], financial events [16] and clinical events [1]. However, existing temporal pattern identification based approaches cannot address all the shortcomings mentioned earlier. For instance, the work of [15] is restricted to univariate time series, while those of [1,12] consider a special type of multiple time series data.

This paper introduces a rough-set based approach to event prediction in multiple time series. This approach adopts a temporal pattern identification strategy and uses two different versions of rough set theory to predict events occurrences and intensities: the event classes and occurrences are predicted based on classical Indiscernibility relation-based Rough Set Approach (IRSA) while the Dominance-based Rough Set Approach (DRSA) is employed to predict the intensity of events. This paper focuses on the theoretical and conceptual aspects of the proposed approach. The application and validation of this approach using real-world data is under progress.

The rest of the paper is organized as follows. Section 2 presents the background on rough set theory. Section 3 introduces the proposed approach. Section 4 provides a framework implementing this approach. Section 5 concludes the paper.

2 Rough Set Theory

2.1 Indiscernibility Relation-Based Rough Set Approach

The Indiscernibility relation-based Rough Set Approach (IRSA) [13, 14] uses equivalence relations to group elements with similar attributes values into indiscernibility classes, and any rough set is characterized by a pair of crisp sets called the lower and the upper approximations. The lower approximation of a rough set contains all the elements that surely belong to the set of interest, where the upper approximation contains all the elements that probably belong to the set of interest.

Let U be a non-empty set of objects (the universe) and D be a non-empty, finite set of attributes such that $q : U \rightarrow V_q$, where V_q is the domain of attribute $q \in D$. With any subset $K \subseteq D$ there is an associated equivalence relation, called K-indiscernibility relation $IND(K)$ such that:

$$IND(K) = \{(x, y) \in U^2 | q(x) = q(y), \forall q \in K\}$$

The relation $IND(K)$ is partitioning U into a set of equivalence classes which is denoted by $U/IND(K)$ or simply U/K. The equivalence classes induced by relation $IND(K)$ are denoted $[x]_K$. Shortly, $[x]_K$ is the equivalence class containing x. In IRSA, any subset $M \subseteq U$ is defined in terms of the elementary sets (equivalence classes) of the partition U/K by lower and upper approximations as follows:

- $K_*(M) = \{x \in U | [x]_K \subseteq M\}$.
- $K^*(M) = \{x \in U | ([x]_K \cap M) \neq \emptyset\}$

The sets $K_*(M)$ and $K^*(M)$ (or simply M_* and M^*) are called the lower and the upper approximations of M, respectively.

The rough approximations obey the following basic law [14]: $M_* \subseteq M \subseteq M^*$. The difference between the upper and lower approximations is called the boundary of M and is denoted by $Bn_K(M) = M^* - M_*$. If $Bn_K(M) = \emptyset$ then M is crisp (exact) set, otherwise M is rough (inexact) set. Each element $x \in U$ is classified with respect to M as *surely* inside M iff $x \in M_*$ or '*probably*' inside M, iff $x \in M^*$. Otherwise x is surely outside M.

2.2   Dominance Based Rough Sets Approach

The Dominance-based Rough Set Approach (DRSA) [6,7] is an extension of IRSA to multicriteria analysis. The working mechanism of the DRSA is a typical machine learning approach: it uses a subset of data (learning set) to deduce relevant insights that can be used to assess new and unseen datasets (see Fig. 1). In this respect, the DRSA is categorized by some authors as a 'preference learning' method because it is used to build a preference model based on a sample of past decisions, via preference representation in terms of several if-then rules, for further prescriptive decision purposes.

Fig. 1. Working mechanism of the DRSA

The information regarding the *decision objects* is often structured in a 4-tuple *information table* $\mathbf{S} = \langle U, Q, V, f \rangle$, where U is a non-empty finite set of objects and Q is a non-empty finite set of attributes such that $q : U \to V_q$ for every $q \in Q$. The V_q is the domain of attribute q, $V = \bigcap_{q \in Q} V_q$, and $f : U \times Q \to V$ is the *information function* defined such that $f(x, q) \in V_q$ for each attribute q and object $x \in U$. The set Q is often divided into a sub-set $C \neq \emptyset$ of *condition attributes* and a sub-set $D \neq \emptyset$ of *decision attributes*, such that $C \cup D = Q$ and $C \cap D = \emptyset$. In this case, $\mathbf{S}$ is called a *decision table*.

In multicriteria decision making, the domains of the condition attributes are supposed to be ordered according to a decreasing or increasing preference. Such attributes are called *criteria*. The proponents of DRSA assume that the preference is increasing with $f(\cdot, q)$ for every $q \in C$. They also assume that the set of decision attributes $D = \{E\}$ is a singleton. The unique decision attribute E makes a partition of U into a finite number of preference-ordered decision classes $\mathbf{Cl} = \{Cl_t, t \in L\}$, $L = \{1, \cdots, n\}$, such that each $x \in U$ belongs to one and only one class.

In DRSA the represented knowledge is a collection of *upward unions* $Cl_t^{\geq}$ and *downward unions* $Cl_t^{\leq}$ of classes defined as follows:

$$Cl_t^{\geq} = \bigcup_{s \geq t} Cl_s, Cl_t^{\leq} = \bigcup_{s \leq t} Cl_s.$$

The assertion "$x \in Cl_t^{\geq}$" means that "x belongs to at least class Cl_t" while assertion "$x \in Cl_t^{\leq}$" means that "x belongs to at most class Cl_t". The basic idea of DRSA is to replace the indiscernibility relation used in the IRSA with a dominance relation. Let $P \subseteq C$ be a subset of condition criteria. The *dominance relation* Δ_P associated with P is defined for each pair of objects x and y as follows:

$$x \Delta_P y \Leftrightarrow f(x,q) \succeq f(y,q), \forall q \in P.$$

In the definition above, the symbol "$\succeq$" should be replaced with "$\preceq$" for criteria which are ordered according to decreasing preferences. To each object $x \in U$, we associate two sets: (i) the *P-dominating set* $\Delta_P^+(x) = \{y \in U : y \Delta_P x\}$ containing the objects that dominate x, and (ii) the *P-dominated set* $\Delta_P^-(x) = \{y \in U : x \Delta_P y\}$ containing the objects dominated by x.

Then, the *P*-lower and *P*-upper approximations of $Cl_t^{\geq}$ with respect to P are defined as follows:

- $\underline{P}(Cl_t^{\geq}) = \{x \in U : \Delta_P^+(x) \subseteq Cl_t^{\geq}\}$,
- $\bar{P}(Cl_t^{\geq}) = \{x \in U : \Delta_P^-(x) \cap Cl_t^{\geq} \neq \emptyset\}$.

Analogously, the *P*-lower and *P*-upper approximations of $Cl_t^{\leq}$ with respect to P are defined as follows:

- $\underline{P}(Cl_t^{\leq}) = \{x \in U : \Delta_P^-(x) \subseteq Cl_t^{\leq}\}$,
- $\bar{P}(Cl_t^{\leq}) = \{x \in U : \Delta_P^+(x) \cap Cl_t^{\leq} \neq \emptyset\}$.

The lower approximations group the objects which certainly belong to class unions $Cl_t^{\geq}$ (resp. $Cl_t^{\leq}$). The upper approximations group the objects which could belong to $Cl_t^{\geq}$ (resp. $Cl_t^{\leq}$).

The *P*-boundaries of $Cl_t^{\geq}$ and $Cl_t^{\leq}$ are defined as follows:

- $Bn_P(Cl_t^{\geq}) = \bar{P}(Cl_t^{\geq}) - \underline{P}(Cl_t^{\geq})$,
- $Bn_P(Cl_t^{\leq}) = \bar{P}(Cl_t^{\leq}) - \underline{P}(Cl_t^{\leq})$.

The boundaries group objects that can neither be ruled in nor out as members of class Cl_t.

The *quality of approximation* of a partition $\mathbf{Cl}$ by means of a set of criteria P is defined as the ratio of all *P*-correctly classified objects to all objects in the system. The accuracy of the rough-set representation of unions of classes is computed as the ratio between the number of objects in the lower approximation and the number of objects in the upper approximation.

The decision attribute induces a partition of U in a way that is independent of the criteria. Hence, a decision table may be seen as a set of 'if–then' decision rules. The condition part specifies the values assumed by one or more criteria, and the decision part specifies an assignment to one or more decision classes. Three types of decision rules may be considered: (i) certain rules generated from the lower approximations of unions of classes, (ii) possible rules generated from the upper approximations of unions of classes, and (iii) approximate rules generated from the boundary regions. Only certain decision rules are considered here. The general structures of this kind of decision rules are as follows:

IF *condition(s)*, THEN *At Most Cl_t*
IF *condition(s)*, THEN *At Least Cl_t*

The decision part of a certain rule takes the form of an assignment to at most class unions or at least class unions.

3   Event Prediction Approach

The proposed approach is composed of three phases: (i) preprocessing, (ii) analysis and inference of prediction rules, and (iii) prediction of events and their intensities. The first phase of the approach concerns the preprocessing of individual time series data in order to transform them into a format adapted to the extraction of prediction rules in the second phase. The main output of the first is an information table. The second phase concerns the inference of decision rules for predicting events and their intensities. The third phase is devoted to events prediction.

3.1   Phase 1: Preprocessing

In multiple time series, complex events result from a combination of different and related individual patterns. Each of these patterns is governed by one (or more) variables. A comprehensive analysis of complex events requires the definition of a common temporal framework. Three steps are required: (i) labeling and segmentation of individual time series; (ii) construction of a common temporal axis; and (iii) construction of the information table.

Labeling and Segmentation of Individual Time Series. First, each time series will be segmented into different elementary 'trendings' and labeled accordingly. Each elementary trending models a single type of variability such as linear increase, linear decrease, stability, etc. Figure 2 presents some elementary trendings. The identification of elementary trendings will rely on existing time series labeling and segmentation algorithms. Figure 3 illustrates graphically the segmentation of individual time series into a collection of elementary 'trendings'. The segmentation operation should be applied with two important constraints: all the temporal axis is covered and the absence of 'holes' between elementary 'trendings'.

Time series labeling techniques assign labels to the different segments of a time series. It can be handled using different classical machine learning algorithms such as c-Means and K-Nearest Neighborhood (KNN) (see e.g. [9]). Time series segmentation is a method of time series analysis in which an input time series is divided into a sequence of discrete segments in order to reveal the underlying properties of its source. Examples of time series segmentation techniques are change-point detection methods including sliding windows, bottom-up, and top-down methods [10], and probabilistic methods based on hidden Markov models [5].

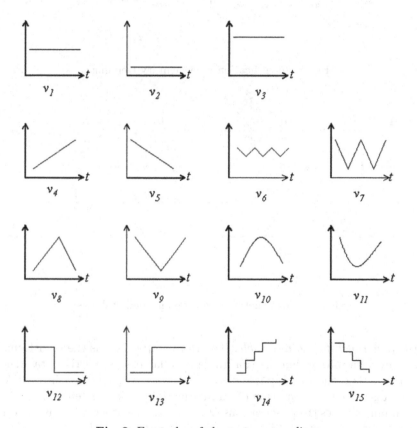

Fig. 2. Examples of elementary trendings

Construction of a Common Temporal Axis. The next step is the construction of a common temporal axis. The common temporal axis is constructed by intersecting the temporal axes associated with the segmented individual times series. The obtained axis is then divided into a series of ordered time segments such that in each time segment, each variable will have only one trending. Figure 4 illustrates graphically the construction of a common temporal axis T.

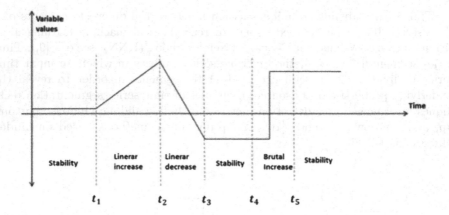

Fig. 3. Identification of elementary trendings

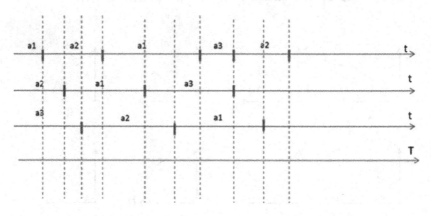

Fig. 4. Construction of a common temporal axis

Construction of Information Table. The third step concerns the transformation of the raw data into an information table. The latter is a matrix data structure that summarizes the raw input data and permits its analysis using IRSA and DRSA. A generic representation of an information table is given in Table 1. The first column specifies the observations $O_i, \cdots, O_p$. The other columns correspond to a set of pairs of the form (T_j, A_k) where T_j $(j = 1, \cdots, N; k = 1, \cdots, M)$ is the jth time period in the common time axis T and A_k is the kth variable (condition attribute); N and M are the number of time periods in T and the number of variables, respectively. The entries of the information table are elementary trendings.

3.2 Phase 2: Inference of Prediction Rules

The objective of the second phase is to infer a collection of decision rules that will be used later (in phase 3) to design the prediction algorithms. There are

Table 1. Generic representation of an information table

Observation	(T_1, V_1)	$\cdots$	(T_1, V_M)	$\cdots$	(T_N, V_1)	$\cdots$	(T_N, V_M)
O_1		$\cdots$		$\cdots$		$\cdots$	
$\cdots$		$\cdots$		$\cdots$		$\cdots$	
$\cdots$		$\cdots$		$\cdots$		$\cdots$	
O_p		$\cdots$		$\cdots$		$\cdots$	

two types of prediction rules that we need to infer. The first type permits to predict the occurrence of events while the second type is devoted to predict the intensity of each event. The prediction of occurrence of events relies on IRSA combined with similarity measures, while the prediction of events intensity relies on DRSA.

Decision Rules for Predicting Events Occurrence. The inference of events' occurrence rules will rely on the IRSA combined with different similarity measures. In IRSA data analysis starts from a data table called a decision table, which columns are labelled by attributes, rows by objects of interest and entries of the table are attribute values. Attributes of the decision table are divided into two disjoint groups called condition and decision attributes, respectively. Each row of a decision table induces a decision rule, which specifies decision if some conditions are satisfied. If a decision rule uniquely determines decision in terms of conditions the decision rule is certain. Otherwise the decision rule is uncertain. Decision rules are closely connected with approximations. Roughly speaking, certain decision rules describe lower approximation of decisions in terms of conditions, whereas uncertain decision rules refer to the boundary region of decisions. The definition of the lower and upper approximations relies on an equivalence relation, called indiscernibility relation, which ensures that objects having the same descriptions are assigned to the same equivalence class. The indiscernibility relation is very restrictive and thus several extension of this relation have been proposed, most of them rely on a similarity relation.

With respect to multiple time series data analysis, decision objects correspond to observations, condition attributes are the considered decision variables and the decision attributes are the event types. One strong difference between the input data used in the IRSA and the one we needed in multiple time series data analysis, concerns the presence of time-varying attributes. The generic structure of the decision table required to be used in multiple time series data analysis is given in Table 2. It consists of the information table obtained at the end of phase 1 with an additional column (last column in Table 2) corresponding to the types of events. This decision table is different to the conventional one used in IRSA. Indeed, in multiple time series data analysis we need to explicitly take into account the temporal dimension with respect to the values of attributes. Accordingly, an extended version of IRSA is needed.

Table 2. Generic representation of decision table

Observation	(T_1, V_1)	$\cdots$	(T_1, V_M)	$\cdots$	(T_N, V_1)	$\cdots$	(T_N, V_M)	(Event, Time)
O_1		$\cdots$		$\cdots$		$\cdots$	$\cdots$	(e_x, t_x)
$\cdots$		$\cdots$		$\cdots$		$\cdots$	$\cdots$	
$\cdots$		$\cdots$		$\cdots$		$\cdots$	$\cdots$	
O_p		$\cdots$		$\cdots$		$\cdots$	$\cdots$	(e_y, t_y)

The extended version of IRSA requires first the definition of a new similarity measure permitting to evaluate the similarity between two multidimensional time series. The similarity relation is a function from $W \times W$ to the range $[0, 1]$ where W is the set of rows in the decision table. The new similarity relation takes as input two vectors W_1 and W_2 of the form

$$((T_1, V_1), \cdots, (T_1, V_M), \cdots, (T_N, V_1), \cdots, (T_N, V_M))$$

and provides a value in $[0, 1]$ indicating the similarity relationship between the vectors W_1 and W_2. This new temporal similarity relation will be used to define the rough approximations of the events in the decision table.

The extended version of IRSA requires also the design of new rule inference algorithms. The inference algorithm should in fact be able to explicitly take into account the temporal dimension that relates the condition attributes.

Decision Rules for Predicting Events Intensity. The inference of events' intensities rules will rely on DRSA. The DRSA is an extension of IRSA to multicriteria classification and looks to assign a set of objects described by a set of criteria (attributes with preference-ordered domains) to some pre-defined decision classes or categories, such that each object is assigned to exactly one class. The decision table used as input to DRSA is similar to the once used in IRSA but the condition attributes and the decision attribute are assumed to be preference-ordered. In this research project, the decision classes correspond to intensities of events as shown in Table 3.

Table 3. Generic representation of decision table for events intensity prediction

Observation	(T_1, V_1)	$\cdots$	(T_1, V_M)	$\cdots$	(T_N, V_1)	$\cdots$	(T_N, V_M)	(Event, Intensity, Time)
O_1		$\cdots$		$\cdots$		$\cdots$	$\cdots$	(e_x, i_x, t_x)
$\cdots$		$\cdots$		$\cdots$		$\cdots$	$\cdots$	
$\cdots$		$\cdots$		$\cdots$		$\cdots$	$\cdots$	
O_p		$\cdots$		$\cdots$		$\cdots$	$\cdots$	(e_y, x, t_y)

The dominance relation used in the DRSA is not appropriate for the analysis of multiple times series data. Thus, we need first to extend the classical dominance relation into a new relation that we will call *temporal dominance* relation. This relation permits to specify the preference relations between vectors of the form

$$((T_1, V_1), \cdots, (T_1, V_M), \cdots, (T_N, V_1), \cdots, (T_N, V_M))$$

This vector is similar to the one given above but the definition of the temporal relation requires that each attribute should be associated with a preference direction, which may be gain or cost.

The new temporal domain relation will be used to design a new method as a temporal extension of the DRSA. The design of the TDRSA requires the definition of new concepts of temporal lower approximations and temporal upper approximations. Furthermore, there will be a need to design new decision rules inference algorithms. The inferred decision rules will relate temporal patterns to events and their intensities.

3.3   Phase 3: Prediction of Events and Their Intensities

The prediction of future events and their intensities using future trendings and estimated data requires the design of new prediction algorithms. These algorithms take the form of rough classifiers; each is defined in terms of a collection of decision rules. The basic hypothesis on which the prediction algorithm will rely is stated as follows: "similar behaviour (i.e. temporal pattern) will most probably lead to the same event". The idea is to scan future times series in order to identify future potential temporal patterns that are similar to the temporal patterns that have preceded (and/or followed) by past events.

A critical question that should be considered at this level concerns the time window that should be considered in order to identify the patterns leading to different events. This window should be defined in such a way that the events can be fully differentiated between each other. The idea that will be investigated in this research project consists in starting by using the smallest time window and then progressively extend this window until all the events have been fully predicted.

4   Framework

A multiple times series analysis framework supporting the different conceptual, theoretical and algorithmic solutions that been indicted in the previous section is being designed and implemented. The conceptual architecture of this framework is given in Fig. 5. As shown in this figure, the framework is composed of two main layers. The first layer is devoted to predict event occurrences while the second layer is aimed to predict the intensity of events. An additional layer of overall validation is added to enhance the framework.

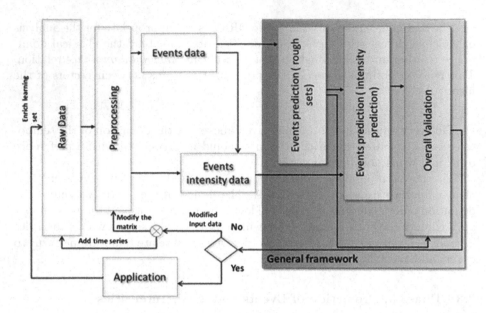

Fig. 5. Architecture of the proposed framework

5 Conclusion

We presented the first results of a rough-set based approach to event prediction in multiple time series. This approach adopts a temporal pattern identification strategy and uses two different and extended versions IRSA and DRSA, which are rough set based approaches. The major advantage of using IRSA and DRSA relies on the fact that they are able to deal with almost any kind of data (symbolic, binary, ordinal and numerical) and their ability to handle missing data.

The application and validation of the proposed approach using real-world data is under progress. The computational behavior and performance of the different algorithms with very large datasets will also be investigated. Additionally, the proposed approach can easily be enhanced by using recent extensions of IRSA and DRSA such as the Variable Consistency Dominance-based Rough Set Approach (VC-DRSA) [8] that enables relaxation of the conditions for assigning decision objects to the lower approximations by accepting a limited proportion of negative examples, which is particularly useful for large decision tables and the Stochastic DRSA [3] relaxes the rough approximations in the DRSA by allowing inconsistencies to some degree.

References

1. Batal, I., Cooper, G.F., Fradkin, D., Harrison, J., Moerchen, F., Hauskrecht, M.: An efficient pattern mining approach for event detection in multivariate temporal data. Knowl. Inf. Syst. **46**, 115–150 (2015)
2. Damle, C., Yalcin, A.: Flood prediction using time series data mining. J. Hydrol. **333**, 305–316 (2006)
3. Dembczyński, K., Greco, S., Kotłowski, W., Słowiński, R.: Statistical model for rough set approach to multicriteria classification. In: Kok, J.N., Koronacki, J., de Mantaras, R.L., Matwin, S., Mladenič, D., Skowron, A. (eds.) PKDD 2007. LNCS (LNAI), vol. 4702, pp. 164–175. Springer, Heidelberg (2007). https://doi.org/10.1007/978-3-540-74976-9_18
4. Erechtchoukova, M.G., Khaiter, P.A., Saffarpour, S.: Short-term predictions of hydrological events on an urbanized watershed using supervised classification. Water Resour. Manage. **30**, 4329–4343 (2016)
5. Fox, E.B., Sudderth, E.B., Jordan, M.I., Willsky, A.S.: An HDP-HMM for systems with state persistence. In: Proceedings of the 25th International Conference on Machine Learning, pp. 312–319. ACM, New York (2008)
6. Greco, S., Matarazzo, B., Slowiński, R.: The use of rough sets and fuzzy sets in MCDM. In: Gal, T., Hanne, T., Stewart, T. (eds.) Advances in Multiple Criteria Decision Making, pp. 14.1–14.59. Kluwer Academic Publishers, Dordrecht, Boston (1999)
7. Greco, S., Matarazzo, B., Slowiński, R.: Rough sets theory for multicriteria decision analysis. Euro. J. Oper. Res. **129**(1), 1 47 (2001)
8. Greco, S., Matarazzo, B., Slowinski, R., Stefanowski, J.: Variable consistency model of dominance-based rough sets approach. In: Ziarko, W., Yao, Y. (eds.) RSCTC 2000. LNCS (LNAI), vol. 2005, pp. 170–181. Springer, Heidelberg (2001). https://doi.org/10.1007/3-540-45554-X_20
9. Harguess, J., Aggarwal, J.K.: Semantic labeling of track events using time series segmentation and shape analysis. In: The 16th IEEE International Conference on Image Processing (ICIP 2009), Cairo, Egypt, pp. 4317–4320. IEEE (2009)
10. Keogh, E., Chu, S., Hart, D., Pazzani, M.: Segmenting time series: a survey and novel approach. In: Machine Perception and Artificial Intelligence, vol. 57, pp. 1 21. World Scientific (2011)
11. Morales-Esteban, A., Martinez-Alvarez, F., Troncoso, A., Justo, J.L., Rubio-Escudero, C.: Pattern recognition to forecast seismic time series. Expert Syst. Appl. **37**, 8333–8342 (2010)
12. Mörchen, F., Ultsch, A.: Discovering temporal knowledge in multivariate time series. In: Weihs, C., Gaul, W. (eds.) Classification – the Ubiquitous Challenge. Studies in Classification, Data Analysis, and Knowledge Organization, pp. 272–279. Springer, Heidelberg (2005). https://doi.org/10.1007/3-540-28084-7_30
13. Pawlak, Z.: Rough sets. Int. J. Inf. Comput. Sci. **11**, 341–356 (1982)
14. Pawlak, Z.: Rough Set: Theoretical Aspects of Reasoning about Data. Kluwer Academic Publishers, Dordrecht (1991)
15. Povinelli, J.R., Feng, X.: A new temporal pattern identification method for characterization and prediction of complex time series events. IEEE Trans. Knowl. Data Eng. **15**(2), 339–352 (2003)
16. Povinelli, R.J.: Time Series Data Mining: Identifying Temporal Patterns for Characterization and Prediction of Time Series Events. Ph.D. thesis, Marquette University, Milwaukee, WI (1999)

Efficient Versus Accurate Algorithms for Computing a Semantic Logic-Based Similarity Measure

Fatma Ezzahra Gmati[1], Salem Chakhar[2(✉)], Nadia Yacoubi Ayadi[3],
Afef Bahri[4], and Mark Xu[2]

[1] COSMOS, National School of Computer Science, University of Manouba,
Manouba, Tunisia
fatma.ezzahra.gmati@gmail.com
[2] Portsmouth Business School and Centre for Operational Research and Logistics,
University of Portsmouth, Portsmouth, UK
{salem.chakhar,mark.xu}@port.ac.uk
[3] RIADI Research Laboratory, National School of Computer Sciences,
University of Manouba, Manouba, Tunisia
nadia.yacoubi.ayadi@gmail.com
[4] MIRACL Laboratory, High School of Computing and Multimedia,
University of Sfax, Sfax, Tunisia
afef.bahri@gmail.com

Abstract. There are three types of Web services matchmakers: logic-based, non logic-based, and hybrid. Logic-based matchmakers employ the semantics of the Web services. Non-logic based matchmakers employ other approaches such as syntactic and structural matching. Hybrid matchmakers combine both approaches. This paper presents and compares two algorithms for computing a semantic logic-based similarity measure in the perspective of Web service matching. The first algorithm offers an efficient solution, while the second algorithm proposes a more accurate result. Both algorithms are evaluated using the SME2 tool. Performance evaluation shows that efficient algorithm reduces substantially the computing time while the accurate algorithm ameliorates considerably the precision of the matching process.

Keywords: Web service · Matchmaking · Similarity measure
Degree of match · Performance

1 Introduction

Web service matchmaking consists in the computation of the similarity between two Web services. It is an important task in Web service discovery and Web service composition. The matchmaking process is generally based on the Web service description; several standards define this description such as WSDL, OWL-S, SAWSDL, the two later include semantics. Many matchmakers that support Web semantics have been proposed in the literature, including [1,3,4,7,9,10,12].

© Springer International Publishing AG, part of Springer Nature 2018
M. Mouhoub et al. (Eds.): IEA/AIE 2018, LNAI 10868, pp. 808–820, 2018.
https://doi.org/10.1007/978-3-319-92058-0_78

Three types of Web services matchmakers can be distinguished [2,11,12]: (i) logic-based matchmakers that employ the semantics of the Web services and set logic-rules and constraints in order to perform the matching; (ii) non-logic based matchmakers that rely on syntactic and structural matching techniques; and (iii) hybrid matchmakers that combine both of the above mentioned matching approaches. Logic-based techniques did not receive much attention and the authors in [9] qualify them as imprecise. However, if the logic-based techniques is considered as a component of a hybrid matchmaker, improving their performances would improve the overall performance of the matchmaker.

To the best knowledge of the authors, the first logic based matchmaker has been proposed in [10]. The authors in [1] improve [10]'s proposal by using bipartite graphs. In this paper, two logic-based algorithms for computing the similarity measure between two Web services are proposed. These algorithms can be seen as an extension of the one proposed in [10]. Both algorithms have been evaluated using the SME2, which is an open source tool for testing different semantic matchmakers. The first algorithm slightly affects the precision of [1]'s algorithm but reduces substantially its computing time. The second algorithm enriches the semantic distance values used in [1] and ameliorates considerably its precision.

The rest of this paper is organized as follows. Section 2 introduces basic definitions and shows how the similarity measure is computed. Sections 3 and 4 present the efficient and accurate algorithms, respectively. Section 5 studies the computational complexity of the algorithms and Sect. 6 evaluates and compares their performances. Section 7 ends the paper.

2   Similarity Measure

2.1   Basic Definitions

A semantic match between two entities frequently involves a *similarity measure*. The similarity measure quantifies the semantic distance between the two entities participating in the match. A similarity measure is defined as follows.

Definition 1 (Similarity Measure). *The similarity measure, μ, of two service attributes is a mapping that measures the semantic distance between the conceptual annotations associated with the service attributes. Mathematically, $\mu : A \times A \rightarrow V$, where A is the set of all possible attributes and V the set of possible semantic distance measures.*

There are different possible definition of set V. In [5], for instance, the mapping between two conceptual annotations may take one of the following values: Exact, Plugin, Subsumption, Container, Part-of and Disjoint.

A preferential total order may now be established on the above mentioned similarity maps.

Definition 2 (Similarity Measure Preference). *Let V be the set of all possible semantic distance values such that $V = \{v_1, v_2, \cdots, v_n\}$. Preference amongst the similarity measures is governed by the following strict order: $v_1 \succ v_2 \succ \cdots \succ v_n$, where $a \succ b$ means that a is preferred over b.*

Definition 3 (Degree of Match). *The degree of match is a function that defines a semantic distance value between two conceptual annotations. Mathematically, $\delta : CA_1 \times CA_2 \to V$, where CA_1 denotes the first conceptual annotation and CA_2 denotes the second conceptual annotation and V is the set of all possible semantic distance values.*

This generic definition of similarity measure extends the one proposed by [5]. Other matchmaking frameworks (e.g. [1,10,13]) utilize an idea similar to μ, but label it differently. The main difference between the above-cited works concerns the way the degree of match is computed. In Sects. 3 and 4, two algorithms for computing the similarity measure are provided. These algorithms improve the one proposed by [1], which is presented in the rest of this section.

2.2 Computing the Similarity Measure

The computing of the similarity measure over two attributes is modeled by [1] as a *bipartite graph matching*. Let first introduce some concepts.

Definition 4 (Bipartite Graph). *A graph $G = (V_0 + V_1, E)$ with disjoint vertex sets V_0 and V_1 and edge set E is called bipartite if every edge connects a vertex of V_0 with a vertex of V_1 and there are no edge in E with both endpoints are in V_0 or in V_1.*

Definition 5 (Matching in a Bipartite Graph). *Let $G = (V, E)$ be a bipartite graph. A matching M of G is a subgraph $G' = (V, E')$, $E' \subseteq E$, such that no two edges $e_1, e_2 \in E'$ share the same vertex. A vertex v is matched if it is incident to an edge in the matching M.*

Let S^R be a service request and S^A be a service advertisement. The matching between $S^R.A_i$ and $S^A.A_j$ (i.e. $\mu(S^R.A_i, S^A.A_j)$) is computed as follows:

1. *Construction of the bipartite graph.* Let CA_0 and CA_1 be the sets of concepts corresponding to the attributes $S^R.A_i$ and $S^A.A_j$, respectively. These two sets are the vertex sets of the bipartite graph G. In other words, $G = (V_0 + V_1, E)$ where $V_0 = CA_0$ and $V_1 = CA_1$. Considering two concepts $a \in V_0$ and $b \in V_1$. An edge between a and b is valued with the degree of match between a and b, i.e., $\delta(a, b)$. Then, a numerical weight is assigned to every edge in the bipartite graph as given in Table 1. These weights verify the following constraints:

$$w_1 \leq w_2 \leq w_3 \leq w_4. \tag{1}$$

2. *Selection of the optimal matching.* A matching is selected only if it fulfills an injective mapping between V_0 and V_1. Figure 1 presents two matchings. The first one respects the injective mapping between V_0 and V_1 while the second does not. A bipartite graph G may contain several possible matchings. In this case, the identification of the *optimal matching* is required. According to [1], the optimal matching is the one that minimizes $\max(w_k)$ with $\max(w_k)$ is the maximum weighted edge in the matching. The final returned degree corresponds to the label of the edge that maximizes $\max(w_i)$ in the obtained matching.

Table 1. Weighting system

Degree of match	Weight of edge
Exact	w_1
Plugin	w_2
Subsume	w_3
Fail	w_4

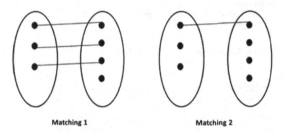

Matching 1   Matching 2

Fig. 1. Matching examples

To select the optimal matching, the authors in [1] propose the use of the Hungarian algorithm. However, the application of Hungarian algorithm using the weighing system given in Table 1 is not possible. This is because the Hungarian algorithm minimizes the sum of weights while the optimal matching is the one that minimizes the maximum weight. The authors in [1] proved that a modification in weights as in Table 2 permits the Hungarian algorithm to identify correctly the optimal matching.

Table 2. Improved weighting system

Degree of match	Weight of edge
Exact	$w_1 = 1$
Plugin	$w_2 = (w_1 * |V_0|) + 1$
Subsume	$w_3 = (w_2 * |V_1|) + 1$
Fail	$w_4 = w_3 * 100$

The computing of the similarity measure $\mu(\cdot, \cdot)$ as described above is formalized in Algorithm 1. The function **ComputeWeights** applies the weight changes as described in Table 2. The function **HungarianAlg** implements the Hungarian Algorithm. The $w(a, b)$ in Algorithm 1 is the weight associated to edge (a, b).

The degree of match $\delta(\cdot, \cdot)$ between two conceptual annotations is established according to Algorithm 2 where: $\equiv$: Equivalence relationship; $\sqsupset_1$: Direct parent/child relationship; $\sqsupset$: Indirect parent/child relationship; and $\sqsubset$: Direct or indirect child/parent relationship.

Algorithm 1. SimilarityMeasure as defined in [1]

Input : $S^R.A_i$, // attribute A_i in requested service.
          $S^A.A_j$, // attribute A_j in advertised service.
Output: $\mu(S^R.A_i, S^A.A_j)$// similarity measure between $S^R.A_i$ and $S^A.A_j$.

1 Graph $G \leftarrow$ EmptyGraph($V_0 + V_1, E$);
2 $V_0 \leftarrow$ concepts of attribute A_i in requested service;
3 $V_1 \leftarrow$ concepts of attribute A_j in advertised service;
4 $(w_1, w_2, w_3, w_4) \leftarrow$ComputeWeights();
5 **for** (each $a \in V_0$) **do**
6   **for** (each $b \in V_1$) **do**
7          $SemanticDistance \leftarrow \delta(a, b)$;
8   **if** ($SemanticDistance =$ Exact) **then**
9              $w(a, b) \leftarrow w_1$
10   **else**
11   **if** ($SemanticDistance =$ Plugin) **then**
12                 $w(a, b) \leftarrow w_2$
13   **else**
14   **if** ($SemanticDistance =$ Subsume) **then**
15                     $w(a, b) \leftarrow w_3$
16   **else**
17                   $w(a, b) \leftarrow w_4$

18 $M \leftarrow$ **HungarianAlg**(G);
19 Let (a', b') denotes the maximal weighted edge in M;
20 $FinalSemanticDistance \leftarrow \delta(a', b')$;
21 **return** $FinalSemanticDistance$;

Algorithm 2. Degree of Match $\delta(\cdot, \cdot)$ as defined in [1]

Input : CA_a, // first concept.
          CA_b, // second concept.
Output: degree of match

1 **if** ($CA_a \equiv CA_b$) **then**
2   **return** Exact;
3 **else if** ($CA_a \sqsupset_1 CA_b$) **then**
4   **return** Plugin;
5 **else if** ($CA_a \sqsupset CA_b$) **then**
6   **return** Plugin;
7 **else if** ($CA_a \sqsubseteq CA_b$) **then**
8   **return** Subsume;
9 **else**
10   **return** Fail;

The optimality criterion used in [1] is designed to minimize the false positives and the false negatives. In fact, minimizing the maximal weight would minimize the 'Fail' labeled edges. However, the choice of $\max(w_i)$ as a final return value is restrictive and the risk of false negatives in the final result is higher. To avoid this problem, the consideration of both $\max(w_i)$ and $\min(w_i)$ as pertinent values in the matching is proposed.

In the two next sections, two different algorithms for the computing the similarity measure are introduced. These algorithms are based on [1]'s approach. The main difference concerns the computation of the degree of match $\delta(\cdot, \cdot)$.

3   Efficient Computation of the Similarity Measure

The semantic distance values are defined similarly to [1] (see Table 1). The improvement concerns the degree of match which is now computed as in Algorithm 3 where: $\equiv$: Equivalence relationship; $\sqsubseteq_1$: Direct child/parent relationship; and $\sqsupseteq_1$: Direct parent/child relationship.

In this version of the algorithm, only direct related concepts are considered for Plugin and Subsume semantic distance values. This change affects the precision of the algorithm since it uses a small set of possible concepts. However, it reduces considerably the computing time. In fact, there is no need to use inference: only facts are parsed in the related ontology, which reduces the complexity of Algorithm 3 (as discussed in Sect. 5). This will necessarily improves the query response time. The proposed algorithm provides a balance between response time and precision, which is valuable in critical situations.

Algorithm 3. Degree of Match $\delta(\cdot, \cdot)$ for an efficient computation of $\mu(\cdot, \cdot)$

```
Input  : CA_R, // first concept.
         CA_A, // second concept.
Output: degree of match
1 if (CA_R ≡ CA_A) then
2 |    return Exact;
3 else if (CA_R ⊑_1 CA_A) then
4 |    return Plugin ;
5 else if (CAS_R ⊒_1 CA_A) then
6 |    return Subsumes;
7 else
8 └    return Fail ;
```

The computation of the similarity measure is the same as in [1] (see Algorithm 1) but the interpretation of the semantic distances is as given in the beginning of this section.

4   Accurate Computation of the Similarity Measure

In this case, six semantic distance values are defined as given in Table 3. The basic idea of this second improvement is that the precision of the algorithm increases with the number of granular values. Then, an extended weighting system is define as in Table 4. These weights verify the following constraints:

$$w_1 \leq w_2 \leq w_3 \leq w_4 \leq w_5 \leq w_6 \tag{2}$$

In this version of the similarity measure, the improvement is also made over the computing of degree of match $\delta(\cdot, \cdot)$, which is now computed according to Algorithm 4 where: $\equiv$: Equivalence relationship (it does not need inference); $\sqsubseteq_1$: Direct child/parent relationship; $\sqsupseteq_1$: Direct parent/child relationship; $\sqsubseteq$: Indirect child/parent relationship; and $\sqsupseteq$: Indirect parent/child relationship.

Table 3. Elements of the semantic distance values set V

V	Semantic distance value
v_1	Exact
v_2	Plugin
v_3	Subsume
v_4	Extended-Plugin
v_5	Extended-Subsume
v_6	Fail

Table 4. Extended weighting system

Degree of match	Weight of edge
Exact	w_1
Plugin	w_2
Subsume	w_3
Extended-Plugin	w_4
Extended-Subsume	w_5
Fail	w_6

Algorithm 4. Degree of match $\delta(\cdot, \cdot)$ for the accurate computation of $\mu(\cdot, \cdot)$

```
Input  : CA_R, // first concept.
         CA_A, // second concept.
Output: degree of match//
1  if (CA_R ≡ CA_A) then
2  |   return Exact ;
3  else if (CA_R ⊏_1 CA_A) then
4  |   return Plugin ;
5  else if (CA_R ⊐_1 CA_A) then
6  |   return Subsume ;
7  else if (CA_R ⊏ CA_A) then
8  |   return Extended-Plugin ;
9  else if (CA_R ⊐ CA_A) then
10 |   return Extended-Subsume ;
11 else
12 |   return Fail;
```

In this algorithm, the consideration of indirect concepts is performed for both Extended-Plugin and Extended-Subsume semantic distance values. Following Definition (2), the following preference order holds:

Exact $\succ$ Plugin $\succ$ Subsume $\succ$ Extended-plug-in $\succ$ Extended-subsume $\succ$ Fail.

Direct relations (i.e. Plugin and Subsume) are preferred to indirect relations (i.e. Extended-Plugin and Extended-Subsume). To apply the Hungarian Algorithm, the weights are modified as in Table 5.

Table 5. Improved weighting system

Degree of match	Weight of edge
Exact	$w_1 = 1$
Plugin	$w_2 = (w_1 * |V_0|) + 1$
Subsume	$w_3 = (w_2 * |V_1|) + 1$
Extended-Plugin	$w_4 = (w_3 * |V_1|) + 1$
Extended-Subsume	$w_5 = (w_4 * |V_1|) + 1$
Fail	$w_6 = w_5 * 100$

The computation of the similarity measure is given in Algorithm 5. This algorithm extends the one proposed by [1] (see Algorithm 1). The function **ComputeWeights** applies the weight changes as described in Table 5. The function **HungarianAlg** implements the Hungarian algorithm. The $w(a, b)$ in Algorithm 5 is the weight associated to edge (a, b).

Algorithm 5. SimilarityMeasure

Input : $S^R.A_i$, // attribute A_i in requested service.
$S^A.A_j$, // attribute A_j in advertised service.
Output: $\mu(S^R.A_i, S^A.A_j)$// similarity measure between $S^R.A_i$ and $S^A.A_j$.

1 Graph $G \leftarrow$ EmptyGraph($V_0 + V_1, E$);
2 $V_0 \leftarrow$ concepts of attribute A_i in requested service;
3 $V_1 \leftarrow$ concepts of attribute A_j in advertised service;
4 $(w_1, w_2, w_3, w_4, w_5, w_6) \leftarrow$ ComputeWeights() ();
5 **for** (*each* $a \in V_0$) **do**
6   **for** (*each* $b \in V_1$) **do**
7          $SemanticDistance \leftarrow \delta(a,b)$;
8   **if** ($SemanticDistance =$ Exact) **then**
9              $w(a, b) \leftarrow w_1$
10   **else**
11   **if** ($SemanticDistance =$ Plugin) **then**
12                 $w(a, b) \leftarrow w_2$
13   **else**
14   **if** ($SemanticDistance =$ Subsume) **then**
15                     $w(a, b) \leftarrow w_3$
16   **else**
17   **if** ($SemanticDistance =$ Extended-Plugin) **then**
18                         $w(a, b) \leftarrow w_4$
19   **else**
20   **if** ($SemanticDistance =$ Extended-Subsume) **then**
21                             $w(a, b) \leftarrow w_5$
22   **else**
23                             $w(a, b) \leftarrow w_6$

24 $M \leftarrow$ HungarianAlg (G);
25 Let (a', b') denotes the maximal weighted edge in M;
26 $FinalSemanticDistance \leftarrow \delta(a',b')$;
27 **return** $FinalSemanticDistance$;

---

5   Computational Complexity

The most expensive operation in Algorithms 1 and 5 is the computing of the degree of match. As shown in [5], inferring degree of match by ontological parse of pieces of information into facts and then utilizing commercial rule-based engines which use the fast Rete [6] pattern-matching algorithm leads to $O(|R||F||P|)$ where $|R|$ is the number of rules, $|F|$ is the number of facts, and $|P|$ is the average number of patterns in each rule. Accordingly, the complexity of Algorithms 2 and 4 is $O(|R||F||P|)$. However, the computing the degree of match according to Algorithm 3 is only $O(|F|)$ since there is not inference.

Let now discuss the algorithmic complexity of [1]'s approach. Let m be an approximation of the number of concepts for the attributes to be compared. Then: (i) the computation of weights is an operation of $O(1)$ complexity; (ii) the construction of the graph involves the comparison of every pair of concepts. It takes then $O(m^2)$ time complexity; (iii) the Hungarian Algorithm has a time complexity of $O(m^3)$; and (iv) the degree of match in Algorithm 2 is $O(|R||F||P|)$.

Generally, m is likely to take small values and it can be considered as a constant. The overall time complexity of [1]'s algorithm is than $O(1 + m^2|F||R||P| + m^3) \simeq O(|F||R||P|)$. Based on the above discussion, the complexity of [1]'s algorithm will be $O(1 + m^2|F| + m^3) \simeq O(|F|)$ when the degree of similarity is computed as in Algorithm 3. The computation of the similarity measure according to Algorithm 5 is the same as [1]'s algorithm, i.e., $O(1 + m^2|F||R||P| + m^3) \simeq O(|F||R||P|)$.

6   Evaluation and Comparison

6.1   Performance Analysis

To SME2 [8] tool has been used to evaluate the performance of the algorithms. The SME2 uses OWLS-TC collections to provide the matchmakers with Web service descriptions, and to compare their answers to the relevance sets of the various queries. The SME2 provides several metrics to evaluate the performance and effectiveness of a Web service matchmaker. The metrics that have been considered in this paper are: precision and recall, average precision and query response time. The definition of these metrics are given in [8].

A series of experimentations have been conducted on a Dell Inspiron 15 3735 Laptop with an Intel Core I5 processor (1.6 GHz) and 2 GB of memory. The test collection used is OWLS-TC4, which consists of 1083 Web service offers described in OWL-S 1.1 and 42 queries.

Figures 2 and 3 show the Average Precision and Recall/Precision plot of the accurate and efficient algorithms, respectively. It can be seen that the accurate algorithm outperforms efficient algorithm with respect to these two metrics. This is due to the use of logical inference, that obviously enhances the precision of the accurate algorithm. In Fig. 4, however, efficient algorithm is shown to be remarkably faster than the accurate algorithm. This is due to the inference process used in accurate algorithm that consumes considerable resources.

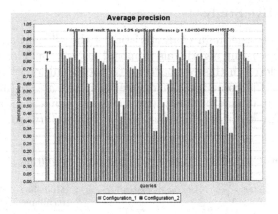

Fig. 2. Average precision

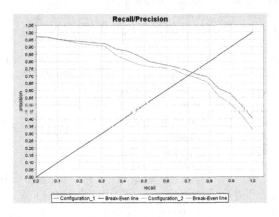

Fig. 3. Recall/Precision

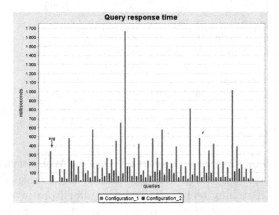

Fig. 4. Response time

6.2 Comparative Study

Table 6 summarizes the main characteristics of the efficient and accurate algorithms and some existing algorithms proposed in [1,5,10]. The following criteria have been considered in this comparison: (i) the definition of the semantic distance set V, (ii) the computing of degree of match $\delta(\cdot,\cdot)$, (iii) the modelling technique of the matching problem, (iv) the level of precision, and (v) the level of complexity. The description of this table is straightforward.

Table 6. Comparison of similarity measure computing algorithms

Approach	Semantic distance	Degree of match $\delta(c_1, c_2)$	Modelling technique	Precision	Complexity
[5]	v_1 = Exact	Exact: $c_1 \equiv c_2$	Unspecified	High	Moderate
	v_2 = Plug-in	Plug-in: $c_1 \sqsubseteq c_2$			
	v_3 = Subsumption	Subsumption: $c_1 \sqsupseteq c_2$			
	v_4 = Container	Container: $c_1 \succeq c_2$			
	v_5 = Part-of	Part-of: $c_1 \preceq {}^a c_2$			
	v_6 = Disjoint	Disjoint: $c_1 \; disj^b \; c_2$			
[10]	v_1 = Exact	Exact: $c_1 \sqsubseteq_1 c_2$	Greedy algorithm	Low	High
	v_2 = Plugin	Plugin: $c_1 \sqsubseteq c_2$			
	v_3 = Subsume	Subsume: $c_1 \sqsupseteq c_2$			
	v_4 = Fail	Fail: $c_1 \; disj \; c_2$			
[1]	v_1 = Exact	Exact: $c_1 \equiv c_2$	Bipartite graph	High	Moderate
	v_2 = Plugin	Plugin: $c_1 \sqsubseteq c_2$			
	v_3 = Subsume	Subsume: $c_1 \sqsupseteq c_2$			
	v_4 = Fail	Fail: $c_1 \; disj \; c_2$			
Efficient algorithm	v_1 = Exact	Exact: $c_1 \equiv c_2$	Bipartite graph	Moderate	Low
	v_2 = Plugin	Plugin: $c_1 \sqsubseteq_1 c_2$			
	v_3 = Subsume	Subsume: $c_1 \sqsupseteq_1 c_2$			
	v_4 = Fail	Fail: $c_1 \; disj \; c_2$			
Accurate algorithm	v_1 = Exact	Exact: $c_1 \equiv c_2$	Bipartite graph	High	Moderate
	v_2 = Plugin	Plugin: $c_1 \sqsubseteq_1 c_2$			
	v_3 = Subsume	Subsume: $c_1 \sqsupseteq_1 c_2$			
	v_4 = Extended-Plugin	Extended-Plugin: $c_1 \sqsubseteq c_2$			
	v_5 = Extended-Subsume	Extended-Subsume: $c_1 \sqsupseteq c_2$			
	v_6 = Fail	Fail: $c_1 \; disj \; c_2$			

[a] part-of relation in the Ontology.
[b] $disj$: There is no relation between the two concepts in the Ontology.

7   Conclusion

Web service matchmaking is an important task in Web service discovery and Web service composition. Early non-logic based matchmakers rely on syntactic and structural matching techniques, which suffer from several shortcomings, especially the high number of false positives and false negatives. Accordingly, different logic-based matchmakers have been proposed (e.g., [1,5,9,10,13]) to overcome these shortcomings. In particular, the authors in [1] propose a bipartite graph-based algorithm that improves considerably the algorithm of [10] by reducing false positives and false negatives in the final results.

This paper presents and compares two algorithms for computing a semantic logic-based similarity measure in the perspective of Web service matching. These algorithms improve the computing of the similarity measure proposed in [1]. Both algorithms have been evaluated using the SME2 tool. The results show that the first algorithm slightly affects the precision of [1]'s algorithm but reduces substantially its computing time, while the second algorithm enriches the semantic distance values used in [1] and ameliorates considerably its precision. In the future, more advanced performance evaluation with large datasets will be conducted.

References

1. Bellur, U., Kulkarni, R.: Improved matchmaking algorithm for semantic Web services based on bipartite graph matching. In: IEEE International Conference on Web Services, Salt Lake City, Utah, USA, 9–13 July 2007, pp. 86–93 (2007)
2. Blake, M.B., Cabral, L., König-Ries, B., Küster, U., Martin, D. (eds.): Semantic Web Services, Advancement through Evaluation. Springer, Heidelberg (2012). https://doi.org/10.1007/978-3-642-28735-0
3. Chakhar, S.: Parameterized attribute and service levels semantic matchmaking framework for service composition. In: Fifth International Conference on Advances in Databases, Knowledge, and Data Applications (DBKDA 2013), Seville, Spain, 27 January–1 February 2013, pp. 159–165 (2013)
4. Chen, F., Lu, C., Wu, H., Li, M.: A semantic similarity measure integrating multiple conceptual relationships for web service discovery. Expert Syst. Appl. **67**, 19–31 (2017)
5. Doshi, P., Goodwin, R., Akkiraju, R., Roeder, S.: Parameterized semantic matchmaking for workflow composition. IBM Research report RC23133, IBM Research Division, March 2004
6. Forgy, C.: Rete: a fast algorithm for the many patterns/many objects match problem. Artif. Intell. **19**(1), 17–37 (1982)
7. Gmati, F.E., Yacoubi Ayadi, N., Bahri, A., Chakhar, S., Ishizaka, A.: A framework for parameterized semantic matchmaking and ranking of web services. In: Proceedings of the 12th International Conference on Web Information Systems and Technologies, pp. 54–65 (2016)
8. Klusch, M., Dudev, M., Misutka, J., Kapahnke, P., Vasileski, M.: SME^2 Version 2.2. User Manual. The German Research Center for Artificial Intelligence (DFKI), Germany (2010)
9. Klusch, M., Kapahnke, P.: The iSeM matchmaker: a flexible approach for adaptive hybrid semantic service selection. In: Web Semantics: Science, Services and Agents on the World Wide Web, vol. 15, pp. 1–14 (2012)
10. Paolucci, M., Kawamura, T., Payne, T.R., Sycara, K.: Semantic matching of web services capabilities. In: Horrocks, I., Hendler, J. (eds.) ISWC 2002. LNCS, vol. 2342, pp. 333–347. Springer, Heidelberg (2002). https://doi.org/10.1007/3-540-48005-6_26

11. Sangers, J., Frasincar, F., Hogenboom, F., Chepegin, V.: Semantic web service discovery using natural language processing techniques. Expert Syst. Appl. 40(11), 4660–4671 (2013)
12. Stavropoulos, T.G., Andreadis, S., Bassiliades, N., Vrakas, D., Vlahavas, I.P.: The tomaco hybrid matching framework for SAWSDL semantic web services. IEEE Trans. Serv. Comput. 9(6), 954–967 (2016)
13. Sycara, K., Paolucci, M., van Velsen, M., Giampapa, J.: The RETSINA MAS infrastructure. Autonom. Agents Multi-Agent Syst. 7(1–2), 29–48 (2003)

Semantic Question Answering System Using Dbpedia

Passent M. ElKafrawy$^{(\boxtimes)}$, Amr M. Sauber, and Nada A. Sabry

Faculty of Science, Department of Mathematics and Computer Science,
Menoufia University, Menofia, Egypt
{basant.elkafrawi,amr,nadaali}@science.menofia.edu.eg

Abstract. Due to the rapid increase of data generated on the web, there is a need for efficient techniques to access required data. Question Answering (QA) is a multi-disciplinary field of information retrieval and natural language processing, which aims at answering users' query written closer to human language. Users can thus submit their requests as they think it and conceptually closer to their intended outcomes. The upcoming trend in query languages, and programing languages in general, towards more human-like language for increased user-friendliness subject to enhanced efficiency with usage of English-like words. In this paper, an architecture of factoid question answering system is presented using Dbpedia ontology. The discussed architecture is tested and results are compared to those of other systems.

Keywords: NLP · Question answering · Question classification
Dbpedia ontology · SVM · Sparql

1 Introduction

Information retrieval systems (IR) have many types, for example, search engines like Google, yahoo and Bing where the user enters a query then a list of reduced links is returned. It is the responsibility of the user to navigate throw the retrieved links and find s\he's own information as needed. Unlike question answering systems that provide the user with the answer directly. Accordingly, it is better to use question answering than search engine. There are two noteworthy difficulties in the ontological question answering systems that should be recognized [1]. Firstly, understanding the desire of the question of the user in the analysis stage. Secondly, making an interpretation of this desire to a correct query adjusted to the formal ontology query schema. Natural language processing technology can resolve the first issue, while the ontology retrieval to find the correct answer can resolve the second. There are different types of queries [2] like: (Factoid queries): WH questions like when, who, where can be answered through simple facts represented in short text answers. 'Who is the president of Egypt?'; (Yes/No queries): 'Is Berlin capital of Germany?'; (Definition queries): 'What is leukemia?'; (Cause/consequence queries): How, Why, What 'what are the consequences of the Iraq war?'; (Procedural queries): 'What are the steps for getting a Master degree?'; (Comparative queries): 'What are the differences between the model A and B?'; (Queries with examples): 'List of hard disks similar to hard disk X'; (Queries

© Springer International Publishing AG, part of Springer Nature 2018
M. Mouhoub et al. (Eds.): IEA/AIE 2018, LNAI 10868, pp. 821–832, 2018.
https://doi.org/10.1007/978-3-319-92058-0_79

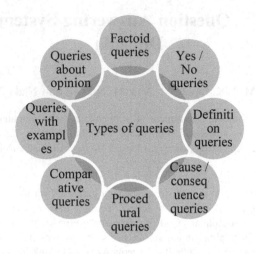

Fig. 1. Types of queries

about opinion): 'What is the opinion of the majority of Americans about the Iraq war?'. As illustrated in Fig. 1.

Factoid queries are chosen to be used in this research, because its answer is often a named entity suitable to the ontology structure. For any question answering system there is a need for a database, from which the system extracts the answer to the query of the user. One of the biggest structured databases is Dbpedia ontology.

Wikipedia is a free online encyclopedia that enables anyone to edit articles. It is the most popular and largest general reference work on the Internet. It is the 5th most visited website according to the statistics of alexa.com (March 2017) [13]. Dbpedia [3] is a project aiming to extract structured information and data from Wikipedia using semantic technology. Its content definition is based on linking concepts using an ontology. Knowledge in Dbpedia is much higher understood by machines and the relations between concepts is highly defined. Dbpedia enables users to ask sophisticated queries against Wikipedia, and to connect the various data sets to Wikipedia information. The latest release of DBpedia till now is DBpedia version 2016-10 The English version of the DBpedia knowledge base currently consists of 6.6M entities of which 4.9M have abstracts, 1.9M have geo coordinates and 1.7M depictions. In total, 5.5M resources are grouped in a consistent ontology, consisting of 840K places (including 513K populated places), 1.5M persons, 286K organizations (including 55K educational institutions and 70K companies), 496K works (including 111K films, 21K video games and 139K music albums), 58K plants, 306K species and 6K diseases [3]. The Dbpedia project utilizes the Resource Description Framework (RDF) as a data model to represent the extracted information from Wikipedia. The RDF data model represents statements about Web resources in the form of subject-predicate-object (triple). This paper is structured as follows; section two describes related work of QA systems. In section three the architecture is discussed in details. The used dataset is described in section four. The experimental results of the system are covered in section five. At the end, conclusion and future work are described in section six.

2 Related Work

The use of QA systems is to retrieve the correct answers to the question of the user from a set of knowledge resources. Many examines are occupied with this task. There are many types of QA like Question Answering on the Web as FAQ Finder [4], which is a question answering system for factual questions over the Web. Its knowledge base is files of frequently asked questions. It retrieves answers that are exist in frequently asked question records but does not concentrate on the age of new answers Moreover; Ask.com [5] uses a technique of template-mapping to determine the type of the question and then a clustering technique to extract multiple answer blocks. Another type of QA is ontology based QA Systems as AQUA [6], which is a question answering system that combines information retrieval mechanism, NLP, logics and ontology in the uniform framework. Its design is to answer questions identified with academic people from its own particular database. The disadvantage of AQUA was that only Academic domain was used. Other domain questions couldn't be answered. PowerAQUA [7], a Multi-Ontology Based Question Answering System that uses natural language input queries and retrieve answers from appropriate distributed resources on the Semantic Web. PowerAQUA uses three components. First, a Linguistic component that takes the query in natural language and interprets it into linguistic triple. Second, Power Map component that determines the kind of ontology from the database. Third, Triple Similarity Services that analyzes the ontologies and produces the suitable result. The drawback of the system is that it can only answer basic linguistic queries. QASYO [1] is another Question Answering System based on YAGO Ontology. QASYO uses various methods to understand NL queries simply and convert them into semantic markup. QASYO system consists of four stages: Question Classifier, Linguistic component, Query generator, and Query processor. IBM Watson (DeepQA) [18] is a question answering system that differs from the proposed system as the questions are framed as statements, but the answers must be phrased as questions. In addition to that it uses machine learning techniques in solving problems and this requires much more data and so more complicated machines with higher specification is required. SELNI [8] which uses Dbpedia ontology in answering users' questions. Its type is a sentence-level question answering system that answers English questions, but its features weren't enough to correctly determine the answer type of the question.

In this study we will deeper investigate the feature set to outperform [8]. The first stage in QA system is question classification stage. The technique in [9] used combination of features that gives high accuracy in classification of question. This technique is used in our proposal to develop a complete QA system with higher accuracy as defined in [9].

3 Proposed System Architecture

The technique is a question answering system based on Dbpedia ontology. It consists of three stages (Question Classification – Question Processing – Query Formulation and Execution) as illustrated in Fig. 2.

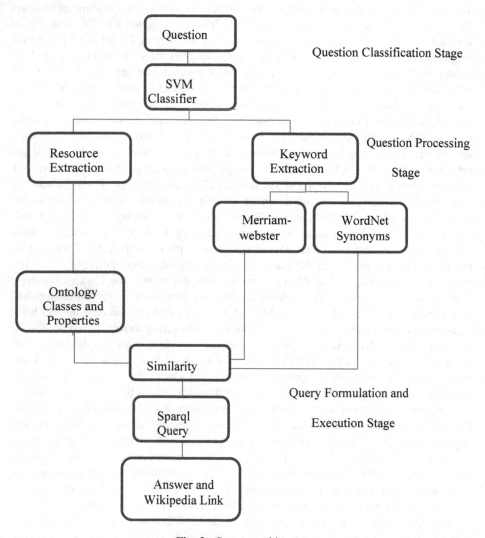

Fig. 2. System architecture

3.1 Question Classification

Question classification has an important role in any QA systems. It categorizes questions into one or more classes depending upon classification technique. For instance,

"Where are the pyramids?" the question classifier task is to specify that the label of the question is "Location". So it determines the answer type which facilitates answering the question. To build such a classifier system, two main challenges should be addressed: (1) what type of classifier to choose and how to train it, and (2) how to extract features and combine them. There are different techniques used for question classification. We choose from them Support Vector Machine (SVM) because it achieves high accuracy of question classification compared to others [9].

The question classes known as (question taxonomy). Lots of question taxonomies have been used in various works, but the majority of current researches depend on a two layer taxonomy suggested by Li and Roth [12].

This taxonomy consists of six coarse-grained classes and fifty fine-grained classes as illustrated in Table 1.

Table 1. Coarse-grained classes and fine-grained classes

Coarse classes	Fine classes
Entity	Food, animal, instrument, body, creative material, color, currency, disease/medicine, event, language, symbol, word, letter, plant, sport, vehicle, product, substance, religion, terminology, technology/method, weather condition, other
Human	Title, description, individual, group
Location	Mountain, state, country, city, restaurant, continent, attraction, body of water, retail, other
Number	Count, code, distance, period, money, ordinal, percentage, date, weight, speed, temperature, volume/size, other
Description	Description, reason, definition, manner
Abbreviation	Abbreviation, expansion

For instance, "What is the capital of India?" LOC is the coarse-grained class which means location and City is the fine-grained class for this question.

Support Vector Machine is a supervised learning method for classifying data. It is especially successful for high dimensional data. There are four types of basic kernel functions: linear, polynomial, sigmoid and radial basis function. Based on experimental results [9] it is noticed that linear kernel had higher performance compared to other types of kernel functions as it is faster than others in large dataset; therefore, linear kernel is chosen to be used.

Features

There are three types of features in question classification: lexical, syntactical and semantic features. To get the best feature space variety of these features were extracted from a question.

Lexical features

Features that are extracted specifically from the question like: N-gram (Unigram–Bigram), WH-words, and Word shapes.

- N-gram is a contiguous series of n words. Unigram (U) is one word and Bigram (B) is two words, where (LB) is limited bigram (the first two words).
- WH-words (WH) are eight types namely what, which, when, where, who, how, why and rest.
- Word shapes (WS) are five types: all digits, upper case, lower case, mixed and other.

Syntactic Features

Features that are extracted from the syntax of the question like: POS Tags, Tagged Unigrams, Headword, and Head rule.

- POS Tags (part of speech tagging) is the process of marking up a word based on both its context and its definition.
- Tagged Unigrams (TU) are the unigrams augmented with POS tags. The classifier used them to consider one word with various tags as two different features.
- Headword (H) is a word in a given question that represents the important information that is being searched for. For instance: What is the capital of Yugoslavia? The headword is Yugoslavia.
- Head Rule (HR): some questions do not contain any head word. Huang et al. in [11] introduced some regular expression patterns to map these types of questions to a pattern and then uses the corresponding pattern as a feature.

Semantic Features

Features that are extracted from the semantic meaning of the words in a question. Semantic features requires data source such as WordNet (http://wordnet.princeton.edu/) or a dictionary for extracting semantic information for questions, like: Hypernyms - Related Words - Question Category - Query Expansion.

- Hypernyms (HY). WordNet is a database of English words that gives a lexical hierarchy which connects a word with higher level semantic concepts namely hypernyms. For instance, a hypernym of "city" is "municipality" of which the hypernym is "urban area".
- Related Words (R): based on [12] gatherings of words were characterized; each word has a category name. If the word in the question was found in one or more gatherings, its relating categories would be added to the feature vector. For instance, if any of the words {birthday, birthdate, hour, day, week, month, year, and decade} was found in a question, at that point its category name, date would be added to the feature vector.
- Question Category (QC): is a semantic feature which was obtained by using WordNet hierarchy depending on the idea in [11]. WordNet hierarchy was utilized to calculate the similarity of the headword exists in the question with each of the classes. The class which has highest similarity is used as a feature and should be added to the feature vector.
- Query Expansion (QE): is a parameter used for weight which decreases by expanding the distance between the original word and a hypernym [9]. For instance, "What is the oldest city in Canada?" (city, 1) (municipality, 0.6) (urban area, 0.36) (geographical-area, 0.22) (region, 0.13) (location, 0.08) (physical-object, 0.05) (physical-entity, 0.03) (entity, 0.02).

A combination of these features was done to obtain higher accuracy.

The features which are extracted from questions will be added to the feature vector with a (feature, value) pair. Instead of using string, each term (feature) is mapped to a unique number, indicating feature number. Furthermore, the class name is also mapped to a unique number. The following form is the same sample from TREC dataset which is translated to the form that is accepted by LIBSVM library.

5 11:4.0 12:4.0 13:2.0 19:2.0 27:1.0 32:1.0 34:1.0 60:1.0 83:1.0 188:1.0

Where the first number (5) indicates the class number and the rest are (feature, value) pairs which are separated by a space while the pairs are separated by a colon. The feature pairs should be sorted in ascending order based on feature number. When all the samples from training and test set are translated to the above format, then classifiers were trained with training set and were tested against the independent test set.

3.2 Questions Processing

In this step resources and keywords were extracted from the question.

Dbpedia spotlight [8] is utilized for extracting resources exist in the question. Dbpedia spotlight is a tool used for automatically annotating mentions of Dbpedia resources in text. Just resource in agreement with the course and the fine classes was chosen.

To extract keywords from a question, these keywords should be nouns or verbs or non-stop words or complex nominals. After the extraction of keywords from the question, the synonyms of these keywords were extracted from a website (merriam-webster.com) [14] because it is a huge thesaurus and dictionary of words. Also, the keywords were enriched by extracting synonyms from WordNet [15], this increases the area used for query formulation. WordNet is an extensive lexical database of English. Nouns, verbs, adverbs and adjectives are gathered into collections of synonyms (synsets), each expressing a different concept.

3.3 Query Formulation and Execution

After determining answer type, resources, keywords and its synonyms. Query Formulation is done by determining ontology classes and properties of the given question. To make this, a Sparql query was built with the resource. Sparql (SPARQL Protocol and RDF Query Language) [16] is a semantic query language used for databases, ready to manipulate and retrieve data stored in Resource Description Framework (RDF) format. The result of the query is an RDF file which contains all ontology properties and classes of that resource.

Similarity between the keywords (and synonyms) in the question and ontology properties and classes was computed using Levenshtein distance algorithm and get the ontology class with the highest similarity to be utilized in the final Sparql query. Levenshtein distance algorithm [8] is a string metric used for measuring the distinction between two sequences. Casually, the Levenshtein distance between two words is the minimum number of single-character edits (deletions, additions or substitutions) to transform one word to the other.

The final Sparql query is built to answer the question from Dbpedia server. This query consists of the resource and the ontology class determined in similarity stage.

4   The Dataset

The dataset which is used in this work is the one created by Li and Roth [10]. This dataset is generally utilized in question classification and known as TREC or UIUC dataset. It consist of 5500 labeled question which is utilized as training set and 500 independent labeled questions which is utilized as test set. Example from this dataset:- NUM: date When was Ozzy Osbourne born?

(NUM: date) is the two layer taxonomy.

5   Experimental Results

The implementation of the system is done using java with set of tools and libraries as Stanford NLP, libsvm, Dbpedia spotlight, snowball, jsoup, WordNet, and Sparql.

In the first stage, support vector machine algorithm is used to train the data. A combination of the features was done in a way to reach acceptable accuracy, which made the classifier more accurate in determining the answer type than that by Tahri and Tibermacine in [8]; where four features were used as the following (unigram – bigram – part of speech

Table 2. Shows the accuracy of support vector machine classifier throw various features.

No.	Features	Dimensions	Accuracy	
			Coarse	Fine
1	U + WS + LB + H + HR + HY	16582	92.4	86.2
2	U + WS + LB + H + HR + QE	20959	92.6	86.8
3	U + WS + LB + H + HR + QC	12774	92.2	85.4
4	U + WS + LB + H + HR + R	12850	92.0	87.4
5	U + WS + LB + H + HR + QE + R	21037	91.8	88.0
6	**U + WS + LB + H + HR + QE + R + QC**	**21039**	**92.0**	**88.4**
7	U + WS + B+H + HR + QE + R + QC	50750	92.8	87.4
8	WH + WS + H + R	2066	88.2	85.8
9	WH + WS + LB + H + R	3076	90.4	86.8
10	WH + WS + H + QE + R	10253	89.4	86.4
11	WH + WS + H + QE + R + QC	10259	89.4	86.2
12	WH + WS + H+HR + QE + R	10290	89.6	86.8
13	WH + WS + LB + H + QE + R	11263	89.6	88.2
14	WH + WS + LB + H + HR + QE + R	11300	90.8	88.2

tags – chunk tags) and reached accuracy of 86:87%. We chose to use a combination of features following the technique in [9]. Table 2 shows these combinations.

After running the 14 experiments of different combination of features we decided to use the following eight features as (unigram – word shapes – limited bigram – headword – head rule – query expansion – related words – question category) because those achieved the highest accuracy of 88.4%.

In the second stage, the resource is extracted from the question. We added another enhancement to the system by the enrichment of keywords extracted from the question by extracting synonyms of these keywords from WordNet. The use of semantic technology gave power to the system, that has not been utilized before.

In the third stage, the Sparql query is built against Dbpedia ontology and results were given back to the user.

However, some questions have not been answered because of the absence of information in Dbpedia ontology.

An example is illustrated in details showing the question answering steps gradually.

Question:
What is the largest city in United States?

1. **Question classification stage**

   Features:
   (What, 1) (is, 1) (the, 1) (largest, 1) (city, 1) (in, 1) (United, 1) (States?, 1) (wordShape:2, 2) (wordShape:1, 5) (wordShape:4, 1) (bigram:What- > is, 1) (rel:What, 1) (rel:be, 1) (rel:presentBe, 1) (rel:singleBe, 1) (rel:city, 2) (rel:country, 1) (rel:list.tar, 9) (rel:loca, 2) (rel:In, 1) (rel:InOn, 1) (rel:term, 1) (DESC:def pattern 1, 1) (headWord:headword:null, 1)
   Coarse class: LOC (location)
   Fine class: city (Individual)

2. **Question processing stage**

   Resource: United_States
   Keywords and synonyms:
   Largest city, big, biggish, goodly, boxcar, bulky, largish, considerable, grand, great, ;handsome, hefty, hulking, heavy, husky, outsize, outsized, oversize, oversized, sizable, sizeable, substantial, tidy, voluminous, declamatory, prominent, with child, expectant, magnanimous, gravid, orotund, enceinte, boastfully, bombastic, tumid.

3. **Query Formulation and Execution stage**

   Some of Ontology Classes:

   (?Property = <http://dbpedia.org/ontology/language>)   (?h = <http://dbpedia.org/resource/Federal_government_of_the_United_States>)
   (?Property = <http://dbpedia.org/ontology/largestCity>) (?h = <http://dbpedia.org/resource/New_York_City>)
   (?Property = <http://dbpedia.org/ontology/leader>)   (?h = <http://dbpedia.org/resource/John_Roberts>)

(?Property = <http://dbpedia.org/ontology/leader>)   (?h = <http://dbpedia.org/resource/Paul_Ryan>)
(?Property = <http://dbpedia.org/ontology/leader>)   (?h = <http://dbpedia.org/resource/Mike_Pence>)
(?Property = <http://dbpedia.org/ontology/leader>)   (?h = <http://dbpedia.org/resource/Donald_Trump>)
(?Property = <http://dbpedia.org/ontology/leaderTitle>) (?h = "President"@en)
(?Property = <http://dbpedia.org/ontology/leaderTitle>)   (?h = "Vice President"@en)

Highest Similarity:
http://dbpedia.org/ontology/largestCity (0.917)
Sparql Query:
SELECT * WHERE {<http://dbpedia.org/resource/United_States> <http://dbpedia.org/ontology/largestCity>?h.}
Answer:
New_York_City
Wikipedia page:
https://en.wikipedia.org/wiki/New_York_City

The question is entered by the user and passed through the system steps. First it is classified according to SVM classifier to Coarse class: LOC and Fine class: city. Then the resource is extracted using Dbpedia spotlight (United_States). After that keywords are extracted from the question and extract their synonyms from merriam-webster.com and WordNet as shown in the example. Sparql query is built to get ontology classes and properties of the resource (United_States) and similarity is computed between the keywords and ontology classes. The highest similarity is (http://dbpedia.org/ontology/largestCity) (0.917). Finally, Sparql query is built using the resource and the ontology class to get the answer (New York) and link to its Wikipedia page.

6 Discussion

Since the proposed system is a question answering system and not only a question classification system. We used the same blueprint in [8] and improved the classifier accuracy which was relatively low (86%) because only four features were used. A different classifier was used with higher performance due to using eight features which were selected by performing multiple experiments on different possible combinations. These features were used instead of the original four. Although some studies [17] used different features (U + H + HY + WS + QC) and claimed to achieve accuracy of 91.1%, however, implementing them on our environment produced accuracy of 86.4% that is why we did not consider them.

Another improvement is done in the query formulation and execution stage by enriching the extracted keywords using WordNet for more synonyms in addition to using (merriam-webster.com) website that utilized previously for increasing synonyms and consequently increasing the semantic capabilities.

We observed that the system performance is determined by the sequence of different techniques and the features used.

7 Conclusion and Future Work

Dbpedia ontology is used in question answering systems. In question classification stage researchers used some features to classify question, but these features weren't enough to determine answer type perfectly. A combination of syntax, syntactic and semantic features was chosen to be used to increase the accuracy of SVM classifier. In question processing stage resources and keywords were extracted. WordNet was used to get more synonyms for these keywords which gave better results. In query formulation and execution stage Sparql is used to extract the answer.

Our future work is to find a huge dataset of questions and compare our results with the results obtained by other systems. Then use this system in building Arabic question answering system using Arabic Dbpedia ontology.

References

1. Moussa, A.M., Abdel-Kader, R.F.: Qasyo: a question answering system for yago ontology. Int. J. Database Theor. Appl. (2011)
2. Yang, L., Ai, Q., Guo, J., Croft, W.B.: aNMM: ranking short answer texts with attention-based neural matching model. In: Proceedings of the 25th ACM International on Conference on Information and Knowledge Management, Indianapolis, IN, USA, pp. 287–296 (2016)
3. Auer, S., Bizer, C., Kobilarov, G., Lehmann, J., Cyganiak, R., Ives, Z.: DBpedia: a nucleus for a web of open data. In: Aberer, K., et al. (eds.) ASWC/ISWC -2007. LNCS, vol. 4825, pp. 722–735. Springer, Heidelberg (2007). https://doi.org/10.1007/978-3-540-76298-0_52
4. Burke, R.D., Hammond, K.J., Kulyukin, V., Lytinen, S.L., Tomuro, N., Schoenberg, S.: Question answering from frequently asked question files: experiences with the FAQ finder system. AI Mag. (1997)
5. Ask.com. Accessed Feb 2013
6. Vargas-Vera, M., Motta, E.: AQUA – ontology-based question answering system. In: Monroy, R., Arroyo-Figueroa, G., Sucar, L.E., Sossa, H. (eds.) MICAI 2004. LNCS (LNAI), vol. 2972, pp. 468–477. Springer, Heidelberg (2004). https://doi.org/10.1007/978-3-540-24694-7_48
7. Lopez, V., Motta, E., Sabou, M., Fernandez, M.: PowerAqua: a multi-ontology based question answering system–v1. OpenKnowledge Deliverable D (2007)
8. Tahri, A., Tibermacine, O.: DbPedia based factoid question answering system. Int. J. Web Semant. Technol. (2013)
9. Loni, B.: A survey of state-of-the-art methods on question classification. Literature Survey. TU Delft Repository (2011)

10. Li, X., Roth, D.: Learning question classifiers. In: Proceedings of the 19th International Conference on Computational Linguistics-vol. 1, pp. 1–7. Association for Computational Linguistics, Taipei (2002)
11. Huang, Z., Thint, M., Qin, Z.: Question classification using head words and their hypernyms. In: Proceedings of the Conference on Empirical Methods in Natural Language Processing. Association for Computational Linguistics, pp. 927–936 (2008)
12. Li, X., Roth, D.: Learning question classifiers: the role of semantic information. In: Proceedings of International Conference on Computational Linguistics, Geneva, Switzerland, pp. 556–562 (2004)
13. www.alexa.com. Accessed Mar 2017
14. https://www.merriam-webster.com/. Accessed Mar 2017
15. https://wordnet.princeton.edu/. Accessed Apr 2017
16. http://dbpedia.org/sparql. Accessed Apr 2017
17. Mishra, M., Mishra, V.K., Sharma, H.R.: Question classification using semantic, syntactic and lexical features. Int. J. Web Semant. Technol. 4(3), 39 (2013)
18. High, R.: The era of cognitive systems: an inside look at IBM Watson and how it works. IBM Corporation, 12 December 2012. Redbooks (2012)

Identifying Similar Sentences by Using N-Grams of Characters

Saïma Sultana and Ismaïl Biskri[✉]

Université du Québec à Trois-Rivières, Trois-Rivières, QC G8Z 4M3, Canada
{Saima.Sultana,Ismail.Biskri}@uqtr.ca

Abstract. Nowadays, detecting similar sentences can play a major role in various fundamental applications for reading and analyzing sentences like information retrieval, categorization, detection of paraphrases, summarizing, translation etc. In this work, we present a novel method for the detection of similar sentences. This method highlights the using of units of n-grams of characters. The online dictionary as well as any search engine are not being used. Hence, this idea leads our method a simplest and optimum way to handle the similarities between two sentences. In addition, the grammar rules as well as any syntax have not been used in our method. That's why, our approach is language-independent. We analyze and compare a range of similarity measures with our methodology. Meanwhile, the complexity of our method is O(N2) which is pretty much better.

Keywords: Similar sentences · N-grams of characters

1 Introduction

Internet and social networks become an increasingly popular source of information, but often difficult to mine due to some limitations of current technologies. Measuring of sentence similarity plays an increasingly important role in sentence related research and applications in tasks such as information retrieval, sentence classification, question answering, machine translation, sentence summarization and so on.

Several approaches have been proposed to speed up information retrieval, reading and analysis. Among them, some are symbolic and logical, based on patterns, others are numerical and empirical, based on co-occurrences and some are a kind of pattern recognition based on algebraic formal models. Those approaches use some special items to make their model dynamic to detect the similarities such as – the grammatical rules or syntax, online dictionary, search engine etc. But using one or two of these items make the whole model more problematic as well as complex for comprehensive usages. Sometimes those approaches might perform poorly on measuring similarities because of data sparseness and the lack of consentience. So, it's very efficient step to skip those mentioned items and implement a simple way to measure similarities.

Akermi and Faiz developed a method that extracts semantic similarity between sentences which is derived by three different stages and those are given below [1]:

© Springer International Publishing AG, part of Springer Nature 2018
M. Mouhoub et al. (Eds.): IEA/AIE 2018, LNAI 10868, pp. 833–843, 2018.
https://doi.org/10.1007/978-3-319-92058-0_80

- Calculate the semantic similarity with the help of their Word Similarity Measure SimFA [2] as well as by normalizing similarity scores. Here, they eliminate the functional words as well as the punctuations.
- Calculate the overall syntactic similarity measure by adding the jaccard coefficient (calculated by including functional words) and the word order similarity.
- Measure sentence similarity by combining the semantic and the syntactic information.

Kumari and K developed a method to identify the numerous semantic relations that exist between two given words, they use a pattern extraction and clustering method [3]. At first they download few web pages from Google and stores it in the database. Then, they use web search engine and retrieves page counts for the two words and also for their conjunctive. They use four popular similarity scores for calculating page counts-based similarity scores. Here, they use a threshold (assumed to be 5) and if the query for page count is less than the threshold, then they set the four co-occurrences is zero in order to reduce the contrary effect due to random co-occurrences. Then, they snippets off the local consentence which contains a window of sentence selected from a web document that includes the queried words and that idea helps them to save the snippets into the database. Thus lexical patterns are extracted from the snippets which are clustered together and also given into the Support Vector Machine (SVM). Finally the SVM acts up on both results of word co-occurrence measures and also pattern clusters in order to calculate semantic similarity between two given words.

Takale and Nandgaonkar presented an approach for measuring semantic similarity between words using the Snippets returned by Wikipedia and the five different similarity measures of association [4]. At first, they downloaded the snippets using simple vocabulary from Wikipedia. Then they preprocessed that snippets gradually which are given below:

- Stop word removing by using Luhn's [5] method.
- Using suffix stripping and stemming by using the algorithm of Porter [6] for extracting some keywords.

Finally, by applying five different strategies - Jaccard, Dice, Overlap, Cosine and simple matching, they find out the semantic similarity of those extracted keywords.

Bollegala, Matsuo and Ishizuka proposed to measure semantic similarity between two words by extracting page counts and snippets using the AND query of the two words from a Web search engine (Google) [7]. Firstly compute the four page counts-based similarity scores of each word-pair in the set of synonymous word-pairs (from Wordnet synsets) by using Jaccard, Overlap, Dice, Point-wise Mutual Information (PMI). Then, extract list of snippets for the AND query of the two words from a Web search engine. By using their proposed pattern extraction algorithm with a set of synonymous and non-synonymous word-pairs, they count the frequency of the extracted patterns respectively. Then they, find out a reliable indicator of synonymy if and only if a pattern appears a statistically significant number of times in snippets for synonymous words then in snippets for non-synonymous words. Afterwards, form a feature vector for both synonymous and non-synonymous word-pair using the pattern frequencies together with page-count based similarity scores respectively [8]. Lastly, integrate all of these similarity scores into support vector machines (SVM) to form a semantic similarity measure by using sigmoid functions to convert the un-calibrated distance into a calibrated posterior probability [9].

According to Islam, Milions and Keselj's method, we get to know about the unsupervised approach for measuring sentence similarity using the tri-gram word similarity [10]. Their main idea is to find for each word in the shorter sentence, some most similar matching at the word level, in the longer sentence. At first they preprocess the two input sentence by removing special characters, punctuations and stop words. Then they count the number of exact matching words between that two processed sentences. Then they remove those matched words from that two processed sentences. If all the matched terms are negative, the program immediately go to the final steps. Otherwise, if there have some matched term, they construct a semantic similarity matrix by calculating semantic relatedness among two words which are getting from the two processed sentences. Here, they use semantic relatedness to find out the frequencies of all the tri-grams that starts and end with the given pair of words with respect to the uni-gram frequencies of the pair. After that, they construct different set of numbers taking each row elements of the matrix and determine a notation to calculate the mean frequency and also the standard deviation of those set. Then they retrieve the set of elements for any row of the matrix, such that each element in the set is larger than the summation of the mean and standard deviation of that row. Thus, the idea is to take into account some most similar matchings unlike in other methods which consider only a single matchings per word. Now choosing the elements of column of the matrix, they create a set utilizing a set-builder notation. After then, they compute the mean of that set. Besides, they estimate the summation of the means of all the rows in the matrix. In the final state, they add the number of exact matching values with that summarization and scale this total score by the reciprocal harmonic mean of that matrix to obtain a normalize similarity score between 0 and 1.

Kondrak develop a notion of n-gram similarity and distance where they illustrate that the edit distance and the length of longest common subsequent are special cases of n-gram distance and similarity respectively [11]. Here, they define a class of word similarity measures which include two widely-used measures – the longest common subsequence ratio (LCSR) and the normalized edit distance (NED) and a series of new measures based on n-grams. As their evaluation methodology is quite similar in all three experiments, so the outline of their experiments is given below:

1. Establish a standard set of word pairs that are known to be related.
2. Generate a much larger set of candidate word pairs.
3. Compute the similarity of all candidate word pairs using similarity measure.
4. Sort the candidate word pairs per the similarity value, breaking ties randomly.
5. Compute the information-retrieval evaluation technique named 11-point interpolated average precision on the sorted list.

Finally, the precision is computed for the recall levels of different level of percentage and then averaged to yield a single number where they uniformly set the precision value at 0% recall to 1 as well as the precision value at 100% recall to 0.

2 Methodology

Our method uses the notion of *n-grams of characters*. This notion has been used in the methodology of [12–15] etc. articles in a respective manner. As we know, an *n-gram* is a contiguous sequence of *n* items from a given sequence of sentence or speech and the items might be letters, characters, words per the application. Because of simplicity as well as scalability, we choose *n-grams of characters* in our technique. Additionally, *n-grams of characters* are natural due to the nature of the sentences to be analyzed. Besides, while *n-grams of characters* used for language modeling, some independent assumptions need to make where those assumptions are important as those can massively simplify the problem of learning language model from large sentence. Furthermore, multilingualism can be deal using this model. Our proposed method is based on some steps. To explain our method precisely we will use an example for each step. Afterward, we will illustrate more about our methodology. The steps of our methodology are given below:

Step 1: Assembling two large datasets from different web pages, journals, blogs, pdf file, doc file, sentence file etc. To better explain, let suppose two short sentences:

Sentence1: Computing.
Sentence2: Recomputing.

Step 2: Preprocessing those raw data-sets i.e. removing special characters, punctuations and stop-words separately. To get better result, converting all upper-case letter into lower case. So, both sentences will be:

Sentence1: computing
Sentence2: recomputing

Step 3: Producing *n-grams of characters* using those data separately and placing those in a set. We tried all the possible size of *n-grams* (i.e. *n-gram* = 1, 2, 3, 4 ...), but lastly, we get the best result using *"trigram"* (using the size of *n-gram* = 3). Mentioned example will be:

Sentence1: 'com', 'omp', 'mpu', 'put', 'uti', 'tin', 'ing'.
Sentence2: 'rec', 'eco', 'com', 'omp', 'mpu', 'put', 'uti', 'tin', 'ing'.

Step 4: Measuring distance between *n-grams* of characters. Basically, the following two distance matrices describe a certain measure of distance between two pair of *n-grams of characters* which lead to measure the similarity between two large sentences precisely. From our previous step, we got the *n-grams* of character of two sentences. Now, the distance between those *n-gram* of characters are given below (Tables 1 and 2):

Table 1. Distance Matrix1

(i, j)	com	omp	mpu	put	uti	tin	ing
com	0	1	2	3	4	5	6
omp	−1	0	1	2	3	4	5
mpu	−2	−1	0	1	2	3	4
put	−3	−2	−1	0	1	2	3
uti	−4	−3	−2	−1	0	1	2
tin	−5	−4	−3	−2	−1	0	1
ing	−6	−5	−4	−3	−2	−1	0

Table 2. Distance Matrix2

(i, j)	rec	eco	com	omp	mpu	put	uti	tin	ing
rec	0	1	2	3	4	5	6	7	8
eco	−1	0	1	2	3	4	5	6	7
com	−2	−1	0	1	2	3	4	5	6
omp	−3	−2	−1	0	1	2	3	4	5
mpu	−4	−3	−2	−1	0	1	2	3	4
put	−5	−4	−3	−2	−1	0	1	2	3
uti	−6	−5	−4	−3	−2	−1	0	1	2
tin	−7	−6	−5	−4	−3	−2	−1	0	1
ing	−8	−7	−6	−5	−4	−3	−2	−1	0

Above mentioned distance matrices are hollow matrixes where we find some explicit matching distance between two *n-grams of characters* denoted by 0. For example - *('com', 'com')* = 0, *('omp', 'omp')* = 0, *('rec', 'rec')* = 0 and so on. The increased positive numeric value of each row from both tables represents a strong positive correlation among two *n-grams of characters* i.e. *('com', 'omp')* = 1, *('eco', 'com')* = 1, *('omp', 'ing')* = 5 and so on. Simultaneously, those positive values signify the distance as well. On the other hand, the increased negative value of each row indicates strong negative correlation between two *n-grams of characters*. For example − *('mpu', 'com')* = −2, *('ing', 'rec')* = −8 etc. As we know, the distance cannot be negative value and to meet the criteria of a matric distance all the off-diagonal entries must be positive value where $a_{ij} > 0$ if $i \neq j$. So, we will remove those negative values afterward. In this way, our two distance matrices satisfy all properties.

Step 5: Removing all negative values from both distance matrices. So, the distance matrices will be (Tables 3 and 4):

Table 3. Matrix1 without negative values

(i, j)	com	omp	mpu	put	uti	tin	ing
com	0	1	2	3	4	5	6
omp		0	1	2	3	4	5
mpu			0	1	2	3	4
put				0	1	2	3
uti					0	1	2
tin						0	1
ing							0

Table 4. Matrix2 without negative values

(i, j)	rec	eco	com	omp	mpu	put	uti	tin	ing
rec	0	1	2	3	4	5	6	7	8
eco		0	1	2	3	4	5	6	7
com			0	1	2	3	4	5	6
omp				0	1	2	3	4	5
mpu					0	1	2	3	4
put						0	1	2	3
uti							0	1	2
tin								0	1
ing									0

Step 6: Measuring the similarity and dissimilarity from these two matrixes. From above two matrices, we get similarities between them if and only if $a_{1ij} = a_{2ij} = $ distance value. For example – the matching true matching values between two matrices are ('com', 'com', 0), ('put', 'uti', 1), and so on. Beside rest of the word pairs with distance values are dissimilar. That means the word 'computing' and 'recomputing' is 62.22% similar. Whether the dissimilarities between them is only 37.78%.

Step 7: Calculating the similarity and dissimilarity scores more preciously by using five popular co-occurrence measures: Jaccard, Dice, Overlap, Cosine and Simple.

Here, the matrices use association ratios between n-grams that are computed using their co-occurrence frequency in datasets. The basic assumption of this approach is that high co-occurrence frequencies indicate high association ratios and high association ratios indicate a semantic relation between n-grams. The five similarity measures proposed here are based on the five commonly used measures of association in information retrieval. The combination of row and column from each matrix used here which are produced from the set of *n-grams of characters* and the counting measure |.| gives the size of the set. The short description of these similarity methods is given below:

Similarity Measuring Methods: Let suppose, the set for Matrix1 is A and Matrix2 is B which are given below respectively:

A = {['com', 'com', 0], ['com', 'omp', 1], ['com', 'mpu', 2], ['com', 'put', 3], ['com', 'uti', 4], ['com', 'tin', 5], ['com', 'ing', 6], ['omp', 'omp', 0], ['omp', 'mpu', 1], ['omp', 'put', 2], ['omp', 'uti', 3], ['omp', tin', 4], ['omp', 'ing', 5], ['mpu', 'mpu', 0], ['mpu', 'put', 1], ['mpu', 'uti', 2], ['mpu', 'tin', 3], ['mpu', ing', 4], ['put', 'put', 0], ['put', 'uti', 1], ['put', 'tin', 2], ['put', 'ing', 3], ['uti', 'uti', 0], ['uti', 'tin', 1], ['uti', 'ing', 2], ['tin', 'tin', 0], ['tin', ing', 1], ['ing', 'ing', 0]}.

B = {['rec', 'rec', 0], ['rec', 'eco', 1], ['rec', 'com', 2], ['rec', 'omp', 3], ['rec', 'mpu', 4], ['rec', 'put', 5], ['rec', 'uti', 6], ['rec', 'tin', 7], ['rec', 'ing', 8], ['eco', 'eco', 0], ['eco', 'com', 1], ['eco', 'omp', 2], ['eco', mpu', 3], ['eco', 'put', 4], ['eco', 'uti', 5], ['eco', 'tin', 6], ['eco', ing', 7], ['com', 'com', 0], ['com', 'omp', 1], ['com', 'mpu', 2], ['com', 'put', 3], ['com', 'uti', 4], ['com', 'tin', 5], ['com', 'ing', 6], ['omp', 'omp', 0], ['omp', 'mpu', 1], ['omp', 'put', 2], ['omp', 'uti', 3], ['omp', tin', 4], ['omp', 'ing', 5], ['mpu', 'mpu', 0], ['mpu', 'put', 1], ['mpu', 'uti', 2], ['mpu', 'tin', 3], ['mpu', ing', 4], ['put', 'put', 0], ['put', 'uti', 1], ['put', 'tin', 2], ['put', 'ing', 3], ['uti', 'uti', 0], ['uti', 'tin', 1], ['uti', 'ing', 2], ['tin', 'tin', 0], ['tin', ing', 1], ['ing', 'ing', 0]}

Now, we will compute five co-occurrences measures using both sets which are drawn below with outcome in Table 5.

(a) *Jaccard coefficient for similarity:*

$$J(A, B) = |A \cap B| / |A \cup B| = |A \cap B| / (|A| + |B| - |A \cap B|)$$

(b) *Jaccard coefficient for dissimilarity:*

$$d_j(A, B) = 1 - J(A, B)$$

(c) *Dice coefficient:*

$$QS = 2C / (A + B) = 2|A \cap B| / (|A| + |B|)$$

(d) *Overlap coefficient:*

$$overlap(X, Y) = |X \cap Y| / \min(|X|, |Y|)$$

(e) *Cosine similarity:*

$$similarity = \cos(\theta) = \frac{A.B}{\|A\|\|B\|} = \frac{\sum_{i=1}^{n} A_i B_i}{\sqrt{\sum_{i=1}^{n} A_i^2}\sqrt{\sum_{i=1}^{n} B_i^2}}$$

(f) *Simple matching:*

$$\textbf{SMC} = \textbf{Number of Matching Attributes / Number of Attributes}$$
$$= (\textbf{M}_{00} + \textbf{M}_{11})/(\textbf{M}_{00} + \textbf{M}_{01} + \textbf{M}_{10} + \textbf{M}_{11})$$

Where:

M_{11} represents the total number of attributes where A and B both have a value of 1.
M_{01} represents the total number of attributes where the attribute of A is 0 and the attribute of B is 1.
M_{10} represents the total number of attributes where the attribute of A is 1 and the attribute of B is 0.
M_{00} represents the total number of attributes where A and B both have a value of 0.

Finally, the measure of similarity and dissimilarity is:

Table 5. Similarity and dissimilarity coefficient

Co-occurrence measures	Values
Jaccard coefficient for similarity	0.6222222
Jaccard coefficient for dissimilarity	0.3777778
Dice similarity coefficient	0.7671233
Dice dissimilarity coefficient	0.2328767
Overlap coefficient	1
Cosine similarity measure	0.7888106
Cosine dissimilarity measure	0.2111894
Simple matching coefficient	0.3835616
Simple matching distance	0.6164384

As per human approximation the two strings – 'computing' and 'recomputing' are quite similar. Using our method, the similarity results using different co-efficient are ≈ 1 [scale: (0, 1)] where Overlap coefficient gives the exact result 1 between two strings 'computing' and 'recomputing'. That means, our result is very close to human estimation. Among those results, only simple matching coefficient shows low similarity value.

3 Experimentations and Results

For our experimentation, we categories the sentences probabilities getting from different web-pages, using four various categorized sentences: 'positive similarities when the similarity of the sentences should be positive (true similarities TS)', 'positive similarities when the similarity of sentences should be negative false (false similarities FS)', 'negative similarities when the sentences should be positive (false dissimilarities FD)', and 'negative similarities when the similarity of sentences should be negative (true dissimilarities TD)'. We have, also compared our results with those obtained by Akermi and Faiz [2] and Takale et al. [4].

We have used a set of 200 sentences in English and in French. We have also take in account different type of sentences: sentences with proper nouns, declarative sentences, imperative sentences, interrogative sentences, sentences with coordination, prepositions, subordinations, sentences with adverbs, passive sentences, etc.

With our approach, we made 49 sentences comparisons. We obtained the following results: 26 true similarities, 18 true dissimilarities, 4 false dissimilarities and 1 false similarity. The accuracy of our methodology is then as it follows:

$True\,Similar\,Rate = \frac{TS}{TS+FD} = 86.67\%$

$True\,Dissimilar\,Rate = \frac{TD}{TD+FS} = 94.74\%$

$Accuracy = \frac{TS+TD}{TS+TD+FS+FD} = 89.796\%$

$Similar\,Predictive\,Value = \frac{TS}{TS+FS} = 96.2963\%$

$Dissimilar\,Predictive\,Value = \frac{TD}{TD+FD} = 81.82\%$

From the above calculations, we can say that the accuracy of our method is 89.796% which is quite satisfying without taking any help of the any online dictionary and any search engine etc. The true similar and dissimilar rates of our method are 86.67% and 94.74% respectively.

Now, we will compare these values of our method with Akermi and Faiz's method [2] as well as Takale et al.'s methodology [4]. We will follow the same rules which are described before to find out the TS, TD, FS and FD respectively.

- Methodology of Akermi and Faiz
  True Similar Rate = 57%
  True Dissimilar Rate == 42.86%
  Accuracy = 50%
  Similar Predictive Value = 50%
  Dissimilar Predictive Value = 50%
- Methodology of Takale & Nandgaonkar
  True Similar Rate = 42.86%
  True Dissimilar Rate = 57%
  Accuracy = 50%
  Similar Predictive Value = 50%
  Dissimilar Predictive Value = 50%

We got the accuracy level of our method is 89.796% and Akermy & Faiz and Takale et al. accuracy level is 50% and 50% respectively. Besides, the rates of true similar and dissimilar are 86.67% and 94.74% respectively. From the method of Akermy and Faiz, the rates of true similar and dissimilar are 57% and 42.86% severally. Besides, from the method of Takale and al., the rates of true similar and dissimilar are 42.86% and 57% respectively. So, we can definitely say that, we get the highest true similar and dissimilar rate as well as the accuracy level is greater than their results. On the other hand, we also noticed that, their method is unable to detect any French sentences or multilingual sentences. Besides, our method is free from these types of limitations.

Above experimentation gave better results to our approach. In addition, our method does not need to follow any grammatical rules, any kind of search engine as well as dictionaries. We can find out the main advantages of our method which are given below:

- Does not follow any dictionary so the processing is quite simple and takes less time. On another hand, using dictionary and search engine sometimes may have problem while exceeding the usage per day i.e. for if the usage of dictionary crossed 500 times per day then it shows error. Finally, some dictionaries might be case sensitive. So sometimes it might be a great problem. In our case, we do not have such dilemma.
- Does not follow the grammar rules, it can learn by itself which could be beneficial for further implementation.
- Does not follow any certain web-pages like Wikipedia, so it could be more versatile and the results would be more authentic.
- Does not depend on some certain search engines like Digg.com as well as Google.com which prevents getting error for over- accessing as well as falsify or exaggerated information.
- The great advantage of our algorithm is multilingualism i.e. our method would be beneficial to find out the similarity between other languages as well as the translated sentences like English $\leftrightarrow$ French. Our method can be used to process any kind of languages like English, French, Chinese, Arabic, Bangla etc. Though this time we tried our method to process English and French sentences, but in near future we will make it more versatile for any kind of languages.

Despite interesting results, we have some limitations with some grammatical rules, especially with passive sentences as in: I am eating rice vs rice is being eaten by me or Carl sounded the alarm due to the panic vs the alarm was sounded by Carl due to the panic. As per our opinion these sentences are similar. However, the values given by Jaccard, Dice, Simple Matching and Cosine similarity are very low.

4 Conclusion

Our approach has been implemented with C# and deliberating the complexity of the algorithm, we deduce that the overall algorithm complexity is $O(N^2)$.

Regardless some limitations, the accuracy level of our method is 89.796% and the true similar and dissimilar rate of our method are 86.67% & 94.74% respectively. These results are very much satisfying comparing to other method.

From above discussion, we can notice that for some certain point our algorithm is unable to give intended result. In our future work, we will expect to use artificial intelligence (AI) to make the similarity detection even more precise.

References

1. Akermi, I., Faiz, R.: An approach to semantic text similarity computing. In: Silhavy, R., Senkerik, R., Oplatkova, Z.K., Silhavy, P., Prokopova, Z. (eds.) Modern Trends and Techniques in Computer Science. AISC, vol. 285, pp. 383–393. Springer, Cham (2014). https://doi.org/10.1007/978-3-319-06740-7_32
2. Akermi, I., Faiz, R.: Hybrid method for computing word-pair similarity based on web content. In: Proceedings of the 2nd International Conference on Web Intelligence, Mining and Semantics. ACM, Craiova (2012)
3. Kumari, P., Ravishankar, K.: Measuring Semantic Similarity between Words using Page-Count and Pattern Clustering Methods (2013)
4. Takale, S.A., Nandgaonkar, S.S.: Measuring semantic similarity between words using web documents. Int. J. Adv. Comput. Sci. Appl. (2010)
5. Rijsbergen, C.J.V.: Information Retrieval. Butterworth-Heinemann, London (1979)
6. Porter, M.F.: An algorithm for suffix stripping. Program **14**(3), 130–137 (1980)
7. Bollegala, D., Matsuo, Y., Ishizuka, M.: WebSim: a web-based semantic similarity measure. In: Proceedings of 21st Annual Conference of the Japanese Society of Artificial Intelligence (2007)
8. Manning, C.: Foundations of statistical natural language processing. Nat. Lang. Eng. **8**(1), 91–92 (2002)
9. Platt, J.: Probabilistic outputs for support vector machines and comparisons to regularized likelihood methods. Adv. Large Margin Classifiers **10**(3), 61–74 (1999)
10. Islam, A., Milios, E., Kešelj, V.: Text similarity using Google tri-grams. In: Kosseim, L. Inkpen, D. (eds.) AI 2012. LNCS (LNAI), vol. 7310, pp. 312–317. Springer, Heidelberg (2012). https://doi.org/10.1007/978-3-642-30353-1_29
11. Kondrak, G.: N-gram similarity and distance. In: Consens, M., Navarro, G. (eds.) SPIRE 2005. LNCS, vol. 3772, pp. 115–126. Springer, Heidelberg (2005). https://doi.org/10.1007/11575832_13
12. Grefenstette, G.: Comparing two language identification schemes. In: Proceedings of JADT 1995 (1995)
13. Damashek, M.: Gauging similarity with n-grams: language-independent categorization of sentence. Science **267**, 843–848 (1995)
14. Huffman, S., Damashek, M.: Acquaintance: a novel vector-space n-gram technique for document categorization. In: NIST Special Publication, National Institute of Standards and Technology, pp. 305–310 (1995)
15. Biskri, I., Delisle, S.: Les n-grams de caractères pour l'aide à l'extraction de connaissances dans des bases de données sentenceuelles multilingues. In: Proceedings of TALN-2001, pp. 93–102 (2001)

Performance Comparison of Intelligent Techniques Based Image Watermarking

Musab Ghadi[1], Lamri Laouamer[1], Laurent Nana[1], Anca Pascu[1],
and Ismaïl Biskri[2(✉)]

[1] Lab-STICC, Université de Brest, CNRS, Université Bretagne Loire, Brest, France
e21409716@etudiant.univ-brest.fr, lamri_laouamer@yahoo.fr,
{Laurent.Nana,Anca.Pascu}@univ-brest.fr
[2] LAMIA, Département de Mathématiques et Informatique,
Université du Québec à Trois-Rivières, Trois-Rivières, Canada
Ismail.Biskri@uqtr.ca

Abstract. The correlations between image characteristics and the Human Visual System (HVS) are investigated in this paper to present their effect on the performance of different image watermarking approaches. The human eye is highly sensitive to various image's characteristics either in spatial domain or in frequency domain. Analyzing these characteristics according to the HVS takes place using different intelligent techniques. These techniques manipulate image characteristics to identify the visual significant locations or coefficients in host image for holding watermark. Inserting watermark in host image through these locations or coefficients would be acceptable with less vulnerability to attacks and causing less noticeable visual distortion on image. Some of intelligent watermarking approaches exploiting the correlation between image characteristics and HVS, are explored and compared for their performance in terms of imperceptibility, robustness and computational complexity.

Keywords: HVS · Watermarking · Intelligent techniques
Imperceptibility · Robustness

1 Introduction

Generating identical and unauthorized digital images becomes prospect with advanced technologies. Indeed, the digital images can be copied, transmitted, and manipulated anonymously. Image watermarking is the process of hiding secret information called watermark in the original image. The original image is readable and visual for all users, while the hidden information is readable and changeable by the authorized user. It may be used to verify the authenticity and the integrity of the host image or to show the identity of its owners [1].

Analyzing the characteristics of digital image, which are homogenous for HVS, is a useful process. This process helps to identify visual significant locations or coefficients in which the watermark could be embedded without causing noticeable visual difference and with robustness to various attacks in the same time.

© Springer International Publishing AG, part of Springer Nature 2018
M. Mouhoub et al. (Eds.): IEA/AIE 2018, LNAI 10868, pp. 844–853, 2018.
https://doi.org/10.1007/978-3-319-92058-0_81

The spatial pixels and the frequency coefficients of the host image have many properties that are correlated to HVS. In the frequency domain, the DWT has been widely employed in watermarking due to its spatial localization and multi-resolution characteristics. The excellent energy compaction for highly correlated image coefficients is one advantage of DCT, imposing watermark invisibility and robustness [2]. The obtained singular values from SVD process have many advantages for image watermarking system. These values specify the luminance of the image and are corresponding pair of singular vectors reflecting the geometry of the image. Aforementioned properties support inserting watermark robustly into singular values with low variation on their original values [3].

In spatial domain, the spatial pixels of digital image provided information for many characteristics that are in relationship with HVS. Color, luminance, contrast, brightness, darkness, image surface and background are set of characteristics that can be obtained by analyzing the values of spatial pixels. These characteristics are used to identify visual significant locations in host image that help to design image watermarking with acceptable imperceptibility and robustness rates.

In most developed HVS based image watermarking systems, the intelligent techniques are incorporated. They are used to optimize some parameters, in order to adapt embedding strength or to define most significant visual locations/coefficients for holding watermark data.

This paper presents the significant relationships between some image characteristics and HVS. It shows the benefits of using different intelligent techniques in analyzing these characteristics in target to achieve good performance for any image watermarking approaches. The performance of these models in terms of robustness, imperceptibility, and computational complexity are compared.

The paper is organized as follows: the correlation between some image characteristics and HVS is illustrated in Sect. 2. Section 3 explores some image watermarking approaches incorporating HVS characteristics and intelligent techniques. Section 4 introduces a performance comparison between these watermarking approaches in terms of robustness, imperceptibility, and computational complexity. At the end, Sect. 5 concludes this paper.

2   Image Characteristics Related to the Human Visual System

The texture is a complex visual pattern consisting of mutually related pixels that give an information about the color, brightness, darkness, and image surface and background. All of these characteristics are correlated to HVS and can be represented by calculating some statistical features like entropy, skewness, and kurtosis. Examining the relationships between these features helps to define highly textured regions in host image, which are more suitable for holding watermark. Inserting watermark in visual significant regions in host image leads to high imperceptibility and robustness against various attacks [4].

The color is another image characteristic correlated to HVS. The human eye is less sensitive to the blue color than red or green colors [5]. Hence, increasing the pixels values of blue color in which the watermark is being embedded, the original image is not distorted visibly.

The DCT coefficients carry many characteristics that are in relationship with the HVS, due to the high correlation between DCT coefficients drawn from adjacent DCT blocks. The DC coefficient for any image block expresses the brightness and the darkness characteristics of that region, while the difference value between the DCT coefficients of adjacent blocks expresses texture characteristic. High difference value expresses more texture than low difference value. Increasing the value of a DCT coefficient according to the others enhances the imperceptibility but may not enhance the robustness. As well, adjusting slightly the values of high DC coefficients which correspond to the significant visual locations will not cause noticeable visual distortion of the image. Also, embedding watermark in these locations enhances robustness against different attacks.

SVD provides many attractive properties correlated to HVS. Singular values, which are obtained from SVD process, stand for the luminance of the image while variance measures the relative contrast and smoothness of the intensity in the image. If a small data is added to an image, large variation of its singular values does not occur [3]. Moreover, SVD has many properties that are very much desirable for designing watermarking algorithms that are particularly robust to geometric attacks [3].

Some parameters of the multi-resolution decomposition of the image using DWT are correlated to the HVS. DWT provides a proper spatial localization and decomposes an image into horizontal, vertical, and diagonal dimensions representing low and high frequencies [1]. The energy distribution is concentrated in low frequencies, while the high frequencies cover the missing details. Since the human eye is more sensitive to the low frequency coefficients, then distributing the watermark on high frequency coefficients causes less visual distortion in image.

3   Intelligent Techniques Based Image Watermarking

Many image watermarking approaches proposed in the literature take into account some image characteristics that are correlated to HVS. Different intelligent techniques are used to analyze these characteristics and offer many benefits, including improving the performance of watermarking in terms of robustness and imperceptibility.

The correlation between DCT coefficients of adjacent blocks is exploited in [6] to define the visual significant locations in host image for embedding watermark. The Artificial Bee Colony (ABC) technique is used as a meta-heuristic optimization method for optimizing watermark embedding process. The goal of this optimization is to achieve maximum level of robustness and lower level of image distortion. A new fitness function is proposed to optimize the embedding parameters in order to provide required convergence for the optimum values.

The attractive properties of singular values are exploited in [4] to compute the activity factor for each processed image block using a weight parameter (α). The blocks with good visual masking effect are selected for embedding watermark. The embedding intensity parameter (β) is also used to control image quality. The Genetic Algorithm (GA) is used to optimize the values of (α and β) in order to improve the robustness and imperceptibility rates.

The Fuzzy Inference System (FIS) and Back Propagation Artificial Neural Network (BPANN) algorithm are integrated in [7] to optimize the intensity factor (α), which is used to balance between the robustness and the imperceptibility rates. The FIS manipulates the texture and brightness characteristics of DCT coefficients to find a basis used to select high textured and high luminance blocks in the host image. The DCT coefficients of the selected blocks are used as a training data for centroid method based BPANN to find the optimum weight factor for the embedding process. Using centroid method based BPANN enhanced the robustness and imperceptibility ratios.

The varying gray-scale of spatial pixels and the statistical redundancy in DWT are two ambiguity problems that affect the image perceptual quality after embedding the watermark. The properties of singular values and DWT are exploited in [8] to design a reference watermarking model able to avoid these problems. The difference value between the maximum and minimum values of gray-scale pixels is used as a threshold to approximate one band of DWT into upper and lower sets. One band of DWT is used as a reference image, while the upper and lower sets are used as weight factors in the embedding process to improve image quality. The watermark is embedded in singular values using the weight factors without causing noticeable visual difference.

The sensitivity of human eye to the blue color and to the brightness is also exploited to define visual significant locations in host image for holding watermark with less quality distortion. Indeed, there is no standard thresholds for the blue color and DC coefficient to say that this location in host image could accept more data without causing noticeable visual distortion. Rough set theory is applied in [9] to approximate the image blocks into upper and lower sets using two theoretical based thresholds which are related to the values of blue color and DC coefficient. All blocks in the boundary region are used as visual significant blocks for adding watermark data. The spatial pixels in these blocks are increased in a level that guarantees less visual distortion and withstands various attacks.

The FIS is applied in [10] to calculate the orthogonal moments of the host image and to calculate the quantization factor for each moment. Indeed, the orthogonal moments describe the fine image information and can be used as significant visual moments to hold the watermark. The quantization factors of these moments are optimized using GA to improve the robustness and imperceptibility rates. The obtained optimized values of quantization factors are used as basis to decide the amount of bits that can be embedded in each moment without causing noticeable visual difference.

In [2] the BPANN is applied to draw a connection between the DCT coefficients of adjacent blocks. The inequality relationship between the real and the predicted values is exploited to insert the watermark bit with least visual distortion. The minimum perceptual threshold (Just-Noticeable Difference(JND)), minimum clearance and adequate offset are set of parameters used to preserve the limit distortion and to decide the embedding strength.

Examining the relationships between set of statistical features in host image helps to define visual significant locations for embedding watermark. These features are in relationship with the HVS and give information about the brightness, darkness, image surface and background in each image region. The Frequent Pattern (FP) mining method is applied in [11] to find the most relevant features that frequently occur together within a host image. The highly correlated features compose a frequent pattern. All blocks that satisfy this pattern are considered as the strongly textured blocks and are used for embedding watermark with low image quality distortion and acceptable resistance against different attacks.

The Formal Concept Analysis (FCA) is another data analysis method used in [12] to examine the relationships between the same features as those used in [11]. FCA manipulates the features and the image blocks to find the set of all blocks that share a common subset of features and the set of all features that are shared by one of the blocks. The result of this manipulation is set of formal concepts, each consists of an extent (a set of blocks) and an intent (a set of features). The constructed formal concepts give an indication about the set of blocks that satisfy the maximum number of features. These blocks are considered as the most visual significant blocks and are used for embedding watermark.

Multi-Criteria Decision Making (MCDM) is an approach to solve problems that are characterized as a choice among many alternatives to find the best one based on different criteria and decision-maker's preferences. Technique for Order Preference by Similarity to Ideal Solution (TOPSIS) is an MCDM method. It has been used in [13] to define the visual significant blocks in host image according to a set of statistical features. It examines the relationships between these statistical features by calculating the closeness value of each block to the positive ideal solution (visual significant case) and to the negative ideal solution (visual insignificant case). Then, it ranks all blocks in a preference order using the resulted closeness values to the highest texture level. The highest ranked blocks are referenced as the significant textured blocks that are selected for embedding watermark with high imperceptibility and robustness rates.

The specifications of the illustrated watermarking approaches are presented in Table 1. The types of targeted images, the type of watermark, the domain (spatial or transform), the blindness and the looseness are set of features considered to describe each of the proposed approaches.

The values of the different features in Table 1 show that all of the proposed approaches are lossy and target natural gray-scale or color images. Some of the proposed approaches like [2, 4, 6, 7] have used 1-bit binary image as a watermark to proof the authenticity of image by embedding the watermark in the host image, while the approach proposed in [10] has used message bits with different

Table 1. Specifications of several proposed medical images watermarking approaches

Proposed approach	Types of targeted images	Type of watermark	Embedding domain	Blindness	Lossy or lossless
Hsu et al. 2015 [2]	Natural gray-scale images	1-bit binary image (0 or 1)	2D-DCT	Blind	Lossy
Han et al. 2016 [4]	Natural gray-scale images	1-bit binary image (0 or 1)	SVD and 2D-DCT	Blind	lossy
Abdelhakim et al. 2017 [6]	Natural gray-scale images	1-bit binary image (0 or 1)	2D-DCT	Blind	Lossy
Jagadeesh et al. 2016 [7]	Natural gray-scale images	1-bit binary image (0 or 1)	2D-DCT	Blind	Lossy
Kumar et al. 2017 [8]	Natural gray-scale images	8-bit binary image (0 or 255)	DWT and SVD	Semi-blind	Lossy
Ghadi et al. 2016 [9]	Natural color images	8-bit gray-scale image (0-255)	Spatial domain	Semi-blind	Lossy
Papakostas et al. 2016 [10]	Natural gray-scale images	Message bit lengths (100 bit, 300 bit or 500 bit)	Spatial domain	Blind	lossy
Ghadi et al. 2016 [11]	Natural gray-scale images	8-bit gray-scale image (0-255)	Spatial domain	Semi-blind	Lossy
Ghadi et al. 2017 [12]	Natural gray-scale images	8-bit gray-scale image (0-255)	Spatial domain	Semi-blind	Lossy
Ghadi et al. 2017 [13]	Natural gray-scale images	8-bit gray-scale image (0-255)	Spatial domain	Blind	Lossy

lengths to proof image's authenticity. The rest of approaches have used 8-bit gray-scale image as a watermark to proof image's authenticity.

The type of used watermark in every approach has an impact on the BER and NC ratios. The probability to get erroneous bits after extracting gray-scale watermark from attacked image becomes higher than the probability to get erroneous bits after extracting a binary watermark from attacked image.

For embedding domain feature, the approaches proposed in [2,4,6–8] were designed using frequency domain while the others were designed using spatial domain. For the blindness feature, the approaches proposed in [8,9,11,12] have extracting the watermark in semi-blind manner while the others have extracting the watermark in blind manner.

Table 2 presents a summary of the illustrated approaches from the perspective of the benefits of using intelligent technique. The intelligent technique used, the image characteristics that are correlated to HVS and the benefits of using the intelligent technique are precised in this table.

4   Performance Comparison

Table 3 presents performance comparison of the image watermarking approaches presented in the previous section. The comparison study takes into account the results achieved by each approach in terms of imperceptibility, robustness, and computational complexity. The measures that are selected to evaluate the performance of the presented watermarking approaches in Sect. 3 are selected according to the available data.

The computation complexity for each illustrated approach in Table 3 is computed after considering the computational complexities for the set of functions that are used in the given approach. All of the proposed approaches have been tested for their performance on host images I, of size $M \times N$. M is the height of image and N is the width of image. As far as the computational complexity is considered, the value considered for each approach is the upper limit of the execution time (i.e. the time complexity in the worst case).

The results in Table 3 show that none of the proposed watermarking approaches has the best performance for all the comparison metrics. Nevertheless, the method proposed in [13] is the one providing the best performances for most of the comparison criteria.

In terms of watermark imperceptibility, all watermarking approaches worked well to preserve low visual distortion on image after inserting watermark. The achieved PSNR in each watermarking approach is in the range 39.7–53 dB.

In terms of watermark robustness, most of the proposed watermarking approaches worked fine to protect watermark against different kinds of attacks. In approaches of [4,7–9,11–13] the BERs were good. For approaches of [2,6,10], the BER reaches high values (respectively 43%, 50% and 35%). These BERs show that these watermarking are not robust.

As the BER, the NC value provides another solution to measure the robustness of watermark against different attacks. In the comparison results, the NC values did not show any conflict with the achieved BERs values.

For the computational complexity, approaches of [2,4,6,7] have higher complexity $O((M \times N)^2 \log_2(M \times N))$ than the other approaches. The computational complexity of [8] approach equals $O(\min(M \times N^2, M^2 \times N))$, while it equals $O(M \times N)$ in the rest approaches. The approaches of [2,4,6,7] use 2D-DCT as embedding domain, and it is known that 2D-DCT process is more complex and time-consuming than DWT and SVD.

Table 2. Summary of the presented image watermarking approaches in this section.

Approach	Intelligent technique used	Image characteristics correlated to HVS	Benefits of using intelligent technique(s)
Hsu et al. 2015 [2]	BPNN	The correlation between the DCT coefficients of adjacent blocks expresses the texture	BPNN explored the correlation between the DCT coefficient to increase the value of one DCT coefficient according to the other to improve the imperceptibility and robustness rates
Han et al. 2016 [4]	Genetic algorithm	The singular values represent the luminance	Optimizing the values of embedding parameters improved the robustness and the imperceptibility rates
Abdelhakim et al. 2017 [6]	Artificial Bee Colony	The texture property obtained from the difference value between the DCT coefficients of adjacent blocks	Optimizing two embedding parameters led to obtain maximum level of robustness and lower level of image distortion
Jagadeesh et al. 2016 [7]	FIS and BPANN	The texture and brightness properties obtained from DCT coefficients	FIS constructed a basis for selecting the high textured and high luminance blocks for holding watermark. BPANN optimized weight factor of embedding process to improve the robustness and imperceptibility rates
Kumar et al. 2017 [8]	Rough set theory	The properties of singular values and DWT bands	Rough set approximated one DWT band into upper and lower sets. The upper and lower sets are used as weight factors in embedding process to improve image quality. Watermark is also embedded in the singular values to improve the imperceptibility and robustness rates
Ghadi et al. 2016 [9]	Rough set theory	The sensitivity of human eye to the color representations and to the brightness obtained from DC coefficient	Approximating image blocks into upper and lower sets helped to define set of significant visual blocks for embedding watermark with less visual distortion and good resistance to various attacks
Papakostas et al. 2016 [10]	FIS and GA	Orthogonal moments of the spatial pixels of image that represent the fine image information	FIS generated the quantization factors of orthogonal moment to control the embedding strength of the watermark, while the GA optimized these factors to find the maximum number of bits that can be added to the image without causing visual distortion
Ghadi et al. 2016 [11]	Frequent patterns mining	The sensitivity of human eye to the texture property (brightness, darkness, image surface and background)	FP mining process identified highly correlated features that defined visual significant locations in host image for embedding watermark with low image distortion and high robustness
Ghadi et al. 2017 [12]	FCA	The sensitivity of human eye to the texture property (brightness, darkness, image surface and background)	FCA helped to identify significant visual blocks for embedding watermark with high imperceptibility and robustness rates
Ghadi et al. 2017 [13]	MCDM	The sensitivity of human eye to the texture property (brightness, darkness, image surface and background)	TOPSIS examined the relationships between the texture features to identify the significant visual locations for watermark embedding with high imperceptibility and robustness rates

Table 3. Performance comparison between the image watermarking approaches presented in the previous section.

Approach	Imperceptibility	Robustness		Computational complexity
	PSNR dB	BER	NC	
Hsu et al. 2015 [2]	40	15–43%	×	$O((M \times N)^2 \log_2(M \times N))$
Han et al. 2016 [4]	46	×	93%	$O((M \times N)^2 \log_2(M \times N))$
Abdelhakim et al. 2017 [6]	39.7–46.7	1–50%	×	$O((M \times N)^2 \log_2(M \times N))$
Jagadeesh et al. 2016 [7]	47	×	73–100%	$O((M \times N)^2 \log_2(M \times N))$
Kumar et al. 2017 [8]	52.7	7–13%	70–87%	$O(\min(M \times N^2, M^2 \times N))$
Ghadi et al. 2016 [9]	45.5	16–17%	99%	$O(M \times N)$
Papakostas et al. 2016 [10]	40	19–35%	×	$O(M \times N)$
Ghadi et al. 2016 [11]	43.5	16–20%	99%	$O(M \times N)$
Ghadi et al. 2017 [12]	45.5	11	99%	$O(M \times N)$
Ghadi et al. 2017 [13]	53	1–3	80–97%	$O(M \times N)$

5 Conclusion

This paper presented the significant correlations between some image characteristics and the HVS, as well as their effect on the performance of image watermarking approaches. The spatial pixels and the transformed coefficients obtained from DCT, DWT or SVD of digital image carry many useful properties that are in relationship with the HVS. Examining the relationships between these characteristics and HVS using many intelligent techniques gives three advantages for the field of image watermarking. Firstly, the intelligent techniques make it possible to identify visual significant locations or coefficients in host image to insert watermark with less image distortion and high robustness. Secondly, some intelligent techniques in some proposed watermarking approaches help to find basis for the limit number of bits that can be added to the image without causing visual distortion. Thirdly, some intelligent techniques help to derive and to optimize some strength parameters that are extracted from image characteristics to control embedding strength, and then to improve the imperceptibility and robustness rates.

References

1. Qasim, A.F., Meziane, F., Aspin, R.: Digital watermarking: applicability for developing trust in medical imaging workflows state of the art review. Comput. Sci. Rev. **27**, 45–60 (2018)
2. Hsu, L.-Y., Hu, H.-T.: Blind image watermarking via exploitation of inter-block prediction and visibility threshold in DCT domain. J. Vis. Commun. Image Represent. **32**, 130–143 (2015)
3. Lai, C.C.: An improved SVD-based watermarking scheme using human visual characteristics. Optics Commun. **284**, 938–944 (2011)
4. Han, J., Zhao, X., Qiu, C.: A digital image watermarking method based on host image analysis and genetic algorithm. J Ambient Intell. Human Comput. **7**, 37–45 (2016)
5. Findik, O., Babaolu, I., lker, E.: Implementation of BCH coding on artificial neural network-based color image watermarking. Int. J. Innov. Comput. Inf. Control. **7**(8), 4905–4914 (2011)
6. Abdelhakim, A., Saleh, H., Nassar, A.: A quality guaranteed robust image watermarking optimization with artificial bee colony. Expert Syst. Appl. **72**, 317–326 (2017)
7. Jagadeesh, B., Kumar, R.P., Reddy, C.P.: Robust digital image watermarking based on fuzzy inference system and back propagation neural networks using DCT. Soft. Comput. **20**, 3679–3686 (2016)
8. Kumar, S., Jaina, N., Fernandes, S.L.: Rough set based effective technique of image watermarking. J. Comput. Sci. **17**, 121–137 (2017)
9. Ghadi, M., Laouamer, L., Nana, L., Pascu, A.: Fuzzy rough set based image watermarking approach. In: Proceedings of the International Conference on Advanced Intelligent Systems and Informatics, vol. 533, pp. 234–245 (2016)
10. Papakostas, G.A., Tsougenis, E.D., Koulouriotis, D.E.: Fuzzy knowledge-based adaptive image watermarking by the method of moments. Complex Intell. Syst. **2**, 205–220 (2016)
11. Ghadi, M., Laouamer L., Nana, L., Pascu, A.: A robust associative watermarking technique based on frequent pattern mining and texture analysis. In: Proceedings of the 8th International ACM Conference on Management of computational and Collective Intelligence in Digital Ecosystems, pp. 73–81. ACM (2016)
12. Ghadi, M., Laouamer, L., Nana, L., Pascu, A.: A robust watermarking system based on formal concept analysis and texture analysis. In: Proceedings of the International Florida Artificial Intelligence Research Society Conference AAAI, pp. 682–687 (2017)
13. Ghadi, M., Laouamer, L., Nana, L., Pascu, A.: A joint spatial texture analysis/watermarking system for digital image authentication. In: Proceedings of the International Workshop on Signal Processing Systems, pp. 1–6. IEEE (2017)

Artificial Intelligence, Law and Justice

Case Law Analysis with Machine Learning in Brazilian Court

Rhuan Barros[1($\boxtimes$)], André Peres[1], Fabiana Lorenzi[2,3], Leandro Krug Wives[4],
and Etiene Hubert da Silva Jaccottet[5]

[1] IFRS - Campus Porto Alegre, Av. Cel. Vicente, 281, Porto Alegre, RS, Brazil
rhuanbarros@gmail.com, andre.peres@poa.ifrs.edu.br
[2] Universidade Luterana do Brasil (ULBRA), Canoas, RS, Brazil
[3] Instituto Federal de Educação, Ciência e Tecnologia do Rio Grande do Sul (IFRS),
Campus Canoas, Canoas, Brazil
fabilorenzi@gmail.com
[4] Universidade Federal do Rio Grande do Sul (UFRGS),
Av. Paulo Gama, 110, Porto Alegre, RS, Brazil
leandro.wives@ufrgs.br
[5] Centro Universitário Ritter dos Reis - Laureate International Universities,
Porto Alegre, RS, Brazil
jean395@gmail.com

Abstract. This paper aims the application of the knowledge discovering process in a judicial decisions database with the goal of unveiling the tendency of opinion Brazilian courts have, in relation to the favored party, employee or employer. Supervised machine learning techniques were used to classify documents. Such predictive model reached scores of more than 90% of ranking decision accuracy resulting in solid information about the tendency of each judge. Thus, this project contributes with a software that allows law firms to obtain information in a fast visual and exploratory way enabling them to focus and make more efforts in finding more effective legal strategies, than in jurisprudential research.

Keywords: Law · Artificial intelligence · Legal · Machine learning

1 Introduction

The use of quantitative methods for problem-solving occurs in several areas such as Economics, which applies econometrics to evaluate theoretical methods. In the law field, [1] coined the term "jurimetrics" which represents the union among juridic theory, computational methods and statistics with the goal of exploring jurisprudence and producing descriptive analysis and predictive studies [2].

Simultaneously, jurimetrics has become the focus of a rising interest in studies by the Brazilian Law researchers. The research of [3] analyzed manually 1044 sentences looking for real data related to juridic safety at establishing values

© Springer International Publishing AG, part of Springer Nature 2018
M. Mouhoub et al. (Eds.): IEA/AIE 2018, LNAI 10868, pp. 857–868, 2018.
https://doi.org/10.1007/978-3-319-92058-0_82

for moral damages by the judicial authority. Besides that, there was big difficulty to access the immense quantity of decisions that deal with moral damages
estimation.

Finally, it is possible to understand that jurists face their daily problems
with an even bigger issue that is the extraction of valuable information in an
effective way from the Brazilian judicial body decisions. This is partly because
these systems were developed in the 1990s from an infrastructure perspective
prior to the development of "Big Data" and "Cloud Computing" concepts. In
fact, the needs of that time were different and did not require large storage
capacity or processing, since most court documents were still written on paper.

In the meantime, new technological solutions are being implemented with the
aim of increasing judicial efficiency. Thus, in 2011 the National Justice Council
initiated the implementation of the Electronic Judicial Process, which allows
the prosecution of the legal case digitally in a computer system [4]. Currently,
more than 8 million cases are pending in this system, and more than 100 million
cases are in progress in the courts [4], partially digital. Thus, it is possible to
observe how the bodies of digital documents kept already demand a significant
amount of storage in the proportion of terabytes, not taking on account all the
new documents and judicial decisions published daily.

However, little was invested in new tools for the exploration, visualization,
and analysis of this publicly accessible corpus. In fact, the tools remain the same,
only sustaining legacy systems. These computer systems were developed by each
Court with the purpose of allowing the research in its judgments base. They
usually have several key-word searches in fields text and selection of judging
section, and as a result, they present a list with thousands of pages. Users must
repeat their query several times, making small changes in the query criteria, and
searching for the answers according to new items of interest [5]. Even with these
solutions, there is still the issue of visualization, since each result is presented
in a text block of approximately 6 lines containing the decision menu. The law
firms must read a large amount of results in order to find the relevant items.

In this context, the business problem is how to know with confidence what
is the Court judging tendency that will judge one individual process. It would
not be interesting to make a decision based only on a subjective opinion on
work experience. Therefore, in this situation, the legal director seeks to surround
himself or herself, with the maximum of evidence to support his/her decision to
accept or not a million-dollar agreement, for example. Thus, to conduct this
evidence-based search, lawyers spend hours conducting case-by-case research to
substantiate their claims, using online search tools provided by the courts which
are outdated, disorganized, confusing and superficial.

Dealing with this, a methodology was applied to process thousands of judicial
decisions of the Regional Labor Court of the 3rd Region, located in the State
of Minas Gerais, Brazil. We used text mining technologies for the extraction
and processing of documents, as well as, natural language processing in order
to build a representative model for automatic classification of documents. Thus,
such a representative model was developed with artificial intelligence training by

supervised learning using annotated judicial decisions to infer the most important features for document classification. This classifier presented more than 86% accuracy for document classification.

This paper presents a study that aims to contribute to the development of software that allows law firms to obtain information more efficiently in less time, which will allow them to focus their efforts on tasks of greater intellectual demand, such as strategically evaluating the best way to bring the claim to the Court. This software also helps higher courts to maintain greater control over the application of jurisprudence by lower courts, in addition to reducing the amount of searches by legal firms in their databases.

This paper is organized as follows: next section describes the background needed to better understand the paper context.

2 Background

This section presents a brief explanation of the fundamental giving concepts needed to understand the work.

2.1 Big Data

Big Data is a term used to describe large volumes of content - usually in quantities measured by terabytes or petabytes, that companies want to track and analyze [6]. Unstructured data is the largest component in this set that is only partially archived [7].

2.2 Process of Knowledge Discovery in Databases

Knowledge discovery in databases, KDD, is a field of computer science that studies how to extract useful knowledge from large collections of data. In 1996, representatives of a group of companies came together to form CRISP-DM, an acronym for CRoss-Industry Standard Process for Data Mining, which aimed to develop documentation and workshops in order to propose standardization to the knowledge discovery process in databases. At that time, there were no documented tools, solutions or processes that guided companies and researchers on better practices. Finally, in 1999 the CRISP-DM Guide 1.0 [10] was released.

The CRISP-DM Guide presents an iterative process composed of several phases, ranging from understanding business needs, to data modelling and application [11]. Figure 1 shows the cycle process proposed by the group with the following phases:

– **Business Understanding:** understanding the value of the knowledge to be generated by the business perspective, in order to align the project with the organization's strategic goals.

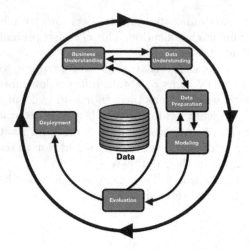

Fig. 1. Diagram of the process of knowledge discovery in databases using CRISP-DM [10]

- **Data Understanding:** it starts with data collection and initial exploration which allows the identification of quality problem and also the measurement of statistical knowledge about the data mass. This phase can identify if the data can actually answer the business questions and also identify the significant variables;
- **Data preparation:** the goal of this phase is to preprocess the data to make it relevant and consistent related to the knowledge-seeking task. This phase is extremely necessary because data can often be incomplete, inconsistent, or even prone to errors;
- **Modeling:** this phase consists in choosing methods and parameterization for pattern extraction, classification, segmentation, regression or association of items, which will generate new knowledge about the importance of each of the variables for the expected final result;
- **Evaluation:** in this phase, the recognized standards, association rules, and all generated knowledge are analyzed to verify their real utility. Statistical measures can also be applied as well as visualizations to help discovering the usefulness of the data.
- **Deployment:** it consolidates all processes in a report form and publication of knowledge, or in computational system incorporation of the modeling.

2.3   Information Retrieval

The retrieval of information in search engines is based on the correspondence between the keywords and the terms in the documents. A document that has a more frequent search term, is generally more related to the research [12].

To perform the ordering of the results, it is necessary to mark a weight for each term in the documents collection. The simplest proposal is to consider the number of occurrences of the term in each document as Term Frequency (TF) [12].

However, not all words in documents are important. There are words like prepositions that do not need to be indexed. In addition, there are words, such as "auto" in an auto industry collection, that will pretty much have that word in all documents. To mitigate this effect, it is important to reduce the weight of these words as their frequency increases in the collection. Therefore, the proposal is defined as the Document Frequency variable (DF), consisting of the number of documents that contain the term. Thus, the variable is introduced as Inverse Document Frequency (IDF) so that the IDF of a rare term is high and a frequent term is low [12].

The combination is given by TF-IDF$_{t,d} = TF_{t,d} \times IDF_t$.

This index indicates a weight that, **high:** when the term often occurs in a small number of documents, **low:** when the term occurs a few times in a document or if occurs in many documents or **low:** when the term occurs virtually in all documents.

2.4 Machine Learning and Its Limitations

The development of quantitative research in big judicial decision volumes would demand the concentrated effort of a big analysts team, not only to perform the initial analysis, but also to execute the maintenance of outcomes as the time goes by. In order to overcome this barrier, the Machine Learning technique may be used for training a software, so it could perform some tasks of judicial decision classification in a shorter time.

To perform this training, it's necessary to feed the algorithm with a judicial decision base annotated by specialists. This process comprises a judicial decision reading done by a human being, and the insertion of a label. In the case of this research, the label contains the information on who won the case. Employee or employer. After, this database is processed by a Machine Learning algorithm, which generates a model. This model, by means of random samples processing, mathematics transformations and the statistical analysis of words that are in each judicial decision, identifies patterns and summarizes it in a general math model, which is used to perform predictions and identify this very same patterns in new judicial decisions [26].

However, the Machine Learning techniques are subject of certain limits, such as for instance, the "bias", or tendency inserted by the machine learning algorithm, which, in order to develop a model needs to perform some suppositions, generalizations and reduce the research space size. Besides that, the accuracy of the model will considerably decrease, if the quantity of labeled documents for one of the two categories is a lot bigger than for the other [27].

2.5 Jurisprudence and Concepts Related to Law

Jurisprudence is the courts decisions set, in the exercise of law enforcement. It represents the court's view, at a given moment, on the legal issues brought to trial [13]. In this way, a labor judicial process begins in 1st Degree being sentenced by a singular judge. The parties that are not in agreement with the decision can appeal and apply to the Courts, also called the 2nd Degree of jurisdiction.

The Regional Labor Courts are composed by several judges, who are organized in Appeal Teams with 3 judges. Thus, when the appeal is forwarded to the Court, it is randomly distributed to one of the Appeal Teams to be performed by a collegiate judging. The Regional Labor Court of the 3rd Region, for instance, is consisted of 10 Appeal Teams.

In addition, a judgment is constituted by the Class members vote who have received the case to be judged and by the judgment containing the collegiate decision. It is also made up of a summary of the matter and conclusion of the judgment [14]. In this way, the summary is composed of key words to facilitate the jurisprudential research, besides being composed by terms contained in the legal thesaurus.

3 Related Work

Several studies agree that keyword search has several counterpoints and cannot meet the explosion of digital age relating to legal documents and, is also technologically insufficient [5,15,17,26].

Another area of study with increasing focus is the answer to legal questions [19,20]. The goal is to train a searching robot embedded in a conversational system and a legal database, so it could answer to questions formulated in natural language.

The Brazilian context [21] Apud [5] presented a proposal for indexing jurisprudential documents using Case-based Reasoning (CBR). The author coined the term Intelligent Jurisprudence Research (IJR) to name the case recovery process and the described results were superior than the results obtained by traditional methods.

Another interesting work was presented in [22], where the author compared the quality of automatic classification to the manual classification, already in execution, from an existing ontology.

4 Brazilian Case Law Search Systems

Currently, the jurisprudential search is performed by the law firms and jurists through Google search and also in the websites of each court. In addition, in the last few years other sites have appeared adding judicial decisions and providing them in their research tools.

All specialized sites provide keyword searching, enable the use of logical operators, provide selection of judgmental bodies, and the ordering by relevance and by date. In relation to the ordering of results, little information is presented about the algorithm, that is, the criterion used to perform the presentation of the documents. In addition, none of them present the data through graphs and views, nor does it providing visual aid to facilitate understanding of the documents or resources for data mining.

The available searching tools provided by public agencies are technologicaly outdated Besides, they present disorganized and confusing outcomes since the consulting performed with identical key-words originated from different computers produce different results. Table 1 presents the systems comparison.

Table 1. Comparison of Brazilian case law search systems

Website	Keyword	Word semantic root	Logical operators	Ontology	Exploration with visual aids	Presentation of the winning party	Protection against search robot (Captcha)
Google	Yes	Partial	Yes	No	No	No	Not detected
Digesto	Yes	Yes	Partial	No	No	No	Not detected
JusBrasil	Yes	Yes	No	No	No	No	Not detected
Court of the 3rd Region	Yes	No	Yes	No	No	No	Yes, after a few attempts
Court of the 4rd Region	Yes	No	Yes	No	No	No	Yes, after a few attempts

5 Development of the Proposed Software

This work seeks to meet the particular business problem that is how to know with confidence what is the opinion trend of a Class of Judges. For this, the goal of data mining was defined to identify and classify the decisions related to the part favored in the decisions.

5.1 Extraction of Documents

Afterwards, a script was developed to copy all the URIs contained in the sitemap files and to filter only those that correspond to the documents of the Regional Labor Court of the 3rd Region. With these results, it was possible to start the web scraping process of HTML pages containing the decision documents. We focus on documents from 2017.

5.2 Data Understanding

It was observed that each Panel of Judges presents a diverse linguistic style, such as different words to indicate the winning party, and there are summaries in which there is no information about the beneficiary of the decision. Thus, it was necessary to perform the extraction of the entire content of the judgments, which contains all the necessary information.

In this way, the decisions were grouped by each Class of Judges, because decisions of the same Class maintain the writing style of their relatively uniform decisions.

These tasks were needed in order to reduce the insertion of errors in the Machine Learning classifier. Since the algorithm is based on words that are found to create the model of prediction, it is important to guarantee that, the dataset of learning represents adequately the aimed classes to be classified.

5.3   Annotation of Documents

Initially, the goal was to read the entire content of the decisions and write down the winning party. However, we realized that all documents contain a brief summary of the judgment, indicating the part that was benefited. Thus, the processing was performed in the documents to extract only the final part of the decisions containing the information needed to understand the favored party. A spreadsheet has been generated with the following items: the small part of the decisions, the URL with the entire content for consultation, the field for the expert writing the beneficiary and type of appealing part, company or employee, or both. We considered only documents that presented a winning party (Table 2).

Table 2. Example annotated documents translated to English

End of decision	Recurrent	Granted	Part
... in a meeting held today unanimously, was informed of the embargoes of the declaration; **in merit, without disagreement, denied them provision**...	SERVUS LTDA	0	2
... at a meeting held today unanimously, rejected the preliminary of inadmissibility of the appeal raised by the claimant, heard of the ordinary appeal of the claimant and, **in merit, without disagreement, denied him provision**...	João	1	1

Moreover, the extracted documents contain the decision and its grounds, as well as the names of the applicants and defendants. However, the proposed classifier must present the information about the winning party in relation to the company or employee. Thus, the mining result must show if the applicant is a company or an employee and if the appeal was granted. We removed the documents where both employee and company appealed. Therefore, the experts carried out manual annotation of 600 documents from three different Classes of Appeal in relation to the type of applicant and, also in relation to the judgment deferral to the applicant.

5.4   Machine Learning Models

First, a predictive model was developed to detect the cases in which both the employee and the company appealed to, in order to remove them from the dataset. This task was performed with the string size calculation, since the strings that both resorted on average have more than double the amount of characters.

A prediction model was developed based on the "K-Nearest Neighbors" algorithm (k-NN), which presented 84% accuracy. Afterwards, the results in which both appealed, approximately 1/3, were taken from the dataset.

Secondly, training was done with the resulting dataset for classification between employee and employer, with the extraction of features through the TF-IDF index and Bayesian Networks. Thus, this model reached 92% accuracy.

In this phase, the dataset was preprocessed with the withdrawal of stop-words from the Portuguese language, and all the trainings were performed considering 1/3 of the test dataset.

Finally, the decisions were processed with the extraction of features through the TF-IDF index and Bayesian Networks to identify the grant of the decision to the applicant. This model reached 90% accuracy. In addition, such a model was trained individually in each Recursal Class and, in conjunction with the others, to be possible to ascertain possible overtraining, which was not identified, since the cross-tests among classes presented practically the same results with variation of approximately 3%.

6   Results

More than 10,000 judicial judgments published in 2017 were carried out from the ten Classes of Judges that compose the Regional Labor Court of the 3rd Region and processed with the proposed Machine Learnings models, which classified the type of claimant as a company or employee, and the appeal granting or denial for each decision. With this dataset was possible to determine the court's current view of the legal issues brought to its judgment. This view presents the proportion of granted requests in relation to the amount of appeals filed by each party.

As shown in Fig. 2, 61% of the total number of appeals filed by the claimants were totally or partially granted. 58% of the total number of appeals filed by the defendants were totally or partially granted. We observed that the Court appreciated the causes of both parties in approximately the same way, going against popular knowledge that "The Labor Court has always leaned more towards the worker side" [24, 25].

We also observed that the judging tendency of some individual Classes is different from the Court's general average. For example, Fig. 3 shows the results from two different classes of judges. We can see that the 9th Class (left) granted 30% more resources to employees than to companies, while the 1st Class (right) granted 18% more resources to companies than to employees. These results corroborate the idea that there are different tendencies in the Brazilian courts in relation to the favored party being employees or employers.

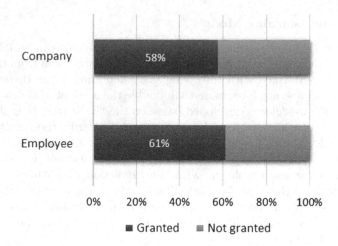

Fig. 2. Comparison of the results of the Regional Labor Court of the 3rd Region

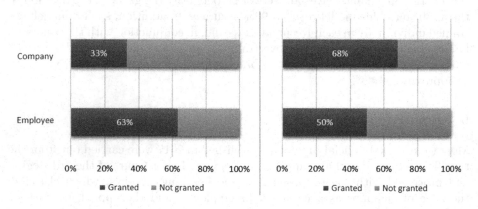

Fig. 3. Comparison of the results of the Regional Labor Courts of the 3rd Region

7   Conclusion and Future Work

It has developed a case law analysis project with a Machine Learning technique to present relevant information about the winners of the causes without the need to manually read the entire documents. Through supervised learning it was possible to obtain high scores of accuracy in the classification of documents.

Finally, it is possible to conclude that, there are really differences of understanding between Recurrent Classes, some supporting more the employees than companies and vice versa. In the meantime, these differences are standardized in the general context of the Court, which presents an independent uniform view of the party ensuring the jurisprudence for the whole society which resorts to the expert to settle their issues.

In addition, the project provides enough knowledge to meet the business objective that is the opinion trend of a Class of Judges. In this way, law firms can evaluate different strategies according to the Class of Judges that have been distributed or even work towards the realization of an agreement before the final judgment.

On the other hand, every Machine Learning model is subject to the bias or tendency inserted by the algorithm. However, the project was designed to minimize the insertion of elements that could decrease accuracy or cause over-training.

As future work, it would be interesting to carry out the processing of documents to identify the legal matters that each Class of Judges has granted in order to be able to construct a probabilistic model of success in court cases.

Acknowledgement. In memory of Etiene Hubert da Silva Jaccottet, the most charismatic person ever known. Word that comes from the Latin that represents the extraordinary and divine gift that he had to fascinate people. May his soul rest in peace.

References

1. Loevinger, L.: Jurimetrics–The Next Step Forward. 33 Minn. L. Rev. 455. HeinOnline (1948)
2. Jaeger Zabala, F., Silveira, F.F.: Jurimetria: Estatstica Aplicada Ao Direito/Jurimetrics: Statistics Applied in the Law. Revista Direito e Liberdade, vol. 16, no. 1, p. 87103 (2014)
3. Hirata, A., et al.: Dano moral no Brasil. Pensando o Direito, vol. 37, Secretaria de Assuntos Legislativos do Ministerio da Justica (2010)
4. Montenegro, M.C.: PJe atinge a marca de 7,4 mi de processos judiciais - Portal CNJ (2016). http://www.cnj.jus.br/noticias/cnj/81864-pje-atinge-a-marca-de-7-4-mi-de-processos-judiciais. Accessed 12 Sept 2017
5. Constancio, A.S.: Ontologia para um Motor de Busca Semantica para Recuperacao Jurisprudencial no Brasil. Master's thesis (2017)
6. Akerkar, R.: Big Data Computing. CRC Press, Boca Raton (2013)
7. Gandomi, A., Haider, M.: Beyond the hype: big data concepts, methods, and analytics. Int. J. Inf. Manag. **35**(2), 137–44 (2015)
8. Erl, T., Khattak, W., Buhler, P.: Big Data Fundamentals: Concepts, Drivers & Techniques. Prentice Hall Press, Englewood (2016)
9. Pierson, L.: Data Science for Dummies. Wiley, Hoboken (2015)
10. Chapman, P., Clinton, J.: CRISP-DM 1.0: Step-by-Step Data Mining Guide. CRISP (2000)
11. Becker, K.: Slides de aula Processo de KDD. UFRGS (2017)
12. Christopher, D.M., Prabhakar, R., Schtze, H.: An Introduction to Information Retrieval, vol. 151, p. 177. Cambridge University Press, Cambridge (2008)
13. TSE - Tribunal Superior do Trabalho. Perguntas frequentes - Pesquisa de jurisprudencia. http://www.tse.jus.br. Accessed 12 Sept 2017
14. STF - Supremo Tribunal Federal: Glossario Juridico :: STF - Supremo Tribunal Federal. [s.d.]. http://www.stf.jus.br/portal/glossario/. Accessed 12 Sept 2017
15. Borden, B.B., Baron, J.R.: Finding the signal in the noise: information governance, analytics, and the future of legal practice. Richmond J. Law Technol. **20**(2), 7–14 (2014). TC Williams School of Law University of Richmond

16. Koniaris, M., Anagnostopoulos, I., Vassiliou, Y.: Evaluation of diversification techniques for legal information retrieval. Algorithms **10**(1), 22 (2017). Multidisciplinary Digital Publishing Institute
17. Zhang, N., Pu, Y.-F., Wang, P.: An Ontology-Based Approach for Chinese Legal Information Retrieval (2015)
18. Jo, D.W., Kim, M.H.: A framework for legal information retrieval based on ontology. J. Korea Soc. Comput. Inf. **20**(9), 87–96 (2015)
19. Adebayo, K.J., Di Caro, L., Boella, G., Bartolini, C.: An Approach to Information Retrieval and Question Answering in the Legal Domain (2016)
20. IBM: ROSS Intelligence Artificial Intelligence in Legal Research. Blue Hill Research (2017). http://www.rossintelligence.com. Accessed 12 Sept 2017
21. Weber, R.: Intelligent jurisprudence research: a new concept. In: Proceedings of the 7th International Conference on Artificial Intelligence and Law, pp. 164–72. ACM (1999)
22. Ferauche, T., de Almeida, M.A.: Aprendizado de Classificadores de Ementas da Jurisprudencia do Tribunal Regional do Trabalho da 2 Regiao-SP. In: VI Workshop de pesquisa do Centro Estadual de Educaão Tecnológica Paula Souza-SP-Brasil (2011)
23. Chen, Y.-L., Liu, Y.-H., Ho, W.-L.: A text mining approach to assist the general public in the retrieval of legal documents. J. Assoc. Inf. Sci. Technol. **64**(2), 280–90 (2013). Wiley Online Library
24. Divisao de Comunicacao do CSJT: CSJT divulga dados sobre arrecadaçao e despesa em resposta a noticia sobre custo da JT - Noticias Lançamento - CSJT (2017)
25. Rogerio Barbosa: ConJur - Justica do Trabalho deixa de privilegiar empregado em acoões trabalhistas (2012)
26. Ashley, K.D.: Artificial Intelligence and Legal Analytics: New Tools for Law Practice in the Digital Age. Cambridge University Press, Cambridge (2017)
27. Kubat, M.: An Introduction to Machine Learning. Springer, Cham (2016). https://doi.org/10.1007/978-3-319-20010-1

Meticulous Transparency—An Evaluation Process for an Agile AI Regulatory Scheme

David Benrimoh[1,2(✉)], Sonia Israel[1,2,3], Kelly Perlman[1,2,4],
Robert Fratila[1,2,4], and Matthew Krause[1,2,4]

[1] McGill University, Montreal, Canada
{david.benrimoh, sonia.israel, kelly.perlman,
robert.fratila, matthew.krause}@mail.mcgill.ca
[2] aifred health, Montreal, Canada
[3] Douglas Mental Health University Institute, Montreal, Canada
[4] Montreal Neurological Institute, Montreal, Canada

Abstract. Artificial intelligence (AI) poses both great potential and risk, as a rapidly developing and generally applicable technology. To ensure the ethical development and responsible use of AI, we outline a new ethical evaluation framework for usage by future regulators: *Meticulous Transparency* (MT). MT allows regulators to keep pace with technological progress by evaluating AI applications for their capabilities and the intentionality of developers, rather than evaluating conformity to static regulations or ethical codes of the underlying technologies themselves. MT shifts the focus of ethical evaluation from the technology itself to instead *why* it is being built, and potential consequences. MT assessment is reminiscent of a Research Ethics Board submission in medical research, with required explanation depending on the potential impact of the AI system. We propose the use of MT to transform AI-specific ethical quandaries into more familiar ethical questions, which society must then address.

Keywords: Assessment framework · AI ethics · Intentionality
Meticulous transparency

1 Introduction

This paper proposes a framework, which we call Meticulous Transparency (MT), for the evaluation of ethical implications of artificial intelligence (AI) technologies, which could be used by regulators. We begin with a discussion of what AI is, how it differs from other transformative technologies, and why this may be grounds for engaging in proactive regulation. We then describe different kinds of ethical problems that are relevant to AI and propose categories for these problems. MT is introduced through our discussion of difficulties in the formulation of AI ethics as well as our categorization of AI ethics problems. We then expand and discuss implementation.

First, an important note on terminology: when discussing AI ethics, the term 'transparency' is often used, in a narrow sense, to refer to the interpretability of an AI's decision-making process. Here, we use 'transparency' in a wider sense, capturing not

© Springer International Publishing AG, part of Springer Nature 2018
M. Mouhoub et al. (Eds.): IEA/AIE 2018, LNAI 10868, pp. 869–880, 2018.
https://doi.org/10.1007/978-3-319-92058-0_83

only the interpretability of the technology, but also the motivations for its development, its implementation, and its interaction with people and social systems.

Prominent thinkers contend that AI technology, much like the advent of the Internet, will represent a step-change for our society with a point of clear discontinuity between the past and the future (Russell et al. 2015). These technologies can bring about widespread, dramatic improvement in daily life, while also presenting humanity with significant, often unanticipated, challenges. Frequently, these challenges are addressed retrospectively, limiting our ability to prevent initial negative consequences and to comprehensively manage ongoing regulation. An instance of this is in nuclear technology, where regulations to control the spread and number of nuclear weapons came years after their initial deployment (the first nuclear weapon was used in 1945 but the Non-Proliferation Treaty was only signed in 1968).

How might AI be different than other step-change technologies and perhaps more in need of proactive regulation? To address this question, let us first define the capabilities of current AI systems. An AI system is any software that can learn information not explicitly programmed by its developers. We restrict our discussion of AI to artificial neural networks, specifically *deep learning networks*, which is one of the most commonly used approaches today. Advances in this field have built the foundations of systems that can recognize images, beat the world champion in the game of 'Go', autonomously drive vehicles, amongst many other applications (Chen et al. 2015; Kavukcuoglu et al. 2010). Most *deep learning* systems rely on extensive training to discover associations between different features. However, once trained, a given *deep learning* system does not readily generalize to other domains. This means that current systems are unable to use past knowledge in order to solve new problems, although this is a prominent area of research (Zoph et al. 2016). As such, AI systems remain far from true human-level intelligence. Their outputs are heavily influenced by the objectives and potentially the biases of their human developers. Bearing this in mind, assessing AI ethics therefore requires consideration of computer programs that learn associations; parse data into increasingly abstract representations; classify these representations; and in certain cases, recommend or act according to those classifications.

AI systems are widely applicable to many domains. Paired with the pervasive and increasing digital footprint of consumers, the rapid development of AI can incite trepidation and optimism. By making use of the massive amounts of data produced by our digital society, AI has the potential to help us vastly increase our ability to anticipate and respond to challenges, both large and small. Along with their attendant financial incentives, these potential benefits mean that the pursuit, development, and deployment of AI is unlikely to slow down soon. AI is likely to be ubiquitous, and will provide companies and governments with the ability to analyze the copious amounts of data that we produce to understand, track, predict, and manipulate our behavior in unprecedented ways. Such systems will likely be incorporated into the fabric of our society and our decision-making processes. As such, without proactive regulation, we risk allowing potentially flawed applications to exert great power through subtle means. We argue that the power of AI—combined with its current dependence on humans to set objectives and parameters—compels for imperative, feasible, and effective regulation. Regulating AI developers will ultimately regulate AI itself, mitigating negative outcomes.

2 Ethical Problems in AI

As a general note on objectives, we would like to point out that this paper is not intended to make normative claims about what is 'right' and 'wrong'. Though we do make some of these claims, they are intended to provide substance for discussion and are not the end of the paper in and of themselves. And though one might argue that naught may be truly free from value, such socially impactful value assignments ought to be determined by the aggregate of society. Our overarching goal is to understand and to classify the kinds of ethical problems that arise with AI technology, and to propose a framework in which they can be evaluated effectively.

Since AI is a general problem-solving technology, it can be applied with great success to many different challenges, even those of an ethically questionable nature. AI is a technology dependent on the data from which it learns in complex and sometimes unpredictable ways (Nguyen et al. 2015). As such, even when applied to less morally ambiguous problems, AI can produce biased solutions, which may have deleterious consequences. Let us explore some examples of what we consider to be *ethically concerning applications* and *biased solutions*.

Here, *ethically concerning applications* refers to the application of AI to solving a problem that, due to ethical concerns, ought not be solved by that (or possibly any) technology. As we will discuss, MT is a more utilitarian than deontological framework; as such, these *ethically concerning applications* are not applications that are currently illegal or considered unethical under any existing ethical frameworks; rather, they are applications of AI that might lead to greater harm than benefit, or whose benefits are accrued only by a small group while its harms are distributed widely. While contentious, we argue that a classic example of an *ethically concerning application* is the development of lethal autonomous weapons systems—seemingly agreed upon by thousands of AI/robotics researchers who have signed the Institute for Life's open letter on these weapons systems. It is currently unclear whether nations developing these weapons intend to find a framework to regulate such AI systems, though ethicists have devised strategies for surmounting the barriers to regulation (Wallach 2016).

Another example of *ethically concerning applications* is the use AI technology to produce advertisements of harmful substances, potentially targeted to vulnerable groups. If a company selling alcohol tasks an AI system with maximizing product sales, and provides it with reams of consumer data to learn from, it is highly likely that the AI system will succeed in its task. There is a very real public health concerns that arises from more effectively targeted alcohol marketing, given that the WHO estimates alcohol caused 5.9% of deaths globally in 2012. In addition, there is a very real chance that the machine, in its optimization of the problem, will learn to target persons suffering from alcohol use disorder and persons struggling with depression or other mental illnesses (Tiku 2017).

Biased solution situations are more complex, but also potentially more dangerous as they are harder to identify. This is because the problem being addressed by the AI system may be completely reasonable, leading regulators, consumers, or even the developers themselves to be fooled into believing there is no ethical issue. What is important to understand before we describe examples of these *biased solutions* is the cardinal rule of AI: "garbage in, garbage out". Using poor quality data for system training will produce poor quality predictions in the general population, especially when the training sample is not representative of that population. Without certain algorithmic upgrades, an AI system is unable to detect biases or errors in the data that is used for its training, and will accordingly learn and express the biases present in the original dataset (Hardt et al. 2016). For example, we can examine experiences with recidivism prediction algorithms. An analysis of a recidivism prediction algorithm found it to be unfairly biased against African Americans (Larson et al. 2016). If any judge or parole board were to use this model in making their decision about whether or not to release a prisoner, they would be further contributing to such bias should they keep the prisoner incarcerated. This leads to a positive feedback loop—an acceleration and augmentation of the power of systemic biases—perversely justified by recourse to the faulty notion that the AI is a machine and therefore "impartial". Given that developers choose the data that is being fed to a model, an AI can easily adopt the biases of its developers.

This issue is compounded by the fact that it is very difficult for humans to examine an artificial neural network and truly understand why it made the decision that it did. This is called the *black box* problem. However, we take issue with this term. The connections between artificial neurons (weights) that led to the decision are available to be analyzed. The problem lies in the interpretation of these weights. Humans have some similar difficulties explaining their own decisions, often resorting to rationalizations or justifications to explain choices (Jarcho et al. 2011). However, we can at least produce a narrative when questioned by a court or review board, and can be held accountable for our actions. An AI system cannot currently produce such a narrative, nor can it be credibly held accountable for its actions. There are now some techniques, such as kernel analysis (Montavon et al. 2011) and sensitivity occlusion (Zeiler and Fergus 2014), in use that allow at minimum an understanding of what factors the machine considered to be salient in making its decision. We will return to the importance of these later. However, the fact remains that many AI systems are not capable of providing explanations for their behavior that would satisfy most people, especially in situations where an automated decision may lead to harm to persons or property. Applying these powerful decision-making systems to matters of life and death, employment, and other important socioeconomic matters could have negative transformative effects that perpetuate cycles of oppression or make it easier for states to control their citizens—or companies their consumers.

Questions of privacy and personal data ownership arise as well. With the ability of AI systems to detect relationships between variables, there is an incentive for companies and government to collect as much data as possible on consumers and citizens. Social media posts, pictures, how long we spend on a webpage, our smartphone sensor information— these are all examples of data that we do not expect to be used to predict, control or modify our behaviors. However, an AI system applied to such data can do just that—use the immensity of our data footprints to build models of our identity, and manipulate these with precision and automation on a scale not previously anticipated.

Presently, little legislation exists that prevents companies and governments from applying this kind of data analysis and decision-making with AI. All the data used for these purposes are, after all, freely (though not always consciously) made available by consumers. People are often not explicitly consenting in an informed manner to the use of their data in this way. In fact, we likely cannot consent in an informed way to all possible uses of the words or pictures that we put on social media—and yet we choose to post anyway. Regulation like the General Data Protection Regulation in the EU may stop the use of EU citizen data for purposes these citizens do not explicitly consent to; however this would not stop the application of an AI trained with data from another jurisdiction being used for potentially unethical purposes within the EU. As such even where there is regulation to regulate the use of data, the use of AI is not similarly regulated, and regulations are not consistent across jurisdictions. In addition, laws regulating data privacy do not regulate the quality of the analyses data is subjected to, allowing for *biased solutions* to emerge.

This exposes a central problem in regulating AI: the concepts and procedures used to regulate human endeavors break down in the face of new possibilities caused by the rapid progress of AI technology. Based on the examples above and on the work of others (Wallach and Allen 2010; Hughes 2017), there is a strong case to find a way to regulate and guide the development of this disruptive technology in a manner that maximizes its benefits and minimizes its harms (IEEE 2016). Various international (Asilomar AI Principles 2017; IEEE 2016) and industry-based groups (Intel 2017; ITIC 2017) have been working on producing ethical AI principles. However, without a firm and empowered regulatory framework, we cannot hope to adequately guide the development of such a multiform, widely available technology. Importantly, there exists the ever-present concern that industries cannot be trusted to regulate themselves, as some uses for AI that are ethically questionable may also be highly lucrative. As such, regulating AI requires political will as well as shifts in perspective and strategy to adapt regulation in an agile fashion that can accommodate rapid technological progress. The form of governance structures that should be implemented for AI regulation, including their jurisdictions and enforcement powers, are beyond the scope of this paper. Instead, we address another question: once we have decided to regulate AI, what framework will we use to assess and audit individual AI applications? Here we propose such a framework, called Meticulous Transparency (MT). MT focuses on regulating *why* instead of *what*—on consequences and intentionality, rather than conformity to existing legal or ethical standards, which may be insufficient to assess new technological applications. MT seeks to transition from a deontological, or rule-based regulatory and ethical system, to a utilitarian one, which focuses on consequences of technologies (though we note that these consequences, once articulated, will sometimes be judged under deontological ethics). Another key focus of MT is on the intentions behind a given application.

3   What Is Meticulous Transparency?

Meticulous Transparency (MT) is a framework articulated in the language of AI to be used by regulators in judging the ethical implications of AI technologies. MT takes the form of a directed ethical analysis of a given product. MT is also a tool that can be used by developers to produce ethical analyses of their products, though it is imprudent to assume that simply having developers produce MT assessments will be sufficient to ensure compliance with ethical norms, especially when multiple developers are tasked with independently producing parts of a larger project (Zevenbergen et al. 2015). As such, an MT analysis must be completed for each product before it ever reaches consumers.

An MT analysis is aimed at addressing the two problematic types of situations described above—*ethically concerning applications* and *biased solutions*. To achieve this, MT analyses must demonstrate clearly the intentions behind a product (to address *ethically concerning applications*), include a sophisticated discussion of the data sources used (to address *biased solution* situations), and describe possible consequences of the product. Conceptually, this type of analysis would be similar to an ethics board application familiar to any academic researcher. An application must establish the rationale for a project (intentions), defend the methods (data sources and interpretability), and discuss positive and negative impacts (consequences). These reports could then be used in evaluating regulatory approval of a given technology within the specified scope of use. These are reports about complex subjects and are not meant to reflect the "ground truth" but to allow for standardized assessment.

Meticulous transparency is meticulous in the sense that it requires a high degree of detail and explanation, as well as documentation that would have to be made available to regulators and the public. The degree of explanation and rigor required in the reporting would be proportional to two variables: the autonomy of the technology (i.e., to what extent can an AI system make decisions without a human being part of the process) and its potential impact (i.e., is the AI system making life-or-death recommendations? Will it have a significant impact on social dynamics?). AI autonomy can be assessed using frameworks such as the BIOSS protocol (available at http://www.bioss.com/ai/).

For a sense of the detail required, a good model would be to examine research ethics board applications commonly used in medical research. After WWII, concerns of unethical experimentation led to the development of a framework for regulating research involving human subjects. This has resulted in the requirement for all research involving humans (from questionnaires to clinical trials) to adhere to international ethical principles, such as the Declaration of Helsinki (World Medical Association 2013), and to be assessed by research ethics boards. Low-risk projects (such as questionnaires) often require abridged applications, while high-risk research (such as clinical trials) require more thorough documentation. We suggest applying similar standards to AI applications. In our experience, this documentation is not prohibitively time-consuming or difficult to complete and provides regulatory boards with standardized assessments that can be evaluated with a mix of a concern for consequences and a deference to existing ethical and legal codes.

This discussion of explanatory rigor is important because *transparency* is a useful concept only insofar as we know what to expect to understand from such a transparent communication about a project. For example, is it sufficient for a search engine company to disclose: "we are collecting information about your internet use habits to train our systems to better meet your needs."? Or should the company be required to disclose that it is collecting information about the kinds of websites visited, video content watched, products purchased online, and that it is using this data to train an AI system to provide personalized advertisements, timed to match usual shopping behaviors, for a commission? The ethical implications of this latter, more complete description might give pause to consumers and to those studying the effects of mingling social media networks with AI (Zeng et al. 2010).

4 Components of an MT Assessment

Here we will discuss the details of an MT assessment. It is important that this assessment be completed by the company or entity which will be selling the finished product. It will also be important for the MT assessment to be reviewed at regular intervals or after shifts in product direction. Finally, any company or entity using an AI system ought to complete an MT assessment should their use of the product differ in any way from that specified in the developer's MT assessment. An MT assessment should contain the following sections:

A Complete Description of the Purpose of the Product. Such description should be provided in fine detail and must reflect the intentions of those selling the product. A company developing targeted advertisements would need to explain first that their goal is to increase revenue for the marketed brands, and then explain in detail the markets being targeted, the products being prioritized, and some of the specific training parameters that are being used in model training. Intellectual Property (IP) protection would certainly give developers the right to keep values of hyperparameters and some input features obscured, as these form the basic IP of the product. However, other values, such as the possible output variables, most input variables, and a description of common input-cluster-output associations would be critical to provide (e.g., if a system's output is commonly targeting alcohol towards people with inputs suggestive of depressive features, this should be recorded and addressed). Some of this information may not be available prior to model training, and thus should be provided to regulators as soon as it is available via an addendum to the original MT assessment. We note that the IEEE has similarly identified the importance of intentionality (IEEE 2016).

Scope of Use. The platforms and reach of the product should be carefully documented. For example, a product present in smartphones and aimed at children will have different ethical implications from a platform present in stores that uses internal camera footage to predict customer flow. In fact, even a system that examines internal versus external (e.g., inside a store versus outside a store) commercial camera footage will have different privacy implications.

Data Sources and Bias Control. To reduce the occurrence of *biased solutions*, the provenance, quality, and characteristics of data used to train the model must be clearly discussed, as a prerequisite to product approval. For example, the developers of an application using phone sensor data to provide information about shopping habits must report how this information is collected, which sample population it is drawn from, any biases introduced by this sample (i.e., if it is only data from phones used by women in an upper-class neighborhood), its basic descriptive statistics (to allow the regulatory body to examine risk of bias), as well as any algorithmic or data curation steps taken to reduce bias. In interpreting risk of bias, one would need to examine the data sample and compare it to the intended market or target population and scope of use. In this example, if the product was being sold to retailers whose market was young, upscale female shoppers, then there would be a reduced risk of bias. If the target population was different than the sample population, or if we return to the above example of recidivism prediction, then there should be more scrutiny over choice of data sources as risk for bias would be much greater.

Human Interpretability. While the current state of technology does not allow access to a reliable narrative account of the decision processes of AI systems, standards based on best practice (and specific to the context) should be set and enforced when it comes to interpretability. For example, all companies could be required to produce saliency and receptive field maps for their networks (when this is meaningful for their application). When used appropriately, these can give us a sense of which factors the machine considered to be most salient in making its decisions (Luo et al. 2017; Pan and Jiang 2016). A clear plan for introducing these features should be included in every MT assessment, and all products should be required to meet current best practice standards. Standards of interpretability and relevant metrics ought to improve with new advances in technology over time.

The Projected Risks and Benefits of the Product. While this section is more speculative than the others, it serves two important functions. Firstly, it gives the developers a chance to explore at least some of the "known knowns" and perhaps identify some of the "known unknowns" when it comes to the impact of their product, and spurs similar reflection in regulatory bodies. Secondly, it gives regulators a chance to see how seriously a developer has considered the consequences of their product. Risks and benefits should be segregated by degree, and whenever possible, up-to-date research should be used to justify assumptions or projections.

Monitoring and Contingency Plans for Adverse Events. Like producers of medication or food, before a developer is willing to put an AI system on the market, they must accept some responsibility for the downstream effects that it may have. For example, a targeted advertising company should have a system in place for monitoring, in aggregate, what kinds of products are being marketed to which kinds of consumers. Accordingly, they should have a plan for how to intervene if unethical behavior occurs (we return to the example of alcohol being marketed to people who may be depressed). Though not all adverse events can be predicted, this exercise effectively assigns developers with responsibility for their products' impacts, and allows them to practice responding to adverse scenarios.

MT is philosophically novel because it abandons the path of trying to understand and legislate AI technologies through the deontological approach of existing ethical and legal codes, which often conceptually lag behind new technologies. Instead, MT provides a framework for regulators and developers to evaluate why these AI technologies are being used as well as potential consequences. As such, MT is more agile than standard rule-based approaches, allowing developers and regulators to progress with the pace of new technology because they are not asking "what is it?" but instead "what can it do?". The potential consequences of any AI technology can then be judged (perhaps based solely on the consequences or within the framework of prevailing moral and ethical systems of thought), allowing civil society to make decisions about the kinds of products with which it wishes to engage. Let us consider an example of why this switch to utilitarianism and away from deontological thinking is significant. There may be nothing illegal about a store using camera footage of customers—who have implicitly consented to being filmed by entering the store—in order to deduce their wealth from clothing and facial features (Bjornsdottir and Rule 2017), and then sending suggestions of products tailored to their socioeconomic status to their store account. Doing so may not even violate all ethical systems consistently. However, there exist many ethical objections to a system that purposefully identifies a person's social class, links this data to a potentially identifiable account, and uses that to manipulate their behavior. In a utilitarian-based MT framework, objections based on the consequences of the technology would allow regulators to block deployment without the need to refer to existing legal frameworks that address precisely the technology in question.

5 Notes on Implementation

MT assessments would need to be carried out early in the development cycle, with updates and resubmissions as development progresses. Application to new markets or to new populations would require a new proposal, and companies would need to stay informed about advances in interpretability and algorithmic bias control. AI systems, by design, learn and change with time. How does an MT application help ensure that an AI system will act in an ethical manner, given the fact that it can change and adapt its behaviour? While this does pose a challenge, we reiterate the fact that an AI system is not totipotential- it cannot become anything or develop any behaviour. It is restricted to a range of possibilities, based off of the data it is given to work with and the training objectives it has been set. Because MT assessments require developers to reflect on precisely these elements of the system, we believe they will help to mitigate the risk of an AI system learning its way beyond ethical bounds. Mitigation is not cancellation, and AI systems may still learn behaviours that violate ethical codes- but here MT requires constant vigilance and a plan on the part of developers to monitor the AI system as it behaves in the world and have contingency plans for behaviour falling outside of ethical norms. While MT does not completely solve these problems, it provides a framework for their assessment so that developers and society do not use AI systems without extensive reflection as to their ethical implications. As developers monitor their AI systems, they would need to file new insights into their ethical implications as addenda to an initial MT assessment, ensuring that boards are kept up-to-date on the impacts of systems they have approved. This would help create a culture of outcome-monitoring which should prove beneficial to the ethical and transparent deployment of AI systems.

Data curatorship would also need to become a stronger focus of companies and governments using AI systems. AI development has often focused on using whatever data is available at hand. This is appropriate in some cases, such as marketing, as the market targeted by the AI system is often identical with the sample data used for training. In other cases, such as the recidivism example above, biased data selection leads to dangerous machine bias. We believe that the MT framework will spur developers onto the path of more careful data selection, and urge companies to invest in the creation and curation of datasets that are designed to answer the question that their product is trying to address.

It is important to remember that MT is not a value system; it does not contain within it guidance on moral judgements. This means that two different MT evaluations may produce the same data with respect to what an AI system is being used for, but those evaluating this data may come to different conclusions with respect to whether the system meets ethical norms. However, a common evaluation framework should facilitate the development of ethical norms for AI and will serve to crystallize the discussions of ethical review boards so that they can make coherent ethical judgements regarding these rapidly changing technologies.

Which types of AI application ought to be assessed via MT? We have proposed that any AI system that interacts with people, autonomously makes decisions, or indirectly assists in making decisions about people (i.e. a recidivism predictor) would benefit from an MT assessment. However, how "meticulous" the MT evaluation would be for a given system would depend directly on two factors: the magnitude of its potential effect on persons, and how autonomous it is. The most extreme example would be lethal autonomous weapons, which can take life (high magnitude of effect) fully autonomously. We feel that a lengthy, involved MT assessment would be warranted for this technology. On the other end of the spectrum, an AI secretarial assistant would undergo a much more rapid MT assessment. The question of updates must also be considered: how often must an MT assessment be completed, given that AI systems can be rapidly updated? This would likely be set by individual review boards after an initial MT assessment, with the amount of divergence from what was set out by the developers in the initial assessment either triggering a fell new assessment or a simple update report. Clearly, MT would apply only to commercial, government, or research uses of AI. Those developing AI technologies as private citizens could not be covered by this framework in a meaningful way. In addition, as an MT assessment is context sensitive, a developer using a pre-existing AI technology would still need to complete an MT assessment describing how that previously built technology is being applied in a new context.

Staffing of MT review boards should be handled in a similar fashion to current human research ethics review boards. In many cases, current boards could, with the addition of relevantly trained members, become the MT review board. Companies would have internal boards; universities and governments would also employ their own boards. Those sitting on the boards should include someone with working knowledge of AI technology, and those with knowledge about sector-specific legal and ethical considerations. More explicitly, while the composition would vary by context, as a general rule, review boards ought to include an ethicist or lawyer, experts with domain knowledge of the problem being addressed, someone with knowledge of AI technology, and a member of the public affected by the application (e.g., a consumer, a patient, an employee, etc.). The value of the MT assessment is that it provides a written, structured record for a review board, which means that members of that board will not necessarily need to be experts in the specific technologies used. The existence of such a record will also provide a legal document for use in auditing if an ethical violation occurs. There may be fair concern on the part of companies when it comes to protecting trade secrets that give their products value. However, MT only requires the release of information about the data and the intentions of training, not the release of the data itself or of in-house training scripts. As such, the impact on IP should be minimal. There is an opportunity for our society to act proactively so as to steer the direction of AI technologies towards ethically serving our most pressing needs. The Meticulous Transparency assessment proposed here provides an agile evaluation framework to be used by a strong future regulatory system to achieve these goals.

Acknowledgments. We are grateful to Dr. Wendell Wallach (Yale University) and to Dr. Jason Behrmann (aifred health), whose comments improved this article.

References

Asilomar AI Principles. https://futureoflife.org/ai-principles/. Accessed 24 Oct 2017

The Bioss AI Protocol. http://www.bioss.com/ai/. Accessed 16 Jan 2018

Bjornsdottir, R.T., Rule, N.O.: The visibility of social class from facial cues. J. Pers. Soc. Psychol. **113**(4), 530–546 (2017)

Chen, C., Seff, A., Kornhauser, A., Xiao, J.: DeepDriving: learning affordance and direct perception in autonomous driving. In: IEEE International Conference on Computer Vision, pp. 2722–2730. IEEE Computer Society, Washington, DC (2015)

Hardt, M., Price, E., Srebro, N.: Equality of Opportunity in Supervised Learning. arXiv:1610. 02413 (2016)

Hughes, G.: Montreal AI pioneer warns against unethical uses of new tech. CBC News (2017)

Artificial Intelligence–The Public Policy Opportunity. http://blogs.intel.com/policy/files/2017/10/ Intel-Artificial-Intelligence-Public-Policy-White-Paper-2017.pdf. Accessed 16 Oct 2017

The IEEE Global Initiative for Ethical Consideration in Artificial Intelligence and Autonomous Systems. http://standards.ieee.org/develop/indconn/ec/autonomous_systems.html. Accessed 20 Jan 2016

Information Technology Industry Council AI Policy Principles. https://www.itic.org/resources/ AI-Policy-Principles-FullReport2.pdf. Accessed 20 Sept 2017

Open Letter on Autonomous Weapons. https://futureoflife.org/open-letter-autonomous-weapons. Accessed 29 Oct 2017

Jarcho, J.M., Berkman, E.T., Lieberman, M.D.: The neural basis of rationalization: cognitive dissonance reduction during decision-making. Soc. Cognit. Affect. Neurosci. **6**(4), 460–467 (2011)

Kavukcuoglu, K., Sermanet, P., Boureau, Y.-L., Gregor, K., Mathieu, M., Cun, Y.L.: Learning convolutional feature hierarchies for visual recognition. In: Advances in Neural Information Processing Systems, vol. 1, pp. 1090–1098 (2010)

Larson, J., Mattu, S., Kirchner, L., Angwin, J.: How We Analyzed the COMPAS Recidivism Algorithm. ProPublica (2016)

Luo, W., Li, Y., Urtasun, R., Zemel, R.: Understanding the effective receptive field in deep convolutional neural networks. arXiv:1701.04128 (2017)

Nguyen A, Yosinski J, Clune J.: Deep neural networks are easily fooled: high confidence predictions for unrecognizable images. arXiv:1412.1897(v4) (2015)

Pan, H., Jiang, H.: A deep learning based fast image saliency detection algorithm. arXiv:1602.00577 (2016)

Russell, S., Dewey, D., Tegmark, M.: Research priorities for robust and beneficial artificial intelligence. AI Magaz. **36**, 105–114 (2015)

Tiku, N.: Welcome to the Next Phase of the Facebook Backlash. Wired (2017)

Wallach, W., Allen, C.: Moral Machines: Teaching Robots Right from Wrong. Oxford University Press, New York (2010)

Wallach, W.: Toward a ban on lethal autonomous weapons: surmounting the obstacles. Commun. ACM **60**(5), 28–34 (2016)

World Medical Association: World Medical Association Declaration of Helsinki: ethical principles for medical research involving human subjects. JAMA **310**(20), 2191–2194 (2013)

Zeng, D., Chen, H., Lusch, R., Li, S.H.: Social media analytics and intelligence. IEEE Intell. Syst. **25**(6), 13–16 (2010)

Zevenbergen, B., Mittelstadt, B., Véliz, C., Detweiler, C., Cath, C., Savulescu, J., Whittaker, M.: Philosophy meets internet engineering: ethics in networked systems research. In: GTC Workshop Outcomes, pp. 1–37. Oxford University, Oxford (2015)

Zoph, B., Yuret, D., May, J., Knight, K.: Transfer learning for low-resource neural machine translation. arXiv:1604.02201 (2016)

Montavon, G., Braun, M.L., Müller, K.-R.: Kernel analysis of deep networks. J. Mach. Learn. **12**, 2563–2581 (2011)

Zeiler M. D., Fergus, R.: Visualizing and understanding convolutional networks. arXiv:1311.2901(v3) (2013)

Towards a New Approach to Legal Indexing Using Facets

Michelle Cumyn[1(✉)], Michèle Hudon[2], Sabine Mas[2],
and Günter Reiner[3]

[1] Université Laval, Québec, Canada
michelle.cumyn@fd.ulaval.ca
[2] Université de Montréal, Montréal, Canada
[3] Universität der Bundeswehr, Hamburg, Germany

Abstract. This paper presents work in progress to design and test a new model for indexing judicial decisions using facets. We have created a prototype database with a sample of 2 500 judicial decisions in the fields of administrative law, labor law and the law of obligations. The decisions are indexed using four facets (Person, Action, Thing, Context) and two classes (Legal category, Remedies and sanctions). We will test the prototype to compare its performance with that of a standard database. It is hoped that our model will support the full or partial automation of legal indexing and provide a structure for AI applications in the legal domain.

Keywords: Database · Facet analysis · Indexing · Legal decision
Document retrieval

1 Introduction

1.1 Context

Writing in England in 2000, Peter Birks remarked that "[t]he biggest problem facing the common law at the beginning of the new century is the information overload. [...] Almost every decision of the courts is now accessible. This puts the traditional methods of the common law under tremendous stress." (Birks 2000, p. xxix)

Quebec is a relatively small jurisdiction, yet the number of judicial decisions published by the Société québécoise d'information juridique (Soquij) now exceeds 1.5 million. Approximately 100 000 new decisions are added each year. In the days when cases were printed in the law reports, a great many were left out. Case editors carefully selected those worthy of publication. Today, nearly all judicial decisions are included in the various legal databases. Users rely on computer-assisted research tools to help them select relevant decisions. Improving the performance of these tools is a necessity and a challenge.

Because judicial decisions are available for free, start-ups and established AI firms with expertise in other domains are beginning to enter the lucrative market for legal research services. The free databases provided by the Canadian Legal Information Institute (CanLII) and by Soquij (citoyens.soquij.qc.ca) are satisfactory for some

© Springer International Publishing AG, part of Springer Nature 2018
M. Mouhoub et al. (Eds.): IEA/AIE 2018, LNAI 10868, pp. 881–888, 2018.
https://doi.org/10.1007/978-3-319-92058-0_84

purposes. The expensive and sophisticated databases designed for legal professionals by Westlaw (Thomson Reuters), LexisNexis and Soquij are striving to keep ahead of the game.

The classification and indexing schemes developed in the old paper law reports were adapted as the computer-assisted index search was introduced in the 1970es by editors such as Westlaw and Lexis. Even today, established editors continue to prepare case digests (*ie* summaries) and to classify them using an elaborate key, because the index search is still considered by experts to be the most effective tool for document selection, at least in theory. In practice though, "manual indexing is only as good as the ability of the indexer to anticipate questions to which the indexed document might be found relevant. It is limited by the quality of its thesaurus. It is necessarily precoordinated and is thus also limited in its depth. Finally, like any human enterprise, it is not always done as well as it might be" (Dabney 1986, p. 14). Moreover, the index search appears rigid and conservative to many users (Delgado and Stefancic 1989; Peoples 2005, p. 662).

When it appeared in the 1980es, the full-text search was an immediate success: "the lawyer searching for precedent may devise a search as complex or as simple as he or she likes. [...] Computer searching frees legal researchers from [Westlaw's] rigid categories and puts them in touch with a postmodern world of cases and phrases limited only by their imagination and ability to formulate search commands with the aid of Boolean logic" (Delgado and Stefancic 2007, pp. 309–310). Full-text searching has become the dominant legal query; users rarely browse the elaborate tools still available in traditional databases (Ferrer et al. 2011, p. 180). Confidence in the full-text search is probably misplaced, since studies have long shown that its performance is poor. According to one study, less than 20% of relevant decisions are retrieved through a full-text search (Dabney 1986, p. 15; Mart 2010, pp. 226–228).

There have been some improvements. Several databases incorporate a rudimentary thesaurus that automatically expands a query to synonyms and near-synonyms (Broughton 2010, p. 36). Search results are then sorted by order of relevance, which is assessed using criteria such as court level, date of publication, number of search term occurrences within the same document, and search term occurrences within the document summary, title or index (Bing 1981, pp. 157–160). In some databases, cases are rated by legal experts, and the rating is used to determine relevance. Citators are a useful tool, enabling one to complete a search by adding decisions that cite a decision one has found.

Further steps to enhance full-text searches in legal databases will likely see the introduction of legal ontologies and relevance feedback (Schweighofer and Geist 2007; Turtle 1995). Feedback can be used in different ways, but a straightforward example would be that documents previously downloaded by users with similar queries are given more weight. This development may be problematic because algorithms that measure relevance based on user feedback are not controlled by a legal expert, nor by the user. It is said that users rarely look beyond the first page of results. Cases pushed further back will be neglected, and this may bias legal decisions that rely only on documents at the top of the list.

In designing a research tool for lawyers, it is important to consider their specific needs. Search results are used in structuring legal arguments, and lawyers need to fit them in to their prior knowledge of the field (Komlodi and Soergel 2002). The research interface should be as simple as possible, because lawyers seldom find the time to learn the use of complex tools (Kuhlthau and Tama 2001; Makri et al. 2008, p. 614). According to our preliminary analysis of query logs provided to us by Soquij, users predominantly design their search to match a description of the problem involved in a legal dispute (eg. fall, ice, sidewalk). Fewer queries (28%) include the abstract concepts that one finds in legal indexes and classifications to name legal categories, rules or standards (eg. municipal law, negligence, foreseeability).

Some scholars are concerned that the full-text search using factual elements discourages more creative forms of reasoning based on abstraction and analogy. This concern is not new. The same point was made by Holmes in 1920: "There is a story of a Vermont justice of the peace before whom a suit was brought by one farmer against another for breaking a churn. The justice took time to consider, and then said that he had looked through the statutes and could find nothing about churns, and gave judgment for the defendant." Nowadays, one might find a decision about churns.

Nevertheless, it would be surprising if the full-text search had not altered the habits and thinking of lawyers, or put their methods at risk, as Birks surmised. In our view, computer-assisted legal research should support the articulation of facts and legal concepts in designing a query.

1.2 Research Goals

There is growing dissatisfaction with legal information management systems, whose underlying structure has not evolved very much since the 1980es. The development of ontologies to support innovation in other domains suggests that legal research tools are also in need of a new conceptual structure (Casellas 2011, pp. 4–5).

Our research program investigates a model that would enhance the performance of legal databases by improving the computer-assisted index search, using facets. We have produced a prototype database named Gaius in accordance with this model. It requires the manual indexing of judicial decisions with a controlled vocabulary. Index terms are assigned to one of six facets or classes. The results screen generated by a query reveals the index terms that co-occur within decisions of the results list. This enables users to add or subtract terms and thus to experiment with different combinations, until the query reflects exactly their needs. It is possible to combine index terms with a full-text search. An example of the results screen from our prototype is provided below (Fig. 1).

We believe that our prototype will outperform existing databases in speed, relevance and completeness of document retrieval. It is hoped that our model will support the full or partial automation of manual indexing, a task usually still performed by humans with legal training. Finally, the structure revealed by our model might form the basis for other AI applications.

2   Work in Progress

2.1   Designing Our Model

The method of facet analysis was conceived by S. R. Ranganathan in the 1930s and formed the basis for the Colon Classification (Ranganathan 1933). Ranganathan believed that every subject matter or unit of knowledge can be broken down according to five broad dimensions or facets: (1) personality (entities or things), (2) matter (materials or constituents of things), (3) energy (actions or activities), (4) space, and (5) time (see Broughton 2001, p. 70). Ranganathan's facets revolutionized the field of knowledge organization and inspired the Bliss Bibliographic Classification, which extended the number of facets to 13: thing, kind, part, property, material, process, operation, patient, product, by-product, agent, space and time (Broughton 2001, p. 79).

The precise nature and functions of facets remain ambiguous to this day. Facets have been studied and used in knowledge organization for 80 years. Today, their popularity and diverse applications make them difficult to define (Côté-Lapointe and Mas 2017). Facets are often mentioned in connection with browsing tools that use categories of search terms, making it possible to combine terms from different categories and to filter results. E-commerce applications are typical examples. Library websites use catalogue fields in a similar fashion (*eg.* author, title, date of publication, location, and subject). Some scholars find issue with such a broad definition of facets, however. Facets were originally designed to represent the subject matter or intellectual content of a document, not its formal attributes (Broughton 2001, pp. 71–72). Although they can always be adapted to specific domains, facets reflect a structure that claims to be fundamental.

Even within the strict conception of facets, it is unclear whether they reveal semantic or syntactic relations (Hudon and El Hadi 2017, pp. 13–15; Maniez 1999, p. 253ff). To illustrate this point, let us apply Ranganathan's facets to the concepts that compose the following scripts:

– Last week, Gill damaged her computer when she slipped on an icy sidewalk.
    Personality: woman, computer
    Matter: ice, damage
    Energy: walking, slipping
    Space: *sidewalk*
    Time: last week
– Melissa has a contract with the city to pave the sidewalks on Main St.
    Personality: woman, contract, city, *sidewalk*
    Energy: paving
    Space: Main St.

In a semantic approach to facet analysis, a given concept must be assigned permanently to a facet, based on its meaning: it is necessary to decide once and for all whether a sidewalk is an entity or a place. Following a syntactic approach, a concept may not always belong to the same facet. An advantage of facets is precisely their ability to represent a variety of relations between concepts. Walking on a sidewalk (a thoroughfare) is different from building a sidewalk (an entity or thing).

Broughton sought to implement the Bliss Classification in the legal domain by building a thesaurus using facets, for the purpose of indexing and retrieving legal documents of the law firm Norton Rose (Broughton 2010). Similarly, Scott and Smith created a legal thesaurus using a faceted scheme for Sweet & Maxwell (Scott and Smith 2010). These do not appear to have been an overwhelming success.

Our approach has been to mediate between the fundamental structure devised by experts in knowledge organization and lawyers' own understanding of their discipline. Ranganathan's facets remind us of the Roman jurist Gaius' famous tripartite division, which continues to provide a structure for legal knowledge even today. In his *Institutes*, Gaius declared that "all our law is about persons, things or actions" (Birks 1997, p. 5). We worked with lists of terms derived from legal classifications and indexes, thesauri and query logs and tested the use of various facets in indexing judicial decisions, until we were satisfied that we had found the combination which best represents both the factual basis of a legal problem and its solution. The fundamental facets of Ranganathan and Gaius were most useful in analyzing the problem, rather than its solution, and the following facets were chosen for that purpose:

F1: Person   Gaius: Person   Ranganathan: Personality

F2: Action   Gaius: Action   Ranganathan: Energy

F3: Thing   Gaius: Thing   Ranganathan: Personality

F4: Context   Ranganathan: Matter
                                       Ranganathan: Space
                                       Ranganathan: Time

The following classes were used to describe the solution discussed or applied in a judicial decision:

F5 Legal category

F6 Remedies and sanctions

The content of both classes resembles that of traditional legal classifications. They are not true facets in the narrow sense, but may be considered such in the broad sense discussed above.

2.2   Building the Prototype Gaius

After designing our model, we drafted an indexing policy that carefully defines the six facets or classes. Using open source software and libraries, we built a Web application prototype that serves as an indexing tool and database. This application was built with Python programming language and the Django framework. Its research interface allows indexers to visualize the indexing of prior decisions. The prototype contains 2 500 judicial decisions from Quebec (written in French for the most part) that were sampled in the fields of administrative law, labor law and the law of obligations. These were chosen because they represent common law and civil law, statute law and case law, public law and private law, provincial law and federal law. Our prototype uses a controlled vocabulary or thesaurus which we have developed incrementally under the supervision of an expert librarian. Our vocabulary is consistent with the syntactic approach to facet analysis outlined above. Indexed terms (in French) are drawn from the thesaurus, which also contains basic semantic relations (general term, specific term, synonym or near-synonym). Terms used to index a decision must be inserted into the appropriate facets. The indexing is presently being completed by lawyers who have received training in document analysis and indexing.

3   Steps Ahead

After the indexing is completed, we will design the research interface to make it more friendly for users. Facets will allow users to filter results, and full-text searching will also be available, alone or in combination.

The next step will be to conduct a user study in order to test the prototype. The study will be designed using quantitative and qualitative approaches, after examining similar studies in the field. In our study, tasks will exemplify different research needs, for instance: searching for a precedent; reasoning by analogy; finding applications for an abstract rule or legal concept. Participants will be asked to complete some tasks using the prototype, and others with a version that will resemble a standard database. Performance in document retrieval will be compared with respect to speed, relevance and completeness.

Finally, the use of our model for automated or semi-automated indexing will be considered. Established editors continue to use human indexing (albeit computer-assisted), despite its cost, because fully automated indexing does not yet meet their standards. Although the automated application of a faceted scheme represents a challenge, an expert system can be devised to suggest index terms belonging to each facet, to be validated, modified or rejected by a human classifier (Ingwersen and Wormell 1992, pp. 191–192). Facets may also form the basis for designing an interactive research interface that can question and guide the user (id., p. 199). Our structured vocabulary may facilitate the construction of legal ontologies (Casellas 2011, c. 4).

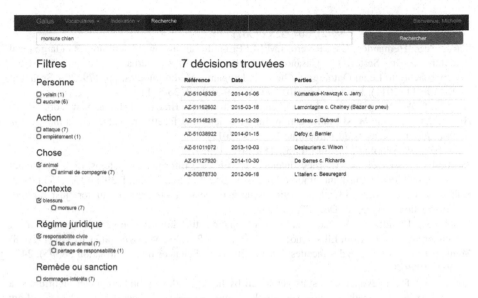

Fig. 1. Research interface

Acknowledgments. This research program is funded by the Social Sciences and Humanities Research Council of Canada (2015–2020). We are grateful for the research assistance of Christophe Achdjian, Dominique Boulanger, Cécile Gaiffe, Marjorie Gauchier, Joanie Gosselin-Lepage, Béatrice Lecomte, Erin Sandberg, Forrest Wakarchuk and Iryna Zazulya. Thanks to Alexandre Fortier, our expert librarian, David Lesieur, our programmer and Charles Tremblay-Potvin, our project coordinator.

References

Bing, J.: Text retrieval in Norway. Program **15**(3), 150–162 (1981)

Birks, P.: Definition and division: a meditation on *institutes* 3.13. In: Birks, P. (ed.) The Classification of Obligations, pp. 1–35. Clarendon Press, Oxford (1997)

Birks, P. (ed.): English Private Law. Oxford University Press, Oxford (2000)

Broughton, V.: Faceted classification as a basis for knowledge organization in a digital environment; the Bliss Bibliographic Classification as a model for vocabulary management and the creation of multi-dimensional knowledge structures. New Rev. Hypermedia Multimedia **7**(1), 67–102 (2001)

Broughton, V.: The use and construction of thesauri for legal documentation. Legal Inf. Manage. **10**(1), 35–42 (2010)

Casellas, N.: Legal Ontology Engineering. Springer, Dordrecht (2011)

Côté-Lapointe, S., Mas, S.: Facettes et archives: modalité et applications. La Gazette des archives 248 (forthcoming) (2017)

Dabney, D.P.: The curse of thamus: an analysis of full-text legal document retrieval. Law Libr. J. **78**, 5–40 (1986)

Delgado, R., Stefancic, J.: Why do we tell the same stories? Law reform, critical librarianship, and the triple helix dilemma. Stanford Law Rev. **42**(1), 207–225 (1989)

Delgado, R., Stefancic, J.: Why do we ask the same questions? The triple helix dilemma revisited. Law Libr. J. **99**(2), 307–328 (2007)

Ferrer, Á.S., Hernández, C.F., Rivero, J.M.M.: From thesaurus towards ontologies in large legal databases. In: Sartor, G., Casanovas, P., Biasiotti, M.A., Fernandez-Barrera, M. (eds.) Approaches to Legal Ontologies: Theories, Domains, Methodologies, pp. 179–200. Springer, Dordrecht (2011). https://doi.org/10.1007/978-94-007-0120-5_11

Holmes, O.W.: The path of the law. Collected Legal Papers. Brace and Howe, New York (1920)

Hudon, M., El Hadi, W.M.: Introduction. La classification à facettes revisitée. De la théorie à la pratique. Les cahiers du numérique **1**, 9–23 (2017)

Ingwersen, P., Wormell, I.: Libri **42**(3), 184–201 (1992)

Komlodi, A., Soergel, D.: Attorneys interacting with legal information systems: tools for mental model building and task integration. Proc. Am. Soc. Inf. Sci. Technol. **39**(1), 152–163 (2002)

Kuhlthau, C.C., Tama, S.L.: Information search process of lawyers: a call for 'just for me' information services. J. Doc. **57**(1), 25–43 (2001)

Makri, S., Blandford, A., Cox, A.L.: Investigating the information-seeking behaviour of academic lawyers: from Ellis's model to design. Inf. Process. Manage. **44**(2), 613–634 (2008)

Maniez, J.: Du bon usage des facettes. Documentaliste - Sciences de l'information **36**(4/5), 249–262 (1999)

Mart, S.N.: The relevance of results generated by human indexing and computer algorithms: a study of west's headnotes and key numbers and LexisNexis's head-notes and topics. Law Libr. J. **102**(2), 221–249 (2010)

Peoples, L.F.: The death of the digest and the pitfalls of electronic research: what is the modern legal researcher to do? Law Libr. J. **97**(4), 661–679 (2005)

Ranganathan, S.R.: Colon Classification. Madras Library Association, Madras (1933)

Scott, M., Smith, N.: Legal Taxonomy From Sweet & Maxwell. Legal Inf. Manage. **10**(3), 217–222 (2010)

Schweighofer, E., Geist, A.: Legal query expansion using ontologies and relevance feedback. In: 2nd Workshop on Legal Ontologies and Artificial Intelligence Techniques, LOAIT, pp. 149–160. Stanford University (2007)

Turtle, H.: Text retrieval in the legal world. Artif. Intell. Law **3**, 5–54 (1995)

Artificial Intelligence and Predictive Justice: Limitations and Perspectives

Marc Queudot and Marie-Jean Meurs[✉]

Université du Québec à Montréal, Montréal, QC, Canada
meurs.marie-jean@uqam.ca

Abstract. One of the main barriers to effective prediction systems in the legal domain is the very limited availability of relevant data. This paper discusses the particular case of the Federal Court of Canada, and describes some perspectives on how best to overcome these problems. Part of the process involves an automatic annotation system, supervised by a manual annotation process. Several state-of-the-art methods on related tasks are presented, as well as promising approaches leveraging recent advances in natural language processing, such as vector word representations or recurrent neural networks. The insights outlined in the paper will be further explored in a near future, as this work is still an ongoing research.

Keywords: Legal artificial intelligence · Predictive justice
Natural language processing · Machine learning

1 Introduction

The search for techniques to predict justice court decisions has been going on for decades. In 1963, Loevinger described a new science called *Jurimetrics*, concerned among other matters, by "the formulation of a calculus of legal predictability" [14, p. 8]. More recently, Zambrano [26] argued that the ability to accurately predict the probable outcome of a court decision would help lawyers to define their legal strategies, and would also help to relieve congestion in courts since some hopeless cases will be dropped. Our work comes at a time where, according to Richard Tromans in his introduction to Legal AI [23], the legal field begins to adopt software solutions that rely on Machine Learning and Natural Language Processing (NLP). Our work will focus on predictive systems, i.e. predicting the probable outcome of court cases. In this area, many startups like Juristat, Lex Predict or Lex Machina, as recensed by Zambrano [26], offer this service to their client. However, the legal field would benefit from more accessible systems that leverage recent advances in sentiment analysis. Access to complete sets of case law is paramount for predictive justice algorithms. Legal decision-making is a process relying heavily on the rule of precedent, even within one case file. The same judge or adjudicator (prothonotary or judge for the Federal Court) may rely on prior decisions, where he or she can find statements

© Springer International Publishing AG, part of Springer Nature 2018
M. Mouhoub et al. (Eds.): IEA/AIE 2018, LNAI 10868, pp. 889–897, 2018.
https://doi.org/10.1007/978-3-319-92058-0_85

of facts and legal reasoning to frame his or her reasons for an order or a judgment. Algorithms can learn to identify common threads and patterns in order to establish a predictive analysis for issues of decisions by adjudicators, provided the precedents constitute a large enough and as complete as possible set of case law.

However, access to complete sets of case law is a thorny issue with the Federal Court of Canada, as its public and free website database is incomplete and not up-to-date. For instance, performing a search for all decisions issued in a case such as Osmose-Pentox, Inc. v. Société Laurentide, Inc., yield roughly 11 decisions, yet when consulting the files history, we find that some decisions dated 2003 and 2005 have been rendered but do not appear in the search. This is illustrative of a much wider problem. Indeed, missing decisions can be accessed through online private and pay-per-use databanks like Westlaw (Law Source) or Quicklaw. Online databanks such as these have proprietary rights on indexed court decisions, and will not give massive access to their databanks. Therefore, access to complete and updated court decisions issued by the Federal Court is tributary of the investment public authorities are willing to put on the website, and in particular the indexing of court decisions in a format readily accessible to the public and researchers. The scope and effectiveness of the predictive algorithm is, as a result, impaired in its capacity to learn and draw inferences with a high probability. Creating our own indexed databases could be a solution, but it would require a staggering amount of resources both financial and in man power, not to mention time-consuming.

The goal of this work is to overcome the difficulties associated with the data access, to provide good quality predictions on justice court decisions. The paper is organized as follows: Sect. 2 presents an overview of various works summarizing the current state-of-the-art in the field, Sect. 3 describes the corpus used for the experiments, Sect. 4 explains our approach while planned experiments are reported in Sect. 5, and finally Sect. 6 concludes.

2   Previous Work

Sulea et al. [21] made predictions on decisions from the French Supreme Court using ensembles of Support Vector Machine (SVM)[7] classifiers. Their dataset contains fields, among others, for the case description and a label of the ruling. They evaluate their approach using the F1-measure. F1-measure is a metric to measure the performance of a system that balances two components. The first one is the number of cases it found from all the ones it was supposed to, while the second one measures the proportion of cases it correctly classified. More details on these metrics will be given in Sect. 4. They achieve an F1-measure of 98,6% in predicting the ruling of cases when such rulings are organized in six classes. This score drops to 95.8% when eight classes are used. In their previous work [22], the authors explained that the labels were derived from the Conclusion(s) (outcome) meta-data field of the database they used. In their first experiment, they used the 200 most frequent outcomes, by selecting only its first word. For the second experiment they used the 200 most frequent outcomes, without filtering on the first word. This process produced respectively 6 and 8 classes, on which they performed their classification experiments. Katz et al. [12] predicted rulings of the United States Supreme Court using Random Forest (RF) [6] classifiers. They found that this algorithm "outperformed [...] support vector machines and feed-forward artificial neural network models" [12, p. 7] in their experiments using the Supreme Court Database[1]. Another benefit of using RF is their ability to perform incremental learning, i.e. improve the model performance when new data are available, without re-training the whole model. They have an interesting approach for evaluating the performance of their system: in addition to using standard metrics, they also develop a baseline algorithm. This baseline "algorithm" always predicts the class most ruled by the Supreme Court judges over the previous years. They found that their approach mostly outperformed the baseline once the training data were of sufficient volume. Aletras et al. [3] classified decisions of the European Court of Human Rights (ECtHR) on matters concerning 3 distinct articles of the European Convention on Human Rights. They obtained good results on their two class classification (either violating or not violating the convention) by engineering a *topic* features by aggregating semantically close n-grams. Although all these studies produce interesting results, it is important to note that the jurisdictions of the legal systems whose decisions they predict are relatively limited. The United States Supreme Court and the European Court of Human Rights only deal with issues regarding their respective constitutions, and [3] further reduced this scope to only 3 articles. The context is different for the French Supreme Court which only judges on matters of law and its application, as opposed to the study of both facts and law in lower level courts. After Bengio et al. trained word embeddings [5] for the first time in 2003, Mikolov et al. popularized them with the introduction of word2vec [15], a toolkit to train or use pre-trained word-embeddings. Ever since, word embeddings representations pre-trained on big amounts of data such as GloVe [16] have been providing state-of-the-art results in a wide range of semantic tasks [19]. Experiments training cross-lingual embeddings were also successful, allowing to use the huge datasets available in English to improve the performance of models in other languages. In his survey of cross-language embeddings, Ruder et al. [18] described the different approaches developed in recent years. Radford et al. [17] show that even the best vector representations, namely skip-thoughts [13], are still outperformed by supervised models. They reference the work of Dai and Le [8], which fine-tunes a pre-trained unsupervised language model to achieve state-of-the-art performance on some classification datasets, and Dieng et al. [9] that combine unsupervised language modeling with topic modeling and small supervised feature extraction to improve the performance of their model. To deal with inputs of variable length such as text, Recurrent Neural Networks (RNNs), a class of neural networks, have been developed, and in particular Long Short-Term Memory (LSTM) [11] networks which bring performance optimizations. Radford et al. trained a particular kind of LSTM called Multiplicative

---

[1] United States Supreme Court decisions dataset http://scdb.wustl.edu/.

LSTM (mLSTM), which use a more input-dependent hidden state transition than regular LSTMs. The conclusion of Radford et al.'s work is that language models trained on a big corpus of books cannot be expected to carry enough information to perform well on more specific tasks like review classification, namely sentiment analysis. The next section describes the dataset that we used.

3   Dataset

The dataset consists of all the decisions taken by the Federal Court of Canada (more than 45 000) that were available on the official Federal Court website[2] in August 2017. The decisions can be rendered either in English or French, but have to be traduced upon request and usually are. As a result, most of the decisions are available in both languages. However, 5% of the decisions are only available in English, and 1.2% only in French. Table 1 presents these statistics on the dataset. The rulings are formated as free texts but include the following information before the argument: date and place of ruling, name of the judge or prothonotary, and names of the parties involved in addition to several identifiers. The main part of the decision is the argument, in which the facts are exposed, relevant laws are cited, and reasoning behind the ruling is detailed. Then, one finds the ruling itself, usually in the last paragraph before stating the information found in the header, plus the names of the people who appeared in the trial, and the solicitors of record.

Table 1. Statistics on the dataset

	Occurrences	% of the total number of decisions
Distinct decisions	46 369	100%
English-only decisions	2 329	5%
French-only decisions	602	1.2%
Number of different judges[a]	41	-

[a]This statistic comes from the Federal Court website.

4   Methodology

We gathered the decisions from the website, combined the French and English versions of the same decisions, and indexed them using Apache Lucene[3]. This allowed us to use the Apache Solr[4] search engine in a preliminary exploration phase. The decisions of the Federal Court are not annotated, so we can not apply supervised learning techniques on this corpus as it is. The lack of structure in

---

[2] http://cas-cdc-www02.cas-satj.gc.ca/fct-cf/.
[3] https://lucene.apache.org/core/.
[4] https://lucene.apache.org/solr/.

the dataset makes it difficult to extract the ruling as categorical variable but the ruling is in the text of the decision, even though there is no established format or way of expressing the ruling. However, a few similar sentences covered a large fraction of the expressed rulings. Using regular expressions, we were able to categorize 12 136 documents. Regular expressions work by matching patterns in text using a particular syntax, and returning the portions of text found this way. We have defined two categories: **granted** and **dismissed**. We select the first one when the judge or prothonotary grants to the plaintiff what they requested, and the other when their request is rejected. We added a third one, "**unknown**", to indicate that we could not choose either class because the regular expressions did not match anything. The specific regular expressions we used are shown in Figs. 1 and 2. The first regular expression in Fig. 1 looks for a portion of text that begins by *orders that* and ends with *dismissed*, regardless of the case. In the second one, we look for a portion of text beginning by *application* followed by none to forty characters, and then *is dismissed*. The third one is the exact part of text it looks for, and the following are equivalent in French. The regular expressions for the **dismissed** class are built in the same way, but the keyword *dismissed* is replaced by *granted*.

```
(?i)orders that(.*)dismissed
application [\w ]{0,40}is dismissed
judicial review is dismissed
(?i)ordonne[ ]?:(.*)rejeté(e)?
demande [\w ]{0,40}est rejetée
```

Fig. 1. Regular expressions for the **dismissed** class

```
(?i)orders that(.*)granted
(?i)application [\w ]{0,40}is granted
judicial review is granted
(?i)ordonne[ ]?:(.*)accueilli(e)?
(?i)demande est accueillie
```

Fig. 2. Regular expressions for the **granted** class

To evaluate the classes extracted by using regular expressions, we plan to manually annotate about 1 000 decisions, randomly selected. Three human experts are currently annotating these documents. We will use the class chosen by the majority and compute the Kappa score [24] to measure the likelihood of these results occurring by chance. This will allow to validate our results in two ways. First, we will compare the classes provided by automatic extraction, with those from the manual annotation process. We will then be able to compute the Precision, Recall and F-measure of our class extraction system. In the context of binary classification, i.e. discriminating positive from negative examples, *precision* is defined as the following: out of the examples that are positive, how many have been identified as such. With True Positive (TP) being the number of positive examples classified as such, and False Positive (FP) the number of negative examples classified as positive, its formal definition is:

$$precision = \frac{TP}{TP + FP}$$

In the same context, *recall* is, out of all the positive examples, how many have been classified as such. With True Negative (TN) being the number of negative examples correctly classified and False Negative (FN) the number of positive examples classified as negative, the formal definition of recall is:

$$recall = \frac{TN}{TP + FN}$$

F-measure, also called F1-score is used to balance *precision* with *recall*. It does so with an harmonic mean of both:

$$F_1 = 2 \cdot \frac{precision \cdot recall}{precision + recall}$$

The metrics mentioned above will allow us to evaluate both the dismissed and granted class annotations performed with regular expressions, but also the ones tagged as unknown. These will be given a special attention to better analyze their structure and characteristics. This will allow the craft of better regular expressions, to classify a bigger proportion of documents into the dismissed and granted classes. The corpus of automatically categorized documents shows a strong imbalance: 2 208 siding with the plaintiff (positive) and 9 928 siding with the defendant. Class imbalance is a common problem for classifiers. In their study of the effect of class distribution on classifier learning, Weiss *et al.* [25] shows that "the naturally occurring class distribution often is not best for learning". If this noticed imbalance proves to be similar to the one found in the manually annotated dataset, we will undersample the majority class up to the size of the minority class to obtain a balanced dataset as recommended by Weiss *et al.*, and successfully applied in several studies [4]. The following experiments attempt to classify decisions, which have been stripped from words which are instant give-away of the class. This approach has been proposed by Sulea et al. [21] in an attempt to approximate a more realistic setting where lawyers give a quick introduction to the case as an input to the algorithm.

5   Planned Experiments

We will compare several representations of one document. The baseline classifier uses a Bag Of Words (BOW) to represent documents. In this representation, each word encountered in the corpus is used to build a dictionary. Then, each document is represented by a vector that counts the number of occurrences of each word. It has the advantage of being a simple representation, well suited to be a baseline. While BOW computes the simplest possible score for a word (the number of occurrences), Term Frequency- Inverse Document Frequency (TF-IDF) [20] computes another score that balances the frequency of a word appearing in the document with its frequency in the corpus. This is to avoid putting the emphasis on words present in too much documents, or too few, which do not help to discriminate documents. Our next step will be to use pre-trained Skip-Thoughts [13] vector representations. We expect these representations to allow our classifiers to outperform the naive ones we tried so far. Radford et al. [17] used mLSTM to classify sentiments from Amazon reviews. As part of the Deep Learning group of algorithms, mLSTM learns the features to describe the documents along with a way to map these features to the class (which is the only part classical Machine Learning algorithms do). Provided we can find a big enough law related dataset, we want to experiment feeding this dataset to a mLSTM similar to the one Randford et al. built, thus creating a language model more adapted to our task.

6 Conclusion

We accessed a public dataset of court decisions which consists of text decisions written in English and in French. We extracted categorical values using a rule-based approach, with the intent of using them as the class of the documents in supervised learning approaches. We will validate this process by manually annotating a portion of the dataset. Then, we will build baseline systems using simple document representations and classical machine learning algorithms. To the best of our knowledge, these are the methods used in state of the art prediction of justice decisions. We will then leverage pre-trained language models to use as documents representations in order to improve the performance of our classification algorithms. We will compare these results with most recently developed mLSTM network architectures on a combination of law related corpora. Doyon [10] argues that case law should be openly accessible to anyone, either law professionals or not. Quebec Court of Appeal aggreed with the editor Wilson & Lafleur Ltée in 2000 [2] when they asked of Société Québécoise d'Information Juridique (SOQUIJ)[5] that they provide them with the all the court decisions ruled in Quebec courts. Canada Supreme Court later ruled [1] that the decisions themselves did not fall under copyright laws, and for this reason, it should be allowed to copy them. In practice, accessibility of legal corpora to the public is limited, which in turn hinders research that could benefit society itself by making law more accessible.

Reproducibility. To ensure full reproducibility and comparisons between systems, our source code will be publicly released as an open source software the following repository: https://github.com/BigMiners.

---

[5] SOQUIJ website: http://soquij.qc.ca/.

Acknowledgments. We thank José Bonneau for his description of the difficulties in accessing legal court decisions. We also thank Diego Maupomé and Antoine Briand for their valuable comments.

References

1. CCH Canadienne Ltée c. Barreau du Haut-Canada, 2004 CSC 13. https://scc-csc.lexum.com/scc-csc/scc-csc/fr/item/2125/index.do
2. Wilson & Lafleur inc. c. Société Québécoise d'Information Juridique, j.E. 2000-17728 (C.A.)
3. Aletras, N., Tsarapatsanis, D., Preoţiuc-Pietro, D., Lampos, V.: Predicting judicial decisions of the european court of human rights: a natural language processing perspective. PeerJ Comput. Sci. **2**, e93 (2016)
4. Almeida, H., Meurs, M.J., Kosseim, L., Butler, G., Tsang, A.: Machine learning for biomedical literature triage. PLOS ONE **9**(12) (2014)
5. Bengio, Y., Ducharme, R., Vincent, P., Jauvin, C.: A neural probabilistic language model. J. Mach. Learn. Res. **3**(Feb), 1137–1155 (2003)
6. Breiman, L.: Random forests. Mach. Learn. **45**(1), 5–32 (2001)
7. Cortes, C., Vapnik, V.: Support-vector networks. Mach. Learn. **20**(3), 273–297 (1995)
8. Dai, A.M., Le, Q.V.: Semi-supervised sequence learning. In: Advances in Neural Information Processing Systems, pp. 3079–3087 (2015)
9. Dieng, A.B., Wang, C., Gao, J., Paisley, J.: TopicRNN: a recurrent neural network with long-range semantic dependency. arXiv preprint arXiv:1611.01702 (2016)
10. Doyon, J.M.: Accessibilité aux jugements et droit d'auteur. CPI 20(3) (2008). http://www.lescpi.ca/s/2773
11. Hochreiter, S., Schmidhuber, J.: Long short-term memory. Neural Comput. **9**(8), 1735–1780 (1997)
12. Katz, D.M., Bommarito II, M.J., Blackman, J.: A general approach for predicting the behavior of the supreme court of the United States. PLoS ONE **12**(4), e0174698 (2017)
13. Kiros, R., Zhu, Y., Salakhutdinov, R.R., Zemel, R., Urtasun, R., Torralba, A., Fidler, S.: Skip-thought vectors. In: Advances in Neural Information Processing Systems, pp. 3294–3302 (2015)
14. Loevinger, L.: Jurimetrics: the methodology of legal inquiry. Law Contemp. Probl. **28**(1), 5–35 (1963)
15. Mikolov, T., Sutskever, I., Chen, K., Corrado, G.S., Dean, J.: Distributed representations of words and phrases and their compositionality. In: Advances in Neural Information Processing Systems, pp. 3111–3119 (2013)
16. Pennington, J., Socher, R., Manning, C.: Glove: global vectors for word representation. In: Proceedings of the 2014 Conference on Empirical Methods in Natural Language Processing (EMNLP), pp. 1532–1543 (2014)
17. Radford, A., Jozefowicz, R., Sutskever, I.: Learning to generate reviews and discovering sentiment. arXiv preprint arXiv:1704.01444 (2017)
18. Ruder, S.: A survey of cross-lingual embedding models. arXiv preprint arXiv:1706.04902 (2017)
19. Schnabel, T., Labutov, I., Mimno, D., Joachims, T.: Evaluation methods for unsupervised word embeddings. In: Proceedings of the 2015 Conference on Empirical Methods in Natural Language Processing, pp. 298–307 (2015)

20. Spärck Jones, K.: IDF term weighting and IR research lessons. J. Doc. **60**(5), 521–523 (2004)
21. Sulea, O.M., Zampieri, M., Malmasi, S., Vela, M., Dinu, L.P., van Genabith, J.: Exploring the use of text classification in the legal domain. arXiv preprint arXiv:1710.09306 (2017)
22. Sulea, O.M., Zampieri, M., Vela, M., van Genabith, J.: Predicting the law area and decisions of french supreme court cases. arXiv preprint arXiv:1708.01681 (2017)
23. Tromans, R.: Legal AI - A Beginner's Guide. Technical report, Tromans Consulting (2017). https://blogs.thomsonreuters.com/legal-uk/wp-content/uploads/sites/14/2017/02/Legal-AI-a-beginners-guide-web.pdf
24. Viera, A.J., Garrett, J.M., et al.: Understanding interobserver agreement: the kappa statistic. Fam. Med. **37**(5), 360–363 (2005)
25. Weiss, G.M., Provost, F.: The effect of class distribution on classifier learning: an empirical study. Rutgers University (2001). http://citeseerx.ist.psu.edu/viewdoc/summary?doi=10.1.1.28.9570
26. Zambrano, G.: Précédents et prédictions jurisprudentielles à l'ère des Big Data: parier sur le résultat (probable) d'un procès (2015). https://hal.archives-ouvertes.fr/hal-01496098. Accessed 28 Jan 2018

Identification of Sensitive Content in Data Repositories to Support Personal Information Protection

Antoine Briand[1], Sara Zacharie[1], Ludovic Jean-Louis[2], and Marie-Jean Meurs[1(✉)]

[1] Université du Québec à Montréal, Montréal, QC, Canada
meurs.marie-jean@uqam.ca
[2] Netmail Inc., Montréal, QC, Canada
ludovic.jean-louis@netmail.com

Abstract. This article presents a two-step approach focusing on the identification of sensitive data within documents. The proposed pipeline first detects the domain of a document, then identifies the sensitive information it contains. Detection of domains allows to better understand the context of a documents, hence supports the disambiguation of potentially sensitive information. The prototype considers three domains: health, business and "other". The system developed for the domain detection step is built and evaluated on a corpus composed of clinical notes, and articles about business or art from Forbes, Reuters, and The New York Times. The identification of sensitive information relies on a Conditional Random Fields (CRF) model.

Keywords: Compliance · Domain detection
Named-Entity Recognition · Natural language processing
Personal Health Information · Sensitive information

1 Introduction

Guidelines are set to ensure regulatory compliance that organizations must follow to handle and correctly secure the data they produce. Considering the large amount of data from many different sources they have to deal with, this is a real challenge in terms of data supervision and security. The definition of sensitive information differs depending on the field of activity concerned. In the case of a company, data such as e-mail addresses, bank card numbers or information about various kind of amounts are considered sensitive. Regarding medical data, it is necessary to identify specific entities, such as names of disease, diagnosis, doctor or health insurance number. An overview of the international standards and regulations related to compliance is reported in [10], along with the recommended processes and requirements according to the domain of application. In Canada, the Personal Information Protection and Electronic Documents Act

© Springer International Publishing AG, part of Springer Nature 2018
M. Mouhoub et al. (Eds.): IEA/AIE 2018, LNAI 10868, pp. 898–910, 2018.
https://doi.org/10.1007/978-3-319-92058-0_86

(PIPEDA)[1] is the primary source of regulations governing the management of private data. PIPEDA is a federal privacy law for private-sector organizations. It sets out the guidelines for how businesses must handle personal information of their employees.

Over the past few years, many cyber-attacks have affected data privacy. In 2013, Yahoo! suffered a massive data breach[2] with more than 1 billion accounts exposed, information including names, phone numbers, dates of birth, passwords and security questions have leaked. Later in 2014, another leak occurred[3] but according to the company, no credit card or banking information were exposed. It was mainly names, email addresses, phone numbers, dates of birth, hashed passwords and some answers to security questions, from at least 500 million user accounts. At the end of 2016, Uber CEO explained that hackers had grabbed personal data of more than 57 million customers worldwide, including 7 million drivers[4]. Mostly names, email addresses and phone numbers had leaked, along with 600,000 U.S driver's licence numbers. In September 2017, one of the major credit reporting agencies, Equifax, went through a data breach[5]. Hackers had access to information of about 143 million American consumers from mid-May to July 2017. Several information leaked, among them names, social security numbers, birth dates, addresses and in some case even driver's licence numbers. Credit numbers were stolen from about 209,000 persons, and it also impacted Canada and United Kingdom. In November 2017, a contractor from the Defense Department of USA left data from a spying program exposed on Amazon Web Services[6]. Apparently, data were uploaded to an Amazon S3 storage instance and set in public. A team of security researchers then discovered that data linked with the global spying operation were publicly available on Amazon Web Services servers. The data consist of at least 1.8 billion online messages from people all around the world. While some of them seemed to be random and harmless, others were highly related to security, with political posts in locations such as Iraq, Pakistan, or even ISIS an other jihadist groups. These are only few recent examples of sensitive data leaks and security issues. Given the risks for individuals and organizations, protecting the privacy by preventing data loss and theft is critical.

On the legislative level, various acts have been proposed to regulate the protection of sensitive data. In the United States, the regulation considers various sorts of sensitive data, resulting in several acts. The Health Insurance Portability and Accountability Act (HIPAA) [2] is one of the most important source of regulation, which provides guidelines for health-related information and lists 18 Protected Health Information (PHI). Those PHI refer to any information about

---

[1] http://laws-lois.justice.gc.ca/eng/acts/P-8.6/.

[2] https://www.nytimes.com/2016/12/14/technology/yahoo-hack.html.

[3] https://uk.businessinsider.com/yahoo-hack-by-state-sponsored-actor-biggest-of-all-time-2016-9.

[4] https://www.bbc.co.uk/news/amp/technology-42075306.

[5] https://www.consumer.ftc.gov/blog/2017/09/equifax-data-breach-what-do.

[6] https://siliconangle.com/blog/2017/11/19/defense-department-contractor-leaves-spying-program-data-exposed-aws-instances/.

health status and health care provided by an institution to an individual. In the European Union, the main source of regulation is the General Data Protection Regulation (GDPR)[7].

The goal of the work presented here is to design a system supporting data compliance and security in large scale data repositories. In our context, data can be located in different countries, and the system must be adaptable to various regulations. The proposed system takes into account documents with unstructured content, *i.e.* structured data such as database repositories are not part of our study.

Several challenges are posed by securing sensitive data in large heterogeneous repositories. Dealing with heterogeneous content such as clinical notes, reports, or any type of semi- or un-structured files (database dump, xml files, etc.) makes it difficult to know what types of data need to be processed. Therefore, it is also difficult to define what types of sensitive information must be protected. For instance, clinical notes almost always contain sensitive health-related information (*e.g.* treatments, biological results, etc.) rather than less specific information (*e.g.* credit card numbers, dates of birth, names and first names, etc.). This work presents a two-step pipeline towards supporting compliance and privacy protection. The prototype system is easily adaptable to various domains, and capable of detecting sensitive information across various type of documents, covering the sensitive information listed in PIPEDA and HIPAA. The pipeline first predicts the domain of a document to know what types of sensitive information need to be detected, and then uses a domain-dedicated statistical model to extract all the sensitive information contained in a document.

The paper is organized as follows: Sect. 2 presents a short overview of various works summarizing the current state-of-the-art in the field, Sect. 3 describes the corpora used for the experiments, Sect. 4 explains our approach while experiments and results are reported in Sect. 5. Conclusion and future work are described in Sect. 6.

2 Previous Work

Detection of sensitive information is closely related to the Named Entity Recognition (NER) task. In natural language processing, a Named Entity (NE) [6] is a textual object that can be roughly designated by a proper name. Standard types of NE are Person, Location, and Organization. For example, *Barack Obama* is a NE of type Person. In addition to this list of NE standard types, both numeric (*e.g.* Money, Number, Ordinal, Percentage) and temporal (*e.g.* Date, Time, Duration, Set) entities are also considered as NE. In our work, the concept of NE is extended to also cover various types of sensitive information. In many cases, a sensitive information is an instance of a NE type, *e.g.* a given date of birth is an instance of the standard NE type Date, and the name of a patient is an instance of the standard NE type Person. The utilization of similar methods for identifying both sensitive information and NER is hence relevant.

---

[7] https://gdpr-info.eu/.

In this Section, we give an overview of works done on NER tasks in the context of sensitive information detection.

Pattern matching is often based on hard-coded rules using regular expressions to detect structured sensitive information. In the context of health related documents, some of the teams in i2b2/UTHealth Shared Task [9] enhanced their systems with such pattern matching rules. This approach has several limitation, and often results in potential detection of many false positive entities while missing critical true positive ones. For instance, the sequence of 9 digits defining the Canadian Social Insurance Number or the 16 digits used for credit card numbers require numerous and highly precise rules to be properly detected – e.g. based on simple character-level patterns, 0000000000000000 would be considered as a credit card number. Moreover, this approach does not take the context in which an entity appear into account, providing no support for disambiguation strategies. It is hence a solution to be used along with other methods.

For the 2013 CLEF eHEALTH Task-1a (identification of disorders from medical electronic records), Bodnari et al. [1] developed a supervised Conditional Random Field (CRF) based model using a knowledge base from specialized bio-medical terminologies and Wikipedia. They used the MIMIC II database version 2.5 [7], divided in a training set of 200 documents and a test set of 100 documents. While their system obtained promising results in a relaxed context (partial matching), strict matching is still difficult to achieve. To evaluate the overall performance of a system, it is common to use the following metrics : Precision, Recall and F1-Score. For the task NE detection, our system assigns a class (a NE type) to a word or group of words in a sentence. The classes provided by the system can then be compared to the judgment of experts in the field who manually annotated the corpus. For this purpose, true positive, true negative, false positive and false negative are defined. In the case of NER, the "positive" means that the NE type has been correctly assigned and "negative" means that the annotated word is not that NE type. The words "false" and "true" refer to the truthfulness of the decision. The performance evaluation metrics Precision, Recall and F1-Score are calculated as follows:

$$Precision = \frac{TruePositive(TP)}{TP + FalsePositive(FP)} \qquad Recall = \frac{TP}{TP + FalseNegative(FN)}$$

$$F1 = 2 \times \frac{Precision \times Recall}{Precison + Recall}$$

Depending on the type of entities, ensemble systems (systems composed of several subsystems) are a good choice to increase the overall F1 Score. For example, in [11], Yang Hui et al. present the winning system of the 2014 i2b2 de-identification task. Based on the i2b2-2014 corpus composed of clinical notes, the authors built an ensemble system based on machine learning techniques, rules and keywords. The combination of these techniques is relevant for the detection of PHI because the same entities can be ambiguous and have different shapes, e.g. "3041023MARY" is composed of two PHI entities with 3041023 being the identifier of a MEDICALRECORD and *MARY* referring to an HOSPITAL.

Building a set of rules and dictionaries containing those writing variation helps a lot machine learning based systems.

Academic and industrial researchers are very interested in these complex tasks of de-identification and prevention of data leakage. This enthusiasm, coupled with the numerous massive leaks discussed in the Introduction Section, gives rise to the creation of commercial offers to protect companies and individuals against these risks. Recently, Google introduced a pattern matching based approach that identifies files containing sensitive information stored in the Google cloud storage. The so-called Google Data Loss Prevention (DLP) API[8] is sold as capable of detecting 50 types[9] of sensitive data. The system relies on a set of services, including text data mining systems. All these systems are currently proprietary and only available on Google Cloud. In addition to the detection of sensitive data, the DLP API also offers ways to control the diffusion of these data, and to delete the identified data. However, since these systems are proprietary, one cannot know how they handle the detection, which is somewhat contradictory in the context of private and sensitive data detection. On the contrary, our system will be open-source: it will not require users to rely on it blindly, and will allow adaptation to other contexts.

3   Datasets

As previously described, systems detecting sensitive information usually rely on algorithms trained on rich datasets. In this Section, we present the datasets we used in this work. We considered documents from various sources: i2b2 [9], a health-care oriented dataset described in Sect. 3.1, and a large enterprise email dataset presented in Sect. 3.2. To contextualize the detection, we built a manually annotated corpus for automatically detecting the domain of a document. This corpus is described in Sect. 3.3.

3.1   I2b2

In order to have a medical data repository containing health-related information, we used i2b2. Those Deidentified Clinical Records are provided by the i2b2 National Center for Biomedical Computing. This dataset was originally released for the Shared Tasks organized by Dr. Ozlem Uzuner, i2b2 and SUNY, concerning Challenges in NLP for Clinical Data. The i2b2 dataset is composed of 1,304 medical files concerning 296 diabetic patients, including details on admission notes, discharges summaries and correspondences between medical doctors. For the tasks it was originally designed for, the dataset is divided in 790 documents for the training set and 514 documents for the test set. In the context of our work, we decided to keep this distribution. The Personal Health Information (PHI) in i2b2 follows a category system of *types* and *sub-types*. The complete

---

[8] https://cloud.google.com/dlp/.

[9] https://cloud.google.com/dlp/docs/infotypes-reference.

list can be found in [9]. Realistic surrogates have been used in place of the real
PHI initially contained in the dataset in order to protect persons privacy. Table 1
shows the distribution of PHI in the corpus in terms of number of occurrences for
each type and sub-type. We can note that some entities are underrepresented in
the dataset. For instance, `Location-Country` and `Location-Other` count only
66 and 134 occurrences respectively in the training set for a total of 17,389
PHI-occurrences.

Table 1. PHI distribution in i2b2.

PHI type	PHI sub-type	Training set	Testing set
DATE		7,505	4,980
NAME	DOCTOR	2,885	1,912
	PATIENT	1,316	879
	USERNAME	264	92
AGE		1,233	764
CONTACT	PHONE	309	215
	FAX	8	2
	EMAIL	4	1
	URL	2	0
ID	MEDICALRECORD	611	422
	IDNUM	261	195
	DEVICE	7	8
	BIOID	1	0
	HEALTHPLAN	1	0
LOCATION	HOSPITAL	1,437	875
	CITY	394	260
	STATE	314	190
	STREET	216	136
	ZIP	212	140
	ORGANIZATION	124	82
	COUNTRY	66	117
	OTHER	134	13
PROFESSION		234	179
Total		17,389	11,462

3.2 Enterprise Emails

This work is done in a context of an industrial partnership. The partner company needs to mine a large dataset of emails from which sensitive information
must be detected. The email dataset is composed of more than 3.5 millions of

Table 2. Statistics on enterprise email.

# of users	504
# of messages	1,657,108
# of attachments	1,914,107
Total number of documents	3,571,215

documents. About 1.6 millions are messages and others 1.9 millions are attachments. The dataset has been collected from about 500 employees of a public organization during a two-year period, from February 2006 to December 2008. About 63% of the messages have between 1 and 3 attachments, while 35% have no attachment. The 2% remaining messages have between 4 to 170 attachments. The largest account has 37,591 messages whereas the smallest one has 4,660. On average, there are 12,267 messages per employee. Finally, the dataset is neither annotated nor de-identified, and contains real sensitive information about the organization employees. This dataset is confidential, and the property of the company, therefore, we will not be allowed to share it.

3.3 Domain Detection Corpus

To support a fine-grained detection of ambiguous sensitive information in documents, it is useful to know the scope of the entities they could contain before mining them. Towards this goal, we developed a machine learning based system capable of detecting domains. As proof-of-concept, the system currently targets two domains: health, business, and the remaining documents are classified as others. To train this system, we built a manually annotated corpus.

This corpus is composed of 680 documents split in 520 documents for the training set and 160 documents for the test set. In the training/test sets, the health-related documents were randomly selected from the i2b2 training/test set, and the set of articles of the Forbes "health" category. The business-related documents are articles selected randomly from the "business" category of Forbes, the New York Times, and Reuters, from December, 15th 2017 to January, 19th 2018. The documents of the "other" category are also articles from the New York Times and Reuters in the "art" category.

Table 3 provides the number of documents and the size of the vocabulary for each subset of the domain detection corpus while Table 4 describes the document distribution by category.

4   Methodology

Our approach relies on two steps. First, the proposed pipeline identifies the domain of the document. We found that the domain of documents provides clues on the type of sensitive information they include. For instance, financial documents are unlikely to contain personal health-related information (*e.g* social

Table 3. Statistics on the domain detection corpus.

Train	Total number of documents	520
	Number of (unique) words	9,331
Test	Total number of documents	160
	Number of (unique) words	3,241

Table 4. Documents distribution by category.

Train	Number of *health* documents	160
	Number of *business* documents	160
	Number of *health* and *business* documents	100
	Number of *other* documents	100
Test	Number of *health* documents	40
	Number of *business* documents	40
	Number of *health* and *business* documents	40
	Number of *other* documents	40

security numbers or medical record number). This first step supports the extraction process by determining the list of sensitive information in relation to the detected domain. The pipeline currently targets two specific domains: business and health. A given document can belong to both business and health domain, and documents not related to these domains are assigned the "other" category. To classify documents in one of these domain, we developed a machine learning based classifier further described in Subsect. 4.1.

The second step is the extraction of the sensitive information included in the documents. For this step, the pipeline relies on CRFs and pattern matching. By experimenting with Stanford CoreNLP toolkit [5], we used the CoNLL model [3] to annotate standard NEs, and we built a model trained on i2b2 to detect health-related information. In order to refine the entity detection, we also use a pattern matching approach for specific entities such as URL, email, phone number, Social Security Number (SSN), credit card and postal code. Based on these models, the sensitive types of information our pipeline identifies are the following: age, city, country, date, doctor name, hospital, idnum (any ID related to an identifiable individual), location, medical record, organization, patient name, phone, profession, state, username, zip code, URL, email, phone number, SSN, credit card and postal code. Some of these types of information are not highly sensitive if considered separately. However, connecting several of them could allow to identify an individual, and this is why they are considered as sensitive information.

4.1   Domain Detection

The first step of the pipeline implements a machine learning approach in order to classify the documents by topics. We compared several algorithms, namely a Support Vector Machine (SVM), a Random Forest, a k-Nearest Neighbors (kNN), a Naive Bayes and a multilayer perceptron (MLP). In order to do so, we used Scikit-learn[10], a Python-based machine learning toolkit. The experiments were run using the corpus for domain detection described in Subsect. 3.3. To ensure reproducibility, parameters for some algorithms we used are listed hereafter:

SVM: penalty = "l2", loss = "squared_hinge", multi_class = "ovr";
Random Forest: n_estimators = 5 (number of trees in the forest), criterion = "gini" (to measure the quality of a split, we use the Gini impurity);
k-Nearest Neighbors (kNN): n_neighbors = 4, metric = "minkowski" (distance metric, equivalent to the standard Euclidean metric here).

4.2   Annotation of Enterprise Emails

As the dataset of enterprise emails is a large dataset, we cannot manually annotate all the documents. In order to build a smaller gold standard corpus, we decided to automatically annotate the whole dataset (messages and attachments) first with 3 annotators: the CoNLL model, the CRF model built on i2b2, and the pattern matching based annotator for specific entities. Then, we use a selection process to retrieve relevant documents, *i.e.* documents containing sensitive data, which will be manually annotated. This selection process is described hereafter.

Selection of Relevant Documents. Dealing with large corpora is a challenge. When it comes to training/evaluating NER systems, one needs a corpus where sensitive data are annotated. Since we cannot manually annotate millions of documents, we set up an automatic system for selecting the most relevant documents to be manually annotated, *i.e.* documents containing PHI and other sensitive data. A random selection from the entire corpus would not provide us with enough of these specific documents, so we built a selection step that filters documents based on the potential sensitivity of their content. To do so, we rely on already trained annotators to find NEs in the documents. Depending on the performance of the annotators, this approach raises a concern: since annotators rely on machine learning based models that are recall oriented, many automatically annotated NEs are false positives. We end up with hundreds of millions of annotations, and a few million of false positives. In order to refine this detection, the selection process considers the most frequent vocabulary that surrounds each type of NE. Once this vocabulary is collected, all NEs surrounded by a vocabulary that is too far from the most common vocabulary of their type are deleted. The final goal is to obtain an automatically annotated corpus, with NE

---

[10] http://scikit-learn.org/.

annotations of reasonable quality. Once these steps are completed, we select the number of documents that we want to manually annotate. The selection process keeps the proportions of the types of annotations found in the preceding steps. The selected document are then converted to the Brat Standoff format[11]. Brat is a widely used open-source manual text annotation tool. It consists of a web interface where each human expert can annotate the corpus. Multiple experts can annotate the same document in order cross-validate the annotations. The document selection steps are described in Fig. 1.

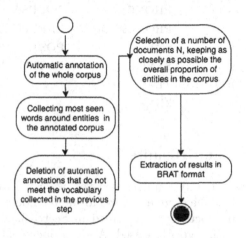

Fig. 1. Document selection steps.

Annotation Procedure. In order to manually annotate the subset of enterprise emails composed of relevant documents selected from the procedure described in Subsect. 4.2 we first established the scope of the NEs we wanted to manually annotate. Table 5 presents the list of these NEs along with the automated annotator providing them.

The CREDIT_CARD entity matches all types of the following credit cards: American Express, Maestro Card, Mastercard, Visa Card, BCGlobal, Carte Blanche Card, Diners Club Card, Discover Card, Insta Payment Card, JCB Card, KoreanLocalCard, Laser Card, Solo Card, Switch Card, Union Pay Card, and the PHONE entity matches all types of the following patterns: 1(222)2222222, +1(222)222−2222, +1 222 222 2222, (222)222−2222, 222 2222222. The automated annotators output the NE but also several other components: its NE type, and its position in terms of character offset (begin and end).

At least three human annotators will manually annotate each selected document to ensure the reliability of the annotation. Based on Landis, J. Richard, and Gary G. Koch [4], we want to use the Kappa coefficient as a measure of agreement between the annotators during the ongoing manual annotation. We use the BRAT interface [8] as an assistant tool for this step.

---

[11] http://brat.nlplab.org/standoff.html.

Table 5. Annotations provided by the CRF and pattern matching annotators.

CRF model		Regexes
AGE	NUMBER	URL
CITY	ORDINAL	EMAILS
COUNTRY	ORGANIZATION	PHONE
DATE	PATIENT	SSN_CA
DOCTOR	PERCENT	SSN_FR
DURATION	PHONE	SSN_USA
FAX	PROFESSION	CREDIT_CARD
HOSPITAL	SET	POSTAL_CODE_CA
IDNUM	STATE	POSTAL_CODE_US
MEDICALRECORD	TIME	
MONEY	ZIP	

5   Experiments and Results

Since the pipeline is not fully implemented yet, we can only present hereafter few preliminary results. The system created for domain detection was evaluated on the test set of 160 documents described in Sect. 3.3. Table 6 presents the results obtained for each algorithm used. A given document can belong to the health, business, other, or both health and business categories. The highest F1 is reached with SVM for the business category while the MLPClassifier provides the highest F1 for the health category.

Once a document has been assigned a domain, the annotator dedicated to this domain is run on its content. Health related documents are annotated with the CRF model trained on the i2b2 training set, and business related documents

Table 6. Results of the evaluated algorithms on the task of domain detection.

		Precision	Recall	F1 score
kNN	Health	0.966	0.700	0.812
	Business	0.789	0.938	0.857
SVM	Health	0.984	0.762	0.859
	Business	0.813	0.925	**0.865**
RandomForest	Health	0.787	0.600	0.681
	Business	0.793	0.812	0.802
MLPClassifier	Health	0.986	0.875	**0.927**
	Business	0.743	0.975	0.843
Naive Bayes	Health	0.985	0.838	0.905
	Business	0.705	0.988	0.823

Table 7. Results of the CRF model on i2b2.

Named entity	Precision	Recall	F1
AGE	0.9431	0.7724	0.8492
CITY	0.8584	0.5272	0.6532
COUNTRY	0.9412	0.1495	0.2581
DATE	0.9787	0.9590	0.9688
DOCTOR	0.9070	0.6274	0.7418
HOSPITAL	0.9297	0.6454	0.7619
IDNUM	0.9608	0.7101	0.8167
MEDICALRECORD	0.9786	0.8889	0.9316
PATIENT	0.9295	0.5556	0.6954
PHONE	0.8682	0.7089	0.7805
PROFESSION	0.5000	0.0685	0.1205
STATE	0.9128	0.7771	0.8395
USERNAME	1.0000	0.9778	0.9888
ZIP	1.0000	0.9420	0.9701

are annotated with the CoNLL model. Documents that belong to both classes are annotated with both annotators, and documents of the "other" class are annotated with the CoNLL model as a default option. A preliminary evaluation of the approach has been performed on documents of the i2b2 test set, detected as health related. Sensitive data of 14 types are considered. The results presented in Table 7 show that a high F1 score is achieved on most of the types except Profession and Country, which are underrepresented NEs in the entire set of sensitive information as unerlined in Subsect. 3.1. The NEs of types Username, ZIP, Date and MedicalRecord are the highest-ranked ones with a F1 Score of 98.88%, 97.01%, 96.88% and 93.16% respectively. These promising results will be complemented with results on documents related to business and both classes.

6   Conclusion and Future Work

The reported work presents a two-step approach to detect sensitive information in documents. The first step consists of detecting the domain of a document, then the second step performs the detection of sensitive information in the appropriate context, *i.e.* taking into account the domain of the document. As a proof of concept, the approach is currently implemented for health or business related documents, using the CoNLL model based annotator by default, and a CRF model trained on i2b2 for detection of health related NEs.

The corpus built for domain detection is quite small so we plan to use a subset of the "Reddit comments 2007–2015" dataset. This dataset is composed by 1.7 billion comments, and includes every publicly available Reddit comment from October 2007 until May 2015. The subset we plan to use contains one month of comments, and is composed of approximately 350,000 comments. More precisely, we target the most popular 3 subreddits discussing each domains we are interested in: health, business, and finance. For each of these subreddits, we have selected the 1,000 most relevant comments by applying our selection procedure described in Subsect. 4.2. These 9,000 documents are currently being manually annotated in order to build a gold standard corpus. This corpus will be used to evaluate our pipeline, and will be shared with the community as an annotated corpus of sensitive information.

Acknowledgment. As part of this work, the Deidentified Clinical Records used were provided by the i2b2 National Center for Biomedical Computing funded by U54LM008748 and were originally prepared for the Shared Tasks for Challenges in NLP for Clinical Data organized by Dr. Ozlem Uzuner, i2b2 and SUNY.

References

1. Bodnari, A., Deleger, L., Lavergne, T., Neveol, A., Zweigenbaum, P.: A Supervised named-entity extraction system for medical text. In: CLEF (Working Notes) (2013)
2. Centers for Medicare & Medicaid Services and others: The Health Insurance Portability and Accountability Act of 1996 (HIPAA) (1996). http://www.cms.hhs.gov/hipaa
3. Finkel, J.R., Grenager, T., Manning, C.: Incorporating non-local information into information extraction systems by gibbs sampling. In: Proceedings of the 43rd annual meeting on association for computational linguistics, Association for Computational Linguistics, pp. 363–370 (2005)
4. Landis, J.R., Koch, G.G.: The measurement of observer agreement for categorical data. Biometrics **33**, 159–174 (1977)
5. Manning, C., Surdeanu, M., Bauer, J., Finkel, J., Bethard, S., McClosky, D.: The stanford CoreNLP natural language processing toolkit. In: Proceedings of 52nd Annual Meeting of the Association for Computational Linguistics: System Demonstrations, pp. 55–60 (2014)
6. Nadeau, D., Sekine, S.: A survey of named entity recognition and classification. Lingvisticae Investigationes **30**(1), 3–26 (2007)
7. Saeed, M., Villarroel, M., Reisner, A.T., Clifford, G., Lehman, L.W., Moody, G., Heldt, T., Kyaw, T.H., Moody, B., Mark, R.G.: Multiparameter intelligent monitoring in intensive care II (MIMIC-II): a public-access intensive care unit database. Crit. Care Med. **39**(5), 952 (2011)
8. Stenetorp, P., Pyysalo, S., Topić, G., Ohta, T., Ananiadou, S., Tsujii, J.: BRAT: a web-based tool for NLP-assisted text annotation. In: Proceedings of the Demonstrations at the 13th Conference of the European Chapter of the Association for Computational Linguistics, Association for Computational Linguistics, pp. 102–107 (2012)
9. Stubbs, A., Kotfila, C., Uzuner, Ö.: Automated systems for the de-identification of longitudinal clinical narratives: overview of 2014 i2b2/UTHealth shared task track 1. J. Biomed. Inf. **58**, S11–S19 (2015)
10. Tarantino, A.: Governance, Risk, and Compliance Handbook: Technology, Finance, Environmental, and International Guidance and Best Practices. Wiley, New York (2008)
11. Yang, H., Garibaldi, J.M.: Automatic detection of protected health information from clinic narratives. J. Biomed. Inf. **58**, S30–S38 (2015)

Erratum to: Recent Trends and Future Technology in Applied Intelligence

Malek Mouhoub, Samira Sadaoui, Otmane Ait Mohamed,
and Moonis Ali

Erratum to:
M. Mouhoub et al. (Eds.): *Recent Trends and Future*
Technology in Applied Intelligence, **LNAI 10868,**
https://doi.org/10.1007/978-3-319-92058-0

In the original version of the book, the following belated corrections have been incorporated:

In chapter "Auto-detection of Safety Issues in Baby Products", The original version of the paper had listed incorrect precision values for the different classifiers in Table 4 and Fig. 2. These have been updated to the correct precision values.

In chapter "A Rough Set Approach to Events Prediction in Multiple Time Series", the middle name of Wided Lejouad Chaari was incorrect. The middle name has been corrected from "Lajoued" to "Lejouad".

The updated online version of these chapters can be found at
https://doi.org/10.1007/978-3-319-92058-0_49
https://doi.org/10.1007/978-3-319-92058-0_77
https://doi.org/10.1007/978-3-319-92058-0

Author Index

Printed in the United States
By Bookmasters